1 MONTH OF
FREE
READING

at

www.ForgottenBooks.com

By purchasing this book you are eligible for one month membership to ForgottenBooks.com, giving you unlimited access to our entire collection of over 1,000,000 titles via our web site and mobile apps.

To claim your free month visit:

www.forgottenbooks.com/free960488

ISBN 978-0-260-62710-0
PIBN 10960488

JOURNALS

OF THE

Legislative Assembly

OF THE

PROVINCE OF ONTARIO

FROM THE 10TH FEBRUARY TO 8TH APRIL, 1926,
BOTH DAYS INCLUSIVE

*IN THE SIXTEENTH YEAR OF THE REIGN OF OUR
SOVEREIGN LORD KING GEORGE V*

BEING THE

Third Session of the Sixteenth Legislature of Ontario

SESSION 1926

PRINTED BY ORDER OF THE LEGISLATIVE ASSEMBLY

VOL. LX

PROVINCE OF ONTARIO

TORONTO
Printed and Published by Clarkson W. James, Printer to the King's Most Excellent Majesty
1 9 2 6

PRODUCED BY
The
United Press
LIMITED
TORONTO
CANADA

INDEX

TO THE

SIXTIETH VOLUME

16 GEORGE V, 1926

AGRICULTURAL DEVELOPMENT ACT:
Questions *re* Farm loans under, 95, 138.

AGRICULTURE:—See *Royal Agricultural Fair.*

AGRICULTURE, DEPARTMENT OF:
Question as to Department keeping record and issuing certificates for seed grain, 68, 95.
Bill (No. 88), introduced respecting, 27. Second Reading, 53. House in Committee on, 71. Third Reading, 260. R.A., 278. (16 Geo. V, c. 19.)

AGRICULTURE AND COLONIZATION COMMITTEE:
To be appointed, 9. Appointed, 25.
Report presented, 55.

AGRICULTURAL ENQUIRY COMMITTEE:
1. Second Report presented, 146. (*Sessional Papers No. 48.*) Referred to Printing Committee, 146. (Appendix No. 1.)
2. Question as to cost of, 41.
3. Motion *re* presentation of report, 270. Debate adjourned, 271, 273. Resolution carried, 274.

AGRICULTURE, MINISTER OF:
Report presented, 240. (*Sessional Papers No. 21.*)

AGRICULTURE, STATISTICS:
Report presented, 240. (*Sessional Papers No. 22.*)

AIRDROME, SAULT STE. MARIE:
1. Question as to building of, 77 78.
2. Question as to estimated cost of, 78.

AIRPLANES:
1. Question as to purchase of U.S. Navy planes, 150, 191.
2. Question as to number owned by Government, 104.

ALFRED, POLICE VILLAGE OF:
Petition for Act respecting, 14. Reported, 128. Bill (No. 24), introduced and referred to Private Bills Committee, 129. Reported, 175. Second Reading, 185. House goes into Committee on, 197. Third Reading, 209. R.A., 276. (16 Geo. V, c. 74.)

ALGOMA:
Expenditure on Capital Account, 164.

ALGOMA:
Expenditure on certain roads in. Return presented, 85. (*Sessional Papers No. 38.*)

APPLE MARKETING:
Question as to date of announcement *re* marketing of, by Department of Agriculture, 158.

ARNPRIOR, TOWN OF:

Petition for Act respecting consolidation of floating indebtedness, 12. Reported, 54. Bill (No. 2), introduced and referred to the Railway and Municipal Board, 56. Reported and referred to Private Bills Committee, 142. Reported, 175. Second Reading, 185. House goes into Committee on, 197. Third Reading, 209. R.A., 277. (16 Geo. V, c. 75.)

ART PURPOSES:

Committee appointed to direct expenditure for, 16.

ASSESSMENT LAW:

1. Bill (No. 85), introduced to amend, 27. Second Reading and referred to Municipal Committee, 81 Reported, 220.

2. Bill (No. 132), introduced to amend, 130. Second Reading and referred to Municipal Committee, 155. Reported, 220.

3. Bill (No. 144), introduced to amend, 144. Second Reading and referred to Municipal Committee, 155. Reported, 220.

4. Bill (No. 146), introduced to amend, 146. Order for Second Reading discharged and Bill withdrawn, 185.

5. Bill (No. 147), introduced to amend, 154. Second Reading and referred to Municipal Committee, 173. Reported, 220.

6. Bill (No. 161), introduced to amend, 183. Second Reading, 205. House goes into Committee on, 211. House again in Committee on, 256. Third Reading, 262. R.A., 279. (16 Geo. V, c. 55.) (Embodied in Bill No. 189.)

7. Bill (No. 189), *The Assessment Act, 1926*, introduced and read a first and second time, 227. House goes into Committee on, 242. Third Reading, 263. R.A., 280. (16 Geo. V, c. 55.)

8. Petitions presented for amendment to the, 199.

ASSOCIATION OF ACCOUNTANTS AND AUDITORS IN ONTARIO:

Petition for Act to incorporate, 42. Reported, 86. Bill (No. 23), Introduced and referred to Private Bills Committee, 89. Reported, 143. Second Reading, 161. House goes into Committee on, 187. Third Reading, 209. R.A., 277. (16 Geo. V, c. 124.)

ATHLETIC COMMISSION:
Report presented, 58. (*Sessional Papers No. 36.*)

AUDITOR, PROVINCIAL:
Report presented, 240. (*Sessional Papers No. 27.*)

AUDITS:

1. Question as to audits carried on by the Government, 150.

2. Question as to how far back special audits have been conducted, 147.

3. Question as to when system of audits was established, 148.

4. Question as to audits made in departments other than by Provincial Auditor, 270. (See order for Return.)

5. Question as to who were Provincial Auditors when defalcations occurred, 147.

AUSTIN AND NICHOLSON:

Return presented, 271. (*Sessional Papers No. 57.*)

AUTOMOBILE LICENSES:

Question as to revenue from, 59.

AYLMER, TOWN OF:

Petition for Act respecting, 13. Reported, 86. Bill (No. 5), introduced and referred to the Railway and Municipal Board, 91. Reported and referred to Private Bills Committee, 118. Reported, 175. Second Reading, 185. House goes into Committee on, 197. Third Reading, 209. R.A., 276. (16 Geo. V, c. 75.)

BALA, TOWN OF:

Petition for an Act respecting, 19. Reported, 88. Bill (No. 33), introduced and referred to Private Bills Committee, 92. Reported withdrawn and fees less actual cost of printing remitted, 143.

BANTING RESEARCH FUND, GRANT TO:—See *Physicians and Surgeons, College of.*

BARRIE AND ORILLIA HIGHWAY:

1. Question as to cost of maintenance, etc., 202.

2. Order for a Return, 202.

BEACHVILLE WHITE LIME CO.:

Question as to supply of material, Highway, Oxford County, 201.

BECK, THE LATE HONOURABLE SIR ADAM, K.C.M.G.:

House adjourns in memory of, 11.

BEEKEEPING:

Question as to how many persons registered under *Foul Brood Act, 1925*, 111.

BEER:—See *under Liquor*.

BELLEVILLE SCHOOL FOR THE DEAF:

Question as to tender for flour supply, 101.

BEVERAGE TAX:

Question as to what new appointments were made for collection of, 39.

BIRTHS, MARRIAGES AND DEATHS:

Report presented, 145. (*Sessional Papers No. 14.*)

BLOOR STREET, WIDENING OF:

See *Toronto, City of*.

BOARD OF PAROLE:—See *Parole*.

BONDS, PROVINCIAL:

Return *re* purchase of, 85. (*Sessional Papers No. 39.*)

BRANTFORD, CITY OF:

Petition for an Act respecting, 13. Reported, 87. Bill (No. 11), introduced and referred to Private Bills Committee, 89. Reported, 175. Second Reading, 185. House goes into Committee on, 197. Third Reading, 209. R.A., 276. (16 Geo. V, c. 77.)

BRASS, JOHN AND OTHERS:

Motion *re* wages for work on Caledon Hill Road, 202.

BREWERIES:

Question *re* prosecution of, 122.

BRITISH MORTGAGE AND LOAN CO. OF ONTARIO:

Petition for Act to carry on under the *Loan and Trust Companies Act*, 14. Reported, 87. Bill (No. 32), introduced and referred to Private Bills Committee, 90. Reported, 126. Second Reading, 137. House goes into Committee on, 140. Third Reading, 187. R.A., 276. (16 Geo. V, c. 121.)

BUDGET:—See *Supply*.

BURLINGTON BEACH ACT:

Bill (No. 62), introduced to amend, 163. Second reading, 180. House in Committee on, 188. House again in Committee on, 258. Third reading, 261. R.A., 279. (16 Geo. V, c. 11.)

BURNS, JAMES:

Questions as to, 122.

BY-ELECTIONS:—See *Elections*.

CABINET MINISTERS:

Question *re* visits to Europe. See *Ministers*.

CALEDON HILL ROAD WORK:

Motion *re* payment of wages to John Brass and others, 202.

CAMPBELLFORD PULP MILL:

Question as to Provincial ownership of, 131.

CATTLE:

Question as to freight rates on feeder, 66.

CEMETERY ACT:

1. Bill (No. 75), introduced to amend, 20. Second reading, 50. House goes into Committee on, 53. Order for Third reading discharged and Bill withdrawn, 255.

2. Bill (No. 128), introduced to consolidate and amend, 119. Second reading, 140. House goes into Committee on, 145. House again in Committee on, 256. Third reading, 263. R.A., 280. (16 Geo. V, c. 63.)

CHICAGO WATER DIVERSION:

Resolution *re* control of, 274.

CHILDREN'S PROTECTION ACT:

Report presented, 240. (*Sessional Papers No. 19.*)

CHIPPEWA POWER:

Question as to expenditure on Hydro Development, 179.

Question as to water rental at, 124.

CHURCH UNION:—See *United Church of Canada*.

CIVIL GOVERNMENT:—See *Supply*.

CIVIL SERVICE COMMISSIONER:

Report presented, 271. (*Sessional Papers No. 59.*)

CIVIL SERVICE, INSIDE:

Question as to number in inside service in Toronto, 179.

CIVIL SERVICE SUPERANNUATION BOARD:—See *Public*.

CONTRIBUTIONS, BILL TO PROHIBIT POLITICAL:—See *Political Contributions.*

CONVICTIONS:—See *Summary Convictions.*

COOKE, HON. J. R.:

    1. Question as to moneys drawn by, from Hydro-Electric Power Commission and from Provincial Treasury, 111.

    2. Question as to moneys drawn by, from Hydro-Electric Power Commission and from Provincial Treasury, 139.

    3. Question as to reply to Question (No. 131), March 15th, 161.

CORN BORER ACT:

    1. Bill (No. 123), introduced to amend, 119. Second reading, 145. House goes into Committee on, 153. Third reading, 261. R.A., 278. (16 Geo. V, c. 61.)

    2. Question as to how many councils have passed by-laws respecting, 38.

CORONERS ACT:

    Bill (No. 93), introduced to consolidate and amend, 43. Second reading, 81. House goes into Committee on, 114. House again in Committee on, 255. Third reading, 261. R.A., 278. (16 Geo. V, c. 33.)

CORPORATION TAX ACT:

    Question as to revenue received under, 150.

COUNSEL, AMOUNTS PAID TO, RE LITIGATION, SEPARATE SCHOOLS:

    Return presented. (*Sessional Papers No. 45.*)

CROWN-ATTORNEYS ACT:

    Bill (No. 92), introduced to consolidate and amend, 43. Second reading, 81. House goes into Committee on, 113. Third reading, 216. R.A., 278. (16 Geo. V, c. 32.)

CROWN LANDS IN NORTHERN ONTARIO:

    Question as to license granted companies to build railway over, 68.

CROWN WITNESSES ACT:

    Bill (No. 83), introduced to consolidate and amend, 22. Second reading, 70. House goes into Committee on, 83. Third reading, 260. R.A., 278. (16 Geo. V, c. 36.)

CURRENT REVENUE OF PROVINCE:

    Question as to amount and expenditure, 171.

CURRY, JOHN, ESTATE OF:

    Petition for an Act to enable the Executor to make a grant to the proposed Essex Borders Utilities Commission General Hospital, 13. Reported, 54. Bill (No. 6), introduced and referred to Commissioners of Estates, 56. Reported against by Commissioners of Estates, 153. Fees, less actual cost of printing, remitted, 246.

DOGS, TAX ON, AND PROTECTION OF SHEEP:—

Bill (No. 140), introduced respecting, 144. Second reading, 156. House goes into Committee on, 163. Third reading, 209. R.A., 276. (16 Geo. V, c. 62.)

EAST BLOCK:—See *Administration Building, Queen's Park.*

EASTDALE:—See *East York, Township of.*

EAST KENT:

Question as to resignation of member for, 30.

EASTVIEW, TOWN OF:

Petition for Act respecting, 15. Reported, 55. Bill (No. 39), introduced and referred to Private Bills Committee, 57. Withdrawn and fees, less actual cost of printing, remitted, 246.

EAST YORK, TOWNSHIP OF:

Petition for Act to incorporate as Town of Eastdale, 14. Reported, 87. Bill (No. 27), introduced and referred to Private Bills Committee, 91. Reported, 190. Second Reading, 204. House goes into Committee on, 211. Third Reading, 240. R.A., 277. (16 Geo. V, c. 106.)

EDUCATION:

Petition *re* Rural School Boards, 54.

Report of Department presented, 240. (*Sessional Papers No. 11.*)

Regulations and Orders-in-Council, under authority of Act, presented, 19. (*Sessional Papers No. 31.*)

Return presented, to an Order of the House, showing Legislative grants for 1925, paid to Rural Public and Separate Schools in counties, 12. (*Sessional Papers No. 30.*)

Section 27, Education Act, report presented, 198. (*Sessional Papers No. 54.*)

School Trustees, Township Board of, Bill (No. 67), introduced respecting, 11. Order for second reading discharged and Bill withdrawn, 211.

EDUCATION, DEPARTMENT ACT:

Bill (No. 69), introduced to amend, 15. Second reading, 21. House goes into Committee on, 50. Third reading, 260. R.A., 277. 16 Geo. V, c. 66.)

ELECTIONS:

Question, Cost of re-election of Cabinet Ministers in 1923, 69.

Question, *re* Holding of General Election, 94.

Notifications of vacancies by resignation, 3, 4, 5.

Notification of vacancy by death, 2, 3.

Question *re* Prime Minister's reason for not bringing on by-elections, 79.

EXPENDITURE:

Question, *re* expenditure on Capital and Ordinary Accounts each year from year 1914, 160.

EXTRAMURAL EMPLOYMENT OF SENTENCED PERSONS:

Report of Committee presented, 272. (*Sessional Papers No. 61.*)

FARM LOANS:

Question respecting, 95, 138.

FATAL ACCIDENTS TO INFANTS:

Act respecting damages: See *Accidents*.

FILM: Moving Picture.

Motion on, withdrawn, 186.

FINES AND FORFEITURES ACT:

Bill (No. 84), introduced to consolidate and amend, 22. Second reading, 70. House goes into Committee on, 83. Third reading, 260. R.A., 278. (16 Geo. V, c. 37.)

FIRE INSURANCE:

1. Question respecting property of the Province of Ontario, 146.

2. Question respecting Hydro-Electric Power Commission of Ontario, 121.

FIRE RANGING:

Question respecting cost of, 172.

FISH AND GAME:

Committee to be appointed, 9. Appointed, 26. Report, 176. (Appendix No. 1). (*Sessional Papers No. 49.*)

See *Game and Fish Departmental Report.* (*Sessional Papers No. 9.*)

FORD CITY:

Petition for an Act respecting the Town of, 14. Reported, 55. Bill (No. 34), introduced and referred to Private Bills Committee, 57. Reported, 246. Second reading, 247. House goes into Committee on 260. Third reading, 263. R.A., 280. (16 Geo. V, c. 79.)

FORT WILLIAM, CITY OF:

Petition for an Act respecting, 13. Reported, 54. Bill (No. 13), introduced and referred to Private Bills Committee, 57. Reported, 190. Second reading, 204. House goes into Committee on, 211. Third reading, 240. R.A., 277. (16 Geo. V, c. 80.)

FORT WILLIAM, ELECTORAL DISTRICT OF:

Question *re* expenditure on Capital Account, 164.

FOUL BROOD ACT:

See under *Beekeeping.*

FOXES IN CAPTIVITY:

Bill (No. 186), introduced to protect property in, 227. Second reading, 241. House goes into Committee on, 243. Third reading, 263. R.A., 280. (16 Geo. V, c. 65.)

FREIGHT RATES ON FEEDER CATTLE:

Question, 66.

GALT, CITY OF:

Petition for an Act respecting, 14. Reported, 88. Bill (No. 36), introduced and referred to Private Bills Committee, 90. Reported, 126. Second reading, 137. House goes into Committee on, 140. Third reading, 187. R.A., 276. (16 Geo. V, c. 81.)

GAME:

Petition of A. E. Jones, *et al.*, 42.

GAME AND FISHERIES ACT:

Bill (No. 185), introduced to amend, 227. Second reading, 241. House goes into Committee on, 243. Third reading, 263. R.A., 280. (16 Geo. V, c. 64.)

GAME AND FISHERIES DEPARTMENT:

Report presented, 174. (*Sessional Papers No. 9.*)

GANANOQUE, TOWN OF:

Petition for Act respecting, 13. Reported, 86. Bill (No. 16), introduced and referred to Private Bills Committee, 91. Reported, 126. Second reading, 137. House goes into Committee on, 140. Third reading, 187. R.A., 276. (16 Geo. V, c. 82.)

GASOLINE AND OIL:

1. Report of Commission *re* prices, 41. (*Sessional Papers No. 33.*)
2. Question *re* cost of Commission, 139.
3. Question *re* expenditure for Government aeroplanes, 104.

GASOLINE TAX:

1. Question *re* collection of revenue, 31, 105.
2. Question *re* new appointments in connection with, 39.

3. Question *re* returns under, 265.

4. Question *re* payment for collection under, 31, 105.

5. Question *re* application for refunds by Farmers under, 124.

6. Question *re* revenue from, 59.

GIRLS' HOME AND PROTESTANT ORPHANS' HOME:

Petition for an Act to amalgamate, 13. Reported, 87. Bill (No. 10), introduced and referred to Private Bills Committee, 90. Reported and fees, less actual cost of printing, remitted, 115. Second reading, 136. House goes into Committee on, 140. Third reading, 187. R.A., 276. (16 Geo. V, c. 119.)

GORDON H. H.:

Question *re* appearing for C. A. Matthews, 93.

GOVERNMENT CONTROL AND SALE OF LIQUOR:—See under *Liquor*.

1. Question respecting, 40, 94.

2. Question, *re* Government plan, 40, 94.

GOVERNMENT MINISTERS:—See under *Ministers*.

GOVERNMENT SAVINGS OFFICE:

Question *re* deposits, 136.

GRANTHAM, TOWNSHIP OF:

Petition for Act respecting, 14. Reported, 128. Bill (No. 31), introduced and referred to Private Bills Committee, 129. Reported, 154. Second reading, 161. House goes into Committee on, 173. Third reading, 187. R.A., 276. (16 Geo. V, c. 83.)

GREAT LAKES:—See under *Water, Diversion of*.

GREY AND BRUCE LOAN COMPANY AND THE OWEN SOUND LOAN AND SAVINGS COMPANY:

Petition for Act to amalgamate, 13. Reported, 86. Bill (No. 3), introduced and referred to Private Bills Committee, 90. Reported, 114. Second reading, 125. House goes into Committee on, 130. Third reading, 186. R.A., 276. (16 Geo. V, c. 123.)

GREY CENTRE:

Question as to resignation of Member for, 29.

GROUND HOG:

Question *re* tenders for Pulp and Timber Limits, 44.

GUELPH, CITY OF:

Petition for Act respecting, 24. Reported, 88. Bill (No. 35), introduced and referred to Private Bills Committee, 91. Reported, 143. Second reading, 161. House goes into Committee on, 173. Third reading, 209. R.A., 276. (16 Geo. V, c. 84.)

HABEAS CORPUS ACT:

Bill (No. 171), introduced to amend, 199. Second reading, 210. House goes into Committee on, 171. Third reading, 262. R.A., 279. (16 Geo. V, c. 27.)

HALIBURTON, WHITNEY AND MATTAWA RAILWAY:

Petition for Act respecting, 14. Reported, 54. Bill (No. 26), introduced and referred to Committee on Railways, 57. Reported, 118. Second reading, 137. House goes into Committee on, 140. Third reading, 187. R.A., 276. (16 Geo. V, c. 109.)

HAWKERS AND TRANSIENT TRADERS LICENSING ACT:

Bill (No. 142), introduced respecting, 144. Second reading, and referred to Municipal Committee, 155. *Not reported.*

HEALTH, PROVINCIAL BOARD OF:

Report, 145. (*Sessional Papers, No. 14.*)

HEARST, TOWN OF:

Question *re* building of Government Agricultural Barn, 110.

HIGHWAY LAWS AMENDMENT ACT, 1924:

Question *re* Townships paid Grants under, 105.

Question *re* construction and work of Advisory Board, 158.

HIGHWAY TRAFFIC ACT:

1. Bill (No. 145), introduced to amend, 144. Second reading, 156. House goes into Committee on, 163. Third reading, 209. R.A., 276. (16 Geo. V, c. 58.)

2. Bill (No. 148), introduced to amend, 155. Second reading, 162. House goes into Committee on, 173. House again in Committee, 213. Third reading, 261. R.A., 278. (16 Geo. V, c. 58.)

HIGHWAY, VEHICLES ON:—See *Public Vehicles.*

HIGHWAYS:

1. Return *re* expenditure on Provincial, 51. (*Sessional Papers No. 35.*)

2. Motion *re* men's wages Caledon Hill job, 202.

3. Motion *re* protection labouring men's wages, 225.

4. Question, *re* additional mileage, 195.

5. Question *re* payments for maintenance, 40.

6. Question *re* expenditures in Oxford County, 105, 201.

7. Question, Revenue through Department, 31, 59.

8. Question *re* cost of keeping clear of snow, 160.

HOUSE, THE:

1. Divisions of, 18, 116, 180, 198.

2. Adjourns one or more days, 271.

3. Sits after midnight, 180.

4. Proclamation calling, 1.

5. In memory of the late Honourable Sir Adam Beck, K.C.M.G., 11.

6. Out of respect for the late Arthur H. Sydere, Clerk of the House, 52.

7. Government Orders to be taken on Mondays, 16.

8. To have two sittings daily 209, 272.

9. Motion *re* reduction of Members of, 225.

10. Prorogation, 283.

HUNTSVILLE, TOWN OF:

Petition for Act respecting, 42. Reported, 129. Bill (No. 41), introduced and referred to Private Bills Committee, 130. Reported, 221. Second reading, 241. House goes into Committee on, 242. Third reading, 263. R.A., 280. (16 Geo. V, c. 85.)

HYDRO-ELECTRIC POWER COMMISSION OF ONTARIO:

1. Question *re* electric power development in Northern Ontario by, 69.

2. Question *re* fire insurance, 121.

3. Question *re* railways operated by, 132.

4. Question *re* Power Extension Fund, 123.

5. Question *re* rental for water used at Queenston-Chippawa plant, 124.

6. Question *re* appointments of Messrs. Magrath and Maguire, 139.

7. Question *re* moneys drawn by Hon. J. R. Cooke since appointment, 111, 139.

Return *re* insurance, 180. (*Sessional Papers No. 51.*)

Report presented, 240. (*Sessional Papers No. 26.*)

Petition for an Act to authorize transfer of Radial Railways to corporation of the City of Toronto, 203. Bill (No. 180), referred to Private Bills Committee, 203. Reported, 246. Second reading, 247. House goes into Committee on, 260. Third reading, 263. R.A., 281. (16 Geo. V, c. 113.)

HYDRO-ELECTRIC RAILWAY ACT: 1914:

Bill (No. 166), introduced to amend, 190. Second reading, 205. House goes into Committee on, 212. Third reading, 262. R.A., 279. (16 Geo. V, c. 18.)

HYDRO SYSTEMS:

Return *re* available supply of power, 84. (*Sessional Papers No. 37.*)

I
MMIGRATION AND COLONIZATION:

Question regarding, 65.

INFANTS, FATAL ACCIDENTS TO:—See under *Accidents.*

INSPECTOR OF LEGAL OFFICES:

Report presented, 137. (*Sessional Papers No. 5.*)

INSURANCE ONTARIO ACT:

Bill No. 178, introduced to amend, 200. Second reading, 210. House in Committee on, 224. House again in Committee on, 258. Third reading, 262. R.A., 280. (16 Geo. V, c. 49.)

INSURANCE:

1. Question *re* revenue from Insurance Companies under Corporation Tax Act, 150.

2. Question *re* salary and statements by superintendent of, 171.

3. Question *re* amount carried on property of Province, 146.

INSURANCE AND FRIENDLY SOCIETIES:

Report presented, 198. (*Sessional Papers No. 6.*)

INTERNATIONAL WATERWAYS:—See under *Water.*

INVESTIGATION OF INDUSTRIAL DISPUTES:

Bill (No. 98), introduced respecting, 58. Order for Second reading discharged and Bill withdrawn, 244.

J
ACKSON, LEWIS COMPANY, Contractors, New Administration Building:

Question *re* bondsmen for, 162.

JARVIS, AMELIUS:

Question *re* total expenditure, Government prosecution of, 164.

JOHNSON, STRACHAN, K.C.:

Question *re* legal fees paid to, 226.

JUDGES' ORDERS ENFORCEMENT ACT, 1926:

Bill (No. 79), introduced, 21. Second reading, 70. House goes into Committee on, 83. Third reading, 260. R.A., 278. (16 Geo. V, c. 26.)

JUDICATURE ACT:

Bill (No. 172), introduced, 199. Second reading, 210. House goes into Committee on, 222. Third reading, 262. R.A., 279. (16 Geo. V, c. 22.)

JURORS ACT:

Bill (No. 102), introduced, 72. Second reading, 97. House goes into Committee on, 99. Third reading, 261. R.A., 278. (16 Geo. V, c. 24.)

JUSTICES OF THE PEACE:

Bill introduced informally, 8.

JUSTICES OF THE PEACE ACT:

Bill (No. 82), introduced to consolidate and amend, 22. Second reading, 70. House goes into Committee on, 83. Third reading, 260. R.A., 278. (16 Geo. V, c. 28.)

KAPUSKASING:

Question *re* tenders for pulp and timber limits, 44.

KENORA:

Question *re* resignation of Member for, 30.

KENORA, ELECTORAL DISTRICT OF:

Question *re* expenditure on Capital Account, 164.

KITCHENER, CITY OF:

Petition for an Act respecting, 24. Reported, 128. Bill (No. 37), introduced and referred to Private Bills Committee, 129. Reported, 143. Second reading, 151. House goes into Committee on, 162. Third reading, 187. R.A., 276. (16 Geo. V, c. 86.)

KITCHENER, LUTHERAN SEMINARY:—See under *Evangelical*.

LABOUR:

1. Committee to be appointed, 9.

2. Appointed, 26.

3. Report of Department presented, 156. (*Sessional Papers No. 10.*)

4. Question *re* contractors defaulting in paying, 159.

LABOURING MEN, PROTECTION OF, DEPARTMENT OF HIGHWAYS:
Motion respecting, 225.

LANDS, VESTING CERTAIN, IN HIS MAJESTY:

Bill (No. 169), introduced, 199. Second reading, 210. House goes into Committee on, 222. Third reading, 262. R.A., 279. (16 Geo. V, c. 14.)

LANDS ACT, PUBLIC:

Bill (No. 73), introduced to amend, 17. Second reading, 50. House goes into Committee on, 71. Third reading, 260. R.A., 277. (16 Geo. V, c. 8.)

Bill (No. 182), introduced to amend, 208. Second reading, 221. House goes into Committee on, 242. Third reading, 262. R.A., 280. (16 Geo. V, c. 8.)

LANDS AND FORESTS:

Report presented, 239. (*Sessional Papers No. 3.*)

1. Question *re* announcement respecting tenders for pulpwood lands at political meeting, Port Arthur, 43, 47.

2. Question *re* contracts given McNamara Construction Company, 66, 108.

3. Return *re* Austin and G. B. Nicholson *re* trespasses, 271. (*Sessional Papers No. 57.*)

4. Question *re* investigation by Public Accounts Committee, 150.

5. Question *re* purchase of lands at Sault Ste. Marie for Government services, 81.

6. Question *re* pavements built by Department of, 147.

LAND TAX AMENDMENT ACT, 1926, PROVINCIAL:

Bill (No. 150), introduced, 155. Second reading, 161. House goes into Committee on, 174. Third reading, 261. R.A., 279. (16 Geo. V, c. 7.)

LA SALLE, TOWN OF:

Petition for an Act respecting, 42. Reported, 55. Bill (No. 50), introduced and referred to Private Bills Committee, 58. Reported, 175. Second reading, 185. House goes into Committee on, 197. Third reading, 209. R.A., 277. (16 Geo. V, c. 87.)

LEDGER, TOWNSHIP OF:

Question *re* cutting of pulpwood in, 148.

LEGAL BILLS COMMITTEE:

1. Committee to be appointed, 9.

2. Appointed, 26. Report, 259.

LEGAL OFFICES:

Report presented, 137. (*Sessional Papers No. 5.*)

LEGISLATIVE ASSEMBLY:

Proclamation convening, 1.

Vacancies in, 2.

Question *re* seats vacant, etc., 28.

Question *re* reasons for not filling vacancies, 79.

Question *re* members interested in contractors supplying Government, 92.

LEGISLATIVE ASSEMBLY ACT:

Bill (No. 86), introduced to amend, 27. Second reading, 210. House goes into Committee on, 222. Third reading, 262. R.A., 279. (16 Geo. V, c. 5.)

LEGISLATIVE SECRETARY:—See *Northern Ontario.*

Return of Requirements and Resources of, for Northern Ontario, 100. (*Sessional Papers No. 42.*)

McBRIDE, KENNETH:

Question *re* payment of gratuity in connection with death of, 111.

McCarthy, D. L., K.C.:

Question *re* legal fees paid to, 226.

McNamara Construction Company:

1. Return *re* tenders, 272. (*Sessional Papers No. 58.*)

2. Questions *re* Government contracts given to, 66, 108.

3. Question as to how many years contracts been awarded to, 109.

Magistrates' Act:

Bill (No. 90), introduced to consolidate and amend, 27. Second reading, 70. House goes into Committee on, 84. House again in Committee on, 255. Third reading, 260. R.A., 278. (16 Geo. V, c. 29.)

Manitoulin:

Return *re* expenditure on roads, 85.

Marriage Act:

Bill (No. 158), introduced to amend, 179. Second reading, 196. House goes into Committee on, 207. Third reading, 261. R.A., 279. (16 Geo. V, c. 43.)

Married Women's Property Act:

Bill (No. 89), introduced to amend, 27. Second reading, 70. House goes into Committee on, 96. House again in Committee, 255. Third reading, 261. R.À., 278. (16 Geo. V, c. 44.)

Mattagami River:

Question *re* tenders for pulp and timber limits, 44.

Matthews, Charles:

Question *re* counsel appearing for, before Public Accounts sub-Committee, 93.

Metal Sales Act:—See under *Unwrought Metal.*

Midland, Simcoe Railway Company:

Petition for an Act respecting, 42. Reported, 88. Bill (No. 51), introduced and referred to the Railway Committee, 90. Reported, 119. Second reading, 137. House goes into Committee on, 140. Third reading, 187. R.A., 276. (16 Geo. V, c. 110.)

MINES, DEPARTMENT OF:

Report presented, 156. (*Sessional Papers No. 4.*)

MINIMUM WAGE BOARD:

Report presented, 145. (*Sessional Papers No. 47.*)

MINISTERS OF THE CROWN:

Question *re* interests in Joint Stock Companies, 92.

Question *re* visits to Europe, 38.

Question *re* salaries paid to, 66.

Question *re* travelling expenses, 112.

MONEY, RAISING ON, CREDIT:—See *Consolidated Revenue Fund.*

MOTHERS' ALLOWANCE ACT:

Question *re* how many widows received help, 268.

MOTHERS' ALLOWANCE COMMISSION:

Report presented, 271. (*Sessional Papers No. 60.*)

MOTOR VEHICLES:—See *Public Vehicles.*

MOUNT MCKAY AND KAKABEKA FALLS RAILWAY COMPANY:

Petition for an Act respecting, 13. Reported, 86. Bill (No. 8), introduced and referred to the Railway Committee, 91. . Reported, 119. Second reading, 137. House goes into Committee, 140. Third reading, 187. R.A., 276. (16 Geo. V, c. 111.)

MOVING PICTURE:

Question *re* cost and maintenance of plant, 200, 201.

Question *re* Indoor Sports film withdrawn, 269.

MOVING PICTURES:

Motion *re* film, 186.

MUNICIPAL LAW:

1. Bill (No. 64), introduced to amend, 155. Order for second reading discharged and Bill withdrawn, 222.

2. Bill (No. 74), introduced to amend, 20. Order for second reading discharged and Bill withdrawn, 225.

3. Bill (No. 97), introduced to amend, 52. Second reading and referred to Municipal Committee, 84. Reported, 220.

4. Bill (No. 111), introduced to amend, 98. Second reading and referred to Municipal Committee, 108. Reported, 220.

5. Bill (No. 112), introduced to amend, 100. Second reading and referred to Municipal Committee, 116. Reported, 220.

6. Bill (No. 113), introduced to amend, 100. Second reading and referred to Municipal Committee, 125. *No report.*

7. Bill (No. 118), introduced to amend, 115. Second reading and referred to Municipal Committee, 140. Reported, 220.

8. Bill (No. 119), introduced to amend, 115. Second reading and referred to Municipal Committee, 151. Reported, 220.

9. Bill (No. 126), introduced to amend, 119. Second reading and referred to Municipal Committee, 151. *No report.*

10. Bill (No. 129), introduced to amend, 127. Second reading and referred to Municipal Committee, 140. Reported, 220.

11. Bill (No. 133), introduced to amend, 130. Second reading and referred to Municipal Committee, 155. *No report.*

12. Bill (No. 134), introduced to amend, 138. Order for second reading discharged and Bill withdrawn, 152.

13. Bill (No. 135), introduced to amend, 138. Order for second reading discharged and Bill withdrawn. 152.

14. Bill (No. 137), introduced to amend, 138. Second reading and referred to Municipal Committee, 151. Reported, 220.

15. Bill (No. 139), introduced to amend, 144. Second reading and referred to Municipal Committee, 156. *No report.*

16. (Bill No. 141), introduced to amend, 144. Second reading and referred to Municipal Committee, 155. Reported, 220.

17. Bill (No. 155), introduced to amend, 176. Second reading and referred to Municipal Committee, 210. Reported, 220.

18. Bill (No. 159), introduced to amend, 179. Second reading, 196. House goes into Committee on, 205. Third reading, 262. R.A., 279. (16 Geo. V, c. 52.)

19. Bill (No. 164), introduced to amend, 183. Second reading, 196. House goes into Committee on, 206. Third reading, 262. R.A., 279. (16 Geo. V, c. 52.)

20. Bill (No. 183), introduced to amend, 208. Second reading, 221. House goes into Committee on, 242. Third reading, 262. R.A., 280. (16 Geo. V, c. 52.)

21. Bill (No. 188), introduced, "The Municipal Act, 1926," 227. Second reading, 227. House goes into Committee on, 243. Third reading, 263. R.A., 280. (16 Geo. V, c. 52.)

22. Committee to be appointed, 9. Appointed, 25. Report, 157, 190, 220.

MUSEUM, ROYAL ONTARIO:—See under *Royal.*

NATIONAL COUNCIL OF Y.M.C.A.:

Petition for an Act respecting, 42. Reported, 87. Bill (No. 53), introduced and referred to Private Bills Committee, 89. Withdrawn and fees, less actual cost of printing, remitted, 246.

NEGLECTED CHILDREN:—See under *Children.*

NIAGARA FALLS:
Question *re* cost of illumination of, 105.
Report of Queen Victoria Park Commission, 51, 198. *(Sessional Papers Nos. 34 and 52.)*

NICHOLSON, AUSTIN AND G. B.:—See under *Lands and Forests.*

NIPIGON LAKE:
Question *re* pulpwood tenders, 46.

NIPIGON REGION:
Question *re* cutting pulpwood in, 149, 268.

NIPISSING CENTRAL RAILWAY:
1. Question *re* expenditure on extension to Rouyn, 195.
2. Question *re* ownership and extension into Rouyn Mining Region, 47.
3. Question *re* construction from Swastika and Rouyn Gold Mines, 110.

NORFOLK NORTH:
Question as to resignation of member, etc., 29.

NORTH HURON:
Question *re* issue of beer permits in, 122.

NORTHERN DEVELOPMENT AND COLONIZATION ROADS BRANCH:
Report presented, 198. *(Sessional Papers No. 53.)*

NORTHERN ONTARIO:
1. Bill (No. 116), introduced to provide for development of, 107. Second reading, 125. House goes into Committee on, 153. Third reading, 261. R.A., 278. (16 Geo. V, c. 10.)
2. Bill (No. 160), introduced to make further provision for development of, 183. Resolution introduced, 203. Second reading, 204. House goes into Committee on, 212. Third reading, 262. R.A., 279. (16 Geo. V, c. 9.)
3. Moneys voted for, 203.—See under *Lieutenant-Governor.*
4. Questions *re* Legislative Secretary for, 48, 49, 59.
5. Question *re* expenditure on roads by electoral districts, 134.
6. Question *re* how much expended for roads, bridges and administration in, 68.
7. Motion, appropriation should be approved by House in estimates before expended. Withdrawn, 186.
8. Question *re* electric power developed in, 69.
9. Return of requirements and resources by Legislative Secretary of, 100. *(Sessional Papers No. 42.)*

NORTH YORK, TOWNSHIP OF:
Petition for an Act respecting, 13. Reported, 54. Bill (No. 14), introduced and referred to Private Bills Committee, 57. Reported, 178. Second reading, 185. House goes into Committee on, 197. Third reading, 209. R.A., 277. (16 Geo. V, c. 107.)

O AKLEY, GEORGE:

Question *re* stone-work for new Government Building, 102.

Question *re* contract for East Block, 67.

OIL, ROAD:

Question *re* purchase of, 103.

Question *re* use of, in New Ontario, 149.

OJIBWAY, TOWN OF:

Petition for an Act respecting, 13. Reported, 86. Bill (No. 7), introduced and referred to Private Bills Committee, 91. Withdrawn, and fees, less actual cost of printing, remitted, 246.

ONTARIO ATHLETIC COMMISSION:

Report presented, 58. (*Sessional Papers No. 36.*)

ONTARIO COMPANIES ACT:

1. Bill (No. 127), introduced to amend, 119. Second reading, 140. House goes into Committee on, 145. House again in Committee on, 256. Third reading, 261. R.A., 278. (16 Geo. V, c. 48.)

2. Bill (No. 168), introduced to amend, 191. Second reading, 205. House goes into Committee on, 212. House again in Committee on, 257. Third reading, 262. R.A., 279. (16 Geo. V, c. 48.)

ONTARIO ELECTION LAWS:—See under *Election Laws.*

ONTARIO GAME AND FISHERIES ACT:—See under *Game and Fisheries.*

ONTARIO GOVERNMENT DISPENSARIES:—See under *Liquor.*

ONTARIO HABEAS CORPUS ACT:—See under *Habeas Corpus.*

ONTARIO INSURANCE ACT:—Bill to amend. See *Insurance.*

ONTARIO INSURANCE ACT—UNDER SECTION 73.

Report presented, 116. (*Sessional Papers No. 43.*)

ONTARIO, NORTH, RIDING OF:

Return *re* appointments in, 141. (*Sessional Papers No. 46.*)

ONTARIO RAILWAY AND MUNICIPAL BOARD:

Report presented, 240. (*Sessional Papers No. 24.*)

ONTARIO SUMMARY CONVICTIONS ACT:—See under *Summary Convictions.*

ONTARIO TELEPHONE ACT:

Bill (No. 101), introduced to amend, 71. Second reading, 97. House goes into Committee on, 99. Third reading, 261. R.A., 278. (16 Geo. V, c. 51.)

PETERBORO ELECTRIC RAILWAY:
Question as to Province paying losses of, 131, 160.

PETITIONS:
1. Children's Protection Act, 220.
2. Game, 42.
3. Highways, Provincial, 272.
4. Rural School Boards, 54, 199.
5. United Church of Canada Act, 126, 142, 163, 178, 182, 190, 199, 220, 272.
6. Wolf Bounties, 272.

PHYSICIANS AND SURGEONS, GRANT TO BANTING RESEARCH FUND:—See under *College of Physicians and Surgeons.*

PICTURE FILMS:—See under *Films.*

PLANNING AND DEVELOPMENT ACT:
Bill (No. 100), introduced to amend, 71. Second reading, 98. Reported 157. House goes into Committee on, 189. Third reading, 209. R.A., 277. (16 Geo. V, c. 54.)

PLEBISCITE, 1924:
Question *re* cost of, 161.

POLICE BENEFIT FUND, OTTAWA:—See under *Ottawa.*

POLICE BENEFIT FUND, TORONTO:—See under *Toronto.*

POLICE MAGISTRATES:
Question *re* conviction under O.T.A., 165.

POLITICAL CONTRIBUTIONS:
Bill (No. 131), introduced to prohibit giving by brewers, etc., 127. Second reading and referred to Special Committee, 151. *Not reported.*

PORT ARTHUR, CITY OF:
Petition for an Act respecting, 14. Reported, 87. Bill (No. 18), introduced and referred to Private Bills Committee, 89. Reported, 178. Second reading, 185. House goes into Committee on, 197. Third reading, 209. R.A., 277. (16 Geo. V, c. 90.)

PORT ARTHUR, ELECTORAL DISTRICT OF:
Question *re* expenditure on Capital Account, 164.

POUND NET LICENSES:
Return presented, 85. (*Sessional Papers No. 40.*)

POWER COMMISSION ACT:
Bill (No. 124), introduced to amend, 119. Order for second reading discharged and Bill withdrawn, 204.
Bill (No. 163), introduced to amend, 183. Second reading, 205. House goes into Committee on, 212. Third reading, 262. R.A., 279. (16 Geo. V, c. 17.)

PSYCHIATRIC HOSPITALS:—See under *Hospitals*.

PUBLIC ACCOUNTS:

1. Committee to be appointed, 9. Appointed, 25.
2. Motion fixing date of first meeting, 98.
3. Certain questions *re* Lyons Fuel & Supply Co. referred to, 107.
4. Report, 244, 245. (*Appendix No. 3.*)
5. Minority report not properly lodged, 251.
6. Accounts presented, 127. (*Sessional Papers No. 1.*) Referred to Committee, 127.
7. Committee authorized to sit concurrently with meetings of Legislature, 177.
8. Motion adding members to, 113.

PUBLIC AUTHORITIES PROTECTION ACT:

Bill (No. 87), introduced to consolidate and amend, 27. Second reading, 70. House goes into Committee on, 97. House again in Committee on, 254. Third reading, 261. R.A., 278. (16 Geo. V, c. 30.)

PUBLIC HIGHWAYS, IMPROVEMENT OF:—See under *Highways*.

PUBLIC LANDS ACT:—See under *Lands*.

PUBLIC LIBRARIES ACT:—See under *Libraries*.

PUBLIC PARKS ACT:

Bill (No. 138), introduced to amend, 144. Second reading and referred to Municipal Committee, 161. Reported, 190. House goes into Committee on, 206. Third reading, 240. R.A., 277. (16 Geo. V, c. 57.)

PUBLIC SCHOOL TRUSTEES, TOWNSHIP BOARDS:—See under *Schools*.

PUBLIC SERVICE SUPERANNUATION BOARD:

Report presented, 180. (*Sessional Papers No. 50.*)

PUBLIC SERVICE SUPERANNUATION FUND:

Question *re* payments, 170.

PUBLIC SERVICE WORKS ON HIGHWAYS ACT:—See under *Highways*.

PUBLIC VEHICLES ACT:

Bill (No. 149), introduced to amend, 155. Second reading, 162. House goes into Committee on, 174. House again in Committee on, 257. Third reading, 261. R.A., 279. (16 Geo. V, c. 59.)

PUBLIC WORKS:

Report presented, 156. (*Sessional Papers No. 8.*)

PUBLIC WORKS ON HIGHWAYS:

Question *re* Members of Legislature interested in contracts on, 28.

16. As to tenders for construction of new Administration Building, 32.

17. As to tenders received for limits in Lake Nipigon region, 46.

18. As to Councils passing by-laws in pursuance of the Corn Borer Act, 1925, 38.

19. As to how many members of the Government have been to Europe since becoming Ministers, 38.

20. As to what new appointments were made for collecting the gasoline and beverage taxes, 39.

21. As to consideration by Government of a policy of Government control of the sale of liquor, 40.

22. As to whether speeches were made by the Minister of Lands and Forests in New Ontario, 47.

23. As to promise to pay half cost of paving Wellington Street, Sault Ste. Marie, and successful tenderer for work, 80.

24. As to purchase of lands at Sault Ste. Marie for Court House extension, and aerodrome site, 81.

25. As to plan of Government *re* Government control of liquor traffic, 40.

26. As to amount paid by Province for highways maintenance, 40.

27. As to ownership of the Nipissing Central Railway, and extension in Rouyn Mining Region, 47.

28. As to tenders for 1925 supply of flour for the School for Deaf, Belleville, 101.

29. As to cost to Province of the Agricultural Enquiry Committee, 41.

30. As to whether Mr. F. H. Keefer took part in Dominion election in Northern Ontario ridings, 48.

31. As to date of appointment of Mr. F. H. Keefer to the Legislative Secretarial post for Northern Ontario, and payment of salary, 49.

32. As to amount of money paid to Mr. Keefer, Legislative Secretary for Northern Ontario, 59.

33. As to revenue from automobile, truck and motor bus licenses and gasoline tax, 59.

34. As to what persons or organizations made recommendations for Waterloo County appointment, 41.

35. As to date of appointment of the English-French Enquiry Commission, 60.

36. As to number of pupils in attendance at English-French Training Schools, 264.

37. As to what English-French Schools were visited by Inspectors in 1925, 63.

38. As to conferences with British officials and others respecting immigration, 65.

61. As to what contracts have been awarded the Walsh Construction Co. for road building, 101.

62. As to whether Mr. Gordon appeared as counsel for Mr. Charles Matthews, 93.

63. As to whether Mr. T. A. Lennox appeared as counsel for Mr. Peter Smith, 93.

64. As to Lyons Fuel Supply Co. soliciting business from persons having Government contracts, 107.

65. As to whether Hon. Jas. Lyons is president of the Sault Ste. Marie Coal & Wood Co., and if said company supplied coal to Lake Superior Pulp and Paper Co., 107.

66. As to whether Hon. Jas. Lyons is still president of the Lyons Fuel & Supply Co., and as to goods supplied by the company to Department of Lands and Forests, 107.

67. As to holding a general election, 94.

68. As to the cost of construction of English-French Training School at Embrun, 102.

69. As to tender of Geo. Oakley & Son for stone work for new Government Building, Queen's Park, 102.

70. As to amount of fire insurance carried on property of the Province of Ontario, 146.

71. As to amount of fire insurance carried on property of the Hydro-Electric Power Commission, 121.

72. As to beer permits issued in ridings without the approval of the sitting member, 94.

73. As to a policy respecting regulation of the liquor traffic, 94.

74. As to an announcement respecting policy on liquor traffic, 94.

75. As to enquiries respecting persons to whom beer licenses were issued, 95.

76. As to how many years the McNamara Construction Co. received contracts from the Government, 109.

77. As to Nipissing Central Railway extension from Swastika to Rouyn, Que., 110.

78. As to kind of roofing specified to be used on new Administration Building, 103.

79. As to keeping records and issuing certificates by Department of Agriculture respecting seed grain, 95.

80. As to number of farm loans advanced by the Government in 1924, 95.

81. As to position held by A. B. Connell with Department of Lands and Forests at Sault Ste. Marie, 103.

82. As to profits of liquor dispensaries each year since established, 96.

83. As to whether there have been any changes in beer regulations, 96.

84. As to prosecutions of Ontario breweries, 122.

85. As to how many beer permits were issued in North Huron, 122.

86. As to what commissions were appointed by the late Government, 265.

87. As to quantity of road oil purchased by the Department of Lands and Forests and Northern Development Branch, 103.

88. As to expenditure on capital account in Northern Ontario Districts since the Government assumed office, 164.

89. As to amount of claim for extras in connection with Sudbury-Coniston Road, 104.

90. As to expenditure for gasoline and oil for Government aeroplanes, 104.

91. As to Government building an agricultural barn at Hearst, 110.

92. As to how many aeroplanes are owned by the Province, 104.

93. As to what Act or regulation contribution was made by the Government for street paving at Sault Ste. Marie, 111.

94. As to removal of aluminum plant from Massena to Lake St. John, 104.

95. As to payment by the Province towards Niagara Falls illumination, 105.

96. As to cost of collecting gasoline tax, 105.

97. As to Attorney-General and case of Rex vs. James Burns at Petrolia, 122.

98. As to registration of beekeepers under the Foul Brood Act, 1925, 111.

99. As to expenditure on Provincial highways within Oxford County, 105.

100 As to ownership of the Peterborough Electric Railway, 131.

101. As to ownership of the Campbellford pulp mill, 131.

102. As to electric railways operated by the Hydro-Electric Power Commission, 132.

103. As to townships complying with the Highway Laws Amendment Act, 1924, 105.

104. As to convictions made for premises holding beer permits, in Toronto, Hamilton and Windsor, 132.

105. As to convictions recorded for selling, having or keeping over-strength beer in Toronto, Hamilton and Windsor, 133.

106. As to convictions for breaches of the O.T.A. for each fiscal year since 1919-20, 122.

107. As to prescriptions issued by physicians, 123.

108. As to establishment and amount of Hydro-Electric Power Extension Fund, 123.

109. As to audits of Government departments other than those made by the Provincial Auditor, and as to any misappropriation of funds, see Order for Return, 270.

163. As to the amount contributed by the Government to the Public Service Superannuation Fund, 170.

164. As to details of Special Warrants, page N-25 (Department of Provincial Treasurer), Public Accounts, 171.

165. As to details of Special Warrants, page M-11 (Department of Labour), Public Accounts, 171.

166. As to amount of current revenue each year since 1919, 171.

167. As to purchase of moving-picture plant, 200.

168. As to salary, etc., of Superintendent of Insurance, R. Leighton Foster, 171.

169. As to estimates and expenditures for fire ranging, 172.

170. As to cost of radio publicity in connection with the visit of Mr. Rothaphel and his company (Roxy and his gang), 267.

171. As to expenditure on the Chippewa Hydro-Electric Power Development, 179.

172. As to estimates and expenditure for the Moving Picture Bureau, 201.

173. As to details *re* company cutting pulpwood on Cons. 6, 7, 8, 9, Nipigon Township, 268.

174. As to purchase of United States naval airplanes from the Laurentide Air Service, 191.

175. As to how many liquor dispensaries and their location, 191.

176. As to maintenance of Provincial Highways in Oxford County, 201.

177. As to number of widows receiving assistance under the Mothers' Allowance Act, 268.

178. As to maintenance of the provincial highway between Barrie and Orillia. (Order for return) 202.

179. As to permits issued for exportation of pulpwood to the United States, 226.

180. As to the expenditure *re* the proposed extension of the Nipissing Central Railway to Rouyn District, 180.

181. As to the employment of Thomas Tooms in the Treasury Department, 202.

182. As to additional mileage added to provincial highways under present Government, 195.

183. As to money spent on trunk road running west from Sault Ste. Marie, 269.

184. As to exhibition film known as "Indoor Sports," 269.

185. As to existence of the Aero Film Company, Limited, 269.

186. As to guarantee by the Province of radial railway bonds, 196.

RENFREW, TOWN OF:

Petition for an Act respecting the Victoria Hospital at, 176, and read under suspended Rule, 176. Bill (No. 61), introduced on suspended Rule and referred direct to Private Bills Committee, 177. Reported, 221. Fees remitted, less penalties and actual cost of printing, 221. Second reading, 241. House goes into Committee on, 242. Third reading, 263. R.A., 280. (16 Geo. V, c. 118.)

REPRESENTATION ACT:

Bill (No. 173), introduced to amend, 199. Second reading, 210. Referred to Special Committee, 200. Reported, 251. House goes into Committee on, 252. Third reading, 263. R.A., 280. (16 Geo. V, c. 2.)

Special Committee appointed re Bill (No. 173), 200. Report, 251.

REQUIREMENTS AND RESOURCES:—See under *Northern Ontario Legislative Secretary.*

RETURNS ORDERED:

1. Showing correspondence relative to an agreement between the Department of Lands and Forests and G. B. Nicholson and Austin and Nicholson, 106.

2. Showing copies of contracts made by the late Government and E. W. Backus in regard to trespasses, 106.

3. Showing all correspondence between Government and persons being lessees of pulp and timber limits, watersheds of Kapuskasing, Ground Hog and Mattagami Rivers and Lake Nipigon, 113.

4. Showing cost of maintenance of Barrie-Orillia Highway for each of the past four fiscal years, 202.

5. Showing all correspondence respecting contracts Nos. 706, 709 and 720 referred to in Public Accounts, page J-15, 196.

6. Showing information as to audits other than those of the Provincial Auditor carried on in Government Departments or Institutions under their control, 270.

7. Showing amount expended on Colonization Roads in Algoma, Sudbury, Sault Ste. Marie, etc., 85. (Ordered, March 6th, 1925, p. 81.)

8. Showing what amounts paid to legal counsel in litigation re Separate Schools, 141. (Ordered March 20th, 1925, p. 157.)

9. Showing maximum available supply of electric power in each of the systems, Niagara, etc., 84. (Ordered February 20th, 1925, p. 36.)

10. Showing the amount of money paid for fire insurance by the Hydro-Electric Power Commission, 180. (Ordered March 26th, 1925, p. 82.)

11. Showing information furnished to Legislature as to requirements and resources of electoral districts in the Provincial Judicial Districts by the Legislative Secretary, 100. (Ordered March 27th, 1925, p. 187.)

RURAL, SEPARATE AND PUBLIC SCHOOL GRANTS TO:—See *Education.*

SALE OF LIQUOR, GOVERNMENT CONTROL:—See under *Liquor.*

SANATORIA FOR CONSUMPTIVES:

1. Bill (No. 153), introduced to amend, 158. Order for second reading discharged and Bill withdrawn, 186.

2. Bill (No. 121), introduced to amend, 116. Second reading, 145. House goes into Committee on, 152. Third reading, 261. R.A., 278. (16 Geo. V, c. 72.)

SARNIA, CITY OF:

Petition for an Act respecting, 97. Reported, 129. Bill (No. 59), introduced and referred to Private Bills Committee, 130. Reported, 246. Second reading, 247. House goes into Committee on, 260. Third reading, 263. R.A., 281. (16 Geo. V, c. 92.)

SAULT STE. MARIE, CITY OF:

Petition for an Act respecting, 42. Reported, 129. Bill (No. 52), introduced and referred to Private Bills Committee, 130. Reported, 221. Second reading, 241. House goes into Committee on, 242. Third reading, 263. R.A., 280. (16 Geo. V, c. 93.)

1. Question *re* Wellington Street pavement 80, 110.

2. Question *re* cost of Trunk Road running west of, 269.

SAULT STE. MARIE, ELECTORAL DISTRICT OF:

1. Question *re* expenditure on capital account, 85, 164.

2. Question *re* cost of Government aerodrome, 78.

3. Question *re* contract for Government aerodrome, 77, 78.

SCHOOL LAWS ACT:

Bill (No. 151), introduced to amend, 155. Second reading, 173. House goes into Committee on, 206. Third reading, 261. R.A., 279. (16 Geo. V, c. 67.)

SCHOOLS, LEGISLATIVE GRANTS TO:—See under *Education.*

SCHOOL TRUSTEES, TOWNSHIP BOARDS OF:—See *Education.*

SECRETARY AND REGISTRAR:

Report presented, 240. (*Sessional Papers No. 55.*)

STANDING ORDERS:

1. Committee to be appointed, 9. Appointed, 24.
2. Report of, 54, 86, 128.
3. Time extended for presenting Petitions, 55, 88.
4. Time extended for presenting Private Bills, 55, 88.

STATISTICS BRANCH:—See under *Agriculture, Ontario, Department of.*

STATUTE DISTRIBUTION:

Report presented, 128. (*Sessional Papers No. 44.*)

STATUTE REVISION:—See under *Revision.*

STOCK COMPANIES, SHAREHOLDERS IN:

Question *re* consent of Minister for searches, 49.

STORMONT:

Question *re* issuing Beer permits in riding of, 165.

STRATFORD, CITY OF:

Petition for an Act respecting, 14. Reported, 87. Bill (No. 28), introduced and referred to Private Bills Committee, 89. Reported, 115, Second reading, 136. House goes into Committee on, 140. Third reading, 187. R.A., 276. (16 Geo. V, c. 95.)

SUBURBAN BUSINESS, CONSUMERS' GAS COMPANY:—See under *Toronto.*

SUDBURY:

Return *re* expenditure on roads, 85. (*Sessional Papers No. 38.*)

SUDBURY TO CONISTON ROAD:

Question *re* claim for extras in connection with, 104.

SUMMARY CONVICTIONS ACT:

Bill (No. 177), introduced to amend, 200. Second reading, 210. House goes into Committee on, 223. Third reading, 262. R.A., 280. (16 Geo. V, c. 31.)

SUPERINTENDENT OF INSURANCE:—See under *Insurance.*

SUPPLY:

1. Motion to go into, 117.
2. Budget delivered and debate on, 128; adjourned, 128, 156, 177.
3. Amendment proposed, increasing revenue by Government control of liquor, 146, defeated, 180.
4. Estimates presented, 127, 191, 205. (*Sessional Papers No. 2.*)
5. House goes into Committee of Supply, 181.
6. Order for House to again go into Committee of Supply and amendment proposed *re* adoption of systematic scheme of provincial taxation, 197. Defeated, 198.

7. House again goes into Committee of Supply, 189, 198, 207, 213, 214, 215, 216, 217, 218, 219.

8. Resolutions reported, and concurred in, 228, 229, 230, 231, 232, 233, 234, 235, 236, 237, 238.

9. Motion to go into Committee of Ways and Means, 239. Goes into Committee, 239. Resolutions reported, 239.

10. Bill of Supply (No. 190), introduced. Second and third readings, 239. R.A., 281. (16 Geo. V, c. 1.)

SURROGATE COURTS ACT:

Bill (No. 157), introduced to amend, 179. Second reading, 196. House goes into Committee on, 207. Third reading, 261. R.A., 279. (16 Geo. V, c. 23.)

SYDERE, ARTHUR H.:

House adjourned out of respect for memory of the late Clerk, 52 .

TAX, BEVERAGE AND GASOLINE:

Question *re* collection of, 31, 105.

TAX ON DOGS AND PROTECTION OF SHEEP:—See under *Dogs*.

TECK, TOWNSHIP OF:

Petition for an Act respecting, 20. Reported, 55. Bill (No. 47), introduced and referred to Private Bills Committee, 57. Reported, 97. Second reading, 106. House goes into Committee on, 113. Third reading, 186. R.A., 275. (16 Geo. V, c. 96.)

TELEPHONE ACT:—See under *Ontario Telephone Act*.

TEMISKAMING AND NORTHERN ONTARIO RAILWAY COMMISSION:

1. Report presented, 240. (*Sessional Papers No. 23.*)

2. Question *re* issue of bonds by, 136.

TEMISKAMING & NORTHERN ONTARIO RAILWAY:

1. *Re* ownership Nipissing Central Railway, 47.

2. *Re* extension from Swastika to Rouyn, 119, 195.

TEMPERANCE ACT:—See under *Ontario*.

THORA, TOWNSHIP OF:

Petition for an Act respecting, 14. Reported, 87. Bill (No. 29), introduced and referred to Private Bills Committee, 90. Reported, 143. Second reading, 161. House goes into Committee on, 173. Third reading, 187. R.A., 276. (16 Geo. V, c. 97.)

TILLEY, W. N., K.C.:

Question *re* legal fees paid to, 226.

TIMBER LIMITS:

Question *re* tenders for, in Kapuskasing, Ground Hog and Mattagami watersheds, 44.

Question *re* tenders in Lake Nipigon, Thunder Bay District, 46.

TISDALE, TOWNSHIP OF:

Petition for an Act respecting, 100. Reported, 129. Bill (No. 60), introduced and referred to Private Bills Committee, 130. Reported, 221. Second reading, 241. House goes into Committee on, 242. Third reading, 263. R.A., 280. (16 Geo. V, c. 98.)

TOOMS, THOMAS:

Question *re* employment in Treasury Department, 202.

TORONTO, CITY OF:

1. Petition for an Act respecting, 13. Reported, 54. Bill (No. 12), introduced and referred to Private Bills Committee, 57. Reported 246. Second reading, 247. House goes into Committee on 259. Third reading, 263. R.A., 277. (16 Geo. V, c. 99.)

2. Petition for an Act respecting Board of Education insurance, 14. Reported, 87. Bill (No. 20), introduced and referred to Private Bills Committee, 90. Bill withdrawn, and fees, less actual cost of printing, remitted, 246.

3. Petition for an Act to own and operate ferry service, 15. Reported, 54. Bill (No. 38), introduced and referred to Private Bills Committee, 57. Reported, 157. Second reading, 173. House goes into Committee on, 188. Third reading, 209. R.A., 277. (16 Geo. V, c. 100.)

4. Petition for an Act respecting certain grants, 42. Reported, 88. Bill (No. 54), introduced and referred to Private Bills Committee, 89. Reported, 190. Second reading, 204. House goes into Committee on 211. Third reading, 240. R.A., 280. (16 Geo. V, c. 101.)

5. Petition for an Act respecting suburban business of Consumers' Gas Company, 42. Reported, 88. Bill (No. 55), introduced and referred to Private Bills Committee, 98. *Not reported.*

6. Petition for an Act respecting special surplus account, Consumers' Gas Company, 42. Reported, 88. Bill (No. 56), introduced and referred to Private Bills Committee, 98. *Not reported.*

7. Petition for transfer of certain radial railways from Hydro-Electric Power Commission to, and read under suspended Rule, 203. Bill (No. 180), introduced on suspended Rule and referred direct to Private Bills Committee, 203. Reported, 246. Second reading, 247. House goes into Committee on, 260. Third reading, 263. R.A., 281. (16 Geo. V, c. 113.)

8. Bill (No. 184), introduced respecting, and Royal Agricultural Winter Fair Association, 208. Second reading, 221. House goes into Committee on, 242. House again in Committee on, 258. Third reading, 263. R.A., 280. (16 Geo. V, c. 20.)

9. Bill (No. 187), introduced respecting widening of Bloor Street, 227. Second reading, 241. House goes into Committee on, 257. Third reading, 263. R.A., 280. (16 Geo. V, c. 102.)

TORONTO EAST GENERAL HOSPITAL:
Petition for an Act to incorporate, 13.   Reported, 86.   Bill (No. 4), introduced and referred to Private Bills Committee, 91.   Reported, 115. Fees, less actual cost of printing, remitted, 115.   Second reading, 136. House goes into Committee on, 162. Third reading, 261. R.A., 278. (16 Geo. V, c. 116.)

TORONTO POLICE BENEFIT FUND:
Petition for an Act respecting, 20.   Reported, 87.   Bill (No. 43), introduced and referred to Private Bills Committee 90.   Bill withdrawn, and fees, less actual cost of printing, remitted, 246.

TORONTO TRANSPORTATION COMMISSION:
Question re payment of licenses, 269.

TORONTO UNIVERSITY:—See under University of Toronto.

TORONTO, WESTERN HOSPITAL:
Petition for an Act to amalgamate with Grace Hospital, Toronto, 20.   Reported, 55.   Bill (No. 42), introduced and referred to Private Bills Committee, 57. Reported, 98. Fees, less actual cost of printing, remitted, 98. Second reading, 108. House goes into Committee on, 130. Third reading, 186. R.A., 276. (16 Geo. V, c. 117.)

TOWNSHIP BOARDS OF PUBLIC SCHOOL TRUSTEES:—See under Education.

TRAFFIC HIGHWAY ACTS:—See under Highways.

TRAVELLING EXPENSES:—See under Ministers.

TRANSIENT TRADERS, LICENSING OF:—See under Hawkers.

TRUSTEE ACT:
Bill (No. 70), introduced to consolidate and amend, 15.   Second reading, 69.   House goes into Committee on, 96.   House again in Committee on, 253. Third reading, 261. R.A., 278. (16 Geo. V, c. 40.)

UNITED CHURCH OF CANADA ACT:
Petition for an Act to amend, 42.   Reported, 87.   Bill (No. 22), introduced and referred to Private Bills Committee, 92.   Reported, 246. Second reading, 247. House goes into Committee on, 259. Third reading, 263. R.A., 280. (16 Geo. V, c. 114.)

WALKERVILLE, TOWN OF:

Petition for Act respecting, 42. Reported, 55. Bill (No. 48), introduced and referred to Private Bills Committee, 82. Reported, 175. Second reading, 185. House goes into Committee on, 197. Third reading, 209. R.A., 277. (16 Geo. V, c. 103.)

WALSH CONSTRUCTION COMPANY:

Question *re* contracts awarded to, by Minister of Lands and Forests, 101.

WARRANTS, SPECIAL:

Question *re*, 170, 171.

WATER, DIVERSION AT CHICAGO FROM GREAT LAKES SYSTEM:

Resolution objecting to, 274.

WATER FLOW AT CHICAGO:

Resolution *re* control of, 274.

WATERFORD, VILLAGE OF:

Petition for an Act respecting, 19. Reported, 87. Bill (No. 15), introduced and referred to Private Bills Committee, 90. Reported, 114. Second reading, 125. House goes into Committee on, 130. Third reading, 186. R.A., 276. (16 Geo. V, c. 104.)

WAYS AND MEANS:—See *Supply.*

WELLAND AND PORT COLBORNE RAILWAY:

Petition for an Act to incorporate, 12. Reported, 54. Bill (No. 1), introduced and referred to Railway Committee, 56. Reported, 118. Second reading, 137. House goes into Committee on, 152. Third reading, 187. R.A., 276. (16 Geo. V, c. 112.)

WESTON, TOWN OF, AND THE TORONTO TRANSPORTATION COMMISSION:

Petition for an Act respecting the Township of York, 14. Reported, 55. Bill (No. 19), introduced and referred to Private Bills Committee, 57. Reported, 246. Second reading, 247. House goes into Committee on, 259. Third reading, 263. R.A., 280. (16 Geo. V, c. 105.)

WHITBY AND DARLINGTON TOWNSHIPS:

Return, relating to formation of new union school section, 99.

WHITEFISH BAY:

Return *re* Issue of Pound Net Licenses, 85. (*Sessional Papers No. 40.*)

WHITNEY BLOCK:—See *Administration Building.*

WIDENING OF BLOOR STREET:—See *Toronto.*

WIDOWS, RIGHTS OF, IN DECEASED HUSBAND'S ESTATES:
Bill (No. 130), introduced respecting, 127. Second reading, 151, and referred to the Legal Committee, 151. Reported 259. Ordered that Bill be withdrawn, 259.

WILLS ACT:

Bill (No. 174), introduced to amend, 200. Second reading, 211. House goes into Committee on, 222. Third reading, 262. R.A., 279. (16 Geo V, c. 39.)

WINDSOR RIDING OF:

Question *re* issuing of Beer permits in, 164.

WORKMEN'S COMPENSATION ACT:

1. Bill (No. 68), introduced to amend, 11. Second reading, 21. House goes into Committee on, 131. *Bill withdrawn.*

2. Bill (No. 179), introduced to amend, 200. Second reading, 210. House goes into Committee on, 223. Third reading, 262. R.A., 280. (16 Geo. V, c. 42.)

WORKMEN'S COMPENSATION BOARD:

Report presented, 239. (*Sessional Papers No. 28.*)

Y.M.C.A.:—See under *National Council.*

YORK, TOWNSHIP OF:

Petition for an Act respecting, 14. Reported, 87. Bill (No. 25), introduced and referred to Private Bills Committee, 91. Reported, 182. Second reading, 196. House goes into Committee on, 211. Third reading, 240. R.A., 277. (16 Geo. V, c. 108).

Petition for an Act to incorporate as Town of York, 24. Reported, 88. Bill (Nô. 44), introduced and referred to Private Bills Committee, 92. Reported, 182. Withdrawn, 182. Fees, less actual cost of printing, remitted, 182.

YORK, EAST, TOWNSHIP OF:—See under *East York.*

YORK, NORTH, TOWNSHIP OF:—See under *North York.*

YOUNG, McGREGOR, K.C.:

Question *re* legal fees paid to, 226.

LIST OF SESSIONAL PAPERS

PRESENTED TO THE HOUSE DURING THE SESSION.

Title.	No.	Remarks.
Accounts, Public.....................................	1	*Printed.*
Agriculture, Department of (Minister), Report..........	21	*Printed.*
Agriculture, Department of (Statistics), Report.........	22	*Printed.*
Agriculture Enquiry Committee, Report...............	48	*Printed.*
Appointments in Riding of North Ontario..............	46	*Not Printed.*
Auditor's Report....................................	27	*Printed.*
Children's Protection Act, Report.....................	19	*Printed.*
Civil Service Commissioner, Report....................	59	*Not Printed.*
Education, Report...................................	11	*Printed.*
Education, Department of Act, Section 27..............	54	*Not Printed.*
Education, Orders-in-Council.........................	31	*Not Printed.*
Estimates...	2	*Printed.*
Extra-mural Employment, Report.....................	61	*Not Printed.*
Game and Fisheries, Report..........................	9	*Printed.*
Game and Fisheries Committee, Report...............	49	*Printed.*
Gasoline and Oil Prices Commission, 1924..............	33	*Not Printed.*
Health, Report of Board (Births, Marriages and Deaths).	13–14	(14) *Printed.*
Highways, Expenditure on Provincial, Return..........	35–38	*Not Printed.*
Hospital and Charitable Institutions, Report...........	17	*Printed.*
Hospital for Insane, Feeble-minded Epileptics..........	15	*Printed.*
Hydro Commission, Insurance, Report.................	51	*Not Printed.*
Hydro-Electric Power Commission, Report.............	26	*Printed.*
Hydro System's Available Supply of Power.............	37	*Printed.*
Insurance and Friendly Societies, Report..............	6	*Printed.*
Labour Department, Report..........................	10	*Printed.*
Lands and Forests Department, Report...............	3	*Printed.*
Lands and Forests Department and Nicholsons, Return...	57	*Not Printed.*
Legal Offices, Report................................	5	*Printed.*
Library, Report.....................................	32	*Not Printed.*
Litigation, Amount to be paid to Counsel, etc., *re* Ottawa Separate Schools....................................	45	*Not Printed.*
Loan Corporations, Report...........................	7	*Printed.*
McNamara Construction Company, Return.............	58	*Not Printed.*
Mines Department, Report...........................	4	*Printed.*
Minimum Wage Board, Report........................	47	*Printed.*
Mothers' Allowance Commission, Report...............	60	*Not Printed.*

Title.	No.	Remarks.
Nicholson, A. and G. B., and Lands and Forests Department, Return	57	*Not Printed.*
Northern Development and Colonization Roads, Report	53	*Printed.*
Northern Ontario, Legislative Secretary, Requirements and Resources, Return	42	*Not Printed.*
Ontario Athletic Commission, Report	36	*Not Printed.*
Ontario Insurance Act, 1924, Orders-in-Council	43	*Not Printed.*
Ontario Railway and Municipal Board, Report	24	*Printed.*
Ontario Temperance Act, Report	20	*Printed.*
Ontario Veterinary College, Report	29	*Printed.*
Parole and Probation Board, Report	16	*Printed.*
Police Commissioner, Report	56	*Not Printed.*
Pound Net Licenses, Re-issuing of, Return	40	*Not Printed.*
Prisons and Reformatories, Report	18	*Printed.*
Provincial Bonds Purchased, Report	39	*Not Printed.*
Public Service Superannuation Board, Report	50	*Not Printed.*
Public Works, Report	8	*Printed.*
Queen Victoria Park Commission, 1924, Report	34	*Printed.*
Queen Victoria Park Commission, 1925, Report	52	*Printed.*
Roads, Expenditure in Algoma, Sudbury, etc., Return	38	*Not Printed.*
Rural, Public and Separate Schools, Grants to, Return	30	*Not Printed.*
School Sections 1 and 5, Whitby and Darlington Townships, Return	41	*Not Printed.*
Secretary and Registrar, Report	55	*Not Printed.*
Sentenced Persons Act, Report	61	*Not Printed.*
Statutes, Distribution, Report	44	*Not Printed.*
Temiskaming and Northern Ontario Railway, Report	23	*Printed.*
Toronto, University of, Report	12	*Printed.*
Workmen's Compensation Board, Report	28	*Printed.*

LIST OF SESSIONAL PAPERS

Arranged in Numerical Order with their Titles at full length; the name of the Member who moved the same, and whether ordered to be printed or not.

No. 1 | Public Accounts of the Province for the year ending October 31st, 1925. Presented to the Legislature, March 11th, 1926. *Printed*.

No. 2 | Estimates—Supplementary, for the service of the Province for the year ending October 31st, 1926. Presented to the Legislature, March 11th, 1926. *Printed*. Further Supplementary Estimates for the year ending October 31st, 1926. Presented to the House, March 26th, 1926. *Printed*. Estimates for the year ending October 31st, 1927. Presented to the Legislature, March 29th, 1926. *Printed*.

No. 3 | Report of the Department of Lands and Forests for the year 1925. Presented to the Legislature, March 31st, 1926. *Printed*.

No. 4 | Report of the Department of Mines for the year 1925. Presented to the Legislature, March 18th, 1926. *Printed*.

No. 5 | Report of the Inspector of Legal Offices for the year 1925. Presented to the Legislature, March 12th, 1926. *Printed*.

No. 6 | Report of the Superintendent of Insurance for the year 1925. Presented to the Legislature, March 26th, 1926. *Printed*.

No. 7 | Report of the Registrar of Loan Corporations for the year 1925. Presented to the Legislature, March 26th, 1926. *Printed*.

No. 8 | Report of the Department of Public Works for the year 1925. Presented to the Legislature, March 18th, 1926. *Printed*.

No. 9 | Report of the Department of Game and Fisheries for the year 1925. Presented to the Legislature, March 22nd, 1926. *Printed.*

No. 10 | Report of the Department of Labour for the year 1925. Presented to the Legislature, March 18th, 1926. *Printed*.

No. 11 | Report of the Department of Education for the year 1925. Presented to the Legislature, March 18th, 1926. *Printed*.

No. 12 | Report of the Board of Governors of the University of Toronto for the year 1925. Presented to the Legislature, February 11th, 1926. *Printed*.

No. 30 | Return to an Order of the House, that there be laid before this House a return of the Legislative grants for the year 1925 paid to Rural Public and Separate Schools in the Counties and Districts, and to Urban Public and Separate Schools in the Counties and Districts which, in accordance with the provisions of the amendment to the Schools Act, passed in 1922, were classed as Rural Schools and received grants as such. Presented to the Legislature, February 11th, 1926. Mr. Belanger. *Not Printed.*

No. 31 | Copies of the Regulations and Orders-in-Council made under the authority of the Department of Education Act, or of the Acts relating to public schools, separate schools or high schools. Presented to the Legislature, February 16th, 1926. *Not Printed.*

No. 32 | Report of the Librarian on the state of the Library for the year 1925. Presented to the Legislature, February 16th, 1926. *Not Printed.*

No. 33 | Report of G. T. Clarkson, Esq., appointed by Commission, dated June 5th, 1925, to enquire whether the prices at which gasoline and oils are sold to the people of Ontario are just and fair. Presented to the Legislature, March 7th, 1926. *Not Printed.*

No. 34 | Report of the Queen Victoria Niagara Falls Park Commission. Presented to the Legislature, February 22nd, 1926. *Printed.*

No. 35 | Return to an Order of the House, dated 3rd April, 1925, That there be laid before the House a Return, showing:—1. What was the total expenditure on account of Provincial Highways from the inception of the Provincial Highways System up to December 31st, 1924. 2. Of the expenditure stated in reply to Question No. 1, what amounts have been refunded to Ontario by (a) county municipalities, (b) cities, (c) by the Dominion Government. 3. Of the expenditure stated in reply to Question No. 1, what amounts have been levied upon but remain unpaid by (a) county municipalities, (b) cities, and (c) the Dominion Government. 4. Of the expenditure stated in reply to Question No. 1, what further amounts will be levied upon (a) county municipalities, (b) cities, (c) the Dominion Government. 5. What is the total amount of expenditure on Provincial Highways remaining after all deductions, to be borne by the Provincial Government. 6. Of the expenditure stated in reply to Question No. 1, what amount was expended upon repair and maintenance, as distinguished from construction. 7. Of the expenditure stated in reply to Question No. 1, what amounts have been refunded to Ontario by (a) county municipalities, (b) cities, and (c) by the Dominion Government. 8. Of the expenditure stated in reply to Question No. 6, what amounts have been levied upon, but remain unpaid, by (a) county municipalities, (b) cities, (c) the Dominion Government. 9. Of the expenditure stated in reply to Question No. 6, what further amounts will be levied upon (a) county municipalities, (b) cities, (c) the Dominion Government. 10. What is the total amount of expenditure on Provincial Highways for maintenance remaining after all deductions, to be borne by the Provincial Government. 11. Of the total expenditure by the Government upon highways in the Province of Ontario, what amount has been paid out of current revenue and what amount has been capitalized. 12. During the years 1921, 1922, 1923, what amount of the annual expenditure was paid out of revenue and what amount capitalized. 13. Against the capitalized debt in respect of the expenditure upon roads, have any sums been credited from any source whatsoever; if so, what amounts, from what source. 14. Of the capitalized debt in respect of roads, has there been any scheme or plan to retire this debt by a sinking fund or by annual payments. If so, what is the amount of the annual payment at the present time necessary to retire this debt. If no such plan has been in operation, what would be the annual sum necessary to retire the Government's capital expenditure upon roads, if such plan was adopted and over how many years would such plan run. Presented to the Legislature, February 22nd, 1926. Mr. Wallis. *Not Printed.*

No. 36   Report of the Ontario Athletic Commission for the year 1925. Presented to the Legislature, February 25th, 1926. *Not Printed.*

No. 37   Return to an Order of the House, dated February 20th, 1925, That there be laid before this House a Return showing:—1. What was the maximum available supply of electric power in each of the systems, Niagara System, St. Lawrence System, Rideau System, Ottawa System and the Central Ontario and Trent Systems, as operated under the Hydro-Electric Power Commission for Ontario in each of the years, 1919, 1920, 1921, 1922, 1923 and 1924. 2. What was the total distribution of electrical power by the Hydro-Electric Power Commission for Ontario in each of the said systems for each of said years. 3. What was the total demand upon the Hydro-Electric Power Commission for Ontario for electrical power in each of said systems in each of said years. 4. What further electrical power is procurable by Hydro-Electric Power Commission for Ontario in each of the above systems when the developments already undertaken or under construction are completed. 5. What is the maximum supply of electrical power procurable by the Hydro-Electric Power Commission for Ontario in each of said systems with the present developments completed and operating to full capacity. 6. What was the total combined supply of electrical power furnished by the Hydro-Electric Power Commission for Ontario from all of said systems combined in the year 1924. 7. What was the total demands for electrical power upon the Hydro-Electric Power Commission for Ontario in all of said systems combined for the year 1924? 8. What was the total amount of electrical power used through the Hydro-Electric Power Commission for Ontario in all of said systems combined in the year 1924. 9. What additional amount of electrical power is it estimated by the Hydro-Electric Power Commission for Ontario will be procured from the proposed development of power from the St. Lawrence River. 10. What is the estimated cost of the Hydro-Electric

Power Commission for Ontario of the proposed power developments contemplated by the Hydro-Electric Power Commission for Ontario on the River St. Lawrence. Presented to the Legislature, March 2nd, 1926. Mr. Sinclair. *Printed.*

No. 38   Return to the Order of the House, dated March 6th, 1925, That there be laid before this House a Return, showing what amount has been expended by the Province of Ontario, in (*a*) the provisional electoral district of Algoma; (*b*) the provisional electoral district of Sudbury; (*c*) the provisional electoral district of Sault Ste. Marie; (*d*) the provisional electoral district of Manitoulin, on account of (1) colonization roads, (2) roads under authority of by-laws, (3) trunk roads, (4) work or construction of any other kind, authorized or coming under the Northern or Northwestern Ontario Development Act, in each of the following years: 1905, 1906, 1907, 1908, 1909, 1910, 1911, 1912, 1913, 1914, 1915, 1916, 1917, 1918, 1919, 1920, 1921, 1922, 1923 and 1924; also the provisional electoral district of Nipissing for 1924, and the provisional electoral district of Sturgeon Falls for 1924. Presented to the Legislature, March 2nd, 1926, Mr. Mageau. *Not Printed.*

No. 39   Return to the Order of the House, dated March 20th, 1925, That there be laid before this House a Return, showing:—1. What amount of Provincial bonds has been purchased by the Government since January 1st, 1920. 2. In each purchase of bonds, what was (*a*) the date of purchase; (*b*) the date of maturity of bonds; (*c*) the interest rate of bonds; (*d*) the price paid for the bonds; (*e*) the person or firm through whom the purchase was made. Presented to the Legislature, March 2nd, 1926. Mr. Doherty. *Not Printed.*

No. 40   Return to the Order of the House, dated March 27th, 1925. Order of the House for a Return to be laid before this House showing all communications, letters and documents of all kinds passing between Mr. Trotter, of Little Current; David Irving, Fish Inspector, Little Current; Mr. Hawkins, of Blind River and the Department of Game and Fisheries, or any other Department of the Government, in connection with the issuing of pound net licenses in White Fish Bay. Presented to the Legislature, March 2nd, 1926. Mr. Sinclair. *Not Printed.*

No. 41   Return to the Order of the House for a Return showing all correspondence, documents, memorandums, petitions or papers of any kind, and in any way relating to the formation of a new union school section out of part of School Section No. 1 in East Whitby Township and part of School Section No. 5 in Darlington Township, now or at any time in the hands of the Minister of Education, or in any part of the Department of Education. Presented to the Legislature, March 4th, 1926. Mr. Sinclair. *Not Printed.*

No. 42   Return to the Order of the House for a Return showing all the information furnished to the Legislature as to the requirements and resources of the electoral districts in the provisional Judicial districts of Ontario by the Legislative Secretary for Northern Ontario, as required of him under "The Legislative Secretary for Northern Ontario Act, 1924," the times at which the same was furnished, and to which Minister the same was furnished, and showing, also, what duties in addition to those required by said Act were imposed upon the Legislative Secretary for Northern Ontario by Order-in-Council, letter or otherwise, the time when same were imposed, and the Report or Reports of the said Legislative Secretary for Northern Ontario upon the performance of the same. Furnished to the Legislature, March 4th, 1926. Mr. Sinclair. *Not Printed.*

No. 43   Copies of Orders-in-Council pursuant to section 73 of The Ontario Insurance Act, 1924. Presented to the Legislature, March 9th, 1926. *Not Printed.*

No. 44   Report on the Distribution of the Revised and Sessional Statutes for the year 1925. Presented to the Legislature, March 17th, 1926. *Not Printed.*

No. 45   Return to the Order of the House, dated March 20th, 1925, that there be laid before this House a Return, showing:—1. What is the amount or amounts paid by the Government of the Province of Ontario since the 1st of January, 1912, to date, to counsel, solicitors and other parties, mentioning the names of such counsel, solicitors and other parties, with the dates of the divers payments so made, in any of the proceedings in the following litigation, *viz.:* (1) *Re* Mackell *vs.* Board of Trustees of the Catholic Separate Schools of the City of Ottawa; (2) Motion to commit chairman of said Board for alleged contempt of Court; (3) Board of Trustees *vs.* The Quebec Bank and the Bank of Ottawa; (4) Board of Trustees *vs.* The Separate School Commission of Ottawa to have it declared that the Act of the Legislature of Ontario, being 5 George V, chapter 45, be declared *ultra vires;* (5) Board of Trustees *vs.* The Quebec Bank and the Corporation of the City of Ottawa; (6) Board of Trustees *vs.* Bank of Ottawa and othres; (7) Board of Trustees *vs.* Quebec Bank and others; (8) Board of Trustees *vs.* Murphy and others; (9) Consolidated case, Board of Trustees *vs.* Quebec Bank and others; (10) Reference to Appellate Division of the Supreme Court of Ontario; (11) Any amount paid by way of fees to counsel or solicitors for preparation and drafting of Act of the Legislature, and more particularly the Act of 5 George V, chapter 45, and 7 George V, chapters 59 and 60; (12) in all proceedings held before the First Division Court of the County of Carleton to garnishee moneys alleged to belong to said Board of Trustees and detained by the Corporation of the City of Ottawa; (13) generally, all sums paid by any of the Departments of the Government of this Province to counsel, solicitors, draughtsmen, agents and other parties in connection with any of the above litigations and matters. Presented to the Legislature, March 15th, 1926. Mr. Belanger. *Not Printed.*

PAPERS ORDERED BUT NOT BROUGHT DOWN.

JOURNALS

OF THE

LEGISLATIVE ASSEMBLY

OF THE

PROVINCE OF ONTARIO

WEDNESDAY, FEBRUARY 10TH, 1926.

PROCLAMATION.

H. COCKSHUTT.

CANADA.

PROVINCE OF ONTARIO.

GEORGE THE FIFTH, by the Grace of God, of the United Kingdom of Great Britain and Ireland, and of the British Dominions beyond the Seas, KING, Defender of the Faith, Emperor of India.

To Our Faithful, the Members elected to serve in the Legislative Assembly of Our Province of Ontario and to every of you—GREETING.

WILLIAM F. NICKLE, WHEREAS it is expedient for certain causes and Attorney-General. considerations to convene the Legislative Assembly of Our Province of Ontario, WE DO WILL that you and each of you and all others in this behalf interested, on WEDNESDAY, the TENTH day of FEBRU-ARY, A.D. 1926, at OUR CITY OF TORONTO, personally be and appear for the DESPATCH OF BUSINESS, to treat, act, do and conclude upon those things which in Our Legislature of Our Province of Ontario by the Common Council of Our said Province may, by the favour of God, be ordained. HEREIN FAIL NOT.

IN TESTIMONY WHEREOF, we have caused these Our Letters to be made Patent, and the Great Seal of Our Province of Ontario to be hereunto affixed. WITNESS, His Honour HENRY COCKSHUTT, LIEUTENANT-GOVERNOR of Our Province of Ontario, at Our Government House, in Our City of Toronto, in Our said Province, this TWENTY-THIRD day of DECEMBER, in the year of Our Lord one thousand nine hundred and twenty-five, and in the Sixteenth year of Our Reign.

By Command,

    C. F. BULMER,
        Clerk of the Crown in Chancery,
                Ontario.

Wednesday, the Tenth day of February, 1926, being the first day of the Third Meeting of the Sixteenth Legislature of the Province of Ontario for the Despatch of Business pursuant to a Proclamation of His Honour Henry Cockshutt, Lieutenant-Governor of the Province.

PRAYERS   3 O'clock P.M.

Mr. Speaker informed the House that he had received notifications of vacancies which had occurred since the last Session of the House, for the following Electoral Districts:—

    London.
    Cochrane.
    Centre Grey
    Kenora.
    Norfolk, North.
    Simcoe, South and
    Kent, East.

To the Honourable Speaker of the Legislative Assembly of the Province of Ontario:

We, the undersigned W. C. Chambers, Member for the said Legislative Assembly for the Electoral Division of West Wellington, and R. N. Berry, Member for the said Legislative Assembly for the Electoral Division of Haldi-mand, do hereby notify you that a vacancy has occurred in the representation in the said Legislative Assembly for the Electoral Division of London, by reason of the death of the Honourable Sir Adam Beck, Member elect for the said Electoral Division of London.

And we, the said W. E. Chambers and R. N. Berry, Members of the Assembly aforesaid, hereby require you to issue a new Writ for the Election of a Member to fill the said vacancy.

IN WITNESS WHEREOF, we have hereunto set our hands and seals on this First day of December, in the year of our Lord one thousand nine hundred and twenty-five.

<table>
<tr><td>Signed and sealed in
the presence of</td><td></td><td></td></tr>
<tr><td></td><td>(Sgd.)   W. C. CHAMBERS,</td><td>[L.S.]</td></tr>
<tr><td>C. C. HELE.</td><td>(Sgd.)   R. N. BERRY.</td><td>[L.S.]</td></tr>
</table>

To the Honourable the Speaker of the Legislative Assembly of the Province of Ontario:

Sir,—I hereby declare my intention of resigning my seat in the Legislative Assembly for the Electoral Division of Cochrane.

And I do hereby resign the same.

And I make this declaration and resignation under my hand and seal in the presence of the undersigned witnesses.

Signed and sealed on this Twenty-ninth day of September, A.D. 1925.

Signed and sealed in our presence the day and year above written.

Witnesses:

NELSON PARLIAMENT,
G. F. SUMMERS.   MALCOLM LANG.   [L.S.]

Owen Sound, Ont.,
October 6th, 1925.

To the Honourable the Speaker of the Legislative Assembly of Ontario:

I hereby declare my intention of resigning my seat in the Legislative Assembly of Ontario, for the Electoral District of Centre Grey, and I do hereby resign the same.

And I make this declaration and resignation under my hand and seal, and in the presence of the undersigned witnesses.

Signed and sealed in our presence at Owen Sound, the day and year above written.

Witnesses:

JNO. F. P. BIRNIE, of Owen Sound,
F. G. MACKAY, of Owen Sound.   D. CARMICHAEL.   [L.S.]

Fort Frances, Ont.,
October 7th, 1925.

Joseph Thompson, Speaker, Ontario Legislature,
   Toronto, Ont.

DEAR MR. THOMPSON,
Please accept my resignation as Member of the Ontario Legislature on account of accepting nomination for the Federal House.

Yours sincerely,

PETER HEENAN.   [L.S.]

Witnesses:

J. D. PRESTON, Loco. Eng., Kenora,
E. R. FINCH, Loco. Eng., Kenora.

Simcoe, Ont.,
October 8th, 1925.

To the Honourable the Speaker of the Legislative Assembly of the Province of Ontario:

Sir,—I hereby declare my intention of resigning my seat in the Legislative Assembly for Ontario, for the Electoral Division of North Norfolk.

And I do hereby resign the same.

And I make this declaration and resignation under my hand and seal in the presence of the undersigned witnesses.

Signed and sealed on this Eighth day of October, A.D. 1925.

Signed and sealed in our presence the day and year above written.

Witnesses:

C. A. TERHUNE,   [L.S.]
A. A. WINTER.   [L.S.]   GEO. D. SEWELL.   [L.S.]

Toronto, October 16th, 1925.

To the Honourable the Speaker of the Legislative Assembly of Ontario:

Sir,—I hereby declare my intention of resigning my seat in the Legislative Assembly of Ontario for the Electoral District of Simcoe, South.

And I do hereby resign the same.

And I make this declaration and resignation under my hand and seal in the presence of the undersigned witnesses.

Signed and sealed in our presence at the City of Toronto, County of York, the day and year above written.

H. M. ROBBINS,
C. C. HELE, of Toronto.   W. EARL ROWE.   [L.S.]

To the Honourable the Speaker of the Legislative Assembly of Ontario:

Sir,—I hereby declare my intention of resigning my seat in the Legislative Assembly for East Kent.

And I do hereby resign the same.

And I make this declaration and resignation under my hand and seal in the presence of the undersigned witnesses.

Signed and sealed on the Twenty-sixth day of November, A.D. 1925.

Signed and sealed in our presence the day and year above written.

C. H. EASSON,
M. NICHOLSON.   MANNING W. DOHERTY.   [L.S.]

The House then adjourned during pleasure.
And after some time the House resumed.

His Honour Henry Cockshutt, Lieutenant-Governor of the Province, then entered the House, and being seated on the Chair on the Throne, was pleased to open the Session by the following gracious Speech to the House:—

Mr. Speaker and Gentlemen of the Legislative Assembly—

It is my privilege to welcome you to the discharge of your Legislative duties at the Third Session of the Sixteenth Legislature of this Province.

Our grateful acknowledgments are due to Almighty God for the abundant harvest of the past year, as well as for the many other blessings we enjoy as a people.

Since you last met, our great Empire has experienced a severe loss through the death of the Queen Mother, whose gracious influence and ennobling qualities have so long endeared her to the British peoples. The many touching evidences of sympathy for His Majesty the King, and the other members of the Royal family, showed how widespread and deeprooted are the ties of affection by which the Empire is united.

It is reassuring to observe the signs of returning prosperity in this Province, largely due to the improved condition of Agriculture, which I trust will prove helpful to the whole Dominion.

.   In the interests of Agriculture, plans are under consideration for stimulating immigration, mainly from the British Isles. Special efforts will be made to encourage the bringing out of boys adaptable for farm work. Increasing attention is being devoted to the marketing of our agricultural products. It is recognized that the maintenance of high uniform quality is one of the main essentials. With this in view, legislation will be introduced for the further improvement of our dairy products. The action of the Government in reducing the rate of interest on farm loans has proven of great advantage to borrowers.

During the recess the Agricultural Inquiry Committee continued its labours and embodied the result in a further report dealing with co-operation and national marketing. This report contains a number of important suggestions looking towards the more advantageous disposal of the principal farm products. These valuable contributions to the information upon these subjects will be submitted to you for your consideration.

It is satisfactory to observe the progress of Education as shown by the generous public support it receives, the larger attendance of pupils and the increased supply of properly qualified teachers. Your attention will be directed again to the suggestion for the formation of Township School Boards, in the hope that the public discussion of this subject may lead to the adoption of means of reducing the cost of education to the rural tax payer. A systematic and thorough investigation has been instituted into the teaching of the English and French languages, and will be continued during the present school year. I am glad to observe that an opportunity to promote co-operation, where possible, with the Imperial authorities along educational lines has been afforded by an exchange of Inspectors, which should lead to advantageous results.

Ontario has experienced a distinct public loss through the death of the Honourable Sir Adam Beck, who was so long and so prominently identified with the development of Hydro-Electric Power. The work of the late Chairman of the Commission was highly valued, and so well in hand that the Commission, as reconstructed, will be able to continue this essential service to the Province with unimpaired efficiency and usefulness.

The development of power at Queenston having been carried to a successful completion during the past year, other sources of supply are now being considered to meet the growing needs of the Province. My Ministers are pressing

for the recognition of the right of the Province to proceed with the initial development of the St. Lawrence River. Meanwhile, they are hopeful that an amicable
arrangement will be effected shortly with our sister Province of Quebec whereby
the waters of the Ottawa River along the inter-provincial boundary will be
rendered available for development.

The efforts of the Department of Labour to improve the conditions of
employment in industrial establishments are meeting with encouraging co-operation. I am glad to observe the advance made in the prevention of accidents in
factories, and the continued improvement in general working conditions. The
business policy of the Government, in the development of our natural resources,
has already brought advantageous results, and its expansion and stabilization
will be of material benefit to the whole people of Canada.

Arrangements now being completed will ensure extensive industrial developments in our northern districts. It has been considered wise in utilizing our
forest resources to adopt approved methods of conservation in order that this
great source of natural wealth may, as far as practicable, be perpetuated. It
is a matter of much satisfaction that the loss from forest fires has been greatly
diminished, and that the air service is proving of valuable assistance in this
connection.

Another important step in advance by the Mining industry is marked by
the increased production of the past year. Ontario is maintaining and improving
its prominent position among the gold-producing communities. We are now
supplying nine-tenths of the world's requirements of nickel. Our silver fields
are yielding large and profitable returns, while new and valuable deposits of
ore are being discovered. It is significant that, notwithstanding this extensive
development, only a relatively small portion of the vast mineralized areas of
this Province has been explored.

Valuable work is being accomplished by the Department of Health through
co-operation with a number of national organizations for the promotion of better
conditions in the Province, and by assisting local communities in solving their
health problems. I am glad to observe the marked decrease in acute com-
municable disease, and the reduction of the hazards to health in industrial occupations. Important gains have been made in the usefulness of the Department
by the establishment of the Dental Branch and the assumption of the School
Medical Service.

By the thorough revision of the accounting methods of the Provincial
Secretary's Department, improvements have been effected, which expert investigation proved to have been necessary for a considerable number of years. The
Department has lately completed and opened the Boys' Training School at
Bowmanville, and thus has placed in practical operation the plans for the welfare of under-privileged youths. Another important work accomplished is the
establishment of the Reception Hospital, which will prove a valuable auxiliary
to the existing institutions for the treatment and cure of the mentally afflicted.

Highways are yearly playing a more important part as an economic factor
in the community. Under the administration of the Department of Highways,
a well-planned system of hard-surfaced roads is being developed on an economical

basis, which places this Province in an advantageous position. The improvement of the highways has led to the further development of the tourist traffic, which has been enhanced by disseminating information as to the attractions of Ontario, and by giving increased attention to the comfort and convenience of our visitors. The response is most satisfactory, and justifies the expectation that an energetic continuation of the effort to attract tourists will produce results of great commercial value.

Further efforts to establish a market for Canadian fuels in this Province have met with encouraging results. There is good ground for the hope that under favourable conditions as to transportation we will become independent eventually of foreign sources of supply.

Since the appointment of the Commission for the revision of the Statutes, a number of the laws have been carefully reviewed by the Commission. The results of these labours have been embodied in legislation to give effect to various suggested amendments. Several consolidating measures will also be submitted to you.

Noteworthy progress has been made in the improvement of the Provincial finances. With the advance already made, we are now within measurable distance of restoring the balance between ordinary revenue and expenditure. The question of the ultimate redemption of the existing debt, together with the adoption of a definite policy to the same end for future commitments, is receiving the earnest attention of my Ministers. At an early date the Public Accounts will be laid before you, and also the details of contemplated expenditures.

Among the measures which will be brought before you are Bills: To improve the quality of Dairy products; to amend the Workmen's Compensation Act; to amend the Land Tax Act; to amend the Minimum Wage Act; respecting the Development of Northern and North Western Ontario; to revise and consolidate the Election Act and the Voters' Lists Act, and for other purposes.

In conclusion, I desire to commend to your earnest attention the various measures and projects to meet the requirements of this Province; and I trust that, under the blessing and guidance of Providence, your deliberations will promote the welfare and happiness of our people.

His Honour the Lieutenant-Governor was then pleased to retire.

————

Mr. Speaker then reported, That, to prevent mistakes, he had obtained a copy of His Honour's Speech, which he read.

————

On motion of Mr. Ferguson, seconded by Mr. Henry, a Bill was introduced intituled "An Act respecting the Administration of Oaths of Office to persons appointed as Justices of the Peace," and the same was read the first time.

On motion of Mr. Ferguson, seconded by Mr. Henry.

Ordered, That the Speech of His Honour the Lieutenant-Governor, to this House, be taken into consideration To-morrow.

On motion of Mr. Ferguson, seconded by Mr. Henry.

Resolved, That Select Standing Committees of this House, for the present Session, be appointed for the following purposes:—1. On Privileges and Elections; 2. On Railways; 3. On Miscellaneous Private Bills; 4. On Standing Orders; 5. On Public Accounts; 6. On Printing; 7. On Municipal Law; 8. On Legal Bills; 9. On Agriculture and Colonization; 10. On Fish and Game; 11. On Labour; which said Committees shall severally be empowered to examine and enquire into all such matters and things as shall be referred to them by the House, and to report from time to time their observations and opinions thereon, with power to send for persons, papers and records.

The House then adjourned at 3.30 p.m.

THURSDAY, FEBRUARY 11TH, 1926.

PRAYERS.   3 O'CLOCK P.M.

The following Petitions were severally brought up and laid upon the Table:—

By. Mr. Vaughan, the Petition of Robert Cooper and others of Welland.

By Mr. Thompson (Lanark), the Petition of the Corporation of the Town of Arnprior.

By Dr. Jamieson, the Petition of the Grey and Bruce Loan Company, Owen Sound, and Owen Sound Loan and Savings Company of Owen Sound.

By Mr. Keith, the Petition of Joe H. Harris and others of Toronto; also, the Petition of the Township of North York; also, the Petition of the Town of Weston; also, the Petition of the Township of East York.

By Mr. McKnight, the Petition of the Corporation of the Town of Aylmer.

By Mr. Wilson (Windsor), the Petition of Verene May McLeod of Toronto and Gladys Alma Curry of New York; also, the Petition of the Town of Ojibway.

By Mr. Spence, the Petition of the Mount McKay and Kakabeka Falls Railway Company.

By Mr. Harcourt, the Petition of Vigfus Einarson and others of the Village of Rosseau.

By Mr. Nesbitt, the Petition of the Protestant Orphans' Home and the Girls' Home of Toronto; also, the Petition of the City of Toronto; also, the Petition of the Board of Education for the City of Toronto.

By Mr. MacBride, the Petition of the City of Brantford.

By Mr. Spence, the Petition of the City of Fort William.

By Mr. Gray, the Petition of the Town of Gananoque.

By Mr. Keefer, the Petition of the City of Port Arthur.

By Mr. Lewis, the Petition of the C. M. & G. Investments, Limited, of Toronto.

By Mr. Proulx, the Petition of the Police Village of Alfred Board of Trustees.

By Mr. Monteith, the Petition of the City of Stratford.

By Mr. Widdifield, the Petition of the Township of Thorah.

By Mr. Pinard, the Petition of the City of Ottawa.

By Mr. Graves, the Petition of the Township of Grantham.

By Mr. Homuth, the Petition of the Town of Ford City; also, the Petition of the City of Galt.

By Mr. McBrien, the Petition of the City of Toronto.

By Mr. Weichel, the Petition of the Lutheran Evangelical Seminary of Canada.

By Mr. Keith, the Petition of the Township of York.

By Mr. Mark, the Petition of the Haliburton, Whitney and Mattawa Railway Company.

By Mr. Monteith, the Petition of the British Mortgage Loan Company.

By Mr. Belanger, the Petition of the Town of Eastview.

By Mr. Elliott, the Petition of the Corporation of the City of London.

The following Bills were severally introduced and read the first time:—

Bill (No. 65), intituled "An Act to amend The Royal Ontario Museum Act." *Mr. Ferguson.*

Ordered, That the Bill be read the second time on Monday next.

Bill (No. 66), intituled "An Act to amend the Public Libraries Act." *Mr. Ferguson.*

Ordered, That the Bill be read the second time on Monday next.

Bill (No. 67), intituled "An Act to provide for Township Boards of Public School Trustees." *Mr. Ferguson.*

Ordered, That the Bill be read the second time on Monday next.

Bill (No. 68), intituled "An Act to amend the Workmen's Compensation Act." *Mr. Nickle.*

Ordered, That the Bill be read the second time on Monday next.

The Order of the Day for the Consideration of the Speech of His Honour the Lieutenant-Governor at the opening of the Session having been read,

Mr. Bradburn moved, seconded by Mr. Berry,

That an humble Address be presented to His Honour the Lieutenant-Governor, as follows:—

To His Honour, Henry Cockshutt, Lieutenant-Governor of our Province of Ontario.

We, His Majesty's most dutiful and loyal subjects, the Legislative Assembly of the Province of Ontario, now assembled, beg leave to thank Your Honour for the gracious speech Your Honour has addressed to us.

And a Debate having ensued, it was, on the Motion of Mr. Sinclair,

Ordered, That the Debate be adjourned until Tuesday.

On motion of Mr. Ferguson, seconded by Mr. Henry,

That out of respect to the memory of the late the Honourable Sir Adam Beck, K.C.M.G., for some years Member of the Executive Council of the Province of Ontario and Chairman of the Hydro-Electric Power Commission of Ontario, when this House adjourns to-day it do stand adjourned until Monday next, the 15th instant, at three o'clock in the afternoon.

The Provincial Secretary presented to the House, by command of His Honour the Lieutenant-Governor:—

Report of the University of Toronto Board of Governors for the year ending 30th June, 1925. (*Sessional Papers, No. 12.*)

Also—Return to an Order of the House, that there be laid before this House a return of the Legislative grants for the year 1925 paid to Rural Public and Separate Schools in the Counties and Districts and to Urban Public and Separate Schools in the Counties and Districts which, in accordance with the provisions of the Amendment to the Schools Act, passed in 1922, were classed as Rural Schools and received grants as such. (*Sessional Papers, No. 30.*)

The House then adjourned at 4.55 p.m.

MONDAY, FEBRUARY 15TH, 1926.

PRAYERS.   3 O'CLOCK P.M.

The following Petitions were severally brought up and laid upon the Table:—

By Mr. Berry, the Petition of the Village of Waterford.

By Mr. Elliott, the Petition of the Municipal Council of the Corporation of the City of London.

By Mr. Nesbitt, the Petition of the Toronto Western Hospital.

By Mr. Wilson (Windsor), the Petition of The Essex Border Utilities Commission.

By Mr. McBrien, the Petition of the Toronto Police Benefit Fund.

By Mr. McBrien, the Petition of Walter F. Campbell and others.

By Mr. Kennedy, the Petition of the Municipal Corporation of the Township of Teck.

The following Petitions were read and received:—

Of Robert Cooper and others of Welland, praying that an Act may pass incorporating the Welland and Port Colborne Railway Company.

Of the Corporation of the Town of Arnprior, praying that an Act may pass for the purpose of consolidating the floating debt and authorizing the said Corporation to raise a loan on the credit of debentures.

Of the Grey and Bruce Loan Company of Owen Sound and the Owen Sound Loan and Savings Company, praying that an Act may pass validating, ratifying and confirming an agreement to amalgamate.

Of Joe H. Harris and others of the City of Toronto, praying that an Act may pass to incorporate the Toronto East General Hospital.

Of the Corporation of the Town of Aylmer, praying that an Act may pass authorizing the consolidation of certain indebtedness.

Of Verene May McLeod of Toronto and Gladys Alma Curry of New York, praying that an Act may pass authorizing the payment of certain monies by the Executor of the John Curry Estate to the Essex Border Utilities Commission for Hospital purposes.

Of the Corporation of the Town of Ojibway, praying that an Act may pass permitting the Municipal Corporation of the Town of Ojibway to separate from the Corporation of the County of Essex for Municipal purposes.

Of the Mount McKay and Kakabeka Falls Railway Company, praying that an Act may pass permitting an extension of time for the completion and operation of their railway.

Of Vigfus Einarson and others of the Police Village of Rosseau, praying an Act to pass incorporating certain areas as an incorporated village.

Of the Protestant Orphans' Home and the Girls' Home, both of the City of Toronto, praying that an Act may pass for the purpose of amalgamating the Homes as one corporation.

Of the City of Brantford, praying that an Act may pass authorizing certain amendments to money by-laws; also, appointments to Hospital Board of Governors.

Of the City of Toronto, praying that an Act may pass authorizing certain grants; also, to authorize passage of by-laws *re* debenture issues; and also, to ratify and confirm a certain by-law *re* construction of sewers.

Of the City of Fort William, praying that an Act may pass validating a certain by-law.

Of the Corporation of the Township of North York, praying that an Act may pass authorizing Council to pass certain by-laws *re* sewers, garbage collection and incinerators; also, to confirm a certain money by-law.

Of the Corporation of the Town of Gananoque, praying that an Act may pass confirming and validating certain by-laws.

Of the Corporation of the City of London, praying that an Act may pass validating and confirming certain by-laws; also, to permit the Housing Commission to sell certain properties; also, for authority to fix assessments, etc.

Of the City of Port Arthur, praying that an Act may pass confirming certain by-laws; also, granting certain fixed assessments; also, to validate sales of certain lands and amend Public Parks By-laws.

Of the Corporation of the Town of Weston, praying that an Act may pass ratifying a certain agreement and permit passage of by-laws authorizing borrowing of money.

Of the Board of Education for the City of Toronto, praying that an Act may pass authorizing the said Board to create by resolution a fund to be known as "The Board of Education Insurance Fund."

Of the C. M. & G. Canadian Investments, Ltd., praying that an Act may pass enabling the petitioner to make certain investments.

Of the Police Village of Alfred, praying that an Act may pass validating and confirming a certain by-law.

Of the Township of York, praying that an Act may pass authorizing the passage of certain by-laws.

Of the Haliburton, Whitney and Mattawa Railway Company, praying that an Act may pass authorizing the building of an additional section of the Railway.

Of the Township of East York, praying that an Act may pass to Incorporate the Township as a Town to be known as Eastdale.

Of the City of Stratford, praying that an Act may pass authorizing the Corporation to prepare and submit to the citizens a by-law for the purchase of a gas plant.

Of the Township of Thorah, praying that an Act may pass confirming a certain money by-law.

Of the City of Ottawa, praying that an Act may pass authorizing the borrowing of money; also, to carry out certain work under the Local Improvement Act.

Of the Corporation of the Township of Grantham, praying that an Act may pass to validate and confirm certain by-laws.

Of the British Mortgage Loan Company, praying that an Act may pass permitting the Company's name to be changed; also, allowing the Company to carry on business under the Loan and Trust Companies Act.

Of the Corporation of the Town of Ford City, praying that an Act may pass incorporating the Town into a City to be known as Ford City.

Of the City of Galt, praying that an Act may pass validating and confirming a by-law.

Of the City of Toronto, praying that an Act may pass authorizing the City to acquire, own and operate vessels for transportation of passengers to and from Toronto Island.

Of the Evangelical Lutheran Seminary of Canada, praying that an Act may pass amending Act 3, George 5, Chap. 145, intituled "An Act to Incorporate the Evangelical Lutheran Seminary of Canada."

Of the Town of Eastview, praying that an Act may pass validating a by-law, and also confirming an agreement between the Petitioners and Bretislav Pliske.

The following Bills were severally introduced and read the first time:—

Bill (No. 69), intituled "An Act to amend the Department of Education Act." *Mr. Ferguson.*

Ordered, That the Bill be read a second time To-morrow.

Bill (No. 70), intituled "An Act to consolidate and amend the Trustees Act." *Mr. Nickle.*

Ordered, That the Bill be read a second time To-morrow.

Bill (No. 71), intituled "An Act to amend the Unwrought Metal Sales Act, 1924." *Mr. McCrea.*

Ordered, That the Bill be read a second time To-morrow.

On motion of Mr. Ferguson, seconded by Mr. Henry,

Ordered, That a Select Committee of Fourteen Members be appointed to prepare and report, with all convenient speed, a list of members to compose the Select Standing Committees ordered by this House, to be composed as follows:—

Messrs. Ferguson, Henry, Price, Black, MacDiarmid, Ireland, Weichel, McKeown, Pinard, Clarke (Northumberland), Mewhinney, Kemp, Lethbridge and Nixon.

On motion of Mr. Ferguson, seconded by Mr. Henry,

Ordered, That a Select Committee of Ten Members be appointed to act with Mr. Speaker in the control and management of the Library, to be composed as follows:—

Messrs. Nickle, Carr, Owens, MacBride, Elliott, Sweet, Belanger, Sangster, Raney and Widdifield.

On motion of Mr. Ferguson, seconded by Mr. Henry,

Ordered, That a Select Committee be appointed to direct the expenditure of any sum set apart by the Estimates for Art purposes, to be composed as follows:—

Messrs. Martin, Goldie, Lewis, Clarke (Brockville), Monteith, Keith, Proulx, Nixon and *Freeborn.*

On motion of Mr. Ferguson, seconded by Mr. Henry,

Ordered, That, beginning on Monday next, and on each succeeding Monday for the remainder of the Session, Government business shall be placed upon the Order Paper.

On motion of Mr. Ferguson, seconded by Mr. Henry,

Ordered, That this House do forthwith resolve itself into a Committee to consider a proposed resolution respecting the University of Toronto.

Mr. Ferguson acquainted the House that His Honour the Lieutenant-Governor, having been informed of the subject matter of the proposed Resolution, recommends it to the consideration of the House.

The House then resolved itself into the Committee.

(In the Committee.)

Resolved, That for the purpose of giving financial assistance to the University of Toronto to purchase property required for the erection of new departmental buildings, the Treasurer of Ontario be authorized, commencing with the year 1925-26, out of the Consolidated Revenue Fund, to make twenty annual payments of Thirteen thousand four hundred and eighty dollars and seventy-five cents ($13,480.75) each to the University of Toronto.

Mr. Speaker resumed the Chair; and Mr. Black reported, That the Committee had come to a certain Resolution.

Ordered, That the Report be now received.

Mr. Black reported the Resolution as follows:—

Resolved, That for the purpose of giving financial assistance to the University of Toronto to purchase property required for the erection of new departmental buildings, the Treasurer of Ontario be authorized, commencing with the year 1925-26, out of the Consolidated Revenue Fund, to make twenty annual payments of Thirteen thousand four hundred and eighty dollars and seventy-five cents ($13,480.75) each to the University of Toronto.

The Resolution having been read the second time, was agreed to, and referred to the Committee of the Whole House on Bill (No. 72), Respecting the payment of an annuity to the University of Toronto.

The following Bill was then introduced and read the first time:—

Bill (No. 72), intituled "An Act to provide for the payment of an annuity to the University of Toronto." *Mr. Price.*

Ordered, That the Bill be read a second time To-morrow.

The House then adjourned at 3.35 p.m.

TUESDAY, FEBRUARY 16TH, 1926.

PRAYERS.   3.00 O'CLOCK P.M.

Mr. Speaker presented to the House:—

Report of the Librarian on the state of the Library. (*Sessional Papers, No. 32.*)

The following Bill was introduced and read the first time:—

Bill (No. 73), intituled "An Act to Amend the Public Lands Act." *Mr. McCrea.*

Ordered, That the Bill be read a second time To-morrow.

The Order of the Day for resuming the Adjourned Debate on the Motion for the consideration of the Speech of His Honour the Lieutenant-Governor, at the opening of the Session, having been read,

The Debate was resumed,

And after some time,

Mr. Raney moved, seconded by Mr. Nixon,

That the Debate be adjourned till to-morrow.

And the motion having been submitted was lost on the following division:—

YEAS.

Belanger.	Fisher.	Mewhinney	Sinclair.
Biggs.	Kemp.	Nixon.	Taylor.
Clarke.	Lethbridge.	Raney.	Tellier.
(Northumberland.	McCallum.	Ross.	Widdifield—15.

NAYS.

Armstrong.	Elliott.	Jamieson.	Monteith.
Belford.	Ferguson.	(Simcoe)	Nesbitt.
Berry.	Finlayson.	Johnston.	Nickle.
Black.	Garden.	Keefer.	Owens.
Bradburn.	Godfrey.	Keith.	Patterson.
Callan.	Goldie.	Kennedy.	Pinard.
Chambers.	Gray.	(Temiskaming)	Price.
(Oxford)	Hambly.	Lewis.	Rankin.
Chambers.	Harcourt.	Lyons.	Spence.
(Wellington)	Henry.	McBrien.	Stedman.
Clarke.	Hill.	McCausland.	Stuart.
(Brockville)	Hillmer.	McCrea.	Sweet.
Colliver.	Ireland.	McKeown.	Trewartha.
Cooke.	Irvine.	McKnight.	Weichel.
Currie.	Jamieson.	Mark.	Wigle—57.
Edwards.	(Grey)	Milligan.	

And the Debate having resumed, Mr. Raney moved in amendment, seconded by Mr. Widdifield,

That the following words be added to the motion: "And to add that this House desires at this time to give expression to its firm adherence to the following principles:—

That the basis upon which government rests under our institutions is that the majority must prevail;

That the people of Ontario having by their votes declared for prohibition of the traffic in intoxicating liquor, prohibition must prevail until the people by their votes pronounce against it.

That no self-respecting government could do otherwise than accept the situation as above stated;

That the question of the prohibition of the traffic in intoxicating liquor ought not to be a question between political parties, but ought to be dealt with entirely on the basis of the will of the people as expressed by their votes by referenda or plebiscites on the subject.

That it is the duty of this Legislature to strengthen any weaknesses that may, from time to time, be revealed in the Ontario Temperance Act, and that it is the duty of the Government to use its best efforts to give the law active, vigorous and efficient enforcement."

And a Debate arising, it was, on the motion of Mr. Ferguson,

Ordered, That the Debate be adjourned until Thursday.

The Provincial Secretary presented to the House, by command of His Honour the Lieutenant-Governor:—

Regulations and Orders-in-Council made under the authority of the Department of Education Act, or of the Acts relating to public schools, separate schools or high schools. (*Sessional Papers, No. 31.*)

The House then adjourned at 10.20 p.m.

WEDNESDAY, FEBRUARY 17TH, 1926.

PRAYERS.   3 O'CLOCK P.M.

The following Petitions were severally brought up and laid upon the Table:—

By Mr Keith, the Petition of the Municipal Council of the Township of York.

By Mr. Weichel, the Petition of the Corporation of the City of Kitchener.

By Mr. McKeown, the Petition of the City of Guelph.

The following Petitions were read and received:—

Of the Village of Waterford, praying that an Act may pass to validate and confirm certain by-laws and to authorize levy of rates.

Of Walter F. Campbell and others of Bala, praying that an Act may pass authorizing the change of date of nomination and election for the Municipality of Bala.

Of the Toronto Western Hospital, praying that an Act may pass authorizing the amalgamation of the Toronto Western Hospital and Grace Hospital.

Of the Toronto Police Benefit Fund, praying that an Act may pass validating and confirming amendments affecting pensions.

Of the Essex Border Utilities Commission, praying that an Act may pass to authorize proceedings prior to the construction of the Grand Marais sewer; also, to amend a certain by-law; also, to equalize the rate of taxation and to make debentures a joint liability of the Essex Border Municipalities.

Of the Municipal Council of the City of London, praying that an Act may pass permitting the Council to borrow $350,000.00 and to issue debentures therefor.

Of the Corporation of the Township of Teck, praying that an Act may pass authorizing the passage of a by-law fixing the poll-tax assessment.

The following Bills were severally introduced and read the first time:—

Bill (No. 74), intituled "An Act to amend the Consolidated Municipal Act, 1922." *Mr. Nesbitt.*

Ordered, That the Bill be read the second time To-morrow.

Bill (No. 75), intituled "An Act to amend the Cemetery Act." *Mr. Nickle.*

Ordered, That the Bill be read the second time To-morrow.

Bill (No. 76), intituled "An Act to amend the Vendors and Purchasers Act." *Mr. Nickle.*

Ordered, That the Bill be read the second time To-morrow.

Bill (No. 77), intituled "An Act respecting Private Detectives." *Mr. Nickle.*

Ordered, That the Bill be read a second time To-morrow.

Bill (No. 78), intituled "An Act to amend the Commissioners for Taking Affidavits Act." *Mr. Nickle.*

Ordered, That the Bill be read a second time To-morrow.

Bill (No. 79), intituled "The Judges' Orders Enforcement Act." *Mr. Nickle.*

Ordered, That the Bill be read a second time To-morrow.

Bill (No. 80), intituled "An Act to amend the Devolution of Estates Act." *Mr. Nickle.*

Ordered, That the Bill be read a second time To-morrow.

The following Bills were severally read the second time:—

Bill (No. 71), To amend the Unwrought Metal Sales Act.

Referred to a Committee of the Whole House To-morrow.

Bill (No. 65), To amend the Royal Ontario Museum Act.

Referred to a Committee of the Whole House To-morrow.

Bill (No. 66), To amend the Public Libraries Act.

Referred to a Committee of the Whole House To-morrow.

Bill (No. 68), To amend the Workmen's Compensation Act.

Referred to a Committee of the Whole House To-morrow.

Bill (No. 72), To provide for the Payment of an Annuity to the University of Toronto.

Referred to a Committee of the Whole House To-morrow.

Bill (No. 69), To amend the Department of Education Act.

Referred to a Committee of the Whole House To-morrow.

———————

The House then adjourned at 5.25 p.m.

THURSDAY, FEBRUARY 18TH, 1926.

PRAYERS.   3 O'CLOCK P.M.

The following Petitions were severally brought up and laid upon the Table:—

By Mr. Willson (Niagara Falls), the Petition of the Township of Stamford.

By Mr. Wilson (Windsor), the Petition of the Corporation of the Town of Lasalle.

By Mr. Lewis, the Petition of John Stein, William Innes *et al* of the Village of Richmond Hill.

By Mr. Finlayson, the Petition of the Midland Simcoe Railway Company.

By Mr. Ecclestone, the Petition of the Municipal Corporation of the Town of Huntsville.

By Mr. Finlayson, the Petition for incorporation of the National Council of Young Men's Christian Associations of Canada.

The following Bills were severally introduced and read the first time:—

Bill (No. 81), intituled "An Act to consolidate and amend the Administration of Justice Expenses Act." *Mr. Nickle.*

Ordered, That the Bill be read the second time To-morrow.

Bill (No. 82), intituled "An Act to consolidate and amend the Justices of the Peace Act." *Mr. Nickle.*

Ordered, That the Bill be read the second time To-morrow.

Bill (No. 83), intituled "An Act to consolidate and amend the Crown Witnesses Act." *Mr. Nickle.*

Ordered, That the Bill be read the second time To-morrow.

Bill (No. 84), intituled "An Act to consolidate and amend the Fines and Forfeitures Act." *Mr. Nickle.*

Ordered, That the Bill be read the second time To-morrow.

The Order of the Day for resuming the Adjourned Debate on the Motion for the consideration of the Speech of His Honour the Lieutenant-Governor, at the opening of the Session, having been read,

The Debate was resumed,

And after some time,

Mr. Ferguson moved, seconded by Mr. Henry,

That all the words in the amendment after the second word "that" in the first line be omitted and the following be substituted therefor:—

"This House desires furthermore to assure Your Honour that it is of opinion that, in the enactment of important public legislation, the principle of Responsible Parliamentary Government, on which our British democratic institutions rest, should be observed in order that such legislation should have the undoubted sanction and support of the people, as expressed through their representatives in the Legislature, to the end that all such legislation should possess the authority and support necessary to command due respect and observance by the community."

And a Debate arising, it was, on the motion of Mr. Homuth,

Ordered, That the Debate be adjourned until Tuesday.

The House then adjourned at 9.55 p.m.

FRIDAY, FEBRUARY 19TH, 1926.

PRAYERS.   3 O'CLOCK P.M.

The following Petitions were severally brought up and laid upon the Table:—

By Mr. Wilson (Windsor), the Petition of the Corporation of the Town of Walkerville.

By Mr. Garden, the Petition of Herbert William Campbell of Hamilton and others.

By Mr. Haney, the Petition of the City of Sault Ste. Marie.

By Mr. McBrien, the Petition of the City of Toronto.

By Mr. Nesbitt, two Petitions of the City of Toronto.

By Mr. Belford, the Petition of A. E. Jones, of Castleton, and others, with respect to the Game Laws of the Province.

The following Petitions were read and received:—

Of the Corporation of the City of Kitchener, praying that an Act may pass, validating a certain by-law.

Of the Township of York, praying that an Act may pass to provide that there shall be submitted to the municipal electors of the Township of York a question concerning incorporation as a Town.

Of the City of Guelph, praying that an Act may pass permitting the Housing Commission to sell certain properties; also, to authorize the issue of debentures; also, to validate an agreement between the Hydro Power Commission and the City of Guelph re the transfer of Guelph Radial Railway.

Mr. Henry, from the Select Committee appointed to prepare and report with all convenient speed lists of members to compose the Select Standing Committees ordered by this House, begs leave to present the following lists as their Report:—

COMMITTEE ON STANDING ORDERS.

Messrs. Acres, Armstrong, Belford, Berry, Biggs, Brackin, Edwards, Freeborn, Graves, Hambly, Haney, Hill, Hillmer, Irvine, Jamieson (Simcoe West), Johnston, Lewis, McKeown, McKnight, McBrien, Martin, Nixon, Oakley, Owens, Patterson, Pinard, Proulx, Raney, Sinclair, Stedman, Stuart, Sweet, Trewartha, Vaughan, Wallis, Weichel, Widdifield, Wilson (Windsor)—38.

The Quorum of said Committee to consist of seven Members.

COMMITTEE ON PRIVATE BILLS.

Honourable Mr. Ferguson, Messrs. Armstrong, Belanger, Berry, Black, Brackin, Bradburn, Bragg, Callan, Chambers (Wellington), Chambers (Oxford), Clarke (Brockville), Clarke (Northumberland), Colliver, Cooke, Currie, Eccleston, Edwards, Elliott, Fallis, Fenton, Finlayson, Fisher, Garden, Gray, Graves, Haney, Harcourt, Henry, Hillmer, Homuth, Ireland, Joynt, Keefer, Keith, Kemp, Kennedy (Peel), Lethbridge, Lewis, McBrien, McCausland, McCrea, McKeown, Macdiarmid, Mageau, Mahoney, Mark, Martin, Mewhinney, Milligan, Morel, Nesbitt, Nickle, Nixon, Oakley, Oke, Owens, Pinard, Price, Proulx, Raney, Rankin, Ross, Sinclair, Spence, Stedman, Sweet, Taylor, Thompson (Lanark), Trewartha, Vaughan, Wallis, Weichel, Widdifield, Wigle, Wilson (Windsor), Willson (Niagara Falls)—77.

The Quorum of said Committee to consist of nine Members.

COMMITTEE ON RAILWAYS.

Honourable Mr. Ferguson, Messrs. Acres, Belanger, Belford, Berry, Biggs, Black, Bowman, Bradburn, Callan, Carty, Chambers (Wellington), Clarke (Brockville), Clarke (Northumberland), Colliver, Currie, Ecclestone, Fallis, Fenton, Fisher, Gray, Hambly, Haney, Harcourt, Hillmer, Homuth, Ireland, Irvine, Jamieson (Simcoe), Joynt, Keith, Kennedy (Temiskaming), Kennedy (Peel), Lyons, McBrien, McCallum, McCrea, McKnight, Macdiarmid, Mageau, Mahoney, Mark, Mewhinney, Milligan, Monteith, Morel, Nesbitt, Nickle, Oakley, Oke, Owens, Patterson, Pinard, Price, Proulx, Ross, Sangster, Spence, Stuart, Sweet, Taylor, Vaughan, Wallis, Wilson (Windsor), Willson (Niagara Falls), Wright—66.

The Quorum of said Committee to consist of nine Members.

COMMITTEE ON MUNICIPAL LAW.

Honourable Mr. Ferguson, Messrs. Acres, Armstrong, Belanger, Belford, Berry, Biggs, Black, Brackin, Bradburn, Bragg, Callan, Carty, Carr, Chambers (Wellington), Clarke (Brockville), Cooke, Currie, Ecclestone, Elliott, Fenton, Finlayson, Fisher, Freeborn, Garden, Godfrey, Goldie, Gray, Graves, Henry, Hill, Hillmer, Homuth, Ireland, Jamieson (Grey), Jamieson (Simcoe), Keefer, Kemp, Kennedy (Peel), Lethbridge, Lewis, Lyons, McBrien, McCallum, McCausland, McCrea, McKeown, McKnight, MacBride, Mageau, Mahoney, Martin, Mewhinney, Monteith, Nesbitt, Nickle, Nixon, Oakley, Oke, Owens, Patterson, Pinard, Price, Proulx, Raney, Rankin, Ross, Sinclair, Stedman, Stuart, Tellier, Thompson (Lanark), Trewartha, Vaughan, Wallis, Weichel, Wigle, Wilson (Windsor), Wright—79.

The Quorum of said Committee to consist of nine Members.

COMMITTEE ON AGRICULTURE AND COLONIZATION.

Honourable Mr. Ferguson, Messrs. Acres, Armstrong, Belanger, Belford, Black, Bowman, Bragg, Callan, Carty, Chambers (Wellington), Chambers (Oxford), Colliver, Cooke, Ecclestone, Elliott, Fallis, Fenton, Godfrey, Goldie, Gray, Hambly, Henry, Hill, Hillmer, Irvine, Jamieson (Grey), Jamieson (Simcoe), Johnston, Joynt, Keith, Kemp, Kennedy (Temiskaming), Kennedy (Peel), Lethbridge, McCallum, McKnight, Macdiarmid, Mageau, Mahoney, Mark, Martin, Mewhinney, Morel, Nixon, Oke, Patterson, Proulx, Rankin, Ross, Sangster, Stedman, Stuart, Taylor, Tellier, Thompson (Lanark), Trewartha, Vaughan, Wallis, Weichel, Widdifield, Wigle, Wright—63.

The Quorum of said Committee to consist of nine Members.

COMMITTEE ON PUBLIC ACCOUNTS.

Honourable Mr. Ferguson, Messrs. Acres, Belanger, Belford, Berry, Biggs, Black, Bowman, Bradburn, Callan, Carr, Clarke (Brockville), Clarke (Northumberland), Currie, Ecclestone, Edwards, Elliott, Finlayson, Fisher, Freeborn, Garden, Godfrey, Graves, Gray, Haney, Harcourt, Henry, Hill, Hillmer, Homuth, Ireland, Jamieson (Grey), Keefer, Keith, Kemp, Kennedy (Temiskaming), Lethbridge, Lewis, Lyons, McCausland, McCrea, McKeown, MacBride, Mageau, Mewhinney,

Morel, Nesbitt, Nickle, Nixon, Oakley, Oke, Owens, Patterson, Price, Proulx, Raney, Rankin, Sinclair, Tellier, Thompson (Lanark), Vaughan, Wallis, Weichel, Widdifield, Wigle, Wilson (Windsor)—67.

The Quorum of said Committee to consist of seven Members.

COMMITTEE ON PRIVILEGES AND ELECTIONS.

Honourable Mr. Ferguson, Messrs. Bradburn, Carr, Currie, Carty, Ecclestone, Elliott, Fisher, Freeborn, Garden, Goldie, Graves, Haney, Homuth, Keefer, Keith, Kemp, Lethbridge, Lewis, Lyons, McCausland, McCrea, McKeown, MacBride, Macdiarmid, Mageau, Milligan, Morel, Nesbitt, Nickle, Oakley, Owens, Pinard, Price, Proulx, Raney, Sinclair, Tellier, Thompson (Lanark), Trewartha—40.

The Quorum of said Committee to consist of nine Members.

COMMITTEE ON FISH AND GAME.

Honourable Mr. Ferguson, Messrs. Armstrong, Belford, Black, Bowman, Bradburn, Bragg, Callan, Clarke (Northumberland), Colliver, Cooke, Currie, Ecclestone, Fenton, Finlayson, Garden, Goldie, Graves, Gray, Hambly, Haney, Harcourt, Hill, Homuth, Ireland, Jamieson (Grey), Keefer, Keith, Kennedy (Temiskaming), Lyons, McCrea, McKeown, McKnight, Macdiarmid, Mageau, Mark, Martin, Mewhinney, Morel, Oke, Pinard, Price, Ross, Spence, Stedman, Stuart, Taylor, Tellier, Thompson (Lanark), Vaughan, Wallis, Weichel, Widdifield, Wigle, Willson (Niagara Falls), Wright—56.

The Quorum of said Committee to consist of seven Members.

COMMITTEE ON LEGAL BILLS.

Honourable Mr. Ferguson, Messrs. Biggs, Brackin, Finlayson, Fisher, Haney, Keefer, McBrien, McCrea, McKeown, MacBride, Milligan, Nesbitt, Nickle, Nixon, Owens, Price, Proulx, Raney, Sinclair, Wilson (Windsor)—21.

The Quorum of said Committee to consist of five Members.

COMMITTEE ON LABOUR.

Honourable Mr. Ferguson, Messrs. Berry, Bradburn, Callan, Carr, Garden, Godfrey, Homuth, Keith, McCallum, MacBride, Mewhinney, Nesbitt, Oakley, Pinard, Sangster, Spence, Vaughan, Weichel, Wright—20.

The Quorum of said Committee to consist of seven Members.

COMMITTEE ON PRINTING.

Honourable Mr. Ferguson, Messrs. Belanger, Biggs, Callan, Carr, Currie, Fallis, Freeborn, Gray, Irvine, Jamieson (Grey), Lewis, MacBride, Price, Proulx, Sinclair, Stedman, Thompson (Lanark), Wigle, Willson (Niagara Falls)—20.

The Quorum of said Committee to consist of five Members.

Resolved, That this House doth concur in the foregoing Report.

The following Bills were severally introduced and read the first time:—

Bill (No. 85), intituled "An Act to amend the Assessment Act." *Mr. Nesbitt.*

Ordered, That the Bill be read the second time on Monday next.

Bill (No. 86), intituled "An Act to amend the Legislative Assembly Act." *Mr. Nickle.*

Ordered, That the Bill be read the second time on Monday next.

Bill (No. 87), intituled "An Act to consolidate and amend the Public Authorities Protection Act."

Ordered, That the Bill be read the second time on Monday next.

Bill (No. 88), intituled "An Act respecting the Department of Agriculture." *Mr. Martin.*

Ordered, That the Bill be read the second time on Monday next.

Bill (No. 89), intituled "An Act to amend the Married Women's Property Act." *Mr. Nickle.*

Ordered, That the Bill be read the second time on Monday next.

Bill (No. 90), intituled "An Act to consolidate and amend the Magistrates Act." *Mr. Nickle.*

Ordered, That the Bill be read the second time on Monday next.

Bill (No. 91), intituled "An Act to improve the Quality of Dairy Products." *Mr. Martin.*

Ordered, That the Bill be read the second time on Monday next.

———

Mr. Lethbridge asked the following Question:—

1. What members of the present Legislature have, to the knowledge of the Government, either directly or as a member of a partnership or joint stock company, an interest in any contract in connection with the erection of the new East Block in Queen's Park. 2. What is the amount of the contract and what is the contract for in each case.

The Minister of Public Works and Highways answered in the following words:—

1. No member of the Legislature has any contract either directly or indirectly with the Government for the erection of the new East Block in Queen's Park. The Government awarded the contract for the erection of the new East

Block by public tender to The Jackson-Lewis Company, Limited. The Government is advised that The Jackson-Lewis Company, Limited, sublet the stonework on such building to Geo. Oakley & Son, Limited, Stone Contractors, of which firm Geo. Oakley, Esquire, Member for Riverdale, is said to be a shareholder. 2. Answered by 1.

Mr. Raney asked the following Question:—

1. How many seats in this House are now vacant. 2. What are the ridings that are not represented. 3. What was the date of the resignation or death, as the case may have been, in each case. 4. How many of the former representatives were supporters of the Government. 5. How many of the Opposition. 6. Is the Government aware that the Legislative Assembly Act requires that a warrant for a new election shall issue immediately upon a seat in the Legislature becoming vacant. 7. Is the Government aware that this provision of the statute is for the protection of the Opposition in the Legislature.

The Prime Minister answered in the following words:—

1, 2 and 3. All the official information asked for by these questions was given to the House by Mr. Speaker, on February 10th. (See Votes and Proceedings, pages 2, 3, 4 and 5.) 4 and 5. The information asked for in these questions is already well known to the public and to the House, and is not a matter of official record. 6. No. 7. No.

Mr. Kemp asked the following Question:—

1. What members of the present Legislature have had or now have, to the knowledge of the Government, interests, direct or indirect, in contracts on the highways or other public works of the Province. 2. What were or are the contracts in which they were severally interested and in what amounts severally.

The Minister of Public Works and Highways answered in the following words:—

1. None. 2. Answered by No. 1.

Mr. Widdifield asked the following Question:—

1. Did the Government leave the issue of beer permits to standard hotels to the Ontario Board of License Commissioners. 2. Were such permits granted as a matter of course to the holders of standard hotel licenses. 3. Did the Government itself issue all other beer permits. 4. If so, what member of the Government. 5. Why was not the issuing of all beer permits left to the Board of License Commissioners.

The Attorney-General answered as follows:—

1. Substantially so. 2. Not in all cases. 3 and 4. No. 5. It was the Attorney-General's desire to keep in close touch with the working out of the measure.

———————

Mr. Sinclair asked the following Question:—

1. When did the member for Centre Grey resign. 2. When was the resignation deposited with the Clerk. 3. What is the date of his notice of the resignation to the Speaker. 4. What is the date of the issue of the Speaker's warrant for a new election in that riding.

The Prime Minister answered as follows:—

1. This information was given to the House by Mr. Speaker on February 10th. (See Votes and Proceedings for that date.) 2. The resignation was originally deposited with the Speaker who immediately communicated it to the Clerk of the Crown in Chancery. 3. Same answer as the answer to Question 1. 4. The Speaker does not issue a warrant for a new election, nor can an election be held under the Speaker's warrant. The Legislative Assembly Act authorizes the Speaker to address his warrant to the Clerk of the Crown in Chancery for the issue of a writ for an election.

———————

Mr. Bragg asked the following Question:—

1. When did the member for Cochrane resign. 2. When was the resignation deposited with the Clerk. 3. What is the date of his notice of the resignation to the Speaker. 4. What is the date of the issue of the Speaker's warrant for a new election in that riding.

The Prime Minister answered as follows:—

1. This information was given to the House by Mr. Speaker on February 10th. (See Votes and Proceedings for that date.) 2. The resignation was originally deposited with the Speaker who immediately communicated it to the Clerk of the Crown in Chancery. 3. Same answer as the answer to Question 1. 4. The Speaker does not issue a warrant for a new election, nor can an election be held under the Speaker's warrant. The Legislative Assembly Act authorizes the Speaker to address his warrant to the Clerk of the Crown in Chancery for the issue of a writ for an election.

———————

Mr. Mewhinney asked the following Question:—

1. When did the member for North Norfolk resign. 2. When was the resignation deposited with the Clerk. 3. What is the date of his notice of the resignation to the Speaker. 4. What is the date of the issue of the Speaker's warrant for a new election in that riding.

The Prime Minister answered as follows:—

1. This information was given to the House by Mr. Speaker on February 10th. (See Votes and Proceedings for that date.) 2. The resignation was originally deposited with the Speaker who immediately communicated it to the Clerk of the Crown in Chancery. 3. Same answer as the answer to Question 1. 4. The Speaker does not issue a warrant for a new election, nor can an election be held under the Speaker's warrant. The Legislative Assembly Act authorizes the Speaker to address his warrant to the Clerk of the Crown in Chancery for the issue of a writ for an election.

Mr. Clarke asked the following Question:—

1. When did the member for East Kent resign. 2. When was the resignation deposited with the Clerk. 3. What is the date of his notice of the resignation to the Speaker. 4. What is the date of the issue of the Speaker's warrant for a new election in that riding.

The Prime Minister answered as follows:—

1. This information was given to the House by Mr. Speaker on February 10th. (See Votes and Proceedings for that date.) 2. The resignation was originally deposited with the Speaker who immediately communicated it to the Clerk of the Crown in Chancery. 3. Same answer as the answer to Question 1. 4. The Speaker does not issue a warrant for a new election, nor can an election be held under the Speaker's warrant. The Legislative Assembly Act authorizes the Speaker to address his warrant to the Clerk of the Crown in Chancery for the issue of a writ for an election.

Mr. Sangster asked the following Question:—

1. When did the member for Kenora resign. 2. When was the resignation deposited with the Clerk. 3. What is the date of his notice of the resignation to the Speaker. 4. What is the date of the issue of the Speaker's warrant for a new election in that riding.

The Prime Minister answered as follows:—

1. This information was given to the House by Mr. Speaker on February 10th. (See Votes and Proceedings for that date.) 2. The resignation was originally deposited with the Speaker who immediately communicated it to the Clerk of the Crown in Chancery. 3. Same answer as the answer to Question 1. 4. The Speaker does not issue a warrant for a new election, nor can an election be held under the Speaker's warrant. The Legislative Assembly Act authorizes the Speaker to address his warrant to the Clerk of the Crown in Chancery for the issue of a writ for an election.

Mr. Clarke asked the following Question:—

1. When did the member for South Simcoe resign. 2. When was the resignation deposited with the Clerk. 3. What is the date of his notice of the resignation to the Speaker. 4. What is the date of the issue of the Speaker's warrant for a new election in that riding.

The Prime Minister answered as follows:—

1. This information was given to the House by Mr. Speaker on February 10th. (See Votes and Proceedings for that date.) 2. The resignation was originally deposited with the Speaker who immediately communicated it to the Clerk of the Crown in Chancery. 3. Same answer as the answer to Question 1. 4. The Speaker does not issue a warrant for a new election, nor can an election be held under the Speaker's warrant. The Legislative Assembly Act authorizes the Speaker to address his warrant to the Clerk of the Crown in Chancery for the issue of a writ for an election.

Mr. Bragg asked the following Question:—

1. What is the total amount of revenue collected to October 31st, 1925, by the Minister of Public Works and Highways under the Gasoline Tax Act, 1925. 2. Has this fund so collected been paid into the office of the Minister of Public Works and Highways. 3. Has a separate accounting department been established in the office of the Minister of Public Works and Highways to receive and account for said tax. 4. How much of said fund has been paid over by the office of the Minister of Public Works and Highways to consolidated revenue. 5. What was the total cost of collecting said tax for said period, including inspectors and all services required to collect the same. 6. How many purchasers, as defined in said Act, paid said tax to the Minister of Public Works and Highways during said period.

The Minister of Public Works and Highways answered as follows:—

1. $2,014,728.67. 2. Yes. 3. No. 4. $1,974,434.10. 5. $40,603.19. 6. All users of gasoline in the Province of Ontario.

Mr. Sinclair asked the following Question:—

1. What is the total amount of revenue collected to October 31st, 1925, under the Luxury Tax, October, 1925, upon each of the following beverages taxed by said Act:—(a) Beverages containing more than one-half of one per cent. by volume at sixty degrees Fahrenheit of absolute alcohol, and not more than 2½ per cent. by volume at sixty degrees Fahrenheit of absolute alcohol; (b) wine containing more than 2½ per cent. by volume at sixty degrees Fahrenheit of absolute alcohol; (c) beverages taxable by said Act and not included in classes "A" and "B." 2. What was the total cost to the Province for collecting the taxes under said Act to October 31st, 1925, including inspectors and all services required to collect the same.

The Provincial Treasurer answered as follows:—

1. (a) $236,829.07; (b) $53,433.38; (c) $80,490.18.   2. $32,254.94.

Mr. Mewhinney asked the following Question:—

1. Were tenders called for by the Government for the construction of the new Administration Building and the supply of material as one contract.   2. Were tenders called for by the Government for parts of the work and material on said building.   3. What tenders were · received by the Government.   4. For what parts of said building was each tender accepted.   5. Who were the successful tenderers on said building, for what part thereof, and the price at which the tender was accepted.

The Minister of Public Works and Highways answered as follows:—

1. No.   2. Yes.   3. See Schedule attached.   4. See Schedule attached. 5. See Schedule attached (pages 63, 64).

LIST OF TENDERS

EAST BLOCK—PARLIAMENT BUILDINGS

BULK		TENDERS
Stuart & Sinclair, Limited, Hamilton:—		
Steel construction, using Queenston & Oolitic stone..	$1,460,290	
Deduct for steel..............................	200,000	
	$1,260,290	
For granite base, add.........................	29,250	
		$1,289,540
Using Credit Valley stone in field, add $45,000....	$1,505,290	
For granite base, add.........................	13,000	
		1,518,290
Using Queenston stone throughout, add $185,000..	$1,645,290	
For granite base, add.........................	25,250	
		1,670,540
Using Credit Valley stone throughout, add 305,000.	$1,765,290	
For granite base, add.........................	9,000	
		1,774,290
W. H. Yates Construction Co., Hamilton:—		
Steel construction, using Queenston & Oolitic stone..	$1,375,000	
For granite base, add.........................	29,250	
		1,404,250
Using Credit Valley stone in field, add $45,000....	$1,420,000	
For granite base, add.........................	13,000	
		1,433,000
Using Queenston stone throughout, add $185,000..	$1,560,000	
For granite base, add.........................	25,250	
		1,585,250

Using Credit Valley stone throughout, add 305,000. $1,680,000
For granite base, add..........................   9,000

―――― $1,689,000
If the Massilon steel joist construction is used in place of
   construction as specified, deduct $40,000...............   1,335,000
For Kalamine windows, Fireproof Door Co................   60,000
For Steel Austral windows, Architectural Bronze Co., add
   $12,000...   72,000
For Fenestra steel windows, Metal Window & Steel Products,
   deduct $15,600...   44,300
Unit price for extra excavations $2 per cubic yard.
Unit price for extra concrete, erection of forms and rein-
   forcing $11 per cubic yard.
Reinforced concrete design, using Queenston &
   Oolitic stone.............................. $1,267,000
Using Queenston stone throughout, add.......... 185,000

――――   1,452,000
T. A. Brown & Co., Brantford:―
Steel construction, kind of stone not mentioned.....   1,555,000
Kind of metal sashes not mentioned.

H. A. Wickett & Co., Toronto:―
Steel construction, using Queenston & Oolitic stone.. $1,470,680
   Add for granite base.......................... 29,250

――――   1,499,930
Using Credit Valley stone, Oolitic stone............ $1,515,680
   Add for granite base.......................... 13,000

――――   1,528,680
Using Queenston stone throughout................ $1,645,680
   Add for granite base.......................... 25,250

――――   1,670,930
Using Credit Valley stone throughout.............. $1,765,680
   Add for granite base.......................... 9,000

――――   1,774,680
If Massilon steel joist construction is used, deduct $59,705 from
   any of the above.
Add for metal windows:
   McFarlane-Douglas, Ottawa, kalomined weather stripped....   69,750
   Campbell, all metal......................................   70,835
   Architectural Bronze, all metal..........................   61,175
   Can. Metal, Fenestra, all metal..........................   44,370
   A. B. Ormsby, kalomined steel sash.....................   63,350

Russell Construction Co., Toronto:―
A. Steel construction, using Queenston & Oolitic
   stone..................................... $1,414,713
   Including granite base.......................   1,443,963
B. Reinforced concrete construction, Queenston &
   Oolitic stone............................. 1,428,513
   Including granite base.......................   1,457,763
C. Massilon Joist construction, Queenston & Oolitic
   stone..................................... 1,384,487
   Including granite base.......................   1,413,737

2 J.

Steel Construction, using Credit Valley field & Oolitic stone	$1,459,713	
Including granite base		$1,472,713
Reinforced concrete construction, Credit Valley & Oolitic stone	1,473,513	
Including granite base		1,486,513
Massilon Joist construction, Credit Valley & Oolitic stone	1,429,487	
Including granite base		1,442,487
Using Queenston stone throughout (steel construction)	1,599,713	
Including granite base		1,624,963
Using Queenston stone throughout (reinforced concrete)	1,613,513	
Including granite base		1,638,763
With Massilon Joist construction	1,569,487	
Including granite base		1,594,737
Using Credit Valley stone throughout (steel construction)	1,719,713	
Including granite base		1,728,713
Using Credit Valley stone throughout (concrete construction)	1,733,513	
Including granite base		1,742,513
Massilon Joist construction	1,689,487	
Including granite base		1,698,487

Jackson-Lewis Co., Limited, Toronto:—

Reinforced concrete, using Queenston stone & Oolitic stone	$1,300,367	
For granite base add	29,500	
		1,329,867
Using Credit Valley & Oolitic stone	$1,345,667	
For granite base, add	13,100	
		1,358,767
For all in Queenston stone	$1,486,367	
For granite base, add	29,500	
		1,515,867
For all Credit Valley stone	$1,607,367	
For granite base, add	9,100	
		1,616,467

NOTE:—$54,000 is included in this tender for hollow metal, double hung windows. If Fenestra windows are used, deduct $9,630. If gypsum blocks are used for floor fillers and partitions, deduct $63,000.

$44,370 is included in these prices for Fenestra steel windows.

For Ormsby's Kalamine windows, add	$18,980
If Can. Ornamental Iron, add	20,350

Dickie Construction Co., Limited, Toronto:—

    Steel construction, Queenston & Oolitic stone....... $1,426,000
    For granite base, add........................ 32,000

                                              $1,458,000

    For Credit Valley and Oolitic stone, add $48,000.... $1,474,000
    For granite base, add........................ 15,000

                                              1,489,000

    For Credit Valley stone throughout, add $30,000... $1,726,000
    For granite base, add........................ 9,000

                                              1,735,000

    For Queenston stone throughout, add $200,000..... $1,626,000
    For granite base, add........................ 27,000

                                              1,653,000

    For reinforced concrete construction, using Queenston
        stone and Oolitic stone..................... 1,411,000
    For reinforced concrete, as per Engholmes' plan.... $1,381,800
    If metal ceilings are lathed on top, add......... 9,600

                                              1,391,400

    Using Massilon Joists with metal lath ceiling....... 1,370,000
    For Austral windows, Architectural Bronze........ 70,600
    For Campbell, all metal...................... 81,500
    For Can. Metal Window and steel products........ 48,000
    For Hollow metal, double hung.................. 59,000
    For Kalamined, double hung................... 70,000

Anglin-Norcross, Limited, Toronto:—

    Steel construction, using Queenston stone throughout $1,683,000
    For granite base, add........................ 25,250

                                              1,708,250

    For reinforced concrete construction, deduct $87,000 $1,596,000
    For granite base, add........................ 25,250

                                              1,621,250

    Structural steel, using Massilon joist, deduct....... 69,000   1,614,000
    For granite & Oolitic, in place of Queenston in basem,
        add.................................... 25,250   1,708,250

    For Queenston & Oolitic stone, deduct $185,000.... $1,498,000
    For granite base, add........................ 25,250

                                              1,523,250

    For granite in place of Queenston & Oolitic up to
        basement window heads, balance of Queenston
        and Oolitic, deduct $155,750 (all granite base). 1,527,250
    For Credit Valley stone throughout, add.......... $1,811,000
    For granite base, add........................ 25,250

                                              1,836,250
    For Credit Valley & Oolitic stone, deduct......... $140,000   1,543,000

Johnstone Bros., Brantford:—

Tender 1. Steel construction, using Oolitic limestone
    trim and Queenston limestone field with Kala-
    mine windows............................... $1,451,437
    Add for granite base.......................... 1,480,687

Tender 2. Concrete construction with stone and
   windows as Tender 1...................... $1,366,216
  Add for granite base......................... $1,395,466
Tender 3. Steel construction with Massilon bar
   joists and stone and windows as Tender 1...... 1,410,505
  Add for granite base.........................   1,439,755
Tender 4. If Oolitic limestone trim is used with
   Credit Valley Ashlar field to steel construction.. 1,496,437
Tender 5. If granite base is used with Tender 4...   1,509,437
Tender 6. Concrete construction, using Oolitic lime-
   stone trim with Credit Valley Ashlar field...... 1,411,216
Tender 7. If granite base is used with Tender 6...   1,424,216
Tender 8. Steel construction with Massilon bar
   joists, if Oolitic limestone trim is used with
   Credit Valley Ashlar field.................... 1,455,505
Tender 9. If granite base is used with Tender 8...   1,468,505
Tender 10. Steel construction, using Queenston lime-
   stone for the entire building................. 1,636,437
Tender 11. If granite base is used with Tender 10..   1,661,687
Tender 12. Concrete construction if Queenston lime-
   stone is used throughout.................... 1,551,216
Tender 13. If granite base is used with Tender 12..   1,576,466
Tender 14. Steel construction with Massilon bar
   joists, if Queenston limestone is used throughout 1,595,505
Tender 15. If granite base is used with Tender 14..   1,620,755
Tender 16. Steel construction, if Credit Valley is
   used throughout........................... 1,756,437
Tender 17. If granite base is used with Tender 16..   1,765,437
Tender 18. Concrete construction, if Credit Valley is
   used throughout........................... 1,671,216
Tender 19. If granite base is used with Tender 18..   1,680,216
Tender 20. Steel construction with Massilon bar
   joists, if Credit Valley is used throughout...... 1,715,505
Tender 21. If granite base is used with Tender 20..   1,724,505
If Campbell metal windows, model 97, are used,
   instead of Kalamine windows, add to Tenders 1 to
   21, inclusive............................. 12,311
If Fenestra architectural windows and casements are
   used, instead of Kalamine windows, deduct
   from Tenders 1 to 21, inclusive.............. 14,157
If Steel Austral windows are used, instead of Kalamine windows, add to Tenders 1 to 21, inclusive 3,373

PARLIAMENT BUILDINGS—EAST BLOCK

Separate Tenders for Steel

John P. Hepburn, Toronto.................................... 260,722
McGregor & McIntyre, Toronto............................... 202,150
Canadian Bridge Co., Walkerville............................ 194,900
Hamilton Bridge, Hamilton.................................. 188,645
Dominion Bridge, Toronto................................... 196,700
Dominion Bridge (Massilon bars)............................ 172,825

PARLIAMENT BUILDINGS—EAST BLOCK

List of Tenders for Heating

B. J. Miller & Co., Toronto.	$159,190
McKinley & Northwood, Ottawa.	188,891
Fiddes & Hogarth, Toronto.	161,825
Sheppard & Abbott, Toronto.	140,000
Drake Avery Co., Windsor.	159,322
W. J. McGuire Co., Toronto.	153,758
Bennett & Wright, Toronto.	150,190
Purdy Mansell, Ltd., Toronto.	128,992

List of Tenders for Plumbing

B. J. Miller & Co., Toronto.	58,600
Wright Bros., Ltd., Toronto.	38,990
W. J. McGuire, Ltd., Toronto.	41,900
Sheppard & Abbott, Ltd., Toronto.	42,542
Purdy Mansell, Ltd., Toronto.	39,977

List of Tenders for Electric Wiring

Bennett & Wright, Toronto.	37,108
Roxboro-Dean, Ltd., Toronto.	37,500
Patterson Electric Co., Toronto.	37,700
Canada Electric Co., Toronto.	37,777
Can. Comstock Co., Toronto.	38,963
Harry Alexander, Ltd., Toronto.	39,800
John Everard Myers, Toronto.	41,595
Harris & Marston, Toronto.	47,695

PARLIAMENT BUILDINGS—EAST BLOCK

List of Tenders for Vault Doors

J. & J. Taylor, Limited, Toronto:—

No. 64-D vault door.	$115 per set
No. 65-D vault door.	110 per set
No. 72-A vault door.	380 per set

Goldie & McCullough, Ltd., Galt:—

No. 261 vault door.	$150 per set
No. 258 vault door.	122 per set

PARLIAMENT BUILDINGS—EAST BLOCK

Contracts Awarded to Date

The Jackson-Lewis Company, Limited:—

Contract for concrete foundations, reinforced concrete skeleton construction, cut stone, brickwork, roof and metal work, tile and flooring and granite steps to entrances. . . . $1,439,197 00

Purdy Mansell, Limited:—
 Contract for heating and ventilating..................... $128,992 00

Wright Bros.:—
 Contract for plumbing............................ 38,990 00

Bennett & Wright Co.:—
 Contract for electric wiring........................... 36,742 74

Consolidated Plate Glass Co.:—
 Contract for glazing of windows....................... 21,051 00

Architectural Bronze & Iron Works:—
 Contract for metal windows........................... 58,625 00

Canadian Ornamental Iron Works Co.:—
 Contract for steel stairs.............................. 22,900 00

Goldie & McCullough, Galt:—
 Contract for vault doors............................. 5,612 00

Mr. Mewhinney asked the following Question:—

1. How many councils have passed by-laws in pursuance of the Corn Borer Act, 1925.   2. How many inspectors so appointed have consulted the Provincial Entomologist of the Department of Agriculture in regard to the eradication of the corn borer.   3. In how many cases has action been taken by inspectors so appointed to carry out the instructions of the Provincial Entomologist.

The Minister of Agriculture answered as follows:—

1. None.   2. None.   3. Answered by one, except that apart from inspectors the Provincial Entomologist and officers of the Department have given instructions and information extensively through the seed corn areas and these have been taken advantage of to a considerable extent on a voluntary basis.

Mr. Carty asked the following Question:—

1. How many members of the present Government have been to Europe since they became Ministers of the Crown.   2. Which members.   3. What was the length of absence in each case.   4. What was the expense to the Province in each case.

The Prime Minister answered as follows:—

Honourable Chas. McCrea, Minister of Mines, visited Great Britain for the purpose of directing the attention of the British investing public to the great natural resources and mining possibilities of Northern Ontario, from April 23rd, 1924, to June 13th, 1924.   Expenses, $3,000.00.

Honourable John S. Martin, Minister of Agriculture, visited Wembley Exhibition as a Commissioner representing the Province, and visited Denmark to enquire into general agricultural methods, rural education and co-operative effort in the production and marketing of farm products. Expenses, $2,000.00.

Honourable Forbes Godfrey, Minister of Health and Labour, represented the Government at the International Labour Conference, Geneva, in June, 1925; absent seven weeks. Expenses, $1,500.00.

Honourable Lincoln Goldie, Provincial Secretary, visited Europe in 1925; was absent seven weeks, but did not go on official mission and consequently the trip cost the Province nothing.

Honourable G. Howard Ferguson, the Prime Minister, visited Europe in 1925 and was absent ten weeks. He had no official mission and consequently the trip cost the Province nothing.

Mr. Homuth asked the following Question:—

1. What new appointments were made for the purpose of collecting (a) the Gasoline Tax; (b) the Beverage Tax. 2. What is the salary of each appointee.

The Provincial Treasurer answered as follows:—

1. (a) None.

1 (b) and 2. The following persons were appointed for the purpose of collecting the Beverage Tax:—

	Salary.
J. M. Clark, Chief Inspector	$229 00 per month
R. Burrows, Inspector, Toronto	158 33 " "
J. T. Nidd, Inspector, North Bay	150 00 " "
J. F. Harper, Inspector, Hamilton	150 00 " "
A. Hergott, Inspector, Kitchener	150 00 " "
J. W. McConnell, Inspector, Windsor	150 00 " "
D. Sharpe, Inspector, Niagara Falls	150 00 " "
A. J. Ferguson, Inspector, Fort William	150 00 " "
W. H. Derrick, Inspector, Burritt's Rapids	150 00 " "
M. T. Pinkerton, Inspector, Ottawa	130 00 " "
L. Girouard, Inspector, Ottawa	130 00 " "
J. Hitzroth, Inspector, Hamilton	130 00 " "
B. Smith, Inspector, Toronto	130 00 " "
R. J. Hanna, Inspector, Toronto	130 00 " "
O. R. Dew, Inspector, Toronto	130 00 " "
F. G. Davies, Inspector, Toronto	130 00 " "
J. S. Hunt, Inspector, Toronto	130 00 " "
P. A. Richards, Inspector, Toronto	130 00 " "

NOTE:—A number of others were temporarily employed in the original organization and collection during the summer season.

Mr. Raney asked the following Question:—

1. Has the Government or the Prime Minister given consideration since the, last session of the Legislature to (a) a policy of Government control of the sale of intoxicating liquor, or (b) to a beer or wine and beer licensing system. 2. Has information been collected along either of these lines. 3. Has a Bill been drafted (a) for submission to the Legislature, or (b) as a basis for discussion before the electors. 4. Has the Government or the Prime Minister given consideration since the last session of the Legislature to a place of local option for the control of the sale of intoxicating liquor.

The Prime Minister answered as follows:—

As the answer to these questions might be construed to be a declaration of Government policy regarding the problem of the sale of intoxicating liquors for beverage purposes the questions are improper.

———————

Mr. Widdifield asked the following Question:—

What, in a brief statement, was the plan of Government control of the liquor traffic which the Government had in mind to bring into existence if the popular majority on the plebiscite in October, 1924, had been in favour of a policy of Government control.

The Prime Minister answered as follows:—

The general plan is briefly set out in the second question submitted to the electors, which read as follows:—

"Are you in favour of the sale as a beverage of beer and spirituous liquor in sealed packages under Government control?"

The final determination of the details of the plan were left in abeyance pending the expression of the people's will.

———————

Mr. Sinclair asked the following Question:—

1. What is the amount of money paid by the Province of Ontario out of the revenues of the Province for maintenance purposes of highways in Ontario during the last fiscal year. 2. To what classes of highways was this applied. 3. What was the amount paid in respect of each such class. 4. Is any portion of this received by the province from municipalities, or repayable by municipalities to the province.

The Minister of Public Works and Highways answered as follows:—

1. $2,466,859.15. 2. Provincial highways, county roads, provincial county roads, township roads. 3. Provincial highways, $963,139.42; county roads,

$708,663.54; provincial county roads, $394,485.16; township roads, $400,571.03.
4. Provincial highways, from counties, $192,627.86; from cities, $30,931.98—
$223,559.84.

Mr. Clarke asked the following Question:—

1. What is the total cost to the Province of Ontario to date of the Agricultural Enquiry Committee appointed April 17, 1924. 2. How much of said amount has been paid for the following: (a) allowance to members; (b) travelling expenses of members; (c) secretary's salary and travelling expenses; (d) printing and stationery. 3. By what authority have sessions been held since the opening of the 1925 Session of the Legislature. 4. How much is now due and owing by the Province of Ontario on account of this committee.

The Minister of Agriculture answered as follows:—

1. $21,011.48. 2. (a) $13,553.00; (b) Nil; (c) $4,920.25; (d) $150.62. 3. At the request of the Government. 4. This information is not available. Accounts are not quite all in.

Mr. Homuth asked the following Question:—

1. From what person or organizations were recommendations for the following appointments in Waterloo County received, and what was the date of each: (1) C. H. Mills, local High Court Registrar; (2) W. A. Kribs, Sheriff; (3) Mr. Scully, Registrar of the Surrogate Court; (4) Mrs. Clark, Division Court Clerk, Galt.

The Attorney-General answered as follows:—

It is not the policy of the Government to give this information as "communications recommending persons for appointments are treated as confidential."

The Provincial Secretary presented to the House, by command of His Honour the Lieutenant-Governor:—

Report of G. T. Clarkson, Esq., appointed by Commission, dated June 5th, 1925, to enquire whether the prices at which gasoline and oils are sold to the people of Ontario are just and fair. (*Sessional Papers No. 33.*)

The House then adjourned at 4.20 p.m.

MONDAY, FEBRUARY 22ND, 1926.

The following Petitions were read and received:—

Of the Municipal Corporation of the Township of Stamford, praying that an Act may pass authorizing the Corporation to pass certain by-laws respecting construction of sewers.

Of the Corporation of the Town of Lasalle, praying that an Act may pass validating certain by-laws passed respecting the payments for watermains.

Of John Stein, William Innes and others, of Richmond Hill, praying that an Act may pass amending the United Church of Canada Act.

Of the Municipal Corporation of the Town of Huntsville, praying that an Act may pass validating an agreement and a certain by-law.

Of the Midland Simcoe Railway Company, praying that an Act may pass extending the times for the construction and completion of their railway.

Of Herbert William Campbell, of Hamilton, and others, praying that an Act may pass incorporating the Association of Accountants and Auditors of Ontario.

Of the Corporation of the Town of Walkerville, praying that an Act may pass to validate a certain by-law; also, to amend Section 7, Chapter 134, of the Town of Walkerville Act.

Of the City of Sault Ste. Marie, praying that an Act may pass validating certain by-laws and confirming certain tax sales and deeds.

Of the National Council of the Young Men's Christian Association, praying that an Act may pass respecting incorporation.

Of the Corporation of the City of Toronto, praying that an Act may pass concerning the issue of debentures for the purpose of raising money for grants to hospitals and other purposes.

Of the Corporation of the City of Toronto, praying that an Act may pass respecting separate accounting for operations within City limits and operations outside City territory by the Consumers Gas Company.

Of the Corporation of the City of Toronto, praying that an Act may pass respecting audits of the books of the Consumers Gas Company.

Of A. E. Jones and others, of Castleton, Northumberland County, with respect to the Game Laws of Ontario.

The following Bills were severally introduced and read the first time:—

Bill (No. 92), intituled "An Act to consolidate and amend the Crown Attorneys Act." *Mr. Nickle.*

Ordered, That the Bill be read the second time to-morrow.

Bill (No. 93), intituled "An Act to consolidate and amend the Coroners Act." *Mr. Nickle.*

Ordered, That the Bill be read the second time To-morrow.

Bill (No. 94), intituled "An Act to consolidate and amend the Constables Act." *Mr. Nickle.*

Ordered, That the Bill be read the second time To-morrow.

Bill (No. 95), intituled "An Act respecting the Red Lake Mining Division. *Mr. McCrea.*

Ordered, That the Bill be read the second time forthwith.

———

The following Bill was read a second time:—

Bill (No. 95), respecting Red Lake Mining Division.

Referred to a Committee of the Whole House To-morrow.

———

Mr. Kemp asked the following Question:—

1. Did the Minister of Lands and Forests announce the result of the opening of tenders for about 9,000 square miles of pulpwood lands at a meeting held at Port Arthur on the 23rd day of October last in the interests of Mr. Langworthy, the Conservative candidate in the late Dominion elections. 2. Were the time and place of the announcement chosen with the object of influencing the electors of Port Arthur to vote for Mr. Langworthy. 3. Why was not the announcement made in the usual way from the Minister's office in Toronto.

And the Minister of Lands and Forests replied as follows — :

1. No. The Minister, however, announced that the Department had given approval to certain offers for the sale of pulpwood cordage off certain lands at the head of the lakes. 2. No. 3. There is no such established custom.

Mr. Tellier asked the following Question:—

1. How many tenders were received by the Government for the pulp and timber limits in the watersheds of Kapuskasing, Ground Hog and Mattagami Rivers (District of Cochrane), in response to the advertisement for tenders to close September 10th, 1925.   2. What was the total area upon which tenders were asked.   3. Who were the tenderers whose tenders were accepted.   4. When were the tenders accepted.   5. What area was allotted to each successful tenderer. 6. What was the price of the successful tenderer in each case for each kind of timber.   7. Who were the unsuccessful tenderers and what was the price each of them offered for each kind of timber, and the area upon which each of them tendered.

And the Minister of Lands and Forests replied as follows:—

1. Three.   2. Tenders were asked upon the basis of cordage and the area was described only for the purpose of indicating the watershed and approximate territory out of which the wood was to be taken, and to enable the tenderers to estimate, when making tenders, the costs of operation.   3. Spruce Falls Company, Limited.   4. November 14th, 1925.   5. The contract provides for a supply of wood at a price per cord.   No specific area is allotted.   To protect the Crown in its undertaking to furnish a supply of wood, a certain area is set aside by the Crown upon which it is estimated such supply exists.   The Company is required to apply annually for a permit to operate on a specific location within that territory.   The Minister may, if in the interests of the Crown, withhold such permit and require the Company to cut elsewhere.

6.

	Bonus	Upset	Dues	Total
Spruce pulpwood............$ 15		$ 50	$1 40	$2 05
Balsam.........................		50	70	1 20
Poplar.........................		10	40	50
Jack Pine......................		10	40	50
Jack Pine logs.................		3 50	2 50	6 00

7. (a) The Hawk Lake Lumber Co. bid only on 81 sq. miles.

	Bonus	Upset	Dues	Total
Spruce pulpwood............$ 06		$ 50	$1 40	$1 96
Balsam.................... 06		40	70	1 16
Poplar.................... 06		10	40	56
Jack Pine................. 10		10	40	60
Jack Pine logs............... 1 00		3 50	2 50	7 00

No deposit—tender irregular.

(*b.*) J. W. Killam & W. D. Ross.

Alternative bid No. 1—742 square miles.

	Add Bonus	Upset Bonus	Dues	Total
Spruce pulpwood.............$1 25	$ 50	$1 40	$3 15
Balsam.........................	40	70	1 10
Poplar.........................	10	40	50
Jack Pine......................	10	40	50
Jack Pine logs.................	3 50	2 50	6 00

Under this bid applicants proposed to extend present plant to increase pulp production only and largely for export.

Alternative bid No. 2—1,228 square miles.

	Add Bonus	Upset Bonus	Dues	Total
Spruce pulpwood.............$1 15	$ 50	$1 40	$3 05

Other wood and timber same as in bid No. 1.

Under this bid part pulp and part paper only to be produced.

Alternative bid No. 3—2,989 square miles.

	Add Bonus	Upset Bonus	Dues	Total
Spruce pulpwood.............$1 05	$ 50	$1 40	$2 95

Other wood, no price bid.

Apparently the same as in bids 1 and 2.

Under this bid part pulp and part paper only to be produced—with other proposals.

The tenderers who made the foregoing bid recite that they control the Metagami Pulp Company, now in a receiver's hands, and that they contemplate the formation of a new company to acquire the old company and carry on the business. About one-half a million dollars of the liabilities of the Metagami Company is owing to settlers, small merchants and operators in Northern Ontario. The Department required the tenderers to undertake to settle these claims before being given further supplies of Crown timber to enable them to rehabilitate the insolvent company. This they refused to do. Moreover, they refused to comply with the requirement of the Department, that all their raw materials should be completely manufactured into paper in Ontario. For these reasons the above tenders were not considered to comply with the requirements of the advertisement for tenders, and therefore were not in form to be acted upon by the Department.

Mr. Tellier asked the following Question:—

1. How many tenders were received by the Government for the pulp and timber limits in the Lake Nipigon Region (District of Thunder Bay) in response to the advertisement for tenders to close September 10th, 1925. 2. What was the total area upon which tenders were asked. 3. Who were the tenderers whose tenders were accepted. 4. When were the tenders accepted. 5. What area was allotted to each successful tenderer. 6. What was the price of the successful tenderer in each case for each kind of timber. 7. Who were the unsuccessful tenderers and what was the price each of them offered for each kind of timber and the area upon which each of them tendered.

And the Minister of Lands and Forests replied as follows:—

1. Four tenders were received, one complying with the conditions required and enclosing necessary deposits; two tenders were received without the necessary deposit; one tender was received and subsequently withdrawn. 2. Tenders were asked for bids for the right to cut wood at a price per cord from any portion of an area of approximately 6,394 square miles, such portion to be determined from time to time by the Department. 3. (a) Thunder Bay Company, Limited; (b) Nipigon Corporation, Limited; (c) Provincial Paper Mills, Limited; (d) Fort William Pulp & Paper. 4. October 21st, 1925. 5. (a) No area was allotted to tenderers, the Crown undertaking to permit the Thunder Bay Company to cut 5,830,000 cords from locations to be fixed by the Department, annually, on territory comprising approximately 1,555 square miles; (b) No area was allotted to the Nipigon Corporation, the Crown undertaking to permit it to cut 5,842,000 cords from locations fixed by the Department, annually, within the territory comprising approximately 1,568 square miles; (c) No area has been allotted to the Provincial Paper Mills, the Crown undertaking to permit the Company to cut 1,755,563 cords from locations to be fixed, annually, by the Department within the territory comprising approximately 1,296 square miles; (d) No area was allotted to the Fort William Pulp & Paper Company, the Crown undertaking to permit the Company to cut 5,200,000 cords from locations to be fixed, annually, by the Department within a territory approximately 1,566 square miles.

6. Thunder Bay Co., Limited:—

(a)

	Add Bonus	Upset Bonus	Dues	Total
Spruce pulpwood.............$ 06		$ 05	$1 40	$1 96
Balsam pulpwood.................		40	70	1 10
Poplar pulpwood.................		10	40	50
Jack Pine pulpwood...............		10	40	50
Jack Pine logs per M. ft...........		3 50	2 50	6 00

(b) Nipigon Corporation, Limited:—

	Add Bonus	Upset Bonus	Dues	Total
Spruce pulpwood.............$ 08		$ 50	$1 40	$1 98
Balsam pulpwood.................		40	70	1 10
Poplar pulpwood.................		10	40	50
Jack Pine pulpwood...............		10	40	50
Jack Pine logs per M. ft...........		3 50	2 50	6 00

(*c*) Provincial Paper Mills, Limited:—

	Add Bonus	Upset Bonus	Dues	Total
Spruce pulpwood............	$ 05	$ 50	$1 40	$1 95
Balsam pulpwood.................		40	70	1 10
Poplar pulpwood.................		10	40	50
Jack Pine pulpwood..............		10	40	50
Jack Pine logs per M. ft...........		3 50	2 50	6 00

(*d*) Fort William Pulp & Paper Company:—

	Add Bonus	Upset Bonus	Dues	Total
Spruce pulpwood............	$ 10	$ 50	$1 40	$2 00
Balsam pulpwood.................		40	70	1 10
Poplar pulpwood.................		10	40	50
Jack Pine pulpwood..............		10	40	50
Jack Pine logs per M. ft...........		3 50	2 50	6 00

7. (*a*) Young & McEvoy on behalf of McDougall Brothers, wrote a letter requesting that the timber on a portion of the area indicated in the published map be reserved for their tie plant. (*b*) Twin Falls Lumber Company wrote but enclosed no cheque.

Mr. McCallum asked the following Question:—

1. Did the Minister of Lands and Forests make a series of speeches in New Ontario during the months of August, September and October last on behalf of Conservative candidates in the last Dominion elections. 2. How many such speeches did he make. 3. Did he, during these months, make promises or announcements intended to influence electors to vote for the Conservative candidates. 4. What were such promises and announcements.

And the Minister of Lands and Forests replied as follows:—

1. Yes. 2. Several. 3. He discussed matters of Provincial activities and general development of Northern Ontario. 4. Answered by 3.

Mr. Raney asked the following Question:—

1. Does the Government of Ontario own the Nipissing Central Railway. 2. Did the Government authorize the Nipissing Central Railway Company to take proceedings in the courts to establish the right of the Company to extend its line of railway over the Crown lands of the Province of Quebec into the Rouyn mining region. 3. Does the Province of Quebec oppose such extension of the Ontario Government Railway over its Crown lands. 4. Did the Ontario Government instruct counsel to argue before the Supreme Court of Canada that it is obligatory upon the Dominion Government to give its consent to the exten-

sion of the said railway line over the Crown lands in Quebec upon an application by the railway company.   5. Has the Supreme Court decided that it is discretionary with the Dominion Government to grant or refuse such consent.   6. Does the Province of Quebec contend that the Dominion Government has no jurisdiction to authorize such extension.   7. Has an appeal been taken to the judicial committee of the Privy Council from the Supreme Court of Canada.   8. In the event of the judgment of the Supreme Court being affirmed, does the Ontario Government intend to ask the Dominion Government to over-ride the objections of Quebec.   9. If not, what is the purpose of the litigation.   10. What has been the cost of the litigation to this date.

And the Prime Minister answered as follows:—

1. The Nipissing Central Railway is owned by the people of Ontario and operated by the Temiskaming and Northern Ontario Railway Commission, under a charter granted by the Dominion   2. The proceedings in Court were instituted by a reference submitted by the Governor-General in Council to the Supreme Court of Canada.   3. The Government of Quebec denies the right of the Dominion Government to grant permission for the extension of the Railway over the Crown lands of Quebec, and denies the power of the Dominion Parliament to give such authority.   4. Instructions given to counsel were given by the Nipissing Central Railway, and such instructions at the present time are confidential.   5. The Supreme Court of Canada has upheld the validity of Section 189 of the Dominion Railway Act, under which authority was sought to extend the Railway and the Supreme Court has further affirmed that it is not obligatory upon the Dominion Government to exercise the authority conferred by the said Section, subject to the following reservations, that: "The Company is constituted and its powers are conferred by Parliament which, as a condition to the taking of Crown lands, has required the consent of the Governor-in-Council, who thus, as the donee of Parliament, is entrusted with the power, to be exercised as an incident of the good government of the country; there is a duty to consider and to exercise sound discretion, but it is a duty involving political rather than legal responsibility, and in respect to the execution of which the Governor-in-Council is not answerable to the judicial tribunals. The condition which requires consent imports no more than an incidental power of regulation, and it cannot be assumed that the Government would exercise this power in a manner to frustrate the execution of the statutory project."   6. Yes. 7. Yes.   8. The future course of action has not been decided.   9. To determine the questions submitted by the Governor-General in Council.   10. There has been no cost as yet to the Province, and the expectation is that the Railway Company will pay its own expenses.

———

Mr. Kemp asked the following Question:—

1. Did Mr. F. H. Keefer, Legislative Secretary for Northern Ontario, take any part in the late Dominion elections in Northern Ontario ridings.   2. How many speeches did he make at meetings held in the interests of Conservative candidates.   3. Did the Province pay him a salary at the rate of $6,000 per year while he was doing this work.   4. Did he charge the Province with his travelling expenses during this time.   5. In what ridings and for what candidates did he make speeches.

And the Prime Minister replied as follows:—

1. Yes; only in the Dominion Electoral Riding where he resides, and in the capacity of an elector thereof. 2. Eight. 3. He received his salary for his official duties only. 4 No. 5. The Dominion Electoral Riding of Port Arthur. Candidate, W. F. Langworthy, K.C.

Mr. Kemp asked the following Question:—

1. What was the date of the appointment of Mr. F. H. Keefer to the Legislative Secretarial post for Northern Ontario. 2. Was he paid the salary of $6,000 a year from the 16th of July, 1923. 3. Was that the day the present Government came into office. 4. Under what authority was he acting from the 16th day of July, 1923, until the date of his appointment pursuant to the Act creating the office, on the 17th of April, 1924. 5. What service did Mr. Keefer perform during those nine months. 6. Was he paid his salary from month to month during those months. If so, out of what appropriation. 7. Did the auditor assent to such payments.

And the Prime Minister replied as follows —

1. The appointment dated from July 16th, 1923, as authorized by Section 5, Chapter 6, 14 George V. 2. Yes, but not until authority was given by the Legislature, by Sections 3 and 5, Chapter 6, 14 George V. 3. Yes. 4. Under the instructions of the Government that legislation would be passed relating thereto. 5. The same service that he continued to render after the above mentioned Act was passed. 6. No. 7. This question is answered by the reply to Question No. 6.

Mr. Tellier asked the following Question:—

1. Has an Order-in-Council been passed by the Government, requiring that before searches can be made in the office of the Provincial Secretary as to officers and shareholders in joint stock companies, in Ontario, and the holdings of such in said companies, the Minister of the Department must give his consent. 2. If so, when was it passed.

And the Provincial Secretary replied as follows:—

1. No. An Order-in-Council was passed on the 23rd April pursuant to Section 33 of The Ontario Companies Act, which provides that "no person, except with the consent of the Minister, shall be privileged to make or procure a copy or copies of any lists of shareholders filed in the office of the Provincial Secretary" under the said Act. Such Order-in-Council does not interfere in any way with searches of the company files in the office of the Provincial Secretary. 2. Answered by No. 1.

The following Bills were severally read the second time:—

Bill (No. 73), To amend the Public Lands Act.   *Mr. McCrea.*

Referred to a Committee of the Whole House To-morrow.

Bill (No. 75), To amend the Cemetery Act.   *Mr. Nickle.*

Referred to a Committee of the Whole House To-morrow.

Bill (No. 76), To amend the Vendors and Purchasers Act.   *Mr. Nickle.*

Referred to a Committee of the Whole House To-morrow.

Bill (No. 77), Respecting Private Detectives.   *Mr. Nickle.*

Referred to a Committee of the Whole House To-morrow.

Bill (No. 78), To amend the Commissioners for taking Affidavits Act.   *Mr. Nickle.*

Referred to a Committee of the Whole House To-morrow.

The House resolved itself into a Committee to consider Bill (No. 65), To amend the Royal Ontario Museum Act, and, after some time spent therein, Mr. Speaker resumed the Chair; and Mr. Jamieson (Grey) reported, That the Committee had directed him to report the Bill without any amendment.

Ordered, That the Bill be read the third time To-morrow.

The House resolved itself into a Committee to consider Bill (No. 66), To amend the Public Libraries Act, and, after some time spent therein, Mr. Speaker resumed the Chair; and Mr. Jamieson (Grey) reported, That the Committee had directed him to report the Bill without any amendment.

Ordered, That the Bill be read the third time To-morrow.

The House resolved itself into a Committee to consider Bill (No. 69), To amend the Department of Education Act, and, after some time spent therein, Mr. Speaker resumed the Chair; and Mr. Jamieson (Grey) reported, That the Committee had directed him to report the Bill without any amendment.

Ordered, That the Bill be read the third time To-morrow.

The House resolved itself into a Committee to consider Bill (No. 71), To amend the Unwrought Metal Sales Act, and, after some time spent therein, Mr. Speaker resumed the Chair; and Mr. Jamieson (Grey) reported, That the Committee had directed him to report the Bill without any amendment.

Ordered, That the Bill be read the third time To-morrow.   .

The House resolved itself into a Committee to consider Bill (No. 72), To provide for the Payment of an Annuity to the University of Toronto, and, after some time spent therein, Mr. Speaker resumed the Chair; and Mr. Jamieson (Grey) reported, That the Committee had directed him to report the Bill without any amendment.

Ordered, That the Bill be read the third time To-morrow.

The Provincial Secretary presented to the House, by command of His Honour the Lieutenant-Governor:—

Report of the Commissioners for the Queen Victoria Niagara Falls Park, 1924. (*Sessional Papers No. 34*).

Also, Return to an order of the House, dated 3rd April, 1925, that there be laid before the House a Return showing—1. What was the total expenditure on account of provincial highways from the inception of the Provincial Highways System up to December 31st, 1924. 2. Of the expenditure stated in reply to Question No. 1, what amounts have been refunded to Ontario by (a) county municipalities, (b) cities, (c) by the Dominion Government. 3. Of the expenditure stated in reply to Question No. 1, what amounts have been levied upon but remain unpaid by (a) county municipalities, (b) cities, and (c) the Dominion Government. 4. Of the expenditure stated in reply to Question No. 1, what further amounts will be levied upon (a) county municipalities, (b) cities, (c) the Dominion Government. 5. What is the total amount of expenditure on provincial highways remaining after all deductions, to be borne by the Provincial Government. 6. Of the expenditure stated in reply to Question No. 1, what amount was expended upon repair and maintenance, as distinguished from construction. 7. Of the expenditure stated in reply to Question No. 1, what amounts have been refunded to Ontario by (a) county municipalities, (b) cities, and (c) by the Dominion Government. 8. Of the expenditure stated in reply to Question No. 6, what amounts have been levied upon, but remain unpaid, by (a) county municipalities, (b) cities, and (c) the Dominion Government. 9. Of the expenditure stated in reply to Question No. 6, what further amounts will be levied upon (a) county municipalities, (b) cities, (c) the Dominion Government. 10. What is the total amount of expenditure on Provincial highways for maintenance remaining after all deductions, to be borne by the Provincial Government. 11. Of the total expenditure by the Government upon highways in the Province of Ontario, what amount has been paid out of current revenue and what amount has been capitalized. 12. During the years 1921, 1922, 1923, what amount of the annual expenditure was paid out of revenue and what amount capitalized. 13. Against the capitalized debt in respect of the expenditure upon roads, have any sums been credited from any source whatsoever; if so, what amount, from what source. 14. Of the capitalized debt in respect of roads, has there been any scheme or plan to retire this debt by a sinking fund or by annual payments. If so, what is the amount of the annual payment at the present time necessary to retire this debt. If no such plan has been in operation, what would be the annual sum necessary to retire the Government's capital expenditure upon roads if such plan were adopted and over how many years would such plan run. (*Sessional Papers No. 35.*)

The House then adjourned at 5.12 p.m.

TUESDAY, FEBRUARY 23RD, 1926.

PRAYERS.   3 O'CLOCK P.M.

The following Petition was brought up and laid upon the Table:—

Mr. Clarke (Northumberland W.), of the ratepayers of the Township of Hamilton and others *re* Rural School Boards.

The following Bills were severally introduced and read the first time:—

Bill (No. 96), intituled "An Act to amend the Ontario Temperance Act." *Mr. Pinard.*

Ordered, That the Bill be read the second time on Friday next.

Bill (No. 97), intituled "An Act to amend the Consolidated Municipal Act.' *Mr. Wright.*

Ordered, That the Bill be read the second time on Friday next.

Question No. 45. Re Ministers being members of Joint Stock Companies, withdrawn.

On motion of Mr. Ferguson, seconded by Mr. Nickle,

Ordered, That out of respect to the late Arthur Henry Sydere, Esq., an Official of this House since Confederation and for many years Clerk of the Legislative Assembly, when this House adjourns to-day it do stand adjourned until Thursday next, the 25th inst., at Three o'clock in the afternoon.

The following Bills were severally read the second time:—

Bill (No. 91), To improve the Quality of Dairy Products. *Mr. Martin.*

Referred to a Committee of the Whole House Thursday next.

Bill (No. 88), Respecting the Department of Agriculture. *Mr. Martin.*

Referred to a Committee of the Whole House Thursday next.

The House resolved itself into a Committee to consider Bill (No. 75), To amend the Cemetery Act, and, after some time spent therein, Mr. Speaker resumed the Chair; and Mr. Black reported, That the Committee had directed him to report the Bill with certain amendments.

Ordered, That the Amendments be taken into consideration forthwith.

The Amendments, having been read the second time, were agreed to.

Ordered, That the Bill be read the third time on Thursday next.

The House resolved itself into a Committee to consider Bill (No. 95), Respecting the Red Lake Mining Division, and, after some time spent therein, Mr. Speaker resumed the Chair; and Mr. Black reported, That the Committee had directed him to report the Bill without any amendment.

Ordered, That the Bill be read the third time forthwith.

The Bill was then read the third time, and passed.

The Order of the Day for resuming the Adjourned Debate on the Motion for the consideration of the speech of His Honour the Lieutenant-Governor, at the opening of the Session, having been read,

The Debate was resumed,

And, after some time, it was, on the motion of Mr. Keefer,

Ordered, That the Debate be adjourned until Thursday next.

The House then adjourned at 6 p.m.

THURSDAY, FEBRUARY 25TH, 1926.

PRAYERS.   3 O'CLOCK P.M.

The following Petition was read and received:—

Of the ratepayers of the Township of Hamilton, praying that no change be made in the present system of Rural School Boards.

———

Mr. Lewis, from the Standing Committee on Standing Orders, presented their First Report, which was read as follows and adopted:—

Your Committee have carefully examined the following Petitions and find the Notices as published in each case sufficient:—

Of Robert Cooper and others of Welland, praying that an Act may pass to incorporate the Welland and Port Colborne Railway Company.

Of the Corporation of the Town of Arnprior, praying that an Act may pass for the purpose of consolidating the floating debt, and authorizing a loan on credit of debentures.

Of Verene May McLeod of the City of Toronto, and Gladys Alma Currie of New York, praying that an Act may pass authorizing the payment of certain moneys to the Essex Border Utilities Commission General Hospital.

Of Vigfus Einarson et al. of the Village of Rosseau, praying that an Act may pass incorporating certain areas as an incorporated village.

Of the City of Toronto, praying that an Act may pass authorizing certain grants, also to authorize the passage of by-laws re debenture issues and to ratify and confirm a certain by-law re construction of sewers.

Of the City of Fort William, praying that an Act may pass validating and confirming certain by-laws.

Of the Township of North York, praying that an Act may pass authorizing Council to pass certain by-laws re sewers, garbage and incinerators, also to confirm a certain by-law.

Of the Haliburton, Whitney and Mattawa Railway Company, praying that an Act may pass authorizing the building of an additional section of the Railway.

Of the Corporation of the City of Toronto, praying that an Act may pass authorizing the City to own and operate vessels for transportation of passengers to and from Toronto Island.

Of the Municipal Corporation of the Town of Eastview, praying that an Act may pass confirming and ratifying a by-law, also ratifying and confirming an agreement between the Petitioner and Bretislav Pliske.

Of the Toronto Western Hospital, praying that an Act may pass validating and confirming an agreement of amalgamation of Grace Hospital and Toronto Western Hospital.

Of the Township of Teck, praying that an Act may pass authorizing the passage of a by-law fixing the Poll-tax Assessment.

Of the Town of Ford City, praying that an Act may pass incorporating the Town into a City.

Of the Town of Weston, praying that an Act may pass to ratify and confirm a certain agreement, also to permit passage of certain by-laws.

Of the Essex Border Utilities Commission, praying that an Act may pass authorizing proceedings prior to construction of the Grand Marais sewer and to amend a by-law, also to give authority to equalize rate of taxation, and to make certain debentures a joint liability of the Essex Border Municipalities.

Of the Town of LaSalle, praying that an Act may pass validating by-laws passed respecting payments for watermains.

Of the Town of Walkerville, praying that an Act may pass validating a certain by-law, also to amend a certain Act passed affecting Town of Walkerville debentures.

Your Committee recommend that Rule No. 51 of Your Honourable House be suspended in this, that the time for presenting Petitions for Private Bills be extended until and inclusive of Friday, the 5th day of March next, and that the time for introducing Private Bills be extended until and inclusive of Friday, the 12th day of March next, and the time for receiving Reports of Committees on Private Bills be extended until and inclusive of Thursday, the 18th day of March, 1926.

Ordered, That the time for presenting Petitions for Private Bills be extended until and inclusive of Friday, the 5th day of March next.

Ordered, That the time for introducing Private Bills be extended until and inclusive of Friday, the 12th day of March next.

Ordered, That the time for receiving Reports of Committees on Private Bills be extended until and inclusive of Thursday, the 18th day of March, 1926.

Mr. Trewartha, from the Standing Committee on Agriculture and Colonization, presented their First Report.

His Honour the Lieutenant-Governor entered the Chamber of the Legislative Assembly and took his seat upon the Throne.

Mr. Speaker then addressed His Honour as follows:—

May it please Your Honour.

The Legislative Assembly of the Province, having at its present Sittings passed a certain Bill, to which, on behalf and in the name of the said Assembly, I respectfully request Your Honour's Assent.

———

The Clerk Assistant then read the Title of the Act that had passed, as follows:—

An Act respecting the Red Lake Mining Division.

To this Act the Royal Assent was announced by the Clerk of the Legislative Assembly in the following words:—

In His Majesty's name, His Honour the Lieutenant-Governor doth assent to this Act.

His Honour was then pleased to retire.

———

The following Bills were severally introduced and read the first time:—

Bill (No. 1), intituled "An Act to incorporate the Welland and Port Colborne Railway Company." *Mr. Vaughan.*

Referred to the Committee on Railways.

Bill (No. 2), intituled "An Act respecting the Town of Arnprior." *Mr. Thompson.*

Referred to the Railway and Municipal Board.

Bill (No. 6), intituled "An Act to enable the Executors of the late John Curry to make a certain gift out of his estates to the Building Fund of the Proposed Essex Border Utilities General Hospital." *Mr. Wilson (Windsor).*

Referred to the Commissioners of Estates Bills.

Bill (No. 9), intituled "An Act to incorporate the Village of Rosseau." *Mr. Harcourt.*

Referred to the Committee on Private Bills.

Bill (No. 12), intituled "An Act respecting the City of Toronto." *Mr. Nesbitt.*

Referred to the Committee on Private Bills.

Bill (No. 13), intituled "An Act respecting the City of Fort William." *Mr. Spence.*

Referred to the Committee on Private Bills.

Bill (No. 14), intituled "An Act respecting the Township of North York." *Mr. Keith.*

Referred to the Committee on Private Bills.

Bill (No. 19), intituled "An Act respecting the Town of Weston, the Township of York, and the Toronto Transportation Commission. *Mr. Keith.*

Referred to the Committee on Private Bills.

Bill (No. 26), intituled "An Act respecting the Haliburton, Whitney and Mattawa Railway Company." *Mr. Mark.*

Referred to the Committee on Railways.

Bill (No. 34), intituled "An Act to incorporate the City of Ford City." *Mr. Homuth.*

Referred to the Committee on Private Bills.

Bill (No. 38), intituled "An Act respecting the City of Toronto." *Mr. McBrien.*

Referred to the Committee on Private Bills.

Bill (No. 39), intituled "An Act respecting the Town of Eastview." *Mr. Belanger.*

Referred to the Committee on Private Bills.

Bill (No. 42), intituled "An Act respecting the Amalgamation of the Toronto Western Hospital with Grace Hospital. *Mr. Nesbitt.*

Referred to the Committee on Private Bills.

Bill (No. 47), intituled "An Act respecting the Township of Teck." *Mr. Kennedy (Temiskaming).*

Referred to the Committee on Private Bills.

Bill (No. 50), intituled "An Act respecting the Town of LaSalle." *Mr. Wilson (Windsor).*

Referred to the Committee on Private Bills.

Bill (No. 98), intituled "An Act respecting the Investigation of Industrial Disputes within the Province." *Mr. Homuth.*

Ordered, That the Bill be read the second time To-morrow.

Bill (No. 99), intituled "An Act to amend the Vital Statistics Act." *Mr. Gray.*

Ordered, That the Bill be read the second time To-morrow.

———————

The Provincial Secretary presented to the House, by command of His Honour the Lieutenant-Governor:—

Sixth Annual Report of the Ontario Athletic Commission. (*Sessional Papers, No. 36.*)

———————

The Order of the Day for resuming the Adjourned Debate on the Motion for the consideration of the Speech of His Honour the Lieutenant-Governor, at the opening of the Session, having been read,

The Debate was resumed,

And after some time, it was, on the motion of Mr. McBride,

Ordered, That the Debate be adjourned till Tuesday next.

———————

The House then adjourned at 5.45 p.m.

FRIDAY, FEBRUARY 26TH, 1926.

PRAYERS.   3 O'CLOCK P.M.

The following Petition was brought up and laid upon the Table:—

By Mr. Pinard, the Petition of the Ottawa Police Benefit Fund Association.

———

Mr. Kemp asked the following Question:—

1. What amount of public money has been paid to Mr. A. H. Keefer, Legislative Secretary for Northern Ontario (a) for salary, (b) for travelling expenses, (c) for any other reason, from the 16th of July, 1923, to this date. 2. Has Mr. Keefer a railway pass or passes covering the Province of Ontario.

The Prime Minister replied as follows:—

1. (a) $15,500.00, being payments on account of salary, at $6,000 per annum, during a period of over two and one-half years. (b) $924.50, including expenses in Washington for one month in 1923, opposing the abstraction of water from the Great Lakes by the Chicago diversion; expenses in Washington for nearly two months in 1924 on the same mission, and expenses in Washington for one week in 1925 in the same connection, also expenses for one week in Michigan City, Indiana, in 1925, attending conference; for one week in St. Paul, Minnesota, and one week in Detroit in 1926, attending conferences regarding the lake ports and harbours; also other expenses on official business in Toronto and elsewhere. The above disbursements did not include any payments for railway fares over any line upon which he as a member of the Legislature has free transportation. (c) $4,985.81, being disbursements for rent of office, stenographers and other usual office expenses. 2. Yes, in common with all other members of the Legislative Assembly.

———

Mr. Bragg asked the following Question:—

1. What was the total revenue during the last fiscal year to the Province of Ontario from automobile licenses, truck licenses, motorbus licenses and franchises and gasoline tax. 2. What is the amount of revenue from each source. 3. What other revenue was received by or through the Department of Highways for the use of the Province during said period as a revenue applicable towards maintenance of highways in Ontario.

The Minister of Public Works and Highways replied as follows:—

1. $7,421,632.58. 2. Auto permits, $4,441,348.02; truck permits, $954,931.63; public vehicles (franchise), $50,918.83; gasoline tax, $1,974,434.10. 3. Motor Vehicles Branch, other revenue, $191,794.90; miscellaneous revenue, $870,708.07. N.B.—This amount includes refunds, rents and sales of materials, which are in reality a set-off against expenditure. One item, cement sacks refund, has for years been placed in ordinary revenue, although the major proportion would seem to come from capital. The major proportion of this receipt will in future be credited to Capital Account. All revenue is paid into and becomes part of the Consolidated Revenue Fund.

Mr. Belanger asked the following Question:—

1. On what date was the English-French Enquiry Commission appointed.
2. Who are the members and officials of the Commission.   3. What is the scope
of the Commission's instructions.   4. Is the enquiry to comprise an investigation
into: (1) the efficiency of the teaching of French; (2) the schools wherein French
is a subject of study and which fall without the purview of Regulation 17; (3)
the personnel and methods and inspection; (4) the sufficiency of present provisions for training bilingual teachers.   5. On what date did the Commission
begin its work.   6. (1) Is the Commission required to report on a set date; (2)
if so, when; (3) if not, what instructions were given it as to the time when a
report will be required; (4) if no instructions were given as to the report, when is
such report expected.   7. (1) Has the Commission been given a list of particular
schools that are to be visited; (2) if so, what schools are comprised in such list;
(3) if so, what determined the choice of the schools comprised in said list.   8.
What schools have been visited by the Commission to date of return.   9 (1)
Do all the members of the Commission visit each class-room at the same time;
(2) if not, what method is followed.

· The Prime Minister replied as follows:—

1. October 21st, 1925.   Note: The examination of the schools could not
be very well undertaken in the Spring after the close of the Session because,'
after Easter, the schools are engaged in a review of the work of the year and in'
examinations. It could not be undertaken earlier in the Fall because the men
desired for the Board could not be obtained. 2. (1) Members of the Board:
Dr. F. W. Merchant, Chief Director of Education for Ontario; His Honour
Judge Scott, of Perth; Mr. Louis Cote, Barrister, Ottawa; (2) Officials: English
Secretary, Dr. W. J. Karr, Director of Rural School Organization, Department
of Education; French Secretary, Mr. A. J. Beneteau, B.A., French Master of
the English-French Training School, Sandwich. 3. To make a comprehensive
and thorough survey of the schools of the Province attended by pupils who speak
the French languages with a view: (1) To determine the general efficiency of
these schools; (2) To ascertain whether the regulations embodied in Circular 17
have been effective in securing for all the pupils a practical working knowledge
of English without interfering with adequate instruction in French; (3) To
devise means for improving the instruction in these schools; (4) To formulate
plans for securing a more constant supply of qualified teachers. (See attached
letter of instructions to the Chairman of the Board.) 4. (1) Yes; (2) Yes;
(3) Yes; (4) Yes. 5. November 11th, 1925. 6. (1) (2) (3) No instructions in
this regard have been given to the Board. An exact date for the completion
of the enquiry cannot be given. There are about 1,000 classrooms in which
French is a subject of instruction in the Public and Separate Schools of the
Province, and a very large proportion of these must be examined if the investigation is to be comprehensive and thorough. From the experience of the Board
up to date it has been found that the pupils in from two to four classrooms can
be examined in a day, depending upon whether the schools are rural or urban
and upon the school grades examined. 7. No. The Board makes special enquiry
from the Inspectors in French-speaking districts and obtains from them a list
of the schools attended by French-speaking pupils. 8. 128 classrooms in the
Counties of Essex and Kent have been examined. The following is a list:—

| Separate Schools | Number of |
Rural:	Classrooms
2, 5, 8 Anderdon	2
8 Sandwich	2
3 Rochester	2
3B Colchester	1
11 Anderdon	1
8, 20 Colchester N	3
6 Tilbury N	1
3 Tilbury E	1
1 Maidstone	1
17 Rochester	1
6 Sandwich W	1
2 Tilbury N	1
7 Tilbury N	1
4 Sandwich W	1
2 Sandwich S	2
6 Maidstone	1
1 Tilbury N	3
3 Sandwich E	1
10, 11 Tilbury N. and Rochester	1
11 Tilbury N	1
9, 14 Rochester and Tilbury N	1
6 Rochester	2
3 Maidstone	1
7 Dover	1
3 Dover	2
9 Dover	1

Urban:	
Amherstburg	4
Belle River	5
Ford	20
La Salle	3
Riverside	7
Sandwich	9
Tecumseh	9
Tilbury	7
Windsor	13

| Public Schools | Number of |
Rural:	Classrooms
2, 5 Anderdon	1
8, 9 Sandwich W	1
1 Maidstone and Rochester	1
6 Rochester	1
3 Tilbury N	1
9 Tilbury N	1
6 Anderdon	2
2 Sandwich W	1
7 Sandwich W	1
5 Sandwich E	2
6 Sandwich E	1
4 Dover	2

9. (1), (2) The methods of examining the schools have been left to the
judgment of the Board. It is understood that, under the direction of the Board,
the Secretaries shall take part in the examination of the pupils. The Secretaries
have been selected with a view to their ability to do this work. Dr. Karr has
had wide experience as a teacher in the schools of the Province. He has been
principal of rural and city public schools. He was for a time English Master in
the English-French Training School at Ottawa, and for several years Assistant
Master in the Normal Schools at North Bay and Ottawa. He is a graduate in
Arts and Pedagogy of Queen's University. Mr. Beneteau is particularly qualified
as examiner in French. He was brought up in a French-speaking family, his
father being for many years a teacher in the English-French public schools.
He holds a First Class professional certificate, and is a graduate of Queen's
University. He has given special attention to the study of French, graduating
with honours in this department at the University. He has also taken special
courses in French at McGill University. He was for a time a teacher in an
English-French rural school. Since 1912 he has been French Master in the
English-French Training School at Sandwich. For the last five years he has
also acted as an Inspector of English-French schools in Essex and Kent.

Letter appointing Dr. Merchant as Chairman of the English-French School
Enquiry Board:—

Toronto, October 21st, 1925.

Dear Sir:—

I desire to have an investigation made of those schools in the Province
attended by pupils who speak the French language. The investigation conducted
by you between 1910 and 1912 arose, as you are aware, from complaints of the
general inefficiency of those schools. Following that enquiry, the present
regulations, embodied in Circular No. 17, were adopted. The purpose of these
regulations was to ensure that all pupils should receive a practical working
knowledge of the English language without interfering with adequate instruction
in French or depriving French-speaking children of training in their mother-
tongue. These regulations have been in operation now for over twelve years
and I am desirous of obtaining accurate information respecting their practical
working especially in respect to the efficiency of pupils in the English and French
languages.

Under the circumstances, I wish you to undertake this investigation and
I have asked His Honour Judge Scott, of Perth, and Louis Cote, Esquire, Barrister, of Ottawa, to join with you in making the enquiry. A comprehensive
and thorough survey of the situation should be carried out with a view of determining the efficiency of the schools, means for improving the instruction, and
plans for securing a more constant supply of qualified teachers for the schools.
The enquiry may be made in the manner believed by the Board, of which you
will act as chairman, to be best adapted to reach the end in view, and all necessary
assistance required to do the work will be provided.

Yours truly,

Minister of Education.

F. W. Merchant, Esq., LL.D., D.Paed.,
Chief Director of Education,
Toronto.

Mr. Belanger asked the following Question:—

1. What English-French schools were visited during 1925 by (1) School Inspector Walsh; (2) School Inspector Lapensee. 2. What total amounts were paid during 1925 in salaries and expenses of all kinds to (1) School Inspector Lapensee; (2) School Inspector Walsh. 3. (1) Has School Inspector Walsh submitted to the Department of Education a translation in French verse of English Nursery Rhymes for use in the English-French schools of his inspectorate; (2) has the Department of Education authorized the use of such translation in the English-French schools; (3) has the Department of Education authorized the payment of any sum to cover the cost of printing such translation.

The Prime Minister replied as follows:—

1. (1) Inspector Walsh visited and officially reported upon 26 English-French schools during 1925 in the Townships of Alfred, Cambridge, Clarence, Cumberland, Gloucester, Plantagenet North and South, Roxborough and Russell. See attached list. (2) Inspector Lapensee visited and officially reported upon 26 English-French schools during 1925 in the Townships of Alfred, Cambridge, Clarence, Cumberland, Gloucester, Plantagenet North and South, Roxborough and Russell. See attached list. Other English-French schools than those reported upon officially have been visited by Inspectors Walsh and Lapensee, but admission was refused by the Trustees. In addition to their regular duties, Inspectors Walsh and Lapensee are also assisting Separate School Inspectors who have a large number of teachers under their supervision. 2. (1):—

Mr. Joseph Lapensee:

Salary paid for calendar year 1925	$3,000	00
Services, Vankleek Hill Summer Model School	330	00
Travelling expenses, Vankleek Hill Summer Model School	61	40
Inspection expenses for calendar year 1925	271	01
Total	$3,662	41

(2) Mr. J. C. Walsh:

Salary paid for calendar year 1925	$3,000	00
Inspection expenses for calendar year 1925	352	05
Total	$3,352	05

3. (1) No. But Mr. Walsh states that the translation of certain nursery rhymes from the Public School Primer and from other sources was made by him and submitted to Dr. Waugh, the late Chief Inspector of Public and Separate Schools, who gave him permission to distribute it as an experiment among teachers of the English-French schools in his inspectorate. The purpose of the translation was not so much to teach French reading as to assist the pupils in getting at the meaning of the English text through the French translation. (2) No. (3) Yes. In November, 1923, an account for 200 copies of the translation for $15.00 was presented from The Ottawa Printing Company, through Inspector Walsh. This was paid by the Department of Education.

English-French schools visited and officially reported upon during 1925 by Inspector Lapensee:—

January, 1925—June, 1925		September, 1925—December, 1925	
Alfred	3	Gloucester	6
"	6	"	14
"	7	"	17
	9	"	27
	11	Roxborough	12
	13	"	16
"	14		
Cambridge	4		
"	5, 9		
"	6		
"	15		
Clarence	4		
"	17		
"	20		
Cumberland	7		
Plantagenet S	4		
Plantagenet N	7		
"	9		
Russell	4		
"	16		

Total number of schools visited and officially reported upon during the year 1925 by Inspector Lapensee—26.

English-French schools visited and officially reported upon during 1925 by Inspector Walsh:—

January, 1925—June, 1925		September, 1925—December, 1925	
Gloucester	6	Alfred	7
"	14	"	7, 8
"	17	"	14
"	27	Cambridge	5, 9
Plantagenet S	7	"	6
Roxborough	12	"	15
"	16	Clarence	17
		"	18
		Cumberland	7
		Plantagenet S	4
		"	15
		Plantagenet N	7
		Russell	4
		"	6
		"	7
			8
			13
			14
		"	16

Total number of schools visited and officially repo:ted upon during the year 1925 by Inspector Walsh—26.

Mr. Belanger asked the following Question:—

1. Has the Prime Minister or any other member of the Ontario Government held any conferences with any member or members or officials of the British Government, steamship companies, railroad companies, immigration or colonization societies or other bodies concerning the promoting and directing of immigration and colonization movements into Ontario. 2. If so, when and between what parties were such conferences held. 3. If so, have definite or tentative schemes, arrangements or agreements been approved providing for the recruiting, transportation, reception and distribution of immigrants and settlers in Ontario. 4. In the affirmative, what are the main features, terms and provisions of such schemes, arrangements and agreements.

The Minister of Agriculture replied as follows:—

1. The Prime Minister conferred with the Overseas Settlement Committee when in London, England. He also had informal discussions with some members of the British Government about general conditions in Canada, and particularly in the Province of Ontario, and as to what plans might be developed that would be to the advantage of the Province. Conferences and discussions also took place with Miss Margaret Bondfield, Under Secretary of Labour for the British Government, and Mr. G. F. Plant, Secretary of the Overseas Settlement Board, when they were in Canada in the Fall of 1924. Conferences also took place between the Prime Minister and members of the Government and the Agent-General for Ontario last Fall when the latter was in Toronto, and the Agent-General for Ontario has had conferences with representatives of the Overseas Committee of the British Government from time to time. 2. There is no record as to exact dates or individuals as the conferences were mainly of an informal character. 3 and 4. A definite agreement is now being negotiated in reference to bringing out boys as farm apprentices, but until it is concluded and copies are received on this side, it will be impossible to give exact details.

Mr. Bragg asked the following Question:—

1. What action has the Department of Agriculture taken upon the Report of the Standing Committee on Agriculture and Colonization adopted by the Legislature on April 8th, 1925, page 276, of the Journals 1925, by way of implementing the recommendations of the Agricultural Inquiry Committee, in regard to assisting farmers to secure a greater supply of limestone for their farms. 2. Will a report of such action be presented to the House this Session.

The Minister of Agriculture replied as follows:—

1. In pursuance of the report mentioned, the Department of Agriculture has given a great deal of attention to the question of the use of lime on Ontario farms. Further experiments have been conducted, a soil survey has been completed, and a new Bulletin, giving the latest and best available information, has been issued. Agricultural representatives have carried on a large amount of educational work. The Department, however, has found no general demand for any additional facilities for the granting of loans for purchase of lime. 2. No report beyond the above statement of facts would appear to be necessary.

3 J

Mr. Bragg asked the following Question:—

1. Have the freight rates on feeder cattle carried from public stockyards to farms for finishing purposes been reduced as requested by the resolution of this Legislature, dated March 31st, 1925. 2. When was the resolution placed before the railways operating in Ontario. 3. What action has the Department of Agriculture taken to secure the results aimed at by said resolution. 4. Will a report of the negotiations in connection with this question be made to the Legislature during the present session.

The Minister of Agriculture replied as follows:—

1. No. 2. and 3. The entire case, including the attitude of the Legislature, was placed before the Dominion Railway Board by officials of the Department of Agriculture associated with the Eastern Canada Live Stock Union in Toronto on January 21st last. No judgment has been announced by the Board, but there is understood to be good prospects of a favourable decision. 4. If a decision is reached before the House rises, the Minister will report to the House.

———————

Mr. Sinclair asked the following Question:—

1. What contracts were let to the McNamara Construction Company during the last fiscal year. 2. What is the total price of each contract. 3. What contracts let in previous years have the said company been working on during the last fiscal year. 4. What is the total amount paid to said company during the last fiscal year.

The Minister of Lands and Forests replied as follows:—

1. None. 2. Answered by No. 1. 3. (a) No. 33, Porcupine bituminous penetration pavement, Timmins to South Porcupine; (b) No. 16, Sudbury concrete roadway from Sudbury to Coniston. 4. Paid on Contract No. 33, $140,889.16; paid on Contract No. 16, $188,399.05. Total, $329,288.21. Under Contract No. 17, covering road from Creighton to Copper Cliff let by public tender to the Labarge Lumber Company, who afterward sub-let to the Mc-Namara Construction Company, there was paid under instructions from the Labarge Lumber Company, $85,488.85.

———————

Mr. Fenton asked the following Question:—

1. Did all the members of the Government collect salaries at the rate of $8,000 a year from the 1st of November, 1924 (in addition to their sessional indemnities of $2,000 per year), under the Act of the last Session of the Legislature assented to in April of 1925. 2. If not, what Ministers did not.

The Prime Minister replied as follows:—

1. Under the provisions of Chapter 9, 15 George V, the salaries of Ministers holding Portfolios were fixed at $8,000.00 per annum, as and from November 1st,

1924, and were paid accordingly, with two exceptions. 2. The Minister of Education has not accepted any salary for his services in that capacity since he became Minister. Neither has the Minister of Health accepted any salary for his services in that capacity since he became Minister of Health.

———————

Mr. Lethbridge asked the following Question:—

1. What was the total expenditure by the Government in the prosecution of directors of the Home Bank. 2. What lawyers were employed by the Government in these cases. 3. How much was paid to each of them.

The Attorney-General replied as follows:—

1. $160,955.22. 2 and 3. D. L. McCarthy, K.C., $75,000.00; McGregor Young, K.C., $20,000.00; Lawson, Armstrong & Sinclair, $1,075.00; Reid, Wallbridge & Gibson, Vancouver, B.C., $476.34; Burne & Walkem, Vancouver, $75.00; Blake & Redden, London, Eng., £435 4s. 8d.; Tupper, Bull & Tupper, Vancouver, $424.92.

———————

Mr. Kemp asked the following Question:—

1. Have George Oakley and Son, Ltd., a contract in connection with the new east block which the Government is erecting in Queen's Park. 2. What is the amount of their contract. 3. What is it for. 4. Is Mr. George Oakley, the member of this House for Riverdale, the president of the said company.

The Minister of Public Works and Highways replied as follows:—

1. The information asked for in this question was given to the House on February 19th. (See Votes and Proceedings, page 53.) 2. This is not a matter of official record. 3. Same answer as the reply to Question No. 1. 4. This information is obtainable from the records in the Department of the Provincial Secretary.

———————

Mr. Carty asked the following Question:—

1. How many beer permits have been issued for the riding of Dundas. 2. What are the names and addresses of the persons to whom the same were granted. 3. Were the applications for these permits or any of them approved by Mr. Aaron Sweet, the representative of Dundas. 4. If not all of them, how many of them were approved by him.

The Attorney-General replied as follows:—

1. Eleven. 2. Boyce, Jos., Shop, South Mountain; Duval, E., Shop, Morrisburg; Weagant, A. B., Shop, Morrisburg; Suffel, B., Hotel, Iroquois; Flynn, Jas., Hotel, Chesterville; Barrigar, F. R., Hotel, Mountain; McCloskey,

F., Hotel, Chesterville; Robinson, F. W., Hotel, Morrisburg; Haley, C., Hotel, Iroquois; Mowat, G. F., Hotel, Winchester; Ouderkirk, H. M., Hotel, Morrisburg. 3. If so, he has not expressed himself. 4. Answered by No. 3.

Mr. Belanger asked the following Question:—

1. Has a license been granted by the Government to a company or companies to build a railway or railways over Crown lands in Northern Ontario. 2. To whom has such license been granted. 3. Where and when is the same proposed to be built. 4. With what railways already built will the same connect. 5. At what point or points will the same connect with existing railways.

The Minister of Lands and Forests replied as follows:—

1. Permission granted to Spruce Falls Company, Limited, to construct logging railroad for transporting company's logs from a point at or near Smoky Falls to a point at or near the Town of Kapuskasing, on the Transcontinental railroad, subject to the issue of a formal license under such terms and conditions as may be determined by the Province. 2, 3, 4 and 5. See answer to No. 1.

Mr. Mewhinney asked the following Question:—

1. What action has been taken by the Department of Agriculture in regard to seed grain machinery as recommended in the report of the Standing Committee on Agriculture and Colonization and adopted by the Legislature on April 8th, 1925 (page 276 of the Journals, 1925). 2. Will a report of such action be presented to the House this Session.

The Minister of Agriculture replied as follows:—

1. Considerable information has been accumulated as to available seed-cleaning machinery and a Seed Demonstration Train of three cars, equipped with the best available machinery, will tour Eastern Ontario for five weeks, commencing March 1st. 2. Yes.

Mr. Fisher asked the following Question:—

1. How much money was spent during the last fiscal year under the North and Northwestern Development Acts. 2. How much was spent for roads. 3. How much was spent for bridges. 4. How much was spent for buildings. 5. How much was spent in directing and administering the expenditures.

The Minister of Lands and Forests replied as follows:—

1. $3,562,147.66. 2. $2,825,119.03. 3. $353,621.64. 4. $20,990.49. 5. $57,784.27.

Mr. Bragg asked the following Question:—

1. How much electric power is being developed in New Ontario by the Hydro-Electric Power Commission. 2. Has any survey been made to show how much undeveloped power is available. 3. How much power is being developed by private companies.

The Prime Minister replied as follows:—

1. 75,000 horse-power. 2. Yes. 3. 380,383 horse-power, being the aggregate installation of machinery at the various power developments made by private parties on lands in fee and under leasehold.

Mr. Sinclair asked the following Question:—

1. What was the total cost to the Province of Ontario of all the by-elections necessary in 1923 upon the cabinet ministers seeking re-election as members of the Legislature after their appointment to cabinet positions.

The Attorney-General replied as follows:—

1. The accounts of the Returning Officers amounted in all to the sum of $5,699.89. This amount does not include the travelling expenses of officers nor the cost of furnishing forms, etc., which are kept in stock. Owing to the belief that these elections would take place by acclamation the cost was reduced to a minimum by eliminating every proceeding which would not be necessary except in the case of the holding of a poll. The amount above mentioned does not include the cost to the municipalities of revising the lists which it is estimated would amount to about an equal amount to the expense to the Province. Had contests taken place the cost to the Province would have been in the neighbourhood of from $30,000 to $40,000. The cost of polling apart from mileage and printing of ballot papers amounts to about $30.00 in the case of each poll so that this item alone in an average district would amount to about $2,000 and in a constituency such as Parkdale, East or West York, would amount to about $6,000 in each case.

Mr. Lethbridge asked the following Question:—

1. Were the beer permits treated at first as party patronage. 2. Are they still so treated.

The Attorney-General replied as follows:—

1. No. 2. No.

The following Bills were severally read the second time:—

Bill (No. 70), To consolidate and amend the Trustees Act. *Mr. Nickle.*

Referred to a Committee of the Whole House on Monday next.

Bill (No. 79), The Judges' Orders Enforcement Act. *Mr. Nickle.*

Referred to a Committee of the Whole House on Monday next.

Bill (No. 80), To amend the Devolution of Estates Act. *Mr. Nickle.*

Referred to a Committee of the Whole House on Monday next.

Bill (No. 82), To consolidate and amend the Justices of the Peace Act. *Mr. Nickle.*

Referred to a Committee of the Whole House on Monday next.

Bill (No. 83), To consolidate and amend the Crown Witnesses Act. *Mr. Nickle.*

Referred to a Committee of the Whole House on Monday next.

Bill (No. 84), To consolidate and amend the Fines and Forfeitures Act. *Mr. Nickle.*

Referred to a Committee of the Whole House on Monday next.

Bill (No. 87), To consolidate and amend the Public Authorities Protection Act. *Mr. Nickle.*

Referred to a Committee of the Whole House on Monday next.

Bill (No. 89), To amend the Married Women's Property Act. *Mr. Nickle.*

Referred to a Committee of the Whole House on Monday next.

Bill (No. 90), To consolidate and amend the Magistrates Act. *Mr. Nickle.*

Referred to a Committee of the Whole House on Monday next.

————————

The House resolved itself into a Committee to consider Bill (No. 76), To amend the Vendors and Purchasers Act, and, after some time spent therein, Mr. Speaker resumed the Chair; and Mr. Jamieson (Grey) reported, That the Committee had directed him to report the Bill with certain amendments.

The Amendments, having been read the second time, were agreed to.

Ordered, That the Bill be read the third time on Monday next.

————————

The House resolved itself into a Committee to consider Bill (No. 77), Respecting Private Detectives, and, after some time spent therein, Mr. Speaker resumed the Chair; and Mr. Jamieson (Grey) reported, That the Committee had directed him to report the Bill without any amendment.

Ordered, That the Bill be read the third time on Monday next.

The House resolved itself into a Committee to consider Bill (No. 73), To amend the Public Lands Act, and, after some time spent therein, Mr. Speaker resumed the Chair; and Mr. Jamieson (Grey) reported, That the Committee had directed him to report the Bill without any amendment.

Ordered, That the Bill be read the third time on Monday next.

The House resolved itself into a Committee to consider Bill (No. 88), Respecting the Department of Agriculture, and, after some time spent therein, Mr. Speaker resumed the Chair; and Mr. Jamieson (Grey) reported, That the Committee had directed him to report the Bill without any amendment.

Ordered, That the Bill be read the third time on Monday next.

The House then adjourned at 4.20 p.m.

MONDAY, MARCH 1ST, 1926.

PRAYERS.   3 O'CLOCK P.M.

The following Petition was brought up and laid upon the Table:—

By Mr. Pinard, the Petition of the Municipal Corporation of the City of Ottawa.

The following Petition was read and received:—

Of the Ottawa Police Benefit Fund Association, praying that an Act may pass authorizing the Association to undertake any class of insurance for which a Fraternal Society may be licensed.

The following Bills were severally introduced and read the first time:—

Bill (No. 100), intituled "An Act to amend the Planning and Development Act." *Mr. Owens.*

Ordered, That the Bill be read the second time To-morrow.

Bill (No. 101), intituled "An Act to amend the Ontario Telephone Act." *Mr. Nickle.*

Ordered, That the Bill be read the second time To-morrow.

Bill (No. 102), intituled "An Act to amend the Jurors Act." *Mr. Nickle.*

Ordered, That the Bill be read the second time To-morrow.

Bill (No. 103), intituled "An Act to revise and amend the Election Laws.'' *Mr. Nickle.*

Ordered, That the Bill be read the second time To-morrow.

Bill (No. 104), intituled "An Act to consolidate and amend the Voters List Act." *Mr. Nickle.*

Ordered, That the Bill be read the second time To-morrow.

———

The Prime Minister read the following letters and statement to the House:—

March 1st, 1926.

DEAR MR. FERGUSON:

The numerous questions placed upon the Order Paper recently, making enquiries of a general character in reference to business relations between the Lyons Fuel and Supply Company, Limited, of which I am a shareholder and President, and customers that the Lyons Fuel and Supply Company, Limited, may be doing business with are evidently placed there with the idea of establishing in the minds of the public, by inference, that the position of Minister of Lands and Forests, that I occupy, is being used to the advantage of the Lyons Fuel and Supply Company, Limited.

May I point out to you, Sir, that the Lyons Fuel and Supply Company, Limited, was established in a small way in July, 1913, I being in direct charge from its inception until 1923. The business commenced as a general fuel business, and has been increased and enlarged from year to year as conditions and circumstances would permit until it is recognized now as a general wholesale and retail fuel and builders supply business with business relations extending from the Atlantic to the Pacific, but trading particularly in Northern Ontario with mining companies, lumbering companies, pulp and paper companies, municipal corporations, and the general public.

You will recall that last year when the question of the advisability of members of the Legislature who were shareholders in joint stock companies doing business with the Government was discussed that I willingly stated on the floor of the House that as far as I was concerned that I would undertake to see that no further business was transacted by the Lyons Fuel and Supply Company, Limited, with the Government while I was a member of the House, and I notified the Lyons Fuel and Supply Company, Limited, accordingly.

You will appreciate the fact that, where a well established business has been built up through years of effort with large industrial concerns, to discontinue such a business would bring disastrous results, and you will also realize, I hope, that to comply with the unprecedented requests and submit to the public the business transactions of any established business with its customers would be just as disastrous.

It is not my desire to embarrass you or your Government in any way, or to retard by any action of mine the progress that your Government is making in re-establishing prosperity and confidence in the minds of the people, and a realization of the necessity of responsible Government, and, as I cannot undertake to discontinue the business relations of the Lyons Fuel and Supply Company, Limited, with its established customers, I beg, Sir, to tender herewith my resignation as Minister of Lands and Forests in your Government. May I express to you my sincere appreciation of the confidence you have placed in me by appointing me to the position, and I have endeavoured to reciprocate by serving loyally and efficiently.

Yours very truly,

(Sgd.) JAMES LYONS.

Hon. G. H. Ferguson,
    Prime Minister of Ontario,
        Parliament Buildings.

———

Toronto, March 1st, 1926.

DEAR MR. LYONS:

I am in receipt of your letter of to-day's date, tendering your resignation as Minister of Lands and Forests in the present Government.

In accepting your resignation, I desire to express the deepest regret that your splendid ability as an administrator will no longer be available to the Province.

I thoroughly appreciate your view of the situation and your determination that no opportunity shall be given to those opposed to this administration to cast reflection upon yourself and upon the Government.

I have the utmost confidence in your integrity and refuse to believe that you at any time, or in any way, made use of your position as a Minister of the Crown to further your personal interests, either through your connection with the Lyons Fuel and Supply Company, or in any other manner. The fact that the customers of your business are to be largely found in Northern Ontario amongst the various business organizations, who are more or less dependent upon or have some relations with the Government, has rendered your position as head of a Department whose activities have chiefly to do with the north country, a most delicate and difficult one, and lends itself to those who may desire through innuendo or contortion to mislead the public and discredit yourself and the administration.

While I regret that these circumstances have arisen, may I say that I fully concur in the conclusion you have reached and the action you have taken.

The cordial relationship that has always existed between yourself and the other members of the Government will increase our regret that you are no longer to be associated with us.

Yours very truly,

(Sgd.) G. H. FERGUSON.

Hon. Jas. Lyons,
    Minister of Lands and Forests,
        Parliament Buildings.

––––––––––

The principle of the independence of Parliament is one of the most firmly established and most important safeguards of our representative institutions. Originally asserted as a protection against encroachments by the Crown, it has been continued as a check upon Governments representing the authority of the Crown. It is designed to insure that Governments will not by the distribution of favours exercise undue influence over legislators. The principle comes to us with the sanction of long established usage and is necessary to uphold the honour, the dignity and the authority of Parliament. Yet it has been found in actual practice that the rule cannot be rigidly enforced without some reasonable modifications. For this reason we have in the law the provision that a member of the Legislature shall not be disqualified by reason of being a shareholder in an incorporated company, which has business relations with the Government. Then, in 1894, it was found that the Honourable E. H. Bronson, a member of the Government, had incurred disqualification because he was interested financially in a license to cut timber. The Government of Sir Oliver Mowat initiated legislation to remove disqualification and to continue Mr. Bronson, in his seat. A few years afterwards it was found that some of the supporters of the Government came under disqualification because being proprietors of newspapers they had accepted Government money for advertising. This disability was removed by special legislation. Again in 1914, it appeared that members who in their professional capacity rendered service to the Dominion Government, thereby incurred disqualification. The members immediately affected were the member for Grenville, and the then Leader of the Opposition, Mr. N. W. Rowell. In both these cases, relief was afforded by amending legislation. As recently as last Session, the member for West Hastings learned with surprise that he had incurred disqualification because a purchase of goods had been made from his place of business for Government purposes. The same situation was revealed with regard to the Hon. F. C. Biggs, through a sale of property to the Government, and in both cases remedial legislation was enacted. I think it will be recognized that it never was the intention of the Legislature that any of these exceptions should conflict with the principle of parliamentary independence but rather that they should make the principle workable and applicable to modern conditions of business. The desire of all who have the public interest at heart will be to maintain the high standing of our parliamentary institutions and to avoid in every way the possibility of reproach or even suspicion against any members of this House.

The determination of this Government has always been not only that there shall be no wrong-doing, but that nothing shall be permitted that can be so construed as to create suspicion or shake public confidence in the integrity of the Government or any of its members. It is of the utmost importance that public men should be above the shadow of suspicion.

There is a tendency to-day with a certain element of the public and a section of the press by suggestion and misrepresentation and allegation, without foundation, from motives best known to themselves, to cast discredit and even villify those engaged in the public service. It is most deplorable, but none the less true, that this condition restrains many public-spirited, outstanding business men from entering public life and giving the Province and the country the benefit of their ability and training.

In the case of Mr. Lyons, I desire to say that I have every confidence in his integrity. Owing to the very nature of his private business and the constituency which it serves, and upon which it depends for its existence, the opportunity is afforded for the creation of suspicion. There are three features of this relationship that I would like to draw to the attention of the House.

Firstly,—A great deal of public work in the way of road construction and otherwise, is carried on under the immediate direction of the Northern Development Branch. Engineers are in charge of these various works. From time to time supplies are required by them, and while they may be within the law and justified in a legal sense, in purchasing from the Lyons Fuel and Supply Company where their prices are lowest, yet with the head of this company as a Minister of the Crown, it is not only dangerous, but a highly improper practice.

When the matter came up in the House a year ago Mr. Lyons gave to his firm instructions that no further goods must be sold by his company for use on these works, and I understand that these instructions have been carried out.

Secondly,—Then there is the case of sales to independent contractors who have secured their contracts by public tender, and are ordinarily entitled to buy supplies where they wish. There could be nothing inherently or legally improper where the Lyons Fuel and Supply Company sells under such circumstances. Yet there is the opportunity for those desiring to direct criticism at the Minister or the Government which casts suspicion on such transactions, and it is better in the public interest that such sales should not take place.

There is a third phase of the subject where the Lyons Fuel and Supply Company have been doing business with lumber companies and mining organizations over a long period of years. I think no one would suggest that these business relations should be severed. They began before the Minister occupied any public position and will doubtless continue on a strictly business basis whether he be Minister or not. Yet, Mr. Lyons, keenly sensitive of his personal honour, feels that in view of active criticism, intended to injure both him and the Government, he should no longer continue in a position that makes these activities possible.

The Minister of Lands and Forests read the following statement to the House:—

As a result of the statement that has just been made to the House by the Prime Minister, I feel that the Honourable Members will grant me their attention for a few minutes that I may take advantage of the opportunity to outline my reasons for my part in the action which has been taken.

After many years of personal effort and close attention I developed, from a very small beginning, a large wholesale and retail fuel and builders supply business with well established connections throughout the Province of Ontario and throughout Canada. The bulk of this business is carried on with business concerns in Northern Ontario. While my family and myself have a controlling interest in the company other parties have a substantial interest.

Following the general election of 1923 the Prime Minister invited me to take a seat in his cabinet as Minister of Lands and Forests, an honour which I appreciated and accepted. I did so believing that with my knowledge of, and experience in, Northern Ontario I would be able to contribute very materially to the development of that very important part of the Province.

Honourable members will recall that prior to my election as member for Sault Ste. Marie, I had had no governmental or parliamentary experience, although I had taken locally at the Soo an active part in political, benevolent and other activities of a public nature there. After entering the Government the exacting administrative demands of my Department absorbed practically my entire time with the result that the control and management of the Lyons Fuel and Supply Company, Limited, a joint stock company, was entrusted to my son and other paid members of the organization.

When last year as a result of a question by an honourable member of this House the attention of the House was directed to the allegation that the Lyons Fuel and Supply Company, Limited, had supplied certain goods to the Province notwithstanding that these purchases were made by resident engineers and others of the Northern Development Branch on a competitive basis, and were not dealt with by me in the Department, I readily saw the impropriety of the incident and acquiesced in the position taken by the Prime Minister when he intimated that members of the House who had substantial holdings in joint stock companies should avoid doing business with the Province.

Honourable members with public experience will realize that in the administration of a Department it is impossible for one member to have an intimate personal knowledge of the details of routine in other Departments, neither time nor opportunity would permit. Each Minister knows generally the routine of affairs of his Department, and relies on the faithful administration of his colleagues, and the exercise of their energies, efforts and abilities.

Since the beginning of the present Session it must have been apparent to honourable members of this House who read with care the proceedings of the House that efforts were being made by cunningly devised questions to create suspicion against me and to embarrass the Government by implying publicly that the Lyons Fuel and Supply Company, Limited, had corruptly sold to those who had contracts with the Government, particularly with my Department, and with firms and persons doing business as Government licensees, or with indirect Government Association. I had never for a moment entertained the idea that such dealings would be challenged. If I had I would never have entered the Government. I was satisfied I was within my legal rights. The business of the Lyons Fuel and Supply Company, Limited, could not continue to exist if it were cut off from all its well established business connections. Its main activities have been and are with the lumbering, mining, the pulp and paper, and contracting organizations of the north.

When in due course the Prime Minister conferred with me as to what had transpired without hesitancy I emphasized the necessity of continuing these long established business relations and to sell to such organizations as it had always done unless the business were to be wound up or ultimately go to ruin; furthermore, I frankly told him if I had to choose between the company abandoning its activities or resigning as Minister, it was inevitable that I should resign. I could not afford to throw to the winds the work of a lifetime merely to gratify an ambition to assist in public affairs as a member of the Government.

Reluctantly, therefore, but without complaint, I place my resignation at the disposal of the Prime Minister for I am determined that no suspicion shall rest upon the Government from any business connection or from the administration of my Department, or from the control of matters peculiarly within my knowledge.

The occurrence cannot however from my personal point of view stop with the acceptance of my resignation. I desire the Public Accounts Committee to investigate, and investigate fully, every transaction the Lyons Fuel and Supply Company, Limited, had with these firms or persons that could on public grounds be challenged. I will place at the disposal of the Committee the books of the company, and the members of the staff, and naturally I shall be ready to be examined on oath respecting every transaction. I have faith and confidence that every dealing will be found honest and square.

Without complaint I admit that it is sound from a public point of view and necessary to the proper administration of a Department of Government that nothing should be done or permitted that would justify anyone stating that any financial benefits unduly accrued during the carrying out of a public trust.

As Minister my relations with the honourable members have been most pleasant, and I entreat none to let personal regard stay his action to secure information. I was a servant of the state, and the representatives of the people have a right, yes, a duty, to scrutinize my stewardship. My regret is that my lack of parliamentary experience, and failure to appreciate the complex workings of Parliament and Governmental departments, has brought suspicion and attendant difficulty. I am at the disposal of the Public Accounts Committee and until its hearings begin I hope that I shall not have to say more.

Mr. Mewhinney asked the following Question:—

1. Who was the contractor who constructed the aerodrome at Sault Ste. Marie in 1924. 2. Did he purchase materials from the Lyons Fuel and Supply

Company, Limited. 3. If so, what materials and what was the total amount paid to the Company for the same.

The Prime Minister replied as follows:—

1. General contractor: J. J. Fitzpatrick. Other contractors: Steel—Hamilton Bridge Works Co., Sarnia Bridge Co.; heating and plumbing—Dunseath & McClary; office and store room—Soo Lumber & Mill Co.; electric wiring, etc.—Greenwood Electric; painting—William Lightfoot. 2 and 3. The Government does not interfere with contractors in purchasing their materials where they desire.

Mr. Kemp asked the following Question:—

1. Did the Government build an aerodrome at Sault Ste. Marie. 2. If so, at what cost. 3. Were tenders called for. 4. Who was given the contract. 5. What was the lowest tender. 6. What was the amount of this contract. 7. What was the amount actually paid for this work. 8. Where are the items to be found in the Public Accounts, giving pages, names and amounts. 9. Did the Lyons Fuel and Supply Company, Limited, furnish any of the material for the work, and at what cost.

The Prime Minister replied as follows:—

1. Yes. 2. $131,357.51. 3. Yes. 4. J. J. Fitzpatrick, general contract. 5. That of J. J. Fitzpatrick. 6. $61,100.00, in addition to certain unit prices for rock and earth excavation and concrete foundations. 7. $80,781.32. (*Note.*—In addition to the general contract to Fitzpatrick, there were contracts made with the lowest tenderers after due advertisement for: Steel work—Hamilton Bridge Works, and Sarnia Bridge Co ; heating and plumbing—Dunseath & McClary; office and store rooms—Soo Lumber & Mill Co. Ltd.; electric supplies and wiring—Greenwood Electric; painting, etc.—William Lightfoot.) 8. Information cannot be given until presentation of Public Accounts. 9. See Journals, 1925, page 278.

Mr. Kemp asked the following Question:—

1. What was the architect's estimate of the cost of the Government aerodrome at Sault Ste. Marie. 2. What was the contract price for the work. 3. Who were the contractors.

The Prime Minister replied as follows:—

1. See Journals, 1925, page 278. 2. General contract price, $61,100.00, plus unit prices on excavation and concrete work. Steel contracts—Hamilton Bridge Co., $15,173.00; Sarnia Bridge Co., $4,452.00; heating and plumbing—Dunseath & McClary, $18,190.00; lumber for store room and offices—Soo Lumber & Mill Co., $2,628.87; electric wiring, etc.—Greenwood Electric, $375.00; painting, etc.—William Lightfoot, $249.00. 3. Answered by No. 2.

Mr. Raney asked the following Question:—

What were the Prime Minister's reasons for not bringing on the elections to fill the seven vacant seats in the House, as required by the Statute.

The Prime Minister replied as follows:—

It is well known that it is not unusual for seats in the Legislature to remain vacant throughout a Session. When the House met on February 14th, 1922, there were two vacant seats owing to the deaths of the members for Russell and for Southeast Toronto, Seat "A." One of these vacancies occurred early in December and the Speaker was notified of it on the 21st December, 1921. There was ample time before the meeting of the House to have had the necessary by-elections to fill these seats. Moreover, the clauses of the Legislative Assembly Act forbidding a by-election during the Session do not apply to vacancies caused by death. Yet, the House sat through the Session of 1922 with these two seats vacant, and no by-election was held until the 23rd of October, 1922, nearly a year after the seats were opened. Both of these vacant seats had formerly been represented by members who opposed the Government and the effect of holding them vacant was to give the Administration a numerical majority in the House, where otherwise it would have been without a majority. The case where a Government deliberately keeps seats vacant in the House for its own political advantage is very different from the case where no possible advantage can come to a Government through not holding by-elections. In October last five members of the Assembly resigned their seats for the purpose of taking part in the Federal general election as candidates. At that time the country was plunged into the most strenuous campaign of this generation, resulting subsequently :n a prolonged political crisis through the determination of the Government to remain in office. Under these circumstances, it was felt that it would be impossible to obtain an expression of opinion on Provincial issues, obscured as they were by the political turmoil, and that it was undesirable to bring on by-elections which were not likely to receive proper attention from the electorate, but would serve only to add to the general confusion. Moreover, the season of the year had become so advanced that in some parts of the vacant constituencies it would be physically impossible for the electors to reach the polls or even to be advised, without great expense and risk, that an election was in progress. The result of holding elections under such circumstances would be practically to disfranchise many electors thus affected. Besides this, there is the general concensus of opinion that election campaigns in the winter season should be avoided as being not only inconvenient to the public, but as affording an opportunity for irregularities which could be guarded against under ordinary conditions. The Government had in mind, also, the fact that there was no public demand at that time for the by-elections. It is true that some of the Ridings could have been opened without inconvenience to anyone, but among these Ridings are the ones that were formerly represented by supporters of the Government. It was felt that to hold the elections in these Ridings and to defer them in others which had formerly been represented by the Opposition would bear upon the face of it the appearance of discrimination, and that the Government ought to forego any advantage it might receive from bringing on the elections that were possible so that the appearance of unfairness might be avoided. There were other considerations involved. One of these is the recognized principle of holding by-elections simultaneously where possible, when there are a number of vacancies. This principle could not have been observed had the

Government decided to bring on the by-elections. Another consideration is the desirability of not encroaching upon the time necessary for preparation for the Session. A campaign just before the Session would tie up public business at an inopportune time. As is well known, the law forbids the issue of a Writ for an Election when the Legislature is sitting, except under very unexceptional circumstances. The object of this law is to avoid political conflict in the Province while the House is in Session, and obviously this is a salutory principle which could not have been respected had the Government determined to fill all the vacant seats. It must be remembered, also, that the result of the by-elections could not affect the standing of the Government in the House or in the Province, but, on the contrary, the Government's chances of improving its position by holding the by-elections were as five to two in its favour, because five of the seats were Opposition seats which might be won, whereas only two of the seats were previously Government seats. For all these reasons the Government felt and still feels that it acted in accordance with the best precedents, that it had the approval of the public in the course it pursued, and that it could not have done otherwise in the general interest.

Mr. Ross asked the following Question:—

1. Did the Minister of Lands and Forests offer the City of Sault Ste. Marie to pay half the cost of paving Wellington Street in that City. 2. Is Wellington Street a residential street. 3. Did residents of that street petition against the work. 4. Are there two other parallel streets within about 100 yards. 5. Did the Minister of Lands and Forests open the tenders. 6. Was the McNamara Construction Company the successful tenderer. 7. What was the amount of its tender. Was it the lowest tender. 6. Did the company do the work. 9. What was the amount actually paid to them for the work. 10. How much did the Government pay. 11. Did the Lyons Fuel and Supply Company, Limited, or Hon. James W. Lyons or any member of his family, supply the cement or tiles for the work. 12. How much cement and what quantity of tiles respectively were supplied, at what price and what was the total amount paid by the McNamara Construction Company to the Lyons Fuel and Supply Company, Limited, or to James W. Lyons or to any member of his family in respect of this work.

The Prime Minister replied as follows:—

1. The Minister upon request from the Mayor of Sault Ste. Marie agreed to pay a portion of the cost of paving a part of Wellington Street in Sault Ste. Marie referred to as provided under the Act and in pursuance of the policy adopted and followed for some years. 2. In part. 3. No. 4. No. 5. Tenders were asked for and received by the City of Sault Ste. Marie for the work referred to. The Minister had stipulated that the Department must approve of the type of road and the cost, if it was expected to contribute. The Mayor evidently misunderstood this requirement and sent the tenders to the Minister to be opened by him. 6. Yes. 7. $50,498.00; Yes. 8. Yes. 9. $50,002.64. 10. Nothing paid but the amount to be paid is $19,132.54. 11. The Government cannot undertake to supply information as to the materials purchased, or the price paid by the contractor who has not a contract with the Government. 12. answered by No. 11.

Mr. Taylor asked the following Question:—

1. Did the present Government purchase land in Sault Ste. Marie to extend the court house grounds. 2. If so, how much land was purchased, from whom, and at what cost. 3. Did the present Government purchase land in Sault Ste. Marie for an aerodrome site. 4. If so, how much land, from whom was it purchased, and at what cost. 5. Did the present Government purchase land in Sault Ste. Marie to extend the jail property. 6. If so, how much land, from whom purchased, and at what cost. 7. Did the present Government pay half the cost of paving Wellington Street in Sault Ste. Marie. 8. What was the length of the pavement. 9. What was the amount paid by the Government. 10. Does the Hon. James Lyons, Minister of Lands and Forests, reside in Sault Ste. Marie. 11. Did he recommend the expenditures above mentioned. 12. What other capital expenditures have been made by the present Government in the City of Sault Ste. Marie.

The Prime Minister replied as follows:—

1. The attention of the Government was drawn by Mayor Dawson to the desirability of purchasing the remaining vacant corner lot adjacent to the Court House so that it might not be built upon but reserved for the future needs of the Crown, and the Government purchased it. 2. One lot 110 feet fronting on Queen Street and 151 feet depth on Elgin Street, from W. J. Thompson at $25,000. (Assessed value $33,000.) 3. Yes. 4 (a) 2.1 acres of land, 1.7 acres water lot; (b) Margaret and Isabella Cameron; (c) $15,000.00. 5. Yes. 6. 2.8 acres from Margaret Ann Ireland and Welburn G. Atkin, $4,500.00, said purchase having been requested by resolution of the City Council of Sault Ste. Marie. 7. No. 8. and 9. Out of a total expenditure of $50,002.64 by the City of Sault Ste. Marie for the construction of a portion of the trunk road, 5,026.6 feet in length, running through Sault Ste. Marie, the Government undertaking to contribute, pursuant to the Statute, $19,132.54. 10. Yes. 11. Only such expenditures as came under the control of the Department of Lands and Forests. 12. Northern Development, store-house, $2,659.52; Aerodrome and Northern Development, administrative and forestry offices, $131,357.51; parking stage for twenty hydroplanes, $32,046.40.

The following Bills were severally read a second time —:

Bill (No. 85), To amend the Assessment Act.

Referred to the Municipal Committee.

Bill (No. 92), To consolidate and amend the Crown Attorneys Act.

Referred to a Committee of the Whole House To-morrow.

Bill (No. 93), To consolidate and amend the Coroners Act.

Referred to a Committee of the Whole House To-morrow.

Bill (No. 94), To consolidate and amend the Constables Act.

Referred to a Committee of the Whole House To-morrow.

————————

The House then adjourned at 5.35 p.m.

================

TUESDAY, MARCH 2nd, 1926.

Prayers.   3 O'Clock P.M.

The following Petition was brought up and laid upon the Table:—

By Mr. Haney, the Petition of the Corporation of the City of Sarnia.

————————

The following Bills were severally introduced and read the first time:—

Bill (No. 48), intituled "An Act respecting the Town of Walkerville." *Mr. Wilson (Windsor)*.

Referred to the Committee on Private Bills.

Bill (No. 105), intituled "An Act to amend the Local Improvement Act." *Mr. Willson (Niagara Falls)*.

Ordered, That the Bill be read a second time To-morrow.

Bill (No. 45), intituled "An Act respecting the Essex Border Utilities Commission." *Mr. Wilson (Windsor)*.

Referred to the Committee on Private Bills.

Bill (No. 106), intituled "An Act to amend the Local Improvement Act." *Mr. Macdiarmid*.

Ordered, That the Bill be read a second time To-morrow.

The House resolved itself into a Committee to consider Bill (No. 91), To improve the Quality of Dairy Products, and, after some time spent therein, Mr. Speaker resumed the Chair; and Mr. Jamieson (Grey) reported, That the Committee had directed him to report the Bill with certain amendments.

Ordered, That the Amendments be taken into consideration forthwith.

The Amendments, having been read the second time, were agreed to.

Ordered, That the Bill be read the third time To-morrow.

The House resolved itself into a Committee to consider Bill (No. 79), The Judges' Orders Enforcement Act, and, after some time spent therein, Mr. Speaker resumed the Chair; and Mr. Jamieson (Grey) reported, That the Committee had directed him to report the Bill without any amendment.

Ordered, That the Bill be read the third time To-morrow.

The House resolved itself into a Committee to consider Bill (No. 80), To amend the Devolution of Estates Act, and, after some time spent therein, Mr. Speaker resumed the Chair; and Mr. Jamieson (Grey) reported, That the Committee had directed him to report the Bill without any amendment.

Ordered, That the Bill be read the third time To-morrow.

The House resolved itself into a Committee to consider Bill (No. 82), To consolidate and amend the Justices of the Peace Act, and, after some time spent therein, Mr. Speaker resumed the Chair; and Mr. Jamieson (Grey) reported, That the Committee had directed him to report the Bill without any amendment.

Ordered, That the Bill be read the third time To-morrow.

The House resolved itself into a Committee to consider Bill (No. 83), To consolidate and amend the Crown Witnesses Act, and, after some time spent therein, Mr. Speaker resumed the Chair; and Mr. Jamieson (Grey) reported, That the Committee had directed him to report the Bill without any amendment.

Ordered, That the Bill be read the third time To-morrow.

The House resolved itself into a Committee to consider Bill (No. 84), To consolidate and amend the Fines and Forfeitures Act, and, after some time spent therein, Mr. Speaker resumed the Chair; and Mr. Jamieson (Grey) reported, That the Committee had directed him to report the Bill without any amendment.

Ordered, That the Bill be read the third time To-morrow.

The House resolved itself into a Committee to consider Bill (No. 90), To consolidate and amend the Magistrates Act, and, after some time spent therein, Mr. Speaker resumed the Chair; and Mr. Jamieson (Grey) reported, That the Committee had directed him to report the Bill without any amendment.

Ordered, That the Bill be read the third time To-morrow.

The following Bills were severally read a second time:—

Bill (No. 97), To amend the Consolidated Municipal Act.

Referred to the Municipal Committee.

Bill (No. 81), To consolidate and amend the Administration of Justice Expenses Act.

Referred to a Committee of the Whole House To-morrow.

The Provincial Secretary presented to the House, by command of His Honour the Lieutenant-Governor:—

Return to the Order of the House, dated February 20th, 1925, that there be laid before this House a Return showing: 1. What was the maximum available supply of electric power in each of the systems, Niagara System, St. Lawrence System, Rideau System, Ottawa System and the Central Ontario and Trent System as operated under the Hydro-Electric Power Commission for Ontario in each of the years, 1919, 1920, 1921, 1922, 1923 and 1924. 2. What was the total distribution of electrical power by the Hydro-Electric Power Commission for Ontario in each of the said systems for each of said years. 3. What was the total demand upon the Hydro-Electric Power Commission for Ontario for electrical power in each of said systems in each of said years. 4. What further electrical power is procurable by the Hydro-Electric Power Commission for Ontario in each of the above systems when the developments already undertaken or under construction are completed. 5. What is the maximum supply of electrical power procurable by the Hydro-Electric Power Commission for Ontario in each of said systems with the present developments completed and operating to full capacity. 6. What was the total combined supply of electrical power furnished by the Hydro-Electric Power Commission for Ontario from all of said systems combined in the year 1924. 7. What was the total demand for electrical power upon the Hydro-Electric Power Commission for Ontario in all of said systems combined for the year 1924. 8. What was the total amount of electrical power used through the Hydro-Electric Power Commission for Ontario in all of said systems combined in the year 1924. 9. What additional amount of electrical power is it estimated by the Hydro-Electric Power Commission for Ontario will be procured from the proposed development of power from the St. Lawrence River. 10. What is the estimated cost of the Hydro-Electric Power Commission for Ontario of the proposed power developments contemplated by the Hydro-Electric Power Commission for Ontario on the River St. Lawrence. (*Sessional Papers, No. 37.*)

Also—Return to the Order of the House, dated March 6th, 1925, that there be laid before this House a Return showing what amount has been expended by the Province of Ontario in (*a*) the provisional electoral district of Algoma; (*b*) the provisional electoral district of Sudbury; (*c*) the provisional electoral district of Sault Ste. Marie; (*d*) the provisional electoral district of Manitoulin, on account of (1) Colonization roads, (2) roads under authority of by-laws, (3) trunk roads, (4) work or construction of any other kind, authorized or coming under the Northern and Northwestern Ontario Development Act, in each of the following years: 1905, 1906, 1907, 1908, 1909, 1910, 1911, 1912, 1913, 1914, 1915, 1916, 1917, 1918, 1919, 1920, 1921, 1922, 1923 and 1924; also the provisional electoral district of Nipissing for 1924, and the provisional electoral district of Sturgeon Falls for 1924. (*Sessional Papers, No. 38.*)

Also—Return to the Order of the House, dated March 20th, 1925, that there be laid before this House, a Return showing: 1. What amount of provincial bonds has been purchased by the Government since January 1st, 1920. 2. In each purchase of bonds, what was (*a*) the date of the purchase; (*b*) the date of maturity of the bonds; (*c*) the interest rate of the bonds; (*d*) the price paid for the bonds; (*e*) the person or firm through whom the purchase was made. (*Sessional Papers, No. 39.*)

Also—Return to the Order of the House, dated March 27th, 1925, Order of the House for a Return to be laid before this House showing all communications, letters and documents of all kinds passing between Mr. Trotter, of Little Current, David Irving, Fish Inspector, Little Current, Mr. Hawkins, of Blind River, and the Department of Game and Fisheries or any other Department of the Government, in connection with the issuing of pound net licenses in White Fish Bay. (*Sessional Papers, No. 40.*)

The Order of the Day for resuming the Adjourned Debate on the Motion for the consideration of the Speech of His Honour the Lieutenant-Governor, at the opening of the Session, having been read,

The Debate was resumed,

And after some time, it was, on the motion of Mr. Clarke (Northumberland),

Ordered, That the Debate be adjourned.

The House then adjourned at 6.05 p.m.

WEDNESDAY, MARCH 3RD, 1926.

The following Petition was brought up and laid upon the Table:—

By Mr. Kennedy (Temiskaming), the Petition of the Township of Tisdale.

———

The following Petition was read and received:—

Of the Municipal Corporation of the City of Ottawa, praying that an Act may pass respecting fixed assessments for hotels.

———

Mr. Lewis, from the Standing Committee on Standing Orders, presented their Second Report, which was read as follows and adopted:—

Your Committee have carefully examined the following Petitions and find the Notices as published in each case sufficient:—

Of the Municipal Corporation of the Town of Aylmer, praying that an Act may pass authorizing the consolidation of a certain indebtedness.

Of the C. M. & G. Canadian Investments, Limited, praying that an Act may pass enabling the petitioner to make certain investments.

Of the Grey and Bruce Loan Company and Owen Sound Loan and Savings Company, Owen Sound, praying that an Act may pass validating, ratifying and confirming an Agreement amalgamating the said companies and granting all powers of a trust corporation.

Of the Mount McKay and Kakabeka Falls Railway Company, praying that an Act may pass permitting an extension of time for completion and operation of their railway.

Of the Town Council of Ojibway, praying that an Act may pass, permitting the said town to separate from the Corporation of the County of Essex for municipal purposes.

Of the Town Council of Gananoque, praying that an Act may pass validating and confirming certain by-laws.

Of Joseph H. Harris and others of Toronto, praying that an Act may pass to incorporate the Toronto East General Hospital.

Of Herbert William Kendall of Hamilton and others, praying that an Act may pass incorporating the Association of Accountants and Auditors in Ontario.

Of the Village Council of Waterford, praying that an Act may pass validating and confirming certain by-laws, also authorizing levy of certain rates.

Of the Township Council of East York, praying that an Act may pass to incorporate the Township as a Town.

Of the Protestant Orphans' Home and the Girls' Home of Toronto, praying that an Act may pass amalgamating the Homes as one Corporation.

Of the City Council of Port Arthur, praying that an Act may pass confirming certain by-laws granting fixed assessments, also to validate sales of certain lands, also to amend Public Parks by-laws.

Of the City Council of London, praying that an Act may pass validating and confirming certain by-laws, also authorizing the Housing Commission to sell certain properties and for authority to fix certain assessments.

Of the City Council of Brantford, praying that an Act may pass authorizing certain amendments to money by-laws, also appointments to Hospital Board of Governors.

Of the Toronto Police Benefit Fund, praying that an Act may pass validating and confirming amendments affecting pensions.

Of the Board of Education for the City of Toronto, praying that an Act may pass authorizing the said Board to create by resolution, a fund to be known as "The Board of Education Insurance Fund."

Of the City Council of Stratford, praying that an Act may pass authorizing said city to prepare and submit to the citizens a by-law for the purchase of gas plant.

Of John Stein, William Innes and others of Richmond Hill, praying that an Act may pass amending the United Church of Canada Act.

Of the Township Council of Thorah, praying that an Act may pass, confirming a certain money by-law.

Of the National Council of Y.M.C.A., praying that an Act may pass permitting the Council to become an incorporated body.

Of the British Mortgage Loan Company of Ontario, praying that an Act may pass granting statutory power to carry on as a Trust Company under the Loan and Trust Corporations Act and authority to change name of company.

Of the Township Council of York, praying that an Act may pass authorizing the said Council to pass by-laws concerning a Department of Industry, Junk Licenses and Tobacco Licenses, a Board of Commissioners of Police and to confirm and validate by-laws *re* sewers.

Of the City Council of Ottawa, praying that an Act may pass authorizing the borrowing of money; also to carry out certain work under the Local Improvement Act.

Of the City Council of Galt, praying that an Act may pass validating and confirming a by-law.

Of the Township Council of York, praying that an Act may pass to provide for the electors being asked to express their opinion as to incorporating the Township as a Town.

Of the City Council of London, praying that an Act may pass permitting the Corporation to borrow $350,000.00, and to issue the debentures therefor.

Of the City Council of Toronto, praying that an Act may pass respecting the Consumers' Gas Company maintaining separate accounts for city business and territory outside the Corporation.

Of the City Council of Toronto, praying that an Act may pass respecting the audit of the books of the Consumers' Gas Company.

Of the City Council of Toronto, praying that an Act may pass permitting the passage of by-laws, confirming payments of grants to St. Michael's Hospital, and the Sick Children's Hospital.

Of the City Council of Guelph, praying that an Act may pass permitting the sale of houses; also, to issue debentures and validate an agreement between the Hydro Power Commission and the City of Guelph respecting the transfer of the Guelph Radial Railway.

Of the Midland Simcoe Railway Company, praying that an Act may pass granting an extension of time for the construction and completion of their railway.

Of Walter F. Campbell and others, praying that an Act may pass changing the time of nomination and elections for the Bala Municipal Council.

Your Committee recommend that Rule No. 51 of Your Honourable House be further suspended in this, that the time for presenting Petitions for Private Bills be further extended until and inclusive of Friday, the 12th day of March, instant, and that the time for introducing Private Bills be further extended until and inclusive of Friday, the 19th day of March, instant.

Ordered, That the time for presenting Petitions for Private Bills be extended until and inclusive of Friday, the 12th day of March next.

Ordered, That the time for introducing Private Bills be extended until and inclusive of Friday, the 19th day of March next.

The following Bills were severally introduced and read the first time:—

Bill (No. 28), intituled "An Act respecting the City of Stratford." *Mr. Monteith.*

Referred to the Committee on Private Bills.

Bill (No. 23), intituled "An Act to incorporate the Association of Accountants and Auditors in Ontario." *Mr. Garden.*

Referred to the Committee on Private Bills.

Bill (No. 54), intituled "An Act respecting the City of Toronto." *Mr. McBrien.*

Referred to the Committee on Private Bills.

Bill (No. 11), intituled "An Act respecting the City of Brantford." *Mr. MacBride.*

Referred to the Committee on Private Bills.

Bill (No. 107), intituled "An Act to amend the Ontario Temperance Act." *Mr. Currie.*

Ordered, That the Bill be read a second time To-morrow.

Bill (No. 108), intituled "An Act to provide for Government Control and Sale of Liquor." *Mr. Currie.*

Ordered, That the Bill be read a second time To-morrow.

Bill (No. 18), intituled "An Act respecting the City of Port Arthur." *Mr. Keefer.*

Referred to the Committee on Private Bills.

Bill (No. 109), intituled "An Act to amend the Local Improvement Act." *Mr. Wright.*

Ordered, That the Bill be read a second time To-morrow.

Bill (No. 53), intituled "An Act respecting the National Council of the Young Men's Christian Associations of Canada, Province of Ontario." *Mr. Finlayson.*

Referred to the Committee on Private Bills.

Bill (No. 51), intituled "An Act respecting the Midland Simcoe Railway Company." *Mr. Finlayson.*

Referred to the Committee on Railways.

Bill (No. 32), intituled "An Act respecting the British Mortgage Loan Company of Ontario." *Mr. Monteith.*

Referred to the Committee on Private Bills.

Bill (No. 36), intituled "An Act respecting the City of Galt." *Mr. Homuth.*

· Referred to the Committee on Private Bills.

Bill (No. 10), intituled "An Act respecting the amalgamation of the Girls' Home and the Protestant Orphans' Home." *Mr. Nesbitt.*

Referred to the Committee on Private Bills.

Bill (No. 15), intituled "An Act respecting the Village of Waterford." *Mr. Berry.*

Referred to the Committee on Private Bills.

Bill (No. 3), intituled "An Act respecting the Grey and Bruce Loan Company and the Owen Sound Loan and Savings Company." *Mr. Jamieson (Grey).*

Referred to the Committee on Private Bills.

Bill (No. 43), intituled "An Act respecting the Toronto Police Benefit Fund." *Mr. McBrien.*

Referred to the Committee on Private Bills.

Bill (No. 20), intituled "An Act respecting the Board of Education for the City of Toronto." *Mr. Nesbitt.*

Referred to the Committee on Private Bills.

Bill (No. 30), intituled "An Act respecting the City of Ottawa." *Mr. Pinard.*

Referred to the Committee on Private Bills.

Bill (No. 29), intituled "An Act respecting the Township of Thora." *Mr. Widdifield.*

Referred to the Committee on Private Bills.

Bill (No. 17), intituled "An Act respecting the City of London." *Mr. Elliott.*

Referred to the Committee on Private Bills.

Bill (No. 46), intituled "An Act respecting the City of London." *Mr. Elliott.*

Referred to the Committee on Private Bills.

Bill (No. 35), intituled "An Act respecting the City of Guelph and the Guelph Radial Railway Company." *Mr. McKeown.*

Referred to the Committee on Private Bills.

Bill (No. 16), intituled "An Act respecting the Town of Gananoque." *Mr. Gray.*

Referred to the Committee on Private Bills.

Bill (No. 8), intituled "An Act respecting the Mount McKay and Kakabeka Falls Railway Company." *Mr. Spence.*

Referred to the Committee on Railways.

Bill (No. 5), intituled "An Act respecting the Town of Aylmer." *Mr. McKnight.*

Referred to the Railway and Municipal Board.

Bill (No. 4), intituled "An Act to incorporate the Toronto East General Hospital Association." *Mr. Keith.*

Referred to the Committee on Private Bills.

Bill (No. 25), intituled "An Act respecting the Township of York." *Mr. Keith.*

Referred to the Committee on Private Bills.

Bill (No. 27), intituled "An Act respecting the Town of Eastdale." *Mr. Keith.*

Referred to the Committee on Private Bills.

Bill (No. 7), intituled "An Act to separate the Town of Ojibway from the County of Essex for Municipal purposes." *Mr. Wilson (Windsor).*

Referred to the Committee on Private Bills.

Bill (No. 44), intituled "An Act to provide for the incorporation of the Township of York as the Town of York." *Mr. Keith.*

Referred to the Committee on Private Bills.

Bill (No. 33), intituled "An Act respecting the Town of Bala." *Mr. McBrien.*

Referred to the Committee on Private Bills.

Bill (No. 21), intituled "An Act respecting the C. M. and G. Canadian Investments, Limited." *Mr. Lewis.*

Referred to the Committee on Private Bills.

Bill (No. 22), intituled "An Act to amend the United Church of Canada Act." *Mr. Lewis.*

Referred to the Committee on Private Bills.

———

Mr. Widdifield asked the following Question:—

1. What members of the Legislature have been, to the knowledge of the Government, or of any member of the Government, since they became members of the House, also members of joint stock companies or partnerships that have furnished supplies to contractors or otherwise, for use on provincial highways or other public works. 2. What members of the Legislature (if any) have themselves, personally, furnished supplies to contractors, or otherwise, for such purposes. 3. What were the supplies, to what amount and value, and to whom furnished in each case.

The Prime Minister replied as follows:—

It must be perfectly obvious that it is not possible for the shareholders of a company to have a personal knowledge of all the details of the multiplicity of business transactions in which the company engages. Much less is it possible for the Government to be aware of all the transactions of the companies with which all the members of the Legislature are associated. The business transactions between incorporated companies and contractors are not reported to the Government, or within its official knowledge.

———

Mr. Kemp asked the following Question:—

1. Have any of the present Ministers of the Crown, since they became members of the Government, been members of joint stock companies or partnerships (a) that have supplied goods to the Government, (b) that have had contracts with the Government, (c) that have supplied goods to lessees from the Government of timber or pulpwood areas. 2. Are any of the Ministers now

members of any such joint stock company or partnership. 3. What Minister, and of what companies or partnerships, is or has he been a member, and to what lessees from the Government have goods been so supplied.

The Prime Minister replied as follows:—

This question is answered by the reply to question No. 46.

———

Mr. Taylor asked the following Question:—

1. Did Mr. Gordon appear as counsel for Mr. Charles Matthews on his examination as a witness before a sub-committee of the Committee on Public Accounts in April, 1925. 2. Had Mr. Matthews asked for counsel. 3. Did the Government pay Mr. Gordon's fee. 4. How much did he charge. 5. How much was he paid.

The Provincial Treasurer replied as follows:—

1. Yes, Mr. Harold H. Gordon, Barrister, Toronto, appeared as counsel for Mr. C. A. Matthews at the unanimous request of the Public Accounts Committee. 2. The family and friends of Mr. C. A. Matthews were notified by the Chairman that the Public Accounts Committee were desirous that counsel be supplied, which resulted in Mr. Harold H. Gordon being nominated by the family. He proceeded with the Committee to Kingston and represented Mr. Matthews when he was being examined. 3. Yes. 4 and 5. Mr. Gordon rendered a bill of $200.00 for his services and $10.30 for expenses, both of which were paid by the Province. (*Note.*—See Minutes and Proceedings of the Public Accounts Committee, 1925, pages 125, 240-245.)

———

Mr. Taylor asked the following Question:—

1. Did Mr. T. H. Lennox, K.C., appear as counsel for Mr. Peter Smith on Mr. Smith's examination as a witness before a sub-committee of the Committee on Public Accounts in April, 1925. 2. Did Mr. Smith ask for the protection of counsel before the committee. 3. Has it been usual for witnesses appearing before the committee to be represented by counsel. 4. Was counsel ever before heard for a witness before the Committee on Public Accounts. 5. If so, when and in what inquiry. 6. Did the Government pay Mr. Lennox's fee. 7. How much did he charge. 8. How much was he paid.

The Provincial Treasurer replied as follows:—

1. Yes. 2. The Public Accounts Committee unanimously agreed to furnish counsel to Mr. Peter Smith. Mr. Smith and his friends were notified and designated Mr. T. H. Lennox, K.C., to act for him before the special committee. 3. The Public Accounts Committee have full discretion in such matters. 4 and 5. This question could only be answered by an exhaustive examination of the Records of the Public Accounts Committee, which are now available to the

members of this House and the public generally. 6, 7 and 8. Mr. Lennox rendered a bill for $200.00 for services and $12.00 for expenses, which were paid by the Province. (*Note.*—See Minutes and Proceedings of the Public Accounts Committee, 1925, pages 125, 240-245.)

Mr. Raney asked the following Question:—

1. Has the Prime Minister given consideration to the holding of a general election for this Assembly this year.

The Prime Minister replied as follows:—

As already intimated, a question to which the reply involves a declaration of policy cannot properly be addressed to the Government and is contrary to parliamentary practice.

Mr. Ross asked the following Question:—

1. Were beer permits issued by the Attorney-General in any riding represented in this House by a Conservative without the approval of the sitting member. 2. If so, in what ridings, and what permits.

The Attorney-General replied as follows:—

1. Yes. 2. Impossible to answer this question. The Attorney-General kept no record of expressions of approval or disapproval as to his wisdom in the exercise of his discretion.

Mr. Lethbridge asked the following Question:—

What, in a short statement, was the policy for the regulation of the liquor traffic which the present Prime Minister had in mind when he announced, in May, 1922, that he had a policy which would appeal to every broad-minded, reasonable man in the Province of Ontario and would at the same time meet with the approval of every real temperance man in the Province.

The Prime Minister replied as follows:—

This question is answered by the reply to Question No. 67.

Mr. Raney asked the following Question:—

Will the Government announce a definite policy on the liquor question before it appeals to the electorate in a general election.

The Prime Minister replied as follows:—

As already intimated, a question to which the reply involves a declaration of policy cannot properly be addressed to the Government and is contrary to parliamentary practice.

Mr. Lethbridge asked the following Question:—

1. Were inquiries made by the Government before issuing 4.4 beer permits whether applicants had been convicted of breaches of the Ontario Temperance Act. 2. Were licenses issued to persons who had been so convicted. 3. If so, what are the names and addresses of the persons to whom such licenses were issued.

The Attorney-General replied as follows:—

1. Not always. 2. In some cases. 3. Impossible to answer as the records of the Department have not this information.

Mr. Bragg asked the following Question:—

1. Have the Agricultural representatives been instructed by the Department of Agriculture to keep records and issue certificates of proof of origin of seeds and grain, as recommended in the report of the Standing Committee on Agriculture and Colonization and adopted by the Legislature on April 8th, 1925 (page 276 of the Journals, 1925). 2. If so, are these records being returned to the Department.

The Minister of Agriculture replied as follows:—

1. Owing to the fact that the inspection and grading of seed is a matter of Federal legislation and administration, it has not yet been found practicable to instruct the Agricultural representatives as suggested by the Standing Committee on Agriculture and Colonization. 2. Answered by No. 1.

Mr. Bragg asked the following Question:—

1. How many farm loans were advanced by the Government in 1924. 2. How many were advanced in 1925. 3. What was the total amount loaned in each of these years.

The Minister of Agriculture replied as follows:—

1. The loans paid by the Agricultural Development Board for the fiscal year ending October 31st, 1924, numbered 819. 2. For the fiscal year ending October 31st, 1925, the number was 701. 3. 1924, $3,200,000; 1925, $2,700,000.

Mr. Fenton asked the following Question:—

1. What have been the profits of the liquor dispensaries each year since they were established.

The Attorney-General replied as follows:—

1919 (seven months), $376,094.02; 1920, $820,540.38; 1921, $702,064.68; 1922 (ten months, change of year), $768,996.59; 1923, $988,453.42; 1924, $877,294.29; 1925, $846,823.00.

Mr. Widdifield asked the following Question:—

1. Have there been any changes in the beer regulations. 2. If so, what changes. 3. Are customers still required to sit at tables. 4. Must bars still be boarded up.

The Attorney-General replied as follows:—

1. No. 2, 3 and 4. Answered by No. 1.

The House resolved itself into a Committee to consider Bill (No. 81), To consolidate and amend the Administration of Justice Expenses Act, and, after some time spent therein, Mr. Speaker resumed the Chair; and Mr. Jamieson (Grey) reported, That the Committee had directed him to report the Bill without any amendment.

Ordered, That the Bill be read the third time To-morrow.

The House resolved itself into a Committee to consider Bill (No. 89), To amend the Married Women's Property Act, and, after some time spent therein, Mr. Speaker resumed the Chair; and Mr. Jamieson (Grey) reported, That the Committee had directed him to report the Bill without any amendment.

Ordered, That the Bill be read the third time To-morrow.

The House resolved itself into a Committee to consider Bill (No. 70), To consolidate and amend the Trustees Act, and, after some time spent therein, Mr. Speaker resumed the Chair; and Mr. Jamieson (Grey) reported, That the Committee had directed him to report the Bill with certain amendments.

Ordered, That the Amendments be taken into consideration forthwith.

The Amendments, having been read the second time, were agreed to.

Ordered, That the Bill be read the third time To-morrow.

The House resolved itself into a Committee to consider Bill (No. 87), To consolidate and amend the Public Authorities Protection Act, and, after some time spent therein, Mr. Speaker resumed the Chair; and Mr. Jamieson (Grey) reported, That the Committee had directed him to report the Bill without any amendment.

Ordered, That the Bill be read the third time To-morrow.

———————

The following Bills were severally read a second time :—

Bill (No. 101), To amend the Ontario Telephone Act.

Referred to a Committee of the Whole House To-morrow.

Bill (No. 102), To amend the Jurors Act.

Referred to a Committee of the Whole House To-morrow.

Bill (No. 99), To amend the Vital Statistics Act.

Referred to the Legal Committee.

———————

The House then adjourned at 5.20 p.m.

===============

THURSDAY, MARCH 4TH, 1926.

PRAYERS.   3 O'CLOCK P.M.

The following Petition was read and received :—

Of the City of Sarnia, praying that an Act may pass respecting the purchase of Sarnia Street Railway stock.

———————

Mr. Nickle, from the Standing Committee on Private Bills, presented their First Report, which was read as follows and adopted :—

Your Committee beg to report the following Bills without amendment :—

Bill (No. 9), An Act to incorporate the Village of Rosseau.

Bill (No. 47), An Act respecting the Township of Teck.

4 J

Your Committee beg to report the following Bill with certain amendments:—

Bill (No. 42), An Act respecting the amalgamation of The Toronto Western Hospital and Grace Hospital.

Your Committee would recommend that the fees less the actual cost of printing be remitted on Bill (No. 42), "An Act respecting the amalgamation of The Toronto Western Hospital and Grace Hospital," on the ground that it is one relating to a charitable institution.

Ordered, That the fees less the actual cost of printing be remitted on Bill (No. 42,) "Respecting the Amalgamation of The Toronto Western Hospital and Grace Hospital."

The following Bills were severally introduced and read the first time:—

Bill (No. 56), intituled "An Act respecting the Special Surplus Account of Consumers' Gas Company of Toronto." *Mr. Nesbitt.*

Referred to the Committee on Private Bills.

Bill (No. 55), intituled "An Act respecting the Suburban Business of the Consumers' Gas Company of Toronto." *Mr. Nesbitt.*

Referred to the Committee on Private Bills.

Bill (No. 110), intituled "An Act to amend Section 16 of the University Act." *Mr. McBrien.*

Ordered, That the Bill be read the second time To-morrow.

Bill (No. 111), intituled "An Act to amend the Consolidated Municipal Act, 1922." *Mr. Wright.*

Ordered, That the Bill be read the second time To-morrow.

On motion of Mr. Sinclair, seconded by Mr. Clarke (Northumberland),

Ordered, That in view of urgent matters to come before the Public Accounts Committee, this House authorizes the calling of the Public Accounts Committee for the transaction of business on Friday the 12th day of March next, at 10 a.m.

The following Bills were severally read the second time:—

Bill (No. 100), To amend the Planning and Development Act.

Referred to the Municipal Committee.

Bill (No. 105), To amend the Local Improvement Act.

Referred to the Municipal Committee.

Bill (No. 106), To amend the Local Improvement Act.

Referred to the Municipal Committee.

Bill (No. 103), To revise and amend the Election Act.

Referred to a Special Committee.

Bill (No. 104), To consolidate and amend the Voters' List Act.

Referred to a Special Committee.

On motion of Mr. Nickle, seconded by Mr. McCrea,

Ordered, That Bill (No. 103), "An Act to revise and amend the Election Laws," and Bill (No. 104), "An Act to consolidate and amend the Voters' List Act," be referred to a Special Committee consisting of Messrs. Nickle, McBrien, Keefer, Thompson (Lanark North), Jamieson (Grey South), Wilson (Windsor), Sinclair, Tellier, Nixon and McCallum.

The House resolved itself into a Committee to consider Bill (No. 102), To amend the Jurors Act, and, after some time spent therein, Mr. Speaker resumed the Chair; and Mr. Jamieson (Grey) reported, That the Committee had directed him to report the Bill with certain amendments.

Ordered, That the Amendments be taken into consideration forthwith.

The Amendments, having been read the second time, were agreed to.

Ordered, That the Bill be read the third time To-morrow.

The House resolved itself into a Committee to consider Bill (No. 101), To amend the Ontario Telephone Act, and, after some time spent therein, Mr. Speaker resumed the Chair; and Mr. Jamieson (Grey) reported, That the Committee had directed him to report the Bill without any amendment.

Ordered, That the Bill be read the third time To-morrow.

The Provincial Secretary presented to the House:—

Return to the Order of the House for a Return showing all correspondence, documents, memorandums, petitions or papers of any kind, and in any way relating to the formation of a new union school section out of a part of School Section No. 1 in East Whitby Township and part of School Section No. 5 in Darlington Township, now or at any time in the hands of the Minister of Education or in any part of the Department of Education. (*Sessional Papers*, *No. 41.*)

Also—Return to the Order of the House for a Return showing all the information furnished to the Legislature as to the requirements and resources of the electoral districts in the provisional judicial districts of Ontario by the Legislative Secretary for Northern Ontario, as required of him under "The Legislative Secretary for Northern Ontario Act, 1924," the times at which the same was furnished, and to which Minister the same was furnished, and showing also what duties in addition to those required by said Act, were imposed upon the Legislative Secretary for Northern Ontario by Order-in-Council, letter or otherwise, the time when the same were imposed, and the Report or Reports of the said Legislative Secretary for Northern Ontario upon the performance of the same. (*Sessional Papers, No. 42.*)

The Order of the Day for resuming the Adjourned Debate on the Motion for the consideration of the Speech of His Honour the Lieutenant-Governor, at the opening of the Session, having been read,

The Debate was resumed,

And after some time, it was, on the motion of Mr. Mewhinney,

Ordered, That the Debate be adjourned.

The House then adjourned at 10.25 p.m.

FRIDAY, MARCH 5TH, 1926.

PRAYERS.   3 O'CLOCK P.M.

The following Petition was read and received:—

Of the Township of Tisdale, praying that an Act may pass validating certain by-laws.

The following Bills were severally introduced and read the first time:—

Bill (No. 112), intituled "An Act to amend the Consolidated Municipal Act, 1922." *Mr. Wigle.*

Ordered, That the Bill be read the second time on Monday next.

Bill (No. 113), intituled "An Act to amend the Consolidated Municipal Act, 1922. *Mr. Oakley.*

Ordered, That the Bill be read the second time on Monday next.

Bill (No. 114), intituled "An Act to amend the Local Improvement Act."
Mr. McBrien.

Ordered, That the Bill be read the second time on Monday next.

Bill (No. 115), intituled "An Act respecting Damages with regard to Fatal
Accidents to Infants." *Mr. Keefer.*

Ordered, That the Bill be read the second time on Monday next.

Mr. Clarke asked the following Question:—

1. Who tendered for the 1925 supply of flour for the School for the Deaf
at Belleville. 2. What was the price quoted by each tenderer. 3. Who was
the successful tenderer. 4. What was the price paid to the successful tenderer.

The Prime Minister replied as follows:—

1. Ogilvie Flour Mills Co., Limited, Montreal, and Hughes & Co., Belleville.
2. Ogilvie Co., $8.20 per bbl. in car-load lots; Hughes & Co., $10.37 in any
quantity. 3 and 4. Contract awarded Hughes & Co. at price tendered on the
recommendation of the Deputy Minister and the Superintendent of School
that there was no storage for a car-load lot and that a year's supply in advance
was liable to spoil.

Mr. Lethbridge asked the following Question:—

1. What contracts for road building have been awarded by the Minister
of Lands and Forests to the Walsh Construction Company. 2. What were the
original contract prices pursuant to tender in each case. 3. What were the
amounts actually paid in each case. 4. What persons acted for the Company
in making and carrying out the contracts with the Government. 5. What other
persons were known to the Minister as having an interest in the Company or
its profits.

The Minister of Lands and Forests replied as follows:—

1. (*a*) Grading 18¼ miles on Haviland Bay Road; (*b*) Grading and gravelling 5 miles on the North Bay-Latchford Road; (*c*) Cutting, stumping, grubbing
and burning 17 miles on the Field-Martin River Road. 2. (*a*) Unit prices based
on estimated quantities for grubbing, excavation and culverts, $56,617.00;
(*b*) Unit prices based on estimated quantities for clearing, grubbing, earth and

rock excavation, gravelling, crosslaying, etc., $41,167.00; (c) Unit prices based on estimated quantities for cutting, stumping and grubbing, $18,720.00. 3. (a) $61,109.68; (b) $50,510.12; (c) $1,565.64. 4. R. Walsh. 5. No one.

Mr. Proulx asked the following Question:—

1. What is the cost of the construction of the English-French Training School Building at Embrun. 2. Were tenders called for, and if so how many tenders were received by the Public Works Department, and what were the respective amounts of these tenders. 3. Which tender was accepted. 4. Were there any extras allowed to the contractor and, if so, what was the total cost of same.

The Minister of Public Works and Highways replied as follows:—

1. $15,562.43. 2. Yes; 4 tenders for building; 2 tenders for heating and ventilating; (a) Stuart & Sinclair, Ltd., Hamilton, Ontario, solid brick construction, $13,935.00; wood construction, $13,200.00; (b) A. Amyot & J. E. Amyot, 178 Rideau Street, Ottawa, solid brick construction, $14,950.00; wood construction, $13,930.00; (c) Loiselle & Dignard, Embrun, Ontario, solid brick construction, $15,345.00; brick veneered, $14,800.00; (d) Cloutier & Grenon, Casselman, Ontario, $16,000.00. Tenders for heating and ventilating: (a) McKinley & Northwood, Ottawa, Ontario, $997.00; (b) Pease Foundry Co., per Ottawa Agency, W. H. Murphy, $1,070.00. 3. Stuart & Sinclair, Ltd., for all brick construction; McKinley and Northwood for installation of heating and ventilating system. 4. Yes, $630.43.

Mr. Kemp asked the following Question:—

1. Did Mr. George Oakley, the member for Riverdale, confer with the Prime Minister or the Minister of Public Works before tendering on behalf of his company, George Oakley and Son, Limited, for the stone work of the new Government building in Queen's Park. 2. Is the Government aware that George Oakley and Son, Limited, is a family company, consisting of the member for Riverdale and members of his family. 3. Did the Government or any member of the Government express disapproval, either before the contract for the stone-work of the said building was awarded to George Oakley and Son, Limited, or afterwards, of such contract. 4. Did the Government after the said contract was awarded to George Oakley and Son, ask Mr. Oakley to vacate his seat in the Legislature.

The Minister of Public Works and Highways replied as follows:—

1. Some time before the type of construction was decided upon, the Prime Minister and the Minister of Public Works discussed with Mr. George Oakley, who is one of the largest stone dealers and foremost experts in that line in Canada, the possibility of using Ontario stone in the new building. 2. The Government is not aware as to who are the stockholders of George Oakley and Son, Limited. 3. The Government holds the General Contractor responsible for the work, and was not aware as to what sub-contractors were being given work by him. 4. No.

Mr. Sinclair asked the following Question:—

1. What kind of roofing was specified to be used upon the roof of the new Administration building. 2. Who supplied the roofing. 3. Was the roof built and the material for it supplied by contract after tenders were called for.

The Minister of Public Works and Highways replied as follows:—

1. Felt and gravel. 2. This work was included in the general contract of Jackson Lewis Company. 3. Answered by the reply to Question No. 2.

Mr. Homuth asked the following Question:—

1. What position did A. B. Connell hold with the Department of Lands and Forests at Sault Ste. Marie. 2. Does he still hold that position. 3. If not, was he dismissed. 4. What was the reason for his dismissal.

The Minister of Lands and Forests replied as follows:—

1. District Forester. 2. No. 3. He resigned. 4. Answered by 3.

Mr. Freeborn asked the following Question:—

1. How much road oil was purchased by the Department of Lands and Forests and the Northern Development Branch during the past fiscal year. 2. How much for the previous year. 3. From whom was the oil purchased.

The Minister of Lands and Forests replied as follows:—

1. None. 2. None. 3. Answered by replies to Questions 1 and 2.

Mr. Kemp asked the following Question:—

1. What was the amount of the claim for extras in connection with the Government road from Sudbury to Coniston. 2. Who made the claims. 3. How much was paid for extras on this work and to whom.

The Minister of Lands and Forests replied as follows:—

1. $3,375.72. 2. MacNamara Construction Company. 3. $2,770.56; paid to the MacNamara Construction Company.

———

Mr. Kemp asked the following Question:—

1. What was the expenditure for the past fiscal year for gasoline and oil for the Government aeroplanes. 2. From whom were the gasoline and oil purchased.

The Minister of Lands and Forests replied as follows:—

1. $16,268.30. 2. Imperial Oil, Limited.

———

Mr. McCallum asked the following Question:—

1. How many aeroplanes are owned by the Province. 2. When were they purchased. 3. From whom. 4. At what prices. 5. Were the machines new or second-hand.

The Minister of Lands and Forests replied as follows:—

1. 18. 2. 1 H.S. 2 L., April, 1924; 8 H.S. 2 L., May, 1924; 2 H.S. 2 L., July, 1924; 1 H.S. 2 I.., September, 1924; 1 Loening, November, 1924; 4 H.S. 2 L., April, 1925; 1 Loening, June, 1925. 3. 10 H.S. 2 L., from Laurentide Air Service; 6 H.S. 2 L., from F. G. Ericson; 1 Loening, from H. Rogers; 1 Loening, from Great Lakes Airways. 4. 10 H.S. 2·L., complete at $5,500; 2 H.S. 2 L., less engines, at $500 each; 4 H.S. 2 L., less engines, at $800 each; 1 Loening, complete, at $6,500; 1 Loening, complete, at $5,000. 5. 16 H.S. 2 L., new; 2 Loenings, slightly used.

———

Mr. Sangster asked the following Question:—

1. Has the Government any intimation that the aluminum plant at Massena is to be moved to the Lake St. John district. 2. If so, what disposition will be made of the 60,000 horsepower now used by this Company.

The Prime Minister replied as follows:—

1. As this plant is situated in the State of New York, the Government has no official knowledge of the matter. 2. Answered by the reply to Question No. 1.

Mr. Sangster asked the following Question:—

What does the Province pay towards the illumination of Niagara Falls.

The Minister of Public Works and Highways replied as follows:—

As part of the Government's general publicity campaign for Ontario, an agreement was entered into between the Cities of Niagara Falls, New York; Niagara Falls, Ontario, and the Park Commission to illuminate the Falls, the cost being borne by the parties in the proportion of 8/12ths by Niagara Falls, New York; 1/12th by Niagara Falls, Ontario, and 3/12ths by the Park Commission. The Commission's share of capital cost was $13,245. The Commission's share of maintenance for 1925 was $2,505.

Mr. Sangster asked the following Question:—

1. Did the Government pay anything for the collection of the Gasoline Tax. 2. If so, how much.

The Minister of Public Works and Highways replied as follows:—

This question was answered February 19th. (See Votes and Proceedings, page 57).

Mr. Ross asked the following Question:—

1. What was the expenditure on that portion of the provincial highways within the County of Oxford for the fiscal years of 1922-3, 1923-4, and 1924-5, respectively. 2. What salaries were paid to permanent road officials in Oxford County for maintenance during those years, naming the officials.

The Minister of Public Works and Highways replied as follows —:

1. 1923, $249,979.52; 1924, $286,538.31; 1925, $151,782.18. 2. None.

Mr. Ross asked the following Question:—

1. How many townships have complied with the "Highway Laws Amendment Act, 1924," and were paid grants. 2. What was the total amount paid. 3. How many townships have not complied. 4. Do all these still perform statute labour. 5. Is it the wish of the Department to have all townships participate in this assistance.

The Minister of Public Works and Highways replied as follows:—

1. 275. 2. This information is not available because the grants are not payable until 1926. 3. 103. 4. The Department is advised that a considerable number of townships have abolished statute labour, but have not as yet passed the necessary by-laws to enable them to obtain the 30 per cent. payable by the Government. 5. Yes.

On motion of Mr. Sinclair, seconded by Mr. Bragg,

Ordered, That there be laid before this House, a Return showing an agreement made on or about August 4th, 1922, between the Department of Lands and Forests and George B. Nicholson and Austin and Nicholson, in regard to trespasses set out in detail in said agreement and the disposition of the same by adjustment.

On motion of Mr. Raney, seconded by Mr. Widdifield,

Ordered, That there be laid before this House, a Return of copies of the contracts made (*a*) by the late Government with Mr. E. W. Backus in respect of the English Pulpwood Circuits and by the present Government with The Thunder Bay Paper Co., The Provincial Paper Co., The Fort William Paper Co., The Nipigon Fibre Co., respectively, in respect of The Nipigon Pulpwood Limits and (*b*) the advertisements and conditions of sale under which the said contracts in each case were made.

The following Bills were severally read a second time:—

Bill (No. 109), To amend the Local Improvement Act.

Referred to the Municipal Committee.

Bill (No. 9), To incorporate the Village of Rosseau.

Referred to a Committee of the Whole House on Monday next.

Bill (No. 47), Respecting the Township of Teck.

Referred to a Committee of the Whole House on Monday next.

The House then adjourned at 4.10 p.m.

MONDAY, MARCH 8th, 1926.

PRAYERS.   3 O'CLOCK P.M.

The following Bills were severally introduced and read the first time:—

Bill (No. 116), intituled "An Act to provide for the Development of Northern Ontario. *Mr. Ferguson.*

Ordered, That the Bill be read the second time To-morrow.

The following Questions were by Order of the House referred to the Committee on Public Accounts:—

Mr. Kemp—1. Has the Lyons Fuel & Supply Co., Ltd., of Sault Ste. Marie, solicited business from companies, firms or individuals having business relations with the Department of Lands and Forests. 2. Has Hon. James Lyons or the Lyons Fuel & Supply Co., Ltd., since Mr. Lyons became a Minister of the Crown, supplied persons or companies to whom Mr. Lyons, as Minister of the Crown, has given contracts for road construction, with cement, gravel, oil, coal, tents or other goods. 3. If so, to what persons or companies. 4. Has Mr. Lyons or the Lyons Fuel & Supply Co., Ltd., since Mr. Lyons became a Minister of the Crown, supplied goods to pulp and paper companies or lumber companies who have been tenderers for pulpwood or timber areas. 5. If so, what persons or companies.

Mr. Kemp—1. Is Hon. James Lyons, Minister of Lands and Forests, the president of the Sault Ste. Marie Coal & Wood Co., Ltd. 2. Did he and members of his family acquire a controlling interest in the company. 3. If not a controlling interest, what interest. 4. When was the interest acquired. 5. Had or has the said coal company a contract with the Lake Superior Pulp & Paper Company for coal. 6. What is the amount of the contract. 7. Was the Lake Superior Pulp & Paper Company a successful tenderer for pulpwood limits since Mr. Lyons became a Minister of the Crown. 8. When and what limits. 9. Had or has the Minister's coal company contracts with other companies having business relations with the Department of Lands and Forests. 10. What companies. 11. How much coal has the Minister's company supplied to the Lake Superior Pulp & Paper Company since he became its president. 12. How much to other pulp and paper companies.

Mr. Kemp—1. Is the Honourable James W. Lyons, the Minister of Lands and Forests, still the president of the Lyons Fuel and Supply Company of Sault Ste. Marie. 2. Do he and members of his family still own a controlling interest in that company. 3. Are the books and invoices of the Lyons Fuel & Supply Company, Limited, available, showing the purchases by the Department of Lands and Forests, from the Lyons Fuel & Supply Company, Limited, of gravel, cement, tile and coal to the amount of $17,920.99 (Journal, Legislative Assembly of Ontario, 1925, at page 145). 4. Were these goods sold by the Lyons Fuel & Supply Company, Limited, to the Government at wholesale or retail prices.

5. Are there books and invoices in the Department of Lands and Forests showing these transactions.   6. Has the Minister of Lands and Forests accounted to the Province for the profit he and other members of his family made on these transactions.

The following Bills were severally read the second time:—

Bill (No. 111), To amend the Consolidated Municipal Act, 1922.

Referred to the Municipal Committee.

Bill (No. 115), Respecting Damages with regard to Fatal Accidents to Infants.

Referred to the Legal Committee.

Bill (No. 42), Respecting the amalgamation of the Toronto Western Hospital and Grace Hospital.

Referred to a Committee of the Whole House To-morrow.

The Order of the Day for the second reading of Bill (No. 114), To amend the Local Improvement Act, having been read,

Ordered, That the Order be discharged, and that the Bill be withdrawn.

Mr. Kemp asked the following Question (No. 6):—

1. What Government contracts have been given by the Department of Lands and Forests to the McNamara Construction Company or to the McNamara Construction, Ltd.   2. What was the amount (*a*) of the tender, and (*b*) of the amount actually paid by this Department in each case.

The Minister of Lands and Forests replied as follows:—

1. (*a*) Contract No. 16, Sudbury, dated June 28th, 1924, the construction of a concrete roadway from Sudbury to Coniston; (*b*) Contract No. 33, Porcupine, dated September 25th, 1924, construction of a bituminous penetration pavement from Timmins to South Porcupine.   2. (*a*) Particulars of the tender for the Sudbury to Coniston roadway are given in reply to Question on February 27th

1925. (See Journals, page 60, 1925). Amount paid, $384,626.80; (*b*) tender for pavement from Timmins to South Porcupine by schedule as follows:—

Earth excavation	$1 00	cu. yd.
Rock excavation	7 00	cu. yd.
Penetration pavement 16 feet wide	93	sq. yd.
Macadam base, 8 inches	70	sq. yd.
Concrete in culverts	20 00	cu. yd.
6-inch agricultural tile in place	80	cu. ft.
Gravel placed where directed	3 00	cu. yd.
Crushed stone where directed	5 00	cu. yd.
Scarifying and reshaping sub-grade	5	sq. yd.
Scarifying and consolidating ex-macadam base	10	sq. yd.
12-inch concrete pipe in place	1 50	cu. ft.
24-inch concrete pipe in place	3 00	cu. ft.
Dry rubble masonry end walls	5 00	
Trimming and levelling earth shoulders	10	
Trimming and leveling stone shoulders	10	cu. ft.
Straw 3-inch in depth	10	
Clearing	100 00	acre
Grubbing	200 00	acre
Stone shoulder 12-inch wide 6 inch deep	20	cu. ft.

Amount paid, $258,754.48.

Mr. Ireland asked the following Question (No. 76):—

1. For how many years has the McNamara Construction Company received contracts from the Province. 2. What contracts did they receive in each year and for what amount.

The Minister of Public Works and Highways replied as follows:—

1. The McNamara brothers, George and Fred McNamara, who are the principals of the McNamara Construction Company, have received contracts from the Province during a period in excess of five years. 2. (*a*) Contracts were awarded to McNamara Brothers and Thornton:

Year	Contract	Amount paid Contractor.
1921	295	$100,096 11
1922	600	91,821 01
1922	606	74,165 34
1922	710	36,214 00
1923	794	81,378 71
1923	827	49,518 33
1923	943	9,099 92
1923	960	126,027 75
1923	Bridge on Toronto-Hamilton Highway at Oakville	66,043 68
		$634,364 85

(b) Contracts awarded to McNamara Construction Company, which continued the business of the former organization and is apparently under the same control: 1924, Sudbury-Coniston Road, $384,626.80; 1924, Timmins-South Porcupine Road, $258,754.48.

Mr. Tellier asked the following Question (No. 77):—

1. When was construction commenced on the extension of the Nipissing Central Railway from Swastika to the Rouyn Gold Mines in Quebec. 2. How many miles have been constructed. 3. How many miles remain to be constructed. 4. What was the cost of the materials and equipment distributed along the proposed right-of-way in Quebec Province. 5. What disposition was made of these. 6. What was the loss sustained by the Province by reason of the abandonment of the work in Quebec Province, including labour in distributing supplies and materials and labour in gathering the same again, depreciation in value and loss of supplies and materials so distributed. 7. Were all the supplies, material and equipment distributed along the proposed right-of-way in Quebec recovered and salvaged.

The Prime Minister replied as follows:—

1. March 11th, 1925, starting from Larder Lake. 2. About 12 miles, including two sidings. 3. About 27 miles. 4. $89,637.52. 5. Dynamite, construction equipment, rails, cars, etc., still on proposed right-of-way. Some of the materials and supplies have been sold; the remainder are being brought back for disposition. 6. Any loss sustained by reason of the abandonment of the work in the Province of Quebec cannot be definitely determined until ultimate disposition of the materials and equipment has been made, but it is expected the loss will be comparatively small. 7. All supplies, material and equipment which have not been sold will be recovered and salvaged, except a small quantity of perishable supplies.

Mr. Kemp asked the following Question (No. 91):—

1. Did the Government build an agricultural barn at Hearst. 2. Who was the contractor. 3. What was the original contract price. 4. What was the actual cost to the Province of the completed building. 5. Did the Lyons Fuel and Supply Co., Ltd., or any member of that company supply any of the material for the work. 6. If so, what material and in what amount.

The Minister of Lands and Forests replied as follows:—

1. Yes. 2. (a) Metal Shingle & Siding Co., Preston, Ont., structural steel work; (b) E. T. Charters, Sault Ste. Marie, erecting and supplying part materials; (c) Reed & Sons, Cochrane, electric wiring; (d) Beatty Bros., Fergus, fittings and equipment. 3. (a) $2,752.18; (b) $9,863.00; (c) $280.00; (d) $830.05; total, $13,725.23. 4. (a) $2,752.18; (b) $10,814.00; (c) $280.00; (d) $1,277.16; day labour, granary, $340.00; total, $15,463.34. 5. The Government is not aware as to where the contractor purchased his supplies. 6. Answered by the reply to Question No. 5.

Mr. Ross asked the following Question (No. 93):—

Under what Act and Section thereof or Government regulation was the contribution made by the Government to the street paving done in the City of Sault Ste. Marie.

The Minister of Lands and Forests replied as follows:—

14 George V, Chapter 14, Sec. 2.

Mr. Ross asked the following Question (No. 98):—

1. How many persons keeping bees registered under "The Foul Brood Act, 1925." 2. What amount has been received in fees. 3. For what purposes was this money used. 4. How many inspectors were employed. 5. Were all registered apiaries inspected. 6. How many apiaries were found infected. 7. Were these destroyed, and, if so, what was the estimated value. 8. Was any compensation paid.

The Minister of Agriculture replied as follows:—

1. 5,238. 2. $5,813.00. 3. This was necessarily turned in as revenue, but a much larger sum was expended in combatting foulbrood. 4. Seventy-nine, part-time. 5. No, only such apiaries as were believed to require attention. 6. 4,567 colonies in 733 apiaries. 7. 1,595 infected colonies were destroyed, but there is no estimate as to value. 8. No.

Mr. Sinclair asked the following Question (No. 110):—

1. To whom was the gratuity of $1,000, in connection with the death of Kenneth McBride, paid, as voted in item 135-2 of the further supplementary estimates, 1925.

The Minister of Lands and Forests replied as follows:—

As these moneys were for the benefit of an infant, they were paid into the Supreme Court of Ontario to the credit of the Kenneth McBride Gratuity Fund, following the usual practice.

Mr. McCallum asked the following Question (No. 112):—

1. What moneys have been drawn by Hon. J. R. Cooke (a) from the Hydro-Electric Power Commission since his appointment as a commissioner; (b) for the fiscal year ending on the 31st of October, 1923; (c) for the fiscal year ending on the 31st of October, 1924; (d) for the fiscal year ending on the 31st of October,

1925; (e) from the 1st of November, 1925, to the answer of these questions. 2. What moneys have been drawn by him during this same time from the treasury of the Province of Ontario. 3. On what accounts respectively were the said moneys drawn in each case.

The Prime Minister replied as follows:—

1. The Honourable Mr. Cooke received remuneration as a member of the Hydro-Electric Power Commission at the rate of $6,000.00 per annum from the 16th July, 1923, to the 31st October, 1924, and from the 1st November, 1924, to date at the rate of $8,000.00 per annum; paid out of the Hydro-Electric Power Commission funds and not chargeable to the Province. 2. Mr. Cooke also received the usual indemnity payable to all members of the Legislature by the Province. 3. Answered by the replies to Questions Nos. 1 and 2.

Mr. McCallum asked the following Question (No. 113):—

1. How much money has been drawn from the provincial treasury by each member of the Government since the present Government came into office for travelling expenses.

The Prime Minister replied as follows:—

1. For fiscal year, 1925: Hon. Mr. McCrea, $950; Hon. Mr. Lyons, $900; Hon. Mr. Price, $700; Hon. Mr. Martin, $975; Hon. Mr. Goldie, $400; Hon. Mr. Nickle, $35.20; Hon. Dr. Godfrey, $1,500 which amount includes part of expenses in connection with trip to Geneva Labour Conference. For previous years, see page 154 Journals of the House, 1925.

Mr. Taylor asked the following Question (No. 114):—

1. What is the total amount that has been paid to the Government of Ontario under the settlement made with the Shevlin-Clarke Company in 1922. 2. Is the said company at present indebted to the Province under the said settlement. 3. If so, in what amount and since when. 4. Has any change been made in the terms of the said settlement. 5. If so, what change. 6. Has the company suggested any change. 7. If so, what was the request.

The Minister of Lands and Forests replied as follows:—

1. $951,605.70. 2. No. 3. Answered by No. 2. 4. No. 5. Answered by No. 4. 6. Yes. 7. Requested that a reduction in Surety bond be considered to the extent that might be consistent with remaining liability.

On motion of Mr. Raney, seconded by Mr. Lethbridge,

That the members of the House whose names follow be added to the Committee on Public Accounts: D. M. Ross, D. J. Taylor, John Carty, M. A. McCallum, J. A. Sangster, J. A. Pinard, W. H. Fenton, R. L. Brackin, W. J. Bragg.

And, after some time, the Motion was, by leave of the House, withdrawn.

On the motion of Mr. Sinclair, seconded by Mr. Proulx,

Ordered, That there be laid before this House, a Return showing all correspondence, telegrams or other communications, passing between the Government or any member thereof, or any official or employee thereof, and any company, person or persons being either purchasers or lessees or intended purchasers or lessees, of timber or pulp limits or water powers, and any correspondence in relation to the same from or with municipalities interested in the same, in regard to the pulp and timber limits in the watersheds of Kapuskasing, Ground Hog and Mattagami Rivers (District of Cochrane), tenders to close September 10th, 1925, the pulp and timber limits in the Lake Nipigon Region (District of Thunder Bay) tenders to close September 10th, 1925.

The Order of the Day for the third reading of Bill (No. 81), To consolidate and amend the Administration of Justice Expenses Act, having been read,

Ordered, That the Order be discharged, and that the Bill be forthwith again referred to a Committee of the Whole, with instructions to amend the same.

The House resolved itself into a Committee, severally to consider the following Bills:—

Bill (No. 9), To incorporate the Village of Rosseau.

Bill (No. 47), Respecting the Township of Teck.

Mr. Speaker resumed the Chair; and Mr. Black reported, That the Committee had directed him to report the several Bills without Amendments.

Ordered, That the Bills reported be severally read the third time To-morrow.

The House resolved itself into a Committee to consider Bill (No. 92), To consolidate and amend the Crown Attorneys Act, and, after some time spent therein, Mr. Speaker resumed the Chair; and Mr. Black reported, That the Committee had directed him to report the Bill without any amendment.

Ordered, That the Bill be read the third time To-morrow.

———————

The House resolved itself into a Committee to consider Bill (No. 93), To consolidate and amend the Coroners Act, and, after some time spent therein, Mr. Speaker resumed the Chair; and Mr. Black reported, That the Committee had directed him to report the Bill with certain amendments.

Ordered, That the Amendments be taken into consideration forthwith.

The Amendments, having been read the second time, were agreed to.

Ordered, That the Bill be read the third time To-morrow.

———————

The House then adjourned at 4.45 p.m.

===============

TUESDAY, MARCH 9TH, 1926.

PRAYERS.   3 O'CLOCK, P.M.

The following Petitions were severally brought up and laid upon the Table:—

By Mr. Wigle, the Petition of William J. Stevenson and others, members of the congregation of the Presbyterian Church at Clinton, Ontario.

By Mr. Chambers (Wellington North), the Petition of R. J. Scott and others, members of the congregation of St. Andrew's Presbyterian Church, Moorefield, Ontario.

By Mr. Jamieson (Grey), the Petition of the members and adherents of the Priceville Presbyterian Congregation.

———————

Mr. Nesbitt, from the Standing Committee on Private Bills, presented their Second Report which was read as follows and adopted:

Your Committee beg to report the following Bills without amendment:—

Bill (No. 3), An Act respecting the Grey and Bruce Loan Company and the Owen Sound Loan and Savings Company.

Bill (No. 15), An Act respecting the Village of Waterford.

Your Committee beg to report the following Bills with certain amend-ments:—

Bill (No. 4), An Act to incorporate the Toronto East General Hospital Association.

Bill (No. 10), An Act respecting the amalgamation of the Girls' Home and the Protestant Orphans' Home.

Bill (No. 28), An Act respecting the City of Stratford.

Your Committee would recommend that the fees, less the penalties and the actual cost of printing, be remitted on Bill (No. 4), "An Act to incorporate the Toronto East General Hospital Association"; and on Bill (No. 10), "An Act respecting the amalgamation of the Girls' Home and the Protestant Orphans' Home" on the ground that they are ones relating to charitable institutions.

Ordered, That the fees, less the penalties and the actual cost of printing, be remitted on Bill (No. 4), An Act to incorporate The Toronto East General Hospital Association.

Ordered, That the fees, less the penalties and the actual cost of printing, be remitted on Bill (No. 10), An Act respecting the amalgamation of The Girls' Home and The Protestant Orphans' Home.

———

The following Bills were severally introduced and read the first time:—

Bill (No. 117), intituled "An Act to amend the Local Improvement Act." *Mr. McBrien.*

Ordered, That the Bill be read the second time To-morrow.

Bill (No. 118), intituled "An Act to amend the Consolidated Municipal Act, 1922." *Mr. Finlayson.*

Ordered, That the Bill be read the second time To-morrow.

Bill (No. 119), intituled "An Act to amend the Consolidated Municipal Act, 1922." *Mr. McBrien.*

Ordered, That the Bill be read the second time To-morrow.

Bill (No. 120), intituled "An Act to amend the Hospitals and Charitable Institutions Act." *Mr. Goldie.*

Ordered, That the Bill be read the second time To-morrow.

Bill (No. 121), intituled "An Act to amend the Sanatoria for Consumptives Act." *Mr. Goldie.*

Ordered, That the Bill be read the second time To-morrow.

Bill (No. 122), intituled "An Act respecting Dentistry." *Mr. Ferguson.*

Ordered, That the Bill be read the second time To-morrow.

The following Bill was read a second time:—

Bill (No. 112), To amend the Consolidated Municipal Act. *Mr. Wigle.*

Referred to the Municipal Committee.

The Provincial Secretary presented to the House, by command of His Honour the Lieutenant-Governor:—

Report of the Ontario Parole Board for the year ending October 31st, 1925. (*Sessional Papers, No. 16.*)

Also—

Copies of Orders-in-Council pursuant to section 73 of The Ontario Insurance Act, 1924. (*Sessional Papers, No. 43.*)

Mr. Raney requested the ruling of the Speaker on the relevancy of the Amendment to the Amendment.

The Speaker ruled that the Amendment to the Amendment was in order being relevant to the Amendment.

The Order of the Day for resuming the Adjourned Debate on the Motion for the consideration of the Speech of His Honour the Lieutenant-Governor, at the opening of the Session, having been read,

The Debate was resumed,

And after some time,

The Amendment to the Amendment, having been put, was carried.

The main Motion, as amended, having been then submitted, was carried.

And it was

Resolved, That an humble Address be presented to His Honour the Lieutenant-Governor, as follows:—

To His Honour, Henry Cockshutt, Lieutenant-Governor of our Province of Ontario.

We, His Majesty's most dutiful and loyal subjects, the Legislative Assembly of the Province of Ontario, now assembled, beg leave to thank Your Honour for the gracious speech Your Honour has addressed to us, and to add that "This House desires furthermore to assure Your Honour that it is of opinion that, in the enactment of important public legislation, the principle of Responsible Parliamentary Government, on which our British democratic institutions rests, should be observed in order that such legislation should have the undoubted sanction and support of the people, as expressed through their representatives in the Legislature, to the end that all such legislation should possess the authority and support necessary to command due respect and observance by the community."

The Address, having been read the second time, was agreed to.

Ordered, That the Address be engrossed and presented to His Honour the Lieutenant-Governor by those Members of this House who are Members of the Executive Council.

On motion of Mr. Price, seconded by Mr. Godfrey,

Ordered, That this House will on To-morrow resolve itself into the Committee of Supply.

Ordered, That this House will on To-morrow resolve itself into the Committee of Ways and Means.

The House then adjourned at 11.30 p.m.

WEDNESDAY, MARCH 10TH, 1926.

PRAYERS.   3 O'CLOCK P.M.

Mr. Speaker then informed the House:—

That the Clerk had received from the Railway and Municipal Board, their Report in the following case:—

Bill (No. 5), Respecting the Town of Aylmer.

The Report was then read by the Clerk at the Table, as follows:—

To the Honourable, The Legislative Assembly of the Province of Ontario.

Upon reference under Rule 61a of your Honourable House to the Ontario Railway and Municipal Board of Bill (No. 5) 1926, entitled "An Act respecting the Town of Aylmer," the Board begs leave respectfully to report that in the judgment of the Board it is reasonable that such Bill should be passed by your Honourable House.

All of which is respectfully submitted,

A. B. INGRAM, *Vice-Chairman.*

J. A. ELLIS, *Commissioner.*

Dated at Toronto,
the 9th day of March, A.D. 1926.

Ordered, That Bill (No. 5), Respecting the Town of Aylmer, be referred to the Committee on Private Bills, with instructions to consider the same with reference to the suggestions of the Railway and Municipal Board thereon.

———

Mr. Gray, from the Standing Committee on Railways, presented their Report which was read as follows and adopted:

Your Committee beg to report the following Bill with certain amendments:—

Bill (No. 26), An Act to extend the time for the completion of the Haliburton, Whitney and Mattawa Railway.

———

Your Committee beg to report the following Bills without amendment:—

Bill (No. 1), An Act to incorporate The Welland and Port Colborne Railway Company.

Bill (No. 8), An Act respecting the Mount McKay and Kakabeka Falls Railway Company.

Bill (No. 51), An Act respecting The Midland Simcoe Railway Company.

The following Bills were severally introduced and read the first time:—

Bill (No. 123), intituled "An Act to amend the Corn Borer Act." *Mr. Martin.*

Ordered, That the Bill be read the second time To-morrow.

Bill (No. 124), intituled "An Act to amend the Power Commission Act." *Mr. Willson (Niagara Falls).*

Ordered, That the Bill be read the second time To-morrow.

Bill (No. 125), intituled "An Act to amend the Local Improvement Act." *Mr. Garden.*

Ordered, That the Bill be read the second time To-morrow.

Bill (No. 126), intituled "An Act to amend the Consolidated Municipal Act, 1922." *Mr. Armstrong.*

Ordered, That the Bill be read the second time To-morrow.

Bill (No. 127), intituled "An Act to amend the Ontario Companies Act." *Mr. Nickle.*

Ordered, That the Bill be read the second time To-morrow.

Bill (No. 128), intituled "An Act to consolidate and amend the Cemetery Act." *Mr. Nickle.*

Ordered, That the Bill be read the second time To-morrow.

Mr. Raney raised a Point of Order that the Legislative Practice was not being conducted conformably to Constitutional Parliamentary Practice in connection with certain Questions and Answers.

And Mr. Speaker addressed the House as follows:—

Two points for determination arise in connection with the point of order submitted by the Honourable Member for East Wellington, as follows:—

1. Is it in order to ask a question, the reply to which involves a declaration of policy.

2. Does the reply to either of the questions submitted involve such a declaration.

With reference to point number 1, I draw attention to the following declaration on page 74 of the Members' Manual:—

"Question addressed to a Minister should relate to the affairs with which he is officially connected, or to a matter of administration for which he is responsible, but he is not required to answer any query asking for an expression of his opinion upon matters of policy."

I refer also to the following from page 248 of May's Parliamentary Practice, Eleventh Edition:—

"Within these lines an explanation can be sought regarding the intentions of the Government, but not an expression of their opinion upon matters of policy."

On March 14th, 1912, the Speaker of this House ruled as follows regarding certain Questions under consideration:—

"Further, they involve matters of inference and of opinion and lead up to or profess to lead up to and deal with a question of policy of the Government which the Minister (is) asked to announce, discuss and declare. Any one of these reasons would be sufficient to condemn the inquiry."

On the 11th April, 1912, this House adopted the following resolution:—

Resolved, "That under the Rules and procedure of this House, questions put to members must not put forward any debatable facts, nor any matter that will involve opinion, argument or inference, nor can any fact be stated, nor any opinion or intention as to matters of policy; nor should any question be put upon a matter which is not within the recognition of the House."

For all these reasons I am convinced that it is a clear violation of the Rules of Parliamentary procedure and of the established practice of this House to ask a question involving a declaration of policy.

The second point which arises is whether the reply to the questions submitted involves a declaration of policy. It is obvious that any answer given to these questions might be construed as indicating a policy, or an opinion, or an intention as to matters of policy, and the questions for that reason are contrary to the Rules of the House and the practices of Parliament.

I am not aware that any request has been made to have these questions ruled out of order, but since the Honourable Member for East Wellington has raised the point of order, I am bound to rule that a question of this nature could have been excluded from the Order Paper by the Speaker or ruled off at any time. I have, however, refrained from enforcing the Rules as to questions in a strict and exacting manner, but have preferred to rely upon the good sense of members in framing such questions, and the spirit of mutual consideration which should characterize the relations between both sides of the House. The fact that a question is admitted to the Order Paper does not mean that its regularity is conceded, or that the Government is not within its rights in drawing attention in its reply to any irregularity that exists. On the whole, the Speaker feels that it would be more in the interests of the decorum of the House, and would tend to avoid undesirable controversy, if members would endeavour to refrain from submitting to the Speaker questions which are outside the Rules and the Practice of Parliament.

The honourable gentleman for East Wellington has advised me that he understood the Chair to rule on a similar question on February 19th that the question was competent, but that the Speaker had no authority to compel the Government to make an answer to it. I do not agree with this recollection of what occurred. On the occasion mentioned I read to the House the following extract from a volume entitled "The Speaker of the House," written by Michael MacDonagh:—

"Once an indignant member appealed to the Speaker against the immovable silence of the Prime Minister, Mr. Asquith, with respect to a certain question. 'Has not a private member the right to ask a Minister any question relating to his Department?' 'Certainly,' said the Speaker, 'Hon. Members have the right to ask questions,'—here Mr. Lowther was interrupted by the cheers of the Hon. Member and his friends,—'but,' he proceeded drily, 'that does not necessarily mean that Ministers are obliged to answer them.'"

I would simply point out that the right to ask questions, which is not disputed, does not involve the right to ask any question whether it is in order or not.

Mr. Nixon asked the following Question (No. 71):—

1. What is the total amount of fire insurance carried on the property of the Hydro-Electric Power Commission of Ontario. 2. What was the total amount of fire insurance premiums paid by the Hydro-Electric Power Commission for the past fiscal year. 3. Who were the agents who placed this insurance. 4. Who are the agents who are now looking after fire insurance for the Hydro-Electric Commission.

The Prime Minister answered as follows:—

1. In the records of the Commission, fire and liability insurance are grouped together and make a total of $12,258,204, up to October 31st, 1925. 2. Fire and liability, $154,338.17. 3. Practically all insurance was placed through the Municipal Underwriters, Limited, as brokers. This company is controlled by The Ontario Municipal Electrical Association, through directors nominated by the said Association, and all the profits are disposed of in the interests of the said Association and the municipalities represented. 4. The same answer as is given in reply to Question No. 3.

Mr. Nixon asked the following Question (No. 84):—

1. How many Ontario breweries have been prosecuted since the new beer law came into force for selling over-strength beer.   2. What breweries were so prosecuted.   3. When and where and what penalties were imposed.

The Attorney-General replied as follows:—

1. Two.   2 and 3. The Fort Frances Brewing and Malting Company. November 27th, 1925, at Fort Frances. Dismissed. Lake Ontario Brewing Company, Limited. February 15th, 1926, at Smith's Falls. Dismissed.

Mr. Widdifield asked the following Question (No. 85):—

1. How many beer permits were issued in North Huron.   2. Was Mr. John Joynt, the sitting member, consulted.   3. Were any issued of which he did not approve.   4. If Mr. Joynt was not consulted, who was.

The Attorney-General replied as follows:—

1. Eleven, all Standard Hotels.   2. No.   3. If so, he has not expressed himself.   4. Officers of the Department.

Mr. Mewhinney asked the following Question (No. 97):—

1. Was the attention of the Attorney-General directed at any time to a case "Rex vs. James Burns" at Petrolia.   2. Did the Attorney-General give any advice or instructions to the Crown Attorney as to changing the charge to be laid against James Burns.   3. Did the Attorney-General receive any complaints as to the way this case was handled by his officers.   4. Did the Attorney-General send someone to make an investigation of the handling of this case. 5. If so, whom.   6. Was a report made.   7. What was the report.

The Attorney-General replied as follows:—

1. Yes.   2. No.   3. Yes.   4. Yes.   5. Inspector E. D. L. Hammond. 6. Yes.   7. The report was a confidential one of an officer to his superior and it is not in the public interests to disclose what same contained.

Mr. Ross asked the following Question (No. 106):—

1. How many convictions were there for breaches of the Ontario Temperance Act in each fiscal year beginning with 1919-1920.   2. How much was collected in fines for each of these years.

The Attorney-General replied as follows:—

1. By provincial officers: 1919-20, 2,786; 1920-21, 4,448; 1921-22, 3,102; 1922-23, 3,229; 1923-24, 3,482; 1924-25, 3,599. The Department has no record of prosecutions by other than provincial officers. 2. Paid to the Province: 1919-20, $273,647.14; 1920-21, $811,087.56; 1921-22, $377,477.56; 1922-23, $379,509.31; 1923-24, $420,868.67; 1924-25, $365,446.82. Paid to the municipalities: 1919-20, $573,676.29; 1920-21, $677,697.50; 1921-22, $364,925.80; 1922-23, $414,776.33; 1923-24, $475,754.83; 1924-25, $387,405.98. *Note:* The amounts stated to be paid to municipalities are compiled from returns from Municipal Treasurers.

Mr. Raney asked the following Question (No. 107):—

1. Since the coming into force of the Act of last year limiting the number of prescriptions by any one physician in any month to thirty, has that number of prescriptions been exceeded by any Ontario physicians. 2. If so, how often. 3. How many different physicians have failed to observe this law. 4. How many physicians have exceeded the number of 40 in a month; how many, 50; how many, 60; how many, 70; how many, 80. 5. How many have exceeded 40 in more than one month; how many, 50; how many, 60; how many, 70; how many, 80. 6. Have any of these men been prosecuted and, if so, how many and where.

The Attorney-General replied as follows:—

1. Yes. 2. Sixty-seven. 3. Sixty-six. 4. Over 40, one; over 50, 60, 70 or 80, none. 5. None. 6. One, at Lindsay. *Note:* The statutory limitation of thirty (30) upon Dispensaries was put into effect in July, 1925, time being required to prepare new prescription forms and pads. The data above relates to the seven months beginning July, 1925; February, 1926, data is not ready yet. There are nearly 4,000 physicians in this Province.

Mr. Sinclair asked the following Question (No. 108):—

1. When was the Hydro-Electric Power Extension Fund referred to in Chapter 21, Section 2, of the Ontario Statutes, 1921, opened in the books of the Province by the Treasurer of Ontario. 2. What sums have been placed to the credit of said fund as required by Section 3 of said Statute and any amendments thereto. 3. What grants have been made from said fund as provided by Sections 4 and 5 of said Act and amendments thereto.

The Prime Minister replied as follows:—

1. The Hydro-Electric Power Extension Fund has not been established for the reason that the legislation purporting to constitute the fund was not found to be workable. 2. Answered by the reply to Question No. 1. 3. The bonuses to Rural Transmission Lines have been paid out of the Consolidated Revenue as authorized by Estimates passed by the House. No payments were made before the present Government assumed office, but since that time, the bonuses paid have amounted to $1,507,442.99.

Mr. Bragg asked the following Question (No. 111):—

1. How many applications for refunds by farmers have been made under the Gasoline Tax Act, 1925. 2. What is the total amount of money which has been refunded to date as a result of such applications.

The Minister of Public Works and Highways replied as follows:—

1. 1,758.   2. $19,650.70.

Mr. Lethbridge asked the following Question (No. 117):—

1 Does the Hydro-Electric Commission pay any rental for water used at the Queenston-Chippewa plant. 2. If so, how much, and what are rentals used for.

The Prime Minister replied as follows:—

1. The Hydro-Electric Power Commission is liable for rentals for water used at the Queenston-Chippewa plant, and is prepared to pay such rentals when the rate of such rentals and the basis of measurement now under negotiation are determined upon.

Mr. Lethbridge asked the following Question (No. 118):—

1. What was the estimated cost of the new Administration Building in Queen's Park when the work was commenced. 2. What is the present estimated cost.

The Minister of Public Works and Highways replied as follows:—

$2,000,000.00. As the Government decided to use all Ontario stone, this was increased by $186,000.00. 2. Answered by No. 1.

Mr. Taylor asked the following Question (No. 128):—

1. What was the architect's original estimated cost of the new East Block now in course of construction in Queen's Park. 2. What is his present estimate of the cost of the completed work.

The Minister of Public Works and Highways replied as follows:—

Same as No. 118.

The following Bills were severally read the second time:—

Bill (No. 113), To amend the Consolidated Municipal Act, 1922.

Referred to the Municipal Committee.

Bill (No. 15), Respecting the Village of Waterford.

Referred to a Committee of the Whole House To-morrow.

Bill (No. 3), intituled "An Act respecting the Grey and Bruce Loan Company and the Owen Sound Loan and Savings Company."

Referred to the Committee of the Whole House To-morrow.

Bill (No. 116), intituled "To provide for the Development of Northern Ontario."

Referred to the Committee of the Whole House To-morrow.

The House resolved itself into a Committee to consider Bill (No. 94), To consolidate and amend the Constables Act, and, after some time spent therein, Mr. Speaker resumed the Chair; and Mr. Black reported, That the Committee had directed him to report the Bill without any amendment.

Ordered, That the Bill be read the third time To-morrow.

The House resolved itself into a Committee to consider Bill (No. 78), To amend the Commissioners for taking Affidavits Act, and, after some time spent therein, Mr. Speaker resumed the Chair; and Mr. Black reported, That the Committee had directed him to report the Bill with certain amendments.

Ordered, That the Amendments be taken into consideration forthwith.

The Amendments, having been read the second time, were agreed to.

Ordered, That the Bill be read the third time To-morrow.

The House then adjourned at 5.45 p.m.

THURSDAY, MARCH 11TH, 1926.

PRAYERS.   3 O'CLOCK P.M.

The following Petitions were severally brought up and laid upon the Table:—

By Mr. Ross, Petition of Wm. R. McDonald and others of the congregation of the Kintore Continuing Presbyterian Church; also, Petition of Alex. Murray and others of the congregation of Knox' Presbyterian Church, Embro, Ontario.

By Mr. Taylor, Petition of Board of Managers and Session of Minority Members of the former Division Street Presbyterian Church, and Knox Presbyterian Church, Owen Sound, Ontario.

By Mr. Raney, Petition of certain citizens of the City of Toronto, asking reduction of taxation on improvements.

———————

The following Petitions were read and received:—

Of William J. Stevenson and others of Clinton Presbyterian Church, praying that an Act may pass to amend the United Church of Canada Act.

Of A. Hammond and others of St. Andrew's Presbyterian Church, Moorefield, praying that an Act may pass to amend the United Church of Canada Act.

Of Archie MacCuaig and others of Priceville Presbyterian Church, praying that an Act may pass to amend the United Church of Canada Act.

———————

Mr. Nickle, from the Standing Committee on Private Bills, presented their Third Report, which was read as follows and adopted:—

Your Committee beg to report the following Bills without amendment:—

Bill (No. 16), An Act respecting the Town of Gananoque.

Bill (No. 32), An Act respecting The British Mortgage Loan Company of Ontario.

Bill (No. 36), An Act respecting the City of Galt.

The following Bills were severally introduced and read the first time:—

Bill (No. 129), intituled "An Act to amend the Consolidated Municipal Act, 1922." *Mr. Mahoney.*

Ordered, That the Bill be read the second time To-morrow.

Bill (No. 130), intituled "An Act respecting the Rights of Widows in the Estates of their Deceased Husbands." *Mr. Fisher.*

Ordered, That the Bill be read the second time To-morrow.

Bill (No. 131), intituled "An Act to prohibit Political Contributions by Brewers, Distillers, Standard Hotel Keepers, Public Contractors, Crown Lessees, and certain Corporations." *Mr. Raney.*

Ordered, That the Bill be read the second time To-morrow.

———

Mr. Goldie presented to the House, by command of His Honour the Lieutenant-Governor:—

Public Accounts of the Province of Ontario for the twelve months ending October 31st, 1925. (*Sessional Papers, No. 1.*)

———

Ordered, That the Public Accounts of the Province be referred to the Standing Committee on Public Accounts.

———

Mr. Ferguson delivered to Mr. Speaker a message from the Lieutenant-Governor, signed by himself; and the said message was read by Mr. Speaker, and is as follows:—

H. COCKSHUTT.

The Lieutenant-Governor transmits Supplementary Estimates of certain sums required for the service of the Province for the year ending 31st October, 1926, and recommends them to the Legislative Assembly.

GOVERNMENT HOUSE,
   Toronto, March 11th, 1926.

(*Sessional Papers, No. 2.*)

Ordered, That the message of the Lieutenant-Governor, together with the estimates accompanying the same, be referred to the Committee of Supply.

The Order of the Day for the House to resolve itself into the Committee of Supply, having been read,

Mr. Price moved,

That Mr. Speaker do now leave the Chair and that the House do resolve itself into the Committee of Supply.

And a Debate having ensued, it was, on the motion of Mr. Pinard,

Ordered, That the Debate be adjourned until Tuesday next.

The Provincial Secretary presented to the House, by command of His Honour the Lieutenant-Governor:—

Report on the Distribution of the Revised Statutes and Sessional Statutes to October 31st, 1924. (*Sessional Papers, No. 44.*)

The House then adjourned at 5.55 p.m.

FRIDAY, MARCH 12TH, 1926.

PRAYERS.   3 O'CLOCK P.M.

Mr. Lewis from the Standing Committee on Standing Orders, presented their Third and Final Report which was read and adopted:—

Your Committee have carefully examined the following Petitions and find the Notices as published in each case sufficient:—

Of the Board of Trustees of the Police Village of Alfred, praying that an Act may pass validating and ratifying a by-law.

Of the City Council of Kitchener, praying that an Act may pass validating a by-law.

Of the Township Council of Grantham, praying that an Act may pass to validate and confirm certain by-laws.

Of the Evangelical Lutheran Seminary of Canada, praying that an Act may pass to amend the Act, 3 George V, chap. 145, intituled "An Act to Incorporate Evangelical Lutheran Seminary of Canada."

. Of the Township Council of Stamford, praying that an Act may pass amending the Township of Stamford Act, 1924, chapter 126, authorizing the Corporation to pass by-laws *re* construction of sewers.

Of the Town Council of Huntsville, praying that an Act may pass validating an Agreement between His Majesty the King and the Town of Huntsville and also to confirm a by-law.

Of the City Council of Sault Ste. Marie, praying that an Act may pass validating certain by-laws, also to confirm tax sales and deeds issued by the Corporation.

Of the City Council of Sarnia, praying that an Act may pass respecting Stock or First Mortgage Bonds of the Sarnia Street Railway Company.

Of the City Council of Ottawa, praying that an Act may pass respecting fixed assessment for hotels.

Of the Ottawa Police Benefit Fund Association, praying that an Act may pass authorizing the Association to undertake any class of insurance for which a fraternal society may be licensed.

Of the Township Council of Tisdale, praying that an Act may pass to invalidate a certain by-law.

———————

The following Bills were severally introduced and read the first time:—

Bill (No. 24), intituled "An Act respecting the Village of Alfred." *Mr. Proulx.*

Referred to the Committee on Private Bills.

Bill (No. 37), intituled "An Act respecting the City of Kitchener." *Mr. Weichel.*

Referred to the Committee on Private Bills.

Bill (No. 31), intituled "An Act respecting the Township of Grantham." *Mr. Graves.*

Referred to the Committee on Private Bills.

Bill (No. 40), intituled "An Act to amend the Act to Incorporate the Evangelical Lutheran Seminary of Canada." *Mr. Weichel.*

Referred to the Committee on Private Bills.

Bill (No. 49), intituled "An Act respecting the Township of Stamford." *Mr. Willson (Niagara Falls).*

Referred to the Committee on Private Bills.

5 J.

Bill (No. 41), intituled "An Act respecting the Town of Huntsville." *Mr. Ecclestone.*

Referred to the Committee on Private Bills.

Bill (No. 52), intituled "An Act respecting the City of Sault Ste. Marie." *Mr. Haney.*

Referred to the Committee on Private Bills.

Bill (No. 59), intituled "An Act respecting the City of Sarnia." *Mr. Haney.*

Referred to the Committee on Private Bills.

Bill (No. 58), intituled "An Act respecting the City of Ottawa." *Mr. Pinard.*

Referred to the Committee on Private Bills.

Bill (No. 57), intituled "An Act respecting the Ottawa Police Benefit Fund Association." *Mr. Pinard.*

Referred to the Committee on Private Bills.

Bill (No. 60), intituled "An Act respecting the Township of Tisdale." *Mr. Kennedy (Temiskaming).*

Referred to the Committee on Private Bills.

Bill (No. 132), intituled "An Act to amend the Assessment Act." *Mr. Weichel.*

Ordered, That the Bill be read the second time on Monday next.

Bill (No. 133), intituled "An Act to amend the Consolidated Municipal Act, 1922. " *Mr. McBrien.*

Ordered, That the Bill be read the second time on Monday next.

The House resolved itself into a Committee, severally to consider the following Bills:—

Bill (No. 42), Respecting the Amalgamation of the Toronto Western Hospital and Grace Hospital.

Bill (No. 15), Respecting the Village of Waterford.

Bill (No. 3), Respecting the Grey and Bruce Loan Company and the Owen Sound Loan and Savings Company.

Mr. Speaker resumed the Chair; and Mr. Jamieson (Grey) reported, That the Committee had directed him to report the several Bills without Amendments.

Ordered, That the Bills reported be severally read the third time on Monday next.

––––––––––

The Order of the Day for the House to resolve itself into a Committee of the whole to consider Bill (No. 68), To amend the Workmen's Compensation Act, having been read,

Ordered, That the Order be discharged, and that the Bill be withdrawn.

––––––––––

Mr. Biggs asked the following Question (No. 100):—

1. Does the Province still own the Peterborough Electric Railway. 2. What has been the total loss in the operation of this road, year by year. 3. Has there been any provision for sinking fund or depreciation, and, if so, what. 4. What does the Government propose to do with this road.

The Minister of Public Works replied as follows:—

1. Yes, this Railway is operated by the Hydro-Electric Power Commission on behalf of the Province. 2. 1918, $12,323.41; 1919, $20,779.07; 1920, $21,205.87; 1921, $33,031.15; 1922, $29,408.24; 1923, $30,475.05; 1924, $35,968.94; 1925, $36,860.44. There was a surplus of $1,848.84 in the first twenty months of operation ending the 31st October, 1917. Allowing for this surplus, the net deficit is $218,221.33. 3. Various amounts have been set aside for renewals during this period, aggregating $30,430.53. 4. For the present continue operation.

––––––––––

Mr. Biggs asked the following Question (No. 101):—

1. Does the Province still own the Campbellford Pulp Mill. 2. Has it been operated since this Government came into office. 3. If so, by whom and with what result, so far as profit or loss is concerned.

The Minister of Public Works replied as follows—:

1. Yes. 2. The Mill has been operated by the Hydro-Electric Power Commission. 3. It is not considered in the public interest at the present time to state the results of the operation of this Mill, as the Commission is contemplating the sale of the property.

Mr. Biggs asked the following Question (No. 102):—

1. How many electric railways are being operated by the Hydro-Electric Power Commission and where are they. 2. Which of these roads was operated last year (a) at a profit, (b) with a deficit, and what was the profit or deficit in each case. 3. Was anything set aside for sinking fund or depreciation in any of these cases; if so, in which cases and what amounts were so set aside.

The Minister of Public Works replied as follows:—

1. The following electric railways are operated by the Hydro-Electric Power Commission:—Sandwich, Windsor and Amherstburg Railway; Guelph Radial Railway; Toronto and York Radial Railway; Peterborough Radial Railway. 2. Results of operation during 1925:—Sandwich, Windsor and Amherstburg Railway, surplus, $64,434.94; Guelph Radial Railway, deficit, $18,437.12; Toronto and York Radial Railway, deficit, $247,122.27; Peterborough Radial Railway, deficit, $36,860.44. 3. Guelph, Windsor and Amherstburg Railway, surplus of $64,434.94 set aside for renewals; Peterborough Radial Railway, $5,622.82 included in deficit above shown, set aside for renewals; other railways mentioned, no provision for renewals.

Mr. Freeborn asked the following Question (No. 104):—

1. How many convictions were made during the latter half of 1925 (a) in the City of Toronto, (b) in the City of Hamilton, (c) in the City of Windsor, for premises in respect of which permits to sell Government beer had been issued pursuant to the law of the last Session of the Legislature. 2. How many of such premises were standard hotels. 3. In how many cases was there more than one such conviction in respect of such premises. 4. In how many such cases were the beer permits cancelled.

The Attorney-General replied as follows:—

1. Toronto, 24; Hamilton, 4; Windsor, 3. 2. Toronto, 23; Hamilton, 4; Windsor, 2. 3. Six. *Note:* In these cases, although the convictions were for the same premises, they were against different proprietors. 4. One. *Note:* As the permit is issued to the individual for the premises, where the proprietors changed the permit automatically expired when he left the premises. With regard to the cases where it was the first offence, the permits were not cancelled, as it was thought that the penalty imposed was sufficient punishment, particularly in view of the fact that in many cases the liquor sold was only slightly over strength.

Mr. Freeborn asked the following Question (No. 105):—

1. How many convictions were recorded (a) in the City of Toronto, (b) in the City of Hamilton, (c) in the City of Windsor, during the last half of 1925 for selling, having or keeping over-strength beer. 2. In how many such cases were the brewers who had supplied the over-strength beer prosecuted. 3. What were the names of the breweries that were so prosecuted.

The Attorney-General replied as follows:—

1. Toronto, 24; Hamilton, 4; Windsor, 3. 2 and 3. None. *Note:* The strong beer which is sold illegally seldom bears any label or mark by which the brewer can be identified. When it does bear such mark it has been found impossible to prove that the purchase was made from the brewer.

Mr. Pinard asked the following Question (No. 122):—

1. Was one, W. B. Cleland, ever in the employ of the Ontario Government Dispensaries. 2. If so, between what dates and what were his duties. 3. What was his salary. 4. For what reason did he retire or resign. 5. Did W. B. Cleland have direction or supervision of ordering supplies of liquor. 6. What contracts did W. B. Cleland place for liquors. 7. Did any of these contracts continue after Mr. Cleland resigned or retired. 8. What brands of liquors have since been purchased through Mr. Cleland as agent, representative or broker, and from what persons or companies. 9. From what person, companies or firms has liquor been purchased, upon which purchases W. B. Cleland advised or acted as agent, representative or broker, and what brands of liquor were so purchased.

The Attorney-General replied as follows:—

1. Yes. 2 and 3. May 1st, 1919, to October 31st, 1920, as General Manager of the Ontario Government Dispensaries with a salary of $10,000 per annum. On October 31st, 1920, relinquished position of General Manager to become Supervisor of the Ontario Government Dispensaries on part time, at a salary of $3,000, and finally resigned from the service of the Dispensaries entirely on May 31st, 1921. 4. His resignation was voluntary and by his own preference. 5. Yes. 6. All contracts that were made during the time he was General Manager and Supervisor. 7. Yes. 8 and 9. Mr. Cleland represents Macdonald, Greenlees & Williams, Limited, of Leith, Scotland, but orders were placed direct with such firm. The brands of liquor purchased from such firm have been and are "Old Parr," "Thomson's Grand Highland Liqueur" and "Sandy Macdonald."

Mr. Jamieson (West Simcoe) asked the following Question (No. 123):—

1. What was the total expenditure by the Department of Public Works, Colonization Roads Branch and Department of Northern Development in Northern and North Western Ontario by electoral districts for the fiscal years 1919 to 1925, inclusive.

The Minister of Public Works and Highways replied as follows:—

1. The following expenditures include expenditures for construction and maintenance of Roads, Bridges, Drainage, Court Houses, Registry Offices, Gaols, Lock-ups, Normal, Agricultural, Continuation and Training Schools, Experimental Farms, Creameries, Returned Soldiers' Settlement; the assistance of settlers by way of loans; relief to fire sufferers; and the provision of feed, cattle, seed grain and agricultural implements.

Electoral Districts	Year Ended 31st Oct., 1919	Year Ended 31st Oct., 1920	Year Ended 31st Oct., 1921	Year Ended 31st Oct., 1922
Kenora	$62,977 84	$115,880 72	$130,512 58	$147,280 75
Port Arthur	55,988 29	60,432 25	70,425 39	77,167 03
Fort William	77,188 63	78,534 69	93,687 88	130,992 11
Rainy River	170,222 09	103,445 63	162,639 48	129,543 10
Sault Ste. Marie	80,692 06	28,061 32	198,020 81	247,130 95
Algoma	204,972 19	247,645 32	153,361 12	148,689 30
Sudbury	297,292 58	92,809 64	75,340 75	117,509 97
Manitoulin	10,634 28	71,361 08	114,597 78	141,962 44
Sturgeon Falls	76,899 05	91,785 94	145,386 71	94,944 81
Nipissing	61,940 85	65,594 60	98,531 48	129,563 43
Renfrew North	38,826 09	44,206 87	32,852 13	54,472 17
Parry Sound	137,753 42	134,237 96	133,027 19	182,833 57
Muskoka	72,596 25	107,750 90	112,940 78	165,455 59
Temiskaming	234,830 29	146,844 19	228,769 14	196,035 35
Cochrane	365,110 19	322,703 07	366,973 02	487,994 81
Simcoe (Dept. N.D. only)	15,510 94	43,246 84	722 51	....
Administration (Dept. N. D. only)	18,457 81	23,424 09	21,566 09	27,550 61
Sundry Surveys	....	....	6,170 74	....
	$1,981,892 85	$1,777,965 11	$2,145,525 58	$2,479,125 99
Miscellaneous Services (Dept. of Northern Develop. only):				
Experimental Farms	$12,992 49	$6,795 38	$5,210 70	$30,278 16
Assistance of Settlers: Feed Shortage	....	....	60,056 87	57,841 20
Assistance of Settlers: Fire Relief	....	....	....	....
Assistance of Settlers: Saw Mills	....	....	....	....
Creameries	7,915 32	7,011 97	7,470 13	11,305 86
Seed Grain	7,322 04	35,439 22	12,640 51	37,174 84
Agricultural Implements	....	....	....	....
Cattle Purchase	18,720 61	405 45	968 55	1,523 38
Schools and other Public Buildings	....	3,773 45	....	17,353 85
Returned Soldiers' Settlement Account	366,085 13	202,465 24	4,274 65	3,169 35
Settlers' Loan Account	44,456 01	64,317 82	115,775 18	248,358 12
Total Miscellaneous Services	$457,491 60	$320,208 53	$206,396 59	$407,004 76
Total Expenditures	$2,439,384 45	$2,098,173 64	$2,351,922 17	$2,886,130 75

Electoral Districts	Year Ended 31st Oct., 1923	Year Ended 31st Oct., 1924	Year Ended 31st Oct., 1925	Total Amount
Kenora......................	$249,946 07	$141,054 57	$218,676 91	$1,066,329 44
Port Arthur.................	195,023 32	369,887 95	348,436 70	1,177,360 93
Fort William................	152,235 35	180,756 49	179,792 42	893,187 57
Rainy River................	162,038 09	87,310 31	92,397 08	907,595 78
Sault Ste. Marie............	135,187 37	245,402 30	289,501 78	1,223,996 59
Algoma.....................	189,511 41	131,006 30	120,919 92	1,196,105 56
Sudbury....................	201,212 49	547,147 54	611,064 57	1,942,377 54
Manitoulin..................	226,535 42	91,279 28	101,625 12	757,995 40
Sturgeon Falls..............	106,269 17	88,714 81	89,979 07	693,979 56
Nipissing...................	219,563 26	141,112 52	210,795 22	927,101 36
Renfrew North..............	63,774 74	40,362 86	68,664 29	343,159 15
Parry Sound................	244,605 45	244,045 07	210,083 75	1,286,586 41
Muskoka...................	263,310 65	167,565 72	150,697 32	1,040,317 21
Temiskaming...............	630,630 69	646,592 61	531,477 86	2,615,180 13
Cochrane...................	757,191 84	761,233 60	1,027,050 79	4,088,257 32
Simcoe (Dept. N.D. only)....	....	....	....	59,480 29
Administration (Dept. N.D. only).....................	32,901 03	37,489 85	47,997 29	209,386 77
Sundry Surveys.............	....	....	....	6,170 74
	$3,829,936 35	$3,920,961 78	$4,299,160 09	$20,434,567 75
Miscellaneous Services (Dept. of Northern Develop. only):				
Experimental Farms.........	$11,036 39	$14,226 51	$46,145 07	$126,684 70
Assistance of Settlers: Feed Shortage...............	6,254 51	37 00	26 91	124,216 49
Assistance of Settlers: Fire Relief....................	282,060 99	47,038 51	....	329,099 50
Assistance of Settlers: Saw Mills....................	4,503 55	6,678 10	3,696 62	14,878 27
Creameries.................	3,975 63	89 00	1,950 00	39,717 91
Seed Grain.................	35,698 75	7,662 69	6,450 15	142,388 20
Agricultural Implements.....	46,771 37	17 55	2 64	46,791 56
Cattle Purchase.............	....	....	23,811 57	45,429 56
Schools and other Public Buildings.....................	32,137 77	3,076 87	430 80	56,772 74
Returned Soldiers' Settlement Account..................	2,832 28	1,653 23	....	580,479 88
Settlers' Loan Account.......	167,308 92	97,513 72	120,256 74	857,986 51
Total Miscellaneous Services..	$592,580 16	$177,993 18	$202,770 50	$2,364,445 32
Total Expenditures.......	$4,422,516 51	$4,098,954 96	$4,501,930 59	$22,799,013 07

Mr. Widdifield asked the following Question (No. 124):—

1. What is the total amount of tax on race track wagers that has been collected by the Province each year since the tax was instituted.

The Provincial Treasurer replied as follows:—

1. 1922, $2,212,220.00; 1923, $1,821,963.72; 1924, $1,794,052.55; 1925, $1,703,716.85.

——————

Mr. Widdifield asked the following Question (No. 125):—

1. What is the total amount of the tax on racing associations that has been collected by the Province each year since the tax was instituted.

The Provincial Treasurer replied as follows:—

1. 1911, $15,790.25; 1912, $17,290.25; 1913, $17,200.00; 1914, $42,250.00; 1915, $42,350.00; 1916, $136,265.00; 1917, $100,723.50; 1918, $160.00; 1919, $100.00; 1920, $770,410.00; 1921, $770,440.00; 1922, $769,910.48; 1923, $670,774.53; 1924, $848,495.00; 1925, $998,690.40.

Mr. Ross asked the following Question (No. 126):—

1. What was the amount on deposit in the Government Savings Offices on the 31st of October in each year since these offices were established.

The Provincial Treasurer replied as follows:—

October 31st, 1922, $2,688,087; October 31st, 1923, $13,682,990; October 31st, 1924, $22,013,860; October 31st, 1925, $19,222,689.

Mr. Nixon asked the following Question (No. 134):—

1. Have any bonds been issued by the T. & N. O. Railway Commission under the enabling Act of the last Session (1925, chapter 22). 2. If so, to what amount. 3. If the money produced by these bonds had been raised by the sale of Ontario bonds according to the former practice, what would have been the effect on the Treasurer's statement as to (a) the Province's expenditure for the year 1924-25, (b) the increase of the Provincial debt.

The Minister of Public Works and Highways replied as follows:—

1. No. 2 and 3. These questions are answered by the reply to Question 1.

The following Bills were severally read the second time:—

Bill (No. 4), To incorporate the Toronto East General Hospital.

Referred to a Committee of the Whole House on Monday next.

Bill (No. 10), Respecting the amalgamation of the Girls' Home and the Protestant Orphans' Home.

Referred to a Committee of the Whole House on Monday next.

Bill (No. 28), Respecting the City of Stratford.

Referred to a Committee of the Whole House on Monday next.

Bill (No. 26), To extend the time for the completion of Haliburton, Whitney and Mattawa Railway.

Referred to a Committee of the Whole House on Monday next.

Bill (No. 1), To incorporate the Welland and Port Colborne Railway Company.

Referred to a Committee of the Whole House on Monday next.

Bill (No. 8), Respecting the Mount McKay and Kakabeka Falls Railway Company.

Referred to a Committee of the Whole House on Monday next.

Bill (No. 51), Respecting the Midland Simcoe Railway Company.

Referred to a Committee of the Whole House on Monday next.

Bill (No. 16), Respecting the Town of Gananoque.

Referred to a Committee of the Whole House on Monday next.

Bill (No. 32), Respecting the British Mortgage Loan Company of Ontario.

Referred to a Committee of the Whole House on Monday next.

Bill (No. 36), Respecting the City of Galt.

Referred to a Committee of the Whole House on Monday next.

The Provincial Secretary presented to the House, by command of His Honour the Lieutenant-Governor:—

Report of the Inspector of Legal Offices for 1925.

(*Sessional Papers, No. 5.*)

The House then adjourned at 4.25 p.m.

MONDAY, MARCH 15TH, 1926.

PRAYERS.   3 O'CLOCK P.M.

The following Petitions were severally brought up and laid upon the Table:—

By Mr. Sinclair, the Petition of James J. Leask and others, members of certain congregations of the Presbyterian Church in Canada.

———————

The following Bills were severally introduced and read the first time:—

Bill (No. 134), intituled "An Act to amend the Consolidated Municipal Act, 1922." *Mr. Lewis.*

Ordered, That the Bill be read the second time To-morrow.

Bill (No. 135), intituled "An Act to amend the Consolidated Municipal Act, 1922." *Mr. Keith.*

Ordered, That the Bill be read the second time To-morrow.

Bill (No. 136), intituled "An Act to amend an Act relating to Hospitals and Charitable Institutions." *Mr. Lewis.*

Ordered, That the Bill be read the second time To-morrow.

Bill (No. 137), intituled "An Act to amend the Consolidated Municipal Act, 1922." *Mr. Currie.*

Ordered, That the Bill be read the second time To-morrow.

———————

Mr. Ross asked the following Question (No. 127):—

1. What was the amount of loans outstanding (a) under the Agricultural Development law, and (b) as short-term farm loans, on the 31st of October in each year since the law was passed. 2. What have been the losses to this date.

The Prime Minister replied as follows:—

1. (a) October 31st, 1922, $1,187,143.32; October 31st, 1923, $4,132,987.55; October 31st, 1924, $7,207,043.78; October 31st, 1925, $9,584,176.21; (b) October 31st, 1922, $150,230.00; October 31st, 1923, $279,673.40; October 31st, 1924, $231,402.74; October 31st, 1925, $199,744.37. 2. (a) $943.82; (b) definite losses to the extent of approximately $1,000.00 have been made by two associations, but no adjustment has as yet been made with the Province.

Mr. Fenton asked the following Question (No. 129):—

1. What length of time elapsed between the date of Sir Adam Beck's last attendance at a meeting of the Hydro-Electric Power Commission and the date of the appointment of Messrs. Magrath and Maguire to the Commission. 2. How was the Commission constituted during this time. 3. Who (if anyone) sat on the Commission during these months with the third Commissioner, Mr. Cooke. 4. Under what authority. 5. How many meetings of the Commission were held during these months.

The Prime Minister replied as follows:—

1. Thirty-eight days. During the illness of the late Sir Adam Beck, meetings of the Commission were held at his home in London until August 5th. On September 12th Mr. Magrath was appointed to the Chairmanship. 2. From the time the last meeting of the Commission was held until the death of Sir Adam Beck on August 15th, the Commission was composed of Sir Adam Beck and the Honourable J. R. Cooke. From the time of the death of Sir Adam until the appointment of Mr. Magrath on September 12th, Mr. Cooke was the sole member of the Commission. 3. As stated in the reply to Question No. 2, Mr. Cooke was the sole Commissioner during the period mentioned. 4. This is answered by the reply to Question No. 3. 5. No meetings of the Commission were held during the period mentioned.

Mr. McCallum asked the following Question (No. 131):—

1. What moneys have been drawn by Hon. J. R. Cooke since the present Government came into office, apart from his indemnity as a member of the House and from his salary as a commissioner (a) from the Treasury of Ontario, (b) from the funds of the Hydro-Electric Power Commission.

The Prime Minister replied as follows:—

(a) Nothing beyond allowances which every member of the Legislature is entitled to receive; (b) nothing.

Mr. Clarke asked the following Question (No. 137):—

1. What was the cost to the Province of Ontario of the Commission appointed June 5th, 1925, to enquire whether the prices at which gasoline and oils are sold to the people of Ontario are just and fair, which commission report was presented to the House February 19th last as Sessional Papers No. 33.

The Prime Minister replied as follows:—

There has been no final settlement as yet as to the cost of this inquiry. An advance of $2,000.00 has been made on account of expenses.

The following Bills were severally read the second time:—

Bill (No. 129), To amend the Consolidated Municipal Act, 1922. *Mr. Mahoney.*

Referred to the Municipal Committee.

Bill (No. 122), Respecting Dentistry. *Mr. Ferguson.*

Referred to a Committee of the Whole House To-morrow.

Bill (No. 127), To amend the Ontario Companies Act. *Mr. Nickle.*

Referred to a Committee of the Whole House To-morrow.

Bill (No. 128), To consolidate and amend the Cemetery Act. *Mr. Nickle.*

Referred to a Committee of the Whole House To-morrow.

Bill (No. 118), To amend the Consolidated Municipal Act, 1922. *Mr. Finlayson.*

Referred to the Municipal Committee.

The House resolved itself into a Committee severally to consider the following Bills:—

Bill (No. 10), Respecting the amalgamation of the Girls' Home and the Protestant Orphans' Home.

Bill (No. 28), Respecting the City of Stratford.

Bill (No. 26), To extend the time for the completion of the Haliburton, Whitney and Mattawa Railway.

Bill (No. 8), Respecting the Mount McKay and Kakabeka Falls Railway Company.

Bill (No. 51), Respecting the Midland Simcoe Railway Company.

Bill (No. 16), Respecting the Town of Gananoque.

Bill (No. 32), Respecting the British Mortgage Loan Company of Ontario.

Bill (No. 36), Respecting the City of Galt.

Mr. Speaker resumed the Chair; and Mr. Finlayson reported, That the Committee had directed him to report the several Bills without Amendments.

Ordered, That the Bills reported be severally read the third time To-morrow.

The House resolved itself into a Committee to consider Bill (No. 81), To consolidate and amend the Administration of Justice Expenses Act, and, after some time spent therein, Mr. Speaker resumed the Chair; and Mr. Finlayson reported, That the Committee had directed him to report the Bill without any amendment.

Ordered, That the Bill be read the third time To-morrow.

———————

The Provincial Secretary presented to the House:—

Return to the Order of the House, dated March 20th, 1925, that there be laid before this House a Return showing—1. What is the amount or amounts paid by the Government of the Province of Ontario since the 1st of January, 1912, to date, to counsel, solicitors and other parties, mentioning the names of such counsel, solicitors and other parties, with the dates of the divers payments so made, in any of the proceedings in the following litigation, *viz.*—(1) *Re* Mackell *vs.* Board of Trustees of the Catholic Separate Schools of the City of Ottawa; (2) Motion to commit chairman of said Board for alleged contempt of Court; (3) Board of Trustees *vs.* The Quebec Bank and the Bank of Ottawa; (4) Board of Trustees *vs.* The Separate School Commission of Ottawa to have it declared that the Act of the Legislature of Ontario, being 5 George V, chapter 45, be declared *ultra vires*; (5) Board of Trustees *vs.* The Quebec Bank and the Corporation of the City of Ottawa; (6) Board of Trustees *vs.* Bank of Ottawa and others; (7) Board of Trustees *vs.* Quebec Bank and others; (8) Board of Trustees *vs.* Murphy and others; (9) Consolidated case, Board of Trustees *vs.* Quebec Bank and others; (10) Reference to Appellate Division of the Supreme Court of Ontario; (11) Any amount paid by way of fees to counsel or solicitors for preparation and drafting of Act of the Legislature, and more particularly the Act of 5 George V, chapter 45, and 7 George V, chapters 59 and 60; (12) in all proceedings held before the First Division Court of the County of Carleton to garnishee moneys alleged to belong to said Board of Trustees and detained by the Corporation of the City of Ottawa; (13) generally, all sums paid by any of the Departments of the Government of this Province to counsel, solicitors, draughtsmen, agents and other parties in connection with any of the above litigations and matters. (*Sessional Papers, No. 45.*)

Also—Return to the Order of the House, dated March 20th, 1925, that there be laid before this House, a Return showing—1. What appointments to public positions have been made by the present Government in the riding of North Ontario. 2. Were the appointments so made, or any of them, and, if any of them, which of them, suggested or recommended by Mr. Daniel Watson Walls, the defeated Conservative candidate at the election of June, 1923. (*Sessional Papers, No. 46.*)

———————

The House then adjourned at 4.20 p.m.

TUESDAY, MARCH 16TH, 1926.

PRAYERS.   3 O'CLOCK P.M.

The following Petition was brought up and laid upon the Table:—

By Mr. Finlayson, Petition of Norman Campbell and others, members of the Congregation of Guthrie Presbyterian Church.

———

The following Petitions were read and received:—

Of Wm. R. McDonald and others of Kintore Continuing Presbyterian Church; also, the Petition of Alex. Murray and others of Knox Presbyterian Church, Embro; also, the Petition of the Board of Managers and Session of the minority members of the former Division Street Presbyterian Church and Knox Presbyterian Church, both of Owen Sound, respecting the United Church of Canada Act.

Of certain citizens of Toronto, praying that an Act may pass to amend the Assessment Act.

———

Mr. Speaker then informed the House:—

That the Clerk had received from the Railway and Municipal Board, their Report in the following case:—

Bill (No. 2), Respecting the Town of Arnprior.

The Report was then read by the Clerk at the Table, as follows:—

To the Honourable, The Legislative Assembly of the Province of Ontario.

Upon the reference under Rule 61*a* of your Honourable House to The Ontario Railway and Municipal Board of Bill (No. 2), 1926, entitled "An Act respecting the Town of Arnprior," the Board begs leave respectfully to report that in the judgment of the Board it is reasonable that such Bill, in so far as it provides for the consolidation of a floating debt, should be passed by your Honourable House as amended.

The largest proportion of the floating debt of $16,750 referred to in the Bill, is for works of a permanent character, and the balance is for expenditures which, in the ordinary course, should have been paid out of taxes. For this reason the Board is of the opinion that the debentures should be made payable in not more than fifteen years from the date of issue.

All of which is respectfully submitted.

A. B. INGRAM, *Vice-Chairman.*

J. A. ELLIS, *Commissioner.*

Dated at Toronto,
this 15th day of March, A.D. 1926.

Ordered, That Bill (No. 2), Respecting the Town of Arnprior, be referred to the Committee on Private Bills, with instructions to consider the same with reference to the suggestions of the Railway and Municipal Board thereon.

———————

Mr. Nickle, from the Standing Committee on Private Bills, presented their Fourth Report which was read as follows and adopted:

Your Committee beg to report the following Bill without amendment:—

Bill (No. 37), An Act respecting the City of Kitchener.

Bill (No. 21), An Act respecting C.M. & G. Canadian Investments, Limited.

Your Committee beg to report the following Bills with certain amendments:—

Bill (No. 23), An Act to incorporate the Association of Accountants and Auditors in Ontario.

Bill (No. 29), An Act respecting the Township of Thorah.

Bill (No. 35), An Act respecting the City of Guelph and the Guelph Radial Railway Company.

Your Committee would recommend that the fees less the actual cost of printing be remitted on Bill (No. 33), "An Act respecting the Town of Bala" the same having been withdrawn by the promoters thereof.

Your Committee would recommend that notwithstanding Rule 51 of Your Honourable House the time for receiving Reports of Committees on Private Bills be extended to and inclusive of Tuesday the thirtieth day of March, 1926.

Ordered, That the fees, less the actual cost of printing, be remitted on Bill (No. 33), An Act respecting the Town of Bala.

Ordered, That the time for receiving Reports of Committees on Private Bills be extended to and inclusive of Tuesday the thirtieth day of March, 1926.

———

The following Bills were severally introduced and read the first time:—

Bill (No. 138), intituled "An Act to amend the Public Parks Act." *Mr. McBride.*

Ordered, That the Bill be read the second time To-morrow.

Bill (No. 139), intituled "An Act to amend the Consolidated Municipal Act, 1922." *Mr. Elliott.*

Ordered, That the Bill be read the second time To-morrow.

Bill (No. 140), intituled "An Act to impose a Tax on Dogs and for the Protection of Sheep." *Mr. Martin.*

Ordered, That the Bill be read the second time To-morrow.

Bill (No. 141), intituled "An Act to amend the Consolidated Municipal Act, 1922." *Mr. Mahoney.*

Ordered, That the Bill be read the second time To-morrow.

Bill (No. 142), intituled "An Act respecting the Licensing of Hawkers and Transient Traders." *Mr. Nickle.*

Ordered, That the Bill be read the second time To-morrow.

Bill (No. 143), intituled "An Act to amend the Ontario Election Act." *Mr. Wilson (Windsor).*

Ordered, That the Bill be read the second time To-morrow.

Bill (No. 144), intituled "An Act to amend the Assessment Act." *Mr. McBrien.*

Ordered, That the Bill be read the second time To-morrow.

Bill (No. 145), intituled "An Act to amend the Highway Traffic Act." *Mr. Nickle.*

Ordered, That the Bill be read the second time To-morrow.

The following Bills were severally read the second time:—

Bill (No. 123), To amend the Corn Borer Act.

Referred to a Committee of the Whole House To-morrow.

Bill (No. 121), To amend the Sanatoria for Consumptives Act.

Referred to a Committee of the Whole House To-morrow.

———

The House resolved itself into a Committee to consider Bill (No. 127), To amend the Ontario Companies Act, and, after some time spent therein, Mr. Speaker resumed the Chair; and Mr. Jamieson (Grey) reported, That the Committee had directed him to report the Bill without any amendment.

Ordered, That the Bill be read the third time To-morrow.

———

The House resolved itself into a Committee to consider Bill (No. 128), To consolidate and amend the Cemetery Act, and, after some time spent therein, Mr. Speaker resumed the Chair; and Mr. Jamieson (Grey) reported, That the Committee had directed him to report the Bill with certain amendments.

Ordered, That the Amendments be taken into consideration forthwith.

The Amendments, having been read the second time, were agreed to.

Ordered, That the Bill be read the third time To-morrow.

———

The Provincial Secretary presented to the House, by command of His Honour the Lieutenant-Governor:—

Report of the Provincial Board of Health for the year 1925. (*Sessional Papers, No. 14.*)

Report of the Minimum Wage Board for the year 1925. (*Sessional Papers, No. 47.*)

———

The Order of the Day, for Mr. Speaker to leave the Chair and that the House do resolve itself into the Committee of Supply, having been read,

The Debate was resumed,

And after some time,

Mr. Brackin moved, in amendment, seconded by Mr. Pinard,

That all the words of the motion after the first word "that" be struck out and the following inserted: "This House regrets that the financial statement by the Honourable the Provincial Treasurer indicates a large deficit last year of approximately $5,000,000.00 and forecasts a deficit next year of at least $1,500,000.00, and this House, recognizing the necessity of other sources of revenue, urges upon the Government the adoption at this Session of a system of sale of spirituous and malt liquors in the Province under Government control with provision for local option, believing, as this House does, that such a system will divert to the Treasury of the Province the millions of dollars now annually going into the pockets of illicit vendors of liquor and will prove of great assistance in wiping out the business of bootlegging, illicit manufacture and smuggling of spirits, with all their attendant evil consequences."

And a Debate having ensued, it was, on the motion of Mr. Lewis,

Ordered, That the Debate be further adjourned until Thursday next.

———————

The House then adjourned at 10.35 p.m.

═══════════════

WEDNESDAY, MARCH 17TH, 1926.

PRAYERS.   3 O'CLOCK P.M.

Mr. Jamieson (Grey) presented the Report of the Agricultural Enquiry Committee on Marketing of Agricultural Products.

Ordered, That the Report be adopted and referred to the Committee on Printing.   (*Sessional Papers, No. 48*).

———————

The following Bill was introduced and read the first time:—

Bill (No. 146), intituled "An Act to amend the Assessment Act."   *Mr. Mahoney.*

Ordered, That the Bill be read the second time To-morrow.

———————

Mr. Nixon asked the following Question (No. 70):—

1. What is the total amount of fire insurance carried on the property of the Province of Ontario. 2. What was the total amount of fire insurance premiums

paid by the Province for the past fiscal year. 3. Who were the agents who placed this fire insurance. 4. Who are the agents who are now looking after fire insurance for the Province.

The Minister of Public Works and Highways replied as follows:—

1. $4,360,736.00. 2. $31,650.61. 3. The business was placed by the Departments through local insurance agents in various parts of the Province to the number of more than 200. 4. The same reply as is given to Question No. 3.

Mr. Fenton asked the following Question (No. 115):—

1. Who were the Provincial Auditors when the shortages and defalcations occurred that have been discovered in different Departments of the Government. 2. What changes, if any, have been made in the Audit Department in consequence of the disclosures.

The Provincial Treasurer replied as follows:—

1. James Clancy, from August, 1905, to October 31st, 1920; G. A. Brown, from November 1st, 1920, to present date. 2. The staff of the Audit Office has been increased sufficiently to enable it to carry on a detailed audit of all the receipts of the Province.

Mr. Lethbridge asked the following Question (No. 116):—

1. How far back has the special audit that the Government has been conducting extended in each Department that has been under investigation. 2. Has it extended through or into (a) the administration of Sir William Hearst; (b) the administration of Sir James Whitney.

The Provincial Treasurer replied as follows:—

1. Attorney-General's Department, 1921; Department of Education, 1919; Health and Labour Department, 1923; Lands and Forests Department, 1922; Mines Department, 1922; Provincial Secretary's Department, 1914; Provincial Treasurer's Department, 1906; Agriculture Department, 1920; Provincial Highways Department, 1917. 2. Answered by the reply to Question No. 1.

Mr. Kemp asked the following Question (No. 119):—

1. How many miles of pavement have been built by the Department of Lands and Forests. 2. How many miles were built by that Department under former Governments, and where, and at what cost. 3. How many miles by that Department under the present Government, and where, and at what cost. 4. In what cities or towns in New Ontario has the Government paid a part of the cost of laying down pavements. 5. What number of miles and at what cost to the Province and in what year was the work done in each place.

The Minister of Lands and Forests replied as follows:—

1. 45.49 miles. 2. Swastika-Kirkland Lake, seven miles water bound macadam, $119,631.48; Severn-Gravenhurst, twelve miles water bound macadam, $165,232.44; Soo-Sudbury Trunk Road (Soo-Garden River Section), 3.13 miles bituminous surfacing, $48,354.34; Bracebridge-Falkenburg, four miles water bound macadam, $49,454.32. (The above are existing roads superficially resurfaced). 3. Timmins-South Porcupine, 6.12 miles, $258,754.48; Sudbury-Coniston, 6.88 miles, $384,626.80; Creighton-Coppercliff, 6.36 miles, $135,063.00. (The above are pavements with permanent foundations). 4 and 5. Fort Frances, .308 miles, $5,522.20 (1924); Sault Ste. Marie, 1.01 miles, $33,038.57 (1924); Sault Ste. Marie, 2.35 miles, $36,304.38 (1923); Sault Ste. Marie, .952 miles, $19,132.54 (1925); Timmins, .702 miles, $9,940.36 (1925); Timmins, .829 miles, $47,689.09 (1925).

Mr. Fenton asked the following Question (No. 133):—

1. When was the system of audit (or lack of audit) of Public Accounts, which the present Government found in existence when it came into office in 1923, established. 2. What Government was then in office. 3. Was there any substantial change in the system (a) under Government of Sir James Whitney; (b) under Government of Sir William Hearst. 4. If so, what was the change, and when was it made.

The Provincial Treasurer replied as follows:—

1. The audit system was established by legislation in 1886. (49 Vic., Chap. 4). 2. The Mowat Government. 3. No. 4. Answered by the reply to Question No. 3.

Mr. Sinclair asked the following Question (No. 136):—

1. Was a permit granted to any person or persons or company to cut 15,000 cords of pulpwood in the Township of Ledger in the Nipigon District. 2. To whom was it granted. 3. Were tenders called before so granting. 4. At what price was the permit granted. 5. How was the price based. 6. Was the Legislative Secretary consulted before the permit was granted. 7. Did he give his approval.

The Minister of Lands and Forests replied as follows:—

1. Yes. 2. Nipigon Corporation, Limited. 3. Public tenders were advertised for, up to the 10th September last, for the right to cut pulpwood up to the requirements of the various tenderers at a price per cord upon several areas outlined in the Lake Nipigon region. The price offered by the highest tenderer was fixed as the price which all of the companies should pay for the amount of wood necessary to meet their requirements. The Township of Ledger was included in the area upon which the Nipigon Corporation, Limited, tendered.

This township, with others, was subsequently excluded from the territory from which the Nipigon Company are to cut their wood. The company expected when tendering that this township would be included in the territory and when their tender was accepted they planned to cut 50,000 cords from this locality, because it was close to their present plant and was required to supply their immediate needs. To meet this situation, and enable them to secure ample wood for this season's operation, permission was granted by Order-in-Council to cut only 15,000 cords on such portions of Ledger Township as the Minister might designate, on the same terms as covers their entire agreement. (See Votes and Proceedings, 1926, page 78). 4. See answer to No. 3. 5. See answer to No. 4. 6. No. 7. See answer to No. 6.

Mr. Bragg asked the following Question (No. 138):—

1. Is the Government aware that 1,988 cords of pulpwood or any portion thereof cut from the east half of Lot 8, Concession 8, Township of Nipigon, District of Thunder Bay, sold by tender August 8th, 1922, to be cut by April 30th, 1923, and extended to April 30th, 1925, was exported to the Central Paper Co. and the Detroit Sulphide Co. during the seasons of 1923 and 1924.

The Minister of Lands and Forests replied as follows:—

No.

Mr. Sangster asked the following Question (No. 139):—

1. Is the Government aware that 1,632 cords of pulpwood or any portion thereof cut from the east half of Lot 5, Concession 6, Township of Nipigon, and sold as non-exportable, was exported in 1923 and 1924 to the Detroit Sulphide Co. and the Central Paper Co.

The Minister of Lands and Forests replied as follows:—

No.

Mr. Taylor asked the following Question (No. 140):—

1. Is oil used on the roads in New Ontario. 2. If so, does the Government contract for this work. 3. What is the system. 4. Who are the contractors.

The Minister of Lands and Forests replied as follows:—

1. No. 2. 3 and 4. Answered by the reply to Question No. 1.

Mr. Kemp asked the following Question (No. 141):—

1. Has the Government, in the investigations that it has been carrying on since it came into office, discovered any thefts of public money or property or defalcations of public servants prior to the coming into office of the Government of Mr. Drury. 2. How far back has a systematic audit been made by the present Government in the different departments, respectively, naming the Department and giving the year in each case.

The Provincial Treasurer replied as follows:—

1. Yes. 2. Same reply as was given to Question No. 116.

Mr. Carty asked the following Question (No. 142):—

1. Did the Government purchase any airplanes from or through Jack V. Elliott, or Jack V. Elliott, Ltd. 2. If so, how many and at what prices. 3. Were any of the airplanes that were purchased by the Government formerly the property of the United States Navy Department. 4. If so, through whom were these planes purchased.

The Minister of Lands and Forests replied as follows:—

1. No. 2. Answered by No. 1. 3. Yes. 4. Laurentide Air Service.

Mr. Kemp asked the following Question (No. 144):—

1. What revenue did the Government receive in 1925 from fire, life, casualty and marine insurance companies under the Corporations Tax Act. 2. What revenue did the Government receive in 1925 from fire, life, casualty and marine insurance companies in license fees. 3. What was the number of employees of Insurance Department (a) in 1920, (b) in 1925. 4. What revenue was received in 1925 from trust companies and loan companies which are under the supervision of Insurance Department. 5. What was cost of Insurance Department in 1925. 6. What amount of taxes was collected from unlicensed fire insurance companies in 1925.

The Prime Minister replied as follows:—

1. $859,256.06. 2. $68,322.50. 3. (a) Seventeen, (b) nineteen. 4. $12,238.50. 5. $48,621.99. 6. $1,918.63.

Mr. Carty asked the following Question (No. 145):—

1. Has the investigation which the Government has been making into the Public Accounts included the Department of Lands and Forests. 2. If so, for what years.

The Provincial Treasurer replied as follows:—

1. Yes. 2. 1922, 1923, 1924, 1925. Outstanding accounts are now being investigated. Messrs. Harbinson & Allen brought the audit up from 1920 to 1922.

———

The following Bills were severally read the second time:—

Bill (No. 37), Respecting the City of Kitchener.

Referred to a Committee of the Whole House To-morrow.

Bill (No. 21), Respecting C.M. & G. Canadian Investments, Limited.

Referred to a Committee of the Whole House To-morrow.

Bill (No. 119), To amend the Consolidated Municipal Act, 1922.

Referred to the Municipal Committee.

Bill (No. 126), To amend the Consolidated Municipal Act, 1922.

Referred to the Municipal Committee.

Bill (No. 130), Respecting the Rights of Widows in the Estates of their Deceased Husbands.

Referred to the Legal Committee.

Bill (No. 136), To amend an Act relating to Hospitals and Charitable Institutions.

Referred to the Municipal Committee.

Bill (No. 137), To amend the Consolidated Municipal Act, 1922.

Referred to the Municipal Committee.

Bill (No. 131), To prohibit Political Contributions by Brewers, Distillers, Standard Hotel Keepers, Public Contractors, Crown Lessees and certain Corporations.

Referred to the Special Committee consisting of Messrs. Nickle, McBrien, Keefer, Thompson (Lanark North), Jamieson (Grey South), Wilson (Windsor), Sinclair, Tellier, Nixon and McCallum, appointed to revise and amend the Election Laws Bill (No. 103); and an Act to consolidate and amend the Voters' Lists Act, Bill (No. 104).

The Order of the Day for the second reading of Bill (No. 117), To amend the Local Improvement Act, having been read,

Ordered, That the Order be discharged, and that the Bill be withdrawn.

The Order of the Day for the second reading of Bill (No. 134), To amend the Consolidated Municipal Act, 1922, having been read,

Ordered, That the Order be discharged, and that the Bill be withdrawn.

The Order of the Day for the second reading of Bill (No. 135), To amend the Consolidated Municipal Act, 1922, having been read,

Ordered, That the Order be discharged, and that the Bill be withdrawn.

The House resolved itself into a Committee to consider Bill (No. 1), To incorporate the Welland and Port Colborne Railway Company and, after some time spent therein, Mr. Speaker resumed the Chair; and Mr. Jamieson (Grey) reported, That the Committee had directed him to report the Bill without any amendment.

Ordered, That the Bill be read the third time To-morrow.

The House resolved itself into a Committee to consider Bill (No. 121), To amend the Sanatoria for Consumptives Act, and, after some time spent therein, Mr. Speaker resumed the Chair; and Mr. Jamieson (Grey) reported, That the Committee had directed him to report the Bill without any amendment.

Ordered, That the Bill be read the third time To-morrow.

The House resolved itself into a Committee to consider Bill (No. 122), Respecting Dentistry, and, after some time spent therein, Mr. Speaker resumed the Chair; and Mr. Jamieson (Grey) reported, That the Committee had directed him to report the Bill without any amendment.

Ordered, That the Bill be read the third time To-morrow.

The House resolved itself into a Committee to consider Bill (No. 123), To amend the Corn Borer Act, and, after some time spent therein, Mr. Speaker resumed the Chair; and Mr. Jamieson (Grey) reported, That the Committee had directed him to report the Bill with certain amendments.

Ordered, That the Amendments be taken into consideration forthwith.

The Amendments, having been read the second time, were agreed to.

Ordered, That the Bill be read the third time To-morrow.

The House resolved itself into a Committee to consider Bill (No. 116), To provide for the Development of Northern Ontario, and, after some time spent therein, Mr. Speaker resumed the Chair; and Mr. Jamieson (Grey) reported, That the Committee had directed him to report the Bill without any amendment.

Ordered, That the Bill be read the third time To-morrow.

The House then adjourned at 5.35 p.m.

THURSDAY, MARCH 18TH, 1926.

PRAYERS.   3 O'CLOCK P.M.

The following Petitions were severally brought up and laid upon the Table:—

By Mr. Raney, Petition of certain citizens of the City of Toronto, asking reduction of taxation on improvements.

Mr. Speaker informed the House:—

That the Clerk had received from the Commissioners of Estate Bills, their Report in the following case:—

Bill (No. 6), "To enable the Executor of the late John Curry to make a certain gift out of his estate to the building fund of the proposed Essex Border Utilities Hospital."

The Report was then read by the Clerk at the Table as follows:—

We, the Right Honourable Sir William Mulock, Chief Justice of Ontario, and the Honourable David Inglis Grant, Justice of the High Court Division of the Supreme Court of Ontario, having had referred to us as Commissioners of Estate Bills, Bill (No. 6), entitled "Bill to enable the Executor of the late John Curry to make a certain gift out of his estate to the building fund of the proposed Essex Border Utilities Hospital," beg to report as follows:—

The executor of said will has submitted to us a verified copy of the will in question from which it appears that the estate of the said John Curry is not to be distributed until the expiration of twenty-one years from his death which occurred on or about the 11th day of May, 1912, and that at the time of such distribution, infants under the age of twenty-one years may be entitled to a substantial portion thereof.

The will does not authorize any portion of the testator's estate being devoted to the purpose contemplated by the Bill in question. In as much therefore as such appropriation of funds of the estate of the testator would be contrary to his intention, and also may affect the rights of possible infant beneficiaries under the will, we are of opinion that it is not reasonable that the Bill should pass into law.

Witness our hands this 15th day of March, 1926.

W. MULOCK,

D. INGLIS GRANT,

Commissioners of Estate Bills.

Mr. Nickle, from the Standing Committee on Private Bills, presented their Fifth Report which was read as follows and adopted:

Your Committee beg to report the following Bill without amendment:—

Bill (No. 31), An Act respecting the Township of Grantham.

Your Committee beg to report the following Bill with certain amendments:—

Bill (No. 57), An Act respecting the Ottawa Police Benefit Fund Association.

The following Bills were severally introduced and read the first time:—

Bill (No. 147), intituled "An Act to amend the Assessment Act, 1926." *Mr. Weichel.*

Ordered, That the Bill be read the second time To-morrow.

Bill (No. 64), intituled "An Act to amend the Consolidated Municipal Act, 1922." *Mr. Nickle.*

Ordered, That the Bill be read the second time To-morrow.

Bill (No. 63), intituled "An Act to consolidate and amend the law respecting the Improvement of Public Highways." *Mr. Henry.*

Ordered, That the Bill be read the second time To-morrow.

Bill (No. 148), intituled "An Act to amend the Highway Traffic Act." *Mr. Henry.*

Ordered, That the Bill be read the second time To-morrow.

Bill (No. 149), intituled "An Act to amend the Public Vehicles Act." *Mr. Henry.*

Ordered, That the Bill be read the second time To-morrow.

Bill (No. 150), intituled "The Provincial Land Tax Amendment Act, 1926." *Mr. Ferguson.*

Ordered, That the Bill be read the second time To-morrow.

Bill (No. 151), intituled "An Act to amend the School Laws." *Mr. Ferguson.*

Ordered, That the Bill be read the second time To-morrow.

The following Bills were severally read the second time:—

Bill (No. 132), To amend the Assessment Act.
Referred to the Municipal Committee.

Bill (No. 133), To amend the Consolidated Municipal Act.
Referred to the Municipal Committee.

Bill (No. 141), To amend the Consolidated Municipal Act.
Referred to the Municipal Committee.

Bill (No. 144), To amend the Assessment Act.
Referred to the Municipal Committee.

Bill (No. 142), Respecting the Licensing of Hawkers and Transient Traders.
Referred to the Municipal Committee.

Bill (No. 139), To amend the Consolidated Municipal Act, 1922.

Referred to the Municipal Committee.

Bill (No. 140), To impose a Tax on Dogs and for the Protection of Sheep.

Referred to a Committee of the Whole House To-morrow.

Bill (No. 145), To amend the Highway Traffic Act.

Referred to a Committee of the Whole House To-morrow.

The Order of the Day for the second reading of Bill (No. 125), To amend the Local Improvement Act, having been read,

Ordered, That the Order be discharged, and that the Bill be withdrawn.

The Provincial Secretary presented to the House, by command of His Honour the Lieutenant-Governor:—

Annual Report of the Minister of Mines. (*Sessional Papers, No. 4.*)

Also, Annual Report of the Department of Labour. (*Sessional Papers, No. 10.*)

Also, Annual Report of the Minister of Public Works. (*Sessional Papers, No. 8.*)

The Order of the Day, that Mr. Speaker do now leave the Chair and that the House do resolve itself into the Committee of Supply, having been read,

The Debate was resumed,

And, after some time, it was on the motion of Mr. Lewis,

Ordered, That the Debate be further adjourned until Tuesday next.

The House then adjourned at 5.50 p.m.

FRIDAY, MARCH 19TH, 1926.

PRAYERS.   3 O'CLOCK P. M.

The following Petitions were severally brought up and laid upon the Table:—

By Mr. Sinclair, the Petition of members of the congregation of the Presbyterian Church of Wick, Ontario.

———

Mr. McKeown from the Standing Committee on Municipal Law, presented their First Report which was read as follows and adopted:

Your Committee have carefully considered the following Bill and beg to report the same with certain amendments:—

Bill (No. 100), An Act to amend the Planning and Development Act.

———

Your Committee have carefully considered the following Bill and beg to report the same without amendment:—

Bill (No. 136), An Act to amend the Hospitals and Charitable Institutions Act.

———

Mr. Nickle, from the Standing Committee on Private Bills, presented their Sixth Report which was read as follows and adopted:

Your Committee beg to report the following Bills with certain amendments:—

Bill (No. 17), An Act respecting the City of London.

Bill (No. 30), An Act respecting the City of Ottawa.

Bill (No. 38), An Act respecting the City of Toronto.

———

The following Bills were severally introduced and read the first time:—

Bill (No. 152), intituled "An Act to amend the Hospitals and Charitable Institutions Act." *Mr. Wigle.*

Ordered, That the Bill be read the second time on Monday next.

Bill (No. 153), intituled "An Act to amend the Sanatoria for Consumptives Act." *Mr. Wigle.*

Ordered, That the Bill be read the second time on Monday next.

Mr. Taylor asked the following Question (No. 120):—

1. How many members are on the Highway Advisory Board. 2. (*a*) What are their names; (*b*) in what counties do they live. 3. In how many counties have recommendations been made. 4. How many counties in the Province have adopted the Board's recommendations for revision of the County Road Systems. 5. (*a*) In what counties have there been a reduction in mileage; (*b*) how much reduction in mileage. 6. (*a*) In what counties has mileage been added that was not formerly in the county road system; (*b*) how much mileage in each county. 7. How much has been paid to each member of the committee since the committee was appointed. 8. (*a*) How much has been paid to each for expense; (*b*) how much for general expenses.

The Minister of Public Works and Highways replied as follows:—

1. Three members with the Minister and the Deputy Minister of Highways *ex-officio.* 2. (*a*) Hon. F. G. Macdiarmid, Mr. T. J. Mahoney, Mr. A. M. Rankin; (*b*) Elgin, Wentworth, Frontenac. 3. Thirty-seven. 4. Thirty-seven. 5. (*a*) Brant, Bruce, Carleton, Dufferin, Elgin, Essex, Frontenac, Grey, Haldimand, Halton, Hastings, Huron, Kent, Lambton, Lanark, Leeds and Grenville, Lennox and Addington, Lincoln, Middlesex, Norfolk, Northumberland and Durham, Ontario, Oxford, Peel, Perth, Peterborough, Prescott and Russell, Prince Edward, Renfrew, Simcoe, Stormont, Dundas and Glengarry, Victoria, Waterloo, Wellington, Wentworth. 5. (*b*) 2,095 miles. 6. (*a*) and (*b*). Brant, 7.5; Bruce, 10.0; Carleton, 7.4; Dufferin, 5.7; Elgin, 13.5; Essex, 24.0; Frontenac, 6.0; Grey, 31.0; Haldimand, 1.0; Halton, 1.0; Hastings, 36.0; Huron, 24.0; Kent, 20.3; Lambton, 15.3; Lanark, 38.0; Leeds and Grenville, 24.5; Lennox and Addington, 1.2; Lincoln, 8.5; Middlesex, 10.5; Norfolk, 23.5; Northumberland and Durham, 4.5; Ontario, 17.0; Oxford, 4.3; Peel, 4.0; Perth, 19.5; Peterborough, 8.0; Prescott and Russell, 0.7; Prince Edward, 11.0; Renfrew East, 19.0; Simcoe, 1.0; Stormont, Dundas and Glengarry, 44.0; Victoria, 3.6; Waterloo, 25.8; Welland, 1.5; Wellington, 46.0; Wentworth, 8.5; York, 72.0. 7. $1,605.00, $1,350.00, $1,455.00, respectively. 8. (*a*) and (*b*) Nothing in addition to amounts shown as replies to No. 7. (Sec. 2, ss. 8*b* of the Act.)

Mr. Nixon asked the following Question (No. 121):—

1. On what date was the announcement made *re* marketing of apples by the Department of Agriculture. 2. How many barrels of apples were purchased and marketed by the Department. 3. (*a*) How much per barrel was paid; (*b*)

how much was realized per barrel; (c) what was the expense per barrel. 4. How many barrels were exported. 5. In what counties, and from whom. and how many barrels in each case purchased. 6. Were the whole 25,000 exported. 7. If not, why not.

The Minister of Agriculture replied as follows:—

1. Early in the fall it appeared that Ontario had one of the best crops of apples in the history of the Province, partly due to the work carried on by the Government in encouraging better orcharding methods. In order that producers might receive a fair return, and to avoid a glut on the local markets, the Department undertook to assist in marketing the crop to the extent of the exportation of 25,000 barrels. Minimum prices were set, with results that were decidedly beneficial and had a steadying influence on the whole apple market. Announcement made September 18th, 1925. 2. The apples remained in the possession of the growers, or their associations, but were shipped under the inspection and supervision of the Ontario Department of Agriculture, and under the price guaranteed to the extent of 7,069 barrels and 7,146 boxes. 3. (a) The minimum prices guaranteed were as follows:—

	No. 1 per Barrel	No. 2 per Barrel	In Boxes
Greening and Baldwin.....	$4 00	$3 00	$1 50
King and Russet..........	4 50	3 75	1 65
Spy and McIntosh........	5 00	4 00	1 85

(b) This varied with the different shipments arriving at different times under different market conditions; (c) The expense also varied with different shipments and involves too much detail to be embodied in the answer to the question. 4. 7,069 barrels and 7,146 boxes. 5. The details of the shipments made under the Government's guarantee are on file in the Department of Agriculture and available to any parties interested, but are too elaborate to be embodied in the answer to the question. 6 and 7. See answers to Nos. 1 and 4. The severe early frost, which destroyed the greater portion of the Northern Spy crop, made it undesirable to export the total quantity originally intended. Furthermore, market conditions had so much improved under the combined influence of the action of the Department and the decrease in the available supply that the growers were able to dispose of their balance at satisfactory prices.

Mr. Biggs asked the following Question (No. 143):—

1. How many road contractors have defaulted in paying their labour (a) in 1924, (b) in 1925. 2. What were their contracts. 3. What are the amounts unpaid to workingmen.

The Minister of Public Works and Highways replied as follows:—

1. (a) One; (b) four. 2. Nos. 1131, 1134, 1176, 1210, 1211, 1223, 1225. 3. Amounts claimed by workmen—$288.33, $1,098.43, $312.79, $4,227.59 and $1,276.02.

Mr. Ross asked the following Question (No. 148):—

1. What was the cost to the Province of keeping the provincial highways clear of snow for the last fiscal year (a) for equipment, (b) for labour. 2. What has been the cost for the present year up to the 1st of March under each head. 3. Is twenty per cent. of this expense charged to the counties.

The Minister of Public Works and Highways replied as follows:—

1. (a) $11,358.42 for new equipment; (b) $44,259.43 for labour, fuel, etc. 2. November 1st, 1925, to March 1st, 1926: (a) $3,278.41 for new equipment; (b) $25,495.90 for labour, fuel, etc. 3. Twenty per cent. of cost of operation is charged to counties. But no percentage on equipment.

Mr. Raney asked the following Question (No. 150):—

1. What was the expenditure of the Province (a) on capital account; (b) on ordinary account, for each fiscal year, beginning with 1914.

The Provincial Treasurer replied as follows:—

1. This information can be obtained from the Public Accounts for each year.

Mr. Raney asked the following Question (No. 151):—

1. Have the tax payers of Ontario paid the losses, aggregating $218,221.00 (see Votes and Proceedings, 1926, page 216), on the operation of the Government-owned Peterborough Electric Railway since the road was acquired in 1918. 2. If not, who has paid them.

The Prime Minister replied as follows:—

1. No. 2. The different portions of the Central Ontario System are operated as one entire System, and the losses on any portion of the System are taken care of out of the general earnings.

Mr. Carty asked the following Question (No. 152):—

1. Who are the bondsmen for the Jackson-Lewis Company contract for the new Administration Building in Queen's Park. 2. What is the amount of the bond.

The Minister of Public Works and Highways replied as follows:—

1. Guarantee Company of North America, Head Office, Toronto. 2. $719,561.00.

Mr. Kemp asked the following Question (No. 155):—

1. What was the total cost to the Province of the plebiscite vote of October, 1924.

The Prime Minister replied as follows:—

1. This information can be obtained from the Public Accounts.

Mr. McCallum asked the following Question (No. 156):—

1. What were the allowances referred to in Number 22 of Votes and Proceedings, for the 15th of March, 1926, that were drawn by Hon. J. R. Cooke from the Provincial Treasury since the present Government came into office. 2. What were the amounts and dates.

The Prime Minister replied as follows:—

1. As previously stated, no allowances were drawn by the Hon. Mr. Cooke, save such allowances as every member of the Legislature is entitled to receive. 2. The only payment made was for sessional mileage in 1924, and the amount was $24.40. For the Session of 1925, Mr. Cooke declined to accept mileage.

The following Bills were severally read the second time:—

Bill (No. 23), To incorporate the Association of Accountants and Auditors in Ontario.

Referred to a Committee of the Whole House on Monday next.

Bill (No. 29), Respecting the Township of Thorah.

Referred to a Committee of the Whole House on Monday next.

Bill (No. 35), Respecting the City of Guelph and the Guelph Radial Railway Company.

Referred to a Committee of the Whole House on Monday next.

Bill (No. 31), Respecting the Township of Grantham.

Referred to a Committee of the Whole House on Monday next.

Bill (No. 138), To amend the Public Parks Act.

Referred to the Municipal Committee.

Bill (No. 150), The Provincial Land Tax Amendment Act, 1926.

Referred to a Committee of the Whole House on Monday next.

Bill (No. 149), To amend the Public Vehicles Act.

Referred to a Committee of the Whole House on Monday next.

Bill (No. 148), To amend the Highway Traffic Act.

Referred to a Committee of the Whole House on Monday next.

Bill (No. 143), To amend the Ontario Election Act.

Referred to the Special Committee consisting of Messrs. Nickle, McBrien, Keefer, Thompson (Lanark North), Jamieson (Grey South), Wilson (Windsor), Sinclair, Tellier, Nixon and McCallum, appointed to revise and amend the Election Laws Bill (No. 103); and an Act to consolidate and amend the Voters' Lists Act, Bill (No. 104); and an Act to prohibit Political Contributions by Brewers, Distillers, Standard Hotel Keepers, Public Contractors, Crown Lessees and certain Corporations, Bill (No. 131).

The House resolved itself into a Committee to consider Bill (No. 4), To incorporate the Toronto East General Hospital, and, after some time spent therein, Mr. Speaker resumed the Chair; and Mr. Jamieson (Grey) reported, That the Committee had directed him to report the Bill without any amendment.

Ordered, That the Bill be read the third time on Monday next.

The House resolved itself into a Committee to consider Bill (No. 37), Respecting the City of Kitchener, and, after some time spent therein, Mr. Speaker resumed the Chair; and Mr. Jamieson (Grey) reported, That the Committee had directed him to report the Bill without any amendment

Ordered, That the Bill be read the third time on Monday next.

The House resolved itself into a Committee to consider Bill (No. 21), Respecting C.M. & G. Canadian Investments, Limited, and, after some time spent therein, Mr. Speaker resumed the Chair; and Mr. Jamieson (Grey) reported, That the Committee had directed him to report the Bill without any amendment.

Ordered, That the Bill be read the third time on Monday next.

The House resolved itself into a Committee to consider Bill (No. 140), To impose a Tax on Dogs and for the Protection of Sheep, and, after some time spent therein, Mr. Speaker resumed the Chair; and Mr. Jamieson (Grey) reported, That the Committee had directed him to report the Bill with certain amendments.

Ordered, That the Amendments be taken into consideration forthwith.

The Amendments, having been read the second time, were agreed to.

Ordered, That the Bill be read the third time on Monday next.

The House resolved itself into a Committee to consider Bill (No. 145), To amend the Highway Traffic Act, and, after some time spent therein, Mr. Speaker resumed the Chair; and Mr. Jamieson (Grey) reported, That the Committee had directed him to report the Bill without any amendment.

Ordered, That the Bill be read the third time on Monday next.

The House then adjourned at 3.55 p m.

MONDAY, MARCH 22ND, 1926.

PRAYERS.   3 O'CLOCK P.M.

The following Petition was brought up and laid upon the Table in substitution for that read and received on February 18th, 1926:—

By Mr. Lewis, the Petition of E. Scott and others, praying that an Act may pass amending the United Church of Canada Act.

The following Bills were severally introduced and read the first time:—

Bill (No. 62), intituled "An Act to amend the Burlington Beach Act." *Mr. Ferguson.*

Ordered, That the Bill be read the second time To-morrow.

Bill (No. 154), intituled "An Act to amend the University Act." *Mr. Ferguson.*

Ordered, That the Bill be read the second time To-morrow.

Mr. Kemp asked the following Question (No. 88):—

1. What has been the total expenditure on capital account since the present Government assumed office, down to the end of the last fiscal year, in (a) the electoral district of Sault Ste. Marie; (b) the electoral district of Kenora; (c) the electoral district of Algoma; (d) the electoral district of Cochrane; (e) the electoral district of Rainy River; (f) the electoral district of Port Arthur; (g) the electoral district of Fort William.

The Prime Minister replied as follows:—

1. The following expenditures include capital outlay for construction and maintenance of Roads, Bridges, Drainage, Court Houses, Registry Offices, Gaols, Lock-ups, Normal, Agricultural, Continuation and Training Schools, Experimental Farms, Creameries, Returned Soldiers' Settlement; the assistance of settlers by way of loans; relief to fire sufferers; and the provision of feed, cattle, seed grain and agricultural implements; fire ranging, forest ranging, surveys and clearing town sites: (a) Sault Ste. Marie, $735,991.86; (b) Kenora, $551,945.20; (c) Algoma, $354,539.80; (d) Cochrane, $1,877,252.09; (e) Rainy River, $264,504.46; (f) Port Arthur, $814,530.64; (g) Fort William, $439,652.79.

Mr. Carty asked the following Question (No. 132):—

1. What was the total expenditure by the Government in the prosecution of Aemilius Jarvis, Peter Smith and Andrew Pepall for alleged offences in connection with bond transactions, including the attempt to have Pepall deported from the United States. 2. What Ontario lawyers were employed by the Government in these cases. 3. How much was paid to each of them.

The Attorney-General replied as follows:—

1. $52,666.48. 2. and 3. Messrs. Hogg & Hogg, Ottawa, $4.27; Messrs. Cunningham & Smith, Kingston, $5.00; J. A. Ritchie, Esquire, K.C., Ottawa, $31.87; Messrs. Tilley, Johnson & Co., Toronto, $20,000.00; Messrs. Young & McEvoy, Toronto, $2,750.00. Note: In addition to the above amounts, Mr. McGregor Young, K.C., was paid a lump sum for his services in connection with Home Bank prosecutions, including services in the Peter Smith and Aemilius Jarvis cases. It is impossible to state the exact amount that should be assigned to these two cases.

Mr. Widdifield asked the following Question (No. 146):—

1. How many beer permits have been issued for the riding of Windsor. 2. Did the applications for these permits or some of them reach the Attorney-General through Mr. Wilson, the representative of the riding of Windsor in the Legislative Assembly. 3. How many of such applications came through Mr. Wilson. 4. Did any of such applications come to the Attorney-General through a committee. 5. If so, how many. 6. Who were the chairman and secretary of the committee.

The Attorney-General replied as follows:—

1. One hundred and sixty-three. 2. and 3. Applications for permits reached the Board of License Commissioners by hundreds through the mails and by personal delivery and there is no way of checking adequately the sources from which they came. 4. No. 5. and 6. Answered by No. 4.

Mr. Widdifield asked the following Question (No. 147):—

1. How many beer permits have been issued for the riding of Stormont. 2. Did the applications for these permits or some of them reach the Attorney-General through Mr. Milligan, the representative of the riding of Stormont in the Legislative Assembly. 3. How many of such applications came through Mr. Milligan. 4. Did any of such applications come to the Attorney-General through a committee. 5. If so, how many. 6. Who were the chairman and secretary of the committee.

The Attorney-General replied as follows:—

1. Twenty-eight. 2. and 3. Applications for permits reached the Board of License Commissioners by hundreds through the mails and by personal delivery and there is no way of checking adequately the sources from which they came. 4. No. 5. and 6. Answered by No. 4.

Mr. Raney asked the following Question (No. 149):—

1. Are there some Police Magistrates in Ontario before whom it is almost impossible to get a conviction for an offence against the Ontario Temperance Act. 2. What action, if any, has the Attorney-General taken in the cases of these officials. 3. What action does he propose to take.

The Attorney-General replied as follows:—

1. No. 2. and 3. Answered by No. 1.

Mr. Kemp asked the following Question (No. 153):—

1. Who is the head (under the Attorney-General) of the Ontario liquor dispensaries. 2. What is his salary. 3. When did he first become associated with the dispensaries. 4. In what capacity and at what salary. 5. How long has he been at the head of the dispensaries.

The Attorney-General replied as follows:—

1. Mr. A. H. Birmingham is General Manager of the Ontario Government Dispensaries, which are conducted under the Board of License Commissioners for Ontario, of the Attorney-General's Department. 2. $5,500. 3. May, 1919. 4. As Secretary-Treasurer, at $3,600 salary. 5. General Manager since November 1st, 1920, salary then $4,600.

Mr. Widdifield asked the following Question (No. 154):—

1. How many beer permits have been issued for the riding of Southeast Toronto. 2. Did Mr. John A. Currie and Mr. E. W. J. Owens, the representatives of that riding in the Legislative Assembly, or either of them, communicate to the Attorney-General, or to anyone authorized to issue such permits, their approval of the permits so issued in Southeast Toronto, before the same were issued. 3. If Mr. Currie and Mr. Owens, or one of them, did not approve of all the said permits, how many did they approve of. 4. Were the applications for such permits submitted to a committee before the permits were issued.

The Attorney-General replied as follows:—

1. One hundred and forty. 2. Occasionally Mr. John A. Currie or Mr. E. W. J. Owens communicated to the Attorney-General that consideration should be given to the application of this or that constituent who was urging expedition, or that there was merit in the recognition of his application. 3. No record was kept of the applications that were mentioned by either Mr. John A. Currie or Mr. E. W. J. Owens. 4. No.

Mr. Kemp asked the following Question (No. 158):—

1. Was the sum of $250 paid to the Attorney-General as money that had been paid to an officer of the provincial police as an intended bribe. 2. Who was the man who paid the money to the officer, and when was it paid. 3. Has he been prosecuted. 4. If so, with what result.

The Attorney-General replied as follows:—

1. The Commissioner of Police deposited for safekeeping with the Attorney-General a certain $250.00 left for an officer of the Provincial Police Force as an intended bribe. 2. The said sum of $250.00 was left by one, Charles Jennings, on 8th August, 1925. 3. and 4. A warrant for arrest has been issued, but has not been executed owing to inability to locate the said Jennings.

Mr. Kemp asked the following Question (No. 159):—

1. Was an attempt made to bribe Inspector Lougheed of the provincial police, stationed at Windsor, by giving him $500. 2. Was this money handed over by Inspector Lougheed to the Attorney-General. 3. Who was the person who paid the money to Inspector Lougheed, and what was the date of the payment. 4. Was an information laid against him, and if so, when, where and by whom. 5. Did he leave the country. 6. Did he return. 7. What has happened to the case.

The Attorney-General replied as follows:—

1. No. 2, 3, 4, 5, 6 and 7. Answered by No. 1.

Mr. McCallum asked the following Question (No. 160):—

1. From what persons, firms or companies did the Government purchase liquors for the dispensaries during the past fiscal year. 2. What was the total amounts of purchases in each case. 3. Were some of the purchases made through agents. 4. Who were the agents.

The Attorney-General replied as follows;—

1. J. Hennessey & Co., Cognac, France; E. Remy Martin & Co., Cognac, France; Godet Freres, La Rochelle, France; Frapin & Co., Segonsac, Cognac, France; Martell & Co., Cognac, France; J. G. Monnet & Co., Cognac, France; Jules Robin & Co., Cognac, France; Pommery Fils & Cie, Reims, France; Societe Vinicole de Champagne, Reims, France; Charles Heidsieck, Reims, France; Pol Roger & Cie, Epernay, France; Bertrand de Mun & Co., Reims, France; W. & A. Gilbey, Ltd., London, England; Field Son & Co. of London, London, England; Jas. Buchanan & Co., Ltd., Lon., Eng.; Gordon Dry Gin Co., Ltd., London, England; Sir Robt. Burnett & Co., London, England; J. W. Nicholson & Co., Ltd., London, England; J. DeKuyper & Son, Rotterdam, Holland; Erven Lucas Bols, Amsterdam, Holland; The Old Bushmills Distillery Co., Ltd., Belfast, Ireland; E. & J. Burke, Ltd., Liverpool, England; Mitchell & Co. of Belfast, Ltd., Belfast, Ireland; The Dublin Distillers Co., Ltd., Dublin, I.F.S.; Distillerie de la Benedictine, Fecamp, France; Marie Brizard & Roger, Bordeaux, France; P. Pastene & Co., Montreal, Que.; Quebec Liquor Commission, Montreal, Que.; Niagara Falls Wine Co., Niagara Falls, Ont.; E. & J. Burke, Ltd., Liverpool, England; Sherriff & Co. (Jamaica) Ltd., Glasgow, Scotland; Daniel Finzi & Co., Kingston, Jamaica; Compania Ron Bacardi, Havana, Cuba; J. Wray & Nephew, Kingston, Jamaica; Martini & Rossi, Torino, Italy; Noilly Pratt & Cie, Marseilles, France; Bulloch Lade & Co., Glasgow, Scotland; Chivas Bros., Ltd., Aberdeen, Scotland; Wm. Teacher & Sons, Glasgow, Scotland; Macdonald, Greenlees & Williams (Distillers), Ltd., Leith, Scotland; Macdonald, Greenlees & Williams (Distillers), Ltd., London, England; Distillers Agency, Ltd., Edinburgh, Scotland; Jas. Buchanan & Co., Ltd., Glasgow, Scotland; Jno. Dewar & Sons, Ltd., Perth, Scotland; John Haig & Co., Ltd., Markinch, Scotland; Mackie & Co., Ltd., Glasgow, Scotland; Mitchell Bros., Ltd., Glasgow, Scotland; J. & G. Stewart & Co., Ltd., Glasgow, Scotland; Whyte & Mackay, Ltd., Glasgow, Scotland; Jno. Walker & Sons, Kilmarnoch, Scotland; Ainslie Heilbron, Ltd., Glasgow, Scotland; J. & G. Stodart, Ltd., Glasgow, Scotland; Wm. Grant & Sons, Dufftown, Scotland; Hill Thomson & Co., Edinburgh, Scotland; Robt. Porter & Co., Ltd., London, England; Read Bros., Ltd., London, England; W. A. Ross & Bro., Ltd., Liverpool, England; Gooderham & Worts, Ltd., Toronto, Ont.; Hiram Walker & Sons, Ltd., Walkerville, Ont.; Jos. Seagram & Sons, Ltd., Waterloo, Ont.; Consolidated Distilleries, Ltd., Montreal, Que.; Wisers Distillery, Ltd., Prescott, Ont.; Dr. J. B. Seigert & Son, Trinidad, B.W.I.; Dominion Distillery Products, Ltd., Montreal, Que.; Dominion Brewery, Ltd., Toronto, Ont.; O'Keefe's Beverages, Ltd., Toronto, Ont.; John Labatt, Ltd., London, Ont.; Brading Breweries, Ltd., Ottawa, Ont.; Carling Export Brewery, Ltd., London, Ont.; Grant Spring Brewery Co., Ltd., Hamilton, Ont.; Hamilton Brewing Association, Ltd., Hamilton, Ont.; Capital Brewing Co., Ltd., Ottawa, Ont.; Walkerville Brewery, Ltd., Walkerville, Ont.; The Lake Ontario Brewing Co., Ltd., Kingston, Ont.; Port Arthur Beverage Co., Ltd., Port Arthur, Ont.; Cosgrave Export Brewery Co., Ltd., Toronto, Ont.; British-American Brewing Co., Ltd., Windsor, Ont;

Kakabeka Falls Brewing Co., Ltd., Fort William, Ont.; The Huether Brewery
Co., Ltd., Kitchener, Ont.; Drug Trading Co., Ltd., Toronto, Ont. 2. J.
Hennessey & Co., 4,650 cases, Cognac 40-ounce; E. Remy Martin & Co,, 1,475
cases, Fine Champagne Cognac 40-ounce; 200 cases, V.S.O.P. Cognac 40-ounce;
10 hogsheads Cognac.   Godet Freres, 850 cases, Cognac 40-ounce; 150
cases, 40-year Old Cognac 40-ounce; 10 hogsheads Cognac.   Frapin & Co.,
50 cases, X.O. Cognac 40-ounce.   Martell & Co., 400 cases, Cognac 40-ounce.
J. G. Monnet & Co., 1,200 cases, Cognac 6-ounce; 200 cases, Cognac 40-ounce.
Jules Robin & Co., 50 cases, Cognac 40-ounce.   Pommery Fils & Cie, 40 cases,
Pommery champagne, 26-ounce; 70 cases, Pommery champagne, 13-ounce.
Societe Vinicole de Champagne, 60 cases, Mumm champagne, 26-ounce; 70 cases,
Mumm champagne, 13-ounce. Charles Heidsieck, 10 cases, C. Heidsieck champagne, 26-ounce; 10 cases, C. Heidsieck champagne, 13-ounce. Pol Roger & Cie,
40 cases, Pol Roger champagne, 26-ounce; 45 cases, Pol Roger champagne,
13-ounce.   Bertrand de Mun & Co., 10 cases, Clicquot champagne 26-ounce;
10 cases, Clicquot champagne 13-ounce.   W. & A. Gilbey, Ltd., 275 cases,
gin 40-ounce; 2,700 cases, rum 40-ounce; 1,200 cases, Spey Royal Scotch 40-
ounce; 22 hogsheads, Spey Royal Scotch. Field Son & Co. of London, 300 cases,
Booth's gin 40-ounce; Jas. Buchanan & Co., Ltd., 400 cases, Coates' gin 40-ounce;
Gordon Dry Gin Co., Ltd., 1,100 cases, gin 40-ounce; Sir Robt Burnett & Co.,
1,500 cases, gin 40-ounce; J. W. Nicholson & Co., Ltd., 800 cases, gin 40-ounce;
J. DeKuyper & Son, 2,000 cases, gin 40-ounce; Erven Lucas Bols, 25 cases,
gin 40-ounce; The Old Bushmills Distillery Co., Ltd., 225 cases, Irish whiskey
40-ounce; E. &. J. Burke, Ltd., 850 cases, rum 40-ounce; 1,500 cases, Irish
whiskey 40-ounce; Guinness stout, quarts, 640 dozens; Guinness stout, pints,
900 dozens; Guinness Stout, nips, 240 dozens.   Mitchell & Co. of Belfast, Ltd.,
1,200 cases, Irish whiskey 40-ounce; The Dublin Distillers Co., Ltd., 50 cases,
Irish whiskey 40-ounce; Distillerie de la Benedictine, 40 cases, liqueur 36-ounce;
Marie Brizard & Roger, 30 cases, liqueur 36-ounce; P. Pastene & Co., 15 cases,
Bitters 36-ounce. Quebec Liquor Commission, 5 cases, Liqueur 36-ounce;
1 case, Angostura Bitters, 9-ounce; 6 cases, Bacardi rum 26-ounce; 25 cases,
Vermouth 36-ounce.   Niagara Falls Wine Co., 375 cases. Native Wine 40-ounce;
Sherriff & Co. (Jamaica), Ltd., 400 cases, rum 40-ounce; Daniel Finzi & Co.,
500 cases, rum 40-ounce; 2 puncheons rum. Compania Ron Bacardi, 10 cases,
rum 26-ounce; J. Wray & Nephew, 1 puncheon rum; Martini & Rossi, 50 cases,
Vermouth 36-ounce; Noilly Pratt & Cie, 85 cases, Vermouth 36-ounce; Bulloch
Lade & Co., 200 cases, Bulloch Lade 40-ounce; Chivas Bros., Ltd., 400 cases,
Royal Strathythan 40-ounce; Wm. Teacher & Son, 2,800 cases, Highland Cream
40-ounce; Macdonald, Greenlees & Williams (Distillers), Ltd., 1,550 cases,
G.H.L. 40-ounce; 4,450 cases, Sandy Mac. 40-ounce; 2,850 cases, Old Parr
40-ounce. Distillers Agency, Ltd., 1,300 cases, King George 40-ounce; Jas.
Buchanan & Co., Ltd., 1,050 cases, Black & White Scotch 40-ounce; Jno. Dewar
& Sons, Ltd., 2,550 cases, Dewar's Special Liqueur Scotch 40-ounce; John Haig
& Co., Ltd., 1,850 cases, Haig's Gold Label 40-ounce; 50 cases, Haig's Dimple
26 ounce; Mackie & Co., Ltd., 100 cases White Horse Scotch 40-ounce; Mitchell
Bros., Ltd., 300 cases, Heather Dew 40-ounce; J. G. Stewart & Co., Ltd., 1,050
cases Usher's Green Stripe 40-ounce; Whyte & Mackay, Ltd., 8 hogsheads,
Whyte & Mackay Scotch; Jno. Walker & Sons, 1,100 cases, J. Walker Red
Label 40-ounce; Ainslie Heilbron, Ltd., 50 cases, King's Liqueur Scotch 40-ounce;
J. & G. Stodart, Ltd., 350 cases, R.O.H. Scotch 40-ounce; Wm. Grant & Sons,
1,000 cases, Best Procurable Scotch 40-ounce; Hill Thomson & Co., 2,000 cases,
Queen Anne Scotch 40-ounce; 25 hogsheads Hilltop Scotch. Robert Porter & Co.,

Ltd., 560 dozen, Guinness Stout quarts; 980 dozen Guinness Stout pints; 180 dozen, Guinness Stout nips; 100 dozen, Bass Ale quarts; 120 dozen, Bass Ale pints; 60 dozen, Bass Ale nips. Read Bros., Ltd., 100 dozen, Guinness Stout quarts; 320 dozen, Guinness Stout pints; 120 dozen, Guinness Stout nips; 1,900 dozen, Bass Ale quarts; 1,520 dozen, Bass Ale pints; 420 dozen, Bass Ale nips. W. A. Ross & Bro., Ltd., 100 dozen, Guinness Stout quarts; 120 dozen, Guinness Stout pints; 60 dozen, Guinness Stout nips; 600 dozen, Bass Ale quarts; 784 dozen, Bass Ale pints; 120 dozen, Bass Ale nips. Gooderham & Worts, Ltd., 50 cases, gin 40-ounce; 225 cases, rye 40-ounce; 69 cases, Canadian Scotch 40-ounce; 40 drums, alcohol. Hiram Walker & Sons, Ltd., 10,775 cases, rye 40-ounce; 914 cases, rye 20-ounce; 3,105 cases, rye 6-ounce; 18 barrels rye; 75 drums alcohol. Jos. E. Seagram & Sons, Ltd., 2,150 cases, rye 40-ounce; 2 barrels rye. Consolidated Distilleries, Ltd., 2,100 cases, rye 40-ounce; 125 cases, rye 20-ounce; 300 cases, rye 6-ounce; 185 cases, Canadian Scotch 40-ounce; 150 cases, gin 40-ounce; 83 drums alcohol. Wisers Distillery, Ltd., 45 cases, rye 40-ounce; 25 cases, rye 26-ounce; 25 cases, rye 20-ounce; 5 cases, rye 6-ounce. Dr. J. B. Seigert & Son, 10 cases, Angostura Bitters 8-ounce; Dominion Distillery Products, Ltd., 50 cases, Canadian Scotch 40-ounce; Dominion Brewery, Ltd., 3,115 dozen beer quarts; 1,270 dozen beer pints. O'Keefe Beverages, Ltd., 9,325 dozen beer quarts; 2,020 dozen beer pints. John Labatt, Ltd., 21,490 dozen beer quarts; 12,480 dozen beer pints. Brading Breweries, Ltd., 207 dozen beer quarts; 140 dozen beer pints. Carling Export Brewery, Ltd., 75 dozen beer quarts; 60 dozen beer pints. Grant Spring Brewery Co., Ltd., 1,850 dozen beer quarts; 675 dozen beer pints. Hamilton Brewing Association, Ltd., 345 dozen beer quarts; 540 dozen beer pints. Capital Brewing Co., Ltd., 25 dozen beer quarts. Walkerville Brewery, Ltd., 75 dozen beer quarts; 2,060 dozen beer pints. The Lake Ontario Brewing Co., Ltd., 230 dozen beer quarts; 80 dozen beer pints. Port Arthur Beverage Co., Ltd., 100 dozen beer quarts; 55 dozens beer pints. Cosgrave Export Brewery Co., Ltd., 2,295 dozen beer quarts; 1,082 dozen beer pints; British-American Brewing Co., Ltd., 175 dozen beer pints; Kakabeka Falls Brewing Co., Ltd., 15 dozen beer pints; The Huether Brewery Co., Ltd., 150 dozen beer pints; Drug Trading Co., Ltd., 61 gallons, 65 O.P. alcohol; 7 pints absolute alcohol. 3. Yes. 4. Gillespies & Co., Montreal, Que., for J. Hennessey & Co., Martell & Co., Jas. Buchanan Co., Ltd., Sherriff & Co. (Jamaica), Ltd.; D. O. Roblin, Toronto, for E. Remy Martin Co., Daniel Finzi & Co., Compania Ron Bacardi, John Haig & Co., Ltd.; A. A. Charbonneau, Montreal, for Godet Freres; Wm. Mara & Co., Toronto, for Frapin & Co., Pol Roger & Cie, Hill Thomson & Co., Read Bros., Ltd.; John Hope & Co., Montreal, for Martell & Co., Field Son & Co. of London, J. DeKuyper & Son, E. & J. Burke, Ltd.; K. I. Litster, Toronto, for Jules Robin & Co.; Law Young & Co., Montreal, for Pommery Fils & Cie, Gordon Dry Gin Co., Ltd., Noilly Pratt & Cie, Jno. Walker & Sons; S. B. Townsend & Co., Montreal, for Societe Vinicole de Champagne; Darling & Eadie, Montreal, for Charles Heidsieck; John Guest, Toronto, for Bertrand de Mun & Co., Wm. Teacher & Sons; C. P. Douglas, Toronto, for W. & A. Gilbey, Ltd., Robt. Porter & Co., Ltd.; J. M. Douglas & Co., Montreal, for Sir Robt. Burnett & Co., The Old Bushmills Distillery Co., Ltd., Jno. Dewar & Sons, Ltd., W. A. Ross & Bro., Ltd.; J. H. Calvert, Toronto, for Mitchell & Co. of Belfast, Ltd., Mitchell Bros., Ltd.; A. W. Scales, Toronto, for The Dublin Distillers Co., Ltd., L. A. Howard, Toronto, for J. Wray & Nephew; Lawrence Wilson & Co., Montreal, for Martini & Rossi; Consolidated Distilleries, Ltd., Montreal, for Bulloch Lade & Co.; A. T. Hill, Ottawa, for Chivas Bros., Ltd.; J. A. Taylor, Montreal, for Distillers Agency, Ltd.; Turton, Ltd., Montreal, for

Mackie & Co.; Colin Campbell, Montreal, for J. G. Stewart Co., Ltd.; W. W. Veitch, Montreal, for Whyte & Mackay, Ltd.; David M. O'Meara, Toronto, for Ainslie Heilbron, Ltd.; W. H. Matthews, Toronto, for J. & G. Stodart, Ltd.; Gooderham & Worts, Ltd., Toronto, for Wm. Grant & Sons; J. W. Wupperman Angostura Bitters Agency, Inc., New York, N.Y., for Dr. J. B. Seigert & Son; Boivin Wilson & Co., Montreal, for Read Bros., Ltd.   N.B.—All other purchases were made direct from companies.

Mr. Widdifield asked the following Question (No. 161):—

1. How many beer permits have been issued for the riding of St. Catharines. 2. Did the applications for these permits or some of them reach the Attorney-General through Mr. E. C. Graves, the representative of the riding of St. Catharines in the Legislative Assembly. 3. How many of such applications came through Mr. Graves. 4. Did any of such applications come to the Attorney-General through a committee. 5. If so, how many. 6. Who were the chairman and secretary of the committee.

The Attorney-General replied as follows:—

1. Seventy-one. 2 and 3. Applications for permits reached the Board of License Commissioners by the hundreds through the mails and by personal delivery and there is no way of checking adequately the sources from which they came. 4. No. 5 and 6. Answered by No. 4.

Mr. Taylor asked the following Question (No. 162):—

What are the details of the item of "Special Warrants, $122,620.41," appearing at page B 10 (Department of the Prime Minister) of the Public Accounts.

The Prime Minister replied as follows:—

Details are given on the same page of the Public Accounts under the heading "Special Warrants."

Mr. Carty asked the following Question (No. 163):—

1. Does the statement at page B 2 of the Public Accounts of $212,319.80, as the total of payments for the year under the Ontario Public Service Super-annuation Act, mean that this amount is charged to capital account.

The Prime Minister replied as follows:—

The Government contribution to the Public Service Superannuation Fund is paid out of Ordinary Revenue and charged accordingly (see page N 4 of the

Public Accounts). The grant is paid into a special fund, along with the contributions of the Service, which is treated as Capital (see page 59 of the Public Accounts). Payments to the beneficiaries are made out of the Special Fund and are therefore charged against Capital, although the actual source of the money in the first instance was Ordinary Revenue and the contributions of the Service. The balance over and above the yearly payments to beneficiaries remains in the Fund to take care of future requirements.

Mr. Taylor asked the following Question (No. 164):—

What are the details of the item "Special Warrants, $67,754.94," appearing at page N 25 (Department of the Provincial Treasurer) of the Public Accounts.

The Prime Minister replied as follows:—

Details are given on the same page of the Public Accounts under the heading "Special Warrants."

Mr. Taylor asked the following Question (No. 165):—

What are the details of the item "Special Warrants, $103,989.32," appearing at page M 11 (Department of Labour) of the Public Accounts.

The Prime Minister replied as follows:—

Details are given on pages M 10 and 11 of the Public Accounts under the heading "Special Warrants."

Mr. Freeborn asked the following Question (No. 166):—

1. What has been the current revenue of the Province for each fiscal year, beginning with 1919. 2. What has been the ordinary expenditure for each of those years.

The Prime Minister replied as follows:—

This information can be obtained from the Public Accounts for each year.

Mr. Clarke asked the following Question (No. 168):—

1. What is the salary of R. Leighton Foster, Superintendent of Insurance. 2. Does he receive any fees or remuneration other than salary. 3. What insurance experience had Mr. Foster before being appointed Superintendent of Insurance. 4. Is Mr. Foster responsible to the Attorney-General's Department. If not, to what Department. 5. Had Mr. Foster the sanction of his Minister for

the public speeches he made during 1924-1925. 6. Has Mr. Foster's Minister seen the judgment of the Hon. Mr. Justice Riddell in *re* the Ontario Insurance Act and General Accident Assurance Company of Canada. If not, will the Minister read the same and inform this House if the conduct of the Superintendent of Insurance in this case was with his approval. 7. Has Mr. Foster, as Superintendent of Insurance, a *quasi*-judicial position. If so, having regard to the Hon. Mr. Justice Riddell's judgment in *re* Ontario Insurance Act and General Accident Assurance Company, does the Minister concerned consider Mr. Foster qualified to perform these duties under the circumstances.

The Attorney-General replied as follows:—

1. $4,700. 2. No. 3. Four years general law practice; three years sessional Assistant Law Clerk, Legislative Assembly; two years, Secretary, Special Legislative Committee on Insurance Legislation; two years' close association with administration of Insurance Department. 4. Yes, to the Attorney-General, who is the Minister in charge of the Department of Insurance. 5. This question is too indefinite to permit of a definite answer. 6. Yes. For a full understanding of the decision of the Court, the judgment of the Hon. Mr. Justice Riddell, as well as that of the Hon. Mr. Justice Masten, should be read in full. The latter does not make any adverse comment upon the action of the Superintendent and points out that the proceeding was the first of its kind and that the Superintendent had probably been misled by procedure under analagous American Statutes. The Court did not overrule the Superintendent, but remitted the case to him for trial. 7. (*a*) Yes; (*b*) yes, see answer to Question 6.

Mr. Nixon asked the following Question (No. 169):—

1. What were (*a*) the estimates, (*b*) the expenditures for fire ranging each year, beginning with the fiscal year of 1918-1919.

The Minister of Lands and Forests replied:—

The information asked for in this question is furnished in the Estimates and the Public Accounts for the various years indicated.

The following Bills were severally read the second time:—

Bill (No. 57), Respecting the Ottawa Police Benefit Fund Association.

Referred to a Committee of the Whole House To-morrow.

Bill (No. 17), Respecting the City of London.

Referred to a Committee of the Whole House To-morrow.

Bill (No. 30), Respecting the City of Ottawa.

Referred to a Committee of the Whole House To-morrow.

Bill (No. 38), Respecting the City of Toronto.

Referred to a Committee of the Whole House To-morrow.

Bill (No. 151), To amend the School Laws.

Referred to a Committee of the Whole House To-morrow.

Bill (No. 147), To amend the Assessment Act.

Referred to the Municipal Committee.

Bill (No. 110), To amend Section 16 of the University Act.

Referred to a Committee of the Whole House To-morrow.

The House resolved itself into a Committee severally to consider the following Bills:—

Bill (No. 29), Respecting the Township of Thorah.

Bill (No. 35), Respecting the City of Guelph and the Guelph Radial Railway Company.

Bill (No. 31), Respecting the Township of Grantham.

Mr. Speaker resumed the Chair; and Mr. Finlayson reported, That the Committee had directed him to report the several Bills without Amendments.

Ordered, That the Bills reported be severally read the third time To-morrow.

The House resolved itself into a Committee to Consider Bill (No. 136), To amend an Act relating to Hospitals and Charitable Institutions, and, after some time spent therein, Mr. Speaker resumed the Chair; and Mr. Finlayson reported, That the Committee had directed him to report the Bill without any amendment.

Ordered, That the Bill be read the third time To-morrow.

The House resolved itself into a Committee to consider Bill (No. 148), To amend the Highway Traffic Act, and, after some time spent therein, Mr. Speaker resumed the Chair; and Mr. Finlayson reported, That the Committee had directed him to report the Bill with certain amendments.

Ordered, That the Amendments be taken into consideration forthwith.

The Amendments, having been read the second time, were agreed to.

Ordered, That the Bill be read the third time To-morrow.

The House resolved itself into a Committee to consider Bill (No. 149), To amend the Public Vehicles Act, and, after some time spent therein, Mr. Speaker resumed the Chair; and Mr. Finlayson reported, That the Committee had directed him to report the Bill without any amendment.

Ordered, That the Bill be read the third time To-morrow.

The House resolved itself into a Committee to consider Bill (No. 150), The Provincial Land Tax Amendment Act, 1926, and, after some time spent therein, Mr. Speaker resumed the Chair; and Mr. Finlayson reported, That the Committee had directed him to report the Bill without any amendment.

Ordered, That the Bill be read the third time To-morrow.

The Provincial Secretary presented to the House, by command of His Honour the Lieutenant-Governor:—

Annual report of the Game and Fisheries Department, Ontario, 1925. (*Sessional Papers, No. 9.*)

The House then adjourned at 4.35 p.m.

TUESDAY, MARCH 23RD, 1926.

PRAYERS.   3 O'CLOCK P.M.

The following Petitions were severally brought up and laid upon the Table:—

By Mr. Bragg, Petition of the Municipal Council of the Township of Cartwright *re* Township School Boards.

By Mr. Lewis, Petition of G. G. Grant and others, praying that an Act may pass amending the United Church of Canada Act; also, Petition of St. Andrew's Presbyterian Congregation, Maple Valley, Ontario, praying that an Act may pass amending the United Church of Canada Act.

———

Mr. Nickle, from the Standing Committee on Private Bills, presented their Seventh Report which was read as follows and adopted:

Your Committee beg to report the following Bills without amendment:—

Bill (No. 5), An Act respecting the Town of Aylmer.

Bill (No. 11), An Act respecting the City of Brantford.

Bill (No. 24), An Act respecting the Board of Trustees of the Police Village of Alfred.

Bill (No. 40), An Act to amend the Act to incorporate the Evangelical Lutheran Seminary of Canada.

Bill (No. 49), An Act respecting the Township of Stamford.

———

Your Committee beg to report the following Bills with certain amendments:—

Bill (No. 2), An Act respecting the Town of Arnprior.

Bill (No. 48), An Act respecting the Town of Walkerville.

Bill (No. 50), An Act respecting the Town of LaSalle.

Your Committee would recommend that the fees, less the penalties and the actual cost of printing, be remitted on Bill (No. 40), "An Act to amend the Act to incorporate the Evangelical Lutheran Seminary of Canada," on the ground that it is one relating to an educational institution.

Ordered, That the fees, less the penalties and the actual cost of printing, be remitted on Bill (No. 40), "An Act to amend the Act to incorporate the Evangelical Lutheran Seminary of Canada."

Mr. Black presented report of the Fish and Game Committee of the Ontario Legislature;

Ordered, That the report be adopted and referred to the Committee on Printing. (*Sessional Papers, No. 49.*)

The following Bill was introduced and read the first time —   :

Bill (No. 155), intituled "An Act to amend the Municipal Act." *Mr. McBrien.*

Ordered, That the Bill be read the second time To-morrow.

On motion of Mr. Thompson (Lanark), seconded by Mr. Willson (Niagara Falls),

That notwithstanding the time for presenting Petitions for Private Bills has elapsed, leave be given to present a Petition of the Town of Renfrew for an Act respecting the Victoria Hospital and that the same be now read and received.

The following Petition was then read and received:—

The Petition of the Town of Renfrew, respecting the Victoria Hospital, praying that an Act may pass to ratify and confirm a certain debenture.

On motion of Mr. Thompson (Lanark), seconded by Mr. Willson (Niagara Falls),

That notwithstanding the time for introducing Private Bills has elapsed, leave be given to introduce a Bill entitled "The Victoria Hospital at Renfrew Act, 1926," and that the same be now read a first time and do stand referred direct to the Committee on Private Bills irrespective of report from Standing Orders or posting in the lobby as required by the Rule in that case made and provided.

The following Bill was then introduced and read the first time:—

Bill (No. 61), intituled "The Victoria Hospital at Renfrew Act, 1926."

Referred to the Committee on Private Bills.

On the motion of Mr. Ferguson, seconded by Mr. Nickle,

Ordered, That leave be granted to the Standing Committee of Public Accounts to hold meetings of the said Committee concurrently with the meetings of the Legislature, for the balance of the Session, as said Committee may deem necessary for the despatch of its business.

On the motion of Mr. Nickle, seconded by Mr. Ferguson,

Ordered, That the Special Committee, consisting of Messrs. Nickle, McBrien, Keefer, Thompson (Lanark North), Jamieson (Grey South), Wilson (Windsor), Sinclair, Tellier, Nixon and McCallum, appointed to revise and amend the Election Laws Bill (No. 103); and an Act to consolidate and amend the Voters, List Act, Bill (No. 104); and an Act to prohibit Political Contributions by Brewers, Distillers, Standard Hotel Keepers, Public Contractors, Crown Lessees and certain Corporations, Bill (No. 131); and an Act to amend the Ontario Election Act, Bill (No. 143), have leave to sit and carry on its business concurrently with the Sittings of the House.

The Order of the Day, that Mr. Speaker do now leave the Chair and that the House do resolve itself into the Committee of Supply, having been read,

The Debate was resumed,

And, after some time, it was, on the motion of Mr. Oke,

Ordered, That the Debate be further adjourned until To-morrow.

The House then adjourned at 11.10 p.m.

WEDNESDAY, MARCH 24TH, 1926.

PRAYERS.   3 O'CLOCK P.M.

The following Petitions were severally brought up and laid upon the Table:—

By Mr. Kennedy (Peel), Petition of the United Congregation of Claude, Ontario.

By Mr. Widdifield, Petition of the Continuing Presbyterian Church of Beaverton, Ontario.

———————

The following Petition was read and received:—

Of Ephraim Scott and others, praying that an Act may pass amending the United Church of Canada Act.

———————

Mr. Nickle, from the Standing Committee on Private Bills, presented their Eighth Report which was read as follows and adopted:

Your Committee beg to report the following Bill without amendment:—

Bill (No. 14), An Act respecting the Township of North York.

Your Committee beg to report the following Bill with certain amendments:—

Bill (No. 18), An Act respecting the City of Port Arthur.

———————

The following Bills were severally introduced and read the first time:—

Bill (No. 156), intituled "An Act respecting Psychiatric Hospitals." *Mr. Goldie.*

Ordered, That the Bill be read the second time To-morrow.

Bill (No. 157), intituled "An Act to amend the Surrogate Courts Acts."
Mr. Nickle.

Ordered, That the Bill be read the second time To-morrow.

Bill (No. 158), intituled "An Act to amend the Marriage Act."   *Mr. Nickle.*

Ordered, That the Bill be read the second time To-morrow.

Bill .(No. 159), intituled "An Act to amend the Municipal Act."   *Mr. Nickle.*

Ordered, That the Bill be read the second time To-morrow.

———

Mr. Lethbridge asked the following Question (No. 135) —:

1. How many civil servants were there in the inside service in Toronto at the end of each fiscal year beginning with the year 1914. 2. How many are there now.

The Prime Minister replied as follows:—

1.—	1920	1921	1922	1923	1924	1925
	1309	1498	1603	1664	1731	1686

These figures are approximate only.

No figures have been compiled prior to 1920.

2.—   March 10th, 1926
                     1698

———

Mr. Kemp asked the following Question (No. 171):—

What has been the total expenditure on the Chippewa Hydro-Electrical Power Development to date.

The Prime Minister replied as follows:—

The expenditures in connection with the Queenston-Chippewa Development at the close of the last fiscal year amounted to $78,805,585.03.   The Plant is now earning Interest and Sinking Fund on the investment.

The following Bills were severally read the second time:—

Bill (No. 62), "To amend the Burlington Beach Act." *Mr. Ferguson.*

Referred to a Committee of the Whole House To-morrow.

Bill (No. 154), "To amend the University Act." *Mr. Ferguson.*

Referred to a Committee of the Whole House To-morrow.

The Provincial Secretary presented to the House, by command of His Honour the Lieutenant-Governor:—

Annual Report of the Public Service Superannuation Board for year ending October 31st, 1925. (*Sessional Papers No. 50.*)

Also, Return to the order of the House, dated March 26th, 1925.

That there be laid before the House a Return showing: 1. What amounts of money have been paid by the Hydro-Electric Power Commission for fire insurance premiums each year during the past ten fiscal years. 2. What amounts have been received by the Commission during the same period from the insurance companies for losses by fire. 3. What amounts of money have been paid by the Province of Ontario for fire insurance premiums each year during the past ten fiscal years. 4. What amounts have been received by the Province of Ontario during the same period from the insurance companies for losses by fire. (*Sessional Papers No. 51.*)

The Order of the Day, for resuming the Adjourned Debate on the motion that Mr. Speaker do now leave the Chair and that the House do resolve itself into the Committee of Supply, having been read,

The Debate was resumed,

And after some time,

And the House having continued to sit until Twelve of the Clock midnight,

THURSDAY, 25TH MARCH, 1926.

The Debate was continued,

And, after some time,

The amendment, having been put, was lost upon the following division:—

YEAS.

Bélanger.	Homuth.	Proulx.	Weichel.
Brackin.	McCausland.	Tellier.	Wilson.—10.
Currie.	Pinard.		(Windsor)

NAYS.

Armstrong.
Belford.
Biggs.
Black.
Bradburn.
Bragg.
Callan.
Carr.
Chambers.
(Oxford)
Chambers.
(Wellington)
Clarke.
(Brockville)
Clarke.
(Northumberland)
Colliver.
Cooke.
Ecclestone.
Edwards.
Elliott.
Fallis.
Fenton.
Ferguson.

Finlayson.
Fisher.
Freeborn.
Garden.
Godfrey.
Goldie.
Gray.
Graves.
Hambly.
Haney.
Harcourt.
Henry.
Hill.
Hillmer.
Ireland.
Irvine.
Jamieson.
(Grey)
Jamieson.
(Simcoe)
Joynt.
Keefer.
Keith.
Kemp.

Kennedy.
(Peel)
Kennedy.
(Temiskaming)
Lethbridge.
Lewis.
Lyons.
McCallum.
McCrea.
McKeown.
McKnight.
MacDiarmid.
Mahony.
Mark.
Martin.
Mewhinney.
Milligan.
Monteith.
Morel.
Nesbitt.
Nickle.
Nixon.
Oakley.
Oke.

Patterson.
Price.
Raney.
Rankin.
Ross.
Sangster.
Sinclair.
Spence.
Stedman.
Stuart.
Sweet.
Taylor.
Thompson.
(Lanark)
Trewartha.
Vaughan.
Wallis.
Widdifield.
Wigle.
Willson.
(Niagara Falls)
Wright.—84.

The main motion having been put was carried, and the House accordingly resolved itself into the Committee.

(*In the Committee.*)

Resolved, That there be granted to His Majesty, for the services of 1926, the following sum:—

126. To defray the expenses of the Insurance Department...... $4,775 00

Mr. Speaker resumed the Chair; and Mr. Jamieson (Grey) reported, That the Committee had come to several Resolutions; also, That the Committee had directed him to ask for leave to sit again.

Ordered, That the Report be received To-morrow.

Resolved, That the Committee have leave to sit again To-morrow.

The House then adjourned at 9.00 a.m.

THURSDAY, MARCH 25TH, 1926.

PRAYERS.   3 O'CLOCK P.M.

The following Petitions were read and received:—

Of C. G. Grant and others; also, of the Congregation of St. Andrew's Presbyterian Church, Maple Valley, praying that an Act may pass amending the United Church of Canada Act.

Of Cartwright Township Council; also, of Clarke Township Council; also, of the Public School Supporters of School Section No. 12, Darlington Township, respecting Township School Boards.

To the Honourable the Legislative Assembly of the Province of Ontario.

Mr. Nickle, from the Standing Committee on Private Bills, presented their Ninth Report which was read as follows and adopted:

Your Committee beg to report the following Bill with certain amendments:—

Bill (No. 25), An Act respecting the Township of York.

Your Committee would recommend that the fees less the actual cost of printing be remitted on Bill (No. 44), "An Act to provide for the incorporation of the Township of York as the Town of York," the same having been withdrawn by the promoters thereof.

Mr. Kennedy (Peel) moved, seconded by Mr. Currie:

That no fine shall be charged against any Bill introduced on or before the 4th day of March for any extension of time for introducing Private Bills or on account of not having been introduced during the first seventeen days of the Session and no fine shall be charged for any extension of the time for receiving reports from Committees on any Bill which was due to be heard by the Committee on or before the 11th day of March and any such fine already paid in connection with such Bills shall be remitted.

Ordered, That the fees, less the penalties and the actual cost of printing, be remitted on Bill (No. 44), an Act to provide for the incorporation of the Township of York as the Town of York.

Ordered, That no fine shall be charged against any Bill introduced on or before the 4th day of March for any extension of time for introducing Private Bills or on account of not having been introduced during the first seventeen days of the Session and no fine shall be charged for any extension of the time for receiving reports from Committees on any Bill which was due to be heard by the Committee on or before the 11th day of March and any such fine already paid in connection with such Bills shall be remitted.

The following Bills were severally introduced and read the first time:—

Bill (No. 160), intituled "An Act to make further provision for Northern Ontario Development." *Mr. Ferguson.*

Ordered, That the Bill be read the second time To-morrow.

Bill (No. 161), intituled "An Act to amend the Assessment Act." *Mr. Nickle.*

Ordered, That the Bill be read the second time To-morrow.

Bill (No. 164), intituled "An Act to amend the Consolidated Municipal Act, 1922." *Mr. Henry.*

Ordered, That the Bill be read the second time To-morrow.

Bill (No. 163), intituled "An Act to amend the Power Commission Act." *Mr. Price.*

Orderιd, That the Bill be read the second time To-morrow.

————————

On motion of Mr. Price, seconded by Mr. Ferguson :

Ordered, That this House do forthwith resolve itself into a Committee to consider certain proposed Resolutions respecting the borrowing of money for the public service.

Mr. Ferguson acquainted the House that His Honour the Lieutenant-Governor, having been informed of the subject matter of the proposed Resolutions, recommends them to the consideration of the House.

The House then resolved itself into the Committee.

(In the Committee.)

Resolved: 1. That the Lieutenant-Governor in Council be authorized to raise by way of loan a sum of money not exceeding forty million dollars ($40,000,000) for all or any of the purposes following, that is to say: For the public service, for works carried on by commissioners on behalf of Ontario, for the covering of any debt of Ontario on open account, for paying any floating indebtedness of Ontario, for the carrying on of the public works authorized by the Legislature and for redeeming in whole or in part the outstanding debentures of the Province of Ontario that have been issued free of succession duty.

2. That the aforesaid sum of money may be borrowed for any term or terms not exceeding forty years, at such rate as may be fixed by the Lieutenant-Governor in Council and shall be raised upon the credit of the Consolidated Revenue Fund of Ontario and shall be chargeable thereupon.

3. That the Lieutenant-Governor in Council may provide for a special sinking fund or instalment annuity bonds with respect to the issue herein authorized, and such sinking fund may be at a greater rate than the one-half of one per centum per annum specified in subsection 2 of section 4 of the Provincial Loans Act.

Mr. Speaker resumed the Chair; and Mr. Jamieson (Grey) reported, That the Committee had come to certain Resolutions.

Ordered, That the Report be now received.

Mr. Jamieson (Grey) reported the Resolutions as follows:—

Resolved: 1. That the Lieutenant-Governor in Council be authorized to raise by way of loan a sum of money not exceeding forty million dollars ($40,000,000) for all or any of the purposes following, that is to say: For the public service, for works carried on by commissioners on behalf of Ontario, for the covering of any debt of Ontario on open account, for paying any floating indebtedness of Ontario, for the carrying on of the public works authorized by the Legislature and for redeeming in whole or in part the outstanding debentures of the Province of Ontario that have been issued free of succession duty.

2. That the aforesaid sum of money may be borrowed for any term or terms not exceeding forty years, at such rate as may be fixed by the Lieutenant-Governor in Council and shall be raised upon the credit of the Consolidated Revenue Fund of Ontario and shall be chargeable thereupon.

3. That the Lieutenant-Governor in Council may provide for a special sinking fund or instalment annuity bonds with respect to the issue herein authorized, and such sinking fund may be at a greater rate than the one-half of one per centum per annum specified in subsection 2 of section 4 of the Provincial Loans Act.

The Resolutions having been read the second time, were agreed to, and referred to the Committee of the Whole House on Bill (No. 162), for raising money on the Credit of the Consolidated Revenue Fund.

The following Bill was then introduced and read the first time—:

Bill (No. 162), intituled "An Act for raising money on the Credit of the Consolidated Revenue Fund." *Mr. Price.*

Ordered, That the Bill be read the second time To-morrow.

The following Bills were severally read the second time:—

Bill (No. 5), Respecting the Town of Aylmer.

Referred to a Committee of the Whole House To-morrow.

Bill (No. 11), Respecting the City of Brantford.

Referred to a Committee of the Whole House To-morrow.

Bill (No. 24), Respecting the Board of Trustees of the Police Village of Alfred.

Referred to a Committee of the Whole House To-morrow.

Bill (No. 40), To amend the Act to incorporate the Evangelical Lutheran Seminary of Canada.

Referred to a Committee of the Whole House To-morrow.

Bill (No. 49), Respecting the Township of Stamford.

Referred to a Committee of the Whole House To-morrow.

Bill (No. 2), Respecting the Town of Arnprior.

Referred to a Committee of the Whole House To-morrow.

Bill (No. 48), Respecting the Town of Walkerville.

Referred to a Committee of the Whole House To-morrow.

Bill (No. 50), Respecting the Town of La Salle.

Referred to a Committee of the Whole House To-morrow.

Bill (No. 14), Respecting the Township of North York.

Referred to a Committee of the Whole House To-morrow.

Bill (No. 18), Respecting the City of Port Arthur.

Referred to a Committee of the Whole House To-morrow.

The Order of the Day for the second reading of Bill (No. 146), To amend the Assessment Act, having been read,

Ordered, That the Order be discharged, and that the Bill be withdrawn.

The Order of the Day for the second reading of Bill (No. 152), To amend the Hospitals and Charitable Institutions Act, having been read,

Ordered, That the Order be discharged, and that the Bill be withdrawn.

The Order of the Day for the second reading of Bill (No. 153), To amend the Sanatoria for Consumptives Act, having been read,

Ordered, That the Order be discharged, and that the Bill be withdrawn.

_____

Mr. Fisher moved, seconded by Mr. Proulx,

That in the opinion of this House, moneys granted under the Northern and Northwestern Ontario Development Act should be used only after appropriations from said grant have been approved of by this House in estimates for the current year, showing the work proposed to be done and the estimated cost thereof.

The motion was by leave of the House withdrawn.

_____

On motion of Mr. Nesbitt, seconded by Mr. Gray,

Resolved: That in the opinion of this House it is expedient for the encouragement of British industry and for national and educational purposes that persons licensed to exhibit moving pictures in Ontario should be restrained from confining such exhibitions to pictures produced elsewhere than in the British Empire and that to this end regulations should be made restricting the exhibition in Ontario of pictures of non-British origin to a percentage diminishing with each year until not more than twenty-five per centum of the pictures exhibited in any one year shall be pictures produced elsewhere than in the British Empire and that the Board of Censors be instructed to report on the practicability and extent of such restrictions.

And, after some time, the motion was, by leave of the House, withdrawn.

_____

The following Bills were read the third time and passed:—

Bill (No. 9), To incorporate the Village of Rosseau.

Bill (No. 47), Respecting the Township of Teck.

Bill (No. 42), Respecting the amalgamation of the Toronto Western Hospital and Grace Hospital.

Bill (No. 15), Respecting the Village of Waterford.

Bill (No. 3), Respecting the Grey and Bruce Loan Company and the Owen Sound Loan and Savings Company.

Bill (No. 10), Respecting the amalgamation of the Girls' Home and the Protestant Orphans' Home.

Bill (No. 28), Respecting the City of Stratford.

Bill (No. 26), To extend the time for the completion of the Haliburton, Whitney and Mattawa Railway.

Bill (No. 8), Respecting the Mount McKay and Kakabeka Falls Railway Company.

Bill (No. 51), Respecting the Midland Simcoe Railway Company.

Bill (No. 16), Respecting the Town of Gananoque.

Bill (No. 32), Respecting the British Mortgage Loan Company of Ontario.

Bill (No. 36), Respecting the City of Galt.

Bill (No. 1), To incorporate the Welland and Port Colborne Railway Company.

Bill (No. 37), Respecting the City of Kitchener.

Bill (No. 21), Respecting C. M. & G. Canadian Investments, Limited.

Bill (No. 29), Respecting the Township of Thorah.

Bill (No. 31), Respecting the Township of Grantham.

Bill (No. 136), To amend an Act relating to Hospitals and Charitable Institutions.

The House resolved itself into a Committee to consider Bill (No. 23), To incorporate the Association of Accountants and Auditors in Ontario, and, after some time spent therein, Mr. Speaker resumed the Chair; and Mr. McKeown reported, That the Committee had directed him to report the Bill with amendments.

The Amendments, having been read the second time, were agreed to.

Ordered, That the Bill be read the third time To-morrow.

The House resolved itself into a Committee to consider Bill (No. 57), Respecting the Ottawa Police Benefit Fund Association, and, after some time

spent therein, Mr. Speaker resumed the Chair; and Mr. McKeown reported,
That the Committee had directed him to report the Bill with amendments.

The Amendments, having been read the second time, were agreed to.

Ordered, That the Bill be read the third time To-morrow.

The House resolved itself into a Committee to consider Bill (No. 17),
Respecting the City of London, and, after some time spent therein, Mr. Speaker
resumed the Chair; and Mr. McKeown reported, That the Committee had
directed him to report the Bill with amendments.

The Amendments, having been read the second time, were agreed to.

Ordered, That the Bill be read the third time To-morrow.

The House resolved itself into a Committee to consider Bill (No. 30),
Respecting the City of Ottawa, and, after some time spent therein, Mr. Speaker
resumed the Chair; and Mr. McKeown reported, That the Committee had
directed him to report the Bill with amendments.

The Amendments, having been read the second time, were agreed to.

Ordered, That the Bill be read the third time To-morrow.

The House resolved itself into a Committee to consider Bill (No. 38),
Respecting the City of Toronto, and, after some time spent therein, Mr. Speaker
resumed the Chair; and Mr. McKeown reported, That the Committee had
directed him to report the Bill with amendments.

The Amendments, having been read the second time, were agreed to.

Ordered, That the Bill be read the third time To-morrow.

The House resolved itself into a Committee to consider Bill (No. 62), To
amend the Burlington Beach Act, and, after some time spent therein, Mr.
Speaker resumed the Chair; and Mr. McKeown reported, That the Committee
had directed him to report the Bill without any amendment.

Ordered, That the Bill be read the third time To-morrow.

The House resolved itself into a Committee to consider Bill (No. 110), To amend Section 16 of the University Act, and, after some time spent therein, Mr. Speaker resumed the Chair; and Mr. McKeown reported, That the Committee had directed him to report the Bill without any amendment.

Ordered, That the Bill be read the third time To-morrow.

———————

The House resolved itself into a Committee to consider Bill (No. 100), To amend the Planning and Development Act, and, after some time spent therein, Mr. Speaker resumed the Chair; and Mr. McKeown reported, That the Committee had directed him to report the Bill without any amendment.

Ordered, That the Bill be read the third time To-morrow.

———————

The House, according to Order, again resolved itself into the Committee of Supply.

(*In the Committee.*)

Resolved, That there be granted to His Majesty, for the services of 1926, the following sums:—

125. To defray the expenses of the Attorney-General's Department.................................... $41,868 57

Mr. Speaker resumed the Chair; and Mr. McKeown reported, That the Committee had come to several Resolutions; also, That the Committee had directed him to ask for leave to sit again.

Ordered, That the Report be received To-morrow.

Resolved, That the Committee have leave to sit again To-morrow.

———————

The House then adjourned at 6.10 p.m.

═══════════════

FRIDAY, MARCH 26TH, 1926.

PRAYERS.   3 O'CLOCK P.M.

The following Petitions were severally brought up and laid upon the Table:—

By Mr. Raney, the Petition of the Lathers' International Union, Local No. 97; also, the Petition of the Machinists' International Association No. 371

(Railroad Shops); also, the Petition of the Brotherhood of Locomotive Engineers, Parkdale Division No. 295; also, the Petition of the Waiters and Cooks Local No. 300.

The following Petition was read and received:—

Of members of the congregation of Claude United Church, respecting the United Church of Canada Act.

Mr. McKeown, from the Standing Committee on Municipal Law, presented their Second Report which was read as follows and adopted:

Your Committee have carefully considered the following Bill and beg to report the same without amendment:—

Bill (No. 138), An Act to amend the Public Parks Act.

Mr. Nickle, from the Standing Committee on Private Bills, presented their Tenth Report which was read as follows and adopted:

Your Committee beg to report the following Bill with certain amendments:—

Bill (No. 27), An Act respecting the Township of East York.

Your Committee beg to report the following Bills without amendment:—

Bill (No. 13), An Act respecting the City of Fort William.

Bill (No. 54), An Act respecting the City of Toronto.

The following Bills were severally introduced and read the first time —   :

Bill (No. 165), intituled "An Act to amend the Power Commission Act." *Mr. Cooke.*

Ordered, That the Bill be read the second time on Monday next.

Bill (No. 166), intituled "An Act to amend the Hydro-Electric Railway Act, 1914." *Mr. Cooke.*

Ordered, That the Bill be read the second time on Monday next.

Bill (No. 167), intituled "An Act to amend the Loan and Trust Corporations Act." *Mr. Nickle.*

Ordered, That the Bill be read the second time on Monday next.

Bill (No. 168), intituled "An Act to amend the Ontario Companies Act."
Mr. Nickle.

Ordered, That the Bill be read the second time on Monday next.

Mr. Ferguson delivered to Mr. Speaker a message from the Lieutenant-Governor, signed by himself; and the said message was read by Mr. Speaker, and is as follows:—

H. COCKSHUTT. ·

The Lieutenant-Governor transmits Further Supplementary Estimates of certain sums required for the service of the Province for the year ending 31st October, 1926, and recommends them to the Legislative Assembly.

GOVERNMENT HOUSE,
    Toronto, March 25th, 1926.

(Sessional Papers, No. 2.)

Ordered, That the message of the Lieutenant-Governor, together with the estimates accompanying the same, be referred to the Committee of Supply.

Mr. Carty asked the following Question (No. 174):—

1. How many airplanes that had been previously the property of the United States Navy Department were purchased by the Department of Lands and Forests from the Laurentide Air Service. 2. What were the descriptions and what prices were paid to the Laurentide Air Service.

The Minister of Lands and Forests replied as follows:—

1. Thirteen. 2. H.S. 2-L. flying boats; $5,500.00 each, delivered at Ramsay Lake near Sudbury.

Mr. McCallum asked the following Question (No. 175):—

1. How many liquor dispensaries are there and where are they located. 2. What are the names of the employees, with salaries, at each dispensary.

The Attorney-General replied as follows:—

1. There are eight liquor dispensaries: (1) 154 Wellington Street West, Toronto; (2) 1271 Dundas Street West, Toronto; (3) 29 Charles Street, Hamilton;

(4) 425 Talbot Street, London; (5) 30 Sandwich Street West, Windsor; (6) Market Square, Kingston; (7) 92 Kent Street, Ottawa; (8) 109 Simpson Street, Fort William.

Answer, No. 2:—

Head Office: Per Year

Arthur H. Birmingham	$5,500 00
James A. McGeachie	3,000 00
Peter Beaton	2,600 00
Charles G. Desjardins	2,200 00
Thomas D. Crighton	2,600 00
Edward A. Leech	2,600 00
Bertram J. Savage	2,300 00
David D. Shaw	2,100 00
James S. Jones	2,000 00
Maurice J. Carroll	1,900 00
William A. Murray	1,750 00
Gordon D. King	1,700 00
William Robinson	1,650 00
James H. Moultrie	1,550 00
Harold G. Barton	1,525 00
Robert Jeffrey	1,500 00
William Nelson	1,375 00
Victor Sutherland	825 00
Samuel Dick	780 00
Frederick Porter	575 00
Miss Gladys Fawssett	1,200 00
Miss Marguerite Abbott	1,150 00
Miss Dorothy Brent	1,000 00
Miss Marjorie McKee	925 00
Miss Mary K. Padget	780 00

Head Office (Censor's Department):   Per Year

William W. Donaldson	$3,000 00
Howard C. Buffam	1,700 00
Miss Winifred C. Young	1,050 00
Miss Joan D. Browne	975 00
Miss Vera Hare	925 00
Miss May I. Macdonald	900 00
Miss Marjorie Reding	900 00
Miss Rita Hall	900 00
Miss Norma J. Blatchford	900 00
Miss Gladys Latimer	850 00
Miss Grace Gardiner	825 00
Miss Muriel Shaw	780 00
Miss Helen Corbett	780 00
Miss Margaret J. Buchanan	780 00

Central Warehouse: Per Year

George Snider	$3,000 00
William Johnston	1,900 00
Matthew Johnson	1,550 00
Milton Holliday	1,600 00
John S. Wilson	1,600 00
Robert S. Bain	1,500 00
Frederick Lacey	1,500 00
Robert West	1,500 00
William Shaw	1,450 00
Charles J. Graham	1,350 00
James L. Johnston	1,350 00
Edward Roberts	1,350 00
George Gray	1,350 00
Albert Ainsworth	1,350 00
James T. Mann	1,350 00
James Duncan	1,350 00
Paul McColl	1,350 00
John McLean	1,350 00
David Hogg	1,350 00
Thomas J. Roberts	1,350 00
John H. Woods	1,350 00
Frederick W. Race	1,350 00
Daniel I. Druce	1,325 00
Thomas Grant	1,300 00
Nelson F. Elliott	1,300 00
John Read	1,300 00
Gordon McManus	650 00
Miss May Adams	780 00
Mrs. Rose Raven	780 00

Dispensary No. 1:   Per Year

Archibald K. Coulthard	$2,850 00
Edward J. Murphy	1,820 00
Frederick E. Wilford	1,700 00
Alexander H. Robertson	1,650 00
Irving D. Forbes	1,550 00
Frank McKenna	1,550 00
Robert Fenton	1,450 00
Harry Elliott	1,400 00
Arthur S. Pitcher	1,450 00
Alex. N. Smillie	1,375 00
John Bradley	1,350 00
Frederick Moorecroft	1,350 00
Walter Pickard	1,350 00
David Adamson	1,325 00
Alex. Sutherland	1,050 00
Miss Agnes Manion	1,050 00
Miss Minnie Woodhouse	1,025 00
Miss Nellie Wynne	1,025 00
Mrs. Marie C. Good	1,000 00
Miss Florence E. Scott	950 00
Miss Edythe MacKenzie	850 00

Dispensary No. 2:   Per Year

   Kingsley C. Brooke............................ $2,500 00
   Charles G. Motton............................ 1,600 00
   Rogers Helsdowne............................. 1,350 00
   James Tebble................................. 1,350 00
   Robert S. Boult.............................. 1,350 00
   Charles C. Chappell.......................... 1,300 00
   Miss Sadie Walsh............................. 1,000 00

Dispensary No. 3:   Per Year

   William Cleland.............................. $3,000 00
   Harry Strickland............................. 1,950 00
   Harold Edwards............................... 1,690 00
   Albert J. Dimmick............................ 1,430 00
   Archibald T. Pollock......................... 1,430 00
   Robert Crossan............................... 1,430 00
   Thomas Tebbutt............................... 1,430 00
   Thomas Patterson............................. 1,350 00
   George Pilton................................ 1,350 00
   Miss Erie Card............................... 1,000 00
   Miss Bessie Robinson......................... 925 00

Dispensary No. 4:   Per Year

   Frank N. Turville............................ $2,500 00
   William D. McDonald.......................... 1,475 00
   George Hexter................................ 1,430 00
   John Worrall................................. 1,430 00
   Christopher Lethbridge....................... 1,350 00
   Minard H. Elliott............................ 1,350 00
   Mrs. Allison E. Craig........................ 1,100 00
   Miss Anna M. Lawless......................... 900 00
   Miss Rhea V. Fitzpatrick..................... 900 00
   Miss Margaret Wilson......................... 780 00

Dispensary No. 5:   Per Year

   Archibald Gray............................... $2,500 00
   Alfred R. Kitts.............................. 1,500 00
   Edward J. Thomas............................. 1,450 00
   David G. Davies.............................. 1,350 00
   Angus Roy.................................... 1,350 00
   David Branion................................ 1,300 00
   Thomas E. Donald............................. 1,300 00

Dispensary No. 6:   Per Year

   James W. Rigney.............................. $3,000 00
   George J. Cooper............................. 1,700 00
   John J. Hyland............................... 1,475 00
   William J. Dunn.............................. 1,430 00
   Richard R. Clarke............................ 1,350 00

Dispensary No. 7:   Per Year

Daniel Beaton	$3,000 00
Wesley Anderson	1,400 00
Peter Patenaude	1,350 00
Robert O. Askin	1,350 00
Miss Grace L. Evans	850 00
Miss Florence Kerr	825 00

Dispensary No. 8:   Per Year

Kenneth G. Austin	$2,500 00
Jesse W. Winters	1,650 00
James Slater	1,500 00
David S. Burnside	1,500 00
Harley B. Anderson	1,450 00
Richard Gosling	1,430 00

Mr. Raney asked the following Question (No. 180):—

1. What has been the total expenditure for labour and materials in connection with proposed extension of the Nipissing Central Railway to the Rouyn District in Quebec, including the expenditure for that part of the line in Ontario. 2. What have been the expenses to this date of the legal proceedings that have been brought to determine the right of the Province of Ontario to build this railway over Crown lands in Quebec Province.

The Prime Minister replied as follows:—

1. The total expenditure to date has been $517,856.86. This provides twelve miles of railway in the Province of Ontario now in operation, passing through a mining country practically all staked out. In this area important developments are anticipated during the coming season towards which the existence of the railway will largely contribute. 2. $5,195.85 which is included in the sum mentioned in the answer to Question No. 1.

Mr. Bragg asked the following Question (No. 182):—

1. In what counties in the Province of Ontario have additions been made in the mileage of provincial highways since the present Government took office, and what was the mileage added in each of said counties.

The Minister of Public Works and Highways replied as follows —:

1. No additions have been made, but the Department has taken over the Toronto and Hamilton highway which has the following mileage:—York, 5.19; Peel, 9.38; Halton, 15.55; Wentworth, 5.16. Total, 35.28 miles.

Mr. Sangster asked the following Question (No. 186):—

1. What radial railways has the Government of the Province of Ontario at any time guaranteed bonds for. 2. What is the amount in each case. 3. Where work has been done and money expended and the road abandoned, will the Government pay the bonds.

The Prime Minister replied as follows:—

1. See Public Accounts, page 52. 2. Answered by the reply to Question No. 1. 3. When such a question comes up for consideration, the Government will decide upon its course of action.

———————

On motion of Mr. Carty, seconded by Mr. Fenton,

Ordered, That there be laid before this House, a Return of contracts, numbers 706, 719 and 720, referred to at page J 15 of the Public Accounts for 1924, and of all correspondence with reference thereto.

———————

The following Bills were severally read the second time:—

Bill (No. 157), "To amend the Surrogate Courts Act." *Mr. Nickle.*

Referred to a Committee of the Whole House on Monday next.

Bill (No. 158), "To amend the Marriage Act." *Mr. Nickle.*
Referred to a Committee of the Whole House on Monday next.

Bill (No. 25), "Respecting the Township of York."
Referred to a Committee of the Whole House on Monday next.

Bill (No. 159), "To amend the Municipal Act." *Mr. Nickle.*
Referred to a Committee of the Whole House on Monday next.

Bill (No. 156), "Respecting Psychiatric Hospitals." *Mr. Goldie.*
Referred to a Committee of the Whole House on Monday next.

Bill (No. 164), "To amend the Consolidated Municipal Act, 1922." *Mr. Henry.*

Referred to a Committee of the Whole House on Monday next.

The House resolved itself into a Committee, severally to consider the following Bills:—

Bill (No. 5), Respecting the Town of Aylmer.

Bill (No. 11), Respecting the City of Brantford.

Bill (No. 24), Respecting the Board of Trustees of the Police Village of Alfred.

Bill (No. 40), To amend the Act to incorporate the Evangelical Lutheran Seminary of Canada.

Bill (No. 49), Respecting the Township of Stamford.

Bill (No. 2), Respecting the Town of Arnprior.

Bill (No. 48), Respecting the Town of Walkerville.

Bill (No. 50), Respecting the Town of La Salle.

Bill (No. 14), Respecting the Township of North York.

Bill (No. 18), Respecting the City of Port Arthur.

Mr. Speaker resumed the Chair; and Mr. Black reported, That the Committee had directed him to report several Bills without amendments and several with amendments.

The Amendments, having been read the second time, were agreed to.

Ordered, That the Bills reported, be severally read the third time on Monday next.

The Order of the Day for the House to resolve itself into the Committee of Supply, having been read,

Mr Ferguson moved,

That the Speaker do now leave the Chair and that the House do resolve itself into the Committee of Supply.

The motion having been put, Mr. Sinclair moved in amendment, seconded by Mr. Belanger.

That all the words after the first word "that" be struck out and the following substituted therefor:—

"This House regrets that the Government has failed to adopt a systematic scheme of provincial taxation, and recommends that a committee of inquiry be appointed to sit during the recess to investigate provincial taxation, taking into consideration its encroachment upon municipal taxation, and to report to this House at its next Session."

A Debate ensued,

And after some time, the amendment having been put, was lost.

The main motion was then put and carried.

And the House accordingly resolved itself into the Committee.

(*In the Committee.*)

Resolved, That there be granted to His Majestv, for the services of 1926, the following sums:—

To defray the expenses of the Game and Fisheries Department... $41,809 00

Mr. Speaker resumed the Chair; and Mr. Black reported, That the Committee had come to several Resolutions; also, That the Committee had directed him to ask for leave to sit again.

Ordered, That the Report be received on Monday next.

Resolved, That the Committee have leave to sit again on Monday next.

The Provincial Secretary presented to the House, by command of His Honour the Lieutenant-Governor:—

Report of the Registrar of Loan Corporations for 1925. (*Sessional Papers*, *No. 7.*)

Also, Report of the Superintendent of Insurance and Registrar of Friendly Societies for 1925. (*Sessional Papers, No. 6.*)

Also, Report of the Commissioners for the Queen Victoria Niagara Falls Park, 1925. (*Sessional Papers, No. 52.*)

Also, Report of the Department of Northern Development and of the Colonization of Roads Branch, for 1925. (*Sessional Papers, No. 53.*)

Also, Copies of Orders-in-Council in accordance with the provisions of Section 27, of the Department of Education Act. (*Sessional Papers, No. 54.*)

The House then adjourned at 6.10 p.m.

MONDAY, MARCH 29TH, 1926.

PRAYERS.   3 O'CLOCK P.M.

The following Petitions were severally brought up and laid upon the Table:—

By Mr. Sweet, Petition of Joseph London and others *re* Rural School Boards; also, Edmund Thompson and others *re* Township School Boards; also, the Petition of the Counties' Council of the United Counties of Stormont, Dundas and Glengarry *re* Children's Protection Act.

By Mr. Widdifield, Petition of members and adherents of the United Church of Beaverton, Ontario.

The following Petitions were read and received:—

Of T. C. Windatt and others of Beaverton Presbyterian Church, praying that an Act may pass to amend the United Church of Canada Act.

Of the Waiters and Cooks Local; also, of the Brotherhood of Locomotive Engineers, Parkdale Division, No. 293; also, of the Machinists International Association, No. 371; also, of the Lathers International Union, Local No. 97, praying that an Act may pass to amend the Assessment Act.

The following Bills were severally introduced and read the first time:—

Bill (No. 169), intituled "An Act to vest certain lands in His Majesty." *Mr. Henry.*

Ordered, That the Bill be read the second time on Tuesday next.

Bill (No. 170), intituled "An Act to amend the Public Service Works on Highways Act, 1925." *Mr. Henry.*

Ordered, That the Bill be read the second time on Tuesday next.

Bill (No. 171), intituled "An Act to amend the Ontario Habeas Corpus Act." *Mr. Nickle.*

Ordered, That the Bill be read the second time on Tuesday next.

Bill (No. 172), intituled "An Act to amend the Judicature Act." *Mr. Nickle.*

Ordered, That the Bill be read the second time on Tuesday next.

Bill (No. 173), intituled "An Act to amend the Representation Act." *Mr. Henry.*

Ordered, That the Bill be read the second time on Tuesday next.

Bill (No. 174), intituled "An Act to amend the Wills Act." *Mr. Nickle.*

Ordered, That the Bill be read the second time on Tuesday next.

Bill (No. 175), intituled "An Act to amend the Adoption Act." *Mr. Nickle.*

Ordered, That the Bill be read the second time on Tuesday next.

Bill (No. 176), intituled "An Act to amend the Hospitals and Charitable Institutions Act." *Mr. Nickle.*

Ordered, That the Bill be read the second time on Tuesday next.

Bill (No. 177), intituled "An Act to consolidate and amend the Ontario Summary Convictions Act." *Mr. Nickle.*

Ordered, That the Bill be read the second time on Tuesday next.

Bill (No. 178), intituled "An Act to amend the Ontario Insurance Act, 1924." *Mr. Nickle.*

Ordered, That the Bill be read the second time on Tuesday next.

Bill (No. 179), intituled "An Act to amend the Workmen's Compensation Act." *Mr. Nickle.*

Ordered, That the Bill be read the second time on Tuesday next.

Bill (No. 181), intituled "An Act to validate the grant from the College of Physicians and Surgeons of Ontario to the Banting Research Endowment Fund." *Mr. Lewis.*

Ordered, That the Bill be read the second time on Tuesday next.

On the motion of Mr. Henry, seconded by Mr. Nickle,

Ordered, That a Select Committee of fifteen members be appointed to consider and fill in the schedule in Bill (No. 173), "An Act to amend the Representation Act," with all convenient speed, to be composed as follows:—

Messrs. Ferguson, Henry, Price, Macdiarmid, Bradburn, Clarke (Northumberland), Homuth, Keith, Mewhinney, Mahoney, Milligan, Monteith, Nixon, Taylor and Vaughan.

Mr. Nixon asked the following Question (No. 167):—

1. When was the moving picture plant purchased and from whom, and at what price. 2. What expenditures have been made upon it (*a*) on capital account, (*b*) for maintenance.

The Minister of Public Works and Highways replied as follows:—

1. November, 1923, from the late James J. Connolly for $30,000. 2. (*a*) $12,917.13; (*b*) $5,736.65.

Mr. Nixon asked the following Question (No. 172):—

1. What were (*a*) the estimates; (*b*) the expenditures for the Moving Picture Bureau for each year, beginning with fiscal year of 1918-1919.

The Provincial Treasurer replied as follows:—

1—	(*a*)	(*b*)	
1919...Films..........	$42,000 00	$40,002 05	
1920...Films.........	133,150 00	137,725 48	
" ...Contingencies..	63,000 00	5,633 81	
1921...Films.........	125,000 00	85,919 20	
" ...Contingencies..	13,150 00	5,254 50	
1922...Films..........	125,000 00	106,119 48	
" ...Contingencies..	10,150 00	8,484 38	
1923...Films..........	90,000 00	89,989 25	which includes $24,558, purchase of Studio, Trenton.
" ...Contingencies..	5,500 00	8,633 39	
1924...Films.........	90,000 00	58,236 89	which includes $5,442, final payment on Studio and $579 Lantern Slide Dept. (New).
" ...Contingencies..	5,500 00	8,400 00	
1925...Films..........	60,000 00	121,433 94	which includes:
			Still Picture Dept... $7,888 12
			Lantern Slide Dept. 3,316 05
			Projection Machines 4,704 66
			Radio Publicity.... 10,283 48
			Film & Slide Co., purchase of Film Library.......... 25,000 00
" ...Contingencies..	10,000 00	18,376 06	

Mr. Ross asked the following Question (No. 176):—

1. What amount was expended in 1925 for maintenance of provincial highways in Oxford County. 2. What payments in salary and expenses were made to temporary or permanent employees who supervised and performed this work. 3. What are the names of such employees and what amounts were received by each. 4. Who supervised the removal of snow from the highway during the winter of 1925-6 and what remuneration·did such supervisor receive. 5. Did the Beachville White Lime Company supply any material for maintenance requirements on provincial highway in Oxford County during 1925. (*a*) If so, what material and quantity; (*b*) What price was paid for same.

The Minister of Public Works and Highways replied as follows:—

1. $5,440.51.   2. $1,648.22.   3. L. McAllister, $100.05; M. McDonald, $112.90; A. Ludlow, $121.00; R. W. Dickie, $764.40; I. Lawrence, $298.50; I. W. Barnard, $26.25; G. B. Ryan, $67.75; I. G. Turnbull, $144.25; C. Cameron, $4.12; G. F. Turner, $4.50; S. Van Koughnet, $4.50.   4. Patrolman, A. Ludlow, $35.00; Patrolman, R. W. Dickie, $114.00; Patrolman, I. G. Turnbull, $13.20; snow plough operators, W. W. Mercer, $143.15; S. Van Koughnet, $30.15. 5. Yes; (a) five tons of screenings; (b) twenty-five cents per ton, $1.25.

Mr. Nixon asked the following Question (No. 181):—

1. Was Thomas Tooms, member of the last Legislature representing Peterborough West, employed in the Treasury Department last year.   2. Did any member of the Legislature request his dismissal.   3. What member.   4. Was he dismissed.   5. Were Mr. Toom's services satisfactory.

The Provincial Treasurer replied as follows:—

1. Yes.   2. No.   3. Answered by No. 2.   4. No.   5. Yes.   Mr. Tooms was temporarily employed on Luxury Tax collection, but, owing to the decline of revenue at the close of the summer season, his services were dispensed with along with ten other temporary inspectors.

On motion of Mr. Homuth, seconded by Mr. Callan,

That in the opinion of this House, the claims of John Brass and the other labouring men who worked last summer for T. J. McLean, road contractor, on the Caledon Hill job on the Middle Road between Orangeville and Brampton, ought to be paid by the Government, at the amounts at which they may be judicially ascertained, upon the men executing assignments of their claims to the Government.

The motion of Mr. Homuth was, by consent of the House, withdrawn.

On motion of Mr. Ross, seconded by Mr. Nixon,

Ordered, That there be laid before the House, a Return showing cost of maintenance of the provincial highway between Barrie and Orillia for each of the four past fiscal years, how much was paid for salaries and services, and to whom in each year, and how much for materials, and to whom.

On motion of Mr. McBrien, seconded by Mr. Lewis,

That notwithstanding the time for presenting Petitions for Private Bills has elapsed, leave be given to present a Petition of the City of Toronto for an Act to authorize the transfer of certain Radial Railways from the Provincial Hydro-Electric Power Commission of Ontario to the Corporation of the City of Toronto, and that the same be now read and received.

The following Petition was then read and received:—

The Petition of the City of Toronto, to authorize the transfer of certain Radial Railways from the Provincial Hydro-Electric Power Commission of Ontario to the Corporation of the City of Toronto, and that the same be now read and received.

On motion of Mr. McBrien, seconded by Mr. Lewis,

That notwithstanding the time for introducing Private Bills has elapsed, leave be given to introduce a Bill entitled "An Act to authorize the transfer of certain Radial Railways from the Provincial Hydro-Electric Power Commission of Ontario to the Corporation of the City of Toronto," and that the same be now read a first time and do stand referred direct to the Committee on Private Bills irrespective of report from Standing Orders or posting in the lobby as required by the Rule in that case made and provided.

The following Bill was then introduced and read the first time:—

Bill (No. 180), intituled "An Act to authorize the transfer of certain Radial Railways from the Provincial Hydro-Electric Power Commission of Ontario to the Corporation of the City of Toronto. *Mr. McBrien.*

Referred to the Committee on Private Bills.

On motion of Mr. Ferguson, seconded by Mr. Henry,

Ordered, That this House do forthwith resolve itself into a Committee to consider certain proposed Resolutions respecting the borrowing of money for the public service.

Mr. Ferguson acquainted the House that His Honour the Lieutenant-Governor, having been informed of the subject matter of the proposed Resolutions, recommends them to the consideration of the House.

The House then resolved itself into the Committee.

(*In the Committee.*)

Resolved, In addition to the amounts provided by the Northern and North-western Ontario Development Acts, heretofore enacted, there shall be set apart out of the Consolidated Revenue Fund the sum of Five Million Dollars ($5,000,000.00), and the same shall be applied for the purposes set out in the said Acts and in the Soldiers' and Sailors' Land Settlement Act or any of them.

Mr. Speaker resumed the Chair; and Mr. Rankin reported, That the Committee had come to certain Resolutions.

Ordered, That the Report be now received.

Mr. Rankin reported the Resolutions as follows:—

In addition to the amounts provided by the Northern and Northwestern Ontario Development Acts, heretofore enacted, there shall be set apart out of the Consolidated Revenue Fund the sum of Five Million Dollars ($5,000,000.00), and the same shall be applied for the purposes set out in the said Acts and in the Soldiers' and Sailors' Land Settlement Act or any of them.

The Resolutions having been read the second time, were agreed to, and referred to the Committee of the Whole House on Bill (No. 160), To make further provision for Northern Ontario Development.

————————

The Order of the Day for the second reading of Bill (No. 124), To amend the Power Commission Act, having been read, and Mr. Speaker ruling that the Bill was out of order.

Ordered, That the Order be discharged, and that the Bill be withdrawn.

————————

The following Bills were severally read the second time:—

Bill (No. 27), Respecting the Township of East York.

Referred to a Committee of the Whole House To-morrow.

Bill (No. 13), Respecting the City of Fort William.

Referred to a Committee of the Whole House To-morrow.

Bill (No. 54), Respecting the City of Toronto.

Referred to a Committee of the Whole House To-morrow.

Bill (No. 160), To make further provision for Northern Ontario Development.

Referred to a Committee of the Whole House To-morrow

Bill (No. 168), To amend the Ontario Companies Act.

Referred to a Committee of the Whole House To-morrow.

Bill (No. 167), To amend the Loan and Trust Corporations Act.

Referred to a Committee of the Whole House To-morrow.

Bill (No. 161), To amend the Assessment Act.

Referred to a Committee of the Whole House To-morrow.

Bill (No. 162), For raising money on the credit of the Consolidated Revenue Fund.

Referred to a Committee of the Whole House To-morrow.

Bill (No. 165), To amend the Power Commission Act.

Referred to a Committee of the Whole House To-morrow.

Bill (No. 166), To amend the Hydro-Electric Railway Act, 1914.

Referred to a Committee of the Whole House To-morrow.

Bill (No. 163), To amend the Power Commission Act.

Referred to a Committee of the Whole House To-morrow.

Mr. Ferguson delivered to Mr. Speaker a message from the Lieutenant-Governor, signed by himself; and the said message was read by Mr. Speaker, and is as follows:—

H. COCKSHUTT.

The Lieutenant-Governor transmits Estimates of certain sums required for the service of the Province for the year ending 31st October, 1927, and recommends them to the Legislative Assembly.

GOVERNMENT HOUSE,
Toronto, March 29th, 1926.

(*Sessional Papers, No. 2.*)

Ordered, That the message of the Lieutenant-Governor, together with the Estimates accompanying the same, be referred to the Committee of Supply.

The House resolved itself into a Committee to consider Bill (No. 159), To amend the Municipal Act, and, after some time spent therein, Mr. Speaker resumed the Chair; and Mr. Black reported, That the Committee had directed him to report the Bill without any amendment.

Ordered, That the Bill be read the third time To-morrow.

The House resolved itself into a Committee to consider Bill (No. 164), To amend the Consolidated Municipal Act, 1922, and, after some time spent therein, Mr. Speaker res med the Chair; and Mr. Black reported, That the Committee had directed him to report the Bill without any amendment.

Ordered, That the Bill be read the third time To-morrow.

The House resolved itself into a Committee to consider Bill (No. 151), To amend the School Laws, and, after some time spent therein, Mr. Speaker resumed the Chair; and Mr. Black reported, That the Committee had directed him to report the Bill with certain amendments.

Ordered, That the Amendments be taken into consideration forthwith.

The Amendments, having been read the second time, were agreed to.

Ordered, That the Bill be read the third time To-morrow.

The House resolved itself into a Committee to consider Bill (No. 138), To amend the Public Parks Act, and, after some time spent therein, Mr. Speaker resumed the Chair; and Mr. Black reported, That the Committee had directed him to report the Bill without any amendment.

Ordered, That the Bill be read the third time To-morrow.

The House resolved itself into a Committee to consider Bill (No. 154), To amend the University Act, and, after some time spent therein, Mr. Speaker resumed the Chair; and Mr. Black reported, That the Committee had directed him to report the Bill with certain amendments.

Ordered, That the Amendments be taken into consideration forthwith.

The Amendments, having been read the second time, were agreed to.

Ordered, That the Bill be read the third time To-morrow.

The House resolved itself into a Committee to consider Bill (No. 156), Respecting Psychiatric Hospitals, and, after some time spent therein, Mr. Speaker resumed the Chair; and Mr. Black reported, That the Committee had directed him to report the Bill with certain amendments.

Ordered, That the Amendments be taken into consideration forthwith.

The Amendments, having been read the second time, were agreed to.

Ordered, That the Bill be read the third time To-morrow.

The House resolved itself into a Committee to consider Bill (No. 157), To amend the Surrogate Courts Act, and, after some time spent therein, Mr. Speaker resumed the Chair; and Mr. Black reported, That the Committee had directed him to report the Bill without any amendment.

Ordered, That the Bill be read the third time To-morrow.

The House resolved itself into a Committee to consider Bill (No. 158), To amend the Marriage Act, and, after some time spent therein, Mr. Speaker resumed the Chair; and Mr. Black reported, That the Committee had directed him to report the Bill without any amendment.

Ordered, That the Bill be read the third time To-morrow.

The House, according to Order, again resolved itself into the Committee of Supply.

(*In the Committee.*)

Resolved, That there be granted to His Majesty, for the services of 1926, the following sums:—

127.   To defray the expenses of the Education Department.. $73,200 00

136.   To defray the expenses of the Miscellaneous........   48,500 00

129.   To defray the expenses of the Public Works Department.. 1,400,917 17

130.   To defray the expenses of the Highways Department..   5,075 00

131.   To defray the expenses of the Health Department.....   4,150 00

132.   To defray the expenses of the Labour Department....   51,000 00

133. To defray the expenses of the Provincial Treasurer's
     Department................................. $48,750 00

134. To defray the expenses of the Provincial Secretary's
     Department................................ 159,738 85

135. To defray the expenses of the Agriculture Department.   71,721 00

Mr. Speaker resumed the Chair; and Mr. Black reported, That the Committee had come to several Resolutions; also, That the Committee had directed him to ask for leave to sit again.

Ordered, That the Report be received To-morrow.

Resolved, That the Committee have leave to sit again To-morrow.

———

The House then adjourned at 11.45 p.m.

════════════════════

TUESDAY, MARCH 30TH, 1926.

PRAYERS.   3 O'CLOCK P.M.

The following Petitions were severally brought up and laid upon the Table:—

By Mr. Sweet, Petition of the Ratepayers' and Trustees' Association for the Township of Williamsburg.

By Mr. Bowman, Petition of the South Manitoulin Wool Growers' Association.

———

The following Bills were severally introduced and read the first time:—

Bill (No. 182), intituled "An Act to amend the Public Lands Act." *Mr. Ferguson.*

Ordered, That the Bill be read the second time To-morrow.

Bill (No. 183), intituled "An Act to amend the Consolidated Municipal Act, 1922." *Mr. Henry.*

Ordered, That the Bill be read the second time To-morrow.

Bill (No. 184), intituled "An Act respecting the Royal Agricultural Winter Fair Association and the City of Toronto." *Mr. Henry.*

Ordered, That the Bill be read the second time To-morrow.

The following Bills were read the third time and passed:—

Bill (No. 140), To impose a Tax on Dogs and for the Protection of Sheep.

Bill (No. 145), To amend the Highway Traffic Act.

Bill (No. 35), Respecting the City of Guelph and the Guelph Radial Railway Company.

Bill (No. 5), Respecting the Town of Aylmer.

Bill (No. 11), Respecting the City of Brantford.

Bill (No. 24), Respecting the Board of Trustees of the Police Village of Alfred.

Bill (No. 40), To amend the Act to incorporate the Evangelical Lutheran Seminary of Canada.

Bill (No. 49), Respecting the Township of Stamford.

Bill (No. 2), Respecting the Town of Arnprior.

Bill (No. 23), To incorporate the Association of Accountants and Auditors. in Ontario.

Bill (No. 57), Respecting the Ottawa Police Benefit Fund Association.

Bill (No. 17), Respecting the City of London.

Bill (No. 30), Respecting the City of Ottawa.

Bill (No. 38), Respecting the City of Toronto.

Bill (No. 100), To amend the Planning and Development Act.

Bill (No. 48), Respecting the Town of Walkerville.

Bill (No. 50), Respecting the Town of La Salle.

Bill (No. 14), Respecting the Township of North York.

Bill (No. 18), Respecting the City of Port Arthur.

On motion of Mr. Ferguson, seconded by Mr. Henry,

Ordered, That on Wednesday and Thursday next there shall be two sittings of the House; the first to begin at eleven in the forenoon, Mr. Speaker to leave the chair at one of the clock until three without the question being put, and the second sitting to begin at three of the clock in the afternoon.

The following Bills were severally read the second time:—

Bill (No. 178), "To amend the Ontario Insurance Act, 1924."   *Mr. Nickle.*

Referred to a Committee of the Whole House To-morrow.

Bill (No. 179), "To amend the Workmen's Compensation Act."   *Mr. Nickle.*

Referred to a Committee of the Whole House To-morrow.

Bill (No. 169), "To vest certain lands in His Majesty."   *Mr. Henry.*

Referred to a Committee of the Whole House To-morrow.

Bill (No. 173), "To amend the Representation Act."   *Mr. Henry.*

Referred to a Committee of the Whole House To-morrow.

Bill (No. 171), "To amend the Ontario Habeas Corpus Act."   *Mr. Nickle.*

Referred to a Committee of the Whole House To-morrow.

Bill (No. 172), "To amend the Judicature Act."   *Mr. Nickle.*

Referred to a Committee of the Whole House To-morrow.

Bill (No. 86), "To amend the Legislative Assembly Act."   *Mr. Nickle.*

Referred to a Committee of the Whole House To-morrow.

Bill (No. 155), "To amend the Municipal Act."   *Mr. McBrien.*

Referred to the Municipal Committee.

Bill (No. 181), "To validate the Grant from the College of Physicians and Surgeons of Ontario to the Banting Research Endowment Fund."   *Mr. Lewis.*

Referred to a Committee of the Whole House To-morrow.

Bill (No. 170), "To amend the Public Service Works on Highways Act, 1925."   *Mr. Henry.*

Referred to a Committee of the Whole House To-morrow.

Bill (No. 63), "To consolidate and amend the Law respecting the improvement of Public Highways."   *Mr. Henry.*

Referred to a Committee of the Whole House To-morrow.

Bill (No. 177), "To consolidate and amend the Ontario Summary Convictions Act."   *Mr. Nickle.*

Referred to a Committee of the Whole House To-morrow.

Bill (No. 176), "To amend the Hospitals and Charitable Institutions Act." *Mr. Nickle.*

Referred to a Committee of the Whole House To-morrow.

Bill (No. 175), "To amend the Adoption Act." *Mr. Nickle.*

Referred to a Committee of the Whole House To-morrow.

Bill (No. 174), "To amend the Wills Act." *Mr. Nickle.*

Referred to a Committee of the Whole House To-morrow.

The Order of the Day for the second reading of Bill (No. 67), To provide for Township Boards of School Trustees, having been read,

Ordered, That the Order be discharged, and that the Bill be withdrawn.

The House resolved itself into a Committee, severally to consider the following Bills:—

Bill (No. 25), Respecting the Township of York.

Bill (No. 27), Respecting the Township of East York.

Bill (No. 13), Respecting the City of Fort William.

Bill (No. 54), Respecting the City of Toronto.

Mr. Speaker resumed the Chair; and Mr. Jamieson (Grey) reported, That the Committee had directed him to report the several Bills without amendments.

Ordered, That the Bills reported, be severally read the third time To-morrow.

The House resolved itself into a Committee to consider Bill (No. 161), To amend the Assessment Act, and, after some time spent therein, Mr. Speaker resumed the Chair; and Mr. Jamieson (Grey) reported, That the Committee had directed him to report the Bill without any amendment.

Ordered, That the Bill be read the third time To-morrow.

The House resolved itself into a Committee to consider Bill (No. 162), For raising money on the Credit of the Consolidated Revenue Fund, and, after some time spent therein, Mr. Speaker resumed the Chair; and Mr. Jamieson (Grey) reported, That the Committee had directed him to report the Bill without any amendment.

Ordered, That the Bill be read the third time To-morrow.

The House resolved itself into a Committee to consider Bill (No. 167), To amend the Loan and Trust Corporations Act, and, after some time spent therein, Mr. Speaker resumed the Chair; and Mr. Jamieson (Grey) reported, That the Committee had directed him to report the Bill without any amendment.

Ordered, That the Bill be read the third time To-morrow.

The House resolved itself into a Committee to consider Bill (No. 168), To amend the Ontario Companies Act, and, after some time spent therein, Mr. Speaker resumed the Chair; and Mr. Jamieson (Grey) reported, That the Committee had directed him to report the Bill without any amendment.

Ordered, That the Bill be read the third time To-morrow.

The House resolved itself into a Committee to consider Bill (No. 160), To make further provision for Northern Ontario Development, and, after some time spent therein, Mr. Speaker resumed the Chair; and Mr. Jamieson (Grey) reported, That the Committee had directed him to report the Bill without any amendment.

Ordered, That the Bill be read the third time To-morrow.

The House resolved itself into a Committee to consider Bill (No. 165), To amend the Power Commission Act, and, after some time spent therein, Mr. Speaker resumed the Chair; and Mr. Jamieson (Grey) reported, That the Committee had directed him to report the Bill without any amendment.

Ordered, That the Bill be read the third time To-morrow.

The House resolved itself into a Committee to consider Bill (No. 166), To amend the Hydro-Electric Railway Act, 1914, and, after some time spent therein, Mr. Speaker resumed the Chair; and Mr. Jamieson (Grey) reported, That the Committee had directed him to report the Bill without any amendment.

Ordered, That the Bill be read the third time To-morrow.

The House resolved itself into a Committee to consider Bill (No. 163), To amend the Power Commission Act, and, after some time spent therein, Mr. Speaker resumed the Chair; and Mr. Jamieson (Grey) reported, That the Committee had directed him to report the Bill without any amendment.

Ordered, That the Bill be read the third time To-morrow.

The House, according to Order, again resolved itself into the Committee of Supply.

(*In the Committee.*)

Resolved, That there be granted to His Majesty, for the services of 1926, the following sums:—

137. To defray the expenses of the Prime Minister's Department...............................$1,250,000 00

138. To defray the expenses of the Attorney-General's Department.................................. 3,000 00

139. To defray the expenses of the Education Department... 1,628,095 00

140. To defray the expenses of the Lands and Forests Department.................................. 2,000 00

141. To defray the expenses of the Mines Department... 5,000 00

142. To defray the expenses of the Game and Fisheries Department.................................. 68,500 00

143. To defray the expenses of the Public Works Department... 98,600 00

144. To defray the expenses of the Provincial Treasurer's Department.................................. 19,600 00

145. To defray the expenses of the Provincial Secretary's Department.................................. 35,142 82

146. To defray the expenses of the Agriculture Department... 44,683 00

Mr. Speaker resumed the Chair; and Mr. Jamieson (Grey) reported, That the Committee had come to several Resolutions; also, That the Committee had directed him to ask for leave to sit again.

Ordered, That the Report be received To-morrow.

Resolved, That the Committee have leave to sit again To-morrow.

———

The Order of the Day for the third reading of Bill (No. 148), To amend the Highway Traffic Act, 1923, having been read,

Ordered, That the Order be discharged, and that the Bill be forthwith again referred to a Committee of the Whole, with instructions to amend the same.

The House accordingly resolved itself into the Committee; and, after some time spent therein, Mr. Speaker resumed the Chair; and Mr. Jamieson (Grey) reported, That the Committee had amended the Bill as directed.

Ordered, That the Bill be read the third time To-morrow.

Mr. Raney moved, seconded by Mr. Biggs,

That this House desires to place on record its view that the manner in which questions addressed to the Ministry by members of the Opposition, have been dealt with at this Session of the Legislature constitutes a very grave denial of well-established rights and liberties of members of this House.

The motion of Mr. Raney was by consent of the House, withdrawn.

The House, according to Order, again resolved itself into the Committee of Supply.

(In the Committee.)

Resolved, That there be granted to His Majesty, for the services of 1927, the following sums:—

1. To defray the expenses of the Lieutenant-Governor's Office.. $5,450 00

2. To defray the expenses of the Executive Council Office.. 29,000 00

3. To defray the expenses of the Civil Service Commissioner's Office............................. 9,850 00

4. To defray the expenses of the Hydro-Electric Power Commission of Ontario......................14,175,829 00

5. To defray the expenses of the Bonuses to Rural Primary and Secondary Transmission Lines....... 500,000 00

6. To defray the expenses of the Legislation......... 395,100 00

7. To defray the expenses of the Attorney-General's Office.. 40,200 00

8. To defray the expenses of the Audit of Criminal Justice Accounts.............................. 11,050 00

9. To defray the expenses of the Inspection of Legal Offices.. 23,500 00

10. To defray the expenses of the Land Titles Office... $35,525 00

11. To defray the expenses of the Local Masters of Titles   33,680 00

12. To defray the expenses of the Supreme Court of Ontario......................................   109,700 00

13. To defray the expenses of the Sundry Civil and Criminal Justice.............................   1,298,050 00

14. To defray the expenses of the Administration of Justice in Districts...........................   277,635 00

15. To defray the expenses of the Miscellaneous Services   231,361 00

16. To defray the expenses of the Insurance Department   47,750 00

17. To defray the expenses of the Minister's Office, Education Department........................   91,300 00

18. To defray the expenses of the Public and Separate School Education............................   4,423,060 00

19. To defray the expenses of the Toronto Normal and Model Schools...............................   152,095 00

20. To defray the expenses of the Ottawa Normal and Model Schools...............................   98,900 00

21. To defray the expenses of the London Normal School   53,150 00

22. To defray the expenses of the Hamilton Normal School......................................   45,020 00

23. To defray the expenses of the Peterborough Normal School......................................   41,450 00

24. To defray the expenses of the Stratford Normal School......................................   43,600 00

25. To defray the expenses of the North Bay Normal School......................................   116,600 00

26. To defray the expenses of the English-French Training Schools.................................   148,230 00

27. To defray the expenses of the High Schools and Collegiate Institutes.........................   330,150 00

28. To defray the expenses of the Departmental Museum   12,500 00

29. To defray the expenses of the Public Libraries, Art Schools, Historical, Literary and Scientific Societies   115,900 00

30. To defray the expenses of the Technical Education. $864,200 00

31. To defray the expenses of the Superannuated
    Teachers...................................   50,150 00

32. To defray the expenses of the Provincial and other
    Universities................................   208,810 00

33. To defray the expenses of the Belleville School for
    the Deaf....................................   139,170 00

34. To defray the expenses of the Brantford School for
    the Blind...................................   93,130 00

35. To defray the expenses of the Monteith Northern
    Academy....................................   70,090 00

36. To defray the expenses of the Miscellaneous........   55,500 00

37. To defray the expenses of the Lands and Forests... 2,045,225 00

38. To defray the expenses of the Colonization Roads
    Branch.....................................   576,700 00

39. To defray the expenses of the Mines Department..   348,950 00

40. To defray the expenses of the Game and Fisheries
    Department.................................   515,775 00

41. To defray the expenses of the Public Works Depart-
    ment—Main Office...........................   81,050 00

42. To defray the expenses of the Maintenance and
    Repairs of Government Buildings: Government
    House......................................   43,350 00

43. To defray the expenses of the Parliament and De-
    partmental Buildings.......................   421,076 35

44. To defray the expenses of the Osgoode Hall.......   61,480 00

45. To defray the expenses of the Educational Buildings   14,810 00

46. To defray the expenses of the Agricultural Buildings   8,000 00

47. To defray the expenses of the District Buildings...   9,900 00

48. To defray the expenses of the Miscellaneous.......   68,550 00

49. To defray the expenses of the Public Works and
    Bridges....................................   105,500 00

50. To defray the expenses of the Public Buildings.....   394,000 00

51. To defray the expenses of the Highways Department $443,075 00

52. To defray the expenses of the Health Department. .   749,715 00

53. To defray the expenses of the Labour Department . 2,345,880 00

54. To defray the expenses of the Provincial Treasurer's Department—Main Office......................   112,025 00

55. To defray the expenses of the Succession Duties Branch....................................   112,300 00

56. To defray the expenses of the Amusement Branches   105,625 00

57. To defray the expenses of the Board of Censors of Moving Pictures.............................   24,400 00

58. To defray the expenses of the Motion Picture Bureau   130,400 00

59. To defray the expenses of the King's Printer's Office   36,250 00

60. To defray the expenses of the Fire Marshall Office . .   77,650 00

61. To defray the expenses of the Office of Law Stamp Distributor.................................   3,500 00

62. To defray the expenses of the Department of Public Records and Archives.........................   19,650 00

63. To defray the expenses of the House Post Office....   15,950 00

64. To defray the expenses of the General............   32,150 00

65. To defray the expenses of the Provincial Auditor's Office.....................................   88,750 00

66. To defray the expenses of the Provincial Secretary's Office.....................................   268,125 00

67. To defray the expenses of the Public Institutions— Administration and Inspection..................   93,007 00

68. To defray the expenses of the Board of Parole.....   11,550 00

69. To defray the expenses of the Hospitals and Charities 1,168,650 00

70. To defray the expenses of the Brockville Hospital. .   329,772 00

71. To defray the expenses of the Cobourg Hospital....   133,550 00

72. To defray the expenses of the Hamilton Hospital...   415,650 00

73. To defray the expenses of the Kingston Hospital. . .   263,930 00

74. To defray the expenses of the London Hospital.... $436,460 00

75. To defray the expenses of the Mimico Hospital.... 250,230 00

76. To defray the expenses of the Orillia Hospital..... 355,102 00

77. To defray the expenses of the Penetanguishene Hospital.................................. 134,090 00

78. To defray the expenses of the Toronto Hospital.... 358,902 00

79. To defray the expenses of the Whitby Hospital.... 443,979 00

80. To defray the expenses of the Woodstock Hospital. 89,631 00

81. To defray the expenses of the Guelph Reformatory. 306,010 00

82. To defray the expenses of the Guelph Reformatory Industries.................................. 226,000 00

83. To defray the expenses of the Mercer Reformatory, Toronto.................................... 80,300 00

84. To defray the expenses of the Mercer Reformatory Industries, Toronto........................... 10,000 00

85. To defray the expenses of the Burwash Industrial Farm...................................... 239,700 00

86. To defray the expenses of the Fort William Industrial Farm................................ 35,820 00

87. To defray the expenses of the Boys' Training School, Bowmanville............................... 51,000 00

88. To defray the expenses of the Toronto Reception Hospital................................... 75,000 00

89. To defray the expenses of the Miscellaneous Public Institutions................................ 64,100 00

90. To defray the expenses of the Agriculture Department, Minister's Office....................... 16,625 00

91. To defray the expenses of the Statistics and Publications Office.............................. 19,075 00

92. To defray the expenses of the Agricultural and Horticultural Societies........................ 228,750 00

93. To defray the expenses of the Live Stock Branch... 196,100 00

94. To defray the expenses of the Institutes Branch.... 73,525 00

95. To defray the expenses of the Dairy Branch....... $231,750 00

96. To defray the expenses of the Fruit Branch....... 99,925 00

97. To defray the expenses of the Agricultural Representatives Branch............................. 346,450 00

98. To defray the expenses of the Markets and Co-operation Branch............................. 46,225 00

99. To defray the expenses of the Agricultural Development Board................................ 70,000 00

100. To defray the expenses of the Kemptville Agricultural School................................ 64,000 00

101. To defray the expenses of the Ontario Veterinary College..................................... 37,650 00

102. To defray the expenses of the Western Ontario Experimental Farm, Ridgetown................. 23,000 00

103. To defray the expenses of the New Ontario Demonstration Farm............................... 16,000 00

104. To defray the expenses of the Colonization and Immigration Branch......................... 211,225 00

105. To defray the expenses of the Miscellaneous Services 48,100 00

106. To defray the expenses of the Ontario Agricultural College..................................... 348,640 00

107. To defray the expenses of the Macdonald Institute and Hall.................................... 58,562 00

108. To defray the expenses of the Farm and Departmental Expenses............................. 253,968 00

109. To defray the expenses of the Miscellaneous....... 531,000 00

Mr. Speaker resumed the Chair; and Mr. Black reported, That the Committee had come to several Resolutions; also, That the Committee had directed him to ask for leave to sit again.

Ordered, That the Report be received To-morrow.

Resolved, That the Committee have leave to sit again To-morrow.

The House then adjourned at 10.05 p.m.

WEDNESDAY, MARCH 31st, 1926.

The following Petitions were severally brought up and laid upon the Table:—

By Mr. Vaughan, Petition of the Garrison Road Highway Association; also, L. Douglas, Reeve, and others of the Village of Fort Erie, Ontario; also, H. Hall, Mayor, and others of the Town of Bridgeburg, Ontario.

By Mr. Keith, Petition of Representatives of Knox Church, Sutton, Ontario.

By Mr. Willson (Niagara Falls), Petition of the Municipal Council of the Township of Bertie, Ontario.

The following Petitions were read and received:—

Of the Congregation of Beaverton United Church respecting the United Church of Canada Act.

Of the Dundas County Ratepayers' and Trustees' Association; also, of the Ratepayers' and Trustees' Association of Matilda Township, respecting Township School Boards.

Of the County Councils of Stormont, Dundas and Glengarry respecting the Children's Protection Act.

Mr. McKeown, from the Standing Committee on Municipal Law, presented their Third Report which was read as follows and adopted:—

Your Committee have carefully considered Bills (Nos. 97, 111, 112, 118, 119, 129, 137, 141 and 155), to amend the Municipal Act and such of their provisions as have been approved of have been embodied in a Bill intituled "The Municipal Amendment Act, 1926."

Your Committee have carefully considered Bills (Nos. 85, 132, 144 and 147), to amend the Assessment Act and such of their provisions as have been approved of have been embodied in a Bill intituled "The Assessment Amendment Act, 1926."

Your Committee have carefully considered the following Bills and beg to report the same with certain amendments:—

Bill (No. 105), An Act to amend the Local Improvement Act.

Bill (No. 109), An Act to amend the Local Improvement Act.

————

Mr. Nickle, from the Standing Committee on Private Bills, presented their Eleventh Report which was read as follows and adopted.

Your Committee beg to report the following Bills without amendment:—

Bill (No. 41), An Act respecting the Town of Huntsville.

Bill (No. 52), An Act respecting the City of Sault Ste. Marie.

Bill (No. 60), An Act respecting the Township of Tisdale.

Bill (No. 61), An Act respecting the Victoria Hospital at Renfrew.

Your Committee would recommend that the fees less the actual cost of printing be remitted on Bill (No. 61), "An Act respecting the Victoria Hospital at Renfrew," on the ground that it is one relating to a charitable institution.

Ordered, That the fees, less the penalties and the actual cost of printing, be remitted on Bill (No. 61), "An Act respecting the Victoria Hospital at Renfrew."

————

The following Bills were severally read the second time:—

Bill (No. 184), "Respecting the Royal Agricultural Fair Association and the City of Toronto." *Mr. Ferguson.*

Referred to a Committee of the Whole House To-morrow.

Bill (No. 183), "To amend the Consolidated Municipal Act, 1922." *Mr. Henry.*

Referred to a Committee of the Whole House To-morrow.

Bill (No. 182), "To amend the Public Lands Act." *Mr. Ferguson.*

Referred to a Committee of the Whole House To-morrow.

The Order of the Day for the second reading of Bill (No. 64), To amend the Consolidated Municipal Act, 1922, having been read,

Ordered, That the Order be discharged, and that the Bill be withdrawn.

The House resolved itself into a Committee to consider Bill (No. 86), To amend the Legislative Assembly Act, and, after some time spent therein, Mr. Speaker resumed the Chair; and Mr. Jamieson (Grey) reported, That the Committee had directed him to report the Bill without any amendment.

Ordered, That the Bill be read the third time To-morrow.

The House resolved itself into a Committee to consider Bill (No. 169), To vest certain lands in His Majesty, and, after some time spent therein, Mr. Speaker resumed the Chair; and Mr. Jamieson (Grey) reported, That the Committee had directed him to report the Bill without any amendment.

Ordered, That the Bill be read the third time To-morrow.

The House resolved itself into a Committee to consider Bill (No. 171), To amend the Ontario Habeas Corpus Act, and, after some time spent therein, Mr. Speaker resumed the Chair; and Mr. Jamieson (Grey) reported, That the Committee had directed him to report the Bill without any amendment.

Ordered, That the Bill be read the third time To-morrow.

The House resolved itself into a Committee to consider Bill (No. 172), To amend the Judicature Act, and, after some time spent therein, Mr. Speaker resumed the Chair; and Mr. Jamieson (Grey) reported, That the Committee had directed him to report the Bill without any amendment.

Ordered, That the Bill be read the third time To-morrow.

The House resolved itself into a Committee to consider Bill (No. 174), To amend the Wills Act, and, after some time spent therein, Mr. Speaker resumed the Chair; and Mr. Jamieson (Grey) reported, That the Committee had directed him to report the Bill without any amendment.

Ordered, That the Bill be read the third time To-morrow.

The House resolved itself into a Committee to consider Bill (No. 175), To amend the Adoption Act, and, after some time spent therein, Mr. Speaker resumed the Chair; and Mr. Jamieson (Grey) reported, That the Committee had directed him to report the Bill without any amendment.

Ordered, That the Bill be read the third time To-morrow.

The House resolved itself into a Committee to consider Bill (No. 177), To consolidate and amend the Ontario Summary Convictions Act, and, after some time spent therein, Mr. Speaker resumed the Chair; and Mr. Jamieson (Grey) reported, That the Committee had directed him to report the Bill without any amendment.

Ordered, That the Bill be read the third time To-morrow.

The House resolved itself into a Committee to consider Bill (No. 179), To amend the Workmen's Compensation Act, and, after some time spent therein, Mr. Speaker resumed the Chair; and Mr. Jamieson (Grey) reported, That the Committee had directed him to report the Bill without any amendment.

Ordered, That the Bill be read the third time To-morrow.

The House resolved itself into a Committee to consider Bill (No. 176), To amend the Hospitals and Charitable Institutions Act, and, after some time spent therein, Mr. Speaker resumed the Chair; and Mr. Jamieson (Grey) reported, That the Committee had directed him to report the Bill with certain amendments.

Ordered, That the Amendments be taken into consideration forthwith.

The Amendments, having been read the second time, were agreed to.

Ordered, That the Bill be read the third time To-morrow.

The House resolved itself into a Committee to consider Bill (No. 63), To consolidate and amend the Law respecting the Improvement of Public Highways, and, after some time spent therein, Mr. Speaker resumed the Chair; and Mr..

Jamieson (Grey) reported, That the Committee had directed him to report the Bill without any amendment.

Ordered, That the Bill be read the third time To-morrow.

The House resolved itself into a Committee to consider Bill (No. 170), To amend the Public Service Works on Highways Act, 1925, and, after some time spent therein, Mr. Speaker resumed the Chair; and Mr. Jamieson (Grey) reported, That the Committee had directed him to report the Bill without any amendment.

Ordered, That the Bill be read the third time To-morrow.

The House resolved itself into a Committee to consider Bill (No. 178), To amend the Ontario Insurance Act, 1924, and, after some time spent therein, Mr. Speaker resumed the Chair; and Mr. Jamieson (Grey) reported, That the Committee had directed him to report the Bill without any amendment.

Ordered, That the Bill be read the third time To-morrow.

On motion of Mr. Lethbridge, seconded by Mr. Widdifield,

That the time has come when the law of Ontario ought to recognize community of property between husband and wife to the extent that neither should be free to devise or bequeath at death more than half of the community property to other persons.

And, after some time, the motion was, by leave of the House, withdrawn.

On motion of Mr. Raney, seconded by Mr. Lethbridge,

That the Ontario Temperance Act has done much good by reducing temptation to the youth of Ontario, by producing a more sober citizenship, by lifting homes from squalor, want and crime, and by taking away the legally authorized inducements which formerly existed for drinking in hotels and clubs to the great waste of time, money, energy and efficiency.

That one of the principal difficulties in connection with the enforcement of the present prohibition law arises from the manufacture of intoxicating liquors by breweries, distilleries, and wineries, within Ontario.

That the extensive and well-organized system of smuggling the product of Ontario breweries and distilleries into the United States, that has been openly carried on for several years past in defiance of the constitution and laws of that country, and without interference from the Canadian authorities, is a discredit to Canada.

That this House is of the opinion that the right and most effectual legislative remedy for these and other evils of the liquor traffic is to be found in the prohibition of the manufacture for sale of intoxicating liquor for beverage purposes and all traffic therein, and this House favours the enactment and strengthening of such laws by this Legislature to the full extent of its constitutional authority.

And, after some time, the motion was, by leave of the House, withdrawn.

On motion of Mr. Raney, seconded by Mr. Lethbridge,

That this House regrets that the Department of Highways has not taken adequate steps for the protection of labouring men working for contractors on the provincial highways from loss of wages, through defaults of contractors.

The motion of Mr. Raney was, by consent of the House, withdrawn.

The Order of the Day for the second reading of Bill (No. 120), To amend the Hospitals and Charitable Institutions Act, having been read,

Ordered, That the Order be discharged, and that the Bill be withdrawn.

The Order of the Day for the second reading of Bill (No. 74), To amend the Consolidated Municipal Act, having been read,

Ordered, That the Order be discharged, and that the Bill be withdrawn.

On motion of Mr. Taylor, seconded by Mr. Ross,

Resolved, That in the opinion of this House, in the interests alike of economy, efficiency and convenience, the number of representatives in this House should be reduced to 81, to correspond with the number of members of the Canadian House of Commons from Ontario, and that Ontario ridings for provincial purposes should be made coterminous with Ontario ridings for Dominion purposes.

And, after some time, the motion was by consent of the House, withdrawn.

8 J.

Mr. Kemp asked the following Question (No. 179):—

1. Have permits been given by the present Government for the export of pulpwood to the United States. 2. If so, to what persons, for what kinds of wood and in what quantities. 3. What was the location in each from which the pulpwood was cut, and the name of the licensee.

The Minister of Lands and Forests replied as follows:—

1. Yes. 2. Thos. Woollings, Licensee: Acquired poplar limit on Black and Lee Townships, and there being no home market for such timber, the licensee was granted the right to export in 1922, and as there was certain spruce and balsam scattered amongst the poplar, he was required for clean-up operation to remove same, and was given the right to export. Woollings was operating for the T. & N. O. Railway Commission, on the Commission's Tie Reserve for Jackpine ties, and certain pulpwood mixed in with Jackpine was required to be cut to remove fire hazard, and he was given the right to export such material. Bryson Cobb, Licensee: 15,000 cords of burnt pulpwood, cut from an area south of Ignace Station. Fully 90 per cent. of wood on area was burnt and it was impossible to secure local market, and to salvage material, permission to export was granted. Jas. A. Stewart, Licensee: 15,000 cords of burnt pulpwood, cut from O-5, O-6 and F.P. 4, District of Thunder Bay. This material was badly damaged by fire and local consumers of pulpwood declined to buy, and for purposes of salvaging and revenue to the Crown, permission to export was granted. New Ontario Col. Co., Licensee: 5,100 cords of pulpwood, cut from Haggart and Kendry Townships. This material had been drum-barked, and held in storage for some years, and the company were unable to market locally; same was largely taken from settlers' lands in Haggart and Kendry. Under special agreement made with the Government in 1912, the right to export was permitted. Continental Wood Products Co., Elsas, Ont., Licensee: 100 cords mixed pulpwood (experimental), cut from Trout Chapleau. This material was required by the company for experimental purposes in connection with a system which the company proposes in connection with the development of a Kraft industry in Ontario. The following were granted poplar export privileges owing to the fact that there was no home market for the material, and to prevent fire hazards and deterioration of the woods, permissions to export were granted— A. J. Jordan, Licensee: 6,000 cords of poplar pulpwood, cut from Nairn Township. J. G. O'Connor, Licensee, J. R. Booth, Ltd.,: 1,000 cords of poplar pulpwood, cut from Olrig Township. Mulholland & Co., Licensee, Standard Bank: 10,000 cords of poplar pulpwood, cut from Cox and Waldie Townships. Wahnapitae Power Co., Licensee, Bank of Montreal: 150 cords of poplar pulpwood, cut from Street Township. Lake Superior Corporation, Licensee: 1,800 cords of poplar pulpwood, cut from Hawkins Township. John Clark, Licensee: 162 cords of poplar pulpwood, cut from Grenfell Township. 3. Answered by No. 2.

Mr. Lethbridge asked the following Question (No. 188):—

1. What legal fees have been paid by the present Government to (a) Mr. W. N. Tilley, K.C., Mr. Macgregor Young, K.C., Mr. D. L. McCarthy, K.C., Mr. Strachan Johnson, K.C., or to the firms of which these gentlemen are severally members. 2. In what matters were the said fees respectively paid.

The Attorney-General replied as follows:—

1. and 2. The Attorney-General's Department has made the following payments: W. N. Tilley, K.C., Rex *vs.* A. H. Pepall, $10,000; Rex *vs.* Jarvis and Smith, $10,000; Rex *vs.* C. A. Matthews, $1,500; *re* Judicature Act, reference, $13,000. Total, $34,500. McGregor Young, K.C., *re* Home Bank prosecutions, $20,000; Rex *vs.* A. H. Pepall, $2,750; *re* Judicature Act, reference, $5,000. Rex *vs.* Jarvis and Smith (covered by Home Bank fees). Total, $27,750. D. L. McCarthy, K.C., Home Bank prosecutions, $75,000. Strachan Johnson, K.C., nothing.

———

The following Bills were severally introduced and read the first time:—

Bill (No. 187), intituled "An Act respecting the Widening of Bloor Street in the City of Toronto." *Mr. Nesbitt.*

Ordered, That the Bill be read the second time To-morrow.

Bill (No. 185), intituled "An Act to amend the Ontario Game and Fisheries Act." *Mr. McCrea.*

Ordered, That the Bill be read the second time To-morrow.

Bill (No. 186), intituled "An Act for the Protection of the Property in Foxes kept in Captivity." *Mr. McCrea.*

Ordered, That the Bill be read the second time To-morrow.

Bill (No. 188), intituled "The Municipal Amendment Act, 1926." *Mr. McKeown.*

Ordered, That the Bill be read the second time To-morrow.

Bill (No. 189), intituled "The Assessment Amendment Act, 1926." *Mr. McKeown.*

Ordered, That the Bill be read the second time To-morrow.

———

The following Bills were severally read the second time:—

Bill (No. 188), The Municipal Amendment Act, 1926.

Referred to a Committee of the Whole House To-morrow.

Bill (No. 189), The Assessment Amendment Act, 1926.

Referred to a Committee of the Whole House To-morrow

The Order of the Day for the second reading of Bill (No. 96), To amend the Ontario Temperance Act, having been read,

Mr. Pinard moved,

That the Bill be now read the second time,

And a Debate having ensued,

And, after some time, it was, on the motion of Mr. Ferguson,

Ordered, That the Debate be adjourned.

———————

The Order of the Day for the second reading of Bill (No. 108), To provide for Government Control and Sale of Liquor, having been read,

And the attention of Mr. Speaker having been called to the fact that the Bill interfered with the Revenue and was therefore beyond the jurisdiction of a private member and, his ruling asked for, he said, That he had no alternative but to declare the Bill to be out of order and must therefore be removed from the Order Paper.

———————

The Order of the Day for the second reading of Bill (No. 107), To amend the Ontario Temperance Act, having been read,

Ordered, That the order be discharged and the Bill be withdrawn.

———————

Mr. Black from the Committee of Supply reported the following Resolutions:

125. *Resolved*, That a sum not exceeding Forty-one thousand eight hundred and sixty-eight dollars and fifty-seven cents be granted to His Majesty to defray the expenses of the Attorney-General's Department for the year ending 31st October, 1926.

126. *Resolved*, That a sum not exceeding Four thousand seven hundred and seventy-five dollars be granted to His Majesty to defray the expenses of the Insurance Department for the year ending 31st October, 1926.

127. *Resolved*, That a sum not exceeding Seventy-three thousand two hundred dollars be granted to His Majesty to defray the expenses of the Department of Education for the year ending 31st October, 1926.

128. *Resolved*, That a sum not exceeding Forty-one thousand eight hundred and nine dollars be granted to His Majesty to defray the expenses of the Game and Fisheries Department for the year ending 31st October, 1926.

129. *Resolved,* That a sum not exceeding One million four hundred thousand nine hundred and seventeen dollars and seventeen cents be granted to His Majesty to defray the expenses of Public Works Department for the year ending 31st October, 1926.

130. *Resolved,* That a sum not exceeding Five thousand and seventy-five dollars be granted to His Majesty to defray the expenses of the Highways Department for the year ending 31st October, 1926.

131. *Resolved,* That a sum not exceeding Four thousand one hundred and fifty dollars be granted to His Majesty to defray the expenses of Health Department for the year ending 31st October, 1926.

132. *Resolved,* That a sum not exceeding Fifty-one thousand dollars be granted to His Majesty to defray the expenses of the Labour Department for the year ending 31st October, 1926.

133. *Resolved,* That a sum not exceeding Forty-eight thousand seven hundred and fifty dollars be granted to-His Majesty to defray the expenses of the Provincial Treasurer's Department for the year ending 31st October. 1926.

134. *Resolved,* That a sum not exceeding One hundred and fifty-nine thousand seven hundred and thirty-eight dollars and eighty-five cents be granted to His Majesty to defray the expenses of the Provincial Secretary's Department for the year ending 31st October, 1926.

135. *Resolved,* That a sum not exceeding Seventy-one thousand seven hundred and twenty-one dollars be granted to His Majesty to defray the expenses of the Department of Agriculture for the year year ending 31st October, 1926.

136. *Resolved,* That a sum not exceeding Forty-eight thousand five hundred dollars be granted to His Majesty to defray the expenses of Miscellaneous for the year ending 31st October, 1926.

137. *Resolved,* That a sum not exceeding One million, two hundred and fifty thousand dollars be granted to His Majesty to defray the expenses of Prime Minister's Department for the year ending 31st October, 1926.

138. *Resolved,* That a sum not exceeding Three thousand dollars be granted to His Majesty to defray the expenses of the Attorney-General's Department for the year ending 31st October, 1926.

139. *Resolved,* That a sum not exceeding One million, six hundred and twenty-eight thousand and ninety-five dollars be granted to His Majesty to defray the expenses of Department of Education for the year ending 31st October, 1926.

140. *Resolved,* That a sum not exceeding Two thousand dollars be granted to His Majesty to defray the expenses of the Lands and Forests Department for the year ending 31st October, 1926.

141. *Resolved*, That a sum not exceeding Five thousand dollars be granted to His Majesty to defray the expenses of Mines Department for the year ending 31st October, 1926.

142. *Resolved*, That a sum not exceeding Sixty-eight thousand, five hundred dollars be granted to His Majesty to defray the expenses of the Game and Fisheries Department for the year ending 31st October, 1926.

143. *Resolved*, That a sum not exceeding Ninety-eight thousand, six hundred dollars be granted to His Majesty to defray the expenses of Public Works Department for the year ending 31st October, 1926.

144. *Resolved*, That a sum not exceeding Nineteen thousand six hundred dollars be granted to His Majesty to defray the expenses of Provincial Treasurer's Department for the year ending 31st October, 1926.

145. *Resolved*, That a sum not exceeding Thirty-five thousand, one hundred and forty-two dollars and eighty-two cents be granted to His Majesty to defray the expenses of Provincial Secretary's Department for the year ending 31st October, 1926.

146. *Resolved*, That a sum not exceeding Forty-four thousand, six hundred and eighty-three dollars be granted to His Majesty to defray the expenses of Agriculture Department for the year ending 31st October, 1926.

1. *Resolved*, That a sum not exceeding Five thousand four hundred and fifty dollars be granted to His Majesty to defray the expenses of the Lieutenant-Governor's Office for the year ending 31st October, 1927.

2. *Resolved*, That a sum not exceeding Twenty-nine thousand dollars be granted to His Majesty to defray the expenses of the Executive Council Office for the year ending 31st October, 1927.

3. *Resolved*, That a sum not exceeding Nine thousand eight hundred and fifty dollars be granted to His Majesty to defray the expenses of Civil Service Commissioner's Office for the year ending 31st October, 1927.

4. *Resolved*, That a sum not exceeding Fourteen million one hundred and seventy-five thousand eight hundred and twenty-nine dollars be granted to His Majesty to defray the expenses of the Hydro-Electric Power Commission of Ontario for the year ending 31st October, 1927.

5. *Resolved*, That a sum not exceeding Five hundred thousand dollars be granted to His Majesty to defray the expenses of Bonuses to Rural Primary and Secondary Transmission Lines for the year ending 31st October, 1927.

6. *Resolved*, That a sum not exceeding Three hundred and ninety-five thousand one hundred dollars be granted to His Majesty to defray the expenses of Legislation for the year ending 31st October, 1927.

7. *Resolved*, That a sum not exceeding Forty thousand two hundred dollars be granted to His Majesty to defray the expenses of Attorney-General's Office for the year ending 31st October, 1927.

8. *Resolved,* That a sum not exceeding Eleven thousand and fifty dollars be granted to His Majesty to defray the expenses of Audit of Criminal Justice Accounts for the year ending 31st October, 1927.

9. *Resolved,* That a sum not exceeding Twenty-three thousand five hundred dollars be granted to His Majesty to defray the expenses of Inspection of Legal Offices (including Registry Offices and Division Courts) for the year ending 31st October, 1927.

10. *Resolved,* That a sum not exceeding Thirty-five thousand five hundred and twenty-five dollars be granted to His Majesty to defray the expenses of Land Titles Office for the year ending 31st October, 1927.

11. *Resolved,* That a sum not exceeding Thirty-three thousand six hundred and eighty dollars be granted to His Majesty to defray the expenses of Local Masters of Titles for the year ending 31st October, 1927.

12. *Resolved,* That a sum not exceeding One hundred and nine thousand seven hundred dollars be granted to His Majesty to defray the expenses of the Supreme Court of Ontario for the year ending 31st October, 1927.

13. *Resolved,* That a sum not exceeding One million two hundred and ninety-eight thousand and fifty dollars be granted to His Majesty to defray the expenses of Sundry Civil and Criminal Justice for the year ending 31st October, 1927.

14. *Resolved,* That a sum not exceeding Two hundred and seventy-seven thousand six hundred and thirty-five dollars be granted to His Majesty to defray the expenses of Administration of Justice in Districts for the year ending 31st October, 1927.

15. *Resolved,* That a sum not exceeding Eighty-three thousand five hundred dollars be granted to His Majesty to defray the expenses of Miscellaneous Services for the year ending 31st October, 1927.

16. *Resolved,* That a sum not exceeding Forty-seven thousand seven hundred and fifty dollars be granted to His Majesty to defray the expenses of Insurance Department for the year ending 31st October, 1927.

17. *Resolved,* That a sum not exceeding Ninety-one thousand three hundred dollars be granted to His Majesty to defray the expenses of Minister's Office, Department of Education for the year ending 31st October, 1927.

18. *Resolved,* That a sum not exceeding Four million four hundred and twenty-three thousand and sixty dollars be granted to His Majesty to defray the expenses of Public and Separate School Education for the year ending 31st October, 1927.

19. *Resolved,* That a sum not exceeding One hundred and fifty-two thousand and ninety-five dollars be granted to His Majesty to defray the expenses of Toronto Normal and Model Schools for the year ending 31st October, 1927.

20. *Resolved,* That a sum not exceeding Ninety-eight thousand nine hundred dollars be granted to His Majesty to defray the expenses of Ottawa Normal and Model Schools for the year ending 31st October, 1927.

21. *Resolved*, That a sum not exceeding Fifty-three thousand one hundred and fifty dollars be granted to His Majesty to defray the expenses of London Normal School for the year ending 31st October, 1927.

22. *Resolved*, That a sum not exceeding Forty-five thousand and twenty dollars be granted to His Majesty to defray the expenses of Hamilton Normal School for the year ending 31st October, 1927.

23. *Resolved*, That a sum not exceeding Forty-one thousand four hundred and fifty dollars be granted to His Majesty to defray the expenses of Peterborough Normal School for the year ending 31st October, 1927.

24. *Resolved*, That a sum not exceeding Forty-three thousand six hundred dollars be granted to His Majesty to defray the expenses of Stratford Normal School for the year ending 31st October. 1927.

25. *Resolved*, That a sum not exceeding One hundred and sixteen thousand six hundred dollars be granted to His Majesty to defray the expenses of North Bay Normal School for the year ending 31st October, 1927.

26. *Resolved*, That a sum not exceeding One hundred and forty-eight thousand two hundred and thirty dollars be granted to His Majesty to defray the expenses of English-French Training Schools for the year ending 31st October, 1927.

27. *Resolved*, That a sum not exceeding Three hundred and thirty thousand one hundred and fifty dollars be granted to His Majesty to defray the expenses of High Schools and Collegiate Institutes for the year ending 31st October, 1927.

28. *Resolved*, That a sum not exceeding Twelve thousand five hundred dollars be granted to His Majesty to defray the expenses of Departmental Museum for the year ending 31st October, 1927.

29. *Resolved*, That sum not exceeding One hundred and fifteen thousand nine hundred dollars be granted to His Majesty to defray the expenses of Public Libraries, Art Schools, Historical, Literary and Scientific Societies for the year ending 31st October, 1927.

30. *Resolved*, That a sum not exceeding Eight hundred and sixty-four thousand two hundred dollars be granted to His Majesty to defray the expenses of Technical Education for the year ending 31st October, 1927.

31. *Resolved*, That a sum not exceeding Fifty thousand one hundred and fifty dollars be granted to His Majesty to defray the expenses of Superannuated Teachers for the year ending 31st October, 1927.

32. *Resolved*, That a sum not exceeding Two hundred and eight thousand eight hundred and ten dollars be granted to His Majesty to defray the expenses of Provincial and other Universities for the year ending 31st October, 1927.

33. *Resolved*, That a sum not exceeding One hundred and thirty-nine thousand one hundred and seventy dollars be granted to His Majesty to defray the expenses of Belleville School for the Deaf for the year ending 31st October, 1927.

34. *Resolved*, That a sum not exceeding Ninety-three thousand one hundred and thirty dollars be granted to His Majesty to defray the expenses of Brantford School for the Blind for the year ending 31st October, 1927.

35. *Resolved*, That a sum not exceeding Seventy thousand and ninety dollars be granted to His Majesty to defray the expenses of Monteith Northern Academy for the year ending 31st October, 1927.

36. *Resolved*, That a sum not exceeding Fifty-five thousand five hundred dollars be granted to His Majesty to defray the expenses of Miscellaneous for the year ending 31st October, 1927.

37. *Resolved*, That a sum not exceeding Two million forty-five thousand two hundred and twenty-five dollars be granted to His Majesty to defray the expenses of Lands and Forests for the year ending 31st October, 1927.

38. *Resolved*, That a sum not exceeding Five hundred and seventy-six thousand seven hundred dollars be granted to His Majesty to defray the expenses of Colonization Roads Branch for the year ending 31st October, 1927.

39. *Resolved*, That a sum not exceeding Three hundred and forty-eight thousand nine hundred and fifty dollars be granted to His Majesty to defray the expenses of Mines Department for the year ending 31st October, 1927.

40. *Resolved*, That a sum not exceeding Five hundred and fifteen thousand seven hundred and seventy-five dollars be granted to His Majesty to defray the expenses of Game and Fisheries Department for the year ending 31st October, 1927.

41. *Resolved*, That a sum not exceeding Eighty-one thousand and fifty dollars be granted to His Majesty to defray the expenses of Main Office, Public Works Department, for the year ending 31st October, 1927.

42. *Resolved*, That a sum not exceeding Forty-three thousand three hundred and fifty dollars be granted to His Majesty to defray the expenses of Government House for the year ending 31st October, 1927.

43. *Resolved*, That a sum not exceeding Four hundred and twenty-one thousand seventy-six dollars and thirty-five cents be granted to His Majesty to defray the expenses of Parliament and Departmental Buildings for the year ending 31st October, 1927.

44. *Resolved*, That a sum not exceeding Sixty-one thousand four hundred and eighty dollars be granted to His Majesty to defray the expenses of Osgoode Hall for the year ending 31st October, 1927.

45. *Resolved*, That a sum not exceeding Fourteen thousand eight hundred and ten dollars be granted to His Majesty to defray the expenses of Educational Buildings for the year ending 31st October, 1927..

46. *Resolved*, That a sum not exceeding Eight thousand dollars be granted to His Majesty to defray the expenses of Agricultural Buildings for the year ending 31st October, 1927.

47. *Resolved*, That a sum not exceeding Nine thousand nine hundred dollars be granted to His Majesty to defray the expenses of District Buildings for the year ending 31st October, 1927.

48. *Resolved*, That a sum not exceeding Sixty-eight thousand five hundred and fifty dollars be granted to His Majesty to defray the expenses of Miscellaneous for the year ending 31st October, 1927.

49. *Resolved*, That a sum not exceeding One hundred and five thousand five hundred dollars be granted to His Majesty to defray the expenses of Public Works and Bridges for the year ending 31st October, 1927.

50. *Resolved*, That a sum not exceeding Three hundred and ninety-four thousand dollars be granted to His Majesty to defray the expenses of Public Buildings for the year ending 31st October, 1927.

51. *Resolved*, That a sum not exceeding Four hundred and forty-three thousand and seventy-five dollars be granted to His Majesty to defray the expenses of Highways Department for the year ending 31st October, 1927.

52. *Resolved*, That a sum not exceeding Seven hundred and forty-nine thousand seven hundred and fifteen dollars be granted to His Majesty to defray the expenses of Health Department for the year ending 31st October, 1927.

53. *Resolved*, That a sum not exceeding Two million three hundred and forty-five thousand eight hundred and eighty dollars be granted to His Majesty to defray the expenses of Labour Department, for the year ending 31st October, 1927.

54. *Resolved*, That a sum not exceeding One hundred and twelve thousand and twenty-five dollars be granted to His Majesty to defray the expenses of Main Office, Provincial Treasurer's Department for the year ending 31st October, 1927.

55. *Resolved*, That a sum not exceeding One hundred and twelve thousand three hundred dollars be granted to His Majesty to defray the expenses of Succession Duties Branch for the year ending 31st October, 1927.

56. *Resolved*, That a sum not exceeding One hundred and five thousand six hundred and twenty-five dollars be granted to His Majesty to defray the expenses of Amusement Branches for the year ending 31st October, 1927.

57. *Resolved*, That a sum not exceeding Twenty-four thousand four hundred dollars be granted to His Majesty to defray the expenses of Board of Censors of Moving Pictures for the year ending 31st October, 1927.

58. *Resolved*, That a sum not exceeding One hundred and thirty thousand four hundred dollars be granted to His Majesty to defray the expenses of Motion Picture Bureau for the year ending 31st October, 1927.

59. *Resolved*, That a sum not exceeding Thirty-six Thousand two hundred and fifty dollars be granted to His Majesty to defray the expenses of King's Printer's Office for the year ending 31st October, 1927.

60. *Resolved*, That a sum not exceeding Seventy-seven thousand six hundred and fifty dollars be granted to His Majesty to defray the expenses of Fire Marshall Office for the year ending 31st October, 1927.

61. *Resolved*, That a sum not exceeding Three thousand five hundred dollars be granted to His Majesty to defray the expenses of Office of Law Stamp Distributor for the year ending 31st October, 1927.

62. *Resolved*, That a sum not exceeding Nineteen Thousand Six Hundred and Fifty dollars be granted to His Majesty to defray the expenses of Department of Public Records and Archives for the year ending 31st October, 1927.

63. *Resolved*, That a sum not exceeding Fifteen thousand nine hundred and fifty dollars be granted to His Majesty to defray the expenses of House Post Office for the year ending 31st October, 1927.

64. *Resolved*, That a sum not exceeding Thirty-two thousand one hundred and fifty dollars be granted to His Majesty to defray the expenses of General for the year ending 31st October, 1927.

65. *Resolved*, That a sum not exceeding Eighty-eight thousand seven hundred and fifty dollars be granted to His Majesty to defray the expenses of Provincial Auditor's Office for the year ending 31st October, 1927.

66. *Resolved*, That a sum not exceeding Two hundred and sixty-eight thousand one hundred and twenty-five dollars be granted to His Majesty to defray the expenses of Provincial Secretary's Office for the year ending 31st October, 1927.

67. *Resolved*, That a sum not exceeding Ninety-three thousand and seven dollars be granted to His Majesty to defray the expenses of Public Institutions, Administration and Inspection, for the year ending 31st October, 1927.

68. *Resolved*, That a sum not exceeding Eleven thousand five hundred and fifty dollars be granted to His Majesty to defray the expenses of Board of Parole for the year ending 31st October, 1927.

69. *Resolved*, That a sum not exceeding One million one hundred and sixty-eight thousand six hundred and fifty dollars be granted to His Majesty to defray the expenses of Hospitals and Charities for the year ending 31st October, 1927.

70. *Resolved*, That a sum not exceeding Three hundred and twenty-nine thousand seven hundred and seventy-two dollars be granted to His Majesty to defray the expenses of Brockville Hospital for the year ending 31st October, 1927.

71. *Resolved*, That a sum not exceeding One hundred and thirty-three thousand five hundred and fifty dollars be granted to His Majesty to defray the expenses of Cobourg Hospital for the year ending 31st October, 1927.

72. *Resolved*, That a sum not exceeding Four hundred and fifteen thousand six hundred and fifty dollars be granted to His Majesty to defray the expenses of Hamilton Hospital for the year ending 31st October, 1927.

73. *Resolved,* That a sum not exceeding Two hundred and sixty-three thousand nine hundred and thirty dollars be granted to His Majesty to defray the expenses of Kingston Hospital for the year ending 31st October, 1927.

74. *Resolved,* That a sum not exceeding Four hundred and thirty-six thousand four hundred and sixty dollars be granted to His Majesty to defray the expenses of London Hospital for the year ending 31st October, 1927.

75. *Resolved,* That a sum not exceeding Two hundred and fifty thousand two hundred and thirty dollars be granted to His Majesty to defray the expenses of Mimico Hospital for the year ending 31st October, 1927.

76. *Resolved,* That a sum not exceeding Three hundred and fifty-five thousand one hundred and two dollars be granted to His Majesty to defray the expenses of Orillia Hospital for the year ending 31st October, 1927.

77. *Resolved,* That a sum not exceeding One hundred and thirty-four thousand and ninety dollars be granted to His Majesty to defray the expenses of Penetanguishene Hospital for the year ending 31st October, 1927.

78. *Resolved,* That a sum not exceeding Three hundred and fifty-eight thousand nine hundred and two dollars be granted to His Majesty to defray the expenses of the Toronto Hospital for the year ending 31st October, 1927.

79. *Resolved,* That a sum not exceeding Four hundred and forty-three thousand nine hundred and seventy-nine dollars be granted to His Majesty to defray the expenses of Whitby Hospital for the year ending 31st October, 1927.

80. *Resolved,* That a sum not exceeding Eighty-nine thousand six hundred and thirty-one dollars be granted to His Majesty to defray the expenses of Woodstock Hospital for the year ending 31st October, 1927.

81. *Resolved,* That a sum not exceeding Three hundred and six thousand and ten dollars be granted to His Majesty to defray the expenses of Guelph Reformatory for the year ending 31st October, 1927.

82. *Resolved,* That a sum not exceeding Two hundred and twenty-six thousand dollars be granted to His Majesty to defray the expenses of Guelph Reformatory Industries for the year ending 31st October, 1927.

83. *Resolved,* That a sum not exceeding Eighty thousand three hundred dollars be granted to His Majesty to defray the expenses of Mercer Reformatory, Toronto, for the year ending 31st October, 1927.

84. *Resolved,* That a sum not exceeding Ten thousand dollars be granted to His Majesty to defray the expenses of Mercer Reformatory Industries, Toronto, for the year ending 31st October, 1927.

85. *Resolved,* That a sum not exceeding Two hundred and thirty-nine thousand seven hundred dollars be granted to His Majesty to defray the expenses of Burwash Industrial Farm for the year ending 31st October, 1927.

86. *Resolved*, That a sum not exceeding Thirty-five thousand eight hundred and twenty dollars be granted to His Majesty to defray the expenses. of Fort William Industrial Farm for the year ending 31st October, 1927.

87. *Resolved*, That a sum not exceeding Fifty-one thousand dollars be granted to His Majesty to defray the expenses of Boys' Training School, Bowmanville for the year ending 31st October, 1927.

88. *Resolved*, That a sum not exceeding Seventy-five thousand dollars be granted to His Majesty to defray the expenses of Toronto Reception Hospital for the year ending 31st October, 1927.

89. *Resolved*, That a sum not exceeding Sixty-four thousand one hundred dollars be granted to His Majesty to defray the expenses of Miscellaneous Public Institutions for the year ending 31st October, 1927.

90. *Resolved*, That a sum not exceeding Sixteen thousand six hundred and twenty-five dollars be granted to His Majesty to defray the expenses of Minister's Office, Agriculture Department, for the year ending 31st October, 1927.

91. *Resolved*, That a sum not exceeding Nineteen thousand and seventy-five dollars be granted to His Majesty to defray the expenses of Statistics and Publications Office for the year ending 31st October, 1927.

92. *Resolved*, That a sum not exceeding Two hundred and twenty-eight thousand seven hundred and fifty dollars be granted to His Majesty to defray the expenses of Agricultural and Horticultural Societies for the year ending 31st October, 1927.

93. *Resolved*, That a sum not exceeding One hundred and ninety-six thousand one hundred dollars be granted to His Majesty to defray the expenses of Live Stock Branch for the year ending 31st October, 1927.

94. *Resolved*, That a sum not exceeding Seventy-three thousand five hundred and twenty-five dollars be granted to His Majesty to defray the expenses of Institutes Branch, for the year ending 31st October, 1927.

95. *Resolved*, That a sum not exceeding Two hundred and thirty-one thousand seven hundred and fifty dollars be granted to His Majesty to defray the expenses of Dairy Branch for the year ending 31st October, 1927.

96. *Resolved*, That a sum not exceeding Ninety-nine thousand nine hundred and twenty-five dollars be granted to His Majesty to defray the expenses of Fruit Branch for the year ending 31st October, 1927.

97. *Resolved*, That a sum not exceeding Three hundred and forty-six thousand four hundred and fifty dollars be granted to His Majesty to defray the expenses of Agricultural Representatives' Branch for the year ending 31st October, 1927.

98. *Resolved*, That a sum not exceeding Forty-six thousand two hundred and twenty-five dollars be granted to His Majesty to defray the expenses of Markets and Co-operation Branch for the year ending 31st October, 1927.

99. *Resolved*, That a sum not exceeding Seventy thousand dollars be granted to His Majesty to defray the expenses of Agricultural Development Board for the year ending 31st October, 1927.

100. *Resolved*, That a sum not exceeding Sixty-four thousand dollars be granted to His Majesty to defray the expenses of Kemptville Agricultural School for the year ending 31st October, 1927.

101. *Resolved*, That a sum not exceeding Thirty-seven thousand six hundred and fifty dollars be granted to His Majesty to defray the expenses of Ontario Veterinary College for the year ending 31st October, 1927.

102. *Resolved*, That a sum not exceeding Twenty-three thousand dollars be granted to His Majesty to defray the expenses of Western Ontario Experimental Farm, Ridgetown, for the year ending 31st October, 1927.

103. *Resolved*, That a sum not exceeding Sixteen thousand dollars be granted to His Majesty to defray the expenses of New Ontario Demonstration Farm for the year ending 31st October, 1927.

104. *Resolved*, That a sum not exceeding Two hundred and eleven thousand two hundred and twenty-five dollars be granted to His Majesty to defray the expenses of Colonization and Immigration Branch for the year ending 31st October, 1927.

105. *Resolved*, That a sum not exceeding Forty-eight thousand one hundred dollars be granted to His Majesty to defray the expenses of Miscellaneous Services for the year ending 31st October, 1927.

106. *Resolved*, That a sum not exceeding Three hundred and forty-eight thousand six hundred and forty dollars be granted to His Majesty to defray the expenses of Ontario Agricultural College for the year ending 31st October, 1927.

107. *Resolved*, That a sum not exceeding Fifty-eight thousand five hundred and sixty-two dollars be granted to His Majesty to defray the expenses of Macdonald Institute and Hall for the year ending 31st October, 1927.

108. *Resolved*, That a sum not exceeding Two hundred and fifty-three thousand nine hundred and sixty-eight dollars be granted to His Majesty to defray the expenses of Farm and Departmental Expenses for the year ending 31st October, 1927.

109. *Resolved*, That a sum not exceeding Five hundred and thirty-one thousand dollars be granted to His Majesty to defray the expenses of Miscellaneous for the year ending 31st October, 1927.

The several Resolutions, having been read the second time were concurred in.

The House, according to Order, resolved itself into the Committee of Ways and Means.

(*In the Committee.*)

Resolved, That there be granted out of the Consolidated Revenue Fund of this Province a sum not exceeding Forty-seven millions two hundred and thirty-five thousand six hundred and twenty-four dollars and seventy-six cents to meet the Supply to that extent granted to His Majesty.

Mr. Speaker resumed the Chair; and Mr. Rankin reported, That the Committee had come to a Resolution.

Ordered, That the Report be received forthwith.

Mr. Rankin, from the Committee on Ways and Means, reported a Resolution which was read as follows:—

Resolved, That there be granted out of the Consolidated Revenue Fund of this Province a sum not exceeding Forty-seven millions two hundred and thirty-five thousand six hundred and twenty-four dollars and seventy-six cents to meet the Supply to that extent granted to His Majesty.

The Resolution, having been read the second time, was agreed to.

———

The following Bill was then introduced and read the first time:—

Bill (No. 190), intituled "An Act for granting to His Majesty certain sums of money to defray the expenses of Civil Government for the year ending 31st October, One thousand nine hundred and twenty-six, and for the year ending 31st day of October, One thousand nine hundred and twenty-seven, and for other purposes therein mentioned." *Mr. Price.*

Ordered, That the Bill be read the second time forthwith.

The Bill was then read a second time.

Ordered, That the Bill be read a third time forthwith.

The Bill was then read the third time and passed.

———

The Provincial Secretary presented to the House, by command of His Honour the Lieutenant-Governor:—

Report of the Department of Lands and Forests for 1925. (*Sessional Papers, No. 3.*)

Report of the Workmen's Compensation Board for 1925. (*Sessional Papers, No. 28.*)

Report of the Temiskaming and Northern Ontario Railway Commission for 1925. (*Sessional Papers, No. 23.*)

Report of the Provincial Auditor for 1924-25. (*Sessional Papers, No. 27.*)

Report of the Minister of Education for 1925. (*Sessional Papers, No. 11.*)

Report of the Secretary and Registrar of the Province of Ontario for 1925. (*Sessional Papers, No. 55.*)

Report of Hydro-Electric Power Commission for Ontario for 1925. (*Sessional Papers, No. 26.*)

Report of the Ontario Railway and Municipal Board for 1925. (*Sessional Papers, No. 24.*)

Report under the Children's Protection Act for 1925. (*Sessional Papers, No. 19.*)

Report of the Ontario Veterinary College for 1925. (*Sessional Papers, No. 29.*)

Report of the Minister of Agriculture for the year 1925. (*Sessional Papers, No. 21.*)

Report of the Statistics Branch of the Ontario Department of Agriculture. (*Sessional Papers, No. 22.*)

Report of the Commissioner of Provincial Police Force for 1925. (*Sessional Papers, No. 56.*)

The following Bills were read the third time and passed:—

Bill (No. 138), To amend the Public Parks Act.

Bill (No. 25), Respecting the Township of York.

Bill (No. 27), Respecting the Township of East York.

Bill (No. 13), Respecting the City of Fort William.

Bill (No. 54), Respecting the City of Toronto.

The House then adjourned at 5.50 p.m.

THURSDAY, APRIL 1st, 1926.

Pʀᴀʏᴇʀs.   11 O'Cʟᴏᴄᴋ A.M.

The following Bills were severally introduced and read the first time:—

Bill (No. 191), intituled "An Act to make certain changes in the Law in consequence of the Revision of the Statutes." *Mr. Nickle.*

———

The following Bills were severally read the second time:—

Bill (No. 41), Respecting the Town of Huntsville.

Referred to a Committee of the Whole House To-day.

Bill (No. 52), Respecting the City of Sault Ste. Marie.

Referred to a Committee of the Whole House To-day.

Bill (No. 60), Respecting the Township of Tisdale.

Referred to a Committee of the Whole House To-day.

Bill (No. 61), Respecting the Victoria Hospital at Renfrew.

Referred to a Committee of the Whole House To-day.

Bill (No. 187), Respecting the Widening of Bloor Street in the City of Toronto.

Referred to a Committee of the Whole House To-day.

Bill (No. 185), To amend the Ontario Game and Fisheries Act.

Referred to a Committee of the Whole House To-day.

Bill (No. 186), For the Protection of the Property in Foxes kept in captivity.

Referred to a Committee of the Whole House To-day.

———

The House resolved itself into a Committee severally to consider the following Bills:—

Bill (No. 109), To amend the Local Improvement Act.

Bill (No. 105), To amend the Local Improvement Act.

Bill (No. 41), Respecting the Town of Huntsville.

Bill (No. 52), Respecting the City of Sault Ste. Marie.

Bill (No. 60), Respecting the Township of Tisdale.

Bill (No. 61), Respecting the Victoria Hospital at Renfrew.

Bill (No. 189), To consolidate and amend the Assessment Amendment Act, 1926.

Mr. Speaker resumed the Chair; and Mr. Black reported, That the Committee had directed him to report the several Bills without amendments.

Ordered, That the Bills reported be severally read the third time To-day.

———

The House resolved itself into a Committee to consider Bill (No. 182), To amend the Public Lands Act, and, after some time spent therein, Mr. Speaker resumed the Chair; and Mr. Black reported, That the Committee had directed him to report the Bill without any amendment.

Ordered, That the Bill be read the third time To-day.

———

The House resolved itself into a Committee to consider Bill (No. 183), To amend the Consolidated Municipal Act, 1922, and, after some time spent therein, Mr. Speaker resumed the Chair; and Mr. Black reported, That the Committee had directed him to report the Bill without any amendment.

Ordered, That the Bill be read the third time To-day.

———

The House resolved itself into a Committee to consider Bill (No. 184), Respecting the Royal Agricultural Fair Association and the City of Toronto, and, after some time spent therein, Mr. Speaker resumed the Chair; and Mr. Black reported, That the Committee had directed him to report the Bill without any amendment.

Ordered, That the Bill be read the third time To-day.

The House resolved itself into a Committee to consider Bill (No. 188), To consolidate and amend the Municipal Amendment Act, 1926, and, after some time spent therein, Mr. Speaker resumed the Chair; and Mr. Black reported, That the Committee had directed him to report the Bill with certain amendments.

Ordered, That the amendments be taken into consideration forthwith.

The amendments, having been read the second time, were agreed to.

Ordered, That the Bill be read the third time To-day.

———

The House resolved itself into a Committee to consider Bill (No. 185), To amend the Ontario Game and Fisheries Act, and, after some time spent therein, Mr. Speaker resumed the Chair; and Mr. Black reported, That the Committee had directed him to report the Bill with certain amendments.

Ordered, That the amendments be taken into consideration forthwith.

The amendments, having been read the second time, were agreed to.

Ordered, That the Bill be read the third time To-day.

———

The House resolved itself into a Committee to consider Bill (No. 186), For the Protection of the Property in Foxes kept in captivity, and, after some time spent therein, Mr. Speaker resumed the Chair; and Mr. Black reported, That the Committee had directed him to report the Bill without any amendment.

Ordered, That the Bill be read the third time To-day.

———

The House resolved itself into a Committee to consider Bill (No. 181), To validate the Grant from the College of Physicians and Surgeons of Ontario to the Banting Research Endowment Fund, and, after some time spent therein, Mr. Speaker resumed the Chair; and Mr. Black reported, That the Committee had directed him to report the Bill without any amendment.

Ordered, That the Bill be read the third time To-day.

———

The Order of the Day for the third reading of Bill (No. 110), To amend Section 16 of the University Act, having been read,

Ordered, That the Order be discharged, and that the Bill be withdrawn.

The Order of the Day for the second reading of Bill (No. 98), Respecting the Investigation of Industrial Disputes within the Province, having been read,

Ordered, That the Order be discharged, and that the Bill be withdrawn.

Mr. Lewis, from the Committee on Public Accounts, presented their Report, which was read as follows:—

Your Committee has had produced before it the following accounts, vouchers, correspondence and particulars in connection with the Public Accounts of the Province of Ontario for the fiscal year ended the 31st October, 1925, and also certain accounts, vouchers and auditors' reports in connection with the business dealings of the Lyons Fuel & Supply Company and the Sault Ste. Marie Coal & Wood Company, with any departments of the Government of the Province of Ontario, or with any contractors, licensees or vendors having dealings with any such department, all of which it has carefully examined and considered.

Details in connection with the following items:—

Item of $414,777.09, page G. 34, Public Accounts, to McNamara Construction Company.

Items of $1,845.89, page G. 12, $8,187.32, page G. 30, $816.24, page G. 41, to E. L. Bedford.

Fire insurance carried by the Government and premiums paid thereon.

Item of $900,000, page 14, Public Accounts, receipt by the Province and generally as to Provincial Dispensaries.

Various items under heading of Motion Picture Bureau, pages N. 3, 12, 13, 14, of the Public Accounts, and generally as to the Motion Picture Bureau and Radio Publicity.

Item of $4,827.67, page K. 22, Public Accounts, paid to T. J. McLean on Contract 1223, grading, Brampton-Chatsworth project, Peel Township.

Your Committee dealt with the request of the former Minister of Lands and Forests, Hon. James Lyons, for an investigation of all business transactions of himself or either of the companies in which he is interested with any department of the Government and examined fourteen witnesses in this connection. In addition, the firm of Clarkson, Gordon & Dilworth, Chartered Accountants and Auditors, at the request of your Committee, made an audit of the books of the Lyons Fuel & Supply Company and the Sault Ste. Marie Coal and Wood Company, and presented to the Committee a report of that audit.

Major A. E. Nash, for the Clarkson firm, reported to the Committee that after an exhaustive examination of the books of the two Companies referred to, in which he was assisted by the officials and auditors of the companies, he found the books in good order and his investigation revealed nothing to warrant any suspicion. The investigation conducted by your Committee confirmed this view.

So far as the evidence before your Committee enables the reaching of a conclusion, your Committee feel that the Hon. Jas. Lyons is entitled to a complete and unqualified exoneration from any breach of the Legislative Assembly Act, and that his Companies' business record with relation to the Government and any contractors having business relations with the Government is beyond reproach.

Your Committee investigated the circumstances under which the firm of Geo. Oakley & Sons secured the contract to supply and erect the stonework on the new Whitney Block of the Parliament Building, and found the entire transaction to be quite regular and the contract well carried out with benefit to the Province.

In connection with the investigation into the treatment by T. J. McLean, contractor on the Caledon Road, of the men employed by him, your Committee is pleased to learn that the Honourable the Prime Minister has made an announcement in the House dealing with this matter, which obviates the necessity of any finding or recommendation by your Committee.

Some evidence having been given by one of the witnesses before the Committee reflecting on the efficiency of the Provincial Air Service of the Forestry Branch, your Committee, having heard the evidence of the witness in question and the evidence of Captain Roy Maxwell, Director of the Air Service, are of the opinion that the criticism suggested was not justified by the facts and that the establishment of this branch of the Public Service has been amply justified by the result.

Several other matters were brought before your Committee and were investigated, but in no case did the results of such investigation suggest any action to your Committee.

Your Committee has held, during the Session, sixteen meetings and has examined thirty-one witnesses, list of which is herewith attached, and submit herewith the Minutes of the Proceedings and the evidence given. as taken by the reporter.

Witnesses examined: Hon. Jas. Lyons, Sault Ste. Marie; J. J. Fitzpatrick, Sault Ste. Marie; G. J. Lamb, Sault Ste. Marie; H. D. McNamara, Toronto; G. A. McNamara, Toronto; A. J. McAllister, Sault Ste. Marie; E. J. Hoskins, Sudbury; Claude Findlay, Niagara Falls; Harry C. Lyons, Sault Ste. Marie; E. L. Bedford, Sault Ste. Marie; E. J. Zavitz, Toronto; C. H. Fullerton, Toronto; Geo. Oakley, M.P.P., Toronto; C. Blake Jackson, Toronto; A. E. Nash, Toronto; R. H. Briggs, Toronto; W. R. Maxwell, Toronto; Jno. Brass, Toronto; Mrs. Emily Franklin, Caledon; Kenneth Hannahson, Orangeville; Mrs. Carrie Sutton, Caledon; Richard Russell, Orangeville; A. J. McEnaney, Toronto; Jas. McDevitt, Toronto; R. L. McClintock, Streetsville; Jno. Telford, Toronto; G. E. Patton, Toronto; A. H. Birmingham, Toronto; J. H. Ferguson, Toronto; J. A. LaBerge, Sudbury; W. H. Brown, Toronto.

Resolved, That this House doth concur in the foregoing Report.

Mr. Nickle, from the Standing Committee on Private Bills, presented their Twelfth Report which was read as follows and adopted.

Your Committee beg to report the following Bills with certain amendments:—

Bill (No. 12), An Act respecting the City of Toronto.

Bill (No. 22), An Act to amend the United Church of Canada Act.

Bill (No. 19), An Act respecting the Town of Weston, the Township of York and the Toronto Transportation Commission.

Bill (No. 34), An Act to incorporate the City of Ford City.

Bill (No. 45), An Act respecting the Essex Border Utilities Commission.

Bill (No. 59), An Act respecting the Corporation of the City of Sarnia.

Bill (No. 180), An Act to authorize the transfer of certain radial railways from the Hydro-Electric Power Commission of Ontario to the Corporation of the City of Toronto.

Your Committee would recommend that the fees less the actual cost of printing be remitted on Bill (No. 6), "An Act respecting the John Curry Estate and the proposed Essex Border Utilities Commission General Hospital," the same not having been proceeded with; and on Bill (No. 7), "An Act respecting the Town of Ojibway and its separation from the County of Essex for municipal purposes"; Bill (No. 20), "An Act respecting the Board of Education for the City of Toronto"; Bill (No. 39), "An Act respecting the Town of Eastview"; Bill (No. 43), "An Act respecting the Toronto Police Benefit Fund"; Bill (No. 53), "An Act to incorporate the National Council of Young Men's Christian Associations of Canada," the same having been withdrawn by the promoters thereof; and on Bill (No. 57), "An Act respecting Ottawa Police Benefit Fund Association," the fees and all fines and penalties on the ground that it is one relating to a benevolent institution.

Ordered, That the fees less the actual cost of printing be remitted on Bill (No. 6), "An Act respecting the John Curry Estate and the proposed Essex Border Utilities Commission General Hospital," the same not having been proceeded with; and on Bill (No. 7), "An Act respecting the Town of Ojibway and its separation from the County of Essex for Municipal Purposes"; Bill (No. 20), "An Act respecting the Board of Education for the City of Toronto"; Bill (No. 39), "An Act respecting the Town of Eastview"; Bill (No. 43), "An Act respecting the Toronto Police Benefit Fund"; Bill (No. 53), "An Act to incorporate the National Council of Young Men's Christian Associations of Canada," the same having been withdrawn by the promoters thereof; and on Bill (No. 57), "An Act respecting Ottawa Police Benefit Fund Association," the fees and all fines and penalties on the ground that it is one relating to a benevolent institution.

The following Bills were severally read the second time:—

Bill (No. 22), To amend the United Church of Canada Act.

Referred to a Committee of the Whole House To-day.

Bill (No. 12), Respecting the City of Toronto.

Referred to a Committee of the Whole House To-day.

Bill (No. 19), Respecting the Town of Weston, the Township of York and the Toronto Transportation Commission.

Referred to a Committee of the Whole House To-day.

Bill (No. 34), To incorporate the City of Ford City.

Referred to a Committee of the Whole House To-day .

Bill (No. 45), Respecting the Essex Border Utilities Commission.

Referred to a Committee of the Whole House To-day.

Bill (No. 59), Respecting the Corporation of the City of Sarnia.

Referred to a Committee of the Whole House To-day.

Bill (No. 180), To authorize the transfer of certain radial railways from the Hydro-Electric Power Commission of Ontario to the Corporation of the City of Toronto.

Referred to a Committee of the Whole House To-day.

Mr. Currie, from the Standing Committee on Printing, presented their Reports, which were read as follows:—

The Standing Committee on Printing held its first meeting on March 25th, 1926, in the office of the King's Printer, at 10 a.m., the following members present: Messrs. Currie, Belanger, Gray, Proulx, Wigle, Stedman, Biggs.

By unanimous vote of the Committee Col. J. A. Currie was elected Chairman.

The Committee ordered the King's Printer to procure for members of the Legislature, to the number of 115 copies, the following publications:—

Heaton's Handbook.

Canadian Almanac 1926.

Farm Economy.

The Parliamentary Guide.

Canadian Annual Review

Summary of the Laws of the Province pertaining to mining

A.B.C. Company Incorporations of Ontario.

The Committee ordered "held over" the following publications:—

The Universal Handbook

5,000 Facts about Canada.

Prominent People of Ontario

The Committee ordered departmental reports and sessional papers printed in the quantities below:—

1. Public Accounts...................... ......
2. Estimates........................... ......
3. Lands and Forests................... ......
4. Mines.............................. ......
5. Legal Offices....................... ......
6. Insurance and Friendly Societies....... ......
7. Loan Corporations................... ......
8. Public Works........................ ......
9. Game and Fisheries.................. ......
10. Labour............................ ......
11. Education.......................... ......
12. University of Toronto............... ......
13. Births, Marriages and Deaths......... ......
14. Board of Health.................... ......
15. Hospital for Insane, Feeble Minded Epileptics...................... ......
16. Board of Parole and Probation (With which is included Prisons and Reformatories Report)................ ......
17. Hospitals and Charities.............. ......
18. Prisons and Reformatories........... ......
19. Neglected Children................. ......

20. Ontario Temperance Act.............. ......

21. Department of Agriculture (Minister).. ......

22. Department of Agriculture (Statistics).. ......

23. Temiskaming & N. O. Railway........ ......

24. Ontario Railway & Municipal Board.. ......

25. Elections............................ ......

26. Hydro-Electric Power Commission..... ......

27. Provincial Auditor.................... ......

28. Workmen's Compensation Board....... ......

29. Ontario Veterinary College............ ......

30. Legislative Grants to Public and Rural
    Schools........................... ...... Hold

31. Regulations and Orders-in-Council re
    Education Act..................... ...... Hold

32. Report Regarding the State of the
    Library........................... ...... Not to print

33. Report of Clarkson re Gasoline........ ...... Not to print

34. Report of Niagara Falls Park Com-
    mission........................... ...... Print

35. Return re Expenditure on Provincial
    Highways.......................... ...... Hold

36. Report Ontario Athletic Commission.. ...... Not to print

37. Return re Electric Power.............. ...... Print

38. Return re Works, etc., in the District of
    Algoma and Sudbury............... ...... Not to print

39. Report re the Purchase of Provincial
    Bonds............................. ...... Not to print

40. Return re Correspondence re Whitefish
    Bay.............................. ...... Not to print

41. Return re School Section of East Whitby ...... Not to print

42. Return re Legislative Secretary for
    Northern Ontario.................. ...... Not to print

43. Return re Copies of Orders-in-Council re
    The Ontario Insurance Act......... ...... Not to print

44. Report re Distribution of Revised
    Statutes.......................... ...... Not to print

45. Return re Counsel fees re School Litigation............................ ...... Not to print

46. Return re Appointments in Northern
Ontario.......................... ...... Not to print

47. Report of Minimum Wage Board...... ...... Hold

48. Report Agricultural Commission on
Marketable Products................ ...... Print

49. Report Fish and Game Committee..... ...... Print

50. Report Public Superannuation Board.. ...... Hold

The Committee then adjourned until Wednesday, March 31st at 10 a.m.

(Signed) J. A. CURRIE,
Chairman.

The Standing Committee on Printing held its second meeting on March 31st, 1926, in the office of the King's Printer at 10 o'clock, Col. J. A. Currie, M.P.P., in the Chair.

The Committee ordered the King's Printer to procure for the members of the Legislature, the following publications which were held over at the first meeting:—

The Universal Handbook.

The Committee decided not to purchase the following publications:—

"5,000 Facts About Canada."

"Prominent People of Ontario."

The Committee decided to deal with departmental reports and sessional papers held over from the first meeting as follows:—

No. 7. Report on Loan Corporations.—For Minister to decide.

No. 30. Legislative Grants to Rural and Public Schools.—Not to print.

No. 31. Regulations and Orders-in-Council *re* Education Act.—Not to print.

No. 35. Return *re* expenditure on Provincial Highways.—Not to print.

No. 47. Report of the Minimum Wage Board.—For Minister to decide.

No. 50. Report Public Superannuation Board.—Not to print.

No. 51. Return *re* amount spent by Hydro for Fire Insurance.—Not to print.

No. 52. Report *re* Niagara Falls Park Commission.—Print.

No. 53. Report Department of Northern Development.—Print.

No. 54. Copies of Orders-in-Council in connection with section 27 of Education Act.—Not to print.

After some discussion the Committee passed a recommendation, signed by the chairman, recommending that the several mimeograph, multigraph and other duplicating machines in the service be placed under the direct control of the King's Printer. The recommendation being attached herewith.

————————

The Committee also instructed the chairman to write to Hon. W. H. Price, Provincial Treasurer, pointing out that in the committee's considered opinion that the amount of $15 be placed with the King's Printer for the disbursement of stationery and sundries to members is too small. The Committee suggests that this amount be raised to $25 per session.

The Committee then adjourned.

Resolved, That the House doth concur in the foregoing Report.

————————

Mr. Raney asked to present report of minority members of Public Accounts Committee,

Objection being taken that report was not properly lodged.

Mr. Speaker ruled the matter out of order.

————————

Mr. Henry, from the Select Committee on Bill (No. 173), presents their report which was read as follows and adopted:—

Your Committee beg leave to announce that the decisions of the members of the Committee on all points have been unanimous.

Your Committee have rectified the boundaries of some electoral districts as to which errors occurred in the Act of 1925.

With a view to equalizing the representation of the County of Simcoe and the County of Grey, your Committee recommend the addition of two townships from the present electoral districts of South and West Simcoe, and the creation of a new electoral district of Southwest Simcoe in lieu of the present electoral districts of South and West Simcoe.

Your Committee, having in mind the demand for further representation for new Ontario, have divided the present electoral district of Cochrane into two electoral districts to be known as North Cochrane and South Cochrane respectively.

Your Committee further recommend the continuation in a northerly direction of the boundaries of the present electoral districts of Kenora, Fort William and Port Arthur so as to include, respectively, portions of the District of Patricia.

The following Bill was read the second time:—

Bill (No. 191), To make certain changes in the Law in consequence of the Revision of the Statutes.

Referred to a Committee of the Whole House To-day.

Mr. McBrien, from the Special Committee appointed to consider Bill (No. 103), "To revise and amend the Election Laws," and Bill (No. 104), "To consolidate and amend the Voters' Lists Act," presented the following report:—

Your Committee have carefully considered the said Bills to them referred and have prepared certain amendments thereto respectively.

The House resolved itself into a Committee to consider Bill (No. 103), To revise and amend the Election Laws, and, after some time spent therein, Mr. Speaker resumed the Chair; and Mr. Gray reported, That the Committee had directed him to report the Bill with certain amendments.

Ordered, That the amendments be taken into consideration forthwith.

The amendments, having been read the second time, were agreed to.

Ordered, That the Bill be read the third time To-day.

The House resolved itself into a Committee to consider Bill (No. 104), To consolidate and amend the Voters' Lists Act, and, after some time spent therein, Mr. Speaker resumed the Chair; and Mr. Gray reported, That the Committee had directed him to report the Bill with certain amendments.

Ordered, That the amendments be taken into consideration forthwith.

The amendments, having been read the second time, were agreed to.

Ordered, That the Bill be read the third time To-day.

The House resolved itself into a Committee to consider Bill (No. 173), To amend the Representation Act, and, after some time spent therein, Mr. Speaker resumed the Chair; and Mr. Gray reported, That the Committee had directed him to report the Bill with certain amendments.

Ordered, That the amendments be taken into consideration forthwith.

The amendments, having been read the second time, were agreed to.

Ordered, That the Bill be read the third time To-day.

The House resolved itself into a Committee to consider Bill (No. 191), To make certain changes in the Law in consequence of the Revision of the Statutes, and, after some time spent therein, Mr. Speaker resumed the Chair; and Mr. Black reported, That the Committee had directed him to report the Bill with certain amendments.

Ordered, That the amendments be taken into consideration forthwith.

The amendments, having been read the second time, were agreed to.

Ordered, That the Bill be read the third time To-day.

The Order of the Day for the third reading of Bill (No. 181), To validate the Grant from the College of Physicians and Surgeons of Ontario to the Banting Research Endowment Fund, having been read,

Ordered, That the Order be discharged, and that the Bill be withdrawn.

The Order of the Day for the third reading of Bill (No. 70), To consolidate and amend the Trustees Act, having been read,

Ordered, That the Order be discharged, and that the Bill be forthwith again referred to a Committee of the Whole, with instructions to amend the same.

The House accordingly resolved itself into the Committee; and, after some time spent therein, Mr. Speaker resumed the Chair; and Mr. Black reported, That the Committee had amended the Bill as directed.

Ordered, That the Bill be read the third time To-day.

The Order of the Day for the third reading of Bill (No. 76), To amend the Vendors and Purchasers Act, having been read,

Ordered, That the Order be discharged, and that the Bill be forthwith again referred to a Committee of the Whole, with instructions to amend the same.

The House accordingly resolved itself into the Committee; and, after some time spent therein, Mr. Speaker resumed the Chair; and Mr. Black reported, That the Committee had amended the Bill as directed.

Ordered. That the Bill be read the third time To-day.

The Order of the Day for the third reading of Bill (No. 77), Respecting Private Detectives, having been read,

Ordered, That the Order be discharged, and that the Bill be forthwith again referred to a Committee of the Whole, with instructions to amend the same.

The House accordingly resolved itself into the Committee; and, after some time spent therein, Mr. Speaker resumed the Chair; and Mr. Black reported, That the Committee had amended the Bill as directed.

Ordered, That the Bill be read the third time To-day.

The Order of the Day for the third reading of Bill (No. 78), To amend the Commissioners for Taking Affidavits Act, having been read,

Ordered, That the Order be discharged, and that the Bill be forthwith again referred to a Committee of the Whole, with instructions to amend the same.

The House accordingly resolved itself into the Committee; and, after some time spent therein, Mr. Speaker resumed the Chair; and Mr. Black reported, That the Committee had amended the Bill as directed.

Ordered, That the Bill be read the third time To-day.

The Order of the Day for the third reading of Bill (No. 81), To Consolidate and amend the Administration of Justice Expenses Act, having been read,

Ordered, That the Order be discharged, and that the Bill be forthwith again referred to a Committee of the Whole, with instructions to amend the same.

The House accordingly resolved itself into the Committee; and, after some time spent therein, Mr. Speaker resumed the Chair; and Mr. Black reported, That the Committee had amended the Bill as directed.

Ordered, That the Bill be read the third time To-day.

The Order of the Day for the third reading of Bill (No. 87), To consolidate and amend the Public Authorities Protection Act, having been read,

Ordered, That the Order be discharged, and that the Bill be forthwith again referred to a Committee of the Whole, with instructions to amend the same.

The House accordingly resolved itself into the Committee; and, after some time spent therein, Mr. Speaker resumed the Chair; and Mr. Black reported, That the Committee had amended the Bill as directed.

Ordered, That the Bill be read the third time To-day.

The Order of the Day for the third reading of Bill (No. 75), To amend the Cemetery Act, having been read;

Ordered, That the Order be discharged, and that the Bill be withdrawn.

The Order of the Day for the third reading of Bill (No. 89), To amend the Married Women's Property Act, having been read,

Ordered, That the Order be discharged, and that the Bill be forthwith again referred to a Committee of the Whole, with instructions to amend the same.

The House accordingly resolved itself into the Committee; and, after some time spent therein, Mr. Speaker resumed the Chair; and Mr. Black reported, That the Committee had amended the Bill as directed.

Ordered, That the Bill be read the third time To-day.

The Order of the Day for the third reading of Bill (No. 90), To consolidate and amend the Magistrates Act, having been read,

Ordered, That the Order be discharged, and that the Bill be forthwith again referred to a Committee of the Whole, with instructions to amend the same.

The House accordingly resolved itself into the Committee; and, after some time spent therein, Mr. Speaker resumed the Chair; and Mr. Black reported, That the Committee had amended the Bill as directed.

Ordered, That the Bill be read the third time To-day.

The Order of the Day for the third reading of Bill (No. 93), To consolidate and amend the Coroners Act, having been read,

Ordered, That the Order be discharged, and that the Bill be forthwith again referred to a Committee of the Whole, with instructions to amend the same.

The House accordingly resolved itself into the Committee; and, after some time spent therein, Mr. Speaker resumed the Chair; and Mr. Black reported, That the Committee had amended the Bill as directed.

Ordered, That the Bill be read the third time To-day.

The Order of the Day for the third reading of Bill (No. 94), To consolidate and amend the Constables Act, having been read,

Ordered, That the Order be discharged, and that the Bill be forthwith again referred to a Committee of the Whole, with instructions to amend the same.

The House accordingly resolved itself into the Committee; and, after some time spent therein, Mr. Speaker resumed the Chair; and Mr. Black reported, That the Committee had amended the Bill as directed.

Ordered, That the Bill be read the third time To-day.

————

The Order of the Day for the third Reading of Bill (No. 127), To amend the Ontario Companies Act, having been read,

Ordered, That the Order be discharged, and that the Bill be forthwith again referred to a Committee of the Whole, with instructions to amend the same.

The House accordingly resolved itself into the Committee; and, after some time spent therein, Mr. Speaker resumed the Chair; and Mr. Black reported, That the Committee had amended the Bill as directed.

Ordered, That the Bill be read the third time To-day.

————

The Order of the Day for the third reading of Bill (No. 128), To amend the Cemetery Act, having been read,

Ordered, That the Order be discharged, and that the Bill be forthwith again referred to a Committee of the Whole, with instructions to amend the same.

The House accordingly resolved itself into the Committee; and, after some time spent therein, Mr. Speaker resumed the Chair; and Mr. Black reported, That the Committee had amended the Bill as directed.

Ordered, That the Bill be read the third time To-day.

————

The Order of the Day for the third reading of Bill (No. 161), To amend the Assessment Act, having been read,

Ordered, That the Order be discharged, and that the Bill be forthwith again referred to a Committee of the Whole, with instructions to amend the same.

The House accordingly resolved itself into the Committee; and, after some time spent therein, Mr. Speaker resumed the Chair; and Mr. Black reported, That the Committee had amended the Bill as directed.

Ordered, That the Bill be read the third time To-day.

The Order of the Day for the third reading of Bill (No. 168), To amend the Ontario Companies Act, having been read,

Ordered, That the Order be discharged, and that the Bill be forthwith again referred to a Committee of the Whole, with instructions to amend the same.

The House accordingly resolved itself into the Committee; and, after some time spent therein, Mr. Speaker resumed the Chair; and Mr. Black reported, That the Committee had amended the Bill as directed.

Ordered, That the Bill be read the third time To-day.

The Order of the Day for the third reading of Bill (No. 149), To amend the Public Vehicles Act, having been read,

Ordered, That the Order be discharged, and that the Bill be forthwith again referred to a Committee of the Whole, with instructions to amend the same.

The House accordingly resolved itself into the Committee; and, after some time spent therein, Mr. Speaker resumed the Chair; and Mr. Black reported, That the Committee had amended the Bill as directed.

Ordered, That the Bill be read the third time To-day.

The Order of the Day for the third reading of Bill (No. 63), To consolidate and amend the Law respecting the Improvement of Public Highways, having been read,

Ordered, That the Order be discharged, and that the Bill be forthwith again referred to a Committee of the Whole, with instructions to amend the same.

The House accordingly resolved itself into the Committee; and, after some time spent therein, Mr. Speaker resumed the Chair; and Mr. Black reported, That the Committee had amended the Bill as directed.

Ordered, That the Bill be read the third time To-day.

The House resolved itself into a Committee to consider Bill (No. 187), Respecting the Widening of Bloor Street in the City of Toronto, and, after some time spent therein, Mr. Speaker resumed the Chair; and Mr. Black reported, That the Committee had directed him to report the Bill without any amendment.

Ordered, That the Bill be read the third time To-day.

9 J

The Order of the Day for the third reading of Bill (No. 176), To amend the Hospitals and Charitable Institutions Act, having been read,

Ordered, That the Order be discharged, and that the Bill be forthwith again referred to a Committee of the Whole, with instructions to amend tht same.

The House accordingly resolved itself into the Committee; and, after some time spent therein, Mr. Speaker resumed the Chair; and Mr. Black reported, That the Committee had amended the Bill as directed.

Ordered, That the Bill be read the third time To-day.

The Order of the Day for the third reading of Bill (No. 178), To amend the Ontario Insurance Act, having been read,

Ordered, That the Order be discharged, and that the Bill be forthwith again referred to a Committee of the Whole, with instructions to amend the same.

The House accordingly resolved itself into the Committee; and, after some time spent therein, Mr. Speaker resumed the Chair; and Mr, Black reported, That the Committee had amended the Bill as directed.

Ordered, That the Bill be read the third time To-day.

The Order of the Day for the third reading of Bill (No. 62), To amend the Burlington Beach Act, having been read,

Ordered, That the Order be discharged, and that the Bill be forthwith again referred to a Committee of the Whole, with instructions to amend the same.

The House accordingly resolved itself into the Committee; and, after some time spent therein, Mr. Speaker resumed the Chair; and Mr. Black reported, That the Committee had amended the Bill as directed.

Ordered, That the Bill be read the third time To-day.

The Order of the Day for the third reading of Bill (No. 184), Respecting the Royal Agricultural Fair Association and the City of Toronto, having been read,

Ordered, That the Order be discharged, and that the Bill be forthwith again referred to a Committee of the Whole, with instructions to amend the same.

The House accordingly resolved itself into the Committee; and, after some time spent therein, Mr. Speaker resumed the Chair; and Mr. Black reported, That the Committee had amended the Bill as directed.

Ordered, That the Bill be read the third time To-day.

Mr. Fisher, from the Standing Committee on Legal Bills, presented their First Report, which was read as follows:—

Your Committee have carefully considered Bill (No. 130), Respecting the Rights of Widows in the Estates of their Deceased Husbands, and report the said Bill without amendment for the consideration of the House.

Your Committee have also carefully considered Bill (No. 115), Respecting Damages with regard to Fatal Accidents to Infants, and report the said Bill without amendment for the consideration of the House.

———

The Order of the Day for the House to resolve itself into Committee of the Whole on Bill (No. 130), Respecting the Rights of Widows in the Estates of their Deceased Husbands, having been read,

Ordered, That the Order be discharged, and that the Bill be withdrawn.

———

The Order of the Day for the House to resolve itself into Committee of the Whole on Bill (No. 115), Respecting Damages with regard to Fatal Accidents to Infants, having been read,

Ordered, That the Order be discharged, and that the Bill be withdrawn.

———

The Order of the Day for the second reading of Bill (No. 96), To amend the Ontario Temperance Act, having been read,

Ordered, That the Order be discharged, and that the Bill be withdrawn.

———

The House resolved itself into a Committee, severally to consider the following Bills:—

Bill (No. 22), To amend the United Church of Canada Act.

Bill (No. 12), Respecting the City of Toronto.

Bill (No. 19), Respecting the Town of Weston, the Township of York and The Toronto Transportation Commission.

Bill (No. 34), Respecting the Town of Ford City.

Bill (No. 45), Respecting the Essex Border Utilities Commission.

Bill (No. 59), Respecting the Corporation of the City of Sarnia.

Bill (No. 180), To authorize the transfer of certain radial railways from the Hydro-Electric Power Commission of Ontario to the Corporation of the City of Toronto.

Mr. Speaker resumed the Chair; and Mr. Black reported, That the Committee had directed him to report the several Bills without amendments.

Ordered, That the Bills reported, be severally read the third time to-day.

————————

The following Bills were read the third time, and passed:—

Bill (No. 65), To amend the Royal Ontario Museum Act.

Bill (No. 66), To amend the Public Libraries Act.

Bill (No. 69), To amend the Department of Education Act.

Bill (No. 71), To amend the Unwrought Metal Sales Act.

Bill (No. 72), To provide for the Payment of an Annuity to the University of Toronto.

Bill (No. 73), To amend the Public Lands Act.

Bill (No. 76), To amend the Vendors and Purchasers Act.

Bill (No. 77), Respecting Private Detectives.

Bill (No. 88), Respecting the Department of Agriculture.

Bill (No. 91), To improve the Quality of Dairy Products.

Bill (No. 79), The Judges' Orders Enforcement Act.

Bill (No. 80), To amend the Devolution of Estates Act.

Bill (No. 82), To consolidate and amend the Justices of the Peace Act.

Bill (No. 83), To consolidate and amend the Crown Witnesses Act.

Bill (No. 84), To consolidate and amend the Fines and Forfeitures Act.

Bill (No. 90), To consolidate and amend the Magistrates Act.

Bill (No. 70), To consolidate and amend the Trustees Act.

Bill (No. 87), To consolidate and amend the Public Authorities Protection Act.

Bill (No. 89), To amend the Married Women's Property Act.

Bill (No. 102), To amend the Jurors Act.

Bill (No. 101), To amend the Ontario Telephone Act.

Bill (No. 92), To consolidate and amend the Crown Attorneys Act.

Bill (No. 93), To consolidate and amend the Coroners Act.

Bill (No. 78), To amend the Commissioners for taking Affidavits Act.

Bill (No. 94), To consolidate and amend the Constables Act.

Bill (No. 81), To consolidate and amend the Administration of Justice Expenses Act.

Bill (No. 127), To amend the Ontario Companies Act.

Bill (No. 121), To amend the Sanatoria for Consumptives Act.

Bill (No. 123), To amend the Corn Borer Act.

Bill (No. 122), Respecting Dentistry.

Bill (No. 116), To provide for the Development of Northern Ontario.

Bill (No. 4), To incorporate the Toronto East General Hospital.

Bill (No. 148), To amend the Highway Traffic Act.

Bill (No. 149), To amend the Public Vehicles Act.

Bill (No. 150), The Provincial Land Tax Amendment Act, 1926.

Bill (No. 62), To amend the Burlington Beach Act.

Bill (No. 151), To amend the School Laws.

Bill (No. 154), To amend the University Act.

Bill (No. 156), Respecting Psychiatric Hospitals.

Bill (No. 157), To amend the Surrogate Courts Act.

Bill (No. 158), To amend the Marriage Act.

Bill (No. 159), To amend the Municipal Act.

Bill (No. 164), To amend the Consolidated Municipal Act, 1922.

Bill (No. 160), To make further provision for Northern Ontario Development.

Bill (No. 161), To amend the Assessment Act.

Bill (No. 162), For raising money on the Credit of the Consolidated Revenue Fund.

Bill (No. 165), To amend the Power Commission Act.

Bill (No. 166), To amend the Hydro-Electric Railway Act, 1914.

Bill (No. 167), To amend the Loan and Trust Corporations Act.

Bill (No. 168), To amend the Ontario Companies Act.

Bill (No. 163), To amend the Power Commission Act.

Bill (No. 86), To amend the Legislative Assembly Act.

Bill (No. 63), To consolidate and amend the Law respecting the Improvement of Public Highways.

Bill (No. 169), To vest certain lands in His Majesty.

Bill (No. 170), To amend the Public Service Works on Highways Act, 1925.

Bill (No. 171), To amend the Ontario Habeas Corpus Act.

Bill (No. 172), To amend the Judicature Act.

Bill (No. 174), To amend the Wills Act.

Bill (No. 175), To amend the Adoption Act.

Bill (No. 176), To amend the Hospitals and Charitable Institutions Act.

Bill (No. 177), To consolidate and amend the Ontario Summary Convictions Act.

Bill (No. 178), To amend the Ontario Insurance Act, 1924.

Bill (No. 179), To amend the Workmen's Compensation Act.

Bill (No. 182), To amend the Public Lands Act.

Bill (No. 183), To amend the Consolidated Municipal Act, 1922.

Bill (No. 184), Respecting the Royal Agricultural Fair Association and the City of Toronto.

Bill (No. 173), To amend the Representation Act.

Bill (No. 185), To amend the Ontario Game and Fisheries Act.

Bill (No. 186), For the Protection of the Property in Foxes kept in captivity.

Bill (No. 41), Respecting the Town of Huntsville.

Bill (No. 52), Respecting the City of Sault Ste. Marie.

Bill (No. 60), Respecting the Township of Tisdale.

Bill (No. 61), Respecting the Victoria Hospital at Renfrew.

Bill, (No. 188), To consolidate and amend the Municipal Amendment Act, 1926.

Bill (No. 189), To consolidate and amend the Assessment Amendment Act, 1926.

Bill (No. 105), To amend the Local Improvement Act.

Bill (No. 109), To amend the Local Improvement Act.

Bill (No. 187), Respecting the Widening of Bloor Street in the City of Toronto.

Bill No. (128), To consolidate and amend the Cemetery Act.

Bill (No. 22), To amend the United Church of Canada Act.

Bill (No. 12), Respecting the City of Toronto.

Bill (No. 19), Respecting the Town of Weston, the Township of York and The Toronto Transportation Commission.

Bill (No. 34), Respecting the Town of Ford City.

Bill (No. 45), Respecting the Essex Border Utilities Commission.

Bill (No. 59), Respecting the Corporation of the City of Sarnia.

Bill (No. 180), To authorize the transfer of certain radial railways from the Hydro-Electric Power Commission of Ontario to the Corporation of the City of Toronto.

Bill (No. 103), To revise and amend the Election Laws.

Bill (No. 104), To consolidate and amend the Voters' Lists Act.

Bill (No. 191), To make certain changes in the Law in consequence of the Revision of the Statutes.

Mr. Belanger asked the following Question (No. 36):—

1. How many pupils are in attendance at the English-French Training Schools, comprising the two years of Fifth Class (or Lower School) and the final professional training class at (1) Sandwich; (2) Sturgeon Falls; (3) Embrun; (4) Vankleek Hill; (5) Ottawa.   2. From what home counties and districts do such pupils come, with the number from each county and district to each of the said English-French Training Schools.   3. Since the opening of each of the said schools at (1) Sandwich, (2) Sturgeon Falls, (a) how many pupils left at the end of the first year of the Fifth Class; (b) how many at the end of the second year; (c) how many at the end of the third year who did not teach in any school of Ontario.   4. How many pupils are in attendance at the three English-French Training Schools at Sandwich, Sturgeon Falls and Embrun who are (1) under 14 years of age; (2) 14 years of age; (3) 15 years of age; (4) 16 years of age; (5) 17 years of age; (6) over 17 years of age.

The Prime Minister replied as follows:—

1.

	Academic or Lower School	Professional	Total
(1) Sandwich......................	29	20	49
(2) Sturgeon Falls..................	131	27	158
(3) Embrun.......................	109	0	109
(4) Vankleek Hill..................	0	22	22
(5) Ottawa.......................	0	41	41

2. Sandwich: Essex, 41; Kent, 7; Glengarry, 1. Sturgeon Falls: Nipissing, 56; Sudbury, 39; Algoma, 9; Timiskaming, 17; Cochrane, 7; Parry Sound, 7; Rainy River, 1; Renfrew, 1; Simcoe, 14; Russell, 3; Stormont, 1; Prescott, 1; Essex, 1. Embrun: Russell, 38; Prescott, 35; Glengarry, 16; Stormount, 4; Renfrew, 2; Carlton, 4. Vankleek Hill: Prescott, 22. Ottawa: Carlton, 5; Russell, 26; Glengarry, 2; Prescott, 6; Quebec, 1; Timiskaming, 1.

3. (a) Sandwich, 4; Sturgeon Falls, 40. (b) Sandwich, 2; Sturgeon Falls, 8. (c) Sandwich, 4; Sgurgeon Falls, 0. (Note.—The training school at Sturgeon Falls was burned in 1919 and the records destroyed, thus affecting completeness of statistics of this school.

4.	Sandwich	Sturgeon Falls	Embrun
(1)...............................	0	0	0
(2)...............................	1	7	13
(3)...............................	8	24	24
(4)....	15	57	33
(5)...............................	15	37	20
(6)...............................	10	31	19

Mr. Bragg asked the following Question (No. 55):—

1. How many persons or companies made returns to the Minister of Highways under the Gasoline Tax Act, 1925, up to October 31st, 1925.

The Minister of Public Works and Highways replied as follows:—

One hundred.

Mr. Jamieson (South Grey) asked the following Question (No. 86):—

1. What commissions were appointed by the late Government and what was the total cost of each commission. 2. Who were the members of each commission. 3. What was the per diem allowance of each member. 4. How much was paid to each in addition to their per diem allowance.

The Prime Minister replied as follows:—

1.—

Commissions	Expenditure
Brantford Police Force	$2,529 00
Ontario Hospital, Hamilton	1,609 12
Ontario Hospital, London	433 31
Victoria Industrial School	600 00
Estate, John McMartin	7,575 00
Shooting of E. Bergeron, Windsor	287 50
Liquor Seizure, Chatham	93 53
Charges against O.T.A. Inspectors, Brockville	43 45
Police Magistrate Hastings, Dunnville	2,644 89
Police Magistrate Goodwin, Welland	386 55
Charges re O.T.A. Enforcement, Guelph	169 50
Death of Captain Huston	4,555 67
Natural Gas	99 68
Soldiers' Settlement, Kapuskasing	1,258 39
Crown Timber Licenses	175,181 50
Wages of Employees at Chippawa	375 00
Ontario Public Service	31,013 75
Hydro Radials	537,917 31
University Finances	6,100 15
Examination Irregularities	1,594 62
Hydro-Electric Inquiry	505,322 33
Addington Road	674 52
Rural Credits Committee	2,551 50
Iron Ore Committee	21,284 00
	$1,304,300 27

3 and 4. Brantford Police Force, W. D. Gregory, paid by City of Brantford. Ontario Hospital, J. Snider, $333.75. Ontario Hospital, London, J. MacBeth, $176.06. Victoria Industrial School, Dr. John Waugh, $150 honorarium; Dr. E. J. Pratt, $150 honorarium; Dr. J. W. Barton, $150 honorarium; Judge Mott, $150 honorarium. Travelling expenses, Dr. Partt, $26.30; Dr. Barton, $33.55; Judge Mott, $15.00. Estate of John McMartin, Mr. Justice Middleton, $150 lump sum. Shooting of Ernest Bergeron, His Honour Judge Wallace, $222; $60 per diem. Liquor seizure, Chatham, J. MacBeth, $14. Charges against O.T.A. Inspectors, Brockville, J. Dowsley. Dunnville Police Magistrate, J. A. Patterson, $638.46; $60 per diem. Welland Police Magistrate, His Honour Judge Campbell. O.T.A. Enforcement, Guelph, James Hales, Major-General Elliott. Death of Captain. Orville Huston, J. A. MacIntosh, $1,500.00; $60 per diem. Natural Gas, E. S. Estlin. Soldiers' Settlement, Kapuskasing, W. F. Nickle, K.C., no remuneration accepted; Lt.-Col. J. J. McLaren, $20 per diem; John Sharp, $20 per diem. Travelling expenses, W. F. Nickle, K.C., $109.70; Lt.-Col. J. J. McLaren, $384.23; John Sharp, $399.55. Crown Timber Licenses, Hon. Mr. Justice Latchford, $12,000.00; Hon. Mr. Justice Riddell, $12.000.00—lump sum payments. Wages of Employees at Chippawa, E. Watson, $75.00; W. H. Casselman, $75.00; M. M. McBride, $75.00; J. C. Tolmie, $75.00; E. E. Ross, $75.00. Public Service Commission, W. D. Gregory, $6,140.00; $40 per diem and $5,000 additional; N. Sommerville, $3,280.00; $40 per diem; Dr. H. L. Brittain, $1,480.00; A. Helleyer, $1,780.00; E. A. Pocock, $2,080.00; $20 per diem. Hydro Radial Commission, Mr. Justice Sutherland (Estate), lump sum payments, $6,000.00; W. A. Amos, lump sum payments, $6,000.00; expenses, $1,362.65; F. Bancroft, lump sum payments, $6,000.00; expenses, $245.00; C. H. Mitchell, $6,000.00; expenses, $221.45; A. F. McCallum, lump sum payments, $6,000.00; expenses, $1,967.00. University Finances, J. Alex Wallace, M.P., $800.00 honorarium; C. R. Somerville, $800.00 honorarium; T. A. Russell, $800.00 honorarium; Sir John Willison, $800.00 honorarium; Colonel A. P. Deroche, $800.00 honorarium; Rev. Archdeacon Cody, $800.00 honorarium. Travelling expenses, C. R. Somerville, $152.80; J. Alex Wallace, $184.90; Colonel Deroche, $352.65. Examination Irregularities, J. H. Putman, B.A., $1,200.00; $30 per diem. Hydro-Electric Inquiry Commission, $50.00 a day and $10.00 a day extra for living allowance. W. D. Gregory, $26,320; M. J. Haney, $22,090; L. Harris, $11,820; J. A. Ross, $10,700. Commissioner paid at the rtte of $125 per day. R. A. Ross, $34,125. Addington Road Commission, Gordon Waldron, K.C., $60 per diem, $240.00. Rural Credits Committee, Prof. W. T. Jackson, services, $1,275.00; expenses, $202.58; Thomas McMillan, services, $300.00; expenses, $206.15; M. H. Staples, services, $180.00; expenses, $126.75. Rate of payment, Professor Jackson, $300 per month; Messrs. McMillan and Staples, $10 per diem and travelling expenses.. Iron Ore Committee, George S. Cowie, $2,000.00 lump sum; G. A. Guess, $2,000.00 lump sum; H. E. T. Haultain, $2,000.00 lump sum; R. J. Hunt, $1,000.00 lump sum; J. G. Morrow, $2,000.00 lump sum.

Mr. Lethbridge asked the following Question (No. 130):—

1. What was the total expenditure of funds of the Province in proceedings before the Public Accounts Committee and in the courts to ascertain who

received the $15,000 that was shown by the books of the Home Bank to have been paid out on account of "Special Commissions" in the month of December, 1919. 2. How much money was spent by the Government in an effort to find out who received the sums of $12,000 and $25,000 shown by the books of the Home Bank to have been paid out on account of "Special Commissions" account in the month of September, 1919.

The Attorney-General replied as follows:—

There has been no division or apportionment of the cost of investigating the transactions referred to in this question. They were all the subject of inquiry by the Public Accounts Committee, where every facility was afforded for eliciting the facts.

Mr. Carty asked the following Question (No. 157):—

1. What were the several dates of the road contracts, numbers 706, 719 and 720, referred to at page J 15 of the Public Accounts for the year 1924. 2. Have the said contracts been completed. 3. When were they completed. 4. How much was paid by the Government in each case. 5. Does the Minister of Highways or his deputy know who are the members of the firm referred to at the said page of the Public Accounts for 1924 in connection with the said three contracts. 6. Who are they. 7. Did the Department have communications with both the members of the said firms with reference to the said contracts. 8. If not both, with which of them.

The Minister of Public Works and Highways replied as follows:—

See Return to Order of the House, dated March 26th. All communications were with the Company.

Mr. Nixon asked the following Question (No. 170):—

1. What was the cost to the Province of the radio publicity of 1925 in connection with the visit to Ontario of Mr. Rothapel and his company, known as "Roxy and His Gang." 2. To whom were the different amounts paid. 3. Who, representing the Government, was in charge of this matter. 4. Have the expenses all been paid. 5. Are there claims that have not been paid. 6. If so, by whom, and in what amounts.

The Provincial Treasurer replied as follows:—

1. Net cost approximately $16,000. The following amounts include cost of Radio Publicity and amounts expended in making ten scenic pictures which will eventually be sold. 2. Spent in Ontario: Bell Telephone Co. (Customs Duty on broadcasting equipment), $1,358.00; Bigwin Inn, $921.76; D. H. Haas (motor boat launch), $60.00; E. L. Ruddy (sign), $40.00; Toronto Transportation Commission (bus service), $341.00; R. S. Williams (piano rental and

tuning), $21.00; Canadian Pacific Railway (transportation), $87.00; Thunder Bay Improvement Company (wire and cable), $68.97; Bell Telephone Company (special installation), $10.00; Harbour Commission (for radio engineers—meals), $32.70; Thompson Ahern (customs brokers), $4.50; T. & N. O. Railway, $112.00; Capt. Murdock (motor launch), $35.00; King Edward Hotel, $1,995.60; Canadian National Railways (transportation), $10,452.25; G. W. Brownridge (travelling expenses, cash disbursements), $1,231.52; S. N. Baruch (travelling expenses), $135.00; L. C. Williams (travelling expenses), $93.80; total, $17,000.00. Spent in U.S.A.: American Telephone & Telegraph Company (setting up broadcasting equipment, transporting and linking up land lines with other cities—three broadcasts), $2,625.00; S. N. Baruch (rental portable broadcasting equipment), $2,485.00; (including his salary—three weeks), $735.00; K. Mott (assistant radio engineer), $138.55; J. Schretzmayer (assistant radio engineer), $158.00; L. C. Williams (special cinematographer), $1,050.00; total, $7,191.55. 3. Director, Motion Picture Bureau. 4. No. 5. Yes. 6. H. W. McKirdy, $507.65; Romanelli's Orchestra, $1,375.00; Canadian National Carbon Company, $49.43.

Mr. Homuth asked the following Question (No. 173):—

1. What is the name of the company cutting pulpwood on Concessions Nos. 6, 7, 8, 9 in the Township of Nipigon, Thunder Bay District. 2. Is it an American or Canadian company. 3. What is the name of the President and where does he live. 4. When did they begin to operate and are they operating now. 5. Does it manufacture or export its wood. 6. Does the company pay any dues to the Government. 7. If so, how much have they paid in each of the following years: 1921, 1922, 1923, 1924, 1925. 8. If not, why not.

The Minister of Lands and Forests replied as follows:—

1. Newago Company, Limited, operating on Concessions 6, 7, 8, 9, Nipigon Township, privately owned lands. The pine being the only timber in the Crown was sold under public competition to said company. 2. Cannot say, but company's collateral with Province is guaranteed by a recognized Canadian guarantee bonding company. 3. George W. Mead, Wisconsin Rapids, Wis., also President, Thunder Bay Paper Company, Limited. 4. Operating some years on Patented lands, acquired Crown timber first in 1922. 5. The company manufactures pulpwood from Crown land and exports material only from private lands. 6. Yes. 7. 1921-22, Nothing; 1922-23, $779.50; 1923-24, $7,229.25; 1924-25, $2,283.45. 8. See answer to No. 6.

Mr. Carty asked the following Question (No. 177):—

1. How many widows received help under the Mothers' Allowances Act for the past fiscal year. 2. How many children were concerned. 3. What has been the amount paid, year by year, since the system was established.

The Minister of Health and Labour replied as follows:—

1. Widows, 3,388; mothers with children and incapacitated husbands, 513; deserted mothers, 170; foster mothers to orphans, 114. 2. 12,500. 3. 1921, $774,667.00; 1922, $1,375,980.00; 1923, $1,607,354.00; 1924, $1,707,894.00; 1925, $1,781,281.00.

Mr. Wallis asked the following Question (No. 183):—

1. How much money has been spent to date on the trunk road running west from the City of Sault Ste. Marie.

The Minister of Lands and Forests replied as follows:—

1. Second Base Line, Korah Road, $38,305.00.

Mr. Black asked the following Question (No. 185):—

1. Is the Aero Film Company, Limited, the contracting company for films during 1920, 1921, 1922 and 1923, still in existence. 2. Has the Government been able to collect the $40,000.00 which this company was reported by the auditors to have defrauded the Province. 3. Who were the shareholders in this company. 4. Was Nelson Parliament a stockholder. 5. What members of the Drury Government held stock in this company. 6. Did several members of the Government take trips through Northern Ontario with officials of this company, and departmental employees. 7. Did the Province or the contractor pay expenses of these trips.

The Provincial Treasurer replied as follows:—

1. No. 2. This shortage has not been made good to the Treasury. 3, 4 and 5. No returns have been filed from which this information can be obtained. 6. Yes. (See evidence before Public Accounts Committee as recorded in Journals of the House, 1921, Appendix No. 2.) 7. See evidence above referred to.

Question No. 184, *re* Indoor Sports Film, withdrawn.

Mr. Wallis asked the following Question (No. 187):—

1. Do the Toronto Transportation Commission busses pay the usual license fee. 2. If not, what fee do they pay. 3. What other bus concerns are getting a similar privilege.

The Minister of Public Works and Highways replied as follows:—

1. Yes. 2. Answered by No. 1. 3. Answered by No. 1.

Mr. Chambers (Wellington West) asked the following Question (No. 189):—

1. Has the Honourable W. E. Raney, the member for East Wellington, a financial interest in the Copeland-Chatterson Company, Limited. 2. (a) Is the Honourable W. E. Raney a shareholder in the said company; (b) Is the Honourable W. E. Raney a director of the said company. 3. When did the Honourable W. E. Raney first become: (a) a shareholder in the company; (b) a director of the company. 4. What is the nature of the company's products. 5. Did the company do business with the Government during the time the Honourable W. E. Raney was Attorney-General. 6. Has the company done business with the Government while the Honourable W. E. Raney occupied a seat in this House as the Member for East Wellington. 7. Was this business obtained by public competition or otherwise. 8. Has the company made the returns to the Provincial Secretary required by law. 9. Do these returns show the salary or remuneration paid to the Honourable W. E. Raney as a director. If so, what was the amount. 10. Do these returns show the dividends of the company. If so, what was the rate of dividend paid to the Honourable W. E. Raney.

The Provincial Secretary replied as follows:—

1. Yes. 2. (a) Yes. (b) Yes. 3. The company's return shows Mr. Raney as (a) a shareholder, March 31st, 1907; (b) a director, March 31st, 1907. 4. The objects of the company are to manufacture and sell perpetual ledgers, loose-leaf systems, account books, etc., etc. 5. Yes. 6. Yes. 7. Not by competition, but by orders placed with the company. 8. Yes, with the exception of the years 1922 and 1923, when returns were not filed. 9. No. 10. No.

On motion of Mr. Mewhinney seconded by Mr. Sinclair,

Ordered, That there be laid before this House a Return showing: 1. What audit or audits other than those made by the Provincial Auditor have been carried on in the different departments of the Government and any institution under their control. 2. Was there any misapproprition of funds in any Department or Institution discovered by such audits. 3. If so, what was the amount in each case. 4. Were any employees dismissed on account of irregularities disclosed by such audits. 5. If so, how many.

Moved by Mr. Jamieson (South Grey), seconded by Mr. Black, That this House desires to record its appreciation of the valuable reports made by the Agricultural Enquiry Committee, and also of the efforts of the Committee to bring about an improvement in the production and the marketing of the agricultural resources of the Province. This House approves of the endeavours of the Committee to effect closer co-operation between the various provinces and the Dominion for the furtherance of the plans of the Imperial Government for placing the products of Canada more advantageously before the British consumer. This House is of opinion that the development of the natural resources of the Province, the opening up of mining areas, the improvement of the highways the extension of educational facilities, the distribution of electrical energy in rural districts and the fostering of industrial activities, are all objects that tend to better the condition of agriculture and should be encouraged in the interests of the farming community and will serve to promote the general welfare and prosperity of the country,

And after some time, Mr. Jamieson (South Grey), moved that the Debate be adjourned until Tuesday next.

On Motion of Mr. Ferguson, seconded by Mr. Henry,

That when this House adjourns to-day, it do stand adjourned until Tuesday next, the sixth day of April, at three of the clock in the afternoon.

The Provincial Secretary presented to the House, by command of His Honour the Lieutenant-Governor:—

Report of the Board of License Commissioners for Ontario for 1925. (*Sessional Papers, No. 20.*)

Report upon the Prisons and Reformatories for 1925. (*Sessional Papers, No. 18.*)

Report of the Inspector of Prisons and Public Charities upon the Hospitals and Charitable Institutions for 1925. (*Sessional Papers, No. 17.*)

Report upon the Hospitals for the Insane and Feeble-minded for 1925. (*Sessional Papers, No. 15.*)

Report of the Civil Service Commissioner for Ontario for 1925. (*Sessional Papers No. 59.*)

Report of the Mothers' Allowances Commission. (*Sessional Papers, No. 60.*)

Return to the Order of the House, dated March 5th, 1926,

That there be laid before this House a Return showing an agreement made on or about August 4th, 1922, between the Department of Lands and Forests and George B. Nicholson and Austin and Nicholson, in regard to trespasses set out in detail in said agreement and the disposition of the same by adjustment. (*Sessional Papers, No. 57.*)

Return to the Order of the House, dated April 9th, 1925,

That there be laid before the House a Return showing: 1. What was the total estimated tender of McNamara Construction Company for pavement and shoulders on road from Sudbury to Coniston. 2. What did the work actually cost. 3. What were the tenders of other contractors for this work. 4. What was the total estimated tender of the McNamara Construction Company for pavement from Timmins to South Porcupine. 5. What did the work actually cost. 6. What were the tenders of other contractors for this work. (*Sessional Papers, No. 58.*)

The House then adjourned at 11.00 p.m.

TUESDAY, APRIL 6TH, 1926.

PRAYERS.   3 O'CLOCK P.M.

The following Petitions were read and received:—

Of the Williamsburg Ratepayers' and Trustees' Association, respecting Township School Boards.

Of the South Manitoulin Wool Growers' Association, respecting Wolf Bounties.

Of the Bertie Township Council; also, of the Garrison Road Highway Association; also, of the Village of Fort Erie; also, of the Town of Bridgeburg, respecting Provincial Highways.

Of Representatives of Sutton Knox Church, respecting Church Union.

On motion of Mr. Ferguson, seconded by Mr. Price,

That when this House adjourns, it do stand adjourned until Eleven in the Forenoon To-morrow.

The Provincial Secretary presented to the House, by command of His Honour the Lieutenant-Governor:—

Report of the Commissioner under the Extramural Employment of Sentenced Persons Act, 1921. (*Sessional Papers, No. 61.*)

On motion of Mr. Ferguson, seconded by Mr. Martin,

Ordered, That the full Sessional Indemnity be paid to those members, absent on account of illness, or other unavoidable cause.

The Order of the Day for resuming the Adjourned Debate on the Motion that this House desires to record its appreciation of the valuable reports made by the Agricultural Enquiry Committee, and also of the efforts of the Committee to bring about an improvement in the production and the marketing of the agricultural resources of the Province. This House approves of the endeavours of the Committee to effect closer co-operation between the various Provinces and the Dominion for the furtherance of the plans of the Imperial Government for placing the products of Canada more advantageously before the British consumer. This House is of opinion that the development of the natural resources of the Province, the opening up of mining areas, the improvement of the highways, the extension of educational facilities, the distribution of electrical energy in rural districts and the fostering of industrial activities, are all objects that tend to better the condition of agriculture and should be encouraged in the interests of the farming community and will serve to promote the general welfare and prosperity of the country, having been read,

The Debate was resumed,

And after some time, it was, on the motion of Mr. Ferguson,

Ordered, That the Debate be adjourned until To-morrow.

The House then adjourned at 11.40 p.m.

WEDNESDAY, APRIL 7TH, 1926.

PRAYERS   11 O'CLOCK A.M.

The Order of the Day for resuming the Adjourned Debate on the Motion that this House desires to record its appreciation of the valuable reports made by the Agricultural Enquiry Committee, and also of the efforts of the Committee to bring about an improvement in the production and the marketing of the agricultural resources of the Province. This House approves of the endeavours of the Committee to effect closer co-operation between the various Provinces and the Dominion for the furtherance of the plans of the Imperial Government for placing the products of Canada more advantageously before the British consumer. This House is of opinion that the development of the natural resources of the Province, the opening up of mining areas, the improvement of the highways, the extension of educational facilities, the distribution of electrical energy in rural districts and the fostering of industrial activities, are all objects that tend to better the condition of agriculture and should be encouraged in the interests of the farming community and will serve to promote the general welfare and prosperity of the country, having been read,

The Debate was resumed,

And after some time, it was, on the motion of Mr. Jamieson (South Grey), seconded by Mr. Black,

Resolved, That this House desires to record its appreciation of the valuable reports made by the Agricultural Enquiry Committee, and also of the efforts of the Committee to bring about an improvement in the production and the marketing of the agricultural resources of the Province. This House approves of the endeavours of the Committee to effect closer co-operation between the various Provinces and the Dominion for the furtherance of the plans of the Imperial Government for placing the products of Canada more advantageously before the British consumer. This House is of opinion that the development of the natural resources of the Province, the opening up of mining areas, the improvement of the highways, the extension of educational facilities, the distribution of electrical energy in rural districts and the fostering of industrial activities, are all objects that tend to better the condition of agriculture and should be encouraged in the interests of the farming community and will serve to promote the general welfare and prosperity of the country.

On motion of Mr. Ferguson, seconded by Mr. Sinclair,

Resolved, That in view of the application to the United States Congress for legislation to authorize a further diversion of water by the Chicago Drainage Canal from the Great Lakes system, this House desires to place on record the following facts and considerations:—

The Sanitary District of Chicago has for some years been abstracting large quantities of water which is part of the watershed of the Great Lakes and diverting it to the Gulf of Mexico. The Province of Ontario, as joint riparian owner with the neighbouring States of the American Union, has a direct and vital interest in this matter.

There is in existence a Treaty between Great Britain and the United States, dated January 11th, 1909, which governs international boundary waters.

It has been decided by the Supreme Court of the United States that this Treaty expressly provides against uses affecting the natural level and flow of boundary waters without the authority of the United States or the Dominion of Canada within their respective jurisdictions and the approval of the International Commission.

That the application to the United States Congress for legislation to sanction a further diversion at Chicago is in effect a proposal to violate this Treaty.

That legal actions have been brought by several of the States of the Union to have it declared that the United States Congress cannot pass any Act depriving those States of the advantage of the flow of said water, and that such actions are still pending.

In view of these facts this Legislature is of opinion that attempts to deal with this matter by way of Legislation, without reference to Canada or its interests, are not in accord with the long-established friendly relations that have existed between these two countries and ought to continue.   ·

That this Legislature therefore requests that proper steps be taken to represent to the Government of the United States, through diplomatic channels, the unneighbourly character of the proposed legislation, and the desirability of reaching an early adjustment of the matter by a mutual arrangement in accordance with the terms of the Treaty.

The House then adjourned at 5.40 p.m.

THURSDAY, APRIL 8TH, 1926.

PRAYERS.   3 O'CLOCK P.M.

His Honour the Lieutenant-Governor proceeded in State to the Legislative Assembly and being seated upon the Throne,

Mr. Speaker addressed His Honour in the following words:—

May it please Your Honour:

The Legislative Assembly of the Province, having at its present Sittings thereof passed several Bills to which, in the name and on behalf of the said Legislative Assembly, I respectfully request Your Honour's Assent.

The Clerk Assistant then read the titles of the Acts that have passed, severally as follows:—

An Act to incorporate the Village of Rosseau.

An Act respecting the Township of Teck.

An Act respecting the amalgamation of the Toronto Western Hospital and Grace Hospital.

An Act respecting the Village of Waterford.

An Act respecting the Grey and Bruce Loan Company and the Owen Sound Loan and Savings Company.

An Act respecting the amalgamation of the Girls' Home and the Protestant Orphans' Home.

An Act respecting the City of Stratford.

An Act to extend the time for the completion of the Haliburton, Whitney and Mattawa Railway.

An Act respecting the Mount McKay and Kakabeka Falls Railway Company.

An Act respecting the Midland Simcoe Railway Company.

An Act respecting the Town of Gananoque.

An Act respecting the British Mortgage Loan Company of Ontario.

An Act respecting the City of Galt.

An Act to incorporate the Welland and Port Colborne Railway.

An Act respecting the City of Kitchener.

An Act respecting C. M. & G. Canadian Investments, Limited.

An Act respecting the Township of Thorah.

An Act respecting the Township of Grantham.

An Act to amend an Act relating to Hospitals and Charitable Institutions.

An Act to impose a Tax on Dogs and for the Protection of Sheep.

An Act to amend the Highway Traffic Act.

An Act respecting the City of Guelph and the Guelph Radial Railway Company.

An Act respecting the Town of Aylmer.

An Act respecting the City of Brantford.

An Act respecting the Board of Trustees of the Police Village of Alfred.

An Act to amend the Act to incorporate the Evangelical Lutheran Seminary of Canada.

An Act respecting the Township of Stamford.

An Act respecting the Town of Arnprior.

An Act to incorporate the Association of Accountants and Auditors in Ontario.

An Act respecting the Ottawa Police Benefit Fund Association.

An Act respecting the City of London.

An Act respecting the City of Ottawa.

An Act respecting the City of Toronto.

An Act to amend the Planning and Development Act.

An Act respecting the Town of Walkerville.

An Act respecting the Town of La Salle.

An Act respecting the Township of North York.

An Act respecting the City of Port Arthur.

An Act to amend the Public Parks Act.

An Act respecting the Township of York.

An Act respecting the Township of East York.

An Act respecting the City of Fort William.

An Act respecting the City of Toronto.

An Act to amend the Royal Ontario Museum Act.

An Act to amend the Public Libraries Act.

An Act to amend the Department of Education Act.

An Act to amend the Unwrought Metal Sales Act.

An Act to provide for the Payment of an Annuity to the University of Toronto.

An Act to amend the Public Lands Act.

An Act to amend the Vendors and Purchasers Act.

An Act respecting Private Detectives.

An Act respecting the Department of Agriculture.

An Act to improve the Quality of Dairy Products.

The Judges' Orders Enforcement Act.

An Act to amend the Devolution of Estates Act.

An Act to consolidate and amend the Justices of the Peace Act.

An Act to consolidate and amend the Crown Witnesses Act.

An Act to consolidate and amend the Fines and Forfeitures Act.

An Act to consolidate and amend the Magistrates Act.

An Act to consolidate and amend the Trustees Act.

An Act to consolidate and amend the Public Authorities Protection Act.

An Act to amend the Married Women's Property Act.

An Act to amend the Jurors Act.

An Act to amend the Ontario Telephone Act.

An Act to consolidate and amend the Crown Attorneys Act.

An Act to consolidate and amend the Coroners Act.

An Act to amend the Commissioners for taking Affidavits Act.

An Act to consolidate and amend the Constables Act.

An Act to consolidate and amend the Administration of Justice Expenses Act.

An Act to amend the Ontario Companies Act.

An Act to amend the Sanatoria for Consumptives Act.

An Act to amend the Corn Borer Act.

An Act respecting Dentistry.

An Act to provide for the Development of Northern Ontario.

An Act to incorporate the Toronto East General Hospital.

An Act to amend the Highway Traffic Act.

An Act to amend the Public Vehicles Act.

The Provincial Land Tax Amendment Act, 1926.

An Act to amend the Burlington Beach Act.

An Act to amend the School Laws.

An Act to amend the University Act.

An Act respecting Psychiatric Hospitals.

An Act to amend the Surrogate·Courts Act.

An Act to amend the Marriage Act.

An Act to amend the Municipal Act.

An Act to amend the Consolidated Municipal Act, 1922.

An Act to make further provision for Northern Ontario Development.

An Act to amend the Assessment Act.

An Act for raising money on the Credit of the Consolidated Revenue Fund.

An Act to amend the Power Commission Act.

An Act to amend the Hydro-Electric Railway Act, 1914.

An Act to amend the Loan and Trust Corporations Act.

An Act to amend the Ontario Companies Act.

An Act to amend the Power Commission Act.

An Act to amend the Legislative Assembly Act.

An Act to consolidate and amend the Law respecting the Improvement of Public Highways.

An Act to vest certain lands in His Majesty.

An Act to amend the Public Service Works on Highways Act, 1925.

An Act to amend the Ontario Habeas Corpus Act.

An Act to amend the Judicature Act.

An Act to amend the Wills Act.

An Act to amend the Adoption Act.

An Act to amend the Hospitals and Charitable Institutions Act.

An Act to consolidate and amend the Ontario Summary Convictions Act.

An Act to amend the Ontario Insurance Act, 1924.

An Act to amend the Workmen's Compensation Act.

An Act to amend the Public Lands Act.

An Act to amend the Consolidated Municipal Act, 1922.

An Act respecting the Royal Agricultural Fair Association and the City of Toronto.

An Act to amend the Representation Act.

An Act to amend the Ontario Game and Fisheries Act.

An Act for the Protection of the Property in Foxes kept in Captivity.

An Act respecting the Town of Huntsville.

An Act respecting the City of Sault Ste. Marie.

An Act respecting the Township of Tisdale.

An Act respecting the Victoria Hospital at Renfrew.

The Municipal Amendment Act, 1926.

The Assessment Amendment Act, 1926.

An Act to amend the Local Improvement Act.

An Act to amend the Local Improvement Act.

An Act respecting the Widening of Bloor Street in the City of Toronto.

An Act to consolidate and amend the Cemetery Act.

An Act to amend the United Church of Canada Act.

An Act respecting the City of Toronto.

An Act respecting the Town of Weston, the Township of York and The Toronto Transportation Commission.

An Act respecting the Town of Ford City.

An Act respecting the Essex Border Utilities Commission.

An Act respecting the Corporation of the City of Sarnia.

An Act to authorize the transfer of certain radial railways from the Hydro-Electric Power Commission of Ontario to the Corporation of the City of Toronto.

An Act to revise and amend the Election Laws.

An Act to consolidate and amend the Voters' Lists Act.

An Act to make certain changes in the Law in consequence of the Revision of the Statutes.

To these Acts the Royal Assent was announced by the Clerk of the Legislative Assembly in the following words:—

"In His Majesty's name, His Honour the Lieutenant-Governor doth assent to these Acts."

Mr. Speaker then said:—

May it please Your Honour:

We, His Majesty's most dutiful and faithful subjects, the Legislative Assembly of the Province of Ontario, in Session assembled, approach Your Honour with sentiments of unfeigned devotion and loyalty to His Majesty's person and Government, and humbly beg to present for Your Honour's acceptance a Bill intituled "An Act for granting to His Majesty certain sums of money for the public service of the financial year ending the 31st day of October, 1926, and for the public service of the financial year ending the 31st day of October, 1927, and for other purposes therein mentioned."

To this Act the Royal Assent was announced by the Clerk of the Legislative Assembly in the following words:—

"His Honour the Lieutenant-Governor doth thank His Majesty's dutiful and loyal Subjects, accept their benevolence and assent to this Act in His Majesty's name."

His Honour was then pleased to deliver the following speech:—

Mr. Speaker and Gentlemen of the Legislative Assembly:

In bringing this Session to a close, I desire to thank you for your labours on behalf of the general welfare.

While a number of useful and necessary measures have been adopted, I observe your principal enactments are designed to simplify and clarify the law. Otherwise your efforts have been directed mainly to matters of importance arising out of the administration of the various public undertakings.

Climatic conditions this season have thus far retarded agricultural work, but the industry as a whole is on a firmer footing than it has been at any other time in recent years. The measures you have adopted for the improvement of the dairy industry, for the protection of sheep, and for the restriction of the corn borer, will, I trust, prove to be useful additions to the legislation in the interest of the farming community.

The importance you attach to the progress of agriculture is recognized in the work of the representative committee which has been studying the needs and problems of this essential industry during the past two years. The committee has succeeded in enlisting the co-operation of various allied occupations, and has stimulated an interest in the subject which cannot fail to be beneficial to the rural community as well as to the Province as a whole.

It is satisfactory to observe the unabated growth of the mining activities. Especially in this the case with regard to the production of gold, which is constantly expanding by reason of the extension of existing operations and the opening up of new fields. The leading position of Ontario in the mining of nickel is being well maintained, while silver mining continues to be an important factor.

The additional provision you have made for carrying on the work of development in Northern Ontario is a sound public investment. As a Province we have already received a substantial return for our expenditures in this regard, and still greater results are anticipated in the future.

Timely steps have been taken to increase the resources of the Hydro-Electric Power Commission. The construction of the new transmission line will bring to the central parts of the Province power generated in the Ottawa River. North-western Ontario will experience advantages from the increased development on the Nipigon River. In the rural districts, the extension of electrical services continues to make headway and is proving a valuable auxiliary to agriculture.

Navigation and power development are being menaced more and more by the excessive diversion of the waters of the Great Lakes at Chicago. It has, therefore, become necessary to emphasize again the fact that the control of these waters is a matter of treaty arrangement, and cannot be dealt with otherwise. I am confident that the opinion you have expressed on this subject reflects the sentiment of this Province.

In making provision for the various branches of education you have responded to the well-understood wishes of the people. I congratulate you upon the facilities that are being provided for the training of pupils in the remoter sections of the Province, and in those more sparsely settled districts where the ordinary schools have not been set up. The institution of correspondence courses, and of itinerant schools along the railway lines in the North, is especially worthy of commendation.

Through the increasing activities of the Departments of Health and Labour, services of a highly beneficial character are finding a wider sphere of usefulness. The improvement of conditions of labour, and the close attention to the physical welfare of those engaged in industrial occupations, inure to the advantage of all classes of the community.

An important change has been made in the Legislative Assembly Act by the provision dispensing with the necessity of Ministers seeking re-election on entering the Government, when they do so within three months after a general election. Similar action was taken by the British Parliament some time ago as the practice which formerly existed has become obsolete.

Additional representation which has been given to Northern Ontario reflects the substantial growth of population consequent upon the development of that portion of the Province. By the re-arrangement made elsewhere, the change will not increase the number of seats in the Legislature, but will serve to effect a more equitable distribution of the representation of the people.

The progress that has been made in the direction of restoring the balance between revenue and expenditure is alike encouraging to the Government and re-assuring to the people. I have confidence that by the continued application of efficient methods of collecting the revenue, and close supervision of expenditures, the financial objects my Ministers have in view will speedily be accomplished.

In this connection, I desire to emphasize the value and the importance of the proposals lately made for the retirement of the Provincial debt. There will be general agreement that the time is opportune for making provision for eventually redeeming the outstanding obligations of the Province.

In conclusion, I thank you for the provision you have made for carrying on the various public services, and I trust that, under the blessing and protection of Providence, your labours will conduce to the prosperity of our country, and the welfare of our people in every walk of life.

The Provincial Secretary then said:—

Mr. Speaker and Gentlemen of the Legislative Assembly:

It is His Honour's will and pleasure that this Legislative Assembly be prorogued and this Legislative Assembly is accordingly prorogued.

List of Appendixes

TO THE

Journal of the Legislative Assembly
1926

PROVINCE OF ONTARIO

REPORT

OF THE

Agricultural Enquiry Committee

ON

Marketing of Agricultural Products

SECOND REPORT

Co-operation and National Marketing

Poultry and Dairy Products, Fruit, Livestock,
Meat, Market Garden Produce

THE AGRICULTURAL ENQUIRY COMMITTEE

Hon. Dr. D. Jamieson, M.P.P. (Chairman).

Messrs.: T. A. Thompson, M.P.P. (Lanark).

N. W. Trewartha, M.P.P.

W. D. Black, M.P.P.

Wm. Keith, M.P.P.

M. M. MacBride, M.P.P.

A. Belanger, M.P.P.

J. G. Lethbridge, M.P.P.

P. F. Cronin (Secretary).

CONTENTS—*Continued*

Report of the Agricultural Enquiry Committee, 1925

SCOPE OF THE INVESTIGATION

(1) The Agricultural Enquiry Committee presented to the Legislative Assembly in 1925 a Report in accordance with an Order of the House. A later instruction was to enquire more particularly into marketing methods and the possibility of bringing about effectual co-operation of the different provinces and of the Dominion in a proposed scheme for marketing surplus Canadian agricultural products through a national export Commission. The purpose was to consider the possibility of improving the marketing methods of our agricultural producers with the view of improving returns from the exportable surplusage of Ontario products.

It was considered advisable to appoint a Sub-Committee for such enquiry. The Chairman, together with Messrs. Black, Keith, Trewartha and MacBride, were appointed to consult with business men having special experience in export of agricultural products, and with heads of the foreign freight departments of transportation companies.

It was decided to call into conference representatives of the Departments of Agriculture of other provinces, and take counsel with them concerning the proposals made by. this Committee in 1925 for a Canadian National Export Marketing Commission and of the functions to be performed by such a Commission.

A further branch of the enquiry was into the status of agricultural co-operation in Canada.

AGRICULTURAL MARKETING

(2) To provincial governments the question of policy arises before a decision may be taken on the proposal of a national marketing commission. And so far as the question of policy is concerned, it has been anticipated that provincial governments would desire in the first place to know the attitude of any federal administration. Owing to the political feature of the past year, constructive consultations were not expected between the provinces and the Dominion. The problem of gaining for Canadian agriculture all marketing economies possible and eliminating waste cannot be solved with haste. Given these points due consideration, however, the farm people burdened with railway costs and taxation demand other forward policies than the usual recourse to immigration. Orderly marketing of all perishable products stands first in their opinion as the plan best calculated to serve the interests of the farming community and the country at large.

NATIONAL EXPORT MARKETING COMMISSION

(3) We have come to the conclusion that only an independent and impartial body constituted as a National Export Marketing Commission can establish

upon a satisfactory basis the standards of agricultural products going out of Canada. Under such a Commission a Canadian brand upon food stuffs entitled to carry its recognition abroad into world markets is fundamental. We have found practical unanimity of opinion on the question that Canadian quality shall have the protection of a Canadian brand.

We have heard many protests against trading and marketing practices in abuse of the name Canadian. We have also heard complaints of marketing practices damaging to the good name of Ontario, and detrimental to the reputation of the growers of the Province.

It has been suggested that provinces now in the lead with special products may desire to maintain the identity of such products till they reach the consumer. We are of opinion that a satisfactory national marketing system for the Dominion must retain for such special products the benefit of their origin in a particular province or even district.

IMPERIAL ECONOMIC COMMITTEE

CANADIAN FOODSTUFFS

(4) The outlook for marketing in larger volume in England should be considered representatively and without delay in connection with the work of the Imperial Economic Committee. Producers of foodstuffs within the empire, but not including Great Britain, are to receive the benefit of the Imperial Government grant of one million pounds sterling yearly, the utilization of which has been entrusted to the Imperial Economic Committee.

The Imperial Economic Committee announced its earliest sessions to enquire into the marketing and preparing for market of empire-produced meat and fruit. This Committee at a conference attended by representatives of other provinces considered the Report of the Imperial Economic Committee on meat, and sent out questionnaires among the business classes. It was desired to arrive at a correctly informed understanding of the steps necessary to place the Canadian position fully in the knowledge of the Imperial Economic Committee. Preparation of the Canadian case had been left in the hands of officials, one from the Department of Agriculture, Ottawa, and one from the Department of Trade and Commerce, who appear to have consulted the research office of the packers. It was the routine way of approaching so important an occasion in empire trade history. A statement by Hon. George B. Hoadley, Minister of Agriculture, Alberta, put the larger view of the occasion before this Committee. He said: "My experience in the old country last year is that this is not a beef question. It is not a hog question. It is not a butter question. It is a huge empire question. It is our place in that question. And I cannot help realizing the possibilities that are in Canada for marketing our production largely in Great Britain. It is from that large point of view we have to look at the question."

This Committee is unable to accept the view that official representation on the Imperial Economic Committee was enough. It is not, however, suggested that better personal representatives could have been selected. The occasion was one of most exceptional importance for Canadian agriculture, when farmers and business men of Canada were engaged seriously in taking stock of their position.

This Committee, and an Agricultural Enquiry Committee with similar terms of reference for the Province of Nova Scotia, have gone to the farmers themselves for an understanding of their problems. Co-operative leaders in Quebec, Ontario and the Western Provinces might well have had timely information and advice as to the purpose of the Imperial Economic Committee. The same remark applies to all organizations engaged in the distribution of Canadian foodstuffs.

MARKETING PLANS OF COMPETING COUNTRIES

(5) A resolution was passed by the conference called by this Committee of September 22nd. (Appendix No. 1.) Reference thereto appeared in a communication received from the Dominion Minister of Agriculture, December 12th. The suggestion we made in 1925 of a National Export Marketing Commission, according to all information obtainable, is better suited to Canadian conditions than the New Zealand or Australian control plans. The proposal of a Federal Co-operative Marketing Board reported by the Committee on Agriculture of the U.S. House of Representatives, has had our attention also. All these proposals aim at embracing the necessary machinery for making co-operative marketing of larger financial service to farm people.

All these business policies of countries in competition with Canada may be regarded as conclusive proof that agricultural co-operation, with its great attainments, rests on fact as well as sound theory. The lesson of these policies is that our Federal Government should sympathetically examine the co-operative principle and adopt a policy towards the business of production and distribution in Canada, suited to Canadian conditions.

AGENCY BETWEEN PRODUCER AND CONSUMER

(6) It has been admitted in connection with all recent efforts for more efficient marketing systems in this and other countries that conditions obviously demand a middle agency between the farmer and the consumer in order to assemble, standardize, store and merchandize farm products. In every-day practice, the greater the degree of the co-operative principle employed, the more marketing efficiency is secured with capable management.

CO-OPERATION NEEDED IN ONTARIO

(7) The co-operative movement in Ontario lags notably in the home market, into which abuses have intruded that deny the producer benefit to which he is entitled from retail price levels, and have left an impression on the public mind, injurious to the reputation of some lines of our agriculture. This is more particularly dealt with later. We are of the opinion that knowledge and recognition of export brands would incidentally give the spasmodic movement in favour of grades in domestic markets a real start, and serve the producers' interests more substantially than is anticipated.

A PROVINCIAL CO-OPERATIVE COUNCIL

(8) The Province of Manitoba has set up an advisory Council on Co-operative Marketing, the function of which is to correlate the aims and activities of the

various associations with a Registrar of Associations responsible to the Minister of Agriculture. The Ontario Agricultural Enquiry Committee has carefully considered plans for a co-operative council constituted to represent the co-operative associations now in existence.

We recommend a Co-operative Council for Ontario. Without making definite recommendations at the present time, concerning the constitution and the representative nature of such a council, we are of the opinion that the Wisconsin as well as Manitoba co-operative laws, also the functions of the State of Wisconsin Department of Markets, which is in charge of a Markets Commissioner, should first be carefully studied.

SPECIAL PRODUCTS FEATURED

(9) Reference to specific marketing factors in connection with the perishable products mentioned hereunder has been requested by producers.

The bulk of the poultry and products, dairy products and fruit exported from Ontario, passes outward through the port of Montreal. The Province of Quebec is credited with the export.

(10) POULTRY PRODUCTS.—A satisfactorily expanding department of Ontario farm production and marketing is that of poultry products. The grading of eggs, made compulsory for export, has served as a valuable object lesson. Here we observe for dressed poultry, as well as eggs, the commodity being marketed from dealer to wholesaler and on to the retailer. The co-operative principle is working well in egg circles and in the egg pool. When the consumer shall have grasped as much practical knowledge of co-operation in this branch as obtains throughout the farm community, the jargon of law evasion, or "bootlegging" in the distribution of eggs, will cease to have any meaning, the producer will be benefited by a more stable price, and the consumer will get better value the year round.

It falls outside our scope to suggest remedies for the dumping of inferior foreign eggs on the Canadian market. Statistical evidence makes the fact abundantly clear that the home market has been greatly stimulated by the steadily improving quality of domestic poultry products. The same complaint of dumping applies to the sale in Canada of baby chicks. We can only point out again that the responsibility here rests with the Federal Government.

(11) BUTTER.—In Manitoba we encountered readiness to consider and determine the suggested National Export Marketing Commission. It was contended there, by the authorities consulted, that Ontario butter should be graded uniformly with the product of the western creameries. While the Western Provinces are in a position to place dressed poultry and honey among their exportable commodities, they are especially proud of the uniform quality of their butter. They wish to see it enter the British market with a Canadian brand, but retaining the distinction of its source of origin.

In special cases, Ontario butter makers continue to carry off the highest Canadian honours. Up to the present time, a large volume of Ontario butter could not be presented under a brand that western makers would accept for the Canadian standard.

The points of difference as between East and West are found in the number of small creameries in Ontario and the system of Government cream-grading in Manitoba, Saskatchewan and Alberta. The local market in Ontario absorbs the product of small creameries. The cost of government cream-grading in the Prairie Provinces, which represents approximately one cent to three pounds of butter, is easily absorbed in the per pound price of creamery butter. The system is declared to work quite as well, if anything a little more, to the advantage of the small creamery as compared with the larger class of creamery.

The distances which cream is hauled do not constitute any part of the problem of attaining quality with uniformity.

The Director of Dairying for Ontario informs us that the ground is being thoroughly studied in this Province for the grouping of small creameries and the training and selection of the requisite number of competent graders. In a short time, and as more Ontario butter makers turn attention to expansion in the British market, they may outdistance any other section of the Dominion in contribution of export volume. The purpose of the Ontario Dairy Director is in accord with the demand of many of the largest creameries.

Sir Joseph Flavelle and R. M. Player (Walkerton) gave evidence to the point of increased consumption being the assured corollary of quality production. Sir Joseph Flavelle's emphasis of this most important fact, as well as necessity for unfailing fidelity to quality, had special application to the British market. The small creameries, however, may accept the rule as also applicable to whatever districts they serve.

Protection of the individual can of cream from the producer's hands to the creamery appears to be observed in all dairying sections of the Province, more strictly as the campaign for compulsory grading advances towards complete acceptance. In the West, we were informed, no objection whatever is raised against compulsory grading.

It is our carefully considered opinion that butter-making in Ontario will continue to occupy a subsidiary place until government grading of cream is adopted by legislation.

Importation of Australian butter in volume into the Canadian market under treaty and with the aid of the Commonwealth bounty, which means the addition of so many cents per pound to the price which the imported article would fetch in free competition, may involve a reduction in the retail price level of 4 or 5 cents per pound, and displace a considerable proportion of creamery butter now sold, especially in British Columbia. The Canadian-made butter turned back from the market sought in the West comes upon our eastern market, allowing makers to prepare additional lots of Ontario butter for the British market. As the home market always offers the best price to producers, disturbance of the Canadian butter market by the advantage afforded to distant competitors must affect agricultural co-operators rather unfavourably, while they are still experimenting with co-operation.

NOTE.—Subsequent to the signing of this Report, the Minister of Customs and Excise announced shipments of butter from Australia as acceptable at Canadian ports upon payment of a duty of four cents per pound, representing one cent per pound under the Australian treaty, and three cents under the dumping clause, pending investigation into the tax under the dumping clause and of the bounty paid on butter exported to Canada.

(12) CHEESE.—Cheesemaking has taken a firmer place as the banner industry of Ontario milk producers. Cheese production in 1925 was approximately 175,000,000 lbs., compared with 150,000,000 lbs. in 1924. It is interesting to compare this volume, large as it is, with cheese production in Wisconsin, a state with a population somewhat less than that of Ontario. In 1924, Wisconsin produced 224,000,000 lbs. of Cheddar cheese, in 2,400 factories, of which one-third are co-operatively owned.

This expansion of volume was influenced by the activities of Wisconsin Cheese Producers' Federation, which is considered a model agricultural commodity organization. In 1914 the Federation marketed 6,108,000 lbs. of cheese, and in 1924, 28,496,198 lbs. The history of this Federation holds beneficial lessons for Ontario cheese makers.

Expansion in production of Wisconsin cheese has kept pace with improvement in quality. Cheese is sold under the Wisconsin Federation brands. The success of this organization rests upon the common understanding of thousands of individuals. It was brought about in a comparatively short period, inasmuch as Wisconsin co-operative marketing is a matter of ten years' growth.

(13) APPLES.—Production and marketing interest has quickened within the year in all apple-growing sections, under the stimulation of publicity and timely assistance extended by the Government of this Province. Selling the best varieties on grade is the essential aim.

Norfolk County offers an outstanding instance of an efficient intermediate agency provided by a Growers' Association functioning on a commission basis. The card of membership in the Association reads:

Member's Name

....

This is a barrel of

No. 1   Apples

grown and packed by

NORFOLK FRUIT GROWERS' ASSOCIATION

SIMCOE   ONTARIO   CANADA

The Norfolk pack of apples is unsurpassed for flavour and for keeping qualities, the fruit coming from orchards that are pruned and sprayed according to the most approved methods, and we feel that consumers should know our brand.
We are anxious to maintain our reputation for putting up an honest pack of apples, and believe that by so doing our markets will be further extended.
We cordially request the user of this barrel to write the manager, giving his candid opinion regarding these apples. Kindly refer to the grower's name or number given on this card, and oblige.

Yours very truly,

NORFOLK FRUIT GROWERS' ASSOCIATION,

JAS. E. JOHNSON,
Manager.

Fidelity to the obligations of the Association is practically imposed.

(14) GROWERS' REPUTATION INJURED.—A marketing system which can offer the foregoing guaranty contrasts with conditions in another county, where a grower reported unsold at the end of January one thousand barrels of hand-picked Spies, the market for which has been spoiled by irresponsible selling practices resorted to in the Toronto vicinity, to which drastic remedy might well apply by the Fruit Branch, Ottawa; the Markets Branch, Department of Agriculture, or the municipal authority. But co-operative selling is the logical and ultimate remedy.

One or two men hire a truck, go into one of the adjacent counties, buy the apples lying on some grower's ground, and later pack in barrels with a few layers of Spies or attractive varieties on top. This stuff is peddled in the city to house-holders, or retail dealers, as the farmer's own pack. No personal trace whatever is left by name or address.

In a somewhat different class is the dealer who purchases the product of one or a number of orchards, packs with more or less carelessness or deceptive purpose, and sells both in domestic and outside markets. The grower may be, and in most cases is, wholly blameless even of knowledge of the marketing scheme of the man who distributes his apples. In Manitoba, in Western and Northern Ontario, and in Toronto, we found the entire blame erroneously attributed to the grower for the disappointment of the consumer, who knows all about the superiority of the Ontario apple, but does not know when he is buying a dependably-packed barrel of Ontario apples.

The consumer who buys potatoes by the bag takes chances against like practices, which would be eliminated if responsible grading and marketing were adopted by the producers.

Attention has been called to a practice by which the reputation of Canadian quality oats suffers in export markets. Oats sold in Winnipeg, or other markets, is processed in the United States for cereal factory requirements. The best is used in the preparation of factory commodities, and the refuse exported as Canadian oats.

These are cited as instances pointing to organization and co-operation as the final remedies for present rural marketing disadvantages.

CANADIAN AND U.S. APPLES FOR EXPORT

(15) Railway rates on apples for export from Ontario points have been protested. The transportation companies have met this complaint about the distribution problem by submitting to us a statement compiled by International Apple Shippers' Association, showing shipments of apples in barrels and boxes from Canadian and United States ports with distribution to British and foreign ports; also, statements covering apples and pears shipped over the Canadian Pacific Railway and the Canadian National Railways to Canadian Atlantic ports. In these latter statements the source of origin, whether Canada or the United States, is distinguished. Our railway rates attract considerable shipments through our ports of the fruit of comparatively distant United States growers, consigned abroad. These statistical statements are published as Appendix No. 2.

BACON

(16) Appendix No. 3 contains the paragraphs from the Report of the Imperial Economic Committee, dealing with sources of supply of bacon to the British market. They are in agreement with the 1925 Report of this Committee to the House.

(17) Paragraphs 38, 39, 41, 42 and 43 of the Meat Report of the Imperial Economic Committee contain information for Ontario producers.

CANADIAN FRESH-KILLED BEEF

(18) Correspondence with the Dominion Minister of Agriculture on this head has not brought forth points of common agreement upon future policy towards the business. The Committee is not convinced by the arbitrary stand taken by the Minister against the feasibility of trade in beef killed in Canada, shipped to England and retailed in fourteen days on a par with the "home-killed" beef of Scotch and English butchers. The Minister considers discussion closed on the question: "How should Canada export beef cattle?" by the results of an experiment made under supervision of officers of his Department. The experiment in question was faulty from the point of view of commercial experience. Commercial experiments by the Harris Abattoir Company endeavouring to establish their fresh-killed beef in the English market are admitted to have been made at considerable loss. The outstanding features of the Government experiment in 1923 are familiar to all interested in the cattle industry. J. S. McLean gave his views by request to this Committee in a letter and also by request amplified his observations in a verbal statement. Mr. McLean's attitude is in no sense whatever opposed to the furthest possible development of the export of stores or fat cattle to Britain, or any official efforts looking to more favourable conditions for live stock shipments to the United States. There is obvious disadvantage to a country in shipping its raw material. Mr. McLean's courageous efforts to establish on the English market Canadian fresh-killed meat in competition with the "home-killed" is in the interest of cattle feeders of Ontario who have the feed and the barns for putting superior finish on cattle. No country is better equipped than this Province for grain-finishing beef. British butchers, however, wish to buy prime Ontario beef, fresh-killed, at the current prices quoted for "imported" beef. The same beef they retail as "home-killed." In this connection it is instructive to note that the Linlithgow Report to the Imperial Government on agricultural prices, recognized the point of identification as between "home produced" and "imported" meat. The Argentine "chilled meat" comes under the classification of "imported," but is in point of fact in a different category to Canadian fresh-killed beef.

These distinctions constitute the major difficulty to be overcome. Mr. McLean confidently says: "I think it is the ultimate judgment of the consumer which will govern the practice of the English dealer. I think with the right class of cattle our fresh-killed beef can establish for itself a place in the British market very close up to the price of home-killed beef."

The Harris Abattoir Company intends, as we understand, going on with shipments of beef which, if forwarded from their abattoirs in Toronto or Winnipeg, deserve encouragement to the point of overcoming the improper profit-seeking practice of dealers or butchers in England.

The Minister is in error in supposing this Committee had considered the subject without all available documentary information. He also erroneously assumes this Committee undertook a brief for Mr. McLean. Any publicity in connection with this branch of our enquiry had not Mr. McLean's prior knowledge.

BEEF CATTLE

(19) Difficulties in shipping live cattle to Great Britain represented at our meetings during 1924, appear to have been sensibly modified since the appearance of the former Report of this Committee. System has been brought into play, and the outlet has increased.

Larger shipments marked the calendar year 1925, when 110,868 head, with a declared value of $11,796,383, were exported. Exports from January 1st to January 31st, 1926, were 5,372 head, as compared with 3,479 for the same period of 1925, and 3,020 for the same period of 1924. The value of 1926 shipments is not obtainable.

Members of this Committee inspected various lots of cattle as they went on shipboard, and believe the classes now going forward compare favourably with any shipments in the history of the cattle industry.

Development of this trade has promise of potentiality for practically all provinces of the Dominion.

Ontario farmers, whose barns in size and number are not rivalled elsewhere, are particularly interested in feeding and finishing beef cattle.

It is admitted that Canada's Western ranges constitute the natural cattle-producing region. The experience of cattle men has been that the same steer, if fed for the same time on the same feed, will finish with greater gain in Northern Alberta than anywhere down to Mexico.

This natural advantage, along with removal of the British embargo, has prepared the way for increased enterprise in production, feeding and marketing of Western cattle. An important factor is the success which has attended the feeding of thousands of cattle in open feed lots in Northern Alberta. Most of the selling and buying occurs at the stockyards in Edmonton, Calgary and Winnipeg.

The Dominion Government has endeavoured to encourage eastern farmers to buy on the range. The inducement is seldom availed of, and the proposition is not an entirely practical one.

Purchasers from Great Britain have lately been coming direct into Western stock yards. Canadian Live Stock Producers, Ltd., is a company representing Scottish and Canadian cattle interests. This organization has between 5,000 and 6,000 head on its feeding lots in Alberta and Ontario, whence cattle are continuously forwarded to finishing destination in Scotland, via the port of Quebec in summer and St. John, N.B., in winter. The company works in with the Jensen cattle freighter line, which is not a member of the Canadian Shipping Conference. The "Ontario," first of the Jensen steamers, took on cattle at St. John, January 23rd, for the Canadian Livestock Producers, Ltd., and for Swifts.

NOTE.—This vessel sailed from St. John with 1,077 head of cattle on January 24th, 1926, and ran into storms then prevailing on the North Atlantic. She made an average daily run of ten knots for the first six days, but discovered shortage of coal in the bunkers obliged shutting down speed to six knots. She reached Birkenhead in thirteen days; landed one-half her cattle there, the remainder at Glasgow, all in excellent condition. The bad weather involved loss of thirteen cattle, a small number in the circumstances. With suggestion of minor improvements the ship was passed by the British Agricultural Committee and Board of Trade.

CATTLE MARKETING

(20) A co-operative system of marketing Western cattle for the benefit of producers is being operated successfully by the United Grain Growers. Toronto abattoir interests have gone into the finishing of cattle for their manufacturing requirements in empty barns of Western Ontario farms. Despite the Fordney tariff, different States with surplus corn are regularly buying cattle at Western Canadian yards. In Manitoba, feeders are adopting the open feed lot plan that Alberta has so successfully proved out.

The combined effect of these influences has been to raise western cattle prices.

Another effect is discovered upon the industry of cattle feeding in Ontario, which must operate injuriously to the farmers of our western counties. Ontario farmers, who have the barns and the feed, should secure the best class of feeders, if they expect to make money under advanced and complex conditions.

The dominant purpose of systems in cattle feeding and selling in Western Canada is to pick and sort animals that should make most gain on feed furnished in the countries for which the lots are selected. The buyers who come from England and Scotland have this purpose in view. The idea of the Alberta feeding lot enterprise is to make money on the feed, in addition to building up reserve supply. The cattle pool sorts cattle required by United States feeders in Pennsylvania, Ohio or elsewhere. The pool likewise regularly sorts classes for export to Great Britain, as well as to Continental Europe, which is expected to become a heavy buyer.

There are twenty-seven different classes, and when picked and sorted by experts of competing organized interests represented at the yards, Ontario buyers, who have no organization, necessarily get too many culls.

DEMAND FOR AN ONTARIO CATTLE POOL

(21) Here is a real danger to Ontario pre-eminence in stockers and feeders. This Committee is not prepared to recommend any novel experiments. The conditions foreseen could be met and handled satisfactorily by an Ontario cattle pool effectively supervised. In many phases of our investigations, we have been assisted by representatives of the United Farmers of Ontario Co-operative, and we understand that one successful experiment has been made in purchasing cattle at the Winnipeg yards and selling to farmers in Western Ontario at cost.

The United Farmers of Ontario Co-operative does not look for privileges in connection with its activities in the cattle industry. Without assistance from Government the United Farmers of Ontario could prepare itself as well as any new organization to meet the requirements of the Ontario farmers. Ontario feeders cannot too soon realize that profitable finishing of cattle in the future will depend primarily upon organization and co-operation. In this way an Ontario cattle pool may develop. There is place and demand for it.

Packers and butchers for local killing require grain-finished cattle. The Ontario-fed type is still unexcelled.

OCEAN TRANSPORTATION

(22) Publicity and constructive criticism following the investigations conducted by this Committee during the past two years have helped transporation interests and producers to better mutual understanding. Complaints which originated in Western Ontario did not indicate the exact direction from which improvement could be expected. It was believed that a trading monopoly outside Canada had gained control of cattle transport and that steamship companies were tied up to one influential shipper.

It is satisfactory to be in a position to state that in this Committee's opinion no combine exists to-day.

CANADIAN SHIPPING CONFERENCE

(23) At the beginning of December a new Canadian trans-Atlantic shipping conference was announced, of which the Anchor-Donaldson, C.P.R., Cunard, Furness-Withy, Manchester Line, Head Line, Inter-Continental Transport Services, Thompson and White Star-Dominion Lines are members. All of these lines are not cattle carriers. This Committee has been assured by Col. Gear, Major Curry and other shipping executives in Montreal that the North Atlantic Conference does not function so far as Canadian ships are concerned, and that the Canadian Conference does not set cattle rates.

If the Jensen Canadian Line can cut rates the possibility of doing so should soon become apparent. The steamship companies and the cattle shippers equally desire a continuous supply of suitable cattle for British feeding destinations.

Uncertain conditions under which the cattle carrying trade developed after removal of the embargo militated against this aim. The producing, marketing and shipping organizations now coping with the problem are doing much better.

IRELAND AND CANADA IN CATTLE TRADE

(24) It has been pointed out to us that of the 1,000,000 cattle imported alive into Great Britain in 1924, ninety-three per cent. came from Ireland and seven per cent. from Canada, these being the only countries privileged to land cattle alive in England. The British authorities are not less vigilant because the privilege has been extended to Canada. Dr. J. L. Frood, M.R.C.V.S., representative of the British Ministry of Agriculture and Fisheries in Canada, guards observance of the letter and spirit of British regulations. The federal authorities are vigilant.

Development of the live cattle trade from Canada cannot soon challenge the supremacy of Ireland. Plans of organization there have, however, already taken the general form of Canadian organizations. The main feature is co-operation of Irish producers with English buyers. This plan is quite successfully developing, according to recent reports. Irish members of a co-operative union ship Irish cattle to the English markets and sell direct to English buyers. Each lot of cattle is inspected by co-operative officials prior to forwarding to the port of embarkation. Special boats take the cattle to England and special trains are used in transporting the animals from the port of entry. Sales are supervised by officials of the Country Gentlemen's Association of England, who make collection and remit the net return to the consignors.

It has been represented to this Committee that Canadian feeder cattle have a natural advantage over the Irish bullocks. The Scotch feeders, who are in the business on a large scale, are reported to be satisfied that the Canadian bullock will make greater gain in the same time on the same feed than the Irish bullock, and Scotch feeders prefer them, all things being equal in respect to continuity of supply. The outlook for this trade is now bright.

BETTER CLASS OF CATTLESHIPS

(25) The established shipping companies in business from Canadian ports for fifty years have space under their control to meet any development of the future. They endeavour to serve all shippers. In the absence of co-operative organization, with one powerful shipper competing against a number of weaker individuals, it has happened that when space was in demand all shippers were calling for space options at the same time. Conversely when markets were disturbed all shippers were clamouring to cut down their space orders. This is an illustration of the need for better methods of steadying the market by continuous supply of the right sorts of cattle.

The steamship managers assure us they are in a position to take care of any possible development of the trade henceforth.

An Ontario cattle pool would bring a second line of continuous supply into service. The new Jensen line of exclusive cattle freighters, relying upon reserves of cattle at feeding stations, claims it can divert its ships at sea to special markets. This plan would serve best where all the space has been contracted to one shipper.

GENERAL CARGO AND OCEAN PORTS

(26) General cargo steamers best serve the purposes of smaller shippers. We saw the Anchor-Donaldson S.S. "Carmia" loaded at St. John. A converted passenger ship, on two decks she had excellent accommodation for more cattle than she was carrying, on her trip of January 22nd, viz., 977 head, weighing 600 tons. The ship reported at Glasgow in eleven days with loss of three cattle in exceptionally bad weather in which liners were overdue and much damage caused to shipping.

DEMAND FOR PORT FACILITIES

(27) Development of Canadian ports is concerned when the business of general cargo ships is in question. The greater the number of these vessels loading at Canadian ports, the more Canadian wheat for export will flow through all-Canadian channels. Wheat is generally carried as ballast on these bottoms. Much of the Canadian wheat for export diverted to U.S. ports is accorded low ocean rates, because the ships want it, and can make up for their east-bound rates on the return cargo. The carrying of cattle on general cargo ships is to be encouraged, consonant with reasonable rates. Harbour facilities at the port of St. John should be kept abreast of the shipping business of that port.

PORTS OF MONTREAL AND QUEBEC

(28) An added cost of $2 per car, incidental to the unloading and loading again of cattle in the Montreal yards before going on shipboard, is not to be obviated by Ontario shippers who may divert their summer shipments to the port of Quebec. Members of this Committee have visited the Montreal yards where cattle are rested and fed according to regulation. Details of all costs have been examined. The Committee can see no substantial reason why Ontario shipments may be more advantageously routed than through Montreal. This opinion applies to the practice of continuing scattered shipments as at present or to the organized business of a pool such as we have suggested in paragraph 21.

CARE OF CATTLE ON SHIPS

(29) Government regulations under which cattle are loaded, stalled, bedded and provided for in respect to feed, water, ventilation and space, are satisfactorily strict. The cattle are accompanied by a veterinary paid by the Dominion Government, are under Government observation when they go aboard, and when they land. Cattle shippers nominally engage the cattle attendants for the voyage. In point of fact, these attendants are taken on by an employ-ment agency acting for the shippers. In most cases they are men looking for a free passage or willing to pay a small premium, such as students in summer, and old country men desirous of returning to the United Kingdom in winter. Such attendants cannot be expected to have experience in the care of cattle. One foreman is paid and is expected to keep the help on the job. The attendants are, of course, amenable to the discipline of the ship. In one respect regulations are faulty. There should be one paid foreman for every hundred cattle taken on board. This is the regulation on ships leaving U.S. ports.

ORCHARD AND GARDEN PRODUCE

(30) Closely related to the difficulties complained of in the marketing of fruit are the well-understood handicaps of Ontario orchard and garden produce growers. Touching this issue involves contact with the demand of these growers who have made substantial investments in their business, for protection against the necessarily unknown quantities of foreign produce dumped on local markets about the time Ontario produce is beginning to come in. This in addition to the continuous supplies of southern fruits and vegetables at high prices through the months of non-production here. Complaint of consumers that Ontario apples and garden produce are not featured in home markets is met by the growers' statement that lack of protection forces them into the uncertainties of export trade.

A line of co-operative action has been suggested to these growers through a brokerage organization or bureau for routing and marketing carlot shipments. No definite action has followed the suggestion, and the dominant demand for tariff protection continues to be made with greater insistance. In its former report this Committee noted that its scope is not in the area of practical service. As a preliminary to embarking on a Growers' Brokerage Bureau, a survey would be advisable of the consuming and producing centres for which the plan is in-tended. The Federal and Provincial Departments of Agriculture have branches that together can give direction and assistance in making such a survey.

VALUE OF AGRICULTURAL EXPORTS CONSIDERED

(31) Table of comparative figures for 12 months ended December, years 1924 and 1925, showing the principal Canadian agricultural exports to the United Kingdom referred to in this Report:

Commodities	12 months ended December	
	1924	1925
Cattle, number	79,435	110,868
Cattle, value	$8,402,377	$11,796,383
Butter, pounds	15,236,116	18,682,836
Butter, value	$5,405,608	$6,936,428
Cheese, hundredweights	1,158,005	1,405,799
Cheese, value	$21,198,294	$31,810,061
Eggs, dozen	2,363,170	2,143,090
Eggs, value	$870,339	$885,545
Apples, fresh, barrels	1,392,970	1,237,125
Apples, fresh, value	$6,230,214	$5,481,343
Oats, bushels	23,435,292	20,633,262
Oats, value	$10,852,969	$10,505,801
Bacon and hams, hundredweights	1,119,688	1,305,037
Bacon and hams, value	$19,688,455	$28,466,844
Beef, fresh, hundredweights	63,656	104,224
Beef, fresh, value	$436,429	$802,251

PROTECTION OF SHEEP FROM DOGS

(32) The Director of the Livestock Branch has given this Committee the substance of a clause proposed to be added to the Dog Tax and Sheep Protection Act. It is intended by the addition that the Minister of Agriculture may bring districts where the Act does not apply under its provisions, the Department assuming the duties and obligations of a Municipal Council in respect to unorganized townships brought in, in so far as statutory liability may exist.

The consensus of opinion gathered by this Committee favours imposition of a heavy fine upon the owners of any dog found off the owner's premises between sunset and sunrise, night being the period when practically all damage of this sort is done to sheep. The proposed addition to the Dog Tax and Sheep Protection Act would permit the Department to work out equitable details in the unorganized townships.

RECOMMENDATIONS AND CONCLUSIONS

(33) If the recommendations and conclusions of this Report seem to call for more definite attitude at all points than has been taken by this Committee, it must appear obvious at the same time that the conditions reported upon are developing and even changing in a very remarkable way. This is true of the features of the Canadian cattle industry dealt with, as well as of dairying, poultry raising and fruit growing. In an especial manner it is true of market influences felt by each and all of these branches of Canadian agriculture, that are due mainly to world co-operative movements. So we have come to a point in this country where a more satisfactory position for ourselves in world marketing must be found.

It need not be reiterated that in Ontario as elsewhere, organization, co-operation and standardization cannot progress more rapidly or satisfactorily than producers concerned shall determine to bring about. Whether Canadian producers realize it or not, or fail to realize it as fully as perhaps they should, the fact remains that the agricultural marketing systems either established or proposed by countries in competition with Canada, make the lesson plain to all who study these systems that the next move is up to Canada.

It is part of this very lesson that

(34) ONTARIO REQUIRES A PROVINCIAL CO-OPERATIVE COUNCIL

which, among other functions, shall assist co-operative organizations in bringing into existence necessary intermediate agencies between farmer and consumer in order that perishable products may be better assembled, standardized, stored and merchandized. A Provincial Council appears to us essential in the very structure of co-operation, helpful from the point of view of a national marketing commission, and capable of good service in regard to world marketing as well as in the domestic field of distribution.

A CANADIAN BRAND FOR CANADIAN QUALITY PRODUCTS

(35) The demand of dairymen for a Canadian brand upon cheese and butter is no new idea. And if cheese and butter, why not bacon and prime beef?

(36) Compulsory grading of cream in Ontario will mark a long stride towards volume of uniform quality butter. The dairy industry at this time can do nothing more practical. There is no way by which the dairy situation in Ontario can be better served than by

GOVERNMENT GRADING OF CREAM

which has behind it a representative demand both of dairymen and distributors all over the Province. This demand we believe will very soon have unanimous support based on experience of its benefit.

(37) There may be some question of the propriety of placing among matters of report the complaints covering butter, eggs, fruit, vegetables and other commodities for which protection is held to be the producers' economic right at the hands of the Federal Government. The remedy may come from publicity of all the facts at issue.

The conclusion we have come to that

(38) AN ONTARIO CATTLE POOL

would fit into the rapidly expanding systems of feeding and selling Canadian cattle is addressed to the farmers of Ontario themselves. If they decide to go on into a cattle pool, they will be generally encouraged by the records of livestock buying and selling organizations in other places. They should not have more difficulty than Irish co-operatives in the live cattle industry had in establishing the complementary part of the organization in Great Britain.

More cattle are needed in Ontario. In the Niagara Peninsula, many fruit growers are allowing the natural fertility of their land to decline for lack of cattle in their barns.

(39) The reports issued by the Imperial Economic Committee are of value to Canada and will help farming interests of the Dominion to improve their position on the British market. With the co-operation of the Federal Government and through the agency of

A NATIONAL EXPORT MARKETING COMMISSION

the purpose of the Committee, which is to increase empire trade, must develop along practical lines of policy and action in Canada.

Respectfully submitted,

> D. JAMIESON, Chairman.
> W. D. BLACK.
> M. M. MACBRIDE.
> J. G. LETHBRIDGE.
> WM. KEITH.
> N. W. TREWARTHA.
> T. A. THOMPSON.
> H. BELANGER.

APPENDIX NO. 1

Moved by Hon. George B. Hoadley (Minister of Agriculture of Alberta),

Seconded by Mr. Elie Bourbeau (Chief Dairy Branch, Department of Agriculture of the Province of Quebec),

WHEREAS the Imperial Government granted a sum of one million pounds sterling annually, to foster the marketing in Great Britain, of food-stuffs produced in the Dominions;

AND WHEREAS the utilization of said grant was entrusted to and is under consideration by the Imperial Economic Committee.

THEREFORE, BE IT RESOLVED that the Federal Department of Agriculture be requested by this conference to invite to Canada at the earliest possible date executive members of the Imperial Economic Committee so that producers, co-operative organizations and departments of agriculture in all the provinces of this Dominion may be afforded, in consultation, adequate information concerning the trade advantages and facilities presented to Canada, or that may be developed under the recommendations made by the Imperial Economic Committee.

That arrangements incidental to such invitation be left with the Federal Department of Agriculture.

APPENDIX NO. 2

Summary of apples and pears carried by Canadian Pacific Railway during the year 1924, to the ports of Montreal, Quebec and West Saint John.

Ports of	Apples		Pears		Point of Origin
	Barrels	Boxes	Barrels	Boxes	
Montreal	19,798	276,694	79	54	Canadian
Montreal	1,514	15,183	3,973	6,288	American
Total	21,312	291,877	4,052	6,342	
Quebec	1,556	28,410	....	....	Canadian
Quebec	....	10,283	....	....	American
Total	1,556	38,693	....	....	
West St. John	13,540	46,347	....	....	Canadian
West St. John	......	20,207	....	....	American
Total	13,540	66,354	....	....	

Total, Canadian—34,894 barrels, 351,451 boxes apples.

Total, American—1,514 barrels, 45,673 boxes apples.

Montreal, September 26th, 1925.

Summary of apples and pears carried by Canadian National Railways during the season—
August, 1924, to May, 1925, inclusive, to the ports of Montreal, Quebec, Saint John and Portland,
Me., for export to the United Kingdom.

Ports of	Apples		Pears		Country of Origin
	Barrels	Boxes	Barrels	Boxes	
Montreal............................	21,435	4,344	666	600	Canadian
Montreal............................	24,202	17,784	427	2,673	American
Total........................	45,637	22,128	1,093	3,273	
Quebec.............................	161	....	445	....	Canadian
Quebec.............................	....	6,312	....	....	American
Total........................	161	6,312	445	....	
Saint John.........................	610	1,399	....	....	Canadian
Saint John.........................	....	1,470	....	....	American
Total........................	610	2,869	....	....	
Portland...........................	13,264	....	....	....	Canadian
Portland...........................	68,314	1,512	....	....	American
Total........................	81,578	1,512	....	....	

```
Total Canadian—35,470 barrels,  5,743 boxes apples.
Total American—92,516 barrels, 27,078 boxes apples.
          ───────            ────────
          127,986            32,821 boxes apples.
Total Canadian—1,111 barrels,    600 boxes pears.
Total American—  427 barrels,  2,673 boxes pears.
          ───────            ────────
          1,538 barrels,  3,273 boxes pears.
```
Montreal, October 7th, 1925.

Destination, Port of	Barrels	Boxes
Liverpool......................................	952,421	1,060,459
London..	536,073	1,234,195
Glasgow.......................................	334,563	791,310
Manchester....................................	267,067	147,624
Southampton...................................	104,399	347,236
Other British ports............................	224,490	129,039
Scandinavia...................................	94,578	290,759
Miscellaneous.................................	98,072	646,918
Total...................................	2,611,663	4,647,520

APPENDIX NO. 3

Meat Report of Imperial Economic Committee

V. PIG PRODUCTS

Pork, Bacon and Hams

Empire and Foreign Supplies.

30. Bacon is one of the staple articles in the diet of the British people, and a review of the sources of importation of this and other pig meats will make very evident the dependence of the United Kingdom upon foreign supplies. In 1924 the United Kingdom imported 9,502,000 cwts. of bacon and hams, as compared with an import of 5,713,000 cwts. in 1913, but the statistics are not comparable, since the latter figure does not include imports from the Irish Free State. These amounted in 1924 to 595,000 cwts.

Table V shows how large a part bacon plays in the national meat bill and the extent to which it is obtained from non-Empire sources. Out of £105,447,000 spent in 1924 on imported meats of all classes, no less than £50,848,000, or forty-eight per cent. went to purchase pig products, and of this sum, £40,120,000 went to foreign countries. The bulk of the expenditure was for bacon and hams, although there was an appreciable import of fresh pork, amounting in 1924, to 279,000 cwts. from the Irish Free State, and 534,000 cwts. from the continent.

Market Requirements.

32. In the bacon market of the United Kingdom a very high standard of quality is generally asked for. The demand is principally for bacon in the form of whole Wiltshire sides. These must satisfy certain requirements as to weight, conformation and thickness of fat, and must, in addition, be mildly cured. Although there is a market for a wide range in weights and qualities, nevertheless the great bulk of the demand is for sides weighing from fifty-five to seventy pounds, a sixty-pound side, which is the product of a pig of 200 pounds live weight, being most in favour. Further, the majority of the consuming public prefer bacon that is not too fat; so that sides carrying 1½ inches to 1¾ inches of fat evenly distributed along the back are most in demand. This requirement forms the basis upon which Wiltshire sides are graded, and although the grades may differ in name according to the country from which the product originates, nevertheless they are all established on the same basis, and are well understood by the trade. Furthermore, as the retailer of bacon in the United Kingdom buys the whole side, which he then cuts up and distributes to his customers, he is very desirous of securing Wiltshires with a long middle and a thick streak, thus obtaining the maximum weight in the most valuable part of the carcass. To ensure the fulfilment of these requirements as to weight, finish and shape or conformation, a pig of certain definite proportions and finish, known as a "bacon pig," is needed.

Danish Supplies.

33. In reviewing the sources of supply, we have been impressed with the steadily increasing quantities obtained from Denmark. In 1914 the United Kingdom imported 2,715,000 cwts. from this source, which, up to that time had been the largest Danish contribution known. After 1914 supplies steadily declined until in 1918-19, practically nothing reached the United Kingdom from Denmark, as during the war period Danish supplies were diverted to other markets. Shipments were resumed in 1920, when the United Kingdom received 704,000 cwts. of bacon from Denmark. Danish supplies have increased annually since then, until in 1924 they reached 3,978,000 cwts., which was nearly fifty per cent. more than the previous record of 1914. The by-products of the Danish dairy industry with other home-grown feeding-stuffs, supplemented by imports of small grains, furnish a satisfactory ration for bacon pig production. Furthermore, through the highly developed Danish system of agricultural and co-operative organization, a uniformly high standard of product is maintained. Proximity to market is also a decided advantage, as the bacon can be mildly cured and distributed regularly to consumers in the United Kingdom in a fresh condition. It should also be noted that since Denmark is a very small country, bacon production is there a specialized industry concentrated in a comparatively limited area, and that in consequence, the details of production, manufacture and selling can be, and are well organized.

United States Supplies.

34. The United States is now the second largest source of supply to the United Kingdom market, although prior to 1924 imports from this quarter exceeded those from any other. During the war years, when Danish supplies practically disappeared from the United Kingdom, the United States furnished large quantities, reaching the peak in 1918 with shipments totalling 10,064,000 cwts. Imports have since declined, and in 1924 amounted to only 3,310,000 cwts., a figure which, none the less, is still in excess of the average pre-war shipments from the United States. The class of product received from this source differs somewhat from that received from Denmark, in that, while the latter country is chiefly concerned in the trade in whole Wiltshire sides, the cheaper class of product, such as Cumberland cut, picnic hams, hams and cut meats, is obtained from the United States. The supplies sent across the Atlantic constitute only a very small percentage of the total United States production, and from the American point of view, their chief importance lies in the fact that by the variation of their amount they can be used to steady prices in the large home market.

Canadian Supplies.

38. Canada's chief contribution to the meat supply of the United Kingdom is of bacon and hams, but the volume of trade is still below that of Denmark, although it has lately increased, both absolutely and relatively. This is made evident by a comparison of the percentage changes as shown in table VII. In extension of that table it may be stated that in the first six months of 1925 the total British imports of bacon and hams were 3.5 per cent. less than in the first six months of 1924, but the imports from the Irish Free State decreased by twenty-six per cent. while those from Canada were twenty-six per cent. higher. The imports from the United States decreased by sixteen per cent. and those from Denmark by two per cent.

Comparative Landed Values.

39. We may also usefully compare the landed values of the goods obtained from Canada with those of the goods from other sources of supply. The following table gives the figures for bacon, but not for hams, during recent years.

Comparison of Landed Values of Bacon from Chief Sources of Supply

Bacon from	1909–13 Average	1922	1923	1924	1925 (half-year)
	Per cwt.	Per cwt.	Per cwt. £5.39*	Per cwt. £5.30	Per cwt. £6.09
Irish Free State........	....	....	5.56	5.10	5.61
Denmark.............	£3.42	£7.05	5.56	5.10	5.61
Canada..............	3.11	5.86	4.61	4.65	4.94
United States.........	3.01	4.95	4.07	3.91	4.62

*Based on imports from April to December.

It must be borne in mind, however, that these figures, which have been calculated from the customs returns of the United Kingdom, are based upon values given by importers and must not be taken as necessarily indicating market prices. The values returned by the importers may be based on long-standing contracts, or out-of-date market conditions. They suffice, however, to indicate that, in general, as shown in paragraph 36, Irish bacon commands a higher price than other imported bacons. The figure for the year 1923 is an exception, and is accounted for by the strike during the summer months, which kept supplies off the market during the period of high prices, and thus affected the annual average. As regards Canadian bacon, the figures indicate that the difference in the prices of Canadian and American bacon is now much greater than was the case before the war. As between Canadian and Danish bacon, it is to be noted that in 1909-13, the Canadian product was lower in price than the Danish by 9.1 per cent. and in 1924 by 9.9 per cent. This, however, does not fully bring out the trend of competition and development as between these two sources of supply, for a more detailed study of average values reveals the fact that in 1921 Danish bacon realized 35s. 8d. per cwt. more than Canadian; in 1922, 23s. 8d. more; in 1923, 19s. 0d. per cwt. more, and in 1924 only 9s. 11d. per cwt. more. In the first half of 1925 there was a slight change in tendency, but not enough as yet seriously to modify the general trend.

Recent Canadian Improvement.

41. The recent improvement in the situation is due to an organized effort on the part of the producers, the packers, and the Government in Canada. This has resulted in the improvement of the pigs themselves, a greater uniformity of the product, a milder cure, and a quicker distribution so that the bacon reaches the consumer in the United Kingdom in a fresher condition. The Canadian product is shipped for the most part in the form of whole Wiltshire sides, and now competes more directly with the product from Denmark than with that from the United States. By virtue of her proximity, Denmark can market bacon in the United Kingdom within two weeks of slaughtering, while from Eastern Canada, it takes four weeks and from Western Canada five or six weeks to reach the market. In view of the very decided preference of the British consumer for a fresh mild-cured bacon, this is a heavy handicap, as the Canadian product must necessarily be cured so as to carry for a longer time. It would appear, therefore, that only a more rapid transit, or a more satisfactory method of long-period cure would put Canada on a par with Denmark. Research should be directed to the latter end.

Transport of Canadian Supplies.

42. The question of transport divides itself into the two questions of more rapid transport and a more regular shipping service. What is required is that vessels from Canada should bring bacon to the most suitable ports on the same day each week. This would go far to place Canadian and Danish supplies on a more equal footing in the United Kingdom market. We are not in a position to judge as to the practicability of such an improved shipping service, but we would venture to suggest, as a first step, that the shippers of bacon in Canada should get together and ascertain precisely what is desirable. This could then be presented to the shipping conference. Failing a satisfactory negotiation, the matter could then be carried to the Imperial Shipping Committee with a view to enlisting the influence of that body.

Methods of Curing—Research.

43. There remains the other method of overcoming the present handicap of time and distance under which not only the Canadian, but also other Dominion producers suffer. This is the discovery of some new or improved way of curing which will enhance the keeping qualities of the bacon and still maintain the mildness of flavour so much desired by the British consumer. This would open up possibilities for the bacon trade in the distant parts of the Empire, such as Australia and New Zealand. Scientific research, possibly on a large scale, will be necessary, and although private firms are continually endeavouring to effect improvements in cure, their efforts are inevitably limited. With a problem of this nature, a solution of which would be of the utmost value to Empire trade, we think that provision for research should be made outside the industry itself.

TORONTO, March 15th, 1926.

HONOURABLE DAVID JAMIESON, M.D.,
    Chairman, Agriculture Enquiry Committee,
        Toronto, Ont.

DEAR SIR:—

After a careful perusal of the report embodying the findings and conclusions of the majority of the Agriculture Enquiry Committee, of which I am a member, I feel constrained to lodge certain protests and make the reserves hereinafter set forth.

With the expression of such protests and subject to such reserves, I fully endorse the statements and recommendations elaborated in the report.

1. SCOPE OF THE COMMITTEE.

The Agriculture Enquiry Committee was appointed by the Legislative Assembly of Ontario to investigate conditions and suggest measures, its findings and suggestions to form the basis of legislative and executive endeavours to better agricultural conditions in this Province. It is essentially a provincial committee, standing *in loco* of the Legislature, and its scope and limitations restricted within the legislative powers of the Assembly to which its report is to be submitted and within the administrative powers of the Ontario Government. Findings and suggestions, however accurate and however opportune, that cannot be acted upon by the Legislature of the Provincial Government as being *hors* their constitutional jurisdiction, are outside the Committee's competence. Findings and conclusions embodied in the Committee's report followed by the Assembly's adoption of the report are tantamount to resolutions of the Assembly. Wherefore do I submit that anything which is not a proper subject of a resolution in the Assembly should be eliminated from the Committee's report.

The above principle was recognized by the Committee at the very outset of its investigation in 1924 and it was decided at a meeting of its members and confirmed at a public meeting at St. Catharines—if I rightly recollect—that every member of the Committee would refrain from pressing upon those appearing before it any questions opening up issues of purely federal concern, such as the tariff and kindred questions. It was however decided to allow the witnesses before the Committee complete freedom so as not to embarrass them in the statement of their grievances. Any proper suggestions which were of the exclusive resort of the Dominion Government, the Railway Board or other public bodies, the Committee would pass on to them. The only possible inference is that what applied to the Committee's discussions applied in greater measure to its reports. So it was that, last Session, on my appealing to that ruling, some paragraphs were eliminated from the Committee's first report as originally drafted and others toned down to where further insistence on my part would have appeared captious.

Furthermore, when a report is submitted to the Legislative Assembly, a debate may be opened and pursued on any paragraph and statement therein contained. Any reference therefore to purely federal issues, such as tariff matters, would inevitably result in transferring to the Provincial Legislature the protracted debates of the House of Commons.

In fine, I submit that the touchstone by which must be judged what should and should not be included in the Committee's report is whether the particular question at issue is or is not wholly or partially within the jurisdiction of the Legislative Assembly and the Government of the Province of Ontario; whether it is competent in the Legislature and the Provincial Executive to apply a remedy to the grievance complained of or give effect to the suggestion made, also whether such contents would form the proper subject of a debate in the Assembly.

2. ORCHARD AND GARDEN PRODUCE.

Under the above caption, the Committee's report urges protection upon fruits and vegetables. Last year, I grudgingly allowed a short statement on the issue to be inserted in the Committee's first report. The matter should have rested there, as no further investigation was made along those lines since last session. The insistence of a majority of the Committee to expound on the subject this year is indefensible. The report speaks to the Legislature and to the Government of Ontario and the Legislature and Government are powerless. So, what better purpose can be served by giving the question the publicity of the report than would have been secured by passing on to Ottawa the evidence submitted, as was first agreed upon. I should be sorry indeed if by such indiscreet action, the Committee's otherwise splendid and fruitful work should suffer from an imputation of partisan bias and political tactics.

The merit or demerit of the question is not in point, although it is argued in certain quarters that the consumer not in the well-to-do class should receive some degree of consideration.

3. EGGS AND BABY-CHICKS.

The same remarks apply to the importation of eggs and baby-chicks and the Committee strikes the proper note in pointing out, without more ado, that the question falls outside its scope and that the responsibility rests with the Federal Government. To suggest further improvement of the quality of the home product and show how and where the Legislature and the Ontario Department of Agriculture can stimulate such improvement is well within the Committee's express functions.

It may be pointed out, however, that under the Customs regulations, no free entry is to be accepted for baby-chicks unless they are pure bred; imported for the improvement of stock and carry chick bands showing their quality under the standard laid down by the American Poultry Association. (*Vide* Amended Regulations governing the Free Entry of Pure Bred Domestic Fowls for Improvement of Stock, April 4th, 1925, No. 51).

4. DUMPING.

The report in those statements which I submit are objectionable as being *ultra* the scope of the Committee, frequently uses the term "dumping" indiscriminately to denote large quantities of imports. The word, however, has received both under our own and under other countries' customs laws, a definite technical meaning and its indiscriminate use in the ordinary meaning of vast importations is apt to be misleading.

The Customs Acts, as they now stand, provide against any "dumping" of foreign products.

5. CANADIAN FRESH-KILLED BEEF.

I cannot agree with all the statements of the report concerning the export to the English market of Canadian fresh-killed beef.

To qualify as "arbitrary" the "stand taken by the Minister against the feasibility of trade in beef killed in Canada, shipped to England and retailed in fourteen days on a par with the home killed beef," besides being little euphemistic, is not justified by the facts. The stand taken by the Dominion Department of Agriculture embodies the results of well-conducted—and not "commercially faulty"—experiments as well as of "commercial experiments by the Harris Abattoir admitted to have been made at considerable loss" and of close export investigations into market conditions in England. It is also prompted by a desire to secure for the Canadian farmer the highest possible price for his product and inducing him thereby to greater effort to ensure the expansion of the beef cattle industry.

I agree however with the Committee's commendations of Mr. McLean's courageous efforts, although past experience does not point to a dressed beef export trade bringing profitable results until our exportable surplus shall have increased to sufficient proportions.

6. IMPERIAL ECONOMIC COMMITTEE.

The Committee's report contains strictures on the Dominion Department of Agriculture supposedly for not having given timely information and advice as to the purpose of the Imperial and Economic Committee on marketing and

Preparing for Market of Foodstuffs prepared in the Overseas parts of the Empire, and especially of meat. After minute enquiry, I must register complete disagreement with this statement. Nothing reasonable was left undone to secure adequate expert representation on the Committee or to lay the Canadian viewpoint thoroughly before the Committee. I may say that Mr. McOuat, Canada's representative, was in himself worth a host of representatives and secured in the Committee's report all that Canada sought and more than the Imperial Government was ready to accept, since, in August last, on instructions from the Baldwin Government, there was added to the report a rider to the effect that it was not the intention of the Imperial Government to act upon certain recommendations of the report inserted at the request of the Canadian representative.

At any rate, the criticism is not a constructive one, nor suggestive of any action that may be taken by the Ontario Legislature or the Ontario Government.

7. THE AUSTRALIAN TREATY.

The statement contained in the report concerning the probable effect of the Australian Treaty on the dairy industry in this country is, to say the least, premature. It is mere prospective conjecture based on no data of any kind and most inopportune coming at a time when the question is being made the subject of protracted debate on the floor of the House of Commons. It is not a finding of facts, nor a recommendation for legislative or executive action and entirely without the purview of the Committee's reference. At the time of writing, no appreciable effect of the treaty can be pointed to upon the butter and cheese industry in Canada, although some weeks have passed since the report was adopted by the majority of the Committee.

As to the so-called Australian bounty on the export of butter mentioned in the report, the Committee's statement is not based on existing facts other than a tentative proposal made in the Antipodes, called the Petersen scheme, which neither was initiated by the Government of Australia nor has had its sanction.

However, my objection to discussing in the report the Australian Treaty and its probable effect is not, I repeat, on the merits, but because it is not competent in the Legislature or the Provincial Government to rescind the treaty or change therein a single iota. The subject fills nearly 150 pages of Hansard to date; if the debate is now carried to the floor of the Legislature, who will see the end? The statement that the intention is to give publicity to the matter is—to say the least—a meagre pretext. It first predicates that the Committee's premature judgment is right, that the Treaty is a bad piece of statesmanship and that the members of the House of Commons in every riding are unqualified to take care of what is of their own particular resort.

With those reserves, Mr. Chairman, I heartily endorse the findings, conclusions and recommendations of the Committee and am deeply convinced that the work of the Committee under your able direction will be fruitful of good results to better conditions in different branches of husbandry in this Province.

I trust this letter will be attached to the report as a justification of my position.

Yours sincerely,

A. BELANGER.

On the motion of Mr. Jamieson (South Grey), seconded by Mr. Black,

Resolved, That this House desires to record its appreciation of the valuable reports made by the Agricultural Enquiry Committee, and also of the efforts of the Committee to bring about an improvement in the production and the marketing of the agricultural resources of the Province. This House approves of the endeavours of the Committee to effect closer co-operation between the various Provinces and the Dominion for the furtherance of the plans of the Imperial Government for placing the products of Canada more advantageously before the British consumer. This House is of opinion that the development of the natural resources of the Province, the opening up of mining areas, the improvement of the highways, the extension of educational facilities, the distribution of electrical energy in rural districts and the fostering of industrial activities, are all objects that tend to better the condition of agriculture and should be encouraged in the interests of the farming community and will serve to promote the general welfare and prosperity of the country.

No. 2

Report of the Committee on Fish and Game, 1926

March 2nd.

The Fish and Game Committee of the Ontario Legislature held its first meeting of the 1926 session on March 2nd at 10.30 a.m. in Committee Room Number 1. The members present were: Messrs. Armstrong, Belford, Black, Bradburn, Callan, Colliver, Finlayson, Gray, Hambly, Haney, Harcourt, Hill, Homuth, Keith, Kennedy (Temiskaming), McKnight, Mark, Mewhinney, Pinard, Ross, Spence, Stedman, Stuart, Tellier, Vaughan, Widdifield, Willson. Mr. Black was selected as chairman for the session.

Hon. Charles McCrea, Minister of Game and Fisheries, was present and commended the Committee to the session's work. He pointed out the importance of the Committee's work and commented that in some respects the Game and Fishery Department was a repressive one, since it dealt with laws framed for the preservation of the game and fishery resources, the enforcement of which sometimes brought a little friction.

In this respect Hon. Mr. McCrea acknowledged the co-operation which the Department had received from the members of all parties in the House in the work of enforcement. People sometimes said that the Department should maintain a whole police force and rigidly enforce the law. The expense of such a policy alone made it impossible, and as a substitute there was growing up in the Province a spirit of respect for the laws and of appreciation of the need of observing them. Local fish and game associations, the Minister said, were doing most valuable work in fostering this spirit of co-operation in law enforcement.

Hon. Mr. McCrea commented upon the fact that members of the House were often pressed by their constituents to secure supplies of fish for local streams, to prevent netting and other practices, and to secure strict law enforcement generally. Persons who thus sought to improve local angling overlooked to some extent, the Minister considered, the fact that with the advent of the good roads and the motor car and with the development of tourist traffic, there now was a matter of some fifty anglers for every one who had formerly visited provincial lakes and streams. Hon. Mr. McCrea referred to a meeting which he had held with anglers of the Kingston district, when hoop nets had been blamed for the depletion of fish. The hoop net men had pointed out that for every one angler who had previously visited the district, fifty now came. The situation had been helped, the Minister stated, by arranging for both the hoop net men and the anglers of the district to co-operate in the interests of the district's fish preservation. This co-operation, replacing the former spirit of enmity, was working out most satisfactorily.

The Minister stated, however, that even with the co-operation of the interests concerned it was difficult for the Department to keep pace with the depletion of the waters. He detailed policies which had been adopted with a view to perpetuating the game fish, mentioning the hatchery established at Normandale for the propagation of speckled trout. With parent fish taken from the Nipigon in 1924, the hatchery now had 25,000 of the finest trout one could wish to see any place. During the past year the fish had been stripped for the first time, with the result that 700,000 eggs had been collected. It was hoped to raise from the hatchery 10,000,000 fry for release into the Province's waters.

Hon. Mr. McCrea further stated that during the past year the Department had added to its staff for the first time a professor of biology trained at the University of Toronto. That official had completed his first season with the Department. One of his duties was to see that, when applications were made from local streams for game fish, the streams were suitable for game fish to live in. Many requests were made for game fish simply because the local streams existed and in spite of the fact that the waters were such that game fish could not live in them.

The Minister stated that one of the problems which would be brought before the Committee would be the advisability of extending the closed season on bass to the first of July. He explained the manner in which the black bass during the past season had failed to spawn during their usual period and suggested that the necessity of prolonging the closed season accordingly should be investigated. He pointed out that the bass was one fish which it was difficult for the Department to propagate since it could not be stripped artificially, but must spawn naturally.

Hon. Mr. McCrea also stated that Warden Clunis of Kent County was present to discuss the 200-yard limit on duck shooting; Judge E. B. Fralick to give several suggestions in fish and game interests; and W. A. Clarke of Collingwood to discuss problems of commercial fishing.

HEARING OF PETITIONERS.

Warden Clunis of Kent County brought a petition signed by 500 county residents praying that the regulation in Section 14 of the Act, which forbade the pursuit of ducks more than 200 yards from shore, should be abolished. He discussed the matter in the light of the situation at Rondeau Harbour, where, he stated, hides had been built closely together from which residents fed the ducks and practically tamed them. They followed this policy until they had the ducks coming in for food in thousands daily, when they would hold a hunt which would be simply a slaughter. Warden Clunis had known of as many as 175 birds being killed in a single volley.

The point which Warden Clunis made was the present law restricted duck hunting to the person who could afford to feed and tame the birds in the manner which he had described. He and his fellow-petitioners did not consider that such a condition was just, and urged that the 200-yard limit be removed in order that any person who desired might go out in a boat and enjoy a day's sport.

Mr. Pinard agreed with the Warden that the shooting from hides as it had been described was not sportsmanlike. He considered that the Committee should recommend the abolition of the 200-yard limit and should consider also if it would not recommend the abolition of the hides.

Mr. Vaughan inquired if the residents had not spent large sums upon the Rondeau marsh in order to make it a duck shooting district and if the suggestion to throw it open might not interfere with their rights. Warden Clunis replied that he did not know of any person who had gone to any expenditure. He agreed that the fact that the residents had fed the birds was responsible for the good shooting, since no natural feeding grounds existed in the harbour. He did not believe, however, that the sport should be confined to those who could afford to feed the birds. Mr. Vaughan further pointed out that at present the hides occupy only a small part of the harbour and that nothing prevented residents from entering upon the other parts of the bay for duck hunting purposes.

Mr. Willson agreed that the 200-yard limit might well be abolished and suggested that duck hunting was covered by too many regulations. Whereas the birds were carefully protected up here, they were ruthlessly shot in the Southern States when they migrated. Mr. Willson believed that the law should allow the pursuit of ducks by a row boat.

Chairman Black of the Committee assured Warden Clunis that, while the matter would not be decided at the moment, it would have the careful consideration of the Committee before the close of the session.

JUDGE FRALICK OF BELLEVILLE.

As a huntsman of fifty years' experience, Judge E. B. Fralick of Belleville appeared before the Committee to impress upon the members the value of the Province's fish and game resources. He gave warning that unless laws were changed and rigidly enforced there would not be a deer left between Lake Ontario and North Bay, except upon private preserves. With a view to conservation, he suggested that the shooting of deer in the water be prohibited; that the chasing of them from the water on to the land and the shooting of them thereupon be prohibited; that the sale of venison be prohibited; and that the shooting of any but horned deer be prohibited, since such a law would save human lives in the bush.

W. A. CLARKE OF COLLINGWOOD.

Mr. Clarke introduced himself as one who had made his living for the past sixty years by fishing. He expressed the belief that the most wonderful fresh water fishery in the world had been ruined in Ontario because too small a mesh was imposed upon the pound net men and too great a yardage allowed the gill net men. He also strongly opposed the abolition some years ago of the closed season upon Great Lakes' fishing. The future of the fishing industry, he declared, required that the Government should impose a smaller mesh upon the pound net men. He recommended a mesh of 4¼ inches when tarred. He urged also that the Government use its influence to secure a closed season from the Dominion Government or, if that were found impossible, that it make its licenses not good between October 15th and November 15th.

The Committee thereupon proposed to adjourn to meet again on Thursday morning at 10.30. Mr. Haney, however, stated that he wished to just bring to the attention of the members the matter of the Point Edward Hatchery, which the Dominion Government was proposing to discontinue shortly. . The hatchery, he said, was the only one serving the Lake Huron fishing industry, upon which scores of people depended; and the feeling was unanimous that the Provincial Government should take it over and carry it on. He stated that he would bring the matter up at the next meeting of the Committee.

The Committee then adjourned until Thursday morning at 10.30 a.m.

March 4th.

The Committee on Fish and Game of the Ontario Legislature held its second meeting of the session on the morning of Thursday, March 4th in Committee Room Number 2. The following were present: Messrs. Belford, Black, Callan, Fenton, Graves, Gray, Hambly, Harcourt, Hill, McKnight, Pinard, Stuart, Taylor, Tellier, Weichel, Widdifield, Wright, Haney.

DEPUTATION FROM THE TRENT BRIDGE FISH AND GAME ASSOCIATION.

The Committee heard the representations of Mr. Lane of the Trent Bridge Fish and Game Association, who was introduced by Major Belford, M.P.P., for Northumberland East. Mr. Lane spoke of the lowering of the Trent waters in the spring, saying that the lunge spawn was left hanging on the rice and that the propagation of game fish was made difficult. He advocated also the licensing of guides and the imposition upon them of responsibility for the tourists whom they took out in the matter of law observance. He believed that many tourist abuses in the wasting of fish could be checked if the guide were made responsible.

John Kent also addressed the Committee with special reference to Rice Lake. He urged that the season for pickerel should be made the same as for bass in order that persons could not take the latter fish under the pretence of seeking the former. With Mr. Lane and Mr. Kent the Committee discussed certain general problems. One was the limit on the daily catch. Mr. Kent believed that it should be reduced to two lunge per day, four bass per day, or perhaps six, and to eight pickerel per day. The catch which tourists are allowed to take out of the Province was also considered. Mr. Lane believed that the law allowing a two-day catch to be taken away was proper if it were limited strictly to the last two days' catch. Under present law, he said, the tourists preserved the catch of several days and then took away the two largest, leaving the rest to waste. The matter of trolling and fishing from motor boats was mentioned, in which respect Departmental opinion was given to the effect that the people who fished from canoes actually made better catches than those who used motor boats.

The Committee and Messrs. Lane and Kent discussed the question of the pickerel season. Mr. Kent's suggestion was that no trolling or bait casting should be allowed until June 16th. Departmental opinion urged that if such a recommendation should be made, it should be for a closed season in order that enforcement might be possible. Chairman Black pointed out that any such regulation would have to apply to specific counties in which there was bass and pickerel fishing, since it would be met with disfavour in counties where such fish did not exist to be protected. While upon the subject the Deputy Minister stated to the Committee the lateness with which the bass had spawned during the past season and suggested that the closed season should be extended in all waters to July 1st.

DISCUSSION OF TAKING OVER OF FEDERAL FISH HATCHERIES.

The question of the Province taking over the Federal Government fish hatcheries which were to be discontinued about May 1st was brought up by W. S. Haney, M.P.P. for West Lambton. He spoke with particular reference to the Point Edward hatchery on Lake Huron. He gave the history of the hatcheries, telling how they had been established by the Dominion Government while it had had control of the provincial resources and how the decision to discontinue them had finally been reached since now the Province controlled its fishery resources and reaped the revenue and benefit from them. The Federal authorities, Mr. Haney said, were willing to turn the hatcheries over to the Province in return for their maintenance, which amounted to from $90,000 to $100,000 per year.

With respect to the Point Edward hatchery especially, Mr. Haney said that it was the only one serving the Lake Huron district, and that since its establishment an increasing yield each year had been reaped by those who depended upon the fishing industry. The fishermen of the district believed that if the hatchery were closed, their industry was doomed. Mr. Haney pointed out that a large number of people depended upon the industry and that their investment was considerable. He understood that the government hesitated to define the general principle of taking over the hatcheries, since in some cases they duplicated those which the Province was already maintaining. Mr. Haney believed that if it should be necessary, however, he could make out a good case for the Point Edward hatchery being made an exception.

Mr. W. H. Fenton spoke on behalf of A. J. Fallis, M.P.P. for East Durham, who favoured the continuance of the hatcheries. D. J. Taylor, M.P.P. for North Grey, expressed himself similarly. He understood that one of the difficulties in connection with the hatcheries was that they were not equipped with gravity water feed and that the water bills to the towns in which they were located ran from $1,500 to $4,000 per annum. Mr. Taylor considered that, in view of the benefit which the towns derived from the fishing industry and in view of the benefits which the hatcheries provided, the towns might agree to a lowered scale of water rates in return for having them continued. Mr. C. E. Wright, M.P.P. for Centre Simcoe, said that his riding greatly desired a fish hatchery and would be prepared to supply the water to operate one if any arrangement for one could be made upon such a basis.

Chairman Black stated that the matter was one for a Departmental decision. It was further stated to the Committee that a report was being made to the Minister upon the question of continuing the hatcheries. In response to the request of Mr. Haney that he should have the opportunity of pressing the matter again when the report was completed, Mr. Black stated that since the report was to be made to the Minister he could not give any undertaking to the effect that it should be brought before the Committee. He said, however, that Mr. Haney would be given the privilege of discussing the whole matter at a later date if he so desired.

The Committee thereupon adjourned to meet on Tuesday, March 9th, at 10 o'clock.

March 9th.

The third meeting of the Fish and Game Committee of the Ontario Legisature was held on the morning of Tuesday, March 9th, in Committee Room Number 2. The following were present: Messrs. Armstrong, Belford, Bowman, Callan, Currie, Ecclestone, Finlayson, Graves, Haney, Harcourt, Hill, Homuth, Jamieson (Grey), Keith, Kennedy, McKnight, Mark, Pinard, Ross, Tellier, Weichel, Willson (Niagara Falls), and Wright. In the absence of Mr. Black, Mr. Graves presided.

HEARING OF DEPUTATIONS.

J. R. Humphreys opposed the previous proposal made before the Committee to change the law restricting shooters from having decoys more than 200 yards from a rush bed or shore line. As one who had had considerable to do with the passing of the law in question, he stated that before it had been brought into force shooters with gasolene boats towed skiffs behind them with large flocks of decoys and went out to the only places where ducks could feed in the day time. They anchored the decoys in these places and held up the shooting from low boats, with the result that the ducks were driven away. The 200-yard limit, he said, was ample so that everybody would have some shooting and he strongly protested against any change in the law.

In reply to a question from Colonel Currie as to the effect of the Migratory Bird Act, Mr. Humphreys believed that canvasback ducks had increased materially under it, but that redheads and teal were becoming diminished. He believed that the Northern States were respecting the Act, but that the Southern ones were not. Consideration was promised Mr. Humphreys view.

The Toronto Anglers' Club.

The deputation was introduced by Mr. Finlayson. Its president, C. N. Kennedy, stated that the Association was desirous of working in harmony with the Department for the preservation of the Province's game and fish. The Association, he said, was fully impressed with the value of the Province's fishing and game resources from a commercial viewpoint and was anxious for their conservation. It had no political leanings.

Walter Davidson presented the Association's request for fingerlings rather than fry to be placed in provincial waters for restocking purposes. Experience had shown, he said, that fry were sometimes gobbled up within a few minutes whereas the fingerling stood a better chance of survival. Mr. Davidson suggested also the placarding of streams which were being restocked, in order that anglers might exercise due regard for that fact in visiting them. Mr. Frost spoke of the necessity of maintaining the fisheries of the Province in order to hold the tourist trade. Although tourists could be brought over poor roads for good fishing, he emphasized that they could not be brought over good roads for poor fishing.

Gregory Clark supported the proposal to put back the bass and lunge season to July 1st. He urged also that streams which were being stocked with trout should be closed for the season during which they are being stocked. The proposal, he felt, will meet with the approval of the localities affected, since it would impress upon the residents that a conservation policy was being followed in their interests. Mr. Clarke also urged that the Department undertake biological survey of Simcoe County after the plan followed by Oneida County in New York State, which employed Dr. Clemens. The Anglers' Association suggested Simcoe County, he said, because it was unique in containing waters suitable for every kind of game fish which existed in the Province. A study could be made of the county, of the history of its streams, of why some were denuded of fish which had been well supplied in years past; and of the food requirements and general living requirements of the different species of game fish. The information gathered in such a survey, Mr. Clark declared, would be invaluable and might be made available to private persons who might be interested in restocking a stream or lake in any part of the Province.

Dr. Wilson of the Association spoke strongly in favour of having the Department foster a spirit of law observance amongst the people. He pointed out that

11 J

unless an army of police were employed, which was impossible, the game laws could only be enforced through the co-operation and respect of the citizens. He suggested propaganda in favour of law enforcement, saying that signs to this effect might be placed alongside the fire signs which had been posted throughout the Province. The cost would be trifling and the benefit, Dr. Wilson contended, substantial. He also suggested that the Department should issue propaganda leaflets in favour of conservation and law observance and should attach them to the licenses which it issued.

Mr. Struthers of Horning's Mills was asked to address the Committee on account of his experience in the propagation of trout. He expressed the view that fingerlings were superior to fry for introduction into Ontario waters. Fry, he said, were not usually suitable for introduction into wild waters. He also said that fingerlings had a better chance of maturing if they were put into the water not too late in the season so that they might still feed upon the flies and other surface food and not have to go deep for their living too early. Mr. Struthers emphasized strongly the value of the tourist traffic to the Province.

In bringing the deputation's presentations to a close, Mr. Finlayson commended the idea of a biological survey of Simcoe County. Its cost, which had been estimated at $2,000, he regarded as moderate, and he mentioned in connection with the project also the plans which were under way to establish a game sanctuary in the north part of Simcoe County, taking in the wild waters of that territory. Should the biological survey be carried out, Mr. Finlayson said this game sanctuary would give the Department a closed ground in which to try out experiments which it might desire to undertake in the propagation of fish or of wild bird life, with a view to evolving methods to be practised in the Province generally. If the Anglers' deputation accomplished no more than to influence such a survey, Mr. Finlayson believed that its visit would prove well worth while.

Chairman Graves acknowledged the representations which the deputation had made and assured its members that they would receive the careful consideration of the Committee.

Lee Brown, a fur farmer of the Province, interviewed the Committee relative to the law which restricts the enclosure from which muskrats may be taken during the closed season for breeding purposes. He asked that it be enlarged and suggested one thousand acres as a size which the fur farming industry would benefit from. He also spoke against present fencing requirements. It was pointed out to the Committee that out of 600 fur farms in the Province only Mr. Brown's and one other had complained. To enlarge the enclosure area as Mr. Brown suggested was further declared to be a proposal which would make enforcement of the closed season impossible and likewise the protection of wild game.

The Committee thereupon adjourned to meet Thursday at 10 a.m. It was announced that the next meeting would be the last one for the hearing of deputations.

March 11th.

The fourth meeting of the Committee on Fish and Game of the Ontario Legislature was held at 10 a.m. on the morning of Thursday, March 11th, in Committee Room Number 2. The following were present: Messrs. Belford, Black, Bowman, Bradburn, Callan, Currie, Fenton, Finlayson, Garden, Graves,

Gray, Hambly, Homuth, Jamieson (Grey), Kennedy, McKnight, Pinard, Ross, Spence, Stuart, Stedman, Taylor, Tellier, Thompson (Lanark) Vaughan, Weichel, Widdifield, Wigle, Willson (Niagara Falls), Wright. ˙

HEARING OF DEPUTATIONS.

The Ontario Game and Fish Protective Association had a deputation present. Its president, W. J. Moodey, of Kitchener, explained the interest in game and fish conservation which the Association maintained and expressed its desire to co-operate with the Fish and Game Department to the utmost extent in encouraging obedience to the laws of good sportsmanship and wise conservation. He spoke especially in favour of more small game sanctuaries in the more settled districts. He believed that they would have special utility there because the deer, when forced back into the wilder parts of the Province ran greater risks from wolves. In the more settled districts too a settler could be appointed deputy to the game warden and would take greater interest in the work of conservation because of the local interests involved. Mr. Moodey believed sanctuaries for the propagation of game were justified because of the commercial value to the Province of the tourist trade. Each deer which was brought out by the hunter in the fall, he computed, represented an expenditure of $50, which went down through the various channels of provincial trade.

Mr. Moodey spoke also in favour of increasing minimum fines for certain offences. He pointed out that in some cases the minimum penalty for not taking out a license was the same as the cost of the license. Under such a condition there was every temptation for those who were so inclined to run the risk of not being caught. Mr. Moodey suggested that every hunter coming into the country should be compelled to take out his license at the border.

Secretary J. C. Richardson of the Association spoke with respect to the open season on bass and lunge. He concurred in the suggestion which had been made to set it back to July 1st. He believed also, however, that the pickerel season should be made to coincide in order that persons might not be able to fish for bass on the pretext of fishing for pickerel. Mr. Armstrong believed that prohibition of bait casting and trolling in bass and lunge waters up to the time of the opening of the bass and lunge season would probably be sufficient provision.

W. Pears spoke in favour of the prohibition of the sale of all game. He referred in particular to the sale of rabbit. He also asked for greater penalties for illegal shooting of English pheasants and Hungarian partridge, telling of one case near Midland where 200 birds had been reared and all but fifteen destroyed while their owner had been absent on a deer hunt. Such an occurrence, Mr. Pears averred, called for drastic punishment.

F. W. Watson urged a gun license, to be nominal in the case of farmers. He stressed the revenue which it would bring and the control which it would give over law evasions. The plan of giving municipalities power to introduce one, he said, was not successful, since county councils for political reasons did not adopt it.

Dr. N. A. Powell spoke strongly against granting any protection to the crow or to the red squirrel because of the interests of the bird life of the Province. He spoke in favour then of protection for bears with provision for an open season to coincide with the deer season. He declared the bear guilty of larceny sometimes but otherwise a desirable denizen of the forests. He asked also a closed season for a period of years on beaver and protection of fur-bearing animals while in their dens.

The protection of bear was discussed by Mr. Bowman, who said that in his county the animal was a great nuisance to the farmers. Mr. Fenton spoke in similar vein, saying that if the bear were protected the farmers of the Bruce Peninsula would have to go out of sheep raising.

Dr. Powell's presentation concluded the requests of the deputation. Mr. Black assured the association that its suggestions would be given consideration by the Committee.

During the sitting the question of the present season on deer was raised for discussion by Colonel J. A. Currie. He contended that for the sportsman who went to the woods for a holiday and not necessarily for the sake of the deer it was too late. It took the hunter into the snow season, which was too rigorous for all except hardy hunters and made it unwise for the person of middle age who wanted some woodland life to go out for the hunt. The season favoured poachers, Colonel Currie said. They shot the deer illegally and were able to keep them frozen and sell them to the hunters when they were coming out. He knew from personal knowledge, he said, that this practice was wide-spread. It was not the man who bought his license and paid for the privilege of hunting who was depleting the deer, it was the poacher who was being protected at the expense of the persons who furnished the Departmental revenues. Colonel Currie gave notice that he would seek the changing of the present season to an earlier date.

The Committee thereupon adjourned to meet at the call of the Chairman.

March 18th.

The fifth meeting of the Fish and Game Committee of the Ontario Legislature was held on the morning of Thursday, March 18th, at 10.30 a.m. The following members were present: Messrs. Armstrong, Black, Bowman, Bradburn, Callen, Colliver, Curry, Fenton, Hambly, Harcourt, Hill, Jamieson (Grey), Haney, Kennedy, McKnight, Mark, Spence, Stedman, Taylor, Tellier, Thompson (Lanark), Weichel.

The Committee considered the recommendation which had been made to it at previous meeting.

Bear.

The Ontario Hunters' Game and Fish Protective Association recommended protection. The Committee considered the recommendation and voted that no action be taken.

Beaver.

E. B. Fralick, Esq., of 219 Front Street, Belleville, recommended protection. The Committee considered the recommendation and voted that no action be taken.

A. S. Weir, Esq., of Utterson, Muskoka District, recommended an open season. The Committee considered the recommendation and voted that no action be taken.

Big Game Season.

C. S. Band, Esq., Dominion Bank Building, Toronto, recommended stopping the shooting of doe by allowing the buck only to be shipped when killed. The Committee considered the recommendation and voted that no action be taken.

F. Farwell, Esq., 110 Duchess Street, Toronto, recommended a closed season on does for four or five years. The Committee considered the recommendation and voted that no action be taken.

M. Gratton, Esq., Westmeath, Renfrew County, recommended prohibiting the running of deer with dogs and shortening the season to save his sheep. The Committee considered the recommendation and voted that no action be taken.

M. U. Bates, Esq., Metagama, Algoma District, recommended that the season open on October 10th. With reference to the recommendation, Chairman Black read to the Committee a letter from Mr. Bates describing conditions as they had been on the opening of the season last year. He told of the ground being covered with snow and of a great many of the streams and rivers being frozen up, with consequent rigours and difficulties for sportsmen. The Northern Ontario members of the Committee, including Messrs. Bowman and Kennedy, believed that last season had been exceptional and that the season as it was now fixed was satisfactory to the great majority of northern residents. The Committee decided accordingly but no action could be taken on the recommendation.

The Municipal Council, Township of St. Joseph, St. Joseph's Island, Algoma District, recommended limiting the open season for deer and moose on St. Joseph's Island to fifteen days from November 15th to 30th. As this was a local matter the Committee considered that the local viewpoint should be met and moved that the recommendation be concurred in.

W. H. Argue, Esq., Clerk of Hilton Township, Hiltonbeach, Algoma District, recommended shortening the open season for deer on St. Joseph's Island to two weeks, viz., November 15th to 30th; or closing the season for period; or an alternate open and closed season. Charles Jaggers, Esq., Reeve, Village of Hiltonbeach, Algoma District, recommended shortening the open season for deer on St. Joseph's Island to two weeks, viz., November 15th to 30th; or, closing the season for period; or an alternate open and closed season. Both these resolutions were met by the action which the Committee had taken on the previous one from the Municipal Council of St. Joseph's Township and were concurred in.

A resolution passed by the directors of The Canadian Forestry Association, Ottawa, recommended advancing the opening date for moose and deer to October 15th. The Committee considered the recommendation and voted that no action be taken.

Messrs. George Hudson and Dan Morin, Copper Cliff, Sudbury District, recommended a hunting season from November 1st to 15th. The Committee considered the recommendation and voted that no action be taken.

License.

The Sharbot Lake Game Protective Association recommended that the commercial license for deer be lowered.

Sharbot Lake, Frontenac County, recommended that the Farmers' Licenses be used for domestic purposes only.

The Committee discussed the recommendation. Mr. Thompson argued that there should be no difference between the cost of a deer license for the provincial resident than for the farmer. The present schedule, which charged the former four dollars and the latter one dollar, he said, was indefensible and purely a class distinction. He cited cases in which provincial residents and farmers hunted from the one camp and enjoyed the same sport but paid differing license fees. Mr. Stedman declared that the present method of dividing the Province for settlers license purposes by a railway line was arbitrary and caused dissatisfaction in many places. In some places, he pointed out, neighbours living within a stone's throw of each other paid one four dollars, the other one dollar. Chairman Black suggested that possibly the old system whereby unorganized districts were placed under a license fee of one dollar and organized ones under a license of four dollars should be revised. The Committee decided to refer the whole matter to the Minister for his consideration.

Duck.

J. W. Miller, Esq., agent, C.N.R., Thamesville, recommended that the bag limit be reduced to ten per day and fifty per season. The Committee considered the recommendation and voted that no action be taken.

A petition from residents of Trenton, Hastings County, recommended the amendment of Section 14, subsection 2, by inserting the word monitor in the fourth line. With reference to this recommendation, Mr. Colliver said that the sport was being commercialized in his district and that the people were indignant about it. Shooters were going out on a sunken punt or monitor and slaughtering the birds and selling them to city hotels. Upon the motion of Mr. Colliver, seconded by Mr. Armstrong, the recommendation was concurred in.

J. W. Miller, Esq., agent for C.N.R., Thamesville, recommended the use of boats when hunting ducks.

J. R. Humphries, Esq., Department of Education, Parliament Buildings, recommended the retaining of the 200 yards limit on ducks.

J. F. Fletcher, Esq., County Clerk, Kent County, Chatham, recommended pursuing and shooting ducks in a row boat within any distance limit from shore.

The above recommendations all concerned the 200-yard limit. The Committee discussed the present regulation and was of the opinion that its abolition would both protect the ducks by halting the slaughter of them from blinds on the shore and would at the same time open the sport to a greater number, who could not at present afford to rent the hides which were being commercialized. Upon motion of Mr. Tellier, seconded by Mr. Armstrong, the Committee resolved that the 200-yard limit should be removed.

J. W. Miller, Esq., agent for C.N.R., Thamesville, recommended prohibiting the scattering of grains and cereals for purpose of luring ducks to be slaughtered. The Committee discussed the recommendation and voted that no action be taken.

One Day.

J. W. Miller, Esq., agent for C.N.R., Thamesville, recommended the shotting of ducks from daylight to dark. The Committee considered the recommendation and moved that no action be taken.

Fox.

Dr. Freeman, Inverary, Frontenac County, recommended protection for fox. N. V. Freeman, Battersea, Frontenac County, recommended prohibiting the digging out of fox pups. C. G. Graham, Esq., Peterborough Protective Association, on behalf of Jack Mitchell, Cavin, Durham County, recommended prohibiting the digging out of fox pups. J. F. Fletcher, Esq., County Clerk, Kent County, Chatham, recommended fox hunting, only where there are no deer.

The Committee gave consideration to the above recommendation and voted that no action be taken.

Gun License.

The Ontario Hunters' Game and Fish Protective Association recommended the adoption of a gun license exempting the farmer on his own land. York County Council, through its clerk, R. W. Philips, recommended the same.

The Committee discussed the recommendation. It was pointed out that the agitation for the gun license had come almost solely from the Counties of Lincoln, Welland, and Wentworth, where efforts were being made to propagate the English pheasant and where much annoyance was being caused by the indiscriminate shooting by aliens in the district. To meet the situation the Department submitted the following draft regulations to apply only to the Counties of Lincoln, Welland, and York, which had requested gun license:

"Section 9, subsection 1. Revoke present subsection and substitute the following: Non-residents shall not hunt, take, kill, wound or destroy any animal or bird, or carry or use a firearm or air gun for such purpose, except under the authority of a license and in all actions and prosecutions under this subsection the possession of any firearm or air gun shall be prima facie evidence that the person in possession thereof was hunting or shooting such animal or birds."

It was explained to the Committee that the above regulation would be a general one affecting the Province. The Committee concurred.

Insertion in section 9 of a new subsection "2 A" was suggested as follows: "Notwithstanding the provisions of subsection 2, every person who uses any firearm or air gun for the purpose of hunting or shooting any protected or unprotected bird or animal in the County of Lincoln and Welland and York except under the authority of a license shall be guilty of an offence against this Act, but this subsection shall not apply to farmers residing and hunting on their own farms, and in all actions and prosecutions under this subsection the possession of any firearm or air gun shall be prima facie evidence that the person in possession thereof with hunting or shooting such birds or animals."

The Committee concurred in the suggested subsection.

Insertion in section 48, subsection 1, of a new clause (*g*) was suggested as follows: "To a resident of Ontario   years of age or over to use firearms or air gun for hunting purposes and the fee for such license shall be $, together with a fee of   for the issuing of same."

The Committee concurred in the suggested clause and left to the Department the fixing of the age and fee.

Guides' Licenses.

The Department suggested that section 52 governing guides' licenses be revoked and the following substituted: Section 9, subsection 5: "It shall be unlawful for any person for hire, gain or reward or hope thereof, to guide for hunting, shooting, fishing, except under the authority of a license, which may be issued upon such terms and conditions as may be prescribed by the Lieutenant-

Governor in Council, and any person who engages or employs any person by hire, gain, reward or hope thereof, for the purpose of guiding, hunting, shooting or fishing parties, who is not in possession of a current Guide's License shall be guilty of an offence against this Act."

It was explained to the Committee that the effect of this new subsection would be to throw greater responsibility upon the guide to see that the game laws of the Province were observed. The Committee concurred in the subsection as suggested and Chairman Black read the following as the Order-in-Council which the Government intended to base upon the above amendment. "The undersigned has the honour to recommend that subject to the provisions of section 9, subsection 5, of the Ontario Game and Fisheries Act, that Guides' Licenses be issued at a fee of $2 and such licenses to terminate on December 31st of each year and that authorized issuers of such licenses be paid a commission of fifty cents on each license.

"Each guide shall be furnished with a badge for the current year by the Department, and upon receipt of same the guide shall by virtue of his office have all the powers of a deputy game and fishery warden, as provided for under the provisions of section 62, subsection 3 of the Act.

"Licensed guides will be held responsible for the extinguishing of any fires that may have been kindled by the party employing him upon leaving the same and will be required to report any violations of the Ontario Game and Fisheries Act and regulations to the Department immediately, unless he has lawful excuse for such delay, and in such reports he shall furnish the name and address of the offender, and such other particulars as will lead to the conviction of the party or parties committing the offence.

"Licensed guides neglecting or refusing to comply with these regulations will be subject to the penalties as provided for in section 65, subsection 1, of the Act, together with the cancellation of their license.

"The undersigned further recommends that an Order-in-Council, dated the 20th day of March, 1909, governing the appointing of licensed guides be revoked.

"All of which is respectfully submitted."

Increase of Fines.

Ontario Hunters' Game and Fish Protective Association recommended the increase of fines for contravention of the Fish and Game Act. The Committee discussed the recommendation and voted that no action be taken.

Muskrat.

Maurice Goddard, Esq., Brampton, recommended a closed season for two or three years. Mr. Colliver said that the present season opening on March 1st, was too early for Eastern Ontario, since the country was not open for trapping at that time, and that rats purchased then had been taken illegally. Other members of the Committee said that the present season was suitable to their districts. Mr. Colliver also held that the Province should consider a closed season for muskrats in the near future. He believed that the trappers would approve of one for their own ultimate interests. The committee decided to leave the matter over for a year with the understanding that it be taken up next session and that the trappers be prepared for the move by the members for their ridings in the interval.

Partridge.

Messrs. George Hudson and Dan Morin recommended a closed season for five years. The Committee discussed the recommendation and voted that no action be taken.

Pheasants.

Representations from Lincoln and Welland Counties recommended: (1) A law to apply only in the first instance to the Counties of Lincoln and Welland but to apply to any other county on application by the county council of such county. (2) Four days' shooting each year. (3) A written permit from the land owner or occupier to any one entering his property to shoot or hunt. (4) A license of five dollars per gun (not to include farmers shooting on their own land).

The Committee discussed the recommendation. Colonel Currie was of the opinion that breeders of the birds should be allowed to shoot or take some each year either for their own use or for sale. He held that the time had come to commercialize the propagation of pheasants as a commercial proposition as it was in the old country. Mr. Tellier spoke of the present method of regulating the shooting by Order-in-Council, saying that it was not satisfactory because the local people did not know of the passage of the Order-in-Council, which meant that non-residents motored in and got the birds. He stated that notice of an open season should be published in the local papers of the places affected. The Committee resolved that the matter be left in the hands of the Department as at present and that no action should be taken on the recommendations.

Pests.

The Ontario Hunters' Game and Fish Protective Association recommended the destruction of the crow and red squirrel. The Committee discussed the recommendation and voted that no action would be taken.

Sale of Game.

The Ontario Hunters Game and Fish Protective Association recommended that the sale of all game be prohibited with the possible exception of rabbits. C. S. Band, Esq., Dominion Bank Building, Toronto, recommended the prohibiting of the sale of venison as a commercial enterprise.

Mr. Taylor strongly agreed with the recommendations declaring that to have them concurred in would not be to deprive the general public of venison since the true sportsman always shared his meat with his friends and did not desire to sell it. Colonel Currie agreed also believing that such a move would eliminate much of the present commercialization of farmers' licenses. Colonel Currie also mentioned the lumber companies of the north as not conserving the game of the country in which they operated. Motion of Mr. Taylor, seconded by Colonel Currie, that the sale of big game be prohibited was carried by the Committee.

Sanctuaries.

The Ontario Hunters' and Game and Fish Protective Association recommended more and smaller sanctuaries especially in more settled districts. The Committee considered the recommendation and voted that no action be taken.

Trapping.

William Quinn, Esq., Charlton, Temiskaming District, recommended that farmers have trapping licenses. The Committee discussed the recommendation and voted that no action be taken.

A. S. Weir, Esq., Utterson, Muskoka District, recommended that a trap line for trappers be required. The Committee discussed the recommendation and moved that no action be taken.

FISH.

Closed Season.

J. R. Harkness, Esq., President of Eastern Ontario Fish and Game Protective Association, Lancaster, recommended a closed season for all kinds of fish in the streams of the River-Aux-Raisins and its branches and also Sutherland's Creeks (east of Bainsville) and Finney's Creek during the closed season for small mouthed black bass. The Committee concurred in the recommendation.

The Toronto Anglers' Club recommended that all public waters restocked with fish be closed for one year. The Committee discussed the recommendation and voted that no action be taken.

The Ontario Hunters' Game and Fish Protective Association recommended that the open season for all fish in the Trent waters conform to that for bass. The Committee discussed the recommendation and voted that no action be taken.

Limit of Catch and Season.

The Severn River Improvement Association recommended that the limit of fish permitted an angler's license be reduced.

Morris Ackerman, Esq., Publisher of Ackerman's Sportsman's Guide, Cleveland, Ohio, recommended that the limit of catch upon maskinonge be reduced to two or one.

The Toronto Anglers' Club recommended that the closed season for bass and lunge be extended to July 1st.

The Committee discussed the recommendations. Upon the suggestions for a reduction in the limit of catch, the opinion was that the present limit upon bass was too high. The Committee resolved, accordingly, that the limit of catch upon bass in its opinion should be reduced to five per day. No change was favoured in the present limits for lunge or pickerel.

Upon the question of the bass and lunge season, the Committee favoured the extension of it to July 1st, in order that the bass might have sufficient time to spawn. The Toronto Anglers' Club recommendation for such an extension, accordingly, was concurred in. It was explained to the Committee that the change could only be made for the 1927 season, since the licenses for the coming summer had already gone out.

Season. (Resolutions Regarded as Dealt with in Preceding Resolution.)

F. D. Boggs, Esq., K.C., Cobourg, Northumberland County, recommended that the season for pickerel open June 16th in order to give necessary protection to maskinonge.

T. U. Fairlie, Esq., Director Point-Au-Baril Islanders' Association, recommended the extension of the bass season to June 30th.

The Toronto Anglers' Club recommended the extension of the closed season on bass to July 1st.

Season (Trent Waters). Question of Trolling for Bass and Lunge.

The Committee discussed difficulties in the Kawartha Lakes region which had recently been brought up by Messrs. Bradburn, Belford, and Marks regarding people taking bass and lunge illegally under the pretext of fishing for pickerel. After discussion of ways and means to solve the problem, having regard to enforcement difficulties and the desirability of still allowing residents to fish from the shore and bridges for pickerel for food, Mr. Bradburn moved, Mr. Mark seconded, and the Committee concurred, that fishing from a boat be prohibited in the closed season in the following waters: Sturgeon Lake, Cameron Lake, Balsam Lake, Mud Turtle Lake, Stoney Lake, Chemong Lake, Buckhorn Lake, and what are called the Kawartha Lakes, down the river to Rice Lake and in the whole of Rice Lake. "How far down the Trent River the provision should apply," Mr. Bradburn said, "I am not prepared to say. That is in Major Belford's area. I know that Major Belford was at previous sittings of this Committee and expressed himself in favour of the prohibition of trolling."

Net Fishing.

Upon motion of Colonel Currie, seconded by Mr. Marks, the Committee resolved that no seine net licenses should be granted in April and May in rivers where pickerel and other fish are being artificially propagated.

Gordon Philip, Esq., Secretary-Treasurer of the Western Ontario United Boards of Trade, Windsor, recommended that net fishing in the rivers and streams of the Province during the spawning season be prohibited.

T. U. Fairlie, Esq., Director of the Point-Au-Baril Islanders' Association recommended the prohibition of seine net fishing.

The Committee discussed the above recommendations and voted that no action should be taken upon them.

Operation of Fish Hatcheries.

The advisability of the Provincial Department taking over and operating the fish hatcheries which the Federal Department had signified its intention of discontinuing in May had been brought before the Committee previously. The matter was declared by Colonel Currie to be one about which there was no politics, as it interested both sides of the House. In order that it might be clear that the matter was being approached from this viewpoint, Colonel Currie moved and Mr. Tellier, of the opposite side of the House, seconded the following resolution as expressing the view of the Committee: "The members of this Committee recommend to the Department the advisability of taking over the hatcheries now operated by the Federal Government." The resolution was endorsed by the Committee unanimously.

This item completed the agenda of the Committee for the session. Before adjourning, upon motion of Colonel Currie, seconded by Mr. Bradburn, a unanimous vote of thanks was tendered to Mr. Black for his chairmanship of the sittings.

Report of the Standing Committee on Public Accounts, 1926.

To the Honourable the Legislative Assembly of the Province of Ontario:.

Your Committee has had produced before it the following accounts, vouchers, correspondence and particulars in connection with the Public Accounts of the Province of Ontario for the fiscal year ended the 31st October, 1925, and also certain accounts, vouchers and auditors' reports in connection with the business dealings of the Lyons Fuel & Supply Company and the Sault Ste. Marie Coal & Wood Company, with any departments of the Government of the Province of Ontario, or with any contractors, licensees or vendors having dealings with any such department, all of which it has carefully examined and considered.

Details in connection with the following items:—

Item of $414,777.09, page G. 34, Public Accounts, to McNamara Construction Company.

Items of $1,845.89, page G. 12, $8,187.32, page G. 30, $816.24, page G. 41, to E. L. Bedford.

Fire insurance carried by the Government and premiums paid thereon.

Item of $900,000, page 14, Public Accounts, receipt by the Province and generally as to Provincial Dispensaries.

Various items under heading of Motion Picture Bureau, pages N. 3, 12, 13, 14, of the Public Accounts, and generally as to the Motion Picture Bureau and Radio Publicity.

Item of $4,827.67, page K. 22, Public Accounts, paid to T. J. McLean on Contract 1223, grading, Brampton-Chatsworth project, Peel Township.

Your Committee dealt with the request of the former Minister of Lands and Forests, Hon. James Lyons, for an investigation of all business transactions of himself or either of the companies in which he is interested with any department of the Government and examined fourteen witnesses in this connection. In addition, the firm of Clarkson, Gordon & Dilworth, Chartered Accountants and Auditors, at the request of your Committee, made an audit of the books of the Lyons Fuel & Supply Company and the Sault Ste. Marie Coal and Wood Company, and presented to the Committee a report of that audit.

Major A. E. Nash, for the Clarkson firm, reported to the Committee that after an exhaustive examination of the books of the two companies referred to, in which he was assisted by the officials and auditors of the companies, he found the books in good order and his investigation revealed nothing to warrant any suspicion. The investigation conducted by your Committee confirmed this view.

So far as the evidence before your Committee enables the reaching of a conclusion, your Committee feel that the Hon. Jas. Lyons is entitled to a complete and unqualified exoneration from any breach of the Legislative Assembly Act, and that his companies' business record with relation to the Government and any contractors having business relations with the Government is beyond reproach.

Your Committee investigated the circumstances under which the firm of Geo. Oakley & Sons secured the contract to supply and erect the stonework on the new Whitney Block of the Parliament Building, and found the entire transaction to be quite regular and the contract well carried out with benefit to the Province.

In connection with the investigation into the treatment by T. J. McLean, contractor on the Caledon Road, of the men employed by him, your Committee is pleased to learn that the Honourable the Prime Minister has made an announcement in the House dealing with this matter, which obviates the necessity of any finding or recommendation by your Committee.

Some evidence having been given by one of the witnesses before the Committee reflecting on the efficiency of the Provincial Air Service of the Forestry Branch, your Committee, having heard the evidence of the witness in question and the evidence of Captain Roy Maxwell, Director of the Air Service, are of the opinion that the criticism suggested was not justified by the facts and that the establishment of this branch of the Public Service has been amply justified by the result.

Several other matters were brought before your Committee and were investigated, but in no case did the results of such investigation suggest any action to your Committee.

All of which is respectfully submitted.

ALEX. C. LEWIS,

Chairman.

WITNESSES EXAMINED BY PUBLIC ACCOUNTS COMMITTEE.

Hon. Jas. Lyons, Sault Ste. Marie.
J. J. Fitzpatrick, Sault Ste. Marie.
G. J. Lamb, Sault Ste. Marie.
H. D. McNamara, Toronto.
G. A. McNamara, Toronto.
A. J. McAllister, Sault Ste. Marie.
E. J. Hoskins, Sudbury.
Claude Findlay, Niagara Falls.
Harry C. Lyons, Sault Ste. Marie.
E. L. Bedford, Sault Ste. Marie.
E. J. Zavitz, Toronto.
C. H. Fullerton, Toronto.
Geo. Oakley, M.P.P., Toronto.
C. Blake Jackson, Toronto.
A. E. Nash, Toronto.
R. H. Briggs, Toronto.
W. R. Maxwell, Toronto.
Jno. Brass, Toronto.
Mrs. Emily Franklin, Caledon.
Kenneth Hannahson, Orangeville.
Mrs. Carrie Sutton, Caledon.
Richard Russell, Orangeville.
A. J. McEnaney, Toronto.
Jas. McDevitt, Toronto.
R. L. McClintock, Streetsville.
Jno. Telford, Toronto.
G. E. Patton, Toronto.
A. H. Birmingham, Toronto.
J. H. Ferguson, Toronto.
J. A. LaBerge, Sudbury.
W. H. Brown, Toronto.

EXHIBITS PRESENTED.

Re PROVINCIAL AIR SERVICE HANGAR, SAULT STE. MARIE:

No. 1—Memorandum from W. R. Maxwell to Hon. Jas. Lyons in connection with location of hangar.

No. 2—Memorandum from W. R. Maxwell to Hon. Jas. Lyons in connection with location of site for hangar at Sault Ste. Marie.

No. 3—Quotations on supplies and materials for construction of hangar from Lyons Fuel and Supply Company to J. J. Fitzpatrick.

No. 4—Map showing plan and location of hangar.

Re PURCHASE OF SUPPLIES BY NORTHERN DEVELOPMENT BRANCH:

No. 5—Letter from C. H. Fullerton, Deputy Minister, to G. J. Lamb, Government Engineer, Sault Ste. Marie.

Re CONSTRUCTION OF WHITNEY BLOCK, QUEEN'S PARK:

No. 6—Contract and documents in connection with stone work presented by Geo. Oakley, M.P.P.

Re LYONS FUEL AND SUPPLY CO. AND ST. MARIE COAL AND WOOD COMPANY:

No. 7—Report of investigation of accounts and records by A. E. Nash.

Re FORESTRY AIR SERVICE:

No. 8—Letter dated Aug. 24th, 1925, from L. H. Briggs to Hon. Jas. Lyons.

No. 9—Letter dated Sept. 3rd, 1925, from Hon. Jas. Lyons to L. H. Briggs.

Re CALEDON ROAD—PEEL COUNTY:

No. 10—Letter dated March 1st, 1926, from W. H. Brown, Accountant, Dept. of Highways, to Jno. Brass with cheque for $19.09 attached.

No. 11—Letter dated March 1st, 1926, from W. H. Brown, Accountant, Dept. of Highways, to A. J. McEnaney, with cheque for $2.33 attached.

No. 12—Letter dated March 1st, 1926, from W. H. Brown, Accountant, Dept. of Highways, to Jas. McDevitt with cheque for $1.50 attached.

No. 13—Letter dated March 1st, 1926, from W. H. Brown, Accountant, Dept. of Highways, to R. L. McClintock.

No. 14—Statement of claim by Jno. Telford against T. J. McLean, submitted to Highways Department, Dec. 3rd, 1925.

No. 15—Letter dated March 1st, 1926, from W. H. Brown, Accountant, Highways Department, to J. Telford, with cheque for $30.68 attached.

Re CREIGHTON—COPPER CLIFF ROAD:

No. 16—Agreement dated Sept. 12th, 1924, between J. A. Laberge and McNamara Construction Company.

Minutes and Proceedings

PUBLIC ACCOUNTS COMMITTEE, 1926

Public Accounts Committee Room,
Parliament Buildings,
Toronto, March 12th, 1926.

The Select Standing Committee to whom was referred the examination of the Public Accounts of the Province for the fiscal year 1924-1925 and composed of the following members: Messrs. Acres, Belanger, Belford, Berry, Biggs, Black, Bowman, Bradburn, Callan, Carr, Clarke (Brockville), Clarke (Northumberland), Currie, Ecclestone, Edwards, Elliott, Finlayson, Fisher, Freeborn, Garden, Godfrey, Graves, Gray, Haney, Harcourt, Henry, Hill, Hillmer, Homuth, Ireland, Jamieson (Grey), Keefer, Keith, Kemp, Kennedy (Temiskaming), Lethbridge, Lewis, Lyons, McCausland, McCrea, McKeown, MacBride, Mageau, Mcwhinney, Morel, Nesbitt, Nickle, Nixon, Oakley, Oke, Owens, Patterson, Price, Proulx, Raney, Rankin, Sinclair, Tellier, Thompson (Lanark), Vaughan, Wallis, Weichel, Widdifield, Wigle, Wilson (Windsor)—66, met this day for organization.

Present:—Messrs. Belanger, Belford, Berry, Biggs, Black, Bradburn, Callan, Carr, Clarke (Brockville), Clarke (Northumberland), Eccleston, Edwards, Finlayson, Freeborn, Garden, Graves, Gray, Haney, Harcourt, Hill, Hillmer, Homuth, Ireland, Jamieson (Grey), Keefer, Keith, Kemp, Kennedy (Temiskaming), Lewis, Lyons, Mewhinney, Morel, Nixon, Oakley, Oke, Owens, Patterson, Raney, Sinclair, Tellier, Weichel, Wigle.

Moved by Mr. Graves, seconded by Mr. J. Patterson,

That Mr. A. C. Lewis, Member for North East Toronto, be and he is hereby appointed Chairman of the Public Accounts Committee for the Session of 1926. Carried.

Moved by Mr. Finlayson, seconded by Mr. Jamieson (Grey),

That the Committee proceed with the investigation requested by Hon. James Lyons into the connection of the late Minister, the Lyons Fuel & Supply Company, Ltd., and the Sault Ste. Marie Coal & Wood Company, Ltd., with the Government of the Province of Ontario, and with Government contractors or Crown licensees.

That Messrs. Clarkson, Gordon and Dilworth of the City of Toronto, Chartered Accountants, be instructed to make investigation of the relation of the said late Minister, the Lyons Fuel & Supply Company, Ltd., and the Sault Ste. Marie Coal & Wood Company, Ltd., with all or any branch of the Ontario Government, and with any Government contractors or timber licensees, and that for such purposes the said firm have power and authority to investigate the accounts of the Government and all accounts, vouchers, documents, bank books, bank accounts, papers, letters or memoranda of the said Companies, or either of them, in connection with the above matters, and power to investigate the accounts of the said companies, or either of them, with the Royal Bank of Canada at Sault Ste. Marie, Ontario, or any other bank account that may be necessary for a complete investigation of the said matters.

That the following witnesses be summoned to appear before the Public Accounts Committee: Honourable James Lyons, Charles H. Fullerton, Alex.

McAllister, J. J. Fitzpatrick, E. J. Zavitz, Claude Findlay, James Dawson, George McNamara, Howard McNamara, Harry C. Lyons, E. L. Bedford, Frank LaBarge, R. Walsh, G. J. Lamb.

Moved by Mr. Sinclair, seconded by Mr. Clarke (Northumberland E.),

That E. L. Bedford, of Sault Ste. Marie, be summoned before this Committee at its next meeting to give evidence as to the following payments made to him as appears in the Public Accounts for the year ending October 31st, 1925.

Page G. 12.............................. $1,845.89
Page G. 30.............................. 8,187.32
Page G. 41.............................. 816.24

Moved by Mr. Sinclair, seconded by Mr. Belanger,

That the President and Secretary of the Walsh Construction Co. be summoned before this Committee at its next meeting to give evidence as to the item of $33,674.14 paid to said company appearing on Page G. 34 of the Public Accounts for the fiscal year ending October 31st, 1925, and to produce all books, vouchers and documents relating to the same.

Moved by Mr. Sinclair, seconded by Mr. Clarke,

That H. D. MacNamara and Geo. A. MacNamara, of the MacNamara Construction Co., Ltd., be summoned before this Committee at its next meeting to give evidence as to the item of $414,777.09 paid to said company appearing on Page G. 34 of the Public Accounts for the fiscal year ending October 31st, 1925, and to produce all books, vouchers, and documents relating to the same.

Moved by Mr. Sinclair, seconded by Mr. Clarke,

That Hon. James Lyons, member for Sault Ste. Marie, be summoned before this Committee at its next meeting to give evidence in regard to payments appearing in the Public Accounts for the fiscal year ending October 31st, 1925, as having been made to the Lyons Fuel and Supply Company as follows:

Page G. 32.............................. $1,087.41
Page G. 35.............................. 1,209.60
Page G. 41.............................. 878.75

and to produce all books, vouchers and documents relating thereto.

Moved by Mr. Kemp, seconded by Mr. Nixon,

That George Oakley, M.L.A., C. Blake Jackson and W. W. Sidley be summoned before the Committee at its next meeting to give evidence concerning the new Government Building now in course of construction in Queen's Park, and to produce all books, papers, letters and documents having reference to the relations of the Jackson Lewis Company, Ltd., and George Oakley and Son, Ltd., in relation thereto.

Moved by Mr. Keith, seconded by Mr. Nixon,

That J. H. Ferguson be summoned to appear to give evidence before the Committee at its next meeting concerning the fire insurance carried by the Province, the premiums paid therefor and all facts connected therewith.

Moved by Mr. Sinclair, seconded by Mr. Raney,

That this Committee be called for Monday evening next and thereafter sit daily until the business now before the Committee is disposed of.

It was moved in amendment by Mr. Finlayson, seconded by Mr. Carr,

That the Committee hold their next meeting at 10 a.m. on Wednesday, March 17th.

A vote was polled, and the amendment carried on the following division:—

Yeas:—

Messrs. Belford,
Black,
Bradburn,
Carr,
Ecclestone,
Finlayson,
Garden,
Graves,
Haney,
Hill,
Hillmer,
Ireland,
Keefer,
Keith,
Kennedy (Temiskaming)
Lyons,
Morel,
Oakley,
Owens,
Patterson,
Weichel,
Wigle—22.

Nays:—

Messrs. Belanger,
Biggs,
Clarke (Northumberland),
Freeborn,
Kemp,
Mcwhinney,
Nixon,
Raney,
Sinclair,
Tellier—10.

The Committee then adjourned until Wednesday, March 17th, at 10 a.m.

Public Accounts Committee Room,
Parliament Buildings,
Toronto, March 17th, 1926.

The Committee met at 10 A.M., Mr. Lewis in the Chair.

Present:—Messrs. Belanger, Belford, Berry, Biggs, Black, Bowman, Bradburn, Callan, Carr, Clarke (Brockville), Currie, Ecclestone, Edwards, Elliott, Finlayson, Freeborn, Godfrey, Harcourt, Hill, Hillmer, Homuth, Jamieson (Grey), Keefer, Kemp, Kennedy (Temiskaming), Lethbridge, Lewis, Lyons, McKeown, Mewhinney, Morel, Nesbitt, Nixon, Oakley, Oke, Owens, Proulx, Raney, Rankin, Sinclair, Tellier, Thompson (Lanark), Wallis, Weichel, Widdifield, Wigle.

Moved by Mr. Widdifield, seconded by Mr. Lethbridge,
That Mr. A. H. Birmingham be summoned before the Committee to give evidence in respect of the item of $900,000 appearing as a receipt by the Province at page 14 of the Public Accounts, and generally as to the Provincial Dispensaries.

Moved by Mr. Raney, seconded by Mr. Nixon,
That when the Committee adjourns to-day it stand adjourned to to-morrow at an hour to be named by the Chair, and that thereafter as far as practicable the Committee sit from day to day until the matters now before it, or which may be brought before it, have been disposed of.

An amendment was moved by Mr. C. R. McKeown, seconded by Mr. Currie,

That it is the desire of this Committee to meet as often as possible to complete the work now before, or that hereafter come before the Committee, and that if necessary for that purpose the permission of the Legislature will be asked to sit while the House is sitting, and that to carry that desire into effect meetings of the Committee will be held as frequently as circumstances will permit. Carried.

Moved by Mr. Raney, seconded by Mr. Kemp,

That S. L. Squire, Deputy Minister of Highways, Frank H. Harris, Edmund P. Stewart, Carleton L. Dyer, R. S. Shenstone, W. G. Clysdale and Albert E. Nash be summoned before the Committee to give evidence concerning contracts for certain advertisements that appeared in a certain magazine called "Rural Canada" on page 22 of the issue of that magazine of October, 1919' and concerning payment of the contract price of the said advertisements and that the said witnesses be required to produce all books, letters, papers and documents in their custody, possession or power relating to the said matters.

Mr. Raney then proceeded to read affidavit in support of this motion, when Mr. Finlayson rose on a point of order protesting that Mr. Raney was out of order in reading the affidavit before the motion had been dealt with by the Committee and appealed to the Chairman for a ruling. The Chairman ruled in the affirmative, and Mr. Raney appealed against the ruling. A vote was polled and the Chair sustained in the following division:—

Yeas:—	Nays:—
Messrs. Belford,	Messrs. Belanger,
Black,	Freeborn,
Bradburn	Kemp,
Carr,	Lethbridge,
Currie,	Mewhinney,
Ecclestone,	Nixon,
Edwards,	Oke,
Elliott,	Raney,
Finlayson,	Sinclair,
Harcourt,	Tellier,
Hillmer,	Wallis,
Jamieson (Grey),	Widdifield—12.
Kennedy (Temiskaming),	
Lyons,	
McKeown,	
Morel,	
Oakley,	
Owens,	
Rankin,	
Thompson (Lanark)—20.	

Mr. Raney's motion, on being submitted, was ruled out of order by the Chairman who quoted the following authority in support of his ruling.

The purpose or object of the Public Accounts Committee is well stated in Sir Erskine May's Parliamentary Practice, Thirteenth Edition, page 557, where he says: "The house also appoints at the commencement of every session the committee of public accounts, for the examination of the accounts showing the appropriation of the sum granted by Parliament to meet the public expendi-

ture." A little lower down he also states, "the function of this committee is
to ascertain that the Parliamentary grants for each financial year, including
supplementary grants, have been applied to the object which Parliament
prescribed."

The objection to the motion made by Mr. Raney is founded on the fact
that the transaction he proposes to enquire into does not relate to Parliamentary
accounts in any way whatever.

I think the objection might be founded on the ground that the transaction
is nearly seven years old, but I prefer to put my ruling on the ground that the
matters which he wishes to call in question are private matters between a publisher
and an advertiser, and does not, in any way, concern Parliamentary Votes or
Expenditure. The journal in question, "Rural Canada," was apparently a
private publication soliciting and obtaining advertisements in the usual way
from the public. It is not alleged that the moneys in question were public moneys,
and apparently it is not alleged that they were expended by a public official, or
by anyone in any way connected with the Provincial Government.

The very name of the Committee, "Public Accounts," shows that it is
intended to investigate and make reports on the public moneys of the Province
of Ontario.

I am clearly of opinion that the proposed enquiry is beyond the jurisdiction
of this Committee and cannot be undertaken.

On the appeal of Mr. Raney, a vote was polled and the Chair sustained on
the following division:—

Yeas:—	Nays:—
Messrs. Belford,	Messrs. Freeborn,
Berry,	Kemp,
Black,	Lethbridge,
Bradburn,	Mewhinney,
Carr,	Nixon,
Clarke (Brockville),	Oke,
Currie,	Raney,
Ecclestone,	Sinclair,
Edwards,	Tellier,
Elliott,	Wallis,
Finlayson,	Widdifield—11.
Harcourt,	
Hillmer,	
Jamieson (Grey),	
Keefer,	
Kennedy (Temiskaming),	
Lyons,	
McKeown,	
Morel,	
Oakley,	
Owens,	
Rankin,	
Thompson (Lanark)—23.	

Hon. James Lyons, being duly sworn, was examined by Mr. Finlayson
regarding his connection, also that of The Lyons Fuel & Supply Co., Ltd., and

Sault Ste. Marie Coal & Wood Co. with the Government of the Province of Ontario and with Government contractors or Crown licensees.
The Committee then adjourned until Thursday, March 18th, at 1.30 P.M.

Public Account Committee Room,
Parliament Buildings,
Toronto, March 18th, 1926.

The Committee met at 1.30 P.M., Mr. Lewis in the Chair.
Present:—Messrs. Acres, Belford, Berry, Biggs, Black, Bradburn, Carr, Clarke (Northumberland), Currie, Elliott, Finlayson, Godfrey, Graves, Harcourt, Hill, Hillmer, Jamieson (Grey), Keefer, Keith, Kemp, Kennedy (Temiskaming), Lethbridge, Lewis, Lyons, McKeown, Morel, Nixon, Owens, Patterson, Proulx, Raney, Rankin, Sinclair, Widdifield, Wigle, Wilson (Windsor)—66.
Hon. James Lyons was recalled and further examined by Mr. Finlayson.
The Committee then adjourned until Friday, March 19th, at 10 A.M.

Public Accounts Committee Room,
Parliament Buildings,
Toronto, March 19th, 1926.

The Committee met at 10 A.M., Mr. Lewis in the Chair.
Present:—Messrs. Belanger, Belford, Berry, Black, Bradburn, Callan, Carr, Clarke (Northumberland), Currie, Edwards, Elliott, Finlayson, Fisher, Freeborn, Garden, Graves, Gray, Harcourt, Hill, Hillmer, Homuth, Ireland, Jamieson (Grey), Keith, Kemp, Kennedy (Temiskaming), Lethbridge, Lewis, Lyons, MacBride, Patterson, Proulx, Raney, Sinclair, Tellier, Weichel, Widdifield, Wigle.

Moved by Mr. Raney, seconded by Mr. Widdifield,
That G. W. Brownridge, G. E. Patton, W. H. Graham, J. E. Rutherford, and G. J. L. Jones, be summoned before the Committee for next Wednesday to give evidence with reference to the following items in the Public Accounts for 1925:—

Page N. 3.—Items under heading Motion Picture Bureau.

Page N. 12.—G. W. Brownridge	$1,991.92
	4,126 27
W. H. Graham	1,559 31
Page N. 13.—G. W. Brownridge	1,231 52
	511 21
Page N. 14.—Am. Tel. & Tel. Co	2,625 00
S. N. Baruch	2,485 00
Bigwin Inn	700 00
Bigwin Inn Co	921 76
Gitz-Rice	125 00
K. Halliker and H. H. Caldwell	1,250 00
L. C. Williams	1,050 00

and to produce and show to the Committee all books, papers, receipts, bills and correspondence relating to the said items at pages N. 12, 13 and 14; and to give evidence generally as to the Motion Picture Bureau and Radio Publicity.

Hon. James Lyons was recalled and further examined by Mr. Finlayson and Mr. Sinclair.

The Committee then adjourned until Friday, March 19th, at 8 P.M.

Public Accounts Committee Room,
Parliament Buildings,
Toronto, March 19th, 1926.

The Committee met at 8 P.M., Mr. Lewis in the Chair.

Present:—Messrs. Acres, Belford, Black, Bowman, Callan, Ecclestone, Edwards, Finlayson, Garden, Gray, Harcourt, Hill, Keith, Kemp, Kennedy (Temiskaming), Lyons, Nesbitt, Oakley, Owens, Raney, Widdifield.

Hon. James Lyons was recalled and examined by Hon. Mr. Raney.

The Committee then adjourned until Monday, March 22nd, at 8 P.M.

Public Accounts Committee Room,
Parliament Buildings,
Toronto, March 22nd, 1926.

The Committee met at 8 P.M., Mr. Lewis in the Chair.

Present:—Messrs. Acres, Belford, Black, Bradburn, Callan, Clarke (Northumberland), Currie, Ecclestone, Finlayson, Graves, Gray, Harcourt, Hill, Ireland, Keith, Kemp, Kennedy (Temiskaming), Lethbridge, Lewis, Lyons, McCausland, Oke, Owens, Patterson, Raney, Rankin, Sinclair, Tellier, Thompson (Lanark), Wallis, Weichel, Widdifield, Wigle.

Moved by Mr. Raney, seconded by Mr. Widdifield,

That S. L. Squire, G. Hogarth, W. H. Brown, J. Telford (244 Jane Street, Toronto), Mr. Franklin (Boarding House, Caledon) and his wife, Emma Franklin, Mrs. Sutton (Hotel, Caledon), John Brass (176 George Street, Toronto), C. L. McClintock (Streetsville), S. B. Griggs (R.R. 1 Laurel), David Hunter (R.R.6, Orangeville), Richard Russell (Box 388, Orangeville), Kenneth Hannahson (Orangeville) be summoned before the Committee to give evidence with reference to item T. J. McLean, contract 1223, grading, Peel Township, Brampton-Chatsworth project (page K. 22 of Public Accounts, 1925), $4,827.67, and bring with them and show the Committee all books, accounts, vouchers, papers and correspondence having reference to the said project. Carried.

Moved by Mr. Raney, seconded by Mr. Widdifield,

That William G. Gerhart, Homestead Inspector, Bracebridge; James A. Brown, Port Severn; Mr. Dinsmore, of the Bethune Lumber Co., Huntsville; and W. C. Cain, Deputy Minister of Lands and Forests, be summoned to appear before the Committee and give evidence concerning items at page G. 8 of the Public Accounts for 1925, as follows:—

Wm. G. Gerhart............................ $1,100 00
253 25

and concerning Lot 11 in the 12th Concession, and Lot 11 in the 13th Concession of the Township of Sinclair, and to produce before the Committee all papers and correspondence with reference to the said matters. Carried.

Moved by Mr. Raney, seconded by Mr. Widdifield,
That Mr. Hoskins, District Engineer at Sudbury, R. H. Briggs, 63 Isabella Street, Toronto; Capt. Roy Maxwell be summoned before the Committee and give evidence on the pending inquiry. Carried.

The Committee met at 8 P.M., Mr. Lewis in the Chair.
Mr. J. J. Fitzpatrick, Sault Ste. Marie was sworn and examined by Mr. Finlayson, Mr. Sinclair and Mr. Raney, in connection with the contract for building the aerodrome at Sault Ste. Marie.
Mr. G. J. Lamb, District Engineer, Sault Ste. Marie, was sworn and examined by Mr. Finlayson, Mr. Sinclair, and other members of the Committee, in connection with the purchase of goods and supplies and his duties generally.
Mr. Geo. McNamara was sworn and examined by Mr. Finlayson, Mr. Sinclair and Mr. Raney, in connection with contracts from the Government for building roads.
Mr. Howard McNamara was sworn and examined by Mr. Finlayson.
The Committee then adjourned until 10 A.M., March 24th.

Public Accounts Committee Room,
Parliament Buildings,
Toronto, March 24th, 1926.

The Committee met at 10 A.M., Mr. Lewis in the Chair.
Present:—Messrs. Belford, Berry, Biggs, Black, Bradburn, Callan, Carr, Currie, Elliott, Finlayson, Fisher, Garden, Haney, Harcourt, Hill, Hillmer, Jamieson (Grey), Keith, Kemp, Kennedy (Temiskaming), Lethbridge, Lewis, Lyons, Mewhinney, Owens, Patterson, Proulx, Raney, Rankin, Sinclair, Thompson (Lanark), Weichel, Widdifield, Wilson (Windsor)—66.
Mr. Alex. McAllister, of the Lyons Fuel & Supply Co., Sault Ste. Marie, was duly sworn and examined by Mr. Finlayson, Mr. Sinclair, Mr. Raney and other members of the Committee, concerning the sale of material and supplies by the Lyons Fuel & Supply Co. to the Government of the Province of Ontario and to contractors having Government contracts.
Mr. E. J. Hoskins, District Engineer, Sudbury, was examined by Mr. Finlayson, Mr. Fisher and Mr. Raney in connection with the building of the Sudbury-Conniston and the Copper Cliff-Creighton roads.
The Committee then adjourned until 2.30 P.M.

Public Accounts Committee Room,
Parliament Buildings,
Toronto, March 24th, 1926.

The Committee met at 2.30 P.M., Mr. Lewis in the Chair.
Present:—Messrs. Belford, Berry, Biggs, Black, Bradburn, Callan, Ecclestone, Edwards, Finlayson, Fisher, Godfrey, Graves, Harcourt, Hill, Hillmer, Keith, Kemp, Kennedy (Temiskaming), Lethbridge, Lyons, Morel, Nesbitt, Owens, Raney, Rankin, Sinclair, Widdifield.

Mr. Claude Findlay was duly sworn and examined by Mr. Findlayson and Mr. Fisher in connection with duties as Government Architect on the construction of the aerodrome at Sault Ste. Marie.

Mr. Harry C. Lyons was duly sworn and examined by Mr. Finlayson and Mr. Fisher, in connection with the sale of material and supplies by the Lyons Fuel and Supply Co. to the Government and Government contractors.

Mr. E. L. Bedford was duly sworn and examined by Mr. Finlayson, Mr. Fisher and Mr. Sinclair, in connection with the sale of goods supplied to the Government of the Province of Ontario.

Mr. E. J. Zavitz, Provincial Forester, was duly sworn and examined by Mr. Finlayson, in connection with the erection of the aerodrome at Sault Ste. Marie.

Mr. Chas H. Fullerton, Deputy Minister of the Northern Development Branch, was duly sworn and examined by Mr. Finlayson and Mr. Fisher in connection with the contracts for building Sudbury-Conniston and Copper-Cliff-Creighton roads.

Moved by Mr. Raney, seconded by Mr. Fisher,

That Mr. John L. Lang, Engineer at Sault Ste. Marie, and Mr. Fred Irwin, of Sault Ste. Marie, be summoned to appear before the Committee to give evidence on the pending inquiries asked for by Hon. James Lyons. Carried.

The Committee adjourned until Thursday, March 25th, at 1.30 P.M.

Public Accounts Committee Room,
Parliament Buildings,
Toronto, March 25th, 1926.

The Committee met at 1.30 P.M., Mr. Lewis in the Chair.

Present:—Messrs. Black, Bradburn, Carr, Clarke (Brockville), Ecclestone, Elliott, Finlayson, Garden, Graves, Gray, Haney, Harcourt, Hillmer, Ireland, Kemp, Kennedy (Temiskaming), Lewis, Lyons, MacBride, Nixon, Oakley, Proulx, Raney, Vaughan, Widdifield, Wigle.

Mr. Geo. Oakley, M.P.P., was duly sworn and examined by Mr. Finlayson and Mr. Raney in connection with the sub-contract of Geo. Oakley & Son with the Jackson Lewis Co. for supplying stone for the new Parliament Buildings, Queen's Park.

Mr. C. Blake Jackson was duly sworn and examined by Mr. Raney in connection with the contract of the Jackson Lewis Co. with the Government of the Province of Ontario for building of the new Parliament Buildings, Queen's Park.

Mr. Chas. Fullerton was recalled and further examined by Mr. Fisher, Mr. Raney and Mr. Finlayson.

Mr. E. J. Hoskins was recalled and further examined by Mr. Fisher.

The Committee then adjourned until Friday, March 26th, at 10 A.M.

Public Accounts Committee Room,
Parliament Buildings,
Toronto, March 26th, 1926.

The Committee met at 10 A.M., Mr. Lewis in the Chair.

Present:—Messrs. Acres, Belford, Berry, Biggs, Black, Bradburn, Callan, Carr, Clarke (Brockville), Currie, Edwards, Elliott, Finlayson, Freeborn,

Graves, Harcourt, Hill, Hillmer, Homuth, Ireland, Keith, Kemp, Kennedy (Temiskaming), Lethbridge, Lyons, Mewhinney, Owens, Patterson, Thompson (Lanark), Widdifield.

Mr. A. E. Nash, of the firm of Clarkson, Gordon and Dilworth, being duly sworn, presented a report of his investigation of the accounts and records of the Lyons Fuel & Supply Co., Ltd., and the Sault Ste. Marie Coal and Wood Co., Ltd., and was examined thereon by Mr. Finlayson and Mr. Raney.

Mr. R. H. Briggs, Toronto, was duly sworn and examined by Mr. Raney, Mr. Finlayson and other members in connection with the Forestry Air Service of the Province of Ontario.

Mr. W. R. Maxwell, Director of Provincial Air Service, was duly sworn and examined by Mr. Finlayson, Mr. Raney and other members in connection with the Forestry Air Service.

The Committee adjourned until Saturday, March 27th, at 10 A.M.

———

Public Accounts Committee Room,
Parliament Buildings,
Toronto, March 27th, 1926.

The Committee met at 10 A.M., Mr. Lewis in the Chair.

Present:—Messrs. Belanger, Belford, Black, Callan, Edwards, Finlayson, Freeborn, Haney, Harcourt, Hill, Jamieson (Grey), Kemp, Kennedy (Temiskaming), Lewis, Lyons, Widdifield.

Mr. A. E. Nash was recalled and further examined by Mr. Raney and Mr. Finlayson.

Mr. Raney read the charges of John Brass against T. J. McLean on Contract No. 1223, Brampton-Chatsworth Project, and he and Mr. Finlayson examined the following witnesses thereon: John Brass, Toronto; Mrs. Emmily Franklin, Caledon; Kenneth Hannahson, Orangeville; Mrs. Carrie Sutton, Caledon; Richard Russell, Orangeville; A. J. McEnaney, Toronto; Jas. McDevitt, Toronto; R. L. McClintock, Streetsville.

The Committee then adjourned until Monday, March 29th, at 2 P.M.

———

Public Accounts Committee Room,
Parliament Buildings,
Toronto, March 29th, 1926.

The Committee met at 2 P.M., Mr. Lewis in the Chair.

Present:—Messrs. Belford, Berry, Black, Callan, Carr, Finlayson, Fisher, Graves, Gray, Harcourt, Ireland, Keith, Kennedy (Temiskaming), McKeown, Mageau, Mewhinney, Oakley, Proulx, Sinclair, Vaughan, Widdifield.

Mr. Jno. Telford, Toronto, was duly sworn and examined by Mr. Raney and Mr. Finlayson in connection with the Brampton-Chatsworth Project.

The Committee decided to further investigate the above matter at a meeting to be held the following day.

The Committee then adjourned until 8 P.M.

Public Accounts Committee Room,
Parliament Buildings,
Toronto, March 29th, 1926.

The Committee met at 8 P.M., Mr. Lewis in the Chair.

Present:—Messrs. Belford, Berry, Callan, Edwards, Finlayson, Fisher, Graves, Hill, Hillmer, Keith, Kemp, Kennedy (Temiskaming), Lethbridge, Lewis, McCausland, Mewhinney, Patterson, Proulx, Raney, Widdifield.

Mr. G. E. Patton was duly sworn and examined by Mr. Raney and Mr. Finlayson in connection with various items under the heading of Motion Picture Bureau and generally as to Motion Picture Bureau and Radio Publicity.

Mr. A. H. Birmingham, General Manager, Ontario Government Dispensaries, was duly sworn and examined by Mr. Raney and Mr. Finlayson in connection with $900,000, page 14, Public Accounts, receipt by the Province and generally to Provincial Dispensaries.

Mr. J. H. Ferguson was sworn and examined by Mr. Raney and Mr. Finlayson in connection with Fire Insurance carried by the Government and premiums paid thereon.

The Committee then adjourned until Tuesday, March 30th, at 4 P.M.

Public Accounts Committee Room,
Parliament Buildings,
Toronto, March 30th, 1926.

The Committee met at 4 P.M., Mr. Lewis in the Chair.

Present:—Messrs. Belford, Bradburn, Callan, Carr, Ecclestone, Edwards, Finlayson, Fisher, Freeborn, Hill, Hillmer, Kemp, Kennedy (Temiskaming), Lewis, Lyons, McCausland, MacBride, Morel, Oakley, Patterson, Raney, Vaughan, Widdifield.

Mr. J. A. LeBerge, Sudbury, was duly sworn and examined by Mr. Finlayson, Mr. Raney and Mr. Fisher in connection with the contract for building the Copper Cliff-Creighton Road.

Mr. Geo. A. McNamara was recalled and further examined by Mr. Raney, Mr. Finlayson, Mr. Fisher and other members of the Committee.

Mr. J. H. Ferguson was recalled and further examined by Mr. Raney in connection with Fire Insurance carried by the Government.

The Committee then adjourned until 8 P.M.

Public Accounts Committee Room,
Parliament Buildings,
Toronto, March 30th, 1926.

The Committee met at 8 P.M., Mr. Lewis in the Chair.

Present:—Messrs. Berry, Bradburn, Carr, Ecclestone, Edwards, Finlayson, Fisher, Freeborn, Gray, Harcourt, Hill, Jamieson (Grey), Kemp, Kennedy (Temiskaming), Lethbridge, Lyons, McCausland, Patterson, Raney, Vaughan, Weichel, Widdifield.

Mr. C. H. Fullerton was recalled and further examined by Mr. Fisher, Mr. Raney and Mr. Finlayson in connection with the Sudbury-Conniston, Copper Cliff-Creighton and Timmins-South Porcupine Roads.

Mr. W. H. Brown, Accountant, Department of Public Highways, was duly sworn and examined by Mr. Raney in connection with the contract to T. J. McLean for the Brampton-Chatsworth Project.

The Committee then adjourned until Wednesday, March 31st, at 2 P.M.

Public Accounts Committee Room,
Parliament Buildings,
Toronto, March 31st, 1926.

The Committee met at 2 P.M., Mr. Lewis in the Chair.

Present:—Messrs. Acres, Berry, Black, Bradburn, Callan, Clarke (Brockville), Currie, Ecclestone, Edwards, Elliott, Finlayson, Fisher, Garden, Graves, Gray, Hill, Hillmer, Keith, Kemp, Kennedy (Temiskaming), Lethbridge, Lyons, McCausland, MacBride, Mageau, Mewhinney, Morel, Owens, Patterson. Proulx, Raney, Sinclair, Widdifield, Wigle.

Moved by Mr. Finlayson, seconded by Mr. Black,

That the Minutes of the various meetings of the Committee on Public Accounts be taken as read and approved. Carried.

Moved by Mr. MacBride, seconded by Mr. Finlayson,

That the payment of fees and travelling expenses to witnesses and the amount to be paid in each case be left to the discretion of the Chairman. Carried.

The Chairman presented his report for consideration by the members of the Committee.

Moved by Mr. Black, seconded by Mr. Edwards,

That the report be adopted and presented to the Legislative Assembly.

Mr. Raney, seconded by Mr. Fisher, moved in amendment,

That the motion for the adoption of the report as drafted by the Chairman be amended by substituting therefore an alternative draft report submitted by him.

A vote was polled and the amendment lost on the following division:—

Yeas:—	Nays:—
Messrs. Fisher,	Messrs. Acres,
Kemp,	Black,
Raney,	Bradburn,
Sinclair,	Clarke (Brockville),
Widdifield—5.	Currie,
	Ecclestone,
	Edwards,
	Elliott,
	Finlayson,
	Garden,
	Graves,
	Gray,
	Hill,
	Hillmer,
	Keith,
	Kennedy (Temiskaming),
	McCausland,
	MacBride,
	Morel,
	Owens,
	Patterson,
	Wigle—22.

An amendment to the amendment was moved by Mr. Currie, seconded by Mr. MacBride,

That the following be added to and included in the report submitted by the Chairman.

So far as the evidence before your Committee enables the reaching of a conclusion, your Committee feel that the Hon. Jas. Lyons is entitled to a complete and unqualified exoneration from any breach of The Legislative Assembly Act, and that his companies' business record with relation to the Government and any contractors having business relation with the Government is beyond reproach.

Some evidence having been given by one of the witnesses before the Committee reflecting on the efficiency of the Provincial Air Service of the Forestry Branch, your Committee having heard the evidence of the witness in question and the evidence of Captain Roy Maxwell, Director of the Air Service, are of the opinion that the criticism suggested was not justified by the facts and that the establishment of this branch of the Public Service has been amply justified by the results.

The amendment to the amendment was carried on the following division:—

Yeas:—

Messrs. Acres,
Black,
Bradburn,
Clarke (Brockville),
Currie,
Ecclestone,
Edwards,
Elliott,
Finlayson,
Garden,
Graves,
Gray,
Hill,
Hillmer,
Keith,
Kennedy (Temiskaming),
McCausland,
MacBride,
Morel,
Owens,
Patterson,
Wigle—22.

Nays:—

Messrs. Fisher,
Kemp,
Raney,
Sinclair,
Widdifield—5.

The motion for the adoption of the report with amendments was declared carried.

The Committee then adjourned for the Session.

PUBLIC ACCOUNTS COMMITTEE.

The Committee held its first sitting of the 1926 Session at 10 A.M., Friday, March 12th.

Mr. FINLAYSON: Gentlemen, will you please come to order? The first duty of the Committee, I fancy, is to elect a chairman for this year. Are there any motions?

MR. GRAVES: Mr. Chairman, I take great pleasure in moving; moved by myself, and seconded by Mr. Patterson, that Mr. A. C. Lewis, member for North East Toronto, be and he is hereby appointed Chairman of the Public Accounts Committee for the Session of 1926.

HON. MR. RANEY: Had you better not call the roll?

MR. FINLAYSON: Well, we had better be in order first and appoint a chairman. Any other motions? You have heard the motion, moved by Mr. Graves? All in favour? Carried.

(The Secretary then called the roll).

MR. SINCLAIR: Before any business is introduced, I would like to express my congratulations to you, sir, on being elevated to the honourable position of Chairman of the Public Accounts Committee. There is a tradition somewhere, an unwritten law somewhere, that when a man is promoted to the position of Chairman of the Public Accounts Committee, he is next in order for Cabinet preferment. Now whether this is significant or not I don't know. We have had the honourable member for Simcoe in the chair for two sessions. He steps down. The newspapers carried his photograph that he was in line.

MR. FINLAYSON: Then that settles it.

MR. SINCLAIR: For Minister of Lands and Forests. And this morning you are elevated to the honourable position and next in line for preferment. I may say it will meet with the unanimous approval of this Committee that you are chosen as Chairman. I hope our deliberations will be pleasant and profitable, and, without wishing you any harm, sir, if there is anything in the preferment which is to come to you, I may say members of this Committee will be delighted that you are now advanced and well under way towards that new position.

THE CHAIRMAN (Mr. Lewis): Gentlemen, I appreciate the kindness of Mr. Sinclair in nominating me for a vacancy in the Cabinet, but the vacancy has to occur first.

MR. SINCLAIR: Oh, it is there.

MR. LEWIS: I thought you had it already filled, that one.

MEMBER: There is two to be filled.

THE CHAIRMAN At any rate, I accept the nomination with gratitude. Let me say just before proceeding to business, that I appreciate the honour of being elected to the chairmanship of this very responsible Committee and I just want to suggest that this is the most responsible Committee of the Legislature, with very heavy, onerous duties, and the only way we can get through during the term of the session the work that will be placed before us will be by having co-operation and the best of feeling in conducting the proceedings before the Committee. On behalf of all the members I am going to bespeak from all the members of the Committee their assistance in conducting the affairs of this Committee, so it will be conducted with proper dignity and the business carried to a proper issue, so we will have our report ready before the end of the session.

MR. FINLAYSON: Mr. Chairman, I propose to move a motion, but before doing that I would like to join with Mr. Sinclair in his congratulations to you. Before I say anything about it, may I say this, that for two years I had the honour of presiding at this Committee, and I want to thank, I think, every member of the Committee for their kind co-operation during the whole term. We were not always unanimous; sometimes there were appeals from the Chair, but it was all done in the very best spirit, and I think the Committee accomplished a great deal of good work during that time, and if it did that and if it did clear the air the credit is entirely due to the Committee, and I want to thank the members. As to your position, may I say this: I have sometimes found it may be an honourable position, but it is an exceedingly onerous one. I found the position required an immense amount of work day and night and an immense amount of physical effort, but I think you will find it beyond that, even in the matter of conduct, a very pleasant position indeed. One suggestion, if you will avoid all the errors of your immediate predecessor, I think you will make a very great success as chairman.

I propose to move a motion and before doing so I would like to say one or two words briefly, because I don't think we want to discuss the matter now. I think the Committee will recognize this, that their first duty will be to clear up the matter mentioned by the member for Sault Ste. Marie the other day, which is the result of a series of questions which have apparently emanated from many members and apparently have attracted some attention. It naturally places Mr. Lyons in a rather difficult and unpleasant position and I think it is only fair to him, I think every member of the Committee of all parties in the House will realize we should first clear that up. It is only fair to Mr. Lyons, and I think the efforts of the Committee should be bent first towards cleaning this up, and then take charge of any other matters.

May I tell the Committee this, that I have instructions from the Premier to say, that the matter is brought before the Committee in a full and free manner with the utmost disclosure both on the part of the Government. The Premier thinks it wise that no member of the Cabinet should attend or take any part in it, so that the Committee will feel perfectly free to dispose of the matter in, may I say, a judicial way, because the other day the Leader of the Progressives said it was a court of justice, the Leader of the Government said it was a court of inquiry, and last session the Leader of the Opposition said we had conducted the affairs of the Committee this session on a high plane. I am sure if the Committee approach this matter in that way without Government interference, without party spirit, and with a desire to get at the facts that then we will do so without any trouble.

Now I propose to move a resolution in these words:

(Mr. Finlayson's motion as finally redrafted was as follows:—

Moved by Mr. Finlayson, seconded by Mr. Jamieson (Grey), That the Committee proceed with the investigation requested by Hon. James Lyons into the connection of the late Minister, the Lyons Fuel & Supply Company, Ltd., and the Sault Ste. Marie Coal & Wood Company, Ltd., with the Government of the Province of Ontario, and with any Government contractors or Crown licensees.

That Messrs. Clarkson, Gordon and Dilworth of the City of Toronto, Chartered Accountants, be instructed to make an investigation of the relation of the said late Minister, the Lyons Fuel & Supply Company, Ltd., and the Sault Ste. Marie Coal & Wood Company, Ltd., with all or any branches of the Ontario Government, and with any Government contractors or timber licensees, and that for such purposes the said firm have power and authority to investigate the accounts of the Government and all accounts, vouchers, documents, bank books, bank accounts, papers, letters or memoranda of the said companies, or either of them, in connection with the above matters, and power to investigate the accounts of the said companies, or either of them, with the Royal Bank of Canada at Sault Ste. Marie, Ontario, or any other bank account that may be necessary for a complete investigation of the said matters.

That the following witnesses be summoned to appear before the Public Accounts Committee: Honourable James Lyons, Charles H. Fullerton, Alex. McAllister, J. J. Fitzpatrick, E. J. Zavitz, Claude Findlay, James Dawson,

George McNamara, Howard McNamara, Harry C. Lyons, E. L. Bedford, Frank LeBarge, R. Walsh and G. J. Lamb.

Now may I say to the Committee that this resolution has been drawn by myself, without any instructions or without any collaboration or without any thought with the Premier or with any other member of the Government, and my instructions from the Premier are these: he wants the Committee to feel at perfect liberty to go into the whole matter and no member of the Government will take any part in the deliberations, and the Committee will feel itself to be a court of inquiry, clothed with the fullest possible powers to go into all this matter.

In explanation may I say this, that when I was instructed to do this I tried to look up to see how committees proceeded in other matters before and I cannot find any direct analogy to this. In other cases, I find some member of the opposition brought matters before the attention of the House and it resulted in an inquiry—perhaps something in the nature of a charge, and it was investigated and the man who made the charge moved the resolution in the Committee and it was proceeded with in that way. I cannot find any case where a Minister has said: "I resign my position in the Cabinet; I appeal to the Public Accounts Committee to investigate this." And under these circumstances, I thought it only fair that the Committee should not have any instructions but that a lead must be given, and I thought it only fair that the way to do was to go at it in this way and I thought we would adopt the procedure we found very effective, that is to ask the Clarkson firm to go into it. If the Committee passes this resolution, I would ask Mr. Clarkson, if possible, to delegate Major Nash to conduct the work as he did a year or two years ago, and I think we are on safe ground if we say we will apply to Mr. Lyons first the same methods we applied in the Smith and Ridout cases and those matters of last year and the year before.

I am sure the Committee will all agree with me that the evidence given by Mr. Nash not only before this Committee but at Ottawa and before the higher court on various matters, the commendations he had received from the Bench puts him in an exceptional position, and if the Committee do what they did in previous years they will say go and investigate, and they will look into it and draw to the attention of the Committee every matter you think suspicious, every matter you think should be followed up, and, having placed these matters before the Committee, we can go on.

I don't want anybody to think that this is final or conclusive. There may be many other witnesses to be summoned at a later date, there may be some you want to be summoned now, but it is quite apparent why Mr. Lyons, and Mr. Fullerton, who is in charge of the Northern Development Branch and has knowledge, McAllister, who, as I understand, is one of the officers of the Lyons Supply Co.; Fitzpatrick is the contractor who had charge on the contract of the construction of the aerodrome at Sault Ste. Marie; E. J. Zavitz is the Deputy Minister who has charge of the Forestry Branch under whom the aerodrome was constructed; Mr. Findlay, I am told, is the architect who designed the aerodrome and had charge of construction; Mr. Dawson, I understand, was Mayor of Sault Ste. Marie, and has, I understand, some knowledge; George and H. MacNamara are members of the MacNamara Construction Co.

MEMBER: Did you say Gordon?

MR. FINLAYSON: George. But I would like to assure that there is no effort to shut off anybody else. If to-day or any other day any members want any further witnesses before the Committee, they are quite at liberty of course to do so.   I fancy to-day it will be a matter of organization.   I don't think it is intended to proceed with any witnesses.   I haven't named any dates for these.   I think that is the practice we agreed on last year, name a list of witnesses and pick out days.

Hon. Mr. Lyons: Did you mention Lamb?   Mr. Lamb is the district resident engineer at Sault Ste. Marie.

Mr. Finlayson: What are his initials?

Hon. Mr. Lyons: I think, G. J. Lamb.   He is the district engineer in charge of Northern Development work.

Mr. Finlayson: I will add G. A. Lamb.   And if anybody else wishes to add names. I will be glad to do so.   I was going to suggest the days of the sittings have been Wednesday and Friday.   On Wednesday, perhaps, if we proceed chronologically, we will take up the matter of the Lyons Fuel & Supply Co. account with the Government appearing in last year's accounts, a year ago. Perhaps it would be well to direct our efforts next Wednesday to that and I think it would be convenient to have Mr. Lyons in the box next Wednesday. I don't know whether the Clarkson firm will be able to complete their investigation by that time.

Mr. Chairman, I beg to move the resolution I have read.

Hon. Mr. Raney: I am sure the ex-Minister and the Government desire, I accept their statement that they desire, the fullest inquiry into this matter, and I assume that the form of the resolution adopted was intended to eventuate or enable it to carry out that kind of inquiry.   I venture to suggest to Mr. Finlayson that his resolution is much too narrow, in fact, it scarcely touches the matter that was raised in the House.   "That the Committee proceed with the investigation requested by the Honourable James Lyons into the connection of the Lyons Fuel & Supply Company with the Government of the Province of Ontario."   There may have been some suggestion in some of the questions before the House, one or more of them, as to that, but the burden of the questions, the matters that were raised by the questions, was something wider, because the matters that were raised were the relations of the Lyons Fuel & Supply Co., the relations of the Minister, of the Lyons Fuel & Supply Co. and of the Sault Ste. Marie Coal & Wood Company—Mr. Lyons being president of both these companies—with Government contractors and Crown lessees.   Now, I take it that Mr. Finlayson probably had in mind to cover all these matters. If so, the suggestions I would make—we will have no difficulty I think in perhaps incorporating them.   They would read, just as I suggest here, I have pencilled them out.   What I would suggest.

Mr. Finlayson: That is why I gave copies of the resolution.

Mr. Raney: If members will look at their copies for a moment, this is just as I sat here the last five minutes.

"That the Committee proceed," this is as I suggest it should be, "with the investigation requested by the Honourable James Lyons into the connection of the late Minister, the Lyons Fuel & Supply Co., Ltd." or maybe it ought to be "and" "The Sault Ste. Marie Coal & Wood Company with the Government of the Province of Ontario, or with Government contractors or Crown lessees."

Mr. Finlayson: You want it to read that the Committee proceed with the investigation requested by the Honourable James Lyons into the connection of the late Minister with the Lyons Fuel & Supply Co., and with the Sault Ste. Marie and with the Government of the Province of Ontario.

Mr. Raney: And with the Government of the Province of Ontario. There should not be any and there.

Mr. Finlayson: Yes, but—

Mr. Raney: That the Committee proceed with the investigation requested by the Honourable James Lyons into the connection of the late Minister, the Lyons Fuel & Supply Company, Limited, and the Sault Ste. Marie Coal & Wood Co.

Mr. Finlayson: Is that correct?

Hon. Mr. Lyons: Sault Ste. Marie Coal & Wood Co.

Hon. Mr. Raney: With the Government of the Province of Ontario and with Government contractors and Crown lessees. Now then, similar amendments to the following paragraph.

I entirely agree in what Mr. Finlayson says in so far as the auditors' accountants are concerned. Nobody would suggest any want of fairness on the part of this firm and their work in the past has been eminently satisfactory. That Messrs. Clarkson, Gordon and Dilworth be instructed to make—insert there, "the late Minister."

Mr. Bellanger: The ex-Minister.

Hon. Mr. Raney: The Lyons Fuel & Supply Company—I am the late Attorney-General.

Mr. Finlayson: My friend from Russell confuses you in French, deceased and late Minister.

Hon. Mr. Raney: Lyons Fuel & Supply Co., Sault Ste. Marie Coal & Wood Company, with all or any branches of the Ontario Government and with Government contractors and Crown lessees and that for such purposes the said firm have power and authority to investigate accounts of the Government or all accounts, vouchers, documents, bank books, bank accounts, papers, letters or memoranda of the late Minister and the said companies.

Mr. Finlayson: You had that in before.

Hon. Mr. Raney: Well, this is dealing with the documents. The bank books, papers, letters or memoranda of the late Minister and the said companies in connection with the above matter, and that power to investigate the accounts of the said companies.

Mr. Finlayson: May I suggest to Mr. Raney this. I have no objection whatever to the amendment he suggests that covers the Sault Ste. Marie Coal & Wood Co. or the suggestion he makes to cover the Crown lessees or licensees or contractors. I intended that that should be within the purview of the motion. There is only one other thing strikes me. You will remember, I drew the latter part of it as to the bank books purposely. The way you had drawn it it might send these people up to investigate the late Minister's private bank account at first. Now I don't think that you intend that and I don't think it should be done at first. I am willing to say this to the Committee, if the investigation into the Lyons Fuel & Supply Company, Sault Ste. Marie Coal & Wood Co., or any of these contractors or lessees shows any lead that would justify the search of the Minister's private bank account, his private papers, then I will say "yes, it should be done." But I don't think as a preliminary matter we should search anybody's private bank account, his personal matters, and have them exposed. And what I will agree to is this, and I think the Committee will approve. If Clarksons report they have come across some lead that indicates something that should be searched in the bank account, then as far as I am concerned, I do not speak for Mr. Lyons, I think it should say to them, "Go ahead and proceed then," if it means searching the private bank account, as in the Smith case. Mr. Raney, I think will remember, I think, as I told him at the time, one member of the Committee came along

12 J

two years ago and wanted to search all bank accounts of a Minister of the old Government. I thought it was outrageous, most improper, and the motion was never put, and you will remember we adopted the same procedure with Mr. Drury in the box here. Something was said as to some loan company, Dependable Securities, I think. He said it had not taken place until after he was out of the Government and we took his word for that. I suggest to Mr. Raney that he knows the Clarkson firm; he knows Mr. Nash, whom I hope will be the one, and if he represents to the Committee or to Mr. Raney privately or to me privately that he thinks there is a lead to be followed up, then I think we should do it. But until that is done, I am opposed to searching any. man's private bank account.

Hon. Mr. Raney: There is no reason it could not stand this way, if any question arises such as you suggest that matter may be subject to appeal to the Committee; I am content.

Mr. Finlayson: Quite so.

Mr. Lewis: Let me say the Committee will be sitting dealing with these things and we will do as we did before. If anything comes up, the Committee will direct.

Hon. Mr. Raney: I think the language here is adequate but it is proper for Mr. Finlayson to raise the thing now so that that point may not be foreclosed. So if that question arises the understanding will be it may be raised before the Committee without anybody pleading that this matter is foreclosed.

Mr. Finlayson: I think Mr. Raney and Mr. Sinclair and every member will agree we are safe in Major Nash's hands. When my friend to my right's books were question, and Mr. Nash reported there are a lot of things there and this was at night, that are personal and private, but I cannot see anything suspicious in them, nobody ever thought of going into them, and I think that is the proper practice. I am not speaking on behalf of Mr. Lyons. I am trying to lay down a rule observed two years ago and I feel very strongly.

Hon. Mr. Raney: I suggest additional names, if you will permit. Harry Lyons. That is the name, is it? E. L. Bedford, Fred Labarge.

Mr. Finlayson: You mean the hardware firm, lumber firm?

Hon. Mr. Raney: R. Walsh. Is it Robert or Richard?

Mr. Lewis: You have the addresses?

Hon. Mr. Raney: Well, Mr. Lyons knows them all.

Hon. Mr. Lyons: Well, Walsh, I don't know his first name.

Hon. Mr. Raney: Well, "R" anyway, that is the Walsh Construction Co. They are all in the Department. Harry Lyons, Bedford, Labarge, Walsh. I should think we might get on next Wednesday. Of course, we don't want to bring a lot of witnesses.

Mr. Finlayson: What I thought next Wednesday, it would be convenient to put Mr. Lyons in the box and cover the general ground and that may take the day or the morning. If not, I think a good deal will depend on whether Mr. Clarkson's report is available.

Hon. Mr. Raney: Oh, it would not be available then.

Mr. Finlayson: As is pointed out there are these men in the building.

Hon. Mr. Raney: If he will revise his resolution then and submit it to Mr. Sinclair and myself, I have no doubt we will agree on the phraseology.

Mr. Finlayson: Well, I will submit the resolution and try and redraw it and submit it to you along lines you have suggested.

Mr. Lewis: The suggestions you have just made are the only ones?

Hon. Mr. Raney: I think so.

MR. LEWIS: Well, we have them in.

MR. SINCLAIR: I agree with those who have already spoken in this matter that the object of the investigation is to get at the facts. I do not see eye to eye with the way in which the matter is brought before the Committee. I have been a member of the Public Accounts Committee, I think this is the tenth year, and on any past occasion on which a matter was brought up for investigation, it was brought up on a specific motion by some member of the opposition. It matters, of course, little, who brings up a resolution, but it makes a big difference in the handling of the investigation.

As I understand it, Mr. Lyons will give his evidence, will be examined by a member of the Legislature who is a supporter of the Government, and that will no doubt take considerable time to go over the field. I do feel that perhaps a better investigation could have been had if for instance, myself had put the motion on your paper and had summoned Mr. Lyons and had examined him from the start along lines which I had been thinking upon. However, we will see how this works out.

I can hardly understand the attitude of the Government in bringing it before the Committee in this way. I have been thinking it over for some little time because my honourable friend, Mr. Finlayson, did speak to me a few hours ago about the way of handling it, and at that time I told him I did not think it was the proper way, but if the Government felt they wished to take the risk and responsibility of introducing this matter before the Public Accounts Committee, and taking the examination themselves, I was not going to raise too serious an objection.

After all the matter rests with the Government and to my mind the investigation would come with better grace from those who have been inquiring into this matter for some weeks and months past, and I think the public would have felt better satisfied that the fuller investigation would be held if the examination was conducted in the first instance by those who had been making the inquiry.

Now there is some merit to the introduction of the chartered accountant, Mr. Nash, into this matter. I don't know that it is all merit because if members of the Committee take upon themselves the responsibility of going into these things they may see things which an accountant would not consider as of importance to bring before the Committee. However, as time goes on we will be able to see how this is working out.

There is one other matter, however, that I do want to impress on the Committee, and that is this: we are not going to start to take evidence until next Wednesday. I don't think there is any doubt in the minds of anybody here but what we will adjourn two weeks from that day, the night before Good Friday, in the time honoured custom of getting through by Easter. And there is no reason why we cannot get through the legislative programme by that time, and we could be through by that time if we wanted to.

Now is the Public Accounts Committee going to suffer by reason of that? I feel it will. By the time the House adjourns, with two meetings a week, two hours in the morning, you won't begin to get started at this thing, and we will adjourn and go home, and that will be all there will be to the investigation. I do think that the Public Accounts Committee, with the vast amount of stuff which is before it, should sit pretty nearly every day, and then we won't get through. I know I have many matters to bring up and I am satisfied they will not be thoroughly investigated by my learned friend, Mr. Finlayson. I am satisfied, and I want it to be distinctly understood that when these witnesses come here there is to be ample time for the examination of all these witnesses. and the cross examination on points we want to take up.

So that we should arrange to-day more sittings of the Public Accounts Committee than what we will be allowed on the regular schedule. The honourable the Prime Minister said the other day in the House that this House would sit here as long as there was any business to do, but those of us who have been here former years know with what speed business is done in the last twenty-four hours and an order paper which looks like something is finished and away we go to our homes, and I say, we. don't want that to happen in relation to the Public Accounts Committee.

I just want to reiterate what I said at the start. I don't like the way this. matter is brought in. I had four distinct motions which I intended to move here this morning in relation to this matter. After speaking to Mr. Finlayson,. I changed one of them. I don't know whether my motions are covered by the motions here, and they were specific matters dealing with this year's Public Accounts, specific items mentioned in the accounts, and I feel before we adjourn to-day I should put resolutions on the order paper at any rate, and then if they are not covered by the investigation which does take place it cannot be said the questions are out of order.

MR. FINLAYSON: Before the motion is put, may I say one or two things. I thought I observed all the courtesies in telling you what we proposed to do and furnishing you and Mr. Raney with copies as soon as they were struck off. I appreciate what you say as to the customs of the Committee extending over ten years and I feel that any of us who try to conduct it after two years are perhaps amateurs.

MR. SINCLAIR: No disrespect. I did not mean it that way.

MR. FINLAYSON: I know. The Government are not in any way responsible for the Committee's actions in this matter. The Government are not going to take any attitude. I speak for the Government to this extent; that the Government said Mr. Lyons has requested an investigation; he has named his forum the Public Accounts Committee, which I think everyone will agree is the proper forum; all the Government say is this: let the Public Accounts Committee proceed to investigate that with the fullest powers, exercise all the powers they have. The only thing I have consulted the Government on is this, I said, if I an to conduct the investigation in a leading way I want to have power to do it and I want the Government to say that I can secure the assistance of Messrs. Clarkson &. Co. to proceed with that, and I was glad to see Mr. Raney say as to their standing and the fact that their name on the report will satisfy the Province of Ontario. And I secured the only instructions I have from the Premier to get his permission to the Public Accounts Committee, the Government are satisfied for you to incur the expense of having these people make investigation.

Apart from that, the Premier has given no instructions apart from telling the Committee to go into it and give them a lead. That is the only interest the Government is going to take then in it. No responsibility at all. Done at Hon. Mr. Lyon's request. If any one wants to move substantative motion to it, very well then. If he wants to move for other witnesses after looking over these, nobody will say the matter stands disposed of. It is entirely open, and as far as everybody in the Committee is concerned let new motions be brought in any time.

HON. MR. RANEY: I was going to make that suggestion.

THE CHAIRMAN: I think members of the Committee will remember that in past years motions for the production of witnesses have never been closed out at subsequent meetings.

HON. MR. RANEY: If there is any other aspect, that motions then should be brought forward, after consideration, I think he ought to have the opportunity reserved to him so he will not be prejudiced by his not putting them in now.

MR. FINLAYSON: Only one other thing. You have spoken of the matter of time and necessity of sittings. The reason I suggested going on Wednesday was this: we may have Clarkson's report by that time. I doubt it. But I think we will have enough witnesses to proceed with, and if the Committee wishes to sit ——————, I will apply to the Premier for an order of the House, so we may have—

HON. MR. RANEY: I was going to say, if Mr. Sinclair would bring, when the right time comes, after we have disposed of this, if he will move that this Committee sit on Monday and after that day by day.

MEMBER: That's right; don't get into Latin.

HON. MR. RANEY: I will second the motion. There is no other way we can possibly make headway, because we cannot possibly get through this and other matters in two weeks.

THE CHAIRMAN: The fact that this Committee is convened the day after the Public Accounts were brought down in the House, without waiting for debate to be ended, shows there is perfect freedom and disposition to help the Committee get ahead and clean up. We sat last year and the year before at nights and other occasions. We have to remember there are other Committees that will be sitting Tuesdays and Thursdays and members of this Committee are interested in business before other Committees, and we must consider their rights in the matter.

Sitting when the House is in session can easily be arranged, and there will be no disposition as far as I am concerned, and I know of none on the part of any member to balk any effort to have sittings.

MR. FINLAYSON: Wouldn't it be convenient not to try and tie ourselves up.

HON. MR. RANEY: Leave that time element.

MR. SINCLAIR: I cannot understand why you cannot go on until Wednesday. I could start right now. Probably you haven't given it—I can understand that—I don't see why we cannot be sitting Monday night.

MR. FINLAYSON: The trouble with Monday night is so few members are here.

HON. MR. RANEY: Let them come.

MR. SINCLAIR: It is their duty to be here.

THE CHAIRMAN: The Committee is called for the first time to-day. Many of the members, I am amongst them, have made engagements for Monday.

HON. MR. RANEY: It doesn't matter. There will be other members.

MR. HOMUTH: I quite agree with some of the remarks of the leader of the Liberal opposition. There is one part of this resolution that I cannot just see the sense of and that is with respect to getting Clarkson, Gordon and Dilworth to go into all these accounts concerning the Lyons Fuel & Supply Company until such time as we have some definite lead for them to go ahead and investigate. I cannot see why we should spend money on an investigation that may be absolutely futile. There may be good reason for it. Whereas, if we have witnesses called here and then if there is something regarding their books that should be investigated let us get this firm of accountants to do it.

MR. FINLAYSON: By that time there would be an adjournment.

MR. HOMUTH: No. Why should we be spending a lot of money to have these people audit all these books when there may be no real necessity for that particular part of it, and I don't think that is the way to have these people go ahead and investigate all these accounts until such time as we have something, some lead, for them to go ahead with.

MR. FINLAYSON: I don't want to speak too much, but these various questions are brought down, brought down properly enough and perhaps on reasonable basis, but if you were a Minister of the Crown and if you had a whole lot of questions thrown at you affecting your private business, with all kinds of innuendoes tacked on, every sort of suggestion made, the gossip of the whole Province of Ontario started, you would like Clarksons to say you are an honest man, and the Province of Ontario won't hesitate for a minute to spend a thousand or two thousand dollars to certify that the Lyons Fuel & Supply Co. had been honest, or that he had been crooked or dishonest and should be punished.

MR. HOMUTH: Well, the unfair part of it is some are using the word "dishonest," and it is the last word I think of in connection with members of the Cabinet or Ministers. There is altogether too much of it all through in the whole political situation. It is always this cry or at least innuendo thrown out of "dishonesty" and I don't like it and never did, because it was not the kind of politics I was taught to believe.

MR. FINLAYSON: Well, none of the questions are in your name.

MR. HOMUTH: That is the reason I say I don't think there should be any general investigation of the account of the Lyons Fuel & Supply Company or of the Minister of Lands until such time as this Committee should see some real reason for it.

MR. SINCLAIR: There is considerable merit in what my friend says. I don't know what Clarkson & Company are going to investigate to start with. You say they won't have a report by Wednesday night. What are they going to start on. I must say I cannot see the virtue of that as yet, because unless you have a brief prepared and know certain lines you want to follow up and have them prepared before. But as questions come up here, we, not being book-keepers and men of that type, we might say, "Look that up and see what there is to it. But to suggest that they do now make an investigation of something which we ourselves as yet probably don't know what we are looking for, it seems to me they have a large order on their hands because it is a big concern.

MR. FINLAYSON: In answer, let me say the position is simply this: Mr. Lyons feels keenly, I am speaking not for the Government, but because he tells me that. You can understand any man who has spent his whole life building up a business, got it to a certain stage, and then, attracted by public service, puts the same energy into the public service and neglects his business and gets into trouble, and then in addition to that all this whispering campaign goes on, and I am pleased to be able to say, Mr. Homuth, that none of the questions that make these suggestions are in his name. I think many of the questions perfectly proper, and I know from the little I have gone into it so far will be disposed of very simply and will not require accounting. But there are other questions aimed at facts that looked suspicious on the face and the Minister is entitled to have it cleaned up. But his first impression was to bring all his books and try and have continuous sitting until somebody went through the whole lot. But Mr. Raney or anybody else who has tried to conduct a judicial matter of any kind know what a hopeless matter it is. It is hopeless in court and hopeless before this Committee.

Hon. Mr. Raney: They can only speak as to the books.

Mr. Finlayson: Certainly.

Member: And after that go back through the books if you want something else; send them back again.

Mr. Finlayson: What I propose that if we give them instructions to turn over this series of questions and say here is your brief; here is the basis for investigation. Look up all particulars of this; get us a report. If you find anything suspicious bring it down and tell us. Surely it is the fair thing to do. Mr. Lyons told me if the Committee hesitates to put the Province to that expense he will feel like settling.

The Chairman: We have had it discussed, and the motion has been placed, and suggested amendments by Mr. Raney which are agreed to. Do you want to read it again?

Members: Dispense.

The Chairman: Is it your pleasure this motion be adopted? Carried. Any opposition? I declare the motion carried.

Hon. Mr. Raney: I desire to move, seconded by Mr. Kemp, That S. L. Squire, Deputy Minister of Highways, Frank H. Harris, Edmund P. Stewart, Carleton L. Dyer, R. S. Shenstone, W. G. Clysdale and Albert E. Nash be summoned before the Committee to give evidence concerning contracts for certain advertisments that appeared in a certain magazine called *Rural Canada* on pages 22 and 23 of the issue of that magazine of October, 1919, and concerning payment of the contract price of the said advertisements and that the said witnesses be required to produce all books, letters, papers and documents in their custody, possession or power relating to the said matters.

The Committee will no doubt want some explanation for the reason of this motion. I take it they will be interested to learn that there has been a discovery of the destination of some more of what we call "legals," the thousand dollar bills about which the Committee heard so much in 1924 and about which they heard something last year.

Rural Canada was a publication, not now in existence, a magazine published in this city for some years, including 1919. It described itself as an independent farm journal and its publishers styled themselves, Canada Farmers' Publishing Company. The issue for October, 1919, was, as you recall, the issue for the month of the general election. The edition for that month was a large, special edition, said to have been 175,000 copies, carrying a quantity of Dominion Government advertising and a quantity of Ontario Government advertising, and, in addition, carrying certain political advertising. It carried—

Member: What year?

Mr. Raney: 1919. The issue of the magazine for the month of October, 1919, which, I am told, came out perhaps late in September of that year, being published in advance of the month.

As I say, the magazine carried a quantity of Dominion Government and Ontario Government advertising, Department of Highways of the Province and Department of Agriculture at Ottawa each having large advertisements, the Ontario Department having, I think, a full page, and the Dominion Government, two pages. Then there was a double page advertisment consisting of a photogravure of Sir William Hearst, faced by a photogravure of Mr. Hartley Dewart.

Mr. Finlayson: Is this O.T.A.?

Hon. Mr. Raney: And the photogravure of Sir William Hearst had underneath it a footnote, perhaps I had better read it.

"The Honourable Sir William Howard Hearst, Premier of the rich, old banner Province of Ontario, who enjoys the respect of all and the confidence of the majority because of his rugged honesty, his good government, and his advanced legislation in the cause of temperance and who personally has declared himself to stand and vote against the liquor in the forthcoming referendum."

Then the inscription under Mr. Dewart's photograph was in these terms:

"Mr. Hartley H. Dewart, K.C., Leader of the Opposition in the Ontario Legislature, a clever man with ambitions, does not enjoy the confidence of his own party. Even sitting members, supposed to be under this leadership, have declared that if the House were to have another session, they would not sit under Mr. Dewart, but would take the cross benches. Elected by the liquor men in a bye-election in the riding of South West Toronto. A great promiser— and verily a clever man!"

Now those two photographs, though they appear to the ordinary reader to be published in the ordinary course with these editorial footnotes, were advertisements, and I propose to call witnesses before the Committee to prove that this edition of 175,000 copies of this paper, carrying this political advertisement was under a contract for $5,000 given by the Conservative Association and that the contract price was paid in part . by what are called legals. There were at least two bills of one thousand dollars each as part of the price paid to the publishers of *Rural Canada* for the publication of these advertisements.

MR. HANEY: You are not suggesting liquor money, though, are you?

MR. KEITH: There is not any suggestion this was paid by the Government?

HON. MR. RANEY: No. But the suggestion is, quite frankly, that these legals came from the same place from which the legals came that went to Stratford into Mr. Peter Smith's bank account in December following, in respect of which Smith is now serving a term, as you know, at Kingston. And, as you will recall, the chief item in the circumstantial evidence against Mr. Smith—it was all circumstantial—was the fact that these legals which were not in ordinary circulation, which are only used for bank purposes to adjust balances between banks to close the day, and hardly ever find their way into circulation, that these legals, paid as part of the consideration price for this advertisement were part of the money that came from the Home Bank in September, 1919.

Members of the Committee will recall that there were three large payments out of the Home Bank account marked Special Commissions. The heading of the account was, I think, "S.C.", which was interpreted to mean Special Commissions. The last one of these payments was a payment of $15,000 in December, 1919. Two previous large payments were in December, 1919, were of $12,000 on the 12th, and one of $25,000 on the 23rd of September, which was the same day on which Mr. McGarry accepted the tender of the Home Bank of 94.48, I think it was, for a $4,000,000 loan issued at that time by Mr. McGarry.

There has been a good deal of evidence before the Committee as to a cigar box and a trip in an automobile, supposed to have carried money to the Parliament Buildings, and on on. It seems to me, and I think to others here, that this matter ought to be explored and we ought to bring the people before this Committee who know and these witnesses I have given you include the names of men who do know these facts.

I propose to establish that these photogravures were really advertisements, that the advertisments were inserted under a contract with the publishers of this magazine, made by a Conservative Association, that the contract price was $5,000, that it was paid as I have indicated. The evidence will be it was paid by cheque for $2,500, by two bills of one thousand dollars each, Dominion of Canada bills, and $500 in smaller bills, making a total of $5,000.

That is my motion and if there is no objection, I suppose the order will go. If there is any objection I may take the opportunity of saying something more to the Committee.

THE CHAIRMAN: You are not suggesting a connection with the Government in connection with these payments?

HON. MR. RANEY: I am not, no. I am not suggesting the Government made these payments.

MR. GRAY: I cannot see where this Committee comes in on this, for the publication of these photographs of two men who are already dead, passed and gone. We can go back over the next twenty-five years perhaps with such matters As long as it doesn't affect this Government I cannot see—or hasn't originated with any member of the Government, or any man in touch, or any member of the Government in days gone by, but some Conservative Association. We may do things in the Conservative Association where I come from, and should this Committee waste hours and hours investigating it. And I think there should be some investigation into the political organization of the Opposition. You are going to throw this Committee wide open to such investigations that I don't know where you will get off, and I don't see why we should entertain this motion.

MR. SINCLAIR: Did I understand you to say both these men were dead?

MR. GRAY: Absolutely. Don't you agree with me?

MR. FINLAYSON: We were discussing a few minutes ago the confusion between a late and deceased minister. Now we have got to distinguish between one who is deceased politically and one who is deceased physically. But it does seem to me that there is a good deal in what Mr. Gray says. If we are going to start in a general search of campaign funds for 1919, we are going to open up a fine field. The Committee may know this, that we did not, in our day, go into some bank accounts of members of the last Government that it was suggested we should go into and some of them did open up a field that looked very promising, and looked as if there was a very lead ahead of us. Now those were not as far ago as 1919. These were nearer to 1923 and they led up to very much larger sums than these. There are also, as Mr. Gray suggests, a great many other political campaign funds that may be investigated. We heard two years ago of the campaign funds that were collected for the U.F.O. campaign. We were told who the Treasurer was. We know some moneys went to him. If we are going into all that—

MR. CLARKE: No legal tenders, though, in that bunch.

MR. FINLAYSON: Legal tenders went right into the U.F.O. Minister, direct to the Minister.

MR. CLARKE: Not thousand dollars.

MR. FINLAYSON: Yes, thousands, went right into his own bank account.

HON. MR. RANEY: Exactly the same thing.

MR. FINLAYSON: What I suggest, there has got to be some finality. When my friend, Mr. Raney presided, not as chairman, but as the guiding spirit of this Committee, they laid down definitely the rule, if I had Public Accounts proceedings of three years ago, Mr. Watson ruled you could not go behind the Public Accounts brought before us.

MEMBER: That is the Public Accounts for 1921?

HON. MR. RANEY: We have been doing that every session since.

MR. FINLAYSON: But that is the rule Mr. Watson laid down and the rule your majority passed. Now what I suggest is this: we are not ready to discuss it. If Mr. Raney will allow it to stand over until next meeting we can discuss it and the Committee can think over it. It cannot possibly be gone into for some time, so it won't be prejudiced in any way. I have tried—

HON. MR. RANEY: If you make that suggestion, I won't object at all.

THE CHAIRMAN: I was going to suggest, let us get started on the matter we have passed the motion for. This will not be closed out.

HON. MR. RANEY: I have no objection to this standing over to the next meeting.

MR. FINLAYSON: Perhaps Mr. Raney has accomplished all he wanted with the advertisement he got with the suggestion.

MEMBER: That is not nice at all.

HON. MR. RANEY: I don't mind. But I think the Chairman would agree with me that there might be reasons why in this particular matter I would not give notice in advance, but the same effect is accomplished if I do not press my motion but agree to the suggestion of Mr. Finlayson.

THE CHAIRMAN: I think it should be left in abeyance as to settlement by this Committee as to how far back we are going in this limited time. Well, that is a matter for discussion. Any other business?

MR. SINCLAIR: I would like to put on two or three motions, substantative to the big motion by Mr. Finlayson.

Moved by myself, seconded by Mr. Tellier, that E. L. Bedford of Sault Ste. Marie be summoned before this Committee at its next meeting to give evidence as to the following payments made to him as appearing in the Public Accounts for the year ending October 31st, 1925—page G. 12, $1,845.19; page G. 30, $8,187.32; page G. 41, $816.24.

MR. FINLAYSON: Do you want to put them through to-day?

MR. SINCLAIR: Might as well.

THE CHAIRMAN: This man is already summoned.

MR. SINCLAIR: Well, that is a specific case.

THE CHAIRMAN: Gentlemen, you have heard the motion of Mr. Sinclair, that E. L. Bedford of Sault Ste. Marie be summoned. It is understood when a motion is for the next meeting it will be arranged to meet the convenience of the Committee, in dealing with this. Your pleasure that this should be adopted? Carried.

MEMBER: Who is the seconder?

MR. SINCLAIR: Mr. Tellier.

MR. GRAVES: Wouldn't it be better to have Mr. Clarke? Someone who is here?

MR. SINCLAIR: Well, Mr. Tellier was here. And I would move, seconded by Mr. Clarke,

That Honourable James Lyons, member for Sault Ste. Marie, be summoned before this Committee at its next meeting to give evidence in regard to payments appearing in the Public Accounts for the fiscal year ending October 31st, 1925, as having been made to the Lyons Fuel & Supply Company as follows: Page G. 32, $1,087.41; page G. 35, $1,209.60; page G. 41, $878.75, and to produce all books, vouchers and documents relating thereto.

THE CHAIRMAN: I don't suppose there is any objection to passing this, although it is covered by the general resolution. Your pleasure it be adopted? Carried.

MEMBER: No.

MEMBER: Oh, it is all right. It is covered by the other, but there is no objection.

MR. SINCLAIR: Moved by myself, seconded by Mr. Clarke, That H. D. MacNamara and George A. MacNamara of the MacNamara Construction Co., Limited, be summoned before this Committee at its next meeting to give evidence as to the item of $414,777.09 paid to said company appearing on page G. 34 of the Public Accounts for the fiscal year ending October 31st, 1925, and to produce all books, vouchers and documents relating to the same.

MR. FINLAYSON: I think that if we had an understanding that we would supply resolutions.

THE CHAIRMAN: Well, of course. these resolutions, while they are covered, they are—

MR. SINCLAIR: It is the only proper way to put a motion of this kind on the Public Accounts order paper. You must specify your figure or page.

Moved by myself, seconded by Mr. Belanger, That the President and Secretary of the Walsh Construction Company be summoned before this Committee at its next meeting to give evidence as to the item of $33,674.14 paid to said company appearing on page G. 34 of the Public Accounts for the fiscal year ending October 31st, 1925, and to produce all books, vouchers and documents relating to the same.

THE CHAIRMAN: You have heard the resolution, seconded by Mr. Belanger? All in favour? Carried.

MR. KEMP: Moved by myself, seconded by Hon. Mr. Nixon, That George Oakley, M.L.A., C. Blake Jackson and W. W. Sidey, be summoned before the Committee at its next meeting to give evidence concerning the new Government building now in course of construction in Queen's Park, and to produce all books, papers, letters and documents having reference to the relations of the Jackson-Lewis Company, Limited, and George Oakley and Son, Limited, in relation thereto.

THE CHAIRMAN: Here is a resolution by Mr. Kemp, seconded by Mr. Nixon, That Mr. George Oakley, M.L.A., etc., etc. We haven't had any explanation of the inclusion of these names in discussion. All in favour? Carried.

MR. KEMP. I have a motion here, moved by Mr. Kemp, seconded by Hon. Mr. Nixon, That J. H. Ferguson be summoned to appear to give evidence before the Committee at its next meeting concerning the fire insurance carried by the Province, the premiums paid therefor and all facts connected therewith.

MR. FINLAYSON: Carried. A very proper inquiry.

THE CHAIRMAN: Any opposition? All those in favour? Carried.

MR. FREEBORN: I move, seconded by Mr. Kemp, That the Provincial Auditor and Albert E. Nash be summoned before the Committee to give evidence at its next meeting concerning the Public Accounts of the Province and the special audit that the Government has been conducting.

MR. FINLAYSON· Well, what is it?

HON. MR. RANEY: The special audit the Government has been carrying on for the past two or three years is what I have in mind. Of course I am a party in this matter. I think this Committee would like to know in general, we are not going into detail, how far back this audit has been conducted, in what departments, and what the general result has been, and why the audit departments of this Government for the past few years fell down, as undoubtedly it did, in allowing accounts of the Province of Ontario to get into a deplorable condition. It is something that has been talked of vaguely in the newspapers, and I think it ought to be ferreted out, and the Committee ought to know what the reason is, and who has been responsible.

Mr. Lewis: I was going to suggest that the terms of that motion, to bring all information about special audits and all departments, all branches, it would take this Committee until next session. Wouldn't the same object be reached if the specific questions which you have asked be placed on the order paper and answered by the Government.

Mr. Finlayson: I think my friend who moved the motion has misconceived the situation.

Hon. Mr. Raney: I think it might be more happily worded.

Mr. Finlayson: Mr. Nash isn't the man you want but we will give you the name.

Hon. Mr. Raney: That stands then.

Mr. Clarke: I think we should thoroughly understand when we are going to meet. Judging by the bill of fare we are getting and likely to get at the present first meeting, we would have to have a meeting every day from now until Easter, and I think until the middle of April to exhaust this Public Accounts inquiry. Is it understood we will have daily sittings?

The Chairman: I don't think we can arrange daily sittings.

Mr. Sinclair: I might say that was up for discussion when you were out, and before we adjourned we decided to take that matter up. Now I would move that when this Committee adjourns to-day, it adjourns to meet on Monday evening next, and that thereafter we meet daily. That means at any hour of the day that can be arranged, until the business of the Committee is disposed of.

Hon. Mr. Raney: I will second that.

Mr. Finlayson: I suppose there is no occasion for discussion as to this. It seems that the purpose, object of the Committee, is to get rid of this matter as rapidly as possible, and now there are some preliminary proceedings and some work to be gone through. Mr. Lyons, I think, is naturally the first witness to give evidence. He has got to get certain documents from Sault Ste. Marie.

Hon. Mr. Raney: But there are some other matters.

Mr. Finlayson: No, with all deference, I think that is the first thing the Committee should charge itself with, the finding of the facts in connection with that. Let me assure my friend.

Mr. Clarke: Why not go on with something else?

Mr. Finlayson: I am anxious that the Committee should clean up this Lyons' matter as rapidly as possible. I think every member will say it is due to the Department and due to Mr. Lyons.

Mr. Clarke: Quite true.

Mr. Finlayson: If we meet Wednesday as suggested, we will be given ample apportunity to meet Wednesday afternoon and evening if necessary, and get sanction to sit concurrently with the House if necessary. But the Government have called this two weeks ahead of the practice. The practice of every Government has been that the Public Accounts doesn't function until the debate is—

Mr. Clarke: In two weeks you will be adjourning.

Mr. Finlayson: Every opportunity will be given to go into all these matters and we will sit right along until it is all exhausted.

Mr. Clarke: All right that will do.

Mr. Finlayson: I am glad to satisfy my friend from Northumberland. If he will give instructions to his leader. I ask them if it will not be satisfactory to sit Wednesday. If not I propose to move an amendment.

Mr. Sinclair: I am sorry I cannot agree, but with the vast amount of stuff here, beyond the expectation of any member, we certainly have a tremendous amount of work ahead of us, and there is no reason why we cannot sit Monday night. If it was necessary I could go on right now and examine Mr. Lyons. I have my line of questions ready, and there is no reason why you cannot have your line of questions ready by Monday night. Now that is giving him ample time. The remark that you made that we can sit concurrently with the House is out of the question because surely Mr. Raney and myself must be in the House and we must get time to sit when the House is not in session.

Mr. Finlayson: There are lots of other members of your party.

Mr. Sinclair: I press before your Committee the urgency of this situation. I forget the day on which this was taken up in the House, when the Honourable Mr. Lyons' resignation was accepted. But from then on members have had every opportunity to prepare for this investigation. Everybody who had any thought about the matter could have been prepared for it, and now we are near the middle of the month of March, and, as I said, there is no doubt we will adjourn before Easter, and you can see how little time there is to pick up anything—

Mr. Finlayson: I haven't charge of the conduct of the House.

Mr. Sinclair: I am satisfied if a vote of the members were taken they would say, "We are going to get away by Easter because the Government has no reason to keep us here longer." This is the big business of the session and we have to start before the Budget debate is through. But there is no earthly reason why we cannot go on Monday night, and if Mr. Finlayson is not ready Monday night I am ready and ready to examine Mr. Lyons and take him on, and we can spend three or four hours going into these matters and largely expedite the work of the Committee if we do go on, because it will set Clarkson & Company to work on lines we want them to work on and if we wait until Wednesday there is another whole week gone. Therefore, I must press my motion that this Committee be called for Monday evening next and thereafter sit daily until the business now before the Committee is disposed of.

Hon. Mr. Lyons: As one of the principals in this investigation, and one who perhaps will be subject to a very gruelling and close questioning, which I have no objections to, I feel it is only a matter of fair play and right that I should be given an opportunity to familiarize myself with the details of the accounts that are going to be discussed and on which I will be questioned. There is nothing that I wish to hide in any way, but you will realize I have not been in close touch with my business and I want to be able to give the Committee here honestly and fairly the information that they expect to get and to give it in a reliable way, without any delay and without hesitation, and I hope you will give me that opportunity because of the seriousness of the situation, to avail myself of every opportunity to present the facts as I see them and as I know them, in the best possible way.

Mr. Finlayson: I will move an amendment, but I hope after that statement Mr. Sinclair and Mr. Raney will be satisfied to withdraw that. I do feel if we start to division over a small matter of this kind it is going to introduce into this Committee a spirit we have kept out for a long time, and I do hope in this investigation it will proceed in a fair and judicial manner. I am sure Mr. Lyons' statement will appear reasonable.

MR. GRAVES: It seems to me it is unusual to start this Committee as the motion calls for. All the members of the Committee are anxious to be here at all these sessions, and this springing of a Monday night meeting is more or less unheard of. Many of us have appointments and matters we would like to attend to, and we would like to be here. And Monday night, as everybody knows, is a day when attendance is not up to full strength, and I think surely if we start on Wednesday and meet night after night and day after day it will give the Committee a chance to regulate their engagements, arrange matters, knowing from then on we are going to be more or less necessitated here every day. I would like to be here Monday and many of us would like to be. But not expecting this, many of us have appointments and I don't think it is really necessary to jump into this, something that hasn't been done before, and I think we can get through this work—

MR. FINLAYSON: I hope he will see the propriety.

MR. SINCLAIR: No. The Honourable Mr. Lyons resigned on the 1st of March and these questions were on the order paper for days before that and those are the questions which will be taken up by this Committee. And I further submit with all due deference to my friend here that no appointments that a man has in a social way should take precedence over his business as a member of this House or this Committee. There are some of us who spend day and night, and now we are getting so near the end of the session it is no hardship on a private, ordinary member of the House to buck in a little bit and take part, and so in view of the fact that the late Minister has had all this time to consider these matters, and time before he resigned, and in view of the fact that I am ready now to commence examination if I was permitted to do so and as I expected to do, I must press my motion that this Committee meet Monday night.

MR. GRAVES: I don't want this Committee or this House to figure I ever let social affairs interfere with my business here. My record as an attendant of this Committee will stand with that of anyone. But there are times when you don't expect, and we are not sent here to work night and day, and when I made that suggestion I know there are other people that made engagements, and I am quite prepared to cancel mine, as I have in the past, and I don't want Mr. Sinclair to think that I am asking the privilege of stopping the Committee for some social event. I am quite prepared to be here on Monday night, but I don't think it is necessary.

MR. FINLAYSON: I think the mover and seconder forget one fact, that they are both leaders of parties; they are both provided with secretaries and both paid for their work, and other members are not.

MR. SINCLAIR: Paid very poorly. We are worth a lot more than we are paid.

MR. FINLAYSON: You both live in or near Toronto. I move in amendment that when the Committee adjourns it stands adjourned until Wednesday morning at 10 A.M. to proceed with the Lyons matter.

THE CHAIRMAN: I don't think further discussion is necessary. There is a motion by Mr. Sinclair seconded by Mr. Raney that when the Committee adjourns it stands adjourned to meet again Monday evening, and then from day to day. The amendment by Mr. Finlayson, seconded by Dr. Carr, is that when the Committee adjourns it stands adjourned until Wednesday, March 17. All those in favour of the amendment signify by holding up their hand. Down! Those opposed? I declare the amendment carried.

MR. SINCLAIR: Call the roll.

THE CHAIRMAN: Members will please vote "yea" if they are in favour of the amendment to adjourn Wednesday morning. Those in favour?

MEMBER: Yes or no.

THE CHAIRMAN: Yes or no. Those in favour of the amendment will vote yes.

(During the vote.)

MR. OAKLEY: I understand since I came in that the Committee are desirous of having me appear before them and so I prefer not to give.

MR. FINLAYSON: Not on this matter. Yes or no.

THE SECRETARY: The yeas are 22; the nays, 10.

THE CHAIRMAN: I declare the amendment carried.

The Committee then adjourned to meet again Wednesday, March 17, at 10 A.M.

PUBLIC ACCOUNTS COMMITTEE

The Committee reassembled Wednesday morning, March 17th, at 10 A.M., with Mr. A. C. Lewis in the Chair.

THE CHAIRMAN: Now gentlemen, I think it was understood that when we resumed this morning we proceed with the examination of Mr. Lyons in connection with the questions and the motions for the production of witnesses at our organization meeting. Mr. Lyons is here ready to go ahead. He is here ready for examination. I propose that Mr. Finlayson shall proceed with the examination of Mr. Lyons.

MR. SINCLAIR: Had you given any consideration to whether there would be more meetings than the regular meetings of the Committee?

THE CHAIRMAN: Well, Mr. Sinclair, I think it was generally understood that we would meet not only on Wednesdays and further regular meeting days but whenever we could put in a meeting in order to facilitate. There won't be any disposition to try and keep you from having as many meetings as necessary.

MR. SINCLAIR: I suppose that would be the farthest from your mind?

THE CHAIRMAN: Quite so.

MR. WIDDIFIELD: May I, before we hear Mr. Finlayson, move, seconded by Mr. Lethbridge, that A. H. Birmingham be summoned before the Committee to give evidence in respect to the item of $900,000 appearing as a receipt of the Province at page 14 and generally as to Provincial Dispensaries.

MR. FINLAYSON: Where is the item?

MR. McKEOWN: Middle of the page, $900,000.

MR. SINCLAIR: Dispensaries, that medicine item there.

THE CHAIRMAN: What is your pleasure, gentlemen, with Mr. Widdifield's motion? Those in favour please signify. Carried.

MR. FREEBORN: I would like to move, seconded by Mr. Kemp, that the Provincial Auditor and Albert E. Nash be summoned before the Committee to give evidence at its next meeting concerning the special audit that the Government has been conducting.

THE CHAIRMAN: That is practically the same wording, Mr. Raney, as the other.

HON. MR. RANEY: No, no, objection was made that other resolution—

THE CHAIRMAN: No, but the point that occurred to me when it was presented last meeting was this, it doesn't specify a particular audit.

Hon. Mr. Raney: Special audit?

The Chairman: Concerning the special audit that the Government has been conducting. The Government has been conducting, as I understand, special audit in practically all departments.

Hon. Mr. Raney: Well, we just want to find out in a general way, and I think other members of the Committee do, what the extent of this investigation has been, what departments have been investigated, up to what time, back to what date, and with what result generally. It isn't a detailed matter at all.

Mr. Finlayson: I appreciate the propriety of Mr. Raney asking for information of that kind, but is this the proper place for it? If you asked for a return you will no doubt get it.

Hon. Mr. Raney: You couldn't ask for a return in this matter.

The Chairman: I think it is already covered to some extent by a question on the order paper.

Mr. Finlayson: The function of this Committee is to discuss expenditure made, or receipts. Now this is no question of expenditure or receipt. This is no doubt a very proper inquiry, but I don't think this is the forum where it should be heard. If we go into the question of Government policy, and the Government—I speak without any exact information and I don't think I have any more information than my learned friend—we all know the Government have been conducting extensive audits; we know Major Nash and the Clarkson firm has had charge in one department at least to my knowledge. If we ask Mr. Nash to come here he may be asked to disclose recommendations he has made to the Government on which they may or may not have formed a policy. I don't think it is a proper matter for discussion before the Public Accounts Committee.

Hon. Mr. Raney: When those questions arise, I submit it is time enough to make objection.

Mr. Finlayson: No, if we summon Mr. Nash here we should summon him here in connection with some payment in the Public Accounts.

Mr. Homuth: Summon him in connection with the payment.

Hon. Mr. Raney: That opens the whole matter. We could put on that resolution items of payment that have been made to this firm of auditors; that would open the whole matter.

Mr. Finlayson: I don't know that it would.

The Chairman: Wouldn't you arrive at the same result Mr. Raney if you simply asked the Provincial Treasurer for this information. There would be no objection whatever to giving you the information you asked for.

Hon. Mr. Raney: Well, you could not get it except by oral questions and answers.

Mr. Currie: Is there any name mentioned there, or specific item?

The Chairman: No.

Mr. Currie: Rule it out.

Hon. Mr. Raney: I don't desire to spend time now. If Mr. Finlayson will discuss the matter with the Treasurer perhaps we could find some middle course by which we could get the information we desire.

Mr. Finlayson: I will be very glad to do that. In the meantime it simply stands; is that the arrangement?

Hon. Mr. Raney: That is it. From what happened here at the last meeting of the Committee, both with reference to Mr. Finlayson's statement as to the desire to be exhaustive in all these matters and to cover everything that has come or may come before the Committee before the adjournment of the House; and in view also of the division we had on the last day, when the Committee voted not to on Monday, as Mr. Sinclair and I desired to do, but to hold the first meeting for taking of evidence to-day—in view of those two things, I think we ought to determine now what our time table so to speak is to be, and my suggestion, and if necessary I will make a motion, but it may not be necessary, that when we adjourn to-day the understanding will be we will adjourn until some hour to be named by the Chairman to-morrow, and thereafter we shall sit from day to day, so far as is practical until these matters have all been cleaned up. Now if this is acceptable to the Committee it won't be necessary for me to move a resolution.

THE CHAIRMAN: Well, it is acceptable, with this reservation. This week Private Bills Committee is meeting to-morrow morning. I don't think it is wise that the members who are on both these Committees should be deprived of the opportunity of attending both committees.

HON. MR. RANEY: If you will pardon me, I was going to suggest perhaps we could meet again this evening; if not this evening, to-morrow evening—

THE CHAIRMAN: This evening and to-morrow evening! I don't think it will be possible to have meetings of the Committee. There is the Speaker's dinner this evening. These things are always understood to have precedence.

MR. CURRIE: Permit me to say that the only people who can permit this Committee to meet when the House is in session are the House, and the House is the proper place—

THE CHAIRMAN Quite so, we will have to make recommendation to the House.

HON. MR. RANEY: I am not going to leave this at a loose end. We are not going to float along from day to day if I can avoid it, with one obstacle after another being given as reason for not sitting, so I am going to move, seconded by Mr. Nixon—

That when the Committee adjourns to-day it stand adjourned to to-morrow at an hour to be named by the Chair, and that thereafter as far as practicable, the Committee sit from day to day until the matters now before it or which may be brought before it have been disposed of.

I am quite content to amend that motion so as to provide for our meeting again to-night, but perhaps this is sufficient if we can get meetings every day as far as practical, you will notice I put in. I.want to affirm the principle that this Committee is going to sit continuously day by day just as often as it can until we overtake this business.

MR. FINLAYSON: What Col. Currie has said is quite right. We are more or less under the necessity of governing our meetings by the meeting of the Legislature. We don't know whether the Legislature will sit in the evening, or night, but I do want to say this: as far as I know there is no objection why the Committee should not sit at every available time to catch up to the business we have ahead of us. I think it is quite apparent from the language Mr. Raney used, and I know in Mr. Sinclair's last week, that the House work is ahead of the Committee work and this Committee and the other committees must function as much as possible in order to catch up. And, speaking for myself, and perhaps to a limited extent for our friends, I want to say that there will be no obstacle placed in the way of the Committee sitting every available moment to dispense the business before it. As for having a formal resolution in, I don't see any objection; it simply affirms the desire of the Committee that we go ahead as fast as possible. To be quite frank, as everyone knows, to-morrow night there is a dinner being tendered to the leader of the Government. We are all very anxious to go, and I don't think my honourable friend would try and force us on to-night. If he did we would either have to submit to it or force an adjournment.

Mr. HOMUTH: Invite us to the dinner.

Mr. SINCLAIR: I don't suppose the mover and myself will be invited to this?

Mr. FINLAYSON: I don't suppose there is any reason why we should not have a dinner to all leaders of the House.

THE CHAIRMAN: Please give attention to the wording of this resolution.

Mr. CURRIE: I don't believe, Mr. Chairman, while I quite agree with the resolution and the spirit of it; I think we all agree to it. But I do not feel as a member of this Committee that we should have our hands bound up in a resolution of Mr. Raney's of that character. The Committee can from day to day decide exactly what it is going to do and it is not necessary for this Committee to be ruled or governed by Mr. Raney.

Mr. FINLAYSON: Oh, I don't think there is any attempt—

Mr. CURRIE: Everybody here is anxious to have this thing all off and for that reason I am going to oppose that resolution if I stand alone.

HON. MR. RANEY: Divide the Committee.

Mr. McKEOWN: I feel very much like Mr. Currie. I feel it is up to this Committee at each time of adjournment comes to say when we will meet again, and if we have to meet to-morrow morning let us meet to-morrow. But we will know then and we don't know to-day what position we will be in next Tuesday, and we are not going, at least as far as my vote is concerned, to bind the Committee to say we will meet Tuesday, Wednesday and Thursday next until we know what we are doing.

Mr. FINLAYSON: Move an amendment that it is the desire of the Committee to proceed as rapidly as possible.

Mr. McKEOWN: That it is the desire—

Mr. CURRIE: Add that if necessary the Committee shall ask to sit at night.

Mr. FINLAYSON: Sit as expeditiously as possible to dispose of this business.

Mr. HOMUTH: I don't think that motion of Mr. Raney's does bind the Committee to sit any particular time.

Mr. FINLAYSON: After we have heard the discussion and general unanimity of opinion of getting on, perhaps Mr. Raney will withdraw his motion.

THE CHAIRMAN: Let me say Mr. Raney was not in when I gave Mr. Sinclair, who made a similar inquiry, the assurance that this Committee will be called on every practical day, at whatever hour is selected, as the hour at which we can most easily meet for the purpose of carrying on business. There may be days we won't be able to hold meetings and if the Committee have sufficient confidence in the Chairman to feel he will call a meeting— .

HON. MR. RANEY: I am disposed, if Mr. McKeown will put his motion in form—I think this ought to be made a matter of record—in the way he has stated it verbally, I will be disposed to consent to the amendment. Just pass on to another order of business.

Now there is another matter. I saw from the newspapers that the auditor had been put on the matter, the main subject of this inquiry, asked for by the late Minister of Lands and Forests. Nothing was said about instructions. The Committee hasn't been told, as far as I know, what instructions have been given to the auditor. Are you in a position to inform the Committee what instructions were given.

THE CHAIRMAN: Mr. Clarkson was immediately communicated with following the meeting of the Committee on Friday last and he brought Major Nash back from Ottawa where Mr. Nash was engaged in some government work. Mr. Nash was here on Saturday morning, and left for the Soo, I think, Saturday or Sunday evening. He was furnished with the questions that were placed on the order paper from which this whole question arose, on which Mr. Lyons based his request for a full inquiry. He was furnished with a copy of those questions and directed to go into the books of Mr. Lyons' various companies most thoroughly to investigate all the different lines of activity suggested by the questions placed on the order paper, and to report to the Committee any information he secured as a result of his investigations of the books, and any further investigation he felt was suggested as a result of your investigation.

HON. MR. RANEY: Thank you, but I venture to think—it is not your fault, of course—that those instructions don't quite cover the case, because I happen to know that there were more questions not put on the order paper because of what happened in the House. So the situation is not covered by the questions that have been printed in the Votes and Proceedings. Morever, it seems to me—I may be wrong—but it seems to me that the accountants will be pretty much at sea unless they are given some more definite information as to the line of their inquiries, and I am going to suggest to this Committee the appointment of a sub-committee. This is the resolution as I have drafted it.

Moved by myself, seconded by Mr. Nixon,

That a sub-committee consisting of Messrs. Finlayson, Sinclair, and the mover be appointed with authority to instruct the accountants as to the investigations they are to make in the inquiry asked for by the late Minister of Lands and Forests.

MR. FINLAYSON: Well, it is very flattering of the late Attorney-General to name that committee, and name me as if I were senior member, but let me remind the late Attorney-General of this, that at the last meeting of this Committee, I think it was Mr. Sinclair said: What instructions are going to be given to these auditors, and I said what I thought would answer the purpose: we would furnish them with the questions, copies of every question put on the order paper, and my friend from East Wellington said, "Yes. " It is on the record.

HON. MR. RANEY: Well, I don't recall, of course, what took place. We were taken by surprise with this—

MR. FINLAYSON: No, no.

HON. MR. RANEY: Well, it was not mentioned to anybody until the suggestion was made in question. Will you be good enough to read what I said and we will see just what it was. Even if I did say something, that doesn't bind the Committee, and it doesn't necessarily bind me.

MR. FINLAYSON: I am sure no member wishes to make any suggestion or exercise any control over the auditors, and I felt that when I submitted the name of Clarkson & Company I was submitting a name that would not only have the confidence of this Committee but the confidence of the House and the whole Province of Ontario, and Mr. Raney said that he was delighted with the suggestion, that their name—

HON. MR. RANEY: I have no doubt I approved of the auditors.

MR. FINLAYSON: Well, as to the instructions to the auditors—

HON. MR. RANEY: See what I said.

MR. FINLAYSON: In a minute. If my friend, Mr. Raney, or Mr. Sinclair wish to send any memoranda to the auditors through the Chairman, as to additional matters to be looked into, let it be done to-day. Will that not answer?

Hon. Mr. Raney: Well, that may answer the purpose.

The Chairman: I was going to suggest—in fact Mr. Lyons also made the suggestion I should say that if Mr. Raney or Mr. Sinclair will give us a memo, or any member of the Committee on any particular line of inquiry that they think should be carried on, those instructions will be forwarded to the auditors.

Hon. Mr. Raney: That seems fair, and for the present I think my suggestion can stand.

Mr. Sinclair: Just a word right here. I don't wish to say anything about the accountants that have been chosen. They are an excellent firm of men and they will carry out our instructions to get whatever information is wanted. I think I said the other day that we were going at this wrong end up. I still think so. The Government are going to conduct the investigation. This is on certain questions which have been on the order paper. If this matter had come up in the usual way before the Public Accounts Committee, by some of the opposition members examining Mr. Lyons first, then the points which the auditors would have been asked to look into would have been apparent and the auditors would not have had to go hunting through the books of Mr. Lyons for something that might not be interesting to this Committee and may never give up any evidence. I simply want to put myself on record at the opening of this Committee, that I do not approve of this manner of conducting the examination because it is going to begin at the wrong end and time will tell just where it is going to finish.

Mr. Currie: What would you suggest?

Mr. Sinclair: Well, I would suggest the time honoured custom in Public Accounts Committee, when opposition members examine the Government. That is what the Public Accounts Committee has always done. In this case the Government examines the Government.

Mr. Currie: Well, the Government has virtually dismissed a Minister—

Members: No, no.

Mr. Currie: He is here, on trial. He has resigned. His resignation is in. That is virtually the same thing. And they have stated they are going to make the way open to investigation. Now if you have anything you want investigated, or any questions relative to his books or accounts, produce them in open committee and let them be investigated by the auditor, and bring the auditor here and we will examine him.

Mr. Sinclair: Well, my learned friend always wants to talk at the same time anybody else is talking.

Mr. Finlayson; Habit of the profession.

Mr. Sinclair: And if he can tell me, from his long experience, just what opportunity I will have, and the time at which I will have the opportunity to examine the witnesses, I would be delighted to concur with his views. I just want to say that we are commencing this thing wrong and anything which is commenced wrong, very seldom turns out right.

Mr. Currie: You start any way you want. Tell us how you want to start. You make a few grouches and don't express anything to the Committee.

Mr. Sinclair: I don't know anybody that grouches more than you.

The Chairman: Is there anything else while Mr. McKeown—

Hon. Mr. Raney: Yes, there is the matter that stood over from the last sitting, the matter of the inquiry with reference to the thousand dollar bills that were said to have been paid.

The Chairman: The motion of which you gave notice.

Hon. Mr. Raney: Well, Mr. Finlayson was to have given us his attitude.

Mr. Finlayson: Mr. Chairman, may I have the attention of the Committee for a moment. At the last meeting Mr. Raney moved this resolution:—

"That S. L. Squire, Deputy Minister of Highways, Frank H. Harris, Edmund P. Stewart, Carleton L. Dyer, R. S. Shenstone, W. G. Clysdale and Albert E. Nash be summoned before the Committee to give evidence concerning contracts for certain advertisements that appeared in a certain magazine called *Rural Canada* on pages 22 and 23 of the issue of that magazine of October, 1919, and concerning payment of the contract price of the said advertisements and that the said witnesses be required to produce all books, letters, papers and documents in their custody, possession or power relating to the said matters."

I have read the whole resolution so that the Committee may be reminded of all the facts in connection with it. Now, sir, I wish to rise to a point of order, or at least, perhaps it would be more correct to state it in this way, that I want to make preliminary objection going to the question of jurisdiction, and that should be treated, I suppose, as a preliminary objection and considered first.

The Committee know that this Committee is not a body of any inherent jurisdiction. It is a creature of the Legislature that the Legislature have authorized the Committee to take cognizance of and deal with certain matters. Now what are the matters that the Committee deal with. What is the object of the Committee's existence. What is the reason for which we are created? The name of the Committee surely indicates what we are here for. We are here to go into the Public Accounts of the Province of Ontario; that is the whole purpose and object of this Committee.

I followed the practice of my friend from North East Toronto in the interval and tried to study the matter and tried to understand it, and I have gone to the source he has always gone to, the Imperial House, and I find this: that the practice, as far as Public Accounts, only dates back to 1860, and the first committee then was authorized by the Imperial Legislature, and since then that practice has been conducted all over the British Empire, in every self governing commonwealth, every legislature, and our Legislature, named every year, following the British practice, a Committee to consider the Public Accounts of the Province of Ontario.

Mr. Currie: For that year.

Mr. Finlayson: For that year. There is ample authority on that. Now what is objectionable in this is first, it is an attempt to go back six years, nearly seven years, but I don't press that before the Committee for this reason, that if it were a proper matter of inquiry, or matter over which this Committee had any jurisdiction or control I would not press that. It is merely a technicality, although the Statute of Limitation is six years, and here we are getting beyond six years.

But what I do press, and if necessary will press as vigorously as I can, here we are asked to deal with something that has nothing to do, and entirely foreign for the purpose for which this Committee is created.

I don't want to weary the Committee with a lot of authorities. I have, in the time, collected all the authorities I could find from down to the time of 1860. Before that the practice was when the estimates and the accounts were brought down in the House to consider in the whole House, and it was found to be inconvenient, and found to take up a lot of time, and you know, in a Legislature of five or six hundred people it was found cumbersome and impractical, and therefore the Committee of Public Accounts was instituted.

Mr friend, Mr. Raney, has in this Committee and in the House expressed

his admiration for Sir Erskine May and his complete confidence in his law and
I propose to read what he says. Erskine May, Parliamentary Practice, 13th
Edition, page 557.

HON. MR. RANEY: But that is discredited now.

MR. FINLAYSON: I don't say that; I would hesitate to say that. I am not
so bold as my learned friend to say anything of the kind. I think the action of
the Legislature the other day was following out May's suggestion entirely.

"The House will appoint at the commencement of every session a Committee of Public Accounts for the examination of the accounts, showing the
appropriation of the sums granted by parliament to meet the public expenditure. . . . The function of this Committee is to ascertain that the parliamentary grants for each financial year, including supplementary grants, have been
applied to the object which parliament prescribed and to recheck the official
audit created by the exchequer and the Audit Department's Act, 1866.   But
Committee also scrutinizes the causes which have led to any excesses over
parliamentary grants and the application of savings on the grants made to the
naval and air force department.   The researches made by the Committee and
the publication of their reports ensure on behalf of the House of Commons an
effectual examination of the Public Accounts."

Then, Mr. Todd's work, Parliamentary Government in the Empire. But,
going over the history, he says, Todd's Parliamentary Government, on page 269:
"Motion was carried in the House of Commons providing for the Committee"—

MEMBERS: Dispense, dispense.

MR. FINLAYSON   Perhaps I have convinced my friend I am right. But
what I want to say is this: all through the practice is well established. I don't
think my friend from East Wellington will make any statement to the contrary.
If he does I could give him a long statement from Mr. Gladstone, who says
that the whole function and duty of the Committee is to consider the accounts.
If anyone wanted to be technical. On the table when we came here you found
Public Accounts for the fiscal year ending the 31st of October, 1925. And that
is our privilege. That is the subject matter of our inquiry, and we cannot go
beyond that.

But what I want to point out in this case is, we are asked to conduct a
fishing expedition seven years old, asked to go into not what is done with public
moneys of 1919, but what happened is between an alleged—nothing in the
resolution, you will notice, very carefully; but Mr. Raney in explaining it made
a speech for the benefit of the *Star* and a few other papers that was placarded
all over the Province as propaganda, and he said, these hints at thousand dollars,
these hints at payments, and he gave what he alleged to be certain details of
payments for these advertisements, these advertisements not inserted by the
Province of Ontario, if his statement is right, but by some private person in a
private publication which has now ceased to exist.   Not provincial moneys!
No suggestion even in my honourable friend's statement to the Committee that
it came even directly or indirectly from any provincial source. It was something
that is a private matter between two individuals or corporations or companies
relating to the publication of an advertisement in a private paper.

Now if the Committee are going into that, what is to prevent some member
of this Committee saying I would desire the Committee, and move a resolution
to have the Committee decide whether the member for Wentworth is charging
too much for his cream on the market, or whether he sold eggs at an improper
price to Mary Jones, or any inquiry—

MR. CURRIE: Or how many legals *The Globe* got.

MR. FINLAYSON: Or what is paid for propaganda in *The Globe* or *Star.*

HON. MR. RANEY: Well, Mr. Currie is humorous.

MR. FINLAYSON: May I say this, this same question arose two years ago. I cannot remind Mr. Raney of it because he did not honour us with his attendance.

HON. MR. RANEY: Oh yes, I know all about it.

MR. FINLAYSON: Evidence was given before this Committee in connection with that inquiry which showed the trail of the U.F.O. campaign fund, where they made one of those fly-by-night trips to New York with the Provincial Treasurer and made a clean up of $50,000 over night and we found it was divided in the U.F.O. way, 50 to the treasurer and 50 to the campaign fund. That was our understanding, 50-50, and we still believe that to be right. We know that Mr. Drury admitted that that man was the treasurer of the fund. It was admitted by Mr. Drury, leader of the Government, by Mr. Raney when he gave evidence, that that gentleman was the treasurer of the U.F.O. campaign fund. It was proved to the Committee he went to New York over night with the treasurer and cleaned up $50,000 over night, and we all assumed that was 50-50 for the campaign fund—

MR. CURRIE: I guess those are some of the legals.

MR. FINLAYSON: I don't know and don't care. But we considered that we had a right to go into that and we came to the conclusion we hadn't, no matter whether the U.F.O. campaign fund was as crooked as we believed them to be, no matter—

MR. MCKEOWN: They couldn't be.

MR. FINLAYSON: No matter whether this treasurer of the U.F.O. was given by Mr. Raney's Government an opportunity to make $50,000 in one night's trip to New York, which Mr. Raney said is most objectionable and improper, and it was exactly the way Mr. Ridout was given, and we know how close some of the Ridout money went to the Government and members of the last Legislature. We came to the conclusion on a matter like this the Committee had no jurisdiction to dig into it. It was not a Government fund, the money was made improperly and indefensibly and the Province lost $50,000 and more over the transaction, but it was not something we could send anybody to jail for, and the treasurer of the U.F.O., having made his $50,000, and we had no right to go into it. It was not Government funds. Now the position is exactly the same to-day with this Committee, that there is no proof here, just an inflammatory speech made for newspaper purposes suggesting legals, suggesting something, but not tying it down to anything this Committee can investigate. I would draw your attention to the practice of a more experienced parliamentarian who speaks as an authority, if you will look at the resolution made by Mr. Sinclair, you will find he says, "I wish John Smith called to this Committee in reference to item so and so, page so and so, in reference to the accounts of last year." Mr. Sinclair complains we moved away from it in this case, and we did to this extent, as I told him, I was doing it because I thought it was a novel procedure and done at the request of the late Minister of Lands and Forests. I would submit to the Committee—

MEMBERS: Give us your next authority.

MR. FINLAYSON: No, but if anybody wants to do it, you will find an interesting discussion of it in the *Quarterly Review.* All the authorities are one way and my learned friend won't contradict. I submit to the Chairman, then, that the resolution is out of order. It is entirely beyond the jurisdiction of the Province of Ontario.

Hon. Mr. Raney: I am not very much concerned, frankly, with the precedents of the year 1860. The precedent of this Committee in the year 1924 and the precedent last year and many other precedents I could refer to, if it were thought advisable to take the time, would be entirely sufficient for my purpose.

In 1924 this Committee was very keen, and properly very keen, to discover what had happened to certain legals that went out of the Special Commission Account of the Home Bank in December, 1919, and this Committee called witnesses and discovered that a few days after those legals went out from the Home Bank in December, 1919, seven legals of the denomination of a thousand dollars each were deposited by Mr. Peter Smith in his bank account in Stratford, and that circumstantial evidence, brought out before this Committee, was the basis of Mr. Smith's conviction of the offence of having received $15,000 special commission or commission in respect of these Home Bank transactions. Now that was 1924, five years after the event, and nothing in the accounts of that year remotely touching—

Mr. Finlayson: Will my friend permit an interruption?

Hon. Mr. Raney: No, no, please.

Last year the question was raised again and it was suggested that Peter Smith and Mr. Charles Matthews knew some things about this very question and the moneys that had come, it is said, from the Home Bank to the Parliament Buildings on the same day on which Mr. McGarry had accepted the tender of the Home Bank for the issue of Provincial bonds of $4,000,000, 23rd of September, 1919, just on the eve of the provincial election of that year.

At first the Government, through the Treasurer who was then attending, took the same position Mr. Finlayson is taking now, that that matter ought not to be investigated and for the same reason. I then suggested to Mr. Price that the position was altogether indefensible and I suggested to him before taking the position hard and fast and before taking the division of the Committee he ought to confer with the Prime Minister to ascertain if the Prime Minister would not consent to the evidence of these men being taken. The matter stood over until next meeting and next meeting Mr. Price changed his attitude and agreed there should be a special committee to take this evidence, and a special committee went to Kingston and evidence taken, as much as was allowed to be given by the members of the Government who attended as members of that committee.

Mr. McKeown: Nice slam.

Hon. Mr. Raney: Now Mr. Finlayson says there is no evidence before the Committee. I am going to put some before the Committee. An affidavit—

Mr. Finlayson: Just a minute. You cannot read evidence on a point of order. My friend got in the other day in a left handed way for publication something of this kind, and I felt at the time it was objectionable. But, to-day, I propose to ask the Chairman to rule. I am quite satisfied that discussion take place, but material of this kind—

The Chairman: Let me ask, is your motion before the Committee?

Hon. Mr. Raney: My motion before the Committee is for the summoning of witnesses with regard to certain advertisements that did appear in the publication *Rural Canada* and the payment of them, not only—the resolution speaks not only of an advertisement to which I referred to the other day specifically but speaks of the other advertisements to which I referred also, namely certain government advertisements that appeared in the same issue of the same paper and were also included in the same resolution.

THE CHAIRMAN: "Moved by Mr. Raney, seconded by Mr. Kemp, That S. L. Squire, Deputy Minister of Highways, Frank H. Harris, Edmund P. Stewart, Carleton L. Dyer, R. S. Shenstone, W. G. Clysdale and Albert E. Nash, be summoned before the Committee to give evidence concerning contracts for certain advertisements that appeared in a certain magazine called *Rural Canada* on pages 22 and 23 of the issue of that magazine of October, 1919, and concerning payment of the contract price of the said advertisements and that the said witnesses be required to produce all books, letters, papers and documents in their custody, possession or power relating to the said matters."

Now Mr. Finlayson has made objection to the status of this motion before this Committee and I think it right that we should decide the admissibility of the motion before we proceed to any evidence that you want to give in support of your motion.

MR. CURRIE: That is right.

HON. MR. RANEY: I would think not. I would submit I have a right to put my motion and to support my motion in any way I see fit before you are called upon to rule.

THE CHAIRMAN: No, I think not. I think the custom is for the Chairman to rule.

HON. MR. RANEY: Well, I will tell you what I have. I have the affidavits—

MR. FINLAYSON: No, no.

MR. CURRIE: There is a point of order taken and the argument is on the point of order, not on what is evidence or what he has got. He has got to show this Committee that his motion is in order. Now I am of the belief that this Committee is exceedingly desirous of going into everything in connection with the affairs of the Province, but this Committee has just as much right to summon the editor of *The Globe* here and say, bring all your books and papers, we want to see what legals or what money you got during the election out of campaign funds, or from anybody else as we have to accept this motion of Mr. Raney's. It is exactly on all fours. Now the point of order is taken that the resolution cannot be accepted by this Committee, and it is of no use now, and we could argue, and I claim all parliamentary authorities would be against having this Committee do anything of the kind.

HON. MR. RANEY: I think if the Chairman would pardon me, if I had the floor—

THE CHAIRMAN: You had the floor subject to this, that I still maintain and I rule if necessary that—

HON. MR. RANEY: Don't rule until I finish my arguments. I have a right to discuss a point of order.

THE CHAIRMAN: You have a perfect right to discuss the question of your motion being properly before the Committee, but I do not think that you are within your rights in presenting evidence you were to present following up the motion.

HON. MR. RANEY: I am going to argue the point. I am going to argue the question of my right to read these affidavits. The resolution, as Mr. Finlayson very properly says, doesn't mention legals at all. Nothing is said about thousand dollar legals. Nothing is said about the source from which these legals came. I made that statement verbally to the Committee. I stated to the Committee just now with an absolute precedent this Committee will stultify itself if, after having pursued the Peter Smith inquiry with regard to these legals, as the Committee did and did properly—

MR. CURRIE: Well, but Peter Smith—

HON. MR. RANEY: Pardon me; but having pursued that inquiry, properly, and having succeeded in landing Smith in the penitentiary, as the Government did—

MR. FINLAYSON: No, no, the Government didn't.

HON. MR. RANEY: The Government did, and I applaud them for it. They were quite right in doing it and I have no objection to any course they took at all—

MR. FINLAYSON: The courts did!

HON. MR. RANEY: I am proposing to show by the affidavit I am proposing to read that this case I am putting before the Committee comes squarely within, the precedent established by this Committee in 1924 and re-established in 1925 that the Committee will inquire as to what happened to these legals that went out from the Home Bank in 1919. I will show from evidence that I will adduce— it is already before the Committee; it was last year and the year before—that these legals were not in general circulation—

MR. FINLAYSON: Just a minute; I object. My friend is starting in on a long direction to the newspapers. My friend knows as well as I do or any member, that he is absolutely out of order and hopes in that left handed way to get it in, and I do not propose to let him.

HON. MR. RANEY: We will get to a ruling, if you please.

THE CHAIRMAN: I think I have stated—

MR. FINLAYSON: May I answer? I want to clear the matter up. Any member of this Committee who charges the Committee with stultifying itself, is making a serious charge—

HON. MR. RANEY: I hope the Committee won't stultify itself.

MR. CURRIE: You would go to the bar in the Old Country for half what you said.

MR. McKEOWN: If he were at the bar he would not know where he was.

HON. MR. RANEY: It takes more than a tin colonel to frighten me.

MR. CURRIE: All right; I got you before.

MR. FINLAYSON: Let us proceed to this case; it is serious. My friend's whole object, he knows perfectly well that this resolution is out of order; he knows perfectly well he has no standing, but he is hoping in some left handed way, typical of matters that come from East Wellington, that he will in some way get into the paper something that will cast suspicion over a whole lot of people. It may hit a hundred other people, but it doesn't matter as long as it blackens up public men. What I propose is that this Committee treat themselves as a self-respecting court, as a court conducting a judicial inquiry, not conducting campaign slander. It is an attempt in a left handed way to mention a number of gentlemen whom Mr. Raney knows know nothing about this matter at all, and mention their names, and suggest. And if we propose to go on with this where will we possibly end? If you want an analogy the analogy is where we declined to follow up two years ago. Mr. Raney's treasurer got $50,000 over night with his connivance—

HON. MR. RANEY: Why didn't you?

MR. FINLAYSON: Because it was not legal. Why not ask Mr. Nixon? Because Mr. Nixon is a friend and relative of one of his colleagues. The whole spirit shows it is a left handed, miserable attempt to besmirch someone's character. What I want to submit to him and to the Committee is there is no analogy in what happened two years ago and what happened one year ago for this reason, that two years ago and one year ago we were investigating certain officials of the Government, a gentleman who sat opposite Mr. Raney in council, his colleague on the Treasury Board. These two gentlemen were responsible for the Treasury and responsible for the finances of the Province and because one of them fell and one of them hasn't fallen yet, this attempt is going to be thrown all over the Province, to besmirch everybody's name. The reason the Committee went into it two years ago, they had before them two men, the Provincial Treasurer and the Deputy Treasurer and that was a proper subject of inquiry. They were public servants paid by this Province, under a trust, and they violated their trust and they fell. Now the next session, my friend says, we carried it a stage farther. True we carried it a stage farther and went down at his request and investigated Smith and Mathews—

HON. MR. RANEY: And you wouldn't let Matthews answer the question.

MR. FINLAYSON: Pardon me; I contradict that directly, and if you look at the record and ask Mr. Oke who sits at the foot of the table and ask Mr. Homuth, independent members, they will tell you we conducted the inquiry in a fair and proper way. What I suggest is this, two years ago we were investigating the finances of the Province and if the Provincial Treasurer accepted money, legals or not legals, from an official or a man he was dealing with and putting them in his own account it was improper and illegal and we didn't prosecute him, we simply investigated the facts and said there they are, and the Crown took it to the courts. Last year, it is true, it was carried a stage farther. Matthews and Smith didn't give evidence before this Committee. Smith didn't give evidence at all because he refused. Smith didn't give evidence simply because he took the stand, "I am advised by my counsel,"—you remember Mr. Dewart was here and said, "Don't give evidence." When he was tendered the Book he refused to give evidence. Last session my friend again was at his propaganda work; he wanted an inquiry at Kingston. He got his inquiry without results whatever, no more than he would get on this occasion.

HON. MR. RANEY: Thanks to you and Mr. Price and Mr. McCrea.

MR. FINLAYSON: Now, my friend has all the remedies. If he wants to get up in the House and make a charge in connection with this matter I am satisfied that the Premier will give him a forum, if he will take his own responsibility. But he won't come here and in a left handed way try and besmirch public names. Why wasn't Smith's name, Jones' name—just the miserable way as the other day he mentioned the member for North Huron and Dundas in such a way that nearly every member of his party came to us and said: "We are ashamed of it."

MEMBER: Who?

MR. FINLAYSON: The men who sit behind him.

MEMBER: No they didn't.

MEMBER: Name them.

MR. FINLAYSON: I will do it. I will give the names if you want it. The point here is simply this. The Committee have no jurisdiction over this. The authorities are all that way. My friend, who is judicial and would cite other authorities if he could find one, cannot present a single authority. And as far as stultifying itself, two years ago and one year ago the Committee were investigating officers of the Government, Treasurer and Deputy Treasurer, the very men into whose accounts this Committee is appointed to look. Last year we carried it perhaps a stage farther but from this resolution we don't know who we are to investigate, a certain magazine, a certain advertisement! If my friend will name any officer of the Government of that day and make a charge he will get a forum and get a Committee and have a trial.

MR. SINCLAIR: Just a word. I love the way the attorney for the Government criticizes the member for East Wellington.

MR. MCKEOWN: We all do.

MR. SINCLAIR: Wait until I get through—in trying, as he says, to get his name in the paper for what he is saying here. My impression is the attorney for the Government does not sit here in any very unbiased manner. I speak very strongly and one can easily see which way his sympathies lie in this matter. Now, if the member for East Wellington has some information which he claims to have which relates to a transaction in 1919, I cannot see the force of the argument of my learned friend. It may be that the evidence which the member for East Wellington has and will produce will lead right up to a part of that $25,000 referred to in the last session in the Public Accounts Committee at last session, and if it does, and if he has evidence leading to that, it is just as relevant—

MR. FINLAYSON: Let him put it on his motion.

MR. SINCLAIR: He has framed his motion in general terms.

MR. FINLAYSON: You know how to frame a motion.

MR. SINCLAIR: I don't wish to make comparisons with my friend from East Wellington.

MR. FINLAYSON: He could frame the resolution if he had the material.

MR. SINCLAIR: If he has this information leading back to that transaction it is just as relevant as the matters which were brought before Public Accounts Committee last year and the other years. We investigated away back to 1919—

MR. FINLAYSON: As to the Treasurer and Deputy Treasurer.

MR. SINCLAIR: —taking any lead that showed itself in order to find out what happened to that $67,000 of commissions—I think that is the amount paid in connection with that loan. Now, if the honourable member for East Wellington has evidence showing that this leads in the same direction and up to the same source it is just as relevant to-day as it was last year and the year before and it is drawing too fine a distinction altogether in relation to this matter which has been before the Public Accounts Committee I think for the last two years at any rate.

Now just a word in regard to this trip of the special committee to Kingston, because—

THE CHAIRMAN: Is that relevant?

HON. MR. RANEY: Go on, take your time.

MR. SINCLAIR: No, I don't suppose it is. But I was a member of that subcommittee and the records show that as soon as you got a question asked that looked as if it would lead to some information, counsel paid for by the Government immediately intervened and said: "Don't answer that question.

THE CHAIRMAN: I don't think that is quite fair to say that—

MR. FINLAYSON: No, these counsel were—

MR. SINCLAIR: Now, I don't propose to let anybody—I say counsel paid by the Government.

MR. FINLAYSON: Province.

MR. SINCLAIR: It went into the Public Accounts and it is there and paid by the Government.

MR. FINLAYSON: Under what authority?

MR. SINCLAIR: I am not saying what authority; I say paid by the Government and they were there and as a result of being there the inquiry was largely fruitless. The honourable member for Simcoe says that it didn't get any information. I disagree with him entirely. It did get valuable information—a cigar box, sufficient to warrant cartoons in the paper——

MR. McKEOWN: That requires a lot.

MR. SINCLAIR: With the honourable member for East Wellington smoking a pipe and myself smoking a cigaret and I think we both plead not guilty to ever having done such a thing in our life. But what I say is that the inquiry, and I only refer to it on account of what the member for Simcoe said, was rendered to a great extent useless on account of the presence of the two counsel who were there.

But getting back to this matter, let me say again that this is just as important a matter to this Committee and to this Legislature and to the Province of Ontario as was the circumstantial evidence we had at the commencement of these other investigations and if this furnishes light and will give any further light in regard to that transaction, this Committee should not stand in the way of the investigation. I am delighted with the attitude of this Committee, verbally spoken, the zeal they show, the desire they show for a full investigation of everything. There is not an honourable member here but says "Amen" every time someone says "full investigation." But immediately they begin to argue open investigation vanishes and every effort is made in argument to negative the words they uttered asking for clear and full investigation. If this Committee wants to put itself on record and carry out the wishes so frequently expressed here by different members of the Government party especially they will say "carried" at once to the resolution moved by the honourable member for East Wellington.

MR. McKEOWN: Just one moment. The Budget debate is on and it seems to me that this political discussion should have been made in the House, not here.

MR. SINCLAIR: Look out what you do.

MR. McKEOWN: And there they would have every chance to spread out as far as they like.

MR. FINLAYSON: Unless somebody jumps in ahead.

MR. McKEOWN: I want to speak to the motion. I have been on this Public Accounts Committee a good many years, I think possibly as many years as any honourable member of the Committee to-day. I don't think I ever knew of a fishing expedition started by this Committee. They speak of what we did two years ago. Two years ago, Mr. Chairman, we were investigating the sale of certain Succession Duty Free bonds. We were investigating an actual payment to the Province of Ontario and where a commission in connection with those bonds went, and to-day if the honourable member for East Wellington wishes to investigate any payment to or from the Province of Ontario, he is perfectly within his rights.

I quite appreciate the address made by the honourable leader of the Liberal opposition when he didn't argue like my friend from East Wellington argued. He said this might get us somewhere, let us look into it and see. We don't know where it leads. And that is not what this Committee is here for. We have not, to my recollection investigated, in our day nor did we prosecute any previously, unless the investigation was tied up somewhere to payments either to or from the Province of Ontario, and apart from that we have no jurisdiction to act. I have paid, and sometimes I don't know where I got my money, I have paid for gasoline. Has any person a right to say you have to come and say before this Committee where you got the money because there was a Government tax of three cents a gallon on it? Surely not. And that would be getting closer to the necessities of this Committee than the suggestion of my honourable friend.

Hon. Mr. Raney: I remind you the first point of order is whether I am entitled to read the affidavit?

Mr. Finlayson: He has ruled.

Hon. Mr. Raney: Then I will appeal from the ruling.

The Chairman: The first point of order was that raised by Mr. Finlayson regarding the admissibility of t' e motion.

Hon. Mr. Raney: But when I was addressing the chair and started to read the affidavit he raised the point of order that I was not entitled to.

The Chairman: I didn't raise the point of order. I said you were not entitled to present your evidence until after we decided as to the admissability of the motion.

Hon. Mr. Raney· Then if you have ruled I will appeal from your ruling. If you have ruled I am not entitled to read this affidavit, I appeal.

Mr. Currie: Don't listen to him.

The Chairman: The motion is the point of order raised by Mr. Finlayson, questioning the admissibility of this motion.

Hon. Mr. Raney: I was addressing you on that point of order. I was interrupted by Mr. Finlayson when I started to read the affidavits. He said I was not entitled to read them. He appealed to you as a point of order that I was not.

The Chairman: You started to read the affidavits and I stopped you, and I said—

Hon. Mr. Raney: Well, if that is the ruling I will appeal from it.

The Chairman: I ruled you could not submit your evidence until after the question of the admissibility of the motion is decided.

Hon. Mr. Raney: You rule, I am not at liberty to read these affidavits?

The Chairman: Yes.

Hon. Mr. Raney: Then I will appeal.

The Chairman: I have decided he shall not proceed with the affidavits until after we have decided the status of the motion. There is an appeal from that order. Shall the ruling of the chair be sustained? Those in favour will vote yes. Those opposed will vote no.

(The Secretary announced the vote: Yeas, 19; Nays, 12.)

The Chairman: Gentlemen, the ruling of the chair is sustained.

Hon. Mr. Raney: Then, Mr. Chairman, I did not finish what I was about to say. You have ruled the affidavits out. I will pursue that matter no further.

Mr. Finlayson: Surely.

Hon. Mr. Raney: Oh, Mr. Finlayson took the better part of an hour in his argument. Mr. Finlayson referred to the proceedings at Kingston.

The Chairman: I think you each, the three of you, have had something to say. Is it relative?

Hon. Mr. Raney: I am proposing to read to the Committee, if I may, there are about a dozen questions and answers just to show what transpired at Kingston.

Mr. McKeown: What has that to do with it?

Mr. Sinclair: Just a parallel case.

Hon. Mr. Raney: Well, if the Chairman rules this may not be pursued by me. He permitted Mr. Finlayson not to exhaust himself.

THE CHAIRMAN: I am not going to rule that you cannot refer to it if you wish. I think you started it, Mr. Finlayson had a say, and—

HON. MR. RANEY: No, I didn't start it.

THE CHAIRMAN: I think you started it by making an interjection.

HON. MR. RANEY: Oh, I said we had gone to Kingston last year.

THE CHAIRMAN: I am not going to rule it out of order. If the Committee wishes to sit all morning and hear something we went through last session. But the Committee should decide because it is material to your motion.

MR. CURRIE: The Committee must be conducted in regular order, while we are quite willing to give every latitude. There are many witnesses here, and we have a long list of witnesses. This is a side issue. Mr. Raney is only blowing bubbles. I think you should give us a ruling on that question whether he is in order with that motion, and not waste all morning talking a lot of nonsense.

HON. MR. RANEY: I will take Mr. Currie's statement and perhaps take the sentiment of the men who voted yes on the last division, and in that view I will accept that without division of the Committee on that point. So I will be content to have your ruling on the main point of order.

THE CHAIRMAN: Gentlemen, when Mr. Raney presented this motion at a meeting of the Committee, he allowed it to stand as in this—or rather he furnished us with copies and said he would bring it up next meeting. I took a copy with me which I have had ever since and read it over carefully. I haven't been a member of this Committee as long as some others, but I have been a member for some years and know something about parliamentary procedure. I didn't go into as many authorities as Mr. Finlayson has produced, but I did go to the library and read Sir Erskine May on such points as this. I felt myself, let me say frankly, that when Mr. Raney admitted it was not connected with Government expenditure or any member of the Government it was very doubtful if we had any jurisdiction.

MEMBER: Government expenditure this year.

THE CHAIRMAN: Or any year. As I am not a lawyer, I took the precaution of having my final decision on the matter typed in order that I might read it, because it is a matter that will perhaps establish a precedent.

"The purpose or object of the Public Accounts is well stated in Sir Erskine May's Parliamentary Practice, thirteenth edition, page 557, where he says: 'The House also appoints at the commencement of every Session, the Committee of Public Accounts for the examination of the accounts showing appropriation of the sum granted by Parliament to meet the public expenditure.'"

A little lower down he also states: "The function of this Committee is to ascertain that the Parliamentary grants for each financial year, including supplementary grants, have been applied to the object which Parliament prescribed."

"The objection to the motion by Mr. Raney is founded on the fact that the transaction he proposed does not relate to parliamentary accounts in any way whatever."

"I think the objection might be founded on the ground that the transaction is nearly seven years old, but I prefer to put my ruling on the ground that the matters which he wishes to call in question are private matters between a publisher and advertiser, and do not in any way concern parliamentary votes or expenditures. The journal in question, *Rural Canada*, was apparently a private publication, soliciting and obtaining advertisments in the usual way from the public. It is not alleged that the moneys in question were public moneys, and apparently it is not alleged that they were expended by a public official or by anyone in any way connected with the Provincial Government."

"The very name of the Committee, Public Accounts, shows that it is intended to investigate and make reports on the public moneys of the Province of Ontario."

"I am clearly of the opinion that the proposed inquiry is beyond the jurisdiction of this Committee and cannot be undertaken."

HON. MR. RANEY: I will appeal from your ruling, Mr. Chairman.

THE CHAIRMAN: That is, my ruling on the admissibility of Mr. Raney's motion. Mr Raney appeals from the chair. Shall the ruling of the chair be sustained? Poll the members. Those voting in favour of sustaining the Chairman's ruling will vote, yes. Those opposed will vote, no.

(The Secretary announced the vote: Yeas, 23; Nays, 11.)

THE CHAIRMAN: I declare the ruling of the chair sustained.

Now we have the resolution by Mr. McKeown, which I understand is to take the place of the one presented by Mr. Raney, if it is satisfactory to him.

HON. MR. RANEY: I will accept that.

THE CHAIRMAN: Moved by Mr. McKeown, seconded by Mr. Currie,

That it is the desire of this Committee to sit as often to complete the work that is before it or that may hereafter come before it, and if necessary the permission of the Legislature will be sought to sit while the House is sitting, and meetings will be held as frequently as circumstances will permit.

MEMBER: Carried.

THE CHAIRMAN: Then I presume we have got through with that and we will proceed with the examination of Mr. Lyons.

Hon. James Lyons called. Sworn.

Examined by Mr. Finlayson.

MR. FINLAYSON: Gentlemen of the Committee, before starting Mr. Lyon's examination in chief may I say this, if any gentleman wishes to ask any question as he proceeds, if he will hand up a slip I will be glad to ask it. If he thinks it should be asked at the moment, very well. But I think we will get along a good deal more rapidly if we proceed in some orderly way. I don't want to shut off anybody, but if anybody has a memo, if they will give me the memo; or, if they want to break in.

I hope the Committee will pardon me if I proceed with matters of Mr. Lyons that may be regarded as more or less personal, but after you hear the whole, it will strike you as somewhat relevant.

Q.—How old are you, Mr. Lyons?

A.—Forty-seven.

Q.—Where were you born?

A.—Virginia, Ontario, in the County of York.

Q.—And when did you go to Sault Ste. Marie?

A.—1900, April.

Q.—For what purpose?

A.—To get a position, to start out in life for myself.

Q.—What did you do there first, Mr. Lyons?

A.—I went there in 1900 and secured a position with the pulp company.

Q.—That is, one of the Clergue enterprises, wasn't it?

A.—Yes.

Q.—As what?

A.—Feeding pulp grinders.

Q.—At what pay?

A.—Twelve and one-half cents an hour.

Q.—And from that what did you proceed to?

A.—I worked at that for a few months and Mason's for a couple of years.

Q.—At the Soo?

A.—At Sault Ste. Marie.

Q.—That is in construction work?

A.—Yes.

Q.—And after that?

A.—Well, then the Clergue industries closed down, I came back to the city of Toronto.

Q.—What year would that be?

A.—1903, I think.

Q.—And what did you do in Toronto?

A.—I secured a position with the Miles Lumber Co. out on Dundas Street.

Q.—As what?

A.—Well, just working around the yard during the winter of 1903 and a while after.

Q.—Following that, what did you do?

A.—In the spring of 1904, I secured a position as manager of the William Davies farm out on the Kingston Road.

Q.—How long did you continue there?

A.—Two years.

Q.—And after that?

A.—I opened up a butcher shop in the city of Toronto, Clinton Street, I think.

Q.—Yes, and what was your next venture?

A.—I went from there to Sault Ste. Marie, or Steelton was really the place, the municipality adjoining Sault Ste. Marie. And I continued in the butcher business by opening up a shop there.

Q.—What year would that be?

A.—1906, I think.

Q.—What was your next, what happened to you next?

A.—I carried on the butcher business there for a couple of years, when I disposed of it.

Q.—And in the interval had you any public position in Steelton?

A.—I was elected as alderman of the town in 1907.

Q.—Again?

A.—In 1908.

Q.—And after that?

A.—I was mayor in 1909, 1910, 1911 and 1912.

Q.—And during that interval what were you doing in a business way?

A.—After I disposed of the butcher business I went into the grocery business and conducted that for, I think about two years, and then I sold that out and I built a large b'ock and I carried on a shoe business in one of the seven stores that were in the block and I sold that out and built another large block. There were four of them, I think, and went into the real estate business.

Q.—How long did you continue to be mayor of Steelton?

A.—Four years.

Q.—Then Steelton was amalgamated?

A.—Well, that occurred, I think, in 1916.

Q.—Were you still in the council?

A.—Well, after, I was mayor in 1912, that was the last year. Then I was off the council I think in 1913 and 1914 and went back in 1915 and 1916.

Q.—Then during that time you were conducting real estate and building?

A.—Well, I carried on the real estate business up, I think, until 1914. In the summer and fall of 1914 I went up to take charge of the fuel business that I had commenced in the fall of 1912.

Q.—Will you tell the Committee the inception of this fuel business, as I understand it that is what has grown into the incorporated companies. Explain that very carefully.

A.—Well, I commenced the fuel business I think late in 1912, I think, perhaps November, due entirely to the fact that the town of Steelton could not secure any fuel whatever to heat its public buildings, and I thought there was an opportunity to engage in the fuel business, and I accordingly ·undertook it. I found more difficulty than I expected after I did undertake it, but, however, after operating for I think almost two years, I had a loss of about $8,000 or $9,000, and I had considerable money tied up and I then quit the real estate business and went up myself in the fall of 1914 and took charge of the yard, and I continued in charge of that until 1923.

Q.—Under what name were you carrying on business?

A.—Lyons Fuel Company, although it was not incorporated until 1916, and I think the only difference was that the name was the Lyons Fuel Company, and when it was incorporated it was changed to Lyons Fuel & Supply Company.

Q.—And that occurred in 1916?

A.—I think in October, 1916, we secured our charter.

Q.—Am I right in this; you took personal charge of the business in 1914?

A.—I think so.

Q.—And did you continue in personal charge down to the time of your election?

A.—Not entirely. I continued in personal charge until 1919, I think, in April, when, due to a rather serious operation, I had a break down and had to leave the office for eight months. Then I went back in October of that year.

Q.—So, apart from the break in 1919, when you were ill, from 1914 to 1923, that was your big undertaking?

A.—Entirely so.

Q.—I don't want you to go into details. Well, you tell the Committee something of the growth and development of that business?

A.—Well, I commenced business, as I said, in a very small way, with, I think, one team of horses and a car-load of coal secured from time to time, with wood necessary to meet the requirements and so on. I found part of our loss was due to the fact that while we sold fuel in winter and could perhaps make expenses in the summer months, when the business was slack we lost perhaps more than we made in the winter. Therefore, when I went there in 1914, after taking the business over that winter, I found that by giving it very careful attention it could be made a financial success, and I determined to try to retrieve the loss I had sustained and to carry on the business myself, in the following spring, 1915. I then undertook to add to the business and keep the organization employed by extending into the supply business and I started then by securing gravel, cement and supplies from time to time, and just enlarge the business year to year as the circumstances and conditions permitted, financial conditions in particular.

Q.—When you speak of financial conditions, was it your own money and savings went into this business?

A.—Oh, yes.

Q.—And before the incorporation, who were the partners in the Lyons Fuel Co.?

A.—Well, the business was started in this way. As I said, we could not secure fuel for the public buildings and a gentleman came to my office one evening and I was discussing the matter and told him what I had in mind, and I said to him, "If you will go up and take charge of this, I will pay you $75 a month and I will give you half the profits and we will run it for a year or two and we will organize a company and you will have your half interest and I will have mine and I will do the financing, and that is just how it started.

Q.—Well, did he remain?

A.—He remained until 1916, I think, and we were incorporated, after I had conducted the business for two or perhaps three years and retrieved the loss we had suffered, and made, perhaps, I think, about $9,000; we organized the company, and he was given half, half of the preferred stock and I was given the other half, and he felt, I think, that perhaps dividends would be slow in being paid and he disposed of his interest to Mr. George Goodwin of Sault Ste. Marie, I think at that time he sold his interest out for fifteen or sixteen hundred dollars and Goodwin or Goodwin's wife or the two of them together had the stock transferred to them from Mr. Dodd, who was the owner of the stock at that time.

Q.—His half holdings were transferred to Goodwin or his wife?

A.—Yes.

Q.—How long did that continue?

A.—It continued right up to the present, any more than I think that when Mrs. Goodwin died that the stock she had in her name was transferred to the children in trust.

Q.—Did he live at the Soo?

A.—Yes.

Q.—Did he take an active part?

A.—None whatever.

Q.—And you say he died?

A.—His wife did.

Q.—Does he still live there?

A.—Well, he did up to a few weeks ago, and his home is there yet, but he is at present down in Florida or Southern States.

Q.—His wife's holdings have gone to the children?

A.—Well, they are held in trust and I assume gone to the children.

Q.—Has he ever had any active control in the company?

A.—None whatever.

Q.—Minority shareholder, isn't he?

A.—Well, he holds, I think, 49 per cent. of the preferred and about 33 per cent of the common, approximately that.

Q.—Well, where had you, let us clear one thing up, has he ever taken any part in your business, any active part?

A.—No, no.

Q.—Has he ever had anything to do with anything, any of those contracts, or matters that are the subject of these questions?

A.—As a matter of fact, he would know little more about the business at any time than perhaps any of you gentlemen.

Q.—May I dispose of it this way. Has he any knowledge of the matter about to be investigated?

A.—No, no, none whatever.

Q.—And did he at any time have any relationship with the contractors or Crown licensees?

A.—No.

Q.—Am I fair in putting it this way. He knew nothing about it and did not participate in any of the dealings with these people?

A.—Yes.

Q.—So he could not give the Committee any information of any kind?

A.—Oh, no.

Q.—During these years after 1914, when you took charge of the business personally, did you continue in the council there?

A.—Well, in 1915 and 1916, I was on the council board again.

Q.—That is, the Soo?

A.—No, that is Steelton, and due to the financial position of the city at that time advocated amalgamation with the Soo. And we had an election and it was carried by a few votes, and from that time it has been Sault Ste. Marie.

Q.—Did you go into the amalgamated council?

A.—No, we completed our year and I stepped out and I had nothing more to do with the municipal affairs until 1922, when I again went on the council board in the City of Sault Ste. Marie for 1922 and 1923.

Q.—So in 1922 and 1923 were your only years of service on the Council of the city?

A.—Yes, that is right.

Q.—And you haven't been on since?

A.—No.

Q.—Now, we get down to the time of your election, 1923, June. Were you actively in charge of the business at that time?

A.—Oh, yes.

Q.—Did your election and your appointment as Minister of the Crown make any difference?

A.—It changed the whole conditions, practically.

Q.—Will you tell the Committee what step you took when you became Minister of the Crown?

A.—Well, in the first place, I had no thought or desire of being a candidate or a member and it was just at the last moment that I did.

MR. FINLAYSON: Felt the public call?

A.—Well, I consented anyway to be a candidate. Then when I was elected the present Prime Minister sent me a wire which was just as unexpected as anything could possibly be and asked me to come to Toronto, and I came down and we discussed the matter of appointing me to the position of Minister of Lands and Forests and I consented to accept his invitation and I went back home, and I thought, not knowing very much about political life, provincial at least, I thought that I could still fill this position satisfactorily and give considerable time to my own business, which I undertook to do. But I found after a very few weeks that it was an absolute impossibility, I couldn't possibly do it, with the result that I left the operation of the business from that time on with my son, Harry, who had little or no experience, because he left High School in 1915 and went overseas and was there until 1919 and he only had a couple of years in the office directing the deliveries of the teams more than anything else, and he and Mr. McAllister, whom I took on the staff in 1922, have been conducting the business from that time on.

Q.—Did McAllister become a shareholder?

A.—No.

Q.—He was just an employe?

A.—Just an employee.

Q.—Your son, Harry, is he a shareholder?

A.—Yes, I gave him a few shares, ten, I think.

Q.—Well, I don't think the Committee is concerned with them. But you found you could not carry out your position in the Crown lands and you had to give it up?

A.—That is right.

Q.—That is, the local business, and when did that take place? You say shortly after.

A.—After I was down here about three months, I concluded I simply had to stop, sever my connection.

Q.—September, 1923?

A.—Along there, some time during the fall.

Q.—In the fall of 1923, you found you had to sever your connection and you did?

A.—Yes.

Q.—Since then have you had anything to do with the active conduct of the business of the Lyons Fuel & Supply Co.?

A.—Outside of looking after the finances and being responsible in a very general way I have had very little to do.

Q.—You mean trying to keep control of the financial end?

A.—Yes.

Q.—To come back. At the time you took charge in 1916, I think?

A.—1914.

Q.—What business were Lyons Fuel & Supply carrying on in 1914?

A.—We were simply selling coal and wood.

Q.—Simply a fuel concern then?

A.—Yes.

Q.—How did you say enlarged that as opportun:ty offered? Will you tell us briefly?

A.—When I took charge I endeavoured to secure more business and I went after it in what I considered a systematic manner and I did enlarge the business and very rapidly.

Q.—What did you branch into?

A.—I branched into more lines of fuel, larger quantities of fuel and into the general builders' supply business, commencing with sand, gravel, cement, lime and going on into other materials and every thing that goes with the general supply business.

Q.—That is when you changed the name to cover that, Fuel & Supply Co.?

A.—Yes.

Q.—That continued until the time you were incorporated. Had you gone further than that when you took charge in 1916?

A.—No.

Q.—What did your charter cover?

A.—I cannot say. It simply covered fuel and builders' supply.

Q.—General?

A.—Yes.

Q.—What was the next step in your business, what else did you take on, what next?

A.—We just kept adding from time to time various lines of builders' supplies, including certain lines of heavy hardware that are used in heavy construction work and in the operation of pulp mills and steel plants and industries of a like nature, and have added from time to time to that particular lines until at the present time we have fairly substantial lines.

Q.—What public do you cater to, and what locality? What is the area of your operations?

A.—Generally speaking, Northern Ontario; that is the field that the greatest attention is given to.

Q.—I would like, if you can; I don't want to go into details, but can you make any comparison, say three years before your election and three years after?

A.—In what way.

Q.—As to, well, say the profits of your business?

A.—The profits?

Q.—I don't want year to year how much, but what relation had they before and after?

A.—Well, I don't care to make any statement if I can avoid it as to our profits in any one year or turn over or anything like that. That is why I resigned, I resigned this position because I refused to divulge my own business. If we take three years previous to my coming down here and the three years since I would say roughly that our profits in the previous three years were about three times as great as they have been since I came down.

Q.—You were elected in 1923, that would be 1920, 1921 and 1922, before and after that?

A.—1923.

Q.—This would cover two periods, first when you had control and second when you were down here, and you say the profits for the first period would be three times the profits for the latter?

A.—Approximately that.

Q.—Perhaps the accountants will be able to substantiate?

A.—I happened to meet Mr. Nash who arrived there Monday with three assistants and I asked him to go very fully into everything covering all these questions, and anticipate other things, from street gossip, I also asked him to give attention to them.

Q.—You say this was—you went up to the Soo when?

A.—Friday.

Q.—When did you return?

A.—Monday.

Q.—When did Mr. Nash come in?

A.—He got in on the 1.10 train and I left on the 3.30.

Q.—So you overlapped a couple of hours?

A.—Well, I just came into the office. I didn't know he was coming in at that time; he just came in when I was there.

Q.—How long did you have conversation?

A.—I would say an hour or an hour and fifteen minutes.

Q.—And he had three assistants?

A.—Yes.

Q.—And did you direct your people to help him?

A.—I gave him opportunity to take every book and every account and our ledgers for the last ten years and anything available and I also brought our auditors up and instructed them to give every assistance they could in any shape, manner or form.

Q.—You mean you introduced your auditors to Mr. Nash?

A.—Yes.

Q.—Did you give me the date of the incorporation?

A.—It was 1916, I think, perhaps October.

Q.—Fall of 1916?

A.—I think so.

Q.—Mr. Lyons, the first matter I think we should touch is this question, this sum of $17,000 that appeared in Public Accounts a year ago, that was mentioned in the House?

A.—Not in one year, I don't think there was $17,000 in one year.

Q.—The total was $17,000?

A.—Including the report of the Public Accounts of 1923 and 1924; I think that is right.

Q.—I see in answer to a question put by Mr. Kemp, the answer is $17,920.

Hon. Mr. Raney: What is the question?

Mr. Finlayson: By Mr. Kemp, Is Hon. James Lyons, Minister of Lands and Forests, still President of the Lyons Fuel & Supply Co., and so on, and the question refers to an amount, $17,920?

The Chairman: That was asked February 26th.

Member: What year?

Mr. Finlayson: This year.

Mr. Finlayson: What you say is that was divided into two amounts?

A.—Well, of course, I don't know what makes up that $17,000, but roughly I think this is the situation—the accounts will show somewhere in the neighbourhood of $4,000 paid our firm in 1923.

Q.—Public Accounts in 1923 show something in the neighbourhood of $4,000?

A.—I think so.

Q.—Under which government did you get that order?

A.—I cannot say as to the details of it all, but I think that the Drury Government purchased from our firm in 1923, something like, I think, $4,000 or $5,000 worth of material.

Q.—That is part of this item of $17,900?

A.—My recollection is that a substantial part of the amount shown on the accounts of 1923 covers materials purchased by the preceding Government.

Q.—Do I put it fairly this way, that the preceding Government, commonly called the Drury Government, had been customers of your firm?

A.—I think we have sold every government, Mr. Finlayson, both Provincial and Federal, practically, since I went to take charge of the business at least.

Q.—And this $14,000 would be the last year's purchase of the Drury Government?

A.—The $14,000?

Q.—The $4,000?

A.—$4,000.

Q.—And you say, previous to that, during the other years of the Drury Government, had you been selling them?

A.—Oh, yes.

Q.—Which branch or department?

A.—Well, we come in contact with only the Northern Development, practically. I think the Public Works purchased coal from us once or twice for the court house or the jail.

Q.—But you had sold previous governments ever since 1914 when you took charge?

A.—Yes.

Q.—Year after year?

A.—I think practically every year.

Q.—And the Drury Government had been customers of yours through the Northern Development Branch?

A.—Yes.

Q.—And that simply continued on with the present Government?

A.—That is quite so.

Q.—And the last year's operation of the Drury Government ran approximately $4,000?

A.—I think between $4,000 and $5,000.

HON. MR. RANEY: Well, you have that all in the Journals of the House last year. I think he is not quite right.

MR. FINLAYSON: Perhaps we can—have you got it?

HON. MR. RANEY: No.

HON. MR. LYONS: What I am trying to make clear is this, I think your Government—

MR. FINLAYSON: It is just a question of amount.

HON. MR. RANEY: Well, maybe so.

MR. FINLAYSON: Well, subject to possible correction as to amount the fact is that the preceding Government and the Drury Government in particular had been customers of yours in considerable amounts?

A.—Reasonable amounts, yes.

Q.—And that was through the same branch, this Northern Development, and continued under the new Government?

A.—I think if you will check up the purchases made by them from the various local firms for material such as we supplied, you will find we supplied the great bulk of the material purchased by them.

Q.—Your sales were peculiarly along the line of the work of the Northern Development?

A.—Yes.

Q.—They were constructing roads and building bridges and even school houses and other public works of that kind?

A.—The only thing I recall, now that you speak of it, outside of building supplies that I sold the Drury Government was a quantity of hay that was shipped down to Manitoulin Island during the season that the drouth destroyed the hay.

Q.—The accounts simply run on?

A.—Yes.

Q.—Was any difference made when you came in?

A.—None whatever.

Q.—Was the officer in charge, the responsible officer at the Soo, the same?

A.—Well, Mr. John Lang was the engineer in charge at the Northern Development work for the Soo district when I came down here. He was only working half time. That is he received pay for half time and would only agree to devote half his time to the work and the other half to his own private business, and after that had gone on for some little time, I concluded it was not the best way to handle the work and we put in a resident engineer who gave all his time and attention to the work. His name was Mr. Lamb. I don't know where he came from or anything about him up to that time.

Q.—Since then the work was continued under Mr. Lamb? Lang gave part of the year?

A.—As long as he was there, he did the purchasing.

Q.—And Mr. Lamb carried on when he succeeded?

A.—I think he carried on practically the same way.

Q.—Did you at any time after your coming into office here see either of these gentlemen as to purchases from your firm?

A.—With instructions? No, never.

Q.—Did you ever at any time give any officer instructions to buy from your firm?

A.—No, no.

Q.—Will you explain to the Committee how these purchases from the Northern Development Branch are made?

A.—Well, after I came in to the Department and was here for some time and had gone into the matter of expenditures and organization of the Department I concluded that the manner in which we were dealing with the whole Northern Development expenditures was not the best, and accordingly we made a change and established resident engineers in various parts of Northern Ontario, and I think we established nine residencies and since then have added one. I think at the present time there are ten men who are given complete charge of the territory under their jurisdiction.

Q.—Before we come down to that, who were they under?

A.—They were under the Department of Lands and Forests, with Mr. Fullerton as Deputy.

Q.—Mr. Fullerton is Deputy—

A.—He was director.

Q.—At that time he was director. Just simply a change in title?

A.—That is all.

Q.—He had complete charge of expenditures under Northern Development?

A.—Yes.

Q.—And he has been with the Department many years?

A.—Yes.

Q.—He grew up with the Department from an engineer?

A.—I think so.

Q.—And you say there are nine or ten resident engineers covering the north country?

A.—That is right.

Q.—And your particular territory in the Soo, Mr. Lamb is?

A.—Mr. Lamb.

Q.—You say you had no discussion or conversation with Mr. Lamb as to purchasing?

A.—As to purchasing from our firm?

Q.—Or any firm?

A.—No.

Q.—Did you give him orders who to buy from?

A.—You mean specific orders?

Q.—Yes?

A.—No.

Q.—Generally?

A.—In talking the matter over with Mr. Lamb, and I think it applies to every engineer, they have charge of that district; they buy their own supplies, that is what we call local requirements. If we require a large quantity of material it is necessary to call for public tenders to take in more than local territory, then we would handle it from this office.

Q.—Ask for tenders?

A.—Yes, but local purchase on what we call local tenders, small quantities of gravel, cement, hardware, lumber, or anything used, they would get prices themselves and make comparisons and make the purchase where they considered it to advantage to make it.

Q.—How is it done as to obtaining favourable figures or competition, what is done as to that?

A.—Well, I understand they got prices from various dealers whenever they required anything.

Q.—That is, competitive prices?

A.—Competitive prices, yes.

Q.—And that is a matter that the engineer has charge of?

A.—Yes.

Q.—That is the same system prevails—

A.—But I do know that is what is carried on.

Q.—That is the same system as any other institution, like a resident engineer of a railway or anything else?

A.—I suppose so.

Q.—I would like to take you over—I have tried to pick out as far as I can from these questions and from my general knowledge of the lumber business and what I can find on the record and who were connected, a number of matters and I would like to go over them with you. What class of corporations or companies or contractors are under your Department, or have dealings with your Department?

A.—Do you mean forests?

Q.—Yes?

A.—Well, sawmills.

Q.—Big class of lumbermen?

A.—Yes.

Q.—Lumbermen of all kinds, they are Crown licensees?

A.—Pulp and paper and water powers, that would practically cover it.

Q.—Well, I suppose in addition there are contractors on roads under the Northern Development?

A.—Well, the contracts would come up in my Department, oh yes.

Q.—Well, what about mining companies?

A.—No.

Q.—They are under the Department of Mines?

A.—Of Mines.

Q.—If the Committee will pardon me, let us run over a number of these things. I asked you to have the Department look up how many timber licensees there are in the Province. You have that figure?

A.—I got those figures last night and they have been forwarded to Mr Nash also and there are according to the report given me last night 400 some odd licensees and twenty-nine concession holders.

Q.—Concession holders?

A.—Pulp and paper.

Q.—Under the new system?

A.—Well, under the old system; a pulp limit as I understand it is considered a concession.

Q.—You distinguish between—

A.—Yes.

Q.—Four hundred odd and twenty-nine concessionaires or roughly **430?**

A.—Four hundred and thirty or 435 all told I believe.

Q.—Let us run down the timber licensees first. Can you tell me how many of these are dealing with you appear on the books of your firm?

A.—I tried to check, Mr. Finlayson, during Saturday, Sunday and Monday, I tried to check as closely as I could, not having this list, the number of people engaged in the lumber and pulp and paper business that are customers of ours, and I think Mr. Nash will check more accurately, and I think perhaps it is thirty all told.

Q.—Out of 430 pulp, paper and lumber concerns, you have dealings with about thirty?

A.—Approximately, yes.

Q.—That is approximately a fair proportion?

A.—Yes.

Q.—Thirty out of 400?

A.—Yes.

Q.—Taking the lumber concerns I have tried to pick out those that operate in your territory. The largest is J. J. McFadden?

A.—J. J. McFadden?

Q.—Yes?

A.—I think he is the largest operator.

Q.—J. J. McFadden is probably the largest operator in Ontario at present?

A.—He and Shevlin Clarke are the two largest.

Q.—And certainly he is the largest in your district?

A.—Oh yes.

Q.—And in addition if my memory is right he has obtained during your incumbency some considerable addition to his territory?

A.—He purchased the Bishop Lumber Co., I think in 1924, late. They took over their operations and secured by public tender four townships in the Mississauga at one time and three at another time which gave him over a hundred million feet of pine then.

Q.—So a man who during your regime has added to his holdings all the Bishop holdings and seven townships has become an immense operator?

A.—Yes, he is a very large operator at the present time.

Q.—And his operators are tributary to the Soo?

A.—Yes.

Q.—What dealings had you with Bishop before Bishop's were taken over by McFadden?

A.—Well, I think we have had an account with the Bishop Lumber Co in every year I think since 1915 and until the day they sold out.

Q.—Will you say what that might mean, a few dollars or a large sum?

A.—Well, it would run into several thousand dollars a year.

Q.—A substantial account yearly?

A.—Yes.

Q.—Well what happened when McFadden took them over?

A.—Well, we could not sell them any longer but in 1925 with the joint operations, or combined operations, we sold J. J. McFadden about $885 worth of stuff.

Q.—Or the total sales to them were $885, what year was that?

A.—That was 1925.

Q.—Before that it was?

A.—Well, we didn't sell McFadden anything of any account. We may have sold him a few dollars now and again. I think if I remember rightly when it was McFadden and Mulloy we used to sell them blacksmith coal and that was the only thing.

Q.—So the largest operators in the Province, immediately tributary to your territory, bought some $880 odd?

A.—Yes, it was much less than we were getting from the Bishop Company before they took it over.

Q.—Now another company, the Searchmount; they are immediately tributary?

A.—Well, they are about twenty-four or twenty-five miles north of the Soo in Algoma.

Q.—They are large?

A.—Yes. They haven't bought anything from us since I have been down here. They did buy considerable.

Q.—I mention that because Mr. Darling stopped me and said it was a lot of damn nonsense.

Q.—The Hope?

A.—Well, the Hope Co. have been in the Soo and previous to my coming here we sold them goods from time to time. Since I came down the total sales in the three years is $161.

Q.—One hundred and sixty-one dollars in nearly three years of your regime. What was it before?

A.—Well, I cannot tell you.

Q.—Approximately what did it run?

A.—Well, they never were very large customers. I didn't go back to get the amount because I didn't have time to do it.

Q.—Take some other companies, the Fort William Paper Company, how is your account with them?

A.—Well, the Fort William Paper Company are located at Fort William.

Q.—And they got recently a pulp concession?

A.—In 1922 when I was there I sold them a little over $11,000 worth of material and in 1923 and 1924 and 1925 and since I have been down here we sold them in three years, $475.

Q.—1922, $11,000; the last three years, $475?

A.—Yes.

Q.—What was the extent of their purchases from the Department recently, they are under this new scheme?

A.—Well, in the sale of pulp limits of September 10, 1925, they secured the right to cut over six million cords of pulp wood.

Q.—One of the other companies, the Thunder Bay Pulp & Paper?

A.—Well, the Thunder Bay Pulp & Paper are located at Port Arthur and they secured the right to cut about 5,800,000 cords of pulp wood in the sale of September, 1924. They have never purchased any goods from our firm of any kind.

Q.—Their purchase was in 1924?

A.—1925.

Q.—And they have never at any time?

A.—No.

Q.—Either before or since?

A.—No.

Q.—Provincial Paper Mills?

A.—Well, they secured the right to cut about two and one quarter million cords of pulp under sale of September 10, 1925, and they have purchased since we have been in business from us about $2,400 worth of material.

Q.—Since you have been in business, any of that since—

A.—Well, some of it is since. I don't know whether it is all or not.

Q.—That is their total purchase anyway?

A.—Yes.

Q.—What about the Nipigon Company?

A.—The Nipigon Fibre Company, well, they secured the right under sale of September 10 to cut 5,800,000 cords of wood and they have never purchased a dollar's worth of material from us in any connection.

Q.—Here is another name, firm, Spruce Falls Company at Kapuskasing; they are the largest concessionaires?

A.—Well, they are going to build the largest mill of any one of the number.

Q.—Their construction work and mill work is right along your line of supplies?

A.—Yes. They secured the right to cut something over 7,000,000 cords of wood for their mill and they have purchased from us in the last three years about $7,000 or $8,000 worth of materials, mostly anthracite coal.

Q.—What about the Mattagami?

A.—They have never been customers of ours.

Q.—Did you have an opportunity to trade with them?

A.—Yes. During last year Mr. McAllister, who looks after almost entirely wholesale coal sales, was in touch with them along with other companies in the north trying to sell them their coal requirements and he was given an order by them for 40,000 tons of coal and up to the time he secured the order I knew nothing about it whatever, it was handled here in Toronto and he came to my office after he had secured the order and told me about it because he said it would require some special financing, that the coal would have to be carried to dock and shipped out as required during the winter months, and he told me he had this order and told me what he had made on it and told me who the firm were he was selling to and I told Mr. McAllister he could not accept that order, that he would have to go back and tell the people he could not take the order.

Q.—That was after the Premier's statement in the House a year ago?

A.—This was last June.

Q.—Forty thousand tons, what would that run into?

A.—It would run into something about $150,000 to them.

Q.—With corresponding profit to you?

A.—Yes.

Q.—Austen and Nicholson are large operators in your neighbourhood, aren't they?

A.—Yes.

Q.—What about them?

A.—We have sold Austen and Nicholson around $4,300 or $4,400 worth ever since we have been in business. The bulk of that was sold, I think, perhaps in the last three years and consisted of three carloads of building or tar paper, sold from time to time.

Q.—That is your total dealings with them?

A.—Yes.

Q.—Abitibi Pulp & Paper are the largest present operators?

A.—One of the largest, if not the largest.

Q.—What about them?

A.—We have sold them $327 worth of goods since we have been in business.

Q.—Three hundred and twenty-seven dollars in ten years. Now I have a list of other lumber companies and large operators, Acme, Graves Bigwood, J. R. Booth—and if any gentleman knowing anything about these companies or any other company would like to ask Mr. Lyons questions about them I will be glad to put the questions immediately while we are on the subject.

MR. CURRIE: Was there any other large lumber company operating in that section that you sold more than $500 worth?

MR. FINLAYSON: If you will allow me to ask two questions first, I will perhaps anticipate. I left a special memo for two names that have been rather conspicuous and notorious, Backus and Shevlin Clarke Co.

MR. CURRIE: Oh all right.

MR. FINLAYSON: What about Backus, for instance?

A.—Well, Backus as an individual doesn't operate anything. There is the Backus-Brookes, I think there is the Fort Frances Pulp & Paper Co. We sold them nothing. The Backus-Brookes, we have sold $1,719.49 worth.

Q.—In how many years?

A.—That is since I came down.

Q.—One thousand seven hundred and nineteen dollars since you came in?

A.—They had a very extensive programme.

Q.—They were not only lumber but they had power operations?

A.—They have constructed the Norman Dam, constructed their pulp, paper, and sulphide mill, and carried on big improvement of the water power during the time those goods were sold.

Q.—And these operations were particularly along your line. They were what you had made a specialty of, that kind of operation?

A.—Yes.

Q.—When you gave me that answer did that include all the corporations you know of Backus controlling?

A.—Well, I don't know; I have heard he was in the Mattagami.

Q.—Well, anything you know of that includes them all?

A.—Yes.

Q.—Fort Frances, Norman Dam, and construction work, and all that?

A.—Well, I have heard he was in the Great Lakes. I don't think we have ever sold them a dollar's worth. I think Backus is connected with them.

Q.—Well, Shevlin Clarke?

A.—We have sold Shevlin Clarke $3,050 worth.

Q.—Since you became Minister?

A.—Yes.

Q.—And before that?

A.—Nothing. Well, I would not say nothing either. It just strikes me as I go along. I had some dealings with them a few years ago and I purchased cement, lumber from them and sold them some—I am not sure about that.

Q.—International Nickel Co. I understand you have been dealing extensively with them?

A.—Well, I don't think we have sold them anything since I have been down here, outside perhaps of one or two thousand dollars worth of stuff, some lines, but I used to sell them large quantities of goods, but I haven't the figures.

Q.—Your office sent me figures of 1919, have you them?

A.—Well, I think 1919 would run over $300,000. I think 1920, around there, would run $100,000, something like that. International Nickel is in the same position. I sold them large quantities and have sold them $60,000, $80,000 worth since I have been down.

Q.—So those large corporations their accounts dwindled all away.

Mr. Currie: Any large lumber companies or mining companies that you haven't named that you sold more than $500 a year to?

A.—What I undertook to do during the short time I was at the Soo was to compile a list of the new wholesale or out of town buyers, that is what we call them, that have been taken on our books since I came down to Toronto in 1923, and the total list runs into 110 or 115 new customers. Out of that 110 or 115 of course is about ninety or more who are merchants, because we sell to merchants, perhaps more than we do to the other people, certain lines of hardware, rubber foot wear, and we sell to merchants all up in Cobalt, Haileybury, and—

Q.—But I refer to companies that would have concessions from the Government. There was no other company that you sold to, any large amount?

A.—Well, I think, the Abitibi Lands and Forests—Now I don't think they have any concession that I know of. They purchased $317 worth. Continental Wood Products purchased $2,770 worth of builders supplies and hardware and two cars of roofing ran into $775. George Farlinger purchased approximately $1,000.

Q.—These aren't people who have dealings with the Government?

A.—Oh yes. these are people who have dealings with the Government. Farlinger has fairly large concessions. Hope Lake Lumber Co., we have sold them all told seventeen or eighteen hundred dollars worth. Milne and Sons, North Bay, they secured a township or two townships or something, they purchased from us $116.50; Nipigon Products Company, that is up at Fort William, I don't know who they are, they purchased $205; Abitibi Electric Development Co., Montreal, I suppose that is the power company in connection with the Abitibi, but I am not sure, purchased coal to the extent of $710. I have given you Backus Brookes. Then there is Dryden Paper Co., that is out in the Kenora district, one car fire brick, $770; Thomas Fallis, large operator at Port Arthur, $61; J. E. Mathieu, Limited, Rainy River, his total purchases run into about $4,500; the Mageau Lumber Co., $136; Marshay Lumber Co., $332. I have given you Provincial and Shevlin Clarke. James Stewart, Port Arthur, $412; Schroeder Mills, $569, which was coal. Now those cover the accounts as I have been able to check them and I think Mr. Nash will check this whole thing very closely and some of my figures are subject to correction by him because I had very limited time, and when you have to go through eight or ten years ledgers to get stuff why you get it rather hurriedly.

Mr. Currie: I think if he will just hand that memo in for information of the members and myself.

The Chairman: We will have that all brought in by the auditor.

Mr. Currie: I think that covers the whole ground.

Mr. Finlayson: Mr. Lyons, have you gone over these firms, partnerships, of those who have had road contracts from the Northern Development?

A.—Yes.

Q.—I have obtained from the records a list of them and I would like to get some information as to them. M. L. McLean, he had a contract on the North Bay and Cobalt highway?

A.—Yes.

Q.—Tell me, that was given under the Northern Development during your incumbency of the office?

A.—Yes.

Q.—Do you know Mr. McLean?

A.—Well, I never knew Mr. McLean until he got this contract, never knew there was such a man until he got this contract. He was low bidder and he got the contract.

Q.—What did the contract—I suppose on a unit basis?

A.—Yes.

Q.—What would it run to roughly?

A.—Well, I think perhaps it would run around $130,000 to $50,000.

Q.—What have your relations been with him?

A.—Well, we sold Mr. McLean—I not only took our own books but I took the trouble of writing a number of these contractors a letter and this letter which I will read with your permission, Mr. Chairman, was written not only to Mr. McLean but it was written to Angus Taylor, who have a contract, written to Grant Brothers, who also have a contract on the North Bay Cobalt road, written to the Walsh Construction Co., who also have some contracts, and the letter that I sent out was identical, the letter was this.

HON MR. RANEY: Wait, are you proposing to prove—

MR. FINLAYSON: I didn't intend Mr. Lyons to answer the question in that way, although I have no objection. What I did propose to ask him was taking out these contractors and asking his dealings.

HON. MR. RANEY: I think he ought to confine himself to what he knows.

THE CHAIRMAN: That is all right.

MR. FINLAYSON: As a direct rule of evidence, I agree. Never mind your letter to them, what are the facts?

A.—The facts are, which I have to get from their letter to give you, that is why I want to read it—

HON. MR. RANEY: Hold on now.

MR. FINLAYSON: Haven't you the facts from your own records?

A.—Yes, but perhaps you will allow me. The assumption is these people have been compelled to buy goods from my firm—

HON. MR. RANEY: I haven't—I don't think, Mr. Finlayson, we don't want to get in—

MR. FINLAYSON: What I did want is, I have picked out the names of firms, contractors on the highway and I propose to get from Mr. Lyons whether he knows these individuals, whether he has any relationship, or whether he has any dealings.

THE CHAIRMAN: I think we will ask Mr. Lyons to answer from his own knowledge.

HON. MR. RANEY: You see if we got what somebody told Mr. Lyons—

THE CHAIRMAN: If Mr. Lyons wishes to bring any evidence from the other side it can be done later on.

HON. MR. LYONS: All I am trying to do is to show the relationship.

MR. FINLAYSON: You want to be fair but there is a rule of law Mr. Raney is appealing to which bans second hand evidence. What I want is not the source of your information but the facts. These people you say you didn't know or didn't until then and had no dealings with them?

A.—I have only met Mr. McLean once since he got the contract.

Q.—Have you any interest in the contract?

A.—None whatever.

Q.—Or any other?

A.—None whatever, in any shape, manner or form, either by myself, through any members of my family, friends, or associations or anything else; you can make that just as broad as you like.

Q.—As broadly as this: Are you prepared to swear that neither directly or indirectly, in trust, nor by any other device, partnership or concealed dealings of any kind have you an interest of any kind in any lumber company, Crown licensee, pulp concessionaire or contractor with the Crown?

A.—Absolutely.

Q.—And that can be made as broad as we like?

A.—As broad as you like.

Q.—How much has he purchased from you?

A.—Approximately $7,000 worth of supplies for his work.

Q.—Take the next one, Grant Brothers Construction Company?

A.—I didn't know them until they secured this contract.

Q.—Were they the lowest tenderer?

A.—Oh, yes.

Q.—What did it amount to?

A.—Their contract?

Q.—Yes.

A.—I don't know, somewhere in the neighbourhood, somewhere around $120,000, or thirty or forty thousand dollars. They purchased from us $1,349.92 worth of goods.

Q.—That is the total?

A.—And according to their letter they purchased—

HON. MR. RANEY: Never mind about that letter, if you please, Mr. Lyons.

Q.—What kind of material was that, can you say?

A.—No, I don't know. It would be perhaps dynamite or—

Q.—Anyway it was the ordinary course of your business?

A.—Yes.

Q.—Now Angus & Taylor Co., they are contractors on the North Bay-Cobalt road?

A.—Yes.

Q.—Is their contract of some volume, approximately?

A.—Yes, they have a ten- or fifteen-mile section.

Q.—How much have they purchased from the Lyons Fuel & Supply Co.

A.—One thousand three hundred and seventy-two dollars and ninety cents.

Q.—On this contract?

A.—Yes

Q.—Do you know the Walsh Construction Co.?

A.—No, I didn't know the Walsh Construction Co. I met Mr. Walsh once after he secured his contract and I have seen him but once since that when I met him in Mr. Lamb's office at the Soo.

Q.—Any sales to them to your knowledge?

A.—We have sold them $1,300 to $1,400 worth of goods.

Q.—One thousand three hundred dollars?

A.—I have letters from Walsh, and letters from Grant, and letters from—well, I will get them in some say.

Q.—Charles ———; that is that barn at Hearst?

A.—He had a contract for the Hearst barn.

Q.—Those are the only contractors on that road work up there apart from the McNamaras?

A.—Unless it is some little, trivial contract, it may be.

Q.—Now, I would like to cover the ground as to your local companies at the Soo. I suppose the largest company is the Algoma Steel Corporation?

A.—Yes, the Algoma Steel.

Q.—They have been customers of yours?

A.—The Algoma Steel have been purchasing from us ever since we were a company.

Q.—Ever since you were doing business?

A.—Yes.

Q.—Can you give me any idea of the volume, year to year?

A.—Well, I think as I checked it up their average sales exceed $40,000 a year.

Q.—Sales? You mean their purchases?

A.—Our sales to them.

Q.—What about since you became Minister, has there been any change?

A.—Well, perhaps it has been less.

Q.—But if there has been any change it has been a reduction?

A.—Yes.

Q.—Algoma Central Railway?

A.—Well, they have been purchasing from year to year from us on for the last, well ever since we have been organized.

Q.—They are old customers?

A.—Yes.

Q.—Dominion Tar?

A.—Yes, they purchased—

Q.—I mean before?

A.—Yes, ever since they have been operating as a company at the Soo.

Hon. Mr. Raney: Tire?

Mr. Finlayson: Dominion Tar & Chemical Co.

Q.—What about the Great Lakes Power?

A.—We have sold the Great Lakes Power Co. material from year to year for a number of years back.

Q.—Any change?

A.—Well, they are not buying as much, as a matter of fact.

Q.—That is due to business conditions?

A.—That is right.

Q.—What about the Lake Superior Pulp & Paper?

A.—Well, the Lake Superior Pulp & Paper have been buying goods from us I think ever since we were organized as a company and before we were organized, ever since I have been up there.

Q.—What would it average, have you any idea?

A.—Oh, it would probably run into $35,000 or $40,000 a year.

Q.—Any increase in business?

A.—There was an increase last year.

Q.—What caused that?

A.—No, not last year, 1924. I think there was an increase.

Q.—Why?

A.—Well, we succeeded in selling them an additional tonnage of coal.

Q.—That would be coal, in the open market?

A.—Yes, coal.

Q.—So that covers the companies that have been doing business around the Soo?

A.—There is the Spanish River Pulp & Paper. Their office is at the Soo and their mills, Espanola and Sturgeon Falls. Our average sales to them over eight or ten years practically is over $60,000 a year. There has not been any change much since I came down; it runs approximately the same.

Q.—What other corporations are there?

A.—We have already mentioned the Monde and the International Nickel and the British American. We have been selling these people from time to time and we have been selling to the contracting concerns in the Soo. I don't think we have missed any of them. When Fraser Bros. were carrying on construction we sold them, ——— Construction Company, and James O. Hayworth who constructed the power house and power canal for the Great Lakes, and we supplied local contractors like Jamieson and Sons when they were in business; McIntyre, Haney and Murray; Fitzpatrick and Gibson, and Brackin and Haney and Mitchell and Cooper, practically all of the contractors.

Q.—Who were in the same line of busines with you at the Soo? Have you competition?

A.—O, yes. I. J. Downey & Sons sell builders supplies, that is their line. They handle a little coal occasionally, a few hundred tons, or perhaps a few thousand tons some years. They don't go into the fuel business very extensively.

Q.—Who are the others, hardware?

A.—Cochrane Hardware.

Q.—They are keen competition?

A.—Very keen. Keys Hardware, James Street Hardware, Plummer Ferguson Hardware, E. S. Bedford. There is another company I have forgotten the name for a moment.

Q.—Take your other lines you spoke of, harness, rubber goods?

A.—Hinesberger Harness Company, Hesson Lumber Co., Sault Lumber & Mill Company.

Q.—I asked you if possible to get me the figures that these competitors of yours supplied to the Northern Development or Forestry branch, that is sub-branches of the Lands and Forests, during your term?

A.—Well, I took from the Public Accounts of 1925 the following.

Q.—That is the current number?

A.—Yes, that is on the table. This includes the purchases made by the Northern Development branch and by the Forestry Branch of the Department of Lands and Forests.

Q.—And what there is there was material which you could have supplied from your concern?

A.—Yes.

Q.—And it covers the Soo?

A.—Yes. This is a list of the local firms at the Soo selling material to the Northern Development and the Forestry Branch of the Department of Lands and Forests that could be supplied by the Lyons Fuel and Supply Co., Ltd. Now it is just possible in that mass of stuff there is some little thing we could not supply, but generally speaking we could supply everything.

Cochrane Hardware, total sales is a little over $28,000.

Q.—That is the last fiscal year?

A.—Yes.

Q.—Hesson Lumber Co., $6,823; Plummer-Ferguson Hardware, $6,017; Ed. Keys Hardware, $552; Soo Lumber & Mill Co., $20,418; Hinesberger, Harness Co., $6,170; E. S. Bedford, $10,849; I. J. Downey Co., $2,927. A total of almost $82,000.

Q.—So during the last fiscal year your competitors at the Soo got from your Department almost $82,000 of business that might have been supplied from your firm?

A.—And on which we didn't have a chance to bid.

Q.—Because of your position?

A.—That is right.

Q.—And during that time your firm supplied nothing?

A.—That is right, nothing whatever, well, with this exception, that before the statement was made in the House there was a small quantity of stuff supplied, I think about $3,000, of which Mr. Sinclair asked for particulars the other day, and which I have here, bearing on that.

Q.—That was supplied prior to the statement in the House last year?

A.—I wrote Mr. Fullerton and I wrote my firm at the Soo. I have the letters if you want them read.

Q.—Mr. Fullerton is in charge of the Northern Development?

A.—Yes. May I read this? This was a letter to the attention of Harry Lyons, Lyons Fuel & Supply Co., Ltd., Sault Ste. Marie, Ont. Toronto, March 16th, 1925.

"Due to a number of questions that have been asked by the members of the House relative to the business done between the Lyons Fuel & Supply Company, Limited, and the Government and the possibility of their using this in an endeavour to leave a bad impression with the people of the Province who do not know the details, I have to advise that from this time on you will not submit prices nor accept business with any Department of the Provincial Government while I am a member of same.

"Please acknowledge receipt of this and oblige,

"Yours very truly,

"Minister."

Q.—And to Fullerton?

A.—This was addressed to G. H. Fullerton, Superintendent of Colonization Roads, Toronto, March 17th, 1925.

"Dear Sir:

"As there is apparently some objection taken by members in the House to the Government buying goods from incorporated joint stock companies where some of the shareholders of the company may be members of the House. The Lyons Fuel & Supply Company, Limited, of Sault Ste. Marie have been doing business with the Provincial Government for many years, but because of this objection I am writing you to advise that I have directed the Lyons Fuel & Supply Co., Ltd., not to accept further business from the Provincial Government while I am a member of the House, and I would be glad if you would advise any of your engineers with whom we may have been doing business that they are not to place any business with the Lyons Fuel & Supply Company, Limited.

Yours very truly,

"Minister."

Mr. Finlayson: Members will perhaps bear with me when I say this, that seems to me to exhaust as far as I am concerned Mr. Lyons' personal aspect and the aspect of his company and his former firm and present incorporated company. There are, I think, six or seven other branches of it I wanted to go into. It is a quarter to one. Does the Committee wish to go on? I am quite willing to go for an hour if you want to. It is in the hands of the Committee.

Mr. McKeown: Move we adjourn.

Hon. Mr. Raney: When to?

The Chairman: Friday morning. I am going to say that subject to possible arranging of time to-morrow. If it is possible, I will undertake to do so.

Mr. Finlayson: We could perhaps sit to-morrow from 1.30 to 3.00. I quite agree with what Mr. Raney says.

The Chairman: I suggest you adjourn at the call of the chair and if we can call a meeting to-morrow, we will do so.

Mr. Sinclair: The difficult we ran into last year, we had a little confusion about it, and I think you will find it good practice to adjourn to a fixed time, and personally I am willing to go on in the morning, or I will go on at half past one.

Hon. Mr. Raney: Why not half past one to three. I think it better to have a definite hour.

The Chairman: If there is no objection?

Hon. Mr. Lyons: Mr. Raney mentioned the possibility of wanting to review further accounts of the Lyons Fuel & Supply while the auditors are up there. If Mr. Raney will send, I would like the names or the accounts, whatever they may be, submitted to them when they are there so they can just exhaust them as fully as possible.

Hon. Mr. Raney: How long do they expect to be there?

A.—They said they expected to be there a week.

Mr. Finlayson: What I was going to suggest on that is, I have had no communication with Mr. Nash at all. I know Mr. Clarkson, the senior member of the firm, told me he would be available to go up there and if necessary go back but he had to go to Ottawa and he would come back but he would leave a staff up there. Mr. Clarkson asked us to make this arrangement, that Mr. Lyon's auditors who are a firm of chartered accounts, would be available with whatever stenographers, typewriters and other facilities and Mr. Lyons at my request wrote a letter, it was given to him, which opened up all their books and opened the bank accounts and everything he wanted to get at.

Now when he will be available I don't know. I fancy Mr. Raney will agree the best thing we can do is to go ahead and exhaust all the evidence we can and then get Mr. Clarkson's report. If there is any list that anyone wants followed up there if they will hand it in to the Chairman, I would suggest the Chairman would then send a telegram to the Soo, directing that that would be pursued.

Hon. Mr. Raney: Well, I should think perhaps, you know, we would know more about what might be required from the accountants after Mr. Lyon's examination in chief, and certainly, we would know more about it after the conclusion of the examination.

Mr. Finlayson: I think so.

Member: I should think Mr. Lyons' examination would be over to:morrow, so that after that his examination would not be very lengthy.

The Chairman: Adjourned until to-morrow afternoon at 1.30 p.m.

PUBLIC ACCOUNTS COMMITTEE.

The Committee sat at 1.30 P.M., Thursday, March 18, 1926, with Mr. Lewis in the Chair.

THE CHAIRMAN: Mr. Finlayson, are you proposing to proceed with examination of Mr. Lyons?

MR. FINLAYSON: Yes, he will be here in a moment. Before he comes, may I say, not because he is not here, but by way of explanation, I see the papers reported me as stating that Mr. Ridout was treasurer of the U.F.O. campaign fund—I think two or three of the papers. I did not make any statement of that kind. Mr. Drury gave the evidence last year as to who was the treasurer, and his trips to New York were entirely separate from the Ridout trips. I think they were equally reprehensible, but I do not want to go into it to-day.

MR. RANEY: If you don't want to go into it, don't talk about it.

MR. FINLAYSON: I am going to make my statement, Mr. Raney, and if you want to interrupt you may get more of this than you want. I know what the point is. All I want to do is in fairness to Mr. Ridout say I never suggested at any time he was treasurer of the U.F.O. campaign fund. It is another man, and if anyone wants to get the name all they have to do is refer to Mr. Drury's evidence last year. Mr. Lyons will be here in a moment. So that the Committee will try to follow the continuity of this matter, it is rather difficult to present it to the Committee in any consecutive way, but what I have tried to do on the last occasion was go over Mr. Lyons' personal standing, then go over the Lyons Fuel and Supply Company. I think we have fairly well covered that. Now to-day I propose to go into what seems to me, after reading over carefully the questions that have been asked, what seems to me to be perhaps the most serious item—that is, it is the largest. A large number of questions have been directed at construction of the aerodrome at Sault Ste. Marie, and many of the questions seem to suggest that expenditure was improper, excessive, and some of them seem to be suggesting that Mr. Lyons has some interest in it or in the contract. Now with the Committee's permission I would like this afternoon to go into that matter. If we have time after that I would perhaps take up the McNamara branch of the case, but first with your approval, sir, I would direct my question toward the aerodrome charges.

HON. MR. LYONS in witness box:

Q.—Will you be good enough to tell me something by way of preliminary, something as to the necessity for an aerodrome or the policy in connection with an aerodrome at the Soo.

A.—Well the building of the aerodrome at the Soo of course was the result of a careful survey of the forest fire patrol service of northern Ontario. When I came in in 1923 we were then in the midst of the worst fire loss the Province of Ontario had ever suffered. In 1923 our fire loss was about 2,120,000 acres. The government of that time, I think, realized that it was impossible to meet the situation with ground organization, because they had undertaken to test out the hydroplane service by giving a contract to the Laurentide Air Service to do certain patrol work in Northern Ontario. This was done on a contract basis. I think the contract prices were $125, $150, and $180 per hour, depending upon the class of machine used.

Q.—That is per flying hour?

A.—Per flying hour. After considering the matter through the balance of 1923, and the early part of 1924, I worked out a scheme which was submitted to the government for approval and was approved of and recommended, that we purchase a number of hydroplanes, and after discussing the matter thoroughly we agreed to purchase what was then available, thirteen hydroplanes. We purchased these at a cost, I think, of $5,500 each. While they were new machines they were war-time machines, which accounts for the very low price, and we put them into service after organizing our patrol force. During 1924 we had an opportunity to try out the value of their services, and during that season I think the machines operated about 2,600 hours and the fire loss was reduced to about 146,000 acres, as compared with 2,120,000 in 1923.

Q.—Now Mr. Lyons so that we can get these figures, or the justification of this policy, I would ask the Committee to be kind enough to let me try to get them. In 1923, what was the cost of the fire protection of the province?

A.—Approximately $1,100,000.

Q.—And you say the loss in 1923 was 2,120,000 acres. Now the total cost in 1924 was what, of fire protection?

A.—About $865,000.

Q.—A reduction from $1,100,000 to $865,000. What did that include? Is that all fire protection? You mention the purchase of these machines.

A.—You mean was the $865,000 all fire protection expense or did it include cost of machines. It would include not only the cost of machines but of the accessories we had to purchase to maintain the service, the cost of any buildings erected that year and the general cost of reorganizing, which was considerable when you consider you have to put gas into Moose Factory and all these northern points.

Q.—So it is fair to say that a considerable amount of it was capital?

A.—Yes, a substantial amount.

Q.—So in 1924 the cost of the fire protection patrol to the Province was $865,000 approximately?

A.—Approximately, yes.

Q.—What was the loss?

A.—Approximately 146,000 acres.

Q.—Now while we are on this, for purposes of comparison can you give me the 1925 figures—the cost?

A.—The cost of the patrol was about $1,181,000.

Q.—What had caused the increase?

A.—We spent about $310,000 in 1925 building an aerodrome and purchasing additional machines and additional equipment.

Q.—So roughly $300,000 odd of that was capital?

A.—That is right.

Q.—Which would bring it down—

A.—To something over $800,000.

Q.—And what was the loss in 1925?

A.—The fire loss was reduced to slightly over 10,000 acres of timber land.

Q.—May I ask the attention of the Committee to these figures because when I heard them they struck me as startling. Nineteen twenty-three fire protection cost $1,100,000 and the loss was 2,120,000 acres; 1924 fire protection, including a large amount of capital was $864,000 and the loss was down to 146,000 acres. In 1925 the total was $1,100,000 with about $300,000 capital, reducing it to $800,000, and the loss was down to 10,000 acres of timber. Acres of timber land?

A.—Yes.

Hon. H. C. Nixon: How does that loss of 1923 compare with the year 1926?

A.—The average loss for five years preceding 1924 was almost a million acres a year.

MR. FINLAYSON: Q.—It is not fair, as Mr. Nixon suggests, to say that two million was entirely representative, because that was an exceptionally bad year, but the average for five years before 1923 was roughly a million acres. Now it is down in 1924 to 146,000 and last year down to 10,000 acres.

MR. KEMP: Is there any difference in the regulation covering the cutting of timber that would have any effect upon that loss?

A.—I would not say so; not noticeably.   The whole thing is a matter of quick detection and prompt action.   If you compare our number of fires one year—1923-24-25—you will find that in 1924 there were more fires than in 1923, but they never got beyond the intial stage.   That is very true of them.

MR. FINLAYSON: Honourable gentlemen of the Committee will follow the reasoning, I think, that although the actual number of initial fires is the same the greater number were stopped in the bud.

MR. SINCLAIR: Is there any record to show the number of fires starting? I think we should have that.

A.—The number of fires in 1923, I think was 1,342, and in 1924, 1,449, and in 1925, 1,140 odd.

MR. FINLAYSON: So that the Committee will see the change is not in the initial fires, but in the combating.

THE CHAIRMAN: These figures are on record?

A.—Yes, they are official.

MR. FINLAYSON: It seems to me the result of this, adopting Mr. Nixon's suggestion, taking the period of five years before this policy was started by Mr. Lyons, the loss being 2,000,000 acres in that year, average over a million acres for five years.   Following up acreage loss alone, it dropped from 146,000 acres in 1924 to about a tenth, and last year to 10,000 acres, a further drop to less then one-tenth; and on the other hand the cost in 1923 was $1,100,000; in 1924, something over $800,000, and last year something over $800,000.   I would like to impress the Committee with that, because it seems to me it is important, and leads up to the way this large expenditure was made at Sault Ste. Marie. Now, Mr. Lyons, if you will be good enough to go on.   You had not completed the figures you were giving as to the purchase of aeroplanes.

A.—When you interrupted me I had reached the point where I had explained our fire loss in acres, and was going to follow that with a statement that, based on the four cords to the acre which is the usual estimate of cordage per acre, I think we would have lost in 1923 about $8,480,000 worth of timber, $1 a cord.

Q.—That is standing?

A.—Yes.

Q.—Is it a reasonable basis?

A.—Yes.

Q.—How does that compare with your sales?

A.—I am using that as a basis.

Q.—That is the basis on which these large pulp companies are purchasing?

A.—Yes.

Q.—The market price for standing pulpwood?

A.—Yes.

Q.—And working out the loss in 1923 how much loss, translating the cordage loss into dollars and cents?

A.—It would be about $8,500,000.

Q.—Does the Committee follow that—$8,500,000 in 1923?

MR. RANEY: We are all here; better get along.

MR. MOREL: That is very small.

MR. LYONS: I am not considering the other merchantable timber, but taking average figures. If we take the result of the saving due, I contend, almost entirely to the institution of the hydroplane service over 1924-25, we will have saved on the same basis of four cords to the acre about 16,000,000 cords, or about $2,000,000 worth of pulpwood in Crown dues on stumpage alone.

MR. FINLAYSON: Taking the actual loss and translating into dollars and putting it over three years' patrol?

A.—Putting it in 1924 and 1925. Based on four cords to the acre the savings to the Province in stumpage and dues is approximately $32,000,000. Of course it was costing us that before on the old system.

MR. FINLAYSON: Far more; last year under the old system $1,100,000.

MR. LYONS: That does not take into consideration the other classes of merchantable timber also saved.

MR. FINLAYSON: Does it take into consideration burning up of soil, the destruction of soil, every other standpoint?

A.—I am simply taking the cordage value.

Q.—As a consequence of this, what policy have you established?

A.—Of course when we put the hydroplanes into use on the new scale we had to create an organization that would take care of them, and we established at Sudbury what is regarded as the eastern base, and from that base there are about, I think, seven machines, or at that time were, operating. We established a western base at Sioux Lookout, and from that there are six or seven machines operating, and we established fourteen or fifteen sub-bases or fuel stations at strategic points where a machine in distress or ordinary patrol might land on some suitable water close to a railway depot where it could secure and where we could deliver our gas supplies economically, and we have these fifteen or sixteen sub-bases and the eastern and western bases to control our operations; but after working that out for a few months we knew of course we would have to establish a headquarters where machines could be overhauled and repaired and reconditioned from time to time. When we had reached that point I instructed Captain Maxwell to make a survey of all the territory in Ontario with a view to recommending the most suitable vicinity at which to establish this headquarters.

Q.—Explain to the Committee who Captain Maxwell is.

A.—Captain Maxwell is in charge of our organization. When we purchased the hydroplanes he was engaged and was formerally engaged with the Laurentide Air Service, and is recognized, I think, as the outstanding air pilot of the Dominion of Canada.

Q.—Before we broke into this you started to make a comparison between what it was costing and under the contract with the Laurentide Service. What is your service costing?

A.—I think the bulk of the flying done by contract was $150.00 an hour. Our cost for flying during 1924 was approximately $43.00 per hour.

Q.—A drop from $150 to $43 per hour. Does that include the capital charges?

A.—That includes all the expenses incidental to the whole operation, worked on a basis of 2,600 flying hours. I think that worked out $42.75 per hour. That does not include depreciation of machines, interest on investment or depreciation on buildings, which will add another $11.00 per hour to that.

Q.—So you reduced it from an average of $150 per hour, under contract system, to what?

A.—Approximately $43.00.

Q.—Does that include depreciation?

A.—$11.00 more.

Q.—Roughly, reduced from $150 to $54 per flying hour. That is the unit?

A.—Yes.

Q.—You said you had engaged Captain Maxwell? I interrupted you.

A.—He made a thorough survey of the Province of Ontario, and there were two points he recommended as suitable for establishment of headquarters. One was Hamilton Bay and the other Sault Ste. Marie. The reason for that is machines are reconditioned during the winter months when not required on patrol and it is necessary to get as early an operation as possible in the spring. Hamilton Bay is open, and St. Mary's River is open perhaps three or four weeks before any of the northern inland lakes, and that is why Sault Ste. Marie was selected, because of that advantage and again because of the fact it is practically in the centre of our northern operations.

Q.—The Sault is open for what reason?

A.—The St. Mary's River is a rapid stream, and there is all the discharge from the pulp mills, the chemical, and the river is frozen over for only a short time.

Q.—In addition the Dominion Government opens it for navigation.

A.—Yes.

Q.—The advantage between the two points was their early and late season. Captain Maxwell made the survey and considered these two points.

A.—And after we decided we would erect the hanger at Sault·Ste. Marie we then undertook to secure a suitable site.

Q.—Well now, did Captain Maxwell put in any report?

A.—Oh, yes.

Q.—Is it on file?

A.—I have a copy of it here I think.

Mr. Finlayson read the report.

Location of Main Base for reconditioning, overhauling and testing of Aircraft and Engines as used in connection with the Forestry Branch Air Service:

After a very careful survey of a possible site for the installation of hangars, etc., in connection with the Air Service, I have come to the following conclusions: two possible places of location:—

Hamilton, Ontario, situated on Burlington Bay.

Sault Ste. Marie, situated on St. Mary's River.

In the selection of the base the following points should be considered— first, location with reference to the summer operation; second, location with reference to the testing of machines; third, location with respect to freight, etc. and fourth, location with respect to personnel.

Burlington Bay adapts itself particularly well in every respect to the testing of machines. The water is open at least four weeks to that of any other northern waters, and the bay is not overcrowded with shipping, etc. The location of this base, however, is too far south with respect to the delivery of machines to the active summer bases which are Sudbury in the eastern section of the Province and Sioux Lookout in the western section of the Province.

It is quite apparent that a base situated midway between these two areas would minimize the necessary cross country flying to and from active flying operations. It would, however, appear that Sault Ste. Marie offers the better all-round inducements. Its position with regard to location enables the flying of machines to their respective operating bases without any loss of time as these machines will leave Sault Ste. Marie and en route will be participating in an active fire patrol.

Secondly, the location on the St. Mary's River, which is open to navigation some two or three weeks previous to the actual opening of the inland lakes, permits machines to be tested from the water and ready for patrol for the early hazard period which begins in the latter part of April and the early part of May.

Thirdly, location with respect to freight: Sault Ste. Marie is situated in an ideal position in this respect in that all gas and oil shipments can be made from Sarnia by boat to the Soo and C.P.R. and other lines have splendid freight facilities at this point.

Fourthly, location with respect to personnel. Success in a flying operation can be attributed to a high class personnel. Naturally the flying personnel after seven months flying operation in various remote areas of the Province will be better satisfied if located in a city of fair size rather than in some small town or village or railroad centre. The city offers entertainment in the winter such as music, winter sports, etc., which all play a part in keeping a staff in a contented mood.

I would, therefore, recommend that if a property can be purchased or rented on the St. Mary's River water front, that a building or buildings can be erected for the housing, reconstruction and erection of machines, and for the dismantling, overhauling and assembling of all motors used in connection with the Forestry Branch Air Service.

Director of Air Service,
W. R. MAXWELL.
Toronto, July 22nd, 1924.

Q.—So you came to the conclusion Sault Ste. Marie was the logical location. And what was done?

A.—After that was decided on we undertook to secure a suitable site, and another very careful survey was made.

Q.—By whom?

A.—By Captain Maxwell. I gave the matter considerable attention myself. And after investigating all the possible sites Captain Maxwell recommended, and I took full responsibility for approving of it, a certain location.

Q.—His report on that is also in wrriting?

A.—Yes.

MEMORANDUM FOR HON. MR. LYONS, MINISTER OF LANDS AND FORESTS.

Further reference is made to our various conversations relative to suitable site for hangar on St. Mary's River water front.

In this connection may I advise, sir, that I secured a boat and made further careful survey which substantiates my previous recommendations made at the time I flew on demonstration flights Sault Ste. Marie, July 1st.

The water lots east of the Imperial Oil dock do not adapt themselves account of shallow, muddy and rock approaches. The necessary dredging operations would indeed be very costly. The lots west of the City dock are quite out of the question account of heavy commercial navigation.

If it is in order, sir, may I recommend that the purchase be made of the lot which is at the foot of Church Street, or just east of Pim Street. After very careful survey and having taken into consideration all phases of operating and reconditioning duties, no other site adapts itself so admirably as this one does. I have been led to believe that the property can be purchased for fifteen thousand dollars. This price, the central location of the lot, and the deep water front advantages, recommends this site as the only and ideal location for a main operating and reconditioning base for the Forestry Branch Air Service.

May I also draw your attention to the fact, sir, that the central location permits the erection of offices, a part of the hangar construction. Would it not be an advantage to have all Ontario Government offices centrally located?

I do not think that motor tests will in any way disturb office duties.

(Sgd.) W. R. Maxwell,
Director of Provincial Air Service.

Toronto, September 3rd, 1924.

Mr. Finlayson: We have a plan of the property here.

The Chairman: Are you going to put these in as exhibits?

Mr. Finlayson: Yes, I want these in as exhibits.

The Chairman: For purposes of exhibits should we not have the original?

Mr. Finlayson: The original is on file in the Department.

The Chairman: If it is satisfactory to the Committee we will take these copies.

Mr. Finlayson: Anybody who wishes to do so can verify them in the Department.

Q.—What size are these lots?

A.—The total area there is approximately four acres. It extends from Queen Street and if any of you people have been in Sault Ste. Marie and know where the Algonquin Hotel is, it is just about a 100 or 150 feet east of the Algonquin Hotel and extends from Queen Street down to the water's edge and right out to the channel. It is one of these lots where the patent extend covering the water lot to the channel, and it is on the west side and runs 14 or 16 feet in width, running from Queen Street to the water's edge and has on the east side of it a street 66 feet wide extending from Queen Street to the water's edge.

Q.—So that this property was recommended by Captain Maxwell, and what steps were taken?

A.—As a matter of fact, it is my candid opinion, there isn't another available property in Sault Ste. Marie at any price.

Q.—What steps were taken to procure it?

A.—The owner was located and the price secured on it, and it was purchased for Fifteen Thousand dollars through the General Insurance Agency, Sault Ste. Marie.

Q.—At $15,000.00?

A.—Yes.

Q.—Does that include both land and water lot?

A.—Yes.

Q.—No buildings on it?

A.—There was an old house on it that was worth very little

Q.—And it had the advantage of a street to the north and a street to the east and west?

A.—Yes.

Q.—So you had access to it all around, and how far out did it go in the water?

A.—Right out into the channel several hundred feet.

Q.—Ample for the purpose?

A.—Oh, yes.

Q.—The property was purchased from whom?

A.—Cameron's.

Q.—Two Miss Cameron's?

A.—Yes.

Q.—And has been owned by them from the time granted by the Crown to the Cameron's in 1858, I think. So you acquired both the land and water lots for $15,000.

A.—Yes.

Q.—Now Mr. Lyons you are a resident of the Sault and have been engaged in real estate; that was a fair and reasonable price?

A.—I would say exceptionally so.

Q.—Exceptionally favourable?

A.—Yes.

Q.—What step was taken next?

A.—It was purchased and we undertook at once to erect a hangar and prepared plans and called for tenders, and when the tenders were received—

Q.—Before we get that far, who prepared the plan?

A.—Mr. Gurley.

Q.—Who is Mr. Gurley?

A.—An architect who was in the Northern Development Branch right here in the building.

Q.—He collaborated with Captain Maxwell I suppose?

A.—Yes.

Q.—You had your architect and an aerial expert prepare your plans?

A.—Yes.

Q.—Then was it advertised? An advertisement for tenders?

A.—I might say both Captain Maxwell and Mr. Gurley made a trip to the United States and inspected quite a number of hangars with a view to getting the very best possible plant that we could build.

Q.—Then you asked for tenders?

A.—We did, yes.

Q.—Where was that advertised?

A.—I would not say offhand, but I think in three or four journals or papers.

Q.—Was the usual time allowed to elapse?

A.—Oh, yes.

Q.—As the result were there a number of tenders came in?

A.—Yes, from five to eight; somewhere along there, I don't know the number.

Q.—Who was the lowest?

A.—Mr. J. J. Fitzpatrick.

Q.—Where does he reside?

A.—At Sault Ste. Marie.

Q.—Before we go on, let us clear up any possible question there? What was Mr. Fitzpatrick's business?

A.—He was a contractor in Sault Ste. Marie for ten or twelve years at least.

Q.—Any relationship with your firm?

A.—None whatever.

Q.—Have you ever had anything in common with him?

A.—Nothing other than selling him goods from time to time ever since he has been in business.

Q.—That is on the open market?

A.—On the open market.

Q.—But have you ever had any business dealings in common?

A.—None whatever.

Q.—He secured the contract. Do you remember the terms?

A.—I think his contract price was $61,100.

Q.—It is given in an answer to a question on the records.

A.—Yes, and then there was a unit price in addition for taking out rock and putting in concrete, because no one could tell how much rock would have to be removed.

Q.—For what purpose?

A.—Putting in a foundation. We made some tests, but from the tests you could not tell whether it was shell rock or hard rock or what it was. ·

Q.—He was given a contract on the usual Departmental form?

A.—Yes.

Q.—Did he put up security?

A.—A marked cheque; I don't know whether there was a bond or not, but a marked cheque for I think $3,000.

Q.—He proceeded with the erection of the aerodrome, I understand?

A.—Yes.

Q.—What was the price?

A.—The total price?

Q.—We have $15,000 for land, I think?

A.—Yes.

Q.—The answer to the question says: $131,351.

A.—That I think is made up of Fitzpatrick's contract, which included the general contract for the building, and that includes steel. I think that was purchased by tender from the Hamilton Bridge Works, or whatever their name may be, and includes the heating, and the plumbing contract and the painting contract.

Q.—Now, in addition to that $131,000, aerodrome, and $15,000 for land, what other amount was paid?

A.—Nothing I recall in connection with the building. We had to build a parking stage.

Q.—Explain to the Committee what it is.

A.—When the planes land in the water and have to be taken out you cannot put them all in the building at once because of the spread of wings. You have to take them apart and take the wings off at least half in order to get them all in, and they all come in late in the fall. Some times they have difficulty in getting away on account of ice, because they are on duty to the last moment. They come into the river there and have to be taken out of the water, and this parking stage, a very large platform, is used for the purpose of running the planes up on to avoid their freezing in, and they are taken apart one by one and put in the building and reconditioned there, and in the spring, commencing now I think, perhaps eight or ten machines now are put on the platform after having been reconditioned, and are ready to slip in the water at a moment's notice.

Q.—What did that cost?

A.—Roughly, $32,000, and that was built largely with our own organization, because the most of pilots in the Air Force are engaged by the year, and due to the fact that the hangar was not ready for use until some time, I think, in March, these pilots had not much to do in the interval, so we employed them building this parking stage and purchased material, and so on.

Q.—So putting it in even figures the aerodrome contract was $131,000, the land $15,000 even and the stage cost $32,000. That would be $178,000.

A.—I think about $180,000 covers the entire cost of land and buildings.

Q.—Does that include interior finish of the buildings?

A.—Oh, yes.

Q.—Will you tell the Committee what you did there?

A.—After the plan was designed for the hangar. It has a very large ceiling, must be thirty feet high, I think, and after that was designed, and the dope-room and machine shop, which takes the southerly end of the building, was put in, we had to put concrete floor or ceiling over the machine shop and dope-room in order to make it so the work could be carried out properly. We then conceived the idea of putting offices above this part of the building, and accordingly proceeded and put offices in there, not expensive at all, because we simply put up studdings and put on beaver board, or some material like that, and used them just in that way. I think the cost of the offices would not exceed $5,000.

Q.—Now what else have you got on the property?

A.—And we used these offices for the Forestry Branch and the Northern Development Branch, which were both paying rent before, and based on the rents we were paying in Sault at that time for the different organizations I have referred to, I think the benefit to the Province is approximately $5,000 a year. In other words, the offices we are occupying in part of this building substitute what we were paying approximately $5,000 a year for.

Q.—That is, you adapted this building upstairs for offices and store-house for the Northern Development Branch and saved a rental of approximately $5,000 at Sault Ste. Marie.

MR. CLARKE (Northumberland):

Q.—That is over and above what you paid before?

MR. FINLAYSON. Do I understand this $5,000 is the total rent you were paying before or a saving of $5,000?

A.—No change.

Q.—That is the rent you were paying before?

A.—Yes, we were paying that out before, but by putting them in this building we haven't to pay that out.

MR. CLARKE: For what it has cost you to erect that, you are saving $5,000 you paid out before?

A.—Yes, and I think the offices cost in the neighbourhood of $5,000 additional.

MR. FINLAYSON: So that by spending $5,000 on the aerodrome properties you were able to save an annual charge of $5,000 rental for different offices the Departments were using up there?

A.—Yes.

Q.—Now will you explain to the Committee the necessity for centralizing your aircraft in an extensive building of this kind for the winter? Why couldn't they be left in their stations all over the Province?

A.—Every machine has to be taken apart and the engines taken out and completely overhauled and the hulls have to be repaired just the same as the hull of a vessel.

Q.—Well anyone who was in the army knows something about that but there are some laymen here who do not understand the necessity for absolute perfection in aircraft.

THE CHAIRMAN: Almost everybody drives a motor car nowadays and knows something of it.

A.—The hulls are strong but delicate; the material is thin and they are covered over with canvas that has to be thoroughly waterproof, and any damage done has to be repaired during the winter, and you have to have a warm, comfortable place to carry it out, because there is the paint to go on and three or four coats of shellac on the canvas, and so on.

Q.—And by centralizing them all you were able to keep your men employed for the winter?

A.—Oh, yes. It had to be done somewhere. And then during the summer months all the engines are overhauled there. An engine operates eighty hours and is taken out, no matter how it is working and is sent back to the shop to be taken apart and overhauled and sent out again.

Q.—In other words, you have surplus engines, and surplus stock is constantly being overhauled.

A.—Exactly.

MR. WIDDIFIELD: What is a dope-room?

MR. FINLAYSON: Not what you think Mr. Widdifield.

A.—It is a room used for mixing the dope they put on the machines and the canvas covering, a special waterproof composition, and has to be handled in a certain way.

THE CHAIRMAN: It is a term inherited from the army.

HON. MR. LYONS: I think we have the only dope-room on the continent where men can work for ten hours at a time.

MR. FINLAYSON: In other words, the dope is applied to the craft and not the person.

MR. CLARKE: In other words, it is 4-4; it does not affect them.

MR. FINLAYSON: Not even invigorating or refreshing. Can you tell me Mr. Lyons, how this aerodrome compares with other similar hangars on the continent.

A.—As a matter of fact I never saw one myself, but I have been told by some American officers and by one or two people from the Old Country that it is the finest hangar they have ever seen anywhere.

Q.—Hangar is a synonymous term for aerodrome?

A.—Yes.

Q.—Now before we go on to this contract will you tell me how long you have been trading with this man Fitzpatrick?

A.—We have been dealing with Mr. Fitzpatrick and the firm Gibson and Fitzpatrick practically ever since we have been selling supplies.

Q.—Have you prepared a statement of sales to Fitzpatrick covering a period of years?

A.—Yes, I have, Mr. Finlayson. I have prepared a statement from our ledgers of sales from 1916 up to and including 1925.

Q.—As I recall, 1916 was the year your company was incorporated.

A.— 1916...................................... $ 418
1917......................................   552
1918......................................   6,126
1919......................................   10,132
1920......................................   2,034
1921......................................   30,822
1922......................................   11,722

```
1923.................................... $  2,134
1924....................................    29,599
1925....................................     9,216
```

Q.—Have you averaged that?

A.—No, I have not.

Q.—Nineteen twenty-three was away below the average.

A.—I think Mr. Fitzpatrick was building a lighthouse and other Dominion buildings in Michipicoten district.

Q.—Since you have been Minister, the 1923 year was below, 1924 above and 1925 below?

A.—All these sales are simply local.

MR. McKEOWN: It is an average of $10,000 a year.

MR. LYONS: They are not sales made to Fitzpatrick on any contract work out of town, but purely local, and some years he would be more successful in getting contracts than in others.

MR. FINLAYSON: Mr. McKeown points out this averaged approximately $10,000 for the period of ten years, and that 1923 was a little over $2,000; 1924, $29,000; and 1925, something over $9,000, so that there has been very little change, apparently. The biggest change was in 1921—$30,800. Going over these figures since 1916 when your company was incorporated, have you ever had in any way an interest in the contracts?

A.—Absolutely none.

Q.—Any interest directly or indirectly with Mr. Fitzpatrick or his firm or anyone connected with him?

A.—Absolutely none.

Q.—Was any inducement, monetary or otherwise, given you or your firm or family or people, directly or indirectly, with this contract? In securing it?

A.—Absolutely none.

Q.—Since it was made?

A.—The only thing would be in profits that might result in transactions of selling him materials.

Q.—But apart from that?

A.—Oh, no.

Q.—And can we, as you said yesterday, make it as broad as we like?

A.—Absolutely.

Q.—Then he started in on the contract, Mr. Lyons, to build the aerodrome. Who was in charge for the Government?

A.—After the contract was let, Mr. Findlay, of Sault Ste. Marie, was put on. He is a very reliable architect. As a matter of fact, his firm secured a thousand dollar prize awarded for the best plan submitted to the Queen Victoria Park Commission for erection of the Administration Building at Niagara. He was the architect in charge of the court house when it was constructed, in 1922-1923 I think, in Sault Ste. Marie.

Q.—That is under the previous Government, Mr. Drury's administration?

A.—Yes, he is I would say an outstanding architect, and was engaged to look after this work at $10.00 per day during the time it was constructed.

Q.—You did not get his exclusive time as supervising architect?

A.—I think he was on the job practically all the time. There was very little doing in Sault Ste. Marie at the time and we put him on at $10 per day. I made the price myself.

Q.—Were payments made on his progress certificates?

A.—Oh, yes.

14 J

Q.—And did he inspect the work all the time?

A.—I think he was there practically all the time.

Q.—What about the final completion of it?

A.—He approved every estimate and the total payments.

Q.—Were all payments made on his certificate?

A.—Yes.

Q.—During the construction of the aerodrome were there ever any difficulties or friction or incident of any kind?

A.—Between the Department and contractor? No.

Q.—Do you know anything about the contractor's purchases from your company?

A.—The total of them?

Q.—You have given the total haven't you?

A.—Over ten years, but on this particular building I haven't the figures, but would say in the neighbourhood of $30,000. I did have the figures some time ago and think I have them in my office now.

Q.—There would be nothing in 1922.

A.—No.

Q.—In 1923 there was nothing. In 1924 you say $29,500 and in 1925 $9,000; that would be nearly $39,000.

A.—Yes, I think perhaps about $30,000 of that or $31,000 was for material used in this building.

Q.—Or in other words, the contractor purchased from the Lyons Fuel and Supply Company, Limited, approximately $30,000 or $31,000 for this aerodrome?

A.—I think that is about right.

Q.—Did you have anything to do with these purchases?

A.—Absolutely nothing.

Q.—Was any arrangement made for purchase?

A.—By me, absolutely none.

Q.—Did he ever see you—ever have any conversation with you as to buying his materials?

A.—Absolutely none.

Q.—What would the material consist of?

A.—Gravel, cement, sand, tile. I think we put on the roof.

THE CHAIRMAN: You mean the waterproof section of the roofing?

A.—We put on roofs; that is part of our business, and have put roofs on the Post Office for the Dominion Government, the High School, Technical School, in fact all the—

MR. FINLAYSON: Let us take these up one at a time. Cement. In this country there are only two sources practically, aren't they?

A.—At the Sault Mr. I. J. Downey and ourselves are the only two firms supplying cement.

Q.—But I mean we get it from Canada Cement or Rogers, isn't that it?

A.—Yes.

Q.—So there are two well-known sources of cement from whom any contractor can buy directly, can't he?

A.—Yes.

Q.—And your profit on cement would be what you could sell him at up there in competition with the other local vendors of the same article.

A.—Yes, the price of cement is fairly well established.

Q.—What is the spread or variation in price?

A.—Well, it might run all the way from about fifteen to forty cents a barrel, depending upon the haulage and conditions under which you had to deliver, and that margin has to take in cost of handling, the financing of it, the loss of cement through sacks destroyed in shipping by boat, and so on.

Q.—You mean the spread from your purchase to your sale price may run fifteen to forty cents depending on the point of delivery?

A.—Yes.

Q.—So if you made fifteen or forty cents on a barrel, that has to cover capital, freight in—

Mr. CLARKE: Not freight in.

Mr. FINLAYSON: Not freight; you buy f.o.b. Soo?

A.—Let us say for argument's sake the laid-down price at the dock is $3.40; then the spread would be anywhere from $3.55 to $3.80 a barrel.

Q.—Which means your handling charge, delivery charge, less breakages?

A.—Return of sacks.

Q.—Capital investment, everything of that kind; and your conditions are the same as the other merchant there, other dealers in cement—you have to meet their competition?

A.—Yes.

Q.—Now go on to gravel.

A.—Gravel is pretty much in the same position. There is only one source of securing gravel at Sault Ste. Marie, and that is that it comes down the river by scow and is delivered on the docks, and the price is the same to Mr. Downey as it is to ourselves.

Q.—That is, neither of you own a gravel pit?

A.—No.

Q.—You have to buy f.o.b. dock?

A.—The Province owns the pit, and these people have an outfit and deliver it at their dock and charge a certain price for it, and we add to that whatever price is necessary in our opinion to meet the conditions and the expense of moving it from that point to wherever it has to go.

Q.—So gravel is in much the same position as cement; there is a standard price and you have to meet the same conditions as your competitor?

A.—Yes.

Q.—The other large item would be the roofing?

A.—Yes.

Q.—That would be specified by the architect?

A.—Yes, the roofing in this case was a standard 20-year roof, I think.

Q.—And that can be purchased from several sources, can't it?

A.—I don't know who all figured on it, but there would probably be two or perhaps three people at Sault Ste. Marie who might supply the same kind of roofing.

Q.—In any case, Mr. Lyons, the roofing prices are well standardized, and competition is keen?

A.—Yes, it is.

Q.—Mr. Clarke asks, was that done by tender?

A.—The roof? I might say to Mr. Clarke that when I was at the Soo this week-end I went into it so I could give information here that any member of our staff might give. We submit a price to every contractor who bid on this work, that we knew of. All the local men secure prices from us for what materials we could supply, and they all quote the same price.

Q.—You mean that when tenders were being asked for by the Government for construction of the aerodrome you gave to people who were tendering the prices?

A.—When a contractor wants to figure on a building, he goes to the supply house, one, two or three, or as many as he wishes, but he secures prices of the different supply houses on the material, the articles he is going to require to construct the building, before he secures the contract, and we submitted these prices to every contractor bidding on the work.

THE CHAIRMAN: At their request.

MR. FINLAYSON: And your prices were the same to Mr. Fitzpatrick and all the others?

A.—Yes.

Q.—And afterwards?

A.—Mr. Fitzpatrick, after securing the contract, did what contractors usually do, he came around and trimmed our fellows five to seven per cent. on the quotation.

Q.—In other words, he got the contract and said, "Before I give you the order what can you do?" Now these are the big items—cement, sand and roofing. What else?

A.—There is tile and brick; I think steel sash.

Q.—Well, tile and brick are standard stock. All these are trade articles and you got the contract in competition with everybody else. Now personally, did you have anything to do with these negotiations?

A.—Absolutely none whatever. As a matter of fact, I went to the Soo on a certain Saturday, and when I was having dinner that day my boy, Harry, told me he had secured the order for some material for the aerodrome, and said, "I just this morning secured the order for the lumber," and he said, "It runs into about $6,300"; and I said, "Who all are bidding on it?" and he said, "I think the Soo Lumber and Hesson." I knew Mr. Hesson usually supplied Fitzpatrick with his lumber, and I said to Harry I thought it would perhaps cause trouble if we got that order for lumber; they would blame me for it, and I asked him to go to Mr. Fitzpatrick and have him to go Mr. Hesson and tell him he would have the order for this lumber if he would meet the Lyons Fuel & Supply Company's price. Harry delivered that message to Mr. Fitzatrick, who went to Mr. Hesson and gave him the order, and until I was up to the Soo last week I thought he had met our price, but I found he had refused to reduce his price, which was $200 higher than ours, because of what I told my son to tell Mr. Fitzpatrick.

Q.—The reason for that, you say, was because Fitzpatrick had been in the habit of dealing with Mr. Hesson for lumber.

A.—And I did not want him to feel we were getting business in any undue way.

Q.—Is there anything else you want to say about the aerodrome contract, Mr. Lyons?

A.—I don't know that there is, Mr. Finlayson.

MR. FINLAYSON: If any gentleman wants to ask a question—no doubt, Mr. Raney will want to cross-examine generally, but before we pass on to another item. Then perhaps we can take up the McNamara matter. Will you tell the Committee, Dr. Lyons, please, something about this McNamara family that seems to have engaged the attention of the inquisitors?

A.—The McNamaras, I think the father and mother went to the Soo some time about the time I did, or a couple of years after. I knew Mr. McNamara,

Senior, there, away back in about 1906, when I think he had a contract under McNamara & Sons from the Town of Steelton, for the installation of a sewer system or part of a sewer system. That is the first time I recall actually knowing him. They carried on business as McNamara & Sons. Then the father died, and they have been carrying on business from time to time since under McNamara Brothers, then I think McNamara and Thornton, and now I believe McNamara Construction Co.

Q.—How long have you had business relations with them?

A.—We have been selling the McNamaras under some title or other ever since we have been in business.

Q.—Away back in 1915 or 1916?

A.—I think in the spring of 1915 was the first substantial business we did with them, when, as I recall, we sold them twenty carloads of sewer pipe for a contract they secured from the city.

Q.—How many brothers are there?

A.—There are three or four.

Q.—How many are interested in this?

A.—George and Howard.

Q.—How old are they—roughly?

A.—Really, they must be pretty much my own age; I would say 45 or along there.

Q.—I thought they were younger than that, from their hockey reputation. They don't play junior any more, eh?

THE CHAIRMAN: These are the boys who used to be the "Dynamite" hockey players—went overseas.

MR. FINLAYSON: The celebrated "Dynamite Twins" when they played hockey effectively. One is out of the weight class now, I observe.

MR. LYONS: Very much.

Q.—Have they lived at the Soo—family grown up there?

A.—Yes.

Q.—A well-known family?

A.—Oh, yes.

Q.—What kind of work have they been engaged in?

A.—General contracting; more sewer work and waterworks and road work than buildings. They have constructed some buildings in the Soo, but their general work has been more along the other line.

Q.—Municipal and government work?

A.—Yes, and a little work for the Algoma Steel Corporation.

Q.—Sewer work, bridge work, roads and pavements?

A.—Pavements, yes.

Q.—Where is their field?

A.—Well, for a number of years their work was entirely local. They were getting what local contracts they could up to 1916, when they went overseas, and they were overseas for I think three years, and when they came back they undertook to carry on their former occupation, and secured work in Sault Ste. Marie, and extended, and went carrying on contract work all over the Province.

Q.—Who have they been contracting for? You say all over the Province. In the older part of the Province?

A.—Yes.

Q.—Who have they been contracting for there?

A.—They have built roads and bridges for the Government. They have had a number of contracts. They have put in waterworks and sewer systems for several municipalities throughout the Province.

Q.—When you say "government," which government do you refer to?

A.—I don't know whether they did any contract work under the Hearst Government, I am sure, but they did a considerable amount under the Drury Government, and have had several contracts under this Government.

Q.—So that it has just been a continuation?

A.—Yes.

Q.—Does that apply to Fitzpatrick, too?

A.—Fitzpatrick has been more of a building contractor. I do not know of any road sork or sewer systems of any size he ever constructed.

Q.—Can you tell me what your firm's dealings with this McNamara family under its various styles have been?

A.—They extended, I think from the spring of 1915 right up to the present, and our transactions with them have been purely local. By that I mean we supplied, when opportunity presented itself, their local requirements. We have never sold them when they were constructing roads or bridges or sewage systems or waterworks systems in other parts of the Province.

Q.—Just when they were in your locality?

A.—That is the idea.

Q.—Just what is the volume, Mr. Lyons?

A.—I had this taken off our ledgers: 1915, $3,403; from 1915 to 1919 we did not do any business with them. That is the period I think they were overseas.

THE CHAIRMAN: Yes, they were.

MR. FINLAYSON: There is a lapse from 1915 to 1919 which covered their period overseas.

THE CHAIRMAN: They were in the army from 1915 to the spring of 1919; I know that.

MR. LYONS: 1919, $9,518.29; 1920, $29,494; 1921, $9,029; 1922, $3,256—hey were down in the older part of the Province then, 1923, we did not sell them anything; 1924, $23,988; 1925, $35,320.

Q.—What was the nature of the goods you supplied them?

A.—Sewer pipe, sand and gravel and cement.

Q.—Supplies for the contracts they were engaged in?

A.—Yes, that is right.

Q.—I don't want to repeat, but all that material is standard stock, is it not?

A.—That is right.

Q.—That can be handled in a dozen supply houses? And every contractor knows to a cent what it cost you?

A.—Pretty well, yes.

MR. CLARKE: Not to a cent.

MR. FINLAYSON: Well, to five cents, then. For Mr. Clarke's sake I will put it up five hundred per cent. So was there anything in the goods you supplied them at any time, particularly in these last two or three years, that was exceptional—that there was room for any monopoly on?

A.—Absolutely none. I have asked Mr. Nash to take off the margins we had on the material supplied, and when the committee get it there will be no doubt as to whether or not it was sold on a competitive basis.

Q.—Did they always make you compete for the business you got?

A.—Take in one case here in 1924, the bulk of that material went into one particular job, and they secured prices from Mr. I. J. Downey, and said that was lower than ours, and when they went to give Mr. Downey the order he refused to deliver the goods, and I have copies of the list. Then they came back to us and tried to get us to reduce the price, which we would not do.

Q.—Is that true of all your dealings? I mean they are on a business basis?

A.—Absolutely.

Q.—Are these people engaged in a business of some volume?

A.—Well, they are carrying on a very large contracting business for the last few years in particular. I think if you take the *Contract Record* you will find they are one of the leading contracting firms in the Province of Ontario.

Q.—Now you speak of George and Howard; are these the only members of the firm, the company, you know?

A.—Yes, the father is dead, and the other boy—I forget his name—left the Sault ten or twelve years ago; I do not know where he is.

Q.—These are the only two you know?

A.—Yes.

Q.—Have you ever been associated with these in any business enterprise?

A.—Absolutely no.

Q.—Have you ever had at any time any interest, directly or indirectly, or trust of any kind in any of their partnerships, firms or incorporations?

A.—Positively none, and you can make that as broad as you like. Never had any suggestion of any, as a matter of fact.

Q.—When you got contracts from them, how were they obtained?

A.—That is, supply material?

Q.—Yes, if they had a contract for a road or sewer or anything like that?

A.—You don't have reference to a contract with the Department?

Q.—I don't care who. When they had a contract with anybody, how did they come to you to get your figures?

A.—On materials, the same as anybody else.

MR. CLARKE: On a business basis.

MR. FINLAYSON: And you had to give prices in competition with others?

A.—Absolutely, yes.

Q.—Does that apply to all your dealings?

A.—As far as I know, yes.

Q.—When they had contracts up in your territory—and when I say that I am not confining it to the Sault, but anywhere under the Lands and Forests Department—under whom would they be operating?

A.—Well, they had two contracts from the Department of Lands and Forests.

MR. CLARKE: What year?

A.—1924. The Sudbury-Conniston road.

MR. FINLAYSON: That is a section on the Sudbury trunk road and the Timmins-South Porcupine road?

A.—Those were the two contracts.

Q.—In the same year?

MR. CLARKE: If I remember right, in 1925 you supplied about $25,000 of material?

A.—Yes.

Q.—What I was about to ask, were their contracts what are called municipal, or government contracts, for that year?

A.—This material I referred to is purely local delivery, Mr. Clarke, and does not cover any work outside the city limits of Sault Ste. Marie.

Q.—In other words, it was not goods supplied for contracts let by your Department?

A.—Absolutely no. We never sold them a dollar's worth.

Q.—Of this $25,000?

A.—None of it whatever.

MR. FINLAYSON:

Q.—So we can put that broadly, can we?

A.—Just as broadly as you like.

MR. CLARK: It just occurred to me the total was larger than some other years.

MR. FINLAYSON: Take these years 1924 and 1925, because there was nothing in 1923; when you supplied that $23,900 in 1924 and $35,000 in 1925, am I correct in the statement that goods representing these two amounts did not go into any Government contract?

A.—Quite so.

Q.—They were for local purposes at the Sault?

A.—That is right.

Q.—So as Mr. Clarke points out, your firm never supplied them with any material that ever went into any Government contract?

A.—I don't think there was a dollar's worth supplied.

Q.—We will be able to verify any details from them, but that is your statement?

A.—Yes.

Q.—They had two contracts on the Timmins road and Conniston road; how were they obtained?

A.—By public tender. When we undertook to build the Sault-Conniston road we advertised for tenders in the usual, regular way, and received a number of tenders.

Q.—Before you go on—as I understand it, that road was divided into sections?

THE CHAIRMAN: The contracts for building that road were let by section?

MR. LYONS: No, it was one contract. One section. The Sudbury-Conniston was one section, roughly seven miles.

MR. FINLAYSON: And you say the seven-mile contract was advertised?

A.—Oh, yes.

Q.—And can you tell me how many tenders were in?

A.—Five or six, perhaps. Four or five, I think that is right.

Q.—Was their tender the lowest?

A.—They were the lowest by severa' thousand dollars.

Q.—Did they put up security in the regular way?

A.—They did.

Q.—Was the contract treated as a routine matter in the Department?

A.—It was treated in just the same way as we treat every contract that comes in.

Q.—Tell me this, Mr. Lyons: what is your practice as to opening tenders?

A.—I did this when I came into the Department: from the first day I made it an established rule that whenever a tender was opened, if it was timber, Mr. Cain should be present, and if roads Mr. Sinton and Mr. Fullerton both.

Q.—You inherited Mr. Cain from a previous administration, the Drury administration, and he is an old civil servant?

A.—And a mighty good one.

Q.—And you inherited Mr. Fullerton also?

A.—And another good one.

Q.—Both good officers of long standing?

MR. CLARKE: Well trained.

MR. FINLAYSON: I do not know whether they go back to the Mowat administration or not. Q.—So your practice was to call in a responsible deputy when tenders were opened? Has that been universal?

A.—Absolutely, in every case, excepting perhaps where there was a little timber lot of 160 acres, or 320 acres; where timber was sold on that that might be dealt with by the Secretary and myself.

Q.—Even then, the Secretary was brought in?

A.—Yes.

Q.—Can I put that broadly, to use your word, that tenders were never opened privately?

A.—Quite so. And moreover, whoever was present had to sign the tenders, saying, "This tender was opened in the presence of" whoever it was.

Q.—Now which was the first of these tenders?

A.—The Conniston one.

Q.—Who was present?

A.—Mr. Fullerton and Mr. Sinton, I think.

Q.—It was the lowest tender and given the contract?

A.—Yes.

Q.—Were there any private negotiations with the McNamaras?

A.—No.

Q.—Or anybody for them?

A.—No.

Q.—Any variation in the contract?

A.—None whatever.

Q.—Was it on the stock departmental form?

A.—Yes.

Q.—And customary security given?

A.—Yes.

Q.—Did they proceed to work?

A.—They did.

Q.—Under what engineer were they?

A.—Well, they carried out their work under Mr. Hosking, who is the resident engineer at Sudbuty, but other engineers were put on under Mr. Hosking there to be in the field all the time, because Mr. Hosking had other activities to look after.

Q.—Tell me about Mr. Hosking. Is he an experienced engineer?

A.—He is, yes.

Q.—And he had charge of the whole Sudbury district?

A.—That is right.

Q.—I understand he had been shifted?

A.—He used to be in the Sault district, but personally I never knew Mr. Hosking until appointed resident engineer at Sudbury.

Q.—He was inherited from a previous administration, too?

A.—Yes.

Q.—And he had charge of the McNamara contract?

A.—Yes.

Q.—Ever any friction or trouble in carrying out this contract?

A.—None I ever heard of.

Q.—Any special incident you had knowledge of?

A.—None I recall, in any way.

Q.—Never had to interfere in any way?

A.—Oh, no.

Q.—So it went on in the ordinary way?

A.—Yes.

Q.—And the contract was carried out?

A.—Yes.

Q.—Payments made on the progress certificates?

A.—That is right.

Q.—No dispute as to accounts or anything of that kind that ever came to you?

A.—I think there was some discussion over some extras, but I do not think I had any discussion in the matter myself. I think the engineers were able to settle it without very much difficulty.

Q.—So the Conniston contract went through as a departmental matter, and you never had occasion to interfere—it never came to you for any settlement or adjustment?

A.—Yes.

Q.—And was it paid in the regular way?

A.—It was.

THE CHAIRMAN: It is three o'clock. I think we will have to adjourn now. The House will be meeting.

MR. FINLAYSON: Until to-morrow morning? What time—10.30, sir?

THE CHAIRMAN: We called it for 10 last morning and there were very few here until half-past ten. I am agreeable to be here at ten if members will be ready to start business.

MR. RANEY: Ten-thirty would be just as bad.

THE CHAIRMAN: To-morrow morning at ten o'clock, gentlemen.

PUBLIC ACCOUNTS COMMITTEE

The Committee met Friday morning, March 19, at 10 a.m. with Mr. Lewis in the chair.

HON. MR. RANEY: Before you proceed with the examination of Mr. Lyons I desire to move, seconded by Mr. Widdifield that G. W. Brownridge, G. E. Patton, W. H. Graham, J. E. Rutherford, and G. J. L. Jones, be summoned before the committee for next Wednesday to give evidence with reference to the following items in the Public Accounts for 1925:—

Page N. 3—Items under heading Motion Picture Bureau.

Page N. 12—G. W. Brownridge	$1,992 92
	4,126 27
W. H. Graham	1,559 31
Page B. 13—G. W. Brownridge	1,231 52
	511 21
Page N. 14—Am. Tel. & Tel. Co	2,625 00
S. N. Baruch	2,485 00
Bigwin Inn	700 00

Bigwin Inn Co........................	$921 76
Gitz-Rice............................	125 00
K. Halliker and H. H. Caldwell..........	1,250 00
L. C. Williams.......................	1,050 00

and to produce and show to the Committee all books, papers, receipts, bills and correspondence relating to the said items at pages N. 12, 13, and 14; and to give evidence generally as to the Motion Picture Bureau and Radio Publicity.

MR. FINLAYSON: Those are all directed at the motion picture?

HON. MR. RANEY: Yes.

THE CHAIRMAN: Gentlemen, you have heard the motion as read by Mr. Raney, seconded by Mr. Widdifield; it is not necessary that I read it again. Shall the motion be adopted? Any opposition? Carried.

HON. MR. RANEY: Then you will notice, Mr. Chairman, I have asked for the summoning of these witnesses for next Wednesday. Now one of them, I am told, is not in Toronto.

MR. FINLAYSON: Which one?

HON. MR. RANEY: Brownridge.

MR. FINLAYSON: Where is he?

A.—I think his headquarters are New York. He may not be even there. It is important that he should be here.

THE CHAIRMAN: He is a departmental official?

HON. MR. RANEY: Yes, but he is resident in Toronto I believe. There is that matter and then there are three other matters that will not require, not all them, I think, a great deal of time. There is the administration building matter, there is the Nash matter and the dispensaries. Now, at the rate we are progressing, this inquiry is going to be long drawn out. Some of these witnesses come from the north country and I don't see how we can hold back everything else for the conclusion of this matter. I think we must sandwich in some of these things from time to time. Perhaps all the more reason for that is to give the accountants time to complete their work. So that my suggestion is we might probably devote next Wednesday to these small matters and make what progress we can with them.

MR. FINLAYSON: I am sure Mr. Raney's suggestion is entirely meant to expedite the work of the Committee and I want to do everything I can to assist, but I am very anxious that we should clean up this particular matter we have started. I don't mean to say if we haven't got material for the Committee to go ahead on that we should not take up some other item.

What I am hopeful of was this, and I am glad you mention it because we may just as well now discuss our procedure, if you were satisfied and Mr. Sinclair, what I thought to do to-day was to try and if possible get through with Mr. Lyons. We will be able to sit practically until one and if necessary in the afternoon, and if necessary to clean up this Lyons matter I don't see why we should not sit in the evening. I will make an effort to do it. My object is I may be able over the week-end to arrange for the witnesses for next week. I hope the chairman will have the report. Have you that report?

THE CHAIRMAN: Not yet.

MR. FINLAYSON: That there will be some report to-day or to-morrow from Mr. Clarkson's firm as to their progress. But even then we have available here the two McNamaras, and departmental officials and I think one or two other witnesses who are on the list in my resolution. I thought if we could get on to-day and during the sittings to-day perhaps—I am not anxious to interfere with your cross-examination or Mr. Sinclair's—but if we could get it done to-day then we could start in on the other witnesses the first of the week and then we could over the week-end summons the ones we want.

HON. MR. RANEY: You mean in this matter?

MR. FINLAYSON: Yes. I will not be long now. I just want to touch upon one or two other matters. I think we have covered the ground that takes time.

HON. MR. RANEY: I was going to say as far as my examination of Mr Lyons is concerned I think the proceedings will be expedited if perhaps that matter were not crowded to-day. Mr. Sinclair, I understand, is willing to go on to-day. I don't see how we can close Mr. Lyons examination. I think we have the statements—

MR. FINLAYSON: I quite appreciate that. I don't mean to say I want to have it recorded as closed. What I mean is his cross-examination on the general motion will be finished and if anything arises out of the accountants' report you naturally have the right—

HON. MR. RANEY: As far as these other matters are concerned I think the witnesses are all available here in Toronto except Brownridge. If the clerk will find out where he is so he may be brought here, so he will be available when he is required, that might get rid of any occasion for discussion.

MR. FINLAYSON: If we are going to say Wednesday for that we are going to sandwich that in.

THE CHAIRMAN: In the meantime we will find out about Mr. Brownridge's whereabouts and how long it will take to get him here and advise you.

HON. MR. RANEY: He is located here, I believe, and I had it suggested to me that he is just now may be in the Western States somewhere.

MR. FINLAYSON: Mr. Regan tells me he is in New York.

MR. REGAN (secretary): I would not say definitely.

MR. FINLAYSON: It is understood with this motion that the Wednesday is not imperative.

HON. MR. RANEY: Yes, that is not imperative.

THE CHAIRMAN: Subject to exigencies.

HON. JAMES LYONS recalled.

MR. FINLAYSON (examining): Mr. Lyons, you have been sworn; this is just the continuation of your examination.

A.—Yes.

Q.—Before we go into other details I would like to clean up one thing. Somebody drew my attention to the fact that one of the papers stated you had ten resident engineers in the Soo. What is the fact?

A.—We have one resident engineer in Sault Ste. Marie and his territory extends from the vicinity of Hornepayne in the west to down in the Webbwood Massey district on the east.

Q.—Where are the ten resident engineers situated?

A.—Well, they are scattered throughout the north, one at the Soo, North Bay, New Liskeard, Cochrane—

Q.—Can you tell us very briefly what changes you have made in the expenditure of public moneys on roads in the north, the system?

A.—Well, after coming in in 1923 and surveying the situation carefully and travelling over practically all of the Northern Ontario work that was being carried on it was my opinion that the organization was a rather loose one and we accordingly undertook to establish a resident engineer located in various parts of the north where they would have jurisdiction over some particular area and be responsible for the work carried out in that particular district. And previous to that, of course, a great deal of the money was spent on the accountable warrants. Foreman and road inspectors had accountable warrants and they simply took the money out and in many cases paid the men and got signed vouchers for it and I didn't think, particularly having regard to some of the reports and conditions that existed that it was good business to continue in that way.

Q.—Where did they report to then?

A.—They reported to Toronto.

Q.—They were under Mr. Fullerton?

A.—Yes, under the department.

Q.—And Mr. Fullerton had charge of the whole Northern Ontario work?

A.—Yes.

Q.—And every foreman on a small job would get—

A.—Not every foreman, but road inspectors and certain foremen had accountable warrants.

Q.—They would get a lump sum for which they would have to account?

A.—Yes.

Q.—And how many of these would there be? I don't mean accurately, but a large number?

A.—Yes, there would be a good number.

Q.—Running into hundreds?

A.—Well, those that would have accountable warrants would not run into hundreds. I cannot say off hand just what it would be.

Q.—And there was no local provision, it all had to be done from Toronto?

A.—Yes.

Q.—So you inaugurated a system of resident engineers?

A.—Yes.

Q.—Who is the money granted to now?

A.—As the matter stands now with the resident engineers we appointed we made it possible for them to issue their own checks signed by the resident engineer and some official in his office covering the pay roll and small amounts covering purchases made locally so that the men employed were able to get their pay at any time. If a man was discharged he could be paid at once, and that is done in every one of the residencies.

Q.—So that the resident engineer has a local account?

A.—Yes.

Q.—For which he can issue cheques countersigned by a proper, that is right And that account is supplemented by money advanced from the Toronto office?

THE CHAIRMAN: Something in the nature of an Impress Account?

A.—Perhaps so.

MR. FINLAYSON: We are all mystified by your term.

THE CHAIRMAN: That is an accounting term.

MR. FINLAYSON: Well, we don't like to jump at it too readily.

Q.—What cheque is there on these engineers? I suppose they are bonded?

A.—Yes.

Q.—To the Department?

A.—That is right.

Q.—In the former way it had not been possible to bond every man?

A.—No, but even if he was bonded the system was so loose that it was not satisfactory in my opinion.

Q.—So you got a resident engineer who is furnished with a bank account who can only draw on cheques countersigned by the accountant and he has to give security to the Crown for any money he handles?

A.—Yes.

Q.—What check have you on that?

A.—We have a travelling auditor who travels from one residency to the other continuously and is able to check up every six weeks or two months on every engineer, audits his accounts, and keeps general supervision over the entire account.

Q.—Well, he is a travelling auditor?

A.—Auditor, yes.

Q.—And his audits cover all your northern staff?

A.—Both Forestry and the Roads.

Q.—Now that covers the accounting end. What supervision have you over the engineer?

A—Well, we have a general supervisor of roads of Northern Ontario, Mr. Alex. McIntyre.

Q.—Is that a new appointment?

A.—Yes.

Q.—The resident engineers are under him?

A.—He goes from one constituency to the other on the construction work and the making of the entire work uniform.

Q.—And both the auditor and supervisor report to your deputy, Mr. Fullerton?

A.—Yes.

Q.—Just to close up one or two other things, I asked you some time ago about Provincial Paper Mills and you were not able to give me the information I asked for about the coal. Have you been able to get it?

A.—I find in 1925 we quoted Provincial Paper Mills on 21,000 tons of coal and did not receive any order for any part.

Q.—Did not receive anything?

A.—No.

Q.—When you say "we" you mean?

A.—Lyons Fuel.

Q.—What about the Abitibi?

A—We quoted the Abitibi on 100,000 tons and did not receive an order for any part of it.

Q.—Do I take it in 1925 you received no order from either?

A.—Quite so, that is for coal.

Q.—What about the Fort Frances Pulp & Paper Co.?

A.—Well, I said the other day that we had not sold them anything I find now, according to the information I got, we quoted them on $640 worth of material in written quotation and received an order out of that for $6.50.

Q.—Is that all you got?

A.—Yes.

Q.—Well, you cleaned up. Mattagami coal—before we go on, some member asked to me to ask—he said he didn't understand what had been said, it has been said too rapidly?

A.—Well, Mr. McAllister was in touch with the officials of the Mattagami—

Q.—That is one of the Lyons Fuel & Supply Co. men?

A.—He generally looks after the wholesale coal business. He was in touch with the officers of the Mattagami Pulp & Paper Co. and in reference to their coal requirements, and he quoted them on 40,000 tons of coal and they told him he could have the order, and he came up to the buildings here to see me because of the fact that the deal was handled here in Toronto, and he came up to see me, which was the first I knew of it, because of the fact that it would require special financing to carry this coal on the dock over the winter period, as it would be delivered from week to week, and told me he had secured this order, who the order was from, and approximately the margin that he was making on it, and I told him that—

Q.—Was it a profitable thing?

A.—Yes, very profitable. I told him that we could not accept the order, that he would have to go back and tell these people we would not take the order.

Q.—Why was that?

A—Well, I told him, and he asked me, of course, why, and I told him that the Mattagami Pulp & Paper Co. were one of the firms that I expected to be tendering on a pulp concession that was being offered for sale by the Province in the Kapuskasing district and I didn't want to have my hands tied in any shape or form by any coal order of that kind and he asked me what he would go back and tell them, and I told him to go back and tell them anything he liked as long as he did not tell them anything I said.

MR. FINLAYSON: I think that cleans up what the member asked you. Have the McNamara firm, McNamara Construction Co., are they a new account for the Government? I mean, so many questions are directed at them I want to find out if they have been contracting with the Crown before your time?

A.—Oh, yes, according to the records they have been contracting with the Provincial Governments since about 1921 or 1921, I think every year.

Q.—That was answered in a question in the House. Are you familiar with the facts?

A.—Well, I did have the facts from the question there but I haven't them in mind.

Q.—When did they start to deal with the Ontario Government?

A.—1921.

Q.—Well, run down from 1921 to date, what have their contracts been? Oh, give us lump sums?

A.—During 1921, including 1921, to, and 1923, that is, for work done with the Drury Government, their contracts amounted to $634,364.83.

Q.—Now since, they have just continued on?

A.—They have had two contracts as I recall it, with the Department of Lands and Forests. They may have had other contracts with the Department of Highways, I don't know.

Q.—But with you they have only had two contracts?

A.—Yes.

Q.—This is right, that they were contracting on what has been referred to as the Kingston road, that is a trunk road?

A.—Yes.

Q.—Leading from where?

A.—Well, it is a section of the Toronto, Sudbury, Soo trunk road.

Q.—That is the road that leads northerly on Yonge Street to North Bay?

A.—It is the only road on which you can get from here to the Soo.

Q.—And this was an extension of it northerly to Cobalt?

A.—It was, now this is the section between Conniston and Sudbury.

Q.—But that is part of the trunk road north?

A.—Yes.

Q.—I think you told us yesterday about the opening of these road contracts, that they were opened by you with who?

A.—In the presence of Mr. Fullerton, and perhaps Mr. Sinton, I am not sure.

Q.—Have you got the tender with you?

A.—No, I haven't.

Q.—But they were let in the regular way?

A.—Yes.

Q.—Now one, or possibly more of these questions are directed at the charge for extras. How much was paid for extras on this work, Sudbury to Conniston, I am referring to a question of Mr. Kemp's. Will you be good enough to explain how these contracts are entered into, what occasion is there for extras?

A.—Well, in this case, I don't know, I don't think I know the first thing about it. I perhaps should have made myself acquainted with the details, but I didn't. I didn't know—

Q.—I am direct'ng my question, Mr. Lyons, towards the particular extras in this case to explain to the Committee the policy of the Department and the basis under which contracts are let. It is done on a unit basis?

A.—We call for tenders for the work and the usual practice is that unit prices are submitted for so much for rock, so much for gravel, so much for concrete, so much for shoulders, culverts, and so on, on a unit basis, and whatever amounts are measured up by the engineer they are paid for on that basis. Now some will run over and some under the estimate.

Q.—Let me clear this up. What are your specifications and your call for tenders based on, on the report of your resident engineer?

A.—Yes.

Q.—Your engineer goes over, in this case the seven mile section, estimates so much rock, so much earth and what he can from his measurements and observations?

A.—That is right.

Q.—That may or may not be right?

A.—Yes.

Q.—What appears to be earth on the surface may turn out to be rock?

A.—Well, it is the usual procedure, I think, followed.

Q.—Yes, I was coming to that, but that is what the facts consist of?

A.—Yes.

Q.—And the engineer cannot test it all accurately?

A.—Quite so.

Q.—And if it turns out there is more rock than he estimates the man is paid for it?

A.—On the basis, yes.

Q.—Is that the general practice of your department?

A.—I think it is the general practice of any department.

Q.—It is standard in your own?

A.—Yes, as a matter of fact I think the specifications and the plans that were adopted in constructing these roads were identical with the Highways Department. I think as a matter of fact we used largely their specifications.

Q.—It has been well standardized?

A.—Yes.

Q.—Now was the McNamara Construction Co., or any of their people, given any instruction at any time?

A.—None whatever.

Q.—Was it ever drawn to their attention any item in connection—

A.—No, I don't think there was—as a matter of fact, those extras, I don't know what they covered. I think the engineers settled that entirely themselves. I don't think that it ever came before me.

Q.—I suppose sometimes if there is a dispute between a resident engineer and the work it may ultimately come to you?

A.—It may be it came for something trivial but I don't just recollect.

Q.—But in any case there was no dispute and no determination of a dispute by you?

A.—No.

Q.—Now that was the Conniston contract, what was the other?

A.—The Timmins South Porcupine.

Q.—Will you tell us what road that is?

A.—That is the one that runs from South Porcupine south and into the town of Timmins and is about seven miles in length, and we called for tenders to complete the construction of that road and received quite a number of tenders, of which McNamara Bros. or McNamara Construction Company, whichever it was, were the lowest bidder by several thousand dollars.

Q.—And they were awarded the contract?

A.—They were awarded the contract.

Q.—They gave the usual security, I suppose?

A.—Yes.

Q.—And entered into the usual form of contract?

A.—They did.

Q.—Was the contract carried out under the engineer's supervision?

A.—It was, yes.

Q —Was there any occasion to consult you about it?

A.—Well, the matter would be discussed from time to time. There is nothing in particular as I recall.

Q.—You have supervision of the work and made trips and saw it but cannot say there ever was any dispute or adjustment between the engineers and the contractors that came before you?

A.—That I had to settle?

Q.—Yes?

A.—I think not.

Q.—May I put it this way, the contract went through in the ordinary way?

A.—Yes, of course there is always more or less discussion between engineers. on nearly everything.

Q.—But that was a matter for them to settle. You never had occasion to interfere?

A.—No, I think not.

Q.—And the remark you made yesterday, as to these contracts, that you had no interest, direct or indirect, applies to them?

A.—To both and to any and all.

Q.—But there are only two McNamara contracts?

A.—Yes.

Q.—Now we take up the question of the street paving at the Soo. A number of questions have been directed, this seems to be Mr. Ross' subject. He is not here. We will go on with it, will we Mr. Raney?

Hon. Mr. Raney: Why, certainly.

Q.—I am asking that because all the questions seem to be in his name.

Hon. Mr. Raney: He is not a member of this Committee I think.

Mr. Finlayson: Isn't he?

The Chairman: No.

Mr. Finlayson (proceeding): Will you explain to the Committee what this street paving consists of?

A.—The Wellington Street?

Q.—Yes, the Wellington street, Sault Ste. Marie?

A.—Well, Wellington Street, Sault Ste. Marie, is commencing at the easterly limits of the city and going through to the westerly limits, must be, well, on to five miles in length, and it is a continuation of the trunk road from Sudbury through to the Soo and beyond, and on a portion of that—

Q.—That would be part of what is sometimes called the Trans-Canada Road?

A.—Well, we hope so.

Q.—Some day, but it is being gradually built up?

A.—Yes.

Q.—In the meantime it is the northerly trunk road, commonly called trunk road up there?

A.—Yes.

Q.—And Wellington Street forms what the Highways call the connecting link through the municipality?

A.—It is. It is practically as straight as you could shoot and it will be for a long distance, I don't know how many miles.

Q.—And it had been treated as a connecting link by the previous Government?

A.—Yes.

Q.—What had been done by the previous administration on it?

A.—Well, in 1923 the Government of the day spent about $45,000 or $48,000, I think on this particular street in the Soo.

Q.—That is on Welington Street?

A.—On Wellington Street.

Q.—Where, in relation to the work that was done under your department?

A.—I would say from a quarter to a half a mile east of where this work was done.

Q.—They were entering the city from the east?

A.—Yes.

Q.—And your work was a continuation of that westerly?

A.—That was westerly.

Q.—Under the Drury administration how was it financed?

A.—The Province paid every dollar.

Q.—The Province paid 100 per cent. And under yours?

A.—And they didn't build a road at that.

Q.—Let us hear what they did?

Hon. Mr. Raney: In the Soo?

Mr. Finlayson: This is the trunk road that leads through the Soo and I am trying to show it had been adopted as a trunk road by your administration and we adopted the policy and extended it westerly. You say the Drury administration had started at the east end?

A.—The distance in the City of Sault Ste. Marie that the Drury Government undertook to build a road and a permanent road was three and about one-tenth miles.

Q.—On Wellington Street?

A.—On Wellington Street.

Q.—The same street?

A.—The same street. And they spent in the neighbourhood of $45,000 or $48,000 and they undertook to build a tar macadam road, and they certainly made a mess of it.

Q.—You say it was in bad condition?

A.—Well, there has been an agitation for two years to make a road out of it.

Q.—How do they finance, what arrangement had they with the city?

A.—Well, Mr. John Lang, who was their part-time engineer for the Northern Development Branch at the Soo, had it no doubt under his supervision but the work was carried out entirely as I understand under the direction of Mr. Fred Irwin, of Sault Ste. Marie, who has no knowledge of building roads.

HON. MR. RANEY: I think we ought to have Mr. Bowman.

MR. FINLAYSON: Get him here. There is no charge against Mr. Bowman.

A.—Oh, absolutely none. I think to be honest, Mr. Cunningham was responsible for the road more than anybody else.

Q.—I am not directing my questions in any charge against Mr. Bowman.

A.—Absolutely none.

Q.—What we are trying to point out is the previous administration started this policy and this was a continuation and Mr. Lyons said $48,000 was spent on this section and it has been in bad shape and there was an agitation for rebuilding. What I am interested in, had they any settled policy on the method of financing?

A.—Of course up to 1923, I think all the expenditures made by the Northern Development Branch were made on a basis of 100 per cent. for whatever work it covered.

Q.—Whatever they did, and—

A.—They paid it all.

Q.—Let me clear that up, was that part of Wellington Street where the Drury administration spent this $48,000, was this in the corporate limits of the city?

A.—Oh, yes.

HON. MR. RANEY: As far as—

A.—Well, running right up into the central part of the city, Mr. Raney. Running right up to Simcoe Street.

HON. MR. RANEY: Up to the place where you took it up?

A.—No, there was an intervening section and we took it up from there on.

MR. FINLAYSON: They had inaugurated this policy and in their day they did it on a basis of 100 per cent. What did you do?

A.—When I came in in 1923 and went over the roads of Northern Ontario I found, taking my own case of the Soo-Sudbury, Timmins-South Porcupine, and Keewatin and places like that—

Q.—North Bay?

A.—North Bay. I felt that while we were justified in doing something to assist in the development of permanent roads in Northern Ontario that we should do it on somewhat the same basis as is done in old Ontario, so we had an amendment made to the Act in 1924 at my suggestion which enabled the Department to make a contribution in any percentage that they saw fit towards the construction of a permanent roadway in any municipality such as Soo Ste. Marie, Sudbury, Timmins, and like places and accordingly from that time on we have dealt with it on that basis.

Q.—What width was the road construction by the Drury administration?

A.—I think it is eighteen feet.

Q.—What did you do?

A.—As a matter of policy?

Q.—Yes?

A.—We undertook to contribute a percentage of the cost of a certain width.

Q.—In this case, what was it?

A.—In this case it was 24 feet.

Q.—And what percentage did you contribute?

A.—Fifty per cent., not including curb or gutters. It is simply for the road itself.

Q.—Intersections?

A.—No.

MR. PATTERSON: Is that 24-foot strip the entire length of the work?

A.—Yes.

Q.—Business part of the town?

A.—Oh, this is not the business section at all.

MR. FINLAYSON: It is the trunk street right through Sault Ste. Marie. It is farther north from the river, to miss the business section, but it is the trunk road right through, recognized by both governments, but it isn't built up with stores.

MR. WIDDIFIELD: Why the space between where the Drury administration left off and you started?

A.—Because it had already been completed by the city.

MR. FINLAYSON: This is just the policy continuing on. We are not quarrelling with the selection of this by the Drury Government. In fact we adopted it. All I want to point out is there is the method. Who was the work done by?

A.—By the City of Sault Ste. Marie.

Q.—And your resident engineer?

A.—We put a man on in part if not all the time to see the work was carried out according to the specifications.

Q.—What kind of road?

A.—Concrete pavement.

Q.—Now one of the questions suggest that some petition was put in against it, is that correct?

A.—No, it is not.

Q.—Will you tell me briefly what happened, so we can clear it up?

A.—Well, the only thing I know of in so far as a petition is concerned is that some of the people sent petitions to the council against being compelled to pay a certain percentage of the city's cost. I think the idea in their mind was that if the Government was paying a portion of the cost they should get the benefit of that entirely.

Q.—In other words, they said, if the Government are paying 50 per cent. the city at large should pay the other?

A.—I think something like that.

Q.—Just to clear up. I am reading here a report in the Sault Ste. Marie *Daily Star*, March 10, 1926, of a meeting of the council at which—

HON. MR. RANEY: That cannot be 1926 surely.

MR. FINLAYSON: Yes.

HON. MR. RANEY: It is just this month.

THE CHAIRMAN: That would be this question of the settlement?

HON. MR. LYONS: I think that resulted from the questions asked for in the House, and that is an explanation of just what did take place.

MR. FINLAYSON (proceeding): "Mr. John L. O'Flynn, K.C., spokesman for the delegation, pointed out that while those interested were anxious not to delay the progress of the work, they protested against the apportionment of the total cost against the abutting property owners. They based their protest on the fact that By-law No. 676, passed in 1912, governed the procedure of the council in so far as it made the city responsible for one-third of the cost of such work."

Q.—The quarrel was as to whether local residents owning property abutting on the street should be forced to contribute. That didn't affect the Government at all?

A.—No, in fact the Government never knew anything about it until just recently.

Q.—Had you any interest in the contract?

A.—None whatever.

Q.—Who did the work?

A.—McNamara Brothers.

Q.—For whom?

A.—For the City of Sault Ste. Marie.

Q.—They were not under you?

A.—No.

Q.—By who were they paid for it?

A.—By the city.

Q.—And who did you make your contribution to?

A.—Well, the contribution I don't think has been made yet. It will be made to the city, unless it has been paid in the last two weeks. There is no dispute about it. It will be paid.

Q.—It is just a matter of your paying us 50 per cent.?

A.—Which amounts to slightly over $19,000.

Q.—On a basis of 50 per cent. for concrete road.

THE CHAIRMAN: How long?

A.—About a mile of it, something like.

MR. FINLAYSON: Had you in any way, directly or indirectly, in any way at all, any interest in this?

A.—None whatever.

Q.—Either with the McNamara people or anything?

A.—None whatever.

Q.—You had no property affected by it at all?

A.—None whatever.

Q.—Anything else you want to say about that, Mr. Lyons?

A.—I don't think there is.

Q.—Soo Coal & Wood Co. There are some questions—

A.—There is the Timmins South Porcupine road.

Q.—McNamaras?

A.—They did that.

Q.—I thought we covered that in the second contract. That was the second contract, McNamara Construction Co.?

A.—I would just like to point out also in that case—

Q.—We have gone back now to the McNamara. Mr. Lyons wants to say something as to the second contract.

A.—What I simply want to say to the Committee if I can is that the work that was carried on under this method in Sault Ste. Marie was not a single instance.

Q.—I see.

A.—The Timmins-South Porcupine road was treated somewhat on the same basis. There is approximately seven miles of pavement between the point that we took the road up in the town of Timmins and where we completed it in the town of South Porcupine.

Q.—When it goes between these two municipalities it is in the township of Tisdale?

A.—Yes, when I came in—

Q.—So you had three municipalities, two towns and—

A.—Well, it is really two municipalities, I think. South Porcupine is part of the municipality of Tisdale. It isn't a separate municipality.

Q.—Oh, I see.

A.—I think I am right in that. When I came in in 1923 and went up to Timmins shortly after I found that they were trying to build a road between those two points, and the Drury Government had spent $109,000 on this seven miles of road and I stopped the work—

Q.—Why?

A.—Because I felt it was practically a waste of money to try and build the kind of road they were endeavouring to build in that particular place.

Q.—What was the material?

A.—Well, it was what you might call a water bound macadam road and having regard for the nature of the rock in that district you cannot make a road that in my opinion will stand up.

Q.—Water bound?

A.—Well, it is simply rock put into place and it may be with water and rolled under heavy pressure.

Q.—To keep it on rock?

A.—Yes, and I stopped the work and we discussed the matter with the officials there from time to time and they were anxious to have a permanent road. They said they had been promised one by the late Government and we wanted to build them a road, but having regard for the Act that was passed I told them candidly we could not do it, that they would have to bear a portion of the cost.

Q.—I suppose this $109,000 had not been all wasted. A certain amount of material was—

A.—Well, it worked in as a basis for the future road. I am not trying to contend it was wasted. That is not the point at all. I just want to show what was being done. So after discussing it with the officials of Timmins and Tisdale we reached a basis of operation which was briefly this, that Tisdale was to contribute ten per cent.

Q.—The township?

A.—The township.

Q.—Tisdale is an exceptional township in this Province. It is enormously wealthy?

A.—Wealthy?

Q.—Yes?

A.—I would say so.

Q.—McIntyre, Porcupine, Hollinger?

A.—Yes.

Q.—And your reasoning was that they should be able with their enormous assets to contribute something?

A.—Yes. They agreed to contribute ten per cent. The town of Timmins agree to contribute ten per cent. of the cost of the road in their town limits. I was not satisfied with that and I told them we would not build the road on that basis and out of the discussion a suggestion came that perhaps the mining companies there would contribute something and I personally took it up with the Hollinger, their engineer there, Mr. —

Q.—Mr. Brigham?

A.—Brigham, yes, and they agreed to contribute $15,000. We worked it out as I recall it on the basis of their earnings. The Dome paid I think $5,000 or $5,500, the McIntyre something and the Hollinger, $1,500, along with the ten per cent. from Tisdale and ten per cent. from Timmins we undertook to build the road, and accordingly called for tenders and let it to the lowest tenderer, which was the McNamara Construction Co.

Q.—That is an example, illustration, of why the Minister in the north has to have power to regulate the contributions that may be made?

A.—Yes.

Q.—It may be a fair rule for the Highways Department in the south to say we will contribute 50 or 40 per cent. but up north it has to vary? Your township of Tisdale—

A.—It was a peculiar situation.

Q.—Tisdale is wealthy and you could go to these three mines and get contributions?

A.—Yes.

Q.—If you hadn't had that power?

A.—We would have had to pay it all ourselves.

Q.—What did your contribution, can you tell me approximately what it amounted it to?

A.—To the town of Timmins?

Q.—After Tisdale paid ten per cent. and Timmins and then these contributions from the mining companies?

A.—Our contribution to the town of Timmins proper was $9,940.36 in one case; $47,689 in another case.

Q.—What I am trying to get at, take your section of roadway separately, in Timmins, partly in Tisdale, to which both made contribution, and the three mining corporations?

A.—Our contribution to that portion of the road between Timmins and South Porcupine was $47,689.09.

Q.—Out of the total expenditure?

A.—Well, I haven't the figures as to that; that was our contribution of making—

Q.—Part of it is in Timmins, part in Tisdale, and these big mines—

Mr. CLARKE: Does that cover Timmins?

A.—That is in the town of Timmins. In the corporate limits. Timmins is a separate corporation. I am speaking of the town of Timmins.

Mr. FINLAYSON: It is really a city, 15,000 people?

A.—That was our contribution to that portion of the road after we had taken into consideration the percentage by the city and by the three mining companies.

Q.—What would it be approximately, fifty per cent. of the total cost?

A.—Oh, it would be more than that. Oh, yes, it would be about, well, it would be 70, I would say, or 75 per cent.

Q.—So that in that case you were trying to work out as Minister and head of the Department some equitable arrangement under the authority of that Act?

A.—That is right.

Q.—In the Soo you felt you were at liberty to pay fifty per cent. Up there?

A.—More.

Q.—You had under the Act these contributions from these people. The previous administration, without attempting to cast any reflection, had it to pay 100 per cent. We paid 60 to 70 per cent. Anything else on that?

A.—We did the same thing out in the town of Fort Frances.

Q.—I hope the Committee will bear with us in this because it is the easiest thing in the world to say why has the Minister power to fix these amounts? Why does he pay fifty per cent. at the Soo and seventy where there are wealthy mining corporations. Gentlemen of the Committee who know the north will know the situation varies all over. If you get a poor township, it may be organized or unorganized, you cannot expect them to put up a five cent piece, but where you get conditions like the McIntyre and Hollinger and Dome, you can fairly ask them for contributions. The City of Sault Ste. Marie can well afford to pay fifty per cent.

A.—Fort Frances. There was just a small piece constructed out there. Our contribution was on the basis of fifty per cent. of the certain width of the roadway.

Q.—Did you do some North Bay too?

A.—No, that is under—

MR. CALLAN: In connection with that Fort Frances, your share wasn't for the total width?

A.—No, just for the centre width, the same as the Soo.

Q.—Same as the Soo. The dispute was not as to what they were paying. but the ratepayers wanted to say because the Government is paying fifty per cent. we as ratepayers should not pay a cent.

A.—We did the same thing at Sudbury on the entrance to the town of Sudbury from the east. There is a connection link there and we contributed fifty per cent. of the cost of a certain width.

Q.—Of the street?

A.—Yes. On the same basis.

Q.—That is, as the Highways?

A.—Well, I don't know exactly what their basis is.

Q.—Well, they pay a percentage of 20 feet, isn't it, Mr. Keith?

MR. KEITH: In Toronto and York, I don't know about the Provincial, the Toronto and York Roads Commission built 20 feet through an urban municipality and any additional width has to be borne entirely by the municipality.

MR. FINLAYSON: However, you have tried to work out a policy there?

A.—Well, I endeavoured to secure financial assistance and co-operation from the municipalities that I thought should be in a position to pay a part of the expenditure.

Q.—Any gentleman want to ask Mr. Lyons anything on that before we pass on?

MR. WIDDIFIELD: I suppose you will appreciate this situation making comparisons of the assistance given under the Drury Government— and comparisons have been made—under the Drury administration, under Mr. Bowman's department and under your own, we can appreciate this that the conditions were relatively pioneer under the early administration. The northern country is developing fast, and it is quite warrantable as that development proceeds, less assistance should be expected from these northern municipalities.

MR. FINLAYSON: I don't want you to think we are contending Mr. Bowman did anything improper or there are any charges, and I think what you say is true. There has got to be development and improvement. As far as Sault Ste. Marie is concerned, the City of Sault Ste. Marie was just as strong in Mr. Bowman's day as in Mr. Lyon's day, and just as well able to pay their share in 1922 as in 1924. But what I am directing my questions at is this, and I hope members will pardon the length of them. Something has been said as to the power of the Minister to make grants being perhaps, well, to put it mildly, an extraordinary power to give the Minister. But I think you and everybody on the Committee who knows all the conditions over the north country, it is a beginning and an initial step in a policy to try and make the cities of the north in places where they are able to do it contribute to the road.

THE CHAIRMAN: I think it fair to say that what Mr. Lyons is outlining is the installation of a new system from that that had been used for years.

A.—And I am simply using the expenditures of the two Governments at Sault Ste. Marie to show clearly if I can that because of my position that I am giving the Soo something some other place is not getting or that the Soo had not got before. I have no quarrel with the expenditure or anything else.

Q.—Just the continuation of the former policy with improvements, what you considered improvements?

A.—Yes.

Q.—Let us take up the Sault Coal & Wood Company. There is a question. Mr. Kemp directed this one. Who is the firm, Sault Coal & Wood Company, who are the controlling people?

A.—Well, the Sault Coal & Wood Company has been established and operating in the Soo for quite a number of years. It was formerly, I think, in the control of Mr. Carney and Mr. Farewell. After Mr. Carney died, Farewell and his close associates controlled it. That went on until 1925 and I believe Mr. Farewell's ill health during the preceding winter compelled him to leave the business in other hands.

Q.—What was their line?

A.—Retail fuel entirely.

Q.—And therefore competitors of your firm?

A.—Yes.

Q.—And when he was away during the winter of 1924, as I understand it, they did not make any money. The management went into new hands with the result that they lost money, and the shareholders decided that they would dispense with the business?

A.—Mr. Farewell, as I understand it, was going to leave it entirely. I heard that the business was likely to be disposed of—

Q.—When was this?

A.—I can't say just when but sometime in 1924. I just heard it as a rumour and I went to Mayor Dawson who was a close friend of several of the shareholders, at least the controlling shareholders, and I told him what I had heard and I said if this business is ever offered for sale I would like to have an opportunity of buying it and I asked him to get in touch with them and find out, and if it was so to get their terms and let me know. He took it up with them at the time and advised me that they had no notion then of disposing of the business. I heard nothing more about it until some time in May or early June of 1925 when I went up to the Soo of a week-end and on Monday morning, Major Dawson called me up and said: "This business is going to be sold and it is going to be sold to-day. You had better come down to my office if you are interested." And I went down to his office about 11 o'clock, which was the first I knew of price or terms or anything else that they wanted.

We discussed terms and payments and I left them by telling them it was impossible for me on that short notice for me to give them a decision in the matter. However, at their directors meeting that afternoon they did not dispose of the business and they came back at six o'clock in the evening and made a proposal to me and they wanted a snap verdict on it, and I asked them time to come back to Toronto in order to consult the manager of the Royal Bank to see if I could finance it. However, I found I could not get the time I required and I thought the matter over for about an hour and I accepted a proposition and I purchased the entire stock both capital stock and the physical stock and assets of the company for a certain sum of money with a very small payment down and agreed to give notes spread over the year to cover the balance, that is the balance of the capital stock, and to pay them outright for the coal stock, or, that is, for the coal that had been put in stock by them since the opening of navigation that year.

Q.—Had they a dock?

A.—They had a dock and we concluded the deal on that basis. I arranged with the Royal Bank the following morning for a loan of $50,000 to pay them for the coal they had brought in since the opening of navigation and for which they had to pay out ready money. I then instructed Mr. Atkin of the Soo, who is my personal solicitor, and instructed him to endeavour to sell about 45 to 48 per cent. of the capital stock and to sell it at a price in excess of what I paid for it because I bought it for considerably less money than par, and to sell enough to raise a certain sum of money to enable me to finance it easier, and to leave the controlling interest in my hands. And he carried that out in a matter of a day or so. As a matter of fact I had an offer of about $20,000 over and above what I paid for the stock the following morning after I purchased it from the people who were trying to buy it before I secured it.

Q.—You purchased the stock on hand. You also purchased one hundred per cent. of the stock of the company?

A.—I did.

Q.—And you have resold part of it since?

A.—It has been resold to residents of the Soo, and their names are all recorded, or should be, in the Department here.

Q.—You have only had the company since June?

A.—That is right.

Q.—And you are one of the officers?

A.—Yes, although I have never been to the yard but once for ten minutes since I owned it.

Q.—The questions seem to be directed at whether you or your family secured a controlling interest in the company. You have told me that is correct?

A.—We have, yes.

Q.—Then, he asks: "Has the said coal company a contract with the Lake Superior Pulp & Paper Company for coal?

A.—That is the Sault Ste. Marie Coal Company?

Q.—I suppose so?

A.—The only coal the Sault Ste. Marie Coal Company sold the Lake Superior Pulp & Paper Company is about 2,800 tons that they supplied for the fuelling of their tugs. Previous to last year the paper company's tugs had had their fuel at a dock over in Soo, Michigan, because there was no dock in Sault Ste. Marie that could accommodate them, but there are docks to fuel large vessels, but not satisfactory to fuel small tugs, and the manager arranged with the manager of the tugs to fuel them at our docks at the same price, of course, which is standard lake price for fuel, we to put up bins and equipment, and the result is we are fuelling them in Sault Ste. Marie, Ontario, instead of having them fuelled in Sault Ste. Marie, Michigan.

Q.—That was the extent of the business?

A.—That is all.

Q.—Had you anything to do with that contract?

A.—Absolutely nothing.

Q.—Did you get anything directly or indirect for it?

A.—Nothing whatever. As a matter of fact it is not a contract, Mr. Finlayson, and the arrangement does not apply to power companies' tugs alone. The equipment is now installed and any tug that can be accommodated by appliances such as we have can and will be fuelled.

Q.—In any case there is a fixed standard price for coal all up the river?

A.—Yes.

Q.—There are hundreds of tugs and thousands of steamers have to be coaled?

A.—Yes.

Q.—And this is a flea bite in the volume of coal?

A.—Yes.

Q.—And the price is fixed by the price at the mine?

A.—Well, there is what you might call an association fuelling price.

Q.—All the price you got was the same as the other?

A.—That is all.

Q.—But by putting in appliances and fixing the docks you were able to accommodate tugs in the river on the Canadian side; they used to go over and get coal on the American side?

A.—That is right.

Q.—What is the amount of the contract? You say there is no contract?

A.—No, we have supplied 2,889 tons, I think that—

Q.—That isn't large?

A.—Oh, comparatively small.

Q.—Doesn't amount to a hill of beans. Was the Lake Superior Pulp & Paper Company a successful tenderer for pulpwood limits?

A.—No, they haven't secured anything.

Q.—When and what limits? The answer, of course, is negative, nothing. Has, or had, the Minister's coal company contracts with other companies having business relations with the Department of Lands and Forests. Mr. Clarke puts it, Did the Minister have any dealings with any coal company?

A.—None whatever.

Q.—How much coal has the Minister's company supplied to the Lake Superior Pulp & Paper Company since he became its president? You gave me those figures?

A.—I don't think I gave you the figures because I don't know. If it refers to the Sault Coal & Wood Company I have given you the figures.

Q.—I must refer to them. That is what it means. What do you mean, Mr. Kemp, by the Minister's company?

MR. KEMP: It has reference to the Lyons Fuel and Supply and the other.

Q.—The only one you mention is the Sault Fuel?

MR. KEMP: Well, it speaks of companies.

Q.—The first question is, Is the Honourable James Lyons the president of the Sault Ste. Marie Coal & Wood Company, Limited. Fuel & Supply Company isn't mentioned. But they did supply—

A.—Two thousand eight hundred.

Q.—After you put in these appliances?

A.—Yes.

Q.—How much to other pulp and paper companies? Do you know whether they are supplying any other?

A.—We are strictly—the Soo Coal & Wood Company is a retail business. It has no rail connections; purely water connection.

Q.—You bring in coal by water and truck it out to local people or if a tug comes along. So that answer to that is in the negative, too?

A.—Yes.

Q.—This stock is widely held over the Soo?

A.—Yes. There are quite a number of shareholders. I think I have a list of them here.

Q.—There seem to be about fifteen outside of your family so far as I can gather. I don't want to go into them. I don't think that is public property. But what I do want to ask is, you sold the stock or part of the stock. When you acquired the whole stock you sold out part of it. Was any of it sold to people who were dealing with your Department, companies, or contractors, lumber companies?

A.—No, I don't think so.

Q.—These names seem to be names of individuals around Sault Ste. Marie?

A.—Yes.

Q.—None are lumbermen?

A.—No.

Q.—Or timber licensees?

A.—No.

Q.—Purely private company, dealing with retail coal supplies?

A.—That is right.

Q.—And as you explain they had a coal dock and they would be an extension to your business?

A.—I think they were the oldest established coal firm in the Soo.

HON. MR. RANEY: Are you putting in the list of shareholders? Do you mind my seeing it?

MR. FINLAYSON: I don't think so. If anybody wants it they can get it over in the Department.

HON. MR. RANEY: Is there any objection to my seeing it?

MR. LEWIS: Oh, there is no objection to Mr. Raney seeing it.

MR. FINLAYSON: I have no objection to any member knowing who the people are.

HON. MR. RANEY: I would rather not look at it if you mean this to be private.

MR. FINLAYSON: I think that cleans up. Perhaps I should ask a general question on that. Was there any consideration or any arrangement direct or indirect, in trust or any other way, in connection with your purchase of this

Sault Company, or any connection with your sale of stock to purchasers of it which in any way relates to any contractor with the Crown, any timber licensee or any pulp concessionaire or anybody?

A.—Absolutely none. It was just a matter of going out and getting a number of citizens to buy some stock that we would like to have associated in the business.

Q.—Not only associated in the business, but they also cut down your investment, too?

A.—Yes.

Q.—Just as material and important, often?

Q.—One other question: Mr. Kemp asks in reference to the agricultural barn at Hearst. Can you tell us about that, Mr. Lyons?

A.—Well, there is nothing much to that, Mr. Finlayson, any more than having regard for the possible agricultural developments in the locality of Hearst that I thought we ought to establish a small demonstration farm there. The Government a few years ago had set aside 800 acres of land there for an experimental farm and I think we disposed of about 600 acres of it and retained 200 acres and undertook to establish a demonstration farm there where we could educate the settlers and give them practical information, and to establish a good line of stock, both cattle, horses, hogs, and sheep, so as to improve the grade of stock in that locality and assist the settlers.

Q.—The Northern Development isn't confined to roads and bridges?

A.—Oh, no.

Q.—You build school houses?

A.—Assist.

Q.—Assist?

A.—We assist in demonstration farm work, establishment of creameries and things of that nature.

Q.—Generally, anything that would lend itself to the development of Northern Ontario?

A.—That is right.

Q.—And in connection with the policy, a previous Government had retained 800 acres?

A.—Yes.

Q.—And you went on to continue that policy and development?

A.—Yes.

Q.—What was done?

A.—Well, we engaged a superintendent to go up there and after advertising for a man and had a good many replies we engaged a Mr. Noble, who went up there and who is still there and will likely be there to carry on the work. We required a barn and we had a plan prepared and we called for tenders and the contract was let and the barn has been completed.

Q.—Who got the contract?

A.—Ed. Charters.

Q.—Has your firm, the Lyons Fuel & Supply Company, supplied any material?

A.—No, we did not supply him with one dollar's worth.

Q.—Haven't supplied him with one dollar?

A.—I have a letter from him here also confirming it.

Q.—Were tenders asked for on the barn?

A.—Yes.

Q.—And the lowest tenderer got the contract?

A.—Yes.

Q.—Carried out?

A.—Carried out.

Q.—And has it been paid for?

A.—I think so.

MR. CLARKE: What was the cost of the barn?

A.—Well, the total cost of the barn, I think, ran into about $15,000.

MR. FINLAYSON: You see it in the answer?

A.—The barn is rather large, Mr. Clarke, because of the fact we wanted to give special attention to the cattle end.

Q.—I think you were introducing stock and improving the grades, bulls for service, and all that?

A.—The intention was to keep breeding stock that would improve the herds of the settlers with practically no cost to them.

Q.—So that you say your firm supplied absolutely nothing?

A.—Nothing whatever.

Q.—I don't know what it is directed at. I don't know what the insinuation or innuendo is. Have you made any money out of it whatever?

A.—No, no, none.

Q.—Handled in a business way?

A.—No.

THE CHAIRMAN: You asked Mr. Lyons if it was handled in a business way and he said "No."

MR. FINLAYSON: I asked you if it was handled in the regular business way of the Department?

A.—Yes.

Q.—Tenders were called for?

A.—Yes.

Q.—The lowest tenderer got the contract?

A.—Yes.

Q.—Gave security?

A.—Yes.

Q.—Carried out?

A.—Yes, no trouble about it.

W. E. N. SINCLAIR, K.C., examining.

Q.—You were Minister of Lands and Forests until March 1?

A.—Yes.

Q.—And on that day you filed your resignation with the Prime Minister?

A.—Yes.

Q.—And it was accepted and appears in the Journals of the House?

A.—That is right.

Q.—And in your resignation you say that the numerous questions placed upon the Order Paper and so on are evidently placed there with the idea of establishing in the minds of the public, by inference, that the position of Minister of Lands and Forests on the Cabinet is being used to the advantage of the Lyons Fuel & Supply Company, Limited, and the questions on the Order Paper created that inference?

A.—Take the Hearst barn we have just dealt with, for one, Mr. Sinclair.

Q.—Well, in what way did any of those questions create an inference that you had profited or your company had profited in any way?

A.—Why, it would give the impression in my opinion that these contracts were being let to certain contractors, some, no doubt, who were favourable to the Lyons Fuel Company and because of that we were getting business out of it.

Q.—But wouldn't the answer to those questions in the regular way in the House have shown the facts?

A.—Well, there are some of those questions if I answered them I would have to give detailed information as to our business transactions. For instance, in connection with the Hearst barn we sold nothing. But in reference to the Lake Superior Pulp & Paper Company I would have to give details in order to answer.

Q.—Details as to what?

A.—Well, our business transactions.

Q.—Details of the transactions of the Lyons Fuel & Supply Company with the Northern Development Branch?

A.—No, no, with companies who are licensees of the Department.

Q.—Only with companies?

A.—Yes.

Q.—Well, what objection would there be to that?

A.—Well, so far as I am concerned, I would not do it, not for any position in the gift of man.

Q.—Wasn't it a matter of public interest?

A.—I would not say so.

Q.—Well, then, your company had been doing business with Government contractors?

A.—Yes.

Q.—No question about that. And until the questions were asked on the order paper you said nothing about it in the House?

A.—About?

Q.—Your dealings with Government contractors?

A.—Oh, no.

Q.—And you didn't resign until the questions were asked?

A.—That is right.

Q.—And the reason you give for resigning is that you would have had to divulge transactions between yourself and contractors with the Government of which you were a member?

A.—As a matter of fact, Mr. Sinclair, when the first two questions, one relating to supplies sold McNamara Brothers in connection with Wellington Street, and the question in connection with supplies sold Fitzpatrick, the contractor on the aerodrome, I took it up with my office to get that information, with the intention of giving it to the House. I received that, I think, on a Tuesday morning, and on Wednesday or Thursday, before the answer would be given on Friday, other questions came up which went deeper into the matter and, as I thought, would indicate that with the information I did give would divulge the business transactions of the Lyons Fuel Company, and I immediately made up my mind I was not going to do it.

Q.—The questions, in other words, gave indication of an outbreak of an epidemic of questions?

A.—Well, an outbreak that in my opinion had nothing to do with the Provincial Department.

Q.—But had to do with dealings of your company with companies having direct relations with the Government?

A.—Yes.

Q.—And you were a Minister of the Government?

A.—Yes.

Q.—And you didn't want to divulge these dealings, and so you resigned.

A.—That is it in a nutshell.

Q.—Now you say that the business relations of your company extend from the Atlantic to the Pacific?

A.—Yes.

Q.—Your head office is at the Sault.   Have you any other offices?

A.—No.

Q.—That is the only office.   And what proportion of your business is outside of Northern Ontario?

A.—Well, not very much.

Q.—Most of it is in Northern Ontario.   And your chief business, as you say in your resignation, is with mining companies, lumbering companies, pulp and paper companies, municipal corporations and the general public?

A.—Yes.

Q.—And mining companies, lumber companies and pulp and paper companies have special dealings at all times with the Government?

A.—Well, not particularly mining companies.   There may be an occasional mining company interested in a waterpower.   Outside of that we would not have any dealings.

Mr. Finlayson: Q.—You mean the Department. Mr. Sinclair said Government.   The witness has answered for the Department.

Mr. Sinclair: Yes. Of these five, which are the chief customers?   There are five classes there?

A.—Of the Lyons Fuel & Supply Company?   Off hand, I would say perhaps the mining companies.

Q.—And next?

A.—Pulp and paper.

Q.—And next.

A.—The lumbering.

Q.—And after that?

A.—General contractors.   Although, if you were to group the general contractors, they would probably, combined, be more than the others are.

Q.—Well, general public and general contractors would come under one head?

A.—Well, that would be much greater than others.

Q.—Would contractors be greater than the ordinary general public dealing with your company?

A.—That is rather difficult to say, because general contractors combined buy a great deal of material.

Q.—And the contractors which you said are largest contractors receive contracts from the Government?

A.—Oh, no.

Q.—Well, what other contractors are there?

A.—Contractors who build schools, town halls, put in sewer systems and do general contracting work.

Q.—How do these contracts compare in volume with road contracts?

A.—For instance, you build a big school and it costs $300,000; that is a pretty substantial contract.

Q. That would be built by a municipality, and not the Northern Development Branch at all.   And no grant from the Government for these schools in Northern Ontario?

A.—Yes.

Q.—A substantial grant?

A.—Yes, but I am just using that as an instance.

Q.—Then your chief business, as you have said, is with these different concerns in these different proportions. And your company had business dealings also with the Northern Ontario Development Branch?

A.—Yes.

Q.—And your company had dealings with companies who had contracts with the Northern Development?

A.—Yes.

Q.—And your company had dealings with companies in search of Government contracts?

A.—Yes, no doubt.

Q.—And pulp and paper companies dealing with the Government?

A.—No doubt.

Q.—So business with your company was largely interlocked with the whole development of the north country?

A.—Quite so.

Q.—Now do you remember last session the Prime Minister referred to this matter of shareholders in companies ceasing to do business through their companies with the Government?

A.—Yes.

Q.—And you say that "As far as I was concerned I would undertake to see no further business was transacted by the Lyons Fuel & Supply Company, Limited, with the Government while I was a member of the House."

A.—Yes.

Q.—And you notified the company accordingly?

A.—I did.

Q.—What notice did you give?

A.—That letter that I read.

Mr. Finlayson: He read the letter to Mr. Fullerton, and also to his own firm.

Mr. Sinclair: Q.—Were dealings with the Government discontinued from receipt of that letter?

A.—Yes, they were.

Q.—And dealings with the Northern Development Branch?

A.—Yes.

Q.—And with Government contractors?

A.—No.

Q.—You did not cease dealing with those who had contracts with the Government?

A.—There was no reference made to Government contractors in the House, either to me or outside the House.

Q.—Did your company cease doing business in pursuance of the notice?

A.—Yes, they did.

Q.—Nothing further was done from the date some time in March of last year?

A.—You asked for some information, and I have it here. On January 20th, 1925, we supplied two yards of gravel, and I think the last thing previous to that was November 22nd, 1924, and then they happened to get two yards of gravel on January 20th. The statement I made in the House was perhaps February or March.

15 J

Q.—Well, following your resignation, you say, "Where a well-established business has been built up through years of effort with large industrial concerns, to discontinue such a business would bring disastrous results, and you will also realize, I hope, that to comply with the unprecedented requests and submit to the public the business transactions of any established business with its customers would be just as disastrous." You felt in your resignation that to discontinue this business would hurt the firm?

A.—Well, I will give you an instance. We had been doing a substantial business every year since 1915 with the Lake Superior Pulp & Paper Company and Spanish River Pulp & Paper Company. Perhaps the outstanding reason was our location. They are at Sault Ste. Marie and so are we. And I would not sever my connection with those firms for any position in the Provincial House.

MR. FINLAYSON: They were the corporation you grew up with?

A.—Yes.

MR. SINCLAIR: Q.—If you discontinued these business relations in 1925, why any fear of these questions asked upon the Order Paper?

A.—We did not discontinue business.

Q.—I thought you said you gave notice to your company and they did discontinue business?

A.—Only in so far as doing business with the Government was concerned.

Q.—That would be limited to the Northern Development?

A.—The Provincial Secretary's Department or Public Works Department; we have supplied coal to the Public Works Department, for the jail at the Sault, Hydro at the Sault, etc.

MR. CLARKE: Q.—During 1925?

A.—Doing it for years. But after I made that statement in the House, that statement was intended to cover and did cover any business relations with the Government in any department from that time.

MR. FINLAYSON: But Mr. Sinclair thought he meant he was discontinuing with the Pulp and Paper Company and Power Company.

MR. SINCLAIR: Q.—Who asked you to discontinue business relations with the pulp and paper companies or any contractors?

A.—Nobody asked me, but these questions that came up indicated I would have to expose my business relations with these companies, which I refused to do.

Q.—And you say: "As I cannot undertake to discontinue the business relations of the Lyons Fuel & Supply Company, Limited, with its established customers, I beg to tender herewith my resignation."

A.—That is right; that is the whole thing in a nutshell.

Q.—All you had ceased doing then was dealing directly with the Government departments?

A.—Yes, that is what I intended to do.

Q.—By last year's Public Accounts, the business I think was $14,000 in the Northern Development Branch?

A.—That was the fiscal year 1923-4.

Q.—And that is all that you were asked to discontinue?

A.—Quite so.

Q.—And that is all you did discontinue?

A.—Yes.

Q.—And yet in the fact of these questions on relations which you were not asked to discontinue you resigned?

A.—Yes, that is right; no other reason, either.

Q.—And what business transactions with your customers would you be obliged to disclose, due to the questions which were asked?

A.—Well, for instance, I do not recall all the questions now, but I think one asked how much coal we had sold paper companies.

Q.—What objection could you have to answering that question?

A.—If I answered that question, the next would be, how much cement and gravel and perhaps oakum, we sold them?

Q.—Couldn't you have done like the Prime Minister—said this did not relate to the public interest and decline to answer?

A.—Perhaps I am a little too independent for that. I had made up my mind to quit, and I quit, and it didn't take more than one second, either.

Q.—You had not thought of resigning before the first of March?

A.—Well, before the preceding Thursday.

Q.—The reason was, you did not want to disclose the relationships between your company and the companies with which your company was doing business?

A.—That is the whole thing in a nutshell.

Q.—You did not want to disclose prices at which you sold goods to contractors, for instance?

A.—No.

Q.—Nor the price at which you sold goods and materials to pulp companies?

A.—That is right.

Q.—And although these people were doing business with the Government, and getting concessions from the Government?

MR. FINLAYSON: Not entirely. This first question is all relating to this street.

MR. SINCLAIR: I wasn't thinking of the street; something bigger than that.

MR. FINLAYSON: They wanted to find out how much he charged for cement going into the street.

MR. SINCLAIR: Q.—You objected to letting the public know what you were charging, for instance, the McNamara Construction Company for certain material?

A.—Certainly.

Q.—Although the McNamara Construction Company were getting all the contracts on the road up there?

A.—No, they were not.

Q.—Well, nearly.

A.—We did not sell the McNamara Construction Company one dollar's worth that went into a Government contract.

Q.—Now we are getting information.

MR. FINLAYSON: No, that all came out yesterday.

MR. SINCLAIR: Q.—And yet you resigned when a question was asked about this very thing?

A.—I certainly did?

Q.—You could have answered and said you sold nothing to the McNamara Construction Company?

A.—I could have, yes.

Q.—Well, then, we haven't found out so far what particular questions were devised to create any suspicion.

A.—I think the general tone of every question is.

Q.—What particular question? You say you are all right with McNamaras. How about Soo Pulp & Paper Company there?

A.—We have been doing business with them since I think about 1915; every year substantial business. I think our average over ten years is something over $40,000 a year, and our average with the Spanish River over the same period is about $62,000 or $65,000 a year.

Q.—Now in the statement which was read in the House by you, along with your resignation, you say that you acquiesced in the position taken by the Prime Minister when he intimated that members of the House who had substantial holdings in joint stock companies should avoid doing business with the Province. It only had relations to dealing with the Province?

A.—Yes, no suggestion was made to me by anyone that would lead me to think otherwise.

Q.—You say you never for a moment entertained the idea that dealings between your company and contractors with the Government would be challenged?

A.—Yes.

Q.—What do you mean by that?

A.—I never for a moment thought anybody would suggest because, for instance, our firm at Sault Ste. Marie, of which I am a shareholder, happened to sell some goods to a contractor who had a contract for building a Government road at Sudbury or North Bay or Cobalt, or anything else, could be considered a matter of wrongdoing.

Q.—Well, who let the contracts, for instance, for building roads in Northern Ontario?

A.—I did, in my Department.

Q.—You were the responsible Minister to let contracts for building roads?

A.—Yes.

Q.—And when a contractor had secured the contract for building a road, you did not see that there was anything improper in yourself turning around and selling this contractor material through your company?

A.—Not myself. Nothing wrong about it, in my opinion.

Q.—And the largest shareholder in the Lyons Company was your wife?

MR. GRAVES: Q.—These contracts, Mr. Lyons, were all let under tender?

A.—Oh, yes.

MR. SINCLAIR: You were the man who let the tender?

A.—Oh, yes.

Q.—You advised So-and-so he was the successful tenderer?

A.—Quite so.

Q.—You felt there was nothing improper in your company dealing with them to whom you as Minister had let the contract?

A.—Quite so, and I still think so.

MR. FINLAYSON: Although, Mr. Sinclair, it may not affect the principle of your question, he did not, as a matter of fact, supply anything to these contractors on the road.

MR. SINCLAIR: Well, probably we will get that now. Q.—Did you supply any material from the company to anyone having contracts with the Government?

A.—We did not supply anything to the McNamara Construction; we did not supply anything to the contractor of the Hearst barn on the North Bay-Cobalt highway. On one section of it that went to Angus & Taylor, out of some $32,000 worth of supplies we sold them $1,342. The Grant Brothers, who had another contract, out of $22,000 worth of supplies purchased by them, we supplied $1,372.

Q.—Who did you supply to?

A.—I am trying to tell you. Grant Bros. in one case, and Angus & Taylor in the other case, and M. L. McLean, who purchased about $11,000 worth of supplies and purchased $700 from us. He had a contract. Then there was Walsh Construction Company which purchased about $12,000 worth, as I recall and about $1,300 from us, and some other firm that bought $11,000 worth and just purchased about $700 from us.

Q.—Then in relation to these questions which were asked regarding the Lyons Company having business with, you say now the company did not have business with them to any great extent?

A.—Yes.

Q.—And still you resigned from a position in the Cabinet for fear you would disclose business relations?

A.—Absolutely.

Q.—Then why couldn't you answer the questions by saying "No" or giving the figures you do to-day?

A.—I would not be an amusement box to anybody to that extent.

Q.—How would that be an amusement box?

A.—It is nothing else, in my opinion.

Q.—Questions were asked on the Order Paper in relation to dealings of the Lyons Fuel & Supply Company with certain contractors?

A.—And pulp and lumber companies they covered the whole field.

Q.—And you say here to-day your dealings with them were very small, and still you resigned?

A.—I did.

Q.—And your reason for resigning is that you did not want to disclose business relations with these companies, which never existed?

A.—Absolutely.

Q.—Then there is no reason for your resignation?

A.—In my opinion there was. There was no legitimate reason, no.

Q.—Taking the wording of your resignation, the inference in the questions, there is nothing in the matters aimed at in the questions?

A.—That is right.

Q.—And still you resigned?

A.—I did.

Q.—For fear you would have to disclose business relations that never existed.

A.—Well, of course they did exist to some extent.

Q.—Existed only to a slight extent.

MR. FINLAYSON: With the contractors, but very largely with the pulp companies and other companies.

MR. SINCLAIR: Just leave me alone.

MR. FINLAYSON: Just let me clear it up. Mr. Sinclair is referring to one thing—

MR. SINCLAIR: I have limited myself to contractors, so far. He said that was the only reason.

MR. FINLAYSON: No, no; he said dealings with the Crown.

THE CHAIRMAN: It is unfortunate Mr. Sinclair was not here during the whole thing.

MR. SINCLAIR: I felt the whole thing was so futile and useless I could not waste the time.

THE CHAIRMAN: Well, most of us feel that way.

MR. SINCLAIR: You resigned because certain questions were placed on the Order Paper. These, you say, carried the inference your company had had dealings with those contracting with the Government. You say to-day that your Company's dealings with these having contracts with the Government are very limited?

A.—You are speaking of road contracts?

MR. FINLAYSON: There are dozens of kinds; the lumber company has a contract.

MR. SINCLAIR: No, they lease limits.

MR. FINLAYSON: Well, that is a contract, and under present conditions very big contracts. The paper companies and mining companies and power companies have.

THE CHAIRMAN: Mr. Lyons made it clear he was ceasing his relations with some particular companies he had been doing business with for a long time.

MR. SINCLAIR: In relation to any company or concern having road contracts, you say that your company's dealings with them were very limited?

A.—Very limited. In comparison with their purchases it was very small.

Q.—Did any of the questions on the order paper in relation to road contractors and your company have anything to do with your resignation?

A.—I took the whole of the questions there together, Mr. Sinclair.

Q.—How great an effect in bringing you to this decision had the questions relating to road contracts?

Q.—Just as much effect in a sense as any other question. The principle was this, in my mind, that I was not going to divulge my company's business relations with any contractors or pulp company or lumber company.

Q.—In the House—but you are doing so here to-day.

A.—To clear the air, and when I get through I will be done.

Q.—In relation to timber companies, what contracts had the Lyons company with any timber company?

A.—I gave the figures very fully the other day.

Q.—Well, were they extensive?

A.—No, small. Roughly it is this: out of 435 licensees or concessionaires in the Province, I think our company is doing business with a total of about thirty, and out of these thirty, something like twenty are new customers, taken on since 1923, and their total purchases since 1923 to the end of 1925 is in the aggregate about $26,000, so that it is very small.

Q.—Then in regard to timber companies having dealings with the Government, your relations are very similar to your dealings with road contractors and otherwise?

A.—Yes, they are.

Q.—Now what other line of Government contractors is there up there with whom you have had dealings?

A.—Well, outside of road contractors, pulp concessionaries and timber licensees, there are none except there might be an odd power company. There is the Abitibi Power Company, for instance, and perhaps some mining companies; I think the International Nickel Company had a lease of power, and we did considerable business with them.

MR. FINLAYSON: The Metagami Company.

MR. SINCLAIR: Am I right in this, in regard to road contracts, timber contracts or any other contracts in which contractors would be dealing with the Government, your dealings with all these contractors have been very limited?

A.—Yes.

Q.—And it is only in relation to these dealings and the inference created by these questions, that you have resigned?

A.—That is right; absolutely.

Q.—And the reason for your resigning was that you did not want to disclose these small dealings which you had had in this limited way with these different companies;

A.—That is absolutely the very reason why I resigned, and there is no other reason for it.

Q.—Why could not that information have been given in answer to these questions?

A.—I suppose it could have been, but I would not do it, Mr. Sinclair, not for any position in the gift of man.

Q.—Now you say, in paragraph 8 (page 123, Votes and Proceedings)—"When in due course the Prime Minister conferred with me as to what had transpired, without hesitancy I emphasized the necessity of continuing these long established business relations and to sell to such organizations as it had always done unless the business were to be wound up or ultimately go to ruin." Then the Prime Minister conferred with you about your dealings in Northern Ontario?

A.—Yes.

Q.—And what you almost described as petty dealings?

A.—Yes.

Q.—And you emphasized the necessity of continuing this small business?

A.—Well, I don't consider business with the Lake Superior Paper Company or Spanish River Pulp & Paper Company as small business. When I made reference to $26,000, I spoke of new customers.

Q.—Well, how much business do you do in a year with the Lake Superior Pulp & Paper Company?

A.—Our average for the last ten years is about $40,000 a year, and with the Spanish River about $65,000; some years up a little, and some down.

Q.—Then it was in particular relation to these two large concerns that your trouble arose?

A.—Yes, and in every company we were doing business with.

Q.—But you have already said you only did business in a small way with these other companies?

A.—Yes.

Q.—So that these two large companies which you have named were the especial ones that got you into trouble?

A.—Yes.

Q.—And it was these dealings you did not want to disclose to the public?

A.—Along with any others.

Q.—But the others were so small.

MR. FINLAYSON: It is the principle of the thing. Next day Mr. Kemp would ask, what does he charge for cement, and how much does he make on it?

MR. SINCLAIR: And the Government have it in their power to say they won't answer.

MR. FINLAYSON: And Mr. Lyons has it in his power to say he won't, and get out.

MR. LYONS: Perhaps the stand taken by me was so unusual it is hard to believe.

MR. SINCLAIR: Probably something to that. At any rate, you told the Prime Minister it was necessary for you to go on doing business?

A.—I did.

MR. FINLAYSON: Business first.

MR. SINCLAIR: Business first and the State next?

MR. LYONS: A.—That is right.

Q.—Although you had been doing this ever since you became Minister?

A.—Oh, yes.

Q.—And no complaint made before these questions were asked?

A.—None whatever.

Q.—There were a few questions asked last year, weren't there?

A.—I think not.

Q.—At any rate, you were perfectly satisfied to go on and do business with these people until these questions were asked?

A.—Oh, yes.

Q.—Did you bring it to the attention of the Prime Minister, or did he bring it to your attention?

A.—It came up in a discussion as to the answers to these questions, and I simply said, "If I have to answer these questions I will quit."

Q.—And did you quit right there?

A.—I did on Monday.

Q.—And these questions were being discussed at the week-end before?

A.—That is right.

Q.—Did the Prime Minister tell you that wasn't good business to do?

MR. FINLAYSON: That is not evidence. My friend knows it is not legal evidence.

MR. SINCLAIR: It is if he wants to answer.

MR. FINLAYSON: It is not evidence under the rules of law. It is hearsay, and then it is objectionable as being communication between two ministers as to policy of a department.

MR. LYONS: There was nothing between the Prime Minister and I that I would hesitate to repeat here.

MR. SINCLAIR: At any rate, you told him you were going on to do business, and it was inevitable that you should resign?

A.—That is right.

Q.—Well, now you say you desire the Public Accounts should investigate and investigate fully everything. Why were you anxious that the Public Accounts should investigate it and not that a simple answer should be given on the Order Paper in the usual way, in the House?

A.—Well, I am getting out of this thing, and the members of this House and the public will be able to get the absolute facts, and in a way that will not be misunderstood, and when I go out of here I will go out with a clean bill of health.

Q.—Without any particular reason for the resignation?

A.—Absolutely, other than I have stated.

Q.—Except that the Prime Minister must have thought these business relations were not just the thing?

A.—It was me who made up my mind about resigning, not the Prime Minister.

Q.—But not until the questions were asked?

A.—After the questions were asked.

Q.—You never considered for a moment there was anything improper in these business transactions?

A.—Absolutely not, and I don't now.

Q.—Then why did you resign?

A.—Simply because I refused to give the information regarding my business or my company's business transactions with any customers of ours.

Q.—But you are giving it to-day?

A.—Yes, I am giving it to-day; we will clear the air.

Q.—But up to the first of March you refused to give the information, and now you are willing to give it.

MR. FINLAYSON: He is giving what he thinks is necessary and proper.

THE CHAIRMAN: You realize the answers given to these questions is only part of the information. This will give the people all the facts.

MR. SINCLAIR: And give the fact that you resigned from the Cabinet, although you thought you had not done anything wrong?

A.—Absolutely, and don't think so yet.

Q.—Who did think you had done anything wrong?

A.—I don't know as anybody did, in particular.

Q.—Then why should you resign if nobody thought there was anything wrong?

A.—Just as I said, I would not divulge the dealings of my company with any of its customers, on the floor of the House.

Q.—You would not, in other words, give a limited answer to a specific question on the floor of the House, but you would give a full answer to unlimited questions in the Public Accounts Committee?

A.—This was my view; if I would answer these questions they would simply be followed by a lot more that would go just a little deeper, and ask for information that was really embarrassing.

Q.—Why could the information be embarrassing if there was nothing wrong in the relationships?

A.—Well, the principle of a man having to dilvulge his business transactions to suit members of the House is something I would not adhere to.

Q.—If the questions got too far afield, you would be justified in saying they had nothing to do with Government business.

A.—Well, perhaps.

Q.—That stand has been taken time and again this last session.

A.—Well, I may have established a precedent.

Q.—They are not trying to get rid of the precedent, are they?

MR. FINLAYSON: He cannot be disturbed; he is well settled.

MR. SINCLAIR: You have given us every reason why you resigned?

A.—Yes, positively, Mr. Sinclair, the only reason under Heaven I resigned for—absolutely.

Q.—That you had been doing nothing wrong?

A.—Nothing wrong whatever.

Q.—Didn't think it was wrong, don't think so now, dealings in a limited way with road contractors?

A.—In a limited and legitimate way, both.

Q.—And dealings in a larger way with the Spanish River Company and the other pulp company up there. Now your company, Mr. Lyons, has been organized about 12 or 13 years?

A.—The charter was taken in 1916, but we had been operating from 1912 without a charter.

Q.—And since your charter, 1915, have you had any increase in your capitalization?

A.—No, there has not been any change in the stock issue at all, and there has been no change in ownership outside the family. I mean, my boy, for instance, was given a few shares, but no shares have been transferred outside of the family.

Q.—Mr. Atkins, the crown attorney, is he a shareholder?

A.—No.

Q.—Mr. Goodwin?

A.—Mr. Goodwin has, I think, 49 per cent. of the preferred and about 35 per cent. of common, and has had it from practically a year or two years after the company was organized.

Q.—In 1916, what line of business did you follow?

A.—Fuel and builders' supplies.

Q.—And how large premises did you occupy?

A.—In 1916, I can hardly say. When we commenced in 1912 and 1913 we had three small lots and a small office about 12 by 14, and at the present time I think there is approximately seven acres of ground and general plant and equipment.

Q.—In what years has the development taken place?

A.—It has just been gradual. I cannot say that one year has been much more than another. Almost every year we have purchased two or three additional lots and perhaps put up some buildings or other, and so on.

Q.—And you have been president throughout, both before aud after you were elected a member of the Legislature?

A.—Yes.

Q.—Can you tell us how much business you did with the Government in the year 1920?

A.—No, I cannot.

Q.—Were you doing it on any extensive scale?

A.—I don't know what we were doing in any particular year without looking it up, but I think you will find, if you look it up, we were supplying the bulk of material from—

Q.—I have looked up some of them, and I don't want you to speak unless you can give me the figures.

MR. FINLAYSON: Perhaps Clarkson's firm will be able to give the exact figures.

MR. SINCLAIR: We might leave it this way, if Mr. Lyons before the Committee gets through can give this, and can give us a statement of the business the Lyons Company did with the Northern Development Branch in the years 1920-25 inclusive.

A.—Or previous, 1919?

Q.—No, 1920 is far enough. And without going into too much detail, Mr. Lyons, if you could indicate what lines these were; I don't want to pick on an axe, and all that, but in a general way. And in the same way, I would like to have the information as to the business done with the Lyons Fuel & Supply Company with companies or contractors dealing with the Government in these same years.

MR. FINLAYSON: When you say "contracts," do you include pulp companies?

MR. SINCLAIR: Divide them if you wish, or lump them.

MR. FINLAYSON: We have gone over them pretty well.

THE CHAIRMAN: You will find it in the evidence; it will be ready by Monday.

MR. LYONS: I was going to say, Mr. Clarkson will exhaust that pretty carefully, Mr. Sinclair, and his statement would be available quicker than mine, and be more accurate, if that is satisfactory.

MR. SINCLAIR: I would suggest a special direction be given the Clarkson firm to get this specific information in tabulated form.

THE CHAIRMAN: It has already been given.

MR. SINCLAIR: That is, relations between the Lyons Fuel & Supply Company and the Government in 1920-21-22-23-24-25, and then the business done with the Lyons Fuel & Supply Company and companies or contractors dealing with the Government in these same years, with a general indication of the lines of goods sold. I can understand we cannot go into too much detail. So that that matter will stand for reference to the auditors, as I understand it.

MR. FINLAYSON: You want that to cover licensees and everything else, do you?

MR. SINCLAIR: Yes, you can put it together or tabulate separately, whichever way they have worked it out.

MR. LYONS: I have a copy of the license holders that was sent Mr. Nash just a few days ago, and he will have that, and he will be able to check from that the accounts we have had.

Q.—He was to go back over a period of years.

A.—And so does the list of license holders.

Q.—Now, in securing business for your house, do you have travellers on the road?

A.—Yes.

Q.—How many do you ordinarily have out?

A.—Four, I think, at the present time.

Q.—And no agents at outside points, or just these travellers?

A.—We have one traveller located at North Bay. That is his headquarters, and he operates out of there.

Q.—And the others operate from the Soo, travelling through the country from time to time, and that is the means of your getting business from—

A.—Anybody. Of course, a great deal of our business up there is with retail merchants. We wholesale to retail merchants.

Q.—You get business on your reputation—like I do?

A.—Yes, only I don't get as much for it.

Q.—I don't know about that. I have to work harder for what I get, that is all.

MR. FINLAYSON: Q.—Do you want these mutual compliments on the record?

MR. SINCLAIR: I don't care. Nothing like advertising yourself.

MR. FINLAYSON: You didn't give your address, that is all.

MR. SINCLAIR: Q.—Now, as Minister of Lands, you have, of course, let contracts?

A.—Yes.

Q.—Contracts for roads?

A.—Yes.

Q.—And buildings?

Q.—And bridges, I suppose, and all that goes into development?

A.—And timber limits and waterpowers.

Q.—And while you have been Minister you have supplied materials to these people to whom you have let contracts?

A.—Our firm has, yes.

MR. RANEY: Might I enquire—something was said about a sitting this afternoon. You cannot sit this afternoon, can you?

MR. FINLAYSON: I am anxious to get on. Why not sit from 2 to 3?

THE CHAIRMAN: Why not sit through until 1.30 and then adjourn?

MR. FINLAYSON: What I am anxious to do particularly is to arrange for witnesses next week. If Mr. Lyons is left over, you won't know what witnesses to have for next week.

MR. SINCLAIR: About to-night, Mr. Finlayson, I would not be here.

MR. FINLAYSON: Wouldn't you be through by 4.30?

MR. SINCLAIR: I hope so.

MR. FINLAYSON: Then let us go on to-night.

THE CHAIRMAN: A schedule of meetings has been drawn up, starting this morning, as near as we can in connection with the House work. We thought we would adjourn from this morning until Monday evening at eight, and then go ahead on Tuesday, either in the morning or between sessions in the afternoon, and carry the thing along.

MR. FINLAYSON: Might I point out the difficulty we are running into. We have a list of about twelve witnesses on this matter, I would think, and they are scattered all over the north country. I would like very much to clean up with Mr. Lyons; sit as long as necessary, early or any other time, and clean it up so as, say, on Monday evening we can start in on the other line. Mr. Sinclair says he will be through this afternoon. If Mr. Raney prefers to go on to-morrow, all right, but if you prefer to sit Monday morning or Monday night, let us start on that branch of it and we can lay out a programme.

MR. RANEY: What is your suggestion, Mr. Chairman?

THE CHAIRMAN: My suggestion is to sit through to-day as late as we can, at the convenience of the various members interested, and adjourn from to-day until Monday evening at 8 o'clock, and hold a meeting Monday evening, and perhaps between morning committee meeting and afternoon session of the House, and then our regular meeting on Wednesday morning. We won't be able to hold meetings outside of Wednesday or Thursday evenings, because the House will probably be sitting, but we will fit in as many meetings as we can next week.

MR. FINLAYSON: I have no objection, but I am anxious to lay out our witnesses for next week. I would like to be able to see this done this week, and then you can have whoever you want, McNamara Brothers or whoever it is, but some have to be brought down from the Sault, and it takes time.

THE CHAIRMAN: They can be summoned for Wednesday morning.

MR. FINLAYSON: We can sit to-night.

MR. SINCLAIR: Better find out from members of the Committee how many would be here.

THE CHAIRMAN: I have been polling the Committee as well as I could, and Friday night is a bad night. Most of them want to go home. They do not want to meet to-night.

MR. FINLAYSON: Friday night meetings won't hurt anybody who is living here or will stay, and we will get a quorum all right. The number taking an interest is comparatively limited. It is not that I want to press it, but what I want to do is to say when we adjourn this week we will start next week on the rest of it, the McNamaras or Fitzpatrick have got to be brought down.

MR. RANEY: You can arrange for next week's programme very easily, I think. I suggest now that Mr. Sinclair conclude his examination and I will be prepared to go on this evening, if the Committee is willing to stay. I have an engagement now, and if you will excuse me, Mr. Sinclair will complete his examination.

Mr. FINLAYSON: The understanding is Mr. Sinclair will finish now and we will go on at eight o'clock, and you can go ahead as long as you like. Are you going to call the Committee to-night?

THE CHAIRMAN: That is to be settled.

Mr. FISHER: There will be a lot of us won't be here to-night.

Mr. FINLAYSON: We can get a quorum, and we have got to get ahead. There are witnesses from all over Northern Ontario, and to-day Mr. Raney has given an order for witnesses from New York, and there are other matters to be disposed of.

Mr. FISHER: Is there any reason Mr. Lyons has to finish? Can't he stand aside?

Mr. FINLAYSON: Yes, if we devote this week to Mr. Lyons, surely we can start in on other witnesses next week. After Clarkson's report is in, Mr. Sinclair may want to ask him again.

THE CHAIRMAN: At any rate, Mr. Raney, we will advise you this afternoon whether it is to-night or Monday, and if it is to-night you will be available?

Mr. RANEY: All right.

Mr. SINCLAIR: Q.—You were saying that when you were Minister of Lands and Forests, you did supply materials to those who had received Government contracts on roads, etc.?

Mr. LYONS: A.—Our company, yes.

Q.—And your company supplied goods to those having pulp concessions and timber licenses?

A.—Yes.

Q.—And your company supplied materials, while you were Minister, to pulp companies and lumber companies who had received contracts from the Government?

A.—Yes.

Q.—And you are going to get me a statement before the Committee gets through of the extent of the business covering these periods that I have mentioned?

THE CHAIRMAN: We have sent word already.

Mr. SINCLAIR: Then I will drop that. Have you a man by the name of Prescott?

A.—Yes.

Q.—What is his business?

A.—He is one of the salesmen.

A.—And before he went to you?

A.—A salesman.

Q.—For what?

A.—He was with the Murray-Alexander people, selling roofing, I think, for a number of years.

Q.—Yes, and what does he sell for you?

A.—Anything we have to sell.

Q.—All your line. And do you handle oil in your business?

A.—No.

Q.—He was with the Murray Oil Company, wasn't he?

A.—No, they are not an oil company; they are roofing. They may sell oil.

Q.—He solicits this business, as a traveller, from companies or business houses or anybody?

A.—Yes.

Q.—In your business you sell roofing?

A.—Yes.

Q.—And in the business relations of the company has the company sold roofing to any contractors having contracts with the Government?

A.—Well, that is pretty hard for me to answer, Mr. Sinclair; only in a very general way. I think last year our sales of roofing and tar paper amounted to about sixty carloads, not at one time, but certain periods, since I have been down here.

MR. FINLAYSON: Q.—They are lumbermen?

A.—We would sell the Lake Superior Power Company for their camps, which use large quantities of tar paper. As to roofs that we have put on, I know we put on the roof of the aerodrome for J. J. Fitzpatrick. I think we put a roof on up at Port Arthur for the C.P.R.; I am not sure about that, but I think we did. We bid on the roof for Backus-Brooke at Kenora, but did not get it, and do put roofs on wherever we can land the job.

MR. SINCLAIR: Q.—Did your company supply the contractor for the East Block of the Parliament Buildings?

A.—Oh, no.

MR. FINLAYSON: The reason, perhaps, is that there is no roof there yet.

MR. SINCLAIR: Well, there will be one, we hope.

Q.—Then you have a man named Wade?

A.—Yes.

Q.—What does he do?

A.—He looks after ties and wood operations. He scales and checks up on operators.

Q.—Who buys the ties?

A.—The Lyons Fuel Company—my lad, Harry.

Q.—How extensive is your business in ties?

A.—I don't suppose it amounts to more than probably $40,000 or $50,000 a year.

Q.—It is just pickup stuff, you might call it. Who buys railway ties?

A.—The C.P.R., most of them, I think.,

Q.—Any dealings with the T. & N. O.?

A.—No.

Q.—Now this Sault Coal Company that we were talking about a little while ago; that was purely a retail business, was it?

A.—Yes.

Q.—And the Lyons Fuel & Supply Company was also a retail coal business?

A.—Retail and wholesale both.

Q.—Your company was retail and wholesale, but the Sault Company was only retail?

A.—That is it.

Q.—They did not sell to the trade outside?

A.—Well, perhaps a carload of coal might be shipped to Thessalon or Bruce Mines, or some little thing like that, but not wholesalers in the sense of the term.

Q.—And what particular advantage was there in your buying this other company?

A.—Well, if you have been in the Soo you will know the Lyons Fuel Company is located in what might be considered the western end of the city, and the Sault Company in the extreme east end of the city, and it was with a view to getting a more equitable distribution at lower and more economical costs that I was anxious to get it.

Q.—And do you handle the retail business from both concerns now?

A.—Oh, yes.

Q.—Keep up two sets of offices and equipment and they run entirely separate?

A.—Entirely separate.

Q.—So that while you are carrying on the same line of business, you have the double overhead?

A.—Yes, but we have the double business.

Q.—And this Sault Coal Company is controlled by your family, similar to the Lyons Fuel & Supply Company—a controlling interest in the stock?

A.—Yes.

Q.—In the Sault Coal Company, what dealing has it had since you took it over, with companies and contractors dealing with the Government?

A.—The only business we have had outside of regular retail business has been supplying coal to the Lake Superior Pulp & Paper Company's docks to the extent of less than $3,000.

Q.—Other than that the business of the Sault Company has been limited entirely to the local trade of the Sault?

A.—No effort made, as far as I know, to do anything else.

Q.—But the other company, the Lyons Fuel & Supply Company, has been and is still handling that nature of business?

A.—The wholesale end? Oh, yes.

Q.—I did not see the list of shareholders. Is G. A. McNamara a shareholder of the Sault Coal Company?

A.—No.

Q.—Now Mr. Atkins, the Crown Attorney, is a shareholder in the Sault Coal Company, isn't he?

A.—Yes. So is Mr. Rowland, of the same firm.

Q.—He took the shares after you had purchased the company; and when was he appointed Crown Attorney?

A.—Well, less than a year ago, I think.

Q.—He was Crown Attorney when he took the shares?

A.—Oh, yes.

Q.—What other coal dealers have you in competition with you there? Are there any extensive concerns?

A.—Oh, yes; Century Coal Company operating a large coal dock and retail business, and there is the Purdy Ice Company and Mr. I. J. Downey & Sons handles a limited amount of fuel, retail only.

Q.—You remember last year in the Public Accounts an item of $14,202.58, goods sold by the Lyons Fuel & Supply Company to the Northern Development Branch?

A.—Yes.

Q.—How were these goods sold?

A.—They were purchased by the resident engineer.

Q.—How does he make these purchases? Does he go around to the stores in the Soo, or advertise, or what?

A.—Well, the most of this stuff is required in the course of a day or two or three days, and what they do is get prices from dealers in the various lines on different goods they want. Most of the stuff we supply is cement and gravel, reinforced concrete sewer pipe.

Q.—Are they bought at the office, or do the travellers bring in this business?
A.—For which?
Q.—That item, the Northern Development. You say the resident engineer—
A.—That would be done entirely by the resident engineer.
Q.—Independent of your travellers? Dealing direct with the house on this?
A.—That is right.
Q.—You say that rates are secured from other concerns besides your own?
A.—I think you will find when Mr. Lamb gives his evidence here that everything has been purchased on a competitive basis.
Q.—I suppose he will be able better to give us the evidence as to the rate these are sold?
A.—Yes.
Q.—Now there is a witness called here to give evidence by the name of Bedford, from the Soo, do you know him?
A.—He is a hardware merchant.
Q.—Retail or wholesale?
A.—Retail.
Q.—And does he have any dealing with your company?
A.—Yes, we sell him, along with the other hardware merchants up there, quantities of goods from time to time.
Q.—I notice that this year in the Public Accounts he has supplied over $20,000 worth of stuff to the Northern Development Branch?
A.—The Cochrane Hardware Supply, $28,000.
Q.—I know, but Bedford this year supplied that amount, and last year almost nothing?
A.—That may be.
Q.—Do you know any reason why he is supplying goods this year and was not last year?
A.—I think a substantial portion of that account of his is made up of reinforced concrete sewer pipe, because I went into it when I was up at the Sault.
Q.—Well, he is a retail hardware man there, and buys largely from your company?
A.—No, no.
Q.—Well, he does buy from your company?
A.—We don't supply him with the bulk of his hardware at all.
Q.—You think the bulk of that is reinforced tile for the roads?
A.—A substantial portion, yes.
Q.—And he would sell that as a retailer, to the Highway Branch?
A.—Yes.
Q.—After he would get that from a wholesale?
A.—Yes.
Q.—Where would he get this tile wholesale?
A.—He bought them from our firm.
Q.—That is, Bedford bought tile from your firm on a wholesale basis and sold them to the Northern Development Branch as a retail dealer?
A.—Yes, I don't know, but I think perhaps the prices he charged the Northern Development Branch were just the same prices, or practically so, that we would have charged them ourselves, or did charge them previously. I have the prices here, and asked Mr. Nash to go into this carefully.
Q.—He did not sell to the Northern Development Branch at the same rate at which you sold him?

A.—No, no. Nor we would not sell to the Northern Development Branch at the same rate we sell him.

Q.—Why?

A.—That is a reasonable thing, I think.

MR. FINLAYSON: That is the trade.

MR. SINCLAIR: Q.—Wouldn't Bedford have to make a profit in handling this stuff which went to the Northern Development?

A.—Yes, but he made it by getting a lower price from us.

Q.—What you say is, you reduce your wholesale price?

A.—No, we didn't; we have a regular wholesale and regular retail price. A wholesale price is a price you give to somebody buying wholesale.

Q.—Well, Bedford could buy from you cheaper than John Jones?

A.—Cheaper than the Algoma Central.

Q.—Or any other hardware merchant in the Soo?

A.—No, at the same price any hardware merchant could, that is all.

Q.—He would have to make a profit on his handling of these goods?

A.—I assume he would, yes.

Q.—And so goods were sold by you to Bedford and by Bedford to the Government?

A.—Yes.

Q.—And in that transfer there would be a profit to Bedford?

A.— I would expect so.

Q.—And if you could afford to sell Bedford at the rate you did, you could afford to sell to the Government at the same rate?

A.—But we did not do it.

Q.—You could afford to?

A.—We did not do it.

Q.—Why don't you?

A.—No wholesaler does that.

Q.—Isn't the Government entitled to buy its goods in the cheapest place possible?

A.—Under certain conditions, yes, but the Government should not get preference over somebody that is buying—

Q.—Well, the wholesale trade say to the Government, "We won't deal with you until our goods have gone through the hands of a retailer?"

A.—No, no.

A.—Well, why does not the Government buy from a wholesaler at wholesale prices?

A.—As far as buying is concerned, there is a wholesale and retail price. Now if the Algoma Central, which buys large quantities of pipe, an order came in to the store for 500 pieces of 13-inch pipe, we charge them the regular, what we call retail, price. If the City of Sault Ste. Marie want pipe—and they purchased $10,000 worth last year—they pay the regular retail established price. Now, if Mr. Bedford wants a price on a car of pipe for retail, he gets a wholesale price. I have the prices here that were charged other people and charged the Government the year before, and would have charged this year if they had bought from us.

MR. MACBRIDE: Is this man Bedford a regular retail merchant dealing with wholesale firms all the time?

A.—Oh, yes.

Q.—So his is a regular line of business?

A.—Oh, yes.

MR. SINCLAIR: Then the goods went from you to Bedford and from Bedford to the Government?

A.—Here is what happened: Mr. Lamb wanted concrete pipe; he went to Mr. Downey, who is in the same business as we are, only not so extensive, and offered him the business, and after a couple of days' thought he refused to accept it. Then Mr. Lamb got prices from out-of-town firms and from Mr. Bedford and others in the Sault. Mr. Bedford, in order to quote Mr. Lamb, got a price from us, and we gave him the regular wholesale price. I don't know, as a matter of fact, what Mr. Bedford sold the pipe for.

Q.—Well, since March, 1925, you had ceased dealing with the Northern Development Branch?

A.—Yes.

Q.—Who got the business?

A.—It was distributed all over—Cochrane Hardware, Plummer-Ferguson Hardware Company, Hesson and Company, Sault Lumber Company, I. J. Downey. Sault Lumber Company bought from Bedford and others. Some of the Cochrane Hardware would be hardware and different things, and so on.

Q.—Now in the Public Accounts last year your item appeared there, I think I referred to it, as something like $14,000. Was that supplied to the Government on a wholesale basis or the retail, similar to Bedford?

A.—You mean now the concrete pipe?

Q.—Anything you sold in that $14,000 before your company ceased dealing with the Department. Did your company sell on wholesale prices or the retail prices?

A.—We sold on what we would call retail prices.

Q.—Competition with other retailers in the Soo?

A.—That is right.

Q.—Although you as Lyons Fuel and Supply Company, Limited, were wholesalers and retailers together, and the Lyons Fuel and Supply Company got the same spread between the wholesale and retail price as Bedford or anybody else?

A.—Yes.

MR. FINLAYSON: You were not here yesterday, but he explained these purchases by the resident engineer are only for filling in. The big things are asked for tenders.

MR. SINCLAIR: I know, it is only an item of $14,000, but Mr. Lyons says that was sold to the Government on a retail basis, although he is a wholesaler and made a spread between the wholesale price and retail price—his company did.

MR. MACBRIDE: He is a retail dealer also.

MR. LYONS: When you get our prices you can find that the spread—call it wholesale or retail or whatever you like—is very small.

MR. SINCLAIR: I am not questioning that, but apparently there is enough spread in it to make it a paying proposition for a man like Bedford to be in it.

MR. LYONS: The wholesale price on concrete pipe is: 10-inch, $1.05, retail, $1.50; 18-inch, $1.40 and $1.75; 24-inch, $3.10 and $3.25; 30-inch, $4 and $4.50; 36-inch, $4.75 wholesale and $5.25 retail. Now these retail prices, Mr. Sinclair, are the exact prices we have charged the Northern Development Branch when they bought from us; that were charged the Algoma Central if they buy from us, or the City of Sault Ste. Marie.

Q.—And the difference between the wholesale and retail price is the profit to the retailer?

A.—Yes.

Mr. Finlayson: Less handling.

Mr. Lyons: In this case the man who buys it wholesale has to finance it and look after the account.

Mr. Sinclair: In connection with Bedford and this tile, you say he bought it from your company?

A.—Yes.

Q.—Was it shipped from your company to Bedford's store or sent direct to wherever the work was being done?

A.—I imagine Mr. Bedford would take it from our yard to the road.

Q.—So all Bedford had to do to make his thirty-five cents or fifty cents a foot, or whatever there was to it, was to draw it from your yard to their road wherever it was?

Mr. Graves: Is there a dollar difference?

Mr. Finlayson: He uses it for an example.

Mr. Lyons: I don't know whether that would take it to the road or not, because I don't know what he charged. I am telling you what our wholesale and retail price is. Bedford may have got a dollar a foot on it for all I know.

Mr. Sinclair: But he would get at least what your retail price was?

A.—He would have a protection of that much per foot.

Q.—And all he had to do was to take it from your wholesale premises to the job, wherever the work was being done?

A.—He would assume ownership and take charge of the pipe at our yard, and from that time he would have to look after it.

Q.—Can you give any reason why Bedford figures largely in the Public Accounts this year and at no previous year?

A.—I suppose for the very same reason all the rest of them do, because there was more business done and more purchasing carried out at the Sault. You will find we built the aerodrome there, and we carried out a substantial road programme, and it increased the purchases, because the total of purchases at the Sault, according to Public Accounts, sold by local firms at Sault Ste. Marie, amounted to about $82,000: Cochrane Hardware Company, $28,000; Hesson and Company, $6,000; Sault Lumber Mills, $20,000; Downey, $3,000, etc. These are all firms supplying the very lines of goods our own firms could supply, every dollar's worth, yet we didn't have an opportunity of bidding on any job.

Q.—In the previous year's Accounts, your company showed about $14,000 and Bedford $1,000?

A.—Bedford showed more than that; about $2,000, I think.

Q.—That is all Bedford comes in for, about $1,000, and your company of course is largely out of it; it would only be from the end of the year until the time the matter came up in the House?

A.—As I say, a substantial amount of his account is concrete pipe.

Q.—And who is charged with these goods, then, that went to Bedford?

A.—Oh, Mr. Bedford.

Q.—Nothing to do with the Department at all?

A.—Nothing whatever.

Q.—I suppose we will have this—?

A.—Oh, yes; there is nothing like that in it. We sold for instance to Bedford a great deal of hardware that does not go to the Northern Development, the same with Keyes and all the rest of it.

Q.—And have you done any more business with Bedford this year than last?

A.—Yes, with all of them. As a matter of fact, this was the first year, 1925, that we added the enlarged line of hardware goods; you see that accounts for larger sales.

Q.—What do you mean by hardware goods?

A.—Take for instance we can supply Bedford with dishes, spoons, knives and forks.

Q.—Small hardware of that kind?

A.—Yes.

Q.—Can you give us any reason why Bedford was not doing business last year on the scale he is doing this year?

A.—I don't know what the total amount of purchases made last year by Mr. Lamb amounted to. They are insignificant, I would say, compared with this year's. Then there was the aerodrome. For instance, this year, take the Hesson Lumber Company, they sold $4,400 to the Northern Development and $2,400 to the Forestry Branch; the Hinsperger Harness Company sold $4,000 to the Northern Development and $400 to the Forestry Branch; Bedford sold about $8,000 to the Northern Development and the balance to the Forestry Branch.

Q.—I have the figures now. In 1924 Bedford's name figured on page 9, F12, of Public Accounts, $162.53, and F33, making roads $579, and your company appeared as getting $14,202.58 at F35 for making roads?

A.—Yes.

Q.—Now this year Bedford in the making of roads account comes in for $10,849 of $579 last year?

A.—He could not come into that for making roads, because his account is split up; the Forestry Branch purchased a couple of thousand dollars worth from him. If you look at F30 you will see it was $8,732.

Q.—I am talking about 1924. Bedford last year and previous years was doing a very limited business with the Northern Development or any other department. This year he is doing quite a little bit. I wanted to know how Bedford came to get in this year when he had not been in before.

A.—For the very reason I was trying to explain. You take the total purchased in 1924 by the Northern Development Branch at Sault Ste. Marie and you will see their total purchases were insignificant, compared with their total purchases for 1925. By that I mean if you look up Hesson you will find, I imagine, his bill is much smaller; Hinsperger Harness Company the same. There is a greater volume of business, consequently Bedford would automatically get more.

Q.—Why would he automatically get more when he was not getting much before?

A.—The same applies to all. They were all getting less before because there was less volume of business. I would have to check it up to give a complete comparison, but I know the buying was heavier than the previous year.

Q.—Bedford would sell at the same rate as other dealers in the Sault?

A.—Oh, yes.

Q.—But had not been getting hardly anything at all?

A.—I don't know how his sales would compare with the other hardware merchants.

Q.—And you don't know to whom the business went that would have gone to the Lyons Company if you had continued doing business with the Government?

A.—No, but I can say this: That we sold the Plummer-Ferguson a considerable amount of hardware; some of it may have gone to the Northern Development Branch, I don't know. We sold Keyes several times more hardware than what his account with the Government is, so that all of his did not go to the Government, that is certain. Downey, we do not sell him much. He is in the same line of business, but that gives you an idea.

Q.—Well, then, it gets down to this: this item of $14,000 which you sold last year to the Government was sold on a retail basis the same as the goods sold by other hardware dealers and dealers of all kinds at the Sault?

A.—Sold on a competitive basis.

Q.—And on a competitive retail basis?

A.—Yes.

Q.—And while you were engaged in the wholesale and retail business you sold to the Government on a competitive retail basis?

A.—Yes. We would not sell the Government concrete pipe on a wholesale basis any more than the Algoma Central.

Q.—You made your profit as a wholesaler dealing with the Government the same as any of the other concerns?

A.—That is right.

Q.—The Lyons Fuel Supply Company supplies goods to the Walsh Construction Company?

A.—We supplied about $1,300 worth out of a total purchase I think of $13,000.

Q.—About 10 per cent. of it. Do you know whether Bedford sold any on this road there?

A.—To Walsh? I have no idea. I think the Cochrane Hardware got a substantial portion of the Walsh business.

Mr. Sinclair: I think, Mr. Finlayson, that probably after some of these other witnesses are called, Mr. Lyons is in the city, there may be a few points we would like to ask him something on, and it might save quite a bit of time just now, after hearing the evidence of some of the other witnesses.

Mr. Finlayson: We want to be reasonable over it, and if anything turns up arising out of the other matters, very well.

Mr. Sinclair: Because I feel now some of this very evidence will come from other witnesses, that probably Mr. Lyons does not know as directly about, and it may make it much easier to ask a few questions.

Mr. Finlayson: Nobody has any desire—I don't want to say you are closed and final.

Mr. Sinclair: No, you cannot close me anyway.

Mr. Finlayson: I move that the Committee adjourn until eight o'clock to-night.

Mr. Sinclair: Is that going to work out to everybody's satisfaction? We don't all need to be here, but will there be enough to do business?

The Chairman: We will have a quorum.

Mr. Finlayson: Mr. Raney will no doubt take up some time, and let us understand this, for Mr. Sinclair's sake, if he does not propose to go on, what is your idea as to next week, Mr. Chairman?

The Chairman: I think for Monday evening we could examine some of these other Crown witnesses.

Mr. Finlayson: We could hardly get Sault witnesses on Monday.

Mr. Lyons: I could have the McNamaras here.

Mr. Finlayson: What I thought of doing would be to call Clarkson's representative, Mr. Nash, as soon as possible, because he will no doubt have statements you will wish to go over, and if he is here for Monday it might be as well to have him Monday evening.

THE CHAIRMAN: There will be a meeting Monday evening at eight o'clock.

MR. MACBRIDE: Mr. Lyons, these merchants who deal in a retail way with products they buy from you in a wholesale way, are they at any expense in the way of handling?

A.—Just the same expense as any retailer.

Q.—When you sell at wholesale, you are saved the expense of handling, and the retailer has to pay it?

A.—Oh, yes.

Q.—So it wouldn't be all profit? He has to put it in stock?

A.—His position in buying from us wholesale is no different from buying wholesale from the Howland Hardware here.

MR. MACBRIDE: He has to do the financing; it is not all profit?

A.—Oh, no.

THE CHAIRMAN: Let me ask every member who possibly can be here to be here to-night at eight o'clock.

The Committee then adjourned.

PUBLIC ACCOUNTS COMMITTEE MEETING

The Committee met again at 8 P.M., with Chairman A. C. Lewis, presiding.

MR. LEWIS: I think we might as well get underway. I understand Mr. Raney is ready to go ahead with the examination of Mr. Lyons.

MR. RANEY: Mr. Lyons, to begin at the beginning, but not to go as far back as Mr. Finlayson did, you were first elected to the Legislature in 1923.

MR. LYONS: Yes.

Q.—And you knew then that a member of the Legislature could not contract with the Government?

A.—I did not know.

Q.—You did not know?

A.—No.

Q.—I have heard you—

A.—I don't know it yet. I think it is quite legal. You are distinguishing between an individual and a company are you?

Q.—No, I have not got to that yet. You knew it was illegal for a member of the Legislature to contract with the Government?

A.—Yes.

Q.—And when you became a Minister, I suppose you realized that a contract between yourself and the Government would be doubly objectionable?

A.—As a matter of fact there never was any contract.

Q.—Never mind that. Just answer my questions. You agree that if a contract between a member of the Legislature and the Government is objectionable, a contract between a member of the Ministry and the Government would be doubly objectionable?

A.—I have never looked at it in that light.

Q.—What do you think now?

A.—Just what I did then.

Q.—What was that?

A.—It would be quite legal.

Q.—Legal for—?

A.—For a member of the Government to have a contract, for a member of the Government who was a shareholder.

Q.—I am not talking about a shareholder. I am talking about a member of the Government. Never mind your part for the present. You knew when you became a member of the Government that it was illegal for a member of the Legislature to have a contract with the Government?

A.—Yes.

A.—And you realized that it would be doubly objectionable for a member of the Government to have a contract?

A.—Yes.

Q.—And much more objectionable for a member of the Government to have a contract with his own department. That would be objectionable?

A.—It would be.

Q.—Now you were and are still a member of the Lyons Fuel & Supply Company?

A.—Yes.

Q.—And you and members of your family control the company?

A.—Yes.

Q.—You are the president, Mr. Goodwin is vice-president and treasurer, and Mr. Morrow, I presume, a clerk?

A.—It is Miss Morrow.

Q.—She is an employee?

A.—Yes. She holds a position for signing cheques.

Q.—She holds a nominal amount of stock, qualified by you?

A.—One share, I think.

Q.—And your son, C. H., is manager?

A.—Yes.

Q.—So that the only director who is not a member of your family or one of the business, is Mr. Goodwin?

A.—That is right.

Q.—He is the vice-president?

A.—Yes.

Q.—Under these circumstances, in the fiscal year 1924, I see your company did a business of $17,920 with the Government?

A.—$14,000, I think.

Q.—$17,000. There is one item of $14,202. Then in the Journals of the House, page 145' you answered the question, was there anything besides that $14,202, by saying there was $3,175 in unpaid bills?

A.—No. That was after the close of the fiscal year.

Q.—I see. Down to the time you answered that question your transactions with the Government had been within $80 of $18,000?

A.—I think that is correct.

Q.—Where those prices wholesale or retail?

A.—They were competitive prices, Mr. Raney, and would be competitive retail prices.

Q.—Competitive retail prices?

A.—Yes.

Q.—And you had something to say to Mr. Sinclair and something similar to Mr. Finlayson about want of appreciation of any impropriety in anything you had done. Do you see now any impropriety in these transactions between your company and the Government before the question was raised in the House last year?

A.—No, I don't think yet there is anything wrong about it at all.

Q.—So that being in control of a joint stock company—might I call it a family company?

A.—Hardly that.

Q.—Hardly that. Being in control of a joint stock company, there is no impropriety, you think, in you, as a Minister of the Crown, dealing with a company of which you were the president and of which you were in control?

A.—Of course I did not have any dealing with the company at all. The merchandise covered in that connection was all purchased by the local resident engineers or other officials of the Department.

Q.—But you were the responsible Minister?

A.—Yes.

Q.—And knew what the engineers did?

A.—To some extent, I suppose.

Q.—And you knew what they were doing?

A.—I did.

Q.—You are not seeking to disclaim responsibility?

A.—Not at all.

Q.—You knew the engineers were purchasing things?

A.—I did.

Q.—You did not protest?

A.—No.

Q.—And you see now no impropriety in that course of action?

A.—I do not, Mr. Raney.

Q.—Are you invoking the technical rule that this company was a joint stock company to which the law did not apply, even though it is a company you control?

A.—I don't just understand.

Q.—You say, you see no impropriety. You mean no legal impropriety, that is what you mean?

A.—I would say both.

Q.—You say both legal impropriety and—

A.—I think that our company, or any other company of which a member of the House happened to be a shareholder, if it did business with any department of the Government in a fair, outstanding, honest, competitive manner, there was nothing wrong.

Q.—That would be, I take it, from your point of view; even if there were no members of this joint stock company but were members of your own family?

A.—Yes.

Q.—Will you distinguish between that situation, where a company is altogether a family company and dealings between an individual and a Minister?

A.—So long as the transaction is carried on in a straight, legitimate way, I see no objection.

Q.—So long as there is competition then, and a competitive price, you would see no objection to James Lyons, as Minister of Lands and Forests, dealing with James Lyons, a merchant of the Soo, in the sum of $18,000 or any other sum?

A.—Not as a merchant, but as a joint stock company.

Q.—Never mind. I know when you have a joint stock company you have an artificial creation. You understand that a joint stock company is an artificial person, and the artificial person, or rather the shareholder is not under the same disability in respect to what we are talking about, as an individual, but as soon as the individual becomes a shareholder in a company, even controlling the company, the principle ceases to apply?

A.—Of course, if James Lyons, Minister, were dealing with James Lyons, merchant, it would be a personal transaction, but if officers of the Department are buying materials or goods from a firm of which James Lyons is a shareholder it is an entirely different proposition.

Q.—Even if James Lyons controls the company?

A.—Yes.

Q.—And nobody else but members of his own family have stock in it?

A.—Yes.

Q.—Well, we get your point of view.

Mr. FINLAYSON: There seems to be ample authority for it.

Mr. RANEY: There seems to be precedent.

Mr. FINLAYSON: And in other cases too.

Mr. RANEY: We will not argue it.

Mr. FINLAYSON: He refers to the law.

Mr. RANEY: The statute is quite clear. We are not talking of the law. We are discussing impropriety. If James Lyons were carrying on this business in the Soo as an individual in his own name then you would think it would be improper for James Lyons, Minister of Lands and Forests, to permit his engineers to have transactions with him?

A.—It would be James Lyons dealing with James Lyons.

Q.—And that would be objectionable?

A.—Yes.

Mr. BLACK: Might I ask a question?

Mr. RANEY: Certainly.

Mr. BLACK: Was this company formed prior to your becoming Minister or later?

Mr. LYONS: It was formed in 1912. The charter was taken out in 1916, and there was no change in the shareholders or stock in that time.

Mr. RANEY: Thank you for the suggestion, Mr. Black. To pursue the matter further. Suppose that if James Lyons was Minister of Lands and Forests, having carried on business as James Lyons, and then he incorporated, with his wife and son and daughter, as a joint stock company, would you think there was impropriety?

Mr. LYONS: If the company was organized for the intent and purpose of creating a means of dealing with the Government I would say it would be wrong.

Q.—That would be whipping the devil from the post?

A.—I would say so.

Q.—Now, I have before me a statement from one of the, what do you call them, the companies that give ratings?

Mr. FINLAYSON: Bradstreets, mercantile agencies.

Mr. RANEY: Mercantile agents. This gives the assets of the Lyons Fuel & Supply Company as of April last year at $227,500.

Mr. FINLAYSON: No, no. Mr. Chairman, I don't know what Mr. Lyons' view is but I think it is most objectionable that we are going into this.

Mr. RANEY: I am asking witness—

Mr. FINLAYSON: You are using something not on the record and it cannot be and you have no right to say, "I have a mercantile report."

Mr. RANEY: I will put the question direct.

Mr. FINLAYSON: I say it is objectionable to discuss ratings and credits, liabilities and assets, and matters of that kind.

. MR. RANEY: I don't intend to ask liabilities. Mr. Lyons opened the door widely by his statement of the large area covered and the great activities of the company and I did not suppose there would be any objection to Mr. Lyons telling us what the assets were and are.

MR. FINLAYSON: It was for this very reason, Mr. Lyons said, you were not here perhaps, he resigned. He objected that his position as Minister of Lands and Forests involved him in discussions of the financial position and details of the firm's affairs. I think it is not only most objectionable, but that it would have no effect whatever on this issue and it looks to me like an attempt to bring in, in a very doubtful way, criticism of a man's financial standing.

MR. LEWIS: Is it going to have a material bearing?

MR. RANEY: If Mr. Lyons objects, I shall not press the question now, whatever I may do when the accountants bring down their statement.

MR. LEWIS: Leave it until we have the accountants' statement.

MR. FINLAYSON: It was understood from Mr. Sinclair there might be something out of the accountants' report he would want to take up and that will apply to you as far as your view is concerned.

MR. RANEY: We will try to get along pleasantly.

MR. FINLAYSON: We have the sweetest disposition in the world. You cannot disturb us.

MR. RANEY: Always, when you have got your own way. To turn to a pleasanter subject. Might I put it in this way, when you became Minister, you assumed a generous attitude towards your adopted place of residence?

MR. LYONS: In what way?

Q.—In a broad way. In a ministerial way?

A.—You refer to Sault Ste. Marie?

Q.—The city.

A.—I cannot say so.

Q.—Well, not many constituencies have been so favoured as yours in the past two or three years?

A.—You will find quite a number in Northern Ontario.

Q.—There are two or three others that I know of but they are fortunate to be represented in a similar manner, if you will pardon my saying so.

A.—You will see that some of the greatest expenditures in any constituency in Northern Ontario were made in Opposition constituencies.

Q.—Let us get down to facts. You bought a Queen Street lot to extend the Court House grounds?

A.—I don't know.

Q.—Your department?

A.—Oh, no.

Q.—Jail property?

A.—Neither that.

Q.—The question was: "Did the present Government purchase land in Sault Ste. Marie to extend the jail property?"

A.—The Government did.

Q.—I mean the Government.

MR. LEWIS: Mr. Lyons took you to mean his Department.

MR. FINLAYSON: That was the word used.

MR. RANEY: (Proceeding with examination.) Yes. It was on your recommendation?

A.—It was not.

Q.—Whose recommendation?

A.—I cannot tell you whose. I think the Minister of Public Works answered the question.

Q.—No. The Prime Minister answered it.

A.—It was the Minister of Public Works who had to do with it.

Q.—It is not in your department?

A.—No.

Q.—Did you have anything to do with the purchase?

A.—Nothing whatever.

Q.—I see Mr. Atkin was one of the gentlemen who owned the property. He is the Crown Attorney there?

A.—He may have had an interest in it.

Q.—Now, one way or another, a lot of money has been spent in the Soo in the past two or three years?

A.—Not an unusual amount.

Q.—Not unusual. Let us see what the amounts were. Here is another question: "Did the present Government purchase land in Sault Ste. Marie for an aerodrome site. If so, how much land, from whom was it purchased and at what cost?" The answer is: "Yes. Two and one-tenth acres of land and one and seven-tenths acres water lot, cost $15,000." That is true?

A.—Yes.

Q.—Besides $25,000 for extending the jail property?

A.—The Government purchased the jail property, yes.

Q.—Have they used it yet?

A.—I have not any idea.

Q.—You know whether it is built on?

A.—I have no idea, you mean the court house?

Q.—Don't you know whether there is any new building on the site?

A.—There has not been any new building. I don't think it was purchased for the purpose of erecting a building.

Q.—The answer to the question is this: "The attention of the Government was drawn by Mayor Dawson to the desirability of purchasing the remaining vacant corner lot adjacent to the court house so that it might not be built on, but reserved for the future needs of the Crown. You knew of that transaction?

A.—I knew of it.

Q.—Was it to you that Mayor Dawson expressed the desirability of purchasing this?

A.—No. It was to Prime Minister Ferguson, I think, in 1923.

Q.—Has anything been done with that piece of property?

A.—No.

MR. FINLAYSON: $2,500 was it not?

MR. LYONS: No, $25,000.

MR. RANEY: One hundred and fifty-one feet depth on Elgin Street; 110 feet frontage on Queen Street, about $280 a foot?

MR. LYONS: Perhaps so.

MR. RANEY: Then $15,000 for an aerodrome site. Then, another, question: "Did the present Government pay half the cost of paving Wellington Street?" Answer, "Yes." That meant $19,000.

MR. LYONS: The answer is not "Yes," that we paid half the cost.

MR. RANEY: For a certain width?

Q.—And then another question is: "What other capital expenditures have been made by the present Government in Sault Ste. Marie?" and the answer is: "Northern Development, store-house, $2,659.52; aerodrome and

Northern Development, administrative and forestry offices, $31,357.51, and parking stage for twenty hydroplanes, $32,046.40." So that I am not far off the mark in saying you were fairly generous?

A.—The whole thing does not amount to as much as you put into the court house.

Q.—The court house is there.

A.—So is the aerodrome.

Q.—If you say you have been ungenerous, I will take the answer.

A.—I have not done as much as I would have liked to.

MR. FINLAYSON: He allowed modesty to rule him.

MR. LEWIS: I think, Mr. Raney, you were out of the room when they went into the question of the aerodrome and we had reports put in.

MR. RANEY: I heard that. (Continuing examination.) Now there was some little doubt, was there not, about the Wellington Street paving, and the Sault Ste. Marie portion of the expenditure.

MR. LYONS: No. I have not heard that.

Q.—You know the Sault *Daily Star*?

A.—I do.

Q.—A pretty good friend of yours?

A.—I would not say so.

Q.—Is it not a supporter?

A.—Sometimes.

MR. FINLAYSON: To the same extent as its namesake in Toronto.

MR. RANEY: Here are the remarks of the Sault *Star*.

MR. FINLAYSON: What date?

MR. RANEY: It is some time in June. I have not the exact date. Some time Wellington Street—

MR. LYONS: I think it was early in May, Mr. Raney. When was the matter settled?

MR. RANEY: It was not settled until June.

MR. LYONS: As between the Department and the city, I think May.

MR. RANEY: The Sault *Star* says: "Sometime Wellington Street will have to be paved. At present, however, it is in fair condition and autoists have three other paved streets by which they can reach Gore Street. These are Albert, Queen and Bay Streets."

A.—That is true.

Q.—"Until the cost of the proposed work is known, it is perhaps out of place to say whether the work should or should not be done this year. The council knows the financial situation better than the ratepayers and is aware also that many citizens view with misgiving any expenditure whatever that can be avoided. If the Province will agree to co-operate later in the building of the pavement, the council should consider deferring the work. For the way to stop piling up debt is to stop." I judge from that statement that the people of the Sault were not all agreed to pay half the cost of this work.

A.—This is the first I have heard of any objection at all, from the *Star* or any other source.

MR. FINLAYSON: Don't overlook the fact that it was a local improvement and the people had a right to stop it if they wanted.

MR. RANEY: Were you aware that this same paper had drawn attention to the fact that through the Government buying so much property the Sault was losing $1,500 a year in taxes?

A.—I never heard of that.

Q.—Here is what the paper says: "The city of Sault Ste. Marie will this year lose $1,500 in taxes as the result of the purchase of a number of properties in the city last year by the Ontario Government. The reason for this is that the Government, while it pays local improvement taxes does not under the law pay general taxes on properties it owns. The properties taken over by the Ontario Government last year, include a lot at the corner of Queen and Elgin Streets, extending the Court House grounds, the site of the aerodrome, and the lots bought to extend the jail property. The interest of the Ontario Government in the Sault is deeply appreciated especially when, as in the case of the aerodrome, it means the employment of a number of men here, but sometimes the city treasurer is inclined to weep the odd tear."

A.—I did not see any tears.

Q.—No? Then we come to the Wellington Street pavement. Tenders were called for?

A.—In the city of Sault Ste. Marie?

Q.—Yes, and the tenders were sent to the chief clerk, I suppose?

A.—I presume so.

Q.—And the city clerk forwarded them to you?

A.—That is right.

Q.—Did you request by letter or otherwise that the tenders should be sent to you?

A.—I did not.

Q.—Did you open them?

A.—In the first place let me read you the first letter I wrote the Mayor in connection with the matter. This was on May 6th. This matter had been under discussion between Mayor Dawson and members of the Council for some time and we had arrived at an understanding as to what should be done in reference to the expenditure by the Government and by the city on the work to be carried out. I wrote on May 6th:—

"Dear Mayor:

"Following our several conversations in reference to your request that the Government contribute a portion of the expense of construction of a pavement on a portion of Wellington Street, which is a continuation of the trunk road from Sudbury to the Sault and beyond, I beg to advise after giving the matter careful consideration that I will agree to contribute fifty per cent. of the cost of a 24-foot pavement, as provided for under the Act, with the understanding that the cost of the pavement is satisfactory to the Department and that no contract will be let and no expenditure made to which the Government is committed until such time as approval has been given by the Department to the contract." That probably led to the tenders coming to me.

Q.—Is that the whole of the letter?

A.—Yes.

Q.—They consented, thinking you wished to make the contract?

A.—I would not say so. Perhaps I may follow up with another letter. Here is the letter Mayor Dawson sent on July 15th:—

"I expected to see you when you were here on Saturday, but missed you. How do you want us to handle the tenders for the Wellington Street pavement? The tenders are to be in the clerk's hands on the 20th. Alderman Brooks reported that you told him you expected the Council to open them. We decided to call a special meeting for Monday night. Shall we award the contract or refer the matter to you before doing so. I would be glad to know your wishes in this matter."

To this, I wrote:

"In reply to your letter of July 15th, I beg to advise you that it does not matter to me who opens the tenders for the road work in question, but it must be strictly understood that the Government will not commit itself to the payment for any portion of the work until such time as the tender has been approved by the Department. I will be very glad to have you open the tenders and advise me promptly, as you will understand that I am particularly anxious that the work carried out in my own district is done so as not to establish a precedent that other places might refer to."

Q.—Yes. You left them free to send the tenders or open them as they saw fit.

A.—Absolutely.

Q.—From the figures published in the Sault *Star* it would appear that the MacNamara tender was not the lowest tender.

A.—Yes.

Q.—The figures I have are: MacNamara, $50,498, and the other prices, were, $50,685, a little more; $50,145, $300 less; $54,184, that is less; $55,723 and $59,501.

A.—As a matter of fact, the Sault *Star* was wrong in the publication of those figures.

Q.—Have you the figures there?

A.—I thought I had, but I have not.

Q.—It may be a typographical error.

A.—Yes. I saw the secretary to have it corrected.

Q.—Well, now, I find another statement in this paper. It says, the date does not appear, probably it was some time in July.

"Work was resumed yesterday pouring concrete on the Wellington Street paving after a lay off on Tuesday as a result of the shortage of cement. The shortage of cement was caused by the tie up in the Welland Canal last week, when traffic was delayed over forty-eight hours by the low water in the canal. One of the boats held up during that period was carrying cement for the Sault, according to the advice received here, and as a result of the delay they were late in arriving here to deliver the cargo."

Then there is a last paragraph:—

"Work was resumed by the contractors, the MacNamara Construction Company, yesterday. The cement is supplied by the Lyons Fuel and Supply Co., whose stock had run out as a result of the hold up."

Q.—Is that true?

A.—I don't know anything about a hold up.

Q.—Did you supply the cement?

A.—Yes.

Q.—Was that brought out in the Committee before?

A.—I doubt if the question was asked.

MR. FINLAYSON: They were contractors for the municipality?

MR. LYONS: Yes.

Q.—Have you the letter in which—to return to the road, you wrote to the clerk of the municipality after you had opened the tenders?

A.—I think I have. May I read the resolution of the Council to confirm what I have said? It is on the 21st of July:—

"That as the Government is assuming forty per cent. of the cost of the Wellington Street pavement and the tenders are based on specifications drafted by our engineer, that in deference to the Government granting this contribution, we submit the tenders to the Department."

Q.—That was before the sealed tenders came down?

A.—Yes. After the tenders were in the office of the City Council. Then I wrote this letter, because the resolution mentioned the Government assuming forty per cent. of the work. That was not correct. I wrote accordingly to Mr. Campbell:—

"I thank you for your letter of July 21st with copy of resolution regarding Wellington Street paving attached. I beg to advise you that the Government is not participating in the payment for this road on a forty per cent. basis of the total cost, but on a basis of fifty per cent. of the cost of a concrete roadway twenty-four feet in width. It may be that forty per cent. as suggested by you would have been less than the amount to be paid on the other basis, but I am anxious not to establish a precedent whereby other municipalities might desire to point to this as a precendent to have their roads constructed on the basis of our paying forty per cent. of the total cost, I hope, therefore, that you will be able to adjust the matter correctly. I am returning herewith the tenders which you were kind enough to forward me and, as confirmed in discussion with your Mayor by telephone, the lowest concrete tender will be satisfactory and if you desire to change your specifications to the Ontario Provincial Highways specifications at the reduced price, it will be entirely satisfactory to me. I also include the letter forwarded to me by the General Accident Assurance Company in connection with the J. J. Fitzpatrick tender."

Q.—The low tender to which you refer was the MacNamara Company?

A.—Yes.

Q.—Now what else did your company supply to the MacNamara contractors on that job besides the cement?

A.—I think we supplied the cement and gravel.

Q.—Gravel, not tile?

A.—I cannot say off-hand. Very little tile, I imagine.

Q.—Do you know what your company's bill was for the supplies furnished to the McNamaras for this work?

A.—I think it was in the neighbourhood of $30,000.

Q.—Were those prices retail or wholesale?

A.—They were competitive retail prices. My recollection of the cement—

Q.—I had rather you did not give recollection. I think you ought to produce the items.

A.—I think Mr. Nash will produce that.

Q.—That will be better. Your recollection is that about $30,000 would cover the whole job?

A.—I think so.

Q.—The contractors' price was around $50,000 in round figures?

A.—Yes, roughly.

Q.—Did you see any impropriety in this transaction?

A.—Oh, my no.

Q.—You could not think of any?

A.—No, could you?

Q.—Unfortunately, I am not giving evidence.

A.—I would like to have your opinion.

Q.—Not now, please. Did the Government know when you resigned that you had supplied the cement for this job?

A.—I don't know if they knew I supplied the cement. They knew I had supplied material.

Q.—Because I find this question was asked: "Did the Lyons Fuel and Supply Company, Limited, or Hon. James W. Lyons, or any member of his family supply the cement or tiles for the work? How much?" and so on. And the answer was: "The Government cannot undertake to supply information as to the materials purchased or the price paid by the contractor who has not a contract with the Government." That was not answered until after you had resigned?

A.—Yes.

Q.—Tell me, if it would not be asking you to repeat yourself, what objection or harm could there be in answering that question?

A.—As a matter of fact, Mr. Raney, I wrote to the office at the Sault and received from them the information, giving details of the materials and the prices charged on the McNamara job on Wellington Street; also on the Fitzpatrick job on the aerodrome and it came into my office on the Tuesday morning preceding the questions on Thursday. If it had not come on Thursday you would have had the answer on Friday.

Q.—There was one question too many.

MR. LEWIS: The last straw that broke the camel's back.

MR. RANEY: Mr. Fitzpatrick came to your company before putting in his tender for the aerodrome?

MR. LYONS: Mr. Fitzpatrick, along with all the other contractors, got prices from us on any material we could supply. I think, Mr. Raney, that the same prices were handed out to every contractor.

Q.—Having procured from your company a tender for the roof, he put in a tender for the whole work?

A.—Yes. Of course, undoubtedly he would get prices from other people as well.

Q.—What was the tender on the roof?

A.—I don't know.

Q.—Can you produce that?

A.—Yes. Our ledger will show exactly.

Q.—What else did you supply?

A.—We supplied the tile.

Q.—Can you give me in rough figures the amount of the roof tender?

A.—I could not.

Q.—Would it be $20,000?

A.—Oh, my no. I suppose it would run $18 or $20 a square. That would be about the regular price for a roof of that kind.

Q.—What would that be?

MR. FINLAYSON: You had better wait for the Clarkson report.

MR. RANEY: What else did you supply?

A.—We supplied the tile; we supplied the brick; we supplied the gravel; we supplied the cement. I think steel sash, and that is about all.

Q.—You supplied almost everything?

A.—Not the steel frame.

Q.—Not the steel frame?

A.—And the steel hammered bridge.

Q.—Was there much besides that you did not supply?

A.—I cannot tell you how much.

Q.—Roughly, how much altogether?

A.—My recollection is $30,000 or $31,000 for the entire amount, including the roof.

Q.—And did your company furnish prices to Mr. Fitzpatrick for other things besides the roof before he put in his tender.

A.—Yes. I think we supplied the prices not only to Mr. Fitzpatrick, but to the other contractors on the materials in that building if they were successful in getting the work.

Q.—Where did he get the glass?

A.—From us, I think

Q.—Brick?

A.—I think so.

Q.—Are you sure?

A.—I am not sure.

Q.—Will you look that up?

A.—I think we supplied him the glass.

Q.—You had nothing personally to do with the transaction.

A.—Nothing.

Q.—You knew of it at the time?

A.—I knew afterwards that Mr. Fitzpatrick purchased a quantity of goods when he came to see me a week or two afterwards.

Q.—And you saw no impropriety in these things?

A.—Absolutely not.

Q.—Did the Government know when you resigned that you had furnished materials to the contractor for the aerodrome?

A.—I think so, yes.

Q.—Do you know why the Government did not tell us about it?

A.—I don't know.

MR. FINLAYSON: That is beyond his knowledge.

Q.—You know a question was asked?

A.—I do.

Q.—The question was asked on the 23rd of February and was answered on the day of your resignation and immediately after your resignation was read. "Did the Lyons Fuel and Supply Company furnish any of the material for the work and at what cost?" And the same question was asked by Mr. McWhinney, "Did the contractor purchase materials from the Lyons Fuel and Supply Company, Limited?" Also, "If so, what materials and what was the total amount paid to the company for same?" The Government answered, "The Government does not interfere with contractors in purchasing their materials where they desire," which was hardly an answer to the question.

A.—I think it was a fair view to take.

Q.—I think you said to Mr. Finlayson that your company did not supply any material to the McNamara people for any of their road contracts outside the city of Sault Ste. Marie?

A.—Yes, I don't think we supplied a dollar's worth.

Q.—You certainly supplied the gravel, and—

MR. FINLAYSON: You said outside the Sault.

Q.—There was a question referred by the House, on the suggestion of the Prime Minister, to the Committee, or rather a series of questions. Perhaps, I had better read them. "Has the Lyons Fuel and Supply Company of Sault Ste. Marie solicited business from companies, firms or individuals having business relations with the Department of Lands and Forests?"

A.—Undoubtedly we have.

Q.—And do I take it that your solicitation of business in the north country

16 J.

was entirely regardless of whether the persons, firms or companies solicited, had or had been having business relations with the Government?

A.—Oh, yes.

Q.—You think it made no difference whatever?

A.—None at all.

Q.—The next question is, "Has the Honourable James W. Lyons or the Lyons Fuel and Supply Company since Mr. Lyons became a Minister of the Crown supplied persons or companies to whom Mr. Lyons, as Minister of the Crown, has given contracts for road construction, with cement, gravel, oil, tents or other goods?"

A.—We have.

Q.—Can you name some of the companies.

A.—There is M. L. MacLean, contractor on the North Bay-Cobalt highway. Out of $22,000 of supplies, we supplied $1,342. There is Grant Brothers, contractors on the Cobalt highway—no, MacLeans was about $700 out of $11,000; to Grant Brothers, we supplied about $1,342 out of $22,000 purchased. There was Angus Taylor of North Bay, on the North Bay and Cobalt road, we supplied there $1,372, I think out of $23,000 or $24,000 purchased. To the Walsh Construction Company, we supplied $1,300 or $1,400 out of $12,000 purchased, and I think that is all.

Q.—All you have in mind at the moment?

A.—Yes.

Q.—The question only refers to road contractors?

A.—Yes.

Q.—"Has Hon. James Lyons, or the Lyons Fuel and Supply Company since Mr. Lyons became a Minister of the Crown, supplied goods to pulp and paper companies or lumber companies who have been tenderers for pulpwood or timber areas?"

A.—Yes, we have.

Q.—Can you name some?

A.—Do you mean those who have secured areas since I came to Toronto or previous?

Q.—Narrow that if you please to those to whom leases were made or contracts given since you became Minister.

A.—I cannot answer, Mr. Raney, as to just those who received areas since I came here but if we took it on the other basis, the number of customers the Lyons Fuel and Supply Company have taken on since I came here who were wholesale or out of town buyers, I think it was about 115 and out of that 115 something like 20 of them are persons or companies who have secured, not since I came here, but at some time, concessions.

Q.—Crown lessees?

A.—Yes, and the total supplied, I think, is in the neighbourhood of $26,000.

Q.—Of course that only applies to new customers.

A.—Yes.

Q.—If you had made the question wider and you had covered all Crown lessees, timber and pulp and paper companies it would have run into a much larger figure?

A.—It would be quite a fair sum.

Q.—Perhaps in the statement from the auditors—?

A.—Yes, I think they are going to give it.

Q.—By the way, two or three cases you referred to before, I am not sure I got it straight, you referred to an instance where you turned down an order for 40,000 tons of coal. What was the reason? They might be tenderers?

A.—I knew they were going to be.

Q.—Where do you draw the distinction? Because any of these companies are prospective contractors with the Government?

A.—Yes.

Q.—All the present contractors and also prospective new contractors?

A.—More or less.

Q.—Why should you draw a line with the Mattagami Company?

A.—Simply for this reason. If this transaction has been disposed of I would have been free to go ahead and sell them coal, but I did not want to be in a position of accepting what was a first order they had ever offered, a large order with this pending. I wanted to be free in the matter.

Q.—In other words, you had it in the back of your head that perhaps this order was intended to influence you?

A.—I cannot say that I had that. I wanted to make certain that it would not.

Q.—Then do you see any risk of a man carrying on business as you were, soliciting orders broadcast from companies having transactions with your department?

A.—I will tell you candidly so far as I am concerned there is absolutely no risk about it. I want to be honest in any business transaction.

Q.—Were Austin Nicholson regular customers of yours?

A.—I suppose their entire purchases from us were about $4,300.

Q.—Covering what time?

A.—Nicholsons have been customers of ours—the $4,300 covered purchases over—

Q.—Forty-three thousand dollars?

A.—No, no, no. There was a car load of roofing paper.

Q.—Did you say the Algoma Steel Corporation was a large customer?

A.—Fairly large. I think they average $40,000 or $50,000 a year for the past ten years.

Q.—The Algoma Central Railway?

A.—Yes.

Q.—How much are they?

A.—I cannot say what that would amount to off hand—sometimes up a few thousands, sometimes down.

Q.—Great Lakes Power?

A.—Yes.

Q.—How did they run?

A.—When they were doing construction work their purchases would be quite high. When they were not doing that the purchases would be small.

Q.—What would you call high?

A.—As I recall it I think that some years their purchases ranged between $18,000 and $20,000.

Q.—They are not a pulp or paper company?

A.—No.

Q.—The Provincial Paper Company at Fort William?

A.—I think their total purchases from us ran into $23,000 or $24,000.

Q.—Were they customers of the Sault Coal and Wood Company?

A.—No.

Q.—What did they buy, coal from the Lyons Fuel and Supply Company?

A.—We quoted them on 21,000 tons of coal last year but did not get any part of the order.

Q.—Are they concessionaires from the Government?

A.—Yes.

Q.—Did they recently receive a concession?

A.—They got rights to cut, September, 1924.

Q.—When did you solicit your order for 21,000 tons of coal?

A.—I think it would be late last fall.

Q.—Can you get the date in the correspondence?

A.—I think so.

Q.—Correspondence about 21,000 tons of coal from the Provincial Paper Mills.

A.—I did not know about it until yesterday as a matter of fact.

Q.—All these pulp and paper companies are liable to come to you at any time to ask for leases of additional pulp areas?

A.—I suppose so.

Q.—What about the Abitibi Pulp and Paper Company?

A.—I think we sold them about $320 worth of stuff.

Q.—You said something about quoting them 100,000 tons of coal. That would be around—?

A.—I think perhaps the price would be around five and a half dollars.

Q.—Half a million dollars?

A.—Yes.

Q.—You solicited that order?

A.—I don't know whether we solicited it or whether they came to us. I did not know about it until yesterday evening.

Q.—When was that?

A.—Last season.   I don't know exactly when.

Q.—They had had leases or concessions from your Department?

A.—No.

Mr. Lewis: Did you get any part of the order you tendered for?

Mr. Lyons: No.

Mr. Raney: The largest contractors with your Department have been the McNamaras?

Mr. Lyons: Not on Government work.

Q.—On road work?

A.—Not on Government road work.

Q.—Who have been the largest?

A.—It would be between Angus Taylor and Grant Brothers—a few dollars difference.

Q.—I see these people ran into $329,000.

A.—Who is that?

Q.—McNamaras.

A.—We did not supply anything like that.

Q.—There are other contractors who had larger contracts than the McNamaras?

A.—I thought you had reference to our sales.

Mr. Raney: No, with the Department. (To stenographer: Cross that out.)

Mr. Raney (Resuming examination): The McNamara people are the largest road contractors since you came into office, with your department?

A.—Yes.

Q.—Their contracts have all been for hard surface roads?

A.—A concrete roadway from Sudbury to Coniston, tar penetration from Timmins to Porcupine.

Q.—Totalling how much?

A.—Sudbury-Coniston, $384,626.80; Timmins-Porcupine, $258,754.48.

Q.—Something over $600,000?

A.—Yes.

Q.—Both contracts on a unit basis?

A.—Yes.

Q.—How could there be extras on a unit basis?

A.—It would be something not provided for in the unit prices.

Q.—I see.

A.—Something unforeseen, I suppose.

Q.—Did the McNamaras have the use of Government equipment for any of the contracts?

A.—I believe they did.

Q.—Large contracts?

A.—I think perhaps both. I am not sure. They had for Sudbury.

Q.—With whom did they arrange that?

A.—With the Department. With Mr. Fullerton.

Q.—What was the basis?

A.—We charged them the same price as when the Public Works rent it. That is my understanding.

Q.—Will you please find out definitely how much the McNamara people paid. You cannot tell how much they used or what they paid?

A.—I have no idea.

Q.—I would like to know what equipment they used and what they paid for it and when they paid for it.

A.—And on what jobs?

Q.—And on what jobs. Let me see. You said the McNamaras had the Sudbury-Coniston contract?

A.—Yes.

Q.—And Timmins-South Porcupine?

A.—Yes.

Q.—And those are the two you have just mentioned?

A.—Yes.

Q.—Did they do the Creighton-Copper Cliff?

A.—Yes.

Q.—Not original contractors?

A.—No.

Q.—They did the Sault job, Wellington Street?

A.—Yes.

Q.—Did they do the Sudbury job?

A.—Which Sudbury job?

Q.—There was some work at Sudbury on a similar basis to that in the Sault?

A.—The Town of Sudbury did that themselves. I think they were doing some similar work on an adjoining street and asked permission to do this themselves.

Q.—Did the McNamaras do the Goulais Bay road?

A.—There was no Goulais Bay. Haviland Bay you mean.

Q.—Is there a Goulais Bay road?

A.—Yes, we did not do any work there. There was the Haviland Bay road. There was a contract on that.

Q.—Who did that?

A.—It was done by the Walsh Construction Company.

Q.—The Timmins road, the McNamaras did that?

A.—Timmins-South Porcupine.

Q.—Inside the Timmins Corporation?

A.—I believe so.

Q.—And the Dome?

A.—I believe so.

Q.—They were not let by your department?

A.—By the Town of Timmins in one case, and the Township of Tisdale in the other.

Q.—You have spoken of the Walsh Construction Company. Do you know who they consist of?

A.—I don't know. I met Mr. Walsh twice, once after he had a contract he came to my office and said when he was going to commence the work. I asked him if he knew anyone at the Sault and he said Mr. Dalton, manager of the Royal Bank.

Q.—All right. Then the Barnett Hearst. We have a question about that. "Did the Lyons Fuel and Supply Company supply any of the material for that?"

A.—No, we did not.

Q.—Here is another question referred by the House to this Committee: "Is the Honourable James Lyons, Minister of Lands and Forests, the President of the Sault Ste. Marie Coal and Wood Company, Ltd.?"

A.—Yes.

Q.—"Did he and members of his family acquire a controlling interest in the company?"

A.—Yes.

Q.—"When was the interest acquired?"

A.—I think early in June, 1925.

Q.—Did I understand you to say to Mr. Finlayson that you bought out all the assets of the company?

A.—I did. Yes.

Q.—And then re-sold the stock?

A.—I bought the capital stock of the company, which is $100,000 for a certain sum of money.

Q.—Do you mind saying how much?

A.—I would sooner not.

Q.—You bought the entire capital stock, all paid up?

A.—Yes. For a certain sum. In addition to that I had to buy the coal and, I think, the horse feed and so on, which did not amount to much—any stuff brought in after the opening of navigation and which they had paid for, running into the neighbourhood of $45,000 or $50 000.

Q.—Was that all paid for in cash?

A.—No. I paid a small sum down on the capital stock and then went into the Royal Bank and borrowed $50,000 to pay for the coal.

Q.—And you sold some of the stock?

A.—I sold somewhere round 45 or 48 per cent. of the capital stock to other parties in Sault Ste. Marie.

Q.—You still owned the controlling interest?

A.—Yes.

Q.—Is that company being operated in conjunction with the Lyons Fuel and Supply Company?

A.—Just as independent as Timothy Eaton's.

Q.—Really in competition?

A.—In a sense.

Q.—I see you are the president; Mr. Atkin, secretary-treasurer; Mr. Dawson, Mayor of the Sault, is one of the directors?

A.—He may be. I really don't know.

MR. FINLAYSON: He is not mayor now, is he?

MR. LYONS: No.

MR. RANEY: And do the McNamaras hold stock?

A.—None whatever.

Q.—Then that company, of course, changed management?

A.—Yes.

Q.—When you purchased it?

A.—Yes.

Q.—And did you get work from the Lake Superior Pulp and Paper Company? Did you get a contract for coal after you purchased?

A.—No.

Q.—What were the facts?

A.—Only that the Sault Ste. Marie Coal and Wood Company supplied 2,889 tons of bituminous coal to their docks for fuelling purposes from time to time during the season of navigation.

Q.—After the purchase?

A.—Yes. Up to that time they had purchased coal over in Michigan because there were no proper appliances in the Sault.

Q.—That is not material. Did you tender for a supply of coal for their pulp mills?

A.—No.

Q.—Did you enter into negotiation with them?

A.—No.

Q.—You did supply about 3,000 tons?

A.—Yes.

Q.—At five or six dollars a ton?

A.—I cannot tell the price. There is a regular Lake Association price for fuel.

Q.—What month was that?

A.—That was July, August, September, October—right through the season.

Q.—There must have been a contract?

A.—There was no contract. They came when they wanted the coal and got it.

MR. FINLAYSON: Bunker coal, is it not?

MR. LYONS: Yes.

MR. RANEY: Where is the Lake Superior Pulp and Paper Company located?

A.—On the Ste. Marie River, beside the ship canal.

Q.—They were successful tenderers for pulp limits?

A.—No.

Q.—Have they transactions with the Department?

A.—I suppose they have minor transactions such as paying stumpage dues and so on, but no transactions in relation to the sale or disposal of timber.

Q.—Because another of the questions referred to this Committee is: "Had or has the Minister's coal company contracts with other companies having business relations with the Department of Lands and Forests?"

A.—What is that?

Q.—I will read it again: "Had or has the Minister's coal company contracts with other companies having business relations with the Department of Lands and Forests?"

A.—It is purely retail.

Q.—This is the only pulp and paper company it has business relations with?

A.—Yes.

Q.—Now, do you know a gentleman, Fred Laberge or Labarge?

A.—Labarge, of Sudbury. Yes.

Q.—Was he active in the last Provincial election?

A.—Not in my constituency. I don't know what he did for McCrea.

Q.—Was the Labarge Lumber Company a tenderer for the Sudbury-Coniston road?

A.—They were I think. No, I beg your pardon.

Q.—Not on that?

A.—No. They bid on the Creighton-Copper Cliff road.

Q.—Did they get a contract?

A.—They did.

Q.—Do you remember the tender.

A.—Yes, I have it here. I don't know, as a matter of fact, which tender was accepted. There were tenders for tar penetration and asphalt penetration. Labarge's tender for tar was $61,165 and for asphalt penetration $59,165. I don't know, Mr. Raney, which one was accepted.

Q.—He was a successful tenderer?

A.—I think it was the asphalt penetration.

Q.—I see the company is not incorporated, so I suppose it is Mr. Labarge?

A.—I think it must be incorporated. They have been doing business for a number of years. I am not sure.

Q.—Yes, I think they may be. Do you know anyone else connected with it?

A.—I don't know. I don't know him very well.

Q.—Has he previous experience in road construction?

A.—I have no idea.

Q.—Had he any equipment for road construction?

A.—I don't know. I think I heard, in a conversation over the telephone, that he said he had somebody who was a partner with him and he was coming to Toronto to consult the Department with reference to the specifications.

Q.—Did he put up a bond?

A.—I think so.

Q.—You don't know?

A.—I am quite sure he did.

Q.—Will you produce the contract with the Labarge Company and the bond?

A.—Yes.

Q.—I should like also if you would produce the different contracts with the McNamara Company and their bonds. Did the Labarge Company do the work?

A.—No, Mr. Raney.

Q.—They turned the contract over to the McNamaras?

A.—They sub-let it or assigned it.

Q.—Do you know anything about that?

A.—No, nothing. Except that it was assigned or sub-let.

Q.—For a consideration?

A.—I don't know. I know there was surprise.

Q.—What were the tenders?

A.—Labarge bid $59,165; McNamara, $59,440; another bid was $59,435.

Q.—Very close?

A.—They are very close and also for tar penetration: Labarge, $61,165; McNamara, $61,190. Warren Brothers bid $61,690 and there was another for $61,435.

Q.—They may have been comparing notes?

MR. FINLAYSON: You would have thought they would have produced better results.

MR. RANEY: Have you ever been told of the consideration from Mc-Namaras to Labarge?

A.—No.

Q.—At any rate the McNamaras did the work and your department settled wi h the McNamaras?

A.—I think perhaps the cheques were made to the McNamaras.

Q.—That would be natural. Now Mr. Bedford, of the Sault Retail Hardware, was mentioned, I think?

A.—Yes.

Q.—And is he a customer of yours?

A.—To some extent.

Q.—After the statement in the House last year that your company would not furnish any more materials to the Government what was done between your company and Bedford?

A.—Nothing in particular.

Q.—Did your department commence to purchase goods from Bedford?

A.—Did our department?

Q.—Yes.

A.—Yes. We did not commence. As a matter of fact I think if you will look it up Bedford's sales were in the neighbourhood of $3,000 before I made the statement in the House. Of course you would not know that.

Q.—There were sales to the Government?

A.—Yes.

Q.—You furnished goods to Bedford and Bedford to the Government?

A.—We sell to Mr. Bedford, Plummer Ferguson, James Street Hardware, Ed. Keys, all Sault merchants. We sell them for general sale, or general resale to the public.

Q.—You told me a while ago that $17,000, almost $18,000 supplied by you to the Government prior to the statement in the House last year were supplied on a competitive retail basis.

A.—Yes.

Q.—Well, then. Did you supply goods after that statement in the House ast year to Bedford and Bedford afterwards supplied the Government?

A.—I think that some of the goods Bedford purchased from us went to the Department of the Northern Development Branch, also some of the goods Plummer Ferguson bought, some from Ed. Keys and some other merchants sold.

Q.—How much in value did you supply Bedford?

A.—I don't know, Mr. Raney. I told Mr. Nash to take particular care to get that amount and what Mr. Bedford purchased from us and work out the merchants who had goods from us.

Q.—You say that several other Sault hardware men also purchased from your company and resold to the Government?

A.—I don't want it put that they were for sale to the Government. They purchased for general resale. Some of the goods may have gone to the Government.

MR. FINLAYSON: They bought them in as stock?

MR. LYONS: Yes.

MR. RANEY: You sold at wholesale prices and they sold to the Government at retail?

A.—I don't know what prices they sold them at. For instance now, Mr. Keys purchased from the Lyons Fuel and Supply Company in hardware about $1,500 or $1,600 and he sold to the Government about $552.

Q.—Give me those figures again.

A.—I think Mr. Keys bought about $1,500 or $1,600 and total sales to the Government during the same period was $552. Plummer Ferguson purchased $15,000 or $16,000 and their sales were $6,000. I cite this to show that it was not direct trading from us to the Department.

Q.—Have you any knowledge or information of commissions having been paid to persons who furnished goods for the aerodrome—by persons who furnished goods?

A.—How do you mean?

Q.—Commissions paid by persons who furnished goods for the aerodrome?

A.—No, I have not.

Q.—Nor for the Hearst farm, or for oil or gasolene?

A.—We do not handle the gasolene.

Q.—I am not identifying anybody. Have you any knowledge of such commissions?

A.—Absolutely none.

Q.—From any source?

A.—No. Take gasolene. We purchased by public tender from the Imperial Oil Company who were the successful tenderers.

MR. RANEY: I think that is all, Mr. Lyons.

MR. FINLAYSON: What about adjournment?

MR. LEWIS: Monday evening at the same hour, eight o'clock?

MR. FINLAYSON: Yes, that satisfies me, if it is convenient to Mr. Raney.

MR. RANEY: Who are called for Monday evening?

MR. FINLAYSON: We have not any report from the Clarkson people. If that is ready I should like to get rid of it.

MR. LEWIS: We are expecting to have some report from them.

MR. FINLAYSON: My own thought was that we could get the McNamaras down. They are working in West Toronto and it might be convenient to get them.

MR. LEWIS: We can get the Department officials at any time.

MR. FINLAYSON: They are like the poor in Scripture, always with us.

MR. RANEY: Is it your thought to proceed with this matter to the exclusion of other things?

MR. FINLAYSON: I thought so. And afterwards take up the Oakley matter. Those two seem to affect the position of members of the House and I think that for that reason they are entitled to precedence. But I will say this, it might happen that we exceed the available witnesses and we might have to wait for some others and then we can agree on what to take up. You suggested that the House might be delayed by it and I am anxious that we should reach the same stage as the House.

MR. RANEY: We can see how we get along.

MR. FINLAYSON: Would you like to have McNamara sometime on Monday?

MR. RANEY: Someone more than that. I would not think that would take a great deal of time.

MR. FINLAYSON: Can we get the men down from the Sault in that time?

MR. RANEY: Bring them all down. Those witnesses won't be long. We can get through those in an evening.

MR. LEWIS: There is McAllister. How many do you want before you have the report of the auditors. When you have that you may want to examine them afterwards.

MR. FINLAYSON: We are not anxious to bring them from the Sault and keep them at the public expense. They could be reached by Monday evening. I will try to arrange for enough witnesses for a reasonable evening on Monday.

MR. LEWIS: Could we not clear up a man like Mr. Bedford, for instance?

MR. LYONS: Take Mr. Bedford. While Mr. Clarkson was not instructed to do it, I asked him as a favour to go into the Bedford accounts and our dealings with him and his with the Northern Development Branch so that you will have the information here.

MR. RANEY: There is this about it. These statements will take a little time for consideration and a little time spent on them may save a good deal of time.

MR. LYONS: I think, Mr. Raney, when Mr. Nash's statement comes in it will clear matters entirely.

. MR. RANEY: I am inclined to think it would be better to suspend the inquiry here and go on with other things that are ready and wait for the report of the accountants and then clean things up.

MR. FINLAYSON: I don't think that is fair to anyone. Take McNamaras, Fitzpatrick and any others we can get.

MR. RANEY: Well, go ahead.

MR. LYONS: I should like Mr. Fitzpatrick as contractor for the aerodrome to come here and tell us his story.

MR. LEWIS: I think if we had McNamara and Fitzpatrick here on Monday it would fill out the evening.

MR. RANEY: I would not think so.

MR. FINLAYSON: I am not interested in family history.

MR. RANEY: Well, if you are going to devote to them Monday evening I have enough to go on with.

MR. LEWIS: We will adjourn then until Monday evening.

PUBLIC ACCOUNTS COMMITTEE.

Monday, March 22, 1926.

The Committee met at 8 p.m., with A. C. Lewis presiding.

MR. LEWIS: Now, gentlemen, if you are ready.

HON. W. E. RANEY: I should like to have three other witnesses summoned, Mr. Hoskins, the district engineer for Sudbury; Mr. L. H. Briggs—

MR. LEWIS: Mr. Raney, would you mind for the better handling of the minutes, putting that in the form of a motion?

MR. FINLAYSON: What are Briggs' initials?

MR. RANEY: L. H.

MR. FINLAYSON: Will you add the name of Roy Maxwell.

MR. RANEY: I move; seconded by Mr. Widdifield, that Mr. Hoskins, district engineer for Sudbury; L. H. Briggs, 63 Isabella Street, Captain Roy Maxwell and Duncan Macdonald, employed by the McNamara Construction Company, be summoned to appear before the Committee.

MR. LEWIS: You have heard the motion. All in favour? Carried.

MR. RANEY: I have another motion, seconded by Mr. Widdifield, that William G. Gerhart, homestead inspector, Bracebridge; James A. Brow, Port Severn; Mr. Dinsmore, Bethune Lumber Company, Huntsville, and W. C. Cain, deputy minister of Lands and Forests, to be summoned to appear before the Committee and give evidence concerning items on page G8 of the Public Accounts for 1925: William G. Gerhart, $1,100 and $253.25, and concerning Lot 11 in the 12th Concession of the Township of Sinclair, and to produce before the Committee all papers and correspondence with reference to such matters.

MR. LEWIS: You have heard the motion by Mr. Raney (reads resolution). All in favour. Shall the motion be adopted. Carried.

MR. RANEY: Moved by myself, seconded by Mr. Widdifield, that S. L. Squire, G. Hogarth, W. H. Brown, J. Telford (244 Jane Street, Toronto), Mr. Franklin (Boarding House, Caledon), John Brass (176 George Street, Toronto), C. L. McClintock (Streetsville), S. B. Greggs (R.R. 1, Laurel), David Hunter (R.R. 6, Orangeville), Richard Russell (Box 388 Orangeville), Kenneth Hannahson, (Orangeville) be summoned before the committee to give evidence with reference to items: J. G. McLean, $1,223, Peel Township, Brampton Chatsworth Bridge, Page K 22 of the Public Accounts 1925, $4,827.67, and bring with them and show to the Committee all books, accounts, vouchers, papers and correspondence having reference to the said project.

MR. LEWIS: You have heard the motion. No opposition. Carried.

Now we have called certain witnesses from out of town to examine in connection with the investigation into the projects of the Lyons Fuel and Supply Company, Limited, and so on. We have with us, I think, Mr. Fitzpatrick, the contractor on the aerodrome at the Sault. Will Mr. Fitzpatrick come forward please.

JAMES J. FITZPATRICK: (Sworn.   Examined by Mr. Finlayson.)

Q.—What is your business, Mr. Fitzpatrick.

A.—General contractor.

Q.—General contractor.   And where do you reside and carry on business?

A.—Sault Ste Marie.

Q.—How long have you been at the Sault?

A.—Twenty-five years.

Q.—How long have you been engaged as a contractor?

A.—Thirteen, nearly fourteen years.

Q.—And what kind of contracting do you undertake?

A.—Mostly buildings.

Q.—You mean houses and stores and that sort of thing?

A.—Schools.

Q.—Who have you been dealing with in that period as owners for whom you were building.

A.—Oh—

Mr. Lewis: He means what class of people.

Mr. Finlayson: City, municipal work?

A.—Yes, quite a bit.

Q.—Any Government work?

A.—Not any Government work until—only from the Federal Government.

Q.—Some Federal contracts?

A.—Yes.

Q.—What other contracts have you had of any size?

A.—I have a list I can read out to you. .

Q.—Just tell us so that we can get an idea of what you do. What is the biggest contract?

A.—The biggest contract is a High School, $140,300.

Q.—That would be for the Board of Education.

A.—Yes, the Public School Board.

Q.—The High School Board?

A.—Yes, the one from the public school board was $81,250, two wings to the centre of the school.

Q.—What other municipal contracts have you had.

A.—Another from the city for a pumping station for $31,000.

Q.—What did the Government work amount to?

A.—$23,170.

Q.—And apart from your work as a general builder—

A.—There is a fire hall, $31,000.

Q.—Now what are you in politics?

Mr. Sinclair: I don't think that is relevant.

Mr. Raney: I think he should answer if he wishes.

Mr. Finlayson: Answer or not as you like.

A.—I am a Conservative.

Q.—And have you had any contracts from the Government, the Ontario Government?

A.—This Government?

Q.—Yes?

A.—The aerodrome.

Q.—Is that the only one?

A.—There were small contracts afterwards, a sewer running into the river.

Q.—From the aerodrome?

A.—Yes, a private sewer. It does not connect with the city sewer.

Q.—In connection with the aerodrome?

A.—It was a separate contract altogether.

Q.—But in connection with the aerodrome property?

A.—Yes.

Q.—How long have you been dealing with the Lyons Fuel and Supply Company?

A.—Since about 1915.

Q.—And what is the volume of your business. How did it run from year to year.

A.—I did not keep track. Round about $30,000 with the brick school—

Q.—Was that all brick?

A.—Yes.

Q.—When was that?

A.—In 1921.

Q.—And running substantially for some years before that and some years after?

A.—When the fire hall was on we bought a good bit of stuff from the Lyons Company for the fire hall.

Q.—When was that?

A.—That would be in 1918, when the war was over.

Q.—Well, did they get the bulk of your business at that time?

A.—Yes.

Q.—Why?

A.—Well we had better prices, good service and I was satisfied and I bought there.

Q.—I see. Now when you were tendering on a contract did you get prices on supplies before you put in a figure?

A.—No, I don't know that we did it that fashion.

Q.—You find what the stuff is worth before putting in?

A.—Yes; I use my own judgment.

Q.—It is a common practice for contractors to get figures on hardware and so on before putting in?

A.—Some of the contractors do that in the Sault.

Q.—They get a figure to supply hardware according to the specifications of the architect?

A.—I don't know that. I sometimes get prices over the telephone and sometimes go up and get it.

Q.—Do you get figures from other firms?

A.—Before I tender?

Q.—You spoke of the Lyons Fuel and Supply Company?

A.—If I put in a tender, whoever I call up I don't call up anyone else. I know the prices pretty well, anyway.

Q.—From your experience you know what it ought to be?

A.—Yes, I know the figures fairly well without calling up.

Q.—Before I get to the aerodrome; have you at any time been connected with Mr. Lyons in any enterprise?

A.—No.

Q.—In any partnership. Has he ever had an interest with you or you with him?

A.—No.

Q.—With the firm or company or in any direct or indirect way?

A.—No. None whatever.

Q.—May I put it in this broad way: You never at any time had any business association with Mr. Lyons apart from the relations of purchaser and vendor in the open market?

A.—None whatever.

Q.—Let us carry it a step further about the aerodrome contract. Is there anything peculiar about that?

A.—Not that I know of.

Q.—Did he or his family or his firm or company have anything to do with that?

A.—Nothing whatever.

Q.—The tenders were asked for, I suppose, in the regular way?

A.—They were advertised.

Q.—Where did you see them?

A.—In the paper at the Sault.

Q.—Asking for tenders?

A.—Yes.

Q.—Did you get plans and specifications?

A.—From Mr. Lamb?

Q.—The resident engineer?

A.—Yes.

Q.—What did you do then?

A.—Went home and figured out the job.

Q.—Did you consult the Lyons Fuel and Supply Company as to furnishing the material?

A.—Over the telephone. I got prices over the telephone.

Q.—When would that be?

A.—Some time around the last of October.

Q.—Of 1924?

A.—Yes. Next day after I got the plans. I got the plans about five to six in the evening.

Q.—A year and a half ago?

A.—Yes.

Q.—And you got the figures from them?

A.—Yes.

Q.—Did you get any written figures?

A.—No. They were given to me over the phone and I wrote them down on the desk at the office.

Q.—Have you got them with you?

A.—I have got a copy.

Q.—Let me see what it is. You say it is a copy. It is on your paper, I see?

A.—Yes, I copied it out of the book.

MR. LEWIS: You took the figures down out of the book?

MR. FINLAYSON: You copied that. It is figures on tiles and so on, different sizes, and roofing, cement, stone, steel sash, glass, doors and fireproof doors?

MR. FITZPATRICK: Yes, big ones.

MR. RANEY: May we see it?

MR. FINLAYSON: Certainly. Here it is.

Examination continued: .

Q.—These were copied out of the book?

A.—Yes.

Q.—That was part of the material on which you made the tender?

A.—Yes.

Q.—Did you base the tender on these figures?

A.—Pretty well.

Q.—Well, then, did you see Mr. Lyons or any of his firm or anyone from him in connection with the tender?

A.—No.

Q.—Was he in the Sault at that time?

A.—No. At least I don't think he was. I don't know.

Q.—You can say you never saw him?

A.—Yes.

Q.—When the tenders closed who were they put in to?

A.—They were addressed to the Minister of Lands and Forests in Toronto here.

Q.—That would be in the Northern Development, in the **Forestry Branch**?

A.—That was where we addressed them. It was specified where to send the tenders.

Q.—You followed instructions and sent them here?

A.—Yes.

Q.—Did you have any arrangement with any other tenderers or know what they were doing?

A.—No.

Q.—Did you go to see Mr. Lyons in connection with it?

A.—No.

Q.—Did you ever see him in connection with the tender?

A.—No, I did not see him.

Q.—Where were you when the tenders were opened?

A.—In Toronto.

Q.—And how did you learn the result?

A.—It appears they wired the Sault.

A.—The Department wired?

A.—I guess so. Mr. Lamb got the wire and called up the house and my eldest son was on a motor trip and the second boy tried to get me on the phone and called Toronto and I was not there, but a party at the house knew where I was and—

Q.—That is not evidence. They got you in Toronto and as a result the news came to you that your tender was accepted?

A.—Yes, the tender was accepted.

Q.—What did you do then?

A.—I told him to get the foreman and tell him to go ahead with the work. He read the telegram over the phone. I told him to get the foreman and tell him to start work right away.

Q.—Did you sign a contract?

A.—I signed a contract at the Sault.

Q.—In the engineer's office?

A.—Yes.

Q.—And gave securities?

A.—Yes, a marked cheque was sent in with the tender.

Q.—How much?

A.—Three thousand dollars.

Q.—Did you furnish security in addition?

A.—Yes.

Q.—A bond?

A.—Yes.

Q.—During this time did you have any conversation or any message from anybody in connection with it?

A.—None whatever.

Q.—Was the tender put in in a purely business way?

A.—Just the same as any other tender.

Q.—No exception of any kind?

A.—None whatever.

Q.—Well then your next step after you signed the contract and put your security in?

A.—The job was started right away and we went ahead.

Q.—Did you know what the other tenders were, Mr. Fitzpatrick?

A.—No, I did not know. I heard afterwards.

Q.—Your contract was $61,100?

A.—Yes.

Q.—Others were $64,000, $65,000, $68,000, $72,000 and $111,000?

A.—I remember the $111,000. That was very high. It stuck in my memory. That was something you would not forget. I don't remember the others.

Q.—There seems to be a difference of $3,000 between yours and the second one?

A.—Yes.

Q.—That was Haney and Brackin?

A.—Brackin and Haney.

Q.—So you got the contract and got to work?

A.—Yes.

Q.—What time did you get to work?

A.—I think it was about the second of the October that the work was started as near as I can remember.

Q.—Before I go on can you tell me roughly the volume of business you had before this?

MR. RANEY: I don't think anyone is inclined to question Mr. Fitzpatrick's standing.

A.—It was not very high. Not an awful lot, $586,100 on seventy-five jobs, not on every job. I had sub-contracts with other firms, carpenters on different jobs and sublet the brick work and mason work.

Q.—Let us get down to the aerodrome work. What steps did you take with the Lyons Fuel and Supply Company as to the material they furnished?

A.—When I went back I went to and bought the material.

Q.—From whom?

A.—McAllister.

Q.—McAllister is the salesman?

A.—Yes, he sells most of the stuff.

Q.—What did you do?

MR. RANEY: Salesman for the Lyons Fuel and Supply Company?

A.—Yes.

MR. FINLAYSON: What did you do with him?

A.—I beat him down all I could on the material and saved quite a bit of money.

Q.—You beat him down and saved on it. How much was the reduction you refer to?

A.—Perhaps $2,000, perhaps it was a little more.

Q.—What was the amount of the order from the Lyons Company in connection with this work?

A.—I cannot tell you, I don't know.

Q.—Can you tell approximately?

A.—If I had known I could have taken that off the bills.

MR. RANEY: Do you keep any books?

A.—I did not take that off. I did not know I was to be asked these things. I just got a wire and I came here.

MR. RANEY: Mr. Lyons says it was $30,000 or $40,000.

A.—I would not contradict it.

MR. FINLAYSON (Proceeding): You cut him down $2,000?

A.—Yes.

Q.—What was the material you bought?

A.—I bought tile there and I bought some brick, not much, very little, and I bought sand and cement and gravel, and I gave him an order for the roofing, and I bought glass there.

Q.—The order for roofing, that was putting the roof on?

A.—Yes. That is their business. They are in that business.

Q.—I suppose the roofing, gravel and cement would be the big items?

A.—Yes, the tile was quite a big item.

Q.—Articles like cement, gravel and roofing are more or less standard, are they not?

A.—Yes, the roofing may vary. This was the cheapest roofing that we put on for some years. The Lyons Fuel Company has put on a lot of roofs. This was the cheapest they put on for me.

Q.—That would depend on the architect's specifications?

A.—Yes.

Q.—Apart from the roof, the brick, cement, tile, gravel—these are stock articles?

A.—Yes, I got $30 a thousand for brick and bought for $25 or $26.

Q.—You know what cement is going to cost, and gravel?

A.—Yes, this was graded gravel. It had to be screened and it was screened on the screens and brought to the job.

Q.—It all comes from one source.

A.—All from the St. Marie River.

Q.—You knew what it would be?

A.—Pretty close.

Q.—The fire brick, gravel, cement—you could figure on that too?

A.—Oh, yes, I could figure that without asking anyone about it.

Q.—There was very little chance for any change?

A.—No.

Q.—Before I am forgetting, was any rebate given to anybody in connection with this?

A.—I don't understand.

Q.—You got the price and beat them down. Did you pay that price?

A.—I paid the price I got when I went back.

Q.—Was there any other consideration?

A.—No, none.

Q.—Did you ever have occasion to discuss it with Mr. Lyons?

A.—Never.

Q.—Did you ever see him in connection with this job?

A.—At the aerodrome I saw him, not for longer than five minutes.

Q.—Did you have any discussion as to what his firm was going to get?

A.—No, none.

Q.—No talk about that at all?

A.—No.

Q.—The stuff was supplied as the contract went along?

A.—Yes.

Q.—The contract was completed?

A.—Yes.

Q.—Any dispute as to prices or extras or anything of that kind?

A.—No. There was some work I thought I should have got, but I did not get it. It only amounted to $25 or $35.

Q.—That is always true. Who was the architect for this?

A.—Mr. Finley.

Q.—A well-known architect?

A.—Yes, I have done a lot of work with him.

Q.—Did you have any disputes that had to be adjusted by the Department?

A.—No.

Q.—Did he, at any time, say anything to you as to where you were getting supplies?

A.—Oh, no.

Q.—Your business relations were the ordinary relations between contractor and architect?

A.—Yes.

Q.—Did the resident engineer have anything to do—you spoke of getting specifications from him?

A.—He just handed out the plans.

Q.—It was not in his Branch?

A.—The plans had to be sent some place and they were sent to the engineer.

Q.—A matter of convenience?

A.—Yes.

Q.—Well, you went ahead. Were there any incidents out of the ordinary in connection with this?

A.—I do not think so.

Q.—Any change in the specifications or plans? There are possibilities of helping the contractors to get extras?

A.—I did not get any.

Mr. Clarke: Any extras?

Mr. Raney: He says there was a matter of $30.

Mr. Finlayson: That was a matter of dispute.

Witness: I did the work and Mr. Finley disputed what my bill was and they did not pay me.

Mr. Finlayson: You claimed extras?

A.—It was an extra but they did not pay so much as I expected.

Q.—Is Mr. Raney correct in saying that that was the only extra on the job?

A.—The job went on quite a while.

Q.—Do you remember any extras?

A.—There was an extra putting in a floor downstairs and one extra fire door, a big door, putting in upstairs.

Q.—I suppose they were put in under the architect's orders?

A.—Yes, and the Government paid me 12 per cent.

Q.—Cost plus 12 for handlng?

A.—Yes.

Mr. Lewis: Under his certificate?

A.—Under Mr. Finley's supervision. He had to O.K. them.

Mr. Finlayson: That is the only extras you remember?

A.—That is all I can remember now.

Q.—So that the contract went along without dispute or incident of any kind?

A.—No trouble at all.

Q.—You were paid in the regular way?

A.—Yes.

Q.—You got security?

A.—Yes.

Q.—I see that although your contract was $60,000 your payment was somewhere approximately $80,000?

A.—Some place there—$80,000 or $81,000.

Q.—That was because your contract for cement was on a unit basis?

A.—The excavation and the cement were on a unit basis.

Q.—The architect's estimate of quantities was out?

A.—Yes, there was a difference.

Q.—Before the tender you put in on a unit basis?

A.—Yes, so much—there was a space to fill out for that.

Q.—And the difference as I understand it was on the unit basis?

A.—Just the unit basis, and so much a yard for concrete, whatever was taken out we were paid for.

Q.—And the architect figured out what you did and gave a certificate and that produced the additional amount?

A.—Yes.

Q.—All right, Mr. Sinclair?

Examination by W. E. N. SINCLAIR.

Q.—Just a question or two. What kind of roof was specified for this building?

A.—I think it was five-ply, built up, fine gravel roof.

Q.—Will you just explain what kind of a roof that is?

A.—It is a roof that is built up one layer after the other until you have five thicknesses and you put a coating of tar in between each layer until it is built up, until you have five thicknesses, and it runs like the shingles of a house. The width is about sixteen inches perhaps and there is fine gravel for the top. We have a certain sized gravel about the size of a marble.

Q.—From whom did you get a figure for the material to go into the roof?

A.—From the Hesson Lumber Company and the Lyons Fuel and Supply Company.

Q.—Was the Lyons Fuel and Supply Company a lower price or a higher price?

MR. RANEY: Hesson, you say?

WITNESS: They were the lowest tenderers.

MR. SINCLAIR: Why did you buy dearer?

A.—They did not put on the roof. They simply sell us the material, but he was going to get somebody from out of town to put the roof on. Now the Lyons Fuel and Supply Company has been putting on the roofs of all the big buildings I have done or built.

Q.—They are the only ones at the Sault who put roofs on?

A.—The Fleckhart Brothers sometimes.

Q.—You did not see him about putting it on and getting a price?

A.—He is too dear.

Q.—Did you get a figure?

A.—No.

Q.—How do you know he is too dear?

A.—I had dealings with him before.

Q.—So you had been before to him. You did not bother with anyone else but the Lyons Company?

A.—And the Hesson.

Q.—But you say the Hesson people could not put it on unless they sent out and brought in a man?

A.—Yes.

Q.—There is a guarantee with the roof?

A.—Yes.

Q.—They would have put it on cheaper?

A.—A little, they would not have saved me much.

Q.—Not very much, but something?

A.—They were $15 and something a square and the Lyons Fuel and Supply Company was paid $16.

Q.—That is a difference of $1 a square?

A.—No, I said $15 something.

Q.—You cannot say exactly?

A.—No.

Q.—It was a large contract?

A.—Yes it is a big building, 80 by 315 feet, I think, but I had no reason not to give it to the Lyons Fuel and Supply Company whether Mr. Lyons was Minister or not. They put on the roof and guaranteed it for twenty years and they have to stand behind the roof.

Q.—Would not the other man have guaranteed the roof?

A.—He might. If something went wrong what was I to do though? Call Mr. Hesson up? He is not a roof man.

Q.—He is a responsible contractor?

A.—He sells lumber. He is a mill man, sashes, doors.

Q.—With regard to the material you purchased, in getting your figures for the materials what companies do you see?

A.—I did not see anybody but the Lyons Fuel and Supply Company to buy tiles, we used their tiles all the time.

Q.—Whom did you see about glass?

A.—McAllister.

Q.—That is the Lyons' representative. Besides the Lyons' man whom did you see about the glass?

A.—I saw Plummer Ferguson.

Q.—A company at the Sault?

A.—Hardware store.

Q.—And how did their figures compare?

A.—Their prices were about thirty-three and one-half cents and the Lyons Fuel and Supply Company was thirty-one.

Q.—Did you see any other dealers other than the Lyons Fuel and Supply Company in all lines of material for this building before you settled?

A.—Before I bought? The gravel I bought direct because it had to be screened. You see if the gravel was not right the architect would not let it be used. It was screened and so it was all right.

Q.—He sells the gravel?

A.—The Lyons Fuel and Supply Company?

Q.—Yes?

A.—Yes.

Q.—Are they the only ones?

A.—Downey too.

Q.—Did you see Downey about the gravel?

A.—No.

Q.—Why not?

A.—Well Downey has a store there and gets gravel and puts it there and he has no screen and at the other place it is screened and comes to the job as it is wanted. I could not take it without being screened. If you want screened gravel you must buy where it is screened.

Q.—You only went to the Lyons Fuel and Supply Company the only one who sells screened gravel?

A.—Yes.

Q.—The only place you could buy it?

A.—That is the only place I could buy it.

Q.—Whom were you talking to over the telephone when you got the first figures before you tendered?

A.—McAllister.

Q.—You never saw any other person except McAllister over the figures?

A.—That is all.

Q.—Either before or after?

A.—You mean for what?

Q.—For prices?

A.—For prices on stuff. I saw Hesson.

Q.—I mean in the Lyons Company. McAllister was the only one in the Lyons Company that you had dealing with?

A.—Yes.

Q.—You did not see any other members of the firm or representatives or anybody else?

A.—No, I bought from McAllister.

Q.—What is his position?

Mr. Finlayson: Salesman.

A.—Salesman. I have been buying from McAllister for years.

Q.—And you beat him down $2,000?

A.—Yes.

Q—Is that $2·000 on his figures or $2,000 on the figures of competitors?

A.—That is $2,000 on his figures.

Q.—He gave you a statement how much the material would be and then you got a $2,000 reduction?

A.—Yes.

Mr. Sinclair: I guess that's all.

Examination by Hon. W. E. Raney.

Q.—Mr. Fitzpatrick, I see some pencilled markings on this paper that you handed in. The paper has quotations from the Lyons Fuel and Supply Company on it?

A.—Yes.

Q.—The first item is tile, 5, 8, 12, 20 cents each and opposite that in pencil, 18 cents?

A.—I got that for 18 cents. I beat him down two cents on the tile prices.

Q.—The price he gave you before your tender was accepted was 20?

A.—Yes.

Q.—Afterwards you went to him and beat him down to 18 cents?

A.—Yes.

Q.—I suppose the major item of expenditure in that matter was cement?

A.—I think it would be tile.

Q.—Perhaps tile; tile and cement would be the larger items?

A.—I guess tile is the biggest.

Q.—Mr. Lyons told us the other night that he had charged retail prices for these articles?

A.—Yes.

Q.—You knew you were paying retail?

A.—Oh, yes.

Q.—This was a large order on cement?

A.—Yes.

Q.—Why didn't you get wholesale prices?

A.—I could not buy cement any cheaper.

Q.—Could you not buy direct from the Canada Cement Company?

A.—I never did.

Q.—Did you try?

A.—No.

Mr. Finlayson: He has to get on the list, and have facilities.

Q—In the matter of roofing, the memorandum says $20 on the square. How many squares where there in this building? If you don't remember exactly—

A.—It was 315 by 80.

Mr. Lewis: Was it flat?

Witness: Yes.

Mr. Lewis: It is not round?

A.—It is up a little.

Mr. Lyons: I think the order was approximately 265 squares.

Mr. Widdifield: Two hundred and fifty-two.

Witness: The roof comes down and runs to the wall, there is a gutter.

Mr. Lyons: It was 265 squares.

Mr. Raney: What was the price the Hesson's quoted you?

A.—I cannot say for sure. It was 15 and somehing.

Q.—And the price quoted by Lyons was $20 a square.

A.—No, no. That was 16.

Q.—I have your memorandum before me, $20 a square, that was the price quoted?

A.—Yes.

Q.—You had a tender from Hesson before?

A.—Before?

Q.—Before you put in the tender?

A.—No, I had not.

Q.—Did you get the prices from Lyons before you put in the tender for the aerodrome?

A.—Yes.

Q.—And also before, from Hesson?

A.—On the roof?

Q.—Yes.

A.—No.

Q.—After you got the contract then you went to Hesson?

A.—No Hesson came to me on the job.

Q.—And Hesson gave a price of $15 and something a square and then you went to the Lyons Fuel and Supply Company and told them "Hesson is giving this and you have got to be somewhere near him"?

A.—I don't know whether it was before. I can't just remember exactly, but I know I beat him down to $16. I don't know what day.

Q.—Your item is $16 in pencil. So that with Hesson's tender before you and this $20 price from the Lyons Fuel and Supply Company you went to Lyons and said, "You have got to make it less" and McAllister said, "I will make it $16"?

A.—Yes. I beat him down $4 on the roof.

Q.—Did you tell the Lyons Fuel and Supply Company Hesson's price?
A.—No.
Q.—That is where you got the benefit?
A.—Yes.
Q.—Then you did not use any fire brick?
A.—Just a few inside the chimney.
Q.—And some common brick?
A.—We used some common on the top of the building.
Q.—Did you beat him down on this?
A.—Yes, I said a few minutes ago from $30 to $26.
Q.—I think it is $26 here. Anyone else give a price on the brick?
A.—No.
Q.—Then steel sash. I see the price is $2,439 and opposite that is $2,939.
That is a drop of $500. Did someone give you a price on that?
A.—Not at that time. No.
Q.—Did anybody at any time give you a price on the steel sash except
the Lyons Company?
A.—That is pretty hard to remember. It is quite a while ago.
Q.—That is what you are here for.
A.—I am on oath here, you know.
Q.—You strike me as trying to remember.
A.—I will try to tell everything I can.
Q.—I can see that. Your face is a good certificate of character.
A.—Thank you. I cannot say about that job. I know we did some work
and got prices for the steel sash.
Q.—You must have had some argument. I notice that he threw off $500
on one item?
A.—I did some talking and I was well able to do it.
Q.—You got $500 on that?
A.—Yes.
Q.—I see you have roller doors. I see they gave you a price, $5,520. Did
anyone else give a price on the doors?
A.—No.
Q.—You must have done some talking there?
A.—Yes. Only one company makes the doors.
Q.—Who is that?
A.—The A. B. Ormsby Company.
Q.—Where are they?
A.—Gosh, I can't say.
Mr. Finlayson: Toronto.
Q.—Why didn't you buy from them?
A.—I called McAllister on the phone and asked him to wire for prices on
the doors. It is something I don't know anything about and I could not figure
it, and he wired.
Q.—When?
A.—When I got the plans.
Q.—Before you tendered?
A.—Oh, yes.
Q.—He wired when?
A.—I don't know about the date. He wired and got the prices and gave
them to me.
Q.—There is $5,000 and something—$5,020. You paid?

A.—Oh yes, I paid. Yes.

Q—Did you find from anyone else what these doors really were?

A—No. There is only one company I know that makes the doors.

Q.—You had no idea whether the doors were worth $5,020 or $4,020?

A.—I did not know. I took a chance.

Q.—And not having any knowledge you thought you would be safer and went and said, "This is $1,000 too much"?

A.—I don't know what I said to him.

Q.—You got $500?

A.—I beat him down.

Q.—Tell me this, and I would like you to think about it, Why did you not order direct from Ormsby yourself?

A.—Because I saw McAllister and asked him to wire. If I asked you that I would not buy from anyone else without going to you first.

Q.—He put it up $500 so that he could take it off?

A.—He had a chance to take it off.

Q.—Why didn't you wire Ormsby and Company yourself?

A.—Well, I don't think I have bought two items direct out of the Sault since I was a contractor. I bought from dealers all the time.

Q.—Who made the steel sash?

A.—I cannot tell you.

Q.—You don't know where that came from?

A.—No.

Q.—You were out to make as much on the contract as you could and these were sizeable items, $3,439, $1,520, according to the first figures and you argued with McAllister and you didn't know what they were worth?

A.—I took quite a while.

Q.—You fought quite a while. Tell me did you get prices from the Cochrane Company on the glass?

A.—When? After I had closed the order from the Lyons Company? They were the lowest price, 31 cents, and the other people were 33½ cents.

Q.—What was the Cochrane Company's price?

A.—They gave me a bulk price on the glass.

Q.—You didn't tell Mr. Sinclair about that?

A.—He did not ask me.

Q.—He asked about other prices on the glass and you said Plummer Ferguson?

A.—I said from the Plummer Ferguson. I had two legitimate prices, the other price came in after the glass was ordered.

Q.—How did it compare with the Lyons' price?

A.—It was lower.

Q.—How much?

A.—I could not say. I am not sure how much.

Q.—See if you can remember. There was a lot of glass required?

A.—Over 4,000 lights.

Q.—You figured out, of course, to see what was the difference between the Cochrane's and the Lyons' price?

A.—I didn't figure at the time.

Q.—But afterwards?

A.—Yes. I was not interested in the Cochrane price.

Q.—What difference was there?

A.—I could not say for sure.

Q.—About how much?

A.—$300 or $400, something like that. That is offhand. I am not positive.

Q.—That is near enough. Then you did the aerodrome sewer?

A.—Yes.

Q.—By tender?

A.—Yes.

Q.—How much was that?

A.—I think the tender was $690. It was a little sewer, running into the river.

Q.—And other tenderers?

A.—Oh, yes, several.

Q.—There were advertisements over the tender?

A.—Yes, I don't know how many.

Q.—How much were you paid?

A.—For the sewer, $690.

Q.—Just the tender?

A.—Yes, no extras.

Q.—The glass you used in the building came from the Lyons Company?

A.—Yes, I bought it from the Lyons Company.

Q.—Did the Cochrane Company have anything to do with it?

A.—Not to my knowledge.

Q.—Why did you say you had not bought from the Cochrane Company?

A.—They charged too much.

Q.—How did they come to put in a price in this case?

A.—A lad came up to the work and handed us a sheet.

Q.—You didn't ask?

A.—No, he came up after the glass was ordered.

Q.—You say it was after the glass was ordered?

A.—Yes, after I had placed the order.

MEMBER: You are not on the jobbers' list as a jobber are you?

A.—No.

MEMBER: The reason you did not get prices direct was because you could not, wasn't it?

A.—I don't know.

MEMBER: If you are not on the jobbers' list you have to do business through an agent?

A.—Why, sure.

MR. WIDDIFIELD: You mentioned a private contract for that sewer in connection with a public enterprise. What does that mean?

A.—Private sewer? It was not connected with the city.

MR. FINLAYSON: It was not a municipal thing. It went to the river.

MR. FINLAYSON (Re-examining).

Q.—Just two or three things. As to the roof. You require roofing on all buildings?

A.—Yes.

Q.—And the roofing is specified by the contract?

A.—Yes.

Q.—And you had to give a guarantee in connection with that building for twenty years?

A.—Generally it is twenty years.

Q.—And in a northern country like that it is quite a risk?

A.—It is a bit hard on the roof some winters.

Q.—And you are responsible financially?

A.—Yes.

Q.—And the Lyons Company gave a guarantee?

Mr. RANEY: And the Hesson Company?

Mr. FINLAYSON: Just let me finish. The Lyons Company were responsible financially and they had supplied the roof for other buildings, schools, high schools, public school, municipal buildings?

A.—Fire hall.

Q.—And they gave you a guarantee?

A.—Yes.

Q.—And they have run along for years satisfactorily?

A.—Yes.

Q.—And you were being relieved of your guarantee by getting a guarantee from a strong financial man?

A.—Yes.

Q.—About the Hesson Company—not their financial ability—they don't put the roof on?

A.—No.

Q.—If any leak developed and the owners complained you would pass it on to the Lyons Company?

A.—For sure.

Q.—But you could not pass it on to Hesson?

A.—I guess I would have had to get up and fix it.

Q.—In your case you were playing safe?

A.—We try in the Sault, on a big job, to play safe on the roof all the time.

COLONEL CURRIE: What kind of a roof was it?

A.—Five-ply, built up.

Q.—Barrett specifications?

A.—Pretty much the same.

Mr. FINLAYSON: They look to the Barrett people probably. The main thing is to have a roof you can look to?

A.—Yes.

Q.—You are not a roofer?

A.—I could put a roof on.

Q.—That is not your trade?

A.—No.

Q.—Nor Hesson's trade?

A—No.

COLONEL CURRIE: You could have been cheated on the roof. They could save a lot by giving you a poor roof?

WITNESS: They could not with the architect up on the roof every day. I will say he was on the job all day long every day.

Examination by Mr. SINCLAIR

Q—Would not a written guarantee from the Hesson Company have been a satisfactory guarantee that you could have enforced in court?

A.—I believe it would be. Yes.

Q—And as it stands you have not a guarantee bond or anything of that kind from the Lyons Company? Just the ordinary guarantee?

A.—Just the ordinary guarantee and they will fix the roof or they will get no more business from me.

Q—If Hesson gave you a written guarantee it would be a guarantee you could enforce in court if the roof went wrong?

A.—Oh, yes.

MR. FINLAYSON: In one case a lawsuit and in the other case a fact.

WITNESS: I buy stuff wherever I like. I am not guided by anyone. I have bought lumber from Hesson and cement from the Lyons Company.

Q.—Why?

A.—Because it suited me.

MR. FINLAYSON: Pass to cement. Sault Ste. Marie is a competitive lake and rail point?

A.—Yes.

Q.—If you got a shipment, a large enough shipment, you could get the benefit of a competitive rate, so that a person who took a boat load of cement could get a possible contract?

A.—Yes.

Q.—And you could not do that?

A.—No.

Q.—But the Lyons Fuel and Supply Company could? They have the dock facilities?

A.—Yes.

Q.—It would have been hopeless for you to have gone to the Canada Cement?

A.—Oh, yes.

Q.—As a matter of fact they were not dealing—

MR. RANEY: Don't coax him too much.

A.—I rather think not. I never tried them. I had no place to store cement either.

Q.—And cement deteriorates?

A.—If it gets hard you are done.

MR. SINCLAIR: Do other dealers at the Sault sell dearer than the Lyons people?

A.—They have.

Q.—No big quantities?

A.—Yes they do.

Q.—How do they get any business, or don't they?

A.—Yes.

Q.—People will pay more than for the Lyons' people cement?

A.—I don't understand you.

Q.—What I mean is this, Mr. Fitzpatrick. Can't you buy a thousand barrels as cheap from anybody else as the Lyons Company at the Sault?

A.—No. Anyway not this time.

Q.—Never?

A.—Well, it all depends on whether they will give prices or not. If the Lyons people sell cheaper than anyone else at the Sault you might buy from the Lyons Company on one job and the next job another Sault man might beat him on price to get the business. There is never any set price all the time.

Q.—Did you get the price of cement from anyone else besides Lyons for this building?

A.—No.

Q.—You did not know then whether the Lyons Company was up or down?

A.—If you had bought as much as I have and bought from Lyons and Downey you would know.

Q.—I want to know if Lyons sells cheaper than Downey or other men?

A.—He has to me in many cases.

Q.—To the general trade?

A.—He does what he can to get the business.

Q.—There are men at the Sault who will pay more for cement than buy from the Lyons Company?

A.—I would not say that. You don't understand. I get a contract in the Sault and perhaps I will buy from Downey cheaper than from Lyons and maybe the next big contract Lyons will beat him and for sure I will buy where I can buy the best.

Q.—In this deal you did not see anyone else?

A.—I could not get a better price from Downey.

Q.—But you have just told me that one day one fellow would be up and the other down and yet you did not see anyone but Lyons?

A.—That is all and I had a good deal.

MR. FINLAYSON: In other words you had been doing busines for fifteen years and knew when you got a good one. You know what the C.U.F.A. is? The Canadian Underwriters Fire Association?

A.—Yes.

Q.—And they fix the specifications for fire doors?

A.—Yes.

Q.—And Ormsby makes the doors to answer to the specification and Ormsby has a jobbers' list?

A.—I suppose so.

MR. RANEY: Please don't tell the witness too much, Mr. Finlayson. I have heard judges say that when counsel leads a witness they disregard the evidence.

MR. FINLAYSON: If these counsel say much more we will have them committed. You know what underwriters are, anyway?

A.—Yes.

Q.—And the specifications for fire doors?

A.—Yes.

Q.—And who sells the doors?

A.—Ormsby sells, I don't know who else.

Q.—Are you on Ormsby's jobbers' list?

A.—No.

Q.—Whom did you have to buy from?

A.—I bought from McAllister. I got the prices on the telephone before I figured the job at all.

Q.—The doors are not like cement?

A.—No, not as easy to figure.

Q.—It was a door for that particular purpose?

A.—Yes. There are all fire doors in the aerodrome now.

MR. LEWIS: Any other member like to ask a question?

MR. TELLIER: What kind of cement was used?

A.—Canada cement.

MR. LEWIS: Any more. Call Mr. Lamb.

Garrett Lamb sworn. Examined by Mr. FINLAYSON.

Mr. Lamb, at present you are district or resident engineer for the Northern Development Branch at the Sault?

A.—Yes.

Q.—What are your qualifications?

A.—I have been engaged in engineering work—

Q —I mean scholastic qualifications. Are you a graduate—

A.—Of Toronto University. Civil engineer.

Q.—I see. How long have you engaged in engineering?

A.—About twenty years including time at school.

Q.—That would mean sixteen years since you graduated?

A.—I graduated in 1915.

MR. FINLAYSON: 1915—

MR. LEWIS: Perhaps I can explain. You worked in between your courses, like a good many engineers?

WITNESS: Exactly.

MR. LEWIS: A few years of practical work and then you take your examination.

MR. FINLAYSON (Proceeding): Tell me your experience since then, Mr. Lamb.

A.—Since 1915?

Q.—Yes.

A.—I worked with M. E. Cooley, engineer, Ann Harbor, in New York.

Q.—Michigan?

A.—New York.

Q.—You mean you were doing work in New York State?

A.—Yes.

Q.—What was the nature of that work?

A.—On the public service railways.

Q.—After that?

A.—I was with the City of Port Arthur, assistant engineer.

Q.—How long?

A.—A year and a half.

Q.—General municipal work?

A.—Yes.

Q.—After that?

A.—I was with the Riordan Pulp and Paper Company.

Q.—How long were you there?

A.—A few months.

Q.—After that?

A.—I was with Frank Barber.

Q.—An engineer in town?

A.—Yes.

Q.—Go quickly over the rest.

A.—I was with Kerry and Chase.

Q.—Hydraulic engineer. And after that to the Department?

A.—Yes.

Q.—When did you make application to the Department?

A.—About the end of April, 1924.

Q.—Who did you apply to?

A.—Mr. Fullerton.

Q.—Deputy minister?

A —Yes.

Q.—And the result?

A.—He sent me to see Mr. Lyons.

Q.—Had you known Mr. Lyons before?

A.—That was the first time I met him.

Q.—Did you have any business connection with his firm or with anybody there?

A.—None whatever.

Q.—Well, then what was the result of the interview with Mr. Lyons in April, 1924?

A.—He told me there were two other applicants who had a better chance and to see him in a few days, so I went looking after another job. I thought he was putting me off.

Q.—That does happen, doesn't it? What then?

A.—I saw Mr. Fullerton and told him that I had been used to doing four men's work. He said, "Did you tell the Minister that?" I think he told him. I was at Timmins when I got a wire from the Sault. Mr. Fullerton was at the Sault and I went there.

Q.—And what became of that?

A.—He wired for me to go to work.

Q.—So you were engaged?

A.—Yes.

Q.—That was in—?

A.—Second of May, 1924.

Q.—You have been on nearly two years?

A.—Two years in May.

Q.—What was your position? Tell the Committee very briefly. What area do you cover?

A.—From Espanola to Hornpayne and from the Sault to Oba, 160 miles east and west and 200 miles north and south.

Q.—Headquarters at the Sault?

A.—Yes.

Q.—Whom did you take over from?

A.—J. Lang.

Q.—What became of him?

A.—He is still at the Sault.

Q.—In the Government employ?

A.—Engineering and contracting.

MR. RANEY: Is that the same name? Is this Mr. Lang?

MR. FINLAYSON: No, this is Lamb. So Mr. Lang's position was the same as yours?

A.—No.

Q.—What is the difference?

A.—When Mr. Lyons took over the Department and became Minister he united three departments, the Northern Development, Colonization Roads and also the Bridges in the north country and Mr. Lang had only charge of the Northern Development Branch.

Q.—Was Lang full time with the Crown?

A.—Part time, I understand.

Q.—Did you go on full time?

A.—Yes.

Q.—Have you told us all the details in connection with your employment?

A.—Everything.

Q.—Any conversation with the Minister or anybody for him as to where you were to get materials or supplies?

A.—No.

Q.—Will you tell the Committee briefly how this is done? What do you purchase locally and under what conditions, and what from Toronto? What are the regulations?

A.—Well there are so many items that have to be treated differently it is hard to explain. Take meat and provisions. Meat particularly. We buy on a standing order. When a camp is opened a certain butcher is given the business and as long as he is satisfactory and gives a right price and good meat we retain him because we cannot keep on jumping from one dealer to another on an item like that. But take bridge steel, reinforcing steel, office supplies and office equipment, they are purchased through the head office in Toronto.

Q.—You have nothing to do with that?

A.—Simply requisitioning it.

Q.—And the Department supply it. You have nothing to do with payment?

A.—The account has to be certified.

Q.—But for local matters such as meat and so on you have to pay at once?

A.—Yes.

Q.—How do you get funds?

A.—We notify the head office.

Q.—Who do you mean, head office?

A.—Mr. Fullerton, the Deputy Minister, all correspondence is with the Deputy Minister.

Q.—You notify him—?

A.—Of the approximate requirements.

Q.—For what period?

A.—A month as a rule.

Q.—At the end of a month you notify him what you will probably require for the next month?

A.—Yes.

Q.—I suppose that in the winter months it is very small and in the summer big?

A.—Exactly.

Q.—How is money supplied?

A.—It is deposited in the Bank of Montreal at the Sault.

Q.—To the credit of—?

A.—The Northern Development Branch.

Q.—Who has the power to check out?

A.—I sign the cheques and they are countersigned by the accountants?

Q.—Well now that would cover the pay roll?

A.—Pay roll—

Q.—And the articles you spoke of like meat and board bill?

A.—Gravel bill, and smaller accounts from settlers, board bills and so on.

Q.—Things that have to be paid in cash, where people cannot afford to wait for the money?

A.—Yes.

Q.—The larger items, how is material for road construction obtained, how do you obtain that?

A.—Well, mostly locally.

Q.—What is the practice? An order is given?

A.—We have a regulation order.

Q.—An order book?

A.—Yes.

Q.—How is it made out?

A.—In triplicate.

Q.—Different colours, I believe. ·And what becomes of the three copies?

A.—One goes to the dealer.

Q.—When he gets the order?

A.—Yes. One is retained at the office until the account comes in and the third one is kept in the book as a record.

Q.—The one that goes to the dealer comes back with the order?

A.—No. He retains it.

Q.—The second is attached to the order and sent where?

A.—To Mr. Fullerton.

Q.—Is it certified by you?

A.—Yes.

Q.—So that the Department have an opportunity to check up the invoice against the order?

A.—Yes.

Q.—And when the goods are delivered who checks?

A.—I had a man doing that specially last year when we had a lot of work, he was a sort of auditor.

Q.—Now were instructions given you at any time as to where you were to deal?

A.—No.

Q.—Was it ever suggested by anyone in the Lyons Fuel and Supply Company that it would be wise to give orders to the Lyons Company?

A.—No, it was not.

Q.—Directly or indirectly?

A.—No.

Q.—When you came there where did you find the Department were dealing, the Branch? They had not been dealing with Lyons Fuel and Supply Company exclusively?

A.—No.

Q.—What others?

A.—A great many others.

Q.—You found they had been dealing with them?

A.—Yes.

Q.—There were many other firms dealing in builders' supplies?

A.—No.

A.—Any others?

A.—One.

Q.—Who was that?

A.—R. J. Downey.

Q.—Is this Downey firm the only competitor Lyons had in the building supplies?

A.—Practically.

Q.—What was the practice as to prices?

A.—I tried to get the price on the phone in most cases, the competitive price, and kept a memorandum of that as long as the deal was on and then destroyed it.

Q.—You telephoned round to get the figures from people in that line and whom did you give the order to?

A.—To the lowest tenderer everything else being equal. Sometimes circumstances arose that made it impossible to do that.

Q.—Other things being equal you gave it to the lowest tenderer?

17 J

A.—Yes.

Q.—And that firm or corporation would get the order?

A.—Yes.

Q.—You would give the order out of the book?

A.—Yes.

Q.—And when the goods came in they were checked up and that was sent to Toronto?

A.—Yes, exactly.

Q.—Where was payment made from?

A.—From Toronto.

Q.—You had nothing to do with the payment?

A.—Sometimes cheques came to our office.

Q.—Payable to the person supplying the goods?

A.—Yes.

Q.—Now was any change made? Did you get any instructions as to who you were to buy from?

A.—In March, 1925, I received orders to do no more business with the Lyons Fuel and Supply Company.

Q.—Have you got that letter?

A.—Yes.

Q.—Let me see it. This is a letter from the Northern Development Branch, re purchases. It reads as follows:

Dear sir,

I have received a memorandum from Hon. Mr. Lyons, Minister of this Department, requesting me to advise any of our officials with whom the Lyons Fuel and Supply Company have been doing business to refrain from making any further purchases from this company, the reason being that serious objection has been made to the Government buying goods from incorporated joint stock companies where some of the shareholders may be members of the Legislature. You will, therefore, govern yourself accordingly.

Yours very truly,
(Sgd.) C. H. Fullerton.

G. J. Lamb,
Sault Ste. Marie,
Ontario.

That is dated 18th March, 1925. Did you make any change after that?

A.—We ceased buying from the Lyons Company.

SAM CLARKE: You did not buy from the Lyons Fuel and Supply Company after that?

A.—No.

MR. FINLAYSON: What effect would that have in a case where builders' supplies were only handled by two concerns?

A.—I suppose we had to pay more for it.

COLONEL CURRIE: You had to pay more for it, of course?

MR. RANEY: Why, Mr. Lamb?

WITNESS: No competition.

MR. FINLAYSON (Proceeding): Before that you got competitive prices from Downey and the Lyons Fuel and Supply Company?

A.—Yes.

Q.—Did Downey get orders from you?

A.—After that?

Q.—Before that?

A.—Yes.

Q.—Right along?

A.—Yes.

Q.—After that were you confined to Downey?

A.—Yes.

MR. CLARKE: Could you not outside the Sault. You were not confined to the Sault?

WITNESS: We bought relatively in small quantities.

MR. CLARKE: I suppose you had big jobs?

WITNESS: Yes, we had. But we have not had any big jobs since that.

COLONEL CURRIE: At any rate all quantities over $500 have to be bought by tender and under $500 the engineer can buy.

WITNESS: I had not instructions, but that is about it substantially.

COLONEL CURRIE: All engineers understand that?

MR. RANEY: How far is it from the Sault to the nearest town where there is competition? Sudbury on the east, I suppose?

WITNESS: Blind River and Thessalon.

MR. FINLAYSON: (Proceeding): What I want first to get at is that the only competitive point would be Sudbury on the east where there is any real competition?

A.—Yes, I suppose so.

Q.—And on the other side?

A.—Port Arthur.

Q.—You spoke of the possibility of cement on Blind River, what about the price?

A.—We would have to pay a little more.

Q.—There is no rail and lake competitive delivery at Blind River?

A.—They could get cement by boat.

Q.—There are very few people who do. Do you know the rates on cement to the Sault from the Canada Cement Company?

A.—No.

Q.—Do you know how it compares with other places?

A.—No.

COLONEL CURRIE: The rate to a point like Blind River is the rate by water plus rail.

MR. FINLAYSON: As a matter of fact for the Committee's information the rates have no comparison and the Sault is most favourable.

MR. LYONS: Canada Cement sells at a 9-cent flat rate by lake and to connect with Alpina the rate from Montreal is 26 or 29. The rate does not enter in.

MR. FINLAYSON: Which puts Blind River off the map. Now you say that this letter is the only written instructions you have ever had of any kind?

A.—Yes.

Q.—Any verbal instructions?

MR. RANEY: Have you the letter there?

MR. FINLAYSON: That is put in. Had you any verbal instructions that you were to give preference to the Lyons Fuel and Supply Company?

A.—No.

Q.—You are a responsible engineer, a graduate of Toronto University?

A.—Yes.

Q.—And your responsibility as an engineer has never been interfered with?

A.—No.

Q.—You have been given a free hand as a responsible engineer?

A.—Yes.

Q.—You know what that means? Does that apply to other concerns from which you might get influenced?

A.—Yes.

Q.—There has never been any attempt to use influence indirectly or in any other way, making it as wide as we can?

A.—No.

Examination by Mr. SINCLAIR.

Q.—You say the only two concerns at the Sault selling builders' supplies are the Lyons Fuel and Supply Company and the Downey Company?

A.—Yes.

Q.—What is included in builders' supplies? Cement—?

A.—And brick, tile, lime, sand, gravel—

Q.—I see, and materials of that kind. And after March 25th all this was purchased from Downey during the whole year?

A.—Yes.

Q.—How much business are you doing up there?

A.—Well, it varies greatly. We did a lot of concrete bridge work in 1924.

Q.—I mean since 1925, since you were dealing with Downey alone?

A.—There was a comparatively small amount.

Q.—I see the Public Accounts give Downey and Son $2,927.28 in the making of roads in the Northern Development Branch?

A.—I think we used cement in three bridges since then.

Q.—And what kind of material did you buy from Bedford and Company?

A.—General hardware and the concrete pipe.

Q.—They handled concrete pipe, but no cement or builders' supplies such as you call them, and when did you start dealing with Bedford?

A.—When I first went there?

Q.—In 1924?

A.—Yes.

Q.—How much dealing did you have in 1924?

A.—Very little in 1924. He could not meet competition.

Q.—And then in 1925? He had changed his heart a little?

A.—Yes.

Q.—And what happened to Bedford to change his heart in 1925?

A.—I don't know. I suppose he could buy better.

Q.—In 1925 his prices were too high?

A.—Yes.

Q.—How did you come to bother with him in 1925 when you could not deal with him in 1924?

A.—We always give them a chance. It is pretty limited. It is only a few hundred dollars.

MR. LYONS: Between $700 and $800. The whole purchases at the Sault that year only amounted to about $11,000.

MR. SINCLAIR: You got $14,000?

MR. LYONS: I mean outside.

MR. SINCLAIR: This last year you were not doing a great amount with Downey and Sons, but Bedford's account gives $8,137.82. How did you happen to get him in line this year to do so much business when last year you could not deal with him?

A.—He could not meet the prices in 1924.

Q.—And this year he could?

A.—Yes.

Q.—How did you find out he had changed his mind?

A.—I suppose he came after me for business. They all do.

Q.—I think you said to my learned friend you generally get your own goods?

A.—In case of a small order.

Q.—What kind of hardware would you get from a man like Bedford for instance?

A.—Pegs, shovels, axes, camp equipment.

Q.—Were you using more in 1925 than in 1924?

A.—Yes.

Q.—How was it you did not use more builders' supplies in 1925 than in 1924?

A.—This year we were cutting out new roads which required putting in camps, utensils and supplies and then again last year was a heavy year in concrete purchases.

Q.—From whom were you buying stuff in 1924 that you bought from Bedford in 1925?

A.—Cochrane Hardware, Plummer Ferguson.

Q.—All of it?

A.—I think they had the business pretty well.

Q.—Anything from the Lyons Company in 1924 that you bought this year, 1925, from Bedford?

A.—Concrete pipe.

Q.—Anything else?

A.—I don't think so.

Q.—Where did he get the concrete pipe from?

A.—From the Lyons Company.

MR. RANEY: What, Bedford?

MR. LYONS: I told you that Mr. Raney. Surely you are not surprised?

MR. RANEY: Yes, I am.

MR. SINCLAIR: You won't grudge me five minutes then?

COLONEL CURRIE: Go after the big stuff.

MR. SINCLAIR (Continuing): The concrete pipe this year was bought from the Bedford firm and Bedford bought from the Lyons people?

A.—Yes.

Q.—And this year by whom was it delivered to the job?

A.—Bedford.

Q.—Not the Lyons people?

A.—Bedford, so far as I know.

Q.—Do you know? Can you swear to it?

A.—No.

Q.—You cannot say whether it was the Lyons' truck or the Bedford truck. What else went into Bedford's account?

A.—Blankets, beds, cooking utensils, nails, I think that is about all.

Q.—Now how big a business does Bedford run? I mean how big a store has he?

A.—It is a first-class store.

Q.—Ordinary retail hardware?

A.—Well, yes, a little above the ordinary.

Q.—How big would it be?

A.—Probably thirty feet frontage.

Q.—Just an ordinary store, and from whom did he get his blankets?

A.—I don't know.

Q.—Was he carrying blankets in 1924?

A.—No.

Q.—And was he carrying beds in 1924?

A.—No.

Q.—And was he carrying cooking utensils in 1924?

A.—Yes.

Q.—He had them anyway, I suppose, a kettle or two, and of course he would have nails, but he had no blankets or beds in 1924?

A.—Not to my knowledge.

Q.—He sold to the Department in 1925 and you cannot tell us how you happened to find Bedford for blankets and beds in 1925 when he had not been selling them in 1924?

A.—It is the custom of dealers to run after me for business. He possibly told me that he would be in a better position to supply our needs this year than in 1924.

Q.—You didn't ask him where he got his beds from?

A.—That does not concern me.

Q.—You don't know?

A.—I suppose he bought them from the Lyons Fuel and Supply Company.

Q.—Do you know?

A.—Yes.

Q.—And where did he get his blankets?

A.—The same place.

Q.—From the Lyons Fuel and Supply Company and they went from Bedford on the account of the Northern Development business. You as resident engineer bought the goods from Bedford?

A.—Yes.

Q.—Bedford bought from Lyons?

A.—I am not concerned where he bought.

MR. RANEY: He said Lyons supplied Bedford.

MR. SINCLAIR: I know, I know. And you bought from Bedford?

A.—Yes.

Q.—You are sure of that?

A.—Yes.

Q.—And the bills were made out to Bedford?

A.—Yes.

Q.—And you did not see any of these things come in on the Lyons truck?

A.—No.

Q.—You were buying these things on what basis, retail, wholesale or what?

A.—Well, I could never find out. I was dealing with firms doing a wholesale and retail business.

Q.—How many beds for instance did you buy in 1925?

A.—About a hundred, possibly.

Q.—And how many blankets?

A.—Six hundred, I should say, speaking from memory.

Q.—Just round number. And you bought these retail at the Sault?

A.—I bought them on a competitive basis.

Q.—You bought them from retailers?

A.—In competition with wholesalers.

Q.—How many did you buy from Bedford?

A.—Possibly 250 or 300.

Q.—That is 300 blankets?

A.—Pairs.

Q.—Six hundred pairs was the total you bought?

A.—Six hundred.

Q.—Was it 600 singles?

A.—Six hundred pairs.

Q.—You bought them from Bedford?

A.—I don't think I bought them all from Bedford.

Q.—What about the beds?

A.—I think I bought fifty from Bedford.

Q.—And fifty from other dealers?

A.—Yes.

Q.—And were they bought on a competitive basis or retail?

A.—In that particular case I had to take them where I could get them. Some of the dealers did not have the particular blankets I wanted to get.

Q.—Did you try to get them wholesale at the opening of the season? You knew how many you wanted?

A —It is a peculiarity about our business that we don't know and in buying a number and keeping them on hand you might have too many. I expected until last year that the work would be done by contract.

MR. FINLAYSON: I can't hear.

MR. LEWIS: He said he expected that the work would have been done by contract.

MR. FINLAYSON: The contract, not for the bridges but for the road work?

A.—Exactly.

MR. FINLAYSON: You had to provide suddenly for them?

A.—Yes, I cannot defend buying pipe from Bedford in a strictly ethical sense, but the work had to be done and I told the agent to see if he could not get the pipe done. I recommended Plummer Ferguson and told him to get a price and he said that Bedford would give us the pipe at the price paid the previous year.

MR. FINLAYSON: Who said that?

A.—The man at the office who was doing the purchasing.

MR. RANEY: Speaking of concrete pipe—

MR. LYONS: Did you not get prices on concrete pipe before Bedford? From other sources?

WITNESS: Yes, I had prices from outside sources.

MR. FINLAYSON: How did they compare?

WITNESS: Outside prices?

MR. FINLAYSON: You exhausted the local market?

MR. CLARKE: Where did you get outside prices?

WITNESS: From the Russell Company, John Russell.

MR. FINLAYSON: Contractor?

MR. RANEY: Toronto?

MR. LEWIS: Yes, of Toronto.

MR. RANEY: Surely the men can make them.

MR. SINCLAIR: Who makes the pipes used there? Does the Lyons Company make them?

WITNESS: Yes.

MR. FINLAYSON: They have to be made at a plant and the Lyons Company have a local plant?

A.—The only one operating.

Q.—So that although the Russell Company are able to make the tile they are at a disadvantage regarding distance? The Lyons Company is the only local firm?

A.—Yes.

MR. RANEY: I see them making pipe along the street. Isn't it an easy thing to make them with the simple materials?

MR. FINLAYSON: Those are without reinforcement. You have to have a steam plant to put in the reinforcing. I think I am correct, am I not?

WITNESS: Yes.

MR. RANEY: I think I have seen them making them with the reinforcement.

MR. FINLAYSON: Not with reinforcement.

MR. LEWIS: Ask Mr. Lamb. He is in a position to know. Do they do it?

WITNESS No.

MR. WIDDIFIELD: There has been an effort to bring out that the Government has lost a lot of money on account of the lack of competition of the Lyons Fuel and Supply Company. Now, perhaps, that is not just exactly right. As a matter of fact you said you had not been doing much business since that letter you received from Mr. Fullerton in March, 1925.

WITNESS: We didn't do much cement work.

MR. WIDDIFIELD: The Government has not lost much then?

WITNESS: This year it is smaller. Last year it would have been a different thing. When we have twenty feet concrete bridges for instance, we try to clean up one district, moving the bridge gang around.

Q.—You have not lost much money by the loss of competition of the Lyons Company?

A.—Not a great deal.

Q.—Since you got the letter in March, 1925?

A.—Not a great deal but we stand to.

Q.—You would not lose much would you? You have got figures from other companies?

MR. RANKIN: There is no one can compete with them.

MR. CLARKE: There are lots of things beside gravel. Six hundred pairs of blankets are a pretty good order. You could get them wholesale from Toronto, from John R. Brock or Macdonald's.

MR. FINLAYSON: He explained that.

MR. RANEY: We are interrupting Mr. Sinclair.

MR. SINCLAIR (Resuming examination): Do you buy any tents?

A.—Yes.

Q.—How many?

A.—Possibly a couple of dozen.

Q.—Who from?

A.—From the Hinchburg Harness Company.

Q.—And where did they come from?

A.—They are made in the Sault.

Q.—Is there anything else in this large item of $8,000 from the Bedford Company you can recall?

A.—No. I think you have covered it pretty well.

Q.—It would not be made up from blankets, beds, cooking utensils and pipe altogether. There would be other things?

A.—Possibly. General hardware of all kinds.

MR. LEWIS: How big an item would this concrete pipe run?

MR. FINLAYSON: Approximately half.

WITNESS: About $4,000.

MR. LEWIS: That was a big item.

MR. FINLAYSON: What would the blankets cost you?

WITNESS: Three dollars and sixty cents.

MR. FINLAYSON: A pair?

WITNESS: Yes.

MR. RANKIN: Pretty dear rate. I buy blankets all the time.

MEMBER: Three dollars and sixty cents is pretty cheap.

MR. SINCLAIR: Everybody join in, $3.60 a pair. Let us have it in capital letters. Some seem to think it is a good buy.

MR. LEWIS: I should think it was rather good.

MEMBER: Very cheap blankets.

MR. SINCLAIR: I suppose you got the beds cheaper than anywhere else? You ought to from a man named Bed-ford.

MR. FINLAYSON: There ought to be a chorus now.

MR. RANEY: I see I shall finish next summer on this job.

MR. SINCLAIR: Can you give a figure on the beds?

WITNESS: I paid different prices for the beds: around $11.

COLONEL CURRIE: Was $3.60 the highest for the blankets?

WITNESS: No, I paid more when I had to get bigger blankets.

COLONEL CURRIE: Three dollars and sixty cents was not the top price?

WITNESS: I think I paid as high as $4.50 for a small order.

MR. FINLAYSON: The same weight?

WITNESS: Heavier blankets.

MR. CLARKE: Wool blankets?

WITNESS: Yes.

MR. CLARKE: All wool?

COLONEL CURRIE: Some.

MR. SINCLAIR: That's all.

MR. RANEY: I don't want anything more.

MR. TELLIER: Did anyone sell cement—Portland?

WITNESS: No.

MR. TELLIER: There are different brands sold?

WITNESS: Yes.

MR. TELLIER: Is there much variation in the prices of the different dealers?

WITNESS: A slight variation.

MR. TELLIER: You have noticed competition in price?

WITNESS: Yes.

MR. FINLAYSON: You say Bedford bought from Lyons, the cement pipe, to sell to you?

WITNESS: Yes.

MR. FINLAYSON: And that was because it was the only plant north of Toronto that made it?

COLONEL CURRIE: The only plant round the Sault?

MR. RANEY: How could he tell?

WITNESS: That I know of.

MR. FINLAYSON: How did those prices compare with those of the Lyons
Fuel and Supply Company the previous year?

A.—The same practically.

Q.—So Bedford got a jobber's rate of some kind I suppose. Those beds
and blankets were bought because of an emergency job?

A.—Exactly.

Q.—You had the job thrown on your hands when you thought it would be
contracted?

A.—Yes.

Q.—And you had to take care of the men?

A.—I certainly did. Yes.

Q.—Did you exhaust the sources of supply before you went to Bedford?

A.—I did.

Q.—To Hinchburg?

A.—Yes.

Q.—Bought them out?

A.—Yes.

Q.—And the others?

A.—Yes.

Q.—You had to take care of the men?

A.—Yes.

MR. CLARKE: Could you go to Mr. Lyons and Mr. Bedford on a 'day's
notice and get 600 pairs of blankets? Did they keep such a stock? It is a
pretty big order?

MR. LYONS: We did.

MR. CLARKE: All the time?

MR. LYONS: Practically.

MR. CLARKE: Sometimes not. I thought you had to give them a week's
notice. It is not so snappy.

WITNESS: When you have nine miles of road to build and you get to
the first of July you cannot let the grass grow under your feet.

MR. LYONS: When you make a comparison of the prices of the blankets
sold by Hinchburg or Bedford we are as cheap as any wholesale house in Toronto.

MR. CLARKE: If they are woollen blankets.

MR. LYONS: They are the same standard.

George McNamara on the stand. Sworn. Examination by Mr. FINLAYSON.

Q.—Mr. McNamara, your home is in Sault Ste. Marie?

A.—It was. Toronto now.

Q.—And what is your firm or company?

A.—McNamara Construction Company, Limited.

Q.—An incorporated company?

A.—Yes.

Q.—With shareholders—?

A.—My brother and myself and his wife and my wife and mother.

Q.—That sounds like a family?

MR. RANKIN: Haven't you a stenographer to make five?

MR. FINLAYSON: It was not necessary. You formerly lived at the Sault?
How long have you been contracting there?

A.—Since 1913.

Q.—Who was the first combination?

A.—I was in with my father. McNamara and Son.

Q.—What was the next affiliation?

A.—McNamara Brothers; father died.

Q.—Your brother and you carried on business?

A.—Yes.

Q.—What was the next step?

A.—We carried on until going overseas and then started as McNamara Brothers in the fall of 1919, until Thornton came in, then McNamara and Thornton.

Q.—Still a partnership?

A.—Yes.

Q.—When did you change?

A.—We carried on until 1924 and then dissolved partnership and carried on as the McNamara Construction Company.

Q.—You incorporated?

A.—Later on.

Q.—When?

A.—That summer.

Q.—And carried on contracting work?

A.—Yes.

Q.—When did you start contracting?

A.—In 1913.

Q.—Now what volume of business have you done since then?

A.—We did a few sewer jobs until the time we went overseas, a few buildings and local jobs at the Sault.

Q.—When you went overseas you were still at it?

A.—We were building railroads.

Q.—Laying railway tracks?

A.—Yes.

Q.—When you came back did you take it up again?

A.—Yes.

Q.—How long were you overseas?

A.—Three years.

Q.—What rank?

A.—I went over as a lieutenant and came back as major.

Q.—And your brother?

A.—He did the same.

Q.—You were constructing light railways in France?

MR. LEWIS: Did you build that down at Bethune?

A.—Yes.

MR. FINLAYSON: It was bad enough.

MR. FINLAYSON: Then you came back again, and in what line have you been since?

A.—General contracting.

Q.—What did you cover?

A.—Bridges, roads, sewers, buildings.

Q.—When you were up at the Sault, was there work around there?

A.—Yes, mostly in the Sault and vicinity, from 1919 to 1923 I think we had something over thirty contracts.

Q.—Approximately what did it run to from 1919 to 1923?

A.—The value of the work for the Drury Government was slightly over a million.

COLONEL CURRIE: Hold on. Let us hear that again.

MR. FINLAYSON: How many contracts did you have with the Drury Government?

A.—Nine.

Q.—What class?

A.—Mostly roads. I think we built twenty-five miles of concrete road and eight of macadam and several other jobs.

Q.—Running into how much?

A.—Over a million dollars.

Q.—Since the present Government came in—?

A.—We tendered on ten jobs, I think for the Northern Development and we got two. We did not get any from the Highways Department but we got a sub from one of them.

Q.—You tendered for ten contracts and got two?

A.—Yes. Those two are the Coniston road and the Timmins-South Porcupine.

Q.—Before I go into this, have you been dealing with the Lyons Fuel and Supply Company?

A.—Yes.

Q.—For how long?

A.—Ever since we have been in business.

Q.—What would your business run per year?

A.—It all depends. We only bought locally when we had work in the Sault.

Q.—Since the present Minister, Mr. Lyons, the late Minister, was head of this Department how many contracts have you had?

A.—Two.

Q.—What amount, if any, did he supply for those?

A.—He did not supply anything.

A.—It has been suggested in some questions that possibly Mr. Lyons had some interest in your firm?

A.—Absolutely no.

Q.—Any percentage, share, commission?

A.—Nothing whatever.

Q.—Did you ever have an interest in any of his concerns?

A.—No.

Q.—One of the questions seems to me to suggest you have an interest, perhaps undisclosed, in the Sault Coal and Wood Company?

A.—Nothing whatever.

Q.—Directly or indirectly?

A.—No.

Q.—You have never had relations with him except business relations with his firm?

A.—That's all.

Q.—I understood you to say that he never supplied you with material for contracts unless they were in the immediate neighbourhood of the Sault?

A.—That's all.

Q.—I asked what they ran from year to year?

A.—It depends on the jobs.

Q.—I see, 1915, three thousand odd dollars and a blank to 1919. You went overseas then; 1919, $9,500; 1920, $29,000; 1921, $9,000; 1922, $3,000; 1923, nothing—

A.—I think we bought more than that from them.

Q.—1924, $23,000; 1925, $33,000. What practice do you follow as to purchases from his firm at the Sault?

A.—We get quotations from him and Downey or anyone else.

Q.—Cement enters largely into the work?

A.—Yes.

Q.—The Committee didn't seem to follow. How is cement handled?

A.—Only two firms, Downey and the Lyons Fuel and Supply Company handle in the Sault. There is a competitive rate given by boat and rail. Up there it paid us to buy from somebody who could bring it up by boat and supply from stock. If we ordered so much and the boat did not get in on time we should have to shut down.

Q.—And if you had 10 per cent. over your requirements were you up against it?

A.—Against loss or disposal?

Q.—What were the prices?

A—There was 15 cents a barrel difference and for that he had to deliver from the boat to the job and we figured we saved money by letting him deliver and if there was any loss he had to take it.

Q.—The Lyons price was 15 cents higher than the Canada Cement and he had to deliver on the job?

A.—They delivered on the job.

COLONEL CURRIE: And took any loss or damage.

MR. FINLAYSON: The spread covered delivery from the dock to the job?

A.—And any loss on cement, and packing trouble and all the rest. We saved five cents a barrel that way.

Q.—What is the competition?

A.—R. J. Downey, St. Mary Cement.

Q.—I mean outside, the Sault against a Michigan point?

A.—Yes.

Q.—It paid you better to deal with them?

A.—Oh, yes.

COLONEL CURRIE: They are the local agents, are they? One for St. Mary and the other Canada Cement, and they could get a better price than yourself?

A.—Yes.

COLONEL CURRIE: Because they are competing on the job?

A.—Yes.

COLONEL CURRIE: That clears up a lot of nonsense.

MR. RANEY: You were talking about his questions as nonsense. That was what Mr. Finlayson had reference to.

MR. FINLAYSON: In addition to the Drury Government contracts and these two from this Government have you had dealings with any other Government?

A.—With the Dominion Government.

Q.—Now let us cover the contracts. The Coniston road. Did you get that in open competition?

A.—Yes.

Q.—Anything irregular about it?

A.—Not a thing.

Q.—Did you pay any consideration to Mr. Lyons or anybody else?

A.—No.

Q.—It was obtained in the regular way?

A.—Just the same as ordinary business.

Q.—And the Porcupine, it applies to that?

A.—The same exactly.

Q.—Let us take up the other. You took the contract from Labarge. Will you please explain it?

A.—We were anxious to get it.

Q.—Why?

A.—We were just completing the Sudbury-Coniston road and had all the equipment within three miles of the spot and we were in the running for the contract and when Labarge got it we got in touch with him.

Q.—Labarge's tender was $59,165 and yours $59,435?

MR. RANEY: Were those unit prices on estimated quantities?

MR. LYONS: That is the total amount, Mr. Raney, worked out on estimated quantities.

MR. RANEY: An estimated quantity?

MR. LYONS: Yes.

MR. FINLAYSON: Your figure was approximately $200 odd higher than his?

MR. RANEY: Have you got the estimates here and the tenders, both?

MR. FINLAYSON: Yes, I think we have. So that as I understand it you were $200 higher and you had just about finished the Coniston job and were anxious to keep your plant near there?

A.—We had our organization there.

MR. FINLAYSON: Hungry for work?

A.—Yes.

Q.—What then?

A.—We got in touch with Labarge and eventually we bought the job outright.

Q.—And took an assignment?

A.—Yes.

Q.—You paid him some consideration, I am not going to ask how much?

A.—We certainly did.

Q.—And was arrangement made with Mr. Fullerton?

A.—We talked it out and he agreed it would be satisfactory providing we carried out according to specifications. Then the bond matter came up and in our arrangements we had to pay for the bond. We found a little later that there were going to be two bonds. He was bonded to the Government and required a bond from us. That meant that we had to pay an extra premium. Mr. Fullerton said he would go into it and eventually said he accepted our bond to complete the job.

Q.—You gave the surety company's bond directly to the Department and Labarge was released from his bond?

A.—Yes.

Q.—Which meant saving one premium?

A.—It amounted to about $600 and two premiums would be absurd. I was looking up a bond from the General Canadian, the whole transaction is set out.

Q.—Labarge assigned the contract to you. In fact he got out and you got in?

A.—They fixed it satisfactorily to the Department.

Q.—Who conducted the negotiations?

A.—With Mr. Fullerton.

Q.—Did you have anything to do with Mr. Lyons?

A.—I don't think we ever spoke to him.

Q.—Have you ever attempted to use any influence?

A.—Absolutely none.

Q.—No Sault influence?

A.—No. As a matter of fact on the Timmins job there was a dispute over some rock and we could not come to an agreement. It was $8,000 and after a battle with Mr. Fullerton we could not get more than $6,000 and we claimed $8,000 and he said the only thing to do was that there was a clause in the contract that if we were not satisfied we could take it up with the Minister but we did not take it up. We settled with him in the best way we could.

Q.—It would be a bad thing to go over the head of the deputy for further dealings. Have you ever had occasion to go to the Minister?

A.—No.

Q.—I refer to Mr. Lyons?

A.—No.

Q.—Now the Labarge contract was accepted by you?

A.—Yes.

Q.—And paid for by the Department?

A.—Yes.

Q.—No material supplied by Lyons for that?

A.—No.

Q.—Now with regard to buying. Labarge has a department at Sudbury?

A.—Yes, supplies and so on.

Q.—And you bought from him?

A.—That was part of the agreement.

Q.—You handled the other contract, the road contract at Wellington Street. Will you explain that?

A.—What do you want to know?

Q.—Who gave the contract?

A.—The City of Sault Ste. Marie.

Q.—They advertised?

A.—Yes.

Q.—And who did you tender to?

A.—The city.

COLONEL CURRIE: Why waste time with the City of Sault Ste. Marie

MR. FINLAYSON: Under whose supervision?

A.—The city engineers.

Q.—Did the Department or the Minister have anything to do with it?

A.—Nothing whatever.

Q.—Payment was made by the City of Sault Ste. Marie?

A.—Yes.

Q.—Have you read over the questions on the order paper as to your dealings?

A.—I have read some of them; not all.

Q.—Has there been anything of any nature improper between you and the Lyons Fuel and Supply Company and the ——— or anyone for him?

A.—Absolutely nothing.

MR. FINLAYSON: All right.

Examination by Mr. Sinclair.

Q.—The road from Coniston to Sudbury, what was the amount of your tender there?

A.—The original tender was $186,000.

Q.—What did it finally cost?. . .
A.—Including unit prices, $380,000.
MR. RANEY: As compared with some $180,000 odd.
MR. SINCLAIR: One hundred and eighty-six thousand dollars only repre-
sents the surface of the road, apart from excavation?
A.—It represents the concrete road and some items.
MR. LYONS: One hundred and eighty-eight thousand seven hundred and
fifty-one dollars and ninety cents.
COLONEL CURRIE: Let us get it square. What interfered to upset the
prices?
MR. SINCLAIR: What did this $188,751 represent at the time of the tender?
A.—It represented what they called for from the tender. It represented
the concrete road and whatever quantities they had in.
Q.—Did you expect to complete the road for that?
A.—Not if they asked us to take out more material.
Q.—What was left open on the specifications?
A.—Nothing. They are the standard specifications.
Q.—Was there a plan of the road before you?
A.—You had to go and look at the road.
Q.—Nothing about how deep you had to excavate?
A.—In the north country it is practically impossible to get satisfactory
cross-sections.
Q.—The $187,000 did not represent anything?
A.—It represented the quantities they worked on.
Q.—Seven miles of concrete road and a certain amount of earth excavation
and rock. It was away below the actual movement.
MR. LEWIS: They take an arbitrary amount on excavation and they submit
that and the tenders are all on the same basis. But it does not fix the actual
amount.
MR. RANEY: Is that quite accurate? Don't the engineers make an estimate
of quantities and then apply the prices to those quantities and you are expected
to get the cost of the work.
MR. MCNAMARA: Those are exactly the same as the rates we offered
for the Drury Government which sometimes ran over 200 per cent. over the
estimated tender.
MR. FINLAYSON: What variations have you had?
WITNESS: We have run over a hundred per cent.
MR. FINLAYSON: On one job?
WITNESS: On the Kingston road $45,000 basis, exactly the same as the
Coniston job; exactly the same tenders to fill in and we were paid $91,821
an excess of $45,825. On the road near Chatham it was $49,518 and the
over-run was $49,518. Those where we were paid unit prices amounted to that.
Other contracts we had ran away over.
MR. SINCLAIR: When you tendered on this road for $187,000 you did
not think you were able to build the road for that?
A.—We said we would build what we said for that.
MR. SINCLAIR: Speaking of unit prices, have you the unit prices here?
A.—No, I have not.
MR. RANEY: The contract gives the price. Let us get the exact amount
paid for the work.
MR. LYONS: Three hundred and eighty-four thousand six hundred and
twenty-six dollars and eighty cents.

COLONEL CURRIE: The total amount?

MR. LYONS: Yes.

WITNESS: The prices are here: Concrete pavement, $2.75; earth excavation, $1.20 a yard; six-inch corner tile, 75 cents; gravel in place, $4.75 and so on; eight-inch concrete pipe, $1; ten-inch concrete pipe, $1.25; twelve-inch, $1.60— about twenty items altogether.

MR. SINCLAIR: Taking those unit prices, Mr. McNamara, you arrive at $188,000 as your contract price?

A.—You are given so many yards of concrete, say, and we multiply it by the prices here and arrive at $186,000, it is exactly like these other places here and it all depends on how much you take out.

Q.—How do you know how many yards you had to take out?

A.—We don't know.

MR. LEWIS: They give unit prices per yard.

MR. SINCLAIR: Why do you tell me $187,000 if you could not tell?

WITNESS: You never did any contracting.

MR. SINCLAIR: A lot of these fellows never practised law, but they laugh at me. Is there any estimate as to the number of cubic feet to take out of rock or anything else?

MR. LEWIS: The Government in submitting specifications estimates there will be a certain number of cubic yards taken out and a certain number of cubic yards placed and then the contractor who is tendering submits unit prices and when the tender is submitted the Department figures out on that and says that the total amount is this.

MR. SINCLAIR: That is what I had in my mind, but these fellows seem to think it funny. The engineers gave you certain figures on which they figured out this $188,000?

A.—Yes.

Q.—And when you come to build the road it is $384,000 on the same unit prices because there was more than they figured?

MR. FINLAYSON: I suppose among that long list of prices there are some items not used at all?

A.—Yes. This tender form is a copy of the standard specifications of the Department of Highways and figured in exactly the same way.

MR. FINLAYSON: Is it not a common practice for them to run greatly over the amount estimated?

WITNESS: There is no comparison building a road up there and down here.

MR. FINLAYSON: No means of knowing what rock is below, or boulders?

MR. RANEY: I think we all understand that. What about the other road?

COLONEL CURRIE: In making out your tender you are in exactly the same position as any other contractor?

WITNESS: Absolutely.

MR. FINLAYSON: There was no guess work, no secrets disclosed to you that if you put in a tender there was not that much rock there and you could take a chance on it. You get paid exactly for the rock there?

WITNESS: Yes, more or less.

MR. SINCLAIR: When was this road advertised for tender?

WITNESS: I don't remember the date. In the spring.

MR. SINCLAIR: What year?

A.—1924.

MR. SINCLAIR: How long after was the contract let?

A.—I could not say, about two weeks I imagine.

Mr. Raney: Perhaps Mr. Lyons could tell that.

Mr. Lyons: Do you know, Mr. Fullerton, how long?

Mr. Fullerton: I think about two weeks.

Mr. Raney: When were advertisements put in?

Mr. Fullerton: Sometime in June.

Mr. Sinclair (Resuming examination): Between the time the tender was in and the time the contract was let what were you doing?

A.—Well, I suppose part of the time I was looking over the road.

Q.—Looking over the road. What for?

A.—To see about the material and so on.

Q.—What I asked you was, between the time you put in the tender and the time the contract was made?

A.—I don't remember.

Q.—Where you doing anything in connection with road work?

A.—On this job?

Q.—On any job?

A.—I don't remember.

Q.—You were not looking around for any gravel?

A.—No.

Q.—No options taken on gravel pits?

A.—I was up looking for gravel before the tenders were put in.

Q.—Did you take any option on any gravel pits?

A.—I made arrangements that if we got the job we could gravel certain places.

Q.—Did you make any definite deals?

A.—I don't think so.

Q.—You won't swear you didn't?

A.—Certainly not.

Q.—How many gravel pits did you look over?

A.—Well, if I looked over any I probably looked over all the pits in that vicinity.

Q.—How many would that be?

A.—Three or four. As a matter of fact we didn't use any of it.

Q.—You looked over some?

A.—Certainly.

Q.—Did you make any arrangements with anyone in particular?

A.—I won't say I didn't.

Q.—Would you say whether you made any arrangements with someone or some arrangement with all?

A.—I don't think I made any arrangements with anyone. I am sure I didn't make any arrangements to take gravel.

Q.—What did you do?

A.—I was up there looking for gravel and seeing if it was for concrete. I don't remember exactly.

Q.—You didn't tell people you were expecting the road contract?

A.—No.

Q.—You didn't tell anyone that?

A.—I knew they were going to go ahead with the road.

Q.—Somebody?

A.—Sure.

Q.—Why were you there?

A.—I was interested in getting the job.

Q.—How far did you go with any sand or gravel pit owner regarding his gravel?

A.—I don't think—

Q.—Will you swear? Lawyers will do the thinking.

A.—I don't remember making any arrangements for gravel. I will swear I did not buy any gravel.

Q.—Did you make any arrangements before the contract was let?

A.—If I got the job, I probably did. I looked at two pits that might be suitable and I may have told both owners that if I landed the job I would be glad to talk.

Q.—Is that as far as you did go?

A.—I believe it was.

Q.—Will you swear that?

A.—Yes.

Q.—You made no arrangements with anyone of any kind?

A.—Not to buy gravel; absolutely. It is a very common practice to look over the job.

Q.—What else were you looking over before the contract was let?

A.—Probably looking over the road.

Q.—Now was there any detour provision in regard to the road?

A.—There was a detour.

Q.—What was that?

A.—A regular detour to get around.

Q —I mean in the specifications; was anything said about a detour?

A.—It was the regular specification if you have to detour a certain way.

Q.—Have you a contract as the contractor that you would have anything to do with the detour?

A.—We had to keep our end of it. The detour was in good shape.

Q.—You had nothing as a contractor having to do with the detour?

A.—The detour was in good shape.

Q.—Had you anything to do with it? I don't care whether the detour was in good or bad shape. Was it mentioned in the specifications about the detour?

A.—I don't think so.

Q.—Was there anything to be paid to you on account of the detour?

A.—No. As I say, it was in good shape.

Q.—Supposing it had got out of shape?

A —The Government probably kept it up.

Q.—Would they?

A.—I suppose so.

Q.—You did not have anything to do with it?

A.—We were not asked.

Q.—Never mentioned to you?

A.—No.

Q.—Was it in any part of the contract that you had to keep the detour?

A.—If there had been anything wrong we would probably have been asked.

Q.—Who by?

A.—The engineers.

Q.—What?

A.—To keep it in running shape.

Q.—Did you have to do it for nothing?

A.—Sure.

Q.—But in figuring for that road you figured something for the detour?

A.—No.

Q.—You figured to do it at a loss?

A.—We figured that we would not have to do anything.

Q.—You figured you would have to look after the detour?

A.—No.

Q.—There was a detour and something might have to be done?

A.—You are trying to tell me how I am to figure our jobs?

Q.—I am trying to get you to tell me. The detour did not enter into your mind at all?

A.—No.

Q.—It was never mentioned by an official of the Government?

A.—No. I only saw it in one of the questions.

Q.—When you took the contract there was nothing said about the detour?

A.—Absolutely no.

Q.—And nothing in the contract about it?

A.—No.

Q.—And nothing spent by you on the detour?

A.—We may have done.

Q.—Did you or didn't you?

A.—We may have done.

Q.—I want something positive.

A.—We may have. We would have to see the superintendent. There was not any amount of any kind spent on the detour.

Q.—You have told us the detour would not require anything and now you tell me that there may have been something.

A.—There may have been a little amount done by the men. I would not say there was not.

MR. FINLAYSON: Do you want the provisions as to detours? Here it is in the standard specifications attached to the contract:

"When the roadway is closed and traffic maintained within the limits of the roadway the contractor shall maintain at his expense a safe detour for traffic unless this duty is specifically assumed by the Department. He shall not close the roadway except on the written order of the engineer. Where the roadway is closed and traffic diverted entirely off the roadway the contractor shall, at his own expense, place and maintain such barricades, signs, lights and watchmen or watchmen as may be necessary to direct the travelling public, which shall include signs and lights at every intersecting road from the commencement of the detour to the point at which such detour joins the trunk road or at such point as the engineer may direct. The contractor shall promptly remove or change all such barricades, signs, lights and watchman and watchmen as the work proceeds or is completed. Signs will be furnished free to the contractor on application to the engineer."

MR. SINCLAIR: How many miles was the detour?

A.—I think about ten or twelve miles.

Q.—You had to look after it?

A.—We put up barricades and so on.

Q.—That would not cost anything?

A.—We cannot do it for nothing.

Q.—Are you sure?

MR. FINLAYSON: There is something else in the agreement:

"Where the roadway is closed and traffic diverted entirely off the roadway to an approved detour which is not a public lane or road, the contractor at his expense shall provide, construct, maintain and remove (unless otherwise provided) the detour and re-establish all original conditions. The detour shall be maintained satisfactorily for public travelling. The contractor shall be liable for all accidents that occur to persons or property on such detour or detours and shall provide, maintain and remove at his own expense such barricades, signs, lights or watchmen as may be requisite for the safety of the public, or as the engineer may direct."

Mr. SINCLAIR: There was a detour then?

A.—There was a detour.

Q.—And you people looked after it. That would cost you something?

A.—Probably it would.

Q.—There is no need to be so scared about it.

A.—I was not, Mr. Sinclair.

Q.—And naturally when you figured on the tender you figured something on the detour?

A.—I was going to explain when we make up tenders we allow for contingencies and so on.

Q.—All goes in?

A.—Sure.

Q.—There is the Creighton-Copper Cliff road. That is the road Labarge got the tender for? Is he a road builder?

A.—I don't know much about him.

Q.—Do you know that he builds roads in the north?

A.—I don't know about roads. I know he built an hotel.

Q.—The only road there would be the road to the dining room. You have been building roads in the north for years?

A.—Only in Sault Ste. Marie.

Q.—Where does Labarge live?

A.—In Sudbury.

Q.—How far from the Sault?

A.—Two hundred miles.

Q.—Had you ever heard of Labarge before?

A.—I never knew him before.

Q.—Did you hear of him as building roads?

A.—No.

Q.—And he got the Creighton-Copper Cliff?

A.—Yes.

Q.—And you bought him out?

A.—Yes.

Q.—What did you pay him?

Mr. FINLAYSON: I don't think that should come out, Mr. Sinclair. I don't think he would want it. I don't think it is material.

Mr. RANEY: We must have the price.

Mr. SINCLAIR: I don't think—

WITNESS: It was a business between ourselves and another contractor. Unless I am ordered—

Mr. SINCLAIR: I am not going to order you.

Mr. RANEY: Then I will appeal to the Committee.

Mr. LEWIS: The amount paid to the Labarge Company personally on their contract? Witness says he feels that it is private business and does not think it should be asked, as not material to the inquiry. It did not affect the price?

WITNESS: No he had already signed the contract with the Government.

MR. RANEY: Is the contract completed?

WITNESS: Yes.

MR. SINCLAIR: What was the original contract price?

MR. LYONS: Labarge and Company, $59,165; St. Denis, $59,435; McNamara, $59,440; Warren Brothers, $61,690. Then there were others, $72,000, $67,000, ten bids in all, the highest $98,000.

MR. RANEY: How much was finally paid for the work?

MR. LYONS: Creighton-Copper Cliff, $135,063.

MR. RANEY: Original price, $59,165.

MR. LYONS: And the price paid for the completed road was $135,063.

MR. RANEY: Of course the price witness paid for the assignment of this contract is absolutely vital.

MR. LEWIS: Why?

MR. RANEY: It is too obvious to be worth discussing.

MR. FINLAYSON: I put it this way: If Mr. Raney can see any object— but to make the bald statement, "It is obvious" and decline to discuss it—

MR. RANEY: It will be clear to the Committee before we get through.

MR. SINCLAIR: The tendered price of Labarge was $59,165 and you tendered on the same job and your price was $59,440, according to Mr. Lyons?

WITNESS: Yes.

MR. SINCLAIR: And when the road was completed it cost $135,063?

MR. RANEY: One hundred and thirty-nine thousand dollars.

MR. LYONS: One hundred and thirty-five thousand dollars.

MR. SINCLAIR: From the time that you tendered on this road and the time Labarge sold to y— ad you go over the road again?

A.—I don't know

Q.—Did you know what Labarge got it for?

A—Yes.

Q.—And you knew what yours was?

A.—Yes.

Q.—And did you go over the figures in the meantime, before you bought over?

A.—I don't think so.

Q.—How long was the time from when the tenders were let to the time you bought from Labarge?

A.—I got in touch right away.

Q.—What do you mean, right away?

A.—Within a couple of days, I think. We were dickering back and forth two or three days.

Q.—How did you find Labarge had the contract?

A.—It was published in the *Record*, or the engineer probably told me. It was public property.

Q.—You say within two or three days afterwards you saw Labarge. Where?

A.—Sudbury.

Q.—I see. You went to see him?

A.—To see if I could make a deal and make some arrangements to get the job.

Q.—And did you think such a thing was possible?

A.—I was going to find out.

Q.—Had you any reason to think it was possible?

A.—I did not know. That is what I went for.

WITNESS: We had all the plant and equipment there and were anxious to land the job.

COLONEL CURRIE: And he hadn't anything?

WITNESS: I don't know what he had. I didn't know what his plans were.

MR. SINCLAIR: Did you know what his equipment was?

A.—He did not tell me.

Q.—And you never knew him before?

A.—I never knew Fred Labarge before.

Q.—How did you find him in Sudbury?

A.—Sudbury is not very large.

Q.—You say you did not know Fred Labarge at all?

A.—I had never met him.

Q.—And you went to see a perfect stranger about getting a contract he had from the Government?

A —As a matter of fact my brother was in Sudbury at the time and called me on the phone and discussed it and he introduced me.

Q.—Your brother knew him and had seen him before you got there?

A.—Yes.

Q.—How long was your brother in Sudbury?

A.—He was working on a Sudbury job.

Q.—And what objection is there to telling me what you paid Labarge for taking over the job?

A —Well, it is more or less a matter of principle. I don't think it is anybody's business but my own.

Q.—What principle is involved?

A.—Well, probably a personal one. I don't think it is anyone's business but my own.

Q.—If it is public business?

A.—If I am ordered I will tell.

MR. FINLAYSON: Let me put it this way. It was an ordinary business transaction you took over and paid a consideration for. In addition you agreed to buy material from him. Now my view is that it is not so material there should be any attempt to hide it. I don't want to ask you to disclose it. I am surprised at the question being pressed, but if you don't do it you are up against comment.

MEMBER: What is the object of this inquiry?

MR. FINLAYSON: If you can tell me the object of this inquiry I shall—

MR. RANEY: I thought it was your inquiry.

MR. FINLAYSON: My friend Mr. Raney admitted that the questions in somebody else's name were his and drawn by him with a deliberate purpose. He has accomplished his purpose and is trying to get a little more advertising, suggesting that it is a horrible thing for this man to decline to answer about his private business and when he is trying to discredit a Minister of the Crown he tries to make it that if the Government cannot be hung on anything else it shall be hung on some justification that they refused to answer a question.

MEMBER: What is the object?

MR. FINLAYSON: I cannot see any object.

WITNESS: I am quite willing so far as that goes. It was $1,500 cash and we agreed to buy from him everything we needed for the Copper Cliff road.

MEMBER: Fifteen hundred. It might have been half a million. (Laughter.)

MR. RANEY: So this is the eminently fair, judicial inquiry we were going to have.

Mr. Finlayson: When somebody sticks to something and then it is blown aside they are annoyed.

Mr. Sinclair: When somebody—

Mr. Finlayson: I think you said yourself it was an improper contract.

Mr. Sinclair: I don't think it is good public business to go on like this.

Mr. Finlayson: I think Mr. Raney—

Mr. Raney: You can't put anything over on me in this inquiry. You have a majority and you can do as you please.

Mr. Finlayson: You are falling down and now you are crying out. It is the public you are appealing to. I think it is time that the author of these questions should say, "I am prepared to apologize."

Mr. Lewis: Mr. Sinclair made a statement that he does not think it is proper that public contracts should be bandied about in this way. I don't think that should go on the record without being noticed. There is no suggestion of impropriety. If there can be any suggestion about that I have not seen it.

Member: Take the Welland Canal.

Mr. Lewis: It is a common practice, particularly where he has a plant handy and wants to keep his men employed. It is done dozens of times each season.

Colonel Currie: By paying $1,500 he saves possibly three or four thousand.

Witness More than that.

Colonel Currie: So you were in pocket?

Witness: And we kept our organization together. The men were employed by the month.

Mr. Raney: Who were the engineers? Who made the estimates, Mr. Lyons?

Mr. Lyons: I think it was Mr. Hoskins. Was it Mr. Hoskins, Mr. Fullerton?

Mr. Fullerton: They came from his office.

Mr. Raney: Will you have whoever made them brought here.

Mr. Sinclair: Did you have any other contracts up there? I understood you to say that you only had two.

Witness: Two from the Government and this assigned one.

Mr. Sinclair: This was a Government one?

Witness: We had it from Labarge.

Mr. Lewis: The evidence is that he had two Government contracts and one from Labarge.

Witness: And one from the City of Sault Ste. Marie.

Mr. Sinclair: You had nothing to do with Wallace Terrace?

Witness: That was the year previous.

Mr. Sinclair: In 1924?

Witness: Yes.

Mr. Sinclair: That was a Sault contract?

Witness: Yes, a Sault contract.

Examination of McNamara by Mr. Raney.

Q.—Mr. McNamara, somebody has sent a memorandum saying that the Coniston-Sudbury road was advertised, tenders were asked by advertisement in the *Contract Record* of June the 11th, 1924?

A.—Probably right.

Q.—That corresponds with your recollection?

A.—Yes.

Q.—My information is that you were up in that district in May of that year looking over the road?

A.—I think it would be early in June.

Q.—Will you say it was not in May?

A.—No.

Q.—That you were there on the 17th of May?

A.—Looking over the road?

Q.—Yes.

A.—No.

Q.—Did you take ratings from any gravel pit owners?

A.—I would not be absolutely certain. Options you mean?

Q.—Yes.

A.—I don't think I did personally; our firm may have.

Q.—How many pits?

A.—We looked at two or three.

Q.—Did you take options on all except the C.P.P.?

A.—No.

Q.—What did you get options on?

A.—Not more than two we dickered with.

Q.—Did you know of any others?

A.—Several.

Q.—Who was one you took an option from?

A.—I know the Priest pit.

Q.—Who made that?

A.—Probably one of the Thorntons.

Q.—Under whose instructions?

A.—I sent a man to look over and see if he could locate gravel and look over the roads.

Q.—Who did you send?

A.—I think Mr. Bird or my brother, I am not sure which.

Q.—Who did he see? How many pit owners?

A.—I saw two of them.

Q.—Who were they?

A.—The Priest pit and Percy Morrison's.

Q.—Did you take ratings from either of these?

A.—We may have. I think we did from Percy Morrison.

Q.—Did you from Priest?

A.—I would not say.

Q.—Were they taken in May?

A.—I don't know.

Q.—Possibly they were?

A.—They may have.

Q.—About the 17th of May?

A —If they were not advertised to June I would not say it was in the midlde of May.

Q.—You have just told me you were up there in May?

A.—I cannot remember.

Q.—Will you say that you were not getting options three weeks before the work was advertised?

A.—I would not say. I don't think so.

Q.—You were not?

A.—I would not swear.

Q.—Where did you gèt the information that the road was to be built?

A.—The Minister made a statement in Sudbury that he was going to build roads.

Q.—When was that?

A.—I don't remember; previous to the time I went there. Previous to the advertisements.

Mr. Finlayson: That was a public speech?

A.—Yes, in Sudbury—that he was going to do considerable work, and I think he mentioned the Sudbury-Coniston road.

Mr. Lyons: I did.

Mr. Raney: How long was that? Before you went to look over the roads?

A.—Yes.

Mr. Lyons: It was early in May.

Mr. Raney: Tenders were called for apparently in June. And where did you see the advertisement for tenders?

A.—Probably in the *Contract Record* or the *Canadian Engineer*.

Q.—Did you see Mr. Hoskins, the district engineer there?

A.—When?

Q.—Before you tendered.

A.—I think we did.

Q.—Did he go over the road?

A.—I think he went over. Yes.

Q.—Was it a mud road or rock road?

A.—Mostly mud.

Q.—Had it not been a gravel road?

A.—There might have been some gravel; in pretty bad shape.

· Q.—Was Labarge looking for the contract?

A.—I had heard Labarge wanted to tender. I don't know.

Q.—Did Labarge tender, Mr. Minister?

Mr. Lyons: No he did not. He talked about it and called me on the phone and, as a matter of fact, he wanted me to delay calling for tenders for another week until he could bid. He said he had some party from Montreal who was going to put in with him. I said we did not want to delay the work. The tenders were to be in on Friday and we said we would delay until Tuesday. The following day he called me up and said he would not bother.

Mr. Raney (Continuing examination): You have given figures with regard to the Sudbury-Coniston road, the amount of the tender and the amount actually paid, and also the road from Timmins to Porcupine. How many miles was the road from Timmins to Porcupine?

A.—About seven miles.

Q.—And the Sudbury-Coniston?

A.—About the same.

Q.—Both concrete roads?

A.—No, one concrete the other macadam.

Q.—Both pavements?

A.—Yes.

Q.—Macadam?

A.—Penetration.

Q.—Hard surface?

A.—Yes.

Q.—Did you also build a piece of road in the Sault?

A.—Yes, Wallace Terrace.

Q.—When?

A.—In 1924.

Q.—Who was that contract made with?

A.—With the City of Sault Ste. Marie.

Q.—How much length of street?

A.—About a mile and a half.

Q.—What kind of road?

A.—Concrete

Q.—What was the tender?

A.—Forty-two thousand dollars.

Q.—What were you paid?

A.—Forty-one thousand dollars something.

Q.—Less?

A.—A little less. No, that ran over five thousand more.

Q.—More?

A.—Yes, $46,000.

Q.—Was that—?

A.—Those figures, I am not certain.

Q.—Was that a city job?

A.—Yes.

Q.—Where did you get your material?

A.—For that job?

Q.—Yes.

A.—We bought most from the Lyons Fuel and Supply Company.

Q.—Cement too?

A.—Yes.

Q.—Then the Wellington Street pavement, that was the same year?

A.—The year after.

Q.—You also bought from the Lyons Company?

A.—We bought where we could buy cheapest.

Q.—From the Lyons Company?

A.—Yes, because he was cheap.

Q.—Wellington Terrace road, where is that? In the Sault?

A.—It is a trunk road out of the Sault.

Q.—Then the Creighton-Copper Cliff, we have been told what the tender was and in your contract with the Labarge Lumber Company what was said about prices, that you were to pay for what you bought from them?

A.—That is where we got stung. We had nothing on prices. We had an agreement that we would buy from them.

Q.—What did you buy?

A.—All we required.

Q.—Cement?

A.—No cement, except culverts. Mostly lumber.

Q.—For what?

A.—For the forms and so forth.

Q.—What else?

A.—Crushed rock, and we buy oil.

Q.—You buy oil, what else?

A.—Cement for the culverts, a very small amount, mostly road oil.

Q.—Did you have to buy that from Labarge?

A.—Alexander Murray.

Q.—What did you buy from Labarge?

A.—I think we bought tile. Lumber was the big item.

Q.—You say you didn't get that at a fair price?

A.—I wouldn't say that. I didn't mean that. We paid what he billed. We didn't get competition.

Q.—How did the tile prices compare?

A.—We didn't get any other prices.

Q.—How would they if you had?

A.—Not very much difference, I think.

Q.—Why did you say, "We were stung"?

A.—I meant we did not make any deal. We just agreed to buy from him.

MR. LEWIS: You don't mean you were stung in the general meaning of the term.

MR. FINLAYSON: He meant bad business.

MR. RANEY: You built for the Township of Tisdale?

A.—Yes. The Government protected on that.

Q.—What was the tender?

A.—Thirty-five thousand nine hundred dollars.

Q.—And what was paid?

A.—Thirty-five thousand nine hundred dollars.

Q.—Just what the tender was?

A.—A straight contract.

Q.—Not an estimate?

A.—Not on unit prices.

Q.—You also built in the same year—when did you build for the Dome?

A.—1925.

MR. FINLAYSON: That was only surfacing, the Dome?

WITNESS: Yes. We agreed to do a certain amount of work and took a chance ourselves on the Dome road.

MR. RANEY: Then the Timmins town road. That was about a mile?

A.—Yes.

Q.—There the Government paid only about half the cost?

A.—I don't know what the Government paid.

MR. LYONS: We paid half.

MR. RANEY: What was the tender there?

A.—Unit prices.

Q.—What was the amount of the tender?

A.—I think we got $40,000 from the city of Timmins. We were paid on unit prices and the prices were practically the same as the Timmins-South Porcupine road, with one or two adjustments for extras largely.

Q.—No estimated quantities in that contract?

A.—There may have been. I would not be sure.

Q.—Your recollection is that the amount was about the same as the tender?

A.—Oh, no. We were paid on unit prices and did not know the quantity.

Q.—What is the relation of your company to the Walsh Construction Company?

A.—No relation.

Q.—Who is Mr. Walsh?

A.—I know Dick Walsh.

Q.—You have no interest in his company?

A.—No, no interest at all.

Q.—You had nothing to do with the Haviland Bay road?

A.—No.

Q.—No interest in the contract at all?

A.—No.

Q.—Or with the job on the Cobalt highway, five miles?

A.—No, we tendered on that but didn't get the job.

MR. FINLAYSON: One thing to clean up. You say the Minister made a speech at Sudbury about those roads?

A.—I believe he did. That is how I heard about it.

Q.—The local people were asking for expenditures on roads?

A.—It was general talk that roads were going to be built early in the season.

Q.—He announced it publicly and you heard from that source. I suppose the whole town of Sudbury knew?

MEMBER: I was there early in May and heard it.

MR. LEWIS: Other contractors were looking there?

WITNESS: Yes.

Examination ended.

Howard McNamara, in witness box. Mr. Finlayson examining.

Q.—What is your full name?

A.—Howard Dennis McNamara.

Q.—Brother of the last witness?

A.—Yes, sir.

Q.—What your brother has told us about the previous composition of your firm, partnership and finally culminating in this company, is correct?

A.—Yes.

Q.—Is there anything you want to add to the history of it?

A.—No, I am out on the work most of the time.

Q.—You are the practical man—foreman?

A.—Yes.

Q.—You have been living at the Sault for a great many years?

A.—Lived in Toronto for some time.

Q.—But before that in the Sault a number of years and started contracting up there?

A.—Yes.

Q.—And continued that until you went into the army?

A.—Yes.

Q.—And then on your discharge went back?

A.—Yes.

Q.—I don't want to go over the whole history of the thing, as with your brother. Your dealings with the Lyons Fuel and Supply Company, were they under your department, or under your brother?

A.—My brother did most of the buying.

Q.—You have been dealing with them ever since you started work?

A.—Yes.

Q.—Why do you deal with them?

A.—We get good prices and good service.

Q.—And you continued that right along?

A.—Right through.

Q.—Is the statement your brother made, that you had nine contracts, involving very large sums, from the Drury Government, and only two from this present Government, correct?

A.—Yes.

Q.—But in addition to the two from the present Government, you also took over the Labarge contract and had this contract, Wellington Street, in the Sault, that the Government contributed to the municipality?

A.—Yes.

Q.—I believe you also had a contract with the Highway Department last year?

A.—Yes.

Q.—An original bid?

A.—Same as the Labarge contract, sublet.

Q.—An assignment, wasn't it?

A.—An assignment, yes.

Q.—But you had one from the Highway Department?

A.—Nine miles.

Q.—Were you not the lowest tenderer for that?

A.—No. As far as we know we were not.

Q.—But you took it over from the lowest tenderer, with the consent of the Highway Department, and carried out the work?

A.—I think we operated it in the other man's name. We did the work and the money was assigned, or something like that.

Q.—That is a common practice?

A.—Absolutely.

Q.—Both assigning and subletting are well recognized practice of construction men?

A.—Yes.

Q.—Tell me, Mr. McNamara, if at any time you or your family or anyone for you or on your behalf had any interest in the Lyons companies?

A.—No, sir.

Q.—As to partnerships and incorporated company?

A.—None at all.

Q.—Does that apply to the Sault Coal and Wood Company?

A.—Nothing to do with it at all.

Q.—Has Mr. Lyons or any of his firm or family had any connection with your business?

A.—None whatever.

Q.—Can you state positively that your dealings have all been in the open market?

A.—Absolutely.

Q.—Nothing hid?

A.—Nothing at all.

Mr. RANEY examining.

Q.—Was there a written contract between the McNamara Company and the Labarge Lumber Company?

A.—I think there was.

MR. LYONS: I have it here.

MR. RANEY: Is this the only contract there was?

A.—I have not seen it.

MR. RANEY: Look at it and tell me.

A.—That is the only contract I know of. I did not have anything to do with it. My brother handled that.

Mr. George McNamara (Recalled).

MR. RANEY: Is this the only contract there was between your company and Labarge?

A.—No, we have a contract with Fred Labarge. This is an assignment. This is not a contract.

Q.—Was there not a written contract?

A.—Yes.

Q.—Where is it?

A.—It may be in the Sault, or it may be here; I would not be sure.

Mr Howard McNamara resumed the witness box.

MR. RANEY: Will you see that contract is produced?

MR. FINLAYSON: I will try to find it.

MR. RANEY: Just don't release him; that is all. What about 10 o'clock Wednesday morning.

MR. CURRIE: Any witnesses here now?

MR. FINLAYSON: No, we are through with witnesses for to-night.

MR. RANEY: Could we take the evidence of the Caledon Mountain matter on Friday—the matter I brought in a little while ago. These are out-of-town witnesses, too.

THE CHAIRMAN: Peel Township.

MR FINLAYSON: Mr. Chairman, I don't want to prevent any member of the Committee bringing on any matter they desire, but I think it only fair, as I said last week, we should clean up this matter and then devote our attention entirely to the matter which will only take a very short time, and then Mr. Sinclair has priority, I suppose, with some of his motions, and then Mr. Raney goes on with his, and we will devote all the time possible to it.

MR. CURRIE: Rush it right through.

MR. FINLAYSON: To-morrow the Private Bills Committee sits, but Wednesday we might have another morning, sit from two to three, and I will be satisfied to go on in the evening.

THE CHAIRMAN: Tuesday, Wednesday and Thursday evenings the House will sit. We can sit Wednesday morning, Thursday between morning Committee and afternoon session of the House. We can sit Friday morning and up until the House meets, and Friday evening .

MR. FINLAYSON: I think we can get on Wednesday evening, perhaps.

MR. BRADBURN: Instead of adjourning at noon, could we have lunch sent down here?

THE CHAIRMAN: Ten o'clock, then, gentlemen, Wednesday morning.

MR. CURRIE: I would ask that you expedite taking of evidence here. We don't want to spend all evening dribble-drabbling. Let the evidence come in and stop this humdrum.

The Committee then adjourned.

PUBLIC ACCOUNTS COMMITTEE.

The Committee met Wednesday morning, March 24, at 10 a.m., with Mr. Lewis in the Chair.

THE CHAIRMAN: Gentlemen, we have several other witnesses present in connection with the matter in which Mr. Lyons is interested, the questions on the order paper directed to him and it is proposed we go ahead this morning and examine these witnesses, and we expect this afternoon that we will have

Mr. Nash's report of the Clarkson firm in connection with the examination of the books, and unless the Committee thinks otherwise I propose we sit this morning and this afternoon and perhaps this evening in order to try and clean up some of the matters we have.

There is such a list of witnesses now, such a number of different matters on which investigations are asked that we must put in some time on it if we are going to get through. Have you any preference?

HON. MR. RANEY: Did you say Mr. Lyons would not be here?

THE CHAIRMAN: No. I expect he will be here. I haven't heard.

MR. FINLAYSON: You mentioned Major Nash's name. I spoke to him a few minutes ago. He tells me he is back and has his material drafted, but he is getting it into shape and I asked him if he would be able to come to the Committee this afternoon. He said he could, personally, but he would prefer to make it this evening. He would have his report in typewritten form then so it could be handed around. And he also asked me to say that he was leaving for Ottawa to-night, but he would be available to the Committee again the first of the week if they thought necessary.

It occurred to me it would be perhaps more convenient for Mr. Sinclair and Mr. Raney if we sat to-night—

MR. SINCLAIR: The House is going to sit to-night.

MR. FINLAYSON: I thought Mr. Speaker had a dinner?

MR. SINCLAIR: He has, but the House is going to sit and get some more of the debate off.

MR. FINLAYSON: Have we permission to have a dinner concurrently with the House? Mr. Nash would prefer to come to-night but he can stretch a point and come this afternoon. Which would be more convenient to you?

MR. SINCLAIR: When the House is sitting I feel I should be in the House. But there are only a few statements I wanted from Mr. Nash arising out of Mr. Lyons' evidence as they were taken in the notes the other day. I take it that statement will be forthcoming?

MR. FINLAYSON: I haven't seen it.

MR. SINCLAIR: When I was examining Mr. Lyons I asked him certain questions but he could not give me the information because he didn't have his books.

THE CHAIRMAN: We immediately wired Mr. Nash and asked him to get that information.

MR. FINLAYSON: Would you prefer this afternoon or this evening?

MR. SINCLAIR: I think it better to give Mr. Nash a little time to put his stuff in shape.

MR. FINLAYSON: Suppose we sit—

HON. MR. RANEY: I want to protest against sittings of this Committee when the debate is on. After we get into the Estimates I am not so particular. I certainly will object to this Committee sitting until this debate is over. The thing is hectic enough as it is.

MR. FINLAYSON: It is hectic because you have piled this stuff on it.

HON. MR. RANEY: Never mind the reasons.

MR. FINLAYSON: Well I am going to give attention to the reasons. These matters have all been piled on us at the last minute. The day before yesterday you introduced a lot of new matter. If we don't sit and dispense with it we will have complaints from you. If we do sit we shall have complaints because we are sitting.

Hon. Mr. Raney: We have the Prime Minister's pledge that the business of this Committee is going to proceed to a finish in the ordinary course and the House will sit until the Committee finishes its work. If the House gets through first its legislative programme it can very easily adjourn over a week to enable the Committee to finish its work.

Mr. Finlayson: Mr. Raney knows how absurd that is, that the House should adjourn for a week and one hundred odd members come back for the convenience of one person. Your protest is against the House being rapid and us being rapid, when, if we—

Hon. Mr. Raney: My protest is against this Committee sitting until the present debate has been concluded.

Mr. Lewis: I don't know that any of us are so interested in the debate. The House is generally half empty.

Mr. Finlayson: I noticed Mr. Raney was not there last week at all.

Hon. Mr. Raney: I was.

The Chairman: The idea of adjourning the House for a week that this Committee might hold sittings sounds all right but I am afraid it would not be practical. You would have very great difficulty in holding interest in this Committee.

Hon. Mr. Raney: Members of the Committee, like members of the House, are paid to attend to the business— .

Mr. Finlayson: As far as I am concerned it doesn't matter a rap. **We** are ready to proceed this afternoon or to-night.

Mr. Sinclair: As far as I am concerned, Mr. Fisher and I can alternate between the House and the Committee, and one watch the House and one watch the Committee.

Mr. Finlayson: Say to-night at seven.

Mr. Sinclair: Better say eight. We have to get an hour for dinner.

The Chairman: We will go ahead now and decide when we come to it.

Hon. Mr. Raney: Is it proposed to call any other witness besides Mr. Nash this afternoon?

The Chairman: We have Mr. Harry McAllister and Harry Lyons. In connection with Mr. Dawson, Mayor of Sault Ste. Marie, I had a wire yesterday stating he would not be able to leave yesterday to be here to-day. I took the liberty of telling Mr. Dawson to await further notice from the Committee because I think members recollect that in the evidence there is very little Mr. Dawson is connected with and I doubted if it was necessary to bring him down.

Mr. Currie: What are you wiring the Soo Mayor for?

The Chairman: He is one asked to be summoned.

Mr. Currie: Has he anything to do with the Public Accounts?

The Chairman: No.

Mr. Currie: Better send for the Mayor of Timbuctoo.

The Chairman: There is a suggestion that he was connected with Mr. Lyons in a business enterprise. I think that has been cleaned up.

Mr. Finlayson: He was on Mr. Raney's list. It is up to Mr. Raney to say.

Hon. Mr. Raney: Was he on my list?

The Chairman: Yes.

Hon. Mr. Raney: I think not.

Mr. Finlayson: Is it satisfactory to drop him?

Hon. Mr. Raney: I don't ask for him.

Alexander McAllister called; sworn.   Examined by Mr. Finlayson.

Q.—What is your first name?

A.—Alexander.

Q —Any other name?

A.—No.

Q.—Where do you live?

A.—Sault Ste. Marie.

Q.—What is your occupation, position?

A.—I am with the Lyons Fuel & Supply.

Q —In what capacity? · ﹕

A.—I have no definite title.

Q.—What are your duties?

A.—My duties are very general, covering sales and other duties around the office.

Q.—What was your occupation before?

A.—Before when?

Q.—Before coming with them?

A.—I was with the Wilput Coke Oven.

Q.—You are an engineer by profession?

A.—Yes, practical.

Q.—And you say your duties with them are general.   What do you mean by that?

A.—I take an active interest in the sales and also other policies of the company, business policies.

Q.—The sales end chiefly?

A.—Yes.

Q.—You look after collections too, and that sort of thing?

A.—Yes.

Q.—Now how long have you been with him?

A.—May 24, 1922.

Q.—Have you any interest in the company?

A.—None at all.

Q.—That is, you are not a shareholder?

A.—Not a shareholder.

Q.—Director?

A.—No.

Q.—Did you receive a salary?

A.—Yes.

Q.—In addition to straight salary do you get anything in the way of commission or anything like that?

A.—No.   Well, at the end of the year I receive a small bonus, the last couple of years, three or four years.

Q.—That depends on work?

A.—Yes.

THE CHAIRMAN: Based on the year's work?

A.—No, it is just a gift from Mr. Lyons.

Q.—Was that common to the rest of the staff?

A.—Yes.

Q.—But you have no commission interest, or no interest as a shareholder, director?

A.—None whatever.

Q.—And since Mr. Lyons has been away from the Soo, since July, 1923, have you had any change in instructions on your conduct of the business?

A.—Please explain more fully.

Q.—Mr. Lyons was up there in control himself?

A.—Yes.

Q.—Until July, 1923?

A.—Yes.

Q.—Then he came to Toronto. Since then he hasn't had active conduct of the business?

A.—No.

Q.—Has the business run on in the same way?

A.—Yes.

Q.—I believe at one time since then you got some instructions from him?

A.—Yes.

Q.—When was that?

A.—That would be in the spring of 1925.

Q.—A year ago?

A.—Yes.

Q.—What were the instructions?

A.—That we must not sell the Ontario Government, any department of the Ontario Government, any materials whatever.

Q.—Well, apart from that have you had any instructions as to sales to governments or to government contractors, licensees, or concessionaires?

A.—You mean as regards to sales?

Q.—Yes?

A.—No.

Q.—That was the only occasion?

A.—Yes.

Q.—Have you ever attempted to use Mr. Lyons' position for the benefit of the business?

A.—Absolutely no.

Q.—Has anybody been canvassed in that way?

A.—None whatever.

Q.—How many salesmen have you?

A.—Two, besides myself.

Q.—They are travellers, are they?

A.—Travellers, yes.

Q.—Are they under you?

A.—Yes.

Q.—What are your instructions to them?

A.—To get out, call on the trade in their certain districts, get all the business they can possibly get—generally sales manager's instructions to salesmen.

Q.—Have you personally ever attempted to use Mr. Lyons' position?

A.—Not at all.

Q.—Has it ever come to your knowledge that your salesmen have?

A.—Not at all, never been mentioned to me.

Q.—Never had any complaints of that kind?

A.—Not at all.

Q.—So that can I put it this way, that the business has been conducted apart from his position here?

A.—Absolutely.

Q.—And ran on the same way as it had before?

A.—Absolutely.

Q.—Any change in policy as to the class of trade you were after?

A.—Yes—not in policy. We have added to our different lines which we have to call on, different lines of trade.

Q.—That is, just ordinary—

A.—Ordinary expansion of business.

Q.—And that had been going on ever since you came with him?

A.—Yes.

Q.—It has been a growing business?

A.—That is why I did come with him.

Q.—Why?

A.—When I came with the Lyons Fuel Company, the instructions, my understanding from Mr. Lyons was that it was his intention to go out after outside business more than he had in the past, and that was why—

Q.—Why you were taken on?

A.—I was taken on.

Q.—Being an engineer, I suppose, you were able to read plans and that sort of thing?

A.—Yes.

Q.—And did you do the tendering on large contracts, figuring?

A.—Yes.

Q.—That is, you would get blue prints, you were able to read them?

A.—Yes.

Q.—Pick off quantities?

A.—Yes.

Q.—Do all the technical end?

A.—Yes.

Q.—Before I go into any particulars, speaking generally have you any knowledge in the Lyons business since 1923 of any dealings directly or indirectly with any contractor or licensee, concessionaire or any corporation or company dealing with the Crown of any advantage being taken of Mr. Lyons' position?

A.—None at all.

Q.—Have you any knowledge of any payments being made directly or indirectly in that connection?

A.—None at all.

Q.—And I can put it broadly that the business is being run by you, and, I understand, Mr. Harry Lyons?

A.—Yes, absolutely.

Q.—And has Mr. Lyons had any conduct of it since then?

A.—None at all, outside of advisory, financial matters.

Q.—His interest in the business has been confined to advice and assistance in the financing?

A.—Absolutely.

Q.—Has he had any active control of the figuring on contracts?

A.—None at all.

Q.—Who does the figuring on contracts?

A.—Generally I do myself.

Q.—And who does the negotiations as to contracts?

A.—I do.

Q.—And have you ever known Mr. Lyons to interfere or give instructions or directions as to that since he became a Minister of the Crown?

A.—Absolutely not.

Q.—May I put it fairly this way, that he just left the business entirely to you and his son, the active part of it?
A.—Yes.
Q.—And his only interest in it has been advice, general advice, or assistance in the banking end?
A.—Yes, absolutely.
Q.—Getting down to particular instances, do you know the McNamara firm?
A.—I do, yes.
Q.—We have heard of two contracts they had with the Crown for road construction?
A.—Yes.
Q.—Conniston road and Timmins road?
A.—Yes.
Q.—Did you have anything to do with that?
A.—None at all.
Q.—Was any of it handled through your firm?
A.—None at all.
Q.—Did you get any allowance from any wholesale house or anyone else from any dealings?
A.—None at all.
Q.—Was there any indirect consideration of any kind accruing to your firm from the McNamara dealings, even if it were through somebody else?
A.—None.
Q.—You know what I mean, it is possible to get a commission that comes from a wholesale house?
A.—None at all.
Q.—And you sold them nothing direct?
A.—None at all.
Q.—Take their other contracts. They had a contract on Wellington Street at Sault Ste. Marie?
A.—Yes.
Q.—Did you have something to do with that?
A.—Yes.
Q.—What did you have to do with that?
A.—We supplied them with gravel and cement.
Q.—That was a city contract?
A.—Yes.
Q.—And how did you do that?
A.—Through bidding on the materials, and got the business.
Q.—Was that in the ordinary course of business?
A.—Yes.
Q.—Anything out of the way in connection with that?
A.—Nothing at all.
Q.—Did Mr. Lyons' company get any benefit except from the ordinary trade?
A.—Just what profits we would make on the material.
Q.—That is all shown in the books?
A.—Oh yes, absolutely.
Q.—Now the aerodrome contract?
A.—Yes.
Q.—You know the contractor, Fitzpatrick?

A.—I do.

Q.—We have heard your firm supplied material for that?

A.—Yes.

Q.—How did you get that?

A.—By the usual way, of going after the business, bidding on it and making the sale.

Q.—Were you shown the plan and specification for the purpose of giving figures?

A.—Yes, I did see them, yes.

Q.—Were you the man to figure on this roof?

A.—Yes.

Q.—The architects plans, I suppose, had attached specifications for the roof?

A.—Yes.

Q.—Did you give one?

A.—Yes.

Q.—Was there any variation or change in it?

A.—From when?

Q.—Well, we heard you gave one figure and later on it was reduced?

A.—Oh yes, it was.

Q.—Explain that?

A.—Well, the architect's plans on that roof were very late coming in and it was my understanding at the time that it was a twenty-year bonded guaranteed roof, five ply, tar, felt and gravel roof, and when the contract was let we discovered that the roof was of the same construction calling for a ten year—instead of being a bonded guarantee it called for a roofer's guarantee only. The cost on a bonded guarantee figures to cover inspection and one thing and another and runs about three dollars per square. And then I figured that the reduction from twenty-year to ten years would be worth another dollar a square and I reduced the price four dollars a square.

Q.—You had thought the bond was supplied by a bond company?

A.—Yes.

Q.—For a twenty-year period?

A.—Twenty-year period.

Q.—That is similar to this Barrett specification?

A.—That is what I thought it was going to be, Barrett specification.

Q.—In that case you would get a bond with the Barrett Company, it that it?

A.—Yes.

Q.—Had you put on a Barrett roof in other cases?

A.—Oh yes.

Q.—You are their agents?

A.—Not now. We were at that time.

Q.—And that involved getting a bond from the Barrett Company?

A.—Yes.

Q.—For which you had to pay premium?

A.—Yes.

Q.—And you found instead of twenty years it was ten and all that was required was the guarantee of a responsible roofer?

A.—Yes.

Q.—And you were able to give that yourself?

A.—Yes, sir.

Q.—And when you found this you made a reduction?

A.—Yes.

Mr. Fisher: And you didn't have a Barrett inspection?

A.—We didn't have a Barrett inspection, no.

Q.—It was cheaper to you?

A.—Their inspection?

The Chairman: This wasn't a Barrett roof.

Mr. Fisher: Wasn't it?

The Chairman: It was a roof specified by the architects. They built by the specifications themselves. They didn't specify Barrett.

A.—I thought we would have to use Barrett specifications and put it on under a twenty-year bonded guarantee which we didn't have to do.

Mr. Finlayson: Or in another words you thought you were putting on a Barrett roof with Barrett specifications and Barrett guarantee?

A.—Yes.

Q.—Which involved twenty years?

A.—Yes.

Q.—And when you found you didn't have to do that you knew you were going to make a saving, the Barrett inspection, the Barrett guarantee, and you yourselves would assume the guarantee but only for ten years?

A.—Yes.

Q.—What did you make it?

A.—Five ply, felt and gravel.

Q.—Supplied by Barrett materials?

A.—Yes.

Q.—So you built of Barrett materials and purchased from Barrett and put it on yourself as you would in the ordinary course of business. So you didn't have to pay premium on the bond and didn't have to get Barrett inspector to come up, but you would have done the work in either case?

A.—Yes.

Q.—So that saving became apparent and you gave Fitzpatrick the benefit?

A.—Absolutely.

Q.—We heard there was certain other changes. Fitzpatrick said he beat you down?

A.—Yes, he did.

Q.—Fire doors?

A.—Yes.

Q.—Tell us, fire doors, I suppose fire underwriters' doors are not a common thing at the Soo?

A.—No.

Q.—And these, I assume, would be great big ones?

A.—Yes.

Q.—Not motor?

A.—No, not motor.

Q.—What size are they?

A.—There is three doors in a span of eighty feet, I think it is. I would not say that eighty feet to be definite, but it is approximately.

Q.—What height?

A.—They will run—I cannot recall that from the plans, but I would judge about thirty to thirty-five feet.

Q.—Anyway these are those big sliding metal doors. Three of them, and they allow a sea plane to come through the doors, and so adjusted that at a certain heat they drop—

A.—No.

Q.—Oh these are not these fire proof?

A.—No, just rolling doors mechanically operated for closing up the main entrance, for bringing planes in and bringing them out.

Q.—A door with narrow slats, just like a roller top desk?

A.—Yes.

Q.—You don't carry them in stock?

A.—Absolutely no.

Q.—Who are they made by?

A.—By several different people; at that time I had quotations from two or three different people. I cannot recall just at the moment.

Q.—Tell us about the change.

A.—At the time we quoted on it originally we didn't have very much time getting any prices and in order to get details as to the erection of these doors— the contractor was calling for prices erected on the doors. I had no idea just what these erection costs would be at the time of putting in my original quotation. To give the contractors a chance to bid on this thing I took the first price I had and played safe on my erection costs and finally I got a price on the doors erected.

Q.—That is when he was putting in his bid, for the purpose of his bid you gave him a figure taken from your list and played safe in the line of erection?

A.—On the erection.

Q.—And he put his bid in on that basis?

A.—Yes. Later I got a price erected by the manufacturers of the doors.

Q.—You got a price on the manufacturer to come up?

A.—Freight paid to the Soo.

Q.—It was lower?

A.—Considerably lower.

Q.—Than your estimate?

A.—Yes.

Q.—As a result of that what did you do?

A.—I lowered my price to Fitzpatrick.

Q.—Now those are the principal changes, aren't they?

A.—I believe so, yes.

Q.—There is no other change?

A.—I think I lowered the price of steel sash.

Q.—For what cause?

A.—The only cause in that was he talked me into it.

Q.—He was a little Yiddish?

A.—Yes.

Q.—And he got you down?

A.—Yes.

Q.—Were those price reductions intended to give him an advantage in bidding?

A.—They were not given him until after the contract was let.

Q.—As a matter of fact they didn't give him an advantage in bidding?

A.—Absolutely not, no.

Q.—They operated the other way. It may have given him an advantage in price, increased his profit?

A.—Well, it is a customary thing as far as the north is concerned when a contractor gets a job then he goes out to buy the materials and as a rule they go after the best price they can get.

Q.—And these reductions were in the ordinary course of business?

A —Oh yes, absolutely.

Q.—Was there any consideration to Fitzpatrick in any way from your company?

A.—None at all.

Q.—Anything given from Fitzpatrick to your company in any way?

A.—Absolutely no.

Q.—Any allowance, commission on the contract, or anything of that kind?

A.—None at all.

Q.—No improper dealings of any kind came to your knowledge, to you or anybody else?

A.—Absolutely not.

Q.—Ordinary business?

A.—Ordinary business.

Q.—What about the company's dealings with other contractors up there? Are there any other government contractors we haven't heard of? We have heard of the McNamaras and the aerodrome?

A.—Would you explain?

Q.—Yes, I don't want to lead you, but tell me generally if you know of any other cases in which the Lyons Company were dealing with any contractors of any kind who had any special rates or cconsideration or received consideration from your company or your company received consideration from them?

A.—None at all. If I understand the question do you want to know whether we have ever had dealings with contractors who have been doing Government contracts?

Q.—I want to know—you are in charge of the sales?

A.—Yes.

Q.—You deal with all contracts?

A.—Yes.

Q.—You have knowledge of everything that has been going on since 'Mr. Lyons left?

A.—Yes.

Q.—Since he became Minister of the Crown in July, 1923, have you ever, either in connection with McNamara, the aerodrome, or any other, on any occasion, observed or know of any consideration being given either way?

A.—None at all.

Q.—Never heard of any?

A.—No.

Q.—Has it all been in the ordinary course?

A.—Business in the ordinary way.

Q.—Just one other thing. Since March a year ago when you received instructions from Mr. Lyons not to sell any department of the Crown you have ceased dealing with this Department?

A.—Absolutely, yes.

Q.—But you have, I understand, sold to some other people who have resold to the Government?

A.—Yes, I think so.

Q.—Have you ever sold particular articles knowing they were going to be turned over or have they just been general sales?

A.—Just general sales.

Q.—We have heard you sold to a man named Bedford?

A.—Yes.

Q.—Who is that?

A.—Hardware merchant.

Q.—Retail?

A.—Retail hardware merchant.

Q.—What have you sold to him?

A.—Considerable heavy hardware, blankets, concrete pipe, and general lines.

Q.—Your connection with him has been running some years?

A.—Oh, yes.

Q.—It has been standing?

A.—Yes.

Q.—When you sell these things to him who do you have to compete with?

A.—We compete with the Cochrane Hardware Company and all the jobbers throughout the Province of Ontario.

Q.—Howlands?

A.—Howlands, yes.

Q.—He is purchasing in the open market?

A.—Absolutely.

Q.—And if you can get the business from him you have to compete with the general wholesale trade?

A.—Yes.

Q.—Cochrane is the big northern hardware you compete with there?

A.—Yes.

Q.—But he also gets from all the jobbers and wholesalers?

A.—Yes.

Q.—You say your account with him has been running for years? In the last year we have heard you sold him some beds, some blankets, some sewer pipe, some of which, part of which, perhaps, went to the Northern Development Branch?

A.—Yes.

Q.—How did you come to sel' him sewer pipe?

A.—He asked us for prices on it and we gave it to him.

Q.—How did you tender? Did he come to you?

A.—Generally by telephone.

Q.—He is in the market for sewer pipe, as a salesman?

A.—What is the question?

Q.—Who are the vendors of sewer pipe up there?

A.—On, there is contractors—

Q.—You don't follow me. .Who do you compete with?

A.—I. J. Downey & Co.

Q.—Are they manufacturers?

A.—No. Sewer or concrete?

Q.—Concrete?

A.—Oh. Well, we are the only manufacturers of concrete pipe north of Toronto.

Q.—Perhaps it is my mistake. Sewer pipe is vitrified pipe shipped in?

A.—Yes.

Q.—Concrete pipe you say, you are the only manufacturers?

A.—Yes.

Q.—It requires a plant?

A.—Yes.

Q.—It is reinforced and has to be put through pressure too?

A.—It has to be put through steam.

Q.—You sell to everybody up there?

A.—Yes.

Q.—And when you gave him a price, what did you give him?

A.—I gave him our wholesale price for resale.

Q.—In other words you put him on the jobbers' list?

A.—Yes.

Q.—Did you know when you were selling to him that it was for a Government contract or what it was for?

A.—Well, I don't know as I did just when he asked for the prices. But I had a good idea it was for the Government.

Q.—Later on, of course, you knew?

A.—Later on I knew about it.

Q.—Where did he get it, what point of delivery?

A.—Oh, he got some in our yards, some we had to deliver.

Q.—What was the difference?

A.—Difference in price?

Q.—Yes?

A.—All depends on where we had to deliver.

Q.—Is it usually delivered?

A.—Oh no, I think we have the only truck in Sault Ste. Marie that is capable of delivering the larger sizes.

Q.—What weight are the larger sizes?

A.—Thirty-six inch runs a ton fifty pounds.

Q.—And where was he using it, this Northern Development work?

A.—Haviland Bay mostly.

Q.—How many miles?

A.—About twenty-seven miles.

Q.—And how is it taken there?

A.—We took it by our truck.

Q.—Twenty-seven miles?

A.—Twenty-seven miles out over the height of land, down the other side of the height of land, the height of land being approximately 600 feet I believe above Sault Ste. Marie and over rocky road.

Q.—Was anybody else able to deliver it?

A.—I don't believe they could have got it delivered.

Q.—Did you make him a proper charge for delivery?

A —Absolutely.

Q.—Was he able to deliver it himself?

A.—Oh, he delivered it himself.

Q.—Then his price would be F.O.B.?

A.—F.O.B. our yards

Q.—But these pipes you alone could deliver, you paid for that?

A.—Yes.

Q.—Tell me this, do I understand in every case the sale was F.O.B. the yard?

A.—Yes.

Q.—But where you delivered there was an extra charge in which you had regard to the distance and the difficulties and time?

A.—Absolutely.

Q.—Was it all on a business basis?

A.—Absolutely.

Q.—In other words, were there any cases in which you knew the Northern Development were going to require a number of pipes and you put it through Bedford's books for concealment?

A.—Absolutely not.

Q.—It was all a straight sale to Bedford?

A.—Yes.

Q.—Bedford sold it where he could?

A.—Absolutely.

Q.—Does that apply to the other articles you sold him?

A.—Absolutely.

Q.—Beds?

A.—I don't know whether he sold the other articles to the Ontario Government or who he sold them, as far as that is concerned.

Q.—You do know of the pipe because you had to deliver?

A.—Yes.

Q.—The others you don't know where he sold?

A.—No.

Q.—Do you know the Government Engineer?

A.—Mr. Lamb?

Q.—Yes?

A.—Yes.

Q.—Have you had any relations with Mr. Lamb by which he has assisted you in securing business?

A.—I haven't talked Government business to Mr. Lamb since Mr. Lyons made the statement in the House and gave instructions not to.

Q.—Before that, was anything ever done towards using him for the purpose of securing business?

A.—Absolutely not.

Cross examination by W. E. N. Sinclair, K.C.

Q.—As I understand it, the Lyons Fuel and Supply Company is a wholesale business and also a retail business?

A.—Yes.

Q.—Who has charge of the wholesale end of the business?

A.—Well, it is a joint—we run the two together.

Q.—What management is there for the wholesale? Just Mr. Harry Lyons and yourself?

A.—Yes.

Q.—And then for the retail?

A.—Mr. Lyons and myself.

Q.—Just the same two. So that this large business, wholesale and retail, is operated by two men?

A.—Yes.

Q.—When you ceased doing business with the Government in 1925 do you know where that business went?

A.—I don't know.

Q.—Don't know who got it?

A.—No.

Q.—And the business you had been doing with the Government was a retail business?

A.—Yes, absolutely.

Q.—In competition with the other retailers in the Soo?

A.—Absolutely.

Q.—And it was the retail business which you ceased doing on instructions from the Minister?

A.—Absolutely.

Q.—You say you had an account with Bedford for some years?

A.—Yes.

Q.—Can you tell me this morning the volume of business you did with him in 1923?

A.—I cannot, no.

Q.—That figure could be got?

A.—Oh yes.

Q.—I would like to have the witness get us a statement of the business— Mr. Nash may have this done, by the Lyons Fuel and Supply Company, either wholesale or retail, with Mr. Bedford in the years, 1923, 1924 and 1925.

MR. FINLAYSON: You want the Bedford business?

MR. SINCLAIR: The business the Lyons Fuel and Supply Company did as wholesalers or retailers with Bedford in 1923, 1924 and 1925.

MR. FINLAYSON: I don't know whether Mr. Nash has it.

MR. SINCLAIR: I don't think Mr. McAllister should be released until he gives us that evidence because he said he had been trading with him for years and I think this Committee should know whether he did more in one year or another.

MR. FINLAYSON: Of course, judging from the evidence that has already been given I think there is no doubt he did more. One answer is they have increased their lines and added different lines of business.

MR. SINCLAIR: Well, the Public Accounts show Mr. Bedford didn't do any business with the Province, practically speaking, until 1925. Now I think it is very material that the evidence of this Committee should show the business that the Lyons people did with Bedford for say those three years.

MR. FINLAYSON: Let it stand until we see what Mr. Nash has.

THE CHAIRMAN: It will be procured.

MR. SINCLAIR: As long as there is a note in the evidence that it will be procured before the Committee rises. I know witnesses cannot give us that off hand.

Q.—Now, you sold cement?

A.—Yes.

Q.—Can you sell cement cheaper than your competitors at the Soo? I don't mean "can." I say do you?

A.—Well, in some cases I guess we do.

Q.—How is that done? I understood there was an arrangement with the cement manufacturers that it was to be sold at a certain price in a certain area?

A.—Absolutely not.

Q.—So you can sell cement if you wish to at a cut price?

A.—Absolutely.

Q.—And how much could you cut the price?

A.—That all depends on how much we are contented—what margin we are content to work on.

Q.—You say there is no arrangement with cement companies by which cement cannot be sold below certain prices?

A.—None.

Q.—It can be sold at any price.

Hon. Mr. Raney: No firm is agent for the Cement Company? You are not any more the agent than Downey? Are you agent for the Canada Cement?

A.—We handle Canada Cement, but we are not exclusive agents.

Mr. Sinclair: In regard to the roof of the aerodrome, the roof which was put on was not a twenty-year guaranteed roof?

A.—No.

Q.—I understood Mr. Fitzpatrick the other night to say it was guaranteed for twenty years.

Hon. Mr. Lyons: I may explain that, if I may. The specifications of the roof is just the same as the specifications covering a twenty-year roof but in the specifications they only asked for a ten years' roofer's guarantee. I don't know whether it was mistake on the part of the architect or whether he thought that was satisfactory, or what. The specifications are just the same as the specifications for a twenty-year roof but the guarantee only asks for ten years instead of twenty. I read the specifications over yesterday myself just to find out.

Mr. Sinclair: My impression is the evidence was to the Committee the other night that it was a twenty-year guaranteed roof.

Mr. Finlayson: You were not in when we started in and I think everybody started on the twenty-year basis and afterwards we got the explanation and I think you were out.

Mr. Sinclair: Anyway, as a matter of fact, you put on a roof guaranteed for ten years?

A.—Yes.

Q.—A roof not guaranteed beyond the written guarantee of the Lyons Fuel and Supply?

Q.—It was not a bonded guarantee or anything of the kind, and was just such a guarantee as anybody doing business would give?

A.—Yes, that is it.

Q.—And when you found that this was to be the guarantee given you reduced the price $4 per square?

A.—Yes.

Q.—And do you remember how your price compared with Hesson's?

A.—No, I do not.

The Chairman: The evidence was Hesson's price was fifteen dollars some odd cents. He didn't remember the cents.

Mr. Sinclair: What paper was actually used putting this roof on?

A.—Barrett paper.

Q.—And laid with tar and five thicknesses?

A.—Five ply, tar and felt.

Q.—Why would the difference account for a difference of $4 per square on a roof such as that?

A.—On account of the inspection fees, the bond, which is all extra expense, which is always added on by the—

Hon. Mr. Lyons: If I may explain. Perhaps many people here won't understand the difference. A bonded guarantee roof is a roof guaranteed by a bonded company just the same way as a bonded company guarantees the completion of a contractor's contract, and of course there is a substantial fee for it—premium. When we bond a roof ourselves we absorb that because the average fellow knows when he puts on a roof on certain specifications he is not going to have trouble with it and he is satisfied to have that responsibility, and we do it ourselves, and that is why we broke away from the Barrett Company, so we would be able to build the same class of roof at less money and give our own guarantee instead of theirs.

Mr. Sinclair: It is not necessary to have a roof put on by the Lyons Fuel and Supply Company bonded by a bond company. It will last for the time without any question. There will be no leaks in it. And, therefore, you can charge $4 per square less than any other roof. You put on this roof at $4 a square less than you first contracted to put it on for?

A.—Yes.

Q.—And the reason given for that is that you did not have to give any guarantee other than the guarantee of the company?

A.—Absolutely.

Q.—And you don't expect that there will be any repairs to make on this roof within the period of ten years?

A.—If there is we will have to do it. I don't expect it.

Q.—You don't expect it, but if you did give a guarantee to a bonded company they would expect to make some repairs to the roof in that time.

Mr. Finlayson: They would make you do it.

Mr. Sinclair: But that is what the charge is made for, a saving of about $1,500, by not having a bonded roof put on?

A.—Yes.

Q.—And the only reason is that instead of a regular bonded guarantee there is the guarantee of the company?

A.—Yes.

Q.—And I suppose the guarantee of one company is as good as the guarantee of another company?

A.—I would not say that.

Q.—The Lyons Company is the only company at the Soo whose guarantee is any good?

A.—I don't say that either.

Member: You put the question to him this way, that any company is as good as another. Well, if a company is financially sound—all companies are not financially sound—one would be as good as another, but all companies are not.

Mr. Sinclair: And the reason given the other night was the guarantee of the Hesson Company was not good?

The Chairman: Let us be correct. What Fitzpatrick said, and I recollect clearly, he didn't want the guarantee of the Hesson Company because in the event of them having to call on them for repairs they would not be in a position to do the repairs. They would have to send for the man who put it on, and he didn't want to deal with two people.

Mr. Sinclair: And, therefore, the Province should pay more for the roofing to get it put on by this company.

Mr. Finlayson: That is a foolish statement. The Province didn't pay more.

Mr. Sinclair: I have a happy faculty of being foolish and that is something you cannot correct. It is born in me.

The Chairman: You wouldn't ask this Committee to believe that the difference in the price Mr. Fitzpatrick got, the fact that he paid more to the Lyons people for his roof than he would have paid to the Hesson after he had his contract accepted by the Government at a certain figure made any difference to the Government.

MR. SINCLAIR: I will answer questions to you when I am subpoenaed. I never do in court and I don't intend to here.

Q.—There are so many things about this I don't understand?

A.—Perhaps if I said this, if I am in order, the Hesson Company don't put on roofs.

HON. MR. RANEY: We understand that.

THE CHAIRMAN: That was the reason Fitzpatrick made for not wanting to take their guarantee. He didn't say they were not a good firm, or not responsible.

MR. SINCLAIR: What other tenderers on this aerodrome got prices from you other than Fitzpatrick?

A.—McIntyre and Kelly Bros., McLarty Bros. I believe Forrest Harton. I don't recall them all.

Q.—And they all got the same prices?

A.—Absolutely, yes.

Hon. W. E. Raney cross examining.

Q.—Did your firm furnish the reinforcing material for the Wellington Street job?

A.—Yes sir.

Q.—That is, it was a steel netting, is it, that goes over the whole street surface?

A.—Yes.

Q.—There was a large quantity?

A.—It is a mesh, it is an expanded metal.

Q.—That is sold, I think, by the hundred square feet, so much a hundred square feet?

A.—Yes.

Q.—What was your price?

A.—I do not recall it off hand.

Q.—I qould like you to find that out for me?

A.—I can.

Q.—When can you get me that information?

A.—I will get it by phone if it is necessary this afternoon.

HON. MR. RANEY: Mr. McNamara hasn't been released?

THE CHAIRMAN: Mr. George McNamara is still available. I understand Howard is left.

HON. MR. RANEY: Which Mr. McNamara had charge?

THE CHAIRMAN: George McNamara.

HON. MR. RANEY: He is available?

THE CHAIRMAN: Yes.

HON. MR. RANEY: And you will get me that information?

A.—I will, yes.

MR. FINLAYSON: How can you get it?

A.—Get it from the ledger sheets.

MR. FINLAYSON: He is asking you what quotation you gave McNamara.

HON. MR. RANEY: What quotation you gave and what price?

A.—I don't know as I can give you the quotation—the original—you had it.

HON. MR. RANEY: Price, that is what I want.

HON. MR. LYONS: We can give the price sold to McNamara.

Hon. Mr. Raney: That is what I want. What you actually sold it for. If you can get me the quotation I would like that too?

A.—Very glad to.

Q.—Did your company sell a couple of trucks to the Government?

A.—No, sir, absolutely not.

Q.—Never at any time?

A.—No, sir.

Q.—The doors on which you quoted for the aerodrome you say you first quoted, we had the other day from Fitzpatrick, $5,020 for the doors?

A.—Is that our original quotation?

Q.—It was furnished by Mr. Fitzpatrick, $5,020?

A.—I don't recall the figure off hand.

Q.—Do you recall when Fitzpatrick came back afterwards he beat you down $500?

A.—I recall he beat me down considerably. I don't know just what it was.

Q.—He fixed the figure at $500. He has it here. This is it written on his own letter head and the typewritten figures are the figures he said you quoted him and the lead pencil figures are the figures he says that were finally arranged. As far as doors were concerned, the original price you gave him before he tendered was $5,020 and after his tender had been accepted he came back to you and you reduced that price to $4,620. That isn't $500. It is $400?

A.—Yes.

Q.—Then he says that originally, before he tendered you quoted $3,439 on the steel sash and afterwards when he came back to you after his tender had been accepted you reduced the price to $2,939, that would be a reduction of $500?

A.—Yes.

Q.—That is right?

A.—I don't know. I assume his figures are correct.

Q.—So on these two items there is a reduction of $900?

A.—Yes.

Q.—On roofing he had quoted you for $20 a square?

A.—Yes.

Q.—And there were 265 squares?

Hon. Mr. Lyons: Two hundred and sixty-five or 266.

Q.—And the price you gave him was $20 a square?

A.—Yes.

Q.—And after his tender was accepted you reduced that to $16?

A.—Yes.

Q.—That would be a difference in price of $1,060?

A.—You are figuring on the basis of 265 squares?

Q.—Yes?

A.—Yes.

Q.—Totalling these it gives you $1,960 as the advantage he had from the prices you gave him after his tender had been accepted over the prices you had given him originally?

A.—Yes.

Q.—If you had given him the prices originally that you gave after his tender was accepted and he had figured on these prices obviously his price to the Government would have been $1,960 less?

A.—I cannot say that.

Q.—Wouldn't you expect that to be so?

A.—I don't think so, no.

Q.—Why not?

A.—If I was contracting myself I would figure on making that little extra.

Q.—Knowing that he is asked to tender on this job?

A.—Yes.

Q.—So much for concrete?

A.—Yes.

Q.—So much for foundation?

A.—Yes.

Q.—So much for the sills?

A.—Yes.

Q.—So much for the roof, doors, steel sash, so much for the different items?

A.—Yes.

Q.—He figures all those times in and he adds so much for profit and that is his tender, isn't that right?

A.—I guess so.

Q.—If he has included in his figures items for about $2,000 more than he will be called upon to pay wouldn't his tender be that much less if he had had the correct figures in the beginning?

A.—I cannot say.

MR. FINLAYSON: If the figures had gone up the Government should have been charged the other way. My friend's experience in contracting is limited. I see Mr. Biggs smiling at these theories.

MR. SINCLAIR: This is not a theory. It is absolute gospel truth. A man takes the costs. He must figure on what costs are given him. Fitzpatrick had the advantage of reduced cost over the other tenderers.

A.—I would like Mr. Sinclair to repeat that.

MR. SINCLAIR: No, this is not your evidence. We make these statements.

HON. MR. RANEY:

Q.—Did your firm furnish the glass for this aerdrome?

A.—We did, yes.

Q.—Where did you get it from?

A.—Cochrane Hardware.

Q.—Was that included in the price you gave Mr. Fitzpatrick originally?

A.—Yes, but I would not swear. I would not say it was. I cannot. I don't recall that was in the original quotation or not.

Q.—Yes, I have it here, $1,932?

A.—Yes.

Q.—Did you give Fitzpatrick a wholesale or retail price on that glass?

A.—Retail price.

Q.—Do you recall what price it was you gave him?

A.—I don't. Just whatever—has he got it extended?

Q.—No, there is no item?

A.—I don't recall the figure, Mr. Raney.

Q.—I think Fitzpatrick did.

THE CHAIRMAN: He said 31 cents as compared with 33½ cents.

Q.—That is right. Thirty-one cents. What would that be?

HON. MR. LYONS: Square foot.

HON. MR. RANEY: But he said another firm had come and had tendered him a lower price.

THE CHAIRMAN: He said the Cochrane that he purchased this glass came along with a lower price.

Hon. Mr. Raney: Explain that matter?

A.—Which?

Q.—Explain the matter of the glass. The Cochrane people apparently made a tender. Fitzpatrick had a lower price than the price you gave, lower lump price?

A.—I can't explain that.

Q.—That in conjunction with the fact that your firm bought the glass from the Cochrane people?

A.—Repeat that?

Q.—Fitzpatrick says that after his tender had been accepted the Cochrane people came to him and tendered on the glass at a price lower than the price you had given. You tell me you purchased the glass from the Cochrane people to fill this contract. I want to know what explanation you have?

A.—Well, I cannot explain why the Cochrane people went to Fitzpatrick after we had secured the order and quoted him on glass. I cannot explain their actions.

Q.—If he cannot explain he cannot, that is all.

Member: Why did he buy from the Cochrane Hardware, if you bought from them?

A.—I bought from the Cochrane Hardware simply to give them the business, providing they would meet the lowest price I had on glass.

Hon. Mr. Raney: What do you mean?

A.—They were after the business, came up to our office soliciting the business.

Q.—What business?

A.—The glass.

Q.—Soliciting what from you?

A.—Soliciting this glass.

Q.—Well, they are a wholesale house too, and you are?

A.—Absolutely.

Q.—And you get your glass from manufacturers?

A.—They made a proposition to us. They said, if we can make a little money on this glass have you any objection to giving us that business. I said none whatever, if your price is as good or even better than the price we have, you will have the business.

Q.—Did you have the glass in stock to fill this order?

A.—No.

Q.—You would have had to order from Belgium?

A.—Absolutely.

Q.—You had quoted at retail price to Fitzpatrick?

A.—Yes.

Q.—And did the Cochrane people have it in stock?

A.—No.

Q.—They would have to get it from Belgium?

A.—Yes.

Q.—Whichever bought it would have to get it from Belgium?

A.—Yes.

Q.—What advantage was there to you in getting the glass through the Cochrane people?

A.—No advantage at all.

Q.—They would have their profit on the transaction?

A.—If they would work in I was willing. I was buying glass at the lowest price I could buy it at. If they could buy it better, it was up to them. It didn't interest me.

Q.—Did they quote you a price?

A.—Yes.

Q.—What was it?

A.—I cannot say.

Q.—Will you find out?

A.—I don't think I will.

Q.—You don't want to disclose.

A.—I don't want to disclose the difference between our buying and selling price.

Q.—You won't tell?

A.—No, I wouldn't.

Q.—Well, I won't try to force you if you don't want to tell. Then why, did you know the Cochrane people had solicited this business from Fitzpatrick?

A.—No.

Q.—It was after he saw them they came to you. Do know whether it was after they had seen Fitzpatrick when they came to you?

A.—I don't know.

Q.—It wasn't you who went to the Cochrane people to buy the glass?

A.—No.

Q.—The Cochrane people came to you to get in on this?

A.—Yes.

Q.—They thought they saw a chance of making a profit?

A.—I guess that was their idea.

Q.—Between the price you had quoted to Fitzpatrick and the price they were able to furnish the glass?

A.—I suppose.

Q.—And they would have to go to the same source to get the glass you would?

A.—Well, I don't know.

Q.—Well, the same people, practically.

A.—They would have to go to the market to buy it.

Q.—Was there a fixed price for glass?

A.—No, not when you get into a volume of that size.

Q.—There is a certain quality of glass?

A.—You call for certain specifications and whoever is the most anxious for the business.

Q.—In 1924 you sold to the Government direct, apparently, from the Public Accounts, about $18,000 worth of goods?

A.—Yes.

Q.—You run both wholesale and retail businesses?

A.—Yes.

Q.—Did you sell to the Government wholesale or retail prices?

A.—Retail prices.

Mr. FINLAYSON: Out of this last question, the Government are not buying in wholesale quantities up there?

A.—No.

Q.—There are just what the trade call sorting orders?

A.—Sorting orders.

Q.—And when driven in to buy a certain order they want it in a hurry?

A.—Yes.

Q.—And they want limited quantities?

A.—Yes.

Q.—And it has to come right out of stock?

A.—Absolutely.

Q.—So when you were selling to the Government at retail prices you were selling the same way as every other store there?

A.—Sure.

Q.—You were selling for job lots, single articles, or fraction quantities right from your shelves?

A.—Yes.

Q.—That you are carrying in stock?

A.—Yes.

Q.—And you are just delivering them wherever they want it?

A.—Yes.

Q.—Ordinary, competitive retail business. Now it may have run into a fair volume but it was made up of an immense number of small orders?

A.—Yes.

Q.—And day after day they would be coming along and buying a few articles, a pick, or a few things they wanted from time to time?

A.—Yes.

Q.—And that is the ordinary retail business?

A.—Yes.

Q.—And you had to compete with the Cochrane Hardware lines, Plummer, Bedford, and all these other concerns?

A.—Absolutely.

Hon. Mr. Raney: Was the glass delivered by the Cochrane Company to your company or direct on the job to the aerodrome?

A.—We delivered it ourselves.

Q.—It was delivered by the Cochrane people to you?

A.—No. I think we took it out of the car.

Q.—You took delivery from the Cochrane people at the station?

A.—Well, I would have to take that up with our shipper.

Mr. Finlayson: Take this glass, running into a considerable volume?

A.—Yes?

Q.—Have you the total figures?

Hon. Mr. Raney: $1,932.

Mr. Fisher: There are not many orders of glass of that amount?

A.—No, very few.

Q.—It would enable anybody to buy it quantity?

A.—Yes.

Q.—And if the Cochrane Hardware had another customer they might be able to make up their carload?

A.—Oh, yes.

Q.—Which is a great advantage?

A.—Yes.

Q.—And if you are buying a half carload or a carload and a half lot of glass or any other article, it is a great advantage to combine your order with Cochranes?

A.—Absolutely yes.

Q.—And wholesale houses like you and Cochranes trade back and forth that way?

A.—Yes.

Q.—If Cochranes had an order for glass and they could combine that with this they are in good shape to go in the market?

A.—Absolutely.

Q.—And you would throw yours into the pot?

A.—Yes.

Q.—That is a very common practice?

A.—Very common.

Q.—And you and the Cochrane people deal back and forth?

Mr. Fisher: Do you know whether Cochranes had any other order?

A.—I cannot say. He just came after the business in a general way.

Member: And he was able to give you a figure that interested you?

A.—Yes.

Mr. Fisher: In regard to these doors, were these doors made to order, or stock doors?

A.—Made to order.

Q.—They would be of an unusual type?

A.—Yes.

Q.—Just three large doors?

A.—Yes.

Q.—There would be a number of firms in Canada that would make that type of door?

A.—There are two or three I believe. There was not a great number if I recall it. Two or three other manufacturers.

Q.—Were you agents for any of these people?

A.—Agents?

Q.—Yes.

A.—Not exclusively, no.

Q.—Or any other way?

A.—Well, we have their price list.

Q.—You didn't have a price list I suppose on doors that are made to order?

A.—Well, no, that is impossible. You have to figure these absolutely separate.

Q.—When Fitzpatrick was making up his tender he asked you for a price?

A.—Yes.

Q.—Was it a price or a contract you had with him? Did you give him a quotation or a firm offer?

A.—I gave him a quotation.

Q.—Did you feel that you were bound to carry that out?

A.—Yes, I was bound to carry out that price for these doors.

Q.—Where did you get your price from?

A.—From two or three different manufacturers.

Q.—At the time you gave him the quotation did you have the figures before you?

A.—Yes.

Q.—What was the lowest figure you had?

A.—I won't say what our lowest figures were.

Q.—Do you mean you won't or you cannot?

A.—I don't feel I should say.

Hon. Mr. Raney: You won't tell.

Mr. Fisher: You had all the figures before you that you ever had?

A.—I won't say that, because at this time, the difficulty in getting prices, these figures, was done a lot by telephone, long distance telephone.

Q.—Did you get figures after you gave him your quotation?

A.—Yes, we did.

Q.—Sure you had any before?

A.—Oh, yes, absolutely.

Q.—And you won't tell us what they were?

A.—No, I don't feel I should.

Q.—Have any understanding with them that if you could get any better price later on you would give him a reduction?

A.—No, I didn't.

Q.—He just took a chance on your quotation?

A.—I don't know what he did. I don't know whether he had other prices or not.

Q.—Is there any reason why he could not got to the manufacturers and get other prices?

A.—No, I don't see why he should be barred from going anywhere.

Q.—Why then would he be interested in coming to you after the contract was awarded? Was he bound to you?

A.—No. He was not.

Q.—Why did he have to dicker with you?

A.—I don't know why.

THE CHAIRMAN: I don't want to interrupt.

HON. MR. RANEY: I think you had better not.

THE CHAIRMAN: I am going to suggest that the other night Mr. Fitzpatrick was being examined and this phase was gone into with Mr. Fullerton and he gave his reasons.

MR. FISHER: As far as you know, Fitzpatrick could get prices just as well as you could from these other people?

A.—I cannot say whether he could or not. If he tried he probably could get them from other people.

Q.—Usually the practice is for these manufacturers to sell direct to any contractors?

A.—I don't know; they always protect the dealer.

MEMBER: Foolish question.

MR. SINCLAIR: This is the second time a man has used the words "foolish question." Professional men come here.

MR. FINLAYSON: I thought any man would know manufacturers have jobbers lists.

MR. FISHER: You never knew of any price lists on goods that were made to order?

A.—No, but any company that gets out two lists, they will quote a dealer cheaper than they will somebody that is going to consume.

Q.—Do you say that as a fact?

A.—I cannot say all companies, but I say a great many companies do.

Q.—Steel doors, there aren't a very great quantity of them used?

A.—I don't know. Not in or particular district.

Q.—You haven't bought a great deal?

A.—Not of that particular type.

Q.—Any of that type?

A.—Not of that type.

Q.—Was there any reason why you should not have get a better price than Fitzpatrick could get himself?

A.—I won't say there is no reason.

Q.—What was the other stuff you quoted to this Fitzpatrick, steel sash? There are half a dozen firms in Canada that make steel sash?

A.—Yes.

Q.—And they are always made to order?

A.—Yes. Not always, no.

Q.—Well, as a rule?

A.—Stock sizes are from standard sizes.

Q.—Well, there aren't very many places in Canada that carry any stock of doors of size?

A.—I believe they do carry standard sizes.

Hon. Mr. Raney: These were specials?

A.—I don't recall.

Mr. Fisher: Where did you get your quotations from in this case?

A.—Several places, several manufacturers.

Q.—Would you like to tell us your lowest quotations?

A.—No.

Hon. Mr. Raney: You won't tell?

Mr. Fisher: And these manufacturers would be selling direct to contractors wouldn't they?

A.—No, not on steel sash. They probably would sell direct but we have a protection on steel sash, jobbers' price.

Q.—It is a very usual thing on buildings for the architect or whoever have charge to advertise for tenders for steel sash?

A.—No, it isn't very usual, I don't recall of ever seeing an architect advertising for steel sash.

Q.—I think if you make inquiries you will find it is the general practice?

A.—Not with any architects I have had dealings with.

Q.—How much steel sash had you handled up to this time?

A.—We have handled a great many.

Q.—Do you buy from one exclusive firm?

A.—No, not if we can get better prices from somebody else.

Q.—Get competition in it?

A.—Well, we haven't had a great deal of competition on steel sash.

Q.—All the same price. Do they all give you the same?

A.—I understood it, did we have much competition in the selling.

Q.—No, in the buying?

A.—It all depends on the size of the contract. If it is a large contract, we do; if it is small the price is pretty general.

Q.—You don't know, I suppose, whether Fitzpatrick got any tenders from anybody else?

A.—I cannot say, no.

Q.—Nothing to prevent him from getting it?

Mr. Graves:

Q.—You have been in the wholesale hardware business for some years?

A.—No, I haven't.

Q.—Well, since 1922?

A.—No.

Q.—Since 1924?

A.—We just took—

Q.—Well, I mean general supply?

A.—Building supplies.

Q.—You know just as well as you are sitting there that Fitzpatrick or any other builder doesn't handle these goods in a wholesale way, can't get the prices you get as a jobber?

A.—No.

Q.—That is the fact?

A.—Yes.

Q.—Why didn't you state the fact. I have been in business for twenty-six years and I have been in business in the north country and I know something about this.

HON. MR. RANEY: Did you make him tell the prices?

MR. GRAVES: I think that is a question you should be ashamed to ask a business man. This had nothing to do with the contract. You might just as well ask what law fee you got.

HON MR. RANEY: I would tell.

MR. GRAVES: In connection with these doors, when you were asked a price first you calculated on having to put these doors in place?

A.—Absolutely, yes.

Q.—And you got a quotation and you made an estimate yourself?

A.—Yes.

Q.—And when you found afterwards that the company would place them themselves and relieve you of the responsibility you were able to make a better price?

A.—Absolutely.

Q.—That was the reason?

A.—Yes.

Q.—Now in connection with prices, they asked you questions here why you changed your price. You have sold goods for less than cost, haven't you?

A.—I have, yes.

Q.—So has every other business man. So if a man comes to you after he gets contract from the Government or anybody else and he had a big order you use your best judgment to get the business?

A.—Yes.

Q.—Is there anything wrong in you making ten per cent. on one article and five on another?

A.—Nothing at all.

Q.—Anything wrong if you wanted to sell Fitzpatrick goods for cost if you wanted to do that?

MR. SINCLAIR: I would think there was.

MR. GRAVES: That is a difference of opinion. You aren't in business.

Q.—In connection with this glass order, Fitzpatrick said he didn't get quotations from the Cochrane Company until after the order was placed?

A.—Yes.

Q.—They tried to make us believe Fitzpatrick gave you the order after he had a quotation for less money. I have done the same thing myself, to make them think they might have done something better, when they might never have got the order. There is nothing peculiar about that?

A.—Nothing peculiar about that.

Q.—I cannot see anything peculiar about any of it, a straight matter of business.

Mr. Fisher: Do you not know it to be a fact that in connection with principal contracts in the city and generally throughout the country that tenders are asked for this steel work, sash and doors and all that sort of thing, and that tenders are made direct by the manufacturers?

A.—I don't know that. I know any buildings we are quoting material on that there is steel sash in we quote on the steel sash.

Q.—Any building of any size they separate the steel sash and the steel doors and they get separate contractors.

A.—Who does?

Q.—The people who have it in charge, usually, the architect?

A.—Any contract I have ever figured on steel sash comes in the general contract.

Mr. Finlayson: I suggest Mr. Fisher go into the library and look at the *Contract Record*.

Mr. Fisher: I know it to be a fact that they can go and get the same prices from half a dozen people.

Hon. Mr. Lyons: You don't know what you are talking about. If you know no more about law than you do about that, you are a fizzle.

Mr. Sinclair: There will be no more evidence taken here until Mr. Lyons takes that back. There is no honourable member of the Bar is going to come into this Committee room and be called such a name as that by any member of this Committee. It is beneath the dignity of a member of the Committee and I ask you to ask the honourable member to withdraw the charge, that if he knows no more law than he does about that, it is a fizzle. It would not be allowed in the House and should not be in this Committee.

The Chairman: I don't see anything unparliamentary about it.

Mr. Sinclair: All right then, if anybody calls you that, I would like to know what you would think of it. If this is the way this Committee is going to act the public might as well know now, how high its findings will be in regard to the charges before this Committee, and we might as well let the public know to-day as any other day, how we are carrying on the business of this Committee.

Mr. Finlayson: This Committee has proceeded very nicely until we got into this mess to-day. Neither you nor Mr. Raney, nor anybody else has got into such a mix-up as we have got into to-day. I am very sorry it has occurred but you can hardly blame any business man of experience or any man of experience around here who know the ordinary conditions under which contracting is done and know what a contractor's list is, and the elementary things handled and waste time of this kind. Anybody can peruse a *Contract Record* to-day or this week and if they can find a tender along this line, it will be something new. I am sorry if anything has been said, and I am sure Mr. Lyons will regret if anything has been said that hurts anybody's professional dignity. I am sorry we have run into this.

Mr. Fisher: As far as I am concerned there has not been any personal feeling anywhere and there is no reflection upon my professional standing that I am worrying at all about. What these gentlemen say does not effect my standing in any way at all. I would say this, I do happen to know a little about this steel contract business and these steel sashes and I am quite satisfied that what I say is absolutely correct because I have seen contracts. For most of the important buildings in this city, if you look at it you will find they call for tenders direct from the manufacturer and get them direct and the thing does not come from any middleman at all.

THE CHAIRMAN: Mr. Fisher's opinion as to how these contracts are secured is his own opinion, but he has no right to insist the witness shall entertain the same opinion. It is all right to ask the witnesses questions and I am not trying to stop him from asking any questions that will bring out the facts, but the whole things arises from the fact that Mr. Fisher thinks he has information on which he bases an opinion.

MR. FISHER: I got along very well with the witness and the witness knows what his own knowledge of the matter is and is giving it.

MR. WIDDIFIELD: Mr.—

THE CHAIRMAN: Now, just a minute, in connection with the unfortunate passage between the witness and Mr. Fisher, I don't think Mr. Fisher is worried about it. Mr. Fisher makes a statement heatedly and Mr. Lyons replied in the heat of the moment and I don't think there is any animus and I am not going to take it that way.

MR. WIDDIFIELD: I am going to appeal for a fair hearing before the Committee. I am going to protest against this one man Committee business. I am not in the legal class, but I am going to protest to the Chairman against the interference of one member of the legal profession who has been interfering throughout the whole progress of the investigation, and I am satisfied, Mr. Chairman, you are going to be fair and if you do take that position, you will have to, I am sure, put a closure on the interference going on in the past. I have not been taking part in the discussion to any extent, but I may, and if I do, I am going to demand a hearing.

THE CHAIRMAN: Mr. Widdifield, you will have no difficulty in asking any questions you want to ask and I don't want you or any other members of the Committee to talk about a one man Committee.

MR. WIDDIFIELD: That is just what we have been having up to to-day.

THE CHAIRMAN: I have been keeping an eye on this and allowing latitude in questions for the purpose of bringing out the facts.

Edward John Hoskins, sworn; Examined by Mr. Finlayson:

Q.—What is your occupation?

A.—An engineer for the Northern Development in Sudbury and Manitoulin Districts.

Q.—Are you an engineer by profession?

A.—Yes.

Q.—Graduate engineer?

A.—Yes, in the old country.

Q.—An English university? And how long have you been engaged as an engineer?

A.—For the last sixteen years.

Q.—And what experience have you had in Ontario? Just general?

A.—Practically ever since I have been in Canada and I have been here sixteen years.

Q.—What class of work?

A.—Railway work, dredging, municipal work, various kinds of engineering.

Q.—Construction work generally?

A.—Yes.

Q.—When did you go with the Ontario Government?

A.—Two years ago next month.

Q.—That would be in April, 1924?

A.—Yes.

Q.—Who had you been with immediately before that?

A.—Haney and Ross, a firm of surveyors in the Sault.

Q.—What position?

A.—I was assistant.

Q.—What position did you secure in the Ontario Government?

A.—District engineer at Sudbury.

Q.—Your district covers?

A.—Sudbury and Manitoulin District.

Q.—Now, were these two McNamara contracts in your jurisidiction?

A.—Yes.

Q.—The other was an assignment of the LeBarge contract?

A.—I understand so.

Q.—Did you prepare the estimates for these contracts?

A.—I did the necessary field work, and sent it down to Toronto office.

Q.—For both?

A.—Yes.

Q.—How do you refer to them?

A.—Sudbury-Coniston Road, and Copper Cliff-Creighton Road.

Q.—All right, will you tell the Committee how that work is done?

A.—Well, we make a survey and a cross-section of the road, fifty feet of a maximum and sometimes less as is needed and then we go into the ditching and the necessary culverts.

Q.—What is the nature of the soil there? Was it a rock formation?

A.—There is some rock on the Sudbury-Coniston Road, but generally it is a clear road.

Q.—Is it possible to tell the exact quantities?

A.—No, it is not.

Q.—What do you do to obtain material from which to make your estimate?

A.—Figure on cross-sections.

Q.—What is the result, can it be relied upon as being accurate?

A.—Well, in most cases they overrun, because unforeseen things turn up and quantities will overrun.

Q.—That is to be expected?

A.—That is to be expected.

Q.—Are the quantities relatively correct? Can we assume that because you figure ten per cent. rock and twenty per cent.—

A.—That is rather difficult because in lots of cases you think the stuff is ordinary dirt and when you start you come to solid rock.

Q.—Is there any way of making sure,—

A.—By taking borings but that is not usual.

Q.—Did you follow in this case the usual practice of the Department?

A.—Yes.

Q.—And how is it hav'ng regard to the usual engineering practice?

A.—It is the usual way of doing things.

Q.—Both the usual departmental and engineering practice?

A.—Yes.

Q.—Good engineering practice?

A.—Yes.

Q.—So in these particular cases, did you carry it out in the usual way?

A.—I did everything that was usual to be done in getting up an estimate for the work.

Q.—Did you have any particular special instructions from the Department?

A.—I was instructed to cross-section the roads.

Q.—Did you see the Minister in connection with it?

A.—No, I believe the Minister was 'n Sudbury in April.

MR. RANEY: Are you speaking of one particular road?

MR. FINLAYSON: Both at present. Do you remember the Minister being there early in the season?

A.—He was there I think practically two days after I went down to take charge. I think he was there on the 28th or 29th of April, 1924.

Q.—Was he at some public meeting there?

A.—Yes.

Q.—Did you attend it?

A.—No.

Q.—Do you know of your own knowledge as to whether any announcement was made as to these roads being undertaken?

A.—Yes.

Q.—What road?

A.—There was a programme laid out by the Minister in which he more or less said certain work would be done on various roads and included a concrete road between Coniston and Sudbury.

MR. RANEY: Were you there?

A.—No.

MR. RANEY: Better not to talk about it, wouldn't it?

MR. FINLAYSON: I don't want you to state what you heard from someone else. Did you make a tour with the Minister over the ground?

A.—No.

Q.—Did you go over the Sudbury-Creighton Mine Road?

A.—Yes.

Q.—Did you go over the Sudbury via Creighton-Chelmsford Road?

A.—Yes.

Q.—Did you go over the road known as the long Lake Road?

A.—Yes.

Q.—Did you go over the road known as the Massey Bay to Sudbury?

A.—No.

Q.—Were you in the party that went over?

A.—Not in the first party.

Q.—There were several. Is this true that the Board of Trade of Sudbury met the Minister?

A.—I think so, yes.

Q.—And did they go over with him and point out what work they wanted or were requesting in the district?

A.—Yes.

Q.—As I understand it, Mr. McCrae was in England at the time and the public bodies and the Board of Trade and Mayor and other corporation officials met the Minister.

A.—Yes.

Q.—And there was a general discussion as to the programme of work. I don't want to lead you but was that the general object of the Minister's visit as far as the public knew?

A.—I don't know what the object of the visit was.

Q.—What was discussed between the Minister and public officials?

A.—Various roads.

Q.—Was that public knowledge?

A.—It became public shortly afterwards.

Q.—And did these officials go around and make an inspection with the Minister of the roads for some of them?

A.—I think they did.

Q.—And I believe you went on some of the trips?

A.—Yes.

Q.—I am told there were several cars in the party running out over these roads?

A.—Yes.

Q.—Is that also true for the road from Sudbury to Coniston?

A.—I don't know whether the Minister went over that road or not.

Q.—However, it is fair to state the Minister made an inspection of the Sudbury District?

A.—Yes.

Q.—And the programme of work for the season was considered?

A.—Yes.

MR. RANEY: This was in April, 1925?

A.—1924.

MR. FINLAYSON: Do you know the dates?

A.—I think I went down on April 26th to take over the work and the Minister was there two or three days after I got there.

Q.—You took over the work on the 26th?

A.—I think so.

Q.—And it would be two or three days after? That seems to correspond with what we have here; the 28th and 29th the Minister was there? Now at that time what were the McNamara firm doing?

A.—I don't know.

Q.—Had they been working there or do you know?

A.—No, I had just moved into the district.

MR. RANEY: When did you go into the district?

A.—26th of April.

Q.—Was that before either of these roads had been built?

MR. FINLAYSON: Oh, yes, this was when they were being considered.

Q.—Were the McNamara Bros. around with this party that you know of?

A.—Not that I know of.

Q.—Do you know if they were working in the neighbourhood?

A.—No.

Q.—Now your specifications and preliminary material for both of these roads were prepared in the usual way?

A.—Yes.

Q.—And sent into the Department?

A.—They were prepared in Toronto the same as the field information was made up and sent down to Toronto and they made up the specifications and the quantities.

Q.—So that the actual compilation of quantities was made in the Department?

A.—Yes.

Q.—But you furnished the field notes from which they were prepared?

A.—Yes.

Q.—And you say that was all done in the regular engineering way?

A.—Yes.

Q.—Now, did you have anything to do with the advertising for tenders?

A.—No.

Q.—Did you see the advertisments out?

A.—I saw the advertisments, yes.

Q.—What did you first have to do with them?

A.—Well, as soon as the advertisments were out, I received quantities and forms of tender and was instructed to give any intending contractors all the information I could, show the roads and everything.

MR. FINLAYSON: Did contractors come up then?

A.—Three or four came up.

Q.—Among others the McNamaras?

A.—Among others the McNamaras.

Q.—Did the McNamara people have any special information over what was available for everybody?

A.—No, more than anybody else.

Q.—Had you ever dealt with them before?

A.—No.

Q.—They were strangers to you?

A.—They were strangers in a business way. I knew them slightly through hockey. I am a hockey fan.

Q.—You had seen the dynamite twins in action as a spectator but profesionally and personally you had nothing to do with them?

A.—I had nothing to do with them.

Q.—Had you anything to do with the tenders?

A.—No.

Q.—What advices did you receive?

A.—When the contract was let I was notified that the McNamara construction company had the contract.

Q.—For which road?

A.—The Sudbury-Coniston road.

Q.—What about the other one?

A.—That came some time later of course and I was notified LeBarge had the contract.

Q.—You say the Sudbury-Coniston one you were notified the McNamaras had the contract?

A.—Yes.

Q.—And did they come up?

A.—Shortly after that.

Q.—Now let us confine ourselves to the Coniston road first, They came up and started to work?

A.—Yes.

Q.—Did it go forward in the regular way?

A.—Yes.

Q.—Were their any incidents in connection with this that you should tell the Committee; you know the object of the inquiry?

A.—Yes; none that I know of.

Q.—Were you ever aware of any facts or circumstances that would lead you to believe there was anything wrong or suspicious?

A.—Absolutely no.

Q.—It was carried out in the ordinary business way? Ever get any instructions to give them preference?

A.—None whatever.

Q.—Did they do a good job?

A.—Certainly did, I saw to that.

Q.—Did they get any preference?

A.—Absolutely none.

Q.—How were they treated as to quantities?

A.—Everything that was coming to them and nothing more.

Q.—Did they have an engineer?

A.—A superintendent, I think he is an engineer.

Q.—And you had control of the work while it went on?

A.—Yes. I might add I had a resident engineer under me who devoted the whole of his time to that road.

Q.—And you inspected it periodically?

A.—I used to see it once a week, but had so much territory to cover I could not devote my whole time to it.

Q.—Did you have a competent man on?

A.—Yes.

Q.—Who made up the quantities?

A.—They were made in the offices in this building. The Northern Development under Mr. Fullerton.

Q.—Who prepared the field material from which the quantities were made up?

A.—A draftsman in my office. We prepared the necessary field notes and sent them in on paper.

Q.—Whose figures were they based on? Yours or local?

A.—Taken through our levels, the lines run in the field plotted on paper and sent in here.

Q.—Who did that?

A.—A young man by the name of Lyons.

Q.—Who is he?

A.—R. T. Lyons, a graduate of Varsity here.

Q.—What was his position with you?

A.—He was known as instrument man.

Q.—He is an engineer but is instrument man?

A.—He did actual field work, plotted out the cross-sections and prepared the material.

Q.—That was sent in to Toronto?

A.—Sent in to Toronto.

Q.—That would be done under your supervision?

A.—I would sign them and send them in.

Q.—How long have you known this Mr. Lyons?

A.—I met him the day I arrived on the job. He was there already doing some work.

Q.—Is he any relation of the Minister?

A.—Absolutely not.

Q.—No connection is there?

A.—Not that I know of. In fact he says not, I asked him.

Q.—Were they given any instruction as in respect to quantities?

A.—No.

Q.—Some comment has been made on the fact that the job overran the tender and worked out above the quantities nearly a hundred per cent. What did he say as to that?

A.—Well, in nearly every contract let the quantities run over and they have to be paid according to final quantities the unit price.

Q.—Is this unusual at all?

A.—I think you will find every contract will show an overrun.

Q.—But in this case was it unusual?

A.—I think not on account of the tremendous amount of work to be done to insure the safety of a road of that type.

Q.—I understood you to say the figures are perfectly honest and the McNamaras earned what they were paid?

A.—Absolutely.

Q.—Some suggestion was made that perhaps they were favoured in connection with a detour?

A.—I don't think there is anything in that.

Q.—Well, were they?

A.—No, they were not because the detour was an existing road, had been there for a good many years and we made them travel round an old road that was in existence and that was all there was to it.

Q.—They would have to put up barricades where you told them?

A.—Yes.

Q.—I see the contract provides for that?

A.—If this road had not been in existence they would have had to make a detour.

Q.—Everybody knew the road was there?

A.—Everybody knew the road was there.

Q.—And they were not given any consideration?

A.—Absolutely none.

Q.—No allowance made for that?

A.—No.

Q.—Didn't get any credit for the detour at all?

A.—Any work they did was under the contract.

Q.—One of the incidents of the contract?

A.—Yes.

Q.—Now, as to the Coniston contract, you say it was a good job and there was no consideration given these people?

A.—Yes.

Q.—Now going on to the other contract, the Copper Cliff-Creighton. You told me you were first notified LeBarge had the contract.

A.—Yes.

Q.—What was the next step?

A.—Well the next thing the McNamaras came to me and said they were going to do the work and I inquired of the Toronto office and found it was sublet to the McNamaras.

Q.—What kind of job is this?

A.—Tar penetration road.

Q.—Approximately the same distance?

A.—Between six and seven miles.

Q.—Have the estimates and quantities been prepared in the same way as the others?

A.—The same way as before. I took the necessary field notes and plotted them and sent in to Mr. Fullerton's office.

Q.—Can I sum it up by saying this was treated as an ordinary contract in the same way as you have described?

A.—Yes.

Q.—That the McNamaras got no special consideration this time?

A.—Absolutely none.

Q.—Was it treated the same way all through?

A.—All through the execution of the contract.

Q.—And when it was completed they were—

A.—A final estimate was made up and they were paid.

Q.—This also seems to have overrun?

A.—Yes, the actual quantities were more than the estimated quantities.

Q.—But you say that is to be expected?

A.—Yes, to be expected.

Q.—Is there any difference between making estimates for highway work in old Ontario and making estimates for road work up there?

A.—Well, conditions are altogether different, more frost to contend with, and in these two places the base was not as good as down east here.

Q.—I am referring more particularly to quantities of rock and different material?

A.—We use the same method.

Q —But the conditions up there are naturally different?

A.—Yes.

Q.—Does that make it easier or more difficult to estimate?

A.—More difficult I would say.

MR. RANEY: Why don't you ask him what the difference is?

MR. FINLAYSON: What is the difference?

A.—There is a difference on account of the state of the roads up there. They are not nearly as good as in Eastern Canada and it costs more to fix them up.

Q.—You mean the roads down here have been travelled for years and people know what they are? Up there it is unknown conditions and following Mr. Raney's suggestion what is the difference as to prevalance of rock or bowlders or things of that kind?

A.—The north country is not like Eastern Canada.

Q.—You don't know what you are going to meet with?

A.—You don't know what you are going to run into.

Q.—These are the only two cases I think, you had anything to do with the McNamaras?

A.—Yes.

Q.—Do you know anything as to supply of material to them, who they bought from?

A.—The only thing I am sure of is the gravel.

Q.—Who did they buy gravel from?

A.—The C.P.R.

Q.—One another thing Mr. Hoskins; referring to these contracts alone but covering contracts generally, contractors and people you are dealing with, have you ever had any instructions to attempt to influence where material was purchased or supplies obtained?

A.—Absolutely not sir.

Q.—Have you ever had any tip it would be wise to tell people it would be wise to buy from the Minister's firm; or anything like that.

A.—No.

Q.—Were you ever interfered with in any way?

A.—Not in any way at all.

MR. FISHER: Mr. Hoskins, I understand that these contracts you were talking about are unit contracts based on fixed quantities. The tenders, I should say, were unit prices, based on fixed quantities.

A.—On quantities shown on a schedule of quantities.   Estimated quantities.

Q.—For the purpose of tendering they were fixed quantities?

A.—For the purpose of tendering an approximate quantity was given, not a fixed quantity.

Q.—Well, the result of the tender would depend on the quantities given wouldn't it?

A.—The lump sum would, yes.

Q.—And the man who got the tender would be the lowest man on these quantities?

A.—Yes.

Q.—Now, these quantities, have you seen them?

A.—Yes.

Q.—Have you got them?

A.—I have not got them here.

Q.—Are they available?

Mr. FINLAYSON: The contracts are here.

THE CHAIRMAN: The contract was not put in.

Mr. FISHER: Is the tender form here?

Mr. RANEY: I suppose what we want is the tender form rather than the contract.

Mr. FISHER: You have seen this?

A.—Yes.

Q.—Are these quantities set out in the tender forms in accordance with your estimate?

A.—Well, the estimate was made up in this building, Mr. Fisher.

Q.—It was based on your—

A.—Based on the field notes I sent in.

Q.—Well, what do you say about them. Are they correct in accordance with your estimates?

A.—I did not make the estimates.

Q.—Didn't you make an estimate of quantities.

A.—Not the original ones, I didn't.

Q.—I thought you said somebody under your direction made the estimate?

A.—No, took the necessary field notes which were plotted and I signed the plans.   If you like to call it cross-sections.

Q.—Somebody made up quantities?

A.—In the Northern Development office.

Q.—Do you know whether right or not?

A.—I didn't check them.

Q.—You didn't check them?

A.—No, they were made up and checked in the offices upstairs.

Q.—You don't know whether the quantities tendered on were in accordance with your field notes or not?

A.—Well, they were taken off my field notes.

Q.—You don't know?

A.—I wouldn't swear to that, no.

Q.—What were the chief classifications?

A.—Well, solid rock and common excavation.

Q.—Only two.

A.—Only two I know of, yes.

Q.—And only two followed in the estimates?

A.—Yes, as far as I know.

Q.—You didn't have any third?

A.—No, not that I am aware of. Solid rock and common excavation or dirt are the only two I remember.

Q.—The only two you allowed?

A.—I cannot tell you off hand unless I look up the final entry.

Q.—Don't you know whether you were allowed anything, also?

A.—They were the only two materials handled anyway, common excavation and solid rock.

Q.—But were they the only two paid for?

A.—They were the only two paid for.

Q.—Now, quantities as actually taken out, exceed the quantities used in the tender?

A.—They did, yes.

Q.—To what extent?

A.—I cannot say exactly what percentage.

Q.—100 per cent.?

A.—Possibly may have been, yes.

Q.—Well, was it 200 per cent.?

A.—Well, I wouldn't say it was 200 per cent.

Q.—The figures I have before me on the Sudbury-Coniston say that tender was $188,000 roughly speaking and the cost $384,000, is the difference entirely accounted for by difference in quantity?

A.—Absolutely yes.

Q.—That is a most extraordinary difference in estimate and quantity, isn't it?

A.—Well, when you come to realize that it is a concrete pavement made out of a cow trail—when I went there first you couldn't drive over that road without going to the axles in clay, and now it is properly paved road, with culverts and everything.

Q.—How do you account for the difference in your estimates?

A.—Well, the amount of work done on it.

Q.—The total quantities differ? Or was there a difference in the different classifications?

A.—Well, I don't quite get your question.

Q.—Well, let us take rock, how much more rock was there than you estimated?

A.—I don't remember off hand, fifteen or sixteen months ago since these things were made up.

Q.—Much more than you expected?

A.—Well, there was on account of proper ditching and cutting down two big hills.

Q.—Was there a larger proportion of rock than you estimated?

A.—Yes.

Q.—The rock proved to be a larger proportion than you had estimated?

A.—But the thing is, Mr. Fisher, I did not do this estimating, not all of it.

Q.—Well, I will take it as the estimate on which the tendering was based?

A.—It is quite evident it did overrun.

Q.—What I want to know is this: it overran on the whole, there is no doubt of that; relatively how did it turn out as between rock and earth?

Mr. Finlayson: Mr. Fisher wouldn't it be better to get this from Mr. Fullerton? The estimates were made in his department and I suppose as a matter of fact Mr. Hoskin never saw the estimates.

WITNESS: I saw the quantities.

MR. FISHER: Would you say they were total quantities based on your field notes?

A.—Yes, I would.

Q.—And then you were on the job and saw the way the thing worked out? Was there more rock found than you estimated?

A.—Must have been because the contractor was not paid for any rock he didn't move.

Q.—Can you tell me off hand what proportion of this work you estimated as rock? and what proportion you estimated as earth?

A.—No, I cannot.

Q.—Did you find an unexpected amount of rock?

A.—In some places we did. Places we thought were dirt happened to be rock when stripped.

Q.—Now, you don't know anything about the tenders?

A.—Absolutely nothing.

Q.—Your field notes were they just diagram forms?

A.—Diagram forms or cross-section paper.

Q.—You didn't make any figures?

A.—Absolutely none.

Q.—Who did those?

A.—They were done in Mr. Fullerton's office. I can't say who did it.

Q.—That is all you can tell us? All right.

MR. RANEY: How much cross-sectioning did you do yourself, Mr. Hoskins?

A.—I didn't do any of it myself.

Q.—None of it at all, then who did?

A.—A young man by the name of R. T. Lyons.

Q.—You gave his name before. He did the whole of it?

A.—The whole of it with the aid of two or three men. He was responsible.

Q.—And how many cross-sections would they make for seven miles?

A.—Well it is rather difficult to say but in cross-sectioning and piece work of that kind, you would take one every fifty feet at least.

Q.—And we are talking about now, the Sudbury-Coniston road, is this a fairly level road?

A.—No, it is uphill and down.

Q.—Some grades, gentle grades I suppose?

A.—Some are and some are not.

Q.—And there had been a road there before?

A.—Well, if you like to call it a road.

Q.—Coniston is a mining centre, is it not?

A.—The smelter of the Mond Nickel Company is there.

Q.—And there was a good deal of travel over this road between Coniston and Sudbury?

A.—Yes.

Q.—This was the direct road?

A.—The nearest road.

Q.—And the one always used?

A.—Yes.

Q.—So you were simply concreting a road that was in use?

A.—Yes.

Q.—Then you put your man Lyons and his assistants on this job to find out what quantities of excavation there would be for the purpose of putting down a concrete pavement and they were told all about what was required?
A.—Yes.

Q.—And their duty would be to take a cross-section every fifty feet at least?
A.—Yes, and where needed they were to take more.

Q.—The substance was for the most part clay?
A.—Yes.

Q.—Long stretches of clay and then stretches of rock perhaps?
A.—Yes, running into small rocky knolls.

Q.—Did the road make detours? Had there been rock cuttings before?
A.—Yes.

Q.—So the road was fairly straight? You could travel it?
A.—It was not straight and it is very crooked right now.

Q.—It follows the course of the old road?
A.—Yes.

Q.—Some rock taken out?
A.—Small portions.

Q.—And you were taking cross-sections every fifty feet and over clay? It would be an easy matter for a man with a pick and shovel, how far would he have to go down to find out?
A.—Oh, for our purposes a foot and a half or two feet.

Q.—It would be a very easy thing to ascertain by opening up the ground for a foot and a half or two feet, what was underneath?
A.—Depends on the time of year, Mr. Raney.

Q.—What time of year was this done?
A.—In May.

Q.—No frost then?
A.—Yes, there was lots.

Q.—You could have deferred it until the frost was out?
A.—My instructions were to get the work done as soon as possible.

Q.—You say there was frost in May?
A.—Oh, yes, there is frost up there in July in the roads.

Q.—There might be possibly?
A.—Every year.

Q.—Were these test pits made on this job?
A.—Not that I am aware of.

Q.—You don't know whether Lyons and his assistant relied on their observation or took test pits?
A.—I don't think they had test pits.

Q.—You didn't take any cross-sections?
A.—No.

Q.—And Lyons brought in his field notes to you?
A.—They were brought in and plotted in my office.

Q.—You didn't know anything of the matter personally?
A.—I went down on inspection trips to see how he was getting on.

Q.—You didn't know anything about the work he had done?
A.—I knew all about it.

Q.—You didn't know anything about the accuracy of it? You said a little while ago you signed it?
A.—I took the responsibility.

Q.—Yes, yes, I know, but did you actually know as a matter of fact, any one of these cross-sections was accurate and truthful?

A.—I had no occasion to doubt them.

Q.—Did you know as a matter of fact, you accepted Lyons' statement of course?

A.—Mr. Lyons has always been—

Q.—But you didn't test them out yourself? You signed the papers and they came to Toronto and you knew the tenders were on the basis of these figures you sent in?

A.—Yes. Well, I didn't send any figures in, I signed the notes plotted on paper, and the estimates were made up in Mr. Fullerton's office.

Q.—What would the sheets show?

A.—Cross-sections and elevations.

Q.—Figures, would they not?

A.—Elevations of the road at various spots.

Q.—And your notes would show rock and earth?

A.—I didn't lay out any fixed cross-sections; that would be done in this office.

Q.—Your notes would show rock and earth?

A.—Yes.

Q.—Then we come to the work; and the work was done?

A.—Yes, sir.

Q.—There was a resident engineer?

A.—Yes.

Q.—Who was he?

A.—D. J. McEachren.

Q.—His duty was to make the actual excavations?

A.—His duty was to lay out the work, and see it was done according to specifications, and to measure it up when done.

Q.—I take it the work was done absolutely according to specifications?

A.—Yes.

Q.—And the only uncertainty would be relative to quantities of rock and earth?

MR. FINLAYSON: Totals as well.

MR. RANEY: Well, now the only uncertainty would be relative quantities of rock and earth—in the work as actually done?

A.—Well there wouldn't be any uncertainty about it at all; everything would be measured up before the contract was let.

Q.—There would be a certain element of uncertainty between the estimates made up here in Toronto and the work actually done by the contractor.

A.—A variation of course.

Q.—And that would be altogether between the quantities of rock and quantities of earth?

A.—Yes, I guess so.

MR. FINLAYSON: Let us clear it up now.

MR. RANEY: Leave me alone with the witness. Now, we had Mr. McNamara here the other day, and he gave us a list of contracts he had executed in the north country, about a dozen altogether during these two years, some for the Government and some for municipalities; and in the Government contracts these three particularly, Sudbury-Coniston, Copper Cliff-Creighton, and South Porcupine-Timmins, the price paid ran in the neighbourhood on an average 100 per cent. above the tender, whereas in the prices paid for the other work done by him there was scarcely any difference in the prices paid. How would you account for that?

THE CHAIRMAN: That comparison you are making is with certain contracts, not with all the other contracts.

MR. RANEY: Could you give any explanation of that?

THE WITNESS: Are you comparing these with roads that the McNamaras did certain work on, roads where the main bid and the final estimate did not overrun?

MR. RANEY: In other cases, besides these three contracts for the most part the price paid was about the same thing as the tender?

A.—Well, I cannot account for it.

Q.—You cannot account for it; well let me give you these figures: Sudbury-Coniston tender on engineer's estimates, $188,751. Price actually paid by the Government, $384,626. That is a difference you see of more than 100 per cent. South Porcupine-Timmins, that is not under your jurisdiction?

A.—No.

Q.—Tender in the same way on unit basis on quantities furnished by the engineer, $132,049; actual cost as paid by the Government, $258,754. Almost 100 per cent. you see. Copper Cliff-Creighton tender $59,165; actual cost as paid by the Government $135,063, being about 120 per cent. above the tender. Now I ask you as an engineer how many years experience have you had?

A.—About sixteen.

Q.—Taking these figures one after the other what is your comment as an engineer upon the efficiency of the engineering, assuming that the prices paid are honest?

A.—Well, as far as those two roads up there are concerned—

Q.—What do you say as to the efficiency of the engineering, assuming that these prices are honest?

A.—Lack information at the start.

Q.—Whose fault would that be?

A.—Well, it might be the man who got the original information didn't have sufficient time to get all that was needed.

Q.—You can understand, of course, Mr. Hoskins, that if a road is to cost $59,000, a government might be willing to take on the work and if it were to cost a $135,000 it might not be willing to take on the work?

A.—I can understand that.

Q.—If a man were doing this, he might only have the price for $59,000 and be put into bankruptcy if it cost $135,000, you can understand that? So that it is a vital thing for an engineer who attempts to give an estimate upon which tenders are to be given on a unit basis to give fair and accurate information: Both have been under the mark. Isn't that right?

A.—I imagine so.

Q.—You would think so? I would think so too. Now you had some experience with this Sudbury-Coniston road on a basis of difference between tender and actual cost—the difference between $188,000 and $384,000—hadn't you?

A.—I had that experience.

Q.—Did you think that was satisfactory engineering after you had had that experience?

A.—Well, yes, because I didn't think a thing was done on the Coniston road that shouldn't have been done for the safety of the road.

Q.—But what about the engineering, that is what I am asking you about; are you satisfied with it?

A.—Yes.

.Q.—You are satisfied with engineering under your supervision in which the quantities are twice the quantities that you estimated.,. Are you. satisfied with that?

A.—Yes.

Q.—You are?

A.—Yes.

Q.—I thought a little while ago you told me you were not?

A.—I am satisfied if the road is standing up. .If these extra quantities had not been made, the road would not have stood up.

Q.—I am told this concrete road was badly cracked after four months?

A.—Did you ever see a concrete road that wasn't?

Q.—I didn't ask you that; it was. badly cracked wasn't it?

A.—Yes.

, Q.—Have you ever considered as an engineer whether that north country and the climate up there are suitable to this class of pavement? Have you ever adv sed as to that?

A.—I never was asked the question.

Q.—What is your opinion about it?

A.—It is not the road that I would recommend in future.

Q.—I thought you would say that. Are you speaking now of concrete pavement from Sudbury to Coniston?

A.—Yes.

. Q.—The road from Copper Cliff to Creighton is what?

. A.—Tar penetration.

Q.—How about that for standing up purposes?

A.—I would say that is the better road for the north country.

Q.—Would you recommend that kind of road for that country?.

A.—Yes, I would.

Q.—But not a concrete road?

A.—No.

Q.—And as a matter of fact the Sudbury-Coniston road is not in good shape now?

A.—It certainly is.

Q.—Badly cracked?

A.—Same kind of crack you find in any concrete pavement.

Q.—But frost conditions are such that concrete pavement would not stand up?

A.—I think it will.

Q.—Why do you condemn it?

A.—Because it is more expensive.

Q.—Because I notice that the concrete road from Sudbury to Coniston cost more than $55,000 a mile. What do you think of that?

A.—I don't think it is excessive.

Q.—Then would you recommend the building of concrete roads in that north country?

A.—No, but I don't think that $55,000 is excessive.

MR. FISHER: The documents handed to me are simply the contracts; the schedules are not here. Now I would like to get some information that perhaps can be got easily. First, the quantities upon which tenders are based, rock and other material, the way they were called; second, the prices of the different tenders for each class of work.

Mr. Finlayson: That is all in.

Mr. Fisher: Perhaps, but we would like to get it. Third, the quantities on which payment was made. Can we have that this afternoon?

The Chairman: Oh, I think so, without any doubt.

Mr. Fisher: I wonder if the Committee thinks it is absolutely necessary to go on. I have to leave.

Mr. Chairman: It is twenty minutes to one; we will go ahead until one o'clock, I think.

Mr. Raney: I suppose if I get through with Mr. Hoskins we can come again for Mr. Fisher's cross-examination?

The Chairman: I think so.

Mr. Fisher: That will be understood.

Mr. Raney: Now you would not think, Mr. Hoskins, that the situation which developed in this Sudbury-Coniston contract, an over-run of more than 100 per cent., was something creditable to your engineer force, would you—something that you would boast of?

A.—I think it would have been far more discreditable if the road had gone to pieces afterwards.

Q.—I am getting back to the cost of the road. The road cost more than 100 per cent. more than the tender. Now the tender was based on your estimates of quantities of rock and earth.

A.—Not on mine.

Q.—I am glad to hear you disclaim responsibility, because I am sure you take a pride in your profession, and I want to know whether you think that result, a cost of $384,000 for a road upon which, the estimates furnished by you, the tender was $188,000—whether that was something that was creditable to you as an engineer?

A.—I don't think it is discreditable.

Q.—Why not?

A.—Because the road is there and standing up.

Q.—I don't care whether the road is standing up or lying down.

A.—Well, that is what I care about.

Q.—My question now has to do altogether with your mistakes—because they were mistakes, weren't they?

A.—No, sir, not mistakes.

Q.—Then what caused the difference between $188,000 tender and $384,000, the price paid?

A.—Because I made the contractor do everything that was necessary to be done on the road, and paid for it on the unit price.

Q.—You had that in mind when you made your field notes and estimates?

A.—I did not.

Q.—You had in mind to make him do everything he was called upon to do?

A.—I did, yes.

Q.—Is it usual for a piece of road work to cost more than 100 per cent. more than the tender?

A.—I would not say it is usual. Nearly all road contracts overrun.

Q.—Five or 10 per cent.?

A.—I think bigger than that.

A.—Can you tell me a case where it has overrun 50 per cent.?

A.—I never really looked up the difference in the original contract and final estimate.

Q.—Or 25 per cent.?

A.—I cannot answer that question.

Q.—You think $55,000 and more is not an excessive price to pay for that road?

A.—Not for the work done on it.

Q.—How do you know what work was done on it, personally?

A.—Because I was over it at least once a week.

Q.—Yes, you said a little while ago your duties called for your presence elsewhere a great part of the time?

A.—Yes, my home is in Sudbury.

Q.—How many hours a week did you put in on the road?

A.—Probably an afternoon a week going over it. When I have a qualified engineer on it I am not supposed to devote the whole of my time to it.

Q.—You did not regard yourself as personally responsible for this work?

A.—I was personally responsible in a way.

Q.—But not in the sense that you were responsible for this overrun—personally?

A.—Well, if there were any doubt about the thing the resident engineer came and consulted me, and I told him to do this or do that.

Q.—Who was he, again?

A.—D. J. McEachren.

Q.—He is the man who was responsible?

A.—He is the man who had charge of the work and devoted the whole of his time to it.

Q.—Apparently there are two men upon whom the responsibility rests—Lyons, the man who did the cross-sectioning?

A.—No, I don't hold him responsible for anything; I take his responsibility.

Q.—Why?

A.—Because I am in charge there, and he works under my instructions.

Q.—We understand that, but under you there were two men responsible for this work: Lyons, who did the cross-sections, and whose work may have been efficient and may not have been efficient—as far as we know now it was perfectly efficient—and McEachren, who did the measurements after the work was put down These were the two men directly responsible under you?

A.—Yes.

Q.—And these are the men personally responsible; you had a supervisory responsibility?

A.—Yes.

Q.—Now how long had the Sudbury-Coniston work been finished before the cross-sectioning was done for the Copper Cliff and Creighton road?

A.—The road was not finished.

Q.—At what stage was the Sudbury-Coniston road when you had instructions to go ahead and cross-section the road from Copper Cliff to Creighton?

A.—It would not be more than 25 per cent. done.

Q.—When was the work Sudbury to Coniston done?

A.—What year? 1924.

Q.—Finished in 1924?

A.—Yes.

Q.—What month of 1924?

A.—I think the road was finally opened on November 17.

Q.—When did you get instructions to go cross-sectioning the Copper Cliff-Creighton road?

A.—I think early in August.

Q.—While the other work was under way. Are you pretty sure? I wish you would fix the time?

A.—I can look it up.

Q.—I wish you would. And when was that contract let?

A.—I think about the first of September; I am not sure.

Q.—And when did work commence on that job? That season, or laid over until 1925?

A.—No, a certain amount was done that fall.

Q.—I suppose work done that fall would be mostly excavation?

A.—And putting in tile draining and culverts.

Q.—All the paving done in 1925?

A.—Surfacing.

Q.—When did you send in your returns of cross-sectioning for the Copper Cliff-Creighton road, to Toronto?

A.—Some time in August, I think.

Q.—The completed field notes?

A —The original field notes.

Q.—Whatever you sent in to Toronto?

A.—Probably took about two weeks to get the necessary information.

Q.—When did you send? Can you let me have that information here this afternoon or evening? I want to know when you sent in—

A.—I would say some time in August.

Q.—The other work was under way then?

A.—Yes.

Q.—Were you watching the Sudbury-Coniston road to see how the actual quantities reported by McEachren were tallying with the estimated quantities?

A.—Well, you see in August there was very little of the Coniston road done.

Q.—But from time to time, as the Coniston-Sudbury road was being made, were you personally watching that point, to see how the quantities the Government was going to be called upon to pay for were tallying with the estimated quantities?

A.—I was noticing they were going to overrun.

Q.—About 100 per cent.?

A.—I wouldn't say what percentage.

Q.—But you saw there was going to be a big overrun?

A.—I did not say a big overrun.

Q.—Who did the field work for the Copper Cliff-Creighton road?

A.—I think Mr. McEachren.

Q.—In the other case it was done by Lyons?

A.—Yes.

Q.—Did you warn McEachren: "Now Mr. McEachren, we have had a serious situation on the Sudbury-Coniston road and there is a heavy overrun of about 100 per cent.?"

A.—I could not tell him that; I knew it was liable to over-run, but I had not the vaguest notion how much.

Q.—I suppose the work is done by sections, isn't it?

A.—No, start at one end and work toward the other.

Q.—That is just what I say; and after say a quarter of the work is done, they are paid for a quarter or thereabouts?

A.—No, there are monthly estimates.

Q.—Well, the monthly estimates would indicate to you, if you chose to examine them, how the quantities being charged for by the contractor were tallying with the estimates, wouldn't they?

A.—Yes.

Q.—Did you try to find out? Did you know they were over-running about 100 per cent.?

A.—Well, some miles might overrun and others not.

Q.—Did you know in August, 1924, there was a heavy overrun on the Sudbury-Coniston road?

A.—No.

Q.—When did you first find out?

A.—In October.

Q.—Did you try to find out before?

A.—Yes.

Q.—When?

A.—I cannot tell you dates.

Q.—Then you were interested?

A.—Of course I was interested.

Q.—As an engineer, your reputation would be at stake, because you are responsible for your subordinates?

A.—Yes.

Q.—And if there was an overrun of 100 to 120 per cent. on either of these jobs it would not be to your credit, would it?

A.—You asked me that question once before.

Q.—I am asking you again, now.

A.—I reply by saying it would be far more to my discredit if the road had fallen down.

Q.—You take that stand?

A.—I take that stand.

Q.—Opinions may differ. I am inclined to think the greater discredit would be if you were responsible—and I am not saying you were—

MR. WILSON: Mr. Chairman, has Mr. Raney's opinion any bearing when examining a witness?

THE CHAIRMAN: We have not closed out opinions; we have had a lot of them.

MR. RANEY: You were more concerned to complete a road that would stand up?

A.—I certainly was.

Q.—And you were not concerned about the cost?

A.—I certainly was.

Q.—So there were these two elements?

A.—Yes.

Q.—And you were concerned when you found out there was this heavy overrun on the Sudbury-Coniston road?

A.—Yes.

Q.—I thought you would be. Well, when you found afterwards there was an overrun of more than 120 per cent. on the Copper Cliff-Creighton road, did that concern you, too?

A.—Yes.

Q.—You could not give me any instance of any other road in your knowledge where there has been an overrun of more than 125 per cent. beyond the engineer's estimates?

A.—No.

Q.—Could you give me a case where the overrun exceeded 10 per cent.?

A.—No, I cannot.

Q.—Well, then, I think you would be inclined to modify your statement made a while ago that it was a common thing to have overruns.

A.—It is a common thing, but I cannot say to what extent.

Q.—It might be 5 or 10 per cent.?

A.—Or 50 per cent.

Q.—Oh, anything; it might be 200 per cent.

MR. FINLAYSON: We will give you examples of some, then.

THE CHAIRMAN: You are asking the witness to give his knowledge of overruns of 25 or 50 per cent., and he says he cannot give any definite figure as to contracts he had been interested in.

MR. FINLAYSON: The Drury Government's standard of overrun was about 400 per cent. We will give some of them.

MR. McKNIGHT: They all cracked to pieces at that.

MR. FINLAYSON: It was rebuilding some of their work we were doing most of the time.

MR. RANEY: Well, you will come back after the adjournment, because Mr. Fisher will probably want you.

MR. FINLAYSON: Let us try to get on. Mr. Fisher has cross-examined this witness, hasn't he?

THE CHAIRMAN: He did examine him, yes. But at any rate you will be available?

A.—Yes.

MR. RANEY: Do you recall, Mr. Hoskins, that some tenderers had some difficulty in getting to see the plans and specifications?

A.—No, sir.

Q.—You don't recall anything of the kind?

A.—No, sir.

Q.—All right.

MR. FINLAYSON: The plans and specifications were in your office, weren't they?

A.—Yes.

Q.—And the advertisements for tenders would instruct people to call and see them?

A.—Yes.

Q.—And is Mr. Raney's suggestion right, that other people had difficulty?

A.—No, everybody who came there had—

MR. RANEY: I accept Mr. Hoskins' statement there was no difficulty.

WITNESS: Anybody who came in could see them, and I told them all I knew.

MR. FINLAYSON: That was the instructions you had?

A.—That was the instructions I received.

Q.—A good deal was said by Mr. Fisher as to relative quantities. The quantities were estimated and the relative varying between stone and dirt you do not know anything about?

A.—No.

Q.—But the general purpose was, these estimates were made up on your man's cross-sectioning and figured out from that, and the relative varying is something you have no knowledge of at all? You do know in the end there was an overrun, but whether rock or dirt pretty hard to tell?

A.—Pretty hard to tell.

Q.—When you say it is a common thing for contracts to overrun, you mean contracts of all kinds?

A.—Of all kinds.

Q.—Anything on the unit basis is bound to overrun?

A.—I think so.

Q.—The amount of overrun varies with locality?

A.—With locality, yes.

Q.—And weather conditions, probably?

A.—Yes.

Q.—And, as you say, would be affected by the time at the disposal of the man who makes the cross-sections?

A.—Yes.

Q.—And in this section he made the cross-section when?

A.—In the spring, and on a road that was a trail before. About fourteen feet wide.

Q.—And had to be widened?

A.—Oh, yes.

Q.—And I understand in the course of this road there were some very heavy grades?

A.—Two to be cut down out of solid rock.

Q.—What reduction?

A.—We reduced them from 15 to 7 per cent.

Q.—In height?

A.—I cannot tell you off hand; five or six feet and twenty-four feet wide.

Q.—In length?

A.—One cut was three or four hundred feet long, I would say.

Q.—And when you get a cut of that kind, nobody can possibly tell whether it is solid rock or partly rock or partly clay?

A.—It is pretty hard to tell until you get into it.

Q.—There is a means of putting down test-pits every few feet, but the time consumed would be enormous and the expense great?

A.—Yes.

Q.—And it wouldn't have made a bit of difference to the final payment, would it?

A.—No, but we would have had more quantities for the contractor to bid on.

Q.—It would have had the advantage that the Government or owner giving the contract would have had a better idea what the probable result would be?

A.—What the probable cost would be

Q.—But it didn't affect the man who tendered?

A.—No, they all tendered under the same conditions.

Q.—And in the result the payment would have been the same no matter who got it?

A.—Yes.

Q.—And the payment made, I understand you to say, you were strong on your engineering to the extent that there were no payments made that were not earned?

A.—Absolutely so.

MR. RANEY: On the reports to him.

MR. FINLAYSON: Well, your weekly visits would check up that?

A.—Yes, actual measurements made on the ground.

Q.—These two rock cuts that you spoke of you could easily check up; your man would give you a figure and you could tell from your knowledge at that stage. So there was no room for fraud?

A.—Absolutely none.

Q.—Something has been said about this overrun of 100 per cent. Have you been building roads?

A.—Well, I have not had very great experience in building roads.

Q.—These are the ones you have had charge of. You don't know what the overruns of others are?

A.—Not that type of road.

Q.—Well, we will get them and be prepared to show an overrun of perhaps 100 up to three or four hundred under the Drury Government. Now it has been said this road cracked. That is to be expected in cement?

A.—You expect that.

Q.—Cement in any country is liable to crack, where there are variations in temperature?

A.—Yes.

Q.—And you provide for that by an expansion joint, where?

A.—Right up and down the middle of the road. At the end of the day's work you put down an expansion joint.

Q.—And these cracks would be what you call hair-lines?

A.—Yes, well the crack up the centre of the road is quite big.

Q.—That is the one you provide for?

A.—Yes, the others are small.

Q.—It does not affect the efficiency of the road a bit?

A.—No.

Q.—And this road you say you are willing to stand by?

A.—Yes.

THE CHAIRMAN: It is in good shape now?

A.—Yes.

MR. RANEY: The rock cuts Mr. Finlayson speaks about, it is obvious to anybody going over the road these rock cuts were there? Or let me put it this way: these rock cuts were covered by the estimates?

A.—Yes.

Q.—Of course they were. Now you say there was frost in the ground when cross-sectioning was done for the Sudbury-Coniston. There was none when the cross-sectioning was done for the Copper Cliff-Creighton road?

A.—No.

Q.—And that was 120 per cent. overrun. How do you explain that?

A.—In the original estimates it was figured for a certain width of road, and during construction of the road it was found desirable to put two-foot shoulders on and widen the road, instead of leaving it sixteen feet.

Q.—Was that an extra?

A.—That was put on a unit basis.

Q.—An extra above the original estimates?

A.—Well, I would say it would be, yes.

Q.—Was it included in the original estimates?

A.—No, the building of the shoulder was not.

Q.—How much would that amount to?

A.—Well, six miles; I cannot tell you off hand.

MR. FINLAYSON: The road was originally designed for sixteen feet in width, tar penetration type, and while the contract was under construction it.

was decided to put a two-foot shoulder on each side and make it a twenty-foot road?

A.—Yes.

MR. RANEY: Of the same material?

A.—No, dirt.

MR. FINLAYSON: Which increased the quantities to be taken out?

A.—Very considerably.

Q.—And increased the quantities of dirt to be added enormously?

A.—It would, yes.

Q.—So that the quantity taken out would be increased, both for rock or dirt, and the quantity to be moved would be increased a great percentage, nearly 25 per cent. for the shoulders.

A.—That explains a lot of the overrun.

MR. WILSON: You are going to adjourn. I would like to call attention to the fact there is only one of Mr. Raney's supporters here, and the Committee attendance on the part of his supporters has not been at all strong. It looks as if there is not much further in it. I appreciate the Government's desire and Mr. Lyons' desire to have it gone into as fully as possible, but why waste time when there are so few taking an interest.

MR. WIDDIFIELD: You have just come. You don't appreciate the facts.

THE CHAIRMAN: We have the witnesses to examine, and we are going to go through and complete the investigation of matters to be brought forward. Whether that is a waste of time is a matter for judgment. How about 2.30?

MR. FINLAYSON: Hadn't we better say two?

THE CHAIRMAN: Well, it is five after one.

MR. RANEY: You can sit until the House meets.

THE CHAIRMAN: No, sit right through. We have a tremendous number of witnesses, and this is only one matter. We could be here for a month yet if we go at the rate we have been going.

The Committee then adjourned at 1.05 until 2.30.

PUBLIC ACCOUNTS COMMITTEE.

Wednesday afternoon, March 24th.

A. C. Lewis, Chairman of the Committee, presiding.

CHAIRMAN: We will not call the roll. The secretary will mark those present, and we are ready to go ahead. I think we might settle the question of meetings now. We were talking of having a meeting to-night, but several of the members have represented that they are going to the Speaker's dinner and most of us wish to be in the House for the conclusion of the budget debate. I don't see how we can arrange for a meeting to-night.

MR. RANEY: Do you understand the debate will close to-night?

CHAIRMAN: I don't say that; but it must be near the end.

MR. FINLAYSON: I don't want to force work on the Committee but the position is simply this: At the last meeting we thought we could clean up the Lyons' matter to-day and with that object in view I telephoned Mr. Nash and asked him if he could come. He said he was working on the report and that it would not be ready this afternoon but might be ready for to-night. If we could sit now and exhaust the witnesses except Mr. Nash and call him to-night and put in what time is necessary on that. I don't want to be unreasonable, but I am anxious to get rid of the matter. I don't want to press my views, but I am very keen on going on to-night and trying to clean the whole matter up.

CHAIRMAN: I sympathize with your idea in wanting to wind this up and I think we have used what expedition we could to that end, but I really don't see, personally I don't see how we can meet to-night.

MR. FINLAYSON: It is hardly fair to Mr. Lyons

CHAIRMAN: I agree with that. We will meet at every convenient moment in order to clean the matter up, but I sympathize with your object. I have representations from members of the Committee who have been very faithful in their attendance and they are not anxious to come to-night and unless the Committee overrides me I don't think we will have a meeting to-night.

MR. FINLAYSON: It is in the hands of the Committee of course. I don't know how they feel about it.

MEMBER: I don't see how we can be at the Speaker's dinner and in the House.

MR. BRADBURN: I agree with Mr. Freeborn.

MAJOR BELFORD: The view of the Committee is rather against you.

MR. FINLAYSON: With regard to Mr. Nash—

MR. RANEY: If you could let us have Mr. Nash's report we might get just as far ahead by seeing the report before he comes here.

CHAIRMAN: Leave it with Mr. Finlayson.

MR. RANEY: Neither Mr. Fisher nor Mr. Sinclair is here. I have to be at the opening of the House.

CHAIRMAN: Perhaps they will be here before you leave.

MR. FINLAYSON: You want to be here when Mr. Fullerton is examined.

MR. RANEY? You say you have not Mr. Walsh or Labarge?

CHAIRMAN: He is sick.

MR. RANEY: Mr. Briggs?

CHAIRMAN: That is in connection with another matter.

MR. RANEY: We are going to be finally rid of this matter practically to-morrow, I think, so that we could subpoena witnesses in the Caledon Mountain matter for Friday.

CHAIRMAN: We have subpoenas in the Oakley case and in the dispensary case.

MR. RANEY: That is mine.

MR. FINLAYSON: The motion he passed the first day.

MR. RANEY: Most of the witnesses in the Caledon Mountain matter are out of town and you have not more than enough time to subpoena them for Friday. You had better let us understand they will have the right of way on Friday.

CHAIRMAN: We shall go into the question of witnesses at the end of the session.

MR. RANEY: You can do that for Friday?

MR. FINLAYSON: Caledon Mountain matter on Friday. Do you want to be present on Oakley?

MR. RANEY: Yes.

MR. LYONS: On the Briggs' matter. Captain Maxwell is at Buffalo and is likely to be in Toronto this afternoon.

CHAIRMAN: I don't think so. They are stuck in the mud and can't get out.

MR. FINLAYSON: We could call it in time to hear him.

CHAIRMAN: They are stuck at Buffalo now.

MR. FINLAYSON: I think Captain Maxwell's evidence is not contentious and we could convene a meeting for him.

CHAIRMAN: He is going on to Red Lake with airplane mail.

Alexander Findlay called, sworn. Examination by Mr. Finlayson.

Q.—Where do you reside. Mr. Findlay?

A.—I have been residing in Niagara Falls since last September.

Q.—Ontario?

A.—Yes.

Q.—What is your profession.

A.—Architect.

Q.—How long have you been practising?

A.—Eighteen years in Ontario and previous experience, about eleven years, in the old country.

Q.—Where have you been practising in Ontario?

A.—Up at Ottawa, Sault Ste. Marie and Niagara Falls.

Q.—In 1924, I believe, you were practising at Sault Ste. Marie?

A.—Yes.

Q.—Were you commissioned to design the aerodrome?

A.—No, sir.

Q.—Who designed it?

A.—It was designed by one of the Department architects.

Q.—What work did you perform in connection with it?

A.—Supervision of the structure.

Q.—Supervision of the erection?

A.—Yes.

Q.—We have been told that J. J. Fitzpatrick was the contractor?

A.—Yes.

Q.—Did you have anything to do with the letting of the contract?

A.—No, sir. It was let before I was employed.

Q.—Had he started work?

A.—He had just started the day before.

Q.—Assembling his plant?

A.—Yes.

Q.—We are not interested in your employ—part time, was it?

A.—Yes.

Q.—And residing at the Sault?

A.—Yes.

Q.—Well, then, will you tell us what you know about the erection of this aerodrome?

A.—Just exactly what questions—

Q.—What work did you perform in connection with it?

A.—I had charge of the erection of the building, the erection and the excavation.

Q.—Were there proper plans and specifications?

A.—Yes.

A.—And a contract?

A.—Yes.

Q.—Given to you?

A.—Yes, I had a copy.

Q.—And was the work carried out entirely under your control?

A.—Yes.

Q.—As supervising architect?

A.—Yes.

Q.—Payments were made under progress certificates?

A.—Yes.

Q.—During the construction of the aerodrome was there ever any interference by anyone?

A.—No.

Q.—Had you any occasion to see the Minister about it?

A.—I saw the Minister when he was at the Sault, but I had no interference in any way I can think of.

Q.—I suppose Mr. Lyons may have been there to see what progress was made?

A.—Yes.

Q.—But apart from a short visit there he took no part in the work?

A.—No.

Q.—Was there ever any interference or suggestion by anybody that you know of?

A.—Not that I know of.

Q.—Did the work go forward in the usual way?

A.—Yes.

Q.—And you gave progress certificates from time to time?

A.—Yes.

Q.—And then a final certificate?

A.—Yes.

Q.—The contract went ahead without incident?

A.—Yes.

Q.—If there was any interference or improper conduct—were you told of any?

A.—I don't know of any.

Q.—The contractor carried out the work?

A.—Yes.

Q.—And you gave a final certificate and passed the work?

A.—Yes.

Q.—All right.

MR. FISHER: You lived in Ottawa quite a while?

WITNESS: Yes.

MR. FISHER: That accounts for your being so good. All right.

CHAIRMAN: Any other questions? All right. Call Mr. Lyons.

Harry Clayton Lyons sworn. Examined by Mr. Finlayson.

Q.—Mr. Lyons, you live in Sault Ste. Marie?

A.—Yes.

Q.—I believe you are a son of the Minister, of Hon. James Lyons?

A.—Yes.

Q.—What is your occupation?

A.—I am employed by the Lyons Fuel and Supply Company.

Q.—Are you an officer, director, shareholders of the company?

A.—Not an officer nor director.

A.—What is your employment?

A.—Well, general supervision of the business in connection with all the branches of it.

Q.—How long have you been with the company in the previous partnership?

A.—Since November—December, 1920.

Q.—1920?

A.—Yes.

Q.—Before that what were you doing?

A.—I had just come back from overseas.

Q.—You were discharged when?

A.—In November.

Q.—1920?

A.—Yes. No 1919, excuse me.

Q —How long were you overseas?

A.—A little over three years some months.

Q.—How old are you?

A.—Twenty-six last January.

Q.—You had a military age and not an actual age. How old were you when you enlisted?

A.—Sixteen.

A.—That is the actual age and not the military age. So that on your return from the service you immediately entered work in your father's company?

A.—Yes.

Q.—And have been there ever since?

A.—Yes.

Q.—You know the McNamara Brothers?

A.—Oh, yes.

A.—I suppose you are interested in hockey at the Sault?

A.—Yes.

Q.—And you could not help knowing them?

A.—Yes.

Q.—They have been contractors round the Sault for many years?

A.—Quite a number.

Q.—Do you know Fitzpatrick?

A.—Yes.

Q.—Dealing with the aerodrome contract had you any thing to do with giving figures to Fitzpatrick?

A.—Not with giving figures. McAllister gave the figures.

Q.—Did you have anything to do with carrying out the contract?

A.—In what way?

Q.—We have heard of some changes in amounts. Did you have anything to do with that?

CHAIRMAN: The purchase figures.

WITNESS: That was an arrangement with McAllister.

Q.—You had nothing to do with that?

A.—In a general way.

Q.—What did you do?

A.—In a general way we discussed the various commodities from time to time and obtained quotations from the manufacturers up until the time it was ready for tenders to be submitted.

Q.—How many bidders were there?

A.—There were five or six I can recall.

Q.—Did you supply figures to all?

A.—Yes.

Q.—And the figures the same?

A.—Oh, yes. The same figures for the same article.

Q.—To all the people?
A.—Yes.
Q.—Was there any special consideration of any kind from Fitzpatrick to your firm?
A.—No.
Q.—Was he treated the same as any other tenderer?
A.—Yes, absolutely.
Q.—During the carrying out of the Fitzpatrick aerodrome tender was there any occasion for obtaining the assistance of your father or discussing it with him?
A.—No.
Q.—It was carried out by you and McAllister?
A.—Yes.
Q.—Taking up the McNamara contract, the first one, the municipal one. He had a contract for Wellington Street?
A.—Yes.
Q.—Have they any interest in your concern?
A.—No.
Q.—Have you any interest in the McNamaras?
A.—No.
Q.—Anybody for you?
A.—No.
Q.—How long have you been dealing with them?
A.—For several years—ever since I have been connected with the business.
Q.—Old customers?
A.—Yes.
Q.—And did you know anything about them obtaining the contract for Wellington Street previous to its being done?
A.—That they had received the contract? No. The first intimation was when it was published in the newspapers.
Q.—Did you have any special contract for supplying them with material or anything?
A.—No.
Q.—What did they do? Get quotations?
A.—Yes, we quoted them. There was a number of contractors bidding and we quoted on the commodities required for the construction of the road.
Q.—Is it true that you gave the same figures to all the tenderers?
A.—Yes, the same figures to everybody.
Q.—As to the other two contracts, the Coniston and Copper Cliff and the Porcupine road—did you have anything to do with them?
A.—Nothing.
Q.—Did you supply material?
A.—No.
Q.—Did you even know of them?
A.—Later on we heard. It was in the press and we knew the contracts had been awarded to the McNamaras.
Q.—Your firm, the Lyons Fuel and Supply Company, had nothing to do with the contracts at all?
A.—No.
Q.—Supplied no material?
A.—No.

Q.—No interest?

A.—None at all.

Mr. Finlayson: All right.

Examination by Mr. Fisher.

Q.—You supplied figures for the tenderers on the aerodrome? Is that what you said?

A.—Yes.

Q.—On what material?

A.—Gravel, cement, tile, brick, roofing material, steel sash, rolling doors and also the lumber.

Q.—Those prices were given before the contract was awarded, were they?

A.—Oh, yes, yes.

Q.—You supplied prices on most of the material that went in?

A.—We supplied prices on practically all the material, yes.

Q.—And did you finally supply material in some of the instances?

A.—Yes.

Q.—There were some instances where you did not?

A.—Yes, there were some instances where we did not.

Q.—What didn't you supply?

A.—We didn't supply the lumber.

Q.—Who got that?

A.—The Hesson Lumber Company.

Q.—Anything else you didn't get?

A.—We didn't get the lime for the mortar. We didn't get the hardware.

Q.—Who got the hardware?

A.—I don't know who got the hardware.

Q.—You did submit prices on that?

A.—Yes, we submitted prices.

Q.—Anything else you didn't get?

A.—I don't recall anything else.

Q.—With these exceptions you supplied everything else?

A.—I don't know what proportion we supplied.

Q.—What do you mean by that?

A.—We supplied what we got orders for.

Q.—I see.

Chairman: What the witness means is that they supplied material of all kinds but whether that was all the contractor purchased or whether he purchased from someone else he does not know. I think Mr. Fitzpatrick's evidence was clear on that.

Mr. Fisher: I suppose it is in evidence how much you did supply?'

Chairman: It is in evidence.

Mr. Fisher: How much?

Witness: I cannot tell.

Hon. Mr. Lyons: It was about $30,000 or $31,000 worth.

Mr. Fisher: We come to the McNamara contract. You said you gave prices to them on something? What was that in connection with?

Witness: In connection with the construction of the Wellington Street road.

Q.—What did you supply, what did you offer to supply there?

A.—Everything that was going to be required.

Q.—What would that be?

A.—Gravel, cement principally, and the expansion joints.···
Q.—That would be pretty nearly everything that went in?
A.—Yes.
Q.—Did you afterwards supply that?
A.—We supplied the gravel and cement, yes.
Q.—All they used?
A.—Well, I don't know about that. We supplied gravel and cement.
Q.—I suppose that is in evidence, how much that was?
CHAIRMAN: Yes, it was all in the other night.
Q.—Do you know how much?
A.—I could not say off-hand. I think in the neighbourhood of $25,000.
Q.—What other jobs of McNamara did you supply?
A.—In what year?
Q.—Any years since this Government came in?
A.—Other jobs since this Government came in?
Q.—Yes.
A.—We supplied some for the road construction on the Wallace Terrace,
Sault Ste. Marie, the year previous to the Wellington Street job.
Q.—What year was that?
A.—That would be 1923, 1924.
Q.—1923 and 1924?
A.—No, 1924.
Q.—Sand and gravel there?
A.—Gravel and cement.
Q.—What else? Any other jobs they had?
A.—That's all.
Q.—At any time?
A.—At any time during that period.
CHAIRMAN: Those two contracts: You supplied the material on the
Wellington Street pavement and the Wallace Terrace. Who let those contracts
to the McNamara Company?
WITNESS: The Corporation of Sault Ste. Marie.
CHAIRMAN: Civic contracts?
WITNESS: Yes, under the supervision of city engineers.

Edmund Lawrence Bedford called, sworn. Examined by Mr. Finlayson.
Q.—Where do you live?
A.—Sault Ste. Marie.
Q.—What is your occupation?
A.—Hardware.
Q.—Wholesale or retail?
A.—Retail.
Q.—How long have you been in business there?
A.—Seven years.
MR. FISHER: Pardon me, have you some other witness to go on with.
I think Mr. Raney and Mr. Sinclair might want to examine this witness.
MR. FINLAYSON: We arranged with Mr. Raney about that just now.
MR. FISHER: I am not instructed in this matter.
MR. FINLAYSON: We made arrangements to protect his interests. There
is little in this witness and it is a matter of covering the ground. Six or seven
years you say?
WITNESS: Seven years.

Q.—You carried on business in your own name?

A.—Yes.

Q.—Nobody else interested?

A.—Yes.

Q.—You manage and control it?

A.—Yes.

Q.—Where do you deal?

A.—Where I can get the best prices.

Q.—Where does that mean?

A.—Sometimes Howlands, Lewis Brothers, Montreal, Lyons Fuel and Supply Company, Canada Paint—

Q.—When you buy from the Lyons Fuel and Supply Company and the Cochrane Hardware you are more or less buying from competitors?

A.—Yes.

Q.—Because both the Lyons Fuel and Supply Company and the Cochrane Hardware have local stores?

A.—Yes.

Q.—And they are local dealers in opposition to you?

A.—Yes.

Q.—They are also wholesale?

A.—Also wholesale.

Q.—I suppose it is natural that you only deal with them when it is worth while?

A.—When it is convenient for me.

Q.—They are jobbers?

A.—They are.

Q.—Which means they can give you a wholesale price?

A.—Yes, they can give a wholesale price.

Q.—And there are occasions when the Lyons Fuel and Supply Company and the Cochrane Hardware compete with Toronto and Montreal houses?

A.—Quite often.

Q.—And sometimes give better prices?

A.—Yes, sometimes they give better prices.

Q.—I suppose the reason is that they can bring it up by boat or—

MR. FISHER: Why not let him give a little evidence himself?

MR. FINLAYSON: I thought I was covering generalities. When it is serious I will be as dignified as you like.

CHAIRMAN: We have not been very strict. We want to get at the facts.

MR. FISHER: It is no use, Mr. Finlayson, giving evidence whether material or immaterial. If it is immaterial what is the use of going on.

CHAIRMAN: I have not been checking anyone up so long as they have been trying to get information.

MR. FISHER: Counsel leading witnesses—

CHAIRMAN: I realize that is so in a court of law.

MR. FINLAYSON: Well, Mr. Bedford, where were we at when this interruption occurred? I was asking you if it was possible for local hardware dealers like the Lyons Fuel and Supply Company and the Cochrane Hardware to compete with the big houses?

WITNESS: Yes, it is.

Q.—Will you satisfy my friend? Explain the reason why it is possible for local firms like these to compete with the larger firms.

A.—They bring goods in in larger quantities. I would have to buy in smaller quantities.

Q.—Have you been supplying the Government of Ontario in purchases of hardware for a number of years?

A.—In 1924 and 1925.

Q.—And before that?

A.—No, I have not.

Q.—What have you supplied?

A.—I have supplied shovels, axes, saws, blankets, concrete pipe, kitchen utensils, camp equipment.

Q.—For whom were they supplied? For what branch?

A.—For the Northern Development Branch.

Q.—Who is in charge of that at the Sault?

A.—Mr. Lamb.

Q.—The resident engineer?

A.—Yes.

Q.—When you got these orders, how were they obtained?

A.—They were obtained sometimes over the telephone; sometimes I went down to the office.

Q.—Sometimes you went down there?

A.—Sure.

Q.—How did you come to go down?

A.—Looking for business.

Q.—You would have to submit prices?

A.—Yes, sir.

Q.—Who did you have to compete with?

A.—Cochrane Hardware, Plummer Ferguson, I presume, and other retail dealers.

Q.—In other words you were competing for the business locally?

A.—Yes.

Q.—Did you get it all or only in part?

A.—I did not I am sorry to say.

Q.—Take up the cement, the cement pipe, who did you get that from?

A.—The Lyons Company.

Q.—Is there any other local source you could get it from?

A.—No, sir.

Q.—Why is that?

A.—It is not manufactured anywhere else north of Toronto that I know of.

Q.—What kind of a plant do they have?

A.—A cement mixer, I presume.

Q.—I presume it is packed or stamped or something—reinforcements put in?

A.—Yes.

Q.—Do they carry stock?

A.—Yes, sir.

Q.—And how did you come to sell the pipe to the Northern Development Branch?

A.—They asked me if I could supply the pipe.

Q.—Then what?

A.—I told them I did not know but that I would find out.

Q.—Who asked you?

A.—Mr. Lamb, I think, gave the first order. They wanted the pipe in a hurry and immediately I found out I could get it I told them so. They asked the price and I gave it and he gave the order for a small quantity.

Q.—Tried you out?

A.—Yes.

Q.—Did that keep on for that season?

A.—I supplied several small quantities and then larger quantities came up and different sizes, sometimes delivered by myself and sometimes out in the country in some cases they took it direct from the Sault themselves.

Q.—You sold to the Northern Development Branch by direct contract between you and them?

A.—Absolutely.

Q.—I am not going to ask you what the profit or spread was. What I want to find out is this: Did you pay the Lyons people directly for it?

A.—Yes.

Q.—And sold directly to the other people?

A.—Yes.

Q.—Did you carry any stock?

A.—I did not carry any stock. It was no use.

Q.—You found out what you needed?

A.—I buy what I need.

Q.—Where did you get it from Lyons?

A.—From their yard, F.O.B. their yard.

Q.—And what did you do? Deliver to where the Government wanted it?

A.—In some cases, and in some cases they picked it up on their own truck.

Q.—We have heard that in some cases the Lyons truck delivered?

A.—Yes.

Q.—Where was that?

A.—The Haviland Bay road.

Q.—How far away is that?

A.—I have never been there. I think it is twenty-seven miles.

Q.—How did their truck come to deliver?

A.—I tried to get other trucks to do the work for me but they could not handle it. The trucks were not large enough for the heavy stuff. The Lyons truck was practically the only one to handle it in the Sault.

Q.—So that you were forced to get the truck?

A.—Yes.

Q.—And did you pay Lyons?

A.—I bought the pipe at the yard.

Q.—What price did you pay there?

A.—I got a quotation on the delivery.

Q.—You paid the price at the yard and got a further quotation for delivery twenty-seven miles away and charged the Government with that plus profit?

A.—Yes.

Q.—Now this profit you made, was that split with the Lyons?

A.—No.

Q.—Did they have any interest in it of any kind?

A.—No, sir.

Q.—Did you use any pull, or influence to get the work?

A.—No. I haven't got any pull.

Q.—So you didn't use any?

A.—I don't know how to get any.

Q.—Well, perhaps, the Committee might give you some evidence about that. Do you know Mr. Lyons personally?

A.—No, sir. I know him to see him. I have never had any conversation with him.

Q.—Did anybody talk to you?

A.—No.

Q.—You know him as seeing him on the streets?

A.—I have heard him speak in the Public Accounts.

Q.—You know him on the street?

A.—I am not personally acquainted with him.

Q.—Are you a supporter of his? You are not an active politician?

A.—No, sir.

Q.—Is it true it was pure business?

A.—Absolutely.

Q.—All the way through?

A.—Yes.

Q.—And those articles you bought from them—you spoke of blankets?

A.—Yes.

Q.—How were they bought?

A.—I got a quotation from different ones and his prices was the best.

Q.—And the other things, you mentioned, hardware—

A.—Saws, axes, general hardware.

Q.—The stuff you bought from the Lyons Company, did not all go to the Government?

A.—Oh, no.

Q.—What about the cement pipe?

A.—That went to the Government.

Q.—And the rest went into stock and if you could sell to the Government, so much the better?

A.—I have got good prices from the Lyons Fuel and Supply Company and replenished my own stock at better prices than anywhere else.

Q.—In other words, it went into stock?

A.—Yes.

Q.—And if the Government wanted some later on they got it the same as any other customers?

A.—If they wanted it and I had it I sold to them if the price was right.

Q.—You told me as to the pipe; tell me as to all the dealings with the Government in any branches, was there any arrangement by which anybody got any consideration?

A.—No, sir.

Q.—Did they ever ask for any?

A.—No, sir.

Q.—Any influence used to get any?

A.—No, sir.

Q.—Purely a business basis?

A.—Pure business.

Examination of Mr. Bedford by Mr. Fisher.

Q.—How long have you been in business at the Sault?

A.—Seven years.

Q.—When did you first sell goods to the Government?

A.—In 1924.

Q.—Can you tell me how much in 1924?

A.—I cannot tell you exactly. I would say between $2,000 and $2,500.

Q.—In 1925 you sold goods to the Government?

A.—Yes.

Q.—How much that year?

A.—Possibly $8,000.

Q.—Still going on selling?

A.—Yes, sir.

Q.—Is the volume increasing?

A.—I have sold a little.

MR. FINLAYSON: 1926 is hardly over yet.

WITNESS: It has not opened yet, for me.

MR. FISHER: What kind of goods did you sell to the Government in 1923?

A.—Some camp equipment, tinware, hardware, graniteware, nails, bolts, locks, knobs, hinges, paint, oil and other articles.

MR. FINLAYSON: That is 1924?

WITNESS: Yes.

MR. FISHER: Were those the chief articles?

A.—Those were the chief articles.

Q.—Did you sell any cement in 1924?

A.—I may have sold a few bags.

Q.—Did you sell any pipe?

A.—I remember selling some brick that year.

Q.—Did you sell any pipe?

A.—No, sir.

Q.—In 1925, what did you sell?

A.—I sold them graniteware, shovels, axes, saws, blankets, concrete pipe and beds.

Q.—How much was the concrete pipe?

A.—I don't know exactly. I presume it would be about $2,500 or $3,000.

Q.—What were the other principal sales?

A.—Shovels, blankets, beds.

Q.—I mean the largest items.

A.—A general line of hardware.

Q.—Any singles item of any size?

A.—Not that I know of.

Q.—Did you sell any cement?

A.—Any cement? A few bags—the odd bag.

Q.—What kind of pipe was this you sold?

A.—Concrete pipe.

Q.—All the pipe used in the Sault is made by the Lyons Fuel and Supply Company is it?

A.—No.

CHAIRMAN: Vitrified.

MR. FINLAYSON: Which is shipped in, of course.

MR. FISHER: There must be a lot of other pipe come into the Sault from outside?

A.—Some sewer pipe, yes.

Q.—The same sort of pipe you sold to the Government?

A.—I don't know of any.

Q.—Any other concrete pipe?

A.—No.

Q.—What other kind 'could they use instead of concrete?

A.—I suppose they could use galvanized pipe.

Q.—They use it, don't they?

A.—I suppose so.

CHAIRMAN: Does not that depend on the contract? That was gone into with Mr. Lamb the other night. There is nothing concealed about the concrete pipe. It was told exactly what it was for and where it was bought.

MR. FISHER: Lyons was the only local source?

CHAIRMAN: The evidence given by Mr. Lamb was that he got the price of the Lyons Fuel and Supply Company who manufacture at the Sault and from J. E. Russell, of Toronto, and that the price and freight made it cheaper to buy at the Sault.

MR. FISHER: Who got the prices?

CHAIRMAN: Mr. Lamb, from Mr. Bedford and from J. E. Russell of Toronto.

MR. FISHER: You were asked to quote on the pipe and you got the prices from the Lyons Fuel and Supply Company?

WITNESS: On the concrete pipe. That was the only place I could get it.

Q.—The Government knew?

A.—I presume they did.

Q.—The only place it could be got?

A.—They had to do it in a hurry.

Q.—So that when the Government engineer asked you to supply they knew you were going to the Lyons Fuel and Supply Company to get it?

A.—I expect they did.

Q.—Sometimes you delivered the pipe yourself?

A.—Yes, sir.

Q.—And sometimes the Lyons people?

A.—Sometimes.

Q.—Why did you say they delivered it?

A.—In the case where they delivered it I could not make delivery in any other way.

Q.—How is that?

A.—I could not get anyone to handle the pipe, it was so heavy and there were no trucks sufficiently large to carry it.

Q.—What was the pipe used for?

A.—For culverts and road work.

Q.—You have sold lots of other pipe for culverts and road work?

A.—I have sold galvanized pipe, yes.

Q.—For culverts and roadways?

A.—Yes.

A.—It is more expensive?

A.—About the same price.

Q.—So that when you were asked to tender the Government would know it would be supplied by the Lyons Fuel and Supply Company and that it could not be supplied by anyone else?

A.—I presume they would know.

Q.—Do you care to say what price you paid?

A.—There is different sizes and prices.

Q.—Do you care to give us any information on that?

A.—I don't know whether I could off-hand.

MR. LYONS: I submitted the price here the other day, Mr. Fisher.

MR. FINLAYSON: I fancy they will be in Mr. Nash's report. He was asked.

CHAIRMAN: It is all in the evidence.

MR. FISHER: Dò you supply goods to others who have contracts with the Government?

WITNESS: I have not been fortunate yet.

Q.—You have never been able to supply any goods to anybody having business with the Government?

A.—No, sir.

Q.—Have you ever been asked to supply?

A.—I have quoted prices.

Q.—To whom did you quote prices?

A.—I quoted some to the McNamara Brothers.

Q.—Of what kind?

A.—On small hardware.

Q.—You have never been asked for any big quantities?

A.—No, sir.

Q.—Did you ever go after it?

A.—No, I have not. We have not had many Government contracts in the place to go after.

Q.—McNamaras—they were not using much hardware?

A.—Nothing much in my line.

MR. FINLAYSON: They did not have any contracts at the Sault.

MR. FISHER: Did you ask prices on this stuff for the aerodrome?

A.—Not the aerodrome; except the finishing of the offices of the Northern Development Branch.

Q.—When was that?

A.—Last spring.

Q.—They asked for prices there?

A.—I sold some articles—locks, hinges.

Q.—What did that amount to?

A.—Not very much. I don't know just how much.

Q.—Up to last year you were not asked to quote anything on the aerodrome?

A.—The aerodrome was only built in 1924.

Q.—When was it going up, in 1924 and 1925?

A.—Yes, in 1924 and 1925.

Q.—And they asked for nothing in 1924?

A.—I sold some nails and drift spikes for the aerodrome platform.

Q.—None of the other fellows who put in tenders got quotations from you?

A.—No, sir.

Q.—They never asked you for it?

A.—No, sir.

Q.—You could have supplied a good deal?

A.—I am very doubtful if I could.

Examination of Mr. Bedford by Mr. Sinclair.

Q.—How much business did you have with the Northern Development Branch in 1924, Mr. Bedford?

A.—Not very much with the Northern Development Branch. I cannot say exactly.

Q.—I think the figures given last night were $700?

A.—Possibly.

Q.—That is round figures. Then in 1925 an item appears in the Public Accounts of $10,849.45 from the Northern Development?

A.—I don't think those figures are right.

CHAIRMAN: I might be able to facilitate it by explaining he is not thinking of the Northern Development alone. A considerable part of his business was with the Forestry Branch. They are two separate organizations.

WITNESS: I won't say the Ontario Forestry and Northern Development is not $10,000.

MR. FINLAYSON: You will remember we added them together the other night.

MR. SINCLAIR: Northern Development Branch; camp and road equipment material and supplies, making of roads, $8,187.32, which is the Northern Development Highways Branch?

WITNESS: Yes.

Q.—You had nothing to do with the forest ranging in 1924 and your total dealings with the whole Northern Development Branch was about $700 and in 1925, on the making of roads alone it was a little over $8,000?

A.—Yes.

Q.—And in 1923, you recall, it was smaller than in 1924?

A.—Yes, sir.

Q.—Can you tell us how your account got so big in one year—1925?

A.—Well, I didn't have so much competition. I could buy better.

Q.—In 1925? Why?

A.—Because the Cochrane Hardware Company in quoting prices to me and the Government gave the same prices.

Q.—You did not get any supplies from the Lyons Fuel and Supply Company?

A.—They did not have anything I required—only small articles.

Q.—Not at all?

A.—No.

Q.—Prior to 1925 you had never been a customer of the Lyons Fuel and Supply Company?

A.—I had bought articles I required when they had them.

Q.—How much?

A.—Small amounts.

Q.—Why?

A.—Because they had articles in my line of business.

Q.—They were carrying it in 1923 or 1924?

A.—Yes.

Q.—The fact that the Lyons Company was not supplying anything to the Government in 1925 had nothing to do with your getting it?

A.—Not that I know of.

Q.—Nothing at all?

A.—No.

Q.—You supplied some beds I believe?

A.—Yes.

Q.—Do you carry them in stock?

A.—No.

Q.—You are a retail hardware man and don't carry beds?

A.—No.

Q.—And the Northern Development engineer went to your store to buy beds, although you don't carry beds?

A.—Yes, sir.

Q.—And you did supply some beds?

A.—Yes.

Q.—How many?

A.—About fifty.

Q.—From whom did you get them?

A.—From the Lyons Fuel and Supply Company.

Q.—And were they delivered to your store or direct to the work?

A.—I took them up at the dock.

Q.—They never got to the Lyons' warehouse?

A.—No.

Q.—You supplied 300 pairs of blankets, was it?

A.—I supplied some blankets.

Q.—How many?

A.—Possibly 300.

Q.—How many blankets did you carry in stock?

A.—None.

Q.—None at all?

A.—No.

Q.—You are a retail hardware man?

A.—Yes.

Q.—The Northern Development in purchasing blankets went to your hardware store where you don't carry blankets, to purchase blankets?

A.—Yes.

Q.—And you got an order from the Northern Development Branch?

A.—Yes.

Q.—And where did you get the blankets to fill the order?

A.—From the Lyons Company.

Q.—And in regard to those beds, how did you know the prices to charge the Department when you did not carry beds in stock?

A.—I got a quotation.

Q. —From whom?

A. —From the Lyons Company.

Q.—You gave the quotation to the Department?

MR. RANEY: Speak a little louder, please.

MR. SINCLAIR: You got a quotation from the Lyons Company on the beds?

A.—Yes.

Q.—When they asked for prices on the blankets how did you know what price to charge?

A.—I got quotations from different firms.

Q.—How many different firms?

A.—From the Hinchberg Harness Company, the Cochrane Hardware and the Lyons Fuel and Supply Company.

Q.—Having got a quotation you gave the price to the Northern Development Branch representative?

A.—Yes.

Q.—And are there men in business at the Sault who would carry blankets as part of their stock in trade?

A.—Those firms I spoke of.

Q.—Not retail?

A.—No.

Q.—If I wanted half a dozen pairs of blankets I could not buy them at the Sault in a retail store?

A.—You might at a dry goods store.

Q.—Is there any place at the Sault where a purchaser could buy beds other than at a hardware store?

A.—It depends on the kind of bed. These kind are camp beds.

Q.—Would the furniture store carry any?

A.—They might carry some; I don't know.

Q.—They are a bed for other people than road builders; they can be used by settlers?

A.—I don't think so.

MR. RANEY: Especially in the north country.

MR. SINCLAIR: What particular virtue have these beds that they are limited only to road builders?

A.—They are practically only used for camps.

Q.—Road builders are not the only people who have camps?

A.—No, the lumber camps, I presume they do.

Q.—Do you mean to say that in a city like Sault Ste. Marie there would be no sale for beds of this kind?

A.—There might be quite considerable.

Q.—And still you cannot tell us whether anybody carried them except the two firms you have mentioned?

A.—No, sir.

Q.—And they carry wholesale, and did you sell the beds and blankets to the Department at wholesale prices or retail?

A.—Retail.

Q.—And how did you find out what the retail prices of beds such as those would be?

A.—Well, I inquired what they sold the beds for.

Q.—From whom?

A.—From the Hinchberg Harness Company.

Q.—You did not say the Hinchberg Harness Company supplied the beds?

A.—I asked for prices.

Q.—They sell the beds?

A.—Yes.

Q.—I understand that before you said you simply asked the Lyons Company?

MR. FINLAYSON: No, he said Hinchberg.

CHAIRMAN: He named the two firms.

WITNESS: I meant I got prices from all.

MR. SINCLAIR: These companies told you what the retail price was on beds and blankets?

A.—No, I don't think so.

Q.—Did any?

A.—Yes.

Q.—Which one?

A.—I think the Lyons Company.

Q.—And so the price at which you sold these beds and blankets to the Government at was fixed by the Lyons Fuel and Supply Company?

A.—Well, they gave me some idea of what they would sell at.

Q.—You say you did not carry any stock, did not know the prices and you got the prices from the Lyons Company?

A.—Yes.

Q.—So they fixed the price at which you sold the goods to the Government?

A.—I don't think they fixed the exact price. I used my own judgment.

Q.—How near the exact price?

A.—Possibly half a dollar.

Q.—That is as near as you can get?

A.—Yes.

Q.—At any rate they had a price they stated at which you could buy?

A.—Yes.

Q.—And they indicated to you a price at which you should sell?

A.—Yes.

Q.—You stated that you had never sold goods to companies doing business with the Government?

A.—Not that I know of.

Q.—But you have been able to supply goods to the Government?

A.—Yes.

Q.—Have you any reason or explanation for this?

A.—Well, I went after the business.

Q.—You went after the business. You never asked any contractor or road builders or pulp companies for any business?

A.—No.

Q.—But you have asked the Government?

A.—I have.

Q.—And when did you first ask the Government for business?

A.—In 1924.

Q.—And how much did you get?

A.—I had about $2,500 worth in 1924.

Q.—With what department?

A.—Ontario Forestry and Northern Development.

Q.—The figures don't show it. Our financial year is up at the end of October, 1924, and your business with the Northern Development was something around $700?

A.—I am speaking of my own business, which ends in December.

Q.—Which means that between 31st of October and the 1st of January there was the remainder?

A.—I suppose so.

Q.—Can you tell us at what date you went after the business from the Government?

A.—I cannot tell you exactly.

Q.—Whom did you go to?

A.—Mr. Lamb's office.

Q.—Anyone else?

A.—Mr. Hyde.

Q.—Who is he?

A.—Superintendent of the construction of the aerodrome platform.

Q.—Who else?

A.—That is all I know of.

Q.—Just those two. And how do you explain the difference that you were more successful in 1925 than in 1924.

A.—In 1924 I had to buy my goods from the Cochrane Hardware.

Q.—Why?

A.—Because there was no person else carried them in the Sault and the Cochrane Hardware would quote the same prices to the Department as to me in order to get the business especially if they knew I was going after the business.

Q.—You could not buy beds from anyone else but the Cochrane Hardware in 1924?

A.—Not that I know of, except the Hinchberg.

Q.—In all that large north country the Cochrane Hardware had the monopoly of beds and blankets up to the end of October, 1924?

A.—Yes.

Q.—Lyons was not in?

A.—No.

Q.—And the other companies were not?

A.—I presume they were.

Q.—Then why did you tell me you were limited to Cochrane?

A.—If I got Hinchberg or Cochrane they would know that I was quoting on this business and they would quote the Department the same as me.

Q.—That is the Cochrane Hardware would give the Department the same price as you would give? This wholesale company would sell to the Government at retail prices?

A.—No, at wholesale.

CHAIRMAN: He said the Cochrane people would quote him the same price as they quoted the Government.

MR. SINCLAIR: You said they would quote the Government the same price as you?

CHAIRMAN: He put it in a different way.

MR. SINCLAIR: Would it not result in the same thing?

A.—It would leave no chance to make a profit. I had to have a percentage on top of the Cochrane price and if I did that I lost the business.

Q.—Our evidence so far has been that whatever the Lyons Fuel and Supply Company sold they sold at retail prices?

A.—Who to?

Q.—To the Government?

A.—Possibly the Lyons Fuel and Supply Company did.

Q.—Were not the Cochrane Hardware selling at retail prices to the Government?

A.—No, they were not. I don't expect they were or I would not have lost so much business in 1924.

Q.—That is the only explanation you can give why the Public Accounts in 1925 show you a fairly good customer with the Northern Development Branch, while in 1924 you did very little business?

A.—I had several opportunities to quote prices in 1924 on goods and I did quote and lost the business.

Q.—When did you first know the Lyons Company were debarred from selling to the Government?

A.—When I read it in the paper.

Q.—When was that?

A.—I don't know exactly—about a year ago.

Q.—Reading that in the paper, what did you do?

A.—In what way?

Q.—Did you think there was a chance for you to get some business?

A.—I thought so, yes.

Q.—Whom did you see?

A.—I did not see anyone except the Government engineer.

Q.—You did not go to the Lyons Company and see what you could get on there?

A.—No, sir.

Q.—When did you first become a customer of the Lyons Fuel and Supply Company?

A.—Sometime last spring.

Q.—About what time?

A.—It may have been April or May.

Q.—You can tell us; you are a business man?

A.—Possibly in April.

Q.—How near to the time when you saw the notice in the paper?

A.—I could not tell you exactly.

Q.—Not far away?

A.—No.

Q.—And as soon as the Lyons Fuel and Supply Company were debarred from doing business with the Government they came to you to get you to buy from them?

A.—No, not as soon, no.

· Q.—Next morning, perhaps?

A.—No, sir.

Q.—How long after?

A.—I don't know.

Q.—You have said you do. Now I want an answer. You told me within a short time?

A.—I told you sometime after, I don't know exactly.

Q.—Two months after?

A.—Possibly.

Q.—Will you swear that for two months after March 25th none of the · Lyons Company came to see you?

A.—I will.

Q.—Not within two months?

A.—Yes.

Q.—So that whatever business you did with the Lyons Fuel and Supply Company was done after the first of June, 1925?

A.—No. I don't think so.

Q.—You said it was not for two months after the Lyons Fuel and Supply Company were debarred from doing business with the Government that they came to you to get you to do business?

A.—I am not sure about dates.

Q.—I want you to he sure.

A.—I cannot be sure.

Q.—You have already said it was two months?

A.—It may have been.

Q.—Was it or was it not?

A.—I don't know.

Q.—Then why didn't you say? Was it one month? Was it before 1st of May they came to see you?

A.—I don't know.

Q.—Have you kept any books on the transactions of goods bought from the Lyons Company?

A.—Yes.
Q.—Where are they?
A.—In the Sault.
Q.—Have you invoices?
A.—Yes.
Q.—They can be produced?
A.—Yes.
Q.—Mr. Chairman, I think he may have to get this. I think we should have something on this.

Mr. Finlayson: I think your question repeated to Clarkson's will cover that point.

Chairman: Perhaps Mr. Nash's statement will show.

Mr. Finlayson: I think the explanation is this: He had been dealing with them for years, but not in any big volume. When they went into the hardware business, then it increased.

Mr. Sinclair: He told me he was not.

Mr. Finlayson: That is a misunderstanding. He meant hardware.

Mr. Sinclair: Up to 1925 what kind of business did you do with the Lyons Fuel and Supply Company?
A.—I had bought a few bags of cement, lime and wood fibre.

Mr. Finlayson: Metal lath?

Witness: Yes.

Mr. Sinclair: In what quantities at any one time?
A.—In small quantities.
Q.—You did not carry any stock because the wholesale house was there?
A.—Yes.
Q.—Up to 1925 your purchases from the Lyons people were comparatively small?
A.—Yes.
Q.—In 1925 they became larger?
A.—Yes.
Q.—And they became larger, you say, because the Lyons people had not been carrying hardware?
A.—Yes.
Q.—When did the Lyons people commence to carry these lines?
A.—The first I bought was in May.
Q.—When did they begin to carry them?
A.—I am not sure.
Q.—You have told us that was your reason why you did not buy from them?
A.—Sometime last year
Q.—You won't say which month?
A.—I don't know when they put in stock.
Q.—They would come to tell you that they had now the goods you bough t in stock?
A.—I started when I knew they had the hardware.
Q.—How did you know?
A.—A man told me.
Q.—When?
A.—Sometime last spring.
Q.—What time last spring?
A.—I cannot tell you.

Q.—You cannot refresh your memory any more than that?

A.—I don't know exactly.

Q.—When you bought goods, anything that was for the Northern Development Branch where were the goods delivered?

A.—Some were delivered to the warehouse of the Northern Development Branch, some to the Algoma Central.

Q.—Any delivered any other place?

A.—Yes.

Q.—Where?

A.—Some on the roads.

Q.—Any delivered to your store?

A.—No.

Q.—They were delivered direct from the Lyons Fuel and Supply Company to the place where they were to be used?

A.—Yes.

CHAIRMAN: By whom?

WITNESS: By ourselves. By myself. By my truck.

CHAIRMAN: You took delivery at the warehouse and carried them to the work?

WITNESS: What goods we were short of.

MR. SINCLAIR: We will come to the articles in time. You had stuff in your store bought and delivered from your own store to the work?

A.—Oh, yes.

Q.—What?

A.—Tools.

Q.—In what quantities?

A.—Small quantities.

Q.—What do you mean—small quantities?

A.—Probably five or six articles.

Q.—There were very small orders on anything you could deliver from your own store?

A.—Yes.

Q.—And when you gave prices to the Government what prices did you give? I don't mean in dollars and cents. Did you sell wholesale or retail?

A.—Retail.

Q.—And of course you bought wholesale?

A.—Yes.

Q.—And when you got an order from the resident engineer how would the order be taken?

A.—Sometimes by telephone; sometimes I got it in his office.

Q.—I suppose he came to the store sometimes?

A.—Sometimes he bought at the store.

Q.—Did you make out a shipping order or bill or something?

A.—Yes.

Q.—How did you make them out?

A.—I got requisitions from the engineer.

Q.—You got a requistion from the engineer for, say, a dozen picks?

A.—Yes.

Q.—And what did you do if you did not have any in the store?

A.—Made out a delivery slip to the Northern Development Branch.

Q.—What do you mean by a delivery slip? Was that an order on Lyons to deliver these goods to the Northern Development?

A.—Oh, no.

Q.—What do you mean then?

A.—A delivery slip I got signed where they were to deliver it.

Q.—Who signed it?

A.—Whoever received the goods. If it was a freight shipment we made out a freight bill.

Q.—In order to get the goods into the truck what did you have to do?

A.—I loaded them up.

Q.—From where?

A.—Some from the Lyons Company, some from the Cochrane Hardware and some from my own store.

Q.—I was dealing specifically with Lyons?

A.—We brought goods to the store and made up the shipment there.

Q.—If they ordered a dozen picks and you did not have them who did you look up?

A.—I got them where I could get the best prices.

Q.—Do they vary from day to day?

A.—Sometimes.

Q.—If Mr. Lamb came in and said he wanted a dozen picks you could not sell them to Mr. Lamb until you had phoned around to the other companies to know what they could sell them for?

A.—Certainly. I looked up the price of the last ones.

Q.—And how did you know what it cost to buy?

A.—I would find out.

Q.—After you had sold to the Northern Development Branch?

A.—You bet I would.

Q.—I see. You buy a dozen picks and say "Here they are" and you put the price on the bill and say they will be so much and then you turn around and find out from the Lyons Company or the Cochrane Hardware how much they cost you?

A.—Yes, sir.

Q.—And suppose they cost more than you sold them for?

A.—I would lose money.

Q.—And that is the way you did business?

A.—Yes.

CHAIRMAN: Do you carry picks in stock?

WITNESS: Yes.

CHAIRMAN: Some orders you would take from stock?

WITNESS: Yes.

MR. SINCLAIR: You have not brought down any invoices, I suppose?

A.—No, I have not. I could have, but I was not asked.

Q.—Did you ever sell any goods on commission?

A.—No, sir.

Q.—You don't do that?

A.—No.

Q.—You buy outright and sell?

A.—Yes.

Q.—You cannot tell us why the resident engineer went to your store to buy blankets?

A.—An inquiry came along with other stuff.

Q.—What other stuff?

A.—Other hardware.

Q.—What other?

A.—Shovels, picks, axes, saws.

Q.—How big an order was there the day the beds were spoken about?

A.—The beds were a separate order.

Q.—I am dealing with the beds separately. Was there anything else ordered at the time the beds were spoken about?

A.—There was quite a lot of goods bought at that time—shovels, picks axes, blankets.

Q.—And the invoice for the beds carries with it these other items?

A.—No the beds are separate. They were not delivered at the same time.

Q.—Had you ever sold beds to the resident engineer before?

A.—No.

Q.—And did he know you did not carry beds?

A.—I don't know whether he did.

Q.—Had you ever sold blankets before?

A.—Not to my knowing.

Q.—You don't advertise blankets for sale?

A.—No.

Q.—Your line of business I suppose you call shelf hardware?

A.—And whatever else I can pick up.

Q.—Just an ordinary hardware business in the Sault?

A.—Yes.

Q.—Can you tell me from memory what time last year you did the biggest business with the Lyons people?

A.—I think it was in May. I think so.

Q.—Can you tell me during what part of 1925 you had the largest business with the Northern Development Branch.

A.—Well, I don't know just exactly what the month was.

Q.—Why did you say the largest month of your dealings with the Lyons people was in May?

A.—I think it was May. I am not sure.

Q.—If not May, what month?

A.—It may have been June.

Q.—Either May or June was the month you did the largest business with the Lyons Company?

A.—I think so.

Q.—Can you tell me what time of the year you did the largest business with the Northern Development Branch?

A.—I think it would be about the same time.

Q.—And the reason you did the largest business with the Lyons people was because you were doing the largest business with the Northern Development Branch at the same time?

A.—Yes.

Q.—And the goods you sold to the Northern Development Branch were largely purchased from the Lyons Company?

A.—Most of them, yes.

Re-examination of Mr. Bedford by Mr. Fisher.

Q.—Did the Lyons Company give you any special prices or did they quote the ordinary wholesale prices?

A.—There was no special price that I know of.

Q.—The ordinary wholesale price?

A.—Yes.

Q.—And you sold at the ordinary retail price?

A.—Yes.

Q.—In 1924 you say you were not very successful because the Cochrane people beat you?

A.—Yes.

Q.—They quoted the same price to you as to the Government?

A.—I expect they did.

Q.—A wholesale price to the Government?

A.—Yes, I think so.

Q.—Did they change their policy in 1925?

A.—I don't know that they did.

Q.—Did they still quote wholesale to the Government in 1925?

A.—I am not sure whether they did or not. I did not get all the business so they must have used the same policy.

Q.—In 1924 you could not get much business because they were quoting below. In 1925 when you were quoting retail you got a considerable amount of the business notwithstanding that policy?

A.—I got some of the business—Yes. I don't just understand the question.

Q.—I was trying to find out why the Cochrane Company was not beating you in 1925 the same as in 1924 if they were quoting wholesale.

Q.—You got wholesale prices and quoted retail, and you say that in 1924 they sold wholesale?

A.—I don't know that there is any set wholesale price.

Q.—I see.

Re-examination of Mr. Bedford by Mr. Finlayson.

Q—You know, I suppose, Mr. Bedford, of your own general knowledge· up there something as to the volume of the work of the Government in 1924 as against 1925?

A.—Yes.

Q.—How did it compare?

A.—In 1925 it was greater.

Q.—The figures show that several firms got altogether $10,000 in 1924 and in 1925 $81,774, so that the volume would be ten times as great?

A.—Yes.

Q.—Eight times as great, I mean. The same people got eight times as much. You knew that in the trade?

A.—Sure

Q.—That would be one reason why you got more in 1925 than in 1924?

A—Yes.

Q.—There was more to be had?

A.—Yes.

Q.—One or two other things. In the fall of 1924 I see there was nearly $2.000 for supplies on the parking stage?

A.—Yes, at the aerodrome.

Q.—You were getting some there? That was stuff ordered from you?

A.—Yes, sir.

Q.—And I think Mr. Lyons' books show that none came from the Lyons Company?

A.—No.

Q.—I want to see if you were right in what you assented to to Mr. Sinclair. The books showed all your purchases, all your sales to the Government. I think nearly two-thirds were purchased from the Cochrane and Howlands?
A.—Yes.

Q.—The goods you sold to the Government that came from the Lyons Company, were only one-third, outside the pipe—a much smaller portion from the Lyons Company?
A.—Yes.

Q.—Somebody said the other night that no retail store carries beds or bedding and to-day you said that perhaps a drygoods man might?
A.—When I spoke of beds and bedding we were speaking of camp beds.
CHAIRMAN: He said blankets.
WITNESS: We were referring to double-decker construction camp beds.
MR. FINLAYSON: And who carries them at the Sault?
A.—I question whether any person does. You are referring to retail?
Q.—I am referring to camp beds. Who carries them, wholesale?
A.—The Lyons Fuel carry them in stock now.
Q.—As to bedding, blankets suitable for camp purposes?
A.—Yes.
Q.—In large quantities?
A.—Yes.
Q.—The dry goods stores could not supply them?
A.—No.
CHAIRMAN: Are they ordinary household blankets?
WITNESS: No, regular camp blankets.
CHAIRMAN: Something like military blankets?
WITNESS: Yes.
CHAIRMAN: The blankets and beds are for a particular class?
WITNESS: Yes.
CHAIRMAN: Not ordinary retail goods?
WITNESS: No.

MR. FINLAYSON: It also appeared from Mr. Lamb's evidence he had blankets from Hinchberg's, only he exhausted their stock?
A.—Yes.
Q.—And he came to fill in afterwards?
A.—Yes.
CHAIRMAN: How do you know?
A.—I don't know. I know I got some of the blanket business.
MR. FINLAYSON: Mr. Lamb told us that his practice when he wanted a list of articles of any extent was to make out a list and send around to the different stores?
A.—Yes.
Q.—And on that list you marked out what you thought you could supply?
A.—Yes.
Q.—With quantities?
A.—Yes.
Q.—That would be a typewritten list would it?
A.—Yes.
Q.—Covering all the supplies he wanted?
A.—Yes.
Q.—And you figured on that in competition with the others?
A.—Yes.

Q.—I suppose there were orders in an emergency when some article or an extra bed or blankets were wanted in a hurry?

A.—Sometimes.

Q.—And you got a telephone message asking for quotations?

A.—Yes.

Q.—But as a general rule when a number of things were wanted a quotation list was sent out?

A.—Yes.

Q.—Had you any—what was your treatment by Mr. Lamb or the Department?

A.—The same as anybody else.

Q.—He used you fairly?

A.—Yes.

Q.—Anything beyond that?

A.—No. I don't think so.

CHAIRMAN: No special consideration?

WITNESS: No, sir.

MR. FINLAYSON: Mr. Zavitz's name is down. I don't know whether anyone wants to call him. We had better clean him up.

Edwin John Zavitz called, sworn. Examined by Mr. Finalyson.

Q.—You are Deputy-Minister in charge of the Forestry Branch?

A.—The Branch of Forestry.

Q.—You have charge of that branch?

A.—Yes.

Q.—What does that branch include?

A.—Forest protection, forest surveys, reforestration and forest investigations.

Q.—You have nothing to do with the sale of timber limits or operations of the licensees?

A.—No.

Q.—And also nothing to do with the pulp concessionaires?

A.—No.

Q.—And I suppose you have nothing to do with road contracts?

A.—No.

Q.—The only thing you know of in connection with this inquiry is as to the aerodrome?

A.—Yes.

Q.—That is under your branch?

A.—Yes.

Q.—I don't want to go into anything except to ask general questions. The aerodrome plans were prepared here?

A.—Yes.

Q.—By whom?

A.—Mr. Gourlay.

Q.—What is his position?

A.—Engineer in the Northern Development. Architect and engineer.

Q.—He collaborated with your department in the preparation of the plans?

A.—Yes.

Q.—We heard the other night that he and Captain Maxwell—he is the head—

A.—Director of the Air Service.

Q.—He and Captain Maxwell made some inquiries and even a trip round to find out the best kind of building to put up?

A.—Yes. They crossed the line and looked over some of the buildings there before the plans were prepared.

Q.—Did they prepare the plans together?

A.—Yes.

Q.—And they were approved by you in the regular way?

A.—Yes, sir. In a general way.

Q.—You are not a flying man?

A.—No, sir.

Q.—Under you they were prepared in a regular way?

A.—Yes, sir.

Q.—And was the contract let?

A.—Yes, sir.

Q.—After proper tenders had been asked?

A.—Yes.

Q.—And the Government regulations were observed as to the advertising?

A.—Yes.

Q.—Were tenders received in a public way?

A.—Yes.

Q.—Were you present when the tenders were opened?

A.—No, sir.

Q.—Who did that?

A.—They were opened as I recall it, in the presence of Mr. Gourlay and the Minister. I am not sure whether Captain Maxwell was there.

Q.—The Minister suggests you were away at the time?

A.—I was away at that time.

Q.—Do you know whether the contract was given to the lowest tenderer?

A.—Yes, sir.

Q.—And an architect was appointed to supervise the construction?

A.—Yes.

Q.—Did he proceed in the usual way?

A.—I think so.

Q.—Payment would be made by progress certificates?

A.—Yes.

Q.—Certified by you?

Q.—Just one general question. Was there any peculiar incident in connection with either the advertisement for tenders or the letting of the contract or in payment?

A.—Nothing that I know of.

Q.—As far as you know it was regular business?

A.—Yes.

A.—And you know of no irregularity or impropriety in connection with the whole matter?

A.—I don't know of any.

Q.—Mr. Raney, any questions?

Mr. Raney: No.

Mr. Finlayson: You, Mr. Fisher? No? All right Mr. Zavitz. I think that exhausts the witnesses, except Mr. Fullerton, whom Mr. Raney has asked for. Are you particular about Labarge?

Mr. Raney: Yes.

Mr. Finlayson: Any other?

Mr. RANEY: I am not particular about Walsh.

Mr. FINLAYSON: Walsh will be dropped.

CHAIRMAN: Labarge will come as soon as the doctor allows him to.

Mr. FINLAYSON: Captain Maxwell—it depends on when he gets here. Well, call Mr. Fullerton.

Charles Herbert Fullerton sworn. Examined by Mr. Finlayson.

Q.—Mr. Fullerton you are Deputy Minister in charge of the Northern Development Branch?

A.—Yes.

Q.—Lands and Forests Department?

A.—Yes.

Q.—Before becoming Deputy Minister you were a director for a good many years? How many years have you been in charge of this branch?

A.—About six years, five and a half I think.

Q.—And prior to that, what were you doing?

A.—I was superintendent on colonization roads.

Q.—For the Ontario Government?

A.—Yes.

Q.—How long have you been in the Government service?

A.—About ten years.

Q.—I believe you are an engineer by profession?

A.—Yes.

Q.—Toronto graduate?

A.—Yes.

Q.—So you are a qualified engineer with how many years' experience in engineering?

A.—Including service here, about twenty-five.

Q.—You have been long enough in the service and having attained the position of Deputy Minister you are above and beyond politics?

A.—I hope so.

Mr. RANEY: Has Mr. Lang been subpoened?

CHAIRMAN: Do you mean the former engineer at the Sault? He is in private practice at the Sault.

WITNESS: Not since 1924 with the Department.

Mr. RANEY: I thought the name Lamb, was Lang.

Mr. FINLAYSON: Now, Mr. Fullerton, you know the general object of this inquiry?

A.—Well, I can guess.

Q.—And dealing with the personal aspect of it first. You have been in charge of this work since June, 1923, when the present minister came into office?

A.—Yes.

Q.—Can you tell me whether he has, or has not, attempted to use any influence to secure business directly, or indirectly, for the Lyons Company?

A.—Not to my knowledge.

Q.—Then I take it he has never attempted that from you?

A.—No.

Q.—Have any instructions come to you—I don't mean formal instructions—suggestions passed on?

A.—No.

Q.—Except the time he notified you to instruct the engineer not to purchase?

A.—That was negative.

Q.—When was that?

A.—About a year ago.

Q.—That is the letter Mr. Lamb produced? On file here?

A.—Yes.

Q.—That was the only occasion that the Minister discussed with you the question of purchasing goods from that company?

A.—Yes.

Q.—Now, dealing with these matters one at a time. Was the aerodrome contract in your department?

A.—No.

Q.—Did you have anything to do with it?

A.—One of our architects was loaned to the Forestry Branch to do some work on it.

Q.—Mr. Gourlay?

A.—Yes.

Q.—Preparing plans and specifications?

A.—Yes.

Q.—After that it was under Mr. Zavitz's branch?

A.—Yes, I had no knowledge of the work at all.

Q.—You know nothing about that at all?

A.—Nothing.

Q.—Let us get to the McNamara contracts. I would like to take up the Coniston road first. Were you in the room when Mr. Hoskins gave evidence?

A.—I don't know whether I was in the whole of the time; part of the time I was.

Q.—Will you tell us how the estimate of quantities on which tenders are asked is prepared?

A.—Cross-sections of the road to be constructed are taken and a ground line established; the width of the road established and from that calculations o the quantities are made.

Q.—Who are the actual measurements and cross-sections made by?

A.—In this particular Sudbury-Coniston job?

Q.—Generally, whose duty is it?

A.—Somebody out in the field.

Q.—Under whom?

A.—Under the district engineer.

Q.—To eliminate one thing: Referring to Mr. Lamb and Mr. Hoskins, are they capable engineers?

A.—Yes.

Q.—Qualified also?

A.—Yes.

Q.—Let us start in on the Coniston road, the same one. In that case who prepared the cross-sections and tracings?

A.—Which cross-sections?

Q.—For the Coniston road. Do you know who did it?

A.—I don't know.

Q.—In what form does it come to you?

A.—Well, the cross-section at each point, whether fifty feet or whatever distance it is, shows the contour of the ground across the road.

Q.—It comes to you on sheets?

A.—Yes.

Q.—The cross-section is mapped out on paper and marked—

CHAIRMAN: On draughting paper.

WITNESS: It is plotted on some kind of paper. It may be on draughting paper or section paper.

Q.—At what intervals are cross-sections made?

A.—Usually fifty feet unless something exceptional interferes.

Q.—Is fifty feet good engineering practice?

/A.—For that class of work, yes.

A.—If the roads present unusual features between cross-sections there should be another one made?

A.—Yes.

Q.—These come down from the field as we have been told, under the resident engineer's certificate?

A.—Yes.

Q.—And what happens to them in your office?

A.—They are taken into the draughting room and a cross-section of the road is made, knowing what the elevation and grade is, and plotted over the cross-sectional lines on the paper and from that the area is taken off the sheets and calculated.

Q.—You use them to plot out contours?

A.—At least somebody does it.

Q.—I don't mean you personally. It is done by competent and experienced men?

A.—Yes.

Q.—Who had charge of that in your branch?

A.—Mr. Simpson is chief engineer. I don't know what draughtsman completed this work.

Q.—How are the quantities worked out?

A.—Well, the cross-sectional area is worked out at each point and then the length is known between points, fifty feet, and the volume of the material to be taken out is calculated. There is a recognized formula for that.

Q.—By adding up the sections you get the bulk, or total road—is that the idea?

A.—That is the way it is done.

Q.—Well, now, what is the next step? After ascertaining the quantities what do you proceed to do next? .

A.—Are you speaking before or after the contract?

Q.—Before. What I want to get is one statement from you as to how this is worked out and then I will ask if that applies to all work. After the draughtsmen's work you make multiplications or additions and you find out what quantities have to be removed?

A.—Yes.

Q.—And then what do you do?

A.—Prepare estimates of cost.

Q.—Do you compete? Do you put in a tender?

A.—We have done in some cases.

Q.—Sometimes you put in a tender against the public?

A.—Yes.

Q.—Always or occasionally?

A.—We have not done it always.

Q.—When these are prepared, what is the next step?

A.—Forms for bidders are prepared and tenders advertised for.

Q.—What is the departmental regulation as to the length of advertising?

A.—That varies; ten days to two weeks.

Q.—Where do you advertise?

A.—Large contracts in the *Canadian Engineer*, the *Contract Record* and in the local paper.

Q.—In this case was that done?

A.—I don't recall; I am certain the *Canadian Engineer* and *Contract Record*. I don't recall whether it was advertised in the local paper or not.

Q.—The tenders come in addressed to whom?

A.—Addressed to the Minister.

Q.—And where do they come to the Department?

A.—Some go to him and some directly to me.

Q.—What is the practice in the Department as to opening the tenders?

A.—The Minister opens them.

Q.—In your presence?

A.—In my presence or the presence of someone else.

Q.—I suppose—your presence—that means your department?

A.—I am speaking for myself. I expect I was there generally always likely, when the tenders were opened.

Q.—Do you remember anything in particular in connection with the preparations of these Coniston road quantities, forms of tender, advertising or opening the tenders? That all went through in the regular departmental way?

A.—I don't remember anything different.

Q.—We heard the McNamara Company got the contract?

A.—Yes.

Q.—Have they been contracting with your department for some time?

A.—Not before that.

Q.—Did they put up the usual security?

A.—Yes.

Q.—Having got the contract did you pass it on to the resident engineer?

A.—The district engineer is notified of the name of the contractor.

Q.—Who is in charge of that?

A.—The district engineer and his staff.

Q.—Do you inspect from time to time?

A.—No.

Q.—Personally?

A.—No.

Q.—We have heard of the Minister being in Sudbury in the spring and discussing with the Board of Trade and some of the officials. Were you there?

A.—I was with him.

Q.—When was that?

A.—That was about the end of April, 1924.

Q.—The 28th we have heard. I believe the Board of Trade and municipal officials met him and made application for Government work in that district?

A.—I don't just know who the representatives were. They were prominent citizens of the town and Board of Trade and Rotary Club and the Mayor of the town was there. I don't know whether they were there in an official capacity.

Q.—Did you go over the ground of the various works?

A.—We went over the Sudbury-Coniston road.

Q.—Did you go over the Creighton-Copper Cliff?

A.—I think we did.

Q.—Were those mentioned as being work for that season at the public meeting?

A.—Yes. The Sudbury-Coniston road was in particular and the other roads were grouped together. I don't know how many were included. I am certain the Creighton-Copper Cliff was one and there was another.

Q.—I am told the ones considered were the road to the Creighton mine from Sudbury via the Creighton mine to Chelmsford; the Sudbury to Long Lake road; from Sudbury out to Massey Bay and the concrete road, Sudbury to Coniston. Was that the programme taken up on the 28th of April?

A.—Yes.

Q.—How many were there at the meeting?

A.—About a thousand.

Q.—Whom did it include?

A.—As many as we could get in the dining room and around the hotel.

Q.—It was a public affair?

A.—Yes.

Q.—The whole of Sudbury knew there was going to be a road programme?

A.—Yes.

Q.—Let us get on. After the work was started do you know anything in connection with the construction of the work? Were you up again?

A.—I did not know until the work was finished.

Q.—Do you know of any incident you should draw to the attention of the Committee that occurred during the construction of the work?

A.—There was not anything that occurred.

Q.—It went on in the regular departmental routine?

A.—Yes.

Q.—Any application for special consideration by the McNamara brothers?

A.—He had a claim for extras, three or four thousand dollars.

Q.—What was done?

A.—Settlement was made. I don't know whether he got two-thirds or half. He got a portion of the claim.

Q.—We have heard you made that?

A.—Yes.

Q.—The Minister had nothing to do with it?

A.—I mentioned to him to—

Q.—You reported?

A.—Yes.

Q.—You actually made the settlement?

A.—Yes.

Q.—We have heard that McNamaras claim a large amount and only got a part?

A.—That is true.

Q.—Apart from that there was no change in the contract?

A.—No.

Q.—Something was said the other night about auditors, a lot of time was taken up.

CHAIRMAN: I don't think there was anything in that, Mr. Finlayson, worth going ahead with. Everybody understands that situation.

Q.—Then payments were made on your certificate?

A.—Payment was made each month.

Q.—Then a final payment?

A.—Yes.

Q.—You have told us everything about the carrying out of the contract?

A.—Everything I have in mind.

Q.—Now something has been said about the fact that the contract tender was $188,000 and the final payment $384,000, an increase of over 100 per cent., what do you say about that?

A.—In what way?

Q.—Is there anything irregular there? Any impropriety?

A.—No impropriety.

Q.—And no irregularity?

A.—No irregularity.

Q.—You say it was quite proper?

A.—Yes.

Q.—What do you say as to such a disparity?

A.—There may have been reasons for it.

Q.—What were they?

A.—I would have to look at the tender form there.

Mr. FISHER: There is an answer to the questions prepared?

Mr. FINLAYSON: Yes.

WITNESS: That was the question Mr. Fisher asked.

Mr. FINLAYSON: Have you a copy? On the left here, these are the itemsr

WITNESS: Yes. Rock, concrete pavement, concrete and culverts and so on, gravel, crushed stones, placing reinforcement, scarifying and reshaping, vitrified pipe, end walls, trimming and levelling earth shoulders—there are twenty-one different classes of items. Several of these were not used at all in this job but those are the standard items for that contract.

Q.—The idea of the twenty-one being in is to try to see there was nothing unforeseen?

A.—Yes.

Q.—And this second column shows the concrete pavement, estimated quantity 65,400, what is that—yards?

A.—Square yards.

Q.—And the, what is the actual amount? Is that shown?

A.—Sixty-four thousand seven hundred and twelve.

Q.—So that you estimated closely on that?

A.—Yes.

Q.—It actually turned out to be a trifle less?

A.—Yes.

Q.—The next item is scarifying and reshaping roadway, 65,400 square yards and the actual quantity 64,712 paid for?

A.—Yes.

Q.—That is a very small decrease. Item 21, earth shoulders?

A.—Thirty-six thousand six hundred and ninety-nine cubic yards.

Q.—And it turned out 36,326?

A.—Yes.

Q.—That is very close too? Where is the big disparity?

A.—In some of the quantities not estimated.

Q.—These three items we have gone over are practically your estimates, and they were correct?

A.—Yes.

Q.—Take Item Number 1; earth excavation. There is no estimated quantity?

A.—No.

Mr. KEITH: Those are on a unit basis?

MR. FINLAYSON: Yes, on a unit basis. Do I understand that the only things you had actual quantities on were concrete pavement, scarifying and reshaping and trimming and levelling earth shoulders, and that those figures were very accurate?

A.—Yes.

Q.—But there were blanks as to earth excavation, and rock excavation were there?

A.—Earth $42,000.

Q.—Why was not that in?

A.—No, 42,000 yards and 5,100 the rock.

Q.—Why were they not estimated at the time tenders were asked?

A.—When we advertised for tenders we drew up a tender form in such a manner that we asked for unit prices and we put in the prices we had estimates on. We only put in quantities we had estimates of. The Minister had undertaken to build this road that season and have it finished by the fall and in order to get the thing started we had to advertise before we received the estimates on these other quantities.

Q.—So that although you knew there would be a large amount of earth and rock excavation you did not know the quantities when you advertised for tenders and you asked for prices but with no estimate of the quantity?

A.—No.

CHAIRMAN: Those unit prices are per yard?

A.—Yes.

Q.—And you got the unit prices on all the twenty-one items?

A.—Yes, on all.

Q.—The only three you had an estimate on were those I have mentioned and they were accurate. Earth excavation is large, rock excavation is a considerable item and placing reinforcements—

A.—As far as that is concerned we had no idea where it would be placed until as construction progressed.

Q.—I can understand that would be difficult to anticipate. But about the others—

A.—We did not receive information from the district officer and we did not want to hold up the advertisements so we had to leave in blanks.

Q.—Is that a common practice?

A.—We endeavour as far as we can to give the contractor some idea of the figures so that he may tender.

Q.—Is this done frequently?

A.—Not frequently. We don't do it always. We try to get quantities if we can and if not we advertise without them. We try to give the contractor a rough idea.

Q.—He goes over the ground and forms his own opinion?

A.—Yes.

Q.—They all have an opportunity to do that?

A.—Yes.

Q.—It naturally results in a vast difference between the tender and the actual payment?

A.—That accounts for the difference.

Q.—Do I put it fairly when I say that the difference of 100 per cent. is caused not by mistakes in quantities but by omission of quantities?

A.—Yes.

Q.—There is a large quantity as to earth and a small quantity as to rock, but the unit is much higher?

A.—Yes.

Q.—And then the concrete and culverts, reinforcements seems to be a large item. Pipe, vitrified pipe, item number 13, that is lineal feet?

A.—One thousand one hundred and fifty-one feet.

Q.—The Lumsden Company, Macdonald, McNamara and Federal Comapny are the four tenderers. Figures are worked out to show the comparison in the Department?

A.—Yes.

Q.—Simply based on Items 3, 9 and 21, is that right?

A.—Yes.

Q.—Well, then, Mr. Fullerton is that any new procedure in the Department?

A.—Which procedure?

Q.—Asking for tenders on a form in which you do not give the rock and earth quantities?

A.—I don't know.

Q.—Did you see this before it went out?

A.—Oh, yes.

Q.—Is this the explanation: You had not had contracts like this before?

A.—That is so.

Q.—What kind had you before?

A.—They were nearly all clearing, stumping, gravelling and crushing rock.

Q.—Opening up roads; individual operations?

A.—Yes.

Q.—And this was the first time you had conducted the unit system?

A.—We adopted it from the Department of Highways.

A.—It came from the Department of Highways?

A.—Yes.

Q.—That is the unit system?

A.—Yes.

Q.—And had you obtained your material from the Highway Department?

A.—What material?

Q.—Specifications, forms of tender and so on?

A.—Yes, we drafted them from their forms. I don't know that they are exactly the same.

Q.—It is a common contract in the Highways Department?

A.—Yes.

Q.—There is an essential difference with the Highways Department as to cement?

A.—Yes.

Q.—Will you explain that?

A.—In the Department of Highways specifications they state they furnish cement to the contractors who obtain contracts for the roads but we decided to put it up to the contractor to purchase his own cement.

Q.—There was a reason for that?

A.—Well, it is up in the north country and we would have to store it and take care of the bags. There would be the question of demurrage and claims and we would have the trouble of handling without much profit. There would be a deterioration in the cement. In case it hardens it is useless.

Q.—In Southern Ontario it is different?

A.—There are places where it can be stored and it can be moved on to the next job.

Q.—In Southern Ontario it is different?

A.—There are places where it can be stored and it can be moved on to the next job.

Q.—Up there your jobs are spread over large areas?

A.—In addition to that it is easy to get cement quickly in Southern Ontario because we are not so far from the place of manufacture.

Q.—You were not taking any chance up there, but were putting it up to the contractor?

A.—Yes.

Q.—The Minister tells me you let the contractor supply tarvia?

A.—Yes.

Q.—Whereas in the Highways they supply it?

A —Yes.

Q.—This contract then was carried out and paid for in the regular way?

A.—Yes.

Q.—Take up the other contract, the Creighton-Copper Cliff, that is the contract assigned from Labarge?

A.—Yes.

Q.—Was that road mentioned at the time by the Minister on April 28th?

A.—Yes.

Q.—The procedure also adopted in this case you have already outlined?

A.—Yes.

Q.—Have you got before you a sheet referring to this? In this I see quite a lot of detail as to estimated quantities?

A.—Yes.

Q.—Why the difference between this and the other?

A.—Well, we had asked the district engineer to obtain quantities on the Creighton-Copper Cliff road and a few days later we received—those are arbitrary quantities.

Q.—The amounts here?

A.—Yes. We did not receive the estimates up there. In order to get out the advertising we put them in. It was the middle of August and we could not wait.

Q.—The other was a hurry in the spring and this was a converse case?

A.—Yes.

Q.—Item three seems to be the first big one, tar penetration and surfacing, estimated quantity 50,000 yards and actual quantity 52,000?

A.—Yes.

Q.—That is quite close. I suppose that is arrived at by taking the length and the width?

A.—We knew the length and width.

Q.—Next one, asphalt penetration, that is a blank, because it was an alternative.?

A.—It was a blank because it was made on tar instead of asphalt.

Q.—Concrete and culverts 350 yards; turned out 820. I suppose that as the work progressed there would be further orders?

A.—I don't know what culverts were there. Those they required we put in.

Q.—Agricultural tile 1,800 lineal feet and actually 9,200?

A.—Well, as far as those quantities are concerned we put in just arbitrary quantities for the purpose of the tender so that we could calculate who would be the lowest tenderer:

Q.—Gravel—none was used apparently?

A.—No.

Q.—Crushed stone, an increase?

A.—As far as the crushed stone is concerned at the time the work was advertised and at the time we went over the road in the spring it was represented that it had been made a stone road some years ago and consequently not much crushed stone would be required but as the work progressed it was essential to use it.

Q.—That was rock used for the foundation?

A.—Yes.

Q.—Scarifying and reshaping 15,000 estimated, and actually 44,000. Trimming and levelling earth shoulders, 32,000. Clearing, grubbing, nothing done. And then some pipe. I suppose your explanation is the same? You were adopting the Highway plan for trying out a new form of contract?

A.—Yes.

Q.—As to this contract was there any dispute or any controversy as to amounts?

A.—The only controversy was with regard to that crushed stone.

Q.—Item Number 8?

A.—Before we went ahead with that and allowed it to be done we had a conference or two and an examination made. I sent the chief engineer there and sent the supervisor of construction to see if there was anything in the claim that extra rock should be put in.

Q.—After the work?

A.—While it was progressing.

Q.—You sent the chief engineer and supervisor, and what did they report?

A.—They reported that it was necessary.

Q.—That would make a large item in the increase?

A.—Yes, about 3,500 extra yards.

Q.—What is it, $5 a cubic yard?

A.—Yes.

Q.—What proportion of the increase would that be roughly?

A.—That would be about $17,500.

Q.—Generally, as to this contract, Mr. Fullerton, was there any other dispute except when you verified that particular change and had an inspection made?

A.—No.

Q.—The figures were arrived at and paid on the certificate?

A.—Yes.

Q.—There was no room for any dispute?

A.—No.

Q.—The other contracts we are interested in are the contracts at Sault Ste. Marie, the street there. What did you have to do with them?

A.—I did not have anything more than looking after the formality when the account came in.

Q.—The Department were paying 50 per cent. of the operation?

A.—Yes.

Q.—Who were you billed by?

A.—By the City of Sault Ste. Marie.

Q.—They billed you for their claim of 50 per cent. on the centre twenty feet?

A.—Of course I had to get a certificate from the district engineer and a copy of the agreement with the City of Sault Ste. Marie and then I passed the account.

Q.—You got a copy of the agreement and the district engineer's report to verify the expenditure and then the city was paid?

A.—Yes.

Q.—You had no dealings with the McNamara people?

A.—No.

Q.—I suppose that applies to the Wallace Terrace?

A.—Yes.

Q.—Simply verification of the contract figures and performance of the work?

A.—Yes.

Q.—Generally, as to these McNamara contracts, these two contracts, was any special consideration given to this contractor by the Department?

A.—In what way?

Q.—Any special consideration other than what he was entitled to?

A.—No.

Q.—All right.

Mr. Fullerton examined by Mr. Fisher.

Q.—Look at Sudbury first. Was that given to the lowest contractor according to your way of figuring?

A.—Yes.

Q.—MacDonald Brothers are dependable contractors, reputable contractors?

A.—I don't know. I think they are from North Bay.

Q.—They were all right so far as you knew?

A.—Yes.

Q.—Do I understand then that you awarded this contract on three items?

A.—Yes.

Q.—There are twenty-one items that went into the making of this road and you awarded the contract on three?

A.—Yes.

MR. FINLAYSON: Was there twenty-one?

MR. FISHER: Twenty-one were considered.

MR. FINLAYSON: They didn't all go in?

MR. FISHER: Twelve items actually did go in. The figure was twenty-one and twelve actually went in and you figured and awarded the tender on three only?

A.—Yes.

Q.—And the others therefore did not have anything to do with the awarding of the contract?

A.—No.

Q.—Take the first, earth excavation. That is a large item?

A.—Yes.

Q.—And it did not make any difference how much earth excavation there was?

A.—No.

Q.—And it did not make any difference how much rock was taken out and what the price was?

A.—No.

Q.—No effect on any of the contracts?

A.—No.

Q.—And the same applies to concrete and culverts and the item of pipe there, Number 5?

A.—Yes.

Q.—The gravel did not have anything to do with getting the contract?

A.—No.

Q.—The crushed stone in place was not considered?

A.—No.

Q.—Nor the placing of reinforcement in the pavement?

A.—No.

Q.—Well, the, what is the next one; vitrified pipe. That did not go in?

A.—Well there was only 1,100 feet of that.

Q.—And Number 20 is what? Rubble masonry. That did not come in?

A.—No.

Q.—And 21, trimming and levelling earth shoulders?

A.—Yes, that did. We applied unit prices to the quantities that we knew.

Q.—You applied unit prices but you only used three quantities?

A.—They were the only ones we knew.

Q.—You started to build the road and in figuring who was entitled to get the contract you considered only the concrete pavement, scarifying and trimming and levelling earth shoulders?

A.—Yes.

Q.—What were these different tenders? How did they work out?

A.—Taking these three quantities employed the unit prices of the contractors were:

Federal Company	$202,758.75
Lumsden Engineering Co	208,244.85
Macdonald Brothers	192,021 90
McNamara	188,751.90

Q.—Have you got any idea how it worked out if you applied all the quantities, all the items, that went into the road. Have you figured it on all the items?

A.—No. We didn't have the quantities. Applying the unit prices to these three quantities made the McNamaras the lowest. There was no other way of determining who should get the contract when they submitted unit prices and we only knew three quantities.

Q.—Why not? You could have estimated the other quantities?

A.—Well, I suppose we could have put in arbitrary quantities, but we didn't have them.

Q.—This engineer said he made cross-sections?

A.—So he did.

Q.—And you could not get that—?

A.—Not before the contract was advertised.

Q.—The contract was advertised when you had only three quantities?

A.—No.

Q.—What would you think of me if I wanted to put up a building and awarded the tender on the foundation and the plumbing?

A.—I suppose that so far as that is concerned it would not matter what I thought.

Q.—Just show the way this thing works. Earth excavation, actual quantity taken out 42,554 yards?

A.—Yes.

Q.—Macdonald was twenty-six cents lower than McNamara on that?

MR. RANEY: Let me interrupt. My examination is going to be somewhat lengthy on some of the matters. I presume Mr. Fisher will keep on until adjournment. I wonder if it could be arranged for me to get away and adjourn Mr. Fisher's examination?

MR. LEWIS: I think there is no question about that. We adjourn until 1.30 to-morrow, but we have summoned several witnesses for then.

MR. RANEY: I could finish later. Very well, then.

MR. FISHER (Continuing): Macdonald was twenty cents lower than McNamara on that. On that one item McNamara was higher than Macdonald, $8,510?

A.—At the time the contract was awarded we did not know that.

Q.—I am asking about it now?

A.—Yes, it was lower.

Q.—According to my arithmetic, $8,510, McNamara would have been higher on earth excavation. Now 2 is rock. McNamara was high on that. His price was $6.50 and Macdonald, $2.50?

Q.—That is right, is it not, Mr. Fullerton?

A.—Yes.

Q.—A difference of $4, McNamara higher than Macdonald. So that applied to the quantity 5,101 yards, McNamara was high $20,404. The next item, concrete pavement, that is one you have estimated on, Number 4. You had 865 in concrete—

A.—Eight hundred and twenty-five.

Q.—Yes. Macdonald, $24; McNamara, $16; a difference of $8?

MR. FINLAYSON: You have them reversed, haven't you? McNamara $24 and Macdonald $16.

Q.—That is a difference of $8 and that makes a difference in that item of $6,600?

A.—Yes.

Q.—The next item is tile in place. Macdonald sixty-five cents, McNamara ninety-five cents. McNamara is higher thirty cents and applying that to the quantity 23,362, McNamara was high $7,008?

A.—Something like that.

MR. FINLAYSON: The best thing would be to check these figures.

MR. RANEY: Give me just the high figures.

MR. FINLAYSON: I would make the suggestion that we try and have this work figured out.

MR. FISHER: I want my figures checked. I should like to run over it.

Q.—The next one, gravel, Macdonald, $3.50; McNamara, $1.75; so that McNamara was $1.75 lower?

MR. LEWIS: Lower? Higher.

MR. FISHER: Macdonald, 3.56; McNamara, $4.75; so that he was high $1.25. $1.25 times 2,996, that is $3,770 on that item McNamara would have been higher than Macdonald?

A.—Something less than that.

Q.—Number 7. Crushed stone placed. Macdonald, $3; McNamara, $4.75; high, $1.75. The quantity is 2,715 yards?

MR. LEWIS: Four thousand seven hundred and fifty-three dollars.

Mr. Fisher: Higher than Macdonald. Next, Item 8, placing reinforcement in pavement, and on that Macdonald's price is ten cents and McNamara seven cents, so that is lower by three cents and the quantity is $582,408.

Mr. Lewis: Seventeen thousand four hundred and seventy-two dollars and twenty-four cents.

Mr. Finlayson: You are a lightning calculator.

Mr. Fisher· Macdonald was high on that $17,472.24. Nine is in.

Mr. Finlayson: You have to give him credit for that. Finish that· Get what that figured.

Mr. Fisher: Number 13, Macdonald $1.90—

Mr. Finlayson: The chairman wants 9. That is 64,712 on which there was Macdonald, thirty-five and McNamara seven cents. That is twenty-eight cents difference. That will be $16,000 difference.

Mr. Fisher: Number 13. Macdonald, $1.90; McNamara, $2.50; a difference of sixty cents and the quantity is 1,151.

Mr. Lewis: Six hundred and ninety dollars and sixty cents.

Mr. Fisher: Twenty next. Macdonald $38 and the other man $9, that is a difference of $29 in favour of McNamara, the quantity, 108.

Mr. Fullerton: About $3,000.

Mr. Lewis: Three thousand one hundred and thirty-two dollars.

Mr. Finlayson: I suggest that somebody might do this with Mr. Fullerton in the Department and have it worked out.

Mr. Raney: I suggest that we ask the reporter to give us the cross-examination to-night. Then you have the whole business.

Mr. Lewis: Just the cross-examination of Mr. Fullerton.

Mr. Fisher: These are the figures: $8,510, $20,204, $6,600, $7,008, $2,996. It is quite evident, is it not, that if this contract had been awarded on the basis of work done it would have gone to Macdonald and not to McNamara?

A.—I don't know that. I have not the quantities. I have just listened to you calculations.

Q.—There was less than $4,000 between them?

A.—Something like that.

Q.—And the only thing in favour of McNamara is the item of $17,000?

Mr. Finlayson: Another item of $3,132, the last item.

Mr. Fisher: With these figures it seems quite evident that if the contract had been awarded on the work done, or a proper estimate of it, that Macdonald would have got the contract and not McNamara. Isn't that a fact?

A.—I don't know. I have your figures but I have not added them.

Q.—Perhaps the best thing is to let Mr. Fullerton check them up. As to the Creighton-Copper Cliff contract. What did you have before you in the way of estimated quantities when you awarded that contract?

A.—We estimated on the quantities opposite the numbers 1, 2,—

Q.—What data had you before you?

A.—We had the length of the road; we had the width and we just approximated the rest for tender purposes.

Q.—You approximated the earth excavation at 500 and it was actually 11,417?

A.—Yes.

Q.—Did you think that an honest presumption?

A.—Yes.

Q.—Did you ever imagine that you were going to get away with that amount of excavation?

A.—Yes.

Q.—You estimated rock at 100 yards?

A.—Yes.

Q.—And it was 3,125?

A.—Yes.

Q.—Did you think that an honest estimate?

A.—It was not an estimate at all. It was an approximate figure to apply to unit prices.

Q.—It was not an approximate estimate of the work. That would be different?

A.—We had no knowledge of what would be required and did not try to estimate how much of these quantities would be done in this job.

Q.—Did you have any quantities that were near to right?

A.—Tiles. They were very closely right. Number 3, tar penetration.

Q.—What else?

A.—Number 10.

Q.—What is this for, 50,000 yards?

Mr. Finlayson: That is an alternative.

Q.—Did that enter into the calculation in awarding the contract?

A.—I think it did. I think all the contractors tendered the same on asphalt as on tar.

Q.—You could not award on two alternatives, not taking both?

A.—If it was the same price for them.

Q.—They didn't do that?

A.—Generally speaking they did. The asphalt was cheaper. It was a lower price on that.

Q.—Here is somebody for instance, Campbell, he estimates on tar penetration ninety-five cents and asphalt he estimates $1.10?

A.—Which one is that?

Q.—That is Campbell?

A.—Yes.

Q.—And McNamara on the other hand estimates that tar penetration is eighty-five and one-half cents and asphalt penetration eighty-two cents, so that one of them estimates asphalt penetration will cost fifteen cents more than the other and McNamara estimates that it would cost three and one-half cents less?

A.—Yes.

Q.—Which one of the jobs was done?

A.—Tar was done.

Mr. Finlayson: Number 3.

Q.—In figuring up the estimate did you take in asphalt?

A.—Yes.

Q.—The asphalt and tar penetration together, you added them?

A.—We did not add the tar and asphalt together. We made two results.

Q.—Suppose you give the results of your figuring as to the tenders.

A.—On the tar or asphalt?

Q.—Take both.

(Mr. Fullerton gave the amounts as tabulated.)

	Tar	Asphalt
Thornton	$99,600.00	$98,600.00
Campbell and Latimer	69,300.00	76,800.00
Gustranel and Zettina	76,116.00	77,616.00
McNamara Construction Co	61,190.00	58,440.00
Labarge and Co	61,165.00	59,165.00
St. Denis and Mooney	61,435.00	59,435.00
Warren Brothers	61,690.00	61,690.00
Grant Brothers	73,415.00	71,415.00
Law Construction Co	73,480.00	72,980.00
Chatooque and Knight	64,775.50	67,025.50

Q.—Who was low? Labarge first, McNamara second. St. Denis and Mooney third; tar. Asphalt, Labarge is low. St. Denis and Mooney second and McNamara third. The contract was given to Labarge?

A.—Yes. Fifty-nine thousand one hundred and sixty-five dollars for asphalt.

Q.—Concrete and culverts estimated quantities, 350 cubic yards?

A.—I don't call the 350 an estimate. It is an arbitrary quantity.

Q.—Item Number 5. Item 6, tile in place, arbitrarily fixed quantity 1,800 and actual quantity, 9,200. What is the tile used for?

A.—Drainage.

Q.—What is this: Gravel placed where directed, Number 7, 500 estimated cubic yards?

A.—We put it on, for fear there might be some gravel.

Q.—There was not?

A.—No.

Q.—Next, crushed stone, 500, arbitrarily fixed, and actual quantity, 3,959 cubic yards. Scarifying in something like what it ought to be, estimated 50,000?

A.—In that case, scarifying and reshaping, that depends on the length and width of the road.

Q.—Anybody could measure the road and figure that?

Mr. FINLAYSON: A whole lot of the tenders are about the same, five cents, five cents, seven cents.

Q.—Levelling shoulders is about the same?

A.—For the same reason. It depends on the road.

Q.—Clearing, two acres. You didn't clear anything?

A.—No.

Q.—Could you not tell in advance?

A.—There was a possibility there might be a diversion of some kind, to straighten out a curve.

Q.—I suppose you had the road laid out before you called for tenders?

A.—In what way?

Q.—You had engineers on the job seeing where to put the road?

A.—Yes, but there was liable to be a slight revision during construction.

Q.—Twelve is grubbing. The same applies to that. You thought there might be and there was not?

A.—Yes.

Q.—You reached a contract on arbitrary figures though some of them could not possibly be like the result?

A.—Except that there were three or four figures not arbitrary, asphalt penetration, 50,000 scarifying and reshaping, and Number 10. Those were large items we pretty well knew.

Q.—Earth excavation, 500 yards, turned out to be 11,417?

A.—Yes.

Q.—Rock excavated, 100, turns out to be 3,125.

MR. FINLAYSON: Labarge and McNamara and the other fellows are exactly the same.

MR. FISHER: That may be. Have you figured out the quantities as each turned out to be, which would be least?

A.—No.

Q.—Will you try?

MR. FINLAYSON: We have tried and it looks as though McNamara should get the contract instead of Labarge.

MR. LEWIS: Are you through?

MR. FISHER: A perusal of this (statement) may disclose a lot of things.

MR. LEWIS: Well, subject to those findings.

MR. FISHER: All right.

The Committee adjourned at 6 P.M. to meet the following day at 1.30.

PUBLIC ACCOUNTS COMMITTEE.

The Committee sat at 1.30 P.M., Thursday, March 25th, 1926. Mr. Lewis in the Chair.

MR. FINLAYSON: I was speaking to my friend, Mr. Fisher, who has been conducting the examination of Mr. Fullerton. I had asked Mr. Fullerton to let Mr. Fisher and myself have copies of his computations, and I understand he was looking for us this morning, but I guess we were both in the Private Bills Committee.

MR. FISHER: Can't he be sent for?

MR. FINLAYSON: Undoubtedly, but Mr. Oakley and Mr. Blake Jackson are here in connection with that other matter.

THE CHAIRMAN: We arranged we could call this meeting particularly to go into that matter to-day and clear up the Lyons matter when?

MR. FISHER: I don't expect to be here to-morrow. I wanted to finish up that matter with Mr. Fullerton. It would only take a very few minutes.

MR. FINLAYSON: It is now twenty minutes to two. The Oakley matter cannot take more than a few minutes.

THE CHAIRMAN: I think it will be over in half an hour.

MR. FINLAYSON: I don't know whether Mr. Fullerton's figures are ready or not.

THE CHAIRMAN: Well, make sure. What time do you want to leave, Mr. Fisher?

MR. FISHER: I don't need to go this afternoon.

THE CHAIRMAN: We arranged with Mr. Raney and Mr. Sinclair yesterday—

MR. FISHER: If you keep me around here, you don't know what trouble I will raise for you.

THE CHAIRMAN: Before we start taking evidence, I think the Committee will agree that if we sit until the House meets, and then to-morrow at 10 o'clock, that is about all we can be expected to do after the late session.

Mr. George Oakley, M.L.A., sworn.

MR. FINLAYSON: You are the member for Riverdale, in the Ontario Legislature?

A.—I am, yes.

Q.—And also, I understand, president of George Oakley, Limited?

A.—George Oakley & Son, Limited.

Q.—I believe that is an Ontario Corporation?

A.—Yes.

Q.—Incorporated under letters patent of the Province?

A.—Yes.

Q.—Can you tell me the object or powers of your company?

A.—Well, the object of our company is the cutting and fashioning of cut stone and marble. We have the right under our charter to go into building supplies or stone or marble properties.

Q.—To own and operate stone or marble properties, and cut and sell stone, is that it? And erect it, too?

A.—Yes.

THE CHAIRMAN: And you could also under your charter go into the general line of builders' supplies?

A.—Yes.

MR. FINLAYSON: When were you incorporated, Mr. Oakley?

A.—In 1911.

Q.—And before that, were you carrying on business as a partnership?

A.—Yes, my father and I carried on a partnership in 1906.

Q.—And in 1911 you were incorporated, and have been carrying on business under the Ontario charter ever since?

A.—Yes.

Q.—What is your position in the company?

A.—I am president and general manager.

Q.—Will you tell us, very briefly, what kind of work your firm are doing?

A.—We have been dealing in cut stone work in connection with many buildings through Toronto, through Ontario and as far east as Halifax.

Q.--Well, what properties have you? What plant?

A.—One plant on Logan Avenue, one on Booth Avenue, both in Toronto. We also have a plant at Point Edward, Ontario. It is not run under the name of George Oakley & Son but Central Canada Cut Stone Company.

Q.—A subsidiary?

A.—Yes.

Q.—I don't want to go over all the building, but what principal buildings in the city have you done stonework on?

A.—Well, we built a great many; for instance, the Manufacturers' Life Building is one of our recent jobs, on Bloor East; the new Toronto union station, the Royal Bank Building at the corner of King and Yonge is one of our buildings, the new Trinity College.

Q.—That will be sufficient. So that in these buildings were you general contractors or simply stone contractors?

A.—Sub-contractors in all cases.

Q.—Do you take general contracts?

A.—No.

Q.—I gathered from what you said about your charter you have not power?

A.—No, we haven't.

Q.—Then you confine yourselves and always have to stone work done on any job?

A.—Yes, stonework and marble.

THE CHAIRMAN: Does that mean just supplying the cut stone?

A.—Supplying and erecting.

MR. FINLAYSON: Now what stone was used in this new East Block?

A.—Queenston limestone.

Q.—An Ontario stone?

A.—Yes, it comes from St. David's, Ontario.

Q.—That is in the Niagara district?

A.—Yes.

Q.—Has this stone been used extensively in Ontario?

A.—It has been used for many years, but not as extensively as in this particular building. It has been used more for base courses, steps and landings.

Q.—Has it ever been used for construction of a large building?

A.—Not outside of some buildings locally over at St. Catharines. There is one fairly good job, but it has never been universally used in superstructures.

Q.—Well, then, this is the first instance where it was used for complete stonework of a large building?

A.—Of a building of this type.

THE CHAIRMAN: Mr. Hoskins, divisional engineer from Sudbury, who was examined yesterday, is enquiring whether he is needed again. He has some work to look after. I asked him to come to-day, but I think he was pretty well covered yesterday.

MR. FISHER: I think something depends on Mr. Fullerton's evidence.

MR. LEWIS: If necessary we can ask him to come back, but I think we are through with him.

MR. FINLAYSON: I understood that way, but if Mr. Fisher thinks he may require him, I don't think we should let him go.

MR. FISHER: When will you know about Mr. Fullerton?

THE CHAIRMAN: We hope to know before we adjourn.

MR. FISHER: Then let him stay for a while.

MR. FINLAYSON: Will you tell the Committee something of the nature of the stone, comparing it with other available building stones for structures of that type?

A.—Well, we in the local market here for years have used American stones, such as Indiana limestone and Ohio sandstone. They are used on account of their cheapness here. That is, the material in itself has very fine working qualities, and we can produce the finest product cheaper than ordinarily done with stone like Queenston.

Q.—Indiana limestone is one of the largest quarries in the world?

A.—Yes, largest dolomitic in the world.

Q.—And a very tractable stone?

A.—Yes.

Q.—And I understand also has the advantage you can get it in very large blocks, in anything you like, almost?

A.—Yes, to suit any detail an architect might desire in the way of large blocks, for columns and caps.

Q.—And well established in the trade all over?

A.—Yes.

Q.—And the other you are competing with?

A.—Ohio sandstone.

Q.—Similar to Indiana limestone?

A.—Only that it is a sandstone and perhaps not quite as adapted to detail work, highly detailed work, as Indiana limestone.

Q.—Are there any other Ontario stones competing?

A.—Credit Valley stone.

Q.—This main building is Credit Valley limestone?

A.—Sandstone.

Q.—What about it?

A.—Well, of course this is a brown stone, and the deposit is practically gone—exhausted. They have in the Credit Valley district new stone, but it is used more in smaller denominations, where they have courses, and use it with a rock-face finish. On account of the hardness of the stone, when you put dressing on it it becomes very expensive.

Q.—Well, we can all tell by appearance the stone in the East Block almost resembles marble.

A.—It has the same qualities as marble; it is a dolomite.

Q.—And what is a marble?

A.—A little farther advanced in its formation. It is hard to say where a hard limestone stops and a marble begins.

Q.—You say it approximates closely to marble?

A.—Very close.

Q.—What about its working qualities?

A.—The working qualities are more expensive than a stone like Indiana limestone.

• Q.—Why?

A.—On account of the hardness of the stone.

Q.—That is more difficult to carve?

A.—Yes.

Q.—What about the quantity of deposit over at St. David's?

A.—It looks, since they were on this job, as if they have a very large deposit there.

Q.—And what effect has the purchase of stone for this building had on the quarry property over there?

A.—Well, the impression now of many architects and builders is that this stone is adaptable to a fine class of good stone work, with the result many jobs are being specified to use Queenston, where it used to be Indiana limestone and Ohio sandstone.

Q.—What effect has it had on local production, that is the owners operating?

A.—Well, previous to this building being let in the Queenston stone, their output was very small. I think perhaps there was not very much money behind the proposition, but since this has come on I would say they produced last year three times as much stone as in any one season. It has opened up the quarry and it is a coming proposition. It has attracted the attention of builders and architects.

Q.—What about the company? Do I understand you they have been strengthened or reorganized?

A.—Strengthened, yes, new capital into the company.

Q.—And has the quarry opened deeper?

A.—Yes.

Q.—So as I gather, you introduced a new building material in Ontario?

A.—No question about it, there is a new industry established in Ontario.

Q.—How was the Ontario market, was there a wealth of material in stone?

21 J

A.—You mean our natural products? No, we haven't great quantities of stone.

Q.—And have we been importing very largely?

A.—Yes, I would say that in our business we import 95 per cent. of our raw material.

Q.—Getting down to this particular contract, Mr. Oakley, did you tender on the general contract?

A.—I tendered as a sub-contractor to several general contractors.

Q.—When the Government asked for tenders, did you tender at all?

A.—No.

Q.—That was a general contract covering excavation and erection of roof, I guess, too?

THE CHAIRMAN: Not the excavation, just the erection.

MR. FINLAYSON: You say you supplied figures, to whom?

A.—The different general contractors figuring on the work.

Q.—Can you tell me how many?

A.—Six or eight, I have some cards here that the general contractor would send out. Here are four forms we figured with.

Q.—The witness hands me a card dated, "Toronto, 3rd March, 1925; We are estimating general contract on the East Block, Parliament Buildings, F. R. Heakes, Architect, and would like to have your estimate on work in your line. If you are figuring on same, note alternatives. Estimate to be in our office not later than March 19, 1925. Jackson-Lewis Co., Limited, Contracting Engineers and Builders."

A.—It says on the stone work in our line.

Q.—It is addressed to George Oakley & Son, Limited, Booth Avenue, Toronto. It seems to be postmarked on the 3rd, too. Now I see another one on the 28th of February from the W. H. Yates Company, also referring to the East Block, Queen's Park, F. R. Heakes, Architect, and then one from Sullivan & Fried, Victoria Street. The card is not dated, but it is postmarked March 1st. Then a fourth card from Anglin Norcross, Limited, dated March 5th, 1925, to George Oakley & Sons, Limited. Are these cards all from general contractors asking you to tender on your own line?

A.—Yes, it is customary with general contractors, when estimating on a large project, to send out cards to different sub-contractors.

Q.—Inviting you to—

A.—Figure on the particular project they are interested in.

Q.—Then I see attached to it what is marked an office copy headed, "George Oakley & Sons, Limited," dated March 19, 1925, "George Oakley & Sons, Limited, Toronto"—what is this?

A.—Our regular form used in connection with all our work.

Q.—You propose to furnish and deliver cut stone according to plans and specifications prepared by the Ontario Public Works and Shop Drawings by the Company, and setting out details for the East Block?

A.—That is a copy of the proposal we send to all general contractors.

Q.—Do you remember how many that was sent to?

A.—I would say eight or ten.

Q.—The same figures sent to them all?

A.—Absolutely.

Q.—And that included the Jackson-Lewis Company?

A.—Yes.

Q.—Now did you enter into a contract with the Jackson-Lewis Company?

A.—I did.

Q.—Is this the contract?

A.—Yes.

Q.—There is a contract here with printed form dated 15th April, 1925, between Jackson-Lewis Company, Limited, and His Majesty King George V, represented in this behalf by the Minister of Public Works for the Province of Ontario, and it recites the contract for the erection of the East Block, and that the Jackson-Lewis Co. has engaged George Oakely & Son, Limited, to do a portion of said work and furnish a portion of said materials hereinafter set forth.

THE CHAIRMAN: The first part is a recital of the fact that there is a contract between Jackson-Lewis and the Government.

MR. OAKLEY: I might say that is the regular sub-contract form used by all general contractors.

MR. FINLAYSON: Looks like an American form: "Know all men by these presents, etc. Stone to be used will be Queenston Limestone." That seems to have been executed in duplicate by your firm, you executing it as president, with Mr. Blake Jackson as president of Jackson-Lewis, and Mr. Sidey as secretary-treasurer. Now, Mr. Oakley, do these documents attached hereto as Exhibit disclose the whole contract, the whole dealings?

A.—It does, yes.

Q.— Did you have any general contract from the Government at all?

A.—No.

A.—I understand your sole dealings were with the Jackson-Lewis Company?

A.—Yes.

Q.—What did you do to carry out this contract?

A.—Under instructions of the Jackson-Lewis Company we received a set of architect's plans from the Public Works here, took them to our office and put them in the hands of our draughtsman.

Q.—Who did you get them from?

A.—From the Public Works Architect. Then we took these plans and made our working drawings, and they in turn were submitted to the Public Works Department for their approval.

Q.—Your working plans were then submitted for the approval of the architect?

A.—Yes. After they were approved they were taken to our shops and the work was executed.

Q.—How was the work executed? Did you do it all?

A.—No, we didn't. We did the part that our shops could handle expeditiously. The aim was to try to get that up in a year's time, although we had a two years' clause in our contract. The purpose of it was to do all the work we could do in our own shop and .then other stonemen I brought them in and submitted the class of work we had, and had them do certain classes of work under our own working drawings and lists.

Q.—When you say other stonemen you don't mean mechanics?

A.—Other cut stone contractors.

Q.—And did you sub-let much of that to others?

A.—Yes.

Q.—When you said two shops?

A.—Our shops in Toronto and one at Point Edward.

Q.—How many men, then, would be engaged on the work? Roughly?

A.—We would have from 120 to 130 or 140 on the pay list.

Q.—Now you say the contract provided a two-year limit for you?

A.—Yes.

Q.—Could you have done it all in that time yourself?

A.—I question very much whether we could have done it in that time. We could not have done it without being in the position we would have to sever all our connections with the general contractors we do business with every day. We would have been tied up exclusively on the job.

Q.—So you say you called in other men in the same line of business? All in Ontario?

A.—I called in all I thought had plants capable of handling that class of work.

Q.—How much did you sub-let?

A.—About 40 to 45 per cent. of the cutting.

Q.—That is the dressing of the stone?

A.—Yes.

Q.—About 40 to 45 per cent. was sub-let? Where did it go?

A.—It went to one firm in London, two firms in Hamilton, and five in Toronto.

Q.—How would you divide it?

A.—Well in making our working drawings this building has great repetition, and we made our drawings and divided them into sections designated by letters, A, B, C, D, E, F, G, and we submitted these different sections to the different cut stone contractors with our own working drawings and our own lists, and they executed that work in their shops and supplied it to us for erection on the building.

Q.—And you gave out 40 to 45 per cent.?

A.—Yes.

Q.—It is pretty well done now so far as stone work is concerned?

A.—Yes.

Q.—Did they carry out their 40 to 45 per cent.?

A.—No, we had to pick up in some places. I would say we picked up another 10 per cent. where some cut stone contractors did not keep up with the general levelling of the building.

Q.—It was forty to sixty? And it became thirty to seventy, is that it?

A.—No, I wouldn't say that—65 per cent.

Q.—You have done about sixty-five and sub-let thirty-five, approximately?

A.—As a final analysis.

Q.—Are you willing to tell the Committee the prices you give the sub-contractors?

A.—I gave it to them on a cubic foot basis. I submitted our estimates to them and showed how we arrived at the price for that kind of work, and told them if they were willing to do that section, I might submit to them at these prices we were willing to let them do it at that.

Q.—Do I understand the same prices you figured on yourselves?

A.—Outside of our working drawings. I had to keep the whole administration of the working drawings and lists and general supervision in my own hands or it would have become unwieldy.

Q.—In the trade is there a stock charge for working drawings—a recognized charge?

A.—Yes.

Q.—What is it?

A.—It would range from seven to ten cents a cubic foot according to amount of detail in it.

Q.—And what did you charge these people?

A.—Ten cents.

Q.—You sub-let this out to these people, sub-contractors, those who did perhaps 35 per cent. of the work, at the same figure you had. This same per cubic foot figure, less the taking care of the working drawings which you fixed at ten cents per cubic foot, which you say is the recognized price in the trade?

A.—Yes.

Q.—And were all the sub-contractors agreeable to that?

A.—Not all that I submitted to. About two said they preferred not to handle that. The reason was it was a new stone, and there was a question in the different stonemen's minds as to how cheaply that could be executed.

Q.—By sub-letting 35 per cent. you expedited the work, and it looks as if you were practically through now?

A.—If we have two weeks good weather we will be finished.

Q.—How long have you been at it?

A.—We stated about the middle of May, 1925.

Q.—So you have done it in a little over ten months?

A.—Yes.

Q.—Instead of two years?

A.—Yes, we had two years.

Q.—How is it as to speed for erection of a building of that kind?

A.—Well, we are very proud of the speed made on the building and it is generally commented upon among men in the trade.

Q.—By way of a record, is it?

A.—Yes.

Q.—And you were enabled to do that by sub-letting it all over, and it went all over the Province to stone merchants who could handle it?

A.—Yes.

THE CHAIRMAN: I understand that you paid them just the same price you got, for the portion of the work they did?

A.—Yes.

Q.—They didn't make the drawings, so you didn't pay for those?

MR. FINLAYSON: There was a standard charge for that including supervision. The work has gone ahead and is practically completed now. How has the stone turned out, first as to appearance?

A.—That is a matter of opinion. Personally I think it is one of the finest looking buildings we have in this country.

Q.—That is an opinion from some one who is predisposed; you are agent for limestone, aren't you?

A.—No, not agents for any stone.

MR. RANEY: No controversy about that, Mr. Finlayson. You are assuming management of my inquiry, I think?

MR. FINLAYSON: Well, we went ahead; this witness was asked for and we waited twenty minutes, I suppose.

MR. RANEY: I think that is my fault, but I am remarking that everybody will agree it is one of the finest looking buildings in Toronto.

THE CHAIRMAN: You won't feel that you were slighted in our going on?

MR. RANEY: No, no, that was my fault; I didn't look at my watch often enough.

MR. FINLAYSON: I don't want to lead you, but I would be glad if you could give me any opinion on the workability of the stone, etc.?

A.—I would say now that the stone, now that it has come into the market, the stone-cutters who worked the stone have become more accustomed to working it, and will produce that stone in the finished product cheaper than they would have done had they never been used to cutting the stone.

Q.—In other words, you have created a body of workmen who can handle that stone?

A.—Yes.

Q.—And I suppose in addition to that you established the cost, not only for yourselves, but also these other working firms, which will naturally produce a market for that stone?

A.—Yes, they have a line now on cost of production.

Q.—What about the opinion of the profession on it?

A.—I have had some of the leading men in the profession comment very favourably on what has been done with the stone.

Q.—Such as who?

A.—Mr. E. J. Lennox one day met me last summer while the job was going on. He stopped me and congratulated me on the job, what we were doing with it, and said he had no idea work of that kind could be executed in a Queenston limestone. I also had Mr. John Pearson, of Darling & Pearson, make a similar statement, with the result that one of the large undertakings now in Darling & Pearson's office, it is Mr. Pearson's intention to take an alternate figure in that particular stone.

Q.—So you think it has established an industry?

A.—I think so, yes.

Q.—Now to clear up one point, did you have any arrangement, directly or indirectly, with the Department or Minister or anybody in connection with this?

A.—Absolutely none.

•   Q.—Have you any interest in the contract of Jackson-Lewis?

A.—None whatever.

Q.—Have you any relationship with them except that disclosed in the contract?

A.—No.

THE CHAIRMAN: Was it specified in the specifications drawn up by the Government that Canadian stone should be used?

A.—Yes, it specified the different types of stone they desired to have figures on.

Q.—And they preferred Canadian stone?

A.—It was the desire of the Government to use an Ontario product.

Mr. Raney examining.

Q.—Mr. Oakley, you are a member of the Legislature, George Oakley, Member for Riverdale?

A.—Yes.

Q.—And are you George Oakley, senior or junior?

A.—I am George Oakley. My father, of course, is dead.

Q.—So there is no George Oakley senior now?

A.—No.

Q.—I need not go into the detail of it, but the company is just your company?

A.—Absolutely, just a family affair.

Q.—Then what was the first you heard about this proposed building, and from whom?

A.—I heard it through the press, that it was proposed the Government were going to build an East Loft.

Q.—When was that?

A.—I think two or three years ago. Perhaps before the Conservative Government came in. I think it was generally known.

Q.—Well what was the first thing you did about it at any time? Who was the first person you saw with reference to it?

A.—We had our man go to the Public Works Department and arrange to get a set of plans when they were calling for tenders.

Q.—When was that?

A.—That would be toward the end of February last year.

Q.—What was it that brought the matter into prominence at that time?

A.—As far as I am concerned? The cards I received from the general contractors saying they were bidding on that type of work and asking for our figures.

Q.—Had you had any communication with anybody about the matter prior to receiving these cards?

A.—I would not like to say definitely about those dates. I will say this: the Minister of Public Works and the Premier said to me one day when the House was in session that they had been discussing the stone situation with Mr. Heakes, the architect, and were desirous of using an Ontario product in their building, and he said they could not come to it between themselves as to whether there was in Ontario a product suitable for that type, and asked me my opinion if there was a stone, and if so, what. I told them there were two stones in Ontario that could be adapted to that building. One was Queenston limestone and the other Credit Valley.

Q.—The Credit Valley is the stone in this building?

A.—Yes, only this is brown and that would be grey.

Q.—How long before was that?

A.—Previous to the specification being written, which would be, I would say, perhaps two weeks previous to that time.

Q.—Some time probably in February or January? •

A.—I don't think in January.

Q.—And where did the interview take place?

A.—As we came out from the Legislative Chamber. Mr. Henry spoke to me there and we went to Mr. Henry's office.

Q.—And the interview was between the Minister of Public Works, the Prime Minister and yourself?

A.—And Mr. Heakes was called in after.

Q.—Was that the only interview?

A.—The only interview.

Q.—At that time had there been an advertisement for tenders for the building?

A.—No.

Q.—That was the first you knew the Government was going ahead with the work?

A.—I would not say that, because the press had had pictures and as you know the unemployed problem was serious at that time, and it was generally in the air that they were going to go ahead with this undertaking.

Q.—Can you recall now when the advertisements appeared?

A.—I would not like to say, but it would be in line with these cards, because they are the result of the advertisements that appeared in the press.

Q.—And you think the advertisement had probably not been issued at the time of the interview you speak of?

A.—I think not.

Q.—Have you the advertisement?

THE CHAIRMAN: It would be in the Department.

MR. RANEY: Was that the only interview that took place between you and a member of the Government?

A.—The only one.

Q.—Did you consider putting in a tender for this?

A.—No.

THE CHAIRMAN: The witness has already testified that according to his charter he is not allowed to take that kind of contract.

MR. RANEY: Only stone work. And that is all you do, anyway?

A.—For stone and marble.

Q.—It is an Ontario charter, isn't it?

A.—Yes.

MR. FISHER: You can do anything under an Ontario charter. The powers are supplemented by the Act.

A.—If our charter gave us the right, we would not do it for business reasons. We deal with general contractors.

MR. RANEY: That is your privilege, of course. There is no difficulty about that. Then when you were asked to give prices you gave prices to the different firms, and I see by the schedule the Credit Valley sandstone would be the most expensive construction?

A.—Yes.

Q.—One million sixty-eight thousand dollars. Then your price for the Queenston limestone for the entire building is specified, $948,000?

A.—Yes.

Q.—That was your tender, so to speak?

A.—Yes, that is the copy you are reading from.

Q.—Really this is a tender given by you to all the tenderers for the building as it was being advertised?

A.—Yes.

Q.—Then I notice in a contract dated 15th April between the Jackson-Lewis Co. and yourself the price is $938,000?

A.—Yes.

Q.—A difference of $10,000?

A.—Yes.

Q.—What is the explanation?

A.—If you will read my proposal you will see I state specifically that we carry the price in our tender to take care of our bond which the specifications call for. It says the contractor must put up a bond. We made it plain to every general contractor that our figure included the bond. When we secured the work with Jackson-Lewis, Mr. Jackson suggesting that he was the man who had to put up the bond, thought we would give him a credit with his tender and he in turn would take care of the bond.

Q.—And that would be $10,000?

A.—That is what I carried for. I think it is 1 per cent., and then if it was to go over—you understand we did not know whether that building would be built in eighteen months or two years.

Q.—That was intended to cover that item in a rough way?

A.—Yes.

Q.—And then you went on with the work? Now how long have you known the Jackson-Lewis Co.?

A.—I would say for eight or ten years.

Q.—Is it a Toronto company?

A.—Yes.

Q.—You know the individuals who compose it?

A.—I know Mr. Jackson very well.

Q.—A Toronto man?

A.—Yes.

Q.—And Mr. Lewis?

A.—There is no Mr. Lewis now. Originally there was a Mr. Lewis—but Mr. Jackson is going to be called and he would be more familiar. He is the member of the firm I had known. I know Mr. Mitchell and Mr. Sidey just by going into his office from day to day, talking business with him.

Q.—Did you discuss with anybody your position as a tenderer through your family company for this sub-contract of $938,000 having reference to your seat in the Legislature?

A.—No, I did not.

Q.—With nobody at all?

A.—No.

Q.—Of course the Government knew right away that you were doing the stone work?

A.—You mean after we got started?

Q.—Yes, yes.

A.—I think all sub-contractors would be known to the Government and the world at large. Because there is a large sign on front of the building which shows all the sub-contractors.

Q.—Nobody suggests there is anything under cover, Mr. Oakley, because it is advertised on the billboard, as you say. Perhaps if this information had been furnished to the House as to your company's contract it might not have been necessary to have had this inquiry before this Committee. Did the Government know what your contract price was?

A.—Not that I know of.

Q.—I want to compliment you before you leave, on your work. As I said in the House last night, it is one of the most beautiful buildings in Canada.

THE CHAIRMAN: I know something about your firm's work. How does your firm in volume of its work compare with the other firms of the same nature?

A.—Well, without being egotistical, we have the largest cut stone plants in this part of the country. Our work, I think, shows that. We ship all the way from Port Arthur in the west to Halifax.

Q.—Would I be making too broad a statement if I said your plant was practically twice as large as any other in Ontario?

A.—Our three plants together would make three times what there is in any other plant.

Q.—You are really the principal contractor in this line of work?

A.—I think so.

Mr. Blake Jackson in witness box. Mr. Raney examining.

Q.—You are resident in Toronto, Mr. Jackson?

A.—Yes.

Q.—How long have you been resident here?

A.—1913 I started in business. Before that I was here going to University.

Q.—And Mr. Lewis is not now connected with the company?

A.—No, he incorporated the company with me, and I bought out the interest, I think in 1917.

Q.—A New York man?

A.—No, an Ontario man, born in Ingersoll; he went to school here with me and since then has gone to the States, so I bought him out.

Q.—Have you had other large contracts?

A.—Yes, quite a number.

Q.—Can you name some of them?

A.—Yes, the Pantages Theatre, Regent Theatre, Muskoka Hospital at Gravenhurst.

Q.—Not as large as this?

A.—No, I don't think they are quite as large.

Q.—I see you are capitalized at $40,000?

A.—Yes.

Q.—With $10,000 paid up?

A.—Yes.

Q.—And your tender for this work was how much?

A.—I have forgotten the exact amount. The main tender was not accepted. The figures were put in various forms, depending on the type of stone.

Q.—Well for the type of stone used, Queenston limestone?

A.—One million four hundred and eighty-six thousand three hundred and sixty-seven dollars.

Q.—And for granite base at $20,500. Was that added?

A.—No.

Q.—So your tender is for $1,486,367?

A.—Yes.

Q.—And of that item of course the major portion was the stone work, sublet to Mr. Oakley's company?

A.—That is right.

Q.—At $938,000. Have you recently taken another contract from the Government on this building?

Mr. Finlayson: That is not a subject of inquiry here, is it?

Mr. Raney: I think so.

Mr. Finlayson: Surely not.

The Chairman: Is it relative, Mr. Raney?

Mr. Raney: Surely. There can be no reason for failing to tell us about it.

The Chairman: The thing is, is it worth while taking up the time of the Committee?

Mr. Raney: No reflection on Mr. Jackson, I take it. We just want to know the facts.

Witness: I signed a contract the other day. I have not sent my copy back, but it is in the course of execution.

Q.—What is that for?

A.—The interior finishing. It takes in plastering, marble, and tile, the interior trim, the cement floors and some interior partitions and some painting.

Q.—What is the total amount of that contract?

A.—About $355,000, in round figures.

Q.—So that it will bring the total of your contracts up to about $1,841,000, in round figures. Was the last contract made I suppose after advertising for tenders?

A.—Yes.

Q.—Did you have any negotiations with anybody with reference to this building, other than those shown in the file, the card to Mr. Oakley before you put in your contract for the stone work?

A.—No, I think the first I knew of it was that there was a building coming out, and when it was advertised we got a set of plans in the usual way and tendered.

Q.—I mean you sent out requests to a number of stone-cutting firms?

A.—Yes, I happen to have the list here.

Q.—Never mind now. You sent out a number of requests for figures on the stone work, and among others you sent out a number of requests for figures on the stone work, and among others you sent a request to the Oakley Company?

A.—Yes.

Q.—Did you have personal interviews with any of these persons to whom you sent these requests?

A.—I don't think I even saw any of them. I may have talked over the telephone to find out exactly what they were including, and following up the tenders, which are a little slow sometimes in getting in, we might have—

Q.—Did you have any interview with Mr. Oakley about this building?

A.—Not that I recall.

Q.—Prior to the time you accepted his proposal for the stone work?

A.—Yes, after the Government told us our tender was being accepted, and they were making a contract with us, then I had consultations with Mr. Oakley as to the handling of the work, and the time we could make, because time was very dependent on the stone work, and naturally I consulted with the sub-contractor as to what he could do.

Q.—Was Mr. Oakley's proposal for stone work the lowest you had from any of the stone-working firms?

A.—Yes.

Q.—And the matter of selection of Queenston limestone—who determined that—the Government?

A.—Yes, we had nothing to do with that.

Q.—You were asked to give alternative figures on several kinds of stone, and you were not consulted as to what the type of stone would be that would be ultimately selected?

A.—No, not at all.

Q.—I notice other tenderers about the same. Your tender was accepted for certain portions of the work. When your present contract has been completed—I mean the new one—will the building be completed?

A.—No, there are some things we have nothing to do with.

Q.—What are the things that will remain to be done after your new contracts have been finished?

A.—The elevators, I think, have not been contracted for, and there has no decorating of walls been provided for yet, and no finishing hardware. The plumbing and heating and electric work we have nothing to do with. I believe that was called for separately and tendered for separately.

Q.—I see according to the answer of the Government to certain questions, in addition to your contract for $1,439,000—is that the figure you gave me?

MR. FINLAYSON: No, $1,836,000.

Mr. Raney: There is Purdy Mansell, $128,992 for heating and ventilating; and Wright Brothers, contract for plumbing, $38,990; Bennett & Wright, electric wiring, $36,742; Consolidated Plate Glass Company, windows, $21,051; Architectural Bronze & Iron Works, $58,625; Canadian Ornamental Iron Works, $22,900; Goldie, McCulloch for folding doors, $5,612. Did you have these figures?

A.—No, I know nothing about these.

Q.—I was just interested to find out about what the entire cost of the building would be. You say when you are through there will still be elevators to do and some other more or less important finishing?

A.—Yes.

Q.—You say the figure for your present contract is how much—the new contract?

A.—Three hundred and fifty-five thousand dollars. There is a discrepancy between our contract and our tender accounted for by the metal windows. They were taken out of our contract.

Q.—What was your last tender?

The Chairman: You mean the tender for the interior work?

Witness: The reason our contract figures do not correspond with the tender figures of $1,486,000, attached to it is a letter, "In attached with our attached tender, we beg to submit the following lump prices our tender is based upon use of metal double-leaded windows as specified, and we have included $54,000 for all windows shown." When our contract was written, the $54,000 was deducted, and the Government bought these windows direct without coming through us, so our contract was $54,000 less than our tender.

Q.—And you would add $54,000 to $439,000 to get the total?

A.—I don't know what they paid for the windows; they bought direct.

Q.—Oh, yes, here it is: Architectural Bronze & Iron Works, contract for metal windows—I assume that is it?

A.—I presume so.

Q.—You say your tender was $54,000?

A.—On a different type of window.

Q.—Because I see the amount here is $58,000?

A.—A different type of window.

Q.—Did you say there was a discrepancy between your later tender and the contract?

A.—No.

Mr. Finlayson: Do you want to call Mr. Sidey?

Mr. Raney: No, I don't want to call him.

Mr. Fisher: Can we go on with Mr. Fullerton?

The Chairman: Can we possibly do it in fifteen minutes?

Mr. Fisher: Well, if it takes twenty it won't hurt.

Mr. Raney: When are you proposing to examine the motion picture people?

Mr. Finlayson: I meant to speak to you about this. Mr. Nash was in Toronto yesterday or day before, and was going to Ottawa, and thought he might return to the city to-night, and if he did would telephone to-night or to-morrow and be here in the morning. He is acting in the Stevens Committee.

Mr. Raney: That would take precedence of the Caledon Mountain matter, is that it?

Mr. Finlayson: Well, yes, I would like to stop expense in that.

Mr. Raney: Well, we won't take long with Mr. Nash.

THE CHAIRMAN: We will have to give a certain amount of consideration to Major Nash, on account of the other work he is engaged on.

MR. RANEY: The expenditure at Orangeville would not amount to much. I won't interfere with the Caledon men.

THE CHAIRMAN: They are summoned.

MR. RANEY: Could we fix the moving picture matter for Monday?

THE CHAIRMAN: I don't see any reason why we cannot.

MR. FINLAYSON: What time Monday?

THE CHAIRMAN: Ten o'clock in the morning. We are going to clean this up.

MR. RANEY: Agreed the moving picture matter will be on Monday?

THE CHAIRMAN: I think we can clean the Lyons matter up in a short time. Now some of these witnesses summoned, for instance that hardware merchant, Bedford, we don't want him again.

MR. RANEY: I don't want him again.

THE CHAIRMAN: I want to discharge them and let them go home.

MR. RANEY: I wanted Mr. McNamara.

THE CHAIRMAN: Yes, he is subject to recall, and Mr. Hoskin, the engineer, you wanted to wait until we have examined Mr. Fullerton. Then Mr. Lamb, engineer from the Soo, I suppose it is not necessary to hold him.

MR. RANEY: I don't want him.

THE CHAIRMAN: Mr. Lamb, you can go home. We just want Mr. Hoskins to wait until the examination of Mr. Fullerton.

MR. FINLAYSON: The understanding, then, is, Mr. Raney, that we have your Caledon Mountain people here to-morrow.

THE CHAIRMAN: They are summoned for to-morrow at ten o'clock. And if Mr. Nash arrives back we will take him on first.

MR. RANEY: Then you had better bring down these Muskoka men, maybe, for Tuesday.

THE CHAIRMAN: We will settle that to-morrow morning.

C. H. Fullerton sworn. Mr. Finlayson examining.

Q.—You were going to do some arithmetic; have you done that?

A.—Yes.

Q.—You were going to figure out what McNamara would be paid and what McDonald would be paid. Will you give us your result? Have you a copy?

A.—Yes.

MR. FISHER: What is the result?

A.—You mean for each item.

Q.—No, the total result?

A.—You want to know whether McDonald or McNamara was lowest.

Q.—What were the totals in each case, taking the actual quantities? What did you pay McNamara?

A.—Three hundred and eighty-four thousand six hundred and twenty-six dollars and eighty cents.

Q.—On the same quantities as taken what would they pay McDonald?

A.—If rental of equipment were the same and quantities the same, McDonald Bros. $856,752.47.

Q.—So McDonald Brothers would have been lower than McNamara by $28,000?

THE CHAIRMAN: Twenty-seven thousand eight hundred and seventy-four dollars.

WITNESS: Had we known the entire quantities.

MR. FISHER: That is the sum that would have been saved the Province if McDonald had got the contract?

A.—That is what we know now.

Q.—Now were there any instructions given to tenderers?

A.—I think there was a form of instruction to bidders gotten out at the time.

Q.—Have you got that?

A.—No, I haven't got that, but it is on file somewhere. They all got the same instructions.

Q.—What were the instructions as to quantities?

A.—They all got the same instructions as to quantities.

Q.—Well, what were they?

A.—That will be on the form of tender and I haven't one here. I gave most of them to you.

Q.—We are talking now of the Sudbury-Coniston work?

A.—Yes, they were given quantities on concrete pavements.

MR. FINLAYSON: That is Item 3?

A.—Item 3.

Q.—Sixty-five thousand four hundred square yards. They were given an estimate of square yards of scarifying and reshaping roadway, that is Item 9, 65,400 square yards. They were given (No. 21) trimming and leveling earthworks, 36,699 lineal feet?

MR. FISHER: You have already told us that on these three quantities the tender was decided?

A.—Yes.

Q.—And no regard paid to prices given for other items?

A.—We had no quantities which we could follow, and the contractors who were tendering knew the quantities that would be decided upon.

Q.—You asked them also for unit prices on nine other items?

A.—Yes.

Q.—And you paid no attention apparently to prices for the other items?

A.—We could not, because we did not know what quantity to apply the other unit prices to.

Q.—Going through all these items I find that McNamaras were low on three as compared with McDonald; that they had the same price for one, and McNamaras were high on eight. Did you notice that at the time?

A.—I don't recall that I noticed at the time. It is nearly two years ago.

Q.—Wouldn't that be a thing that ought to be taken into consideration when you were trying to get the cheapest work done?

A.—No.

Q.—Wouldn't it occur to anybody that if McNamaras were high on eight items they might be high on the whole work?

A.—It might. We cannot apply figures to some hypothetical questions.

Q.—You say you hadn't any quantities. Is that a fact? Just exactly what do you mean? We had an engineer here the other day who gave evidence at some length and said he had been employed to make cross-sections and that he had sent these to this department?

A.—Yes.

Q.—You had that material in your hand at the time of calling for these tenders? I suppose it was possible from these cross-sections to pick up quantities on most items, wasn't it?

A.—Yes; I said yesterday that we didn't have the quantities, and you ask me to-day if it is a fact, and I say it is.

Q.—Is it a fact you had the data in your possession?

A.—No.

THE CHAIRMAN: I think you are a little at cross-purposes, if you don't mind my intervening. The witness said yesterday that while they had ordered these cross-sections in order to get the tenders into the papers and get the road finished in season, they had to make their decision before they received their information from the field, but the information came in afterwards.

MR. FISHER: Is that correct, Mr. Fullerton?

A.—That is exactly correct.

Q.—You did not have these cross-sections when you called for tenders?

A.—No.

Q.—And what you did was simply make an office estimate, the scarifying and pavement are arrived at by multiplying the length of the road by the width of it?

A.—Practically.

Q.—That is all. And the shoulders are done in a similar way. That is all the information any contractor had?

A.—Except what he saw when he went over the road.

Q.—When we got the impression from this engineer the other day that he had prepared data on which these tenders were called, we got a wrong impression?

A.—Well, I think he firmly believed we had that data and used it to get at the quantity for this contract.

Q.—He thought you had it, but you say you had not?

A.—No, we had not.

Q.—You must have been in a great hurry to let that contract?

A.—We wanted to get it done that year, as I said yesterday.

Q.—McNamara's tender on items you took into account was about $188,000?

A.—Yes.

Q.—And it turned out that the other items you did not take into account amounted to $198,000?

A.—Well, I don't know; I did not subtract it.

Q.—I use the figures you gave yesterday?

A.—Well, they would be the same to-day. It would be $195,000 and something.

Q.—So that the items that were not taken into account in letting this contract were larger than the items that were taken into account. The tender forms, were they supplied by the Department?

A.—Yes.

Q.—Were they filled in with quantities when sent out?

A.—Yes.

Q.—I notice that all the tender forms have the quantities filled in with typewriting except McNamara's and it is filled in with ink. There is another like that, I just noticed it now. How do you account for that?

A.—We had to get out some forms; I cannot account for it unless it was a typographical error and we had to put in by pencil or pen.

Q.—Do you know if it was done before it went out?

A.—I am quite sure it was done before it went out, or it would not have gone out. There certainly would not be any object in putting in afterwards.

Q.—Is it usual for you department to let tenders on three items in this way?

A.—Well, it was thought that one at least was one of the great governing items—concrete pavement.

Q.—A comparatively small item, though, compared with the whole?

MR. FINLAYSON: It is the biggest item of the road, isn't it?

MR. RANEY: The largest individual item.

MR. FISHER: Yes, $177,000 as compared with $384,000.

MR. FINLAYSON: I thought you were comparing with other items.

MR. FISHER: Is that good practice, Mr. Fullerton?

A.—Well, if the work is to be done in the season, you have to take the best information you have, to begin with.

Q.—How much late was this information that reached you from the engineer?

A.—I cannot tell you that; I do not know.

Q.—No idea when you got that?

A.—No.

Q.—When were the tenders called for?

A.—I fancy it was about the middle of June. I think I gave Mr. Raney that information the other day, but I have just forgotten.

Q.—Middle of June, you think?

A.—I think it was.

Q.—Well, the cross-sections were taken; we were told they were not in time?

A.—I don't know when they were taken.

MR. FINLAYSON: We were discussing frost in the ground in July.

MR. RANEY: No matter; they were taken.

MR. FISHER: There was a question asked by somebody if there were any extras?

A.—Yes.

Q.—And the reply, I think, showed $3,000—was it?

A.—I think $2,770.56.

Q.—Well, as a matter of fact, the additional amount paid over that which was considered in the tender was $195,000?

A.—Yes. But they were provided for in unit prices.

Q.—Was there a report to Council prepared in this matter?

A.—Which matter?

Q.—This Sudbury-Conniston matter, does it go to Council?

A.—I do not know.

Q.—You know what the practice is?

MR. RANEY: This is a Northern Development matter, and there is a lump sum of $5,000,000 and the Minister spends it just as he pleases.

MR. FISHER: And it is not submitted to the Cabinet at all?

A.—I don't know that.

Q.—You know the practice, I suppose?

A.—I don't know how he arrives at his decision.

Q.—You would know whether there was a report made to Council on this sort of thing?

A.—I know there would be no Order in Council, but I don't know whether he consulted the Cabinet or not.

Q.—You did not prepare any report to the Cabinet?

MR. MACBRIDE: Every member of the House knows the Northern Development is a departmental matter, and has been for years.

MR. FISHER: Did you prepare a report as to this work?

A.—What sort of report?

Q.—Any sort of report, for their information?

A.—No, I don't think I did.

Q.—The quantities you used were approximately correct? There was no overrun in quantity—very little overrun?

A.—Yes.

Q.—All the additional cost came in the items you did not take into account in awarding the tender?

A.—The items regarding which we had no information.

Q.—You were asked the other day whether you were present when these tenders were opened?

A.—Yes.

Q.—What did you say?

A.—Yes.

Q.—You were. And the result, at any rate, is that $26,000 might have been saved if the other fellows had got it. Now just a minute in the other job, the Creighton-Copper Cliff. These quantities were given the tenderers, were they?

A.—I think they were. The arbitrary quantities that we took and the estimated quantities of certain surfacing.

Q.—You say arbitrary quantities, not estimated quantities?

A.—Something that were arbitrary.

Q.—Why didn't you have estimated quantities there?

A.—We had not information when it was advertised.

Q.—You called for tenders without information, on arbitrary quantities?

A.—There is another point to that, too. When we decided to go ahead with that work, it was expected that it was largely a matter of surfacing the Creighton-Copper Cliff road with tar penetration or asphalt. Our information at the time was that the foundation was quite satisfactory, because the road had been stoned once before some years ago, and our information was the road was well drained and would not need much drainage, and that it was in pretty fair shape, and all it would need was surfacing. We went ahead on that basis, and found afterwards the foundation was not what it had been represented to be, and we had to put on shoulders to save the surfacing that was put on, and had to go to some expense with drainage, and had to make some detours that were not contemplated at first, and as result of one of these detours we had to construct a concrete culvert of considerable size.

MR. MACBRIDE: Were these matters reported on by the Department engineers?

A.—As the work progressed, yes.

MR. FISHER: Didn't you have any report before the work started?

A.—In a general way.

Q.—What do you mean—general way?

A.—I don't know that we had one even in a general way from our engineer, but we had information from somebody.

Q.—From whom?

A.—I don't know where we got it, but the information we had generally was that the road was such as I have described.

Q.—The information was from whom?

A.—It didn't prove very good.

MR. MACBRIDE: Mr. Chairman, just a point of order; are we asking the witness for expressions of opinion or evidence?

MR. FISHER: A matter of opinion.

Mr. Raney: He is an expert.

Mr. MacBride: He is a clerk in one of the departments. If you are going to enlarge this enquiry to expressions of opinion, we will be here all summer.

Mr. Fisher: What do you say, Mr. Fullerton?

A.—I am not certain how we got the information, whether from an engineer or some other source.

Q.—Have you any information on file in your office?

A.—I don't know that, because I have not examined these files since then.

Q.—Well, now, was the price based on the quantities given to the successful tenderer? Labarge?

A.—Sixty-one thousand one hundred and sixty-five dollars.

Q.—The contract was based on $61,165?

A.—Yes.

Q.—And what did the work cost? '

A.—One hundred and thirty-five thousand and sixty-three dollars and fifty cents.

Q.—So that your estimate was very much astray?

A.—It was too low.

Q.—There was very close tendering on the job?

A.—Yes.

Q.—I think three of them are within $300?

A.—Yes.

Q.—Actual quantities or estimated quantities might have made a very great difference in the tender, mightn't it?

A.—They may have.

Q.—As a matter of fact, have you figured this the same as you did before?

A.—No, I haven't figured this one.

Q.—Haven't figured, taking the actual quantities, who would be low?

A.—No, I haven't.

Q.—There is quite a similarity in some of the prices in these tenders, isn't there?

A.—I haven't the tenders here; you have them.

Q.—Earth excavation, McNamara and Labarge each $1; rock excavation, 7?

Mr. Finlayson: There were more than these at $1; several of them, aren't there?

Mr. Fisher: Quite a number the same?

A.—I don't know; I haven't seen them.

Mr. Fisher: All right. That is all.

Mr. Raney examining.

Q.—I shall have to ask Mr. Fullerton to come back, because I perhaps desire to cover some points in this matter and into another matter I wish to go rather extensively.

Mr. Bradburn: How long would you be, Mr. Raney?

Mr. Raney: Possibly an hour.

Mr. Bradburn: Because the House is not sitting yet.

Mr. Raney: If you had waited for the cross-sections from the engineer, you would have had all the information necessary to give estimated quantities?

A.—I think so.

Q.—And the estimated quantities that you did give, as Mr. Fisher has pointed out, were very accurate—upon which definite tenders were made?

A.—Yes.

Q.—And if the cross-sections had worked out just as accurately then McDonald Bros. would have had the contract?

A.—Yes.

Q.—Now why did you not wait for the cross-sections?

A.—As I have already pointed out, it was a matter of speeding up the work.

Q.—Well, who instructed you not to wait for the cross-sections?

A.—I got instructions to advertise the work, so the work could be finished that season.

Q.—Did anybody instruct you not to wait for the cross-sections?

A.—Nobody said, "Don't wait for the cross-sections," but I got instructions to advertise the work.

Q.—From whom?

A.—The Minister of the Department.

Q.—Did you point out to him you had not the information necessary to call for tenders?

A.—I don't remember what transpired at the time about that.

Q.—Well, you are an engineer, Mr. Fullerton, and careful of your own reputation, I suppose, and your responsibility was involved in this to a degree?

A.—Well, I don't know whether it was or not.

Q.—You knew you could not get a proper tender unless you had cross-sections?

A.—I knew we would get a proper tender if we advertised certain quantities.

Q.—You knew you could not get a proper tender unless you had cross-sections?

A.—We would have got the same tender that we did get.

Q.—Please answer the question direct. You knew you could not get a businesslike tender unless you had full information including the cross-sections?

A.—I don't know; we would not get exactly the same tender from each of these tenderers.

Q.—Supposing you had not put in any quantities at all, you would have got tenders, I suppose?

A.—Yes.

Q.—And your tenders would have been just as valuable as these tenders proved to be?

A.—I don't know that we would have got tenders any different.

Q.—I did not suggest that. As a matter of fact the quantities you did give were not anything of any consequence, because anybody could multiply the width of the road by seven miles in length and get the information you gave in the specifications?

A.—Well, the contractor would be interested in the length of the road.

Q.—And also the width. And would know these things from the advertisement, I suppose?

A.—Well, we would give him the information.

Mr. Vaughan: Mr. Chairman, I have just arrived and been listening to the member for Wellington, and it appears he is trying to ask and answer the questions both himself. I would like to hear this man answer the questions.

Mr. Raney: I am dealing with an expert who knows his business, I assume. Now I would like you, Mr. Fullerton, to tell us explicitly what the urgency was that caused you to proceed with advertising for tenders without knowing the quantities?

A.—I think I stated before it was the idea of the Department to have the road completed that fall.

Q.—Who told you that?

A.—I stated that here yesterday, that it was the idea of the Department—

Q.—Who is the Department? Who told you that?

Mr. CHAMBERS (Wellington): As an engineer, wouldn't you understand that it had to be speeded up to get through that fall?

A.—No doubt about that, but it was publicly stated by the Minister that road would be completed in the fall.

Mr. RANEY: Did you call his attention to the fact you could not get right results unless you had the cross-sections to work from?

Mr. BLACK: He has already answered that question twice.

WITNESS: I already told you I did not think the tenders would have been any different. I did not put it in any language like that.

Mr. RANEY: How did you put it?

A.—I don't remember conversations with the Minister two years ago.

Q.—Did you call his attention to that?

A.—In what way.

Q.—In anyway? Have you ever before in any case advertised for tenders without having the necessary information?

Mr. FINLAYSON: Perhaps you were not here, but this is the first time they ever used this system.

Mr. RANEY: What system?

Mr. FINLAYSON: Unit system.

WITNESS: Do you want to know if the Minister had all the information?

Mr. RANEY: Yes.

WITNESS: Then the question would be, would the Minister know you did not have the information to give you the quantities?

Mr. RANEY: All right; and what do you say?

A.—Yes.

Q.—And without that knowledge he instructed you to go ahead?

A.—Yes.

Q.—Did you tell Mr. Fisher how long after you had advertised that the cross-sections came in?

A.—I did not know, and I don't know now.

Q.—Do you know whether you found it out before the tenders came in?

A.—I know that I did not.

Q.—How do you know that?

Mr. FINLAYSON: He said that several times.

WITNESS: I know they did not come in in time to be considered with the tenders.

Mr. RANEY: I would like you to produce the tenders and show the date of advertisement and date of tenders and date the cross-sections came in.

Mr. CHAMBERS: If they had come in, you would have got the information better, would you not?

Mr. RANEY: You were not able to tell, on the information you have, when you received the tenders of the McNamara Company and McDonald, which was the lowest?

A.—We were able to tell which was the lowest on the information.

Q.—You were not able to tell which was the lowest tender on that job?

A.—We were not able to tell which was the lowest tender asked for in the advertisement.

Q.—You were not able to tell when the tenders came in which was the lowest tender for that work?

A.—Well, yes.

Q.—You know now that McDonald was the lowest tender, don't you?

A.—We know now.

Q.—Then you assumed that McNamara was the lowest tenderer?

A.—Yes.

Q.—So that you did not know which was the lower tender?

A.—McNamara's was the lowest tender having regard to the information we had, and it could not have been let to anybody else on that information.

Q.—No, but when the contract was let did you have the cross-sections in then?

A.—No.

Q.—Sure?

A.—Yes.

Q.—All the more need for getting that information for me.

MR. CHAMBERS: I might say for the information of the Committee I did work under the Drury Government, and no fault to find, but never had contracts until the contract was finished.

MR. RANEY: And was it Mr. Chambers' experience that he collected twice the amount of his tender?

MR. CHAMBERS: No, it didn't always turn out that way, but we figured on the quantities we got at the time, but invariably they were off one way or the other.

MR. FINLAYSON: That is always true.

MR. RANEY: I think we will wait, Mr. Chairman, until we get these figures, if you please.

WITNESS Which figures?

MR. RANEY: Those I asked for a moment ago.

MR. FINLAYSON: Let us get through with this witness.

MR. RANEY: Well, that is about all I have to ask him; when I get these figures.

MR. FISHER: Perhaps the engineer might tell us what he knows about the—hospital, is it?

MR. BLACK: We want to get through with one thing first.

MR. RANEY: On the Copper Cliff road, could you let me see the arbitrary quantities of which you speak, on which you asked for tenders, and the statement of actual quantities?

WITNESS: You have the tenders there, Mr. Fisher, on the Creighton-Copper Cliff road.

MR. RANEY: I should not be able to make anything of this in the next few minutes; you better go on, Mr. Finlayson.

Mr. Finlayson examining.

Q.—This unit system, you explained, was the first time you had tried it out?

A.—On a job of this magnitude, I think, yes.

Q.—You told us you had used the standard classification used by the Highway Department?

A.—Generally speaking, yes.

Q.—Adapted that for your purpose?

A.—Yes.

Q.—And it is the same system under which the Highway Department received tenders?

A.—Yes.

Q.—And it is a very common engineering practice, isn't it?

A.—Yes.

Q.—Variations occur up to several hundred per cent., sometimes, don't they?

A.—Yes.

Q.—In the case of the former government, I understand some of them ran 300 per cent. variation?

A.—I believe they did.

MR. MACBRIDE: Can we get an instance of that?

MR. FINLAYSON: We will give the tabulation, showing some three or four hundred per cent., not one but dozens.

MR. MACBRIDE: I think we ought to have it.

MR. FINLAYSON: Have you some figures there?

A.—These are figures obtained from the Department of Highways.

Q.—Under what Government?

A.—I don't know when the work was done.

Q.—Doesn't it show the year?

A.—Yes.

Q.—What year?

A.—Well, I have a contract here in 1922.

Q.—Who was the contractor?

A.—McNamara Bros. & Thornton.

Q.—From whom?

A.—The Government.

Q.—Which department?

A.—Highways, $17,125.30.

Q.—And what was the payment?

A.—Seventy-four thousand one hundred and sixty-five dollars and thirty-four cents.

Q.—A jump from $17,125 to $74,165 in 1922, and that on the unit system?

A.—Yes.

MR. FISHER: Was there an addition to the work there?

A.—I do not know.

Q.—You don't know whether mileage was added?

A.—I know the total mileage was two miles, but I don't know whether that was an extension of the contract or not.

MR. FINLAYSON: What other have you got there, if they are interested in this?

A.—Well, concrete pavement, No. 600.

Q.—What year?

A.—Spring of 1923.

Q.—Is that a highway—No. 600?

A.—Yes. The tender amounted to $45,996 and the amount paid was $91,821.

MR. RANEY: You don't know anything about the facts in the case, I suppose?

A.—Nothing further than that.

Q.—That is on the unit basis, too?

A.—So far as I know.

MR. FINLAYSON: Have you some others there?

A.—Well, there is Contract 960, Department of Highways, the tender bid amounted to $65,915.20, and the total estimate $126,027.75.

Q.—That is the payment, is it?

A.—Yes.

MR. RANEY: There again you don't know anything about the explanation?

A.—In addition to these figures I have given, the materials were largely supplied by the Department of Highways.

MR. FINLAYSON: The practice of the Department is to supply cement or tar or asphalt?

A.—Yes.

Q.—Whereas the practice in your Department is that the contractor supplies that, doesn't he?

A.—Yes.

Q.—So in the case of Highways there could be no variation of cost by cement or surfacing material? That does not enter into the contract? That is supplied by the Department?

A.—Yes, in the Department of Highways.

MR. FISHER: I suppose the general explanation in these cases was that they tendered for a certain length of road and were given an additional length.

MR. FINLAYSON: I don't think that is the case in any one of them.

MR. FISHER: Would the witness know?

MR. FINLAYSON: I will state this to the Committee. I think that everybody knew the variation on unit tendering is very great, and there is always uncertainty, as Mr. Chambers said a minute ago, and that is particularly true in Northern Ontario, where you do not know what you are going to find below the surface, but if the Committee are impressed by this apparent discrepancy that seems to have caused some interest, I will endeavour to get an engineer from the Highway Department who will explain this. One hundred per cent. sounds big, and these remarks about engineering. The whole thing is that it was a new form—the Northern Development adopting the unit system. Perhaps the practice will improve as they go on. Undoubtedly it will, but a discrepancy of 100 per cent. occurs in this unit tendering everywhere. If the Committee are interested, I will be glad to furnish material.

MR. FISHER: It all depends on how good your original estimates are, whether you base them on real estimates or something else.

MR. FINLAYSON: That is one feature, but the big feature is if a discrepancy occurs in an item like rock, that runs into a big price, you are going to double it right off; and if you do not take rock into consideration at all it is going to be—

MR. FISHER: It is fair comment to say this: Undoubtedly the practice is better to have as accurate estimates as possible, and in this case it was apparently rushed under this new system, but the discrepancy does not mean very much.

MR. MACBRIDE: I have tried to follow the evidence with a common-sense view. I think we are wasting a lot of valuable time on this matter and getting us nowhere. I say that with all respect to every member of the Committee. Perfectly obvious tenders were called some time in June, 1925, for the purpose of constructing a roadway from Conniston to Sudbury. The lowest tender was that of McNamara for the concrete work. The Department through its engineers made an estimate of the probable cost. Anyone who knows anything at all about that country knows that any contractor, any engineer would be bound to run into unexpected difficulty. Now for some reason or other the road had to be rushed to completion, because the tenders were called in June, the contract let in July and completed probably that year.

Shouldering and doing drainage and other work it was found it ran $28,000 over the amount estimated in the Department. If McDonald had got the work it would have probably run over the same amount. I know from my experience in the House, of five or six years, we had that same incident time after time when this Government was in power.

MR. RANEY: But if McDonald had got the contract it would have been $28,000 less.

MR. MACBRIDE: Not necessarily. They would have run into trouble. ound to make a difference.

MR. RANEY: When do you go on to-morrow?

MR. BLACK (in Chair): To-morrow morning at ten o'clock, I understood the Chairman to say.

MR. RANEY: The other matter I want to take up with Mr. Fullerton I can take up again. The matter of the Sault road, etc.

MR. FINLAYSON: Let us have a memorandum of any papers you want.

MR. RANEY: I don't think I will require any papers.

MR. FINLAYSON: You said you were trying out the unit system in Northern Ontario?

A.—Yes.

Q.—And it was a novel practice as far as you were concerned? As far as the Department was concerned, you had not been letting contracts that way

A.—Not on permanent roads.

Q.—And like every other new matter you had more or less to feel your way?

A.—Yes.

Q.—And supply them with the information you could?

A.—Yes.

Q.—And in addition to that, you were handicapped by the fact that the season in the north is very much shorter than here?

A.—Yes.

Q.—You say frost is not out of the ground until when?

A.—I have seen frost in the ground in June.

Q.—When does it come again in the fall?

A.—In the woods it remains the year round.

Q.—And places like that you may have frost in the ground in June, and when may you expect it in the fall?

A.—October or November.

Q.—So your season is limited to four working months, isn't it?

A.—Well, sometimes it may be longer than that.

Q.—Three to five, is it?

A.—Yes.

Q.—And that is a matter that you have to have regard to, don't you?

A.—Yes.

Q.—Makes it extremely important to get your contracts let early?

A.—Yes.

Q.—And that is the reason for your rushing this contract?

A.—Yes.

Q.—As far as these tenders are concerned, you have told us it was announced publicly at Sudbury that the work was going to be undertaken?

A.—Yes.

Q.—Of these tenders that we heard of, McDonald's was from North Bay, Labarge from Sudbury, McNamara's at the Sault, and these other firms are northern firms?

A.—I do not recall.

Q.—The Italian ones are, anyway?

A.—Yes.

Q.—So they were all up there, and had opportunity to tender on it?

A.—Yes.

Q.—And their unit price would be furnished from their observation of the ground?

A.—Yes.

Q.—And this unit system is bound to produce disparities, isn't it?

A.—Yes, depending on the judgment of the contractor.

Q.—If a contractor, for instance, can say, "I am sure there is going to be a lot of rock," and he can give a very low price on earth, he can make it up if he has an overrun of rock, can he? All these items make it difficult to tender in that country?

A.—Yes.

Q.—Particularly where you cannot put down test pits on account of frost?

A.—Yes.

Q.—It would be an expensive undertaking. Now did you have any other figures there of unit contracts?

A.—I have all the unit contracts of the Sudbury-Conniston road.

Q.—Have you any Highway ones?

A.—I have a report, yes.

Q.—Have you any others beyond those you gave me already?

A.—Yes; Contract No. 939, Grant Brothers, an asphaltic concrete road.

Q.—What year?

A.—Late spring of 1922.

Q.—What was the tender?

A.—Seventy-seven thousand one hundred and fifty-eight dollars.

Q.—And what was the payment?

A.—Two hundred and fifteen thousand four hundred and twelve dollars.

Q.—A jump from $77,158 to $215,412?

A.—Yes.

Q.—That was a unit tender. What was the surface work?

A.—Asphaltic concrete.

Q.—Any others there?

A.—Contract 692; macadam. That must have been laid in the beginning of 1922, because some of the estimates were made in December.

Q.—All right, in Mr. Raney's Government; what was the tender?

A.—Forty-nine thousand one hundred and twenty-seven dollars.

Q.—And what was the payment?

A.—I don't know what was paid upon it. The total was $114,000.

MR. MACBRIDE: What part of Ontario?

A.—Ottawa-Kingston Road.

MR. FISHER: Do you know in any of these cases how much road was tendered on and how much was done?

A.—I don't know absolutely, but I obtained these figures from the Department of Highways, and asked for the length of the road, and they gave me the lengths of the road, and it does not show two different lengths. I conclude, therefore, there were not two different lengths, but the same road—no extension.

MR. LYONS: These figures were asked for to substantiate this method of unit bidding, and as far as I am able to ascertain it was carried out the same way as these, and the excess amounts are due to excess quantities over the quantities in the original tender.

MR. MACBRIDE: We had an instance outside my own city, the first year the Drury Government began to construct highways; ran into extra drainage. A perfectly good road, the Minister was not to blame; the condition had to be met.

Q.—What was the overrun?

A.—Considerable. Ran into a bog.

MR. FINLAYSON: Any others?

A.—Contract 302; Dufferin Construction Company, 1922; the Dundas Highway. Tender bid, $187,994, and total estimate, $601,877.39.

Q.—A jump from $187,000 to $601,877, considerably over 300 per cent.

MR. LYONS: It might be interesting to know that that just covered thirteen miles down here, so the Sudbury-Conniston was a cheaper road.

MR. FINLAYSON: Suppose a man put in a bid that worked out around the time, it might work out anything afterwards. Any more there?

A.—Dufferin Construction Company, Hamilton-London macadam road, 1921, tender bid, $49,035; total estimate, $162,067.09.

Q.—Nearly 400 per cent.

A.—No. 627, 1922, Niagara Falls-Simcoe, tender bid, $98,750; total estimate, $144,246.02.

Q.—That was a different construction company also.

A.—No. 132, Warren Bituminous Company, bitulithic pavement, Kitchener-Dundas; tender bid, $118,768.50; total estimate, $271,651.33, and the distance was slightly less than a mile and three-quarters.

Q.—What year was that in?

A.—1920.

Q.—Well now, Mr. Fullerton, it is perfectly apparent, is it not, that the unit system is liable to great increases?

A.—Yes.

Q.—Why is it made so flexible?

A.—Well, it is impossible to ask for lump sum bids when you are not certain of lump quantities.

Q.—Would it be possible to obtain a lump sum bid on that road when you were constructing it that year?

A.—It would not have been constructed that year, I think.

Q.—Could any responsible firm of contractors take the responsibility of making a lump sum bid?

A.—With the information we were able to furnish them, no.

Q.—Isn't it apparent every bid would have to be so enormous to be safe?

A.—Nobody would put in a lump sum bid.

Q.—I suppose they could if they wanted to put in an enormous one and play safe, but it would be disregarded, wouldn't it?

A.—No contractor would put in a lump sum bid. He would know it would have to be higher.

Q.—Don't you have a resident engineer and get progress reports?

A.—Yes.

Q.—And in the end is the test not this, the contractor is paid for what he does, on a careful check?

A.—Yes.

Q.—It also has another advantage, that it eliminates extras, doesn't it?

A.—To a great extent.

Q.—And is it standard form of contracting?

A.—Yes.

Q.—Adopted all over, isn't it?

A.—Wherever highways are built.

Q.—Now somebody suggests that $27,000 might have been saved by giving it to McDonald. It is easy to be wise after?

A.—Yes.

Q.—And that may or may not be true?

A.—I think it is true.

Q.—It is true, but it might have worked out the other way?

A.—Depending on the quantities taken out.

Q.—The unit system even if you have the most careful preparation of cross-sections and estimating, could always work out that way? I mean if you have two close bids and it happens that the one which is a little bit higher, after you figure it out afterwards might easily vary ten or twenty per cent.?

A.—Yes. On new work like that it is not the same as city pavement, because in city pavement the foundation is usually there; there is not much excavation, and here is something absolutely new—you do not know what is there.

Q.—That is, there is a great uncertainty?

A.—There never could be an absolutely correct estimate made.

Q.—Was this solid rock or boulders, or both?

A.—Both, and only two classifications.

Q.—And then some surface mud or dirt?

A.—Yes.

Q.—Now on the other contract, the Creighton-Copper Cliff road, there were extras, were there not—unforeseen work?

A.—Yes.

Q.—You mentioned a culvert?

A.—Yes.

Q.—And some diversions?

A.—Two.

Q.—And also, I think, some drainage, wasn't there?

A.—Yes.

Q.—Do these run into large sums?

A.—Quite a lot of earth excavation.

Q.—And they would only develop as the work proceeded? So no matter how careful your cross-sectioning might have been, you would still be liable to these increases?

A.—If we cross-sectioned on the old location entirely, it would not take care of it.

Q.—As the engineer says, it would pay to have a little diversion here to straighten this out?

A.—Yes.

Q.—That is the advantage of the unit system, that you can give a man an order to go ahead?

A.—Yes.

Q.—And that caused the large increase in this case?

A.—Yes.

Mr. Hoskins (recalled). Mr. Fisher, examining.

Q.—Can you tell us when you sent forward your cross-sections?

A.—I cannot remember the date, Mr. Fisher, but I am under the impression I received orders early in May to cross-section that road.

Q.—When did you finish?

A.—It would probably take two weeks to do it, with the outside work; two or three weeks.

Q.—How many miles was that road?

A.—Seven miles. Two or three weeks would probably do the outside work, and a week inside.

Q.—About four weeks altogether, and when did you send forward the cross-sections?

A.—I cannot say, but I could find out.

Q.—Will you send that to the Committee when you get back?

A.—I could, sir, but they would have a record upstairs.

MR. FINLAYSON: Mr. Fullerton made a note of that, and he will get it.

MR. FISHER: When you gave evidence the other day, you were under the impression your cross-sections were here?

A.—I was, yes.

Q.—How did you get that impression?

A.—I did not keep track of dates, and probably did not notice the date of the first notice calling for tenders.

Q.—There could not have been very much difference?

A.—I cannot say; I have no record of the dates.

MR. MACBRIDE: How long ago now since you were on this work?

A.—Two years ago next May.

MR. BLACK (in chair): To-morrow morning at 10 o'clock.

The Committee adjourned at 3.50 P.M.

PUBLIC ACCOUNTS COMMITTEE.

Friday Morning, March 26th.

The Committee met at 10 A.M. with A. C. Lewis, Chairman, presiding.

MR. RANEY: What are you going on with Mr. Lewis?

MR. LEWIS: We have Mr. Nash here.

MR. RANEY: Did the secretary speak about a witness?

MR. LEWIS: Yes, the man says he is ill and I would not want to bring him here, Mr. Brown, from Severn Mills.

MR. RANEY: I suppose we will sit to-morrow?

MR. LEWIS: Do you think we will need to?

MR. RANEY: There is quite a lot of matter to go into yet.

MR. LEWIS: Will we get a quorum? We will see about it later. Order, gentlemen.

MR. FINLAYSON: Call Mr. Nash. Mr. Nash telegraphed yesterday from Ottawa that he would be available to-day. He has to go away again and I have been discussing with Mr. Lewis the most convenient way of disposing of the matter. I venture this suggestion, that Mr. Nash give evidence generally to-day and his report be received and I will go over it with him. In addition to the report there is a mass of detail that I have not got through and Mr. Raney has not had a chance to go through and he has pointed out to me that he could not be expected to cross-examine at present as it would be a waste of time. I wish to suggest that I might go over this in a general way with Mr. Nash and then it can be left and he can be recalled. Could you be here next week?

MR. NASH: I would sooner come back to-night.

MR. FINLAYSON: To-night will suit me but I want to give Mr. Raney an opportunity.

MR. RANEY: We will see as it develops.

MR. NASH: I am really due in Ottawa on Monday.

MR. FINLAYSON: We will find out what suits your convenience Mr. Nash.

Albert E. Nash (sworn; examined by Mr. Finlayson).

Q.—Mr. Nash, you are a member of the firm of Clarkson, Gordon and Dilworth?

A.—Yes, I am.

Q.—Chartered accountants?

A.—Yes.

Q.—And you have been acting for the Crown in many liquidations?

A.—Yes, investigations.

Q.—And you have assisted this Committee on many previous occasions?

A.—Yes, I have.

Q.—You received some instructions from the Committee as to investigating the Lyons Fuel and Supply Company?

A.—I did, yes.

Q.—What was given to you as the ground work, or foundation, for the investigation?

A.—We were asked to make an investigation of the accounts.

Q.—What material was handed to you?

A.—From the Committee?

Q.—Yes.

A.—I received all the questions that had been asked in the House in connection with the Lyons Fuel and Supply Company.

Q.—And the answers?

A.—And the answers so far as given.

Q.—You were furnished with a resolution?

A.—Yes.

Q.—And in pursuance of that what did you do?

A.—We went to Sault Ste. Marie on Sunday week last and returned from there on Tuesday last spending some nine days at the Sault. I was in the Sault part of four days.

Q.—And you had a staff of accountants with you?

A.—Yes.

Q.—How many?

A.—Three besides myself.

Q.—And do you present a report?

A.—Yes, I hand you a special report dealing with the matter in general terms.

Q.—What is the date?

A.—It is dated 24th of March.

Q.—Dated 24th of March; put in as Exhibit 7.

MR. RANEY: Is that the whole report or the first part?

MR. FINLAYSON: I think you will find that one is a report and then there are statements. Is there anyone representing Mr. Sinclair? I have a set for him.

MR. RANEY: Better keep that. Give that to me.

MR. FINLAYSON: That is in as an exhibit.

CHAIRMAN: Number 7.

MR. FINLAYSON: Perhaps it will be convenient to read it over.

MR. NASH: It is dated 24th March, 1926, and reads as follows:

"Alex Lewis, Esq., M.L.A., Chairman, Public Accounts Committee, 1926, Province of Ontario, Parliament Buildings, Toronto:

DEAR SIR:

In accordance with instructions from your Committee, dated March 12th, 1926, we have made an investigation of the accounts and records of the Lyons Fuel and Supply Company, Limited, and the Sault Ste. Marie Coal and Wood Company, Limited, for the purpose of determining the relationship of the Honourable James Lyons, or his companies with all or any branches of the Ontario Government contractors, vendors or timber licensees. We report as follows:

SCOPE OF INVESTIGATION.

The work covered by us included the following:

(a) *Lyons Fuel and Supply Company, Limited.*

1. Analysis of the balance sheets and profit and loss account for the years 1921 to 1925, inclusive, prepared from audited statements of the company, and a comparison of the 1924 and 1925 statements with the books of the company to satisfy ourselves that the books and records produced to us were the actual operating and financial books of the company.

2. A scrutiny and abstract of the directors' and shareholders' minutes and of the by-laws since the inception of the company and an analysis of the shareholdings.

3. A general examination and scrutiny of the general ledger of the company to ascertain whether there were any extraordinary or unusual accounts or transactions.

4. A careful scrutiny of the Accounts Receivable Ledger for the years 1923, 1924 and 1925, and preparation of a list of customers of the company, who, from our investigation and enquiries made of the company's officials appeared to have any business dealings with the company or any of its departments.

5. A scrutiny of cheques, etc., paid through the company's bank account to satisfy ourselves that there were no improper payments or payments except in the ordinary course of business, and a test comparison of these charges to the company's cash book.

6. A scrutiny of cash receipts from the 1st July, 1923, to 31st December, 1925, to ascertain if there were any unusual items.

7. A test of the sales slips and copies of invoices to the sales books to determine that all sales were properly recorded.

8. A scrutiny of the Purchase Ledger from January, 1924 to December, 1925.

9. Enquiry into the salary and personal accounts in the company's books of the Honourable James Lyons and members of the family and other officials of the company.

10. An analysis of the investment account as shown on the company's books as at 31st December, 1925.

11. A thorough test of the prices charged by the company to a representative list of companies and persons doing business with the Government or holding timber licenses and a comparison of prices charged to these companies and

persons with prices charged to other customers, and with the company's whole-sale lists.

12. Special inquiry into the company's transactions in the purchase and sale of pulpwood, to determine with what concerns and under what conditions the company transacted its business.

(b) Sault Ste. Marie Coal and Wood Company, Limited.

Our investigations of the company's books and records covered substantially the same routine as outlined above. Mr. Lyon's interest in this company dates from the 1st of May, 1925.

(c) Other Companies.

As we found that the Honourable James Lyons or the Lyons Fuel and Supply Company had certain small stock holdings with other companies, we thought it only proper to inquire into his relations with these companies. These companies were as follows:

> Lethbridge Brick Company, Limited. (Inactive since 1920.)
> National Discount Corporation, Limited.
> Soo Films, Limited.
> Northern Canada Supply Company.
> Soo Boat Works. (In receiver's hands.)

From our inquiries we elicited nothing to show that these companies had any business relations with the Government with the exception of the Northern Canada Supply Company.

(d) Personal Bank Accounts.

We did not examine the personal bank accounts of the Honourable James Lyons. There was nothing in the investigation of the Lyons Fuel and Supply Company, Limited, or the Sault Ste. Marie Coal and Wood Company, Limited, which would appear to call for any such examination.

STATEMENTS.

We have prepared statements showing from the years 1920 to 1925, inclusive, net sales of the Lyons Fuel and Supply Company, Limited, and Sault Ste. Marie Coal and Wood Company, Limited, to:

(*a*) Various departments of the Provincial Government.

(*b*) Companies, contractors and individuals having dealings with the Provincial Government or holding timber licenses or concessions.

These statements have been prepared from the books of the company. Every effort has been made to include in them all those companies and persons who had dealings with the Provincial Government within the six-year period, but in order to be certain that all such companies and persons have been included, it would be necessary for the Public Accounts of the Province and other records of the various departments of the Government to be examined in detail and compared with the company's ledgers. This work has not so far been completed as time would not permit, but we have no reason to believe that the completion of this work would materially add to the statements.

I would like to add in connection with that, that we have gone back into the Public Accounts of 1923 and nothing we found would indicate that it would be necessary to go back further, but we can go back further if so instructed.

A scrutiny of the statements will reveal the names of no new customers of the company having business dealings with the Government. Since July, 1923, the Lyons Fuel and Supply Company, Limited, has opened approximately 117 new accounts (exclusive of local retail accounts) of which 38 were with companies or persons doing business with the Government or timber licensees.

We are not including in this report any statements of the operation or profits of the Lyons Fuel and Supply Company, but the records of that company disclose the fact that the profits for the last three years were substantially lower than the preceding two years. In view of the nature of the investigation, we think it proper to mention this fact but do not draw any conclusion from it.

Neither are we including in this report any details of prices charged by the company but statements have been prepared of all price tests made by us and our examination has not disclosed any unusual profits on business done with companies or persons doing business with the Government or with timber licensees.

We found the books of both companies to be well kept. All information which we required was given to us and all records of the companies for more than six years were available to us. The companies' officials and auditors were placed at our disposal and assisted us whenever required.

GENERAL.

The directors and officers of the Lyons Fuel and Supply Company, Limited, in 1925 were as follows:

> Hon. James Lyons, President.
> G. W. Goodwin, Vice-President and Secretary-Treasurer.
> H. C. Lyons, Assistant Secretary-Treasurer.

The controlling interest in the company is held by the Hon. James Lyons and members of his family.

The directors and officers of the Sault Ste. Marie Coal and Wood Company were as follows:

> Hon. James Lyons, President.
> W. G. Atkin, Secretary-Treasurer.
> A. Sinclair.
> J. Dawson.
> Angelina Lyons.

The controlling interest in the company is held by Hon. James Lyons and members of his family.

> Yours respectfully,
> (Sgd.) CLARKSON, GORDON AND DILWORTH."

MR. FINLAYSON (resuming examination): Now, Mr. Nash, in addition to that, you furnish three statements, do you not?

A.—Three statements, Mr. Finlayson.

Q.—What is Number One?

A.—The first statement is a statement of sales by the Honourable James Lyons' companies to Government departments from 1920 to 1925, inclusive.

Q.—That is apparently tabulated. The first column is 1920, the next 1921, 1922, 1923, 1924, 1925 and in the last column is the total. Then it is divided the other way?

A.—To show to what branch of the Government the sales were made.

Q.—I see. What is this below?

A.—The same information on the books of the Sault Ste. Marie Coal and Wood Company, only in 1925, because I understand that his interest in the company only dates from June, 1925.

Q.—Only one year?

A.—We did not have the books prior to Mr. Lyons' interest in the company.

MR. RANEY: Take 1925, I see there you have the sum of $704.95.

WITNESS: Yes.

CHAIRMAN: Court House fuel.

MR. FINLAYSON: Does that mean that the goods were supplied that year?

WITNESS: The goods were supplied. It is possible the figures may not agree exactly with the Public Accounts, because they closed their books on the 31st December and the Public Accounts closed on 31st October.

CHAIRMAN: I suppose also that might account for the $704, it might have been supplied from the early months of the year.

WITNESS: It was supplied since Mr. Lyons became interested in the company in June, 1925.

MR. RANEY: That was from the Lyons Fuel and Supply Company?

WITNESS: I beg your pardon. I am wrong. It was supplied in 1925.

MR. FINLAYSON: It appears then that the Lyons Fuel and Supply Company have been supplying the Government continuously from 1920 to 1924 with this one item in 1925?

A.—They have, yes.

Q.—The totals for the years 1920 are $198.68; for 1921, $3,503.12; for 1922, $909.78; for 1923, $5,217.69; for 1924, $20,079.29; and for 1925, $704.95, so that the grand total for the six years is $30,613.50?

A.—That's right.

Q.—Are these items spread out over all the departments of the Government?

MR. RANEY: All what?

MR. FINLAYSON: Departments.

MR. RANEY: I think only two departments stand out and there is a small item for the Department of Marine and Fisheries that ought not to be there.

MR. FINLAYSON: Is that Game and Fisheries?

WITNESS: We took the description from the books of the company.

MR. RANEY: Marine and Fisheries, that is Dominion, of course.

WITNESS: That is our information.

MR. FINLAYSON: It was in 1921, they supplied goods to the Ontario Government Hatchery. It should be Game and Fisheries. Marine and Fisheries is not an official name anyway.

CHAIRMAN: That is right, Marine and Fisheries.

MR. FINLAYSON: For a period of six years there was a total of $30,613.50 supplied to the Ontario Government by Mr. Lyons?

A.—Direct to the Ontario Government.

Q.—And Statement Number Two?

A.—That is a statement of sales to companies or contractors doing business with the Government or timber licensees by Hon. James Lyons' companies.

Q.—Let me first understand what was the scope of it. It covered contractors such as road contractors?

A.—Road contractors, general contractors, companies, wholesale or retail in the Sault and timber licensees. It covered everybody we could find that had business dealings with the Government.

22 J

Q.—I see a large number of them described as vendors. If you will look in column three, Mr. Raney.

WITNESS: Vendors is the name used to describe people who sold to the Government, whether wholesale or retail.

MR. RANEY: You had better describe what you mean by licensee.

WITNESS: Timber licensee.

MR. RANEY: That would be—

MR. FINLAYSON: Lumber company.

WITNESS: We had supplied to us from the Government a list of all timber licensees.

MR. RANEY: Does licensee include not only timber licensees, but pulp and wood licensees?

WITNESS: Yes.

MR. FINLAYSON: The term licensee includes anyone with a concession from the Government, whether timber or pulpwood?

WITNESS: Yes.

MR. FINLAYSON: And vendor?

A.—Vendor is anybody who sold goods to the Government.

Q.—How did you get that?

A.—Partly from the Public Accounts Committee, partly from information in the books and in some cases, locally.

Q.—For instance, half-way down you have C. W. Cox of Port Arthur, given as a licensee?

A.—Yes.

Q.—And then you have the Algoma Steel Company given as a vendor. What was their relationship?

A.—I cannot tell you their exact relationship.

Q.—It means they sold steel or something to the Government?

A.—They sold goods to the Government.

Q.—If a man sold a bill of groceries he is a vendor?

A.—Yes, we have included him in the list.

Q.—If John Smith sold groceries to the Government and also purchased from the Lyons Fuel and Supply Company you have included him here?

A.—Yes, we have gone so far as to show a ton of coal in one case.

Q.—You must have made an elaborate study of the Public Accounts?

A.—We made as much as time would permit, we were anxious to disclose every possible fact.

Q.—I am not complaining. I never contemplated that you would get all this.

CHAIRMAN: It is just as well to have it all and then we have full information.

MR. FINLAYSON: I see Goudreau Gold Mines. How do you put them in. Have they bought a gold mine from the Government and so you put them in?

WITNESS: I don't recollect the item. If I turned to the account, I could tell you.

Q.—I just wanted to try and understand. So that everybody in Northern Ontario who sold the Government $5 worth of groceries and dealt with the Lyons Company you searched their accounts?

A.—Yes.

Q.—For this period?

A.—As far as we could find.

MR. RANEY: You went on the principle that you were expected to tell the Committee the names of all persons having transactions with the Government?

WITNESS: Who, in turn, had dealings—

MR. RANEY: Who in turn had dealings with the Lyons Fuel or Supply Company or the Sault Ste. Marie Coal and Wood Company?

WITNESS: That is right.

MR. RANEY: I think that is right.

MR. FINLAYSON: I am not complaining.

CHAIRMAN: That was to be the scope of the inquiry.

MR. FINLAYSON: For instance, J. A. Hennessy is a butcher?

WITNESS: I don't know.

MR. LYONS: Yes.

MR. FINLAYSON: You seem to have covered the ground pretty well.

MR. RANEY: By contractor, I suppose you mean a road contractor?

WITNESS: In some cases, building contractors.

MR. RANEY: Where does the McNamara Company appear for instance?

MR. FINLAYSON: About the middle of the second page.

MR. RANEY: What do the different stars mean?

WITNESS: Where we have made price tests.

MR. FINLAYSON: Mr. Nash, is it fair to put it this way, this second statement covers not only lumber companies and pulp contractors, but also vendors of every kind and description to the Government whom you could find were on the books of the Lyons' companies?

A.—So far as we could find.

Q.—Where did you get the information to say whether these people were contractors with the Government?

A.—We searched the Public Accounts Committee for some period; we made a close examination of the company's ledger and inquired into each account where we thought there might be a connection and in some cases we rang up the people and asked had they any business with the company's officials or in any other way and also with the Government and when the reply was "yes"——

Q.—Does that statement in your opinion cover the full field of Government lessees, concessionaires and contractors?

A.—Substantially, I would say, yes.

Q.—Is there any way of summarizing the result?

A.—On page three the totals are given year by year.

Q.—That is the totals?

A.—Yes.

Q.—Well, before going into this, have you any observations to make on it?

A.—I think perhaps, Mr. Finlayson, the observations that are noted on page three. I note in the first place that in all cases marked X test of prices charged was made. In making price tests we had in mind the questions asked in the House, and secondly, the people who had the larger volume of business with the Lyons' companies.

Q.—You tried to cover the ground in connection with the questions?

A.—Yes.

Q.—And also those particular cases that indicated a volume of business?

A.—Yes.

Q.—In "B" I note there the company had received a certain advance on pulpwood purchased—"The accounts of the company show that at 31st December, 1925, the company had received $35,000 advances on pulpwood purchased by the Lake Superior Paper Company for future delivery."

A.—That does not appear in the total, because the sale was not made until 1926.

MR. RANEY: Is the Lyons Fuel and Supply Company a dealer in pulpwood?

WITNESS: Yes.

MR. RANEY: And this means they had a contract with the Lake Superior Paper Company for a considerable quantity for 1926 delivery and against this pulpwood contracted for the Lake Superior Paper Company had advanced $35,000 as a credit to the Lyons Company?

WITNESS: That is right.

MR. RANEY: Against wood to be delivered?

WITNESS: Yes.

MR. FINLAYSON: A common contract. When woods are in transit they have to make an advance to the vendors?

WITNESS: I think that is a common practice.

MR. FINLAYSON: Then I note "C," "While practically no sales were made to the International Nickel Company from 1920 to 1923 the company sold $174,640.50 to the Nickel Company in 1919."

A.—I made that point because the statement might seem unfair to Mr. Lyons without it. The Nickel Company in 1925 is the purchaser of a very substantial amount from Mr. Lyons.

MR. RANEY: Where is that?

CHAIRMAN: On the first page, close to the bottom.

WITNESS: $68,000 in 1924 and nothing from 1920 to 1923.

MR. RANEY: There had been substantially no purchases from 1920 to 1923 and in 1924 there was purchased $68,000 and in fairness to Mr. Lyons, you point out that before the time you began your investigation, in 1919 there was the large item of $178,000?

WITNESS: Yes.

MR. FINLAYSON: What is that for? Do you remember?

WITNESS: I can get it.

MR. FINLAYSON: Mr. Lyons tells me it is coal.

MR. RANEY: That was in 1919?

MR. FINLAYSON: Both cases. The explanation is this: those are the years in which he got the contract?

A.—Yes.

MR. RANEY: He being the tenderer on the contract each year and those two years he landed it?

MR. FINLAYSON: The other years were the lean years. I note "D," "The increase in sales in the year 1925 is partly due to the fact that the company started to do business in hardware and van goods in this year." You make that note in fairness because it ppears there is a growth of business in 1924-25 and it is largely in hardware and van goods.

MR. RANEY: What are the increases?

WITNESS: There are a great many hardware people there all through the statement. Note "E," "The officials of the company informed us that the supplies sold to Mitchell and Cooper in 1921 in connection with the building of the Technical School would mount to approximately $100,000." The ledger sheets of this particular company in Mr. Lyons' books were not available. They had been produced in Toronto in a case Mr. Lyons had in the courts, and for that reason we were not able to get the additional amount of sales. We put in the statement of sales we could find.

MR. RANEY: Where is the item?

WITNESS: On the top of that page.

MR. RANEY: That does not make any difference. It is not in the purview.

WITNESS: Note "F." "Sales to new customers having business dealings with the Government amounted in 1924 and 1925 to $59,900."

MR. FINLAYSON: In 1924 and 1925?

A.—Yes.

MR. FINLAYSON: And that amount would be larger if we went back to 1923?

A.—Yes. And then the last note refers to the Sault Ste. Marie Coal and Wood Company.

MR. RANEY: For the rest, the statement speaks for itself.

MR. FINLAYSON: I would like to say one thing about Statement 3. I am suggesting to Mr. Raney that Statement 3 is very elaborate and will take a long time to go over it. I have just glanced over it and it covers apparently a long series of price tests Mr. Nash made with anybody whose business dealings with the Government were indicated in the questions or where there was a large volume of trade and in that there is a mass of information, an immense amount of detail that I don't think it either necessary or desirable to discuss in public. I don't think it would be fair to the company. Mr. Lyons says he had no objection to any member of the Committee seeing it but thinks after that it will be apparent that it should not be published. For that reason I have suggested to Mr. Raney that if he will be good enough to look over it to-day and Mr. Nash would come back—

MR. RANEY: It will make particularly fine Sunday reading. There is no desire on my part to embarrass Mr. Lyons, and I will certainly limit any questions I have to ask with regard to all these statements to matters I deem to be absolutely in the interest of the inquiry.

MR. FINLAYSON: Well then, let me ask one or two general questions—but first of all, about coming back.

CHAIRMAN: Let us settle that right now. Mr. Nash says he can remain to-morrow.

MR. FINLAYSON: What about the first of the week?

WITNESS: I am supposed to return to Ottawa on Monday.

MR. FINLAYSON: Can you come to-morrow morning?

A.—Yes.

MR. RANEY: I think I could be ready by to-morrow morning.

MR. FINLAYSON: I think it better to leave it all until to-morrow morning. Then, Mr. Nash, to-morrow morning at 10 o'clock.

CHAIRMAN: Order, please. As these names are called will you please stand: Mr. Franklin, Mrs. Franklin, Mrs. Sutton, John Brass, S. B. Griggs, David Hunter, Richard Russell, Kenneth Hahnson.

MR. RANEY: Will you also please call A. J. McEnaney and J. McDevitt. They are not on the list. I want them added. McDevitt is 208 Humberside and McEnaney 193 Humberside, Junction 6711.

MR. FINLAYSON: I may mention one thing: Captain Maxwell is here as a witness and he is on a flight from New York to Red Lake and I understand a witness named Briggs is here.

MR. RANEY: Yes, Briggs is here.

MR. FINLAYSON: The number of days suitable for flying are limited and I don't want Captain Maxwell back.

MR. RANEY: When can Captain Maxwell come back?

MR. LYONS: Not for ten days or two weeks.

MR. FINLAYSON: If he goes to Red Lake and back it will be two weeks.

MR. RANEY: He would want to be here when Mr. Briggs is being examined. When does he want to leave?

MR. FINLAYSON: This morning.

MR. RANEY: I will call Mr. Briggs now if you say so. The other witnesses are not very far away.

MR. FINLAYSON: Is the Briggs matter long?

MR. RANEY: Very likely.

MR. FINLAYSON: I have a bill in the next room and I will be right back. It is not contentious.

Lawrence H. Briggs (sworn; examined by Mr. Raney).

Q.—Mr. Briggs, what is your business or occupation?

A.—Automobile mechanic.

Q.—How old are you?

A.—Forty-five years of age.

Q.—Where did you learn your business?

A.—In England.

Q.—What apprenticeship?

A.—I had an apprenticeship with the Daimler Motor Car Company of Coventry.

Q.—How many years?

A.—Five years.

Q.—What age were you when you went in?

A.—Eighteen.

Q.—And then how long did you remain with them?

A.—Seven years.

Q.—And then you were twenty-five. Then what happened?

A.—I went to Southport, with the Vulcan Motor Company.

Q.—How long were you there?

A.—I was about two years there.

Q.—Then where?

A.—I came out to Canada.

Q.—You were nine years in England on automobile engines, learning to be an automobile engineer?

A.—I had already learned when I went to the Vulcan. I had charge of a department there.

Q.—Both?

A.—Yes.

Q.—Have you papers as an engineer from England?

A.—I have but I have not them with me.

Q.—Then you came to Canada?

A.—Yes.

Q.—When you were twenty-seven?

A.—Round about that.

Q.—Then what?

A.—The first position I had was with the Vinot Motor Cab Company in Montreal.

Q.—How long?

A.—About fourteen months.

Q.—What was your position?

A.—Foreman of the assembling shop.

Q.—Then what?

A.—I came to Toronto in 1910 and get a position with the Toronto Taxicab Company on Jarvis Street in charge of the repairs.

Q.—How long were you there?

A.—About three years.

Q.—Then what?

A.—I went to the Curtis Motor Company in Buffalo.

Q.—How long were you there?

A.—About a year, when the war broke out.

Q.—What position had you there.

A.—I just had an ordinary position in the shop as assembler.

Q.—Then what?

A.—I enlisted in 1914.

Q.—Did you go overseas?

A.—Yes.

Q.—In what force?

A.—With the division munition park of the C.E.F.

Q.—In what position?

A.—As an automobile mechanic.

Q.—How long were you overseas?

A.—One and a half years.

Q.—What happened?

A.—I went to France.

Q.—What happened there?

A.—I was wounded and discharged as unfit for further service.

Q.—You lost part of one of your feet?

A.—Yes.

Q.—Then what?

A.—I came back to the Curtis Company.

Q.—Where?

A.—At the school in Long Branch.

Q.—In Toronto.   How long were you there?

A.—About nine months.

Q.—Then what?

A.—I re-enlisted in the R.A.F.   I was the first man to enlist in Canada in that.

Q.—And then what?

A.—I was given charge of engine instruction in Toronto University.

Q.—On aeroplane instruction; how long?

A.—Until August, 1918.

Q.—How many years?

A.—From January, 1917, when the R.A.F. was inaugurated.

Q.—And did the flying men go through your hands there?

A.—All of them.

Q.—You instructed them?

A.—Not personally.   I had charge of that particular department.   We had about fifteen instructors.

Q.—You were the head?

A.—Yes.

Q.—After that, what did you do?

A.—I was released to take charge of the engine assembling tests of the Sunbeam engine at the Willy-Overland factory for the Government, in Toronto.

Q.—And how long were you in that position?

A.—Well, I took it in August and the war finished in November. I was kept there six months after the war finished and then I stayed on with them when they went on the production of automobiles.

Q.—Then what?

A.—I re-enlisted in the Canadian Air Force in 1920.

Q.—And what after that?

A.—I was there two years. I did not do anything then until I joined the Provincial Air Service, forestry ranging, in 1924.

Q.—What month?

A.—April, 1924.

Q.—And you are in the Ontario Air Service now?

A.—No.

Q.—When did you cease?

A.—In September, 1925.

Q.—Did you write a letter to the Minister of Lands and Forests in August, 1925?

A.—Yes.

Q.—The letter will be in the Department.

Mr. Lyons: I have it here.

Q.—Is this the letter you wrote?

A.—Yes, sir.

Q.—Sault Ste. Marie, August 24th, 1925. You were still in the Air Service then?

A.—Yes.

Q.—But had received notice of dismissal?

A.—Yes.

Q.—The letter is addressed to the Hon. James Lyons, Minister of Lands and Forests, Toronto, and reads as follows:

Dear Sir:

"I respectfully desire to call your attention to the very serious and costly mistakes in the overhaul and maintenance of 'Liberty' engines at the Sault Ste. Marie airdrome. A change was made at the commencement of the season in the oiling system that has already resulted in a few engines being entirely written off and none with this alternative has attained eighty hours of flying time."

Chairman: Alteration, I think, not alternative.

Mr. Raney: It should be alteration.

"Resulting in tremendous monetary loss to engines and damage to machines, costly re-installing of engines in out-of-way places, and jeopardizing of the lives of the crews operating machines with these altered engines, and regardless of the results, engines are being shipped out in this way. Myself and others warned against this at the time the alteration was made, as perfect lubrication was impossible by this foolish system adopted. I have very strenuously opposed this and several other crude and dangerous methods of operation with the result that I am discharged by W. R. Maxwell at the instigation of S. A. Thompson. Vast sums of money are needlessly wasted in these methods, and the above is only one of the many changes I wish to bring to your notice. Would you please see me personally here at the Sault or send a representative and go with me through the shops and verify the statements. Trusting these charges to be accepted in the spirit they are made, 'In the interest of the service,' and that I may be favoured with a reply per return, awaiting your instructions,

Yours very truly,

L. H. Briggs."

Then you received a reply to that letter which I will show in a moment?
A.—Yes.
Q.—This letter is from the Department of Lands and Forests and is dated Toronto, September 3rd, 1925. It reads:

Dear Mr. Briggs:
"I may say in reply to your letter of August 24th, that I have forwarded copy to Captain Maxwell and to Mr. Zavitz, and have asked for a written report in connection with the matters referred to. As soon as I have their reply, I will, if necessary, take the matter up with you further.

"You state in the last paragraph of your letter that this is only one of the many charges that you desire to bring to my notice and with a view to getting all the facts in the case, I would appreciate it very much if you would let me have the additional information you possess so that I may give it my attention.

"I am glad that you are writing in the interest of the service and apparently not dissatisfied because you have been discharged, and I believe that it would have been more in the interest of all concerned had you forwarded this information when it first came to your attention.

"Trusting that you will let me have the additional information you possess immediately so that I can give it prompt attention.

Yours very truly,
(Signed) JAMES LYONS (Minister)."

Q.—Did you go to see Mr. Lyons by appointment?
A.—Yes, I came to see him the minute I got back from the Sault to Toronto.
Q.—In the meantime if I may take you over this letter of yours to Mr. Lyons: "I desire to call attention to the very serious and costly mistakes in the overhaul and maintenance of 'Liberty' engines at the Sault Ste. Marie airdrome." What was the matter referred to?
A.—The oiling system in particular.
Q.—Of the engines?
A.—Yes.
Q.—What is the type of engine that is used by the Government?
A.—Liberty.
Q.—Liberty engine?
A.—Yes.
Q.—Installed in what do you call the machines?
A.—H.S. 2 L.
Q.—That does not convey much?
A.—That is the type of machine.
Q.—What would you call it? Are they hydroplanes?
A.—Flying boats.
Q.—Are they hydroplanes?
A.—They are hydro-airplanes.
Q.—What is the difference between a flying boat and a hydroplane?
A.—One is a flying boat pure and simple; what its name implies, a boat with wings to make it fly. The other is a flying plane with floats that skims over the water.
Q.—When were they purchased, before or after you came to the service?
A.—I think before I came.
Q.—Were they at the Sault before you came?
A.—No.

Q.—They came afterwards?

A.—I did not move to the Sault until the winter of 1924.

Q.—When do you say you went into the service?

A.—In April of 1924.

Q.—Between April and the end of the year where were you?

A.—On operations, forestry operations, at Timagami and Orient Bay.

Q.—Were there flying machines there?

A.—Yes, certainly.

Q.—Were those flying machines now at the Sault there?

A.—Yes.

Q.—When did they come into the service?

A.—I think when we were at Timagami; I was not turned on engines and I think they were flying at Orient Bay.

Q.—How far is that from the Sault?

A.—About 500 miles.

Q.—You were at Timagami for the season of 1924?

A.—We were changed from Timagami to Orient Bay about August.

Q.—Were you in charge of a boat at Orient Bay?

A.—Only one, one engine.

Q.—And you were there for the remainder of that season?

A.—Yes.

Q.—When were the machines brought into the Sault?

A.—I was on the first flown into the Sault, rather the second one, November, 1924. That was the first of November.

Q.—When was the aerodrome ready for occupation at the Sault?

A.—Sometime in February or the first week in March, 1925.

Q.—And where were the machines housed in the meantime?

A.—They were anchored on the river.

Q.—Before we proceed to inquire about these flying boats, you know where they came from originally? Were they new?

A.—No they are not new. The H.S. 2 L's were built during the war. They were built by the United States Navy Department; they were built by different contractors.

Q.—Had they been used before they were purchased by the Government?

A.—I understand that the first nucleus—

MR. FINLAYSON: Never mind if you only understand.

WITNESS: I am not guessing. I understand that the first machines we got at Sudbury were taken from the Laurentide Air Service.

MR. RANEY: How old were the machines to your knowledge when they came?

A.—Well they were built in 1917, eight years then.

Q.—What do you say as to the other machines? Are they modern machines, speaking in the sense of air service, or obsolete?

A.—Obsolete.

Q.—Are they building them now?

A.—No.

Q.—How long is it since they were built?

A.—There has not been a flying boat constructed in the last three years.

CHAIRMAN: How long?

WITNESS: Three years.

MR. RANEY: How long is it since this particular type of flying boat was discontinued?

A.—Not after 1917; not after the war.

Q.—How many were built altogether?

A.—About 5,000.

MR. FINLAYSON: Does he know what he is talking about because he is all wrong. Do you swear there was none built?

WITNESS: No H.S. 2 L's.

MR. FINLAYSON: You swear that?

WITNESS: Yes.

MR. FINLAYSON: Nowhere?

WITNESS: Certainly.

MR. RANEY: You will have a chance to cross-examine him. I see in the report of the Minister of Lands and Forests for 1923 that reference is made to the air patrol. Do you know the author of this part of the report?

A.—I was not paying attention.

Q.—I say in the report of the Minister of Lands and Forests for 1923, the section devoted to the air patrol, do you know who was the author of that report?

A.—I think I have seen it. It is Mr. Johnson's report?

MR. FINLAYSON: What would a mechanic know of that?

WITNESS: I have seen it. It has been lying around.

MR. FINLAYSON: He understands it is by Mr. Johnson.

MR. RANEY: Have you papers as an automobile engineer for Canada?

WITNESS: As an air engineer.

MR. RANEY: I see at the top of page 179 of this air patrol report, whether by Mr. Johnson or someone else, section 5, he says a special type of machine should be designed for this class of work as the machines available at the present time are not entirely suitable in that operating cost is high and performance low. What do you say about that?

A.—That is quite correct, but in justice to the Department they did not have any other machines available when they bought those. I don't want to say anything against them in that way.

Q.—We are trying to deal with facts. Do you know, as an expert in this line, whether any H.S. 2 L's have been built during the past six or eight years?

A.—I don't think any have been built since. There may have been one or two assembled from the parts lying around at different plants, but none actually built.

Q.—What do you say as to the size of these machines?

A.—Well they are very large machines but not larger than they ought to be to make them necessary to fly.

Q.—For the weight of the machine?

A.—For the machine the H.S. 2 L is a very capable machine.

Q.—Is it suitable for this kind of flying?

A.—It does the work, but it is not suitable.

Q.—Why?

MR. FINLAYSON: This man is a mechanic.

MR. WIDDIFIELD: Then he ought to be competent to answer the question.

MR. RANEY: You can go ahead when I am through.

MR. FINLAYSON: Get an expert for expert evidence.

MR. RANEY: What do you say as to the suitability of these flying boats for fire patrolling?

A.—I say that they could get a much more suitable machine.

Q.—Of what type?

A.—Seaplane.

Q.—Larger or smaller?

A.—Smaller.

Q.—How much smaller?

A.—Seventy-five per cent.

Q.—What about the cost of operating these machines?

A.—Well, how far do you mean Mr. Raney, do you mean—

Q.—Compare the cost of operating these flying boats and the smaller machines you refer to.

A.—There is practically no comparison at all.

Q.—What is the consumption of gasolene per hour of your flying boats? ·

A.—About thirty gallons an hour.

MR. FINLAYSON: Do you swear that? You had better make a note and be careful.

MR. RANEY: What is the cost, the number of gallons for a hydroplane, for the smaller machine?

A.—Nine or ten.

MR. FINLAYSON: Do you say the H.S. 2 L takes thirty gallons an hour?

WITNESS: You must understand in that Mr. Finlayson, that there is quite a little consumption in warming up and getting away.

MR. FINLAYSON: You are talking about flying hours.

MR. RANEY: If you will leave him alone you will have full opportunity later. It has been said here Mr. Briggs that the cost per flying hour of the present service is $46 without overhead and $53 with the overhead?

MR. LYONS: Fifty-four dollars.

MR. RANEY: Forty-three dollars a flying hour without overhead and $54 an hour with overhead. What do you say about that?

WITNESS: How many hours is that supposed to cover?

MR. RANEY: The whole season.

WITNESS: For 1924 with an average of 2,000 hours salaries alone would come to more than $43 an hour.

Q.—Have you calculated the actual cost per flying hour in the present service?

A.—No, sir, I don't know what flying hours they have had.

Q.—You say about 2,000 hours?

A.—On the average, yes.

Q.—Can you give the Committee any information as to the cost per flying hour of the present service?

A.—I have no idea of the overhead. I cannot do that.

Q.—Leave out the overhead.

A.—It is not possible at $50 an hour.

Q.—Leaving out the overhead and taking out everything else what in your opinion is the cost?

A.—I should imagine—

MR. FINLAYSON: Don't imagine.

WITNESS: I will say that with the salaries, gasolene and oil consumption and camp expenses, it would run nearer $100 than $50.

MR. FINLAYSON: Leave out the overhead.

MR. RANEY: Leave the witness alone. Tell me what is your estimate of the cost of flying service an hour leaving out the overhead?

A.—I would not make an estimate. I am not in a position to do that. I will say that for 2,000 hours of flying service the salary cost would be more than $50 an hour.

Q.—Salaries are part of overhead?

A.—I don't know anything about that. You can't fly a machine without anybody in it.

Q.—Do you know what gasolene cost?

A.—Not the contract price. I know it cost a lot to deliver.

Q.—Why?

A.—In many cases it is a long rail haul and then after taking it from the railroad it has a long way to go to the lakes.

Q.—Motorboat haul?

A.—Yes.

Q.—What about the size of the aerodrome if the machines had been of the smaller type you speak of?

A.—Well, the airdrome was built for the H.S. 2 L's.

Q.—Then it would be four times too large?

A.—Not four times.

CHAIRMAN: Mr. Raney is quite right. He said that the machines could have been reduced by 75 per cent., which means that it is four times as large.

MR. RANEY: If that is so the aerodrome is about four times as large as it need be for the protection of machines of the right type?

A.—That is if you have only the same quantity of machines.

Q.—Now come back to the specific thing you started out to tell Mr. Lyons about. "I respectfully desire to call attention to the very serious and costly mistakes in the overhaul and maintenance of Liberty engines at the Sault Ste. Marie aerodrome." What was the mistake you had in mind?

A.—The mistake of oiling in the crankshaft.

Q.—In the crankshaft there are holes on the left-hand side of the crankshaft, a number of holes drilled in for lubrication?

A.—Just one for each bearing.

Q.—And these holes were blocked up, you say, and other holes opened on the other side of the crankshaft?

A.—Yes.

Q.—When was that done?

A.—Immediately we started to overhaul the machines for the coming season.

Q.—What year?

A.—The winter of 1924-25. I would like to say right here that Captain Maxwell at the time I told him about it said they had done two or three of the engines previously in the Laurentide Air Service, so he naturally thought it was a good improvement.

Q.—What was the object sought to be attained in this change of the lubricating system?

A.—To keep the oil cleaner and prevent any carbon getting into the crankshaft.

Q.—Did you register any opinion on it at the time?

A.—I had registered my opinion. I spoke to the men about it.

Q.—Who was the man in charge?

A.—At that time, Gordon Hutt.

Q.—Was this done at his instance or Captain Maxwell's?

A.—I don't know.

Q.—Did you speak to him—Mr. Hutt?
A.—Yes.
Q.—What did you say?
A.—I said it would not work.
Q.—Then you warned him?
A.—Yes.
Q.—Of the change in the engines?
A.—Yes.
Q.—How many are there?
A.—I could not say. About twenty.
Q.—For how many machines?
A.—Fourteen machines.
Q.—That is to say you have spare engines?
A.—Yes, so that when they are taken out to be reconditioned another one can be put into place.
Q.—The engines require to be reconditioned about how often?
A.—Every eighty hours of flying time.
Q.—During the winter of 1924-25 were all the engines changed in that way?
A.—Yes.
Q.—Was a test made to see how the new plan would work?
A.—They were not all changed. They were not all finished by the time the machines were going out.
Q.—Nearly all?
A.—A big percentage.
Q.—Were any tests made to see how the change would work?
A.—Not beyond a few minutes round on the block.
Q.—Well, after all, or nearly all of the Liberty engines were changed what were they worth?
A.—I could not tell.
Q.—About how much?
A.—About $2,000 each.
MR. FINLAYSON: A mechanic knows a lot about this.
MR. RANEY: Don't worry; he ought to know something about it.
WITNESS: It depends on the cost of production. The cost originally was $12,000 or more.
Q.—Each engine?
A.—Yes.
Q.—Only a small production you mean?
A.—There was quite a large one.
Q.—What do I understand from that? What is the statement about the cost?
A.—The engine is a war type engine and naturally they are down to old engines now and they can be bought quite reasonably.
Q.—I suppose the Government can show what it paid for them. These engines having been changed in this way, what happened to them when the flying season started? When did it start?
A.—I cannot say. I was in the shop at the time. I think the machines went to Sudbury first.
MR. FINLAYSON: This is all supposition.
MR. RANEY: In 1925?
A.—I was on the last machine to leave the shop to go to operations.
Q.—What do you mean—operations?

A.—Forest patrol.

Q.—How many men do these machines carry?

A.—Four.

Q.—How many usually go?

A.—Three.

Q.—The pilot the observer and—

A.—The engineer.

Q.—And you go as the engineer. Can you drive a machine?

A.—Yes. I am not a licensed pilot and not allowed to.

Mr. Finlayson: This man is a mechanic.

Mr. Raney: Let him alone.

Mr. Finlayson: You ask him if he has been driving machines many times?

Mr. Raney: Have you driven?

Witness: Not very often. I have relieved the pilot a little. It is a heavy job driving four or five hours in the air.

Q.—What happened when the machines were altered and went into the air? What was the first thing that happened?

A.—In my own particular case they burned out the bearings and smashed the connecting rod.

Q.—Stay there, about the practice, who went with you?

A.—Mr. Oakes, the pilot; Mr. Sanderson, the observer, and myself as engineer.

A.—And you started from the Sault to go to?

A.—Sault Lake.

Q.—A distance of round about five or six hundred miles in round figures. What date?

A.—I could not say for certain.

Q.—Have you got the record?

A.—Not here?

Q.—In August?

A.—No, July.

Q.—Now what happened? Had the engine been in the air after the change?

A.—Yes, about fifty hours of flying.

Q.—What happened on the trip?

A.—The reason we made the trip was because the engine was not satisfactory and they were having great difficulty to get off the water. We wasted an hour in one instance. They argued that it was the rigging and my argument was that it was the engine. Thompson ordered us to Sault Lookout to have the rigging changed. We left about two o'clock in the afternoon. We just got about sixty miles from the station at Orient Bay when without any warning the oil pressure went out, showing on the guage and I asked Oakes to make for the lake.

Q.—That was so that you could land?

A.—Yes. Just as he turned the crash happened. The connecting rod broke, the oil had got so hot the engine was on fire.

Q.—What did you do?

A.—We could do nothing. We got the fire extinguisher out and extinguished the fire immediately we got to the water.

Q.—You made the water, by gliding I suppose?

A.—Yes. I was successful in getting the fire out without serious damage to the machine.

Q.—The machine, was it repairable or destroyed?

A.—The machine was not damaged.

Q.—I mean the engine?

A.—It was absolutely written off, only a little salvage on it.

Q.—You had to send back to the Sault and have another engine brought up?

A.—Yes, sir. We were sixty miles from the base.

Q.—From the Sault?

A.—From Orient Bay.

Q.—How far from the Sault?

A.—It is 400 miles.

Q.—Did you have to have the engine brought from Orient Bay or the Sault?

A.—From the Sault.

Q.—And you had to wait until it arrived?

A.—Yes.

Q.—Was that the first of these changed engines that had gone wrong?

A.—I don't think so. I think Mr. Thompson had one.

Q.—You were in the shops?

A.—No I was out at Orient Bay.

Q.—What was the next thing that happened?

A.—We got another engine and got it installed and that was the time I was discharged.

Q.—I see.

A.—The engine arrived on the night train at Orient Bay and I went down and got it off at 10.30, put it on the boat, took it to the lake and stayed on the job until it was installed. Two days after I was coming out of the tent at five after eight in the morning and Thompson was outside with his watch and said, "We start work at eight." I had been working two nights previously and two days and Thompson said I would not be required after the end of the month. Naturally I felt very sore and told him what I thought. He wrote to Captain Maxwell and possibly explained the situation but I think he must have exaggerated.

Q.—You were dismissed?

A.—Yes.

Q.—How many engines went bad?

A.—I cannot say. When I got back I would say there were nine or ten.

Q.—Out of business?

A.—Yes.

Q.—Do you know how many accidents occurred of the character of the one you have told us about?

A.—I don't know how many. Thompson had one, a new engine I handled went somewhere.

Mr. Finlayson: Do you know about this or is it hearsay?

Witness: Certainly, I was at the Sault when I left Orient Bay.

Mr. Raney: Don't be too nervous.

Mr. Finlayson: I am not nervous.

Mr. Raney: He ought to know about it.

Mr. Finlayson: Getting a discharged mechanic to give expert evidence; you know this man is guessing and talking and theorizing.

Mr. Raney: What happened to the engine you installed after the accident?

Mr. Finlayson: Does he know of his own knowledge?

Chairman: Do you know?

Witness: Yes.

Mr. Raney: Answer the question.

Witness: That engine went the same way; the same accident exactly. I don't know how many hours it flew. The wire came through, the engine was smashed.

Mr. Finlayson: That shows he does not know of his own knowledge.

Mr. Raney: How many engines do you know of going in this way after the change.

Mr. Finlayson: Of his own knowledge.

Witness: I could prove I know if I am allowed to ask a question.

Mr. Raney: Never mind Mr. Finlayson. How many engines were out of business?

A.—I could not say how many. I know eight or nine at the Sault, including three at Orient Bay.

Q.—Put out of business?

A.—Yes.

Q.—And how many of these engines were so badly injured that they were of no further use?

A.—I cannot say.

Q.—How many repairable?

A.—All repairable to the extent that you could buy new parts.

Q.—Practically, how many were repairable?

Mr. Finlayson: All, he says.

Witness: If you bought new parts, which would include the crankcase.

Chairman: You are speaking of the one that went wrong?

Witness: That was in very bad shape, the salvage possibly only a few cylinders and valves and stuff like that.

Mr. Raney: Was your engine brought to the base?

Witness: Yes, I dismantled it at the Sault.

Mr. Finlayson: It is in use again now.

Mr. Raney: They saved the parts that could be saved?

Witness: No parts could be saved that were broken.

Mr. Raney: What was done with respect to the other engines that had not been destroyed or injured in this way?

Witness: I don't get you.

Mr. Raney: We have the fact that the crankcase had been changed by blocking up the holes on one side and opening them on the other side.

Mr. Black: You say the crankcase and he says the crankshaft?

Mr. Raney: I mean the crankshaft.

Mr. Black: There is a vast difference.

Mr. Raney: What happened to those machines? They were all put back to the original condition?

A.—Yes.

Q.—All the holes that had been opened were blocked up and the old holes that had been blocked up were reopened?

A.—Yes. I might explain right here that when the holes were drilled on the opposite side of the shaft when the engine got any speed it was impossible for the oil to come out, it does not matter what the pressure is, just as when you swing a bucket of water round the centrifugal force will keep it in in the same way.

Q.—Did you argue that out with the man in charge?

A.—I had had the same trouble with the Willys-Overland five years ago.

Q.—You knew the crankshaft was properly made?

A.—Yes.

Mr. Widdifield: He was an expert engineer.

Q.—Do you know what was the real reason for your dismissal?

A.—No, sir, I do not.

Q.—You were never told?

A.—No.

Q.—Did you ask anybody?

A.—No, I believe I did say to Mr. Lyons when I was here in his office I really did not know what I was discharged for.

Q.—What did he say?

A.—Mr. Lyons did not say anything about it. He left it to Captain Maxwell, naturally, who should be taken on and who should not. I am not blaming Mr. Lyons.

Q.—Were you the only man discharged?

A.—Yes, sir.

Q.—You say in your letter: "A change was made at the commencement of the season in the oiling system that has already resulted in a few engines being entirely written off and none with this alteration has attained eighty hours of flying time." Is that true?

A.—Before I left the Sault Captain Maxwell said that some had attained eighty hours.

Mr. Finlayson: We will give a list of the whole service if you like.

Mr. Raney: "Resulting in tremendous monetary loss." Let us see what the new parts cost. A crank case, I understand is $800?

Chairman: In the letter I understand he said the change had resulted in a number of the machines being entirely written off. This evidence does not support that.

Mr. Raney: What do you say about that?

Witness: The particular engine I had was. There was very little salvage.

Q.—What about parts for the Liberty engine, is there difficulty in getting them?

A.—That I cannot say.

Q.—How long is it since they were made?

A.—There are none made, I think, by the original makers.

Q.—"Resulting in tremendous monetary loss to engines and damage to machines in out-of-way places"—I suppose that is a factor?

A.—Mine was an out-of-the-way place, five or six hundred miles from the Sault.

Q.—How many days would the crew be detained?

A.—I was eight days before I got the engine.

Q.—And were the pilot and observer there?

A.—Yes.

Q.—Kept there eight days?

A.—Yes.

Q.—"Jeopardising of the lives of the crews,"—was that true?

A.—Certainly, with the engine breaking up like that. If we had had another half-mile to go we could not have made the water.

Q.—What would have happened?

A.—We should have landed in the bush.

Q.—What would have happened then?

Mr. Finlayson: They would have injured some branches and trees.

Mr. Raney: You would not have wanted to be on the machine?

A.—Not if we could have helped it. I may say that nobody gets away from the water unless it is absolutely necessary. We always keep to the water-course.

Q.—"Myself and others warned against this at the time the alteration was made, as perfect lubrication was made impossible by this foolish system adopted. I have very strenuously opposed this and other crude and dangerous methods of operation with the result that I am discharged."

A.—I might say, Mr. Raney, that when I saw Hon. Mr. Lyons he was very nice to me and said that he could say not anything until he got the written report.

Q.—Did you ever hear of a written report afterwards?

A.—No.

MR. RANEY: Have you one?

MR. FINLAYSON: We will give our evidence.

MR. RANEY: If you decline to give it now probably I will have to recall the witness.

MR. FINLAYSON: He is here for causing trouble; he will be available.

MR. RANEY: How many machines were out of commission at one time at Orient Bay?

A.—There was only one when I left; I know there were three afterwards.

CHAIRMAN: Do I understand that you were discharged almost immediately after the machines which had been changed went into the service. After these machines which had the oiling system changed, how long after that was it before you were discharged?

WITNESS: Quite a long time. I was discharged on the fifth of August.

MR. RANEY: When did your service come to an end?

A.—On the fifth of September.

Q.—How many machines were put out of business before you left in September?

A.—I cannot say how many.

Q.—How many do you know of?

A.—I know of three at Orient Bay.

Q.—How many more?

A.—I don't know where they were; one or two in different places. Captain Maxwell will bear me out in that. We were working night and day getting the engines out.

Q.—What do you say about co-operation between the Air Service and the Fire Ranging staff?

A.—Always a little at loggerheads.

Q.—Take Timagami station for instance. What about it?

A.—I will have to explain that right from the beginning.

Q.—Do you know the facts?

A.—Yes.

Q.—Go ahead by way of illustration.

MR. FINLAYSON: Is the Service to be brought into question? No doubt there are occasional differences between a novel and an old established branch. Is that to be brought into question and policy discussed by a mechanic before the Committee?

MR. RANEY: Go on witness, please.

MR. FINLAYSON: I leave it to the Committee. It seems to me a waste of time and bad for any service. It is just as if we got an office boy from your office to discuss friction between you and someone.

MR. RANEY: This gentleman is not an office boy.

MR. FINLAYSON: That is the relationship exactly. He is a mechanic working on the ground. What does he know?

MR. RANEY: Let us get on. Were you at Timagami? I should like you to denote what was the failure of co-ordination of these two services and the general efficiency or inefficiency.

MR. FINLAYSON: The result of the forest protection service for the past two years is simply marvellous and I didn't think it should be called into question by some discharged mechanic.

MR. RANEY: You raised the question yourself in your examination of Mr. Lyons. If you had not done so I would not now.

MR. FINLAYSON: On this point?

MR. RANEY: You introduced the whole question.

MR. FINLAYSON: You are bringing a discharged mechanic, with animus no doubt—

MR. RANEY: Go on, discredit him.

MR. FINLAYSON: Those are the facts. Any man may be unfortunate and incapable and get discharged.

MR. RANEY: Pardon me. You say that being incapable he was discharged. That was never suggested Mr. Chairman, he says—

MR. FINLAYSON: I don't care a rap what he says; when it gets down to suggesting that two branches of the Service are not co-ordinated I think it should be obtained from someone who might know something about it.

CHAIRMAN: Unless it has some direct bearing on the inquiry—

MR. RANEY: I would not bring it unless I thought it had some bearing.

MR. WIDDIFIELD: I am a member of this Committee. I want to hear the evidence.

CHAIRMAN: There is no need to get excited. We are not going to close off anything relevant.

MR. WIDDIFIELD: Mr. Finlayson talks about him being a discharged mechanic. The fact that he is discharged is opportune perhaps to bringing out the evidence and that is what the Committee wants to know. I object to three or four talking at once. I want to hear the evidence and I think the interrogator and the witness should be left alone for the time being.

MR. FINLAYSON: Mr. Widdifield, I am not—

MR. RANEY: When Mr. Finlayson was examining witnesses I have not interrupted.

CHAIRMAN: I don't think he did.

MR. RANEY: Ever since this examination started there has been an attempt to injure this witness, calling him names, a mere mechanic, a discharged mechanic.

MR. FINLAYSON: I never said a mere mechanic.

MR. RANEY: I ask you to rule, Mr. Chairman, that Mr. Finlayson must leave him alone and examine him when his turn comes.

MR. FINLAYSON: Sit down for a minute and let me get a word in. I only wanted to point out to the Committee that if we are going into the question of co-ordinating the service there is a proper way of doing it.

CHAIRMAN: It seems to me that we should not prevent Mr. Raney pursuing this line of investigation if he thinks it is relative to the subject he has brought forward. I was going to say that Mr. Widdifield is getting on dangerous ground when he says what he wants to do as a member of the Committee. We are not dealing with it in that way.

MR. CALLAN: What in your opinion caused the failure at Sault Lookout?

WITNESS: Lack of lubrication.

MR. CALLAN: Could you give me a sketch of how the lubrication system works?

WITNESS: Yes.

MR. RANEY: Let him do it now. It is an important matter. It had caused the loss of $50,000.

CHAIRMAN: Of course, Mr. Briggs could not give an estimate of that.

WITNESS: I don't think I should give evidence against people in the force.

CHAIRMAN: I think you are trying to give what you know.

MR. RANEY: Will you explain for Mr. Callan?

CHAIRMAN: May I suggest drawing a large plan of the crankshaft and piston rods connecting.

(Diagram is drawn.)

MR. RANEY: Stand up and tell the Committee.

(Witness explains diagram.) He points out where holes are drilled so that oil can be forced by pressure through the shaft.

CHAIRMAN: The same as an automobile.

MR. CALLAN: Inside the shaft?

WITNESS: Yes, and then up the pipe to the cam shaft. When the engine gets up speed, 2,000 revolutions, not quite, 1,400 revolutions per minute, when it gets up that speed and the hole is drilled on the other side the centrifugal force would keep it in.

MR. RANEY: You must have the oil working with the centrifugal force and not against it?

WITNESS: It was a good idea to have the holes on the other side because it would prevent a lot of carbon getting in and keep the shaft cleaner.

MR. CALLAN: What is the size of the hole?

WITNESS: About one-eighth outlet; the hole through the shaft is about a quarter.

MR. CALLAN: What diameter is the pipe that holds the oil?

WITNESS: Every time this goes to the hole it shoots through.

MR. CALLAN: Is there not a possibility of that pipe becoming clogged?

WITNESS: No, because the oil is filtered before it is turned into circulation. It goes through a screen.

MR. CALLAN: There is no solid matter. Is there not a possibility regardless of which side of the shaft that oil was placed that there might be a possibility of that hole becoming blocked up?

WITNESS: It has grown very hot on occasions and burned out the bearings.

MR. CALLAN: What is the shaft made of?

WITNESS: Steel.

MR. CALLAN: What are the bearings made of?

WITNESS: White metal; babbitt metal.

MR. CALLAN: Is there a possibility that the babbitt metal may get into the hole and restrict it?

WITNESS: It is a possibility overcome by the pressure of the feed of the oil.

MR. CALLAN: Regardless of what side the oil goes is there that possibility?

WITNESS: Yes, the babbitt can get into the hole but not sufficient to stop oil circulation.

MR. RANEY: It means that you must keep examining.

WITNESS: After every eighty hours of flying.

MR. CALLAN: That's all.

CHAIRMAN: It is the same system on most of the automobiles for oiling.

MR. RANEY: To avoid further friction I will not pursue the subject of Timaga.ni. There is another thing I want to touch on with this witness. The statement is that in 1923 two million acres of the wooded wealth of Ontario was destroyed and that last year, 1925, only 10,154, and the improvement is startling and staggering and so on. Was there any difference between the seasons 1923 and 1925?

WITNESS: Yes.

Q.—What is the difference?

A.—One was dry and two were wet.

Q.—1924 and 1925 were wet?

A.—Yes.

Q.—Take 1925, when did your machines first leave the water?

A.—I could not be exact to the day—In May.

Q.—When they first left the water for fire patrol?

A.—Right on then.

Q.—Was it 1924 that was wetter than 1925?

A.—I don't think there was very much difference.

Q.—What was the extent of the fire patrol in 1924 and 1925 as compared with 1923? Was it as large in those two years?

A.—I don't know what was the time in 1923. It was common talk it was a dry season.

Q.—What about the necessity for an air patrol in 1924 and 1925?

A.—There is always a necessity for an air patrol. You can't get away from that. It is the only system for spotting fires.

Q.—But compared with a dry season was there as much or not?

A.—I think that for eight weeks we never flew at all.

Q.—That is what I am trying to get at. In what year?

A.—In 1925.

Q.—Why was that?

A.—It was a wet season.

Q.—Wet woods. What months would that be?

A.—The months would be May, June and July.

Q.—You hardly flew at all in July?

A.—The pilot I was with did quite a bit of flying. I think we had the record up to that time. But we were doing quite a bit of surveying and photographing.

Q.—Not fires?

A.—We had some fires because we had a large district.

Q.—But very little for May, June and July of 1925?

A.—Very little.

MEMBER: Is that an examination to show why the Department makes a good showing.

MR. RANEY: Take the witness, Mr. Finlayson.

MEMBER: We have to take the questions for what they are worth. Supposing a man is dismissed has he a right to come before the Committee like this? Is every man discharged by Captain Maxwell to come here and try and destroy the system altogether?

MR. LYONS: I have no objection to Mr. Briggs or anyone giving his views. All I ask is an opportunity to present the facts which will make him look so ridiculous it will make him wish he never appeared here.

MR. FINLAYSON: I suppose gentlemen, there is this view: This is not the army. Those who were in the army know that this kind of thing would not be entertained. We are a public body and I think we should allow reasonable latitude for a discharged man's feelings, and I fancy that the Committee and the public generally will know what is to be expected—

MR. RANEY: Go ahead; don't abuse the witness.

MR. FINLAYSON: You have ordered me several times and you ordered Mr. Graves. I hestitate to order.

MEMBER: I object to wasting my time here.

MR. FINLAYSON: You have to take these things as they come.

Mr. Briggs examined by Mr. Finlayson.

Q.—Mr. Briggs, when did you enter the Government service?

A.—In April, 1924, I think it was April, March 20th the letter was dated.

Q.—Never mind, April will do. Before that—I was not here when you gave the first part of your evidence—you served in France?

A.—Yes.

Q.—As mechanic?

A.—As mechanic in the Divisional Ammunition Park.

Q.—You were in the D.A.C.?

A.—The A.S.C.

Q.—You were not in the Flying Corps?

A.—No, sir.

Q.—And when did you start this? When did you get into this branch? Were you ever in the air service?

CHAIRMAN: After he was discharged—he lost part of his foot and came back—he came to Canada and joined in 1917 in the R.A.F. as a mechanic and was with them in various capacities for the balance of the war.

Q.—Your service was in the Army Service Corps?

A.—Yes.

Q.—And you came back here. You had other experience and qualified as a mechanic?

A.—Yes.

Q.—You went into the Department service in April, 1924?

A.—Yes, in the Forestry Branch.

Q.—You were there as a mechanic?

A.—Yes.

Q.—And the duty of a mechanic is to keep the machines in order?

A.—Yes.

Q.—And it is limited to that?

A.—Except at the time when we are assembling in the shops.

Q.—Your work is mechanical?

A.—Yes.

Q.—Pure and simple, and you don't profess to be a forestry expert?

A.—No, sir.

Q.—Nor to have any knowledge of that branch of the service?

A.—No.

Q.—What were we wasting time about?

A.—We all have a general knowledge.

Q.—I know we all have opinions.

A.—Not opinions. I mean we all know a little about the rest of the service. We don't interfere with it and have nothing to do with it.

Q.—So you don't have opinions of value on anything but mechanical duties?

A.—Yes.

Q.—Since you left the service, you were organizing something?

A.—I was endeavouring to organize a company to construct machines in Canada.

Q.—That fell through, I believe.

A.—No.

Q.—You formed one?

A.—It did not fall through.

Q.—It has never gone through?

A.—It may do.

CHAIRMAN: It may?

WITNESS: Yes.

Q.—You are trying to organize a company to sell to the Forestry Branch?

A.—No.

Q.—Have you not tried to sell them a flying service?

A.—No, sir.

Q.—I have the correspondence here on that. Were you not negotiating with the president of the Curtis Company, or the vice-president, for a flying service?

A.—To supply machines.

Q.—And also a flying service?

A.—Not for the Forestry Branch.

Q.—Any branch?

A.—Yes, the Federal Government.

Q.—And you were trying to sell a flying service to them?

A.—Yes.

Q.—And you were telling the officers of the Curtis Company, you would get a flying service?

A.—No, that was not gone into.

Q.—Just for a minute now. Never mind the correspondence. You can hand that over if you like.

A.—That was as far as it went.

Q.—Did you tell one of the officers you could sell the Ontario Government a flying service per hour?

A.—No, I said we might do eventually.

Q.—That is one of your purposes now?

A.—Not now. That is all washed out for the present.

Q.—But you have still hopes of a flying service at so much per hour?

A.—I am out of that now.

Q.—What are you in?

A.—As a matter of fact I have entered negotiations to go into business on my own.

Q.—You have been negotiating ever since you left?

A.—Every man has something to do. I have to live.

Q.—And living involves negotiating and you have been negotiating ever since you left and one of the negotiations looked to the selling of a Curtis service to the Government?

A.—Selling the machines.

Q.—And also supplying a flying service?

A.—That could not be done.

Q.—You hoped it could?

A.—I talked of the possibility.

Q.—And did you not tell one of the officers of the Curtis Company that you could get the Ontario Government to give $300?

A.—Not $300. The price mentioned would be around $50.

Q.—We are told it was $300?

A.—No one would pay $300 an hour for flying.

Q.—What did the Laurentide get?

A.—I don't know.

Q.—$250?

A.—I don't know.

Q.—What is the cost to the Dominion Government?

A.—Well, there is a different organization.

Q.—Answer the question.

A.—I don't know.

Q.—Did you mention the possibility of getting the Ontario Government to pay $300 an hour?

A.—No, and I would not attempt to sell it them. Round about $45 or $50 I would want to sell.

Q.—How do you arrive at that?

A.—That is a pretty long story.

Mr. Raney: You are qualifying him as an expert.

Mr. Finlayson: I think he admits it.

Mr. Raney: It is not impossible.

Mr. Finlayson: Now since you have been discharged, you have not done any work since?

A.—I have done a little work. I have overhauled a few cars on my own.

Q.—A few motor cars?

A.—Yes. I have not done many.

Q.—How many?

A.—Two.

Q.—Two motor cars. You work as a mechanic?

A.—I have not done regular work since I left the service seven months ago.

Q.—I am satisfied with that. Except for overhauling two motor cars, since you left you have devoted yourself to this work you are bringing before the Committee?

A.—Pardon me—

Q.—Who have you been collaborating with about this?

A.—What work?

Q.—This you bring before the Committee?

A.—I have not seen anybody.

Q.—You must have seen somebody?

A.—I was introduced to Mr. Raney a couple of days ago.

Q.—How was that arranged?

A.—It was not arranged at all. It just happened.

Q.—It just happened that you were introduced to Mr. Raney and these matters are before the Committee; otherwise you have done nothing. All right. Now your work at the Sault was work in the winter. You had been working in the shop?

A.—Yes.

Q.—Grinding valves and so on?

A.—Yes. That is I was most of the time grinding valves.

Chairman: That is the principal part of the overhauling.

Q.—I see; grinding valves, that was your job. Did you do anything else?

A.—All kinds of work.

Q.—There are experts' jobs around the shop, you did not do them?

A.—I did a little.

Q.—Is it not true that your work was physical work—the grinding of valves?

A.—Not all the time.

Q.—Nearly all the time?

A.—I did welding work and overhauling motors, once with a man named Sam McCaulay.

Q.—But apart from that one occasion you were engaged in the grinding of valves?

A.—I was not engaged in grinding valves.

Q.—You were working at grinding valves? That was your occupation. I believe you helped the carpenter a little?

A.—I might have.

Q.—I suppose they used men according to their ability?

A.—Not according to ability.

Q.—Not according to your ability.

MR. RANEY: Did you not hear him say that he was at Toronto University, and that all the flying men passed through his hands.

MR. FINLAYSON: Who were you under?

A.—Gordon Hutt.

Q.—Who was superintendent of the shop?

A.—Mr. Thompson. Hutt was sub-foreman and Thompson, superintendent.

Q.—And he put you to the work he thought you could do?

A.—What he thought I should do.

Q.—And he thought that you should grind valves and that other men should do the delicate work?

A.—Yes.

Q.—Now, you say you were offering some observations on the machines, on the Liberty engines?·

A.—Yes. .

Q.—Are they not the result of all the mechanical skill of North America?

A.—Yes.

Q.—And produced in enormous quantities?

A.—Yes.

Q.—They are the finest thing produced by the combined American shops?

A.—By the combined engineers of the world.

Q.—And the result of study of—

A.—All conditions.

Q.—If you will listen for a minute, of all the American scientists who were directed to this work by the American government?

A.—Yes.

Q.—And is considered one of the finest machines in the world?

A.—It was.

Q.—And is still in use all over the world?

A.—Yes.

Q.—And it was produced in such quantities that there are still some in stock?

A.—I don't know of any stocks. I believe they are hard to get.

Q.—Hard to get?

A.—I think so.

Q.—Don't you know that there are many still uncrated and being used for other devices?

A.—They are all used stuff and, pardon me—

Q.—There are Liberty engines never uncrated—

Mr. RANEY: Let him give his evidence.

Q.—And it is possible to replace engines?

A.—Yes.

MEMBER: Is that new or overhauled?

WITNESS: Overhauled.

Mr. FINLAYSON: New engines, never touched.

Mr. RANEY: Witness says different.

WITNESS: We have not had any new ones.

Mr. FINLAYSON: You don't know from general information. Liberty engines are being used all over the world?

WITNESS: No, sir.

Q.—You say it is not?

A.—It may be, but not to any general extent.

Q.—The flying world?

A.—They have got the engines and have to use them up.

Q.—Do you know what the Liberty engine is worth new?

A.—What they are supplied for I don't know.

Q.—Supplied new?

A.—Around $12,000 or $14,000.

MEMBER: Are you guessing at the prices?

WITNESS: Those engines were made in tremendous quantities.

Q.—Have you any proof? You would not swear?

A.—No, sir.

MEMBER: Then why do you say?

Mr. FINLAYSON: As a matter of fact, he is miles out.

WITNESS: That is the price ruling to-day.

Q.—Do you want to swear to production prices?

A.—No.

Q.—Let us test the man. You said $12,000. Now do you swear to that?

A.—I didn't swear. I said I imagined they cost about $12,000.

Q.—$18,000 is the exact price.

A.—Well then, if they cost that, $12,000 is a reasonable price to-day.

CHAIRMAN: Just a minute. Don't get making mistakes in the evidence. The evidence you gave to Mr. Finlayson was that they cost so much under mass production, about $12,000, and used engines about $2,000.

WITNESS: That is what I did say and you remind me I should not say, "I understand."

Mr. GRAVES: I should like to ask this question. Is this an investigation to make inquiries concerning supposed irregularities of a Minister who resigned or is it an investigation into the inefficiency of some particular man or department. At this rate, we will be here for ever. I thought this was an investigation of a Minister who resigned.

CHAIRMAN: Mr. Graves, that is not quite correct. It was an inquiry Mr. Lyons asked. This is a man Mr. Raney brought before the Committee, with a couple of witnesses we called, and we were not told what they were going to be—

Mr. RANEY: I said, I was going to confine myself to matters before the Committee, but Mr. Finlayson took Mr. Lyons over the air service and a lot

of other branches and in consequence of what Mr. Lyons said about flying cost
being forty odd dollars and as the witness said he told about the change in the
oiling system I thought he was entitled to tell the Committee.

MR. FINLAYSON: Mr. Raney has made a statement absolutely misleading.
He knows his questions put on the order paper in Mr. Kemp's name were directed
on the aerodrome contract. You said that was what you wanted to investigate
and questions were directed at the "enormous" expense and it was necessary to
say something in explanation of why that investment was made and Mr. Lyons
went into the aerial patrol work to show the enormous saving and the cutting
down of operating expense.

MR. RANEY: For goodness sake, go on with the cross-examination.

MR. FINLAYSON: Are you going to withdraw?

MR. RANEY: No, go on.

MR. FINLAYSON: You said that $12,000 was the cost of the Liberty
engine?

A.—Yes.

Q.—Is that wild guess?

A.—Not exactly wild.

Q.—When the total was $18,000?

A.—$12,000 was my suspicion.

CHAIRMAN: Your estimate?

WITNESS: Yes.

Q.—You are only out the difference between $12,000 and $18,000. You
went on to say something about $5,500—

A.—I never said $5,500.

Q.—Did you not say that overhauled engines were $5,500?

A.—I said around $2,000.

CHAIRMAN: That is right.

Q.—Was the $2,000 a guess?

A.—On the Liberty engine?

Q.—On the value now. That is the particular engine in the service?

A.—Yes.

Q.—Do you think they could be bought for $5,000?

A.—No, I said the engines we got.

CHAIRMAN: These were the kind we got.

WITNESS: Not purchased new.

MR. FINLAYSON: What does your $2,000 mean, second-hand engines?

A.—Yes.

Q.—What would you say a new Liberty engine could be bought for?

A.—I would not say.

Q.—Of course. Perhaps you are wise. You say a Liberty engine is not
suitable for this purpose?

A.—I didn't say that.

Q.—You agree it is?

A.—It is a suitable engine for this particular body.

Q.—And those particular bodies are not suitable?

A.—Those particular bodies give good service for what they are.

Q.—You said a four times smaller size was required?

A.—I said they could get a machine more suitable for forestry patrol.

Q.—What kind do you suggest?

A.—I suggest a small type of seaplane.

Q.—Such as what?

A.—Such as Captain Maxwell has brought over.

Q.—What is that worth?

A.—Nine to ten thousand dollars?

Q.—Laid down?

A.—What I was going to suggest was to build them in this country.

Q.—You suggest that the Government should abandon the H.S. 2 L's, and instal these?

A.—I am not making any suggestion, Mr. Finlayson.

Q.—Am I wrong in saying that you made the statement that they were four times too big and the aerodrome was too large? Did you make that charge?

A.—Yes, I said the aerodrome was built to accommodate the H.S. 2 L's.

Q.—Too large?

A.—Not for the H.S.'s.

Q.—You say the H.S.'s are too large?

A.—Yes, you could use smaller.

Q.—For the fire service?

A.—Yes.

Q.—Let us analyse that for a minute. These H.S.'s will carry a whole fire fighting apparatus?

A.—They have done so on occasions.

Q.—Is it not what they are for?

A.—They are used as fire spotters.

Q.—Just a minute, there are two purposes aren't there?

A.—Yes.

Q.—When a fire is seen is not the main thing to do, to put it out?

A.—Certainly.

Q.—And these machines will do both?

A.—The machines won't. We can take a man and equipment to put out the fire.

Q.—Pumps, hose, everything else?

A.—I think I was on the crew of the first machine to do that. That shows I know.

Q.—And that is what they are for, carrying equipment?

A.—Yes.

Q.—And men?

A.—Yes, but they need a lake large enough to get down in.

Q.—Aren't there millions of such lakes in Northern Ontario?

A.—Yes.

Q.—If the fire is near a lake you can land with the H.S. 2 L's, can't you?

A.—If it is a reasonably sized lake.

Q.—They are all big enough for that aren't they?

A.—Not all of them.

Q.—The vast majority?

A.—Yes. But it is possible that you will have a fire not starting near a lake.

CHAIRMAN: Even if the fire started inland, could you not with these machines take fire fighting apparatus to the nearest point?

WITNESS: Yes.

MR. FINLAYSON: And with the smaller machines, you could not do that?

A.—No.

Q.—These are machines required for spotting?

A.—Not for spotting.

Q.—I know what you mean. What rate do they travel?

A.—Sixty miles.

Q.—Eighty?

A.—If the wind is behind them.

Q.—And the other machines can do 200?

A.—No, 125.

Q.—I see. The difference between 80 and 125—

A.—Sixty miles is the rate.

Q.—The difference is not appreciable for this purpose?

A.—It is nearly double, no, more than double.

Q.—Are you giving this in knots or miles?

A.—Miles

Q.—And you say 60 to 80?

A.—Sixty.

Q.—And the others will do 100 to 125?

A.—Yes.

Q.—Do you want to tell the Committee that a machine that will travel 60 to 80 miles per hour and carry three men—some have carried five—and equipment to put out a fire, is not ten times as useful as one travelling 100 to 125 miles per hour with only one man and no equipment?

A.—Not for fire spotting.

Q.—We want to put them out.

A.—There are few occasions when you have to use a machine to put a fire out. I have not had two occasions when that was done in two years.

Q.—I don't want to say anything that will hurt your feelings, but the difference between a superintendent and a mechanic is vast. You want to tell the Committee that the machines, take spotting, which travel 60 to 80 miles an hour are not practically as useful as machines that travel 125 miles an hour?

A.—Not by any means.

Q.—Where does the difference come in?

A.—The great difference is in the cost of operation, for spotting.

Q.—I am talking for spotting. Your small machine travels a little faster but the difference between 60 and 100, does not amount to much?

A.—Supposing I allow that to a certain extent.

Q.—I think it must be apparent that a machine that travels 60 to 80 miles an hour is fast enough for all practical purposes?

A.—Yes.

Q.—And it has a very great advantage if it can carry a crew of men?

A.—If necessary.

Q.—As many as six, five possibly?

A.—It can carry five but cannot get off with them very easily.

Q.—It is easier to rise with one man than five men, certainly, But your H.S. 2 L's can carry five or four men?

A.—Yes.

Q.—And they can leave two men and the necessary equipment to fight a fire?

A.—Yes.

Q.—And can go back and get more equipment?

A.—Yes.

Q.—It is the most effective machine for putting out fires in existence?

A.—No.

Q.—What is more effective?

A.—If you want a machine to carry fire apparatus you can get a better machine, a modern machine.

Q.—If you want to pay the price, I suppose. These are efficient?

A.—Yes, certainly.

Q.—There are more modern machines no doubt, that would cost a fortune to get?

A.—No, sir.

Q.—How much?

A.—We just spoke of $9,000.

Q.—There is a vast difference between $2,000 and $9,000. What will a modern machine, built right up-to-date, with the carrying capacity of the H.S. 2 L's cost?

A.—They would cost $9,000.

Q.—You speak of the Lark, it would not carry with the H.S. 2 L's?

A.—It will carry 800 pounds.

Q.—And what do you say the Lark cost? $9,000? Are you an agent for them? Would you like to take orders for them at that price?

A.—I was figuring over on the other side.

CHAIRMAN: He estimates he could build them for that.

Q.—You have not the means nor the capacity.

A.—I have the capacity and could get the means.

Q.—Why don't you build?

A.—There are no orders for them.

Q.—What do you say the Lark cost?

A.—About $9,000.

Q.—What do they sell them for?

A.—It depends on the engine. Captain Maxwell's may have cost $15,000.

Q.—What would it cost here?

A.—Plus customs.

Q.—What is that?

A.—About forty-five per cent.

Q.—Round about $20,000 here?

A.—That tax is just coming off.

Q.—Just as likely. You may have charge of the Dominion Government and know what nobody else knows. I hope you are going to take off the income tax.

A.—I'd like to.

Q.—Please take off the income tax at the same time. What you are suggesting is that the H.S. 2 L's should be discarded and that machines that cost $20,000 or $22,000 put in their place?

A.—No.

Q.—What are you suggesting then?

A.—I am suggesting nothing.

Q.—The machines are four times too large—do you say that?

A.—No.

Q.—I thought you didn't mean that. You say the aerodrome is too large?

A.—Not for those machines.

Q.—Too large for the service?

A.—Yes, if you used smaller machines.

Q.—As we have large machines and the service may expand it is not a bit too large?

A.—No.

Q.—Let us drop this foolishness. You have had some advice on the price of gasoline. Do you know anything about it?

A.—I don't know what you paid.

Q.—Then we are not going to worry about that.

Q.—Your trouble was with Thompson was it not?

A.—I had no trouble with him.

Q.—He discharged you?

A.—I was discharged.

Q.—He had reported you for discharge the previous year hadn't he?

A.—Yes.

Q.—And Captain Maxwell was good enough to give you another chance?

A.—It was a case of another chance. I was wrongfully discharged.

Q.—His boss reported him for discharge the previous season.

A.—You would like an explanation?

Q.—I want the facts. Answer the question. In the previous season your immediate boss had reported you for discharge?

A.—He discharged me right there.

Q.—And Captain Maxwell took you back and gave you another chance?

A.—I did not know Captain Maxwell did. I had a letter from Thompson that same day.

Q.—And you were given another chance?

A.—Thompson wrote the discharge. I left for Sault Ste. Marie with a machine and we were just starting off when the mail came and there was a letter from Captain Maxwell congratulating me—

Q.—We will give you the benefit of that.

CHAIRMAN: The letter is signed by W. Maxwell and is to Briggs at Orient Bay, October 22nd, 1924. Acknowledgment is made of yours of October 15th. Cheque passed for fifty dollars. Acceptable performance on your machine. Trust you did not run into unfavourable weather.

Q.—Apparently you had Captain Maxwell's goodwill at that time?

A.—I always have had.

Q.—Thompson had discharged you the previous season?

A.—The same season; at the time of that letter.

Q.—Your immediate boss discharged you in 1924 and because Captain Maxwell had some favoured feeling he gave you another chance?

A.—No. Major Thompson's machine came in very dirty and when he found I had not been on that machine for five or six days he took back his word and sent a letter.

Q.—Have you that letter?

A.—No, it was destroyed. He said I was to forget about it.

Q.—You were discharged for allowing a machine to become dirty?

MR. RANEY: He did not say that.

WITNESS: I was not on the machine for five or six days.

Q.—It was one of your machines?

A.—I had been taken off it, and—

Q.—You were discharged?

MR. RANEY: Let him explain.

Q.—You were discharged anyway?

A.—I was not exactly discharged. I had no form of actual discharge. I was told I was not wanted any more.

Q.—I don't, what else anyone would want—

A.—The next minute I was taken on again.

Q.—You were let off and let on again.

Mr. Callan: Did you make any explanation to Mr. Thompson after you were discharged.

Witness: Yes.

Mr. Callan: And were immediately re-hired?

Witness: Not until I got to the Sault and he sent me a letter.

Mr. Finlayson: You were discharged and the management, the O.C., was good enough to give you another chance for some reason. We can put it this way, Thompson and Maxwell were disposed to be friendly?

A.—Maxwell was always, not Thompson.

Q.—Captain Maxwell was friendly?

A.—And always has been. I always got a square deal from Captain Maxwell.

Q.—You have no complaint to make about him?

A.—None at all, no.

Q.—If he discharged you a second time it would not be from any animus or feeling?

A.—Not on the letter he got from Thompson.

Q.—The first time he was willing to overlook it; so much for that. They told him there was trouble over a number of your machines and that was one of the reasons you were discharged?

A.—There was no trouble with the machines; that was the end of the season.

Q.—1924?

A.—Yes.

Q.—In 1925, we understand there were dirty machines again. Is it correct that before your final discharge for being late there had been complaints from Thompson about neglect of work?

A.—No.

Q.—From anybody?

A.—No complaints at all.

Q.—How many engines were lost through dirt?

A.—None.

Q.—You may say that.

A.—I do say that.

Q.—Other people are the judges, of course. You say there was a mistake in drilling these holes?

A.—Yes.

Q.—The Laurentide people who had the service from Mr. Raney's Government, had done the same thing?

A.—So Captain Maxwell told us.

Q.—The Laurentide was managed by competent officials?

A.—Captain Maxwell.

Q.—And other competent people, too?

A.—Major Thompson.

Q.—And they were contractors for the Drury Government?

A.—Yes.

Q.—And they had had a lot of experience with these machines?

A.—Yes.

Q.—And you had not?

A.—Certainly, I had.

Q.—Before going up there?

A.—Yes, certainly.

23 J

Q.—Had you had experience with the H.S. 2 L's, Liberty engines? •

A.—Certainly.

Q.—Where?

A.—In the Canadian Air Force.

Q.—Where was the station?

A.—At Camp Borden.

Q.—Flying boats with Liberty engines?

A.—I was doing the same work there.

Q.—Were you ever operating H.S. 2 L's with Liberty engines?

A.—I was in the repair shop.

Q.—You formed some novel theories there and did you tell Captain Maxwell this was not right?

A.—He would not give me the opportunity.

Q.—You could parade to the O.C.?

A.—He would not see me.

Q.—When did you try?

A.—When I got to the Sault.

Q.—After the trouble?

A.—Yes.

Q.—But when the work started, Captain Maxwell would see you?

A.—Yes. And previously, I saw Hutt to make an appointment, and you yourself told me to see him at Toronto and I didn't see you and—

Q.—Briggs. You started a moment ago to try and say something, that you could never see Captain Maxwell; that is not right?

A.—I tried to see him.

Q.—You stated a moment ago that you tried to see him after your discharge and he would not see you. That is not right.

A.—I stated that I tried several times and never saw him and sent a letter to the Minister.

Q.—When you had this theory about the Laurentide people and the people at the aerodrome being all wrong and a mechanic right, who did you tell?

A.—It was talk all over the shop.

Q.—Who did you tell?

A.—I said to Thompson that it would never work.

Q.—How long had it been working before that?

A.—On two machines that collapsed the same way.

Q.—Do you know this or are you only guessing?

A.—One collapsed in the bush.

Q.—Do you know this?

A.—Certainly, I saw the engine.

Q.—The engine may have collapsed from a thousand causes. You were not on it? I am told it was valve trouble. You thought they were making a mistake and still think so?

A.—I don't think so. I am sure.

MR. RANEY: Were not the crankshafts all changed back?

MR. FINLAYSON: No.

WITNESS: They were being changed when I was at the Sault.

MR. FINLAYSON: You state, "A change was made at the commencement of the season in the oiling system, that has already resulted in a few engines being entirely written off." Is that correct?

A.—Yes.

Q.—You say "entirely written off." Will you swear to that?

A.—Yes. There was a little salvage on the engine.

Q.—Which engine?

A.—The one I had.

Q.—The one they said you let get dirty?

A.—No the one that crashed.

CHAIRMAN: He means the engine of which the connecting rod—

Q.—The whole engine gone?

A.—With a little salvage.

Q.—What do you mean—little?

A.—A few cylinders would be saved.

Q.—How many cylinders are there?

A.—Twelve.

Q.—How many destroyed?

A.—Three.

Q.—Nine saved out of twelve, 75 per cent.?

A.—No, they were not all good.

Q.—You said three gone?

A.—Three gone and several others warped with the heat.

Q.—What did they do with them?

A.—I don't know.

Q.—That is the trouble: you don't know.

CHAIRMAN: You say they were warped so as to be unfit to use?

A.—I was in the shop when they put the test guage on them. They were badly split.

MR. FINLAYSON: What was the trouble?

A.—What trouble?

Q.—The engine trouble?

A.—The trouble was that the oil ceased to flow and the bearings seized.

Q.—How would the heat warp the cylinder?

A.—That is just what would warp it.

Q.—We will let your mechanic's opinion go against my legal opinion. How many other engines were written off?

A.—That was not written off? There was a little salvage. Three cylinders went and the crankshaft.

Q.—The cylinders are only a small item, the bearings, the crankcase—how much are they worth?

A.—I don't know.

Q.—The crankcase, anything else?

A.—Lots of nuts, connecting rods.

Q.—They are not very heavy items?

A.—One hundred dollars, I guess. Am I right Captain?

MR. FINLAYSON: He says you are nowhere near it.

WITNESS: I am not speaking of prices. I said the engine was written off with the exception of a little salvage.

Q.—And you are not quite right. You don't know the prices of the parts. That is not your business?

A.—I have quite a knowledge of prices.

Q.—Well what are they?

A.—Bearings would cost $8 each; seven of those.

Q.—Where are the rest of the many engines written off?

A.—In the Sault.

Q.—How many?

A.—Five in the Sault when I got there.

Q.—What do you know about them?

A.—I saw them all.

Q.—What about them?

A.—Bearings gone; most of the crankshafts damaged.

Q.—"None with this alteration has attained eighty hours of flying time." That is false?

A.—No.

Q.—Let us examine it. Do you want to swear that none with this alteration attained eighty hours of flying time?

A.—I stated that to Captain Maxwell and he said that four or five had attained eighty hours.

Q.—Then it is false?

A.—He did not prove it to me. I saw the engines.

Q.—Your word as a mechanic would be confined to what you saw in the shops?

A.—And what I saw—

Q.—When you were grinding valves you didn't see much?

A.—I was not grinding on this occasion.

Q.—Do you know Number 1791 engine?

A.—I cannot remember the number right off.

Mr. Raney: Let me see the report made. You are not using it now.

Mr. Finlayson: I am using it. Engine 1791; do you remember that?

Witness: I cannot say I do.

Mr. Callan: Is that the serial number?

Mr. Finlayson: Yes. It did ninety-two hours and thirty-five minutes. What do you say as to that?

Witness: I don't know the engine.

Q.—You say none did eighty hours? What about 4188?

A.—I don't know the numbers.

Q.—That did 100 hours and five minutes.

A.—What machine was that?

Q.—That was machine "M."

A.—Those engines are not supposed to do more than eighty.

Q.—You say none of them did it?

A.—You say you have reached 100? I am entitled to ask a question. They should not stay out that long in the service.

Q.—Suppose they did. You say they should not. You told the Minister that none of the altered engines did eighty hours. Just a minute. I am pointing out here one that did 100.

A.—Maybe they had a good engineer.

Q.—I suppose some men can grind valves better than others? Some become experts?

A.—Yes.

Q.—Some day you may attain to that?

Mr. Raney: I don't think Mr. Finlayson need be so insulting. Witness has done magnificent service for this country and there is no reason why, if he comes here, he should not be treated as a gentleman.

Mr. Finlayson: Here is a man who made a statement to the Minister in a letter which apparently started the trouble. He made a testament there and he swore to it and I want to examine him.

Mr. Callan: What date was the letter?

WITNESS: August 24th, 1925.

MR. CALLAN: What date of the record would that be?

MR. FINLAYSON: September, 1925.

CHAIRMAN: I think it is obnoxious to all the members of the Committee. We have got several important inquiries and we have wasted a whole morning on the witness and I don't think any member would say that there is anything in the whole thing.

MR. FINLAYSON: I want to see how honest the man is.

MR. RANEY: I asked Mr. Finlayson to let me see the Government report and he would not, so I may have to recall him.

CHAIRMAN: I understand Mr. Raney asked a moment ago.

MR. FINLAYSON: Come and look at it.

CHAIRMAN: I suggest in connection with that, I don't want to criticize, and we have not stopped the bringing of witnesses, I think a member who summonses witnesses should make sure there is something in what a man will say.

MR. RANEY: Indeed there is something in what this man says.

MR. FINLAYSON: Let us finish it then. Now do you still want to swear to this statement, "None with this alteration has attained eighty hours flying time"?

A.—I do wish to substantiate all that letter except there might have been two—

CHAIRMAN: Mr. Briggs, look, be reasonably fair. Don't get into something—

WITNESS: When I was in the shop after coming from Orient Bay nine engines were shown me smashed up the same way.

MR. FINLAYSON: Let us get this statement. You still want to swear that none of these machines with this alteration attained eighty hours?

WITNESS: Yes.

Q.—You swear that?

A.—With the exception of—

Q.—No, no.

CHAIRMAN: Do you know?

WITNESS: No.

MR. FINLAYSON: Then why do you swear?

MR. RANEY: He is not satisfied he is mistaken.

MR. CALLAN: I am sitting here and want to get the facts. This man, I understand, has made a statement to the Minister that none of the engines went over eighty hours of flying time. Now what proof have you that none of them did outside the engine you went on?

WITNESS: I just admitted there may be an exception.

CHAIRMAN: He admitted he does not know.

MR. CALLAN: What proof have you?

WITNESS: I was on one machine myself.

MR. CALLAN: What about the others?

WITNESS: The other machines, I saw the engines in the shop. I saw the engines personally.

MR. CALLAN: My question is not answered.

WITNESS: I said none had attained eighty hours of flying.

MR. CALLAN: Who keeps this record? Is it the mechanic on the machine?

WITNESS: Yes, on the machine.

MR. CALLAN: But you were only on one? More than—

WITNESS: On two.

MR. CALLAN: It is on the word of the mechanics running the other machines? They told you?

WITNESS: Yes.

MR. FINLAYSON: I have given 1791 Machine K which attained 92.35 hours; 4188, Machine M, 100.05—wrong in that?

WITNESS: That is two.

Q.—You were wrong in those?

A.—I won't swear I am wrong.

Q.—Why did you make the statement to the Minister?

A.—Why did you make the report?

MR. LYONS: I am satisfied to let this remain until we bring the records from the Sault as this man's statements are ridiculous and I am not going to stand for these wild, bombastic statements, if in doing it it takes a whole week.

MR. CALLAN: In this connection does every pilot of every machine file with the head of the Department a record of the flying hours?

MR. FINLAYSON: Yes.

MR. CALLAN: Is that kept on record.

CAPTAIN MAXWELL: Yes. There are records of the pilot, the superintendent and the director since the first of these machines flew for the Government.

MR. CALLAN: Have you that record?

CAPTAIN MAXWELL: Yes.

MR. CALLAN: Can it be brought?

CAPTAIN MAXWELL: Yes, sir.

WITNESS: There is also an engineer's record on each boat and there is a copy kept on file in Captain Maxwell's office.

MR. FINLAYSON: Take engine 222, Machine I, which flew ninety-six hours after this alteration?

WITNESS: You are wrong there—no. Yes.

MR. FINLAYSON: Number 380, Machine E, 89.5 hours after the alteration? That is four?

WITNESS: Yes.

MR. FINLAYSON: Number 2662, Machine F, 95.25 hours?

WITNESS: Yes.

MR. CALLAN: I understand that you are not getting witness to say he knows those specific numbers?

MR. FINLAYSON: He knows how they are kept.

MR. CALLAN: It would be impossible to remember those numbers.

CHAIRMAN: It is a record of the director of a number of flying cases after the alteration. They can be verified by oath.

WITNESS: It depends on the next engine whether I can remember right or not.

MR. FINLAYSON: Engine 2662, Machine F, 95.25 hours?

WITNESS: Yes.

Q.—Engine 471, Machine A, 93.33 hours?

A.—Well, nine engines I saw.

Q.—Have you reason to doubt this statement?

A.—Yes, I have. I saw nine engines out in the shop and they—(end of sentence lost, through noise).

MR. RANEY: They were what?

WITNESS: All smashed up. Here Mr. Finlayson says there are six installed machines did over eighty hours. We didn't have that many machines in operation.

MR. FINLAYSON: What do you mean—smashed up?

WITNESS: Bearings burned up.

Q.—How many lost last year?

A.—I saw nine.

Q.—The truth is they only lost four. Do you know the difference between a major and minor accident?

A.—Yes.

Q.—When you say there were nine major breaks you are wrong?

A.—No.

Q.—All right. Engine 101, Machine J, eighty-six hours and five minutes; 2674, Machine L, eighty hours and ten minutes; 2901, Machine S, eighty hours and twenty-five minutes; 151, Machine R, seventy-seven hours and twenty-five minutes; 2194, Machine A, seventy-four hours and five minutes; 181, Machine N, seventy-seven hours and five minutes; 1791, K, ninety-two hours and thirty-five minutes; 2264, Machine G, fifty-three hours fifty minutes.

WITNESS: At the end of those fifty hours, what happened to them?

MR. FINLAYSON: It was removed to replace for heavy gears, and seventy-seven and seventy-four removed because of shortage of work in the reconditioning shop. Eighty hours is considered good normal flying service?

A.—Yes.

Q.—Under normal conditions at the end of eighty hours it should be turned in for repairs?

A.—For reconditioning.

Q.—Whether there has been an accident or not?

A.—Yes.

Q.—It depends on the exigencies of the service, some may be out longer and some have to come in?

A.—They endeavour to take them out at the end of eighty hours.

Q.—They ran seventy-seven to 100?

A.—My engine did not run seventy-seven.

Q.—I am trying to test your statement: none attained eighty hours of flying service.

MR. CALLAN: Do I understand the record is of the maximum flying hours?

MR. FINLAYSON: Not the maximum. Every one is supposed to go in at the end of eighty hours.

MR. CALLAN: Are those the ones that attained the maximum?

MR. FINLAYSON: Those are the whole lot.

MR. CALLAN: In the service?

MR. FINLAYSON: That cover his description.

MR. RANEY: How many machines are there?

MR. FINLAYSON: Fourteen.

MR. RANEY: There were nine you say, wrecked?

MR. FINLAYSON: He says that.

WITNESS: I didn't say they were wrecked.

MR. FINLAYSON: He is just talking.

WITNESS: I am not just talking.

MR. FINLAYSON: Is it not true your statement is all wrong?

A.—No.

Q.—You still stick to it?

A.—These machines were brought in for conditioning—

Q.—You are not entirely stupid. Try and get away from that. Compose your mind for a minute and listen. Here you state that none with this alteration has attained eighty hours of flying service?

A.—That was August 24th.

Q.—And this report is the following week. Do you still stick to that?

A.—Yes.

Q.—And you state this report is false?

A.—I have not seen it.

Q.—I will show it to you.

A.—Mr. Finlayson, on that date, August 24th, when I wrote that letter, were there machines that had attained eighty hours?

Q.—Those are the hours.

MR. RANEY: At that date?

MR. FINLAYSON: Yes. September 4th. Your letter was at the end of August and this refers to the beginning of September. The Minister was trying to find out if the letter was reliable or not.

WITNESS: I was on the O.G. machine.

CAPTAIN MAXWELL: What year?

WITNESS: Last year, at Orient Bay. It was not removed for heavy gears. It was smashed up.

CAPTAIN MAXWELL: This record is taken from the engine record of competent air engineers.

MR. CALLAN: This witness is on oath and is twenty-one years of age. He has come here and I want to hear his evidence.

MR. FINLAYSON: Do you still want to swear to that?

WITNESS: I have the record of that.

MR. RANEY: You have the record at your house?

WITNESS: Downtown.

MR. RANEY: And it does not accord with the report?

MR. FINLAYSON: The engine he mentions did not fly eighty hours. We don't contend it did.

WITNESS: That engine is shown as taken out for heavy gears. It crashed from want of oil. O.G., that is my machine.

MR. FINLAYSON: There are thirteen machines from seventy-seven to 100 hours and I am asking you if you swear this is false? Answer the question.

A.—I cannot answer the question. The first machine—

Q.—Never mind that. The question ignores the first machine.

A.—Then you mean ignore the whole report?

Q.—Please answer this question. Ignore the first machine, which did not do anything like that.

A.—It crashed and—   . .

Q.—You will answer the question if I have to get an order from the House. Ignore the first machine. I say there are twelve others which did from seventy-seven to 100 hours, all of which, I am told, had this alteration.

A.—Yes.

Q.—Do you contradict that?

A.—That they all had the alteration?

Q.—No. I did not ask you that. Listen. Ignore the first machine. I say there are twelve others which, having this alteration, did from seventy-seven to 100 hours of flying service.

A.—Yes. Not all over eighty.

Q.—Do you contradict that?

A.—No.

Q.—Then your statement is wrong?

A.—No.

CHAIRMAN: You don't realize the significance. You state to the Minister that none of these machines, changed in this manner, had eighty hours of flying service. In view of this report, which you accept, do you want to swear to that?

WITNESS: In view of that report—I didn't then say so—

MR. RANEY: If the report is true you are wrong? You impugn the report?

WITNESS: I take back what I put in that letter.

MR. RANEY: Let us see what the report says about the engine that crashed

WITNESS: That was taken out to change heavy gears.

MR. RANEY: Was that true?

WITNESS: No.

MR. RANEY: 2264, G.C.A.O.G., that was your engine?

WITNESS: Yes.

MR. CALLAN: Was that your engine?

WITNESS: Yes. That was the number. It was not removed to replace heavy gears though.

MR. RANEY: If this is false, perhaps others are.

MR. FINLAYSON: Do you know the number of your engine?

WITNESS: No. I know the number G, flown by George Oakes at Orient Bay.

MR. FINLAYSON: This report was prepared from records at the Sault and you want to withdraw?

WITNESS: I want to withdraw it in parts of the report only.

MR. KEITH: You have no doubt about its correctness?

WITNESS: That simply shows the machine I was in—

MR. FINLAYSON: The hours of twelve flying machines ran from seventy-seven to 100 hours. You don't doubt that, Mr. Keith says?

WITNESS: I will grant you that.

MR. CALLAN: Had all those machines the changed oiling system?

MR. FINLAYSON: Yes, all.

WITNESS: Some crashed from that cause.

MR. FINLAYSON: You may have that opinion. You said none of them did eighty hours?

WITNESS: You make the difference between one and some of them.

MR. FINLAYSON: I suppose this is true: When you were wrong in that your information was not more reliable on the rest of your statements?

WITNESS: My information, Mr. Finlayson, is what I saw.

MR. FINLAYSON: You did not see them all, yet you state: None with this alteration achieved eighty hours of flying service.

WITNESS: I have already disposed of that.

MR. FINLAYSON: Well, I have not.

WITNESS: I want to withdraw to this extent only that you want to point out that none of the engines crashed instead of a few.

MR. CALLAN: You say there is a possibility that the official report of the Department may be wrong?

WITNESS: Yes.

MR. FINLAYSON: There is a possibility. There always is.

MR. CALLAN: I believe there is.

Mr. Keith: In answer to my question he said he did not doubt the correctness.

Witness: It is incorrect.

Mr. Keith: About the twelve machines?

Mr. Raney: How long are we going to sit?

Chairman: I was hoping we were going to clear up this matter. What about another session to-day?

Mr. Finlayson: This witness can be recalled again but Captain Maxwell wants to get away and Mr. Squire is leaving at 5 o'clock.

Mr. Raney: I have to be in the House.

Mr. Finlayson: I should like Captain Maxwell to get away.

William Roy Maxwell sworn. Examined by Mr. Finlayson.

Q.—What is your position?

A.—Director of the Ontario Government Air Service.

Q.—How long have you been flying?

A.—Since 1916.

Q.—In the—?

A.—In the R.F.C., in the R.A.F. and in the R.C.A.F. and merchant.

Q.—In four branches?

A.—In four branches.

Q.—Have you covered all branches of the service?

Mr. Raney: Everybody knows his qualifications.

Chairman: I think he is an acknowledged expert.

Mr. Finlayson: Get down to your own service and this man's complaint. He was under Thompson?

A.—Yes, Thompson is the general superintendent.

Q.—He was under him?

A.—Yes.

Q.—What branch?

A.—He is in charge of the re-conditioning at Sault Ste. Marie.

Q.—Mechanical repair?

A.—Yes.

Q.—Is he a capable man?

A.—He is a very competent, capable man, I understand, in mechanics and theory in so far as aircraft and engines are concerned.

Q.—In 1924 there was some trouble with Briggs?

Mr. Raney: Cannot you refer to Mr. Briggs?

A.—He came to me with an application for work respecting the H.S. 2 L's and showed his credentials. I saw he had an excellent war record and I was favourably impressed. I took him on; in fact an advance was made as I understood he was up against it, to carry him through until he started work. The first mishap with Briggs happened when Kelly damaged the bottom of his boat so that it leaked. The machine was brought on the shore to repair the bottom. Briggs, who I will say did not have a large experience on active flying operations— in the shops, yes, but operations, no—carelessly left his coat on the flying wires and when the engine was started it was sucked into the propellor and destroyed the propellor. A report came in but, as I said before, I felt Briggs had ability and he was not a young fellow, and I thought we should not jump at conclusions. I went personally to the lake, put on the propellor and flew the machine and Briggs back to Sudbury. That apparently started the trouble with Thompson.

Q.—When was that?

A.—In the season of 1924.

MR. RANEY: With whom?

WITNESS: With Major Thompson. Major Thompson will not tolerate carelessness. I think it is possible that is where the trouble started.

MR. FINLAYSON: Is that what he discharged him for?

A.—Not that time. Thompson classified that as carelessness. During that season I received a confidential report from him and so on. I even had Briggs in mind as shop foreman in 1924. I went through the season and in October I wrote for a report off the man Rouse and asked him to give me in writing his personal report of all the air engineers we had in the service. That is the first letter on file.

MR. CALLAN: Who is Rouse?

A.—Rouse is the man in charge of the Sudbury station, a mechanic, and really in charge of the mechanical work in so far as the engines are concerned of the Provincial Air Service. He did not measure up and was reduced. He could not handle men. He is a very good mechanic.

MR. FINLAYSON: We don't want to reflect on other people. We don't want to introduce names that may give a left-handed swipe on someone else. I am not referring to this man, who has presented himself.

WITNESS: It went on until I had a report from Thompson that Brigg's machine was in a filthy condition—the machine, not the engine. It was in a filthy, oily condition and a machine like that does not function as well as it should. In other words, if it is plastered with oil and grease it cannot climb, it cannot perform.

MR. CALLAN: When was that?

WITNESS: In the fall of 1924.

CHAIRMAN: It is part of the duty of the mechanic to keep the machine as well as the engine clean?

WITNESS: The machine is that apart from the power. The engine is the engine. The duty of the mechanic is to keep the machine air-worthy. We have classified them as air engineers instead of mechanics because they have passed examinations presented to, and approved by, the Controller of Civil Aviation at Ottawa. It is in connection with engines and aircraft and they must know how to draw up and rig a machine; know the chief aeronautical terms, and so on. The air engineer keeps the engine ready for flight and the machine ready for flight. Thompson on inspection of his machine found it was terribly dirty. He communicated with me and I said it might not be his fault and that his time had been devoted to something else which would not permit him to take care of the boat, and I believe that inquiry showed this was the case. Briggs had been discharged, but I asked Thompson to reinstate him and he did. Then in 1925 I had several complaints, verbal complaints, from Thompson about Mr. Briggs and it blew up at Orient Bay when I got a series of telegrams about the condition of affairs there with regard to engines and Briggs' refusal to comply with instructions of the general superintendent. If I place a superintendent in a position I have faith in him and naturally what he says should mean something. Briggs refused to come out at the correct time for operations and Thompson dismissed him and I backed Thompson up. That is the story.

MR. FINLAYSON: That is the personal end. What about his complaint of the change made in the oiling system?

WITNESS: If I may, I will be as brief as I can. Mr. Briggs said that if these holes were blocked on the outside no oil would go to the bearings. But even after two years' service in the Laurentide Air Service where this condition was maintained on every engine in the service he says the engines would seize up—

MR. FINLAYSON: Did the Laurentide service adopt this?

WITNESS: It was the idea of Vauchon, an air enginner. His theory, I am not an air engineer so I quote the consensus of opinion in the air service, was that if the holes in the crankshaft were put in the other side the sediment would not be thrown to the bearings thus causing additional friction. Now this system was used in the Laurentide and in 1924 by the Provincial Air Service, this system of oiling.

MR. CALLAN: In that connection Mr. Briggs stated that that oil was filtered and there would be no solid matter. You make the statement that it would throw sediment.

WITNESS: It is true it is filtered but regardless of that there is a certain amount of sediment collects after it has come through the strainer. As previously stated, I am not an air engineer and it is an air engineer's duty—the overhaul and reconditioning.

MR. FINLAYSON: As I understand the Laurentide had made this change?

WITNESS: And I had flown machines with the change.

Q.—With no trouble?

A.—With no trouble.

Q.—It was not entirely new?

A.—Oh no. Machines were delivered to the Provincial Air Service with this change.

MR. CALLAN: That had been in operation?

WITNESS: Yes, from the point of delivery to Sudbury. They were new engines.

MR. CALLAN: How far is that?

WITNESS: About 400 or 500 miles.

CHAIRMAN: Some were delivered with this system in operation?

WITNESS: Yes.

MR. CALLAN: How long is a flight of 400 or 500 miles?

WITNESS: It depends on the weather. I would say that average time runs at seventy to seventy-five miles per hour.

MR. FINLAYSON: He made no complaint in the spring about the work?

A.—No complaint was made to me.

Q.—Is his statement to the Minister correct: the change was made at the commencement of the season?

A.—Does he refer to 1924 or 1925?

MR. RANEY: In between the two seasons.

A.—We carried on the same oiling conditions.

MR. FINLAYSON: In 1924 and 1925 the same?

WITNESS: Yes, some of the engines from the Laurentide came to us in that condition.

CHAIRMAN: It was not a radical departure in the air service?

WITNESS: No. It was a change recommended by the Laurentide Air engineer, Vauchon.

MR. FINLAYSON: This statement that none of the engines attained eighty hours of flying service?

WITNESS: That is entirely untrue. I am satisfied that the engines in the report flew more.

Q.—The twelve machines that I read to him?

A.—Yes.

Q.—They achieved from seventy-seven to 100 hours of flying service?

A.—Yes, sir.

Q.—And all had been altered?

A.—All had been altered. I saw the man who supplied the list of numbers and actual flying times of the engines which had been modified to furnish the statement in connection with Mr. Briggs' letter.

Q.—He says that himself and others warned against this?

A.—I will read a statement about that: "Meeting held in the office of W. R. Maxwell at Sault Ste. Marie at 11.30 A.M., Monday, August 31st.

"The following air engineers were present: T. Woodside, G. R. Hutt, A. E. Hutt, W. G. Chapman, S. McCauley, W. J. Gill, W. G. Thompson, J. C. Rouse and R. H. Fraser.

"The following questions and answers were put to the above-mentioned air engineers:

"Did you hear Mr. Briggs warn against certain alterations being made to engines?

"Answer: Everybody answered, 'No.'

"Did he oppose this and other dangerous methods of change?

"Answer: Everybody answered, 'No.'

"Did he warn against this alteration (oiling system) at the time it was made?

"Answer: Everybody answered, 'No.'

"Did any of you boys hear Mr. Briggs remarks that G. A. Thompson stated that unless he (Briggs) was fired, he would resign.

"Answer: Yes, George Doan."

Those are the questions I applied to these air engineers after this trouble.

MR. CALLAN: After the previous witness was discharged?

WITNESS: Yes.

MR. CALLAN: Don't you think there is a possibility in connection with calling these other employees in connection with an investigation that they would be prompted not to tell for fear it would be detrimental to themselves?

WITNESS: I would not say so. The boys of the Provincial Air Service are a very honourable lot, and our success so far may be attributed to an out-spoken statement of conditions and facts.

CHAIRMAN: In your system of organization you welcome suggestions from the air engineers?

WITNESS: Absolutely. That is what we ask.

MR. CALLAN: I am not a legal man. Assuming that some of the men at the investigation had given answers contrary to that and assuming, on the strength of that, that you had discharged them, is the field very wide for employ-ment in that same class of service in Canada?

WITNESS: As far as air engineers are concerned?

MR. CALLAN: Yes.

WITNESS: Right now, yes. Possibly not so great then. I say they all love the Service and aim to build up the Service in the Province. They were never nervous about overtime. They would be on the job from seven to twelve every night and—

MR. RANEY: Mr. Callan, you will notice I am not objecting to the reading of this letter. I am not making a technical objection, but I want to ask who was there to investigate?

WITNESS: I was at the Sault.

MR. RANEY: And you called the engineers into a conference to investigate?

WITNESS: When I received a copy of the letter I called the man in to investigate.

MR. RANEY: Mr. Briggs was there at the time this conference was called?

WITNESS: I don't know.

MR. RANEY: Yes. He did not leave until September. He was in the aerodrome, working in the shop, working out his month. Did you call him in?

WITNESS: I don't recollect him.

MR. RANEY: Did you ask him anything about this matter? Did you ask him anything about the inquiry?

WITNESS: No, he had made a statement to the Minister.

MR. RANEY: You were conducting an inquiry?

WITNESS: I was asking questions.

MR. RANEY: You did not ask him in front of the other men?

WITNESS: No.

MR. RANEY: You worked in his absence?

WITNESS: Certainly I did.

MR. RANEY: From one answer you discovered that Thompson had a strong feeling against him: "Did any of you boys hear Mr. Briggs remark that G. A. Thompson stated that unless he (Briggs) was fired, he would resign?"

WITNESS: I asked the question and George Doan answered "Yes."

MR. RANEY: If that statement was made there was indication of strong feeling by Thompson against Briggs?

WITNESS: I was trying to find out if there was prejudice.

MR. RANEY: That would indicate prejudice?

WITNESS: I would not say.

MR. RANEY: Unless Briggs was discharged he would resign—that would indicate prejudice against Briggs by Major Thompson?

CHAIRMAN: I would not say so.

CHAIRMAN: In connection with that, I understand from the evidence brought out that Mr. Thompson had taken strong ground that Briggs should be discharged.

MR. RANEY: Quite so. Thompson had recommended Briggs for discharge the previous year on account of the coat incident. You had used superior authority to keep Briggs in place?

WITNESS: In view of the facts of the case.

MR. RANEY: You have heard to-day an explanation that Briggs gave and what happened on the morning that he was notified of his discharge. He had been working two nights before and was five minutes late in turning out for operations and because of that he was told he was discharged.

A.—That is Briggs' story. Thompson has a different story.

Q.—Assuming Briggs' story is true would that be a reasonable ground for Thompson to take?

A.—Certainly not, if he had worked overtime all night; that would not be fair.

Q.—I quite agree you must work on the report of the superintendent, unless you find there are reasons to doubt him and it is a difficult thing to over-ride a superintendent when he recommends a man for discharge. He knows he is being over-ridden. But if the facts were as stated Thompson was doing Briggs an injustice?

A.—As Briggs states it he was.

Q.—As he had previously on the other machine, you came to that conclusion?

A.—Over the telephone.

Q.—Let me ask you, did you know Briggs at all before this time?

A.—The first time was when he applied for a position.

Q.—You knew that he had been in charge of engine instruction at the University over all the men?

A.—Captain Fisher was in charge and Mr. Briggs was an N.C.O. under his instruction.

Q.—He was in charge practically, is that it?

MR. FINLAYSON: No; one was an N.C.O. and the other the officer in charge.

CHAIRMAN: We are not wanting to deprecate Mr. Briggs' knowledge, but there was an officer in charge in all these cases. I would like that to go on record unless we have official evidence to the contrary. He was only nominally in charge.

MR. RANEY: Officially in charge?

MR. FINLAYSON: The officer was officially in charge.

CHAIRMAN: It is like having a superintendent and under him a foreman.

MR. RANEY: You had no doubt as to his capability?

WITNESS: No.

Q.—You knew he had done important service over here in connection with the air service?

A.—It was shown to me in writing from his recommendations.

Q.—And from the age of eighteen until the time you took him, when he was past forty-two or forty-three his whole life had been devoted to gasolene engines?

A.—He told me that.

Q.—I suppose he gave a record of his experience?

A.—He did. I had it with me in the office before we started.

Q.—Can you think of a more thorough record to qualify a man for this kind of work in regard to assuming he was a man for these engines?

A.—It should be a necessary inference.

Q.—Eminently so?

A.—Yes.

Q.—Now coming down to the conference had it not occurred to you that you ought to see Briggs at that time?

A.—No. He had written to the Minister making statements which were false and I was immediately planning my defence.

Q.—Was it really that?

A.—I was supplying a true report.

Q.—Were you looking at it from the view that he had gone over your head to the Minister? "We will see about that," was your point of view?

A.—No. I did not mind that. It has been done before.

MR. CALLAN: The date of Mr. Briggs' letter and the date of this investigation—how do they correspond?

MR. RANEY: The date of the letter from Briggs was 24th August. Just a week later. Come back to the changes on the machines. You are not disputing the fact that the oiling system in these Liberty engines not already changed were changed during the winter of 1924-25 at the airdrome at the Sault?

A.—Yes, we changed them. The Laurentide started the change and those not changed were changed—

Q.—How many did the Laurentide change?

A.—I would not like to say.

Q.—Maybe only two or three? How many were changed at the Sault?

A.—I cannot say.

Q.—The holes on the left-hand side were blocked and new holes opened on the right-hand side?

A.—From the throw side to the inside.

Q.—That would weaken the crankshaft?

A.—No.

Q.—Were all the engines at the Sault changed in that way—the old holes blocked and new ones made?

A.—I would necessarily have to consult the engine log books.

Q.—Do you understand they were changed?

A.—I understand all were to be changed.

Q.—The evidence is that all were changed. Now how many of the engines changed in that way crashed?

A.—If I may refer to ships as crashing and engines as major breaks, four in the season of 1924.

Q.—You knew of four. Were these breakdowns brought on by the change in the oiling system?

A.—That cannot be absolutely proved. It was thought from the condition of certain bearings when the machines came in for overhaul after eighty hours that the system employed was faulty.

Q.—It was found that there had been a mistake in making these changes?

A.—No, because they had the same trouble with the oil with the holes on the other side.

Q.—Not the same trouble?

A.—Absolutely.

Q.—How many cases?

A.—There are many cases in commercial flying.

Q.—Was the change made back and the new holes blocked up?

A.—We went back to the old system.

Q.—When?

A.—Long before Mr. Briggs ever reported to Sault Ste. Marie for dismissal.

Q.—When?

A.—In August.

Q.—Before or after his notice of dismissal?

A.—Before his notice of dismissal.

Q.—The 5th of August. When did you decide to go back? Before the 5th of August?

A.—I would not say until I see the record.

Q.—I am not going to hold you so strictly as Mr. Finlayson did with Mr. Briggs because we all make statements that we afterwards have to qualify. I think even Mr. Finlayson will admit that.

Mr. FINLAYSON: I don't make statements of oath more deliberatley than without them.

Mr. RANEY: We sometimes speak too quickly. I often do.

Mr. FINLAYSON: I will shake hands on that and say we do frequently.

Mr. RANEY: Open confession is good for the soul. About the time of the dismissal of Mr. Briggs you did come to the conclusion that this had been a mistake?

WITNESS: I don't swear to that. It is the consensus of opinion. I am not an air engineer.

Q.—On the advice of the engineers?

A.—Yes.

Q.—At all events the views of the engineers were after the event; it was after this experience they thought they had made a mistake and had better get back?

CHAIRMAN: When you say that you worked on the consensus of opinion of air engineers you are applying that to your own engineers or generally?

WITNESS: That is relative strictly to our own air service.

MR. RANEY: Then you returned to the old system. Any trouble since?

WITNESS: Yes.

Q.—Not as much though?

A.—That is September, October, only two months' operation.

Q.—Of course, Captain Maxwell, we all know that men in the Service, even superintendents make mistakes and act unjustly at times and get prejudiced. Did you know that Captain Thompson had been one of the men who went through the instruction of Mr. Briggs while Briggs was at the University?

A.—Major Thompson is an Englishman, having learned all his aircraft knowledge in England.

Q.—He was passed—got his papers through Mr. Briggs?

A.—No, sir.

Q.—You knew Briggs had papers as an air engineer from England?

A.—I knew he had papers from England.

Q.—You have no reason to doubt his qualifications?

A.—No.

Q.—Would you think it odd for a man with his qualifications to be cleaning and grinding valves?

A.—I only go from the expression of opinion I received from the man in charge, written in October, 1924. That is at the top of the list. If you will refer to the letter.

Q.—That has nothing to do—

A.—It says his ability was not such that he could be entrusted with fine work.

Q.—Whose report was that?

A.—From the shop foreman.

Q.—Mr. Thompson?

A.—No.

Q.—From Mr. Thompson to you?

A.—The signature will tell you from.

Q.—Is not Thompson the man responsible?

A.—Thompson was at operations in the field at that time. T. B. Kelly was acting superintendent.

MR. CALLAN: Did Mr. Thompson have charge of the department at that time?

WITNESS: At this time T. B. Kelly was acting superintendent and the report was sent by Rouse, the mechanical foreman.

CHAIRMAN: Was he under Thompson's orders?

WITNESS: Yes, but Thompson was in the field.

MR. RANEY: I see: "In reply to your letter, am enclosing report from Mr. Rouse on different members of the staff." Rouse was one of the engineers?

A.—Shop foreman. Rouse has equal qualifications with Briggs. He was ten years with the Napier works in England.

Q.—I see, "Briggs has made mistakes and I would not feel inclined to entrust him with particular work." He did not indicate the nature of the mistakes?

A.—No. That is just his own opinion.

Q.—And Rouse was one of the engineers who attended the conference?

A.—If his name is down there.

Q.—At that time was he an ordinary mechanic?

A.—Air engineer in charge of the electrical equipment.

Q.—What was that?

A.—He was a step higher than an air engineer. He had charge of the electrical equipment.

Q.—Is that his position still?

A.—Yes, sir.

Q.—No superiority over Mr. Briggs, but a little higher—different qualifications on account of electrical experience?

A.—Chief inspector.

Q.—So that all these machines where the new holes had been drilled were brought back to the plan upon which they had been originally built. The old holes were re-opened and the new holes blocked?

A.—We have even gone so far as to leave two holes in on each side.

Q.—For experiment?

A.—Yes, for experiment.

Q.—You have opened up the holes you blocked?

A.—And blocked up the holes we opened.

Q.—Would that justify the attitude to Briggs?

A.—Briggs comes back to the shop after these changes have been made and attempts to take credit for them.

Q.—He made a warning?

A.—He made no warning; no man made a warning.

Q.—Just a minute, Captain Maxwell. Thompson was in charge of the shop?

A.—He is the general superintendent.

Q.—Thompson was inimical to Briggs. You knew that?

A.—Well, he says not in the correspondence.

Q.—You know he twice recommended dismissal without cause—

Mr. Finlayson: Not without cause.

Mr. Raney: Did you discuss the matter with Thompson?

Mr. Briggs: I had three weeks argument with Thompson when Thompson came to Orient Bay.

Mr. Raney: Before the change was made did you warn Thompson against making this change?

Mr. Briggs: I told him it would not work.

Mr. Raney: So it was Thompson who recommended the change?

Captain Maxwell: No, sir. It was an air engineer named Vauchon.

Mr. Raney: He made the recommendation?

Captain Maxwell: Absolutely.

Mr. Raney: And you took the responsibility of ordering it to be done on hese machines?

Captain Maxwell: Certainly not. They came to the Service like that.

Mr. Raney: But those which were changed at the Sault. Who gave instructions for those to be changed?

A.—The air engineer in charge—Gordon Hutt.

Q.—You knew of the change?

A.—Naturally.

Mr. Raney (To Mr. Briggs): Did you talk of the change with Hutt?

Mr. Briggs: Yes.

Mr. Raney: And told him it would not work?

Mr. Briggs: Yes.

Mr. Raney: And Thompson?

Mr. Briggs: Yes.

Mr. Raney: Did you know Hutt was recommending the change?

Mr. Briggs: I knew he had Vauchon's idea.

Mr. Raney: So Hutt approved?

Mr. Briggs: I didn't think he approved.

Captain Maxwell re-examined by Mr. Finlayson.

Q.—Thompson is a competent, capable man?

A.—Absolutely.

Q.—He is in charge of this branch of the Service and you act on his recommendations?

A.—When he suggested dismissal I backed my general superintendent up after the three causes for dismissal.

Mr. Raney: After three recommendations for dismissal.

Chairman: The facts speak for themselves.

Q.—Had the change anything to do with Briggs?

A.—Absolutely no.

Mr. Callan: This oil I understand is forced into the bearings, into the shaft. You understand that? What is the power used to force it in there? Is it motor driven?

Witness: Yes, a disc with flanges.

Mr. Callan: Are there any indicators to show the pressure on the pipe from the pump to the bearings?

Witness: Absolutely. And that is why the air engineer travels with the pilot. He has to keep an eye on the instruments. If you have trouble—

Mr. Callan: Just a minute. Is the pulsation indicated?

Witness: An instrument records the pressure, another records the temperature. If the temperature of the oil runs high—

Mr. Callan: Where is the temperature taken from?

Mr. Briggs: From the end of the shaft.

Mr. Callan: Would that go dead?

Mr. Briggs: Yes.

Mr. Callan: You could not close off the engine then?

Mr. Briggs: We do, to glide.

End of examination.

Chairman: I understand Mr. Squire wants to get away.

Mr. Squire: Perhaps Mr. Hogarth, who is Deputy-Minister of Public Works, would do or the chief engineer of our department?

Mr. Raney: Very well.

Chairman: In connection with that is there anything you want to tell the Committee?

Mr. Squire: I think the whole story could be told in a two minutes.

Mr. Raney: Then go ahead.

Chairman: He did not say he wanted to tell it. The meeting is adjourned then until to-morrow.

PUBLIC ACCOUNTS COMMITTEE

March 27th, 1926.

Mr. Lewis, in the Chair.

The Chairman: We will not waste any time this morning; members who are kind enough to stay over and attend a meeting on Saturday morning are entitled to get away as soon as possible. The Secretary has marked the members who are present.

Mr. Finlayson: Is it desired to have a meeting on Monday morning?

Hon. Mr. Raney: Yes, the motion picture witnesses have been summoned for Monday.

Mr. Finlayson: It is the only chance I have to get home; suppose we say Monday at two o'clock, and sit Monday evening if necessary?

The Chairman: Don't you think we will be able to complete this morning.

Hon. Mr. Raney: I think I can, I cannot promise for the rest.   -

Mr. Finlayson: You have no confidence in anybody else?

Hon. Mr. Raney: No.

The Chairman: We will decide to go ahead this morning until one o'clock, and the witnesses who are not called to-day will return on Monday at two o'clock.

Major Nash: Resumed.

Hon. Mr. Raney: Take the first statement of sales made to the Department, of the Provincial Government, take the year 1923?

A.—Yes.

Q.—Do you know whether these orders were, for the most part, after the new government came in, or before the new government came in?

Mr. Finlayson: What are you referring to?

Hon. Mr. Raney: The first statement in the year 1923, the new government came in, in the middle of July?

A.—I will give you that exact information. It commenced in June, 1923.

Q.—Will you tell me how much there was before the middle of July? I will come to that in a moment. What portion of the orders for goods to the Lyons' Company in the year 1923?

The Chairman: By the Northern Development?

Hon. Mr. Raney: Or any other department, were prior to the new government coming into office. Looking at Statement No. 2, there are four or five items I want to get on the notes. Take the case of the E. L. Bedford Hardware Company, 1920, purchased $80?

A.—Yes.

Q.—1921, $106.78?

A.—Yes.

Q.—1922? $108.16?

A.—Right.

Q.—1923. $144.97?

A.—Right.

Q.—1924. $108.73?

A.—Right.

Q.—1925. $8,596.50?

A.—Yes.

Q.—Then take the International Nickel on the same page. They are mine licensees?

A.—Mine licensees.

Q.—In 1921, I see their purchases were $201.81?

A.—Yes.

Q.—In 1924, $68,266.34?

A.—Yes.

Q.—That is all?

A.—That is all except in 1919.

Hon. Mr. Raney: That was a purchase, and that was explained by the Hon. Mr. Lyons by saying he was a tenderer each year for their coal, but did not succeed in landing their order until 1918.

Q.—Then take the Keewatin Lumber Company, they are licensees?

A.—Yes, and vendors.

Q.—There are no purchases from that company until 1925, $7,405.92?

A.—That is right.

Q.—Then MacNamara Brothers, they were purchasers in 1920 for $38,803.71?

A.—Yes.

Q.—1921, $8,496.77?

A.—Yes.

Q.—1922 for $3,305.56?

A.—Yes.

Q.—1923?

A.—Nothing.

Q.—1924, $23,378.84 and in 1925, $38,288?

A.—Yes.

Q.—The Lake Superior Paper Company are licensees?

A.—They are.

Q.—1920 they purchased $11,614.34?

A.—Yes.

Q.—1921?

A.—One thousand three hundred and nineteen dollars and sixty-six cents.

Q.—All these figures I have been reading are the amounts of the purchases by these different companies from the Lyons Supply Co.?

A.—Yes.

Q.—In 1921 Spanish Pulp and Paper Company, $1,319.66; and in 1922, $9,456.64; and in 1923, $17,316.63?

A.—That is right.

Q.—In 1924, $110,646.01?

A.—Yes.

Q.—In 1925, $67,020.94?

A.—That is right.

Q.—Then the next item of the Spanish River Pulp and Paper Company in 1920 their purchases were $144,710.37?

A.—Right.

Q.—Then in 1921? $5,772.70?

A.—Yes.

Q.—In 1922, $39,599.34?

A.—Correct.

Q.—In 1923, $83,354.14?

A.—Right.

Q.—In 1924, $54,695.33?

A.—Right.

Q.—In 1925, $88,403.18?

A.—That is right.

Q.—Then we will take the Spruce Falls Company of Kapuskasing, they are licensees also?

A.—Yes.

Q.—The first good purchases were in 1923, $1,165.50?

A.—Yes.

Q.—Can you give me the date in 1923, they commenced in August, 1923?

A.—Yes.

MR. FINLAYSON: That was a new company just starting about that time?

A.—I am informed that is so.

Q.—The bulk of that is for coal?

A.—All for coal in 1923.

Q.—The subsequent orders the bulk of the account is for coal?

A.—Yes.

HON. MR. RANEY: I thought they were operating for two or three years before that?

A.—I am informed that is so. I have no proof of that. They commenced operating some time in 1923, but I cannot prove that.

MR. FINLAYSON: That is my recollection, but I would not like to be positive.

HON. MR. RANEY: In 1924 their purchases were $13,355.44?

A.—Right.

Q.—In 1925, $25,913.43?

A.—That is right.

Q.—Then the Spanish Mills Company, they are also licensees?

A.—Yes.

Q.—In 1923, they purchased $337.04?

A.—Yes.

Q.—In 1921, $7.50?

A.—Yes.

Q.—In 1922, nothing?

A.—Right.

Q.—In 1923, $7,364.47?

A.—Yes.

Q.—What was the date of that order?

MR. FINLAYSON: I do not want to go back but I would like to ask that one particularly.

HON. MR. RANEY: Wait till I get through and I won't object as soon as I finish this line?

A.—It was October or November, 1923.

Q.—1924, $10,009.92?

A.—Yes.

Q.—In 1925, nothing?

A.—That is right.

MR. FINLAYSON: That company lost their mill or do you know?

A.—I do not know.

HON. MR. RANEY: I think that is all I will trouble you with as far as the Lyons Fuel and Supply Company are concerned. At the foot of the last page you deal with the Sault Ste. Marie Coal and Wood Company, Limited?

A.—Yes.

Q.—The Lake Superior Paper Company are Crown licensees?

A.—Yes.

Q.—In 1925, their purchases were $15,232.43?

A.—That is right.

Mr. FINLAYSON: Have you got their vouchers for this last item of $15,000?

A.—I have the sheet.

HON. MR. RANEY: I think I ought to say in justice to Mr. Lyons that I have gone through Statement No. 3, having to do with the price tests, and I see no ground for criticism and in fact I never heard of any criticisms. I never heard anybody suggest there was any preferential treatments of road contractors or Crown licensees.

THE CHAIRMAN: Or that they had paid little more for their stuff?

HON. MR. RANEY: More or less.

THE CHAIRMAN: I went through it also and I think we will all agree the prices compare favourably.

MR. FINLAYSON: May I make acknowledgment and say I am very glad to note that Mr. Raney is treating it in that fair and reasonable way.

To MR. FINLAYSON: Having regard to your investigations and having regard to the line of cross-examination, is there anything of a suspicious nature in connection with the books of either the Lyons Fuel and Supply Company, or the Sault Ste. Marie Coal and Wood Company?

A.—I did not find anything.

Q.—Is there anything in all your study of these two companies or. Mr. Lyons own matter that led you to be suspicious of his or of his firm's dealings?

A.—No.

Q.—No indication of any improper transaction or of any attempt on his part to use his position as Minister?

A.—No; in answering that so long as I am not going on record that I know what is proper and what is not proper as a Minister. I am not in a position to say what is proper and what is not proper; I found nothing suspicious.

HON. MR. RANEY: You are not passing any judgment on the question of his dealing with Government contractors?

A.—No.

Q.—Or with the Government itself?

A.—No, I am not competent to pass on that.

To MR. FINLAYSON: As a business man, you and your firm have had a vast amount of experience in that line; from a business standpoint, was there anything to indicate anything, but the very fairest of public dealing?

A.—Nothing that I saw.

Q.—You ask me about the Northern Development, June, $946; July, $870; and $1,900 subsequent to July?

HON. MR. RANEY: I will now take up the Caledonia Road matter.

THE CHAIRMAN: I would suggest that before calling your first witness, you might in a few words give us the object of the enquiry, because it was not contained in the motion.

HON. MR. RANEY: You want me to advise the Committee as to the substance? Perhaps I could not better than just summarize a statement by Mr. Brass one of the workmen.

THE CHAIRMAN: It is on his statement that you enquiry is based?

HON. MR. RANEY: Largely. This is a sketch of a statement made by J. Brass, a steam shovel operator employed by the contractor, T. J. McLean, on the work on the Caledon Hill in the summer of 1925. I will omit the first two paragraphs. The third paragraph is shortly as follows:

"There were no regular pay days, the Contractor McLean gave the men cheques on banks where there were no funds. They were paid only small amounts on account of their summer's work. The men complained insistently to Messrs. Fulton and Smeaton who were Government representatives on the job, one an inspector and the other an engineer, and were induced to remain on the job by their promises that the Government would see that they were paid.

"In the meantime while this condition of things existed upwards of $3,600 was paid by the Government, or by the Department to McLean, and was used by him, excepting a small amount for other purposes than the payment of liabilities including wages incurred on the work. That the men working through July, August and September, until the lodging house keepers would give them no further credit, and that their clothing is still being held by the lodging house proprietors for non-payment of board and lodging.

"That on the 28th of September, Brass and McClintock came to Toronto and made their complaint to the officials of the Department and were persuaded by them from taking legal action by promises that the Government would see that they were paid.

"That throughout October, November and December, Brass, McClintock, and others were pressing their claims before the ministers and departmental heads and were being put off from time to time with promises that their claims would be paid.

"That when Brass and McClintock, came to Toronto in September, they had preference claims for wages, against McLean and there was money still in the hands of the Government and this preference was lost because of their acceptance of the assurance by departmental officials that their claims would be claimed by the Government.

"That on the 8th of October, with full knowledge of the facts, the Government paid McLean $1,164. and that no part of this amount went to the men. That in December, when the situation was much more acute, another cheque for $500 was made to McLean by the Department and none of this money went to the working men. That on the first of March, the Department made a distribution of the alleged balance of $623 then in hand, among creditors, with claims aggregating $6,397 and sent Brass a cheque for $19.09 virtually for a summer's work. The other cheques were in ratio."

Mr. Finlayson: What percentage is that?

Hon. Mr. Raney: A little less than 10 per cent.

The Chairman: That was paid to all the creditors?

Hon. Mr. Raney: Yes. "That at the request of the officials of the Department, Brass and McClintock, early in October made a statutory declaration verifying their claims, as follows:

"Brass, $744.70; McClintock, $278.15. That at McLean's instance and without communicating with Brass or McClintock the Department reduced Brass's claim from $744.70 to $196 and McClintock's claim from $278.15 to $211 and that the distribution was on this footing:

"That is to say, Brass's ten per cent. was not computed on his claim, but on the claim as stated by McLean.

"That is the substance of the charge."

THE CHAIRMAN: I thought it was well we should know what the charge was.

HON. MR. RANEY: You are quite right; I will call Mr. Brass.

John Brass, sworn. Examined by Hon. Mr. Raney.

Q.—What is your occupation?

A.—Steam shovel engineer.

Q.—You are an engineer?

A.—Yes.

THE CHAIRMAN: What papers do you hold for that?

A.—Hoisting papers.

MR. FINLAYSON: A stationary engineer's certificate?

A.—Yes.

HON. MR. RANEY: Are you a married man?

A.—Yes.

Q.—How many children have you?

A.—One.

Q.—How old are you?

A.—Thirty-two.

Q.—Do you live in Toronto?

A.—Live in Toronto, but my home is in Hamilton. I live in Toronto most of the time and work here.

Q.—Were you employed last summer?

A.—Chambers, McCaffrey Construction Co., fixing up that shovel that they rented to McLean for the Caledon job.

Q.—You were at work for Chambers and McCaffrey on their steam shovel and then you went with McLean on the Caledon Mountain job as engineer on this steam shovel?

A.—Yes.

Q.—Who was your assistant?

A.—McClintock, the fireman.

Q.—Tell the Committee your story.

A.—I started to move machinery in on the 29th of June and I got started digging on the 13th of July, about eleven o'clock.

Q.—Did you see McLean himself?

A.—Yes.

Q.—Were you employed by him?

A.—Yes, McLean hired me, he came down to where we were fixing the machine on Sligo Hill about four miles away and he told me he would pay me the same wages as Chambers and McCaffrey were paying me. Two hundred and fifty dollars a month for nine hours a day, and board. Twenty-six days a month.

Q.—You went up there?

A.—I moved the machinery to the mountain on Saturday the 29th of June and I started working on the 13th of July.

Q.—Was the machine driven over the road by yourself on its own power?

A.—Yes.

Q.—You were paid from the time you left Toronto?

A.—From the time I left Sligo Hill.

Q.—How large was the crew at work on this job?

A.—The first two weeks we had fourteen teams and I guess about eight or ten men.

Q.—The work was the cutting down of the grade of the Caledon Mountain?

A.—Yes.

Q.—Mostly steam shovel work and carting away the earth?

A.—Yes.

Q.—Pick and shovel men and your dredge and farmers' teams carting the earth away?

A.—Yes, and men on the dump.

Q.—You began work on June 29th? When did you get your first pay?

A.—The first pay I got from McLean was $15.00, some time in' July.

Q.—In money?

A.—Yes, he said he was getting an estimate through from the Government and he would pay the next week.

Q.—How long had you been at work then?

A.—About a month.

Q.—Had you been trying to get pay before this?

A.—I did not say anything to him on account of the two weeks we were up there waiting to start. I waited to the end of July and I thought he would pay up then and I went to him and he said all the money he had on him was $25.00 and he gave me the $25.00 and he said the Government has held my estimate back but I will pay you all up the first of the week when the estimates go through.

Q.—You gave him back $10.00?

A.—I had $25.00 then.

THE CHAIRMAN: $15.00 before that and then $25.00?

A.—No, I got $25.00.

HON. MR. RANEY: You said in the first place you were paid $15.00?

A.—No; I got $25.00 and the fireman got $10.00.

Q.—Do you know whether the other men were being paid?

A.—McLean told me, don't let any of the other know you are getting money or they will be all after me for money.

Q.—Was there a superintendent on the job?

A.—Yes. Jack Telfer.

Q.—Was McLean there himself a good deal of the time?

A.—Some of the time, he was not there all the time.

Q.—Who was the Government Engineer in charge?

A.—Mr. Fulton.

Q.—Was there an Inspector?

A.—Mr. Smeaton.

Q.—Was Fulton there all the time?

A.—No, he had two other jobs to look after; he would be there and give us the grade.

Q.—Fulton would be there I suppose two or three days a week?

A.—Yes, he was there most of the time.

Q.—How about Smeaton?

A.—He was there all the time.

Q.—When next were you paid?

A.—About two weeks after that I got $30.00 in cash.

Q.—That would be about the middle of August?

A.—Yes.

Q.—Had you in the meantime been making any complaints or making an effort to get your money?

A.—I told the Inspector and Engineer we were not getting our pay and I went to him the next time and I got $30.00 and he said the Highway Department are holding my estimate back.   They are charging me up with a lot of lumber I never got and I did not get all the money, he said that is all I got now, and he says I am going down to see them about how they can charge me up with lumber I never got.

Q.—When did you get anything more after that?

A.—I got a cheque for $40.00 in the Bank in Wingham.

Q.—Was that cheque paid?

A.—About two days after I got a letter from a Notary Public up there that the cheque was protested in the bank, no funds.

Q.—Did you pay the notary's fees?

A.—No.

Q.—You didn't get that $40.00?

A.—I was going to write the notary public, but he wrote his name so that I could not make it out.

Q.—You did not get the $40.00?

A.—The hotel keeper in Inglewood cashed it for me on Saturday and he took it to the bank and put it through the bank, but it came back.

Q.—Did you pay the money back to the hotel keeper?

A.—No, I did not pay it back.   I do not know whether he has got it or not; the last I know about it when I left up there he was going to Brantford or Orangeville to get a lawyer to have me put in jail for giving him the cheque.

Q.—What more did you get?

A.—I got a cheque for $75.00 on the bank in Caledonia; that was Saturday before Labour Day.

Q.—At the end of August?

A.—Yes; I went to McLean the week before and I told him the holiday is coming on and I want to get into Toronto and I want a little money and he said, all right, I will see that you get it and he came around Saturday afternoon and handed me the cheque when I could not get to the bank and I went to this man who cashed it for me.   McLean went to the bank in Caledonia and he said that cheque is all right, I just seen the bank and there is lots of money there.   It will be cashed Tuesday morning, Monday was a holiday.

Q.—You got the money from the hotel man?

A.—I got that money from the hotel man.

Q.—Did he get that money?

A.—I don't know whether he got his.

Q.—Had he got it when you saw him last?

A.—Not when I saw him last, he was going to get a lawyer and have me pinched.

Q.—As far as you know, neither of these cheques have been paid?

A.—I have never heard from them.

Q.—Was that all the money you got on the job?

A.—I have it all down some place.

Q.—Did you get any other payments?

A.—$25.00, $40.00 and $30.00.

Q.—Was this $30.00 cash or cheque?

A.—Cash after I got the cheque and there was $50.00.

THE CHAIRMAN: That was before the cheque?

A.—No, after it.

Q.—It was in your book before?

A.—No, after.

Q.—That $50.00 was cash?

A.—Yes, and $12.50 cash, I got $12.50 the day I got the $75.00. He gave me $25.00 and he said divide that up between you and the fireman.

HON. MR. RANEY: How much was that altogether while you were on the job?

A.—$232.50.

Q.—That includes the $75.00 and the $40.00?

A.—They are no good.

MR. FINLAYSON: They were good to you?

A.—I got it.

Q.—You won't have to go to Kingston, we will give you Government protection.

HON. MR. RANEY: When did you quit?

A.—September 26th.

Q.—Why did you quit?

A.—The board bill was running up and they would not keep us any longer and we were thrown out of the boarding house and we could not live in the bush.

Q.—The boarding house people shut down on you?

A.—Yes.

Q.—What is the amount of your claim?

A.—$744.70. Then if the cheques were made good, they should come out of that.

Q.—Why did you stay on during all these three months?

A.—I seen the inspector and engineer up there and they told me we would get paid; there were bonds on this job. At the time I got the $75.00 the hotel-keeper came to me and he said he had been to the bank and there was no money there and I says, come on to the bank I will go with you and I came back to the job about a quarter to one, and I said, "To hell with it; I am not going to work here any more."

Q.—Who to?

A.—To the men standing around. "No, more money; the first thing we know we will be in Kingston or some place over this job," and Smeaton came up and spoke to me and I started to work about half-past one.

Q.—What did he say to you?

A.—They told me it would be all right, McLean would make it good, and that the Government had money and they had their bonds. He said there was bonds on this job to pay it.

Q.—Had you been told the same thing before by either Smeaton or Fulton?

A.—They said all the time there was money to pay for the job; it was a Government job.

Q.—They told you that all the time?

A.—Yes.

Q.—If you had not had that assurance from Smeaton and Fulton would you have stayed on the job?

A.—I would have been out of there the first of August.

MR. FINLAYSON: That is leading; I am not objecting, but I would rather you would do it fairly.

HON. MR. RANEY: Did all the men quit on the 26th of September?

A.—Some men worked on the culvert; they put in a culvert.

Q.—McClintock and you came to Toronto?

A.—I came on the 28th of September alone.

Q.—Where were your wife and family at this time?

A.—In Hamilton and Toronto.

Q.—Are you a man of means?

A.—Pretty small right now.

Q.—What did you do at Toronto?

A.—I went down and saw Chambers and McCaffrey's office and I saw McCaffrey down there.

Q.—I believe this dredge was rented by McLean from Chambers and McCaffrey?

A.—Yes, I went down and seen them and Mr. McCaffrey phoned up Mr. Hogarth and made an appointment for me to go up and see Mr. Hogarth.

Q.—What did you do?

A.—I went up and saw Mr. Hogarth.

Q.—What took place between you and Mr. Hogarth?

A.—I told them how things were going, and he said, "Your wages will be paid all right." And I said, "What about our board bill?" and he said, "I won't promise your board bill at all, but the wages will be given first consideration and if there is anything left the other claims wil be considered." And I said, "What about going back to work," he said, "You go back there and give McLean another chance." I said, "McLean will do the same thing; he will tell me 'to-morrow,' and to-morrow will never come and he said if he don't pay, let me know." I went back and saw McLean and I told him what Hogarth said, and he said "to hell with you and the Department of Highways too, we don't care for you." I said, "All right," that is what I got and I am going back to Toronto again and I stayed there a week and then came back to Toronto.

Q.—How much did you owe the boarding house people when you left finally?

A.—One week's board. When I was down on the 28th, McLean came down and paid.

Q.—Were you supposed to have your board paid as well as the $250 a month?

A.—$250 and board.

Q.—Did you see Fulton and Smeaton when you went up?

A.—I saw them when I went back and I told them what Hogarth told me and I told them I was not going to start working until I got a settlement.

Q.—What did they say?

A.—They told me if I did not have word from Toronto, they could not say anything about it.

Q.—Then what did you do?

A.—McClintock and Sam Griggs and I came back the following Monday and went up and saw Hogarth again.

Q.—What date was that?

A.—A week after the 28th of September?

Q.—That would be the 1st of October?

A.—That would be the 1st of October.

Q.—Then what did you do?

A.—I went up and saw Hogarth and he told us the same thing.

Q.—What?

A.—That the wages would be paid.

Q.—Did he say who would pay them?

A.—McLean cannot get any more money out of the Highway Department until these wages are settled up and there is money coming to him and he cannot get any more until the wages are paid. I said, "What about seeing a lawyer?"

and he said, "There is no use seeing a lawyer, a lawyer will run away with half your wages." We will do just as good for you as a lawyer and we won't put in any lawyer's bill.

Q.—So you didn't go to see a lawyer?

A.—No.

Q.—Did you know then that you had a preferential claim against any moneys coming to McLean?

A.—I did not know.

Q.—You had not seen a lawyer?

A.—No.

Q.—How was the matter left with Mr. Hogarth?

A.—Hogarth told us when we were going out of the office, go and make up your time and bring it in here. Mr. McLean told me on the job that he was not making money and I know that is not right, and he talked like that about the job but the wages will be paid.

Q.—Was there anybody with you when you went to see Hogarth?

A.—McClintock and Sam Griggs.

Q.—Are they both here?

A.—No, Griggs is not here. McClintock is here.

Q.—You were told to go away and make your time out and bring it back?

A.—Yes.

Q.—Did you do that?

A.—I brought it back.

Q.—How many days after?

A.—About two days after.

Q.—And then what happened?

A.—I waited a few days then.

Q.—Did you make an affidavit as to your claim?

A.—No, I did not make out an affidavit I took it back and Mr. Hogarth was not in and I left it with one of the stenographers and I waited about two days and I went back and saw Mr. Hogarth again and he said go on in and see Squires.

Q.—That is the Deputy Minister?

A.—Yes; and I went in to see Squires and I could not get in. The fellow in the office told me to go up and see Brown the Chief Accountant and I went up there.

Q.—Mr. Hogarth was Chief Engineer?

A.—At that time.

Q.—Mr. Squire was Deputy Minister?

A.—Yes.

Q.—Mr. Brown was Chief Accountant?

A.—Yes.

Q.—So Mr. Squire referred you to Mr. Brown?

A.—Mr. Brown.

Mr. FINLAYSON: You did not see Mr. Squire?

A.—No. Somebody told me to go up to Brown.

HON. MR. RANEY: You and McClintock saw Mr. Brown?

A.—Yes.

Q.—What took place at that interview?

A.—I said, what are we going to do about it; it is time we were getting our wages and he took us into a fellow and had us swear out our time was all right.

Q.—You made out your affidavit of claim?

A.—Yes.

Q.—You asked if you should see a lawyer?

A.—No. He said it was not necessary to see a lawyer. He said put your time in and we will see about this now. It won't take long to settle it up now.

Q.—Then you and McClintock went away again?

A.—Yes, I went home and McClintock went home.

Q.—Early in October?

A.—About the second week in October.

Q.—Then you went back to Hamilton?

A.—Yes.

Q.—Go on and tell us what happened after that, step by step?

A.—I kept going up to see Hogarth and he would tell me to go and see Squires and I could never get in to see Squires. He would be out or something or other. I went there five or six times during October and then I got in to see Squires and Squires said there is a difference between the time here you have got to get McLean in, and see what the difference is and he told me to go up and see Brown.

Q.—Did Squire tell you anything about your being paid?

A.—No, he told us they could not settle up because there was a difference between the time.

Q.—You understood that was the only difficulty?

A.—Yes.

Q.—Go on?

A.—I went up and saw Brown and came out.

Q.—What did Brown say?

A.—Mr. Brown sent me into a fellow who figured what my claim was and what McLean said it was. I took it down to show to Squires and there was somebody in the office and I left it with a fellow outside; I went back two or three times and I went up one day pretty mad, and I walked into Hogarth's office and I said, "Hogarth, can you give me McLean's address?"

Q.—What date would this be?

A.—About a month after.

Q.—Some time in November?

A.—Yes, I could not say the date. Hogarth said Wingham and I said there is no street numbers in Wingham and he said, No we haven't got any street address and he said what are you going to do, and I said I am going to hand it in to a lawyer, and he said, well it won't do you any good, we are looking after this for you and I said, "You have been looking after it quite a while now, and nothing has turned up about it," He said, "A lawyer will take half your money" and I said, "If I had this thing settled up right now I would be willing to give anybody half of it." He says, "You leave it alone and come back here in a couple of days" so I went back in a couple of days and said, "What about it now," and he said, "Well, we have wired McLean and sent him registered mail and phoned him and we are going to send out a messenger after him and if he won't come back we are going to settle up." I went out again and came back a couple of days after and I went into Squire's office and Squire sent me up to Brown. Brown said everything is all right, "He will settle up, all we have to do is to get Hogarth's word and we will settle up." I said, "All right that sounds pretty good," and I went down and Mr. Hogarth was not in and I said, "I am not going to wait about." The money will be all right, I will get my money to-morrow. And I went up to-morrow, and Hogarth said he did not know anything about it, and I told him—

Q.—He said he didn't know anything about it; what Brown had said?

A.—I told him what Brown told me and he said "you go back," and I went out and went into Squires office and Squires was not in. I said to the man there, "You sent me up to Brown, and Brown told me everything was all right and it would be settled up, all they needed was Hogarth's word. He said, "I will phone up Brown and find out," and he phoned up Brown and Brown said, "Yes, all we are waiting on is to get word from Hogarth and it came in this morning, the estimate."

MR. FINLAYSON: You could not hear that?

A.—This is what the fellow told me. I went in and told Hogarth they were waiting on him and he said that estimate has been up there for months. Any time they want my word to settle up, night or day, they can have it. So I came out of there again.

Q.—You hadn't got any money down to that time?

A.—No.

Q.—What next?

A.—From there I went up to see Dr. Godfrey, the Minister of Labour. I went in to see him, but it did not come under the heading of his Department at all and he could not do anything for it. He took my name and address and the amount of the claim and he said he would see Squires about it. I do not know what he did about it.

MR. WIDDIFIELD: It was Dr. Godfrey you saw?

A.—No, somebody in his office. You cannot get in to see them, unless you have a passport.

HON. MR. RANEY: That sounds funny to us, but was not funny to you?

THE CHAIRMAN: We are not laughing at Mr. Brass's position.

HON. MR. RANEY: I know that.

Q.—How were you keeping your family alive at this time?

A.—I had to borrow about $200 to keep us going. I see that one of the members said that the other night they had nothing to eat but cheese and crackers.

THE CHAIRMAN: That was one of the Leaders of the Opposition.

WITNESS: That was a better meal than I have had some days this winter.

HON. MR. RANEY: The people up there were keeping your clothes?

A.—I was not going to take my clothes away and make a crook or liar out of myself.

Q.—We have got down now to a point where the matter rests somewhere between these three gentlemen, Mr. Squire, Mr. Hogarth, and Mr. Brown?

A.—Yes, the week before Christmas I went up and I wanted to get a little money before Christmas; I went up to see Hogarth and he sent me to see Squires and I could not see him and I came up here and I saw Mr. Henry, the Minister.

Q.—Mr. Henry himself?

A.—Yes, I got in to see him and he was very nice, and he says, "There is money down there and I do not see why you cannot get some." And I says, "It is a hell of a thing for a man to be broke around Christmas," and he says, "Yes, it is a bad thing for a man to be broke any time in the year. I will take this up with Mr. Squires." And I said, "I have to see Squires to-morrow after-noon," and he says, "I will try and get in touch with Squires in the morning." I went in the afternoon about two o'clock and waited until about four and got in to see Squires and of course Squires told me then, "I have about $900 here and we will get McLean to sign this cheque and put it all in a pot and divide it up among you."

Q.—How much do you say the claims were?

A.—He did not say; it was $900.

Q.—That $900 was to be put in a pot and divided up?

A.—Yes.

Q.—That is the first time you heard McLean would not be paid in full?

A.—The first time I heard that. So I said to Squires, "I thought on a Government job there was always a bond to protect wages and everything and he said, "This is not a Government job this is a Highway job," and I said, "If it is a Highway job how about us putting a mechanic's lien on that job? and hold up the whole job until it is settled," and he said, "You cannot do that," and I said, "I know we can put a mechanic's lien on a $10,000 house and the moment the lien goes on it has to be paid," and he says, "I know you can put a lien on for a little plumbing," and I said, "What about this," and he said, "This is a Government job," and I started to laugh and I said, "Then the damned Highway and the Government is all the same thing," so I started to laugh.

Q.—What next?

A.—Squires got sore; I do not know but it led to one thing and another and I went out.

Mr. Finlayson: You both got sore?

A.—Yes, and I went out and came up here the Monday after Christmas and went up to see Mr. Henry. There was myself and Cook, and McClintock, and John Telfer.

Mr. Widdifield: Who is Cook?

A.—He is a farmer.

The Chairman: Telfer was the Superintendent?

A.—Yes. We went up to see Henry and went in and the stenographer said, "Who do you want to see?" and I said, "Mr. Henry." Mr. Henry was in and this man came out and she went in the office and came back out and said, "Mr. Henry has a very important engagement until eleven o'clock and he won't be able to see you to-day and he says for you to go down and see Squires." "And I said, "As far as I am concerned there is no use of my going to see Squires; if Mr. Henry has an important engagement on for eleven o'clock he is now forty-five minutes late and a couple of minutes more won't make any difference, to see us fellows, it is now a quarter to twelve." So she phoned up Squires and she told Mr. Squires that Mr. Henry said to send us down there and she says Squires asked if Henry had the money up there to pay these men and she said she didn't know.

The Chairman: That is all the stenographer told you?

A.—Yes. So we went down and Cook went in to see Squires; and I didn't go in to see Squires at all, so I came down to see Mr. Raney at his office and handed it in.

Q.—That is where my trouble began?

A.—That is where you started.

Q.—I think that was the last day of the year, the 30th of December?

A.—It was the Monday after Christmas I think, Mr. Raney.

Q.—I wrote a letter to the Minister on the 30th of December; then you didn't go back any more?

A.—No.

24 J.

Q.—Then I see a letter addressed to you on the 1st of March, as follows:

"Toronto, March 1st, 1926.

"John Brass, Esq.,
    5 Pembroke Street,
        Toronto, Ontario.
Re Contract 1223, T. J. McLean.

Dear Sir:
    The amount of money which was being retained by this Department on the above contract was $623.63. Mr. McLean has now furnished a sworn statement of his liabilities, the total being $6,397.32 and request that we pay out the amount held to the creditors on a pro rata basis which is .097 cents on the dollar, a little less than 10 per cent. We have pleasure, therefore, in enclosing cheque No. 3 to the value of $19.09, being the amount due you on the above arrangement. Your claim as submitted by Mr. McLean is given as $196. Will you please acknowledge receipt of this cheque?"

Signed by Mr. Brown, I suppose, I cannot make out the signature, that is the letter you received?

A.—Yes.

Q.—You received the cheque that day?

A.—Yes.

Q.—What did you do with the cheque? Did you cash it?

A.—No, I did not cash it. I was just figuring out if that is all I am going to get out of it.

Q.—Who authorized the Department to reduce your claim from $744 to $196?

A.—I do not know, I put my affidavit to my claim and McLean made an affidavit too.

Q.—They accepted McLean's affidavit without saying anything to you about it?

A.—Yes, then I should be in gaol, I guess.

Q.—You may get there yet because a man who does not get his pay and grumbles about it may get into trouble?

A.—I had to borrow money to get something to eat.

Q.—You notice this is a nice touch: "We have pleasure, therefore, in enclosing you."

A.—Yes, it doesn't cost anything for them to say that up there.

Letter and cheque marked Exhibit 10.

Mr. Finlayson: How old are you?

A.—Thirty-two.

Q.—You have been working how long?

A.—I started out when I was fourteen years old.

Q.—You have been working for eighteen years?

A.—Yes.

Q.—At various kind of work?

A.—All connected with steam; I spent three years on the North Sea and I have been on construction work.

Q.—How many years have you been on construction work?

A.—Eighteen, three years after that about fifteen. I might as well have missed last year.

Q.—So that you have been fifteen years in construction work in this country?
A.—Yes.
Q.—Has that all been in this country?
A.—No.   I was about one year outside of Detroit.
Q.—Apart from the year in Detroit the rest has been in construction work in Ontario?
A.—Yes.
Q.—Similar work to this?
A.—Working for the railroads and for the Hydro and for contractors.
Q.—Contractors?
A.—Contractors.
Q.—All work of that kind?
A.—Yes.
Q.—All on jobs similar to this unfortunate one?
A.—Sure.
Q.—So that you know pretty well the habits and usages in connection with work of that kind, you know how accounts are paid?
A.—Yes.
Q.—You know that there are regular pay days?
A.—Every job I have been on they used to pay every two weeks, some pay every week, it used to be a month some time ago.
Q.—It used to be a month and lately it was every two weeks?
A.—Yes, sometimes I have been paid every week.
Q.—In any case there were regular stated pay days?
A.—Yes.
Q.—Men get their pay on these pay days and if they do not get it there is something wrong?
A.—Yes.
Q.—You state there are regular pay days and unless a man receives his pay on that day he knows there is something wrong?
A.—Yes.
Q.—That applies to all this construction work?
A.—Yes.
Q.—Have you ever worked on highway jobs before?
A.—Yes.
Q.—For contractors?
A.—Yes.
Q.—And I suppose you know what happens, the contractor pays the men and then he has to look to the Government or whoever he is doing the work for?
A.—Well.
Q.—You have nothing to do with that end of it?
A.—No.
Q.—Anytime you do not get your pay you know there is something wrong with that job?
A.—You would think there would be.
Q.—This particular job you started on the 29th of June?
A.—Twenty-ninth of June.
Q.—And the bargain was you were to get $250 per month and board and you were to work nine hours a day and be paid twice a month?
A.—No set time for pay, but that is what I figured on.
Q.—When the first pay day came you were expecting some money?
A.—Yes, I was expecting some.

Q.—You did not get it?

A.—I did not get any.

Q.—You knew this man McLean was behaving badly?

A.—He was drinking all of the liquor round about the country.

Q.—Was not attending to business?

A.—Was not attending to business.

Q.—So that the trouble was with your employer?

A.—He was not handling his job right or he would come out all right.

Q.—McLean was not handling the job right or he would have come out right?

A.—Sure he would have come out right?

Q.—He was drinking heavily?

A.—About the worst I have ever seen and I have seen some pretty bad.

Q.—You have seen some pretty bad drinkers, but he was the worst you have ever seen?

A.—The worst I have ever seen.

Q.—When did that start, you came on the 29th of June?

A.—Yes.

Q.—He had a celebration for Dominion Day?

A.—Yes, Dominion Day.

Q.—That was the following day?

A.—Yes.

Q.—Two days after he had a celebration on the mountain, two days after you came on the job you knew you were working for a drunkard?

A.—You would think a man who had lots of money to drink whiskey you would think he had lots of money to pay his help.

Q.—That should be true but unfortunately it is not always true. What I am trying to get at is that two days after you started to get to work you knew this man was b having badly?

A.—Yes.

Q.—And that th re would be trouble?

A.—I did not know, I had seen some contractors who used to take a drink and pay their men.

Q.—You have seen contractors who took a drink, but you never saw a contractor act like this man did?

A.—No.

Q.—You knew the moment you started on the job that he was a bad actor?

A.—I would not say I put it down that way, I would not say the man was a bad actor.

Q.—He was a bad drinker?

A.—I found out before I was very long on the job that he was a bad actor.

Q.—You started the 29th of June and you found he was celebrating on Dominion Day and then on the 12th of July again?

A.—Yes.

Q.—All the time in fact?

A.—More or less.

Q.—The work was not being attended to?

A.—No.

Q.—And the job could not run on that way?

A.—No.

Q.—Your own steam shovel was idle?

A.—Part of the time.

MR. CALLAN: I understand the Highway Department had a resident engineer on this job all the time; I want to be fair with Mr. Brass and I want to see that this man gets a fair deal and I am going to see that he gets it. You say to this witness he should know that the work was not going on. There was a resident engineer there.

MR. FINLAYSON: He also should have known.

MR. HANEY: I suppose it is also fair to those gentlemen who hear the evidence to place on record, so far as we are concerned, that after hearing the evidence there is no question in our minds but that this man has been unfairly dealt with.

MR. FINLAYSON: I am not trying to anticipate the judgment of any member of the Committee. I suggest that we get through as rapidly as possible and hear the other side of it.

MR. HANEY: I am making my position clear. Mr. Callan very rightly said that he was here to see that his man got fair play. The inference might seem to be that the rest of us were not anxious that he should get fair play.

MR. CALLAN: No; nothing of the kind.

THE CHAIRMAN: I think there is no question at all but that the sympathies are with these men who did not get their money.

MR. CALLAN: Not having a legal mind, I am not in a position to know that I am right in the position I take.

MR. FINLAYSON: The work was not being attended to?

A.—No.

Q.—Your machine was idle for a long time?

A.—The first two weeks we went along all right and had fourteen teams and then there was no pay day coming and the teams went home, and then we monkeyed along with two and three teams.

Q.—So that at the end of the first pay day some of the teams quit?

A.—Yes.

Q.—They stopped altogether?

A.—Yes.

Q.—Went to other work?

A.—They were farmers around there and they had work of their own.

Q.—Was not there other work you could have gone to?

A.—If I wanted to, I did not want to quit.

Q.—You did not?

A.—No, because I was told around there it was Government work and the pay would be all right.

Q.—So that you were willing to take a chance and be idling along, and hoping that you would get your pay? There was a lot of loafing around?

A —There was, yes.

Q.—There was a large period of the day when you were doing nothing, I am not blaming you, it was not your fault?

A.—No.

Q.—After the first day the teams dropped from fourteen to two?

A.—Yes.

Q.—Two teams would not keep a steam shovel busy?

A.—Not very well.

Q.—Then the two teams quit?

A.—I think two was the lowest we ever had.

Q.—They quit?

A.—No, they stayed on until the finish.

Q.—What part of your time would you be working?

A.—We would get out at seven in the morning and load these two teams and then wait until they got back again and then load them again and we kept on going in that way all day.

Q.—It is quite apparent that the thing was being neglected?

A.—It was known all the way from here to Owen Sound.

Q.—How long did you stay on after this first pay day when it became apparent that he would not pay?

A.—I stayed on until the 26th of September.

Q.—When was this first pay day you missed?

A.—When I went on the first day was about the 1st of August.

Q.—You stayed all through August and September knowing that the thing was not going to pay?

A.—He was coming there every day and going to get more teams, and he got a railroad in there and a hoist on top, and he was going to do away with all the teams. He was going to go ahead.

Q.—What he was doing was drinking?

A.—If he hadn't drank up all the money he got from the Government.

Q.—You had it in your minds that because somebody up there said that because there was a bond it was going to be all right anyway?

A.—Sure.

Q.—If it had been anybody but a Government contractor you would not have stayed?

A.—No.

Q.—Because it was a Government contractor you thought you could stay and take a chance or you thought you were not taking any chance?

A.—I thought if we had a Government in at all that it was half decent to a working man.

Q.—If it had been a railway job or any other kind of job you would have said, "Here I better get out of here and get some work"?

A.—Sure, the first pay day if I did not get any money I would.

Q.—You say the first pay day that was missed if it had been anything but a Government job you would have jumped?

A.—Sure.

Q.—Because it was a Government job you thought there was some claim? It does not matter whether you were right or not it was not your fault?

A.—It was not my fault.

Q.—I want to get at why you state that somebody led you to believe that it was a Government job and there was a bond?

A.—That was the Government engineer.

Q.—There was a strike up there was there not?

A.—Not that I know of.

Q.—Didn't all the Toronto teamsters quit?

A.—He got sixteen from Toronto and he was to pay them every week, and they waited for the pay when the week was up and he did not get the money and they would not go to work and he came to Toronto to get the money and he paid them and they all went back to Toronto.

Q.—All these Toronto teamsters and the local teamsters quit and then he got some from Toronto and they all quit?

A.—Yes.

Q.—It was quite apparent to anybody that there was trouble there?

A.—Yes. It looked as though there was a man trying to handle a job that didn't know anything about it

Q.—Your boss was trying to handle a job that he didn't know anything about?

A.—Yes.

Q.—You kept on working for a man of that kind?

A.—What was I to do? I was so far in.

Q.—It is easy for me to tell you now, but I guess if you were back there again you would leave the job?

A.—I would never have started.

Q.—It is easy for us to be wise and tell you what you should have done; anyway the fact is that although you knew it was a bad outlook you stayed on because somebody told you there was a bond, some magic bond, or power that the Government would do something? I took down what you said, You saw Mr. Hogarth and he said the wages would get first consideration"?

A.—Yes.

Q.—And if there was anything left, that is all Mr. Hogarth ever said to you?

A.—He told me the wages would get first consideration and when I asked him about board he said he could not pay board he said if there was anything left the creditors would come in.

Q.—He never went beyond telling you the wages would get first consideration and if there was anything left that it would be divided in the board bill? That is all the promise you ever had from him?

A.—That is all.

THE CHAIRMAN: The board would go on in as one of the other debts of the Company.

MR. FINLAYSON: Hogarth told you the wages would receive first consideration and then if there was any money left the other creditors would get it?

A.—Yes.

Q.—You went to McLean in June, and you got your first pay the $25 in July and $30 in August, and cheques for $40, and $75, and $12.50, and then $50 in cash, making $232.50?

A.—Yes.

Q.—In addition to that you got a cheque for $19.09?

A.—Yes.

Q.—Have you got that cheque yet?

HON. MR. RANEY: I am holding the cheque for him.

THE CHAIRMAN: I thought that was where it would probably go.

MR. FINLAYSON: Mr. Raney is not holding it for fees you need not worry about that. The cheque will be available if necessary. So that you got in all $251.09? Who was it you had some talk with out there?

A.—The engineer and the inspector.

Q.—Who do you say was the engineer?

A.—Mr. Fulton.

Q.—What did you tell the engineer first?

A.—I told him about the job not going ahead and we were getting no pay.

Q.—He said he would hold up the estimates?

A.—Yes, that is what Hogarth told me.

Q.—That is later on? Fulton was the engineer?

A.—Yes.

Q.—Do you remember Mr. Alder?

A.—I have seen him around.

Q.—Mr. Fulton was an instrument man?

A.—He was a fellow who went around with the machine giving us the grade.

Q.—He gave you the levels?

A.—Yes.

Q.—You say you spoke to him about it and he said he would hold up the estimates?

A.—No. Fulton never told me he would hold up the estimates; Hogarth told me McLean would not get any more money.

Q.—You saw Fulton and he said he would hold up the estimates and there would be no more paid?

Q.—Was not that Fulton?

A.—No, Hogarth. McLean could not get any more money from the Highway Department until the wages were paid, that was on the 29th of September.

Q.—So that as far as Mr. Hogarth is concerned all he told you was that the wages would be given first consideration, and they would hold up McLean's money and he could not get any more money?

A.—Yes.

Q.—Tell us about Mr. Fulton.

A.—I told him two or three times about not getting the pay.

Q —When did you first tell Mr. Fulton?

A.—Right after we did not get paid the first time.

Q.—Which time was that?

A.—After the first pay day came around and we did not get any. I did not say anything about not getting paid before pay day. I expected pay about the 1st of August.

Q.—Some time after August you spoke to Mr. Fulton?

A.—Yes.

Q.—And told him you had not been paid?

A.—Yes.

Q.—That is not his business, you know an instrument man has nothing to do with the pay?

A.—He was going into Toronto all the time and I thought he would tell them in there.

Q.—What did he say?

A.—He said this is a Government job and the men's wages will be paid on it. You don't need to worry about this job.

Q.—"This is a Government job, the men's wages will be paid," do you say he told you that?

A.—Yes, two or three times, and so did Smeaton. "Don't worry about a Government job and the men will get their pay."

Q.—Smeaton told you that?

A.—Yes.

Q.—Did you see Mr. Adler?

A.—No.

Q.—Don't you remember an engineer who came around inspecting?

A.—He was around there but I did not know who he was.

Q.—Did you see him there?

A.—I saw him on the job. I was told he was there.

Q.—Did you ever speak to him about it?

A.—No.

Q.—In other words, you knew who Alder was? He had been pointed out to you as engineer in charge?

A.—He was supposed to be District Engineer.

Q.—He would be the man in charge, the boss there?

A.—I do not know whether he was the boss or not.

Q.—You knew the District Engineer had charge of that work?

A.—I guess he did have charge of it.

Q.—He was there frequently?

A.—Yes, he was there frequently.

Q.—Did you ever speak to him?

A.—No, I did not know the man at all.

Q.—You saw him coming there every day or two?

A.—Yes.

Q.—He was the real boss, he was the fellow they all took off their hats to?

A.—I do not know whether they took off their hats to him. Smeaton and Fulton were the men I would take my orders from. I could not go over their heads.

Q.—I would have thought that after all the trouble and your knowing the boss was drinking you would have done that?

A.—Alderson knew he was drinking as well as I did.

Q.—Did you complain to anybody else except these two?

A.—Not until the 28th of September.

Q.—Have you told us all that occurred between you and Smeaton and Fulton? That is they say it was a Government job and they say there was a bond?

A.—Yes.

THE CHAIRMAN: Was it these gentlemen who mentioned that there was a bond?

MR. WIDDIFIELD: Which one mentioned that there was a bond?

A.—Both.

MR. FINLAYSON: They told you there was a bond for wages?

A.—They told the contractor had to put up so much bond and if they did not finish his job, the bond was there.

Q.—Nobody said the bond was for wages?

A.—Making up anything that is not paid.

Q.—Who said that?

A.—They both told me that the bond was up there and that McLean did not finish his job the Government held the bond and would pay the debts.

Q.—What you understood from that, whether you are right or not, was because it was a Government job and because there was some bond, it was safe for you to stay on the job and not worry about your wages?

A.—Sure.

MR. CALLAN: Do I understand what this bond was?

A.—The contractor is supposed to put up a bond for so much money when he takes the job.

Q.—What for?

A.—To go security that he would finish his job.

Q.—Do I understand that this bond would be used to pay wages?

A.—That is what I understood from the inspector and engineer on the job.

Q.—You would be surprised to know now that it does not?

A.—That is what I found out since.

Mr. Finlayson: What your contention is, Mr. Brass, is that you knew this man was drinking and although you knew the job was neglected; if you had been working for anybody else you would have quit; but because you understood it was a Government job and there was some bond you thought you were safe to stay on? You base that on the fact that Smeaton and Fulton told you it was a Government job and you thought you would be paid? They are the only two; you had not any conversation with Alder?

A.—No.

Q.—You have given me what occurred between you and Hogarth?

Mr. Raney: I produced the cheque that was attached to the letter. It was on another file.

Mr. Finlayson: Hadn't he better cash it?

Hon. Mr. Raney: I do not think he will cash it now. I would not advise him to cash it now. If he wants to cash it it is his affair.

The Chairman: It would not affect his position.

Hon. Mr. Raney: It is more sentiment than anything else.

Witness: If that is all I am going to get for my summer's wages, I am going to get it framed.

The Chairman: That is not all you got?

A.—I got that other little bit.

Mr. Finlayson: You got the $230.50 in addition to that so it is hardly fair to say that is all you got.

Hon. Mr. Raney: It is hardly fair to say he got $230 because he may have to pay the $115 for these cheques.

Mr. Finlayson: I do not think that worries him very much. I am not saying that in a disparaging way. It could not be recovered. You have told us everything that occurred?

A.—Yes.

Q.—You do not contend that there was any promise made by Mr. Henry or Mr. Squires except that the matter would be looked into?

A.—Yes.

Q.—You have told us Mr. Hogarth said the wages would get the first consideration. Do you know how much the board is?

Hon. Mr. Raney: I will call two witnesses on that question.

The Chairman: I am puzzled as to the amount of your claim. You say you started to work on the 29th of June?

A.—Yes.

Q.—You quit in September?

A.—Yes.

Q.—Did you work up until the 26th or were you in the city part of the time?

A.—I came in sometimes on Saturday night.

Q.—That did not interfere with your work on the job?

A.—No.

Q.—That would be three months?

A.—Yes.

Q.—That would be $750?

A.—Yes, at nine hours a day, twenty-six days to the month, but I worked ten and twelve hours.

Q.—More time than twenty-six days to the month?

A.—We worked ten hours instead of nine.

Q.—You were to get a nine-hour day?

A.—Yes.

MR. FINLAYSON: Do you remember telling Mr. Hogarth you were going to Rouyn in September and you could get a job up there?

A.—No, sir. Mr. Hogarth put that in the paper and I want to know how I would be able to go up to Rouyn.

Q.—You were talking about going up to Rouyn?

A.—I could have gone up there, but my clothes were up at the boarding house and I did not have money to buy a new outfit to go to Rouyn.

Q.—When were you offered this job?

A.—In October.

Q.—You hadn't an opportunity of going up there to a job of your own, but you stayed around here to collect this money?

A.—My working clothes were up there.

THE CHAIRMAN: There is no use of your giving that excuse. A suit of overalls would not prevent your going to a job.

HON. MR. RANEY: You told Mr. Finlayson that McLean was drinking very heavily all summer Did Fulton and Smeaton know that?

A.—Everybody knew it from Toronto to Owen Sound that ever passed that job. He was lying on the job and could not get up and was rolling on the ground.

Q.—Did you discuss that matter with Fulton and Smeaton?

A.—Sure, that was the talk every day up there.

Q.—Was there a superintendent on the job besides McLean?

A.—Mr. Telfer. I think he was there about two weeks before Telfer came.

Q.—Telfer was on after that?

A.—Yes.

Q.—He is an efficient man?

A.—Yes.

Q.—Is Telfer here?

HON. MR. RANEY: He has been subpoenaed.

Mrs. Emma Franklin sworn.

HON. MR. RANEY: You keep a boarding house at Caledonia?

A.—I just take in boarders.

Q.—Did Mr. Brass board with you?

A.—Yes.

Q.—You understood McLean was to pay the board bill?

A.—He came in and arranged for the board.

Q.—Mr. McLean arranged for the board?

A.—Yes.

Q.—How much does he owe you?

A.—The first money he paid me he paid with a false cheque for $23.65.

Q.—There were no funds for it?

A.—No.

Q.—The Ocean Blend Tea Company cashed the cheque for me.

Q.—Do you know whether the cheque was ever paid?

A.—No, it has not been paid. We had to pay it here lately.

Q.—Was that all the money you received?

A.—He paid me every week after that himself for a few weeks.

Q.—Does he owe you anything now?

A.—Yes.

Q.—How much?

A.—Thirty-one dollars. The claim he put in is all right; then there is a false cheque besides.

Q.—So that there is $31 owing you and this cheque that you say you had to pay?

A.—Yes.

Q.—Did you get a cheque from the Government?

A.—Yes, for $3.01.

Q.—Did you cash it?

A.—No. My husband has it in his pocket.

Q.—Why didn't you cash it?

A.—I thought I could do it as the rest are doing.

Mr. FINLAYSON: So that there is $31 coming to you and the $23.65 that you had to repay?

A.—Yes.

Q.—Mr. McLean has told the Department that he did not make the contract with you at all; you state he came to you deliberately?

A.—Yes. He came right to the house.

Q.—Told you he would be responsible?

A.—Yes.

HON. MR. RANEY: You have a dividend on $31, but not for the bad cheque?

A.—No.

Kenneth Hannahson sworn.

HON. MR. RANEY: Did you work on this job?

A.—Yes.

Q.—With a shovel or a team?

A.—With a team.

Q.—Did you put in your account?

A.—Yes.

Q.—Who did you give it to?

A.—Mr. Brown in Toronto.

Q.—Did you first give it to Mr. McLean?

A.—No; I never could see McLean the last few weeks we were on the job.

Q.—I see your claim was put in at $221.75?

A.—By whom?

Q.—I assume put in by you at that?

A.—Yes; I had a cheque that was no good. I gave him credit for it when I put in that claim.

Q.—Your claim is really more than that?

A.—The total amount is $295.

Q.—Were you one of those who worked right through?

A.—Yes.

Q.—You were one of the two teams that stayed by the job to the finish?

A.—Yes.

Q.—Your claim was $295?

A.—Yes, I let him down very easy. I was hired at $5.50 a day but I only charged him up with $5.

Mr. FINLAYSON: Who hired you?

A.—McLean himself.

HON. MR. RANEY: I see McLean represented to the Department that your claim was only $111.25?

A.—Yes, that is what he put it in at.

Q.—The Department apparently acted on his statement?

A.—Yes.

Q.—Did you receive the cheque?

A.—Yes, for $10.83.

Q.—Where is it?

A.—With my lawyer up home. I had him write the Department.

Q.—You haven't cashed that?

A.—No.

Q.—Did you come to Toronto to see anybody about this claim?

A.—Yes, a couple of times.

Q.—Did you see Mr. Smeaton and Mr. Fulton?

A.—No, not in particular.

Q.—When you came to Toronto, who did you see?

A.—Mr. Hogarth; but he was not in and I went up to see Mr. Brown.

Q.—When was that?

A.—After we had quit the job sometime in October, the first week in October.

Q.—You saw Mr. Brown and what took place?

A.—He told us the money would be all right and further than that he said he had a cheque going out that day for some amount of money.

Q.—What date was that?

A.—The first week of October.

HON. MR. RANEY: There was a cheque went out on the 8th of October for $1,164.40?

A.—Yes.

Q.—There was a cheque on the 25th of September just before that for $1,144?

A.—Yes.

MR. FINLAYSON: Is that all that took place between you and Mr. Brown?

A.—I wanted to know if there was any way of stopping the cheque and he said no.

MR. RANEY: Did you know then that you had a preference claim for your wages over Chambers and McCaffrey for the loan of their machine?

A.—No, I did not know that.

Q.—Was that the only time you came to Toronto about it?

A.—I was in once or twice after that, I did not see Mr. Hogarth at any time.

Q.—What was the second interview with Mr. Brown?

A.—He did not just say much about it, I had my lawyer write him a letter.

Q.—What did he tell you on the first occasion?

A.—Mr. Brown told me our money would be all right.

MR. FINLAYSON: You say the contract was $5 or $5.50 per day?

A.—I had hired with him for $5.50 a day and then when he was failing to pay and I saw he had his job too cheap and hadn't any equipment when he came on the job I took $5 to get out.

Q.—Why do you say he took it too cheap?

A.—I know. I have been on construction and I know.

Q.—The other witness said the job was all right but the man was all wrong?

A.—There may be a little of that wrong, but the job was too cheap I know.

Q.—What did he have it at?

A.—The grading I was told at thirty-eight cents a yard. That is just what I was told.

THE CHAIRMAN: You were forming your opinion on some information you received?

MR. FINLAYSON: Your figures are not right.

A.—They may not be.

Q.—Anyway you say you were hired at $5.50 and you cut it down to $5?

A.—Yes.

Q.—Let me tell you that when you get a job at a higher figure keep it, because if you get a dividend you lose both ways.

A.—The dividend didn't amount to very much. It would be better at $5.50. It would be a couple of cents, perhaps.

Q.—You would be satisfied if you got $5?

A.—Yes, I did not make any money out of it.

Q.—Five dollars is a very moderate rate for a teamster and a team?

A.—It sure is.

Q.—You stayed on like Brass and took a chance?

A.—Yes.

Q.—You stayed right on to the bitter end?

A.—Yes.

Q.—Notwithstanding there was no pay day and notwithstanding the job was taken too cheap?

A.—No, he used to tell us he would pay us.

Q.—He has never turned you away with a harsh answer? He was a good promiser?

A.—A good promiser.

Q.—You saw Brown in October?

A.—Yes.

Q.—You did not see Hogarth?

A.—No.

Q.—You said you saw him once?

A.—Not to my knowledge.

Q.—You were in to see him with two or three men at one time?

A.—Just one man was ever in with me.

Q.—Mr. Hogarth said you saw him?

A.—Not to my knowledge, Mr. Cook was with me.

Q.—Whoever you did see told you that it was a Government job and that the money would be divided?

A.—No.

Q.—He told you a cheque had gone out that day?

A.—Mr. Brown told us that there was a cheque to McLean that day.

Q.—You were too late for that one? That one was gone?

A.—Yes.

Q.—That was the last cheque that went out?

Hon. Mr. Raney: No, there was a cheque after that in September.

Mr. Finlayson: Don't you remember coming in with Cook?

A.—No, I was only down once with Cook.

Q.—Mr. Hogarth seems to have written a letter immediately afterwards saying that Kenneth Hannahson had a claim for $241, and B. C. Cook had a claim for so and so on this job?

A.—We did not see Mr. Hogarth that day at all.

Q.—Don't you remember him telling you when you were making some claim that you had better see a lawyer, that he could not advise you about it?

A.—No.

The Chairman: Did anybody tell you that?

A.—No.

Q.—The date you saw Mr. Brown, he told you your money would be all right?

A.—Yes.

Q.—Did you come away with the idea that he said your money would be all right because he was sending out a cheque and he could pay you out of the cheque?

A.—I knew if the contractor got the cheque we would never see the money.

Caroline Sutton sworn.

HON. MR. RANEY: You keep hotel at Caledon?

A.—Yes.

Q.—Did some of these men board with you?

A.—Yes, Mr. McLean.

Q.—Were you paid something?

A.—Yes, I was paid.

Q.—Did you get a bad cheque too?

A.—No, I never got any cheque, Mr. McLean always paid me in cash.

Q.—You have a claim here for $150, is that right?

A.—One hundred and twenty-three dollars and fifty cents.

Q.—G. E. Sutton?

A.—No, that is my son.

Q.—Did you get a cheque?

A.—No, I did not put in any claim, that is my son's claim.

Q.—You did not put any claim in?

A.—No, I never bothered, I thought probably Mr. McLean would come along and pay me.

Q.—He had not come along yet?

A.—No.

Q.—What is your claim?

A.—One hundred and twenty-three dollars and fifty cents.

Q.—You haven't been paid anything on account of that?

A.—No, I have the cash here that has been paid.

MR. FINLAYSON: McLean came to you and made arrangments with you himself?

Q.—You are looking to him?

A.—Yes.

Q.—You are still looking to him?

A.—I thought he would pay it but he has not come along yet.

Q.—You think he has just been held up on the way?

A.—Oh, yes.

Richard Russell, sworn.

HON. MR. RANEY: You are a farmer?

A.—No.

Q.—You were working on this job?

A.—Yes.

Q.—With a team?

A.—No, just myself.

Q.—Have you an unpaid claim? For how much?

A.—$137.00.

Q.—Your claim has been cut down by Mr. McLean to $118?

A.—Yes, I got a cheque for $11.49.

Q.—Recently?

A.—Yes.

Q.—As a dividend?

A.—Yes.

Q.—Have you used it?

A.—Yes, I cashed it.

Q.—Did you authorize Mr. McLean to reduce your claim to $118?

A.—No.

Q.—Did you have any talk with Mr. Fulton or Mr. Smeaton while working on this job?

A.—No.

Q.—You just went on faith?

A.—Yes.

Q.—Did you get a bad cheque?

A.—Yes, I have it here.

Q.—How much was that for?

A.—$71.50.

Q.—There were no funds for that?

A.—No.

Q.—That amount was included in your $125?

A.—Yes.

A. J. McEnaney, sworn.

Hon. Mr. Raney: You worked on this job?

A.—Yes.

Q.—With a shovel?

A.—Yes.

Q.—How much were you paid?

A.—I put in a claim for $45.00 and he cut it to $24.00 and I got a cheque for $2.33.

Q.—Is your claim for $45.00 right?

A.—Yes.

Q.—He owes you that much money?

A.—Yes.

Q.—The Government sent you a cheque for $2.33?

A.—Yes.

Q.—Was this the letter and the cheque that came with it?

A.—Yes.

Exhibit Marked 11.

Q.—That was the dividend on $24.00?

A.—Yes.

Q.—Did you authorize anybody to reduce your claim to $24.00?

A.—No.

Q.—Did you go to see anybody about this claim?

A.—Yes. I went to Mr. Hogarth up in the Highway Department and he was not in and we talked to Mr. Brown the accountant.

Q.—When was that?

A.—About October 10th, I think it was.

Q.—What took place?

A.—We talked to him quite a while, and he assured us by what I could see from his talk to get our claim in as quickly as we could. That there was money in there and felt quite sure we would get our pay. We asked him if there was a bond, and he said, "Naturally, there was a bond," which I understood. All he said to us was to get our claim in quickly; therefore, I put it in the next day or so.

Q.—Mr. Telfer is a neighbour of yours?

A.—Yes, I worked with him on the C.P.R. for twenty years. He is trying to be here to-day, but we could not locate him last night. He is to be in to-day sometime.

MR. FINLAYSON: You worked how long?

A.—About five days.

Q.—You put in a claim for $45, that McLean says should be $24.00?

A.—Yes.

Q.—How many days did you work?

A.—Five.

Q.—How much were you to get?

A.—$9.00.

Q.—What is the reason for that?

A.—First, they phoned me for a man and I could not get a man to go at ninety cents an hour.

Q.—Are you an engineer?

A.—Yes, a steam shovel engineer, I never ran Keystone. I went down and got a man named McKie.

Q.—You broke the Keystone?

A.—No.

Q.—Isn't there some trouble between you and McLean?

A.—No, McLean and I are good friends.

Q.—He didn't pay you?

A.—I haven't bothered with about it. Just one time I was in I went to Mr. Brown about it.

Q.—He said to get your claim in quickly?

A.—Yes. I understood, everybody told us that the Government would be good and even when the shovels stopped they asked me to go up and run the shovel and I understood that everybody would get paid.

Q.—I suppose the truth is that locally there was some thought that the Government would pay all these things? And you had a claim in that he cut down from $45.00 to $24.00 and Mr. Brown said, get your claim in and you said, "Is there a bond?"

A.—Yes, he also said there was an amount of money held back, he said $2,400.

James McDevitt, sworn.

MR. RANEY: There is a letter from the accountant of the Department of Highways, enclosing a cheque for $1.50, dated 1st of March. What is your claim?

A.—$108.00.

Q.—What is that for?

A.—For working firing the shovel. The Keystone shovel.

Q.—You were a fireman?

A.—Yes.

Q.—Is that the amount you are entitled to?

A.—I consider so.

Q.—Did you have a contract with McLean?

A.—No, the foreman hired me, Mr. Telfer.

Q.—At what rate?

A.—No rate mentioned.

Q.—He just told you to go on?

A.—Yes.

Q.—What rate are you charging?

A.—Seventy-two cents an hour.

Q.—Is that the regular charge?

A.—I consider it is.

Q.—A fair charge?

A.—Yes.

Q.—Have you been paid anything on account other than this cheque for $1.50?

A.—No.

Q.—How many days did you work?

A.—Fifteen days.

Q.—According to the statement, your account is $108 and it was reduced to $15.50, do you know anything about that?

A.—No.

Q.—Did you authorize anybody to reduce your claim to $15.50?

A.—No.

Q.—You worked for fifteen days?

A.—Yes.

Q.—This is the letter and the cheque you received? Exhibit No. 12?

A.—Yes.

Q.—That is all the payments you ever received?

A.—Yes.

Q.—Did you see anybody about this matter?

A.—No.

MR. FINLAYSON: You say you were hired by the foreman and nothing said about wages?

A.—No, nothing at all.

Q.—That is extraordinary? The foreman was sober?

A.—Yes, I guess he was.

Q.—That means you were to take whatever he put down for you?

MR. CALLAN: Usually in cases like that there is a standard rate of wages.

MR. FINLAYSON: Were you to take whatever he gave you for the class of work you were doing?

A.—I considered there was standard rate, whatever it was.

Q.—The standard rate on that job for work of that class?

A.—Yes.

Q.—Did you take somebody else's place?

A.—McClintock was fireman.

Q.—You only worked on that job for two days?

A.—No, fifteen days.

Q.—On this particular job of firing?

A.—Yes.

Q.—You only fired for two days?

A.—Altogether, no, more than that. The shovels broke down and they were waiting for repairs.

Q.—Mr. McLean has put in that you only worked a couple of days firing and then you worked at labouring work?

A.—I was at other work with a shovel.

Q.—You did not keep any track of the time?

A.—No.

Q.—You do not know how much time you had in firing or how much at labouring, but you claim the same pay?

A.—I claim for firing for the time I am there.

Russell Lloyd McClintock, sworn.

HON. MR. RANEY: You were fireman on the shovel with Mr. Brass?

A.—Yes.

Q.—Who employed you?

A.—I was employed by Mr. McLean.

Q.—At what rate?

A.—Fifty-five cents an hour.

Q.—You put in your claim for $278.15?

A.—$278.15.

Q.—Is that right?

A.—That is correct.

Q.—Have you been paid anything?

A.—Yes, I was paid by three different periods.

Q.—The balance is $278.15?

A.—Yes.

Q.—Did you get a bad cheque?

A.—I got a couple, but I got them both cashed.

Q.—So that the man that cashed the cheque is the loser?

A.—I did not hang around long enough to find whether they were good or bad, I got them cashed quick.

Q.—Is this $278.15 the balance after crediting these two cheques?

A.—Yes.

Q.—These cheques are being treated by you as though they were good?

A.—Yes.

Q.—You were reduced by this statement to $93.00?

A.—$96.00 I thought it was.

Q.—Did you get a cheque?

A.—Yes, I received a cheque for $9.09.

Q.—Where is it?

A.—I have it here in my pocket.

Q.—You had better put it in?

A.—If you gentlemen would like to look at it.

MR. FINLAYSON: I would not give it up, I could cash it.

WITNESS: I will hang on to it for car fare home.

HON. MR. RANEY: I think he had better put them both in for the present. I think they will want to have these cheques framed. Whatever you want to do.

WITNESS: I will give you the cheque and get car fare from you. Do you think it would be satisfactory if I cashed that cheque. I need it, leaving all jokes aside; I need car fare to-night.

MR. FINLAYSON: It does not affect your claim against the Government or anybody else and the cheque is good.

HON. MR. RANEY: You really need it for car fare?

A.—I do.

Q.—Did you have any talk with Mr. Smeaton or Fulton on the job about not being paid?

A.—I was talking to Mr. Smeaton quite often.

Q.—About what?

A.—About the wages not being paid and the way the job was running, and I asked him what he thought of it,

Q.—What did he say?

A.—He said your wages will be all right.   The Government will be good for that.

Q.—They will be good for it?

A.—Yes.

Q.—Did he tell you that more than once?

A.—Different times, different occasions.

Q.—What about Mr. Fulton?

A.—I wasn't talking to Mr. Fulton very much.

Q.—You came down afterwards in October did you not with Mr. Brass?

A.—Yes, to Toronto.

Q.—Did you go with him on several occasions to the Parliament Buildings?

A.—Yes, I was with Mr. Brass five different times.

Q.—Who did you see at the different times?

A.—We met Mr. Hogarth and Mr. Brown and Mr. Squires.

Q.—Tell me, what Mr. Hogarth told you?

A.—Mr. Hogarth said, he thought it would be all right, we would get our money all right, he thought.

Q.—What did Mr. Brown say?

A.—Mr. Brown said pretty much the same.

Q.—What did Mr. Squires say?

A.—Mr. Squires did not say very much but what he did say; he told us at first that the Government did not owe us any money.   He asked us what our business was first and we told him that we came after our money; why he said, "We don't owe you any money," and I said, "That is funny if you don't owe us some money," so then he put up a kind of an argument about the job; . Well, we talked back not very much and then he brought around this pro rata basis. He told us there was so much money, McLean had a certain amount of money there.

Q.—Do you remember the date of this?

A.—I am not just sure.   I think some time in October.

THE CHAIRMAN: After you quit the job?

A.—After we quit the job.   He explained about handing this money out on a pro rata basis.

Q.—Nothing said to you or any of these men about going to a lawyer to protect yourselves?

A.—Not by Mr. Squires.

Q.—Was that discussed with any of them?

A.—Well, Hogarth said once.

Q.—What did he say?

A.—He said he didn't think it was any use going to a lawyer; he thought it would be all right.

Q.—Did you know that against any funds in the hands of the Government your work for wages, would be entitled to be paid first within a certain time, three months, were you told that?

A.—What is that?

Q.—Did anybody tell you at this time that if you had gone to a lawyer and put your claim in you would have had a preference, you would have been paid ahead of anything else?

A.—No, we were not.

MR. FINLAYSON: You were firing on the shovel?

A.—Yes.

Q.—You were hired by McLean at fifty-five cents a hour?

Q.—Why should you get fifty-five cents and this other chap, McDevitt get seventy-two?

A.—That was the rate I was working for at the time with Chambers and McCaffrey.

Q.—That apparently was the rate on which you were hired?

A.—The regular rate is seventy-two cents an hour for firing on any class of steam shovel.

Q.—Why were you getting fifty-five cents?

A.—That is what I hired at myself.

Q.—There is no reason why you should get fifty-five and the other chap, seventy-two, it was the same work?

A.—Pretty much, yes.

Q.—The same class of work?

A.—Yes.

HON. MR. RANEY: I guess if the other fellow gets fifty-five, I guess he will be satisfied.

WITNESS: I should have had seventy-two cents, that is the regular rate.

MR. FINLAYSON: You knew who the district engineer was on the job?

A.—No. I never met him.

Q.—You saw him there?

A.—I saw him.

Q.—The only one you talked to was Mr. Smeaton?

A.—Yes.

Q.—He said, according to you, that the wages would be all right?

A.—Yes.

Q.—No promise or anything? Just expressed the hope they would be all right?

A.—We both hoped together.

Q.—That is all it amounted to?

A.—Yes.

Q.—Then you saw Mr. Squires and he said the Government did not owe you anything and explained about what they would do; they would divide the money pro rata?

A.—On a pro rata basis.

Q.—You saw Mr. Hogarth and spoke to him?

A.—Yes.

Q.—He said the Government would hold what they had on hand?

A.—Yes.

Q.—He tells me you spoke to him about seeing a lawyer and he said you would have to decide that for yourself. Don't you remember speaking to him and he told you, you would have to decide whether you wanted to go to a lawyer or not?

A.—I would not say I remembered hearing that.

Q.—You won't deny it?

A.—No. I will neither deny it or remember it.

Q.—It might have occurred?

A.—I would not swear exactly.

Hon. Mr. Raney: Suppose we adjourn now.

The Chairman: The Committee will adjourn until two o'clock, Monday afternoon.

Adjourned at 12.50 p.m. until 2 p.m. Monday next the 29th of March, 1926.

PUBLIC ACCOUNTS COMMITTEE.

The Committee met on Monday, March 29th, 1926, at 2 p.m., with Mr. Lewis in the Chair.

The Chairman: Gentlemen, we have the members present marked on the list without calling the roll. It saves time. We will go right ahead.

John Telford, called; sworn. Examined by Hon. W. E. Raney.

Q.—John Telford, is it?

A.—Yes, sir.

Q.—Mr. Telford, you were superintendent on that Caledon Hill job?

A.—Yes, sir.

Q.—Last summer?

A.—Yes, sir.

Q.—And I see you sent in a bill to the Department for the claim of your payment against McLean for three months' wages at $225 per month, $675, and some disbursments, making it up to $697, and against that you give a credit of $25.00, leaving a balance of $672.75?

A.—Yes.

The Chairman: Mr. Telford was superintendent for the contractor?

Hon. Mr. Raney: Superintendent for the contractor, yes.

Q.—You say in your letter: "I might say that Mr. McLean and I had no agreement as to what wages were to be, but I have put in my claim at the same rate as the lowest I have received any place I have worked since before the war. The last work I did, previous to that with Mr. McLean, was with the Dominion Construction Company for which I received $225 per month with board."

Q.—Was that right?

A.—Yes, sir. "In the season of 1924, I worked for Mr. H. E. McLean for which I received from $250 to $300 per month and board."

Q.—Was that right?

A.—Yes, sir.

Q.—And you made out your bill on that basis? I see your claim is down on this list that was apparently sworn to by Mr. McLean and sent into the Department, you have put down as the amount claimed by claimants $672.65; that agrees, I think, with this letter, and amount acknowledged by contractor $315, and then you received a cheque, I see, from the Department on the 1st of March for $30.68, being a dividend on the amount that McLean admitted, $315?

A.—Yes, sir.

Q.—Did you authorize anybody to reduce your claim from $672 to $315?

A.—No, sir.

Q.—Do you know how that came about?

A.—No, I don't.

Q.—I see your letter to the Department in which you give particulars of your claim was dated 3rd of December, 1925?

A.—Yes.

Q.—Then this is the letter and the cheque that you received from the Department, I believe on the 1st of March?

A.—Yes, sir.

(Exhibits 14 and 15, letter with the cheque.)

Q.—When did you go on the job?

A.—July 20th.

Q.—Your job was to superintend the work?

A.—Yes, sir.

Q.—And you remained for three months?

A.—Yes, sir.

Q.—Now, you were not paid anything you say except this $25.00 which about covered your disbursements?

A.—That is all.

Q.—Did you ask McLean for money?

A.—No, I did not until after he was through.

Q.—Why didn't you?

A.—Because I would rather have seen him pay the men.

Q.—You knew the men were not being paid?

A.—Yes, sir.

Q.—Did the men come to you and complain?

A.—Yes, they were kicking.

Q.—Did you take the matter up with Mr. Fulton?

A.—Yes, I did.

HON. MR. RANEY: I may say I saw this witness a few minutes ago and he told me he would prefer not to repeat what his conversation between him and Mr. Fulton was, and I see no reason why it should not be repeated and I am going to ask him. Tell me, what took place with Mr. Fulton?

A.—Well, about six weeks after I was on the job, I asked Mr. Fulton if he would find out in the office if the Government was responsible for our wages, so in about a week's time he told me he had seen them, I didn't know who it was.

Q.—He had been to Toronto?

A.—Yes, and he told me those who actually worked on the job will be paid; that is what he told me.

Q.—That is the message Mr. Fulton brought back to you, that the men who worked on the job would be paid?

A.—The men who actually worked on the job.

Q.—Did he tell you his authority?

A.—No.

Q.—But he had been to Toronto?

A.—Yes.

MR. KEITH: Who was Fulton?

THE CHAIRMAN: The level man, instrument man.

HON. MR. RANEY: Engineer.

MR. FINLAYSON: No.

THE CHAIRMAN: This was the instrument man who gave the levels.

MR. KEITH: Was he sent there by the Government or McLean?

A.—He is a Government man.

MEMBER: Superintendent?

HON. MR. RANEY: Assistant to the engineer, that is what he was, I suppose.

MR. FINLAYSON: He is a man who went from job to job, giving levels. He wasn't there steadily on this job.

Hon. Mr. Raney: He was there from time to time.

Q.—Then you came down to Toronto after the work stopped?

A.—Yes.

Q.—The work stopped, I believe, because the boarding house people closed down on the men?

A.—The men all quit.

Q.—And you quit and you came to Toronto?

A.—Yes.

A.—I went to the ——

Q.—About this matter of unpaid wages?

A.—Yes, I went down to the Provincial Highways and saw Mr. Brown.

Q.—The auditor?

A.—Accountant.

Q.—What took place between you and him?

A.—He told me there was $2,300 or $2,400 there of McLean's money and that they would pay that out as far as it went, but no more.   But he says, "Remember, McLean is bonded," giving me to understand the bonding company was responsible for our pay.

Q.—Did you know then that the wages, that the men having claims for wages had preference over other creditors?

A.—Yes, sir, I did.

Q.—Was that discussed between you and Mr. Brown?

A.—Yes, it was mentioned.   I said something about it, after thirty days it became the same as any other debt.   I didn't care to put the man in jail or anything.

Q.—You knew that by taking proceedings before a magistrate in thirty days.   Did you know anything about the bankruptcy law?

A.—No.

Q.—I think it is three months under the bankruptcy law.

A.—I understood it was thirty days.

Hon. Mr. Raney: It is thirty days, I think under the Ontario law. What did he say about that?

A.—I don't remember what he said in particular.

Q.—But you understood you had thirty days in which to make your claim?

A.—Yes.

Q.—And you were liable to lose it unless something was done?

A.—Yes.

Q.—Then you went away?

A.—Yes.

Q.—Then did you go back again to see anybody in the Department?

A.—Yes, I went back several times.

Q.—Did you see anybody else in the Department?

A.—I saw the Deputy Minister the day before Christmas.

Q.—Mr. Squire?

A.—Yes.

Q.—The day before Christmas?

A.—Yes, he told me they couldn't get McLean in here to sign some papers and they couldn't pay anything out until they got him in.   If they could get him in they were going to pay on a pro rata basis.   They couldn't pay until they got McLean into the city to sign off.

Mr. Finlayson: Pay on a pro rata basis?

A.—Yes.

Hon. Mr. Raney: Did he tell you how much was still owing McLean?
A.—No.

Q.—But Brown said $2,300 or $2,400, that was in October?
A.—Yes, sometime in October.

Q.—Were those the only two men you saw?
A.—That is all.

Q.—You saw Brown several times?
A.—Three or four times.

Q.—Did he ever make any different statement about the amount that was coming to McLean?
A.—I think he told me, I think he said a thousand dollars. The last time I was there he said there was only a thousand dollars, if I remember.

Q.—It had been reduced. Well, cheques had been made to him in the meantime. There is no doubt about that.

(Cross examination by Mr. Finlayson).

Q.—You are superintendent?
A.—Yes, sir

Q—And you have been acting as that I judge from your letter a good many years?
A.—Well, supervisor, and road man, and that kind of thing.

Q.—Well, we won't quarrel about the title, but some superior being who had charge of things?
A.—Yes.

Q.—And you speak in this letter as if you had been doing that a great many years?
A.—Yes, sir.

Q.—Before the war?
A.—Yes.

Q.—And you never got less than $225? You had been doing that work before the war?
A.—Yes.

Q.—So you had been doing it for fifteen or twenty years, supervisor, superintendent?
A.—Yes, sir.

Q.—And that meant you had charge of the work under the boss?
A.—Yes, sir.

Q.—So you were on the boss's side?
A.—Yes, sir.

Q.—You were his representative?
A.—Yes, sir.

Q.—And had complete charge of the work, I understand?
A.—That is right.

Q.—Well now, being that kind of a superior man, you knew how these jobs are run, don't you?
A.—Yes, sir.

Q.—They are usually a pay day every two weeks and on this particular job we have heard there never was a pay day?
A.—Yes, sir.

Q.—So you knew perfectly well you were not treating the men, you and the boss together, were not treating the men right?
A.—Yes, sir.

Q.—The men were being ill-treated by you and McLean?

A.—Yes, sir.

Q.—And there never was a pay day of any kind?

A.—Well, some of the men got some money at different times.

Q.—Well, we heard they got some bad cheques?

A.—Yes, sir.

Q.—You remember the occasion on which McLean came up and waved a roll of bills and said, "I have got this and none of you will get it?"

A.—No.

Q.—You have heard of it?

A.—No.

Q.—You knew he was drawing money?

A.—Well, he told me several times he had not seen the colour of their money.

Q.—You also knew, the engineers knew, he was drawing money?

A.—I don't think the engineers ever told me.

Q.—Who did?

A.—No person in particular, but I know he paid the men some money a couple of different times.

Q.—That he had paid progress certificates? You would be there when the resident engineer would come around and give him a certificate?

A.—I suppose, but I didn't see him give a certificate.

Q.—No, but you were the man—I understand you are not troubled with the same fault that McLean is, are you?

A.—No, sir.

Q.—You are, to put it positively, you are sober?

A.—Yes, sir.

Q.—That is what I am told, and you were on the job all the time?

A.—Yes, sir.

Q.—So when the boss was off the job with these fits, you were the man that checked up the estimates?

A.—No, I was not even timekeeper.

Q.—But you were the man who was superintendent, when the engineer came around and measured up the work?

A.—Yes.

Q.—So you knew he was getting progress certificates?

A.—Yes.

Q.—And you knew he was being paid regularly on the amount of work done?

A.—Yes.

Q.—Well, this man being drunk, you were in charge, weren't you?

A.—Yes. I don't know that he was drunk so much as reported.

Q.—Well, one of the witnesses on Saturday told us he drank up everything between Toronto and Owen Sound and was never on the job?

A.—That wasn't right.

Q.—That was an exaggeration?

HON. MR. RANEY: Well, it is obvious it was an exaggeration, of course.

MR. FINLAYSON: Anyway, he was acting very badly?

A.—At times, yes.

Q.—And you knew when the engineer came up for the purpose of making progress certificates you had to attend to it?

A.—Yes.

Q.—And you know these progress certificates were given?

A.—I suppose they were.

Q.—And you know that meant a cheque, doesn't it?

A.—Yes.

Q.—You have worked on highway jobs?

A.—Well, it was railroad construction I always worked on.

Q.—Well, it is the same thing?

A.—Every two weeks.

Q.—And the men should be paid every two weeks?

A.—Yes.

Q.—So when the men were not paid and the boss was drunk, you knew there was something wrong?

A.—Yes.

Q.—And notwithstanding that, you continued on?

A.—Yes, sir.

Q.—For three months?

A.—Yes, sir.

Q.—So you missed six pay days?

A.—Yes, sir.

Q.—Do you think that is treating the Government or anybody else fairly?

A.—Why?

Q.—Well, you were representing the boss, and the boss wasn't paying you. You might have told them?

A.—I went to Mr. Fulton and asked him if the Government was responsible.

Q.—When?

A.—That would be a month or six weeks after I started, about the last of August.

Q.—We can understand a working man being misled, but a superintendent isn't misled when he knows his boss is drunk and knows payments are being made to him right along. You never had any idea the Government was going to pay you as well as McLean?

A.—Well, McLean told me he wasn't ——

Q.—You didn't believe that? Be honest? You didn't believe that?

A.—No, I didn't.

Q.—So you knew perfectly well the boss was being paid by the Government and was drinking the money up and the men were not being paid. You didn't expect the Government were going to pay you under those circumstances?

A.—I suppose they knew he wasn't paying the men as well as I did.

Q.—But that was your job. You were superintendent?

A.—But I wasn't supposed to go to the Government.

Q.—I don't think you were. I think you were supposed to go to the boss and get your money when you knew he was being bad. Isn't it the fact you were working for McLean as superintendent?

A.—Yes, sir.

Q.—And he was not on the job and attending to business?

A.—He was on the job most of the time.

Q.—He was not attending to business?

A.—He may not have been all the time.

Q.—And a good many times. You let the time go by. And you knew he was being bad and you come here and want to tell this Committee the Government should pay you and pay him too?

A.—Yes.

Q.—Pay him and pay you, too?

A.—I think the Government is responsible for our wages.

Q.—Notwithstanding the fact that you were superintendent? Why didn't the superintendent see the men were paid?

A.—I couldn't get money from McLean. He said he hadn't seen the colour of their money.

Q.—You knew that wasn't true. Do you come from out there?

A.—No. I live in Toronto.

Q.—Ever work for this man before?

A.—No.

Q.—Ever work for a contractor of that kind before?

A.—Not on the highways.

Q.—Or anywhere?

A.—I followed railroad construction.

Q.—Did you ever work for a contractor who acted that way before?

A.—No.

Q.—So McLean you knew was drinking and the first pay day went by and you saw the engineer estimating the quantity of work done and you knew that meant a progress certificate and you knew that meant cash?

A.—I suppose.

Q.—That is the way it is done. Every superintendent knows that?

A.—They might make out a progress report and hold the money back. I can't say.

Q.—You know when progress certificates are made out that is the basis on which payment is made?

A.—Yes, sir.

Q.—And you knew the man was getting his pay, or you had reason to believe it?

A.—Yes.

Q.—Notwithstanding that you went on and kept the men on?

A.—Yes.

Q.—Wouldn't it have been fair to yourself and the men to say, "Here, there is something wrong here."

A.—What could you do?

Q.—You could have stopped?

A.—I did stop.

Q.—You didn't stop until three months after. You missed six pay days?

A.—Well, I didn't stop, the men stopped.

Q.—You would have gone on?

A.—I went right on.

Q.—There was a strike then?

A.—Yes.

Hon. Mr. Raney: See, he had the assurance of this bond.

Mr. Finlayson: You have been on this work for fifteen or twenty years, as superintendent?

A.—Yes.

Q.—So you knew perfectly well this man was being paid and yet you stayed on for six pay days and got $25.00?

A.—I didn't know perfectly well. I had an idea he was paid.

Q.—So you cannot complain very much yourself. You say that you had been there six weeks, after three pay days?

A.—About that time.

Q.—You spoke to Fulton?

A.—Yes.

Q.—You know Fulton has nothing to do with payments, don't you?

A.—Yes.

Q.—Fulton has nothing to do with payments of any kind. His job is to take levels; give you the lines?

A.—Yes.

Q.—There is an engineer, Alden, who came around?

A.—Yes.

Q.—And above him there is the divisional engineer?

A.—Yes.

Q.—And you never said a word to either of them?

A.—No.

Q.—Fulton had nothing to do with payments.

MR. MAGEAU: Which Fullerton is this?

HON MR. RANEY: Fulton.

MR. FINLAYSON: And about six weeks after that, after missing three pay days, you spoke to Fulton?

A.—Yes.

Q.—How often would Alden be around, the engineer?

A.—Once every couple of weeks.

Q.—He tells me he was there very week at least?

A.—He may have been.

Q.—He says you never spoke to him at all?

A.—No, I didn't.

Q.—Henning, the engineer, was around, every couple of weeks anyway. You never spoke to him about it?

A.—No.

Q.—Wouldn't it have been fair to speak to them?

A.—Well, I didn't think it necessary when I spoke to Fulton, when he took it up in the office.

Q.—You also saw Mr. Hogarth, the engineer. He tells me he was up there and talked to you?

A.—Yes.

Q.—Because McLean was off he talked to you. You were McLean's representative?

A.—Yes.

Q.—The chief engineer came around and you never said a word to him?

A.—No.

Q.—Isn't it perfectly apparent you haven't been fair to them at all?

A.—Well —

Q.—You know the instrument man has nothing to do with the pay, and you had the resident engineer, divisional engineer and chief engineer all seeing you and you never said a word to any of them?

A.—No.

Q.—And were you fair to the men? The men looked to you as the superior gentleman on the job?

HON. MR. RANEY: You will have to pay this, first thing you know.

MR. FINLAYSON: You strike me as being a reasonable sort of man. I cannot understand?

A.—Well, I could not do anything.

Q.—Couldn't do anything?

A.—No.

Q.—Couldn't report the facts to the engineers?
A.—There was plenty reporting that without me.
Q.—But you were the man representing McLean?
A.—Yes.
Q.—Anyway you didn't do it?
A.—Yes.
Q.—And when was this you spoke to Fulton?
A.—About the latter part of August.
Q.—Later than that, wasn't it?
A.—I couldn't say to a day, somewhere around there.
Q.—I understand it was the end of August, is it?
A.—That is what I said.
Q.—End of September?
A.—No.
Q.—When?
A.—About the last of August.
Q.—Well, it would be more than that according to your own figures? **You** say six weeks?
A.—Well, I started in July.
Q.—20th of July?
A.—20th.
Q.—So it would be the end of September?
A.—Well, thereabouts. I cannot tell the dates at all.
Q.—Can you swear to the date you started?
A.—20th of July.
Q.—Did you keep a time book?
A.—No, I didn't get a time book at all.
Q.—Who kept the men's time?
A.—McLean himself and a foreman he had there.
HON. MR. RANEY: Was he sent on the job?
A.—Yes.
MR. FINLAYSON: Who kept the time?
A.—This here foreman, a fellow that was right there on the job all the time.
Q.—This job seems to have been a wonderful job. And you came on the job as superintendent and never said a word about how much you were going to get?
A.—I had reasons for it, too, because, he didn't have a very good foreman.
Q.—What has that to do——
A.—Well, it has a whole lot to do with my rate of wages. I advised him to get a bigger shovel and he told me he was getting a bigger shovel and he was also getting construction cars so I figured when we got bigger shovel and construction cars we would be in a paying basis and get a better rate.
Q.—How could you get a better rate when you never got any rate? Is this true, that you went out there, worked for three months and never had a word between you and the boss as to what you were going to be paid?
A.—Not a word about rate. He said he would pay me as much as anybody else.
Q.—You seem to have been great bargainers. You worked for three months and never a word about pay, and never got a cent except $25.00?
A.—That is all.
Q.—And never made any complaint until about two months had elapsed?
A.—No.

Q.—And then you spoke to the instrument man?

A.—I spoke to the instrument man about six weeks after.

Q.—Well, I understand it was later. I say it was about two months. You won't contradict that because you don't know when?

A.—A month or six weeks.

Q.—Well, you are guessing at this?

A.—Yes, it may have been that long.

Q.—And you asked him if the Government would pay. Now when he came back and said the men who were on the job then and stayed on the job would be paid for the rest of the time?

A.—He said all who actually worked on the job would be paid.

Q.—There were a whole lot that were not working at all, is that it?

A.—No.

Q.—How many were working then?

A.—At that time?

Q.—Yes.

A.—About ten or twelve teamsters, four or five labourers.

Q.—When was that?

A.—September.

Q.—Well, we are told the teamsters were down to two before that?

A.—The latter part ——

Q.—They were gone before that. You remember there were fourteen teamsters started, weren't there?

Mr. Mageau: How many men on the job?

A.—It varied.

Q.—Well, average?

A.—Seven or eight teams.

Q.—Men and all?

Mr. Finlayson: They started with fourteen teams?

A.—Yes.

Q.—And after the first pay day the twelve farm teams left?

A.—Twelve farm teams left?

Hon. Mr. Raney: No, no. He said the number varied.

Witness: I didn't know twelve teams——

Mr. Finlayson: Isn't it right, twelve teams quit and there were only two teams?

A.—No, it is not.

Q.—Well, if you could tell us what day it was in September, we could tell how many teams were working.

A.—There was about twelve teams when I went on first.

Q.—But that was in July?

A.—Yes.

Q.—But six weeks after brought it into September?

A.—There would be eight or ten teams on when I was——

Q.—When?

A.—First of September.

Q.—Let us see. First of September there were four teams; 31st of August there were three teams working. The highest seems to have been six, then four, four, two. If the rest of your information was about as correct as that. You are speaking from memory?

A.—Yes.

Q.—So you may be all wrong?

A.—I may be.

Q.—So when he came back he told you the men who were then working on the job would be paid?

HON. MR. RANEY: No, no.

MR. FINLAYSON: When Fulton came back he told you that men who were working on the job would be paid?

A.—He said those who actually worked on the job would be paid.

Q.—Actually worked then?

A.—Yes.

Q.—Actually worked then would be paid, you say Fulton said?

A.—Yes, sir.

Q.—That is all he said?

A.—Yes.

Q.—So you went on?

A.—Yes.

Q.—That applied to the men?

A.—Yes.

Q.—It wouldn't apply to the superintendent?

A.—Oh, yes.

Q.—You think it would?

A.—Yes.

Q.—Then you came to Toronto. How long would that be when you saw Brown in Toronto?

A.—I saw Brown about the middle of October.

Q.—The work was closed then?

A.—Yes.

Q.—After the work was closed down?

A.—Yes.

Q.—And Brown said there were between $2,300 or $2,400 due him, but no more?

A.—Yes.

Q.—And that might be divided among the creditors?

A.—He said they would pay that out as far as it went.

Q.—Pro rata?

A.—Yes, I suppose, as far as it went but no more.

Q.—They would pay out whatever they had on hand pro rata as far as it went?

A.—Yes. But, he says, remember, McLean is bonded.

Q.—Well, he didn't tell you what the bond was or anything like that? Did you think the bond related to wages?

A.—Yes.

Q.—You know what these bonds are, don't you? I mean you are a superintendent. Have you ever contracted?

A.—No. But I thought the bond, I thought that was what he was bonded for, to make sure the men would be safe and get their money, that was the idea of the bond.

Q.—That was your idea, but we won't quarrel about it. He didn't say that to you?

A.—He told me he thought the bonding company was going to pay. He said, "Remember, McLean is bonded."

■ THE CHAIRMAN: I just want to clear that. Did he tell you that the bonding company was going to pay it?

A.—No.

Hon. Mr. Raney: But, "Remember, McLean is bonded?"

A.—Yes.

Mr. Finlayson: He told you McLean was bonded, which might apply to the finish of the contract, and might leave this money available to divide among you; that was a fair inference; McLean was bonded, but that would leave $2,300 to be divided pro rata among the men?

A.—What I understood was that $2,300 would be divided as far as it went. Then the bonding company would pay the balance.

Q.—Well, he told you $2,300 would be divided pro rata but no more?

A.—They would not pay any more.

Q.—Told you whatever money the Department had on hand they would divide it?

A.—Yes.

Q.—But no more?

A.—Yes.

Q.—So you thought there was $2,300 or $2,400 to be divided up pro rata?

A.—Yes.

Q.—And beyond that there was this mysterious bond they may or may not—

A.—Yes, sir.

Q.—He didn't tell you anything about that except mention it?

A.—Yes.

Q.—Then you went to see Mr. Squire, and he told you they could not get McLean in?

A.—Yes, sir.

Q.—You knew that was right, or you were ready to believe it, and when they could get McLean in they would try and divide the amount among the men?

A.—Yes, sir.

Q.—So the real trouble to the whole thing is McLean, isn't it? He should have paid the men?

A.—Yes.

Q.—And should have paid you. And don't you think you are largely to blame for letting the thing slide in this way?

A.—No, I don't.

Hon. Mr. Raney: Did you have anything to do with paying the men?

A.—No.

Q.—Your work was just to see that the job was done?

A.—Yes.

Q.—To see the men kept working and the job was done?

A.—Yes.

Mr. Keith: You were superintendent, I suppose you employed the men on the job and let them off?

A.—Yes.

Mr. Finlayson: Wouldn't it have been well to let them off when they were not being paid?

The Chairman: Some of these men that were employed on the latter part of the job were acquaintances of yours. Some of the evidence gives me the impression that they knew you?

A.—Yes.

Q.—They had confidence in you?

A.—Yes.

Q.—And that is probably the reason they stayed on the job.

Mr. MAGEAU: What is the amount due to yourself and the men, all told?

THE CHAIRMAN: Perhaps this will give you the information. I haven't totalled the amount, but on the whole summer's work, with the exception of certain payments in cash and certain cheques, not very good, that McLean gave from time to time, most of these men got nothing except ten per cent. cheque which was their pro rata share of what was coming to McLean when the matter came to the attention of the Deputy Minister.

MEMBER: What was the average of men and teams employed on the job?

MR. FINLAYSON: It started with four teams.

HON. MR. RANEY: Started from four and ranged up and down. Men left because they were not being paid. Finally, at the finish there was only two men.

Mr. Finlayson has made a suggestion to me which might result in something in this matter and that is all the witnesses we have except department officials. I intended to call two or three of them but in view of what he says I think we might let this matter stand over until to-morrow morning. I think this Committee is sympathetic.

THE CHAIRMAN: No question of that.

HON. MR. RANEY: And see if we can see our way through this thing. If we cannot we will go on to-morrow.

THE CHAIRMAN: Not to-morrow morning, I think. We will meet to-night and to-morrow afternoon if necessary.

MR. FINLAYSON: Do you want to meet to-night?

HON. MR. RANEY: I wanted to go on with the motion picture thing.

THE CHAIRMAN: In connection with Brownridge, he hasn't been brought here yet.

HON. MR. RANEY: Well, he can get here to-morrow morning.

THE CHAIRMAN: I talked to the Minister. Brownridge is in the middle of a deal in New York for the Department. He will be brought here if you want him.

HON. MR. RANEY: I want him.

MR. FINLAYSON: The Minister thought probably after you had examined Mr. Paton, head of the department, you might not need him.

HON. MR. RANEY: I want Brownridge.

THE CHAIRMAN: If you want him we will bring him here.

MR. FINLAYSON: This will stand until to-morrow morning?

HON. MR. RANEY: Not until to-morrow morning, but to-morrow.

MR. FINLAYSON: To whenever we adjourn. And as Mr. Raney said, it is all new to me and I want to try and understand the matter. Nobody likes to see men kept out of their money. Of course it is delicate.

HON MR. RANEY: I have no doubt all these man were acting in good faith and wanted to help this man, but in the result.

THE CHAIRMAN: No question, the men got a rough deal.

MR. FINLAYSON: The men got a rough deal with this man Telford and somebody else acting carelessly.

HON. MR. RANEY: There is another matter I meant to have spoken about, of which I want to speak. I find in this morning's *Globe* and *Mail and Empire* statements concerning the Crown lands inquiry. I am not accusing anybody of having been a party to putting across a wrong impression. I think maybe the inference is from something I said yesterday.

Let me first call attention to what is said in *The Globe*.

MR. KEITH: Saturday?

Hon. Mr. Raney: Something I said on Saturday. *The Globe* says: "Inquiry exonerates Hon. James W. Lyons of all suspicion; investigation shows nothing questionable in dealings of former Minister.

"Hon. James W. Lyons, former Minister of Lands and Forests, has been completely exonerated of any suspicion of improper conduct as an official of the Crown. At the conclusion of a three weeks' investigation, demanded by him as a result of questions put upon the order paper by Liberal and Progressive members of the Legislature just before his resignation from office. Major D. Nash of Clarkson, Gordon and Dilworth informed the Public Accounts Committee on Saturday that an audit of the Lyons Fuel and Supply Company and the Soo Coal and Wood Company had failed to disclose anything of a questionable nature, while Hon. W. E. Raney said that his own examination of statements has convinced him there was no ground for criticism."

Well, of course, that is quite wrong. The *Mail and Empire* statement was very much the same.

The Chairman: And the *Star*, Saturday night was the same.

Hon. Mr. Raney: Then it is all wrong.

Well, as you recall, this is what happened. When Mr. Nash was put in the box he produced a report and three statements accompanying the report. One of those statements was a statement of past profits, past prices, and Mr. Finlayson asked that that statement be not made public but that Mr. Sinclair and I should look at it and if there was anything we wanted to call attention to we might call attention. I looked at it and I suppose Mr. Sinclair did, and I came to the conclusion that there was nothing that ought to be brought to the attention of the Committee in the statement.

I said to the Committee, you will recall, that this was not one of the matters that was raised in the questions that were asked in the House. No question was raised in the House about prices. I never had heard any suggestion that there had been any preference, that there had been any excess charge in prices or any reduced prices to Government contractors on the roads or timber licensees, nothing of that sort was suggested. Mr. Lyons, in presenting his case, thought it proper, and I think very properly, to give attention, to volunteer along that line, because there might be suspicion, somebody might say there was a rake-off, and to produce this statement, and volunteer, it having nothing to do with the inquiry so far as the questions were concerned.

And I said, and I repeat, there was nothing in that statement that would cast discredit on Mr. Lyons, but that is a long way from saying that the investigation showed nothing questionable in the former Minister's dealings. The matter isn't closed. There are other witnesses to be called, and the whole thing is wide open. I just want to make it clear, the matter is just as wide open now as it was Saturday morning or Friday, and my statement had no reference whatever to any portion of the inquiry except this sheet, this report, of which I said there was no ground for criticism of Mr. Lyons. Because nobody is in this Committee I am sure, to put anything across that isn't justified by the evidence.

The Chairman: What you want to say is that your statement of Saturday, dealt with report number three, dealing with the past operation? Your statement then wasn't just as full as. to-day, or perhaps——

Hon. Mr. Raney: Well, it was full enough, I think.

Mr. Finlayson: I understood Mr. Raney the way the papers did.

THE CHAIRMAN: I did. I thought the inquiry was at an end.

MR. FINLAYSON: This happened: Mr. Fullerton said to me toward the close of the inquiry, some messenger, with some papers, and it was just after you had made that statement, and I sent word back that the matter was over, and I didn't look at what he sent. Now, I don't want to stand on a technicality or anything of that kind. My friend made a statement that apparently we all took up as going further than he intended to go. It isn't one paper; apparently all three of them.

HON. MR. RANEY: Well, there is another paper in town.

MR. FINLAYSON: Well, there is another; the other paper is so much under your control.

HON. MR. RANEY: Well, I am not imputing bad faith to anybody. I guess the press table misunderstood.

THE CHAIRMAN: I am inclined to think that the most of us here thought probably the inquiry was over. I understood after your statement regarding number three statement.

HON. MR. RANEY: But I went on after that to cross-examine.

MR. FINLAYSON: No, I think it was before.

HON. MR. RANEY: No, it was after.

MR. FINLAYSON: Well, we needn't quarrel. Let us understand what it is you want, because I sent word to him that those papers were not wanted.

HON. MR. RANEY: I wanted a tabulation of South Porcupine, tabulation of the tenders the same as we had in the case of the Conniston Road and the Creighton, Copper Cliff Road. He has prepared it.

MR. FISHER: Mr. Fullerton was also to figure out what the road, Copper Cliff, Creighton-Copper Cliff, would have cost, if it had been done by the other tenderers.

MR. FINLAYSON: He sent on Saturday some papers with a message, "This is something asked to be followed up," and I said, "Go and tell Mr. Fullerton the thing is over," and I haven't seen him since, but I will endeavour to get it.

MR. FISHER: I suppose the same thing might be done in this other.

HON. MR. RANEY: That is what I asked for.

MR. SINCLAIR: The same as we did the other day.

MR. FINLAYSON: That is all you want?

HON. MR. RANEY: That is all I think for the present.

MR. FINLAYSON: Then you want to examine Mr. Labarge?

HON. MR. RANEY: Yes, and George McNamara was to come back.

MR. FINLAYSON: He will be here whenever you come back.

HON. MR. RANEY: Some papers he was to get.

THE CHAIRMAN: Yes, he was to produce.

HON. MR. RANEY: Well, I will let Mr. Finlayson know.

MR. LEWIS: Do you want McNamara to-morrow?

HON. MR. RANEY: We are going on with the other inquiry. Better get Mr. Labarge here from the north, but we may not reach them to-morrow.

MR. FINLAYSON: What are we going to do with this chap, McLean. Was he served personally?

HON. MR. RANEY: Oh, what would be the use.

MR. FINLAYSON. It was done at your request.

HON. MR. RANEY: He would only be a waste of time.

MR. FINLAYSON: I don't want any misunderstanding, that is all.

THE CHAIRMAN: What about continued sittings of this Committee?

Hon. Mr. Raney: We had better sit to-night.

The Chairman: You want to sit and get ahead with this motion picture matter?

Hon. Mr. Raney: Yes.

Member: Won't we sit again before to-night?

Mr. Finlayson: We cannot sit before to-night. Two things I want to do is to see Mr. Henry and report what has happened—

The Chairman: Eight o'clock?

Hon. Mr. Raney: Seven thirty if you like. Make a good long sitting.

Member: Make it eight.

Hon. Mr. Raney: Better have Fullerton here. We might get to it.

The Committee then adjourned until evening, Monday, March 29th, at eight o'clock.

PUBLIC ACCOUNTS COMMITTEE.

The Committee resumed at 8 o'clock on the evening of Monday, March 29th, with Mr. Lewis in the chair.

The Chairman: Now I think the understanding was that we go ahead and inquire into the Motion Picture Bureau.

Hon. Mr. Raney: All right.

The Chairman: Who do you call first?

Hon. Mr. Raney: I call Mr. Paton, I think.

Mr. Finlayson: Before we go into that, may I say Mr. MacNamara came to me to-night—

The Chairman: George?

Mr. Finlayson: The first witness. And he left with me his contract with Labarge and a cheque for the final payment. And also there is another item, some figures in reference to reinforcing metal for that Wellington Street. Those were the two items. And I have arranged with Mr. Raney that he is going to look over them.

The Chairman: The document in particular he was to produce was his contract with the Labarge people as I recollect.

Hon. Mr. Raney: There is something else that Mr. Fisher called for. I don't remember, but he will speak for himself.

G. E. Paton called, sworn. Examined by Hon. W. E. Raney, K.C.

Q.—Mr. Paton, you are director of the Motion Picture Bureau?
A.—Yes, sir.
Q.—How long have you occupied that position?
A.—Since June 3, I think, 1922.
Q.—Who was your predecessor?
A.—There was no director before I took on. It was really placed temporarily under a Mr. Elliott who was in charge of theatre inspection; preceding me, I think his name was Dawson.
Q.—When did Elliott leave the service?
A.—In 1923, I think sir, or 1924, I would not say.
Q.—Before the present Government came in?
A.—Afterwards.
Q—Do you know what date?

A.—I think it was about three or four months after the present Government, perhaps six months

Q.—What was his office when he went out?

A.—Director of Amusement Branches, which includes the tax—

Q.—Were you in the Department before you became director?

A.—No, sir.

Q.—You came, then, fresh?

A.—Yes, sir.

Q.—Where had you been before?

A.—Agricultural College at Guelph.

Q.—As teacher?

A.—No, sir, as student; I graduated in 1922.

Q.—So you came fresh to the service in 1922?

A.—1922.

Q.—Your staff consists I see of film editor, Mr. Black?

A.—Yes, sir.

Q.—And an accountant and superintendent of lantern slides, a field man—what do you mean by field man?

A.—Originally a field man used to go around the country putting on moving picture entertainments or rather instruction entertainments for the agricultural representatives. We have a great number of machines scattered throughout the Province.

Q.—And a couple of operators. Then you have temporary service, and temporary services, I find the name G. W. Brownridge, special representative?

MR. FINLAYSON: What page?

HON. MR. RANEY: N 12.

Q.—Where is he the representative?

A.—In New York.

Q.—For what purpose?

A.—For the purpose of distributing our films in the United States theatres.

Q.—Has he any other employment?

A.—No sir. Well, if we want to buy any films he will look out.

Q.—Is he employed by any person else besides the Province of Ontario?

A.—No, sir, just by us entirely

Q.—You took his whole time?

A.—Supposed to, sir, should do

Q.—I am told he is the employee of a theatre company?

A.—Not to my knowledge, sir. I have no knowledge.

Q.—Do you know where he puts up in New York?

A.—Yes, sir. Hotel Commodore.

Q.—That is one of the biggest hotels in New York?

A.—Yes, sir, I think it is. He has a small room on the top floor in which the charges are $4 a day which is a pretty cheap rate. It is his office too.

Q.—Well, living is fairly high nevertheless because I find his travelling expenses—does he travel?

A.—Yes, occasionally outside New York, but mostly his travelling expenses would be his living expenses there.

Q.—Besides $2,000 you pay his living expenses?

A.—Yes, sir, naturally.

Q.—I don't know whether it is naturally or not. Where does he travel to?

A.—Not very far outside New York, sir. Travelling expenses are taken to include hotel expenses—

Q.—And street car fare—

A.—And taxis. Well, he has screenings to do for his pictures. If he is screening his pictures for some man who is to buy them he has to pay the operators.

Q.—This is travelling expenses?

A.—It comes under that heading.

Q.—Not that, surely?

A.—It would come under that. Well, travelling expenses are taken to mean his incidental expenses.

Q.—Have you details of his travelling expenses?

A.—Yes, sir.

Q.—Where are they? Are they here?

A.—Yes, sir.

Q.—I see $4,126 for last year?

A.—Yes, sir.

Q.—Not for last year, for eight months, I think, yes for the year; his travelling expenses are down there, $4,126?

A.—Yes, sir.

Q.—That is about twice his salary?

A.—Yes.

Q.—Now then, you have a camera man? You have several camera men?

A.—Yes, sir.

Q.—Camera man named Graham?

A.—Yes, sir.

Q.—Where is he now?

A.—Up at Red Lake now—

Q.—Did he go up to Red Lake before this inquiry was announced?

A.—Oh yes sir, a long time before. He went up with Mr. Black.

Q.—Have you these vouchers for these travelling expenses?

A.—You will find other travelling expenses as well there, but Brownridge is included.

Q.—But these are G. E. Paton?

A.—Yes, sir, you see it is in my accountable warrant, but you will see inside if you open it, you will see they are for various members of my staff.

Q.—Tell me, what this item travelling expenses covers besides this gentleman's hotel board in New York?

A.—Well, sir, if you will just take any one. Meals, I see here, cabs and other conveyances, stamps, screenings, stenography.

Q.—We won't stop for those now?

A.—No, sir.

Q.—How long has Mr. Brownridge been with the Department?

A.—I think about—I cannot answer that accurately until I looked at the record, but he has been at least a year, more than a year.

Q.—Was it from Mr. Brownridge that the Province, the Government purchased the Trenton plant?

A.—No, sir, it was not.

Q.—Was he connected with that plant?

A.—He was at one time, but he severed his connection some time before we purchased the plant from Connelly.

Q.—What are his duties in New York?

A.—His duties are to get distribution for our pictures.

Q.—What do you mean by that?

A.—Ever since the Bureau started we have been trying to get distribution in the United States and never succeeded.

Q.—For what purpose?

A.—For the purpose of attracting tourists. They are nearly all scenic pictures. At one time we had offers from New York to put our pictures in the theatres if we paid for it, but we hardly thought that was good policy.

Q.—Have you succeeded?

A.—Yes, sir, we have.

Q.—When?

A.—They have been running since about September, I think.

Q.—Of last year?

A.—Yes.

Q.—How long has Brownridge been in New York?

A.—He has been in New York about eight, perhaps nine, about nine months, I think, the first time he went down. We had one of our scenic pictures, Ontario, six of them ran in the Detroit theatres, and they paid us $100 each for them, which is rather—

Q.—Whose idea was this radio publicity?

A.—It was Brownridge's idea, sir.

Q.—Yes, I suppose so. That is what you call it?

A.—Yes sir, at least—well, this is rather a long story. We were seeking release for our pictures. We were also at the same time trying to devise some plan of making pictures that would be acceptable to the American public, something in the pictures that would strike not the American public so much as the American theatre owner. And Brownridge sent up word to me he thought he could get Roxy and his Gang—

Q.—Roxy is the gentleman who in private life is known as Rothfeld?

A.—Rothfeld. Mr. Rothfeld isn't known in Canada, but he is the best known man in the States.

Q.—Oh we hear him sometimes on the radio?

A.—Yes. He is also the manager, he was then, of the Capitol Theatre in New York, which is the largest theatre in the States and I think in the world. So it was really through that channel we first became connected or saw the possibilities of it. We found when he first brought his scheme to me—

Q.—When Brownridge?

A.—Yes. I thought it was too good to be true. However, I made some inquiries and found it was possible, and the American Telephone Company who are beholden to Roxy for his good work on the radio even went so far as to say they would get it at cost price or a little less—

Q.—What was the plan?

A.—The plan was to have Roxy come up here and broadcast three broadcasts about Ontario, in the interval—he only broadcasts once a week—to tour the Province, and in addition to the broadcasting we had in mind getting the news in the American papers, because wherever Roxy moves—

Q.—Well, now, see, did Roxy come?

A.—Yes, sir.

Q.—And his gang?

A.—Yes, sir.

Mr. Finlayson: You asked him to explain it.

Hon. Mr. Raney: Well, I don't want extraneous matters. How many of them came?

A.—I think in all twenty-six, sir. I could refer to—

Q.—When did they come?

A.—On July 1 they arrived in Toronto.

Q.—From where?

A.—From New York. Direct from New York.

Q.—Weren't they here before that? Didn't they come down from Lake of Bays on July 1?

A.—No, sir. It was Dominion Day. I think that is July 1st. It is July 1st they came, I remember, because we didn't know what to do with them, the town was so quiet.

Q.—Were they coming up for a holiday?

A.—No, sir. We asked them to come up and we said we would give them a holiday if they would broadcast about anything—

Q.—How long did they remain?

A.—Three weeks.

Q.—Where did they stay?

A.—At the week ends they stayed at the King Edward, from which we got a special rate, and during the week they were on the trains.

Q.—Did they go to Lake of Bays?

A.—Yes.

Q.—How long were they there?

A.—They were there, I think, offhand, four days. I cannot be certain, but in that neighbourhood.

Q.—And what other town did they visit besides Toronto?

A.—They went from Toronto to Orillia, back from Orillia, they went to Peterborough and toured the Trent Canal. Then they came back and broadcasted. Then they went out again and stopped at Kingston, the Thousand Islands. Then they went up to Ottawa, from Ottawa to Algonquin Park, then to Bigwinn Inn and then back to Toronto.

Q.—Then the end of the first week finds them at Bigwin Inn?

A.—End of the first half week, they were back in Toronto to broadcast. The end of the second week they were at Bigwin Inn.

Q.—I find in the accounts an item of $921 from Bigwin Inn?

A.—Yes, sir.

Q.—How long were they there?

A.—I think about four days. I cannot remember.

Q.—What were they doing there?

A.—They were looking around the scenery and enjoying themselves for the purpose of broadcasting.

Q.—Pardon?

A.—They were taking in the scenery for the purpose of broadcasting.

Q.—Did the Treasury pay their expenses for the whole trip?

A.—Yes, sir; we could not have ever—

Q.—Did you?

A.—Yes, sir.

Q.—And the expenses of Bigwin Inn alone were $920?

A.—Yes, sir. We could not get a special rate from Bigwin Inn at all. It was the only place we could not get a special rate.

Q.—Have all the accounts from this trip come in?

A.—Yes, sir.

Q.—This is the only hotel bill. Were there other hotel bills?

A.—The King Edward bill was paid after the year closed, but it can be produced quite easily.

Q.—What did the whole trip cost?

A.—The cost of the whole was $26,000 round figures, $26,731. But round figures $26,000, of which $1,386 will be returned. It was duty paid on the equipment we brought in, but it will be returned.

MR. FINLAYSON: What amount?

A.—Twenty-six thousand one hundred and twenty-three dollars and seventy-three cents.

Q.—And what will the credit be?

A.—One thousand three hundred and fifty-eight dollars.

HON. MR. RANEY: And the greater part of these accounts did not come in at the end of the fiscal year?

A.—The majority had, but there were three that were not completed.

Q.—Because I find that in answer to a question in the House to-day the answer was, the radio part of the expenses this year, that would be this matter?

A.—Yes.

Q.—Ten thousand three hundred and eighty-two dollars. So that all the expenses of this trip, the whole of the $26,000 odd beyond the $10,283 was paid after the 31st of October?

A.—Yes, sir. In three items I think it was. It was mainly Canadian National Railways, the largest, because they did all the transportation.

Q.—Did they travel by Government car?

A.—No, sir. We had one car with a meal on it, and the other car was an ordinary Pullman.

Q.—You mean it wasn't the Government car?

A—No.

Q.—But you gave the party the facilities of two cars, you chartered two cars from the railway company?

A.—Exactly

Q.—For their use for these three weeks?

A.—Yes

Q.—Pullman car and dining car, lounge car, I suppose?

A.—Well, yes sir

Q.—Have you ever heard this party called the Heinz party?

A.—The what?

Q.—The Heinz party?

A.—No, I haven't.

Q.—Didn't you?

A.—Which party?   .

Q.—This radio party?

A.—The Heinz?

Q.—I have heard it referred to as the Heinz? .

A.—No, I haven't.

Q.—You have never heard it called that.   Did you travel with them?

A.—Yes.

Q.—-Who else besides their own crowd?

A.—We had two camera men.

Q.—Who were they?

A.—One was a camera man we got in New York; the other was our young man, J. G. Rutherford.

Q.—Where is he?

A.—Another one was a man called Williams whom we got in New York:

Q.—What is the salàry of Mr. Rutherford? How much a year do you pay him?

A.—One thousand eight hundred a year.

Q.—And I see you paid Williams, how much?

A.—It is in the account.

Q.—Who made the arrangement with Williams?

A.—Brownridge and Roxy.

Q.—And who?

A.—Rothfeld.

Q.—Why bring a man from New York?

A.—Well, sir, Mr. Rothfeld wanted something that was really good—

Q.—Oh now, you are not depreciating your own camera man?

A.—No, as a matter of fact we put on our young man and he was just as good as the other fellow.

Q.—But Brownridge got you to bring up a man from New York and I see he was paid $150 a week?

A.—Yes, sir.

Q.—That is stiff. Brownridge is a pretty high flyer, isn't he?

A.—He is a good flyer. When they made the productions in Ottawa they, I understand, pay camera men there between $150 and $200 a week. I mean the special productions.

Q.—Who do you mean by Ottawa? The Federal Government?

A.—The Commercial Company in Ottawa.

Q.—Your own man at $150 a month would have done just as well?

A.—Except that he has no publicity value.

Q.—Of course this was a publicity stunt?

A.—Yes, sir.

Q.—Did you travel all the way around?

A.—Yes, sir.

Q.—Who else of the Service?.

A.—When we went to Northern Ontario district, I don't know very well, Mr. Hele and Mr. Grant assisted me on that trip.

Q—Of what department?

A.—Secretary Hele of the Publicity Department. As a matter of fact it really should have been in his department.

Q.—What is his position in the Service?

A.—He is the general secretary, I think.

Q.—Of whom, whose general secretary?

A.—I don't know. I accepted him—I don't know that I can answer that. I don't really know.

Q.—What is the Publicity Department? I don't recognize it. What Minister is it under?

A.—Under Mr. Ferguson.

Q.—And he is of the Prime Minister's office?

A.—Yes, sir.

Q.—And Mr. Grant is also of the Prime Minister's office?

A.—Yes, sir.

Q.—And tell me who else?

A.—That was all the officials we had. Oh, my own department! I had a still man, Mr. Sparling, still pictures.

Q.—And Jones?

A.—No, sir.

Q.—So there were three of you who went with the party?

A.—Only on the Northern Ontario trip the last week

Q.—We have dealt with the first week, Orillia, Peterborough, Trent Canal, Ottawa, Algonquin Park, Bigwin Inn. That is the first week?

A.—Well, the first week and a half, because they came in the middle of the week, you see.

Q.—Yes

THE CHAIRMAN: In connection with Mr. Hele and Mr. Grant accompanying you on the last week, did the Government pay their expenses, do you know?

A.—The only expenses I know of were the expense I paid for my own office and I paid no expenses for them.

Q.—Did you pay any vouchers of any expenses for them?

A.—No, sir.

HON. MR. RANEY: Were they at Bigwin Inn?

A.—No, sir.

MR. FINLAYSON: No, they were on the last week, Northern Ontario.

HON. MR. RANEY: Oh, Northern Ontario. Well, was broadcasting done from all these places, Peterborough, Orillia?

A.—No broadcasting from Orillia; no broadcasting from Peterborough.

Q.—Where was there?

A.—The broadcasting was done every week when we came back to Toronto.

Q.—Where from?

A.—From the Parliament Buildings.

Q.—After you returned?

A.—Yes.

Q.—What did you do at Orillia?

A.—We didn't do anything. They arrived here on the morning and we shipped them straight out to Orillia because there was nothing else for them to do in Toronto. We wanted to get Roxy to mention when he talked over the radio on Sunday—

Q.—Where from?

A.—From the Parliament Buildings

Q.—They came in on Sunday?

A.—In the middle of the week, but the broadcasting was done at the end of the week.

Q.—End of the first week?

A.—End of each week.

Q.—But you went to Orillia?

A.—Yes.

Q.—What did you do?

A.—We looked around.

Q.—That was the time of the Champlain celebration?

A.—Yes.

Q.—You went to the Champlain celebration?

A.—Yes

Q.—Take it in?

A.—Yes.

Q.—What else did you do?

A.—We looked at it and came away.

Q.—Pleasant trip?

A.—It wasn't a very pleasant trip because it was a very cold day and they arrived from New York—

Q.—Well, they didn't have enough clothes. Then you went to Peterborough with these two cars?

A.—Yes.

Q.—What did you do in Peterborough?

A.—In Peterborough we were taken over by the Peterborough Chamber of Commerce—

Q.—Showed you around?

A.—Yes.

Q.—What did you do?

A.—We fished and took pictures.

Q.—What kind?

A.—Moving pictures and still pictures.

Q.—Pleasant time?

A.—Very pleasant indeed. It was very pleasant for them, not for me.

Q.—Then you took in the Trent Canal?

A.—Yes, sir.

Q.—Motor boat?

A.—No. We had Mr. Fraser's yacht, but we had a boat loaned by the Dominion Government, I think called the *Betty Butler.*

Q.—Where did you go in the *Betty Butler?*

A.—I am afraid I cannot give all the places. Mount Julien—I'm afraid I can't tell you.

Q.—This is Roxy and how many?

A.—I should say between twenty-five and thirty.

Q.—Mostly singers?

A.—All kinds, instrumentalists, vocalists—

Q.—Comedy men?

A.—Well, unless you call Gitz-Rice a comedian.

Q.—If he is a comedian. They were mostly performers, artists?

A.—They were really artists.

Q.—Surely, of course they were, high class. And what was the name of this boat?

A.—The *Betty Butler..*

Q.—How long did you stay on the Trent Canal?

A.—I think three days. I think we came back—

Q.—Well, you must have put up at some place besides Peterborough?

A.—We only touched Peterborough and went on to Mount Julien.

Q.—Summer place. How long were you there?

A.—I think it was two nights. I don't remember.

Q.—What did you do there all the time, play croquet? Fish?

A.—Fishing.

Q.—Catch any fish?

A.—Yes, we got some fish. The fish were mentioned over the radio when he talked to the American people.

Q.—How did you get to Kingston, automobile?

Q.—No, we came down to Toronto and started out from Toronto again on the Canadian National Railway.

Q.—Oh, you came back to Toronto?

A.—Yes.

Q.—And stayed at Toronto that night?

A.—Yes, sir.

Q.—King Edward?

A.—Yes.

Q.—Whole party?

A.—Yes, sir.

Q.—Then to the Thousand Islands?

A.—Yes, sir.

Q.—By boat or train?

A.—By train to Kingston, got off at Kingston and the Kingston people had two launches for us, went to the Thousand Islands and back again, got on the train again, went to Ottawa.

Q.—And you did the Thousand Islands?

A.—No, sir, we didn't have time. Just went through.

Q.—What did you do at Ottawa? Just showing the people around the country?

A.—Because if you don't show them the country—

Q.—Ottawa?

A.—Yes.

Q.—What did you do at Ottawa?

A.—We were only there in the afternoon. We went from Ottawa to Algonquin Park.

Q.—Oh yes, of course, any fishing there?

A.—Yes, good fishing.

Q.—Anything else at Algonquin Park?

A.—We broadcasted. No, we gave a concert that evening.

Q.—Your broadcasting machine wouldn't work?

A.—We had hoped by a little portable set to broadcast from places we went. We found we got into large trees and rock—

Q.—Of course it was summer time too, and that is not good broadcasting. At any rate you didn't do any broadcasting?

A.—Not to any extent.

Q.—Until you came to Toronto. Then from Ottawa to Algonquin Park. How long were you there?

A.—One day.

Q.—All drawn on these two cars?

A.—Yes, sir.

Q.—C.P.R.?

A.—C.N.R.

Q.—Then Bigwin Inn for Sunday?

A.—No, we came home for the week end.

Q.—How long at Bigwin Inn?

A.—I think four days.

Q.—No, three days. Rice, three days at $7 a day, $21; and Mr. Rothfeld, $8 a day $24; and Baruck, three days at $7, $21; and Scrlezman. Did that cover meals too?

A.—Yes, I think it does. You will find it by items.

Q.—Let me count them then. There is thirty-two. I see Brownridge was one of the party?

A.—Oh, yes, sir.

Q.—And Rutherford, your camera man?

A.—Yes, sir.

Q.—And I don't see your name here, Mr. Paton?

A.—May I—that isn't it.

Q.—Oh, I forgot. That was the whole party, was it?

A.—Yes, sir.

Q.—Somebody said there were fifty-seven. That was an exaggeration? That was the reason they called it the Heinz party?

A.—Oh.

Q.—But there weren't fifty-seven?

A.—No, sir, nothing like it. There was just the cream of this gang.

Q.—Not the creme de la creme, just the cream. Then you got back to Toronto?

A.—Yes.

Q.—And you did some broadcasting from this building?

A.—Yes, sir.

Q.—On what night?

A.—Every Sunday night.

Q.—You haven't been here one Sunday night?

A.—Yes.

Q.—After Orillia? Then where did you go next?

A.—From Bigwin?

Q.—From Toronto?

A.—We went up to Lake Timagami.

Q.—Same two cars?

A.—Yes.

Q.—And in addition Mr. Grant and Mr.—?

A.—Hele.

Q.—And straight to Timagami without stopping?

A.—Yes, sir, right straight through.

Q.—How long did you stop?

A.—Stopped there a day.

Q.—At the Inn up there?

A.—We didn't need inns because we slept on the cars. The people came back to the cars at night, and they would have their meals at an inn and I think we had our meals at Timagami Inn.

Q.—How long a time were you there?

A.—One day.

Q.—Then where?

A.—Straight up to Nipigon.

Q.—Right through to Nipigon?

A.—Yes.

Q.—Did you get any fish in Timagami?

A.—Yes, some of the party fished and others went straight to the inn.

Q.—Not so good as Nipigon?

A.—Well, Nipigon was the best fishing.

Q.—So Nipigon was the next jump?

A.—Yes.

Q.—How long at Nipigon?

A.—Remainder of the week, I think three days.

Q.—Where is the bill for Nipigon? Have you it here?

A.—No, that bill was paid after the close, but it could be procured.

Q.—Do you know how much that bill is?

A.—I think—

Q.—I would like you to bring in the rest of those bills. Perhaps you cannot get them to-night?

A.—Well, Nipigon would be included in the Canadian National bill.

Q.—Oh, yes?

A.—It would be in that bill.

Q.—Then I will get along with this?

A.—This one here.

Q.—So I see in this bill, this is the general resume of the whole business, $26,123 and all that you paid to the Canadian National Railways was $10,457; that included these two special cars and all your—

A.—Meals.

Q.—On the cars?

A.—And the Nipigon, also Algonquin Park.

Q.—I see the King Edward is here too?

A.—Yes.

Q.—You paid them $1,925?

A.—Yes, we got a special rate from them.

Q.—Well, they must have been there some time; $1,925 is quite a chunk of money?

A.—Well, we had a number of people, you see, there for three week ends and two days beginning—

Q.—Yes. Then I see G. W. Brownridge here, travelling expenses, cash disbursements, $1,231?

A.—That is for the incidental expenses on the trip.

Q.—What would they be?

A.—Baggage transportation, cash payments to where they were necessary.

Q.—Any liquid refreshments in any of these items?

A.—No, sir; certainly not.

Q.—You didn't see anything of that sort?

A.—No, I should think not, sir. It was a Government party. I had to be very careful.

MR. WIDDIFIELD: What do you mean by being careful?

A.—I said to myself beforehand I had to be jolly sure nothing like that occurred.

HON. MR. RANEY: Some statements have come to me?.

A.—Of course they have. A lot of statements came to me that were absolutely unfounded of course. I expected them. You always get stories like that.

Q.—None of these items included any liquid refreshments?

A.—No, sir.

MR. FINLAYSON: You mean liquors?

HON. MR. RANEY: Quite so.

A.—I presumed you mean alcohol.

HON. MR. RANEY: Certainly. Now this is interesting. Where did you go from Nipigon. How long were you there?

A.—Two or three days. We stayed there as long as we could. We jumped from Timagami and got there as fast as the train would take us and stayed there as long as we could just to give ourselves enough time to get back to Toronto to broadcast on Sunday night.

Q.—That was the last Sunday?

A.—Yes.

Q.—What after that? What was the next thing?

A.—We spent the day around Toronto, Christie Street, and went down to Hamilton and broadcasted there for the wounded soldiers in the hospital there at noon hour, and they have their own broadcast there, and we went through to Niagara Falls and then straight through to Detroit. I took them through Detroit because the *Detroit News*, which is one of the best papers outside New York, have a broadcasting station, told me if I took them through Detroit they would give me a broadcast and a lot of publicity, which they did.

Q.—Then from Detroit?

A.—Straight to New York.

Q.—And did you pay the expenses of the party from New York back to New York?

A.—We paid every expense incurred by the party from the time they left New York to the time they got back.

Q.—Now let me see some of these items. Toronto T.T.C. Bus Service?

A.—Yes.

Q.—Three hundred and forty-one dollars?

A.—We went from Toronto to Niagara Falls by bus because we wanted them to see the orchards, wanted to give them that idea. We also used the Toronto Transportation in moving around the city. We went from Sunnyside on it and broadcasted for the *Star* there.

MR. FINLAYSON: For the *Star*?

THE CHAIRMAN: CFCA?

A.—Yes.

HON. MR. RANEY: I see a sizeable item here. S. M. Baruch, $2,485?

A.—Yes.

Q.—Rental of transmitter?

A.—Yes, that was the portable broadcasting set.

Q.—How large a machine is it?

A.—It occupied about half a freight car. It was in one end of the freight car. It took up pretty well all that space.

Q.—What does a machine of that kind cost when new?

A.—I should think in the neighbourhood of—.

Q.—Do you know?

A.—Yes, I know fairly well, because they were inquiring about it. I should think in the neighbourhood of $20,000 to $30,000.

Q.—Did that work at all?

A.—It did, sir, but not in the north.

Q.—Where did it work?

A.—In Toronto.

Q.—Are you quite sure about that?

A.—We got replies from Rhode Island and there was also an item in the local newspapers.

Q.—You broadcasted first from the Parliament Buildings on the first Sunday?

A.—Yes, sir.

Q.—Did one of the Toronto broadcasting stations take on the broadcast for one of the nights?

A.—For two of them, sir.

Q.—Which one?

A.—On Sunday nights, the two last Sunday nights, CKCL and the CFCA on the Thursday night.

Q.—These were all the three broadcasts?

A.—Yes, sir. No. CFCA had one of their own. The *Star*. We gave them a special one of their own when they came.

Q.—CFCA broadcasted from Toronto?

A.—Yes.

Q.—That was not this transmitter?

A.—No, sir.

Q.—Was that the first broadcast?

A.—Yes.

Q.—When was the next Sunday night? From the Parliament Buildings?

A.—The first Sunday night in July.

Q.—Who broadcasted that?

A.—WEAF, the American Telephone Company.

Q.—What transmitter was used?

A.—They brought up their own.

Q.—The one I have been speaking about?

A.—No.

Q.—Not Baruch's?

A.—No. His was just a portable for short distances. WEAF transmitter.

Q.—Did you pay for that?

A.—Yes, sir.

Q.—Is that in the bill?

A.—Not in Baruch's bill.

Q.—Where is it?

A.—American Telephone Co. It is the first one there in the United States payments.

Q.—Bell Telephone Co.?

A.—They are separated in payments into Canada and the States.

Q.—Oh, yes. American Telephone, setting up broadcast equipment, three broadcasts, $2,625?

A.—Yes, sir.

Q.—That was for three broadcasts?

A.—Yes.

Q.—And included the transmitting machine for one broadcast?

A.—Yes, included every thing.

Q.—But they only actually transmitted one of the broadcasts?

A.—No, three, each Sunday night.

Q.—For the first one from Sunnyside you used CFCA?

A.—Yes, sir.

Q.—The second was from the Parliament Buildings. Who broadcasted that, CKCL?

A.—No, the American Telephone Company.

Q.—That is covered by this item, $2,625?

A.—Yes, sir.

Q.—Then the third, how was that?

A.—Same people, American Telephone Company.

Q.—And the fourth one?

A.—Yes, sir, same people. Originally their contract was to broadcast from Toronto, Roxy and his Gang for one hour for three weeks, three consecutive weeks, and link up the eight largest stations in the States.

Q.—Then where was this transmitter of Baruch's used?

A.—On the trip when we were away, when we stopped at Timagami for instance, we took it out and broadcasted and we got results.

Q.—Where?

A.—One place about twenty miles down the line and the other one farther on, the other was about three hundred, I think.

Q.—But it was not a success?

A.—No.

Q.—In fact that machine was never a success?

A.—In Toronto it was.

Q.—When did you use it in Toronto?

A.—When we came back.

Q.—I thought you had given me all the broadcasts?

A.—I said to Baruch, I don't think that thing before us is any good. He said it was. He said, I can't get out because of seepage into the trees and rocks. I said you have got to stay here and you have to show me if this broadcast will work. So we went down to Sunnyside and he set it up.

Q.—Where?

A.—Just beside where the Sunnyside pool is, there is a steel plant, I have forgotten the name, but it was near that.

Q.—What day of the week was this?

A.—I cannot recall.

Q.—This wasn't for a regular—

A.—This was for a test, because I wasn't going to pay him unless I found it would work. It was the night when the swimming pool was open at Sunnyside, because I went over and get Mr. O'Connor and Mr. Gundy and suggested coming over and speaking over the radio, because I wanted to test it. They did so.

Q.—That is Mr. John O'Connor of the Harbour Board?

A.—Yes, he and Mr. Gundy.

Q.—How far did you get afield?

A.—Well, we got, of course it was broadcasted through Toronto, but we also get a letter from Rhode Island.

Q.—Somebody picked it up?

A.—Yes. They were asked to write in and several letters were sent in.

Q.—That was only a test?

A.—A test.

Q.—Just ten or fifteen minutes?

A.—Half an hour.

Q.—What did you put on?

A.—Just Mr. Gundy and Mr. O'Connor.

Q.—Just talking?

A.—Oh, it was just a test.

Q.—To see if you could reach anywhere?

A.—Yes.

Q.—For actual broadcasting this wasn't used at all?

A.—It was used but not successfuly.

Q.—It was a dud?

A.—It was a dud. But I don't think it was entirely its fault because we tested it out and found it would.

Q.—Well, too much rock and seepage. Then, page 13, Mr. Brownridge had $1,231 for incidental expenses?

A.—Yes, sir.

Q.—Did he account for those?

A.—Yes, sir.

Q.—Where are the items of that account? The items of Brownridge's account of $1,231 for travelling expenses?

A.—I think it is included in that.

Q.—Turn me to it: I find you paid to Brownridge one thousand dollars on account of rental of transmitter. I suppose that would be to Baruch?

A.—Baruch would get that, yes.

Q.—That would not be to Baruch besides this other sum?

A.—No, sir.

Q.—Whatever was not included in some other account here was left over as a $1,231 item?

A.—Yes.

Q.—Well, this is still a little vague. For instance, re Huntsville expense, $50, what would that be for?

A.—That is just a setting forth of them. They will be underneath there. All the receipts are there. For instance, Baruch's are here.

Q.—So you paid Baruch $2,485 rental for this transmitter?

A.—Yes, the figure is correct in the account there.

Q.—And there was a radio engineer with it, I believe?

A.—He was a radio engineer.

Q.—Who?

A.—Baruch.

Q.—How much did you pay him?

A.—I don't know off hand, but I think—

Q.—He was one of the party?

A.—Yes, sir.

Q.—And I see he got $700 for his services?

A.—Yes, the arrangement with him was, we rented his transmitter and paid him so much to operate it himself and he had two journeyman boys with him.

Q.—$2,485 to him for rental of his transmitter that wouldn't work, and $700 to him as an engineer?

A.—Yes.

Q.—Then Gitz-Rice? I am told you paid him $125 for writing two stanzas of poetry?

A.—No, sir. He did write some poetry.

Q.—Wasn't that really what you paid him for?

A.—No. He is a very clever writer and when we got back to New-York the films, pictures, were in the rough, just as we took them and he titled a picture for us.

Q.—Now wasn't it really for the poetry you paid him?

A.—No, sir, no. Absolutely not.

Q.—Sure?

A.—Why these title people are paid very highly, that would represent a week's work, that title.

Q.—If that is so, it would be very cheap. Well, you paid him—if you had known what this was going to go into you wouldn't have let yourself into it?

A.—I should think I would. The manager of the Detroit *News* told me it was the best piece of publicity ever put over on the American continent, and I believe him.

Q.—Who are K. Pellicker and Caldwell?

A.—It is a firm of Pellicker and Caldwell.

Q.—Is it Kate Pellicker?

A.—I think it is, she titles a lot of these pictures.

Q.—And she was editing this?

A.—Not Roxy's. That is a series before. That is some old pictures we had here we sent down to New York.

Q.—That had nothing to do with this?

A.—No, sir.

Q.—I see you paid $1,250 and this camera man, Williams, $1,050?

A.—Yes, sir.

Q.—You all had a good time?

A.—I didn't, I was over worked.

Q.—Well, the rest of them had a good time?

A.—Yes, they did. They were supposed to.

MR. McCAUSLAND: You can have it in Ontario yet, you know.

(Cross examination by Mr. W. Finlayson, K.C.)

Q.—This publicity stunt, or publicity matter, is a peculiar field or zone?

A.—Yes, it is.

Q.—These people, Roxy and his Gang, tell me about them. It is selling a name, isn't it?

A.—Well, I think the best way I can tell you is by just showing you this picked up yesterday, the *New York Times* of March 24th, 1926. We just happened on it by chance. We see a large advertisment for arch preservers. Here it is. And underneath it says, "There is probably no more energetic or better loved man in the public eye than Rothfeld, better known to the radio fans as Roxy." Well, that is the man we got.

Q.—What is he advertising there?

A.—Somebody's shoes. That just happened to come by chance.

HON. MR. RANEY: Why did you stop at $26,000?

A.—Before they came up we estimated it would cost about $12,000 apart from the railway expenses and we were not very far short of it, really. The railway expenses come to about $11,000.

Q.—So it is just on your own, you and Brownridge?

A.—No, sir. I would not take it upon himself to recommend a thing like that unless I went into it fairly carefully. We naturally took consultation with Mr. Hele's department and his publicity work, and Colonel Price.

MR. FINLAYSON: Tell me, Roxy is one of the most prominent and best known publicity men in America?

A.—Oh yes, sir, absolutely.

Q.—Do you know what salary he commands, or anything?

A.—I don't know of his salary. I would not like to estimate it. But he certainly—I know his artists get at least $10,000 as a retainer fee. I cannot tell you.

Q.—I am told Roxy's own salary is $2,000 a week?

A.—I would think it would be quite that.

Q.—And he has a connection all over America?

A.—When he left New York station, we had a policeman there and a carpet laid down, and I think next to President Coolidge, he is probably the best known man in the States.

Q.—After the president, he—

HON. MR. RANEY: How does he compare with Babe Ruth?

A.—Well, in the summer time, Babe Ruth—

MR. FINLAYSON: Well, the Babe has failed lately. Roxy controlled the Capital Theatre?

A.—Yes, he is the outstanding man, not only in the radio world, but also in the motion picture business.

Q.—And at present he is building a new theatre in New York?

A.—Yes, he left the Capital Theatre and is building his own seven million dollar place, and a chain of theatres which he will operate himself.

Q.—This seven million dollar theatre and chain of theatres which will be operated in connection with it?

A.—Yes, sir.

Q.—What does his Gang mean?

A.—Well, he presents in the Capital Theatre—he has there a large orchestra and he scours the country, Europe, really most of his artists are European, to get those artists to come, to keep up the prestige of the Capital Theatre, New York, and on Sunday evenings it is his custom to broadcast the best of his artists, and Roxy's Gang is, of course, the outstanding radio entertainment in the world.

Q.—What connection does he have from New York when he broadcasts?

A.—Well, I think I would be safe in saying probably everybody in the States listens to him.

Q.—What chain of broadcasting stations?

A.—Well, if you will just let me refer—

THE CHAIRMAN: You can hear it announced almost every evening, but some members of the Committee may not be fans.

Q.—Well, I never heard of Roxy myself before I came here.

Q.—I'm afraid you are not a fan?

A.—No. Washington, Providence, Boston, Worcester, Detroit, Pittsburg, that is the lot I have here.

Q.—Buffalo?

A.—Buffalo is on the chain.

Q.—That is the WEAF chain?

A.—Yes, the technical name is The Web.

Q.—And WEAR, is it?

A.—Yes.

Q.—They are controlled or managed through the American Telephone?

A.—Yes.

Q.—And they are known as the WEAF connection.

A.—Yes.

Q.—When you listen in you hear WEAF and this chain?

A.—Simultaneous.

Q.—And they are sent out and are broadcasted by all these substations?

A.—Yes.

Q.—And in that way they cover America?

A.—Yes, practically speaking, they cover the whole of the States.

THE CHAIRMAN: WOC, Davenport?

A.—Yes.

MR. FINLAYSON: And his Gang consists of artists?

A.—Oh, absolutely.

Q.—Somebody has given me the figures that the salaries of his Gang were over $5,000 a week?

A.—Oh, quite easily, one that I happen to know gets $500 a week.

Q.—That is, $500 and his present—

A.—Yes.

MR. FINLAYSON: So you were getting the greatest publicity man in America?

A.—Yes.

Q.—You were getting the man and all his artists?

A.—Yes.

Q.—And the man gets $2,000 a week?

A.—I should say easily that.

Q.—And his Gang are over $5,000 a week?

A.—I should certainly say so.

Q.—And then you were getting the benefit of all his connection with his different broadcasting stations?

A.—Yes. With the added fillip that they were going to Ontario, they were in a different country.

Q.—I understand. My recollection is they announced in New York previously, they were going on this trip to Ontario?

A.—Yes. A week before, they told all about it.

Q.—The whole of the United States knew they were coming up to Ontario?

A.—Here is the clippings; it is that thick; those are the clippings from the New York papers, most of them front page, that Roxy and his Gang are going to Ontario. Practically every paper in the United States carried that news. Newspaper men will tell you, you could not have bought that space for thousands —well, they would not have sold it to you, that is all.

Q.—Before they left, a couple of weeks, it was broadcasted all over the United States that they were going to Ontario?

A.—Yes.

Q.—For the purpose of broadcasting?

A.—Yes, sir.

Q.—So that the attention of the radio America was on their trip to Ontario?

A.—Yes, sir.

Q.—And in addition to that, they had this newspaper publicity?

A.—Yes, sir.

Q.—Can you tell me the number of clippings, or anything?

A.—One, two, three, four, five, six—

Q.—Oh, add up the number of pages. What does it amount to?

HON. MR. RANEY: You were describing Canada to New York?

MR. FINLAYSON: Introducing.

HON. MR. RANEY: Jacques Cartier and Champlain.

MR. FINLAYSON: And Roxy.

WITNESS: Oh, about forty-two pages there.

Q.—About forty-two pages of clippings?

A.—Yes.

Q.—Have you any idea of the commercial value, of the advertising value of that?

A.—I could not say. Unless you get the *New York Times* and asked them how much it would cost to put a news item on the front page. You would find it would be pretty expensive.

Q.—Let us get at it this way. How many weeks did you have Mr. Roxy?

A.—Three weeks, sir.

Q.—That would be $15,000. And you had his Gang for how long?

A.—Three weeks.

Q.—That would be, three times two are six thousand—this publicity would run into $40,000 or $50,000, wouldn't it?

A.—Yes, easily. Well, a dollar and a half per line it would be, or something like that.

Q.—What would it run to? Estimate it roughly?

HON. MR. RANEY: Oh, a million dollars or so.

MR. FINLAYSON: Well, we don't exaggerate as well as you.

Q.—It would run over $25,000 easily?

A.—Oh, yes, easily.

Q.—Let us test it. What is a page of the *Saturday Evening Post* worth?

A.—It is now $7,200 one page.

Q.—One page of the *Saturday Evening Post* is $7,200 a week?

A.—Yes, sir.

HON. MR. RANEY: Is the poem here?

A.—No, sir. I will sing it for you if you like.

MR. FINLAYSON: So that, Mr. Paton, your salaries alone would be twenty odd thousand dollars?

A.—Yes, sir.

Q.—Your newspaper publicity would be at least as much?

A.—Yes.

Q.—And you were able to make an arrangement by which these people came for their expenses?

A.—Yes.

Q.—Now, do I understand there were no payments to Roxy or his Gang of any kind?

A.—No payment of any description to Roxy and his Gang, not a cent.

Q.—All you did was treat them as guests of the Province?

A.—Yes, sir.

Q.—Let us run over this itinerary. You say they were European and American?

A.—Yes, sir.

Q.—Any Canadian artists?

A.—Yes, sir.

Q.—And you were fortunate in striking the Champlain celebration in Orillia?

A.—Yes, sir.

Q.—An event of some importance?

A.—Yes, it impressed Roxy very much, because he mentioned it on his broadcast.

Q.—And I believe he mentioned he thought the Champlain monument the finest bit of sculpture work in America?

A.—Yes, sir, he said that.

MEMBER: Whose riding is that in.

Q.—Then you came back to Toronto?

A.—Yes, sir.

Q.—That was broadcast?

A.—Yes, sir.

Q.—Tell me, while I am on that—three weekly broadcasts?

A.—Yes, sir.

Q.—What were the charges made for that in the ordinary way. Suppose you went to WEAF, New York?

A.—I think it was $10,000 for a quarter of an hour.

Q.—Ten thousand for a quarter of an hour?

A.—I think so. I don't know how many stations that would include.

Q.—That would include the whole web?

A.—I don't think they sell that. I think it would just include one station.

Q.—One station would be $10,000 for a quarter of an hour?

A.—I would not like to be definite because I really don't know.

Q.—Suppose I wanted to advertise Campbell's soup, would it be possible to do it?

A.—No, you would have to get up a gang and make yourself popular and get the radio ear before they would let you.

Q.—So the Province of Ontario got at least what would run into several thousand dollars each night they broadcasted?

A.—Yes, sir.

Q.—Would it be an exaggeration to say it would at least cost $15,000 or $20,000 for the hour's broadcast?

THE CHAIRMAN: Total, one hour.

HON. MR. RANEY: I think I found that poem. Here it is.

MEMBER: Sing it.

A.—Roxy and his Gang broadcast from CHNC, Monday night; they pulled a good one in the form of a comic song entitled, "For You I'll Pine, for You I'll Ball Some (Balsam)." That wasn't a song at all; that is simply a joke.

HON. MR. RANEY: This is put here as a song?

A.—No, the song you are referring to probably is a song, "Hullo, Ontario." It is about the sportsman's paradise and catching fish and that kind of thing, which received a good welcome in New York. They got good notice for it.

MR. McCAUSLAND: There is a lot of fishing in New York.

MR. FINLAYSON: So the salaries you think amounted to $21,000 at least?

A.—Yes, sir.

Q.—And the broadcast you say would run how much an hour?

A.—I was supplied with these figures, about $30,000 an hour.

Q.—And you had it for three weeks?

A.—Yes.

Q.—That would be $90,000?

A.—Yes.

Q.—So you got $90,000 worth of publicity there?

A.—Yes.

Q.—Then after seeing Orillia, you came back and that was broadcasted?

A.—Yes.

Q.—That was the initial?

A.—The first one.

Q.—Then you took in Peterborough?

A.—Yes.

Q.—The Trent Valley Canal system?

A.—Yes.

Q.—I believe they described the route by which boats could come in, down the Georgian Bay and out to American waters again?

A.—Yes.

Q.—That was advertising a route that the Dominion Government advertise every year in New York themselves?

A.—Yes.

Q.—And the Dominion Government have a big exhibit at the motor and boat show?

A.—Yes.

Q.—And carry advertising for that in all American sport magazines?

A.—Yes.

Q.—That was in the same line?

A.—As a matter of fact at that motor show a lot of the people who came to the show mentioned that they had heard Roxy talking about the Trent-Valley Canal.

Q.—At the show?

A.—Yes, they mentioned that to the man in charge.

Q.—You were able to check up your advertising values there?

A.—Yes, sir.

Q.—You went to Mount Julien?

A.—Yes.

Q.—And went down the Trent Valley Canal system?

A.—Yes.

Q.—The next was Port Hope?

A.—We picked up Port Hope.

Q.—Went down from the Trent to Port Hope and came back by the Kingston Road?

A.—Yes.

Q.—That was the first week?

A.—Yes.

Q.—Morning and evening of the first week?

A.—Yes.

Q.—And next week you went down to Kingston?

A.—Yes.

Q.—And the Thousand Islands?

A.—Yes.

Q.—Then, I believe you went by the Rideau waters?

A.—Yes.

Q.—Get pictures of the Rideau waters?

A.—Yes.

Q.—After that you went to Ottawa?

A.—Yes.

Q.—And I believe the Ottawa people entertained you?

A.—Yes. The Ottawa Chamber of Commerce; I think the Mayor was there.

Q.—Did you find co-operation from the municipalities all over?

A.—Everybody! In fact, my chief job was to keep telling where we were, we could not go to see their town.

Hon. Mr. Raney: I'll bet you.

Mr. Finlayson: From Ottawa, you ran over on the Canada Atlantic to Algonquin Park?

A.—Yes.

Q.—And I believe, stayed at the Algonquin Inn?

A.—Yes.

Q.—And Bigwin Inn?

A.—Yes.

Q.—Huntsville after that?

A.—Yes.

Q.—And down to Toronto at the week-end?

A.—Yes.

Q.—Your second broadcast in Toronto?

A.—Yes.

Q.—While I am at that, my friend suggests one of your broadcasting apparatus was not very successful.

Hon. Mr. Raney: He said it was a dud.

A.—You said it was a dud and I agreed.

Mr. Finlayson: I understand the .broadcast from the Buildings was remarkably successful?

A.—So successful that the engineers wrote up and asked us what sort of a place we broadcasted from, because it was so well—

Hon. Mr. Raney: That is CKCL?

A.—No, that is WEAF.

Q.—That wasn't Baruch's machine?

A.—No, sir. ⸱

Mr. Finlayson: Tell me, each one of these Sunday evenings it was WEAF?

A.—Yes.

Q.—Which covers the whole North American continent?

A.—Yes, sir.

Q.—So you had on each one of these occasions when Roxy described his week's experiences, you had that whole system at your disposal?

A.—Absolutely, practically everybody in the States.

Q.—A hundred odd million?

A.—Everyone of intelligence.

Q.—All the intelligent ones, yes. And you have tested, I believe, by your reports?

A.—We had hundreds of letters come into the buildings from people all over the States. I have some of them here which I could show you.

Q.—I mean, you have correspondence by the ton?

A.—Oh, yes, tons of it.

Q.—I don't want to go into it, but it covered the whole of the North American continent?

Hon. Mr. Raney: Dispense.

Mr. Finlayson: I will dispense with the reading, but I want to have it treated seriously. Americans pay big money for it; it is a big matter. Roxy is the greatest publicity man of this kind?

A.—Yes.

Q.—What did he estimate his audience was?

A.—Well, a net estimate was five million; the gross about seven million.

Hon. Mr. Raney: I don't believe this ranks with Drury's coal scuttle as a piece of publicity. I don't believe it ranks.

Mr. Finlayson: I'm afraid that never came to New York's attention.

Q.—Then you went back up north?

A.—Yes.

Q.—Lake Timagami?

A.—Yes.

Q.—And then from there you saw Timmins and the Mines?

A.—Yes, sir. The Hollinger.

Q.—And the Hollinger people placed all their ——

A.—Everything.

Q.—Had moving pictures and everything else there?

A.—Yes, sir.

Q.—And then you went from there—you saw the Abittibi?

A.—We went over their plant.

Q.—You saw what is now the largest gold mine in the world, or one of the two?

A.—Yes.

Q.—And saw the Abitibbi Pulp & Paper Co., the largest pulp plant.

A.—Yes.

Q.—From there to Cobalt?

A.—Yes.

Q.—And saw the silver?

A.—Yes.

Q.—Nipissing, a number of the plants?

A.—Yes.

Q.—And from there to Cochrane?

A.—Kirkland Lake. Oh, no, that is—·

Q.—Then Long Lake?

A.—Yes.

Q.—And went over to Orient Bay, Nipigon?

A.—Yes.

Q.—Timagami, Timmins, the Hollinger, Iroquois Falls, the Abitibbi, Cobalt, Long Lake and Orient Bay. You gave the world Northern Ontario, didn't you?

A.—Yes.

Q.—And then you returned and I believe he gave a very rosy description of these big industries and the fishing?

A.—Yes, he worked it in very skilfully.

Q.—Mr. Raney would think he would at the price?

A.—If you are on the radio, he would say we have been in the largest mine and he would say, so and so is going to sing to you now and you ought to have seen him pulling out the fish in Algonquin Park. And it was done skilfully.

Q.—So the serious matter, the description of the industry, and so forth, was interspersed with music?

A.—Yes.

Hon. Mr. Raney: Sandwiched lunch.

Mr. Finlayson: More in the nature of supper?

A.—We had the orchestra play appropriate music and Roxy explain the different places we had been.

Q.—I suppose when you went down the Hollinger at some depth—

A.—Deep bass notes.

Q.—Now you have told us about the broadcast. Tell me what did you do when you were up there?

A.—We were very busy taking moving pictures of the Gang as they were. It is a very hard job to follow the Gang around. You have to make preparation, have to see everything is looking at its best and every man in his proper place, and see the man did not take too much footage.

Hon. Mr. Raney: You had your hands full.

Member: You didn't have any lawyers in the party?

A.—No, sir.

Q.—Did you use Roxy and his entertainers in the pictures you took?

A.—Oh the whole point was to get Roxy and his Gang linked up with the scenery.

Q.—Tell me, you took in all those places, Bigwin Inn, Algonquin Park, Timagami, when you took moving pictures, you had these well known characters?

A.—Yes, that was the idea.

Q.—Then this lettering in would describe who this celebrated character was and he would also talk on fishing or going down the Hollinger Mine, the deepest in the world?

A.—Yes.

Q.—An what quantity of films did you take?

A.—We took—they are titled and ready to go, have been for some time—about ten thousand feet, ten single reel pictures.

Q.—That was a by-product?

A.—Yes, it was a by-product.

Q.—If you had taken this alone you would have had to pay your expenses on that trip?

A.—Yes, sir.

Q.—And in addition to that you took still pictures?

A.—Yes, sir, we distributed 1,500 of those still pictures in the States already.

Q.—And those are available for Ontario Government literature?

A.—Yes, sir.

Q.—I believe a new tourist book is being embellished?

A.—Yes, sir.

Q.—Which gives the benefit of that advertising too?

A.—Yes, sir.

Q.—Pictures of the play grounds of Ontario?

A.—Yes.

Q.—Taken by the very best artists of that kind?

A.—Yes, sir.

Q.—So that, that has a considerable value, hasn't it?

A.—Yes.

Q.—Now this chap Roxy has made himself famous by his enormous fund for disabled soldiers?

A.—Well, he is always doing something. Of course he is a publicity man. He has to keep in the public eye all the time.

Q.—You think philanthropy is second to publicity?

A.—Oh, it is half and half, I guess.

Q.—And I believe he has raised money for Ontario soldiers since?

A.—$20,000.

Q.—As a result of his trip to Ontario, he has raised $20,000?

A.—For Ontario soliders.

Q.—He broadcasted the figures of Ontario's contributions to the war?

A.—Yes.

THE CHAIRMAN: He started a fund to supply radio equipment for them also, didn't he?

A.—Yes, he started a fund to give them all headpieces.

HON. MR. RANEY: I think Mr Price did that.

THE CHAIRMAN: He is Treasurer.

A.—Roxy started it and Mr. Price is appointed secretary.

Q.—Roxy started the fund, which resulted in these men collaborating with Col. Price and $20,000 has been raised for Canadian disabled soldiers?

A.—Yes, sir.

Q.—So that is considerable return from the enterprise?

A.—Yes, sir. We have also got entry for our pictures we never had before.

Q.—I was going to ask you about that. Tell me, before this was it easy to have Canadian reels distributed through American agencies?

A.—It was not, sir. We never could get it done unless we paid out money. The scheme before this that was put before me, that we were to send our negatives to New York and pay the man to print them, bear all the cost, and he would distribute them for us in the theatres if we paid him for that service.

Q.—So before, it was a matter of pay?

A.—It would have been all right if the man did that but if you paid the man to do a thing like that you have no way of checking him up.

Q.—What has been the result of this?

A.—Six of our scenic features have played in Chicago, Detroit and Boston and Philadelphia, in the Roxy theatres, but some were old, re-titled and re-hashed, and on two of them we got $100 rental for that one week, which is a considerable sum for one picture.

Q.—So you have your foot in on the American picture market?

A.—Yes, sir.

Q.—You are selling some of the results from this trip at $100 a week each?

A.—Not from this trip, but old pictures. It was through this we got the introduction.

Hon. Mr. Raney: Hadn't heard of Canada before.

A.—Some of them are very ignorant of it.

Q.—What is that chain?

A.—In September, he will open the largest theatre in the world in the Capital and he will have a chain in connection with it and when he does that our pictures will naturally have entry there and we shall have a revenue from it. I don't mean of Roxy's trip but our pictures of scenery we make from time to time. In other words it has directed attention to our scenic beauties and our pictures are in demand which they never were before.

Q.—So is there a prospect of it being a financial as well as an advertisement and publicity matter?

A.—Well, our man in New York tells me he expected to get $40,000 back for the sale of those ten pictures.

Hon. Mr. Raney: Is this Brownridge?

A.—Yes, sir. I take no responsibility for that. I mean, I will wait until I see the money.

Mr. Finlayson: You are from Missouri.

A.—I think there should be a fair return. If it is not as much as $40,000 it will be getting on that way.

Q.—Do I put it fairly in saying that Brownridge estimates that the pictures taken on this trip will return $40,000 to the Province. You say you don't know whether that is over-enthusiastic, but there is going to be a large return?

A.—Very large return.

Q.—You already have some?

A.—Yes.

Q.—And you hope the trip will be repaid in that way?

A.—Yes.

Q.—So there will be no actual cash outlay if that works out?

A.—Yes.

Q.—This broadcast. We know of WEAF, what other broadcast did you have?

A.—What other?

Q.—From the Prince George what did you do?

A.—Oh, yes, we had CKCL, who very kindly offered us their services and we gladly took them and they broadcasted, and they are a powerful station. They do reach the States.

Q.—Is that free?

A.—Free? I should think it was. ·

Q.—You didn't pay anything?

A.—No, sir.

Q.—Then what else?

A.—We had three radio stations besieging us to do it.

Q.—Sunnyside?

A.—Yes.

Q.—CFCA?

A.—CFCA.

Q.—CKCL?

A.—Yes; sir.

Q.—What is that?

A.—That is Reliable Batteries.

Q.—That is a Canadian Station?

A.—Yes, sir.

Q.—Who is that from?

A.—I should think Ottawa.

Q.—I mean the Province does not pay anything?

A.—No. We had the. three radio stations beseeching us to do it.

Q.—CFCA?

A.—Yes.

Q.—CKCL?

A.—Yes.

Q.—What is that?

A.—Reliable Batteries.

Q.—That is a Canadian?

A.—Yes.

Q.—What is CKNC?

A.—The Canadian National Carbons.

Q.—You had that, too?

A.—Yes, sir.

Q.—What about CKCL?

A.—We had that twice.

Q.—And then until last night, I believe you had CKNC?

A.—That is Canadian National Carbons.

Q.—You wound up with Detroit?

A.—Yes, sir.

Q.—That was on invitation of the *Detroit News?*

A.—Yes.

Q.—That is the great publicity organ of the Central States?

A.—I think it is regarded as one of the soundest newspapers outside New York.

Q.—And in broadcasting they were the pioneers among newspapers?

A.—Yes, they are a very fine organization, most of them Canadians as a matter of fact.

Q.—I believe they have a very powerful station?

A.—One of the most powerful in the United States.

Q.—What did you do with them?

A.—We arrived in Detroit as per invitation and were met by two bands. I think we had between twelve and twenty mounted police to escort us through the streets.

Q.—Necessary?

A.—I think just to make a bigger splash. We got to a club and were given a dinner there and broadcasted from *Detroit News* station. We got three whole columns on the front page of *Detroit News* that day. We got two half columns; we got a couple of columns on page 7 and another on page 11 of the *Detroit News* that day.

Q.—So do you mean to tell me you had six or seven columns in the *Detroit News*?

A.—Yes.

Q.—Several columns on the front page?

A.—Three and a half.

Q.—Give me an idea of what the value of that would be alone?

A.—A newspaper man would tell you that.

THE CHAIRMAN: You cannot buy that sort of space for advertising.

WITNESS: There were interviews with Roxy, what he thought of Ontario and how he enjoyed himself.

Q.—Did he describe his trip?

A.—Yes, sir; and also in the rotogravure section on the following Sunday, that was the display we had on the front page. They would not sell you that.

MR. FINLAYSON: Are these all the artists? Let us admire them.

MR. RANEY: How many millions is that worth? We will pay our national debt before we get through.

MR. FINLAYSON: Is this Mr. Roxy here? You tell me this is a front page of the *Detroit News*, the photo section?

A.—That is in addition to what we got in the daily paper.

Q.—In addition to what you got in the regular issue—all these beautiful young ladies and instruments.

MR. RANEY: Did your wife let you go alone with this crowd?

A.—Yes, sir.

MR. FINLAYSON: That of course could not be obtained in any monetary way, could it?

A.—No, sir, it could not.

MR. RANEY: It is beyond price—beyond rubies.

MR. FINLAYSON: What is the circulation of that paper? Mr. Raney's organ says it is 250,000?

MR. RANEY: We have paid our national debt now and should pay the national debt of the United States.

MR. FINLAYSON: We should be neighbourly. So that you had not only the broadcasting publicity, but the newspaper publicity you have given us in these articles all over and this particular publicity in the *Detroit News*?

A.—Yes.

Q.—Can you tell me anything of the value of the pictures you took on that trip? Here is a test: Before this was started the Ontario Government, under the Drury administration, purchased their own pictures?

A.—Yes, sir.

Q.—What did they pay for them?

A.—They paid various prices, on an average between seventy-five cents as the lowest and I think about $1 a foot for negative and ten cents the lowest we paid for positive.

Q.—Then putting it on the basis the Drury Government paid for pictures, what would the value of the pictures you took on that trip be?

A.—Ten thousand feet at $1; $10,000 for the negative alone.

Q.—And what for positive?

MR. RANEY: This is small change.

MR. FINLAYSON: We are completing our test.

WITNESS: The prints would run between $80 and $100. You order as many prints as you required. .

Q.—Roughly, what would the positive part be?

A.—About ten cents a foot.

Q.—What would that run into? What you took that trip?

A.—One thousand dollars, just for one print only.

Q.—Do I understand you then, that placing the price fixed by Mr. Raney and Mr. Drury on pictures taken in their regime, the pictures taken on this trip would have a value to the Province of $11,000?

A.—Yes, sir.

Q.—And did the Raney-Drury Government ever take pictures of the value of these?

A.—Oh, no, sir.

MR. RANEY: I thought you were appointed by the Drury Government?

A.—I am going to be fair sir, I can't tell a Conservative from a Liberal; my business is making pictures. They never did a publicity campaign, of course, of this kind.

MR. FINLAYSON: Did they ever take pictures of this class for publicity purposes?

A.—No, sir.

Q.—Well, then, the pictures they did take—cheaper pictures you say, if these had been paid for at the Drury regular rates you say they would have cost $11,000?

A.—Yes, sir.

Q.—And they are a permanent asset to the Province?

A.—Yes, sir.

Q.—So that we have covered that ground. Now one or two other things arising out of what my friend asked you. Brownridge does not maintain an office in New York?

A.—No, sir.

Q.—He has a room and runs his work from that?

A.—Yes, sir.

Q.—And you pay his fixed salary and audit his expense?

A.—Yes.

Q.—So that there is no office expense of any kind?

A.—None at all, sir.

Q.—Have you made any estimate of what an office would cost if he had one and ran the business from there?

A.—No experience of offices in New York, sir, and I don't know.

Q.—But this must be infinitely cheaper?

A.—Oh, yes, sir.

Q.—Before 1924 the pictures were purchased?

A.—Yes.

Q.—I see from Government returns that in 1920 the late Government paid— can you tell me how much the late Government paid in 1920 for pictures?

26 J.

A.—One hundred and twenty-one thousand dollars for film alone, and speaking from memory, sir.

Q.—I have it here $127,821.

MR. RANEY: Under your administration?

A.—No, sir; I came on in 1922. They spent $90,000 in 1922.

MR. FINLAYSON: In 1921 what did they pay for pictures?

A.—For film alone, not counting incidental expenses, but pure purchase, $127,821.85.

Q.—That was for films alone, without expenses of the Bureau?

A.—No, just pure films, expenses of the Bureau to be added.

Q.—In 1921 what did they pay for purchase of pictures?

A.—Seventy-two thousand nine hundred and twenty-two dollars.

Q.—And in 1922?

A.—Ninety-eight thousand seven hundred and thirty-four dollars.

Q.—So that in 1920-21-22 we would have $333,649?

A.—No, sir, that includes 1919 and 1918.

Q.—But for these three years $293,000, practically $300,000; nearly $300,000 paid by the late Government for purchasing pictures in three years, or approximately $100,000 a year?

A.—Yes.

Q.—What is the present arrangement?

A.—We make our own pictures.

Q.—What do they cost?

A.—Last year, the first year we had our studio in full operation, and including all costs of operation, the studio cost $68,301.27.

Q.—So do I understand that that includes salaries?

A.—Everything, sir; salaries, maintenance and everything else.

Q.—What were salaries and maintenance before?

A.—We had none, because we bought the films outright.

Q.—You had to have some operating expenses?

A.—Yes, sir, but that comes out of a contingency fund which has no connection with the fund used to purchase film.

Q.—Is this a fair comparison: In three years, 1920-22, the average was slightly less than $100,000 for purchase of films? And since then, by the new method it has been cut down to $68,000 for the total expense of the Bureau?

A.—Total expense of making motion pictures.

Q.—So it is a fair comparison, $100,000 a year under Drury-Raney Government down to $68,000 by the present Government?

A.—Yes, sir.

Q.—How do they compare in volume?

A.—That is difficult to say, because it is difficult to get the records per year, but we have worked it out this way: Last year we produced 112,647 feet of negative, 390,370 feet of positive. Now charging that up at sixty cents a foot for negative, which is less than we ever paid before except during last year, and charging at six cents a foot for positive, which are the current rates I could get now, because things have cheapened in the industry—I could get a contract at these rates—taking these figures that would cost us to purchase the same amount of negative and positive, $91,010.40.

MR. RANEY: You see, Mr. Finlayson, nobody would remember these figures. Why not concede there are improved conditions in the Motion Picture Bureau?

Mr. Finlayson: If you will concede conditions are different from the late regime.

Witness: We saved by making our own pictures this year, $22,000.

Mr. Raney: All right.

Mr. Finlayson: So that on the year you have a reduction of $22,000 under Col Price's administration as against the old?

A.—Yes.

Q.—And in addition to that you have had all this publicity?

A.—That is, of course, on separate charge.

Q.—But you have got the benefit of all this—

A.—Oh, yes, sir.

Q.—So that cutting down the price from $100,000 to some $60,000 odd has not only cut the price down but you say the product is away ahead of what it was before?

A.—Yes, because before we used to pay by the foot, which meant that the urge on the part of the man taking the picture was to turn the crank as long as he could. When making our own picture we can afford to spend a long time on a picture that requires it, because we are not out to get our money back that month for operating expense and can afford to make better pictures for that reason.

Q.—And what was the purchase of the plant down there?

A.—Thirty thousand dollars.

Q.—Total cost?

A.—Yes.

Q.—That is capital?

A.—Yes, sir.

Q.—So that for investment of $30,000 you have reduced the picture production from $160,000 to $60,000 odd and you say that you have control over what you want?

A.—Exactly.

Q.—And in addition you have these wonderful pictures taken last summer all through the north country?

A.—Yes, sir.

Q.—Now what about this tourist trade? Was this directed at the tourist trade?

A.—Yes, it was, sir.

Q.—What does it amount to?

A.—The tourist trade in the Province is estimated by various authorities— of course nobody knows what it is, but *The Globe* says we should spend a million dollars every year advertising for tourists. "Ontario should invest $1,000,000 a year to attract tourists." Article in *The Globe* of May 20.

Q.—What does the Tourist Association say about it?

A.—They see opportunities afforded holiday-seekers not only for enjoyment but investment and settlement, and say a comprehensive advertising campaign would bring lucrative returns. Influx of motorists attaining new records, and estimated 800,000 American cars crossed at Niagara in three months.

Q.—What authority for that?

A.—*Daily Star*, August 26.

The Chairman: I think that is given on the authority of actual figures. Have you read the article?

Witness: That is estimated at Niagara Falls officially.

MR. FINLAYSON: What is the estimate of the amount of money spent by American tourists in Ontario?

A.—"More than $136,000,000 from U.S. in year, says C. W. Stokes, of the C.P.R."

MR. RANEY: We have surely all read about this in the newspapers.

MR. FINLAYSON: We want to get more of it, and justify our—

THE CHAIRMAN: As I recall it, that was a speech by Stokes at a meeting of those interested in the tourist traffic, at some convention.

WITNESS: Canadian Advertisers' convention.

MR. FINLAYSON: This money was all spent on necessary expenses?

A.—Yes, sir; absolutely.

Q.—You were head of the Bureau?

A.—Yes.

Q.—And given an accountable warrant?

A.—Yes, sir.

Q.—Which means you were entrusted with a certain amount of money of the Province for which you were personally responsible?

A.—Yes, sir.

Q.—And you have accounted for it?

A.—Yes, sir.

Q.—To the satisfaction of whom?

A.—The usual channels, the Deputy Minister and Audit Office.

Q.—I see through this memoranda from the Auditor asking for information, and replies to that?

A.—Yes, sir.

Q.—So that the Provincial Auditor was satisfied with the use of this money?

A.—Otherwise it would not be passed.

Q.—And it was passed?

A.—Yes, sir.

Q.—There were some accounts stopped because you wanted to have reductions made?

A.—Some came in that I thought were excessive, and we finally cut down the bill.

Q.—Did you carefully scrutinize and take care of all the accounts?

A.—Yes, I did, sir.

Q.—And are you able to tell the Committee no moneys were improperly expended?

A.—Absolutely, sir.

Q.—And I understand you to assure Mr. Raney no moneys were used for intoxicating liquors?

A.—Yes, sir.

Q.—And that nothing of that kind occurred?

A.—Yes, sir.

Q.—You had particular instructions about that, had you not?

A.—Yes, I had, sir.

Q.—And watched that part of it carefully?

A.—Yes, sir.

Q.—I understand these were high-class artists?

A.—Yes.

Q.—And so it was necessary as guests of the Province to give them proper accommodation?

A.—Yes, sir; we told them we could not give them the accommodation they were used to, but would do the best we could.

Q.—And you got special rates everywhere except Bigwin Inn?

MR. RANEY: No competition there.

WITNESS: They were very full, and very independent anyway.

MR. FINLAYSON: A hotel of their own class, and nothing like it; and that included Huntsville Band and all sorts of things. Are you able to assure the Committee, or are you not—if not, tell us so—that the whole expedition was conducted properly and as an expedition when distinguished artists are the guests of the Province should be?

A.—Yes; I am certain they were extremely easy people to handle. They were, of course, artists and temperamental, and I, of course, thought it was going to be a little difficult, but they were very decent, and if things were a little difficult, and if they had to get off the train and baggage not transported, or if they had to sing that night, they were very agreeable and behaved in a way that made it a pleasure to handle them.

Q.—And there were no incidents in connection with the trip the Province would have reason to be ashamed of?

A.—No, sir; not at all.

MR. RANEY: Now to get our feet down again to solid earth, Mr. Paton, I suppose most of these little paragraphs from the *Radio Digest*, 25th August, present the situation: "Fishing and wilds give Roxy rest—Toronto; Roxy and his Gang, Capital Theatre, New York, idols of many millions of listeners in the eastern half of the country, are just finishing an extended vacation in Ontario, where they travelled about in a private car, visiting the scenes of interest and sampling the fishing and other good things for which Ontario is famous." This is a fair summary of the case, isn't it?

A.—Yes, it is, sir.

MR. FINLAYSON: Everybody's happy now.

MR. RANEY: Now, Mr. Paton has told us such an illuminating tale I am not going to bother anybody else about the story. If you can stop Mr. Brownridge, stop him and save a few dollars.

WITNESS: I telephoned him and he was just on the eve of sending these pictures to-morrow and coming on Wednesday.

MR. RANEY: You stop him and tell him I don't want him.

WITNESS: Thanks very much; it is very good of you.

THE CHAIRMAN: Are you ready to take Mr. Birmingham?

MR. FINLAYSON: I have no instructions.

MR. RANEY: You can take cross-examination later, if you like.

MR. FINLAYSON: It is such a big subject, and my friend is such an expert. There is just one thing I would like on the record in the other matter. I understand Mr. Hall and Mr. Grant paid all their own expenses?

A.—I did not pay any for them.

THE CHAIRMAN: As a matter of fact they did pay their own expenses. They went on their vacation.

THE CHAIRMAN: Mr. Birmingham has asked if there is any objection to having the secretary along with him?

MR. RANEY: Certainly not; it will help the information.

Arthur Birmingham sworn.   Mr. Raney examining.

Q.—What is your business?

A.—General manager of the Ontario Government Dispensaries.

Q.—How long have you occupied that position?

A.—November 1, 1920; prior to that I was secretary-treasurer, from 28th of May, 1919, to 31st October, 1920.

Q.—Your position from 28th of May, 1919, until 31st October?

A.—Secretary-treasurer of dispensaries. I might say for seven months after I was general manager Mr. W. B. Cleland was still there as supervisor, and I think could be considered over me during that period, until Mr. Flavelle retired as chairman.

Q.—You have the distinction of being the only Government department that does not feature itself in the Public Accounts. The only item I find in the Accounts for last year (page 14) covering liquor dispensaries is this: an item of revenue, Dispensaries, $900,000?

A.—Yes, sir; that is the sum of money I handed in from month to month, I think.

Q.—Do you know on what principle your department is exempt from this document—the Public Accounts?

A.—I don't know, sir. I know when you were there, the same as Mr. Nickle, I sent to the Board of License Commissioners a report like this, giving our financial statement every month, giving our profit, operating expenses, salaries, etc.

Q.—That was all there was to it?

A.—Yes, but we are audited by Clarkson and Dilworth.

Q.—I don't want to disclaim any responsibility there may be attaching to myself, but apparently from the beginning, for some reason, this Department of the Government has been exempt from the Public Accounts?

A.—I don't know; I reported to the Board. That is all I know.

MR. FINLAYSON: Isn't it published in the Board's report?

A.—Yes.

MR. RANEY: Certain information is published, but not the same kind of information you would get in Public Accounts. For instance, no salaries, no details.

MR. FINLAYSON: They are audited by Clarkson, like the Hydro.

MR. RANEY: When were the dispensaries opened?

A.—Twenty-seventh or 28th of May, 1919; I am not quite sure.

Q.—That was under Hearst Government?

A.—Yes.

Q.—And the first part year ended with October?

A.—Well, we ended on the 31st day of December.

Q.—That is right; you had a different year?

A.—And then we changed, I think in 1922; we had a ten-month year.

Q.—I remember that. Who was your predecessor?

A.—W. B. Cleland.

Q.—And he was director from the beginning?

A.—He was general manager until the last day of October, 1920.

Q.—And had been from the beginning?

A.—Yes, and he became supervisor for ten months.

Q.—Salary $10,000?

A.—Yes, and reduced to $3,000 when he became supervisor.

Q.—What salary did you start at?

A.—Three thousand six hundred dollars.

Q.—As secretary-treasurer?

A.—Yes.

Q.—And what salary did you start out at as director?

A.—Four thousand six hundred dollars, and now $5,500.

Q.—One increase?

A.—Yes, I think under your regime I got an increase—$200 I think—I don't know the year, and then I got an increase of $500, and then $200 this year.

Q.—So that it is now $5,500?

A.—Yes, sir. I might say before Mr. Cleland was there we had another position, director; that office was abolished when I came in, a $3,000 position.

Q.—You say Mr. Cleland got $10,000?

A.—Yes, sir.

Q.—That was from the beginning. I remember. Yes. You have, I notice, three major departments apparently here in Toronto, the chief censor's department and central office and central warehouse?

A.—Yes, sir; well, the head office and censor's department are really one. The censor's department, over all doctors and dentists, is comprised of a number of girls and three men.

Q.—Have you your report with you?

A.—I placed my report for 1925 in the hands of the Board some time ago, with Clarkson & Dilworth's statement.

Mr. FINLAYSON: What are these three departments?

Mr. RANEY: Censor's department, central office department and central warehouse?

WITNESS: You can say the central department and censor's department are one.

Q.—Who is chief censor?

A.—A. W. Donaldson.

Q.—Salary?

A.—Three thousand dollars a year. He got that when Mr. Flavelle was there and no increase since.

Q.—Who is head of the central warehouse?

A.—George Snyder.

Q.—What is his salary?

A.—Three thousand dollars a year; he got that before I became general manager, the last day. Neither have been increased since I became general manager.

Mr. FINLAYSON: And do liquor department profits carry these?

A.—Oh, yes, our wages are paid twice a month and we write our own cheques.

Mr. RANEY: Have you a copy of your statement for 1925?

A.—I have one of Clarkson, Gordon & Dilworth.

Mr. FINLAYSON: Should we go into that? It is not the Public Accounts we are examining.

Mr. RANEY: What possible objection could there be?

Mr. FINLAYSON: It is not public yet. Mr. Birmingham, is there any objection to its being used?

A.—We are satisfied to have it used. You gentlemen are members. Mr. Hales said give the facts, and I called up Mr. Dingman and said the report was not in, and he said to give the facts. I have one copy and gave the other four to the Board, and presume they went to the Government.

Mr. RANEY: I don't suppose there can be any possible objection to it. It ought to be in Public Accounts. I am not blaming you, Mr. Birmingham, but there is no reason that I know of why this should not be treated like any other department of government and these figures put in Public Accounts.

THE CHAIRMAN: It would probably be only fair to get the sanction of the Board under which Mr. Birmingham works.

MR. RANEY: They cannot possibly have any objection.

MR. FINLAYSON: It is very simple to say that, but we are taking what comes from the particular department. If the Committee want to go into it I do not want to be technical, but I think we ought to get that from his chief. When an officer reports to his chief, a report that has not been sent out by his chief, for some reason Mr. Hales' report is not out yet—I don't know why; it is not Mr. Birmingham's fault, because his material was furnished in January—I don't know what we want to do with it.

MR. RANEY: I don't want to strain anybody's responsibility, and I will go on with the examination, and perhaps to-morrow Mr. Birmingham will let me see the report when he gets consent, and if I want him back I can have him back.

THE CHAIRMAN: I think, perhaps, that would be best.

MR. FINLAYSON: Who is the central manager?

A.—That is myself.

MR. RANEY: I see the general salaries are $10,550?

A.—I only got $5,300 last year. They may have put two inspectors in and taken them out this year. I rather think that would be my own salary, Mr. Geachy's and the two inspectors.

Q.—I see an item, 1924, $13,655 for insurance, I suppose premiums?

A.—Yes, sir.

Q.—Through what agency do you place your insurance?

A.—Well, sir, we placed them through about thirty in Toronto alone. I try to keep this thing divided up. I could not name them, but when I discussed this matter with Mr. Flavelle in the beginning, he said, "Divide it as well as you can" and I have followed that. I think in Fort William I got it with over eight. It is practically on that basis all through—and that would only be $54,000 divided among eight men. We try to keep it divided, and there is no advantage in it for anybody. Our rate is very low. I don't know that I would care to give it so low.

Q.—Well, liquids don't burn readily?

A.—No, and by moving into that building we saved between $7,000 and $8,000 in insurance.

Q.—Yes, it is a good building.

MR. FINLAYSON: What is the total premium?

Thirteen thousand eight hundred and sixty-five dollars and fourteen cents in 1924. That is over the entire dispensaries.

Q.—And what is the amount of the policy?

MR. RANEY: That covers all the dispensaries, I suppose?

A.—The insurance report evidently was not published in 1924. The Board have it, but for some reason it was left out, but they have it in their report from Clarkson, Gordon & Dilworth.

MR. RANEY: How many dispensaries are there?

A.—Eight.

Q.—Two in Toronto. Who is the head of the other one in Toronto?

A.—I am general manager. A. K. Coulthart is manager of No. 1 on Simcoe Street, which is just the same to us as Hamilton. They have a little warehouse of their own and a store.

Q.—What is his salary?

A.—Two thousand eight hundred and fifty dollars.

Q.—Are all the managers of liquor dispensaries on the same footing as to salary?

A.—No, sir; originally all were, I think, $3,000. They are not so great now. For instance Mr. Coulthart has, I think, 39 per cent. of our business and yet does not get as much as some of the older managers; $3,000, London; $2,500 at Dundas Street; $2,500 at Hamilton.

Q.—Do you try to get your ratio with the salaries in this building?

A.—Well, Dr. McCutcheon has been consulted in connection with all our increases and has been down to see me on different occasions. I send my recommendations to the Board, and they, I presume, to the Minister.

Q.—Do you not think your Department ought to be in the Public Accounts?

Q.—I would not like to answer that question. I presume Mr. Hales would be the gentleman to answer that.

Q.—Or the Attorney-General, probably.

MR. FINLAYSON: A matter of policy.

MR. RANEY: Did you have any connection with the 1923 election?

A.—No, sir; when I left politics I left them for good.

Q.—Or 1919?

A.—No.

Q.—But you were before?

A.—I was chief organizer of the Conservative Party from 1913 until the day I came into the place.

Q.—That was in May, 1919?

A.—Yes. Previous to that I was chief organizer in the City of Toronto.

Q.—Since then you have had no connection?

A.—No, sir.

Q.—Now if you let me see your own report and the auditors' report?

A.—Delighted, if I get permission.

Q.—If you let me see these to-morrow that may be all I will require of you to-morrow.

A.—Ten o'clock?

Q.—Don't come here unless I telephone for you.

MR. FINLAYSON: See Mr. Hales and get the permission in the meantime, and he may expedite it by handing the report to you.

MR. RANEY: What I want is the auditors' report and your own.

Julian Harcourt Ferguson sworn. Mr. Raney examining.

Q.—Mr. Ferguson; you are a member of the firm Burns & Ferguson, insurance brokers?

A.—Yes.

Q.—Here in Toronto?

A.—Yes.

Q.—And you have some connection with the Department here, haven't you?

A.—We did some insurance work for them; that is the only connection we have with the Department here. There is no insurance department here that I know of.

Q.—Well the insurance for the Province is in the Department, I suppose, of the Minister of Public Works?

A.—Portions of it are and portions not.

Q.—And you have had some employment with that department?

A.—Not exactly employment. We tendered for certain Government work and received it and our commission for doing that. Whether you consider that employment or not I don't know.

Q.—What was it you tendered for?

A.—Various types of insurance.

Q.—Have you your tender?

A.—We have our letters and correspondence. To make a long story short, during the U.F.O. Government, as a manager of a company, I was induced to act on behalf of the Armour, Bell, Boswell & Cronyn Company, and they informed me they insured certain commodities such as buildings, automobiles, etc. I came to Mr. Biggs and tendered verbally and in writing, and he said he would let us know. That was the first intimation I had the Government placed any insurance. This firm informed me they were insuring automobiles and asked a quotation. I did so verbally, in front of Mr. Biggs, and he informed us he would let us know in a week or so. The next I heard was from Mr. Edgar Watson, a member of Parliament, who walked into my office and informed me he had the placing of insurance of Government automobiles. I checked up the numbers I had from Armour, Bell, Boswell & Cronyn and found they were the same cars. I thought if it was that way I would not give the same quotation, but make more money, so I gave a higher quotation to Mr. Watson than I had quoted Mr. Biggs, because there was not, apparently, any need for as low a quotation as I had quoted previously for Mr. Bell—the Armour, Bell, Boswell & Cronyn people.

Q.—Can you say what it was?

A.—No, but I do know that it was a joke to me to think that Mr. Watson got this insurance on a higher quotation.

Q.—I should think so, too.

MR. FINLAYSON: That was Rev. Mr. Watson?

A.—From Fenelon Falls.

MR. RANEY: Did he profess to act as agent?

A.—He received a commission and had a license, which I told him would be necessary

Q.—What did you pay him?

A.—The usual commission, Mr. Raney, that he was entitled to at that time. The premium was around $3,000 and he possibly received 15 per cent. commission on that.

Q.—And that was on government automobiles, you say?

A.—Yes.

Q.—What year?

A.—About 1922.

Q.—I suppose you knew that that transaction would probably disqualify him, didn't you?

A.—No, I didn't know it; I was just thinking of getting business for my company.

Q.—That is all you were concerned about?

A.—Yes, he had a license, and I had no alternative.

Q.—Were you acquainted with the law governing membership in the House?

A.—At that time, no.

MR. FINLAYSON: You say he took out a license in order to get this particular insurance?

A.—I informed him he would have to have a license.

MR. GRAVES: He is not an insurance man?

WITNESS: He said he could write insurance in his spare time. Well, we are always looking for agents, and they can bring business into our office if they are legitimate, licensed agents.

MR. RANEY: He may have been licensed, but that would not justify him.

A.—As far as I understand it, a man does not get a license just for one transaction.

THE CHAIRMAN: At that t'me the new regulations covering the issue of licenses had not come in.

MR. FINLAYSON You told him he would have to take out a license, and he did that to qualify for this job?

A.—Jack Ramsden got the balance. I quoted for the entire fleet, and it was split in two. Mr. Ramsden got some and Watson the balance.

Q.—Fifty-fifty?

A.—I would not say exactly. That is how I knew the Government got insurance. I afterward left the managerial job of the Royal Indemnity and I informed Burns & Webster, insurance brokers, at their request.

MR. RANEY: Who is the clerk in the Department of the Minister of Public Works who looks after fire insurances?

A.—No clerk that I know.

Q.—Somebody in charge of placing this insurance?

A.—We always got our business through Mr. Henry.

Q.—Direct?

A.—No, but we were informed by various people in the Department. Mr. Squire would tell us, for instance, our proposition had been accepted.

Q.—You are carrying some insurances for the Province now?

A.—Yes, the largest portion of the insurance placed by the Province, as far as I can find out.

Q.—What is the largest amount?

A.—I can give you some idea. Through our office, under our managership, as suggested by Mr. Henry and Mr. Squire, there is $3,488,000 placed on these three buildings—the main Parliament Buildings.

Q.—What do you mean by three main buildings? The annex? What we call the main building? The old building consists of two buildings really, a fireproof and non-fireproof building, the fireproof being the west side and non-fireproof the east?

A.—This new section back here is one building, because cut off to a certain extent, making three separate buildings and three separate rates.

Q.—You have the fireproof building at the west end and the non-fireproof building at the east end, and new building at the north, and the insurance is $3,488,000?

A.—Yes. After I became an insurance broker and joined this firm I still knew this automobile fleet existed. We are brokers and buy where we can buy the cheapest, and at the same time select compan'es that can pay a loss if sustained.

Q.—Tariff and non-tariff?

A.—Mutual and reciprocal; we deal all over the world. We tried several companies, and I knew they were being written by Ramsden and Watson, so with that advantage I asked a certain company for a quotation, and at the expiry date I was a competitor, and competed for these cars, and my quotation was lower—I knew it was lower—and we received the business on the automobiles. Our claims were settled fairly promptly; we were complimented upon them, and I made some enquiries and knew there was some fire insurance in these buildings. I asked them how it was written and have studied the business fairly well.

MR. RANEY: This is going to be a long story. I don't care how you came by the business.

SOME MEMBERS: Some of the rest of us would like to know.

WITNESS: I will show you where they threw money away, and that is very interesting these days. I discussed it with our engineers and took it up with several eminent insurance men of Toronto, and found we could place $1,400,000 more insurance on here, with a much better wording, and cut the rates down. We went to the Fire Underwriters and pointed out facts and figures; and $1,000,000 before we took it over was costing the Government about $7,350 a year. They are now receiving about $1,200,000 for $5,000, and saving $2,000 per annum.

MR. RANEY: The present insurance on these buildings is $3,488,000?
A.—Yes.

Q.—Out of a total insurance carried by the Province of how much?
A.—I don't know. I have never had permission to go through the various departments.

Q.—And you say that until recently the amount carried was much less?
A.—No, I don't say much less. Some thousands. But in order to get the raise I pointed out to Mr. Henry the value of these buildings and expert engineers' advice as to how long they would stand in case of fire. Mr. Henry, I think, took it up with members in the House, and they decided they should carry more than they were carrying, because it was pointed out by us as experts in this business the possibility of a big loss, especially on the main building. We have copies of these reports here. And they decided to carry that amount of insurance, and in doing so they received $1,000,000 for approximately $5,000, instead of paying for one million over $7,000.

Q.—How much of it is placed through your agency?
A.—The whole of it, with this exception: we distribute that to a large number of insurance agents and brokers throughout the entire Province from the commission.

MR. GRAVES: You mean you put that through other insurance agents outside Toronto?
A.—Yes, pretty well all over the Province.

MR. RANEY: How much of it do you distribute?
A.—I submitted a list of names to Mr. Henry and Mr. Squire who I knew were in the insurance business and who had not done anything in the proposition. We did spend some time on the proposition, and Mr. Squire and Mr. Henry pointed—

Q.—Tell me now how much insurance you placed with various other agencies of this $4,388,000?
A.—Approximately 150 agents. For instance, Wood & Kirkpatrick, Toronto; Smith, Mackenzie, Lyon & Harvey, Mewburn and—

Q.—How much of the $3,488,000 have you placed out with other agencies?
MR. HILLMER: How much do you carry directly of this?
A.—Well, I am willing to say half of the three million.

MR. RANEY: I would like the exact figures, if you please.
A.—It is some hours' work. The largest policy any other agent got amounted to $30,000.

Q.—About half was placed with other agencies?
A.—Over half.

Q.—Other agencies got the commission and you did not get any?

A.—No, sir.

Q.—I understand fire commissions run about 30 per cent.?

A.—No, if we place it with another company we pay certain commissions.

Q.—It is common knowledge?

A.—Not common knowledge what I receive, and we don't want to divulge it.

Q.—Well, I am going to ask you, Mr. Ferguson, what the amount of your commission is on the insurance that is handled by your firm for the Government, independently of this you place with outside agencies?

A.—It will take an hour or so to add it up. I would need to get it from my bookkeeper.

Q.—Then I will ask you to come back. Broadly, then, you control the insurance on what we call the Parliament Buildings?

A.—I was told it would be under our supervision for the services we rendered to the Government.

Q.—You control it?

A.—No, because we may be told it is taken away from us.

Q.—But for the present?

A.—Yes, we do to a degree.

Q.—How long has it been in your hands?

A.—Last May, this particular branch.

Q.—Do you have any insurance on the outside properties of the Province—the public institutions in different places?

A.—No, we do not. We got as far as we could. The agents themselves are distributed; they may have some.

Q.—Did you understand my question?

A.—We have none of that outside this main building.

Q.—No insurance on Ontario buildings outside these main Parliament Buildings?

A.—Absolutely none.

Q.—Well, this is something by itself?

A.—There is quite a volume of business placed out of the city with various brokers.

Q.—Have you assisted the Department in connection with insurances, or just as an expert in the way you have told us?

A.—Yes. And in this way we went over insurance we had never placed and had nothing to do with the handling of it, and discovered in Northern Ontario buildings that had not belonged to the Government for six or seven years, and handed over to school boards, were being insured by the school boards of various towns, and they were also being insured by the Government. It practically proved that it was necessary the Government should have some supervision of this insurance. We wrote to these school boards and told them the Government was also insuring their buildings. They laughed at the joke, and then we cancelled the Government policies and received rebates back on the unexpired portions.

Q.—When was this?

A.—Some time during the year.

Q.—During 1925?

A.—I will give you the letter.

MR. FINLAYSON: In other words they were doubled?

A.—And tripled—and some places none at all.

Q.—It would not be good?

A.—I don't think they would be legally liable.

Q.—They might in decency.

Witness reads letter:

Toronto, September 19.

London & Lancashire Insurance Co.,
  14 Richmond Street, Toronto.

Dear Sirs:

Re Cancellations and Policies 11222748 and 11222757, Department of Insurance, Province of Ontario.

We are duly in receipt of your letter of the 18th inst., enclosing cheque in the amount of $17.44 for which we thank you.

Regarding the difference in the amount of return premium due on Policy 11222757, we have checked this up and find your figures are correct.

BURNS & FERGUSON.

Also to Mr. Squire:

"Enclosed find cheque—

MR. RANEY: We don't want that. This insurance business had not been properly looked after?

A.—I never saw worse.

Q.—Very likely it has gone on for twenty years?

A.—It was overlapping for one year.

Q.—Very likely. Do you know the total insurance carried by the Province?

A.—I cannot say.

Q.—I will have to get here whoever in the Public Works Department has charge and bring him here to-morrow.

A.—There are two or three departments. Some is in the Provincial Secretary's Department, some in the Department of Education. Insurance of these buildings is in the Department of Public Works.

MR. RANEY: Mr. Finlayson, will you get me the men in the different Departments, who look after the different buildings? I want to find out what the total amount of insurance is on the property of Ontario, because I have a theory that I want to back up if I can that this Province ought to carry its own insurance. That would cut out some of your business, I know, too.

WITNESS: We have gone into facts and figures and found the losses the companies have paid—

MR. RANEY: That is one of the things I want to find out, how much we have paid in premiums and how much we have received back.

THE CHAIRMAN: That is a question the City of Toronto has been talking for about ten years.

MR. FINLAYSON: Unfortunate we did not do it when we might have, eh?

MR. RANEY: Any time for reform is a good time.

Mr. Finlayson examining.

Q.—You say you saw Mr. Biggs, the Minister of Public Works, and when was that?

A.—1921 or 1922.

Q.—And what did he tell you?

A.—Well he said he had not quite made up his mind, but would consider the tender.

Q.—Did you give him figures?

A.—Oh, yes.

Q.—Do you remember the rate?

A.—No, I was disgusted when we did not get the business, and gave it up as a bad job.

Q.—How long until Rev. Edgar Watson called on you?

MR. RANEY: I don't think he professes to be a clergyman.

MR. FINLAYSON: He is practicing again now. He has resumed. He is practicing religion in the States. His reverence called on you when?

A.—In about a week's time.

Q.—And had you any communication with him before he called?

A.—I had met the gentleman, and he was informed I was in the insurance business.

Q.—What connection was there between your visit to Mr. Biggs and Mr. Watson's visit to you?

A.—None, only that Mr. Watson said I was about the only man in the insurance business he knew in Toronto. He said Mr. Biggs had called him in and given him this insurance.

MR. RANEY: This is clearly hearsay evidence, and Watson is not available. Is this fair to have the witness repeat a conversation that—

MR. FINLAYSON: We have all been doing it. You have enough hearsay evidence in to sink a ship. I submit, Mr. Chairman—

MR. RANEY: My suggestion is that this witness is asked to tell the Committee of a conversation he had with Mr. Watson, who is said not now to be available, which affects Mr. Biggs. Mr. Biggs is here; Mr. Watson is not. Mr. Biggs does not know what Mr. Watson said to this witness, I suppose. Is it fair to bring out that kind of evidence?

MR. FINLAYSON: Mr. Raney calls this witness on an item of insurance, and the moment it becomes at all embarrassing—

MR. RANEY: No, I don't give a hang. If you want to go ahead with the evidence, do so.

THE CHAIRMAN: Mr. Finlayson is asking the witness to give him the substance of his conversation with Mr. Watson, as to how he came to see him. I think I would leave out the questions relating to how Mr. Biggs came to send him in.

WITNESS: Mr. Biggs did not send him in; he came to my house.

THE CHAIRMAN: I don't know that I would close out questioning as to what Mr. Watson told him, but I suggest to Mr. Finlayson not to follow a line of questioning as to whether Mr. Biggs sent him in.

MR. FINLAYSON: Your conversation with Mr. Biggs was first as to automobile insurance?

A.—Yes.

Q.—Relating to the Government fleet of cars?

A.—Yes.

Q.—Over in the garage?

A.—I don't know where they were situated at the time.

Q.—But the Government had a fleet of cars, as now, and you called on Mr. Biggs, the Minister in charge, for the purpose of trying to secure the business on the cars, and you quoted a rate. You don't care to tell us that rate?

A.—I don't remember it.

Q.—Did that cover the whole insurance on the cars?

A.—On all their cars at that time.

Q.—What else occurred between you and Mr. Biggs?

A.—Only that I had an interview and he informed Mr. Bell and myself he would let us know. He was a broker in the firm of Armour, Bell, Boswell and Cronyn.

Q.—So you and Mr. Bell called on Hon. Mr. Biggs, Minister in charge of the cars, and asked for the business?

A.—Yes.

Q.—And gave him a rate of premium?

A.—Yes.

Q.—What did he say?

A.—He said he had not quite decided whether or not he would insure them or whether he would place it just then, but would let us know. I never heard anything further from Mr. Biggs or his Department until Mr. Watson came in.

Q.—The member for North Victoria, who was then a member of the House, supporting the Government of which Mr. Biggs was a member?

A.—Yes.

Q.—And a week after your conversation with Mr. Biggs, Mr. Watson called on you?

A.—About a week.

Q.—You hadn't any message from Mr. Biggs in the meantime?

A.—None at all.

Q.—Your application was under consideration, with the rate quoted?

A.—Yes.

Q.—What occurred between you and Mr. Watson?

A.—Mr. Watson said he had been allotted this insurance to place.

Q.—By whom?

A.—Mr. Biggs.

Q.—That Mr. Biggs had alloted this insurance to place. How much?

A.—From memory, it looked as if the fleet, according to the serial numbers, had been cut in half, or certain types of cars like Ford trucks given to Watson and passenger or pleasure cars given to Ramsden.

Q.—You had not seen Ramsden at this date?

A.—No.

Q.—Mr. Watson called and wanted the insurance, and it seemed to you he had approximately half the covering?

A.—That is right.

Q.—And you quoted him a rate?

A.—He did not ask mè what it would cost, and I gave him what I thought a fair rate.

Q.—That is a retail rate?

A.—I was disappointed Bell had not got it, and—

MR. GRAVES: What do you mean in insurance by fair rates, and tendered rates and so on? Isn't there a regular rate of insurance?

A.—No, sir. You are referring to the tariff rate.

Q.—No, but when you talk about tendering, what do you mean by tendering for the fleet?

A.—Well, there are tariff and non-tariff, and I, as manager, could say exactly what I could write the fleet at. If you were representing a tariff company you knew how to write, and if non-tariff you knew, within a few cents. I was representing my own company and could write my own rate.

Q.—Legislation has gone through now that may interest some of you fellows that have been doing it.

A.—I would not say that. We were right within the law.

MR. FINLAYSON: You quoted Mr. Biggs a rate, and then quoted Mr. Watson, after he told you Mr. Biggs had allotted him this portion of the insurance, a higher rate?

A.—Yes.

Q.—In the same company?

A.—Yes.

Q.—So you had one rate for the Minister and a higher rate for the member?

A.—No, we hadn't. We had one rate for Armour, Bell, Boswell & Cronyn— we considered them in the business. We had been up and seen the deputy several times and sat outside several hours, and when I saw Mr. Watson come in I thought, "Well, I am working for dividends for the company, and there is apparently no competition," and I wrote the rate so-and-so.

Q.—If you cannot remember the figures, approximately how much higher?

A.—I knew it was higher, because I knew I was putting the rate up.

Q.—It was put up to give Watson a rake-off?

A.—Oh, no.

Q.—You increased the rate because you had to deal through an agent?

A.—No, I was dealing through an agent before, and Watson was only a broker or agent, but I increased the rate because I knew I had no competition.

Q.—You figured Watson had placing of the insurance?

A.—Yes, when I was working for Armour, Bell, Boswell & Cronyn I thought there would be proper competition.

Q.—When dealing with the Minister you thought you were giving a competitive rate, but through the member an exclusive privilege if you gave him the job. Approximately what percentage higher would Watson's rate be? Fifteen per cent.?

A.—I cannot tell. The Royal Indemnity Company have amalgamated since with Royal Insurance. I turned them over their record.

Q.—Approximately 15 per cent?

A.—I don't know whether 10 or 5, but I know it was higher, because it was easy.

Q.—He was a mark?

A.—No, the Government was a mark.

Q.—Mr. Biggs may have had some elementary knowledge of insurance, but the clergyman didn't, did he?

A.—No, not any more than a lot of people in the business.

Q.—You mean he knew what lots of people know?

A.—He knew very little about it.

Q.—He knew that he was going to get something out of it?

A.—Yes, he asked me what commission, and I told him 15 per cent.—15 or 20.

Q.—Did he give it to you right off?

A.—He had the list in his hand and told the policy-writing department to write that policy, sign our signature and send it out and the Government's signature was signed. He received $100 or more, I am sure.

Q.—For which the Government had to pay more than they would if Mr. Biggs had had it? More than $100 more?

A.—Yes.

Q.—So that Mr. Watson by some manipulation was able to make $100 out of half the insurance on the fleet of cars?

A.—Yes.

Q.—And was that all you had to do with him? Did he do a thing? Did he handle the policy?

A.—I think he gave me the insurance on his home at Lindsay.

MR. GRAVES: Did he issue these policies?

A.—No, they were written in our office.

MR. FINLAYSON: Who prepared the wording?

A.—They are a standard form.

Q.—But the clerical work?

A.—All done in our office.

Q.—Did Watson do a thing?

A.—No, operated from our office.

Q.—He came in and handed you the insurance and got his $100 later on?

A.—Yes, the only office he had was Burns & Ferguson.

Q.—The insurance on his house, I suppose he got 15 per cent. on that?

A.—Yes, because he had a license.

Q.—You told him there was a law requiring a license? He would not know that?

A.—No.

Q.—Did he grasp that, or did you get a license for him?

A.—He was told he had to pay $3 and fill in a form and he got his license.

Q.—Did you make the form out?

A.—No, he did that.

Q.—Then he came back and got the insurance on his house, less 15 per cent.?

A.—He told me he intended to go into the insurance business; he had time on his hands in Toronto.

Q.—Did you ever have any other business from him?

A.—No.

Q.—So the only transaction he had was what he was handed out by this item of Government insurance, in which he got over $100?

A.—I may be wrong. He got a commission, if I recollect, on Northern Ontario Railway, on a policy from Mr. Smith's Department, the Provincial Treasurer's.

Q.—Did you go after that business first?

A.—No, we had an inspector working on that, and he went up with Watson and showed what we could do with cheque-altering—forging—insurance.

Q.—So that one of your inspectors thought the Province should have insurance against alterations in cheques and went up to see Mr. Smith?

A.—Yes.

Q.—How did Mr. Watson get in on that?

A.—I did not know many members at the time, but had been introduced to Mr. Watson, and our man's name was Watson, and I said, "If you look up Mr. Watson you can be introduced to Mr. Smith," and he introduced him and the policy was written.

Q.—How much did the clergyman make out of that?

A.—He got the usual commission. Over $50.

Q.—So as far as you can remember, Mr. Watson got something over $100 on automobile business and something over $50 on Mr. Smith's business?

A.—Yes.

Q.—These are the only items of business apart from his house you knew him to write?

A.—He may have put another policy in; I would not know. But I am sure here were not over five.

Q.—Can you look it up for us?

A.—I would not like to say I could, so far back.

Q.—Well, Mr. Ramsden was member for South-west Toronto?

A.—Yes.

Q.—How did he come to get in on automobile insurance?

A.—It was given to him to place in the Royal Indemnity Insurance through the Royal Insurance Company, who are affiliated with our company.

Q.—Is he an insurance agent?

A.—Yes, he was for two or three years.

Q.—How much did he get?

A.—I cannot exactly say, but I think Watson had told me it was split between him and Ramsden.

Q.—On the regular U.F.O. fifty-fifty basis?

A.—I think so.

Q.—However, he got something over $100 too?

A.—I presume he did.

Q.—Did he get any other items from you?

A.—No.

Q.—Any other members in on this?

A.—Not that I know. I did not know they were members, if they were.

MR. GRAVES: Mr. Ferguson, in your evidence a while ago you spoke of the amount of money you would save on the insurance on these buildings when transferred to you. You got a lower rate?

A.—Yes.

Q.—Was there any alteration made in the description of the buildings, that you were entitled—

A.—Am I giving information now that will hurt me with my competitors? I don't know that I am compelled to answer a question like that. I don't want to divulge how our office operates, as long as we do things in a proper, business-like manner and save the Government money.

Q.—Usually when there is a change in rate on the property there is change made in the risk, which enables you to get some change in the rate?

A.—I am not going to tell you my secrets of business or my knowledge of the business.

MR. RANEY: I don't think you have any secrets in this Committee, Mr. Ferguson.

A.—I have secrets from my competitors, how I reduced the rate to the Government.

MR. RANEY: One witness told us the fireproof part of the building was carrying heavy insurance and the non-fireproof not enough?

MR. GRAVES: That is all right, but they could put a smaller amount on one and more on another and reduce the aggregate amount and the premiums.

THE CHAIRMAN: The witness' evidence was to the effect that they increased the total amount of insurance.

MR. GRAVES: That is as broad as it is long, because if you charge the same amount of money and lower the rate you can get more insurance. If you have the insurance divided under three different rates and you increase the amount of insurance on the low rate, and reduce it on the high rate, your aggregate when you get through is lower, isn't it?

A.—That is not honest. We don't do that, and we got a lower rate and increased the amount of insurance.

Q.—You have got to do something?

A.—I am not telling you what we did.

MR. FINLAYSON: You gave some figures before that formerly one million cost what?

A.—Approximately $7,000.

Q.—And as result of your changes $1,400,000 cost what?

A.—About $5,000.

MR. GRAVES: Is this in tariff companies?

A.—It is all written at tariff rate. Some companies demanded tariff rate on this building and did quote it. The non-tariff companies got it, but at tariff rate. It is all placed at the published tariff rate by the Tariff Association.

MR. GRAVES: Then you got a reduction on the tariff rate by certain manipulations?

A.—By certain manipulations.

Q.—Non-reciprocal?

A.—No.

Q.—All British or Canadian?

A.—Mr. Henry insisted a certain portion Canadian first, British second, and American companies third, which we did.

MR. FINLAYSON: Do I understand some of these buildings in Northern Ontario are some of them doubly insured, and some trebly?

A.—Yes.

Q.—That means that legally there is no insurance at all?

A.—Not being a lawyer, I cannot say.

Q.—One of the statutory conditions of the policy is that you have to obtain the consent of the company to every other policy?

A.—They had permission to do that, in their policies, but they would not receive the full face value of their policies, but the total amount of such. There is a certain law among the insurance companies, an Insurance Act, which says they will be paid pro rata the proportion in event of a fire.

MR. GRAVES: You must put on all your policies the concurrent insurance, in such and such a company?

A.—Permission is granted to place other insurance, and you do not have to mention the other companies.

Q.—But you have to have that clause on, and if it is not you have to give your concurrent insurance.

MR. FINLAYSON: Did each of these policies contain a notation on the policy that further concurrent insurance was permitted?

A.—I did not see the ones in Northern Ontario.

MR. FINLAYSON: What about McNamara?

MR. RANEY: I want him back. What about it, Mr. Chairman?

THE CHAIRMAN: We won't meet in the morning. We have that important meeting of Private Bills. How about afternoon? I suppose you want to be in the House?

MR. RANEY: There will be estimates. Supposing we have a meeting at four o'clock?

THE CHAIRMAN: We could meet from four to six.

MR. FINLAYSON: Do I understand we are finished with motion pictures, Mr. Raney?

MR. RANEY: That is all I want to call.

MR. FINLAYSON: And dispensaries?
MR. RANEY: No, I want to see the statement.
The Committee then adjourned. (Eleven P.M.)

PUBLIC ACCOUNTS COMMITTEE.

The Committee reassembled on the afternoon of Tuesday, March 30, at 4 P.M., with Mr. Lewis in the Chair.

THE CHAIRMAN: Order, gentlemen, please. Now we have a quorum present and there is no reason for waiting. Members present are marked on the list. We will not bother calling the roll.

MR. FINLAYSON: Before you go on to-day there is one thing I thought I might mention. It occurs to me, perhaps as I acted as Chairman for the last two years, that is the question of a report. We are approaching the end of the session and last year and the year before I think it was left practically to the last day of the session, which was most unfortunate for everyone. I thought I would mention it to the Committee.

What I was going to suggest was this, that the Chairman be asked in the usual way to draught a report. It won't be finished now, of course, but if you have it in hand we can, perhaps, save some of the rush at the last moment that occurred last year.

THE CHAIRMAN: If that meets with the approval of the Committee. Of course, as a matter of fact, I may say I have been keeping a memo of the different things we have been dealing with, with the idea of incorporating them in the report for submission to the Committee when we get to the last sitting, And if that meets with the approval of the Committee I will be glad to do that. outline a report, something on which we can discuss a report at the final meeting.

HON. MR. RANEY: I suppose, perhaps, we can get pretty well through to-day.

THE CHAIRMAN: I think we can.

HON. MR. RANEY: So that we would be in a position to finish up to-morrow and consider a report to-morrow.

THE CHAIRMAN: That is what I thought we could do.

MR. FINLAYSON: I don't know what your idea is but my idea of the Committee is I don't think a partisan finding of any Public Accounts Committee which might be passed by a majority is of very much value. I think anything the Committee can agree on as to recommendation, or as to suggestions for the future, arising out of the observations of the Committee during the season, is very good material to pass on to proper mention for us as we used to say in the army for his necessary action.

But I don't, I never thought any great value attached to a finding of a Committee over a matter that perhaps drifted into a partisan manner before the Committee were finished.

HON. MR. RANEY: I don't think it should be a partisan report, but I think after the time that we have spent with this Committee, and the subjects, that there ought to be a summary of them and not only a summary of the facts, but perhaps some conclusions drawn.

MR. FINLAYSON Anything we can agree on I think it is desirable that we should.

THE CHAIRMAN: As far as my knowledge goes of the operations of the Committee in the past, as a general rule the report has been confined to reporting the subject matter that the Committee has considered. And without, excepting in one or two instances, one or two cases, going into any report as to the result of the investigation. Personally, I don't see much value in that. However—

MR. FINLAYSON: Well, we can leave it in the Chairman's hands to draught something.

THE CHAIRMAN: It is subject to revision by the Committee.

MR. FINLAYSON: Yes.

HON. MR. RANEY: The understanding being we will endeavour to arrive at the report stage to-morrow if possible.

MR. FISHER: I think there should be a special time mentioned when you are going to do that. Some of the members might like to be here.

THE CHAIRMAN: I was hoping we might pretty well wind up, perhaps in this next two-hour session.

HON. MR. RANEY: I don't think that is possible. We can sit this evening.

THE CHAIRMAN: If necessary.

MR. FINLAYSON: Well, I think we might get through.

THE CHAIRMAN: And following we can set a time to-morrow to meet for consideration of a report. Now Mr. Laberge is here and George McNamara is here and I think probably you could clean that up.

Joseph Alfred Laberge called, sworn. Examined by Mr. Finlayson, K.C.

Q.—Mr. Laberge, I believe you are a merchant residing in Sudbury?
A.—Yes.
Q.—What is your business?
A.—Lumbering and contracting.
Q.—What form of contracting?
A.—Business blocks and contracts of that kind.
Q.—Business blocks?
A.—Yes.
Q.—You are a building contractor?
A.—Yes.
Q.—And you also run a hardware store?
A.—No.
Q.—Oh, do you not?
A.—Builders' supplies, lumbering.
Q.—And timber and that sort, I see. Now you tendered on the road that is known as the Creighton-Copper Cliff road?
A.—Yes, sir.
Q.—When was that?
A.—In September some time, the latter part of August. I haven't the date.
Q.—A year ago?
A.—Yes.
Q.—In August, 1925, and I believe your tender was the lowest?
A.—I understand so.
Q.—What was the figure?
A.—The figure was roughly around sixty some odd thousand dollars. It was on unit prices.
Q.—Around $60,000, on a unit basis?
A.—Yes.

Q.—And did you receive notice from the Department that you were the lowest tenderer?

A.—Yes, sir.

Q.—Have you that notice with you? What form did the notice take?

A.—I was advised by letter.

Q.—A letter?

A.—I think it was signed by Mr. Fullerton, Director of the Northern Development Branch.

Q.—Signed by Mr. Fullerton and addressed to whom?

A.—Addressed to myself.

Q.—At Sudbury, I suppose?

A.—Yes.

Q.—What was the effect of that letter?

A.—Notifying me that we had been awarded the contract for the Creighton road.

Q.—Now did you put in a tender independently of everybody else?

A.—Yes.

Q.—And have your own bid?

A.—Yes, sir.

Q.—Nobody in with you in it?

A.—No, sir.

Q.—Did anybody have any interest in it direct, disclosed or undisclosed?

A.—No, sir.

Q.—You did have your own bid?

A.—Yes, sir.

Q.—You put up the security?

A.—Yes, sir.

Q.—Deposited?

A.—Deposited a marked cheque.

Q.—How much?

A.—I don't know.

Q.—Thousand dollars, I think?

A.—I think it was a thousand dollars.

Q.—I think I remember. Anyway you put up a marked cheque of your own. Was that your own funds?

A.—Yes, sir.

Q.—After you had received the notice that you were the lowest tenderer and had been awarded the contract what was the next step?

A.—Just what do you mean?

Q.—What happened in connection with this contract next?

A.—Do you refer to the fact that I sold it?

Q.—Was that the next thing?

A.—Well, I came down here and notified Mr. Fullerton.

Q.—Saw Mr. Fullerton?

A.—Yes, asked him if he would—the McNamara Brothers, Howard rather, came up to see me at Sudbury, wanted to know if I would be interested in selling this contract.

Q.—This is before you came to Fullerton?

A.—Yes. After I was notified I had the contract.

Q.—And before your visit to Toronto McNamara came to you and asked you if you were interested—

A.—If I would sell the contract. We had two or three interviews.

Q.—At that time what were the McNamara firm doing?
Q.—They were working on the Conniston road.
Q.—That is in the neighbourhood?
A.—Yes.
Q.—I see. And what stage was the Conniston job at?
A.—Well, it was in process of construction.
Q.—Was it an early stage, or near a finish?
A.—No, it was nearly finished. This was on in September.
Q.—So McNamara came to you and asked if you would consider selling?
A.—Yes.
Q.—What did you finally agree on?
A.—I agreed to sell.
Q.—What were the terms?
A.—One thousand five hundred dollars.
Hon. Mr. Raney: You have a memo of it there haven't you.
Mr. Finlayson: Have you a copy of that?
A.—Of the agreement of this? Yes.
Q.—This will be Exhibit 16, document on the paper of the McNamara Construction Company.

"In consideration of the sum of Five Hundred dollars ($500) receipt of which is hereby acknowledge and One Thousand dollars to be paid November 1st, 1924, I, J. A. Laberge, agree to assign to you the contract for the Copper Cliff-Creighton Road awarded to me by the Government, it being understood that the McNamara Co. is to furnish security to me for their carrying out the work either by bond or otherwise and to carry out the work according to Department specifications, etc.

McNamara Construction Co. do further agree to buy from me any supplies for this work that we carry in stock.
(Signed) J. A. Laberge,
H. D. McNamara."

Q.—That is your signature?
A.—Yes.
Q.—It is also signed by McNamara on behalf of his company?
A.—Yes, sir.
Q.—Were you paid $500 then?
A.—No, I had been paid $250 a few days previous by Howard.
Q.—That is when you made the bargain?
A.—When we really made the bargain and he consulted his brother, or his brother came up there and they gave me the balance of the $500.
Q.—So you got the $500 in two payments of $250 each?
A.—Yes, sir.
Q.—One slightly before the date of this agreement and the other on the date of this?
A.—Yes.
Q.—So the agreement properly acknowledged $500?
A.—Yes.
Q.—Then the balance of a thousand? Did you get that?
A.—Yes.
Q.—First of November?
A.—No, it was on the third of November.
Q.—So that you got the balance according to the agreement?

A.—Yes, sir.

Q.—So you were paid in full?

A.—Yes, sir.

Q.—Did they carry out the other part of the arrangement that they were to buy supplies as far as possible from you?

A.—Yes, sir.

Q.—What did that consist of?

A.—It consisted of lumber for their forms, for the culverts and tile, some cement, some coal for their rollers, and different items that we sell.

Q.—Well then, did this $1,500 express consideration represent everything you got?

A.—Yes, sir.

Q.—Apart from the ordinary trading profit in supplies?

A.—Yes, sir.

Q.—And did you give them—what prices did you give them on supplies?

A.—Standard price. It was understood that they were to pay at our standard public lists.

Q.—And do I understand you then that not in any way was there any consideration expressed or implied or paid any way except the fifteen hundred dollars?

A.—That was all. No other consideration.

Q.—And this document disclosed the whole contract?

A.—Yes, sir.

Q.—I believe in addition to this you also executed a formal assignment for the Government records?

A.—Yes, sir, that was what I referred to in seeing Mr. Fullerton. That would be an agreement to the Department.

Q.—So after you had seen McNamara you came to see if Mr. Fullerton was satisfied?

A.—Yes.

Q.—What did he say?

A.—He said he was providing McNamara Brothers would put up the necessary bonds to carry out the work.

Q.—Necessary security?

A.—Yes.

Q.—What arrangement did you make with Mr. Fullerton and McNamara as to security?

A.—We went to a bond company and the bond was arranged direct from McNamara to the Department.

Q.—And did McNamara enter into the complete contract with the Department? Which signed the contract with the Department? You or McNamara?

A.—I had put in my first tender, of course.

Q.—I know, but when it came to assigning the actual formal contract?

A.—McNamara did.

Q.—Or did you? Or both?

A.—McNamara did.

Q.—And McNamara furnished the security?

A.—Yes, sir.

Q.—And that let you out?

A.—Yes, sir.

Q.—They returned your deposit to you?

A.—Yes, sir.

Q.—Do you know Mr. Lyons, the Minister?

A.—Yes, sir.

Q.—How intimately?

A.—Well, I just met him during the last year up on one of his visits to Sudbury.

Q.—At the time of these negotiations did you know him?

A.—I had never met Mr. Lyons.

Q.—But the following year, on one of his official visits to Sudbury you met him?

A.—Yes.

Q.—Just presented to him?

A.—Yes.

Q.—That is the only occasion you had anything to do with him?

A.—Yes.

Q.—Did Mr. Lyons or anyone on his behalf have any connection whatever with the assignment to McNamara?

A.—No, sir.

Q.—Did he have any interest in it?

A.—No, sir.

Q.—Did he suggest it or was it suggested from him?

A.—No, sir.

Q.—You have told us all the facts in connection with the assignment?

A.—Yes, sir.

Hon. W. E. Raney, K.C., cross-examining.

Q.—This was the road from Creighton to Copper Cliff?

A.—Yes, sir.

Q.—About seven miles?

A.—About seven miles.

Q.—And the pavement was to be tar penetration, what they call?

A.—Yes.

Q.—Copper Cliff is how far from Sudbury?

A.—Four miles.

Q.—What kind of road is there between Copper Cliff and Sudbury?

A.—Tar macadam.

Q.—How large a place is Copper Cliff?

A.—About 3,500 population; that is approximately.

Q.—And what is the population of Creighton?

A.—Oh, about two thousand.

Q.—What is there at Creighton?

A.—There is a mine there.

Q.—What mine?

A.—Nickel mine.

Q.—And a nickel mine at Copper Cliff?

A.—Smelters.

Q.—Smelters, rather. And there had been a road previously between the two places communicating. This tar penetration was to go down on the old road?

A.—Yes.

Q.—That was a gravel road?

A.—Yes, sir.

Q.—That was not the trunk road?

A.—No, sir.

Q.—It is no part of the trunk road?

A.—Do you mean by trunk road, transcontinental road?

Q.—Through road?

A.—No. This road finished, I think, at O'Donnell which is about three four miles farther than Creighton.

Q.—Well now, the trunk road, I suppose, goes through Sudbury?

A.—Yes.

Q.—Not to Copper Cliff?

A.—Goes through Sudbury, Copper Cliff, but it doesn't got to Creighton.

Q.—Sudbury and Copper Cliff?

A.—Yes.

Q.—Creighton is like an offshoot, spur?

A.—Yes.

Q.—Spur. So this road was really to accommodate Creighton?

A.—Yes, sir.

Q.—It is the road to accommodate Creighton?

THE CHAIRMAN: Are you asking this witness to tell you that the Department built the road for?

HON. MR. RANEY: This road is a special road so far as the concrete is concerned through Copper Cliff to Creighton?

A.—Yes.

Q.—Does it run at right angles with the trunk road?

A.—No. It doesn't.

Q.—At an angle?

A.—I would be possibly two or three miles and more at different places between the two roads.

Q.—So it rather angles off at sharp angle?

A.—Yes.

Q.—And is there a through road beyond Creighton or does it pretty well end at Creighton?

A.—I don't think it goes farther than O'Donnell.

Q.—How far is that on?

A.—Practically four miles.

Q.—Beyond Creighton?

A.—Yes.

Q.—What is there there?

A.—The roast yards of the International Nickel.

Q.—And what population is there there?

A.—Oh I wouldn't say to be exact. I suppose five hundred.

Q.—What experience had you had in road building?

A.—I had some experience in 1911 and again in 1920 and 1921. In 1911, we built the Algoma Eastern, or part of it.

Q.—That is a railway?

A.—Yes.

Q.—Any highway building?

A.—No highway building. In 1920 and 1921 when I was mayor of Sudbury, we built the same class of road.

Q.—Not as contractor?

A.—No, as mayor supervising the work.

Q.—Did you have any equipment when you made this tender?

A.—No.

Q.—Had you had it in mind to tender on the Conniston to Sudbury road?
A.—Yes, I had.
Q.—Why didn't you?
A.—Changed my mind. Just didn't want to tackle it.
Q.—That was the only reason? Just changed your mind?
A.—Yes, sir.
Q.—Did you employ an engineer to go over the Creighton-Copper Cliff road before you put your tender in?
A.—Yes, sir.
Q.—Who did you employ?
A.—Paul Gravell.
Q.—Did you take cross-sections?
A.—No.
Q.—Did you have before you when you put your tender in any cross-sections of the road? You know what I mean, of course?
A.—No, we had the approximate quantities of course.
Q.—Did you compare your figures before putting your tenders in with anybody?
A.—No, sir.
Q.—Did you discuss your figures with any body?
A.—No, sir.
Q.—Who assisted you to prepare them?
A.—Paul Gravell.
Q.—The engineer?
A.—The engineer.
Q.—That is all the assistance you had?
A.—Yes, sir.
Q.—Then Mr. Howard McNamara came to see you to see if you would be willing to assign the contract?
A.—Yes, sir.
Q.—You hadn't had any thought of doing that before?
A.—No, sir.
Q.—Had you made arrangements before you tendered with anybody in respect of the purchase of supplies in case the tender came to you?
A.—No, except with the oil. Of course that was the only thing we had to buy anyway.
Q.—Who did you see about that?
A.—The Imperial Oil Company.
Q.—You got prices from them on the oil?
A.—Yes.
Q.—And you had estimated what quantity you would require?
A.—Yes.
Q.—What did you say your business was in Sudbury?
A.—Lumber and building supplies and contracting.
Q.—Did you take an interest in the last general election?
A.—I always do.
Q.—Did you act as agent for Mr. McCrea?
A.—No.
Q.—Were you active in his interest?
A.—Yes, sir.
Q.—You took an active interest on Mr. McCrea's behalf?
A.—Yes.

Q.—Did you discuss with him road building?

A.—No, sir.

Q.—Or tendering on road contracts?

A.—No, sir.

Q.—How did you arrive at the $1,500 for the assignment of this contract?

A.—Just thought it was worth that and I asked him.

Q.—Was that your first price?

A.—No, we talked other figures, but we came to a compromise.

Q.—What was your first price?

A.—I don't know. It was around $2,000.

Q.—The first price you mentioned?

A.—Yes.

Mr. Fisher: When were these tenders called?

A.—For the beginning of September.

Q.—Was there any time fixed for the completion of the road?

A.—I think there was. But having read both specifications for the Conniston and Creighton, and not having done the work, I am not just positive.

Hon. Mr. Raney: You had specifications for the other job?

A.—Yes, sir.

Mr. Fisher: When was the road finished?

A.—it was completed last year, 1925.

Q.—The tender went in September, 1924?

A.—Yes, sir.

Q.—Never any thought of finishing in 1924?

A.—No, it would be too late.

Q.—Did you take off any quantities as to the work that would have to be done on that road?

A.—No, excepting the quantities that we were given by the engineer.

Q.—What do you mean by that?

A.—Which were approximate.

Q.—What?

A.—Approximate quantities as shown on the forms supplied by the Government.

Q.—We were told the other day that they were not approximate but merely arbitrary quantities.

The Chairman: On this road, I recollect the evidence of Fullerton, it was for certain things, the amount of surfacing, they had approximately correct figures, but on the balance of the items they had an arbitrary figure in order to unit price base on that.

Mr. Fisher: Did you know, Mr. Laberge, that they were not estimates?

A.—No. It was very hard to get a close estimate in such rough country. I know they were not exact by any means, could not possibly be.

Q.—Did you make any estimates yourself as to any quantities?

A.—No, any more than sizing up the proposition in general, as one would naturally do.

Q.—Sizing them up. Did it appear to you those quantities would represent the work that would have to be done?

A.—Approximately, yes.

Q.—They proved very far wrong, did they?

A.—Yes. The quantities overran, as they always do on that class of work in that kind of country.

Q.—They always overrun?

A.—To my knowledge.

Q.—And you expect them to overrun?

A.—Yes.

Q.—Do you expect them to overrun as much as they did in this case?

A.—I am not in a position to say, because I did not prepare the estimates. I don't know what they based them on.

Q.—Well, the arbitrary amount fixed for earth excavation was five hundred cubic yards. There was actually done 11,417 yards. Was that more than you would expect?

A.—Well, of course, that is no doubt occasioned on account of the engineer changing the level of the road, and the drains.

THE CHAIRMAN: Mr. Fisher, I don't want to interfere if you have some particular object, but these facts have been dealt with by the engineer and they are quite willing to discuss them. I don't think you are going to get any place. He is not an expert. He is not an engineer.

MR. FISHER: Well, he says he has had experience.

THE CHAIRMAN: Not in building roads. He says so.

MR. FISHER: He says it is natural, when they change levels that the quantities would overrun as they always do.

MR. FISHER: You would expect they would overrun?

A.—Yes.

Q.—You knew of course that they would not overrun as to some of the items?

A.—Naturally, they must vary. They cannot all overrun to the same degree.

Q.—The surfacing for instance would be about the same?

A.—Because they can arrive at that pretty closely.

Q.—How far is this job from the other one, Sudbury to Conniston?

A.—About five miles, about six miles, rather.

Q.—Generally speaking, the material is the same, rock and that?

A.—Pretty much the same kind of country, yes, although the Creighton road is a rougher country.

Q.—Rougher?

A.—Yes, sir.

Q.—Where did you get your prices for concrete and culverts?

A.—Where did I get it?

Q.—Yes.

A.—Do you mean, how did I arrive at it?

Q.—Yes.

A.—Based on our costs from time to time.

Q.—And you thought it was a fair price?

A.—I thought it was a fair price, yes, sir.

Q.—But you don't know whether it proved to be or not? Did you see the McNamara figures on the other contract before you put in your tender?

A.—No, sir.

Q.—You had not seen those?

A.—No, sir.

Q.—Did you know anything about their figures on this contract, before you put in your tender?

A.—No, sir.

Q.—You sold this for $1,500 and an obligation to take materials from you?

A.—Yes, sir.

Q.—Do you supply materials?

A.—Yes, sir.

Q.—To what extent?

A.—In dollars?

Q.—Roughly?

A.—I don't know, because I don't look after the sales of the company. I knew, I was asked, I was sales manager, I was getting the sales, and I didn't ask before I came just what the amount was.

Q.—And that was a valuable consideration, was it, in signing the contract, to get this work?

A.—Yes.

Q.—And you cannot tell us how much you expect to make out of that?

A.—No, I haven't got any approximate idea in my mind.

Hon. Mr. Raney: Do you know whether your engineer conferred with McNamara Company's engineer?

A.—He couldn't possibly have seen him.

Q.—And you didn't confer with the McNamara engineer?

A.—No, sir.

Q.—Or anybody representing them?

A.—No, sir.

Q.—Or they with your engineer?

A.—No, sir.

The Chairman: In other words, there was no collusion at all?

Hon. Mr. Raney: Mr. Fisher has referred to the quantity of earth excavation, five hundred cubic yards, as compared with the actual quantity, 11,417 yards on this seven mile road. Of course, you know that five hundred yards was not a real estimate at all?

A.—Yes, I thought it was too little.

Q.—You knew it was arbitrary?

A.—That is, I knew, I thought I did, because I was not sure, just sure what level the engineer would demand.

Q.—No matter what the level was, you could not build a road that long with five hundred yards of excavation?

A.—That is just what I wanted to say.

Q.—So that figure of five hundred yards was purely arbitrary?

A.—Yes, it was small.

Q.—Of course, and arbitrary. Then, so far as rock excavation was concerned, I see the actual quantity was 3,125 cubic yards. Do you remember what the arbitrary amount was?

A.—I don't, sir.

Q.—Well, if I tell you that the figures of the Department show it was 100 cubic yards, then you will at once admit to me that that was arbitrary and of no value at all to you so far as quantity was concerned?

Q.—That might depend. If the engineers might have changed their amounts to such an extent.

Q.—You could not on that road, it couldn't be possible, you would have 100 cubic yards?

A.—Yes, it all depends, that road is very rough country.

Q.—That is your answer. Here is another estimate; 1,800 lineal feet of tile, whereas the actual quantity was 9,200?

A.—Yes.

Q.—That must have been arbitrary?

A.—No, because that all depends again on the grade of the road that they decided to make.

Q.—Surely not a difference between 1,800 and 9,200?

A.—It might be quite possible.

Q.—Well, here is another estimate. Five hundred cubic yards of crushed stone. That is an arbitrary quantity. The actual quantity which you find required 3,959, that is to say, 4,000, eight times as much. Isn't it quite obvious 500 cubic yards was quite arbitrary?

A.—No, sir. Same answer as in the other case.

Q.—Are you saying now it is possible this road could have been built on any survey or any engineer's report with an excavation of five hundred cubic yards of earth, one hundred cubic yards of rock and five hundred cubic yards of crushed stone to be placed on the road?

A.—I would say outside of the earth, yes.

Q.—But the earth, though, is impossible?

A.—In my mind that is too small.

MR. FISHER: You hadn't anything before you at all to show you what the grades were going to be?

A.—No.

Q.—Didn't know anything about the road except that it was going to be seven miles long?

A.—Of course, covering the ground we had an idea what it was going to be.

Q.—Yes, you had to get your own idea yourself?

A.—Yes.

Q.—The Department didn't supply you with any idea of how the road was going to be built?

A.—No, except what specifications—

MR. FINLAYSON: This road was between six and seven miles long?

A.—Yes, sir.

Q.—And four miles had been built by the previous government?

A.—Yes.

Q.—And was supposed to be metalled?

A.—Metalled?

Q.—To be covered with crushed rock?

A.—Yes.

Q.—If it had been honestly done, and that metal was there for four miles that only required surfacing?

A.—Yes.

Q.—But I believe it turned out it had never been properly done?

Q.—It wasn't properly, the same as any other road.

Q.—The road metal was not on?

A.—No.

Q.—So when the engineers figured on the quantities they figured that four miles of it was crushed stone, was there?

A.—Yes.

Q.—Which would make four-sevenths of the material should have been there?

A.—Yes.

Q.—But I believe it turned out it had been skimped and wasn't there?

A.—Yes.

Q.—In addition, they changed the levels?

A.—Yes.

Q.—They improved as they went ahead the levels all through?
A.—Yes.
Q.—Which increased excavation and increased the fill?
A.—Yes.
Q.—Which meant you had more earth to move and more rock?
A.—Yes.
Q.—And also changed the location of the road?
A.—Yes.
Q.—Straightened out three places?
A.—Three or four bad curves there.
Q.—Three or four bad curves were improved as the road went ahead?
A.—Yes.
Q.—So that also increased the rock cut, increased the drainage, increased the material?
A.—Yes.
Q.—And increased the price, of course?
A.—Surely.
Q.—You are a practical man, you live in the neighbourhood, you were mayor of Sudbury, are still—
A.—No.
Q.—There for some years, and you are a contractor. Having regard to the improvements in the grade, the improvements in the levels, the cutting out of all these curves and the fact that the rock that was there by the previous government supposed to be there, was not there, was the increase in the price reasonable?
Q.—I believe so, yes.

George McNamara re-called.
THE CHAIRMAN: You are already sworn.
HON. MR. RANEY: You have the bills I believe for this reinforcement material. You purchased reinforcement material from the Lyons Fuel and Supply Company?
A.—Part of it.
Q.—78,459 square feet.
MR. FINLAYSON: This is Wellington Street?
HON. MR. RANEY: This is the Conniston-Sudbury?
WITNESS: No, we didn't buy anything.
HON. MR. RANEY: Oh, this is Wellington Street.
Q.—This bill from the Lyons Fuel and Supply Company for wire mesh for—it looks like—
A.—Reinforcement.
Q.—Wire mesh reinforcement, 78,459 square feet for paving purposes at $2.47 a square foot?
A.—One hundred square feet.
Q.—Total $1,914. Then you show me also a tender from another company Pedlar People, Limited, on a different basis, you say, $2.50 per square foot F.O.B. There was something different about that?
A.—No, that was practically the same except we had to deliver and Lyons delivered on the job.
Q.—So this was practically the same thing?
A.—Only Lyons was considerably cheaper.
Q.—Then another from Biscome?

27 J.

A.—Yes.

Q.—And that worked out rather differently?

A.—It was higher.

Q.—Did you have any others?

A.—I wired several others but they were all higher than that.

Q.—I ask you that because I have a letter from the Sarnia Fence Company. Did they put one in?

A.—That is Biscome's.

Q.—Is that Biscome's?

A.—Yes.

Q.—Biscome is at the Soo?

A.—But he is agent and I wired and they told me to get in touch with Biscome.

Q.—They say they offered to supply you with this reinforcement fabric at $1.90 per square foot?

A.—No, they didn't.

Q.—Where is their tender?

A.—Never no tender from them at any price.

Q.—Biscome put in a tender?

A.—Well, I guess he protected himself. If I remember rightly they told me to get in touch with Biscome, but that price is $2.10?

Q.—Biscome reinforcing material approved by the engineer, $2.10?

A.—Yes, per 100 square feet, that is 100 square feet of reinforcement and the other Lyons quoted on was 100 square of pavement which you have to work out the overlap.

Q.—So you say Biscome's tender worked out—?

A.—Worked out higher and we wouldn't have used it anyway because it isn't the right kind.

Q.—Apparently my information is not correct when the Sarnia people say they tendered our price to the engineer was $1.90?

A.—Absolutely. We never got that tender. We could not have used it anyway.

THE CHAIRMAN: This is on the pavement?

A.—The Soo.

Q.—Municipal contract?

A.—Yes.

MR. FISHER: You tendered on the Sudbury-Conniston road, Mr. McNamara?

A.—Yes, sir.

Q.—At the time you tendered did you have any instructions as to the tendering or any information supplied by the Department?

A.—The usual information on the tender form.

Q.—What quantities did you have?

A.—Well, I don't remember them now. That is two years ago.

Q.—You will remember that they supplied you with quantities on three items?

A.—Something like that, I believe.

Q.—They were altogether twenty-one items?

A.—I don't remember the number.

THE CHAIRMAN: Am I not correct in saying twelve?

MR. FISHER: No. Twelve actually used.

A.—It is the standard specification of the highways.

Q.—Were you informed at the time that the contract would be awarded on the three items in connection with which the quantities were given to you?

A.—We did not have any information except what was in the specifications.

Q.—What was your understanding? Did you understand that the contract would be awarded to the lowest tenderer on the three items?

A.—We understood as it read in the specifications that the low man on whatever was called for would be awarded the contract.

Q.—What do you mean by whatever was called for?

A.—Well, the items that were mentioned.

Q.—But you didn't have quantities on a lot of them?

A.—No, that is often the case.

Q.—When that is the case what is the tender awarded on?

A.—On the quantities that are mentioned.

Q.—Then, did you understand at the time when this contract was given to you that the contract was to be awarded on the three items in connection with which quantities were given?

A.—Had been given?

Q.—Quantities were given only in connection with three items. Did you understand when you put in your tender that the tender would be awarded only on those three items?

A.—That is the only way it could be.

Q.—You understood that?

MR. FINLAYSON: I don't know what he means by understanding. If you want to ask him if there was anything behind the specifications all right, but what he understood—

A.—Those specifications are exactly the same as we have been figuring on the last five years for the Drury Government and the highways.

MR. FISHER: Forms?

A.—Forms and quantities and sometimes we would put in considerable quantities for items that there would be no item whatever in and we put in our price for what we expect providing there was any done and that was what we were paid for on this work. It would be an impossibility on a lot of items to put in the quantity or anything like the quantity until they had torn up the road.

Q.—Did you say the contract could only be awarded on those items where quantities were given?

A.—I don't see any other way to award it.

Q.—On the Sudbury-Conniston road I just wanted one question. I gather from what has been said there was a road of some sort more or less permanent on part of it.

HON. MR. RANEY: It must have been the whole of it.

MR. FISHER: I am sorry, on the Creighton-Copper Cliff?

A.—Yes.

Q.—There was already a road in some part?

A.—There was supposed to be, as we understood it when we tendered on the road and the engineer gave us the information that some time ago, I don't know just how long previous, two or three years ago, there had been a contract given to put in stone which would make a stone base and we were given to understand that stone was there. When we began to rip up the road we found there was absolutely no stone whatever, sand, clay, dirt road.

Q.—How much of the road did that apply to?

A.—Practically the whole road.

Q.—The whole road supposed to be stoned?

A.—Yes, I believe it was stone over the whole road.   Stone base.

Q.—Laberge talked about three miles?

A.—Well, we understand stone was to be put over the whole road.

Q.—Did you see this road before?

A.—Yes, sir.

Q.—And was the stone there?

A.—There was a certain amount of gravel on top but there was no stone base of any kind.   There might have been a scattering of stone on part of it.

Q.—Was the road graded over the whole length?

A.—Oh, yes, but there was no foundation, no stone base.   There might have been in small stretches of it but nothing over any length of it.

Q.—Was the grade changed much after you started to work?

A.—Yes, actually, in one place, what caused a great deal of that extra excavation—there were three places, but one in particular, when they got down to put the road over the bridge.   The bridge was in very bad shape and it would have been only a waste of money to have followed that line.   They diverted the road then the Government built a bridge.

MR. FINLAYSON: You told us before you had been contracting for fifteen or twenty years in this kind of work?

A.—Twelve.

Q.—And I believe your firm has done as much contracting of this kind as any of the firms that are doing the work in Ontario?

A.—We have done quite a bit.

Q.—You are one of the foremost firms.   And what I would like to get at is something on this what seems to mystify my friends, the tender system on units.   Why are tenders taken by units?

A.—It is really the only way it can be done.

Q.—Why?

A.—To begin with it is an impossibility in lots of cases to be able to tell what quantity of material you are going to have to have, and up in the north country it is very hard, it is absolutely impossible on that Creighton road or the Conniston road to tell what quantity of rock, for instance, you are going to strike.   I don't believe if the engineers had taken an estimate it would have been anywhere near the quantities.   I don't believe it is possible.

Q.—We were discussing the practice of tendering on a unit system.   What is the big advantage from the Department's standpoint?   What is the big advantage from the Government's standpoint?

A.—They pay for actually what is taken out.

Q.—Without extras?

A.—Without any extras.   There is no extras.

Q.—So there is no opportunity for a contractor to make up a claim for extras?

A.—Absolutely not.   There is an item in there for every possible unit that could be put in.

Q.—Item for every form of work that could be done?

A.—That could be done on the road.

Q.—And by figuring—whether the quantities are in or not, you put in your figure?

A.—Put in our figure.

Q.—Per ton or whatever it is?

A.—What it is.

Q.—And you are bound to do whatever work is incurred?

A.—Regardless of what it is you have to do it and you get paid at that price.

Q.—And no possibility of any extras?

A.—No extras.

Q.—But it does result in variations?

A.—Nearly always.

Q.—That is the contract usually overruns?

A.—Oh, away over.

Q.—What is the common thing for them to overrun? How much?

A.—Well, we haven't done much for the Highways here but I know for the Drury Government, several of our own cases, we ran away over 100 per cent. and several of the others far more than that, that I know of.

Q.—Is an overrun of one hundred per cent. quite common and to be expected?

A.—To be expected, and more so in the north country because up there where there are culverts to be built, when you start in you cannot tell what drainage system—for instance on the Copper Cliff, you could not tell what tile was required until you got into it and see what draining is required.

Q.—Didn't know whether you were going to run into muskeg or what was there?

A.—No.

Q.—And the drainage must be regulated?

A.—They found it necessary, the engineers, after we were well under way in constructing the road, to build eighteen inch or thirty-six inch pipe away out into the swamp to get drains.

Q.—Off the road?

A.—Off the road altogether otherwise that road would not have been any good.

Q.—You were telling my friend, Mr. Fisher, that a large quantity of this road, or seven miles, was supposed to have been metalled?

A.—Yes.

Q.—And turned out it was not?

A.—Certainly wasn't.

Q.—That deceived everybody?

A.—Yes.

Q.—You thought there was that much stone there that could be handled.

A.—We had been given that information.

Q.—Then we have been told they changed the levels?

A.—There was a number of changes in levels along the road, changing the course.

Q.—General improvements?

A.—As they found necessary to do as they went along.

Q.—The change in levels increased the quantities?

A.—Yes, the biggest was where they found this bridge gave out. When they got ready to built they found the bridge was gone. It was necessary to divert the road, which they did, and put in a permanent bridge.

Q.—What percentage would the diversions of the road—I think there were four or five diversions?

A.—Four, I think.

Q.—What percentage of increase would that cost?

A.—Well, I think that big one would be half nearly of the extra earth.

Q.—You mean the big diversion would increase the percentage fifty per cent.?

A.—I mean it would take nearly half of the extra earth excavation.

Q.—Beyond the estimate?

A.—Yes.

Q.—And the rock?

A.—Well, there was several places—yes, the rock on two of those diversions would take over half.

Q.—So that the result that has startled my friend is something that was reasonably to be expected?

A.—Absolutely.

Q.—And comparing it with the previous government, you say it is moderate, is it?

A.—Yes. At the rate the overruns were down here on this kind of work, why they would have been fifteen times as high because tendering here they had the quantities.

Q.—Down here you know what you are doing?

A.—Yes.

Q.—Up there you don't know what it is?

A.—Different country altogether.

Q.—My friend, Mr. Raney, seemed to be confused. As I remember your evidence, you didn't purchase any material from the Lyons Company for the building of this Conniston or Copper Cliff or South Porcupine?

A.—We didn't purchase a cent's worth of material from Lyons on any government job whatever or any of the three jobs.

Q.—No Lyons' materials went into any of the jobs?

MR. FISHER: It is quite clear there were no plans available?

A.—We never get plans.

Q.—There were no cross-sections?

A.—Well, we never get cross-sections.

Q.—There were not any here?

A.—We don't see any.

Q.—And what you say, it was to be expected there would be a good deal of overrun?

A.—Which?

Q.—It was to be expected for instance on the Sudbury road you would have a considerable quantity of earth excavations?

A.—Yes, if they built the road right they would have to take out considerable earth.

Q.—And in parts you might strike rock?

A.—Well, that would be found out after you got into the job.

Q.—That was to be expected in that country?

A.—There is a lot of rock there, yes.

Q.—It was certain you were going to put in concrete culverts?

A.—No, it was not.

Q.—Weren't you going to put in culverts?

A.—It was a question whether they would put in pipe or culverts.

Q.—You would have to put in some sort of thing?

A.—Either pipe or concrete culverts.

Q.—And you would expect considerable amounts under these items, wouldn't you?

A.—Well, if they put in pipe culverts, of course it would not have run so high. They would not have been so good.

Q.—So it would make a good deal of difference to the Government what the price of the contractor was on all these items?

A.—Yes, it would make a difference.

Q.—And if one contractor happened to be high on all but one of them, or all but two of them, that is a matter they might reasonably have taken into account?

A.—Well, they couldn't, everybody would figure on the items according to what he was figuring, he would want to do them providing there was any done.

Q.—Nobody knew that a good many of those items would have to be done.

MR. FINLAYSON: That is what they are asked for.

MR. FISHER: And where a contractor is awarded a contract on three items and he was high on all the rest except one, it would be evident to the Department that he was going to get a lot more money by reason of the fact that he was high on the others?

A.—Depend on the price and the quantities.

Q.—And your price was higher than the other on all the items that went in except two?

A.—Well, if the price that was in one of the Toronto papers the other night was correct, the figures, the man certainly never figured on having any of that material to take out, that is a sure thing.

Q.—You think he was very low on it?

A.—I know it.

Q.—And he was low on concrete, apparently? His price for concrete was sixteen and yours twenty-four?

A.—Well, that is not the price I saw.

Q.—Twenty-four on the Sudbury-Conniston?

A.—I was referring to the Copper Cliff.

Q.—And he was, you think, unreasonably low on a lot of these figures.

A.—Well, I didn't see them. I don't know what they were.

MR. FINLAYSON: Was there any collusion between you and Laberge over this tender?

A.—Absolutely not.

MR. KEMP: How do you arrive at your unit on the yard basis for moving soil? Is that measured on the wagon or solid?

A.—Solid.

Q.—Is that the same system you always tender on?

A.—Same system.

Q.—For all your tenders?

A.—Yes.

Q.—Same system is in vogue now as under the Drury Government?

A.—Same tender form, I believe, yes.

Q.—And the whole matter would be adjusted between the contractor and the engineer rather than between the contractor and the Government?

A.—Adjusted by the engineer altogether, practically.

MR. FINLAYSON: He is the final arbitrator.

MR. CALLAN: The estimated quantity of earth was 500 yards and the ultimate quantity as measured was 11,400. Assuming you had had this full amount of 11,500 yards in front of you when you tendered, would your price have been the same for that quantity as it would have been for five hundred?

A.—It probably would.

MR. WIDDIFIELD: It isn't reasonable to expect you would; and it would be an advantage to the contractor and all concerned that an approximate estimate be made. How do you account for the spread? You made the statement that there was always a spread in the estimate? Why so? If it be invariable why not allow for that and make the estimate higher in every case?

A.—Well, our price on those jobs, and on any jobs—you take those three jobs we tendered on, whether there was quantities shown on the specifications or not—I think there was one job they were not—our prices have regard for the different localities and conditions, and are practically the same. It is impossible to say now whether if the total amount shown now were given would our price be the same. We would have to take into consideration extra equipment and what we wanted, and the extra time. But our price on the three jobs are, practically, the same having regard for the different conditions.

Q.—Was the equipment you were using on the Conniston road Government equipment?

A.—About $90,000 of the equipment belonged to us and we rented equipment valued at about $10,000 from the Government and paid them $6,000.

Q.—Surely.

A.—Yes. That is what they charged us. They charged us more than the Department of Highways.

Mr. FINLAYSON: In other words, just summing up this. You have, in your long experience, you have arrived at what are standard prices for different classes of work?

A.—Yes.

Q.—And the ones you put in on this job were standard prices?

A.—Yes, and they were used on the three jobs regardless of whether there is quantities or not.

HON. MR. RANEY: I think the only other witness is Mr. Fullerton and I suppose he is coming on this evening.

THE CHAIRMAN: Subject to the figures of Mr. Fullerton—

MR. FISHER: There were some figures we were to have last week.

MR. FINLAYSON: All I can say is some were prepared and then Mr. Raney wanted some more. Perhaps it was my fault. I have been busy to-day, so there would be no misunderstanding I got a memo and based—

HON. MR. RANEY: Mr. Fullerton has what we wanted the other day.

J. H. Ferguson re-called.

THE CHAIRMAN: You are already sworn.

HON. MR. RANEY: You were to have found out for the Committee how much of these Parliament Buildings, because you say there are three, how much of the insurance on these Parliament Buildings is retained by Burns & Ferguson?

A.—$650,450.

Q.—That is quite different from what you said last night?

A.—Well, I would sooner tell you I had more and show you I had less.

Q.—I just wanted—

A.—Approximately half, I said.

Q.—You told us last that your total insurance was $3,444,000?

A.—No, sir, I said $3,488,000.

Q.—And your thought then was about half of that was retained by your firm?

A.—Yes, sir

THE CHAIRMAN: I think we should remember he said he didn't have the exact figures and he said he would estimate half.

Q.—Now you find the exact quantity of insurance retained by your firm is $650,450?

A.—Yes, sir.

Q.—And you say your firm has no interest, receives no benefit from the rest of this insurance?

A.—No, sir.

Q.—What are the commissions then on the quantity of insurance you retain for your own firm?

A.—The premium on that? You probably want the premium?

Q.—Yes.

A.—$3,349.82.

Q.—On $650,000?

A.—Yes, sir.

Q.—That much a year?

A.—No, that is for three years.

Q.—And what is your firm's interests?

A.—Commission? It would be about seventeen per cent.

Q.—That is net, I suppose?

A.—No, that doesn't include my time, an engineer's time and extra help which we employ.

Q.—It includes some overhead, I suppose?

A.—That seventeen per cent.?

Q.—Yes?

A.—Yes. That is not net.

Q.—What is the gross?

A.—The gross would be about twenty-two per cent. of that.

Q.—You deduct certain items and find a net of seventeen per cent.?

A.—Yes, sir. We find our overhead on our office is about eight and one-half per cent.

Q.—You say that is seventeen per cent.?

A.—$3,349.82.

Q.—Of that?

A.—Yes.

Q.—And that is all your advantage in it?

A.—Yes.

Q.—You are not under salary from the Government, that is all the advantage you have?

A.—Yes, sir.

Q.—Then I wanted, Mr. Finlayson, this is the more important matter, the insurance premiums for the past ten years paid by the Government, and the moneys collected from the companies during the same period?

MR. FINLAYSON: You didn't ask me for that?

HON. MR. RANEY: Yes, I did. I wanted the man brought here.

MR. FINLAYSON: You did?

HON. MR. RANEY: I handed Mr. Finlayson the questions I wanted him to answer. You have it here.

MR. FINLAYSON: I didn't get them. This is the first time I have heard about this ten year business.

HON. MR. RANEY: They were on the order paper at one time and they were taken off because it was said the answers involved too much detail.

MR. FINLAYSON: This is the first I have even heard of this ten years.

HON. MR. RANEY: Look in your files.

Mr. Finlayson: I think you are mistaken.

Hon. Mr. Raney: I scored out two of the questions.

Mr. Finlayson: You told me you would like to find out which officer of the department was in charge of insurance?

Hon. Mr. Raney: Then I handed you these questions, two of them scored out.

Mr. Finlayson: Get somebody here.

Mr. MacBride: Are we going to investigate information for the last ten years?

The Chairman: I took up with Mr. Henry the question of securing the attendance of the officers in the department who handle this insurance business. First, I want to say, as I was going to suggest, if when you had put in your resolution calling for the attendance of Mr. Ferguson you had explained exactly what you wanted to get we could have it?

Hon. Mr. Raney: My information was he had the information.

Member: Your information wasn't correct.

The Chairman: Mr. Henry says so far as this building was concerned—I took up the matter with Mr. Henry—so far as this building was concerned, he said the matter was handled with Mr. Squire through Mr. Ferguson, by Mr. Squire, who was then Deputy Minister of Public Works, so far as the insurance generally of the public works is concerned—

Member: Mr. McNaughton?

The Chairman: The man in charge of that particular work. We tried to get Mr. McNaughton's presence but he is ill, we learned when we went out to get him to be present at the Committee.

Hon. Mr. Raney: Mr. Hogarth could get the information for me I think in five minutes. Mr. McNaughton showed me a file which carried this information and if he will send for them—

Mr. Ferguson: I have all Mr. McNaughton has in his files but they don't control or look after all the insurance carried by the Government. There is no department doing—

Hon. Mr. Raney: Well, if I could get the major item. Look at that file? How do you come to have it?

A.—This is an exact copy. We were asked to supervise this insurance, to find out whether anything was wrong with the insurance and found there was and naturally we kept copies of all our records in connection with this building and outside.

Q.—Have you the file Mr. McNaughton brought to my office the other day?

A.—I have a copy of it which will show the insurance handled by his company.

Q.—Mr. McNaughton brought to my office a file he had prepared.

A.—We prepared that for him. I think you will recognize that, showing who our agents are; here is another.

Hon. Mr. Raney: I asked the question. The question was put on the order paper and the answer was prepared, and apparently after the answer had been prepared the Prime Minister, perhaps not knowing of it, said my question was too elaborate, and asked me to simplify. I took it off to put on a simpler one; meantime the material had been prepared for the other. One of the questions asked: What was the total amount of premiums paid by the Province during the past ten years and the answer which was produced on this file of Mr. McNaughton's showed the amount was $98,368.26.

And the other: What was the amount of the money paid by the insurance companies during that time and the answer was $1,708.29.

WITNESS: That isn't correct.

HON. MR. RANEY: Don't you worry. I was not addressing you.

MR. FINLAYSON: What you want to get on the records is—

HON. MR. RANEY: I want to get on the records the figures which will substantiate an argument that this Province ought to carry its own insurance. I am not blaming anybody.

MR. FINLAYSON: No, no. Perfectly proper.

THE CHAIRMAN: The only criticism I have is we could have had it prepared in advance.

MR. MACBRIDE: Mr. Raney has very clearly told us his purpose. He wants to get this information to put it on the records of this Public Accounts Committee for the purpose of advocating that the Province carry its own insurance. But is this the place to do this? Is that the duty of the Public Accounts to do so?

THE CHAIRMAN: I don't think there is any objection to doing it.

MR. FINLAYSON: It is manifestly in the public interest.

MR. MACBRIDE: I have asked for a ruling.

THE CHAIRMAN: I am not going to prevent this information being brought forward and put in the records. If he wants it we will produce it.

MR. FISHER: Do your companies reinsure all these risks?

A.—I presume they do, but I would not like to say because I have nothing to do with the management of the company.

Q.—Do you know whether they reinsure them in Canadian companies or American?

A.—I presume they reinsure them all over the world. That is the general practice.

Q.—All over the world?

A.—Yes, sir. France, Switzerland and Germany.

MR. FINLAYSON: Did you look up the other matter we were talking of finding out, what was paid to Mr. Watson?

A.—I find one item, this is an old book, we destroy these applications for automobile insurance after three years, but we kept this book. On September 13th, Mr. Watson—that is Mr. Edgar Watson.

Q.—What year?

A.—1922. He received a commission, Department of Highways Account, $325.58.

Q.—Department of Highways?

A.—$325.58.

Q.—What did that cover?

A.—The only highways insurance that he placed, that is at that time, was automobile insurance.

Q.—What?

A.—The only highway insurance he would place, that is what, automobile insurance.

Q.—Does that mean that on the insurance that he placed on the motor cars he got $325 for himself?

A.—Yes.

Q.—Less the three dollars for his taking out the insurance license?

A.—I don't know anything about that.

Q.—He had to do that?

A.—He would have to do that.

Q.—What did he get on this other insurance, this cheque?

A.—I cannot find that item.

Q.—What about Mr. Ramsden?

A.—Mr. Ramsden didn't place the business directly with me, therefore we would not pay him commission; if he received any he will probably deny he received it. I know Mr. Watson told me it was split.

THE CHAIRMAN: That is not your own knowledge?

MR. FINLAYSON: We want to be fair. You have no knowledge of any payment to him?

A.—No.

Q.—But you do know Mr. Watson, North Victoria, got $325 in September, 1922, when he was a member?

A.—Yes, sir.

Q.—And that was a premium?

A.—Commission.

Q.—Commission on insurance he placed on Government cars?

A.—Yes.

MR. MACBRIDE: The 13th of September? Was it Friday?

A.—I cannot say.

MR. HILLMER: Do you know from personal knowledge that Mr. Ramsden placed any insurance with any other companies?

A.—I know that practically the half of the automobile that reached the Royal Insurance Company through the Royal Insurance Company where Mr. Ramsden had office space. I know that.

HON. MR. RANEY: You are very eager. You are too sharp on the bit, I think.

A.—We have been brought up here. Our firm has been exhibited to a certain amount of criticism and doubt for saving the Government five thousand on this building and two thousand on your automobile stuff. I think we are entitled to get up—

HON. MR. RANEY: That is all this. We are through with the insurance. We have just the two matters, the Caledon matters. We have the Caledon Mountain matter and we would like these officials.

MR. FINLAYSON: Did you consider the statement the Premier made?

MR. RANEY: I think we would clean it up.

MR. FINLAYSON: I have a memo I will give it to you if you would like to consider it.

MR. RANEY: Well, let them be here to-night if you please.

THE CHAIRMAN: You want Mr. Brown?

MR. RANEY: I want Mr. Brown and Mr. Hogarth and Mr. Squire is not here. And Mr. Fullerton, of course.

The Committee then adjourned until 8 o'clock the same evening.

PUBLIC ACCOUNTS COMMITTEE.

Tuesday, March 30th, 8 P.M.

A. C. Lewis, Chairman of the Committee, presiding.

CHAIRMAN: Now gentlemen, whom do you want to go ahead with first?

MR. FISHER: Can we get through with Mr. Fullerton?

CHAIRMAN: Certainly.

MR. FISHER: It will only take a few minutes, I imagine.

C. H. Fullerton, called; on stand.

CHAIRMAN: Mr. Fullerton has already been sworn.

(Examination by Mr. Fisher).

Q.—Mr. Fullerton, in connection with the Creighton-Copper Cliff road, you were to figure out how the different tenders would have worked out, applying the actual quantities that were paid for. What are your results?

A.—Well, I did not understand it just in that way. I took the actual quantities and found out which would have been the lowest tender had the actual quantities been known and applied the unit prices of the contractors and I worked that one out. That is the only one I have.

Q.—You have the one which would have worked out the lowest?

A.—Yes.

Q.—The man who would have got the tender if you had had the actual quantities. Well, what is the result?

A.—You mean in dollars and cents?

Q.—Yes.

A.—There is another contractor who would have been lower.

Q.—What?

A.—There is another contractor who would have been lower.

Q.—Working out the McNamaras got the contract at the Labarge figures?

A.—Yes.

Q.—What did you pay the McNamaras?

MR. FINLAYSON: I did not understand you meant it in that way. You mean on the assignment?

MR. RANEY: No, no.

WITNESS: I did not mean that.

MR. FINLAYSON: I did not think you did,

CHAIRMAN: What Mr. Fisher meant was the total amount paid to the McNamaras under the contract.

WITNESS: $135,063.50.

MR. FISHER: That is what the contract cost you?

WITNESS: Yes.

Q.—What was the cost if the Warren Bituminous Company had got the contract?

A.—$114,050.86.

CHAIRMAN: That is the total working out the actual quantities at the price they quoted?

WITNESS: Yes. Now, of course, I applied there to both of them the same items for force account and the deduction for equipment rental and that sort of thing.

MR. FISHER: Assuming they had rented the same equipment as the McNamaras?

MR. FINLAYSON: You assumed they would have rented the same material from the Department?

MR. RANEY: He made the conditions correspond.

MR. FISHER: Now, Mr. Fullerton, I have had this worked out and according to the figures given me there would have been six tenderers ahead of Labarge on the actual quantities. Is that right?

A.—I don't know. I don't think so.

Mr. Raney: How many do you make?

Mr. Fisher: Did you figure any of the others?

Witness: Yes.

Mr. Fisher: How many did you figure would have been lower?

Witness: Three.

Mr. Fisher: What are they?

Mr. Finlayson: Do your figures agree with him on the Warren one?

Mr. Fisher: Yes, practically.

Witness: Yes, six, including the McNamaras.

Q.—Would have been lower?

A.—Yes.

Q.—According to my figures the McNamaras would have been the highest of the lot.

A.—No, the McNamaras were lower on that basis.

Q.—Talking about the result? You understand that do you?

A.—Yes.

Q.—You say there would have been six ahead of the Labarge, including McNamara?

A.—Yes.

Q.—What would the McNamara have cost?

A.—$134,094.02.

Q.—Have you got the summary on each item?

A.—Yes.

Q.—Will you give them?

A.—Number one, $11,417; two, $21,875; three, $44,695.98; four, $42,866.32; five, $13,940; six, $7,360; eight, $19,795.

Q.—What about seven?

A.—Nothing for seven. It is a blank.

Q.—Eight is $19,975?

A.—Nine, $2,258.65; ten, $3,360.60; that totals, $123,702.23.

Q.—There was nothing for eleven, twelve, thirteen or fourteen?

A.—Nothing.

Q.—What about thirteen? ·

A.—There was no thirteen.

Q.—This 18, C.I. pipe?

A.—That was an extra.

Q.—You have added extras in?

A.—Yes.

Q.—What is your mark for?

A.—Ten thousand six hundred and thirteen dollars and seventy-nine cents to be added, that makes the $134,000.

Q.—Have you got that separate? Pipe and shoulders were added?

Chairman: He has added on force account, $10,613.79.

Witness: Yes, $10,613.79, that is the force account and equipment rental, $1,222 deducted.

Mr. Fisher: How much does all this amount to?

A.—For the McNamaras? $134,094.

Mr. Fisher: We had it $170,000 something.

Chairman: Let me check your figures.

Witness: Perhaps, if I gave you one of these sheets the same as mine—

Mr. Fisher: I guess you gave us four and three and only should have given us one.

Mr. Raney: That was asphalt penetration?

Witness: Yes, I gave both tar and asphalt.

Chairman: That is what makes the difference.

Witness: They would be on tar.

Chairman: At what price?

Witness: At the tar price—at the lowest price, whichever it was—asphalt.

Chairman: Take out the tar penetration price.

Mr. Fisher: McNamara lower than Labarge. There were six you say who would have been lower on the actual quantities that went into the work?

Witness: Yes.

Mr. Finlayson: That seems to dispose of any question of collusion.

Mr. Raney: Not necessarily.

Mr. Fisher: I don't say anything about collusion. I don't know enough about it to know.

Mr. Finlayson: You giving us all the results certainly disposes of that.

Mr. Fisher: I will not make any remarks that might not be fair.

Mr. Finlayson: We will reserve judgment.

Mr. Fisher: There was another job too—the Timmins-South Porcupine road?

Witness: Yes.

Q.—And the McNamaras got that contract too, did they?

A.—Yes.

Q.—At what price? Were there only two tenderers?

A.—On the Timmins-South Porcupine?

Q.—Yes.

A.—No.

Q.—You have prepared a schedule like in the others?

A.—There were eight tenderers.

Q.—Have you got the schedule?

A.—Yes.

Q.—Can we have a copy?

A.—I have got the office copy.

Q.—Have you two?

A.—No, just the one.

Mr. Raney: We could put that in, I suppose.

Q.—How were the tenders on that job?

A.—The McNamaras were the lowest tenderers on the quantities given.

Q.—Will you give us the figures?

A.—On the tar penetration, $132,000—

Q.—Which was successful?

A.—McNamara.

Q.—Tar penetration went in?

A.—Tar went in.

Q.—Suppose you give us the tar?

A.—One hundred and thirty-two thousand and forty-eight dollars and seventy-nine cents; $136,941.39—

Q.—Who was that?

A.—Grant Brothers. Although tar went in they had the option of tar or asphalt. McNamaras tendered the same on both.

Q.—I suppose you awarded the contract on the tar penetration did you, not on the asphalt?

A.—We picked out the lowest.

CHAIRMAN: I think probably the system is this, speaking subject to correction, when the alternative tenders were quoted they accepted the lowest figure and the contractor would put in whichever he wished, tar or asphalt, but they took the lowest figure.

WITNESS: That is correct.

MR. FISHER: Well, I guess we had better have both figures.

WITNESS: Well, I will name the contractors and will give first the tar and then the asphalt figures opposite each contractor.

CHAIRMAN: Better take them in order.

(Witness reads figures as follow):

	Tar	Asphalt
Curran and Briggs............	$185,540 57	$185,540 57
Chisholm Construction Co.....	145,248 50	No price.
Dominion Construction Co....	193,384 00	193,384 00
Goodson Construction Co......	191,271 00	188,368 42
McNamara Construction Co...	132,049 79	132,049 79
Grant Brothers...............	139,263 51	136,941 39
St. Denis and Mooney........	157,857 59	154,374 41
Warren Bituminous Co........	187,736 57	187,736 57

MR. FISHER: On the quantities tendered, McNamara was low?

A.—Yes.

Q.—Chisholm's were next were they?

A.—Yes.

Q.—Those quantities, were they arbitrary quantities?

A.—No.

Q.—What were these?

A.—They were estimated on the quantities turned in by our engineering staff.

Q.—Well, now, how were they made up? From cross-sections?

A.—From measurements on the ground.

Q.—Sometimes you did have quantities?

A.—Yes.

Q.—These were the quantities the engineers gave?

A.—Yes.

Q.—Well, now, taking the quantities that actually went into the work, what was the result? You paid the McNamaras how much?

A.—Two hundred and fifty-eight thousand seven hundred and fifty-four dollars and forty-eight cents.

Q.—Who would have been lower?

A.—Chisholm.

Q.—What would you have paid him?

A.—Two hundred and seven thousand two hundred and twenty-six dollars and ten cents.

MR. RANEY: Fifty-one thousand dollars difference?

WITNESS: Yes.

MR. FISHER: Can you tell us where the difference arose chiefly?

A.—You mean accounting for the additional quantities?

A.—Yes.

A.—Well, after the whole matter had been settled up I was anxious to know about that time why the quantities were so great, the excess was so great over the original quantities. Of course, I knew this: that comparing work in the northern country, comparatively new ground, with the work in older Ontario there was bound to be some difference. I did not know how great. In Old Ontario, I suppose, all this land has been cleared for a hundred years and in that 100 years it must have changed a great deal, and as the drainage becomes better it becomes consolidated, humus has disappeared, everything in the nature of muck and vegetable growth and all that kind of thing has disappeared and it is pretty hard to make comparisons with work in practically virgin soil. The excess quantities are bound to be much greater where conditions like those in Northern Ontario prevail. Climatic conditions have something to do with it too, and the moisture remains longer in the soil and there is greater settlement. However, I wrote to the district engineer to get his reason why the quantities were greater than he estimated. This was his answer.

MR. FINLAYSON: When was this?

WITNESS: I wrote in January and got this letter on February the 6th. It reads as follows:

Dear sir,

Re Timmins-South Porcupine Road, your letter of January 27th:

The quantities estimated for this road were based on similar types of roads in older Ontario and at the time it was not realized that there was so much difference in the sub-grade. The condition of the sub-grade was directly responsible in every case for the over-running of the estimates. Also owing to the very limited time in which these quantities were taken out and computed it was impossible to investigate the quantities and conditions as thoroughly as they should have been.

The sub-grade at this time was considered sufficiently firm enough for this type of roadway, but when the actual operations were commenced it was found that in a great many places it was too soft and long stretches had to be excavated and filled with rock. Owing to the extremely wet season of 1925 the drainage plans, and the then drainage system, proved absolutely inadequate to properly drain the sub-grade and a great deal of additional drainage was required. The ditches had to be deepened practically along the entire roadway and the off-take ditches correspondingly to be lengthened and deepened. The fill at the McIntyre mine settled considerably more than was anticipated and to bring this up to grade it was necessary to overrun the estimated cost of this section. The fill was over four hundred feet in length and over twenty feet high at its greatest depth.

The rock throughout this section is very flat and without borings it was impossible to estimate the quantity that would likely be encountered with any degree of accuracy.

Owing to the soft, spongy nature of the sub-grade it was necessary to carry the footings of the concrete culvert to a greater depth than was estimated.

The additional agricultural tile was used in draining a great many soft spots that were not considered wet enough to require this during the preliminary investigation. It was found that all the hills required agricultural tile and that the streets throughout the most of South Porcupine were so soft and spongy that they were practically tiled throughout.

Owing to the yielding conditions of the sub-grade it was necessary to use a great deal of extra stone to bring up the depressions that were continually developing, and to insure a firm and solid base throughout. To have kept the finished surface up to the original grade, throughout the entire length of the road, would have required a great many more yards, but it was not considered of sufficient importance to do this and although the amount of stone used was greatly in excess of the estimated quantity yet had the original design been closely adhered to this quantity would have been still greater.

To protect the edge of the bituminous top it was considered necessary that a stone shoulder should be carried throughout the entire length of the road. It had been found that without this shouldering the traffic cut the earth shoulder abruptly down to the base on the edge of the top and caused a break up.

The earth shoulders were included in excavation and as the cost of trimming them and stone shoulders was the same, this was included in one item.

If any similar type of roadway is constructed throughout this district I would suggest that the work be carried on over several years so as to allow each separate of the operations to become consolidated before succeeding ones are laid. By doing this I think a cheaper and better road would be constructed.   (Signed) H. D. Duff, Engineer.

MR. FISHER: When was this road constructed?

WITNESS: During the season of 1925. It was commenced in 1924.

Q.—When were the tenders called for?

A.—August of 1924.

Q.—Who was the engineer?

A.—H. F. Duff.

Q.—What had he done before?

A.—He had handled work in the Northern Development for several years.

Q.—Built some roads?

A.—Yes.

A.—And to what extent had he built roads?

A.—Our expenditure up there must have been $600,000 or $800,000 a year.

MR. FINLAYSON: In his district?

WITNESS: Yes.

MR. FISHER: Can you see any reason why this man would base figures on Southern Ontario?

A.—This was the first hard road he had constructed.

Q.—What other kind of road had he built before?

A.—All gravel roads and clay roads.

Q.—Drainage on them would be the same?

A.—No. He would have to go to greater expense with a road with a hard top. It would cost more to make the foundation for and drain the road upon which an expensive top was being placed.

Q.—A man who had been up there all this time should know that the conditions were considerably different from those in Southern Ontario?

A.—Well, of course, it was his first experience with a hard-top road and his first experience running a ten-ton roller over that kind of soil.

Q.—He did not make much of a success of it?

A.—I am not prepared to say that.

Mr. Fullerton examined by Mr. Raney.

Q.—Mr. Fullerton, you were to have found out for me in respect of the Sudbury-Coniston road the date of the advertisement for tenders, the date of opening and the date of the receipt of the engineer's cross-sections?

A.—I will start with the last one you mentioned. I want to make an explanation with regard to that. When I was last here I was absolutely convinced that these cross-sections did not reach the office before this work was advertised. As a matter of fact I was not certain that they reached the office for a month after the work was advertised and when I went upstairs after leaving this room I mentioned it to one of the officials that I had said we had not received the cross-sections when the work was advertised. He said, "I think you are quite correct." I said, "Hunt it up in the fyle," and he did and he found that these sections had been received on the second of June.

Q.—1924?

A.—1924. Now I can easily understand why I was perfectly certain they had not been received because I find that I had been absent from the office at that time and for some days before and that I did not return to the office until the ninth day of June, a week after they had arrived and on that date instructions were given to prepare the advertising.

Mr. Fisher: What date?

Witness: June the ninth and on the tenth the advertisements were sent to the papers.

Mr. Raney: The tenth of June the advertisements were sent.

Witness: Now you will understand that so far as the staff was concerned that was not routine work. Work that came through in my absence would be handled by the office and taken care of and at that season of the year, of course, everybody was busy getting ready for the season's work and I can easily understand how they came to escape anybody's notice. I am not prepared to say whether that was drawn to my attention.

Q.—Who prepared the advertisements for the tenderers?

A.—I think the chief engineer.

Q.—You don't know what instructions he had?

A.—The instructions he had—

Q.—You don't know?

A.—Yes, I do. Instructions were given to prepare the advertisement.

Q.—You did not give any instructions with reference to the cross-sections— you did not give any instructions with respect to the resident engineer's cross-sections. Those cross-sections ought to have been worked out so as to have made specific quantities for the earth excavation and the rock excavation and so on?

A.—Of course they stood a week until I returned. There was nothing done and I could not expect them to have done anything. They had not received any instructions.

Q.—Did the chief engineer know that the cross-sections had come in?

A.—Yes.

Q.—Surely he would know that in preparing the advertisement he would have to work out the cross-sections to get the quantities?

A.—Yes.

Q.—Why didn't he do it?

A.—He had not been instructed. I had not told him.

Q.—Maybe someone else—

A.—No. If he knew the cross-sections were there he had to have time.

Q.—Why didn't you give instructions?

A.—At the time it was too late to work the cross-sections.

Q.—Didn't he know the work was to be advertised?

A.—He did not know until the tenth.

Q.—The coming in of the cross-sections would be evidence to you, to any intelligent man, there would be an advertisement for tenders?

A.—At some date.

Q.—Wouldn't he inquire, "What are you going to do about these cross-sections"?

A.—He probably did. When I returned on the tenth—

Q.—How long would it take to work out the quantities from the cross-sections?

A.—Well, it would have taken, to make an accurate estimate, probably two or three weeks.

Q.—To make an approximate estimate?

A.—I don't know.

Q.—A day or two?

A.—Impossible.

Q.—How long for an approximate estimate?

A.—Any kind of an estimate that an engineer would be responsible for would take at least ten days or two weeks.

Q.—Any kind would be better than no estimate at all—an approximate estimate would be better than no estimate at all?

A.—I think that is correct.

Q.—So, as a matter of fact you went ahead and advertised the work with no quantities, no engineers' quantities except the concrete pavement, scarifying and reshaping and trimming and levelling earth shoulders, length and breadth of the road, nothing with regard to excavation?

A.—No.

Q.—Well, now, is that all the explanation you have to give of the absence of specifications?

A.—Yes.

Q.—And do you know as a matter of knowledge now, can you tell the Committee now why the cross-sections were not used and why these quantities were not given in the specifications?

A.—Well, because when the cross-sections reached the office I was not there to give any directions.

Q.—Your correspondence would have shown that was to happen in your absence? Were your instructions verbal or written as to the building of the road—the instructions that came to you?

A.—Verbal.

Q.—From whom?

A.—With regard to this road?

Q.—Yes, to you.

A.—They could only come from the Minister.

Q.—When did you get them? When did you know the road was to be built?

A.—I must have known about it in May.

Q.—In the early part of June, when these cross-sections came in, your duties were being performed by the man next under you?

A.—The cross-sections were not being taken by him.

Q.—Your duties were being performed by somebody, what is his name, the chief engineer? He performed your duties? Were you ill?

A.—As far as routine work was concerned—

Q.—Were you ill?

A.—I was in Northern Ontario.

Q.—Did he know the road was to be built?

A.—I think he did.

Q.—Well, then, why was not anything done?

A.—He did not have sufficient information to go ahead.

Q.—The telephone was working I suppose and the telegraph lines were in operation?

A.—In order to make use of the cross-sections, he must know the grade and width of the pavement.

Q.—That would be before him in the material?

A.—No.

Q.—Not the length?

A.—Yes.

Q.—And the breadth?

A.—Yes.

Q.—And the depth?

A.—We didn't have the depth.

Q.—Because you did not work the cross-sections, that was the only reason?

A.—Up to that time the chief engineer did not know the width of the road we had decided to build.

Q.—All that could be found out from you in the north country by letter or telephone or telegraph?

A.—Yes.

Q.—Why was it not? It was apparently some one's neglect or some instructions from someone—one or the other?

A.—The chief engineer or the office staff, when those cross-sections came in, were not seized with the importance—

Q.—You say the chief engineer knew the road was to be built?

A.—Yes.

Q.—And that summer, 1924?

A.—I don't know he knew that.

Q.—I guess we won't get any further into that. You were to give me the same information about the Creighton-Copper Cliff road—the date of the advertisement for tenders, the date of opening of the tenders and the date of the receipt from the resident engineer of the cross-sections.

A.—Well, so far as the receipt of cross-sections of the Creighton-Copper Cliff is concerned, I don't think we received any cross-sections until the work was finished.

Q.—What was the date of the advertisement for tenders?

MR. FINLAYSON: Which road is that?

MR. RANEY: Creighton-Copper Cliff.

WITNESS: I think some time in August. I have not the date. We did not get any cross-sections.

Q.—You say you were going to start on the work that year?

A.—We intended to start that fall.

Q.—Did you, really?

A.—Yes.

Q.—Why? You could not finish in the fall?

A.—No.

Q.—You know you said of the Sudbury-Conniston, "We are going to start and finish in 1924." You could not possibly finish this in 1924?

A.—No.

Q.—What was the tremendous urge about starting this road in 1924?

A.—Well, I suppose local pressure had a good deal to do with it and, of course, it was not expected that it would be the formidable proposition it turned out.

Q.—With reference to the Coniston road you said there was some difficulty with frost in May, in getting the test pits?

A.—I did not tell you that. Hoskins—

CHAIRMAN: That was Mr. Finlayson's evidence.

Q.—Were there test pits in the Sudbury-Coniston road?

A.—I don't know.

Q.—There were cross-sections. How was it cross-sections were not prepared for the Creighton-Copper Cliff road?

A.—My recollection is that the instructions were given to the district engineer to prepare cross-sections of the Creighton-Copper Cliff road, but the man who was sent out to do the work took ill and they were not turned in here in time to advertise the work. I don't know when they were turned in.

Q.—They never came in?

A.—Sometime.

Q.—That was not good engineering practice, not to have turned them in at all?

A.—Yes.

Q.—Well, of course, the contract was let by that time. It was not good practice to go on with the Creighton-Copper Cliff road without cross-sections? It was not good business to advertise until you were able to work out the quantities?

A.—Well, I——

Q.—It is not good business to advertise a road to cost $40,000 or $50,000 a mile until you know something about the quantities?

A.—We did not anticipate that it was going to cost $40,000 or $50,000 a mile.

Q.—Even if it cost only $20,000 a mile?

A.—It would have been better business to secure the cross-sections.

Q.—What was the earth excavation in the Creighton-Copper Cliff road? Five hundred cubic yards?

A.—Yes.

Q.—Who made that arbitrary figure?

A.—I don't recall that.

Q.—You were responsible?

A.—Yes.

Q.—You know it was 500 yards of earth excavation, arbitrary quantity, and it turned out to be 11,400 yards by actual quantity?

A.—Yes.

Q.—That was not good engineering was it?

A.—I don't know whether that is——

Q.—Mark you, now, you are starting out to advertise in August; no difficulty then in getting test pits; no difficulty in making cross-sections was there?

A.—No.

Q.—What was the tremendous urgency in going on with the work before you had cross-sections to work out the quantities?

A.—I suppose it was thought it was practically a matter of putting on an asphalt, tar surface on the existing road.

Q.—The road that was there had been seen?

A.—Yes.

Q.—I see here you have—and this would not apply to that at all—here you have 100 yards, estimated quantity—it should be arbitrary quantity—100 cubic yards of rock to be excavated and on the other hand the actual quantity was 3,125 yards?

A.—Yes.

Q.—That was not good engineering?

A.—I don't know whether——

Q.—It was not engineering at all. It was guessing, not even guessing.

A.—It was a matter of opinion.

Q.—Not a matter of opinion.

A.—It was thought the old road would be satisfactory to put a surface on.

MR. FINLAYSON: The grade was changed.

WITNESS: It was a matter of improving the existing grade.

MR. RANEY: Who instructed you to go on with the Creighton-Copper Cliff without waiting for cross-sections?

A.—Well, that did not come into it. It was because of advertising——

Q.—Who instructed you to advertise without being able to put quantities into the specifications?

A.—Naturally the only place I could get instructions was from the Minister of the Department?

Q.—Yes.

MR. FINLAYSON: Just to clear up the question, I want to be satisfied with the answer. Witness says the only instructions came from the Minister, but he has not said he said, "Go ahead. Advertise without the cross-sections."

MR. RANEY: He instructed you to go ahead without having the quantities worked out?

WITNESS: I wanted to explain that was not one of the conditions of the instructions. The Minister would not give me instructions about that.

MR. RANEY: Would it not—

MR. FINLAYSON: Let witness explain.

WITNESS: The Minister did not put it that way. He did not say, "Not having the cross-sections, Mr. Fullerton, and not having the information, go ahead and advertise."

MR. RANEY: Of course, I know that, but did the Minister know when he instructed you to go on with the advertising of the work that you did not have the information on which to base estimates for the quantities of excavation?

A.—I don't know that.

Q.—Did you point out to him that you did not have the necessary information to frame specifications?

A.—No. What my views were at the time and what my information was and the impression I had was that this was an old stone road that was going to be surfaced with tar or asphalt top and practically very little excavation, rock or otherwise, would be necessary, and I think the Minister had the same view.

Q.—And you put in 500 cubic yards of earth excavation and there were 11,400 and 100 cubic yards of rock and it turned out to be 3,125 and you put in 500 yards of crushed stone where it turned out 3,959 were required?

A.—Yes.

Q.—You would not defend that as good engineering practice?

MR. FINLAYSON: We had two witnesses who said that could reasonably be expected.

WITNESS: I think under the circumstances when it was discovered that the stone was not in the road that was supposed to be and they were putting on the top and a road that had the cross-roads that had and the steep grades, it was probably good engineering practice to make the improvement.

MR. RANEY: Have you heard, Mr. Fullerton, of a practice of avoiding giving exact engineering information in contracts of this kind in respect of certain large items of the work?

A.—No. I don't think so. I have not.

Q.—Never heard?

A.—You mean avoiding on purpose?

Q.—Have you ever heard of cases of that kind where small quantities were given deliberately on what would be the leading items in the work?

A.—No. Not in my experience.

CHAIRMAN: In connection with those arbitrary amounts, I was interested in your explanation that this was supposed to be road that already had stone and you were going to tar the top. Is it a fair inference from your reply to state that the arbitrary amounts were put in to get unit prices for a protecting tender in case you did come across some?

WITNESS: Yes.

MR. RANEY: Take the earth excavation. I notice that the McNamara's tender and the Labarge tender are each one dollar per cubic yard on the Creighton-Copper Cliff.

MR. FINLAYSON: Seven of them are, I think.

WITNESS: Yes.

MR. RANEY: Applying one dollar per cubic yard to the arbitrary quantity, 500 yards, that would bring it to $500?

A.—Yes.

Q.—Another tendered, Grant Brothers' tender, was fifty cents a yard?

A.—Yes.

Q.—And applying the fifty cents tender of Grant Brothers to the number 11,417 yards actually taken out and applying the dollar tender you would have in that item alone a difference of $5,000, nearly $6,000?

A.—Yes, as it works out.

Q.—Do you see my point?

A.—I see the point.

Q.—Those two items, rock excavation and earth excavation dominate the contract?

MR. FINLAYSON: Grant Brothers were not the lowest.

MR. RANEY: Have a little sense of fairness.

MR. FINLAYSON: He makes a statement all wrong. He says they dominated the contract.

MR. RANEY: Take the next. The arbitrary quantity was 100 yards on rock and the actual quantity 3,125 yards?

WITNESS: Yes.

Q.—McNamara's tender on rock excavation is $7 a cubic yard and Labarge is the same?

A.—Yes.

Q.—And Grant Brothers is $3.50?

A.—Yes.

Q.—The Italian firm is $2.50 a yard?

A.—Yes.

Q.—Again applying the $7 a yard to the larger item, the actual item, and applying the $2.50 a yard, you get a very large difference?

A.—Yes.

Q.—And take further down, 1,800 lineal feet, agricultural tile. I suppose that is arbitrary is it?

A.—Yes.

Q.—And the actual quantity is 9,200. I notice McNamara's tender is eighty cents a foot and Labarge is eighty cents a foot?

A.—Yes.

Q.—And the Italian firm twelve cents a foot. There again, you have a very large item, haven't you?

A.—No; 9,200 at twelve cents—

Q.—The difference between twelve and eight cents—that is about $5,000?

MR. FINLAYSON: They could not be bought wholesale at that price.

MR. RANEY: There's the tender. Take the item, Mr. Fullerton, of crushed stone placed where directed; the arbitrary quantity is 500 cubic yards?

A.—Yes.

Q.—And the actual quantity 3,959?

A.—Yes.

Q.—The Labarge price is $6 a cubic yard?

A.—Yes.

Q.—And the McNamara price $5 a cubic yard?

A.—Yes.

Q.—And the Warren Bituminous $1.50?

A.—Yes.

Q.—So that the Labarge tender is four times as large as the Warren Bituminous?

A.—Yes.

Q.—And that is a large item?

A.—Yes.

Q.—Six dollars a cubic yard—3,959—you have almost $24,000, have you not?

A.—Yes.

Q.—As against the dollar and a half of the Warren Bituminous which would be about $6,000?

A.—Yes.

Q.—These items, I take it, account for the difference between the high tenderer and the light tenderer on the actual quantities of material required on the job?

A.—Yes.

Q.—And what is the difference between the Labarge tender as applied to actual quantities and the low tender as applied to actual quantities on this job?

A.—I think about $20,000.

Q.—And these four items I have referred to would more than amount to that sum?

MR. FINLAYSON: It would more than account for it because you have picked out the low ones.

MR. FISHER: In connection with the Sudbury-Coniston road, you let the contract on three items?

WITNESS: Yes.

Q.—Did you look at the price at all for the other items?

A.—I think it is altogether likely that we looked.

Q.—Did you observe that McNamara was high on all the principal items outside of that?

A.—I don't know what I observed at that time. It is two years ago.

Q.—You observe it now?

A.—Yes.

Q.—Would it not occur to anyone looking at the prices that McNamara would be high in carrying out the work?

A.—No. Not without some knowledge of the quantities that would have to be taken out.

Q.—If there were any considerable quantities they were bound to be high?

A.—There would have to be a considerable amount.

Q.—The difference on the three items was $3,270 was it not?

A.—Something like that.

Q.—If you had had any considerable quantity at all on the other items McNamaras were bound to be high. It would have cost more money would it not?

A.—Yes.

Q.—You did not consider that at the time?

A.—I do not recall it.

Examination by Mr. Finlayson.

Q.—Mr. Fullerton, I suppose it is apparent to anybody that after a few months' study of any problem improvements can be made?

A.—No doubt.

Q.—And sitting down with the benefit of a few of His Majesty's counsel and a committee, holes can be picked in anything?

A.—Yes.

Q.—And the fact is that this work was done in Northern Ontario?

A.—Yes.

Q.—Some of it, take one thing—the South Porcupine-Timmins, was being done in a mining area?

A.—Yes.

Q.—Immediately adjoining the McIntyre properties?

A.—Yes.

Q.—The road is the road over which the mines sent bullion to the station. Do you know enough about it to know that?

A.—The Hollinger mine would use a part of it, not the entire length.

Q.—And the McIntyre?

A.—I don't know.

Q.—The road was being built under new and novel conditions for that purpose—for the rapid growth of Timmins and the rapid growth of mining there?

A.—Yes.

Q.—And it was isolated—the farthest north constructed in Ontario? How far north of Sudbury for instance?

A.—I suppose a couple of hundred miles.

Q.—No road in America, or perhaps in the world, has been constructed under conditions of that kind?

A.—I don't know that.

Q.—There is nothing in Ontario like it?

A.—No.

Q.—You had never attempted roads like that in that country before?

A.—No.

Q.—You were two hundred miles north of anything you had done before?

A.—Two hundred and fifty, I guess.

Q.—As far as a road of that class was concerned?

A.—Yes.

Q.—You had built trails, cut down timber and grubbed up a road?
A.—Yes.
Q.—And there had been attempts to fill in the holes and get over gullies before?
A.—Yes.
Q.—They had built to some new mines, but in Northern Ontario there had been no attempt on roads of this kind before?
A.—No.
Q.—And on this particular bit the Drury Government had wasted $109,000?
CHAIRMAN: I would not ask that question.
Q.—They did spend the money there?
A.—Something like that.
Q.—On this particular section. And with your engineer's experience you figured there was something to show for that?
MR. RANEY: I don't like you asking witness to swear to this. I don't mind you making these strong statements.
MR. LYONS: Those are the facts, nevertheless.
MR. FINLAYSON: Is it right there was $100,000 spent?
WITNESS: Yes.
Q.—And you were proceeding to build up a road assuming there was something there; assuming there was a metal road on which they were putting a surface practically? Part of the base was there?
A.—Yes, part of the base was there.
Q.—And nobody could tell how many improvements were necessary?
A.—No.
Q.—It turned out that improvements were necessary as to grades?
A.—Yes.
Q.—It turned out that four deviations had to be straightened?
A.—I don't recall anything about that.
Q.—It also turned out, did it not, that the conditions varied very much beyond what you expected?
A.—Yes.
Q.—One witness this afternoon said he thought the changes which developed as the road went ahead accounted for fifty—
CHAIRMAN: You are dealing with the evidence of the Creighton-Copper Cliff.
MR. FINLAYSON: I am sorry.
MR. RANEY: That would not make any difference.
CHAIRMAN: It would to me. I think it might make some difference to the witness's reply.
MR. FINLAYSON: Is Duff a qualified engineer?
WITNESS: He is not a graduate of the University.
Q.—Is he experienced?
A.—Yes.
Q.—And that letter was written to find out his observations on the increase in cost?
A.—Yes.
Q.—Getting to the other one—he speaks of a fill 400 feet by 20 feet?
A.—That would be the greatest depth of the fill. That is extreme.
Q.—That would disturb calculations?
A.—Well, yes.

Q.—As I judge from his letter that is a result of subsidence and he suggests it would be better to spread operations over two or three years?

A.—I agree with that.

Q.—Now, the variations between the contract and the actual payment— are they unusually large?

A.—No, I don't think they are for that class of work.

Q.—And is the unit system the right system to apply to this class of work in your opinion?

A.—I don't see how any other could be applied.

Q.—For what reason?

A.—Suppose you let a lump sum contract, there would be the great question of extras.

Q.—Every contractor would have to bid so high to protect himself that it would be enormous would it not?

A.—It would not be practicable.

Q.—You believe you are adopting good engineering practice?

A.—Yes.

MR. RANEY: I think that is the end of this matter. Shall we go on with the Caledon Mountain matter?

MR. FINLAYSON: That is the end of the Lyons' matter?

MR. RANEY: I had intended to go into some question of road conditions under the Drury Government. I recognize that it ought to be done. It would involve, perhaps, an extension of two or three hours, or perhaps half a day of these sittings and I am prepared—

CHAIRMAN: We are not going to make a report on the Drury administration.

MR. RANEY: If I don't pursue it I am just observing it must be understood that I am not accepting Mr. Finlayson's statements.

CHAIRMAN: We would not expect that.

MR. RANEY: Shall we take Mr. Brown?

William Henry Brown sworn. Examined by Mr. Raney.

Q.—You are an accountant in the Public Works Department?

A.—In the Department of Public Highways.

Q.—Have you got with you the statement of payments made by you on this work?

A.—To the contractors, yes. We have some certificates, probably better still.

Q.—I want to get the payments made as the work progressed, to MacLean. The work, we are told, started rather early in July?

A.—Yes.

Q.—I notice 13th August?

MR. FINLAYSON: June.

MR. RANEY: Yes, June, early in June. That 13th August, I notice, would be paid in by cheque, $1,446?

WITNESS: McLean drew $1,066.62; $380 was deducted by the Department for team waggons and blankets sold to him.

Q.—Give me those two.

A.—One thousand and sixty-six dollars and sixty-two cents certificate, actually paid to McLean.

Q.—Not paid in cash?

A.—By cheque.

Q.—And something for equipment?

A.—Three hundred and eighty dollars. Those two items make $1,446.62.

Q.—Then on August 28th you paid $1,071?

A.—One thousand and seventy-one dollars and eighty-seven cents.

Q.—On September 25th you paid $1,144.51?

A.—McLean only got $975.56 of that in cash and $168.95 to the General Assurance Company to cover bond.

Q.—And those two items made $1,144.51. Then on October 8th, one month later, the work stopped apparently. Did the work stop?

A.—This certificate calls for payment from September 22nd to September 30.

Q.—Do you know when the work stopped?

A.—I do not.

Q.—We have heard from another witness; $1,164.67, October 8th?

A.—One for $500 and $664.67.

Q.—Then along in December, I think, towards the end of the year, on the 22nd of December, you gave a cheque for $500?

A.—Yes.

Q.—Then there was a charge against you from the Workmen's Compensation Board?

A.—Three hundred and nineteen dollars and thirty-four cents.

Q.—And deducting all these amounts from the amounts standing to his credit for work he had done there was a balance remaining at the end for distribution of $623.63?

A.—Yes.

Q.—Now, that money you proceeded to distribute?

A.—Yes.

Q.—Among the creditors?

A.—Yes.

Q.—And did you prepare this chart of claims? I see a chart of claims against contract Number 1223, T. J. McLean?

A.—Yes.

Q.—I see here, the first item, a claim from a construction company, Chambers, of $1,900; amount acknowledged by the contractor, $820; amount paid, $79.86?

A.—That is the pro rata on a distribution of $623 amongst claims amounting to $6,397.

Mr. FINLAYSON: That was .0974 cents on the dollar.

Mr. RANEY: A little less than 10 per cent. Did you know, Mr. Brown, I suppose you did, that the workmen on this job had a preferential claim, under the Ontario Statutes, for thirty days over other creditors?

A.—Yes.

Q.—And in bankruptcy proceedings, I think you knew, when they do claim, for three months—preferential claim?

A.—I was not aware of that.

Mr. FINLAYSON: That is hardly correct. Under the Dominion Act they have three months prior to the assignment and prior to the order, which may mean anything, if they had not worked in the month before—

Mr. RANEY: In this case when the man left the job if he claimed for preference, under the bankruptcy law, and they put him in insolvency there would be three months—

Mr. FINLAYSON: I don't think your law is quite right.

Mr. RANEY: Under your distribution you treated all creditors alike, apparently?

WITNESS: Yes.

Q.—I may say on the same basis?

A.—The same pro rata basis.

MR. FINLAYSON: The date of distribution was March 1st, I think.

WITNESS: Yes.

MR. RANEY: These men had been nagging you and the Department for six months?

A.—Quite a long while.

Q.—Will you tell me, Mr. Brown, on what authority you reduced this claim of $1,960 to $820?

A.—The whole thing was done on instructions received.

Q.—From whom?

A.—The Deputy Minister.

Q.—You don't know what authority he had?

A.—I only know he had McLean's sworn statement.

Q.—He also had sworn statements of some of the claimants?

A.—Yes.

Q.—And why was McLean's any better than Brass's was?

A.—I don't know.

Q.—All you did was to act on the instructions of Mr. Squire?

A.—Yes.

Q.—I see; take for instance the claim by Barry, $61; nothing was allowed?

A.—No. McLean said he did not do anything.

Q.—And you took his statement?

A.—Yes.

Q.—Don't you think you were incurring a good deal of responsibility?

A.—I did not think so, Mr. Raney.

Q.—Just doing what you were told?

A.—Absolutely.

Q.—Then I see James McDevitt, one of the witnesses before the Committee, 208 Humberside, Toronto, $108 claimed and you allowed him $15.50 and sent a cheque for $1.50?

A.—Yes.

Q.—Because you were told. Had McDevitt made an affidavit?

A.—No.

Q.—Did Brass?

A.—Brass and McClintock.

Q.—You reduced Brass's claim from $774.70 to $196?

A.—I did not reduce it. It was reduced by Mr. McLean.

Q.—You proceeded to distribute on that evidence and sent him a cheque for $19.09 which he is going to have framed?

And then McClintock made an affidavit, claiming $278.15 and you reduced to $93 and sent a cheque for $9.05 and he said he had to apply for street car fare to get home with. The next amount is from Kenneth Hahnson, Orangeville, $221.75, reduced to $111.25 and you sent him $10.83?

A.—Yes.

Q.—"With pleasure"?

A.—It was sent him. It was a pleasure to send something.

Q.—Griggs claimed $264, you reduced it to $162.25 and sent him $15.80?

A.—Yes.

Q.—McLean came to see you?

A.—Yes.

Q.—Did you think him a more reliable man, more to be depended on than the other people who put in claims?

A.—I am not in a position to say that.

Q.—All you can say is that you got the instructions?

A.—Yes.

Q.—I think that is fair. Now I am not proposing—Mr. Finlayson may do so—to ask you what took place between you and those women who came to see you from time to time.

MR. FINLAYSON: Generally my attitude is not to do anything that may prejudice these men getting their money and I don't want to stir up anything. I hope after the Premier's statement some arrangement can be made whereby the men may get their money. I don't want to make any difficulty.

MR. RANEY: I do not think that there is any purpose served by calling any more Department men. I wanted to get the payments made to McLean and the basis of the payments, because they dovetail with the complaints and I wanted to show the distribution, which, of course—but I won't say anything more.

MR. FINLAYSON: Pax vobiscum. Here endeth the lesson on that.

MR. RANEY: I think that is, perhaps, all.

CHAIRMAN: That cleans up the different matters.

MR. RANEY: I hope not to think of anything more.

CHAIRMAN: What about a meeting to-morrow to consider a draft report.

MR. RANEY: I think that is all right. What time do you suggest?

CHAIRMAN: Suppose in the afternoon for an hour.

MR. RANEY: To-morrow will be fairly busy in the House.

MR. FINLAYSON: If the Chairman drafted a report and let you and Mr. Sinclair see it?

MR. RANEY: It is all right, of course. But suppose we meet here.

CHAIRMAN: Suppose we met at 1.30, between the morning and the afternoon sessions of the House; or between the afternoon and evening sessions?

MR. CALLAN: That will give us only ten minutes for lunch.

MR. JAMIESON: There is no evening session to-morrow.

MR. RANEY: We want to get this into the House. The report should be in to-morrow.

CHAIRMAN: Not later than Thursday.

MR. FINLAYSON: Suppose we say 1.30. It should not take long if things run smoothly and if not we can meet in the evening.

CHAIRMAN: There was some talk of this room being engaged for another meeting to-morrow. Make it two o'clock. I think it will be all right to meet here then.

PUBLIC ACCOUNTS COMMITTEE.

The Committee sat on Wednesday, March 31st, 1926, at 2 P.M., Mr. Lewis in the Chair.

MR. FINLAYSON: We have never approved the minutes, hadn't we better have a resolution?

THE CHAIRMAN: The minutes of the meetings have been present always at the succeeding meeting. They haven't been read, nobody has asked for it. It will be in order to have a resolution approving the minutes.

MR. FINLAYSON: I move that the minutes of the various meetings of the Standing Committee on Public Accounts during the Session be taken as read.

MR. BLACK: I second that.

THE CHAIRMAN: Approved? Carried.

MR. RANEY: Mr. Chairman, what about payment of witnesses? Do you require a resolution for that?

THE CHAIRMAN: No, that is looked after by the Department.

MR. RANEY: Well, on what basis are they paid, because these people who have come here and paid their railway fare and travelling expenses ought to get a witness fee, I suppose.

MR. REGAN (Secretary): There has never been any application for fees.

MR. FINLAYSON: We had one case two years ago.

MR. RANEY: I think they ought to be paid.

THE CHAIRMAN: You wouldn't include all these witnesses, because some are not looking for a witness fee, they are getting their expenses. You perhaps have reference particularly to the people who came down on the Caledon Road thing. I don't know any reason why we cannot consider something on that.

MR. MACBRIDE: The men were summoned here and put to expense; they ought to be paid, of course.

THE CHAIRMAN: I don't want a blanket resolution that all witnesses be paid.

MR. RANEY: I think they ought to have some allowance.

THE CHAIRMAN: Will you put it this way, that where, in the judgment of the Chairman, witnesses should be remunerated for their attendance, he be authorized to do so?

MR. RANEY and MR. SINCLAIR: All right.

MR. MACBRIDE moved, seconded by MR. FINLAYSON: That the matter be left to the judgment of the Chairman. Carried.

THE CHAIRMAN: Now, gentlemen, the work of the Committee was completed at the session last night and the Chairman was asked to have a report for submission to the meeting to-day for consideration and I did that and have had it written.

MR. RANEY: Mr. Chairman, before you go on there is something I forgot last night. Mr. Hogarth was to have come along with the original of this return showing insurances. I just want to get that on the record. Did you bring that with you, Mr. Hogarth?

MR. FINLAYSON: I thought we were finished last night.

MR. RANEY: Yes, but I forgot that. I want to get this on the record.

MR. FINLAYSON: I think the understanding was that whatever information was available in the files would be supplied, but we didn't undertake beyond that.

MR. RANEY: Mr. Hogarth, that is from your Department?

MR. HOGARTH: Yes.

MR. FINLAYSON: Let me say this: As I understand it, Mr. Raney had some question on the order paper that stood over for some reason and then it was amended and answered, and something was submitted to you that is not on the records. It is not accurate entirely.

MR. RANEY: Then I had better correct it.

MR. FINLAYSON: It is public now; I don't know that it is desirable.

MR. RANEY: My questions, Mr. Chairman, were these, and they are answered in two sets of figures: What is the total amount of fire insurance premiums paid by the Province for the past ten years? I hold in my hand the answer; if it is to be corrected, I have no objection. The second, What is the total amount paid by the insurance companies to the Province for losses during the same time? Just these two questions.

MR. FINLAYSON: That has never been answered.

MR. RANEY: Never answered in the House, no.

MR. FINLAYSON: Mr. Hogarth tells me there is a mistake in some item, I don't know what it is, and the Department has sent word that if these figures are to be used, they should be obtained correctly. I understand my friend, Mr. Raney, wants to contend that the Province should carry its own insurance—practically what we discussed in the Private Bills Committee this morning in relation to protection, and a very proper subject for argument, perhaps—but I do not think this material is what it should be based on and I don't like it to go out as the findings of the Public Accounts Committee.

MR. RANEY: I have not yet asked that; that is another matter entirely. But why not get the facts established as to what these figures are? You bring out anything else you want. It won't take five minutes.

MR. FINLAYSON: He is not ready for it.

MR. GRAVES: If this is for the purpose of future consideration of a matter of policy, why not leave the matter until you decide to consider it as a matter of policy? Why put in just a statement and forget it for a year or two and then let it drift through the Province.

THE CHAIRMAN: You don't anticipate any difficulty in getting the information you desire?

MR. MACBRIDE: That is why I asked a ruling. If one member of this Committee is permitted to put a question or ask for a return covering any departmental matter, any member of the Committee should have a like privilege, and where would we finish up? I might ask for a report for the last ten years on the Attorney-General's Department and that would lead us, God knows where.

THE CHAIRMAN: Of course, consideration of anything, excepting the report is precluded from to-day's meeting, because the Committee decided last night at the hearing of the final witnesses we were through with this phase of our business. Mr Raney, there is no question, did yesterday afternoon ask for certain information respecting insurance and the understanding was that if that information was in the file of the clerk handling that it would be produced last night. It was not and we understand the information they have is faulty in some respects.

MR. FINLAYSON: Partially.

MR. MACBRIDE: Here is my point. Mr. Raney is evolving a policy, the Province should carry its own insurance, and perfectly right, but suppose I evolve a policy that we abolish the Provincial Police and we would be here for another month.

MR. SINCLAIR: It strikes me, as a lawyer, if certain evidence came up yesterday afternoon or night, and it was understood Mr. Raney was to get a certain statement, the record cannot be complete without it.

MR. FINLAYSON: May I explain that. Mr. Raney put a question on the order paper early in the Session, then withdrew it and the question was substituted, and that question has never been answered, although in the Department the Deputy or Minister or somebody sent to Mr. Raney a memorandum and asked him if that was the material he wanted. The question was not completed, the figures are not accurate; and the Department now say they do not want the figures to go out for purposes of argument.

MR. SINCLAIR: Can't they be corrected before the minutes are completed and incorporated in the evidence?

MR. FINLAYSON: I will ask the Minister if that can be done, but I think everybody will recognize if we are to discuss the general question of whether or not it is good policy for the Government to carry its own insurance, we should have complete data and we won't and cannot have that. Surely the position is this: if the great Province of Ontario, the City of Toronto and the Board of Education of Toronto are going to carry their own insurance, it means all the desirable risks are going to be removed from the insurance companies.

THE CHAIRMAN: Don't let us discuss that.

MR. FINLAYSON: And other people are going to pay high premiums, and that is a big departure in policy and we ought to have all the material to discuss it.

THE CHAIRMAN: So Mr. Raney asked for certain information and the understanding was that, that information was prepared and in the files of one of the clerks. The understanding when we adjourned yesterday was that if the information was so prepared, it would be produced last night. Last night nobody thought of it, but we find it is not prepared, according to the Department's point of view, therefore, it is not ready for production.

MR. RANEY: I don't want to take too much time. I will just drop this in view of that statement that this information is not accurate. I will have to accept that and I can base my argument on some other ground if I want.

THE CHAIRMAN: I do not think you will have any difficulty in getting the information you want.

Now, I have supplied Mr. Raney and Mr. Sinclair and Mr. Finlayson a copy of the report and I will read it for consideration of members of the Committee.

(The Chairman read the report of the Standing Committee on Public Accounts, 1926.)

May I just say in explanation that in preparing this report, I felt a precedence of this Committee was to avoid lengthy reports or findings and recommendations, contentious matters and to make a report simply on what it has done and what evidence has been placed before the Committee and let the report of the evidence speak for itself, and I have endeavoured to do that in drafting this report and I submit that for consideration of the Committee, if it meets with their approval.

MR. RANEY: I suppose someone will make a motion.

MR. FINLAYSON: May I make a suggestion. In the paragraph at the foot of page one, "Your Committee dealt with the request of the former Minister of Lands and Forests for the investigation of all business transactions of himself or other companies in which he is interested, with any Department of the Government." I think we should add "With Contractors."

THE CHAIRMAN: We have that covered in the first paragraph on the same page, Mr. Finlayson. That is the reason I did not repeat it.

MR. MACBRIDE: There was a matter brought before the Committee, perhaps irrelevant, and yet perhaps it may be. One witness attempted to cast aspersion on the forestry air force. I happen to know practically every member of the force. It there is a finer body of men in public service, in Canada or elsewhere from Captain Maxwell down, that perhaps is the finest body of men we have. I think there should be something in the report regarding the service they give to the Province. There is evidence they are saving great amounts to the Province every year in their splendid work, and to have a witness come here and cast aspersion on the force and their morale is a great mistake. You men realize what they are doing in that country, and I think there should be a paragraph relating to the service afforded by the air force. I don't think a member of the Committee can possibly object to that. We have the evidence as to what they are saving.

THE CHAIRMAN: I did not deal with that specifically, because I did not think it was necessary. The evidence heard by the Committee spoke for itself.

MR. MACBRIDE: Young men at Sioux Lookout and Sudbury who all summer long look after that desolate land in which a great proportion of the wealth of the Province is found, and they are risking their lives every day to perform that service, and when we have a witness coming here to give evidence such as was given, I think the Committee owes something to these men.

MR. FINLAYSON: What do you suggest?

MR. MACBRIDE: I suggest that the Chairman be authorized to draft a paragraph recording our confidence and appreciation of the service of all men in the air force.

THE CHAIRMAN: A paragraph could be drafted in three minutes to cover it, if the Committee thinks it necessary. There were only two witnesses heard and I think Mr. Raney and everybody felt the evidence spoke for itself when we got through.

MR. MACBRIDE: My point is, it has gone through Ontario and people read scare heads in the newspapers, and few understand or appreciate what these boys are doing up there. I think we owe all the men in that force our strongest moral support.

MR. FINLAYSON: Make a motion then.

MR. MACBRIDE: I don't care to make a motion, I merely wanted to make a suggestion.

THE CHAIRMAN: Supposing you passed a motion here to give effect of your suggestion and incorporated it in the minutes which will be published along with the report.

MR. MACBRIDE: That would cover it. With the consent of the Committee, I will draft a motion in conjunction with the Chairman.

MR. SINCLAIR: The form of the motion really should come before the Committee. It is hardly regular yet because you haven't moved adoption of your report.

MR. RANEY: Is this going into the report or the minutes?

MR. FINLAYSON: I would put it in the report.

THE CHAIRMAN: Suppose we say something like this: Some evidence having been given by one of the witnesses before the Committee reflecting on the efficiency of the Air Service of the Forestry Branch, your Committee beg to report that having heard the evidence of this witness and Captain Maxwell, director of the service, are of the opinion that the evidence in criticism was not justified and that the services rendered by this Branch have amply justified the establishment of this Branch of the service. Does that cover it? If so, I can draft it in three minutes.

Will this meet the suggestion of Mr. MacBride: "Some evidence having been given by a witness before your Committee reflecting upon the efficiency of the Provincial Air Service of the Forestry Branch, your Committee having heard the evidence of the witness in question and the evidence of Capt. Roy Maxwell, director of the Air Service, are of the opinion the criticism suggested was not justified by the facts, and that establishment of this branch of the public service has been amply justified by the results."

MR. BLACK: I beg to move that the report as read be adopted.

MR. EDWARDS: I second that.

28a J

MR. RANEY: Mr. Chairman, I am not desiring to precipitate an argument. I imagine no argument will be necessary. I am moving an amendment, seconded by Mr. Fisher, that all the words of the draft report as read to the Committee, after the words "To the Honourable the Legislative Assembly of Ontario" be stricken out and the following substituted therefor:

(Mr. Raney here read his proposed alternative report.)

THE CHAIRMAN: Apparently Mr. Raney does not agree with me about keeping contentious matters out of these reports. I am going to suggest that it is useless entering into a long discussion this afternoon as to the relative merits of these reports. We all have the evidence in our minds.

MR. RANEY: Hear, hear!

THE CHAIRMAN: Let us vote on this thing and not have a long discussion.

MR. MACBRIDE: Just a moment. There are members here who have been members of the Public Accounts Committee several years. I am in that position. I think the duty of the Public Accounts Committee is to be non-partisan, and when I heard Mr. Raney open his remarks with the clear statement that he proposed to be non-partisan in his arguments, and as I followed him through, I must say to this Committee I was amazed with the inconsistency between his text and his sermon. I can remember the time of the Lennox charges. Mr. Raney himself was acting for the Government, and he argued then that it was not the right of this Committee to make partisan comments or partisan reports. Here we have the very reverse of the policy, and the principle that he himself enunciated at that time when Attorney-General of the late Government. Now just three instances to show the inconsistence of this entire presentment of his, and prove that it is an appeal to partisan political advantage; not a single mention anywhere in that report of the repeated glaring overruns in road construction under the former administration, and in the evidence there are clear-cut instances of it, instances where there was 100 and over 100 per cent. overrun. If my friend wanted to be fair and non-partisan, as he said in opening, he would have made mention of that fact in the evidence. He ignores that, and I put it to any member of this Committee, any member of the House, and any citizen of the Province, that if he is true to his text, that he wants a non-partisan report, he certainly ought to include instances in the evidence of glaring overrun in connection with road construction during the time he was Attorney-General in the former government. He carefully avoids making any reference to the insurance incident, in which the late member for Victoria, Mr. Edgar Watson, was concerned. There are two instances. He is not quite fair enough to include a reference to the fact that the Prime Minister of this Province from his seat in the House, the moment the Caledon incidents of non-payment of wages were brought to his attention, made a definite and clear-cut undertaking on the part of the Government that these men would receive their wages. Now, Mr. Chairman, my view is that we cannot play petty politics, and least of all, partisan politics, with this enquiry we have been conducting. True, the Conservative Government are in the seats of power to-day. A few short years ago, another government was in the seats of power, and in due course various parties will come into power. We cannot afford to let the Public Accounts Committee at any time become the means of promoting throughout this Province partisan politics and bias against any public man, I don't care what political party he belongs to. Hon. Mr. Lyons started out a poor boy. We have the evidence here. He worked his way up by hard work and honesty of purpose and undoubted integrity, and came to this House a splendid example of the proper duty of a public man, that when questions touching the operations of his firm were put on the Order Paper, he promptly resigned the honourable position he occupied as a Minister of the Crown, and voluntarily submitted himself to this Committee; voluntarily asked that the best firm of chartered accountants in this Province, the same firm that investigated other matters, should examine into his private and public affairs in the most broad and non-partisan manner. That being so, if this Committee are going to come to any finding, and make any comment or conclusion, as a court might, with regard to the evidence, I put it to any fair-minded member of this House, regardless of politics, that the thing we ought to do is exonerate the man in no uncertain terms, if we are going to get into that kind of report. I think, Mr. Chairman, when you read your report, that you were extremely fair, that you were concise, that there was an absence of any attempt to play politics, and I want to express my regret at this petty, picayune—as my friend from East Kent said the other day—attempt to everlastingly throw aspersions at public men in any party. Hon. Mr. Raney knows full well as a lawyer what his privileges are and what his opportunities are. If he, as a member of this Committee, has any basis for his insinuations and his suggested references in that report, why doesn't he stand up on the floor of the House and as a member of the House accept his full responsibility of making charges, if he is not satisfied with the finding of this Committee. He has been given every opportunity to examine every witness he wanted to, bring all the witnesses here he wanted to. In heaven's name, Mr. Chairman, let us bring a little fair sportsmanship into the relationships of members of this House, and between parties in this House, and thereby perhaps serve to elevate the public life in this Province.

MR. FINLAYSON: I don't want to say anything very strong, or anything that at this late stage of the Session will cause any feeling. I thought we were trying to conduct this Committee with dignity. I thought you, sir, had spent a lot of time on it, and various members of the Committee had tried to bring to this enquiry a spirit of fair play, and were trying to do something in the interests of the Province. It might have been said, as it was said at Ottawa, that when a member of the House wants to make a charge he should get up and do the way Mr. Porter did, make his charge and say, "I take the responsibility for that, and I am willing to abide by the result." Instead of that, at the early part of the Session, a miserable lot of questions were put on the Order Paper, containing innuendo and insinuations, not in the names of the men enquiring—Mr. Raney admitted the other day that although the questions were in the name of Mr. Kemp or somebody they were those of Mr. Raney—if I may use a biblical quotation the voice was the voice of Jacob, but the hand was the hand of Esau. Mr. Raney got up in Committee himself and said, as to Capt. Maxwell, "I congratulate you," "I am satisfied with the Clarkson report," and his own organ, *The Star*, said, as every member of this Committee thought, he had exonerated Mr. Lyons, and he said Mr. Lyons' conduct was above reproach, and the incident was closed and he is exonerated, and his own organ said so, and *The Mail and Empire* and *The Globe*, responsible papers, did so, and the whole Province knows that no public Minister of the Crown ever had a more complete vindication and exoneration than the Minister of Lands and Forests has had at the hands of this Committee; and yet at this late stage, when we all thought we came in here to ask you, as Mr. Raney assented to the other night, that it would be a brief report, merely summarizing—I fancy you, as I did before, sir, went through the report for many years to find out the practice, and the practice, not only of this Government but preceding governments, was to merely summarize the evidence and state what the activities of the Committee had been—

and then at the last day of the Session, when we have left the preparation of the report to you, this venomous document is produced here, and I am surprised that some responsible member of the Committee in addition to Mr. Raney lends his name to it. I can only hope he had not read it.

Let me just test it and get down to the facts. These facts were handed to me during the progress of this Committee, and I kept them from the Committee; I thought we were making an enquiry, but when a report like this, showing a petty, small spite indicated in every word of the report, then I say the Committee ought to know this. During 1920, 1921, 1923 and 1924, the man who moves that report was a director and a shareholder and the solicitor in an incorporated company carrying on business year after year with this Province, notwithstanding the fact that Mr. Raney was a member of the Government in 1920-21, and in 1923-24, he was a shareholder and director in a company selling goods to the Province of Ontario, and also, I believe, a solicitor for that company.

MR. CURRIE: What company?

MR. FINLAYSON: Copeland-Chatterson Company, and I read from the returns to the Province that in 1920 the directors among others included William E. Raney, Parliament Buildings. In 1921, the return showed a director was the Hon. William E. Raney of the Parliament Buildings. In 1922-23, the company did not file returns. In 1924, we find the company filed a return, and Hon. William E. Raney, Sun Life Building, is still a director and shareholder; and during all these years the company sold goods to the Province, and the Attorney-General's department, too. Is there any difference in this, between the Hon. Mr. Lyons selling goods to contractors and the Copeland-Chatterson Company, in which Mr. Raney is a director and shareholder, selling to his own department.

HON. MR. LYONS: Yes, Raney is a lawyer.

MR. FINLAYSON: The only difference I see is that one is a merchant from the north and the other a trained lawyer from the south.

MR. MACBRIDE: Mr. Lyons did it openly and above board.

MR. FINLAYSON: And when the leader of the Government said he should not sell it ceased. There is also this, when this investigation started, I said, "I think the best policy is to pursue the same policy as in the Smith and other investigations and include the best firm of chartered accountants," and Mr. Raney said, "Certainly, the name of the Clarkson firm will clear it all up," and when that report came down he said that settled it all, and every reporter here knows he said the report exonerated Mr. Lyons, and we thought the matter at an end. Now in this left-handed way he tried to get a slap at a public man. He says he does not want to start a debate. If he had ordinary courtesy he would have sent a memorandum to me or the Chairman or more particularly to Mr. Lyons.

MR. RANEY: I did not get the report completed until after two o'clock.

MR. FINLAYSON: Even after two o'clock it might have been fair to send it to us. It is a common courtesy observed by public men, is it not?

MR. RANEY: Oh, go ahead.

MR. FINLAYSON: As far as Mr. Lyons is concerned, from beginning to end here is a left-handed attack on a man who dealt fairly and publicly, whose whole accounts were open to investigation by the keenest auditors in this Province, and they reported, and Mr. Raney agrees their figures show, and there is not a single word in your memo in reference to the Clarkson's investigation. Five pages devoted to picking out all the evidence, any single thing that can be thought to be unfavourable or adverse to the late Minister, but not a single word will Mr. Raney give the Province of the report of the Clarkson firm which met with his approval. Five pages devoted to a venomous attack, picking out details, going all over this stuff and picking out anything unfavourable, and then it is thrown at the Committee in this late date and left-handed way, and never a single word about the report of the Clarkson firm or their audit and accounting. Surely, nothing could be more unfair or of which one might be more ashamed. Let us go on just for a moment. The Oakley case. Also an attack on Mr. Oakley. I remember at close of the Committee here when Mr. Oakley gave his evidence, Mr. Raney shook hands with him and congratulated him on his work and his evidence, and told us all it was eminently satisfactory.

MR. RANEY: I said the building was a beautiful building.

MR. FINLAYSON: You went far beyond the building, too. Why don't you say it was satisfactory in bringing in your report.

"The evidence discloses that the George Oakley & Son, Limited, have a sub-contract for the stone work of the new Administration Building in Queen's Park, at the contract price of $835,000. It was admitted before the Committee that the Oakley Company is a family company controlled by Mr. George Oakley, the member representing Riverdale in this House. The Oakley contract is not contrary to law, but in the opinion of your Committee, it too, is an encroachment on the principles of the independence of Parliament and a breach of the spirit of the Legislative Assembly Act. In the view of your Committee, no member of the Legislative Assembly ought to have a contract on any public work of the Province."

If that is true, why didn't Mr. Raney get up and propose a law of that kind when he was head of the department for years? For four years he had in his own control, and direct management—the only lawyer in it; whatever he said went. If he had amended the Act he could not have stayed a director of the Copeland-Chatterson Company supplying goods to his own department. And yet this high moral tone is applied to a man like Mr. Oakley. I have only this to say in conclusion: Mr. Oakley and Mr. Raney are both known in Toronto. Mr. Oakley has been elected in Toronto, and Mr. Raney defeated, and I fancy the electors would be delighted to have an opportunity of judging between these two men.

The Caledon road job. Mr. Raney professed to be a friend of the men. Could he have done anything to prejudice the case more of the men getting their money? Some of the men have a fair claim, as I think, strong. Some of them perhaps loafed on the job. It might be fair comment to say the engineer should have stopped the job at an earlier date than he did. I presented the facts to the Minister and Premier, and was delighted to hear the free statement of the Premier in the House that these men would get sympathetic consideration. What is going to be the effect of this? The $10 or $20 or $30 owing to men up there is being made a matter of party politics. The U.F.O. party are going to try to rehabilitate themselves on a few dollars owed up in the Caledon Mountain.

MR. MACBRIDE: Not the U.F.O.; the unnamed group.

MR. FINLAYSON: Mr. Raney's party are trying to rehabilitate themselves in this. They are going to forget that Mr. Raney was dealing with the Government.

MR. MACBRIDE: I respect the U.F.O. as an organization. I do not recognize the group led by my honourable friend as U.F.O.

MR. WIDDIFIELD: Does the party recognize you?

MR. FINLAYSON: As soon as Mr. Widdifield's interruptions are over I will be glad to go on. Here was a party that was never in as bad repute as they are. All Session they have been attempting to rehabilitate themselves with a temperance issue; trying to forget the sins and crimes for which their leaders are suffering to-day, and such things as this Copeland-Chatterson thing, which I would willingly have hidden, for it was handed to me weeks ago; and now they are trying to rehabilitate themselves on a wage claim. What do they care whether these poor men get their wages or not? Everyone in the Committee was sympathetic, but if they are going to be tied on as exhibits to Mr. Raney's campaign to try and cover himself, the sooner the poor men learn they are going to be used, and not assisted, the better.

Liquor dispensaries. Your Committee is asked to say that the accounts should be published. I don't know why they were not published. All I can suggest is that when Mr. Raney was head of the Department, he did not publish them, and his nominee, Mr. Hales, has carried out his policy still. I don't know whether it is an attack on Birmingham, or Hales, or who.

MR. RANEY: Suppose you assume it is not an attack on anybody.

MR. FINLAYSON: I am willing to assume that for some reason you are trying to get something before the Committee that was not before it, and get a recommendation. The only person who saw the accounts was Mr. Raney. When Mr. Birmingham said, "Here are the accounts," I asked if he had his chief's permission, and next day I telephoned Mr. Hales and Mr. Raney saw the report and nobody else.

MR. RANEY: Nobody saw any such report as printed in the Public Accounts.

MR. FINLAYSON: Well, only you saw that, and this Committee is asked to comment on that. Who he knows it from I don't know or care.

THE CHAIRMAN: I took the trouble to enquire into that next day, and the Attorney-General assured me he had given permission to the License Board and Mr. Birmingham to supply Mr. Raney.

MR. FINLAYSON: Then why should they be dragged into this.

THE CHAIRMAN: I think the Committee are amazed at any recommendation being suggested in connection with the dispensaries, on the meagre examination that took place here and the consent Mr. Raney had to look into the financial statement.

MR. MACBRIDE: When Mr. Raney was Attorney-General, he took the ground that certain information was confidential and could not be divulged in the House, when we asked a question.

MR. FINLAYSON: Whether this is aimed to get rid of Mr. Birmingham or Mr. Hales, I do not know, but apparently he is after somebody, and I don't think either will thank him for what he has done. As I take it, the dispensary has been conducted in a business-like way. The accounts were audited by Clarkson & Company under the regime of Mr. Raney when head of the liquor department—a subject perhaps he is more familiar with than the rest of us. He never published his reports, but the moment he gets out he wants to blame somebody else for not, and we get this left-handed attack at somebody here.

Then an article on radio publicity. What it means I do not know. "The Committee transmits the evidence without comment." It was a "dud," I guess, as campaign stuff. Then we get this long paragraph on Home Bank legals. Surely the Home Bank legals is exhausted. There is no evidence before this Committee to justify it at all. My friend had a chance in the House, and the Premier laughed at him, and let him read all his declarations.

THE CHAIRMAN: Of course, no reference could be included in the report of the Committee, because the Committee refused to consider it, and Mr. Raney afterwards took opportunity to discuss it in the House.

MR. FINLAYSON: These two particular items show the animus of the thing. These poor dispensary people, who are trying apparently to conduct a business which produces a large profit to us, one of them has to be hit at. Another thing is the reckless charges, no more before the Committee than the legals. The legals are not before the Committee. My friend knows that, and knows it was perfectly proper in a legal way they were not before it. They were not a public issue in any sense. It was years old, and even if you take these declarations, they were apparently between a private publisher and private subscriber. My friend took his chance in the House, and when it fell so flat that not even a newspaper paid any attention to it, he tries to get this advertising at this late date. I am sorry to have to talk this way to the Committee, but the animus, the small, petty, party spirit, the attempt to rehabilitate a dead and deceased party over something like this, and try to forget their crimes and punishments and imprisonments, as the member for Brant said a moment ago, if Mr. Raney wanted to be fair, why didn't he mention the most startling thing that came out, that Mr. Watson, U.F.O. member for North Victoria, had obtained $350 on an illegal commission? Poor Mr. Lyons, who did something that was perfectly legal, and Mr. Oakley, who did something that was perfectly legal, can get pages devoted to them, but when the Committee found the other day that Mr. Biggs had arranged with Mr. Watson to get $350 illegally, which would have forfeited his seat in the House, not a word from Mr. Raney about that at all; and when Mr. Raney himself does what Mr. Lyons did as a shareholder of a company, dealing with his own department, I think it will satisfy any member of this Committee this whole matter is surely a matter of petty, party politics.

THE CHAIRMAN: I was going to suggest, before you reply, Mr. Raney, if any member wants to speak.

MR. RANEY: I might have expected this tirade, Mr. Chairman. Almost anything is liable to happen when Mr. Finlayson is in the air. I just want to speak to the personal charge, if I may call it such. When I became a member of the Government, I was a shareholder and director of the Copeland-Chatterson Company, which is a company doing business in Toronto. I have no knowledge that any goods were supplied by that company to the Government during my term in the Government.

MR. FINLAYSON: I can give you the figures, if you like.

MR. RANEY: Wait until I get through. My attention was called, after I had been in the Government a time, I don't know how many months, to the fact that the Copeland-Chatterson Company was seeking government business. I immediately notified the president that I must retire from the board, and immediately resigned my directorate, and was not a director again of the Copeland-Chatterson Company until after my term of office expired.

MR. FINLAYSON: They return you as being one for 1920 and 1921.

MR. RANEY: 1920 was the year after the election. I suppose I was elected in the early part of 1921, and sometime during that year retired, just as soon as I learned—

MEMBER: Did you retain your interest in the firm?

MR. RANEY: Yes.

MR. FINLAYSON: And you are still a director?

MR. RANEY: After my term of office expired I was again elected a director.

MR. FINLAYSON: And sold goods to amount of $2,385 while a director?

MR. RANEY: I had no knowledge of any transaction between that company and the Province of Ontario during the time of my service with the Government.

MR. FINLAYSON: Perhaps Mr. Raney will tell us why Copeland-Chatterson Company did not file returns for 1922.

MR. CURRIE: Are they still doing business with the Government?

MR. RANEY: I had no knowledge until to-day, as supplied by Mr. Finlayson, of any goods sold the government or any branch of it while I was Attorney-General, and the very moment it was intimated to me they were seeking business from the Government, I retired from the directorate.

THE CHAIRMAN: Are you ready for the question?

MEMBERS: Question!

MR. SINCLAIR: In connection with this wordy argument which has taken place, I do not intend to get into that, but I would like to call the attention of the Committee to this, that the report submitted for the consideration of this Committee should not have transgressed in the first place. If they had followed the precedent of Public Accounts Committee reports there would have been no reference to vindication or condemnation of the late Minister of Lands and Forests.

MR. FINLAYSON: There isn't any.

MR. SINCLAIR: Yes, two lines distinctly partisan, exonerating the Minister. Major Nash found the books in order, etc., and "investigation conducted by your Committee confirmed this view." Now if you were strictly following the rules, which you so vigorously argued for, all these words of comment should be stricken out of your report, and you should as a Committee submit a report of the names of the witnesses called and schedule of exhibits and so on and limit yourselves entirely to that, and not make any reference to what your opinion is of the dealings of the late Minister with the Government. If you were on that ground, I could see some merit to the argument directed against the ex-Attorney-General, but having first adopted this course yourselves it certainly comes with very ill grace to attack an amendment such as he has submitted. It is true, it is more in detail, but it is no more offensive than the main report, and the suggestion made by the member for Brantford, made in perfect good faith, an advertising scheme of the air force of the north country. Those of us who have sat on Public Accounts Committee for some years—and I have taken the trouble to look up the reports for years back, and there is not a sign of any reference to a finding until this Government came into office.

THE CHAIRMAN: Did you look up the report of 1922?

MR. SINCLAIR: That was the O.T.A.

MR. FINLAYSON: Whitewashing Mr. Raney.

MR. SINCLAIR: If because one man has a black face, another has a black face, make him still blacker, that is not my view.

MR. FINLAYSON: I agree with a great deal of what Mr. Sinclair said. The reports year after year are all along this line. All he can possibly object to is, "The Committee confirm this view." Mr. Nash made the statements, there is no doubt of that.

MR. SINCLAIR: My argument is, if you are going to reject the amendment of the ex-Attorney-General, you have no right whatever to refer in the slightest way to any evidence given other than to say so-and-so was called, and that we submit herewith the evidence, and leave it to the public to draw their own conclusions from the evidence submitted, rather than to try to create public opinion from what we submit.

Mr. Raney: Even the report added about the flying—

Mr. Sinclair: That paragraph the member for Brantford put in, I knew it was not in keeping with what we do, and I voted for it to get it before the House. I say you have no right to criticize the action of the member for East Wellington if you are going to present such a report as this to the House.

Mr. Currie: Mr. Raney is going to present that to the House as a minority report, so why waste so much time? You say whether you want to vote for the government one or this one.

Mr. Finlayson: If it will answer Mr. Sinclair's purpose, I am willing to leave out the phrase, "The investigation conducted by this Committee confirmed that view."

Mr. Sinclair: There may be other words.

Mr. Raney: We are not going to change our—

Mr. Sinclair: I am not asking you to meet my wishes or anybody else's. I say the tirade directed against the amendment has its foundation in the report of the main Committee, amplified by the member for Brant.

Mr. Finlayson: Mr. Sinclair has been an active member as long as I can go back, and I have always found him disposed to conduct things in a reasonable and fair way, and I know when Chairman he helped me a great deal, and I think there may be something in what he says, and my own view is that that line, "Investigation by the Committee confirmed Mr. Nash's view," if that would meet Mr. Sinclair's wishes, I would say do it.

Mr. MacBride: In connection with the air force, my only thought was for the record and good name of the boys engaged in the air force, and if that will meet his wishes, I will delete that.

Mr. Finlayson: Why should we send out a venomous document like that.

The Chairman: In drawing up this report, I endeavoured to keep away from contentious matters, and refrain from making findings or recommendations. I thought that in the wording of that clause dealing with the investigation into Mr. Lyons' companies, that I was couching it in very reasonable language.

Mr. Currie: But Mr. Chairman, here is a public man in a very high place.

Mr. Chairman: Wait until I read what I wrote. Dealing with the investigation of the Lyons Company affairs, I said in the final paragraph: "Major A. E. Nash, for the Clarkson firm, reported to the Committee that after an exhaustive examination of the books of the two companies referred to, in which he was assisted by the officials and auditors of the companies, he found the books in good order and his investigation revealed nothing to warrant any suspicion." That is his evidence as he gave it the morning he came back, and I added, 'The investigation conducted by your Committee confirmed this view."

Mr. Raney: There is one other thing I want to say. I don't want to make a speech. I wanted to add to the Caledon Mountain matter—this comes from something suggested by the member for Brantford—these words, "Your Committee is pleased to learn that the Prime Minister has made an announcement in the House which it is hoped will meet the case of these men." This has the consent of Mr. Fisher.

Members: Question, question!

Mr. Currie: My view of this thing is perhaps a little different from a great many, even yours, perhaps, Mr. Chairman. Here is a public man openly attacked in the House. No charge was laid, but insinuations bandied around, and he resigned his position as Minister and threw his books and affairs open, and he has made an above-board report to the Committee, and been reported by the auditors and everybody else. Now after that is done, you prepare a non-partisan report and don't say anything that he is vindicated, but simply submit a bare report. Mr. Raney comes in and puts up an amendment to that report, which no doubt he is going to bring into the House as a supplementary or minority report from this Committee, which no doubt he can do. We have gone to work and said nothing about Mr. Lyons; we just drop him cold in the report, and he comes in and charges freely that everything was proved to the hilt. To my mind, I don't think the Committee has done justice to Mr. Lyons, and I think there should be some opportunity given whereby a vote of confidence can be given him. He is now only an ordinary member of the House. Mr. Raney does not deny he is a member now of Copeland-Chatterson, and you know it is difficult for people to realize that companies have done business with the Government. I feel very deeply for Mr. Lyons, and I would not delete a line out of that report. You just leave it, Mr. Chairman, as it is. This Committee has every confidence in Mr. Lyons, and if this was an Ottawa committee, he would have a straight resolution of the committee vindicating him.

MR. RANEY: You can move an amendment to the amendment if you wish.

MR. CURRIE: We want to strike a clear-cut note. We are not going to let the other fellows play all the politics and take it lying down. If Mr. Raney had not introduced his resolution, I would say send in a non-partisan report. But as he introduces an amendment which challenges the good faith of the Committee, we should vindicate Mr. Lyons. I move in amendment to the amendment:

"That so far as the evidence before this Committee enables the reaching of a conclusion, your Committee feel that the Hon. James Lyons is entitled to a complete and unqualified exoneration from any breach of the Legislative Assembly Act, and that his company's business record in relation to the Government and any contractors having business relating to the Government is beyond reproach." Seconded by Mr. MacBride.

MR. FINLAYSON: If that were carried, it would cut out both amendment and report.

MR. CURRIE: No, that goes on the main report.

THE CHAIRMAN: That is, it would be added to the report as submitted by the Chairman.

MR. GRAY: I think that is a little irregular. We should adopt the report of the Committee, and if the Committee sees fit then to adopt an addition, well and good. I think even though the late Government erred in that respect we should not follow their example, but bring in a report according to Hoyle, and pass this as a resolution.

MR. CURRIE: Here is a man put to great expense, who has had to bring witnesses and evidence and documents here, and be kept out of his business, and he is on the rack, and there is not a tittle of evidence against him to show that directly or in any shape or form he did anything wrong—and you bet if they could find out he did anything wrong they would be right here. The Committee is practically at an end, and I would say let the report go as it is, if Mr. Raney had refrained from his minority report, but when a minority report like that is presented, then the Committee must justify Mr. Lyons, and I would strongly urge that the Committee pass that resolution and be done with it.

MR. MACBRIDE: That is my point. If your non-partisan report could be allowed to go unchallenged, all right, but after Mr. Raney's amendment I think it is the duty of the Committee to give Mr. Lyons a complete exoneration.

THE CHAIRMAN: I would like if Mr. Currie and Mr. MacBride would consider this suggestion, that we might vote on Mr. Raney's amendment and if it is unsuccessful you can move that this be added to the report.

MR. CURRIE: You are only splitting hairs.

MR. EDWARDS: Under the circumstances, I was willing to let that report go through, but I don't think in fairness to Mr. Lyons we should do it under the circumstances.

MR. CURRIE: Let Mr. Raney's motion go.

MR. GRAVES: Under the circumstances, and the very fair report you have put in, why should not Mr. Raney withdraw that? Of course I know the purpose, but it might be withdrawn.

THE CHAIRMAN: The vote now is on Mr. Raney's amendment, seconded by Mr. Fisher, that the alternative report presented by him be substituted for the draft report submitted by the Chairman. All those in favour will raise their hands. The amendment is lost.

MR. RANEY: Poll the Committee, Mr. Chairman.

THE SECRETARY: For, 5; against, 22.

THE CHAIRMAN: Mr. Currie moves, seconded by Mr. MacBride, that the clause he read be added to the report submitted by the Chairman, and that that report be adopted. Make it unanimous?

MR. RANEY: Record the same vote, if you like.

MR. LEWIS (Chairman): On the same division.

MR. FINLAYSON: Reversed. Move the Committee adjourn sine die.

INDEX

9243

Lightning Source UK Ltd.
Milton Keynes UK
UKHW010336120219
337137UK00004B/247/P